Houghton
Mifflin
Harcourt

★TEXAS★
Contemporary
World Studies

PEOPLE, PLACES, AND SOCIETIES

HISTORY.

Experience it @

hmhsocialstudies.com

Senior Texas Reviewer

Jesús F. de la Teja

Jesús F. de la Teja is Jerome H. and Catherine E. Supple Professor of Southwestern Studies and Regents' Professor of history and serves as director of the Center for the Study of the Southwest at Texas State University in San Marcos, Texas. He holds a Ph.D. in Latin American History from The University of Texas at Austin, and before coming to the university in 1991 he worked in the Archives and Records Division of the Texas General Land Office. His research interests focus on the northeastern frontier of Spanish colonial Mexico and Texas through the Republic era.

Professor de la Teja is the author of *San Antonio de Béxar: A Community on New Spain's Northern Frontier* (1995); co-author of *Texas: Crossroads of North America* (2004), a college-level survey of the state's history; and editor of *Tejano Leadership in Mexican and Revolutionary Texas* (2010). In addition to his research activities, he serves as a consultant for the Bullock Texas State History Museum in Austin and as book review editor of the *Southwestern Historical Quarterly*. In 2005 Dr. de la Teja became the first-ever state historian of Texas and has also served as a Social Studies Expert Reviewer for the Texas Education Agency.

Texas Review Panel

Valerie Garnier
Social Studies Consultant
Coppell, Texas

Kerry Green
Sunnyvale High School
Sunnyvale, Texas

Kristin Harman
Bailey Junior High
Arlington, Texas

Aderienne Shaw-Kelly
E. B. Comstock Middle School
Dallas, Texas

Contents

UNIT 1 Introduction to Geography 1

Available @

↗ **hmhsocialstudies.com**

- Facts About the World
- Regions of the World Handbook
- Standardized Test-Taking Strategies
- Economics Handbook

In addition to premium video-based resources, **HISTORY** has extensive offerings for teachers, parents, and students to use in the classroom and in their in-home educational activities, including:

▶ *The Idea Book for Educators* is a biannual teacher's magazine, featuring guides and info on the latest happenings in history education to help keep teachers on the cutting edge.

▶ **HISTORY Classroom (www.history.com/classroom)** is an interactive website that serves as a portal for history educators nationwide. Streaming videos on topics ranging from the Roman aqueducts to the civil rights movement connect with classroom curricula.

▶ **HISTORY email newsletters** feature updates and supplements to our award-winning programming relevant to the classroom with links to teaching guides and video clips on a variety of topics, special offers, and more.

▶ **Live webcasts** are featured each year as schools tune in via streaming video.

▶ **HISTORY Take a Veteran to School Day** connects veterans with young people in our schools and communities nationwide.

In addition to **HOUGHTON MIFFLIN HARCOURT**, our partners include the *Library of Congress*, the *Smithsonian Institution*, *National History Day*, *The Gilder Lehrman Institute of American History*, the *Organization of American Historians*, and many more. HISTORY video is also featured in museums throughout America and in over 70 other historic sites worldwide.

Texas Essential Knowledge and Skills

This course is based on the Grade 6 Texas Essential Knowledge and Skills (TEKS) for Social Studies. The TEKS identify the student expectations for this course—the things that you should be able to identify, explain, and accomplish by the end of the year.

Read through these expectations now for a preview of the content you will study this year. Later, as you read this book, you will see TEKS codes listed on the opening pages of chapters and sections. The TEKS codes indicate which TEKS are being covered. Refer back to these pages if you want to see the full text of each TEKS code.

History

TEKS 1 The student understands that historical events influence contemporary events. The student is expected to:

1A trace characteristics of various contemporary societies in regions that resulted from historical events or factors such as invasion, conquests, colonization, immigration, and trade; and

1B analyze the historical background of various contemporary societies to evaluate relationships between past conflicts and current conditions.

TO LEARN MORE: See regional Chapters 6–30. Look especially for sections with "History and Culture," "Today," or country names in their titles.

TEKS 2 The student understands the influences of individuals and groups from various cultures on various historical and contemporary societies. The student is expected to:

2A identify and describe the influence of individual or group achievements on various historical or contemporary societies such as the classical Greeks on government and the American Revolution on the French Revolution; and

2B evaluate the social, political, economic, and cultural contributions of individuals and groups from various societies, past and present.

TO LEARN MORE: See regional Chapters 6–30. Look especially for Biographies features, and sections with "History and Culture," "Today," or country names in their titles.

Geography

TEKS 3 The student uses geographic tools to answer geographic questions. The student is expected to:

3A pose and answer geographic questions, including: Where is it located? Why is it there? What is significant about its location? How is its location related to the location of other people, places, and environments?;

3B pose and answer questions about geographic distributions and patterns for various world regions and countries shown on maps, graphs, charts, models, and databases;

3C compare various world regions and countries using data from geographic tools, including maps, graphs, charts, databases, and models; and

3D create thematic maps, graphs, charts, models, and databases depicting aspects such as population, disease, and economic activities of various world regions and countries.

TO LEARN MORE: See introductory Chapters 1–4 and regional Chapters 6–30. Look especially for sections titled "Physical Geography," Social Studies Skills pages, and visuals such as maps, graphs, charts, and models.

TEKS 4 The student understands the factors that influence the locations and characteristics of locations of various contemporary societies on maps and globes and uses latitude and longitude to determine absolute locations. The student is expected to:

4A locate various contemporary societies on maps and globes using latitude and longitude to determine absolute location;

4B identify and explain the geographic factors responsible for patterns of population in places and regions;

4C explain ways in which human migration influences the character of places and regions;

4D identify and locate major physical and human geographic features such as landforms, water bodies, and urban centers of various places and regions;

4E draw sketch maps that illustrate various places and regions; and

4F identify the location of major world countries such as Canada, Mexico, France, Germany, the United Kingdom, Italy, Spain, Norway, Sweden, Russia, South Africa, Nigeria, Iraq, Afghanistan, Israel, Iran, India, Pakistan, the People's Republic of China, the Republic of China (Taiwan), Japan, North and South Korea, Indonesia, and Australia.

TO LEARN MORE: See introductory Chapters 1 and 4 and regional chapters, Chapters 6–30. Look especially for sections titled "Physical Geography," the map activities in chapter reviews, and the Social Studies Skills pages for Chapters 7 and 10.

TEKS 5 The student understands how geographic factors influence the economic development, political relationships, and policies of societies. The student is expected to:

  5A identify and explain the geographic factors responsible for the location of economic activities in places and regions;

  5B identify geographic factors such as location, physical features, transportation corridors and barriers, and distribution of natural resources that influence a society's ability to control territory; and

  5C explain the impact of geographic factors on economic development and the domestic and foreign policies of societies.

TO LEARN MORE: See introductory Chapters 3 and 5, and regional Chapters 6–30. Look especially at sections titled "Physical Geography," the Chapter 19 Case Study (Oil in Saudi Arabia), and headings that include the terms "Resources" and "Economy."

TEKS 6 The student understands that geographical patterns result from physical environmental processes. The student is expected to:

  6A describe and explain the effects of physical environmental processes such as erosion, ocean currents, and earthquakes on Earth's surface;

  6B identify the location of renewable and nonrenewable natural resources such as fresh water, fossil fuels, fertile soils, and timber; and

  6C analyze the effects of the interaction of physical processes and the environment on humans.

TO LEARN MORE: See introductory Chapters 1, 2, and 3, and the sections titled "Physical Geography," the Geography and History lessons, and the Case Studies in regional Chapters 6–30.

TEKS 7 The student understands the impact of interactions between people and the physical environment on the development and conditions of places and regions. The student is expected to:

  7A identify and analyze ways people have adapted to the physical environment in various places and regions;

  7B identify and analyze ways people have modified the physical environment such as mining, irrigation, and transportation infrastructure; and

  7C describe ways in which technology influences human interactions with the environment such as humans building dams for flood control.

TO LEARN MORE: See introductory Chapters 1 and 3, and regional Chapters 12, 15, 27, and Focus on Technology features.

Economics

TEKS 8 The student understands the factors of production in a society's economy. The student is expected to:

8A describe ways in which the factors of production (natural resources, labor, capital, and entrepreneurs) influence the economies of various contemporary societies;

8B identify problems and issues that may arise when one or more of the factors of production is in relatively short supply; and

8C explain the impact of relative scarcity of resources on international trade and economic interdependence among and within societies.

TO LEARN MORE: See introductory Chapters 3 and 5, and the sections titled "Physical Geography" in regional Chapters 6–30.

TEKS 9 The student understands the various ways in which people organize economic systems. The student is expected to:

9A compare ways in which various societies organize the production and distribution of goods and services;

9B compare and contrast free enterprise, socialist, and communist economies in various contemporary societies, including the benefits of the U.S. free enterprise system;

9C understand the importance of morality and ethics in maintaining a functional free enterprise system; and

9D examine the record of collective, non-free market economic systems in contemporary world societies.

TO LEARN MORE: See introductory Chapter 5, and sections with "Today" or country names in their titles in regional Chapters 6–30.

TEKS 10 The student understands categories of economic activities and the data used to measure a society's economic level. The student is expected to:

10A define and give examples of agricultural, wholesale, retail, manufacturing (goods), and service industries;

10B describe levels of economic development of various societies using indicators such as life expectancy, gross domestic product (GDP), GDP per capita, and literacy; and

10C identify and describe the effects of government regulation and taxation on economic development and business planning.

TO LEARN MORE: See introductory Chapter 5.

Government

TEKS 11 The student understands the concepts of limited and unlimited governments. The student is expected to:

11A identify and describe examples of limited and unlimited governments such as constitutional (limited) and totalitarian (unlimited);

11B compare the characteristics of limited and unlimited governments;

11C identify reasons for limiting the power of government; and

11D review the record of human rights abuses of limited or unlimited governments such as the oppression of Christians in Sudan.

TO LEARN MORE: See introductory Chapter 5 and regional Chapters 6, 13, 14, 17, 18, 19, 23, 27, and 28.

TEKS 12 The student understands various ways in which people organize governments. The student is expected to:

12A identify and give examples of governments with rule by one, few, or many;

12B compare ways in which various societies such as China, Germany, India, and Russia organize government and how they function; and

12C identify historical origins of democratic forms of government such as Ancient Greece.

TO LEARN MORE: See introductory Chapter 5 and regional Chapters 6, 13, 14, 17, 18, 19, 23, 27, and 28.

Citizenship

TEKS 13 The student understands that the nature of citizenship varies among societies. The student is expected to:

13A describe roles and responsibilities of citizens in various contemporary societies, including the United States;

13B explain how opportunities for citizens to participate in and influence the political process vary among various contemporary societies; and

13C compare the role of citizens in the United States with the role of citizens from various contemporary societies with representative and nonrepresentative governments.

TO LEARN MORE: See introductory Chapter 5 and regional Chapters 19 and 27.

TEKS 14 The student understands the relationship among individual rights, responsibilities, duties, and freedoms in societies with representative governments. The student is expected to:

14A identify and explain the duty of civic participation in societies with representative governments; and

14B explain relationships among rights, responsibilities, and duties in societies with representative governments.

TO LEARN MORE: See Chapter 5 and the Celebrate Freedom pages.

Culture

TEKS 15 The student understands the similarities and differences within and among cultures in various world societies. The student is expected to:

15A define culture and the common traits that unify a culture region;

15B identify and describe common traits that define cultures;

15C define a multicultural society and consider both the positive and negative qualities of multiculturalism;

15D analyze the experiences and evaluate the contributions of diverse groups to multicultural societies;

15E analyze the similarities and differences among various world societies; and

15F identify and explain examples of conflict and cooperation between and among cultures.

TO LEARN MORE: See introductory Chapter 4, Focus on Culture features, and sections with "History and Culture," "Today," or country names in their titles in regional Chapters 6–30.

TEKS 16 The student understands that all societies have basic institutions in common even though the characteristics of these institutions may differ. The student is expected to:

16A identify institutions basic to all societies, including government, economic, educational, and religious institutions;

16B compare characteristics of institutions in various contemporary societies; and

16C analyze the efforts and activities institutions use to sustain themselves over time such as the development of an informed citizenry through education and the use of monumental architecture by religious institutions.

TO LEARN MORE: See introductory Chapters 4 and 5 and sections with "History and Culture," "Today," or country names in their titles in regional Chapters 6–30.

TEKS 17 The student understands relationships that exist among world cultures. The student is expected to:

17A identify and describe how culture traits such as trade, travel, and war spread;

17B identify and describe factors that influence cultural change such as improved communication, transportation, and economic development;

17C evaluate the impact of improved communication technology among cultures;

17D identify and define the impact of cultural diffusion on individuals and world societies; and

17E identify examples of positive and negative effects of cultural diffusion.

TO LEARN MORE: See introductory Chapter 4 and regional Chapter 18.

TEKS 18 The student understands the relationship that exists between the arts and the societies in which they are produced. The student is expected to:

18A explain the relationships that exist between societies and their architecture, art, music, and literature;

18B relate ways in which contemporary expressions of culture have been influenced by the past;

18C describe ways in which contemporary issues influence creative expressions; and

18D identify examples of art, music, and literature that have transcended the boundaries of societies and convey universal themes such as religion, justice, and the passage of time.

TO LEARN MORE: See introductory Chapter 4, Connecting to the Arts and Focus on Culture features, and sections with "History and Culture," "Today," or country names in their titles in regional Chapters 6–30.

TEKS 19 The student understands the relationships among religion, philosophy, and culture. The student is expected to:

19A explain the relationship among religious ideas, philosophical ideas, and cultures; and

19B explain the significance of religious holidays and observances such as Christmas, Easter, Ramadan, the annual hajj, Yom Kippur, Rosh Hashanah, Diwali, and Vaisakhi in various contemporary societies.

TO LEARN MORE: See introductory Chapter 4 and regional Chapters 6, 8, 14, 19, 20, 21, 26, 27, 28 and 29.

Science, Technology, and Society

TEKS 20 The student understands the influences of science and technology on contemporary societies. The student is expected to:

20A give examples of scientific discoveries and technological innovations, including the roles of scientists and inventors, that have transcended the boundaries of societies and have shaped the world;

20B explain how resources, belief systems, economic factors, and political decisions have affected the use of technology; and

20C make predictions about future social, political, economic, cultural, and environmental impacts that may result from future scientific discoveries and technological innovations.

TO LEARN MORE: See introductory Chapter 4.

Social Studies Skills

TEKS 21 The student applies critical-thinking skills to organize and use information acquired through established research methodologies from a variety of valid sources, including electronic technology. The student is expected to:

21A differentiate between, locate, and use valid primary and secondary sources such as computer software; interviews; biographies; oral, print, and visual material; and artifacts to acquire information about various world cultures;

21B analyze information by sequencing, categorizing, identifying cause-and-effect relationships, comparing, contrasting, finding the main idea, summarizing, making generalizations and predictions, and drawing inferences and conclusions;

21C organize and interpret information from outlines, reports, databases, and visuals, including graphs, charts, timelines, and maps;

21D identify different points of view about an issue or current topic;

21E identify the elements of frame of reference that influenced participants in an event; and

21F use appropriate mathematical skills to interpret social studies information such as maps and graphs.

TO LEARN MORE: See Section Assessments, Chapter Reviews, Primary Source lessons, Reading Social Studies lessons and activities, Connecting to Math features and the Social Studies Skills lessons and activities.

TEKS 22 The student communicates in written, oral, and visual forms. The student is expected to:

22A use social studies terminology correctly;

22B incorporate main and supporting ideas in verbal and written communication based on research;

22C express ideas orally based on research and experiences;

22D create written and visual material such as journal entries, reports, graphic organizers, outlines, and bibliographies based on research

22E use standard grammar, spelling, sentence structure, and punctuation; and

22F use proper citations to avoid plagiarism.

TO LEARN MORE: See the Section Assessments, the Reading Social Studies lessons and activities, the Social Studies Skills lessons and activities, and Writing Workshops. Look especially for Reviewing Vocabulary Terms and Places, Using the Internet activities, and Focus on Reading, Writing, and Viewing activities.

TEKS 23 The student uses problem-solving and decision-making skills, working independently and with others, in a variety of settings. The student is expected to:

23A use a problem-solving process to identify a problem, gather information, list and consider options, consider advantages and disadvantages, choose and implement a solution, and evaluate the effectiveness of the solution; and

23B use a decision-making process to identify a situation that requires a decision, gather information, identify options, predict consequences, and take action to implement a decision.

TO LEARN MORE: See the Social Studies Skills pages and Chapter Review Social Studies Skills activities for Chapters 5 and 25.

Source: The provisions of this §113.18 adopted to be effective August 23, 2010, 35 TexReg 7232.

Geography and Map Skills Handbook

Contents

Throughout this textbook, you will be studying the world's people, places, and landscapes. One of the main tools you will use is the map—the primary tool of geographers. To help you begin your studies, this Geography and Map Skills Handbook explains some of the basic features of maps. For example, it explains how maps are made, how to read them, and how they can show the round surface of Earth on a flat piece of paper. This handbook will also introduce you to some of the types of maps you will study later in this book. In addition, you will learn about the different kinds of features on Earth and about how geographers use themes and elements to study the world.

Mapping the Earth
Using Latitude and Longitude

A **globe** is a scale model of the Earth. It is useful for showing the entire Earth or studying large areas of Earth's surface.

To study the world, geographers use a pattern of imaginary lines that circles the globe in east-west and north-south directions. It is called a **grid**. The intersection of these imaginary lines helps us find places on Earth.

The east-west lines in the grid are lines of **latitude**, which you can see on the diagram. Lines of latitude are called **parallels** because they are always parallel to each other. These imaginary lines measure distance north and south of the **equator**. The equator is an imaginary line that circles the globe halfway between the North and South Poles. Parallels measure distance from the equator in **degrees**. The symbol for degrees is °. Degrees are further divided into **minutes**. The symbol for minutes is ´. There are 60 minutes in a degree. Parallels north of the equator are labeled with an N. Those south of the equator are labeled with an S.

The north-south imaginary lines are lines of **longitude**. Lines of longitude are called **meridians**. These imaginary lines pass through the poles. They measure distance east and west of the **prime meridian**. The prime meridian is an imaginary line that runs through Greenwich, England. It represents 0° longitude.

Lines of latitude range from 0°, for locations on the equator, to 90°N or 90°S, for locations at the poles. Lines of longitude range from 0° on the prime meridian to 180° on a meridian in the mid-Pacific Ocean. Meridians west of the prime meridian to 180° are labeled with a W. Those east of the prime meridian to 180° are labeled with an E. Using latitude and longitude, geographers can identify the exact location of any place on Earth.

Lines of Latitude

Lines of Longitude

Northern Hemisphere

The equator divides the globe into two halves, called **hemispheres**. The half north of the equator is the Northern Hemisphere. The southern half is the Southern Hemisphere. The prime meridian and the 180° meridian divide the world into the Eastern Hemisphere and the Western Hemisphere. Look at the diagrams on this page. They show each of these four hemispheres.

Earth's land surface is divided into seven large landmasses, called **continents**. These continents are also shown on the diagrams on this page. Landmasses smaller than continents and completely surrounded by water are called **islands**.

Geographers organize Earth's water surface into major regions too. The largest is the world ocean. Geographers divide the world ocean into the Pacific Ocean, the Atlantic Ocean, the Indian Ocean, the Arctic Ocean, and the Southern Ocean. Lakes and seas are smaller bodies of water.

Southern Hemisphere

Western Hemisphere

Eastern Hemisphere

Mapmaking
Understanding Map Projections

A **map** is a flat diagram of all or part of Earth's surface. Mapmakers have created different ways of showing our round planet on flat maps. These different ways are called **map projections**. Because Earth is round, there is no way to show it accurately on a flat map. All flat maps are distorted in some way. Mapmakers must choose the type of map projection that is best for their purposes. Many map projections are one of three kinds: cylindrical, conic, or flat-plane.

Paper cylinder

Mercator projection

Cylindrical Projections

Cylindrical projections are based on a cylinder wrapped around the globe. The cylinder touches the globe only at the equator. The meridians are pulled apart and are parallel to each other instead of meeting at the poles. This causes landmasses near the poles to appear larger than they really are. The map below is a Mercator projection, one type of cylindrical projection. The Mercator projection is useful for navigators because it shows true direction and shape. However, it distorts the size of land areas near the poles.

Conic Projections

Conic projections are based on a cone placed over the globe. A conic projection is most accurate along the lines of latitude where it touches the globe. It retains almost true shape and size. Conic projections are most useful for showing areas that have long east-west dimensions, such as the United States.

Paper cone

Conic projection

Flat-plane Projections

Flat-plane projections are based on a plane touching the globe at one point, such as at the North Pole or South Pole. A flat-plane projection is useful for showing true direction for airplane pilots and ship navigators. It also shows true area. However, it distorts the true shapes of landmasses.

Flat plane

Flat-plane projection

Map Essentials
How to Read a Map

Maps are like messages sent out in code. To help us translate the code, mapmakers provide certain features. These features help us understand the message they are presenting about a particular part of the world. Of these features, almost all maps have a title, a compass rose, a scale, and a legend. The map below has these four features, plus a fifth—a locator map.

❶ Title

A map's **title** shows what the subject of the map is. The map title is usually the first thing you should look at when studying a map, because it tells you what the map is trying to show.

The First Crusade, 1096

Christian lands, 1095
Muslim lands, 1095
First Crusade, 1096–1099

0   100   200 Miles
0   100   200 Kilometers

Projection: Azimuthal Equal Area

North Sea

ENGLAND

HOLY ROMAN EMPIRE

ATLANTIC OCEAN

FRANCE

Lyon

Regensburg

Vienna

Trieste

Genoa

Zadar

Corsica

Rome

Black Sea

Constantinople

SELJUK TURKS

40°N

Sardinia

Mediterranean Sea

BYZANTINE EMPIRE

Edessa

Antioch

Sicily

Tripoli

Crete

HOLY LAND

Acre

Jerusalem

50°N

❷ Compass Rose

A directional indicator shows which way north, south, east, and west lie on the map. Some mapmakers use a "north arrow," which points toward the North Pole. Remember, "north" is not always at the top of a map. The way a map is drawn and the location of directions on that map depend on the perspective of the mapmaker. Most maps in this textbook indicate direction by using a compass rose. A **compass rose** has arrows that point to all four principal directions.

❸ Scale

Mapmakers use scales to represent the distances between points on a map. Scales may appear on maps in several different forms. The maps in this textbook provide a **bar scale**. Scales give distances in miles and kilometers.

To find the distance between two points on the map, place a piece of paper so that the edge connects the two points. Mark the location of each point on the paper with a line or dot. Then, compare the distance between the two dots with the map's bar scale. The number on the top of the scale gives the distance in miles. The number on the bottom gives the distance in kilometers. Because the distances are given in large intervals, you may have to approximate the actual distance on the scale.

❹ Legend

The **legend**, or key, explains what the symbols on the map represent. Point symbols are used to specify the location of things, such as cities, that do not take up much space on the map. Some legends show colors that represent certain features like empires or other regions. Other maps might have legends with symbols or colors that represent features such as roads. Legends can also show economic resources, land use, population density, and climate.

❺ Locator Map

A **locator map** shows where in the world the area on the map is located. The area shown on the main map is shown in red on the locator map. The locator map also shows surrounding areas so the map reader can see how the information on the map relates to neighboring lands.

Working with Maps
Using Different Kinds of Maps

As you study the world's regions and countries, you will use a variety of maps. Political maps and physical maps are two of the most common types of maps you will study. In addition, you will use thematic maps. These maps might show climate, population, resources, ancient empires, or other topics.

Political Maps

Political maps show the major political features of a region. These features include country borders, capital cities, and other places. Political maps use different colors to represent countries, and capital cities are often shown with a special star symbol.

Caribbean South America: Political

The Indian Subcontinent: Physical

ELEVATION

Feet	Meters
13,120	4,000
6,560	2,000
1,640	500
656	200
(Sea level) 0	0 (Sea level)
Below sea level	Below sea level

Projection: Albers Equal-Area

Physical Maps

Physical maps show the major physical features of a region. These features may include mountain ranges, rivers, oceans, islands, deserts, and plains. Often, these maps use different colors to represent different elevations of land. As a result, the map reader can easily see which areas are high elevations, like mountains, and which areas are lower.

Thematic Maps

Thematic maps focus on one special topic, such as climate, resources, or population. These maps present information on the topic that is particularly important in the region. Depending on the type of thematic map, the information may be shown with different colors, arrows, dots, or other symbols.

West Africa: Climate

Climate Types

- Humid tropical
- Tropical savanna
- Desert
- Steppe

Projection: Azimuthal Equal-Area

Using Maps in Geography The different kinds of maps in this textbook will help you study and understand geography. By working with these maps, you will see what the physical geography of places is like, where people live, and how the world has changed over time.

Geographic Dictionary

OCEAN
a large body of water

CORAL REEF
an ocean ridge made up of skeletal remains of tiny sea animals

GULF
a large part of the ocean that extends into land

PENINSULA
an area of land that sticks out into a lake or ocean

BAY
part of a large body of water that is smaller than a gulf

ISLAND
an area of land surrounded entirely by water

ISTHMUS
a narrow piece of land connecting two larger land areas

DELTA
an area where a river deposits soil into the ocean

STRAIT
a narrow body of water connecting two larger bodies of water

SINKHOLE
a circular depression formed when the roof of a cave collapses

WETLAND
an area of land covered by shallow water

RIVER
a natural flow of water that runs through the land

LAKE
an inland body of water

FOREST
an area of densely wooded land

COAST
an area of land
near the ocean

MOUNTAIN
an area of rugged
land that generally
rises higher than
2,000 feet

VALLEY
an area of low
land between
hills or mountains

GLACIER
a large area of
slow-moving ice

VOLCANO
an opening in Earth's crust
where lava, ash, and gases erupt

CANYON
a deep, narrow valley
with steep walls

HILL
a rounded, elevated
area of land smaller
than a mountain

PLAIN
a nearly
flat area

DUNE
a hill of sand
shaped by wind

OASIS
an area in the
desert with a
water source

DESERT
an extremely dry area with
little water and few plants

PLATEAU
a large, flat,
elevated
area of land

Themes and Essential Elements of Geography

by Dr. Christopher L. Salter

To study the world, geographers have identified 5 key themes, 6 essential elements, and 18 geography standards.

"How should we teach and learn about geography?" Professional geographers have worked hard over the years to answer this important question.

In 1984 a group of geographers identified the 5 Themes of Geography. These themes did a wonderful job of laying the groundwork for good classroom geography. Teachers used the 5 Themes in class, and geographers taught workshops on how to apply them in the world.

By the early 1990s, however, some geographers felt the 5 Themes were too broad. They created the 18 Geography Standards and the 6 Essential Elements. The 18 Geography Standards include more detailed information about what geography is, and the 6 Essential Elements are like a bridge between the 5 Themes and 18 Standards.

Look at the chart to the right. It shows how each of the 5 Themes connects to the Essential Elements and Standards. For example, the theme of Location is related to The World in Spatial Terms and the first three Standards. Study the chart carefully to see how the other themes, elements, and Standards are related.

The last Essential Element and the last two Standards cover The Uses of Geography. These key parts of geography were not covered by the 5 Themes. They will help you see how geography has influenced the past, present, and future.

5 Themes of Geography

Location The theme of location describes where something is.

Place Place describes the features that make a site unique.

Regions Regions are areas that share common characteristics.

Movement This theme looks at how and why people and things move.

Human-Environment Interaction People interact with their environment in many ways.

6 Essential Elements

18 Geography Standards

I. The World in Spatial Terms

1. How to use maps and other tools
2. How to use mental maps to organize information
3. How to analyze the spatial organization of people, places, and environments

II. Places and Regions

4. The physical and human characteristics of places
5. How people create regions to interpret Earth
6. How culture and experience influence people's perceptions of places and regions

III. Physical Systems

7. The physical processes that shape Earth's surface
8. The distribution of ecosystems on Earth

IV. Human Systems

9. The characteristics, distribution, and migration of human populations
10. The complexity of Earth's cultural mosaics
11. The patterns and networks of economic interdependence on Earth
12. The patterns of human settlement
13. The forces of cooperation and conflict

V. Environment and Society

14. How human actions modify the physical environment
15. How physical systems affect human systems
16. The distribution and meaning of resources

VI. The Uses of Geography

17. How to apply geography to interpret the past
18. How to apply geography to interpret the present and plan for the future

Become an Active Reader

Did you ever think you would begin reading your social studies book by reading about *reading*? Actually, it makes better sense than you might think. You would probably make sure you knew some soccer skills and strategies before playing in a game. Similarly, you need to know something about reading skills and strategies before reading your social studies book. In other words, you need to make sure you know whatever you need to know in order to read this book successfully.

Tip #1

Read Everything on the Page!

You can't follow the directions on the cake-mix box if you don't know where the directions are! Cake-mix boxes always have directions on them telling you how many eggs to add or how long to bake the cake. But, if you can't find that information, it doesn't matter that it is there.

Likewise, this book is filled with information that will help you understand what you are reading. If you don't study that information, however, it might as well not be there. Let's take a look at some of the places where you'll find important information in this book.

The Chapter Opener
The chapter opener gives you a brief overview of what you will learn in the chapter. You can use this information to prepare to read the chapter.

The Section Openers
Before you begin to read each section, preview the information under What You Will Learn. There you'll find the main ideas of the section and key terms that are important in it. Knowing what you are looking for before you start reading can improve your understanding.

Boldfaced Words
Those words are important and are defined somewhere on the page where they appear—either right there in the sentence or over in the side margin.

Maps, Charts, and Artwork
These things are not there just to take up space or look good! Study them and read the information beside them. It will help you understand the information in the chapter.

Questions at the End of Sections
At the end of each section, you will find questions that will help you decide whether you need to go back and re-read any parts before moving on. If you can't answer a question, that is your cue to go back and re-read.

Questions at the End of the Chapter
Answer the questions at the end of each chapter, even if your teacher doesn't ask you to. These questions are there to help you figure out what you need to review.

Tip #2

Use the Reading Skills and Strategies in Your Textbook

Good readers use a number of skills and strategies to make sure they understand what they are reading. In this textbook you will find help with important reading skills and strategies such as "Using Prior Knowledge," and "Understanding Main Ideas."

We teach the reading skills and strategies in several ways. Use these activities and lessons and you will become a better reader.

- First, on the opening page of every chapter we identify and explain the reading skill or strategy you will focus on as you work through the chapter. In fact, these activities are called "Focus on Reading."

- Second, as you can see in the example at right, we tell you where to go for more help. The Reading Social Studies page at the end of each chapter is a practice lesson that supports the reading skill or strategy for that chapter.

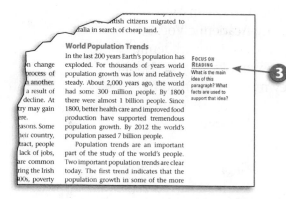

- Third, we give you short practice activities and examples as you read the chapter. These activities and examples show up in the margin of your book. Again, look for the words, "Focus on Reading."

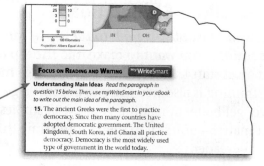

- Finally, we provide another practice activity in the Chapter Review at the end of every chapter. That activity gives you one more chance to make sure you know how to use the reading skill or strategy.

Tip #3

Pay Attention to Vocabulary

It is no fun to read something when you don't know what the words mean, but you can't learn new words if you only use or read the words you already know. In this book, we know we have probably used some words you don't know. But, we have followed a pattern as we have used more difficult words.

- First, at the beginning of each section you will find a list of key terms that you will need to know. Be on the lookout for those words as you read through the section. You will find that we have defined those words right there in the paragraph where they are used. Look for a word that is in boldface with its definition highlighted in yellow.

- Second, when we use a word that is important in all classes, not just social studies, we define it in the margin under the heading Academic Vocabulary. You will run into these academic words in other textbooks, so you should learn what they mean while reading this book.

Tip #4

Read Like a Skilled Reader

You won't be able to climb to the top of Mount Everest if you do not train! If you want to make it to the top of Mount Everest then you must start training to climb that huge mountain.

Training is also necessary to become a good reader. You will never get better at reading your social studies book—or any book for that matter—unless you spend some time thinking about how to be a better reader.

Skilled readers do the following:

1. They preview what they are supposed to read before they actually begin reading. When previewing, they look for vocabulary words, titles of sections, information in the margin, or maps or charts they should study.

2. They get ready to take some notes while reading by dividing their notebook paper into two parts. They title one side "Notes from the Chapter" and the other side "Questions or Comments I Have."

3. As they read, they complete their notes.

4. They read like **active readers**. The Active Reading list below shows you what that means.

5. Finally, they use clues in the text to help them figure out where the text is going. The best clues are called signal words. These are words that help you identify chronological order, causes and effects, or comparisons and contrasts.

Chronological Order Signal Words: *first, second, third, before, after, later, next, following that, earlier, subsequently, finally*

Cause and Effect Signal Words: *because of, due to, as a result of, the reason for, therefore, consequently, so, basis for*

Comparison/Contrast Signal Words: *likewise, also, as well as, similarly, on the other hand*

Active Reading

There are three ways to read a book: You can be a turn-the-pages-no-matter-what type of reader. These readers just keep on turning pages whether or not they understand what they are reading. Or, you can be a stop-watch-and-listen kind of reader. These readers know that if they wait long enough, someone will tell them what they need to know. Or, you can be an active reader. These readers know that it is up to them to figure out what the text means. Active readers do the following as they read:

Predict what will happen next based on what has already happened. When your predictions don't match what happens in the text, re-read the confusing parts.

Question what is happening as you read. Constantly ask yourself why things have happened, what things mean, and what caused certain events. Jot down notes about the questions you can't answer.

Summarize what you are reading frequently. Do not try to summarize the entire chapter! Read a bit and then summarize it. Then read on.

Connect what is happening in the section you're reading to what you have already read.

Clarify your understanding. Be sure that you understand what you are reading by stopping occasionally to ask yourself whether you are confused by anything. Sometimes you might need to re-read to clarify. Other times you might need to read further and collect more information before you can understand. Still other times you might need to ask the teacher to help you with what is confusing you.

Visualize what is happening in the text. In other words, try to see the events or places in your mind. It might help you to draw maps, make charts, or jot down notes about what you are reading as you try to visualize the action in the text.

Social Studies Words

As you read this textbook, you will be more successful if you learn the meanings of the words on this page. You will come across these words many times in your social studies classes, like geography and history. Read through these words now to become familiar with them before you begin your studies.

Social Studies Words

WORDS ABOUT TIME

AD	refers to dates after the birth of Jesus
BC	refers to dates before Jesus's birth
BCE	refers to dates before Jesus's birth, stands for "before the common era"
CE	refers to dates after Jesus's birth, stands for "common era"
century	a period of 100 years
decade	a period of 10 years
era	a period of time
millennium	a period of 1,000 years

WORDS ABOUT THE WORLD

climate	the weather conditions in a certain area over a long period of time
geography	the study of the world's people, places, and landscapes
physical features	features on Earth's surface, such as mountains and rivers
region	an area with one or more features that make it different from surrounding areas
resources	materials found on Earth that people need and value

WORDS ABOUT PEOPLE

anthropology	the study of people and cultures
archaeology	the study of the past based on what people left behind
citizen	a person who lives under the control of a government
civilization	the way of life of people in a particular place or time
culture	the knowledge, beliefs, customs, and values of a group of people
custom	a repeated practice or tradition
economics	the study of the production and use of goods and services
economy	any system in which people make and exchange goods and services
government	the body of officials and groups that run an area
history	the study of the past
politics	the process of running a government
religion	a system of beliefs in a supreme God, gods or spirits, or an ultimate divine power or cosmic principle; includes practices that express those beliefs and perspectives
society	a group of people who share common traditions
trade	the exchange of goods or services

Academic Words

What are academic words? They are important words used in all of your classes, not just social studies. You will see these words in other textbooks, so you should learn what they mean while reading this book. Review this list now. You will use these words again in the chapters of this book.

Academic Words

abstract	expressing a quality or idea without reference to an actual thing		**impact**	effect, result
affect	to change or influence		**implement**	to put in place
agreement	a decision reached by two or more people or groups		**implications**	consequences
aspects	parts		**incentive**	something that leads people to follow a certain course of action
cause	to make something happen		**influence**	the ability to change, or have an effect on
circumstances	conditions that influence an event or activity		**innovation**	a new idea or way of doing something
concrete	specific, real		**method**	a way of doing something
consequences	the effects of a particular event or events		**monumental**	monumental impressively large, sturdy, and enduring
contemporary	modern		**motive**	a reason for doing something
criteria	rules for defining		**neutral**	unbiased, not favoring either side in a conflict
development	the process of growing or improving		**policies**	rules, courses of action
distinct	clearly different and separate		**primary**	main, most important
distribute	to divide among a group of people		**procedure**	a series of steps taken to accomplish a task
effect	the results of an action or decision		**process**	a series of steps by which a task is accomplished
efficient	productive and not wasteful		**purpose**	the reason something is done
element	part		**reaction**	a response to something
establish	to set up or create		**role**	a part or function
execute	to perform, carry out		**structure**	the way something is set up or organized
factor	cause		**traditional**	customary, time-honored
features	characteristics		**values**	ideas that people hold dear and try to live by
function	use or purpose		**vary**	to be different

Making This Book Work for You

Studying geography will be easy for you with this textbook. Take a few minutes now to become familiar with the easy-to-use structure and special features of your book. See how it will make geography come alive for you!

Unit

Each unit begins with a satellite image, a regional atlas, and a table with facts about each country. Use these pages to get an overview of the region you will study.

Regional Atlas The maps in the regional atlas show some of the key physical and human features of the region.

Regional Database See which countries are included in each region and learn some important facts about them with these helpful tables.

Chapter

Each regional chapter begins with a preview of what you will learn and a map of the region. Special instruction is also given in reading and skills.

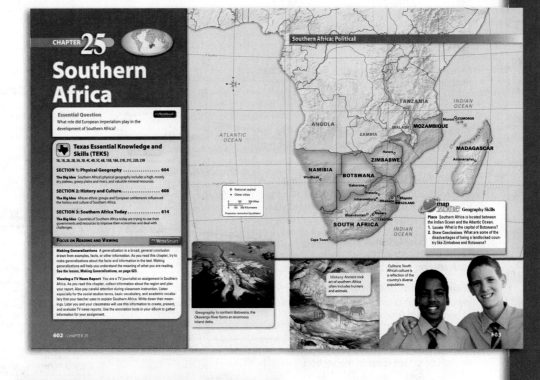

Reading Social Studies

Chapter reading lessons give you skills and practice to help you read the textbook. More help with each lesson can be found in the back of the book. Margin notes and questions in the chapter make sure you understand the reading skill.

Social Studies Skills The Social Studies Skills lessons give you an opportunity to learn, practice, and apply an important skill. Chapter Review questions then follow up on what you learned.

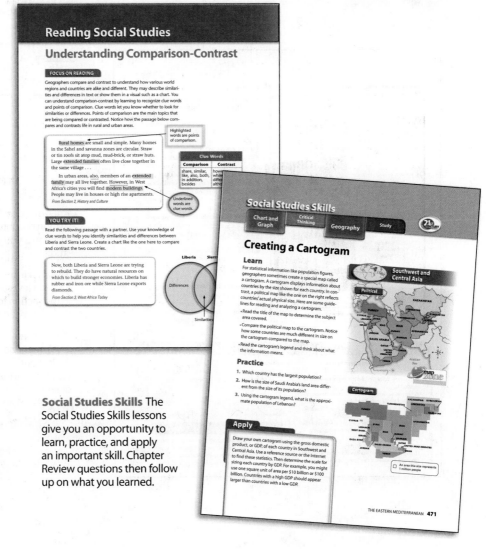

Section

The section opener pages include TEKS codes, Main Ideas, an overarching Big Idea, and Key Terms and Places. In addition, each section includes these special features:

Texas Essential Knowledge and Skills Each section begins with the TEKS codes that are covered in the section.

If YOU Lived There . . . Each section begins with a situation for you to respond to, placing you in a place that relates to the content you will be studying in the section.

Building Background The Building Background connects what will be covered in each section with what you already know.

Short Sections of Content The information in each section is organized into small chunks of text that you can easily understand.

Taking Notes Suggested online graphic organizers help you read and take notes on the important ideas in the section.

SECTION 2

The Caucasus

TEKS 1A, 1B, 2A, 2B, 3A, 3B, 3C, 3D, 4B, 4C, 15B, 18B, 21B, 21C, 22D

What You Will Learn...

Main Ideas
1. Many groups have ruled and influenced the Caucasus during its long history.
2. Today the Caucasus republics are working to improve their economies, but they struggle with ethnic unrest and conflict.

The Big Idea
In an area long ruled by outside groups, the Caucasus republics are struggling to strengthen their economies and to deal with ethnic unrest.

Key Places
Caspian Sea, *p. 427*
Caucasus Mountains, *p. 427*
Tbilisi, *p. 428*
Yerevan, *p. 428*
Baku, *p. 429*

hmhsocialstudies.com
TAKING NOTES
Use the graphic organizer online to take notes on the Caucasus.

If YOU lived there...
You live in Tbilisi, the capital of the country of Georgia. Several years ago, your sister and her college friends joined the Rose Revolution, a political protest that forced a corrupt president to resign. The protestors' symbol was a red rose. Since the protest, you have become more interested in politics.

What kind of government do you want?

BUILDING BACKGROUND Georgia is one of three republics in the area called the Caucasus. In 1991, when the Soviet Union ended, the Caucasus republics gained independence. Since then, the republics have struggled to become democracies with market economies.

History

The Caucasus lies in the rugged Caucasus Mountains between the Black and Caspian seas. Located where Europe blends into Asia, the Caucasus reflects a range of cultural influences. At one time or another, Persians, Greeks, Romans, Arabs, Turks, and Mongols have all ruled or invaded the area. The Russians took control of much of the Caucasus in the early 1800s.

Russian control in the Caucasus did not include what is now western Armenia. The Ottoman Turks held this area. Over time, the Turks grew to distrust the Armenians, however; and in the late 1800s began abusing and killing them. During World War I (1914–1918), the Turks forced all Armenians to leave. Hundreds of thousands of Armenians died during this ethnic cleansing, or attempt to remove an ethnic group. The Turks lost World War I, though, and had to give up western Armenia.

After World War I, Armenia, Azerbaijan, and Georgia gained independence—but not for long. By the early 1920s they were part of the vast Soviet Union. Finally in 1991, when the Soviet Union fell, the Caucasus republics achieved true independence.

READING CHECK **Finding Main Ideas** Why do the countries in the Caucasus reflect a range of cultural influences?

Primary Source

Communist-era Poster

The Soviet Union used posters as propaganda. Propaganda is information designed to promote a specific cause or idea by influencing people's thoughts and beliefs. For example, Soviet posters often promoted the greatness and power of the Soviet state, its leaders, and their Communist policies.

The message of this 1924 poster reads: "Long live the Young Communist League! The young are taking over the older generation's torch!"

The color red in this poster symbolizes communism and the Russian Revolution.

ANALYSIS SKILL **ANALYZING PRIMARY SOURCES**
How do you think the poster's images and message influenced Soviet teens at the time?

The Arts and Sciences
Russia has made great contributions in the arts and sciences. In the performing arts, Russia's ballet companies are world famous for their skill. In music, Peter Tchaikovsky (chy-KAWF-skee) is Russia's most famous composer. His many works include *The Nutcracker* ballet and the *1812 Overture*.

In the material arts, Russia's Fabergé eggs are priceless. Gifts for the czars, these eggs are made of precious metals and covered with gems such as emeralds and rubies. Each egg opens to reveal a tiny surprise.

In the sciences, Russia has contributed to space research. In 1957 the Soviet Union launched Sputnik, the first artificial satellite in space. Russian scientists now help work on the International Space Station.

READING CHECK **Generalizing** How did the end of the Soviet Union affect Russian culture?

SUMMARY AND PREVIEW The history of Russia, from a great empire to a Communist superpower to a new nation, has shaped its rich culture. Next, you will read about life in Russia today.

Reading Check Questions end each section of content so you can check to make sure you understand what you just studied.

Summary and Preview The Summary and Preview connects what you studied in the section to what you will study in the next section.

Section Assessment Finally, the section assessment boxes make sure that you understand the main ideas of the section. We also provide assessment practice online!

Section 2 Assessment

hmhsocialstudies.com
ONLINE QUIZ

Reviewing Ideas, Terms, and Places
1. **a. Define** Who were the **czars**?
   b. Analyze What role did the city of **Kiev** play in Russian history?
   c. Elaborate What problems and events caused the Russian Empire to decline?
2. **a. Identify** Why are Vladimir Lenin and Joseph Stalin significant in Russian history?
   b. Evaluate Do you think life in the Soviet Union was an improvement over life in the Russian empire? Why, or why not?
3. **a. Recall** What is the main religion in Russia?
   b. Summarize How has Russian culture changed since the collapse of the Soviet Union in 1991?

Critical Thinking
4. **Sequencing** Draw a chart like the one here. Use your notes to list the order of the major events leading up to the collapse of the Soviet Union.

FOCUS ON WRITING   *my* WriteSmart

5. **Considering Russia's History and Culture** Look at the locations you listed for Section 1. For the Russian locations, make notes about historical or cultural details you could include in your ad.

Features

Your book includes many features that will help you learn about geography, such as Close-up and Satellite View.

The Mississippi River Delta

From its source in Minnesota, the Mississippi River flows south across the central United States. It ends at the tip of Louisiana, which is shown here. This satellite image shows the area where the Mississippi River meets the Gulf of Mexico. This area is called a delta. A river's delta is formed from sediment that a river carries downstream to the ocean. Sediment is usually made up of rocks, soil, sand, and dead plants. Each year, the Mississippi dumps more than 400 million tons of sediment into the Gulf of Mexico.

The light blue and green areas in this image are shallow areas of sediment. The deeper water of the Gulf of Mexico is dark blue. Also, notice that much of the delta land looks fragile. This is new land that the river has built up by depositing sediment.

Making Inferences What natural hazards might people living in the Mississippi Delta experience?

The river branches out in several places here as it tries to find the shortest way to the ocean.

Satellite View See and explore the world through satellite images.

Close-up

Viking Raids

The Vikings of Scandinavia launched raids on many European settlements in the early Middle Ages. Using powerful longships, Viking warriors attacked towns and villages near coasts and rivers. Vikings even sailed as far as North America in their longships.

A large woolen sail helped increase the ship's speed.

Sometimes as many as 30 oars spanned each side of a longship.

Viking longships were designed the same at each end. As a result, warriors did not have to turn the ship around to make a quick escape.

The longship's shallow design made river travel possible and allowed Viking raiders to sail their ships ashore.

ANALYSIS SKILL **ANALYZING VISUALS**
What aspects of Viking longships might have frightened Europeans who saw them approaching?

NORTH AMERICA / Viking homeland / ASIA / EUROPE / NORTH ATLANTIC OCEAN / AFRICA

NORTHERN EUROPE **369**

Close-up These features help you see how people live and what places look like around the world.

Chapter Review

At the end of each chapter, the Chapter Review will help you review key concepts, analyze information critically, complete activities, and show what you have learned.

THE EURASIAN REPUBLICS **443**

THE EURASIAN REPUBLICS **445**

444 CHAPTER 18

Strategies for English Language Learners

Are you learning English? You can learn social studies and English at the same time. You already know a lot about social studies from knowing what's going on in the world. You can also learn English while learning social studies. Your teacher and other students will be happy to help you. Some of the ideas below will help you get ready to learn English. Some ideas will help you learn better in class and while you read. Other ideas will help you remember and use what you learn.

Get Ready to Learn

You can do these things before you go to social studies class.

Visit Your Classroom and Teacher

Go to your classroom with other students if you can. Look carefully around the room.

- Ask your teacher to tell you the names of things you do not know. You can ask, "What is this?" or "Will we use this in class?" or "What does it do?"
- Learn how to say and read the names of things you will use in class.
- Are there signs on the wall? What do they say? If you do not know, ask your teacher or other students, "What does this say? What does it mean?"
- Remember the words on signs. You may see these same words in other places.

Learn Some Social Studies Words

You will learn a lot of new words in your social studies class. Some of these new words will be social studies words. Other new words may not be social studies words but will still be important to learn.

- Ask your teacher to say and write some words you need to know.
- Ask what the words mean.
- Learn how to say and read the words.

Ask Your Teacher for Help with Reading

Your teacher can help you read your social studies book. He or she can help you learn new words that you need to know before you read.

- Your teacher might give you a list of the important words or ideas you will read or a list of questions to answer as you read.

- Your teacher might give you a graphic organizer to help you understand what you read. A graphic organizer is a drawing that shows how ideas are connected.

Look at Pictures Before You Read

Before you read your social studies book, look at the pictures. It will be easier to read the pages if you already know a little bit from looking at the pictures.

- As you look at the pictures, think about what you already know.

- If there are words with the pictures, read the words. Try to figure out the meaning of the words by what the pictures show.

Read Before Class

Your teacher may tell you what he or she will talk about tomorrow. If you read that part of the book today, you will already know some of what the teacher will say. Then it will be easier for you to understand when the teacher talks.

Before reading a section, look at the information in the Section Opener. This information introduces you to some of the words and ideas you will learn in the section.

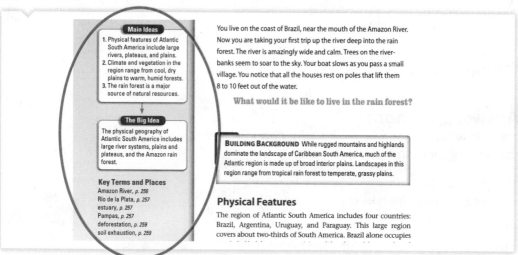

Main Ideas
1. Physical features of Atlantic South America include large rivers, plateaus, and plains.
2. Climate and vegetation in the region range from cool, dry plains to warm, humid forests.
3. The rain forest is a major source of natural resources.

The Big Idea
The physical geography of Atlantic South America includes large river systems, plains and plateaus, and the Amazon rain forest.

Key Terms and Places
Amazon River, *p. 256*
Río de la Plata, *p. 257*
estuary, *p. 257*
Pampas, *p. 257*
deforestation, *p. 259*
soil exhaustion, *p. 259*

You live on the coast of Brazil, near the mouth of the Amazon River. Now you are taking your first trip up the river deep into the rain forest. The river is amazingly wide and calm. Trees on the river-banks seem to soar to the sky. Your boat slows as you pass a small village. You notice that all the houses rest on poles that lift them 8 to 10 feet out of the water.

What would it be like to live in the rain forest?

BUILDING BACKGROUND While rugged mountains and highlands dominate the landscape of Caribbean South America, much of the Atlantic region is made up of broad interior plains. Landscapes in this region range from tropical rain forest to temperate, grassy plains.

Physical Features

The region of Atlantic South America includes four countries: Brazil, Argentina, Uruguay, and Paraguay. This large region covers about two-thirds of South America. Brazil alone occupies

Start Taking Notes Before Class

Taking notes means writing something to help you remember what you read or hear. Do not write all the words you read or hear. Write just the most important words, or make drawings.

- It can be hard to take notes when you listen. It is easier if you start your notes before class, when you read your book.

- Write down important words that you read, or draw something to help you remember important ideas. Leave lots of space on your paper.

- Then, take your notes to class. Use the same paper to take notes when you listen in class. Write more notes in the space you left.

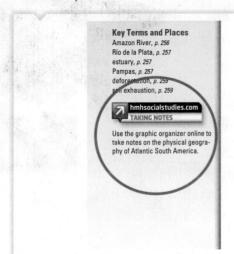

Key Terms and Places
Amazon River, *p. 256*
Rio de la Plata, *p. 257*
estuary, *p. 257*
Pampas, *p. 257*
deforestation, *p. 259*
soil exhaustion, *p. 259*

hmhsocialstudies.com
TAKING NOTES
Use the graphic organizer online to take notes on the physical geography of Atlantic South America.

region range from tropical rain forest to temperate, grassy plains.

Physical Features

The region of Atlantic South America includes four countries: Brazil, Argentina, Uruguay, and Paraguay. This large region covers about two-thirds of South America. Brazil alone occupies nearly half of the continent. Most of the physical features found in South America are found in these four countries.

Major River Systems

The world's largest river system, the Amazon, flows eastward across northern Brazil. The **Amazon River** is about 4,000 miles (6,440 km) long. It extends from the Andes Mountains in Peru to the Atlantic Ocean. Hundreds of tributaries flow into it, draining an area that includes parts of most South American countries.

Because of its huge drainage area, the Amazon carries more water than any other river in the world. About 20 percent of the water that runs off Earth's surface flows down the Amazon. Where it meets the Atlantic, this freshwater lowers the salt level of the Atlantic for more than 100 miles (160 km) from shore.

Get Ready to Ask Questions

You might have questions about what you read before class.

- First, write down your question or words that you do not understand.
- Practice your question.
- Bring your question to class. Listen carefully when the teacher talks about the same thing as your question. Your teacher may answer the question.
- If you still do not have an answer, raise your hand. Ask the question you wrote and practiced.

Get Ready to Answer Questions

Learn these question words: *what, where, when, who, why, how much, is it, will it.* Learn how to answer questions that use each word.

- *What*: Tell the name of a thing.
- *What will happen*, *what happened*: Tell how something changes.
- *Where*: Tell a place.
- *When*: Tell a time (you can also say before or after something).
- *Who*: Tell a person. Your teacher might ask, "Who can tell me . . .?" That means, "Do you know the answer?" If you do, raise your hand.
- *How much*: Tell an amount.
- *Why*: Tell what made something happen, or explain a reason.
- *Is it* or *Will it*: Answer yes or no. You can also give a reason for your answer.

If you do not know the exact words to answer a question, try using words you know to describe your ideas.

While You Learn

You can do these things in your social studies class.

Use What You Know

When you hear or read about something new, think about what you already know.

If a new word sounds like a word you already know, maybe the two words mean almost the same thing. Maybe you already know something about a new idea. Use what you know to help you understand new words and ideas.

Talk to your teacher and classmates about how what you already know relates to what you are learning.

Take Notes During Class

As you learn new words and ideas in class, listen carefully to your teacher and take notes. The type of notes you take will depend on the topic you are learning about. Here are some suggestions:

Write down the main ideas that your teacher explains.

- Write down important words and their meanings.
- Make lists of characteristics, causes, effects, and examples.
- Number the steps in a process.
- Draw pictures.

Put a question mark next to any notes that you do not understand.

Understand Instructions

Instructions tell you how to do something. They are sometimes called directions. You need to follow instructions many times in social studies class. Sometimes your teacher says the instructions. Sometimes you need to read the instructions.

Some instructions have some parts, called steps. Sometimes the teacher or book will use numbers (1, 2, 3 . . .) to tell you the order of steps.

Other times, instructions use words. Learn the words that tell you when to do things: first, then, next, before, after, while, last. Listen and look for these words in instructions. Use them to help you know when to do things.

You can also use these words to give other people instructions. You can use them to write or tell about something you did.

Learn Some Signal Words

Signal words are words that show how ideas are connected. Learn the words below, look for them as you read, and listen for them when people are speaking.

- These signal words show how things are the same or almost the same: *and, also, another, like.*

- These signal words show how things are different: *but, however, although, instead.*

- These signal words show how one thing causes another: *so, because, as a result.*

Look for Different Kinds of Sentences

There are four main kinds of sentences. They are listed below. Look for these kinds of sentences when you are reading. Listen for them when someone else is speaking. Practice using all types of sentences when you are speaking.

Sentence type	Example
Statements end with a period and tell you something.	Thomas Jefferson wrote the Declaration of Independence.
Commands tell you to do something. You will see these sentences when there is something for you to do in the book or when you are doing a project.	State who wrote the Declaration of Independence.
Questions end with a question mark. When you are listening, listen for the speaker to pause after they ask a question. The pause gives you time to think about the question or to give an answer to the question.	Who wrote the Declaration of Independence?
Exclamations show excitement or surprise and end with an exclamation point.	The colonies declared their independence!

Get Help If You Do Not Understand

If you don't understand something that you hear or read, get help.

- Ask your teacher or another student. Raise your hand and ask in class, or wait until the teacher is finished talking.

- If you do not understand a word, try to say the word. Then ask, "What does that word mean?"

- If you do not know how to do something, ask, "How do I do this?"

- If you do not understand an idea or picture, tell what you do know. Then ask about the part you do not understand.

Answer Questions

When your teacher asks you a question, you need to answer. Here are some things that can help you:

- Listen carefully to the question. If you do not understand the words, you can ask, "Could you repeat the question?" or "Can you say that more slowly?"

- Listen for the question word. It tells you what kind of answer to give.

- If the teacher is pointing at something, the question is probably about that thing. You can talk about that thing in your answer.

- Remember what the teacher said before the question. The question might be about what the teacher said. Maybe you can use some of the teacher's words in your answer.

- If you do not know an answer, tell the teacher. You can say, "I don't know" or "I did not understand that very well" or "I don't remember that."

Talk in Groups

In social studies class, you often work with other students. You need to understand what your group should do.

- Read instructions if you have them. You can ask, "Can I have some more time to read?"

- If you do not understand the instructions, you can ask, "Can you help me understand this?"

- Talk about the instructions after you read. Tell what you can do. Ask the other students what they will do.

- As you work, you can ask your partner for help. You can say, "What do we do next?"

- Be sure to help your partner. You can ask, "What can I do to help?"

- If you have an idea, you can say, "I think we should do it this way" or "I have an idea."

Remember and Use What You Learn

You can do these things to help you learn important social studies words and ideas. Do them before class, in class, or after class.

Say It Again (and Again and Again)

One way to learn new words is to repeat them, or say them many times.

- First, make sure that you can say the word correctly.

- Be sure you know what the word means, too. Ask a friend or your teacher if you need to say the word differently or if you do not have the right meaning.

- When you can say the word correctly and know what it means, say the word several times. With a partner, take turns saying the word and telling each other the meaning.

- You will remember better if you say the meaning in your own words. You will remember even better if you say your own sentence that uses the word. Try to say a different sentence each time you repeat.

Use Flash Cards
Flash cards help you learn new words.

- To make flash cards, use some pieces of paper that are all the same size. What words do you need to learn?

- Write one word on a piece of paper. Turn the paper over. Write the meaning of the word. Use your own words or draw pictures to help you remember.

- Write the other words and their meanings on other pieces of paper.

To use flash cards, look at a word. Say what you think it means. Check the back of the paper for the word's meaning. Do this with all your words.

- If you get the meaning right, you may not need to look at that card again.

- If you get some wrong, look at them again and again.

You can use flash cards alone or with a partner.

Tell Somebody
Ask a friend or a person in your family to help you learn. Have the person ask you a question. If you need to learn some social studies words, have him or her ask you what the words mean.

If you need to remember what something in social studies means, have the person ask you. Then use your own words to tell what you know from your book or class. Tell the person what the words mean.

Answer all the person's questions. Helping that person understand helps you understand and remember too.

Make a Picture
Sometimes a picture can help you remember better than words can. You can draw pictures when you take notes. Draw your own picture, or use a graphic organizer.

There are many different graphic organizers. Here are some examples of graphic organizers used in this book.

A **Venn diagram** (Figure 1.A.) shows how two things are the same and how they are different.

- Write how they are different in the two circles.

- Write how they are the same where the two circles come together.

You might be asked to complete a Venn diagram in this book.

A **concept map** (Figure 1.B.) shows how information is connected. Write an important word or idea in the big circle. Draw lines to smaller circles. In the smaller circles, write words that tell more about the idea in the big circle.

Figure 1.A. **Venn Diagram**

Figure 1.B. **Concept Map**

Summarize

Summarizing can help you remember what you read or hear. A summary includes only the most important ideas.

- You can summarize what you read.
- You can summarize what your teacher says in class.

When you summarize, write or say the most important ideas using your own words. You will remember better if you use your own words.

This book has a Visual Summary at the end of every chapter. The Visual Summary has important pictures and ideas from the chapter. Reading the Visual Summary will help you remember better.

Scavenger Hunt

Are you ready to explore the world of geography? *Contemporary World Studies: People, Places, and Societies* is your ticket to this exciting world. Before you begin your journey, complete this scavenger hunt to get to know your book and discover what's inside.

On a separate sheet of paper, fill in the blanks to complete each sentence below. In each answer, one letter will be in a yellow box. When you have answered every question, copy these letters in order to reveal the answer to the question at the bottom of the page.

1 The second key term listed on page 472 is ☐☐☐☐☐☐ .

5 In the English and Spanish Glossary, the second word in the definition of cartography is ☐☐☐☐☐☐☐ .

2 On page 614, the main ideas are followed by The ☐☐☐ Idea. How do the main ideas connect to what is covered in this section?

6 The Skills lesson on page 116 is called ☐☐☐☐☐☐☐ a Problem. What are the four types of skills lessons shown at the top of the page?

3 The title of the map on page 563 is East Africa: ☐☐☐☐☐☐☐☐ .

7 The subject of the Writing Workshop on page 128 is ☐☐☐☐☐☐☐☐☐☐ a Process.

4 The Case Study feature on pages 394–395 is called The Breakup of ☐☐☐☐☐☐☐☐☐☐☐ . What other features can you find in the book?

Fact!

There are about 7 ☐☐☐☐☐☐☐ people in the world today.

Introduction to Geography

Deserts

Huge deserts, such as the Sahara in North Africa, are visible from space and appear yellow and brown.

Oceans

About 71 percent of Earth's surface is covered by vast amounts of salt water, which form the world's oceans.

665.00

Introduction to Geography

Explore the Satellite Image Human-made machines that orbit Earth, called satellites, send back images of our planet like this one. What can you learn about Earth from studying this satellite image?

Frozen Lands

Earth's icy poles are frozen year-round and appear a brilliant white from space. These frozen lands contain much of Earth's freshwater.

A Geographer's World

Essential Question *myNotebook*

How does geography help us understand our world?

Texas Essential Knowledge and Skills (TEKS)

2A, 3A, 3B, 4E, 6C, 21B, 21C, 22A, 22D

FOCUS ON READING AND WRITING *my WriteSmart*

Using Prior Knowledge Prior knowledge is what you already know about a subject. Before you read a chapter, review the chapter and section titles. Then make a list of what you already know. Later, you can compare your prior knowledge with what you learned from the chapter. **See the lesson Using Prior Knowledge on page 23.**

Writing a Job Description Geographers are people who study geography, but what is it exactly that they do? As you read this chapter, you will learn about the work that geographers do. Then you will write a job description that could be included in a career-planning guide. Use the annotation tools in your eBook to gather information for your assignment.

Studying the World Exploring the world takes people to exciting and interesting places.

ANALYSIS SKILL ANALYZING VISUALS

This village is in the country of Nepal. It rests high in the Himalayas, the highest mountains in the world.

What is the land around the village like? How can you tell that people live in this area?

Human Geography
Geography is also the study of people. It asks where people live, what they eat, what they wear, and even what kinds of animals they keep.

Physical Geography Geography is the study of the world's land features, such as this windswept rock formation in Arizona.

3

Studying Geography

TEKS 3B, 21B, 21C, 22A, 22D

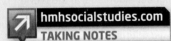
If YOU lived there...

You have just moved to Miami, Florida, from your old home in Pennsylvania. Everything seems very different—from the weather and the trees to the way people dress and talk. Even the streets and buildings look different. One day you get an e-mail from a friend at your old school. "What's it like living there?" he asks.

How will you describe your new home?

BUILDING BACKGROUND Often, when you are telling someone about a place they have never been, what you are describing is the place's geography. What the place looks like, what kind of weather it has, and how people live there are all parts of its geography.

What Is Geography?

Think about the place where you live. What does the land look like? Are there tall mountains nearby, or is the land so flat that you can see for miles? Is the ground covered with bright green grass and trees, or is the area part of a sandy desert?

Now think about the weather in your area. What is it like? Does it get really hot in the summer? Do you see snow every winter? How much does it rain? Do tornadoes ever strike?

Finally, think about the people who live in your town or city. Do they live mostly in apartments or houses? Do most people own cars, or do they get around town on buses or trains? What kinds of jobs do adults in your town have? Were most of the people you know born in your town, or did they move there?

The things that you have been thinking about are part of your area's geography. **Geography** is the study of the world, its people, and the landscapes they create. To a geographer, a place's **landscape** is all the human and physical features that make it unique. When they study the world's landscapes, geographers ask questions much like the ones you just asked yourself.

Geography as a Science

Many of the questions that geographers ask deal with how the world works. They want to know what causes mountains to form and what creates tornadoes. To answer questions like these, geographers have to think and act like scientists.

As scientists, geographers look at data, or information, that they gather about places. Gathering data can sometimes lead geographers to fascinating places. They might have to crawl deep into caves or climb tall mountains to make observations and take measurements. At other times, geographers study sets of images collected by satellites orbiting high above Earth.

However geographers gather their data, they have to study it carefully. Like other scientists, geographers must examine their findings in great detail before they can learn what all the information means.

Geography as a Social Science

Not everything that geographers study can be measured in numbers, however. Some geographers study people and their lives. For example, they may ask why countries change their governments or why people in a place speak a certain language. This kind of information cannot be measured.

Because it deals with people and how they live, geography is sometimes called a social science. A **social science** is a field that studies people and the relationships among them.

The geographers who study people do not dig in caves or climb mountains. Instead, they visit places and talk to the people who live there. They want to learn about people's lives and communities.

READING CHECK **Analyzing** In what ways is geography both a science and a social science?

What Is Geography?

Geography is the study of the world, its people, and the landscapes they create. To study a place's geography, we look at its physical and human features.

The physical features of Algeria include huge deserts full of tall sand dunes.

Many Algerians live in small villages like this one. The village is one of Algeria's human features.

Together, Algeria's physical and human features create the country's landscape.

ANALYSIS SKILL **ANALYZING VISUALS**

What is the landscape of this part of Algeria like?

Looking at the World

Whether they study volcanoes and storms or people and cities, geographers have to look carefully at the world around them. To fully understand how the world works, geographers often look at places at three different levels.

Local Level

Some geographers study issues at a local level. They ask the same types of questions we asked at the beginning of this chapter: How do people in a town or community live? What is the local government like? How do the people who live there get around? What do they eat?

By asking these questions, geographers can figure out why people live and work the way they do. They can also help people improve their lives. For example, they can help town leaders figure out the best place to build new schools, shopping centers, or sports complexes. They can also help the people who live in the city or town plan for future changes.

Regional Level

Sometimes, though, geographers want to study a bigger chunk of the world. To do this, they divide the world into regions. A **region** is a part of the world that has one or more common features that distinguish it from surrounding areas.

Some regions are defined by physical characteristics such as mountain ranges, climates, or plants native to the area. As a result, these types of regions are often easy to identify. The Rocky Mountains of the western United States, for example, make up a physical region. Another example of this kind of region is the Sahara, a huge desert in northern Africa.

Other regions may not be so easy to define, however. These regions are based on the human characteristics of a place, such as language, religion, or history. A place in which most people share these kinds of characteristics can also be seen as a region. For example, most people in Scandinavia, a region in northern Europe, speak similar languages and practice the same religion.

Looking at the World

Geographers look at the world at many levels. At each level, they ask different questions and discover different types of information. By putting information gathered at different levels together, geographers can better understand a place and its role in the world.

ANALYZING VISUALS Based on these photos, what are some questions a geographer might ask about London?

Local Level This busy neighborhood in London, England, is a local area. A geographer here might study local foods, housing, or clothing.

Regions come in all shapes and sizes. Some are small, like the neighborhood called Chinatown in San Francisco. Other regions are huge, like the Americas. This huge region includes two continents, North America and South America. The size of the area does not matter, as long as the area shares some characteristics. These shared characteristics define the region.

Geographers divide the world into regions for many reasons. The world is a huge place and home to billions of people. Studying so large an area can be extremely difficult. Dividing the world into regions makes it easier to study. A small area is much easier to examine than a large area.

Other geographers study regions to see how people interact with one another. For example, they may study a city such as London, England, to learn how the city's people govern themselves. Then they can compare what they learn about one region to what they learn about another region. In this way, they can learn more about life and landscapes in both places.

Global Level

Sometimes geographers do not want to study the world just at a regional level. Instead they want to learn how people interact globally, or around the world. To do so, geographers ask how events and ideas from one region of the world affect people in other regions. In other words, they study the world on a global level.

Geographers who study the world on a global level try to find relationships among people who live far apart. They may, for example, examine the products that a country exports to see how those products are used in other countries.

In recent decades, worldwide trade and communication have increased. As a result, we need to understand how our actions affect people around the world. Through their studies, geographers provide us with information that helps us figure out how to live in a rapidly changing world.

READING CHECK **Finding Main Ideas** At what levels do geographers study the world?

Regional Level As a major city, London is also a region. At this level, a geographer might study the city's population or transportation systems.

Global Level London is one of the world's main financial centers. Here a geographer might study how London's economy affects the world.

Geographers use many tools to study the world. Each tool provides part of the information a geographer needs to learn what a place is like.

ANALYZING VISUALS What information could you learn from each of these tools?

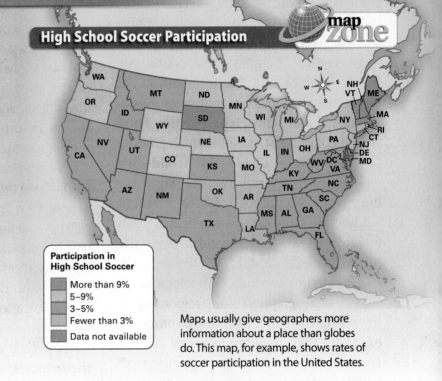

High School Soccer Participation

Participation in High School Soccer

- More than 9%
- 5–9%
- 3–5%
- Fewer than 3%
- Data not available

Maps usually give geographers more information about a place than globes do. This map, for example, shows rates of soccer participation in the United States.

A geographer can use a globe to see where a place, such as the United States, is located.

The Geographer's Tools

Have you ever seen a carpenter building or repairing a house? If so, you know that builders need many tools to do their jobs correctly. In the same way, geographers need many tools to study the world.

Maps and Globes

FOCUS ON READING
What do you already know about maps and globes?

The tools that geographers use most often in their work are maps and globes. A **map** is a flat drawing that shows all or part of Earth's surface. A **globe** is a spherical, or ball-shaped, model of the entire planet.

Both maps and globes show what the world looks like. They can show where mountains, deserts, and oceans are. They can also identify and describe the world's countries and major cities.

There are, however, major differences between maps and globes. Because a globe is spherical like Earth, it can show the world as it really is.

A map, though, is flat. It is not possible to show a spherical area perfectly on a flat surface. To understand what this means, think about an orange. If you took the peel off of an orange, could you make it lie completely flat? No, you could not, unless you stretched or tore the peel first.

The same principle is true with maps. To draw Earth on a flat surface, people have to distort, or alter, some details. For example, places on a map might look to be farther apart than they really are, or their shapes or sizes might be changed slightly.

Still, maps have many advantages over globes. Flat maps are easier to work with than globes. Also, it is easier to show small areas like cities on maps than on globes.

In addition, maps usually show more information than globes. Because globes are more expensive to make, they do not usually show anything more than where places are and what features they have.

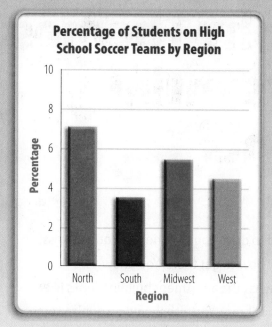

Percentage of Students on High School Soccer Teams by Region

Charts and graphs are also tools geographers can use to study information. They are often used when geographers want to compare numbers, such as the number of students who play soccer in each region of the country.

Maps, on the other hand, can show all sorts of information. Besides showing land use and cities, maps can include a great deal of information about a place. A map might show what languages people speak or where their ancestors came from. Maps like the one on the opposite page can even show how many students in an area play soccer.

Satellite Images

Maps and globes are not the only tools that geographers use in their work. As you have already read, many geographers study information gathered by satellites.

Much of the information gathered by these satellites is in the form of images. Geographers can study these images to see what an area looks like from above Earth. Satellites also collect information that we cannot see from the planet's surface. The information gathered by satellites helps geographers make accurate maps.

Other Geographic Tools

Geographers also use many other tools. To depict aspects of various countries and world regions geographers create maps, graphs, charts, databases, and models. They also use these tools to gather data and compare various world regions. In some cases, the best tools a geographer can use are a notebook and tape recorder to take notes while talking to people. Armed with the proper tools, geographers learn about the world's people and places.

READING CHECK **Summarizing** What are some of the geographer's basic tools?

SUMMARY AND PREVIEW Geography is the study of the world, its people, and its landscapes. In the next section, you will learn about two systems geographers use to organize their studies.

Section 1 Assessment

hmhsocialstudies.com
ONLINE QUIZ

Reviewing Ideas, Terms, and Places

1. **a. Define** What is **geography**?
   b. Explain Why is geography considered a science?
2. **a. Identify** What is a **region**? Give two examples.
   b. Elaborate What global issues do geographers study?
3. **a. Describe** How do geographers use satellite images?
   b. Compare and Contrast How are maps and globes similar? How are they different?

Critical Thinking

4. **Summarizing** Draw three ovals like the ones shown here. Use your notes to fill the ovals with information about geography, geographers, and their tools.

FOCUS ON WRITING

*my*WriteSmart

5. **Describing a Field** Based on what you have learned, what might attract people to work in geography? In your notebook, list some details about geography that might make people interested in working in the field.

Geography Themes and Essential Elements

 TEKS 3A, 3B, 6C, 21B, 21C, 22A, 22D

What You Will Learn...

Main Ideas

1. The five themes of geography help us organize our studies of the world.
2. The six essential elements of geography highlight some of the subject's most important ideas.

The Big Idea

Geographers have created two different but related systems for organizing geographic studies.

Key Terms

absolute location, *p. 12*
relative location, *p. 12*
environment, *p. 12*

hmhsocialstudies.com
TAKING NOTES

Use the graphic organizer online to take notes on the five themes and six essential elements of geography.

If **YOU** lived there...

Your older sister has offered to drive you to a friend's house across town, but she doesn't know how to get there. You know your friend's street address and what the apartment building looks like. You know it's near the public library. You also would recognize some landmarks in the neighborhood, such as the video store and the supermarket.

What might help your sister find the house?

BUILDING BACKGROUND Like drivers, geographers have to know where places are in order to study them. An area's location is only one of the aspects that geographers study, though. In fact, it is only one of the five themes that geographers use to describe a place.

The Five Themes of Geography

Have you ever gone to a Fourth of July party with a patriotic theme? If so, you probably noticed that almost everything at the party was related to that theme. For example, you may have seen American flags and decorations based on the flag's stars and stripes. You may have seen clothes that were red, white, and blue or heard patriotic music being played. Chances are that almost everything at the party reflected the theme of patriotism.

Like party planners, geographers use themes in their work. Geographers do not study parties, of course, but they do note common themes in their studies. Just as a party's theme is reflected in nearly every aspect of the party, these geography themes can be applied to nearly everything that geographers study. The five major themes of geography are Location, Place, Human-Environment Interaction, Movement, and Regions.

The Five Themes of Geography

Geographers use five major themes, or ideas, to organize and guide their studies.

Location The theme of location describes where something is. The mountain shown above, Mount Rainier, is in west-central Washington.

Place Place describes the features that make a site unique. For example, Washington, D.C., is our nation's capital and has many great monuments.

UNITED STATES

Regions Regions are areas that share common characteristics. The Mojave Desert, shown here, is defined by its distinctive climate and plant life.

Movement This theme looks at how and why people and things move. Airports like this one in Dallas, Texas, help people move around the world.

Human-Environment Interaction People interact with their environments in many ways. Some, like this man in Florida, use the land to grow crops.

ANALYSIS SKILL | **ANALYZING VISUALS**

Which of the five themes deals with the relationships between people and their surroundings?

Location

Every point on Earth has a location, a description of where it is. This location can be expressed in many ways. Sometimes a site's location is expressed in specific, or absolute, terms, such as an address. For example, the White House is located at 1600 Pennsylvania Avenue in the city of Washington, D.C. A specific description like this one is called an **absolute location**. Other times, the site's location is expressed in general terms. For example, Canada is north of the United States. This general description of where a place lies is called its **relative location**.

Place

Another theme, Place, is closely related to Location. However, Place does not refer simply to where an area is. It refers to the area's landscape, the features that define the area and make it different from other places. Such features could include land, climate, and people. Together, they give a place its own character.

Human-Environment Interaction

FOCUS ON READING
What do you know about environments?

In addition to looking at the features of places, geographers examine how those features interact. In particular, they want to understand how people interact with their environment—how people and their physical environment affect each other. An area's **environment** includes its land, water, climate, plants, and animals.

People interact with their environment every day in all sorts of ways. They clear forests to plant crops, level fields to build cities, and dam rivers to prevent floods. At the same time, physical environments affect how people live. People in cold areas, for example, build houses with thick walls and wear heavy clothing to keep warm. People who live near oceans look for ways to protect themselves from storms.

Movement

People are constantly moving. They move within cities, between cities, and between countries. Geographers want to know why and how people move. For example, they ask if people are moving to find work or to live in a more pleasant area. Geographers also study the roads and routes that make movement so common.

Regions

You have already learned how geographers divide the world into many regions to help the study of geography. Creating regions also makes it easier to compare places. Comparisons help geographers learn why each place has developed the way it has.

READING CHECK **Finding Main Ideas** What are the five themes of geography?

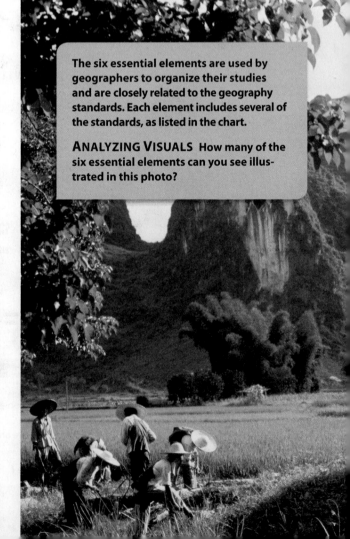

The six essential elements are used by geographers to organize their studies and are closely related to the geography standards. Each element includes several of the standards, as listed in the chart.

ANALYZING VISUALS How many of the six essential elements can you see illustrated in this photo?

The Six Essential Elements

The five themes of geography are not the only system geographers use to study the world. They also use a system of standards and essential **elements**. Together, these standards and essential elements identify the most important ideas in the study of geography. These ideas are expressed in two lists.

The first list is the national geography standards. This is a list of 18 basic ideas that are central to the study of geography. These standards are listed in black type on the chart below.

The essential elements are based on the geography standards. Each element is a big idea that links several standards together. The six essential elements are The World in Spatial Terms, Places and Regions, Physical Systems, Human Systems, Environment and Society, and The Uses of Geography. On the chart, they are shown in purple.

Read through that list again. Do you see any similarities between geography's six essential elements and its five themes? You probably do. The two systems are very similar because the six essential elements build on the five themes.

ACADEMIC VOCABULARY
element part

The Essential Elements and Geography Standards

The World in Spatial Terms

- How to use maps and other geographic representations, tools, and technologies to acquire, process, and report information from a spatial perspective
- How to use mental maps to organize information about people, places, and environments in a spatial context
- How to analyze the spatial organization of people, places, and environments on Earth's surface

Places and Regions

- The physical and human characteristics of places
- How people create regions to interpret Earth's complexity
- How culture and experience influence people's perceptions of places and regions

Physical Systems

- The physical processes that shape the patterns of Earth's surface
- The characteristics and spatial distribution of ecosystems on Earth's surface

Human Systems

- The characteristics, distributions, and migration of human populations on Earth's surface
- The characteristics, distribution, and complexity of Earth's cultural mosaics
- The patterns and networks of economic interdependence on Earth's surface
- The processes, patterns, and functions of human settlement
- How the forces of cooperation and conflict among people influence the division and control of Earth's surface

Environment and Society

- How human actions modify the physical environment
- How physical systems affect human systems
- Changes that occur in the meaning, use, distribution, and importance of resources

The Uses of Geography

- How to apply geography to interpret the past
- How to apply geography to interpret the present and plan for the future

BOOK
Geography for Life

The six essential elements were first outlined in a book called Geography for Life. *In that book, the authors—a diverse group of geographers and teachers from around the United States—explained why the study of geography is important.*

❝Geography *is* for life in every sense of that expression: lifelong, life-sustaining, and life-enhancing. Geography is a field of study that enables us to find answers to questions about the world around us—about where things are and how and why they got there.❞

❝Geography focuses attention on exciting and interesting things, on fascinating people and places, on things worth knowing because they are absorbing and because knowing about them lets humans make better-informed and, therefore, wiser decisions.❞

❝With a strong grasp of geography, people are better equipped to solve issues at not only the local level but also the global level.❞

–from *Geography for Life*,
by the Geography Education Standards Project

ANALYSIS SKILL **ANALYZING PRIMARY SOURCES**

Why do the authors of these passages think that people should study geography?

For example, the element Places and Regions combines two of the five themes of geography—Place and Regions. Also, the element called Environment and Society deals with many of the same issues as the theme Human-Environment Interaction.

There are also some basic differences between the essential elements and the themes. For example, the last element, The Uses of Geography, deals with issues not covered in the five themes. This element examines how people can use geography to plan the landscapes in which they live.

Throughout this book, you will notice references to both the themes and the essential elements. As you read, use these themes and elements to help you organize your own study of geography.

READING CHECK **Summarizing** What are the six essential elements of geography?

SUMMARY AND PREVIEW You have just learned about the themes and elements of geography. Next, you will explore the branches into which the field is divided.

Section 2 Assessment

hmhsocialstudies.com
ONLINE QUIZ

Reviewing Ideas, Terms, and Places

1. a. Locate Choose a city in the United States to locate on a globe. Use latitude and longitude to determine the **absolute location** of the city.
b. Contrast How are the themes of Location and Place different?
c. Elaborate How does using the five themes help geographers understand the places they study?
2. a. Identify Which of the five themes of geography is associated with airports, highways, and the migration of people from one place to another?
b. Explain How are the geography standards and the six essential elements related?
c. Compare How are the six essential elements similar to the five themes of geography?

Critical Thinking

3. Categorizing Draw a chart like the one below. Use your notes to list the five themes of geography, explain each of the themes, and list one feature of your city or town that relates to each.

Theme					
Explanation					
Feature					

FOCUS ON WRITING

my WriteSmart

4. Including Themes and Essential Elements The five themes and six essential elements are central to a geographer's job. How will you mention them in your job description? Write down some ideas.

Posing and Answering Geographic Questions

Learn

Geographers pose and answer geographic questions to figure out how the world works. To better understand location, geographic patterns, and geographic distributions, a geographer might pose and answer:

- Where is it located?
- Why is it there?
- What is significant about its location?
- How is its location related to the location of other people, places, and environments?

The Environment of Texas

Legend:
- Grassland or prairie
- Forest
- Savannah
- Cattle ranching
- Cotton farming
- City

Practice

Use the map of Texas at right to answer the geographic questions below.

1. Where are forests located in Texas?

2. Why do you think Texas farmers are growing cotton in the regions shown on the map?

3. What do you think is significant about the location of cattle ranches in Texas?

4. How is the location of grasslands and prairie related to the location of cattle ranching?

Apply

In addition to maps, you can use graphs, charts, models, and databases to show geographic information. Look at the bar graph in Section 1 of this chapter titled, "Percentage of Students on High School Soccer Teams by Region." Pose and answer the four geographic questions listed above about each region of the United States shown in the graph. What geographic distributions or patterns of high school soccer participation in the United States does the graph show?

The Branches of Geography

 TEKS 2A, 3A, 21B, 21C, 22A, 22D

What You Will Learn...

Main Ideas

1. Physical geography is the study of landforms, water bodies, and other physical features.
2. Human geography focuses on people, their cultures, and the landscapes they create.
3. Other branches of geography examine specific aspects of the physical or human world.

The Big Idea

Geography is divided into two main branches—physical and human geography.

Key Terms

physical geography, *p. 16*
human geography, *p. 18*
cartography, *p. 19*
meteorology, *p. 20*

hmhsocialstudies.com
TAKING NOTES

Use the graphic organizer online to take notes on the branches of geography.

If YOU lived there...

You are talking to two friends about the vacations their families will take this summer. One friend says that his family is going to the Grand Canyon. He is very excited about seeing the spectacular landscapes in and around the canyon. Your other friend's family is going to visit Nashville, Tennessee. She is looking forward to trying new foods at the city's restaurants and touring its museums.

Which vacation sounds more interesting? Why?

BUILDING BACKGROUND Geography is the study of the world and its features. Some features are physical, like the Grand Canyon. Others are human, like restaurants and museums. The main branches of geography focus on these types of features.

Physical Geography

Think about a jigsaw puzzle. Seen as a whole, the puzzle shows a pretty or interesting picture. To see that picture, though, you have to put all the puzzle pieces together. Before you assemble them, the pieces do not give you a clear idea of what the puzzle will look like when it is assembled. After all, each piece contains only a tiny portion of the overall image.

In many ways, geography is like a huge puzzle. It is made up of many branches, or divisions. Each of these branches focuses on a single part of the world. Viewed separately, none of these branches shows us the whole world. Together, however, the many branches of geography improve our understanding of our planet and its people.

Geography's two main branches are physical geography and human geography. Geographers identify and locate major physical and human geographic features of various places and regions in the world. The first branch, **physical geography**, is the study of the world's physical geographic features—its landforms, bodies of water, climates, soils, and plants.

Physical Geography

The study of Earth's physical geographic features, including rivers, mountains, oceans, weather, and other features, such as Victoria Falls in southern Africa

Human Geography

The study of Earth's people, including their ways of life, homes, cities, beliefs, and customs, like those of these children in Malawi, a country in central Africa

Geography

The study of Earth's physical and human geographic features

The Physical World

What does it mean to say that physical geography is the study of physical geographic features? Physical geographers want to know all about the different features found on our planet. They want to know where mountain ranges are, how rivers flow across the landscape, and why different amounts of rain fall from place to place.

More importantly, however, physical geographers want to know what causes the different shapes on Earth. They want to know why mountain ranges rise up where they do and what causes rivers to flow in certain directions. They also want to know why various parts of the world have very different weather and climate patterns.

To answer these questions, physical geographers take detailed measurements. They study the heights of mountains and the temperatures of places. To track any changes that occur over time, physical geographers keep careful records of all the information they collect.

Uses of Physical Geography

Earth is made up of hundreds of types of physical geographic features. Without a complete understanding of what these features are and the effect they have on the world's people and landscapes, we cannot fully understand our world. This is the major reason that geographers study the physical world—to learn how it works.

There are also other, more specific reasons for studying physical geography, though. Studying the changes that take place on our planet can help us prepare to live with those changes. For example, knowing what causes volcanoes to erupt can help us predict eruptions. Knowing what causes terrible storms can help us prepare for them. In this way, the work of physical geographers helps us adjust to the dangers and changes of our world.

READING CHECK **Analyzing** What are some features in your area that a physical geographer might study?

Eratosthenes

(c. 276–c. 194 BC)

Did you know that geography is over 2,000 years old? Actually, the study of the world is even older than that, but the first person ever to use the word *geography* lived then. His name was Eratosthenes (er-uh-TAHS-thuh-neez), and he was a Greek scientist and librarian. With no modern instruments of any kind, Eratosthenes figured out how large Earth is. He also drew a map that showed all of the lands that the Greeks knew about. Because of his many contributions to the field, Eratosthenes has been called the Father of Geography.

Generalizing Why is Eratosthenes called the Father of Geography?

Human Geography

The physical world is only one part of the puzzle of geography. People are also part of the world. **Human geography** is the study of the world's human geographic features—people, communities, and landscapes. It is the second major branch of geography.

The Human World

Put simply, human geographers study the world's people, past and present. They look at where people live and why. They ask why some parts of the world have more people than others, and why some places have almost no people at all.

Human geographers also study what people do. What jobs do people have? What crops do they grow? What makes them move from place to place? These are the types of questions that geographers ask about people around the world.

Because people's lives are so different around the world, no one can study every aspect of human geography. As a result, human geographers often specialize in a smaller area of study. Some may choose to study only the people and landscapes in a certain region. For example, a geographer may study only the lives of people who live in West Africa.

Other geographers choose not to limit their studies to one place. Instead, they may choose to examine only one aspect of people's lives. For example, a geographer could study only economics, politics, or city life. However, that geographer may compare economic patterns in various parts of the world to see how they differ.

Uses of Human Geography

Although every culture is different, people around the world have some common needs. All people need food and water. All people need shelter. All people need to deal with other people in order to survive.

Human geographers study how people in various places address their needs. They look at the foods people eat and the types of governments they form. The knowledge they gather can help us better understand people in other cultures. Sometimes this type of understanding can help people improve their landscapes and situations.

On a smaller scale, human geographers can help people design their cities and towns. By understanding where people go and what they need, geographers can help city planners place roads, shopping malls, and schools. Geographers also study the effect people have on the world. As a result, they often work with private groups and government agencies who want to protect the environment.

READING CHECK **Summarizing** What do human geographers study?

Other Fields of Geography

Physical geography and human geography are the two largest branches of the subject, but they are not the only ones. Many other fields of geography exist, each one devoted to studying one aspect of the world.

Most of these fields are smaller, more specialized areas of either physical or human geography. For example, economic geography—the study of how people make and spend money—is a branch of human geography. Another specialized branch of human geography is urban geography, the study of cities and how people live in them. Physical geography also includes many fields, such as the study of climates. Other fields of physical geography are the studies of soils and plants.

Cartography

One key field of geography is **cartography**, the science of making maps. You have already seen how important maps are to the study of geography. Without maps, geographers would not be able to study where things are in the world.

In the past, maps were always drawn by hand. Many were not very accurate. Today, though, most maps are made using computers and satellite images. Through advances in mapmaking, we can make accurate maps on almost any scale, from the whole world to a single neighborhood, and keep them up to date. These maps are not only used by geographers. For example, road maps are used by people who are planning long trips.

CONNECTING TO Technology

Computer Mapping

In the past, maps were drawn by hand. Making a map was a slow process. Even the simplest map took a long time to make. Today, however, cartographers have access to tools people in the past—even people who lived just 50 years ago—never imagined. The most important of these tools are computers.

Computers allow us to make maps quickly and easily. In addition, they let us make new types of maps that people could not make in the past.

The map shown here, for example, was drawn on a computer. It shows the number of computer users in the United States who were connected to the Internet on a particular day. Each of the lines that rises off of the map represents a city in which people were using the Internet. The color of the line indicates the number of computer users in that city. As you can see, this data resulted in a very complex map.

Making such a map required cartographers to sort through huge amounts of complex data. Such sorting would not have been possible without computers.

Contrasting How are today's maps different from those created in the past?

Meteorology is the study of weather. This meteorologist is using computers to follow and predict the movement of a powerful storm.

Meteorology

Have you ever seen the weather report on television? If so, you have seen the results of another branch of geography. This branch is called **meteorology**, the study of weather and what causes it.

Meteorologists study weather patterns in a particular area. Then they use the information to predict what the weather will be like in the coming days. Their work helps people plan what to wear and what to do on any given day. At the same time, their work can save lives by predicting the arrival of terrible storms. These predictions are among the most visible ways in which the work of geographers affects our lives every day.

READING CHECK **Finding Main Ideas** What are some major branches of geography?

SUMMARY AND PREVIEW In this section, you learned about two main branches of geography, physical and human. In the next chapter, you will learn more about the physical features that surround us and the processes that create them.

Hydrology

Another important branch of geography is hydrology, the study of water on Earth. Geographers in this field study the world's river systems and rainfall patterns. They study what causes droughts and floods and how people in cities can get safe drinking water. They also work to measure and protect the world's supply of water.

FOCUS ON READING
What do you already know about drinking water?

Section 3 Assessment

hmhsocialstudies.com
ONLINE QUIZ

Reviewing Ideas, Terms, and Places

1. **a. Define** What is **physical geography**?
   b. Explain Why do we study physical geography?
2. **a. Identify** What are some things that people study as part of **human geography**?
   b. Summarize What are some ways in which the study of human geography can influence our lives?
   c. Evaluate Which do you think would be more interesting to study, physical geography or human geography? Why?
3. **a. Identify** What are two specialized fields of geography?
   b. Analyze How do cartographers contribute to the work of other geographers?

Critical Thinking

4. **Comparing and Contrasting** Draw a diagram like the one shown here. In the left circle, list three features of physical geography from your notes. In the right circle, list three features of human geography. Where the circles overlap, list one feature they share.

Physical   Human

FOCUS ON WRITING

*my*WriteSmart

5. **Choosing a Branch** Your job description should point out to people that there are many branches of geography. How will you note that?

Chapter Review

Visual Summary

With a partner, read the visual summary below to help you review and discuss the main ideas of the chapter. Be sure to include important vocabulary, terms, and places.

QUICK FACTS

Physical geography—the study of the world's physical features—is one main branch of geography.

Human geography—the study of the world's people and how they live—is the second main branch.

Geographers use many tools to study the world. The most valuable of these tools are maps.

Reviewing Vocabulary, Terms, and Places

Match the words in the columns with the correct definitions listed below.

1. geography
2. physical geography
3. human geography
4. element
5. meteorology
6. region
7. cartography
8. map
9. landscape
10. globe

a. a part of the world that has one or more common features that make it different from surrounding areas

b. a flat drawing of part of Earth's surface

c. a part

d. a spherical model of the planet

e. the study of the world's physical features

f. the study of weather and what causes it

g. the study of the world, its people, and the landscapes they create

h. the science of making maps

i. the physical and human features that define an area and make it different from other places

j. the study of people and communities

Comprehension and Critical Thinking

SECTION 1 *(Pages 4–9)*

11. a. **Identify** What are three levels at which a geographer might study the world? Which of these levels covers the largest area?

    b. **Compare and Contrast** How are maps and globes similar? How are they different?

    c. **Elaborate** How might satellite images and computers help geographers improve their knowledge of the world?

SECTION 2 (Pages 10–14)

12. a. Locate Choose a country to locate on the political map of the world in this book's atlas. Use latitude and longitude to determine the absolute location of the country.

b. Explain Why did geographers create the five themes and the six essential elements?

c. Predict How might the five themes and six essential elements help you in your study of geography?

SECTION 3 (Pages 16–20)

13. a. Identify What are the two main branches of geography? What does each include?

b. Summarize How can physical geography help people adjust to the dangers of the world?

c. Elaborate Why do geographers study both physical and human geographic features of places?

Using the Internet

14. Activity: Using Maps Through your online textbook, explore how maps can help you understand your community and identify its human geographic features. Then search the Internet to find a map of your community. Use the map to find the locations of at least five major human geographic features. For example, you might locate your school, the library, a park, or major highways.

hmhsocialstudies.com

Social Studies Skills

Posing and Answering Geographic Questions *Use the Environment of Texas map from the Social Studies Skills lesson in this chapter to answer the following questions.*

15. Notice the geographic pattern of vegetation in Texas on the map. Why might the region of savannah have less farming and ranching activity?

16. What geographic distribution of cattle ranching can you locate on this map?

17. Choose one feature shown on the map and pose and answer the following questions: Where is

it located?, Why is it there?, What is significant about its location?, How is its location related to the location of other people, places, and environments?

Map Activity

18. Sketch Map Look for and read environmental print to help you sketch a map of your school. Environmental print can be found all around you in the form of labels, symbols, words, or numbers that provide information. Your map should include environmental print such as labels, symbols, words, or numbers in around classrooms and buildings. Use the basic sketch map shown here as an example.

19. Using Prior Knowledge With a partner, create a three-column chart titled, A Geographer's World. In the first column, list what you each knew about geography before you read the chapter. In the second column, list what you each learned about geography. In the third column, list questions that you each still have about geography.

20. Writing Your Job Description Review your notes on the different jobs geographers do. Then use *my*WriteSmart in your eBook to write your job description. You should begin your description by explaining why the job is important. Then identify the job's tasks and responsibilities. Finally, tell what kind of person might do well as a geographer.

Reading Social Studies

Using Prior Knowledge

When you put together a puzzle, you search for pieces that are missing to complete the picture. As you read, you do the same thing when you use prior knowledge. You take what you already know about a subject and then add the information you are reading to create a full picture. The example below shows how using prior knowledge about computer mapping helped one reader fill in the pieces about how geographers use computer mapping.

In the past, maps were always drawn by hand. Many were not very accurate. Today, though, most maps are made using computers and satellite images. Through advances in mapmaking, we can make accurate maps on almost any scale, from the whole world to a single neighborhood, and keep them up to date.

From Section 3, The Branches of Geography

Computer Mapping	
What I know before reading	What else I learned
• My dad uses the computer to get a map for trips. • I can find maps of states and countries on the Internet.	• Maps have not always been very accurate. • Computers help make new kinds of maps that are more than just cities and roads. • These computer maps are an important part of geography.

YOU TRY IT!

Then take turn reading aloud the passage below with a partner. Once you each have read the passage, add what you learned about satellite images to the right column.

Much of the information gathered by these satellites is in the form of images. Geographers can study these images to see what an area looks like from above Earth. Satellites also collect information that we cannot see from the planet's surface. The information gathered by satellites helps geographers make accurate maps.

From Section 1, Studying Geography

CHAPTER 2

Planet Earth

Essential Question

*my*Notebook

How do physical processes and features shape life on Earth?

Texas Essential Knowledge and Skills (TEKS)

6A, 6B, 6C, 7A, 7B, 7C

FOCUS ON READING AND WRITING

my WriteSmart

Using Word Parts Sometimes you can figure out the meaning of a word by looking at its parts. A root is the base of the word. A prefix attaches to the beginning, and a suffix attaches to the ending. When you come across a word you don't know, check to see whether you recognize its parts. **See the lesson Using Word Parts on page 47.**

Writing a Haiku Join the poets who have celebrated our planet for centuries. Write a haiku, a short poem, about planet Earth. As you read the chapter, gather information about changes in the sun's energy, Earth's water supply, and the land's shapes. Then choose the most intriguing information to include in your haiku. Use the annotation tools in your eBook to gather information for your assignment.

Energy from the Sun The planet's movement creates differences in the amount of energy Earth receives from the sun.

ANALYSIS SKILL **ANALYZING VISUALS**

Many of Earth's features are visible from space. This photo, taken from a satellite orbiting the planet, shows part of the North American continent.

Which of Earth's features are visible in this photo?

Land Forces on and under Earth's surface have shaped the different landforms on our planet. Geographers study how mountains and other landforms were made.

Water on Earth Water is essential for life on Earth. Much of the planet's water supply is stored in Earth's oceans and ice caps.

25

Earth and the Sun's Energy

 TEKS 3B, 3C, 6A, 6C, 21B

What You Will Learn...

Main Ideas

1. Earth's movement affects the amount of energy we receive from the sun.
2. Earth's seasons are caused by the planet's tilt.

The Big Idea

Earth's movement and the sun's energy interact to create day and night, temperature changes, and the seasons.

Key Terms

solar energy, *p. 26*
rotation, *p. 26*
revolution, *p. 27*
latitude, *p. 27*
tropics, *p. 29*

hmhsocialstudies.com
TAKING NOTES

Use the graphic organizer online to take notes on Earth's movement and the seasons.

If YOU lived there...

You live in Chicago and have just won an exciting prize—a trip to Australia during winter vacation in January. As you prepare for the trip, your mother reminds you to pack shorts and a swimsuit. You are confused. In January you usually wear winter sweaters and a heavy jacket.

Why is the weather so different in Australia?

BUILDING BACKGROUND Seasonal differences in weather are an important result of Earth's constant movement. As the planet moves, we experience changes in the amount of energy we receive from the sun. Geographers study and explain why different places on Earth receive differing amounts of energy from the sun.

Earth's Movement

Energy from the sun helps crops grow, provides light, and warms Earth. It even influences the clothes we wear, the foods we eat, and the sports we play. All life on Earth requires **solar energy**, or energy from the sun, to survive. The amount of solar energy places on Earth receive changes constantly. Earth's rotation, revolution, and tilt, as well as latitude, all affect the amount of solar energy parts of the planet receive from the sun.

Rotation

Imagine that Earth has a rod running through it from the North Pole to the South Pole. This rod represents Earth's axis—an imaginary line around which a planet turns. As Earth spins on its axis, different parts of the planet face the sun. It takes Earth 24 hours, or one day, to complete this rotation. A **rotation** is one complete spin of Earth on its axis. As Earth rotates during this 24-hour period, it appears to us that the sun moves across the sky. The sun seems to rise in the east and set in the west. The

Solar Energy

Earth's tilt and rotation cause changes in the amount of energy we receive from the sun. As Earth rotates on its axis, energy from the sun creates periods of day and night. Earth's tilt causes some locations, especially those close to the equator, to receive more direct solar energy than others.

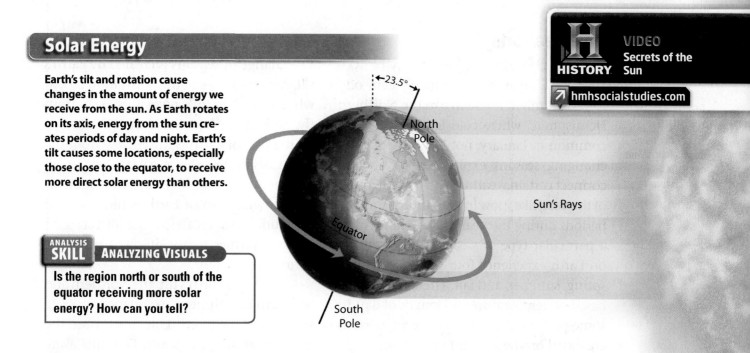

VIDEO
Secrets of the Sun

hmhsocialstudies.com

ANALYSIS SKILL **ANALYZING VISUALS**

Is the region north or south of the equator receiving more solar energy? How can you tell?

23.5°

North Pole

Equator

Sun's Rays

South Pole

sun, however, does not move. It is actually Earth's rotation that creates the sense of the sun's movement.

Earth's rotation also explains why day changes to night. As you can see in the illustration, solar energy strikes only the half of Earth facing the sun. Warmth and light from the sun create daytime. At the same time, the half of the planet facing away from the sun experiences the cooler temperatures and darkness of night. Earth's rotation causes regular shifts from day to night. As a result, levels of solar energy on Earth constantly change.

Revolution

As Earth spins on its axis, it also follows a path, or orbit, around the sun. Earth's orbit around the sun is not a perfect circle. Sometimes the orbit takes Earth closer to the sun, and at other times the orbit takes it farther away. It takes 365¼ days for Earth to complete one **revolution**, or trip around the sun. We base our calendar year on the time it takes Earth to complete its orbit around the sun. To allow for the fraction of a day, we add an extra day—February 29—to our calendar every four years.

Tilt and Latitude

Another **factor** affecting the amount of solar energy we receive is the planet's tilt. As the illustration shows, Earth's axis is not straight up and down. It is actually tilted at an angle of 23½ degrees from vertical. At any given time of year, some locations on Earth are tilting away from the sun, and others are tilting toward it. Places tilting toward the sun receive more solar energy and experience warmer temperatures. Those tilting away from the sun receive less solar energy and experience cooler temperatures.

A location's **latitude**, the distance north or south of Earth's equator, also affects the amount of solar energy it receives. Low-latitude areas, those near the equator like Hawaii, receive direct rays from the sun all year. These direct rays are more intense and produce warmer temperatures. Regions with high latitudes, like Antarctica, are farther from the equator. As a result, they receive indirect rays from the sun and have colder temperatures.

READING CHECK **Finding Main Ideas** What factors affect the solar energy Earth receives?

ACADEMIC VOCABULARY
factor cause

The Seasons

FOCUS ON READING

The prefix *hemi-* means half. What does the word *hemisphere* mean?

Does the thought of snow in July or 100-degree temperatures in January seem odd to you? It might if you live in the Northern Hemisphere, where cold temperatures are common in January, not July. The planet's changing seasons explain why we often connect certain weather with specific times of the year, like snow in January. Seasons are periods during the year that are known for a particular type of weather. Many places on Earth experience four seasons—winter, spring, summer, and fall. These seasons are based on temperature and length of day. In some parts of the world, however, seasons are based on the amount of rainfall.

Winter and Summer

The change in seasons is created by Earth's tilt. As you can see in the illustration below, while one of Earth's poles tilts away from the sun, the other tilts toward it. During winter part of Earth is tilted away from the sun, causing less direct solar energy, cool temperatures, and less daylight. Summer occurs when part of Earth is tilted toward the sun. This creates more direct solar energy, warmer temperatures, and longer periods of daylight.

Because of Earth's tilt, the Northern and Southern hemispheres experience opposite seasons. As the North Pole tilts toward the sun in summer, the South Pole tilts away

The Seasons: Northern Hemisphere

As Earth orbits the sun, the tilt of its axis toward and away from the sun causes the seasons to change. Seasons in the Northern Hemisphere change at about the same time every year.

ANALYZING VISUALS As the Northern Hemisphere experiences winter, what season is it in the Southern Hemisphere?

March 21
SPRING

Winter and Spring The North Pole tilts away from the sun in winter, causing cooler temperatures. In the spring, temperatures gradually rise as the North Pole begins to point toward the sun.

December 21
WINTER

June 21
SUMMER

Summer and Fall Summer's warm temperatures are the result of the North Pole's tilt toward the sun. As we move away from the sun in the fall, temperatures slowly decline.

North Pole

Tropic of Cancer

Equator

Tropic of Capricorn

South Pole

September 22
FALL

from it. As a result, the Southern Hemisphere experiences winter. Likewise, when it is spring in the Northern Hemisphere, it is fall in the Southern Hemisphere.

Spring and Fall

As Earth orbits the sun, there are periods when the poles tilt neither toward nor away from the sun. These periods mark spring and fall. During the spring, as part of Earth begins to tilt toward the sun, solar energy increases. Temperatures slowly start to rise, and days grow longer. In the fall the opposite occurs as winter approaches. Solar energy begins to decrease, causing cooler temperatures and shorter days.

Rainfall and Seasons

Some regions on Earth have seasons marked by rainfall rather than temperature. This is true in the **tropics**, regions close to the equator. At certain times of year, winds bring either dry or moist air to the tropics, creating wet and dry seasons. In India, for example, seasonal winds called monsoons bring heavy rains from June to October and dry air from November to January.

READING CHECK Identifying Cause and Effect What causes the seasons to change?

FOCUS ON CULTURE

The Midnight Sun

Can you imagine going to sleep late at night with the sun shining in the sky? People who live near the Arctic and Antarctic circles experience this every summer, when they can receive up to 24 hours of sunlight a day. The time-lapse photo below shows a typical sunset during this period—except the sun never really sets! This phenomenon is known as the midnight sun. For locations like Tromso, Norway, this means up to two months of constant daylight each summer. People living near Earth's poles often use the long daylight hours to work on outdoor projects in preparation for winter, when they can receive 24 hours of darkness a day.

Predicting How might people's daily lives be affected by the midnight sun?

SUMMARY AND PREVIEW Solar energy is crucial for all life on the planet. Earth's position and movements affect the amount of energy we receive from the sun and determine our seasons. Next, you will learn about Earth's water supply and its importance to us.

Section 1 Assessment

hmhsocialstudies.com
ONLINE QUIZ

Reviewing Ideas, Terms, and Places

1. **a. Identify** What is **solar energy**, and how does it affect Earth?
   b. Analyze How do **rotation** and tilt each affect the amount of solar energy that different parts of Earth receive?
   c. Predict What might happen if Earth received less solar energy than it currently does?
2. **a. Describe** Name and describe Earth's seasons.
   b. Contrast How are seasons different in the Northern and Southern hemispheres?
   c. Elaborate How might the seasons affect human activities?

Critical Thinking

3. **Identifying Cause and Effect** Use your notes and the diagram to identify the causes of seasons.

| Cause |
| Cause | → | Effect: Earth's changing seasons |

FOCUS ON WRITING

my WriteSmart

4. **Describing the Seasons** What are the seasons like where you live? In your notebook, jot down a few notes that describe the changing seasons.

Water on Earth

TEKS 6B, 7B, 7C

What You Will Learn...

Main Ideas

1. Salt water and freshwater make up Earth's water supply.
2. In the water cycle, water circulates from Earth's surface to the atmosphere and back again.
3. Water plays an important role in people's lives.

The Big Idea

Water is a dominant feature on Earth's surface and is essential for life.

Key Terms

freshwater, p. 31
glaciers, p. 31
surface water, p. 31
precipitation, p. 31
groundwater, p. 32
water vapor, p. 32
water cycle, p. 33

hmhsocialstudies.com
TAKING NOTES

Use the graphic organizer online to take notes on Earth's water.

If **YOU** lived there...

You live in the desert Southwest, where heavy water use and a lack of rainfall have led to water shortages. Your city plans to begin a water conservation program that asks people to limit how much water they use. Many of your neighbors have complained that the program is unnecessary. Others support the plan to save water.

How do you feel about the city's water plan?

BUILDING BACKGROUND Although water covers much of Earth's surface, water shortages, like those in the American Southwest, are common all over the planet. Because water is vital to the survival of all living things, geographers study Earth's water supply.

Earth's Water Supply

Think of the different uses for water. We use water to cook and clean, we drink it, and we grow crops with it. Water is used for recreation, to generate electricity, and even to travel from place to place. Water is perhaps the most important and abundant resource on Earth. In fact, water covers some two-thirds of the planet. Understanding Earth's water supply and how it affects our lives is an important part of geography.

Earth's Distribution of Water

Earth's water supply is divided into two main types—salt water and freshwater. Humans, plants, and animals rely on Earth's freshwater supply for survival.

Salt Water

Although water covers much of the planet, we cannot use most of it. About 97 percent of the Earth's water is salt water. Because salt water contains high levels of salt and other minerals, it is unsafe to drink.

In general, salt water is found in Earth's oceans. Oceans are vast bodies of water covering some 71 percent of the planet's surface. Earth's oceans are made up of smaller bodies of water such as seas, gulfs, bays, and straits. Altogether, Earth's oceans cover some 139 million square miles (360 million square km) of the planet's surface.

Some of Earth's lakes contain salt water. The Great Salt Lake in Utah, for example, is a saltwater lake. As salt and other minerals have collected in the lake, which has no outlet, the water has become salty.

Freshwater

Since the water in Earth's oceans is too salty to use, we must rely on other sources for freshwater. **Freshwater**, or water without salt, makes up only about 3 percent of our total water supply. Much of that freshwater is locked in Earth's **glaciers**, large areas of slow-moving ice, and in the ice of the Antarctic and Arctic regions. Most of the freshwater we use everyday is found in lakes, in rivers, and under Earth's surface.

One form of freshwater is surface water. **Surface water** is water that is found in Earth's streams, rivers, and lakes. It may seem that there is a great deal of water in our lakes and rivers, but only a tiny amount of Earth's water supply—less than 1 percent—comes from surface water.

Streams and rivers are a common source of surface water. Streams form when precipitation collects in a narrow channel and flows toward the ocean. **Precipitation** is water that falls to Earth's surface as rain, snow, sleet, or hail. In turn, streams join together to form rivers. Any smaller stream or river that flows into a larger stream or river is called a tributary. For example, the Missouri River is the largest tributary of the Mississippi River.

Lakes are another important source of surface water. Some lakes were formed as rivers filled low-lying areas with water. Other lakes, like the Great Lakes along the U.S.–Canada border, were formed when glaciers carved deep holes in Earth's surface and deposited water as they melted.

Most of Earth's available freshwater is stored underground. As precipitation falls to Earth, much of it is absorbed into the ground, filling spaces in the soil and rock.

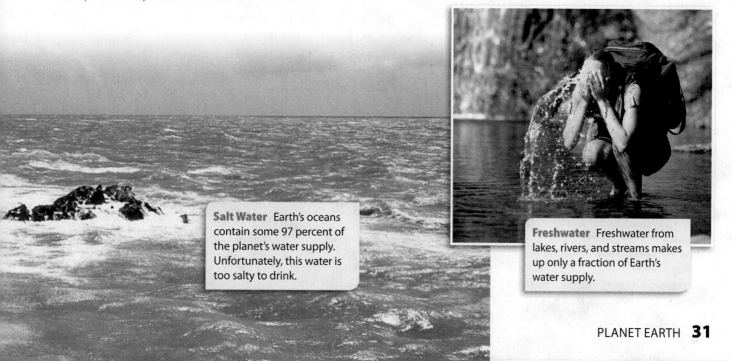

Salt Water Earth's oceans contain some 97 percent of the planet's water supply. Unfortunately, this water is too salty to drink.

Freshwater Freshwater from lakes, rivers, and streams makes up only a fraction of Earth's water supply.

Water found below Earth's surface is called **groundwater**. In some places on Earth, groundwater naturally bubbles from the ground as a spring. More often, however, people obtain groundwater by digging wells, or deep holes dug into the ground to reach the water.

READING CHECK **Contrasting** How is salt water different from freshwater?

The Water Cycle

Energy from the sun drives the water cycle. Surface water evaporates into Earth's atmosphere, where it condenses, then falls back to Earth as precipitation. This cycle repeats continuously, providing us with a fairly constant water supply.

The Water Cycle

When you think of water, you probably visualize a liquid—a flowing stream, a glass of ice-cold water, or a wave hitting the beach. But did you know that water is the only substance on Earth that occurs naturally as a solid, a liquid, and a gas? We see water as a solid in snow and ice and as a liquid in oceans and rivers. Water also occurs in the air as an invisible gas called **water vapor**.

Water is always moving. As water heats up and cools down, it moves from the planet's surface to the atmosphere, or the mass of air that surrounds Earth. One of the most important processes in nature

Condensation occurs when water vapor cools and forms clouds.

When the droplets in clouds become too heavy, they fall to Earth as precipitation.

Runoff is excess precipitation that flows over land into rivers, streams, and oceans.

ANALYSIS SKILL **ANALYZING VISUALS**
How does evaporation differ from precipitation?

is the water cycle. The **water cycle** is the movement of water from Earth's surface to the atmosphere and back.

The sun's energy drives the water cycle. As the sun heats water on Earth's surface, some of that water evaporates, or turns from liquid to gas, or water vapor. Water vapor then rises into the air. As the vapor rises, it cools. The cooling causes the water vapor to condense, or change from a vapor into tiny liquid droplets. These droplets join together to form clouds. If the droplets become heavy enough, precipitation occurs—that is, the water falls back to Earth as rain, snow, sleet, or hail.

When that precipitation falls back to Earth's surface, some of the water is absorbed into the soil as groundwater. Excess water, called runoff, flows over land and collects in streams, rivers, and oceans. Because the water cycle is constantly repeating, it allows us to maintain a fairly constant supply of water on Earth.

READING CHECK **Finding Main Ideas** What is the water cycle?

As energy from the sun heats water on Earth's surface, the water evaporates, or turns to water vapor, and rises to the atmosphere.

Water and People

How many times a day do you think about water? Many of us rarely give it a second thought, yet water is crucial for survival. Water problems such as the lack of water, polluted water, and flooding are concerns for people all around the world. Water also provides us with <u>countless</u> benefits, such as energy and recreation.

Water Problems

One of the greatest water problems people face is a lack of available freshwater. Many places face water shortages as a result of droughts, or long periods of lower-than-normal precipitation. Another cause of water shortages is overuse. In places like the southwestern United States, where the population has grown rapidly, the heavy demand for water has led to shortages.

Even where water is plentiful, it may not be clean enough to use. If chemicals and household wastes make their way into streams and rivers, they can contaminate the water supply. Polluted water can carry diseases. These diseases may harm humans, plants, and animals.

Flooding is another water problem that affects people around the world. Heavy rains often lead to flooding, which can damage property and threaten lives. One example of dangerous flooding occurred in Bangladesh in 2004. Severe floods there destroyed roads and schools, affecting about 25 million people.

Water's Benefits

Water does more than just quench our thirst. It provides us with many benefits, such as food, power, and even recreation.

Water's most important benefit is that it provides us with food to eat. Everything we eat depends on water. For example, fruits and vegetables need water to grow.

FOCUS ON READING

Look at the word *countless* in this paragraph. The suffix *-less* means unable to. What does *countless* mean?

The Benefits of Water

Many people take advantage of the recreational and agricultural benefits that water provides.

Animals also need water to live and grow. As a result, we use water to farm and raise animals so that we will have food to eat.

Water is also an important source of energy. Using dams, we harness the power of moving water to produce electricity. Electricity provides power to air-condition or heat our homes, to run our washers and dryers, and to keep our food cold.

Water also provides us with recreation. Rivers, lakes, and oceans make it possible for us to swim, to fish, to surf, or to sail a boat. Although recreation is not critical for our survival, it does make our lives richer and more enjoyable.

READING CHECK **Summarizing** How does water affect people's lives?

SUMMARY AND PREVIEW In this section you learned that water is essential for life on Earth. Next, you will learn about the shapes on Earth's surface.

Section 2 Assessment

Reviewing Ideas, Terms, and Places

1. **a. Describe** Name and describe the different types of water that make up Earth's water supply.
   b. Analyze Why is only a small percentage of Earth's **freshwater** available to us?
   c. Elaborate In your opinion, which is more important—**surface water** or **groundwater**? Why?
2. **a. Recall** What drives the **water cycle**?
   b. Make Inferences From what bodies of water do you think most evaporation occurs? Why?
3. **a. Define** What is a drought?
   b. Analyze How does water support life on Earth?
   c. Evaluate What water problem do you think is most critical in your community? Why?

Critical Thinking

4. **Sequencing** Draw the graphic organizer at right. Then use your notes and the graphic organizer to identify the stages in Earth's water cycle.

FOCUS ON WRITING *my* WriteSmart

5. **Learning about Water** Consider what you have learned about water in this section. How might you describe water in your haiku? What words might you use to describe Earth's water supply?

Heat from the sun evaporates water on Earth.

↓

↓

↓

The water cycle repeats.

The Land

If YOU lived there...

You live in the state of Washington. All your life, you have looked out at the beautiful, cone-shaped peaks of nearby mountains. One of them is Mount Saint Helens, an active volcano. You know that in 1980 it erupted violently, blowing a hole in the mountain and throwing ash and rock into the sky. Since then, scientists have watched the mountain carefully.

How do you feel about living near a volcano?

> **BUILDING BACKGROUND** Over billions of years, many different forces have changed Earth's surface. Processes deep underground have built up landforms and even shifted the position of continents. Wind, water, and ice have also shaped the planet's landforms. Changes in Earth's surface continue to take place.

Landforms

Do you know the difference between a valley and a volcano? Can you tell a peninsula from a plateau? If you answered yes, then you are familiar with some of Earth's many landforms. **Landforms** are shapes on the planet's surface, such as hills or mountains. Landforms make up the landscapes that surround us, whether it's the rugged mountains of central Colorado or the flat plains of Oklahoma.

Earth's surface is covered with landforms of many different shapes and sizes. Some important landforms include:

- mountains, land that rises higher than 2,000 feet (610 m)
- valleys, areas of low land located between mountains or hills
- plains, stretches of mostly flat land
- islands, areas of land completely surrounded by water
- peninsulas, land surrounded by water on three sides

Because landforms play an important role in geography, many scientists study how landforms are made and how they affect human activity.

READING CHECK **Summarizing** What are some common landforms?

 TEKS 6A

What You Will Learn...

Main Ideas

1. Earth's surface is covered by many different landforms.
2. Forces below Earth's surface build up our landforms.
3. Forces on the planet's surface shape Earth's landforms.
4. Landforms influence people's lives and culture.

The Big Idea

Processes below and on Earth's surface shape the planet's physical features.

Key Terms

landforms, *p. 35*
continents, *p. 36*
plate tectonics, *p. 36*
lava, *p. 37*
earthquakes, *p. 38*
weathering, *p. 39*
erosion, *p. 39*

 hmhsocialstudies.com
TAKING NOTES

Use the graphic organizer online to take notes on Earth's landforms.

Forces below Earth's Surface

Geographers often study how landforms are made. One explanation for how landforms have been shaped involves forces below Earth's surface.

Earth's Plates

ACADEMIC VOCABULARY

structure the way something is set up or organized

To understand how these forces work, we must examine Earth's **structure**. The planet is made up of three layers. A solid inner core is surrounded by a liquid layer, or mantle. The solid outer layer of Earth is called the crust. The planet's **continents**, or large landmasses, are part of Earth's crust.

Geographers use the theory of plate tectonics to explain how forces below Earth's surface have shaped our landforms. The theory of **plate tectonics** suggests that Earth's surface is divided into a dozen or so slow-moving plates, or pieces of Earth's crust. As you can see in the image below, some plates, like the Pacific plate, are quite large. Others, like the Nazca plate, are much smaller. These plates cover Earth's entire surface. Some plates are under the ocean. These are known as ocean plates. Other plates, known as continental plates, are under Earth's continents.

Why do these plates move? Energy deep inside the planet puts pressure on Earth's crust. As this pressure builds up, it forces the plates to shift. Earth's tectonic plates all move. However, they move in different directions and at different speeds.

The Movement of Continents

Earth's tectonic plates move slowly—up to several inches per year. The continents, which are part of Earth's plates, shift as the plates move. If we could look back some 200 million years, we would see that the continents have traveled great distances. This idea is known as continental drift.

Earth's Plates

North American plate

Eurasian plate

Pacific plate

Nazca plate

South American plate

African plate

Indian plate

Australian plate

Antarctic plate

The theory of continental drift, first developed by Alfred Wegener, states that the continents were once united in a single supercontinent. According to this theory, Earth's plates shifted over millions of years. As a result, the continents slowly separated and moved to their present positions.

Earth's continents are still moving. Some plates move toward each other and collide. Other plates separate and move apart. Still others slide past one another. Over time, colliding, separating, and sliding plates have shaped Earth's landforms.

Plates Collide

As plates collide, the energy created from their collision produces distinct landforms. The collision of different types of plates creates different shapes on Earth's surface. Ocean trenches and mountain ranges are two examples of landforms produced by the collision of tectonic plates.

BIOGRAPHY

Alfred Wegener

(1880–1930)

German scientist Alfred Wegener's fascination with the similarities between the western coast of Africa and the eastern coast of South America led to his theory of continental drift. Wegener argued that the two continents had once been joined together. Years of plate movement broke the continents apart and moved them to their current locations. It was only after Wegener's death that his ideas became a central part of the theory of plate tectonics.

The theory of plate tectonics suggests that the plates that make up Earth's crust are moving, usually only a few inches per year. As Earth's plates collide, separate, and slide past each other, they create forces great enough to shape many of Earth's landforms.

ANALYZING VISUALS Looking at the map, what evidence indicates that plates have collided or separated?

When two ocean plates collide, one plate pushes under the other. This process creates ocean trenches. Ocean trenches are deep valleys in the ocean floor. Near Japan, for example, the Pacific plate is slowly moving under other plates. This collision has created several deep ocean trenches, including the world's deepest trench, the Mariana Trench.

Ocean plates and continental plates can also collide. When this occurs, the ocean plate drops beneath the continental plate. This action forces the land above to crumple and form a mountain range. The Andes in South America, for example, were formed when the South American and Nazca plates collided.

The collision of two continental plates also results in mountain-building. When continental plates collide, the land pushes up, sometimes to great heights. The world's highest mountain range, the Himalayas, formed when the Indian plate crashed into the Eurasian plate. In fact, the Himalayas are still growing as the two plates continue to crash into each other.

Plates Separate

A second type of plate movement causes plates to separate. As plates move apart, gaps between the plates allow magma, a liquid rock from the planet's interior, to rise to Earth's crust. **Lava**, or magma that reaches Earth's surface, emerges from the gap that has formed. As the lava cools, it builds a mid-ocean ridge, or underwater mountain. For example, the separation of the North American and Eurasian plates formed the largest underwater mountain, the Mid-Atlantic Ridge. If these mid-ocean ridges grow high enough, they can rise above the surface of the ocean, forming volcanic islands. Iceland, on the boundary of the Eurasian and North American plates, is an example of such an island.

Plates Slide

Tectonic plates also slide past each other. As plates pass by one another, they sometimes grind together. This grinding produces **earthquakes**—sudden, violent movements of Earth's crust. Earthquakes often take place along faults, or breaks in Earth's crust where movement occurs. In California, for example, the Pacific plate is sliding by the edge of the North American plate. This has created the San Andreas Fault zone, an area where earthquakes are quite common.

The San Andreas Fault zone is one of many areas that lie along the boundaries of the Pacific plate. The frequent movement of this plate produces many earthquakes and volcanic eruptions along its edges. In fact, the region around the Pacific plate, called the Ring of Fire, is home to most of the world's earthquakes and volcanoes.

READING CHECK **Finding Main Ideas** What forces below Earth's surface shape landforms?

HISTORY
VIDEO
Earthquakes
hmhsocialstudies.com

Plate Movement

The movement of tectonic plates has produced many of Earth's landforms. Volcanoes, islands, and mountains often result from the separation or collision of Earth's plates.

ANALYZING VISUALS What type of landform is created by the collision of two continental plates?

The separation of plates can allow magma to rise up and create volcanic islands like Surtsey Island, near Iceland.

Plate A

magma

Plate B

Plate A   Plate B

The Himalayas in South Asia resulted from the collision of two massive continental plates.

Processes on Earth's Surface

For millions of years, the movement of Earth's tectonic plates has been building up landforms on Earth's surface. At the same time, other physical environmental processes are working to change those very same landforms.

Imagine a small pile of dirt and rock on a table. If you poured water on the pile, it would move the dirt and rock from one place to another. Likewise, if you were to blow at the pile, the rock and dirt would also move. The same process happens in nature. Weather, water, and other forces change Earth's landforms by wearing them away or reshaping them.

Weathering

One force that wears away landforms is weathering. **Weathering** is the process by which rock is broken down into smaller pieces. Several factors cause rock to break down. In desert areas, daytime heating and nighttime cooling can cause rocks to crack. Water may get into cracks in rocks and freeze. The ice then expands with a force great enough to break the rock. Even the roots of trees can pry rocks apart.

Regardless of which weathering process is at work, rocks eventually break down. These small pieces of rock are known as sediment. Once weathering has taken place, wind, ice, and water often move sediment from one place to another.

Erosion

Another force that changes landforms is the process of erosion. **Erosion** is the movement of sediment from one location to another. Erosion can wear away or build up landforms. Wind, ice, and water all cause erosion.

Powerful winds often cause erosion. Winds lift sediment into the air and carry it across great distances. On beaches and in deserts, wind can deposit large amounts of sand to form dunes. Blowing sand can also wear down rock. The sand acts like sandpaper to polish and wear away at rocks. As you can see in the photo below, wind can have a dramatic effect on landforms.

Earth's glaciers also have the power to cause massive erosion. Glaciers, or large, slow-moving sheets of ice, build up when winter snows do not melt the following summer. Glaciers can be huge. Glaciers in Greenland and Antarctica, for example, are great sheets of ice up to two miles (3 km) thick. Some glaciers flow slowly downhill like rivers of ice. As they do so, they erode the land by carving large U-shaped valleys and sharp mountain peaks. As the ice flows downhill, it crushes rock into sediment and can move huge rocks long distances.

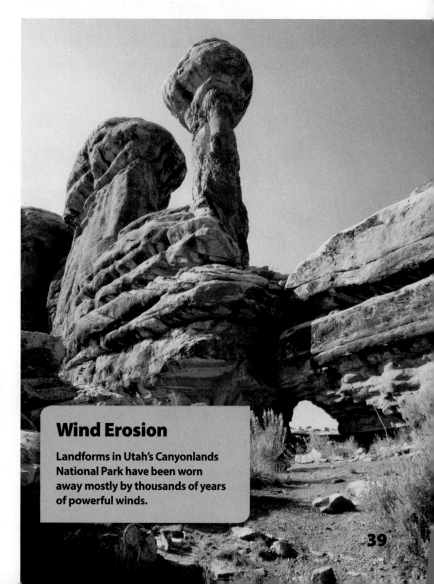

Wind Erosion

Landforms in Utah's Canyonlands National Park have been worn away mostly by thousands of years of powerful winds.

Water is the most common cause of erosion. Waves in oceans and lakes can wear away the shore, creating jagged coastlines, like those on the coast of Oregon. Rivers also cause erosion. Over many years, the flowing water can cut through rock, forming canyons, or narrow areas with steep walls. Arizona's Horseshoe Bend and Grand Canyon are examples of canyons created in this way.

Flowing water shapes other landforms as well. When water deposits sediment in new locations, it creates new landforms. For example, rivers create floodplains when they flood their banks and deposit sediment along the banks. Sediment that is carried by a river all the way out to sea creates a delta. The sediment settles to the bottom, where the river meets the sea. The Nile and Mississippi rivers have created two of the world's largest river deltas.

READING CHECK **Comparing** How are weathering and erosion similar?

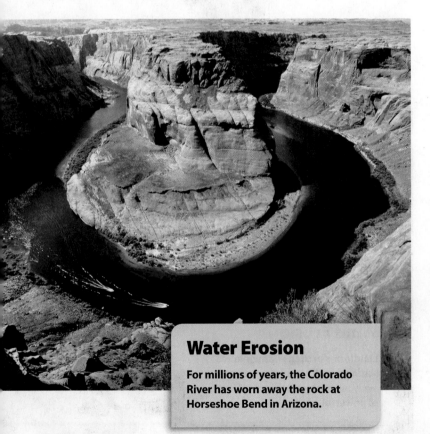

Water Erosion

For millions of years, the Colorado River has worn away the rock at Horseshoe Bend in Arizona.

Landforms Influence Life

Why do you live where you do? Perhaps your family moved to the desert to avoid harsh winter weather. Or possibly one of your ancestors settled near a river delta because its fertile soil was ideal for growing crops. Maybe your family wanted to live near the ocean to start a fishing business. As these examples show, landforms exert a strong influence on people's lives. Earth's landforms affect our settlements and our culture. At the same time, we affect the landforms around us.

Earth's landforms can influence where people settle. People sometimes settle near certain landforms and avoid others. For example, many settlements are built near fertile river valleys or deltas. The earliest urban civilization, for example, was built in the valley between the Tigris and Euphrates rivers. Other times, landforms discourage people from settling in a certain place. Tall, rugged mountains, like the Himalayas, and harsh desert climates, like the Sahara, do not usually attract large settlements.

Landforms affect our culture in ways that we may not have noticed. Landforms often influence what jobs are available in a region. For example, rich mineral deposits in the mountains of Colorado led to the development of a mining industry there. Landforms even affect language. On the island of New Guinea in Southeast Asia, rugged mountains have kept the people so isolated that more than 700 languages are spoken on the island today.

People sometimes change landforms to suit their needs. People may choose to modify landforms in order to improve their lives. For example, engineers built the Panama Canal to make travel from the Atlantic Ocean to the Pacific Ocean easier. In Southeast Asia, people who farm on steep hillsides cut terraces into the slope to

Living with Landforms

The people of Rio de Janeiro, Brazil, have learned to adapt to the mountains and bays that dominate their landscape.

ANALYZING VISUALS How have people in Rio de Janiero adapted to their landscape?

create more level space to grow their crops. People have even built huge dams along rivers to divert water for use in nearby towns or farms.

READING CHECK **Analyzing** What are some examples of humans adjusting to and changing landforms?

SUMMARY AND PREVIEW Landforms are created by actions deep within the planet's surface, and they are changed by forces on Earth's surface, like weathering and erosion. In the next chapter you will learn how other forces, like weather and climate, affect Earth's people.

Section 3 Assessment

Reviewing Ideas, Terms, and Places

1. **a. Describe** What are some common **landforms**?
   b. Analyze Why do geographers study landforms?
2. **a. Identify** What is the theory of **plate tectonics**?
   b. Compare and Contrast How are the effects of colliding plates and separating plates similar and different?
   c. Predict How might Earth's surface change as tectonic plates continue to move?
3. **a. Recall** What is the process of **weathering**?
   b. Elaborate How does water affect sediment?
4. **a. Recall** How do landforms affect life on Earth?
   b. Predict How might people adapt to life in an area with steep mountains?

Critical Thinking

5. **Identify and Describe** Use your notes and the chart below to identify and describe different physical environmental processes and their effects on Earth's surface.

Physical Environmental Process	Effect on Earth's Surface

FOCUS ON WRITING

my WriteSmart

6. **Writing about Earth's Land** Think of some vivid words you could use to describe Earth's landforms. As you think of them, add them to your notebook.

The Ring of Fire

Essential Elements

The World in Spatial Terms
Places and Regions
Physical Systems
Human Systems
Environment and Society
The Uses of Geography

Background Does "the Ring of Fire" sound like the title of a fantasy novel? It's actually the name of a region that circles the Pacific Ocean known for its fiery volcanoes and powerful earthquakes. The Ring of Fire stretches from the tip of South America all the way up to Alaska, and from Japan down to the islands east of Australia. Along this belt, the Pacific plate moves against several other tectonic plates. As a result, thousands of earthquakes occur there every year, and dozens of volcanoes erupt.

The Eruption of Mount Saint Helens One of the best-known volcanoes in the Ring of Fire is Mount Saint Helens in Washington State. Mount Saint Helens had been dormant, or quiet, since 1857. Then in March 1980, it began spitting out puffs of steam and ash. Officials warned people to leave the area. Scientists brought in equipment to measure the growing bulge in the mountainside. Everyone feared the volcano might erupt at any moment.

On May 18, after a sudden earthquake, Mount Saint Helens let loose a massive explosion of rock and lava. Heat from the blast melted snow on the mountain, which

Ring of Fire

- Plate boundary line
- Earthquakes
- Active volcanoes

Major Eruptions in the Ring of Fire	
Volcano	**Year**
Tambora, Indonesia	1815
Krakatau, Indonesia	1883
Mount Saint Helens, United States	**1980**
Nevado del Ruiz, Colombia	1985
Mount Pinatubo, Philippines	1991

Mount Saint Helens, 1980

The 1980 eruption of Mount Saint Helens blew ash and hot gases miles into the air. Today, scientists study the volcano to learn more about predicting eruptions.

mixed with ash to create deadly mudflows. As the mud quickly poured downhill, it flattened forests, swept away cars, and destroyed buildings. Clouds of ash covered the land, killing crops, clogging waterways, and blanketing towns as far as 200 miles (330 km) away. When the volcano finally quieted down, 57 people had died. Damage totaled nearly $1 billion. If it were not for the early evacuation of the area, the destruction could have been much worse.

What It Means By studying Mount Saint Helens, scientists learned a great deal about stratovolcanoes. These are tall, steep, cone-shaped volcanoes that have violent eruptions. Stratovolcanoes often form in areas where tectonic plates collide.

Because stratovolcanoes often produce deadly eruptions, scientists try to predict when they might erupt. The lessons learned from Mount Saint Helens helped scientists warn people about another stratovolcano, Mount Pinatubo in the Philippines. That eruption in 1991 was the second-largest of the 1900s. It was far from the deadliest, however. Careful observation and timely warnings saved thousands of lives.

The Ring of Fire will always remain a threat. However, the better we understand its volcanoes, the better prepared we'll be when they erupt.

Geography for Life Activity

1. How did the eruption of Mount Saint Helens affect the surrounding area?

2. Why do scientists monitor volcanic activity?

3. **Investigating the Effects of Volcanoes** Some volcanic eruptions affect environmental conditions around the world. Research the eruption of either Mount Saint Helens or the Philippines' Mount Pinatubo to find out how its eruption affected the global environment.

Social Studies Skills

Using a Physical Map

Learn

Physical maps show important physical features, like oceans and mountains, in a particular area. They also indicate an area's elevation, or the height of the land in relation to sea level.

When you use a physical map, there are important pieces of information you should always examine.

- Identify physical features. Natural features, such as mountains, rivers, and lakes, are labeled on physical maps. Read the labels carefully to identify what physical features are present.

- Read the legend. On physical maps, the legend indicates scale as well as elevation. The different colors in the elevation key indicate how far above or below sea level a place is.

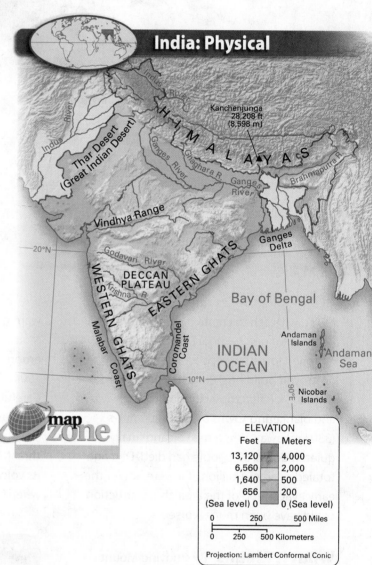

India: Physical

Kanchenjunga
28,208 ft
(8,598 m)

Indus River

Thar Desert
(Great Indian Desert)

HIMALAYAS

Ganges River

Ghaghara R.

Brahmaputra R.

Vindhya Range

Ganges River

20°N

Godavari River

Ganges Delta

WESTERN GHATS

DECCAN PLATEAU

Krishna R.

EASTERN GHATS

Bay of Bengal

Malabar Coast

Coromandel Coast

Andaman Islands

INDIAN OCEAN

Andaman Sea

10°N

90°E

Nicobar Islands

map zone

ELEVATION
Feet	Meters
13,120	4,000
6,560	2,000
1,640	500
656	200
(Sea level) 0	0 (Sea level)

0   250   500 Miles

0   250   500 Kilometers

Projection: Lambert Conformal Conic

Practice

Use the physical map of India at right to answer the questions below.

1. What landforms and bodies of water are indicated on the map?

2. What is the highest elevation in India? Where is it located?

Apply

Locate the physical map of Africa in the atlas in the back of the book. Use the map to answer the questions below.

1. Which region has the highest elevation?

2. What bodies of water surround Africa?

3. What large island is located off the east coast of Africa?

Chapter Review

Visual Summary

Use the visual summary below to help you review the main ideas of the chapter.

QUICK FACTS

The amount of solar energy Earth receives changes based on Earth's movement and position.

Water is crucial to life on Earth. Our abundant water supply is stored in oceans, in lakes, and underground.

Earth's various landforms are shaped by complex processes both under and on the planet's surface.

Reviewing Vocabulary, Terms, and Places

For each statement below, write T if it is true and F if it is false. If the statement is false, write the correct term that would make the sentence a true statement.

1. **Weathering** is the movement of sediment from one location to another.

2. Because high **latitude** areas receive indirect rays from the sun, they have cooler temperatures.

3. Most of our **groundwater** is stored in Earth's streams, rivers, and lakes.

4. It takes 365¼ days for Earth to complete one **rotation** around the sun.

5. Streams are formed when **precipitation** collects in narrow channels.

6. **Earthquakes** cause erosion as they flow downhill, carving valleys and mountain peaks.

7. The planet's tilt affects the amount of **erosion** Earth receives from the sun.

Comprehension and Critical Thinking

SECTION 1 *(Pages 26–29)*

8. **a. Identify** What factors influence the amount of energy that different places on Earth receive from the sun?

   b. Analyze Why do the Northern and Southern hemispheres experience opposite seasons?

   c. Predict What might happen to the amount of solar energy we receive if Earth's axis were straight up and down?

SECTION 2 *(Pages 30–34)*

9. **a. Describe** What different sources of water are available on Earth?

   b. Draw Conclusions How does the water cycle keep Earth's water supply relatively constant?

   c. Elaborate What water problems affect people around the world? What solutions can you think of for one of those problems?

10. a. Define What is a landform? What are some common types of landforms?

b. Explain What are some effects of physical environmental processes on Earth's surface?

c. Elaborate What physical features dominate the landscape in your community? How do they affect life there?

Using the Internet

11. Activity: Researching Earth's Seasons Earth's seasons not only affect temperatures, they also affect how much daylight is available during specific times of the year. Through your online textbook, research Earth's seasons and view animations to see how seasons change. Then use the interactive worksheet to answer some questions about what you learned.

↗ hmhsocialstudies.com

Social Studies Skills

Using a Physical Map *Examine the physical map of the United States in the back of this book. Use it to answer the questions below.*

12. What physical feature extends along the Gulf of Mexico?

13. What mountain range in the West lies above 6,560 feet?

14. Where does the elevation drop below sea level?

Map Activity

Physical Map *Use the map on the right to answer the questions that follow.*

15. Which letter indicates a river?

16. Which letter on the map indicates the highest elevation?

17. The lowest elevation on the map is indicated by which letter?

18. An island is indicated by which letter?

19. Which letter indicates a large body of water?

20. Which letter indicates an area of land between 1,640 feet and 6,560 feet above sea level?

FOCUS ON READING AND WRITING *my* WriteSmart

Using Word Parts *Use what you learned about prefixes, suffixes, and word roots to answer the questions below.*

21. The prefix *in-* sometimes means "not." What do the words *invisible* and *inactive* mean?

22. The suffix *-ment* means "action" or "process." What does the word *movement* mean?

23. Writing a Haiku Look back through your notes about Earth. Choose one aspect of Earth to describe in a haiku. A haiku is a three-line poem that consists of 17 syllables—five in the first line, seven in the second line, and five in the third line. Use *my*WriteSmart in your eBook to write your haiku. Be sure to use descriptive words to paint a picture of planet Earth.

Reading Social Studies

Using Word Parts

FOCUS ON READING

Many English words are made up of several word parts: roots, prefixes, and suffixes. A root is the base of the word and carries the main meaning. A prefix is a letter or syllable added to the beginning of a root. A suffix is a letter or syllable added to the end to create new words. When you come across a new word, you can sometimes figure out the meaning by looking at its parts. Below are some common word parts and their meanings.

Common Roots		
Word Root	**Meaning**	**Sample Words**
-graph-	write, writing	autograph, biography
-vid-, -vis-	see	videotape, visible

Common Prefixes		
Prefix	**Meaning**	**Sample Words**
geo-	earth	geology
inter-	between, among	interpersonal, intercom
in-	not	ineffective
re-	again	restate, rebuild

Common Suffixes		
Suffix	**Meaning**	**Sample Words**
-ible	capable of	visible, responsible
-less	without	penniless, hopeless
-ment	result, action	commitment
-al	relating to	directional
-tion	the act or condition of	rotation, selection

YOU TRY IT!

Use your knowledge of word parts to understand challenging words such as the ones listed below. Work with a partner to read the words. First separate any prefixes or suffixes and identify the word's root. Use the chart above to define the root, the prefix, or the suffix. Then work with your partner to write a definition for each word.

geography	regardless	reshaping	movement	invisible
seasonal	visualize	separation	interact	

CHAPTER 3

Climate, Environment, and Resources

Essential Question

*my*Notebook

What factors shape Earth's different environments?

Texas Essential Knowledge and Skills (TEKS)

3C, 3D, 6A, 6B, 21B, 21C, 22A, 22D

FOCUS ON READING AND VIEWING

my **Write**Smart

Understanding Cause and Effect A cause makes something happen. An effect is the result of a cause. Words such as *because*, *result*, *since*, and *therefore* can signal causes or effects. As you read, look for causes and effects to understand how things relate. **See the lesson Understanding Cause and Effect on page 77.**

Writing a Weather Report You have likely seen a TV weather report, which tells the current weather conditions and predicts future conditions. After reading this chapter, prepare a weather report for a season and place of your choosing. Present your report to the class and then view your classmates' reports.

Climate Earth has many climates, such as the dry climate of the region shown here.

ANALYSIS SKILL **ANALYZING VISUALS**

This photo shows a severe thunderstorm. These storms produce violent weather, such as heavy rainfall and strong winds, which affects people's lives.

How do you think this storm might have affected the people who lived in this area?

Environments Living things, such as this koala, depend on their surroundings.

Natural Resources Earth provides many valuable and useful natural resources, such as oil.

Weather and Climate

 TEKS 6A, 21B, 21C, 22A, 22D

What You Will Learn...

Main Ideas

1. While weather is short term, climate is a region's average weather over a long period.
2. The amount of sun at a given location is affected by Earth's tilt, movement, and shape.
3. Wind and water move heat around Earth, affecting how warm or wet a place is.
4. Mountains influence temperature and precipitation.

The Big Idea

The sun, location, wind, water, and mountains affect weather and climate.

Key Terms

weather, *p. 50*
climate, *p. 50*
prevailing winds, *p. 51*
ocean currents, *p. 52*
front, *p. 53*

hmhsocialstudies.com
TAKING NOTES

Use the graphic organizer online to take notes on the factors that affect weather and climate.

If YOU lived there...

You live in Buffalo, New York, at the eastern end of Lake Erie. One evening in January, you are watching the local TV news. The weather forecaster says, "A huge storm is brewing in the Midwest and moving east. As usual, winds from this storm will drop several feet of snow on Buffalo as they blow off Lake Erie."

Why will winds off the lake drop snow on Buffalo?

BUILDING BACKGROUND All life on Earth depends on the sun's energy and on the cycle of water from the land to the air and back again. In addition, sun and water work with other forces, such as wind, to create global patterns of weather and climate.

Understanding Weather and Climate

What is it like outside right now where you live? Is it hot, sunny, wet, cold? Is this what it is usually like outside for this time of year? The first two questions are about **weather**, the short-term changes in the air for a given place and time. The last question is about **climate**, a region's average weather conditions over a long period.

Weather is the temperature and precipitation from hour to hour or day to day. "Today is sunny, but tomorrow it might rain" is a statement about weather. Climate is the expected weather for a place based on data and experience. "Summer here is usually hot and muggy" is a statement about climate. The factors that shape weather and climate include the sun, location on Earth, wind, water, and mountains.

READING CHECK **Finding Main Ideas** How are weather and climate different from each other?

Sun and Location

Energy from the sun heats the planet. Different locations receive different amounts of sunlight, though. Thus, some locations are warmer than others. The differences are due to Earth's tilt, movement, and shape.

You have learned that Earth is tilted on its axis. The part of Earth tilted toward the sun receives more solar energy than the part tilted away from the sun. As the Earth revolves around the sun, the part of Earth that is tilted toward the sun changes during the year. This process creates the seasons. In general, temperatures in summer are warmer than in winter.

Earth's shape also affects the amount of sunlight different locations receive. Because Earth is a sphere, its surface is rounded. Therefore, solar rays are more direct and concentrated near the equator. Nearer the poles, the sun's rays are less direct and more spread out.

As a result, areas near the equator, called the lower latitudes, are mainly hot year-round. Areas near the poles, called the higher latitudes, are cold year-round. Areas about halfway between the equator and poles have more seasonal change. In general, the farther from the equator, or the higher the latitude, the colder the climate.

READING CHECK **Summarizing** How does Earth's tilt on its axis affect climate?

Wind and Water

Heat from the sun moves across Earth's surface. The reason is that air and water warmed by the sun are constantly on the move. You might have seen a gust of wind or a stream of water carrying dust or dirt. In a similar way, wind and water carry heat from place to place. As a result, they make different areas of Earth warmer or cooler.

Global Wind Systems

Prevailing winds blow in circular belts across Earth. These belts occur at about every 30° of latitude.

ANALYZING VISUALS Which direction do the prevailing winds blow across the United States?

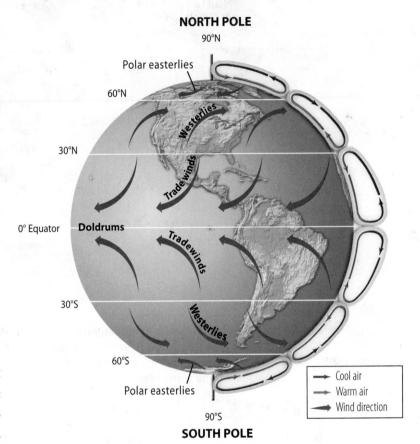

NORTH POLE
90°N
Polar easterlies
60°N
Westerlies
30°N
Trade winds
0° Equator   Doldrums
Tradewinds
30°S
Westerlies
60°S
Polar easterlies
90°S
SOUTH POLE

→ Cool air
→ Warm air
→ Wind direction

Global Winds

Wind, or the sideways movement of air, blows in great streams around the planet. **Prevailing winds** are winds that blow in the same direction over large areas of Earth. The diagram above shows the patterns of Earth's prevailing winds.

To understand Earth's wind patterns, you need to think about the weight of air. Although you cannot feel it, air has weight. This weight changes with the temperature. Cold air is heavier than warm air. For this reason, when air cools, it gets heavier and sinks. When air warms, it gets lighter and rises. As warm air rises, cooler air moves in to take its place, creating wind.

Warm current
Cold current

Arctic Ocean
NORTH AMERICA
North Pacific Ocean
North Atlantic Ocean
EUROPE
ASIA
AFRICA
SOUTH AMERICA
Equator
Indian Ocean
AUSTRALIA
South Pacific Ocean
South Atlantic Ocean
Southern Ocean
ANTARCTICA

map zone
Geography Skills

Movement Ocean currents carry warm water from the equator toward the poles and cold water from the poles toward the equator. The currents affect temperature.

1. **Use the Map** Does a warm or cold ocean current flow along the lower west coast of North America?
2. **Explain** How do ocean currents move heat between warmer and colder areas of Earth?

FOCUS ON READING

What is the effect of Earth's rotation on prevailing winds?

On a global scale, this rising, sinking, and flowing of air creates Earth's prevailing wind patterns. At the equator, hot air rises and flows toward the poles. At the poles, cold air sinks and flows toward the equator. Meanwhile, Earth is rotating. Earth's rotation causes prevailing winds to curve east or west rather than flowing directly north or south.

Depending on their source, prevailing winds make a region warmer or colder. In addition, the source of the winds can make a region drier or wetter. Winds that form from warm air or pass over lots of water often carry moisture. In contrast, winds that form from cold air or pass over lots of land often are dry.

Ocean Currents

Like wind, **ocean currents**—large streams of surface seawater—move heat around Earth. Winds drive these currents. The map above shows how Earth's ocean currents carry warm or cool water to different areas. The water's temperature affects air temperature near it. Warm currents raise temperatures; cold currents lower them.

The Gulf Stream is a warm current that flows north along the U.S. East Coast. It then flows east across the Atlantic to become the North Atlantic Drift. As the warm current flows along northwestern Europe, it heats the air. Westerlies blow the warmed air across Europe. This process makes Europe warmer than it otherwise would be.

Large Bodies of Water

Large bodies of water, such as an ocean or sea, also affect climate. Water heats and cools more slowly than land does. For this reason, large bodies of water make the temperature of the land nearby milder. Thus, coastal areas, such as the California coast, usually do not have as wide temperature ranges as inland areas.

As an example, the state of Michigan is largely surrounded by the Great Lakes. The lakes make temperatures in the state milder than other places as far north.

Wind, Water, and Storms

If you watch weather reports, you will hear about storms moving across the United States. Tracking storms is important to us because the United States has so many of them. As you will see, some areas of the world have more storms than others do.

Most storms occur when two air masses collide. An air mass is a large body of air. The place where two air masses of different temperatures or moisture content meet is a **front**. Cold air masses from the North and warm air masses from the South frequently collide over the United States, producing dramatic storms.

Fronts can produce rain or snow as well as severe weather such as thunderstorms and icy blizzards. Thunderstorms produce rain, lightning, and thunder. In the United States, they are most common in spring and summer. Blizzards produce strong winds and large amounts of snow and are most common during winter.

Thunderstorms and blizzards can also produce tornadoes, another type of severe storm. A tornado is a small, rapidly twisting funnel of air that touches the ground. Tornadoes usually affect a limited area and last only a few minutes. However, they can be highly destructive, uprooting trees and tossing large vehicles through the air.

Tornadoes can be extremely deadly as well. In 1925 a tornado that crossed Missouri, Illinois, and Indiana left 695 people dead. It is the deadliest U.S. tornado on record.

The largest and most destructive storms, however, are hurricanes. These large, rotating storms form over tropical waters in the Atlantic Ocean, usually from late summer to fall. Did you know that hurricanes and typhoons are the same? Typhoons are just hurricanes that form in the Pacific Ocean.

Extreme Weather

Severe weather is often dangerous and destructive. In the top photo, rescuers search for people during a flood in Yardley, Pennsylvania. Below, a tornado races across a wheat field.

53

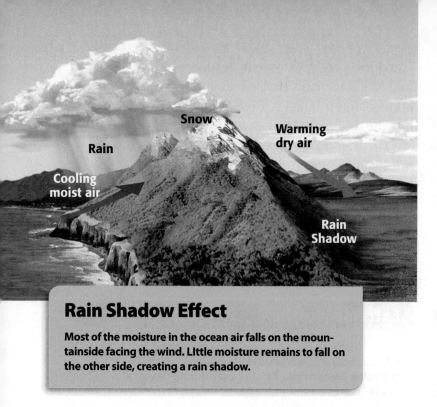

Snow

Rain

Warming
dry air

Cooling
moist air

Rain
Shadow

Rain Shadow Effect

Most of the moisture in the ocean air falls on the mountainside facing the wind. LIttle moisture remains to fall on the other side, creating a rain shadow.

Hurricanes produce drenching rain and strong winds that can reach speeds of 155 miles per hour (250 kph) or more. This is more than twice as fast as most people drive on highways. In addition, hurricanes form tall walls of water called storm surges. When a storm surge smashes into land, it can wipe out an entire coastal area.

READING CHECK **Analyzing** Why do coastal areas have milder climates than inland areas?

Mountains

Mountains can influence an area's climate by affecting both temperature and precipitation. Many high mountains are located in warm areas yet have snow at the top all year. How can this be? The reason is that temperature decreases with elevation—the height on Earth's surface above sea level.

Mountains also create wet and dry areas. Look at the diagram at left. A mountain forces air blowing against it to rise. As it rises, the air cools and precipitation falls as rain or snow. Thus, the side of the mountain facing the wind is often green and lush. However, little moisture remains for the other side. This effect creates a rain shadow, a dry area on the mountainside facing away from the direction of the wind.

READING CHECK **Finding Main Ideas** How does temperature change with elevation?

SUMMARY AND PREVIEW As you can see, the sun, location on Earth, wind, water, and mountains affect weather and climate. In the next section you will learn what the world's different climate regions are like.

Section 1 Assessment

hmhsocialstudies.com
ONLINE QUIZ

Reviewing Ideas, Terms, and Places

1. **a. Recall** What shapes **weather** and **climate**?
   b. Contrast How do weather and climate differ?
2. **a. Identify** What parts of Earth receive the most heat from the sun?
   b. Explain Why do the poles receive less solar energy than the equator does?
3. **a. Geographic Questions** Examine the model of Global Wind Systems in this section. Pose and answer a question about the geographic patterns of winds shown on the model.
   b. Summarize How do **ocean currents** and large bodies of water affect climate?
4. **a. Define** What is a rain shadow?
   b. Explain Why might a mountaintop and a nearby valley have widely different temperatures?

Critical Thinking

5. **Identifying Cause and Effect** Draw a chart like this one. Use your notes to explain how each factor affects climate.

	Effect on Climate
Sun and Location	
Wind	
Water	
Mountains	

FOCUS ON VIEWING

my WriteSmart

6. **Writing about Weather and Climate** Jot down information to include in your weather report. For example, you might want to include a term such as fronts or describe certain types of storms such as hurricanes or tornadoes.

World Climates

If YOU lived there...

You live in Colorado and are on your first serious hike in the Rocky Mountains. Since it is July, it is hot in the campground in the valley. But your guide insists that you bring a heavy fleece jacket. By noon, you have climbed to 11,000 feet. You are surprised to see patches of snow in shady spots. Suddenly, you are very happy that you brought your jacket!

Why does it get colder as you climb higher?

BUILDING BACKGROUND While weather is the day-to-day changes in a certain area, climate is the average weather conditions over a long period. Earth's different climates depend partly on the amount of sunlight a region receives. Differences in climate also depend on factors such as wind, water, and elevation.

Major Climate Zones

In January, how will you dress for the weekend? In some places, you might get dressed to go skiing. In other places, you might head out in a swimsuit to go to the beach. What the seasons are like where you live depends on climate.

Earth is a patchwork of climates. Geographers identify these climates by looking at temperature, precipitation, and native plant life. Using these items, we can divide Earth into five general climate zones—tropical, temperate, polar, dry, and highland.

The first three climate zones relate to latitude. Tropical climates occur near the equator, in the low latitudes. Temperate climates occur about halfway between the equator and the poles, in the middle latitudes. Polar climates occur near the poles, in the high latitudes. The last two climate zones occur at many different latitudes. In addition, geographers divide some climate zones into more specific climate regions. The chart and map on the next two pages describe the world's climate regions.

READING CHECK **Drawing Inferences** Why do you think geographers consider native plant life when categorizing climates?

TEKS 6A, 21B, 21C, 22A, 22D

What You Will Learn...

Main Ideas

1. Geographers use temperature, precipitation, and plant life to identify climate zones.
2. Tropical climates are wet and warm, while dry climates receive little or no rain.
3. Temperate climates have the most seasonal change.
4. Polar climates are cold and dry, while highland climates change with elevation.

The Big Idea

Earth's five major climate zones are identified by temperature, precipitation, and plant life.

Key Terms

monsoons, *p. 58*
savannas, *p. 58*
steppes, *p. 59*
permafrost, *p. 61*

hmhsocialstudies.com
TAKING NOTES

Use the graphic organizer online to take notes on Earth's major climate zones.

World Climate Regions

To explore the world's climate regions, start with the chart below. After reading about each climate region, locate the places on the map that have that climate. As you locate climates, look for patterns. For example, places near the equator tend to have warmer climates than places near the poles. See if you can identify some other climate patterns.

Tropical climate

Climate		Where is it?	What is it like?	Plants
Tropical	HUMID TROPICAL	On and near the equator	Warm with high amounts of rain year-round; in a few places, monsoons create extreme wet seasons	Tropical rain forest
	TROPICAL SAVANNA	Higher latitudes in the tropics	Warm all year; distinct rainy and dry seasons; at least 20 inches (50 cm) of rain during the summer	Tall grasses and scattered trees
Dry	DESERT	Mainly center on 30° latitude; also in middle of continents, on west coasts, or in rain shadows	Sunny and dry; less than 10 inches (25 cm) of rain a year; hot in the tropics; cooler with wide daytime temperature ranges in middle latitudes	A few hardy plants, such as cacti
	STEPPE	Mainly bordering deserts and interiors of large continents	About 10–20 inches (25–50 cm) of precipitation a year; hot summers and cooler winters with wide temperature ranges during the day	Shorter grasses; some trees and shrubs by water
Temperate	MEDITERRANEAN	West coasts in middle latitudes	Dry, sunny, warm summers; mild, wetter winters; rain averages 15–20 inches (30–50 cm) a year	Scrub woodland and grassland
	HUMID SUBTROPICAL	East coasts in middle latitudes	Humid with hot summers and mild winters; rain year-round; in paths of hurricanes and typhoons	Mixed forest
	MARINE WEST COAST	West coasts in the upper-middle latitudes	Cloudy, mild summers and cool, rainy winters; strong ocean influence	Evergreen forests
	HUMID CONTINENTAL	East coasts and interiors of upper-middle latitudes	Four distinct seasons; long, cold winters and short, warm summers; average precipitation varies	Mixed forest

Polar climate

Dry climate

Climate		Where is it?	What is it like?	Plants
Polar	SUBARCTIC	Higher latitudes of the interior and east coasts of continents	Extremes of temperature; long, cold winters and short, warm summers; little precipitation	Northern evergreen forests
	TUNDRA	Coasts in high latitudes	Cold all year; very long, cold winters and very short, cool summers; little precipitation; permafrost	Moss, lichens, low shrubs
	ICE CAP	Polar regions	Freezing cold; snow and ice; little precipitation	No vegetation
Highland	HIGHLAND	High mountain regions	Wide range of temperatures and precipitation amounts, depending on elevation and location	Ranges from forest to tundra

Geography Skills

Regions Note how Earth's climate regions relate to different locations.

1. **Locate** Which climates are found mainly in the Northern Hemisphere?
2. **Identify** What climate does most of northern Africa have?
3. **Make Generalizations** Where are many of the world's driest climates found on Earth?
4. **Interpreting Charts** Examine the chart. Which two climates have the least amount of vegetation?

hmhsocialstudies.com

The Tuareg of the Sahara.

In the Sahara, the world's largest desert, temperatures can top 130°F (54°C). Yet the Tuareg (TWAH-reg) of North and West Africa call the Sahara home—and prefer it. The Tuareg have raised camels and other animals in the Sahara for more than 1,000 years. The animals graze on sparse desert plants. When the plants are gone, the Tuareg move on.

In camp, Tuareg families live in tents made from animal skins. Some wealthier Tuareg live in adobe homes. The men traditionally wear blue veils wrapped around their face and head. The veils help protect against windblown desert dust.

Summarizing How have the Tuareg adapted to life in a desert?

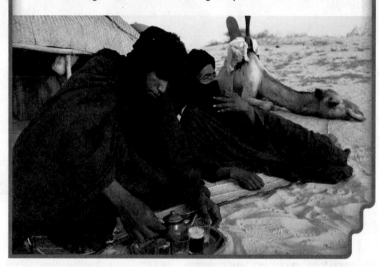

Tropical and Dry Climates

Are you the type of person who likes to go to extremes? Then tropical and dry climates might be for you. These climates include the wettest, driest, and hottest places on Earth.

Tropical Climates

Our tour of Earth's climates starts at the equator, in the heart of the tropics. This region extends from the Tropic of Cancer to the Tropic of Capricorn. Look back at the map to locate this region.

Humid Tropical Climate At the equator, the hot, damp air hangs like a thick, wet blanket. Sweat quickly coats your body.

Welcome to the humid tropical climate. This climate is warm, muggy, and rainy year-round. Temperatures average about 80°F (26°C). Showers or storms occur almost daily, and rainfall ranges from 70 to more than 450 inches (180 to 1,140 cm) a year. In comparison, only a few parts of the United States average more than 70 inches (180 cm) of rain a year.

Some places with a humid tropical climate have **monsoons**, seasonal winds that bring either dry or moist air. During one part of the year, a moist ocean wind creates an extreme wet season. The winds then shift direction, and a dry land wind creates a dry season. Monsoons affect several parts of Asia. For example, the town of Mawsynram, India, receives on average more than 450 inches (1,140 cm) of rain a year—all in about six months! That is about 37 feet (11 m) of rain. As you can imagine, flooding during wet seasons is common and can be severe.

The humid tropical climate's warm temperatures and heavy rainfall support tropical rain forests. These lush forests contain more types of plants and animals than anywhere else on Earth. The world's largest rain forest is in the Amazon River basin in South America. There you can find more than 50,000 species, including giant lily pads, poisonous tree frogs, and toucans.

Tropical Savanna Climate Moving north and south away from the equator, we find the tropical savanna climate. This climate has a long, hot, dry season followed by short periods of rain. Rainfall is much lower than at the equator but still high. Temperatures are hot in the summer, often as high as 90°F (32°C). Winters are cooler but rarely get cold.

This climate does not receive enough rainfall to support dense forests. Instead, it supports **savannas**—areas of tall grasses and scattered trees and shrubs.

Dry Climates

Leaving Earth's wettest places, we head to its driest. These climates are found in a number of locations on the planet.

Desert Climate Picture the sun baking down on a barren wasteland. This is the desert, Earth's hottest and driest climate. Deserts receive less than 10 inches (25 cm) of rain a year. Dry air and clear skies produce high daytime temperatures and rapid cooling at night. In some deserts, highs can top 130°F (54°C)! Under such conditions, only very hardy plants and animals can live. Many plants grow far apart so as not to compete for water. Others, such as cacti, store water in fleshy stems and leaves.

Steppe Climate Semidry grasslands or prairies—called **steppes** (STEPS)—often border deserts. Steppes receive slightly more rain than deserts do. Short grasses are the most common plants, but shrubs and trees grow along streams and rivers.

READING CHECK ▶ **Contrasting** What are some ways in which tropical and dry climates differ?

Temperate Climates

If you enjoy hot, sunny days as much as chilly, rainy ones, then temperate climates are for you. *Temperate* means "moderate" or "mild." These mild climates tend to have four seasons, with warm or hot summers and cool or cold winters.

Temperate climates occur in the middle latitudes, the regions halfway between the equator and the poles. Air masses from the tropics and the poles often meet in these regions, which creates a number of different temperate climates. You very likely live in one, because most Americans do.

Mediterranean Climate Named for the region of the Mediterranean Sea, this sunny, pleasant climate is found in many popular vacation areas. In a Mediterranean climate, summers are hot, dry, and sunny. Winters are mild and somewhat wet. Plant life includes shrubs and short trees with scattered larger trees. The Mediterranean climate occurs mainly in coastal areas. In the United States, much of California has this climate.

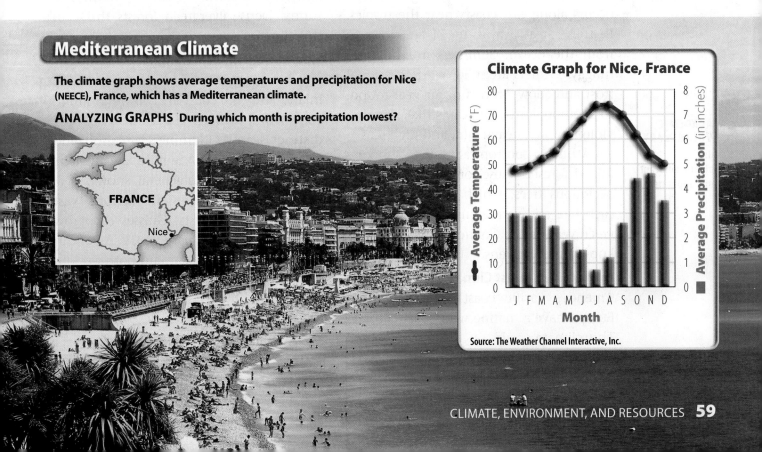

Mediterranean Climate

The climate graph shows average temperatures and precipitation for Nice (NEECE), France, which has a Mediterranean climate.

ANALYZING GRAPHS During which month is precipitation lowest?

FRANCE
Nice

Climate Graph for Nice, France

Source: The Weather Channel Interactive, Inc.

Highland Climates

Mount Kilimanjaro is the tallest mountain in Africa. Although Kilimanjaro is only about 200 miles (320 km) south of the equator, snow blankets its highest peak.

Kilimanjaro rises to 19,341 ft (5,895 m). The snow-covered summit has an ice cap climate.

Climate and plant life ranges from rain forest, to steppe, to desert, to tundra.

A tropical savanna climate is found around the base of Mount Kilimanjaro.

ANALYSIS SKILL **ANALYZING VISUALS**

Which type of climate is found on the top of Mount Kilimanjaro?

Humid Subtropical Climate The southeastern United States is an example of the humid subtropical climate. This climate occurs along east coasts near the tropics. In these areas, warm, moist air blows in from the ocean. Summers are hot and muggy. Winters are mild, with occasional frost and snow. Storms occur year-round. In addition, hurricanes can strike, bringing violent winds, heavy rain, and high seas.

A humid subtropical climate supports mixed forests. These forests include both deciduous trees, which lose their leaves each fall, and coniferous trees, which are green year-round. Coniferous trees are also known as evergreens.

Marine West Coast Climate Parts of North America's Pacific coast and of western Europe have a marine west coast climate. This climate occurs on west coasts where winds carry moisture in from the seas.

The moist air keeps temperatures mild year-round. Winters are foggy, cloudy, and rainy, while summers can be warm and sunny. Dense evergreen forests thrive in this climate.

Humid Continental Climate Closer to the poles, in the upper–middle latitudes, many inland and east coast areas have a humid continental climate. This climate has four **distinct** seasons. Summers are short and hot. Spring and fall are mild, and winters are long, cold, and in general, snowy.

This climate's rainfall supports vast grasslands and forests. Grasses can grow very tall, such as in parts of the American Great Plains. Forests contain both deciduous and coniferous trees, with coniferous forests occurring in the colder areas.

READING CHECK **Categorizing** Which of the temperate climates is too dry to support forests?

ACADEMIC VOCABULARY

distinct clearly different and separate

Polar and Highland Climates

Get ready to feel the chill as we end our tour in the polar and highland climates. The three polar climates are found in the high latitudes near the poles. The varied highland climate is found on mountains.

Subarctic Climate The subarctic climate and the tundra climate described below occur mainly in the Northern Hemisphere south of the Arctic Ocean. In the subarctic climate, winters are long and bitterly cold. Summers are short and cool. Temperatures stay below freezing for about half the year. The climate's moderate rainfall supports vast evergreen forests, or taiga (TY-guh).

Tundra Climate The tundra climate occurs in coastal areas along the Arctic Ocean. As in the subarctic climate, winters are long and bitterly cold. Temperatures rise above freezing only during the short summer. Rainfall is light, and only plants such as mosses, lichens, and small shrubs grow.

In parts of the tundra, soil layers stay frozen all year. Permanently frozen layers of soil are called **permafrost**. Frozen earth absorbs water poorly, which creates ponds and marshes in summer. This moisture causes plants to burst forth in bloom.

Ice Cap Climate The harshest places on Earth may be the North and South poles. These regions have an ice cap climate. Temperatures are bone-numbingly cold, and lows of more than –120°F (–84°C) have been recorded. Snow and ice remain year-round, but precipitation is light. Not surprisingly, no vegetation grows. However, mammals such as penguins and polar bears thrive.

Highland Climates Highland climates are cool to cold climates in mountain areas. They are unique because they contain several climate zones. This is because, as you climb a mountain, the climate changes. Temperatures drop, and plant life grows sparser. Going up a mountain can be like going from the tropics to the poles. On very tall mountains, ice coats the summit year-round.

FOCUS ON READING
What is the effect of elevation on climate?

READING CHECK **Comparing** How are polar and highland climates similar?

SUMMARY AND PREVIEW As you can see, Earth has many climates, which we identify based on temperature, precipitation, and native plant life. In the next section you will read about how nature and all living things are connected.

Section 2 Assessment

hmhsocialstudies.com
ONLINE QUIZ

Reviewing Ideas, Terms, and Places

1. **a. Recall** Which three major climate zones are most closely related to latitude?
   b. Summarize How do geographers categorize Earth's different climates?
2. **a. Define** What are **monsoons**?
   b. Make Inferences In which type of dry climate do you think the fewest people live, and why?
3. **a. Identify** What are the four temperate climates?
   b. Geographic Questions Use the climate graph on page 59 to pose and answer a question about climate patterns in Nice, France.
4. **a. Describe** What are some effects of **permafrost**?
   b. Explain How are highland climates unique?

Critical Thinking

5. **Categorizing** Create a chart like the one below for each climate region. Then use your notes to describe each climate region's average temperatures, precipitation, and native plant life.

| Climate Region | → | Temperature | Precipitation | Plant Life |

FOCUS ON VIEWING

my WriteSmart

6. **Discussing World Climates** Add information about the climate of the place you have selected, such as average temperature and precipitation.

TEKS 6A, 6B, 21B, 21C, 22A, 22D

What You Will Learn...

Main Ideas

1. The environment and life are interconnected and exist in a fragile balance.
2. Soils play an important role in the environment.

The Big Idea

Plants, animals, and the environment, including soil, interact and affect one another.

Key Terms

environment, *p. 62*
ecosystem, *p. 63*
habitat, *p. 64*
extinct, *p. 64*
humus, *p. 65*
desertification, *p. 65*

hmhsocialstudies.com
TAKING NOTES

Use the graphic organizer online to take notes on Earth's natural environments.

Natural Environments

If YOU lived there...

When your family moved to the city, you were sure you would miss the woods and pond near your old house. Then one of your new friends at school told you there's a large park only a few blocks away. You wondered how interesting a city park could be. But you were surprised at the many plants and animals that live there.

What environments might you see in the park?

BUILDING BACKGROUND No matter where you live, you are part of a natural environment. From a desert to a rain forest to a city park, every environment is home to a unique community of plant and animal life. These plants and animals live in balance with nature.

The Environment and Life

If you saw a wild polar bear outside your school, you would likely be shocked. In most parts of the United States, polar bears live only in zoos. This is because plants and animals must live where they are suited to the **environment**, or surroundings. Polar bears are suited to very cold places with lots of ice, water, and fish. As you will see, living things and their environments are connected and affect each other in many ways.

Limits on Life

The environment limits life. As our tour of the world's climates showed, factors such as temperature, rainfall, and soil conditions limit where plants and animals can live. Palm trees cannot survive at the frigid North Pole. Ferns will quickly wilt and die in deserts, but they thrive in tropical rain forests.

At the same time, all plants and animals are adapted to specific environments. For example, kangaroo rats are adapted to dry desert environments. These small rodents can get all the water they need from food, so they seldom have to drink water.

Connections in Nature

The interconnections between living things and the environment form ecosystems. An **ecosystem** is a group of plants and animals that depend on each other for survival and the environment in which they live. Ecosystems can be any size and can occur wherever air, water, and soil support life. A garden pond, a city park, a prairie, and a rain forest are all examples of ecosystems.

The diagram below shows a forest ecosystem. Each part of this ecosystem fills a certain role. The sun provides energy to the plants, which use the energy to make their own food. The plants then serve as food, either directly or indirectly, for all other life in the forest. When the plants and animals die, their remains break down and provide nutrients for the soil and new plant growth. Thus, the cycle continues.

Close-up

A Forest Ecosystem

A forest is one type of ecosystem. The plants and animals in the forest depend on one another and the forest environment for survival.

1 Sunlight is the source of energy for most living things.

2 Plants use the energy in sunlight to make food. They serve as the basis for other life in the ecosystem.

3 Animals such as rabbits eat plants and gain some of their energy.

4 Predators, such as wolves and hawks, eat rabbits and other prey for energy.

5 Larger predators, such as mountain lions, compete for the prey that is available.

ANALYSIS SKILL ANALYZING VISUALS

What might happen in the forest ecosystem above if the number of rabbits fell significantly?

Changes to Environments

The interconnected parts of an ecosystem exist in a fragile balance. For this reason, a small change to one part can affect the whole system. A lack of rain in the forest ecosystem could kill off many of the plants that feed the rabbits. If the rabbits die, there will be less food for the wolves and mountain lions. Then they too may die.

Many actions can affect ecosystems. For example, people need places to live and food to eat, so they clear land for homes and farms. Clearing land has **consequences**, however. It can cause the soil to erode. In addition, the plants and animals that live in the area might be left without food and shelter.

Actions such as clearing land and polluting can destroy habitats. A **habitat** is the place where a plant or animal lives. The most diverse habitats on Earth are tropical rain forests. People are clearing Earth's rain forests for farmland, lumber, and other reasons, though. As a result, these diverse habitats are being lost.

ACADEMIC VOCABULARY

consequences the effects of a particular event or events

FOCUS ON READING

What are some causes of habitat destruction?

Extreme changes in ecosystems can cause species to die out, or become **extinct**. For example, flightless birds called dodos once lived on Mauritius, an island in the Indian Ocean. When people first settled there, they hunted dodos and introduced predators, such as dogs. First seen in 1507, dodos were extinct by 1681.

Recognizing these problems, many countries are working to balance people's needs with the needs of the environment. The United States, for example, has passed many laws to limit pollution, manage forests, and protect valuable ecosystems.

> **READING CHECK** **Drawing Inferences** How might one change affect an entire ecosystem?

Soil and the Environment

As you know, plants are the basis for all food that animals eat. Soils help determine what plants will grow and how well. Because soils support plant life, they play an important role in the environment.

CONNECTING TO Science

Soil Factory

The next time you see a fallen tree in the forest, do not think of it as a dead log. Think of it as a soil factory. A fallen tree is buzzing with the activity of countless insects, bacteria, and other organisms. These organisms invade the fallen log and start to break the wood down.

As the tree decays and crumbles, it turns into humus. Humus is a rich blend of organic material. The humus mixes with the soil and broken rock material. These added nutrients then enrich the soil, making it possible for new trees and plants to grow. Fallen trees provide as much as one-third of the organic material in forest soil.

Summarizing What causes a fallen tree to change into soil?

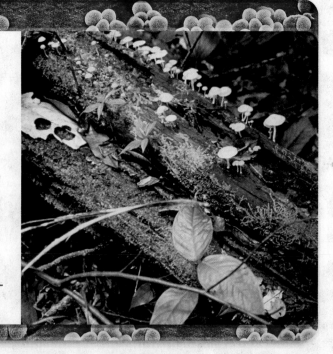

Fertile soils are rich in minerals and **humus** (HYOO-muhs), decayed plant or animal matter. These soils can support abundant plant life. Like air and water, fertile soil is essential for life. Without it, we could not grow much of the food we eat.

Soils can lose fertility in several ways. Erosion from wind or water can sweep topsoil away. Planting the same crops over and over can also rob soil of its fertility. When soil becomes worn out, it cannot support as many plants. In fragile dry environments this can lead to the spread of desertlike conditions, or **desertification**. The spread of desertlike conditions is a serious problem in many parts of the world.

READING CHECK **Analyzing** What do fertile soils contain, and why are these soils important?

SUMMARY AND PREVIEW Living things and the environment are connected, but changes can easily upset the balance in an ecosystem. Because they support plant life, soils are important parts of ecosystems. In the next section you will learn about Earth's many resources.

Soil Layers

The three layers of soil are the topsoil, subsoil, and broken rock. The thickness of each layer depends on the conditions in a specific location.

ANALYZING VISUALS In which layer of soil are most plant roots and insects found?

Topsoil

Subsoil

Broken Rock

Solid Rock

Section 3 Assessment

hmhsocialstudies.com
ONLINE QUIZ

Reviewing Ideas, Terms, and Places

1. **a. Define** What is an **ecosystem**, and what are two examples of ecosystems?
   b. Summarize How do nature and people change ecosystems?
   c. Elaborate Why can plants and animals not live everywhere?
2. **a. Recall** What is **humus**, and why is it important to soil?
   b. Identify Cause and Effect What actions can cause **desertification**, and what might be some possible effects?
   c. Elaborate Why is it important for geographers and scientists to study soils?

Critical Thinking

3. **Identifying Cause and Effect** Review your notes. Then use a chart like this one to identify some of the causes and effects of changes to ecosystems.

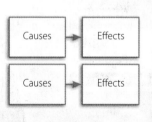

FOCUS ON VIEWING

my WriteSmart

4. **Writing about Natural Environments** Jot down ideas about how different types of weather might affect the environment of the place you chose. For example, how might lack of rain affect the area?

Earth's Changing Environments

PANGAEA

Pangaea About 250 million years ago, all of Earth's continents were connected, forming one giant landmass called Pangaea.

What was North America like 74 million years ago, when dinosaurs roamed Earth? You might be surprised to learn that it was a very different place. Earth's environments are always changing. The map at right shows North America in the age of dinosaurs. Back then, the climate was warm and humid, and large inland seas covered much of the land. The region's plants and animals were completely different. Slowly, however, things changed. Some major event, possibly an asteroid impact, wiped out the dinosaurs. Over time, North America's environments changed into the ones that exist today.

HISTORY

VIDEO
Future Chill

hmhsocialstudies.com

What Survived Dinosaurs, such as the plant-eating ceratopsian at left, are long gone. But insects, such as cockroaches and dragonflies, are still around.

GREENLAND

Labrador Seaway

NORTH

AMERICA

Western Interior Seaway

Hudson Seaway

COAST MOUNTAINS

SIERRA MADRE OCCIDENTAL

ROCKY MOUNTAINS

APPALACHIAN MOUNTAINS

North America in the Dinosaur Age
Over time, Earth's continents slowly moved apart. About 74 million years ago, North America looked like the map at left. Inland seas covered parts of the continent. The map below shows North America today.

NORTH AMERICA TODAY

ANALYSIS
SKILL ANALYZING VISUALS

1. **Name** What mountain ranges covered parts of North America 74 million years ago?
2. **Contrast** Based on the maps above, how has North America changed since the dinosaur age?

Natural Resources

TEKS 3D, 6B, 6C, 21B, 21C, 22A, 22D

What You Will Learn...

Main Ideas

1. Earth provides valuable resources for our use.
2. Energy resources provide fuel, heat, and electricity.
3. Mineral resources include metals, rocks, and salt.
4. Resources shape people's lives and countries' wealth.

The Big Idea

Earth's natural resources have many valuable uses, and their availability affects people in many ways.

Key Terms

natural resource, *p. 68*
renewable resources, *p. 69*
nonrenewable resources, *p. 69*
deforestation, *p. 69*
reforestation, *p. 69*
fossil fuels, *p. 69*
hydroelectric power, *p. 70*

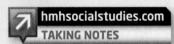
hmhsocialstudies.com
TAKING NOTES

Use the graphic organizer online to take notes on Earth's resources.

If YOU lived there...

You live in Southern California, where the climate is warm and dry. Every week, you water the grass around your house to keep it green. Now the city has declared a "drought emergency" because of a lack of rain. City officials have put limits on watering lawns and on other uses of water.

How can you help conserve scarce water?

BUILDING BACKGROUND In addition to plant and animal life, other resources in the environment greatly influence people. In fact, certain vital resources, such as water, soils, and minerals, may determine whether people choose to live in a place or how wealthy people are.

Earth's Valuable Resources

Think about the materials in nature that you use. You have learned about the many ways we use sun, water, and land. They are just a start, though. Look at the human-made products around you. They all required the use of natural materials in some way. We use trees to make paper for books. We use petroleum, or oil, to make plastics for cell phones. We use metals to make machines, which we then use to make many items. Without these materials, our lives would change drastically.

Using Natural Resources

Trees, oil, and metals are all examples of natural resources. A **natural resource** is any material in nature that people use and value. Earth's most important natural resources include air, water, soils, forests, and minerals.

Understanding how and why people use natural resources is an important part of geography. We use some natural resources just as they are, such as wind. Usually, though, we change natural resources to make something new. For example, we change metals to make products such as bicycles and watches. Thus, most natural resources are raw materials for other products.

Reforestation

Members of the Green Belt Movement plant trees in Kenya. Although trees are a renewable resource, some forests are being cut down faster than new trees can replace them. Reforestation helps protect Earth's valuable forestlands.

ANALYZING VISUALS How does reforestation help the environment?

BIOGRAPHY

Wangari Maathai
(1940–2011)

Can planting a tree improve people's lives? Wangari Maathai thinks so. Born in Kenya in East Africa, Maathai wanted to help people in her country, many of whom were poor. She asked herself what Kenyans could do to improve their lives. "Planting a tree was the best idea that I had," she says. In 1977 Maathai founded the Green Belt Movement to plant trees and protect forestland. The group has now planted more than 30 million trees across Kenya! These trees provide wood and prevent soil erosion. In 2004 Maathai was awarded the Nobel Peace Prize. She is the first African woman to receive this famous award.

Types of Natural Resources

We group natural resources into two types, those we can replace and those we cannot. **Renewable resources** are resources Earth replaces naturally. For example, when we cut down a tree, another tree can grow in its place. Renewable resources include water, soil, trees, plants, and animals. These resources can last forever if used wisely.

Other natural resources will run out one day. These **nonrenewable resources** are resources that cannot be replaced. For example, coal formed over millions of years. Once we use the coal up, it is gone.

Managing Natural Resources

People need to manage natural resources to protect them for the future. Consider how your life might change if we ran out of forests, for example. Although forests are renewable, we can cut down trees far faster than they can grow. The result is the clearing of trees, or **deforestation**.

By managing resources, however, we can repair and prevent resource loss. For example, some groups are engaged in **reforestation**, planting trees to replace lost forestland.

READING CHECK **Contrasting** How do renewable and nonrenewable resources differ?

Energy Resources

Every day you use plants and animals from the dinosaur age—in the form of energy resources. These resources power vehicles, produce heat, and generate electricity. They are some of our most important and valuable natural resources.

Nonrenewable Energy Resources

Most of the energy we use comes from **fossil fuels**, nonrenewable resources that formed from the remains of ancient plants and animals. The most important fossil fuels are coal, petroleum, and natural gas.

Coal has long been a reliable energy source for heat. However, burning coal causes some problems. It pollutes the air and can harm the land. For these reasons, people have used coal less as other fuel options became available.

FOCUS ON READING
In the second sentence on this page, what cause does the word *because* signal? What is the effect of this cause?

Today we use coal mainly to create electricity at power plants, not to heat single buildings. Because coal is plentiful, people are looking for cleaner ways to burn it.

Petroleum, or oil, is a dark liquid used to make fuels and other products. When first removed from the ground, petroleum is called crude oil. This oil is shipped or piped to refineries, factories that process the crude oil to make products. Fuels made from oil include gasoline, diesel fuel, and jet fuel. Oil is also used to make petrochemicals, which are processed to make products such as plastics and cosmetics.

As with coal, burning oil-based fuels can pollute the air and land. In addition, oil spills can harm wildlife. Because we are so dependent on oil for energy, however, it is an extremely valuable resource.

The cleanest-burning fossil fuel is natural gas. We use it mainly for heating and cooking. For example, your kitchen stove may use natural gas. Some vehicles run on natural gas as well. These vehicles cause less pollution than those that run on gasoline.

Renewable Energy Resources

Unlike fossil fuels, renewable energy resources will not run out. They also are generally better for the environment. On the other hand, they are not available everywhere and can be costly.

The main alternative to fossil fuels is **hydroelectric power**—the production of electricity from waterpower. We obtain energy from moving water by damming rivers. The dams harness the power of moving water to generate electricity.

Hydroelectric power has both pros and cons. On the positive side, it produces power without polluting and lessens our use of fossil fuels. On the negative side, dams create lakes that replace existing resources, such as farmland, and disrupt wildlife habitats.

Another renewable energy source is wind. People have long used wind to power windmills. Today we use wind to power wind turbines, a type of modern windmill. At wind farms, hundreds of turbines create electricity in windy places.

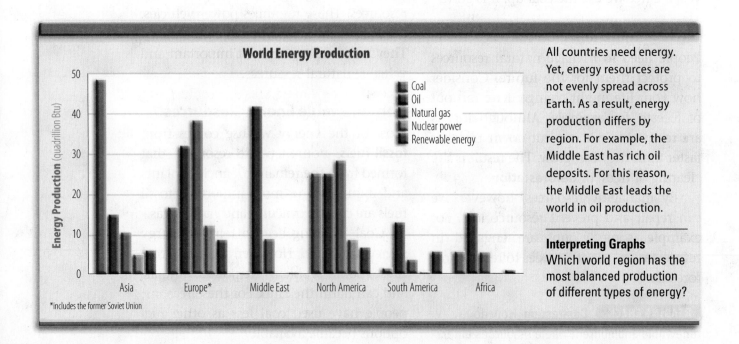

World Energy Production

Energy Production (quadrillion Btu)

- Coal
- Oil
- Natural gas
- Nuclear power
- Renewable energy

Asia   Europe*   Middle East   North America   South America   Africa

*includes the former Soviet Union

All countries need energy. Yet, energy resources are not evenly spread across Earth. As a result, energy production differs by region. For example, the Middle East has rich oil deposits. For this reason, the Middle East leads the world in oil production.

Interpreting Graphs
Which world region has the most balanced production of different types of energy?

A third source of renewable energy is heat from the sun and Earth. We can use solar power, or power from the sun, to heat water or homes. Using special solar panels, we turn solar energy into electricity. We can also use geothermal energy, or heat from within Earth. Geothermal power plants use steam and hot water located within Earth to create electricity.

Nuclear Energy

A final energy source is nuclear energy. We obtain this energy by splitting atoms, small particles of matter. This process uses the metal uranium, so some people consider nuclear energy a nonrenewable resource. Nuclear power does not pollute the air, but it does produce dangerous wastes. These wastes must be stored for thousands of years before they are safe. In addition, an accident at a nuclear power plant can have terrible effects.

READING CHECK **Drawing Inferences** Why might people look for alternatives to fossil fuels?

Mineral Resources

Like energy resources, mineral resources can be quite valuable. These resources include metals, salt, rocks, and gemstones.

Minerals fulfill countless needs. Look around you to see a few. Your school building likely includes steel, made from iron. The outer walls might be granite or limestone. The window glass is made from quartz, a mineral in sand. From staples to jewelry to coins, metals are everywhere.

Minerals are nonrenewable, so we need to conserve them. Recycling items such as aluminum cans will make the supply of these valuable resources last longer.

READING CHECK **Categorizing** What are the major types of mineral resources?

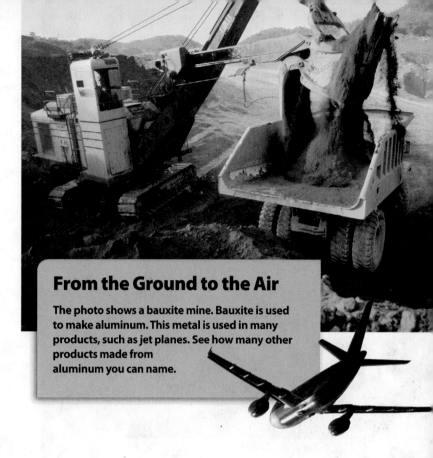

From the Ground to the Air

The photo shows a bauxite mine. Bauxite is used to make aluminum. This metal is used in many products, such as jet planes. See how many other products made from aluminum you can name.

Resources and People

Natural resources vary from place to place. The resources available in a region can shape life and wealth for the people there.

Resources and Daily Life

The natural resources available to people affect their lifestyles and needs. In the United States we have many different kinds of natural resources. We can choose among many different ways to dress, eat, live, travel, and entertain ourselves. People in places with fewer natural resources will likely have fewer choices and different needs than Americans.

For example, people who live in remote rain forests depend on forest resources for most of their needs. These people may craft containers by weaving plant fibers together. They may make canoes by hollowing out tree trunks. Instead of being concerned about money, they might be more concerned about food.

Products from Petroleum

This Ohio family shows some common products made from petroleum, or oil.

ANALYZING VISUALS What petroleum-based products can you identify in this photo?

Resources and Wealth

The availability of natural resources affects countries' economies as well. For example, the many natural resources available in the United States have helped it become one of the world's wealthiest countries. In contrast, countries with few natural resources often have weak economies.

Some countries have one or two valuable resources but few others. For example, Saudi Arabia is rich in oil but lacks water for growing food. As a result, Saudi Arabia must use its oil profits to import food.

READING CHECK **Identifying Cause and Effect** How can having few natural resources affect life and wealth in a region or country?

SUMMARY AND PREVIEW You can see that Earth's natural resources have many uses. Important natural resources include air, water, soils, forests, fuels, and minerals. In the next chapter you will read about the world's people and cultures.

Section 4 Assessment

hmhsocialstudies.com
ONLINE QUIZ

Reviewing Ideas, Terms, and Places

1. a. Define What are **renewable resources** and **nonrenewable resources**?
b. Explain Why is it important for people to manage Earth's natural resources?
c. Develop What are some things you can do to help manage and conserve natural resources?

2. a. Define What are **fossil fuels**, and why are they significant?
b. Summarize What are three examples of renewable energy resources?
c. Compare Regions Look back at the graph of World Energy Production on page 70. How does energy production in the United States compare to energy production in the Middle East?

3. a. Recall What are the main types of mineral resources?
b. Analyze What are some products that we get from mineral resources?

4. a. Describe How do resources affect people?
b. Make Inferences How might a country with only one valuable resource develop its economy?

Critical Thinking

5. Categorizing
Draw a chart like this one. Use your notes to identify and evaluate each energy resource.

	Fossil Fuels	Renewable Energy	Nuclear Energy
	Pros	Pros	Pros
	Cons	Cons	Cons

FOCUS ON VIEWING

6. Noting Details about Natural Resources What natural resources does the place you chose have? Note ways to refer to some of these resources (or the lack of them) in your weather report.

BOOK
Geography for Life

The book Geography for Life *is an overview of geographic perspectives, knowledge, and skills to help readers become geographically literate. Below is a passage from the book about Earth's diverse ecosystems.*

Ecosystems form distinct regions on Earth's surface, which vary in size, shape, and complexity. They exist at a variety of scales, from small and very localized areas (e.g., a single stand of oak trees or a clump of xerophytic[1] grasses) to larger areas with precise geographic boundaries (e.g., a pond, desert biome[2], island, or beach). Larger scale ecosystems can form continent-wide belts, such as the tundra, taiga, and steppe of northern Asia. The largest ecosystem is the planet itself.

However, the stability and balance of ecosystems can be altered by large-scale natural events such as El Niño[3], volcanic eruptions, fire, or drought. But ecosystems are more drastically transformed by human activities....For example, the overgrazing of pasturelands, coupled with a period of drought, can lead to vegetation loss, the exposure of topsoil layers, and massive soil erosion (as occurred in the 1930s Dust Bowl[4]); tropical forest clear-cutting[5] can lead to soil erosion and ecological break-down, as is currently occurring in Amazonia[6].

The Amazon River basin is mostly made up of rainforest ecosystems.

> Notice the wide range of ecosystems described by the author.

> El Niño can affect ecosystems by dramatically increasing rainfall in some regions and causing severe drought in others.

[1] **xerophytic:** adapted to living in a dry, arid habitat
[2] **biome:** a large community of living organisms, such as a grassland or desert
[3] **El Niño:** unusually warm ocean water temperatures that dramatically affect the weather across the Pacific Ocean
[4] **Dust Bowl:** an area in the southern Great Plains that was stricken with drought during the Great Depression
[5] **clear-cutting:** logging an area by removing all of the trees at one time
[6] **Amazonia:** the Amazon River basin in northern South America

ANALYSIS SKILL ANALYZING PRIMARY SOURCES

1. **Describing** What types of details about ecosystems does the author include?
2. **Analyzing** Why do you think humans sometimes have a negative effect on ecosystems?

Social Studies Skills

| Chart and Graph | Critical Thinking | Geography | Study |

Creating and Analyzing a Bar Graph

Learn

Bar graphs are drawings that use bars to show data in a clear, visual format. Use these guidelines to create bar graphs.

- Decide on a topic to illustrate with a bar graph. Then research the data you want to show.

- Identify what the graph will measure and the units of measurement being used. For example, this bar graph is measuring precipitation by climate. The unit of measurement is inches.

- After you have created a bar graph, analyze and compare the data. As you do, note any increases or decreases and look for trends or changes over time.

This bar graph compares the average annual precipitation of six climate regions.

The height of each bar indicates the amount of precipitation.

Average Annual Precipitation by Climate Region

This graph shows precipitation in inches.

The names of the climate regions appear across the bottom.

Practice

1. On the bar graph above, which climate region has the highest average annual precipitation?

2. Which two climate regions have about the same amount?

3. Which climate region receives an average of between 50 and 75 inches of precipitation each year?

Apply

Examine the World Energy Production Today bar graph in Section 4. Then use the graph to answer the following questions.

1. Which region produces the most oil?

2. Which three regions produce little or no nuclear power?

3. Based on the graph, what type of energy resource do most Asian countries likely use?

Chapter Review

Visual Summary

Use the visual summary below to help you review the main ideas of the chapter.

QUICK FACTS

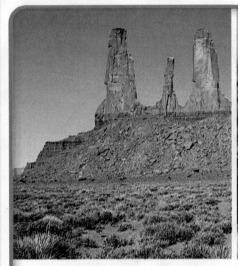

Earth has a wide range of climates, which we identify by precipitation, temperature, and native plant life.

Plants, animals, and the environment are interconnected and affect one another in many ways.

Earth's valuable natural resources, such as air, water, forests, and minerals, have many uses and affect people's lives.

Reviewing Vocabulary, Terms, and Places

Unscramble each group of letters below to spell a term that matches the given definition.

1. **usumh**—decayed plant or animal matter
2. **tahrewe**—changes or conditions in the air at a certain time and place
3. **netorietfaosr**—planting trees where forests were
4. **neticxt**—completely died out
5. **estpep**—semidry grassland or prairie
6. **sifeticatorined**—spread of desertlike conditions
7. **laitemc**—an area's weather patterns over a long period of time
8. **arsmofrtpe**—permanently frozen layers of soil
9. **snonomo**—winds that change direction with the seasons and create wet and dry periods
10. **vansanas**—areas of tall grasses and scattered shrubs and trees

Comprehension and Critical Thinking

SECTION 1 *(Pages 50–54)*

11. **a. Identify** What five factors affect climate?

    b. Analyze Is average annual precipitation an example of weather or climate?

    c. Evaluate Which of the factors that affect climate do you think is the most important? Why?

SECTION 2 *(Pages 55–61)*

12. **a. Recall** What are the five major climate zones?

    b. Explain How does latitude relate to climate?

    c. Geographic Questions Look at the map and chart of World Climate Regions on page 56. With a partner, pose and answer questions about the distribution and patterns of climate regions. Take turns reading aloud and answering the questions in the column headings.

SECTION 3 (Pages 62–65)

13. a. Define What is an ecosystem, and why does it exist in a fragile balance?

b. Explain Why are plants an important part of the environment?

c. Predict What might be some results of desertification?

SECTION 4 (Pages 68–72)

14. a. Define What are minerals?

b. Contrast How do nonrenewable resources and renewable resources differ?

c. Elaborate How might a scarcity of natural resources affect life in a region?

Using the Internet

15. Activity: Experiencing Extremes Could you live in a place where for part of the year it is always dark and temperatures plummet to –104°F? What if you had to live in a place where it is always wet and stormy? Through your online textbook, learn more about some of the world's extreme climates. Then create a poster that describes some of those climates and the people, animals, and plants that live in them.

↗ hmhsocialstudies.com

Social Studies Skills

Creating and Analyzing a Bar Graph *Examine the bar graph titled Average Annual Precipitation by Climate Region in the Social Studies Skills for this chapter. Then create your own bar graph by researching the average annual temperature of each climate region shown in the precipitation bar graph. Use the bar graph you created to answer the following questions.*

16. Which climate region experiences the warmest average annual temperatures?

17. Which climate region experiences the coldest average annual temperatures?

18. What is the difference in average annual temperature between tropical savanna climates and desert climates?

Map Activity

19. Prevailing Winds On a separate sheet of paper, match the letters on the map with their correct labels.

equator	South Pole	westerly
North Pole	trade wind	

→ Cool air
→ Warm air
→ Wind direction

FOCUS ON READING AND VIEWING *my*WriteSmart

Understanding Cause and Effect *Answer the following questions about causes and effects.*

20. What causes desertification?

21. What are the effects of abundant natural resources on a country's economy?

22. Presenting and Viewing a Weather Report
Select a place and a season to write a weather report about. Use *my*WriteSmart in your eBook to describe the weather and predict upcoming weather. Include basic or academic vocabulary from this chapter. Then present your report to the class. To add interest, speak using professional, friendly tone and a variety of sentence types. Make frequent eye contact with your audience. Then listen and take notes as your classmates present their reports. Be prepared to give feedback on the content and their presentations techniques.

Reading Social Studies

Understanding Cause and Effect

FOCUS ON READING

Learning to identify causes and effects can help you understand geography. A **cause** is something that makes another thing happen. An **effect** is the result of something else that happened. A cause may have several effects, and an effect may have several causes. In addition, as you can see in the example below, causes and effects may occur in a chain. Then, each effect in turn becomes the cause for another event.

Cause
Gulf Stream

Effect
Warm water flows along the coast of northwest Europe.

Effect
Warm water raises temperature of the air above.

Effect
Winds blow warm air across Europe.

Effect
Warm winds make Europe warmer.

First cause

Last effect

The Gulf Stream is a warm current that flows north along the U.S. East Coast. It then flows east across the Atlantic to become the North Atlantic Drift. As the warm current flows along northwestern Europe, it heats the air. Westerlies blow the warmed air across Europe. This process makes Europe warmer than it otherwise would be.

From Section 1, Weather and Climate

YOU TRY IT!

Read the following sentences, and then use a graphic organizer like the one below to analyze the cause and effects. Create as many boxes as you need to list the causes and effects.

Mountains also create wet and dry areas. . . A mountain forces wind blowing against it to rise. As it rises, the air cools and precipitation falls as rain or snow. Thus, the side of the mountain facing the wind is often green and lush. However, little moisture remains for the other side. This effect creates a rain shadow.

From Section 1, Weather and Climate

Cause → **Effect** → **Effect** → **Effect**

The World's People

Essential Question

myNotebook

What concepts help geographers understand the world's people?

Texas Essential Knowledge and Skills (TEKS)

4B, 5A, 15A, 15B, 15E, 16A, 16B, 16C, 17A, 17D, 17E, 18A, 18B, 18C, 18D, 19A, 22A, 22D

FOCUS ON READING AND WRITING

my **WriteSmart**

Understanding Main Ideas A main idea is the central idea around which a paragraph or passage is organized. As you read, ask yourself what each paragraph is about. Look for a sentence or two that summarizes the main point of the entire paragraph. **See the lesson Understanding Main Ideas on page 103.**

Creating a Poster Think of some great posters you have seen at the movies, in bus stations, or in the halls of your school. They likely all had a colorful image that captured your attention and a few words that explained the main idea. Read this chapter about the world's people. Then create a poster that includes words and images that summarize the chapter's main ideas. Use the annotation tools in your eBook to gather information for your assignment.

Culture Thousands of different cultures make up our world. Clothing, language, and music are just some parts of culture.

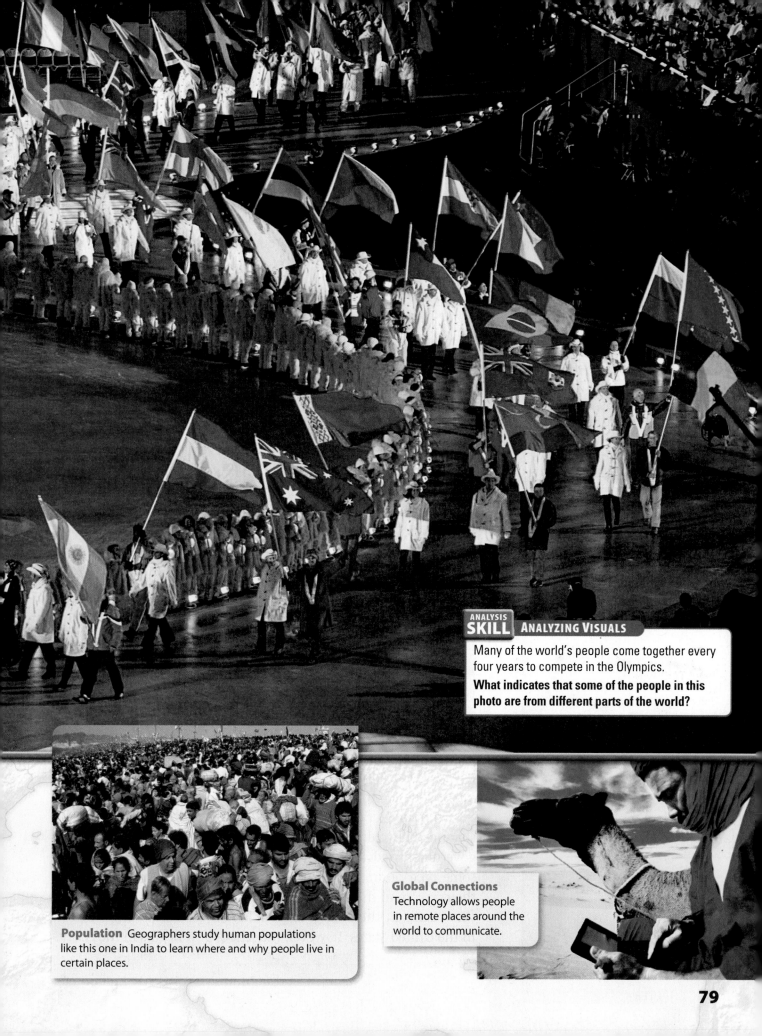

ANALYSIS SKILL **ANALYZING VISUALS**

Many of the world's people come together every four years to compete in the Olympics.

What indicates that some of the people in this photo are from different parts of the world?

Population Geographers study human populations like this one in India to learn where and why people live in certain places.

Global Connections Technology allows people in remote places around the world to communicate.

Culture

 TEKS 15A, 15B, 17D, 17E, 22A, 22D

What You Will Learn...

Main Ideas

1. Culture is the set of beliefs, goals, and practices that a group of people share.
2. The world includes many different culture groups.
3. New ideas and events lead to changes in culture.

The Big Idea

Culture, a group's shared practices and beliefs, differs from group to group and changes over time.

Key Terms

culture, *p. 80*
culture trait, *p. 81*
culture region, *p. 82*
ethnic group, *p. 83*
multicultural society, *p. 83*
cultural diffusion, *p. 85*

hmhsocialstudies.com
TAKING NOTES

Use the graphic organizer online to take notes on culture.

If YOU lived there...

You live in New York City, and your young cousin from out of state has come to visit. As you take her on a tour of the city, you point out the different cultural neighborhoods, like Chinatown, Little Italy, Spanish Harlem, and Koreatown. Your cousin isn't quite sure what culture means or why these neighborhoods are so different.

How can you explain what culture is?

BUILDING BACKGROUND For hundreds of years, immigrants from around the world have moved to the United States to make a new home here. They have brought with them all the things that make up culture—language, religion, beliefs, traditions, and more. As a result, the United States has one of the most diverse cultures in the world.

What Is Culture?

If you traveled around the world, you would experience many different sights and sounds. You would probably hear unique music, eat a variety of foods, listen to different languages, see distinctive landscapes, and learn new customs. You would see and take part in the variety of cultures that exist in our world.

A Way of Life

What exactly is culture? **Culture** is the set of beliefs, values, and practices that a group of people has in common. Culture includes many aspects of life, such as language and religion, that we may share with people around us. Everything in your day-to-day life is part of your culture, from the clothes you wear to the music you hear to the foods you eat.

On your world travels, you might notice that all societies share certain cultural features. All people have some kind of government, educate their children in some way, and create some type of art or music. However, not all societies practice their culture in the same way. For example, in Japan the school year begins in the spring, and students wear school uniforms. In the United States, however, the school year begins in the late

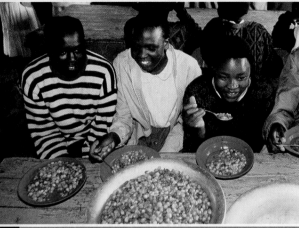

These students in Japan and Kenya have some culture traits in common, like eating lunch at school. Other culture traits are different.

ANALYZING VISUALS What culture traits do these students share? Which are different?

summer, and most schools do not require uniforms. Differences like these are what make each culture unique.

Culture Traits

Cultural features like starting the school year in the spring or wearing uniforms are types of culture traits. A **culture trait** is an activity or behavior in which people often take part. The language you speak and the sports you play are some of your culture traits. Sometimes a culture trait is shared by people around the world. For example, all around the globe people participate in the game of soccer. In places as different as Germany, Nigeria, and Saudi Arabia, many people enjoy playing and watching soccer.

While some culture traits are shared around the world, others change from place to place. One example of this is how people around the world eat. In China most people use chopsticks to eat their food. In Europe, however, people use forks and spoons. In Ethiopia, many people use bread or their fingers to scoop their food.

Development of Culture

How do cultures develop? Culture traits are often learned or passed down from one generation to the next. Most culture traits develop within families as traditions, foods, or holiday customs are handed down over the years. Laws and moral codes are also passed down within societies. Many laws in the United States, for example, can be traced back to England in the 1600s and were brought by colonists to America.

Cultures also develop as people learn new culture traits. Immigrants who move to a new country, for example, might learn to speak the language or eat the foods of their adopted country.

Other factors, such as history and the environment, also affect how cultures develop. For example, historical events changed the language and religion of much of Central and South America. In the 1500s, when the Spanish conquered the region, they introduced their language and Roman Catholic faith. The environment in which we live can also shape culture.

FOCUS ON READING
What is the main idea of this paragraph?

For example, the desert environment of Africa's Sahara influences the way people who live there earn a living. Rather than grow crops, they herd animals that have adapted to the harsh environment. As you can see, history and the environment affect how cultures develop.

READING CHECK **Finding Main Ideas** What practices and customs make up culture?

Culture Groups

Earth is home to thousands of different cultures. People who share similar culture traits are members of the same culture group. Culture groups can be based on a variety of factors, such as age, language, or religion. American teenagers, for example, can be said to form a culture group based on location and age. They share similar tastes in music, clothing, and sports.

Culture Regions

When we refer to culture groups, we are speaking of people who share a common culture. At other times, however, we need to refer to the area, or region, where the culture group is found. A **culture region** is an area in which people have many shared culture traits.

In a specific culture region, people share certain culture traits, such as religious beliefs, language, or lifestyle. One well-known culture region is the Arab world. As you can see at right, an Arab culture region spreads across Southwest Asia and North Africa. In this region, most people write and speak Arabic and are Muslim. They also share other traits, such as foods, music, styles of clothing, and architecture.

Occasionally, a single culture region dominates an entire country. In Japan, for example, one primary culture dominates the country. Nearly everyone in Japan speaks the same language and follows the same practices. Many Japanese bow to their elders as a sign of respect and remove their shoes when they enter a home.

A single country may also include more than one culture region within its borders. Mexico is one of many countries that is made up of different culture regions. People in northern Mexico and southern Mexico, for example, have different culture traits. The culture of northern Mexico tends to be more modern, while traditional culture remains strong in southern Mexico.

A culture region may also stretch across country borders. As you have already learned, an Arab culture region dominates much of Southwest Asia and North Africa. Another example is the Kurdish culture region, home to the Kurds, a people that live throughout Turkey, Iran, and Iraq.

Arab Culture Region

Culture regions are based on shared culture traits. Southwest Asia and North Africa make up an Arab culture region based on ethnic heritage, a common language, and religion. Most people in this region are Arab, speak and write Arabic, and practice Islam.

Cultural Diversity

As you just learned, countries may contain several culture regions within their borders. Often, these culture regions are based on ethnic groups. An **ethnic group** is a group of people who share a common culture and ancestry. Members of ethnic groups often share certain culture traits such as religion, language, and even special foods.

Some countries are home to a variety of ethnic groups. For example, more than 100 different ethnic groups live in the East African country of Tanzania. Countries with many ethnic groups are culturally diverse. A **multicultural society** is a society that includes a variety of cultures in the same area. While multiculturalism creates an interesting mix of ideas, behaviors, and practices, it can also lead to conflict.

In some countries, ethnic groups have been in conflict. In Canada, for example, some French Canadians want to separate from the rest of Canada to preserve their language and culture. In the 1990s ethnic conflict in the African country of Rwanda led to extreme violence and bloodshed.

Although ethnic groups have clashed in some culturally diverse countries, they have cooperated in others. In the United States, for example, many different ethnic groups live side by side. Cities and towns often celebrate their ethnic heritage with festivals and parades, like the Saint Patrick's Day Parade in Boston or Philadelphia's Puerto Rican Festival.

READING CHECK **Making Inferences** Why might multiculturalism cause conflict?

Many people share Arab culture traits. An Omani boy, above, and Palestinian girls, at left, share the same language and religion.

ANALYZING VISUALS What culture traits do you see in the photos?

83

Cultural Diffusion of Baseball

Like many other ideas and customs, baseball has spread around the world through the process of cultural diffusion. Since its beginnings in New York in the 1800s, baseball has spread throughout the United States, into Central and South America, and to Asia.

Spread of baseball
0   1,000   2,000 Miles
0 1,000 2,000 Kilometers
Projection: Miller Cylindrical

ASIA

NORTH AMERICA

PACIFIC OCEAN

UNITED STATES

New York
Origin of baseball

ATLANTIC OCEAN

SOUTH AMERICA

American students first brought baseball to Cuba in the 1800s.

American missionaries introduced baseball to Korea in 1905.

Changes in Culture

You've read books or seen movies set in the time of the Civil War or in the Wild West of the late 1800s. Think about how our culture has changed since then. Clothing, food, music—all have changed drastically. When we study cultural change, we try to find out what factors influence the changes and how those changes spread from place to place.

How Cultures Change

Cultures change constantly. Some changes happen rapidly, while others take many years. What causes cultures to change? **Innovation** and contact with other people are two key causes of cultural change.

New ideas often bring about cultural changes. For example, when Alexander Graham Bell invented the telephone, it changed how people communicate with each other. Other innovations, such as motion pictures, changed how people spend their free time. More recently, the creation of the Internet dramatically altered the way people find information, communicate, and shop.

Cultures also change as societies come into contact with each other. For example, when the Spanish arrived in the Americas, they introduced firearms and horses to the region, changing the lifestyle of some Native American groups. At the same time, the Spaniards learned about new foods like potatoes and chocolate. These foods then became an important part of Europeans' diet. The Chinese had a similar influence on Korea and Japan, where they introduced Buddhism and written language.

Organized baseball began in New York around 1845 and quickly spread around the world.

ANALYSIS SKILL **ANALYZING VISUALS**

Where did baseball begin, and to what parts of the world did it eventually spread?

How Cultural Traits Spread

You have probably noticed that a new slang word might spread from teenager to teenager and state to state. In the same way, clothing styles from New York or Paris might become popular all over the world. More serious cultural traits spread as well. Religious beliefs or ideas about government may spread from place to place. The spread of culture traits from one region to another is called **cultural diffusion**.

Cultural diffusion often occurs when individuals move from one place to another. For example, when Europeans settled in the Americas, they brought their culture along with them. As a result, English, French, Spanish, and Portuguese are all spoken in the Americas. American culture also spread as pioneers moved west, taking with them their form of government, religious beliefs, and customs.

Cultural diffusion also takes place as new ideas spread from place to place. As you can see on the map above, the game of baseball first began in New York, then spread throughout the United States. As more and more people learned the game, it spread even faster and farther. Baseball eventually spread to other world societies. Wearing blue jeans became part of our culture in a similar way. Blue jeans originated in the American West in the mid-1800s. They gradually became popular all over the country and the world.

READING CHECK **Finding Main Ideas** How do cultures change over time?

SUMMARY AND PREVIEW In this section you learned about the role that culture plays in our lives and how our cultures change. Next, you will learn about human populations and how we keep track of Earth's changing population.

Section 1 Assessment

hmhsocialstudies.com
ONLINE QUIZ

Reviewing Ideas, Terms, and Places

1. **a. Define** What is **culture**?
   b. Analyze What influences the development of culture?
   c. Elaborate How might the world be different if we all shared the same culture?
2. **a. Identify** What are the different types of **culture regions**?
   b. Define What is a **multicultural society**?
3. **a. Describe** Identify an example of a cultural trait that has spread. How did that culture trait spread?
   b. Identify Which factors influence cultural change?
   c. Evaluate Do you think that cultural diffusion has a positive or a negative effect? Explain your answer.

Critical Thinking

4. **Finding Main Ideas** Using your notes and a chart like the one here, explain the main idea of each aspect of culture in your own words.

Culture Traits	Culture Groups	Cultural Change

FOCUS ON WRITING

my **WriteSmart**

5. **Writing about Culture** What key words about culture can you include on your poster? What images might you include? Jot down your ideas in your notebook.

Population

 TEKS 4B, 22A, 22D

What You Will Learn...

Main Ideas

1. The study of population patterns helps geographers learn about the world.
2. Population statistics and trends are important measures of population change.

The Big Idea

Population studies are an important part of geography.

Key Terms

population, *p. 86*
population density, *p. 86*
birthrate, *p. 88*
migration, *p. 89*

hmhsocialstudies.com
TAKING NOTES

Use the graphic organizer online to take notes on population.

If YOU lived there...

You live in Mexico City, one of the largest and most crowded cities in the world. You realize just how crowded it is whenever you ride the subway at rush hour! You love the excitement of living in a big city. There is always something interesting to do. At the same time, the city has a lot of crime. Heavy traffic pollutes the air.

What do you like and dislike about living in a large city?

BUILDING BACKGROUND An important part of geographers' work is the study of human populations. Many geographers are interested in where people live, how many people live there, and what effects those people have on resources and the environment.

Population Patterns

How many people live in your community? Do you live in a small town, a huge city, or somewhere in between? Your community's **population**, or the total number of people in a given area, determines a great deal about the place in which you live. Population influences the variety of businesses, the types of transportation, and the number of schools in your community.

Because population has a huge impact on our lives, it is an important part of geography. Geographers who study human populations are particularly interested in patterns that emerge over time. They study such information as how many people live in an area, why people live where they do, and how populations change. Population patterns like these can tell us much about our world.

Population Density

Some places on Earth are crowded with people. Others are almost empty. One statistic geographers use to examine populations is **population density**, a measure of the number of people living in an area. Population density is expressed as persons per square mile or square kilometer.

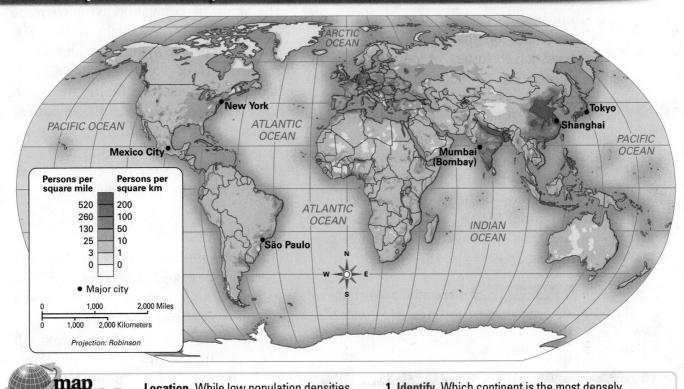

Location While low population densities are common throughout much of the world, South and East Asia are two of the world's most densely populated regions.

1. **Identify** Which continent is the most densely populated? Which is the least densely populated?
2. **Making Inferences** Why might the population density of far North America be so low?

Population density provides us with important information about a place. The more people per square mile in a region, the more crowded, or dense, it is. Japan, for example, has a population density of 880 people per square mile (340 per square km). That is a high population density. In many parts of Japan, people are crowded together in large cities, and space is very limited. In contrast, Australia has a very low population density. Only 6 people per square mile (2 per square km) live there. Australia has many wide-open spaces with very few people.

How do you think population density affects life in a particular place? In places with high population densities, the land is often expensive, roads are crowded, and buildings tend to be taller. On the other hand, places with low population densities tend to have more open spaces, less traffic, and more available land.

Where People Live

Can you tell where most of the world's people live by examining the population density map above? The reds and purples on the map indicate areas of very high population density, while the light yellow areas indicate sparse populations. When an area is thinly populated, it is often because the land does not provide a very good life. These areas may have rugged mountains or harsh deserts where people cannot grow crops. Some areas may be frozen all year long, making survival there very difficult.

For these reasons, very few people live in parts of far North America, Greenland, northern Asia, and Australia.

Notice on the map that some areas have large clusters of population. Such clusters can be found in East and South Asia, Europe, and eastern North America. Fertile soil, reliable sources of water, and a good agricultural climate make these good regions for settlement. For example, the North China Plain in East Asia is one of the most densely populated regions in the world. The area's plentiful agricultural land, many rivers, and mild climate have made it an ideal place to settle.

READING CHECK **Generalizing** What types of information can population density provide?

CONNECTING TO Math

Calculating Population Density

Population density measures the number of people living in an area. To calculate population density, divide a place's total population by its area in square miles (or square kilometers). For example, if your city has a population of 100,000 people and an area of 100 square miles, you would divide 100,000 by 100. This would give you a population density of 1,000 people per square mile ($100,000 \div 100 = 1,000$).

Analyzing If a city had a population of 615,000 and a total land area of 250 square miles, what would its population density be?

City	Population	Total Area (square miles)	Population Density (people per square mile)
Adelaide, Australia	1,198,271	705	1,700
Lima, Peru	9,129,790	1,032	8,847
Nairobi, Kenya	3,363,130	269	12,502

Population Change

The study of population is much more important than you might realize. The number of people living in an area affects all elements of life—the availability of housing and jobs, whether hospitals and schools open or close, even the amount of available food. Geographers track changes in populations by examining important statistics, studying the movement of people, and analyzing population trends.

Tracking Population Changes

Geographers examine three key statistics to learn about population changes. These statistics are important for studying a country's population over time.

Three key statistics—birthrate, death rate, and the rate of natural increase—track changes in population. Births add to a population. Deaths subtract from it. The annual number of births per 1,000 people is called the **birthrate**. Similarly, the death rate is the annual number of deaths per 1,000 people. The birthrate minus the death rate equals the percentage of natural increase, or the rate at which a population is changing. For example, Denmark has a rate of natural increase of 0.05%. This means it has slightly more births than deaths and a very slight population increase.

Population growth rates differ from one place to another. In some countries, populations are growing very slowly or even shrinking. Many countries in Europe and North America have very low rates of natural increase. In Russia, for example, the birthrate is about 10.8 and the death rate is 16.1. The result is a negative rate of natural increase and a shrinking population.

In most countries around the world, however, populations are growing. Mali, for example, has a rate of natural increase of about 3.3 percent. While that may sound

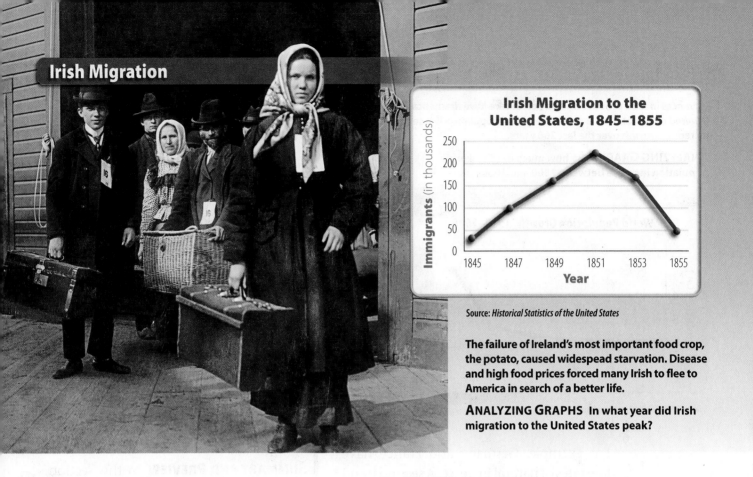

Irish Migration

Irish Migration to the United States, 1845–1855

Immigrants (in thousands)

Year

Source: *Historical Statistics of the United States*

The failure of Ireland's most important food crop, the potato, caused widespead starvation. Disease and high food prices forced many Irish to flee to America in search of a better life.

ANALYZING GRAPHS In what year did Irish migration to the United States peak?

small, it means that Mali's population is expected to double in only 21 years! High population growth rates can pose some challenges, as governments try to provide enough jobs, education, and medical care for their rapidly growing populations.

Migration

A common cause of population change is migration. **Migration** is the process of moving from one place to live in another. As one country loses citizens as a result of migration, its population can decline. At the same time, another country may gain population as people settle there.

People migrate for many reasons. Some factors push people to leave their country, while other factors pull, or attract, people to new countries. Warfare, a lack of jobs, or a lack of good farmland are common push factors. For example, during the Irish potato famine of the mid-1800s, poverty and disease forced some 1.5 million people to leave Ireland. Opportunities for a better life often pull people to new countries. For example, in the 1800s and early 1900s thousands of British citizens migrated to Australia in search of cheap land.

World Population Trends

In the last 200 years Earth's population has exploded. For thousands of years world population growth was low and relatively steady. About 2,000 years ago, the world had some 300 million people. By 1800 there were almost 1 billion people. Since 1800, better health care and improved food production have supported tremendous population growth. By 2012 the world's population passed 7 billion people.

Population trends are an important part of the study of the world's people. Two important population trends are clear today. The first trend indicates that the population growth in some of the more industrialized nations has begun to slow.

FOCUS ON READING
What is the main idea of this paragraph? What facts are used to support that idea?

World Population Growth

Advances in food production and health care have dramatically lowered death rates. As a result, the global population has seen incredible growth over the last 200 years.

ANALYZING GRAPHS By how much did the world's population increase between 1800 and 2000?

World Population Growth, 1500–2000

Source: *Atlas of World Population History*

For example, Germany and France have low rates of natural increase. A second trend indicates that less industrialized countries, like Nigeria and Bangladesh, often have high growth rates. These trends affect a country's workforce and government aid.

READING CHECK Summarizing What population statistics do geographers study? Why?

SUMMARY AND PREVIEW In this section you learned where people live, how crowded places are, and how population changes. Geographers study population patterns and trends to plan for the future. In the next section, you will learn about cultural universals, or the human features that all societies have in common.

Section 2 Assessment

hmhsocialstudies.com
ONLINE QUIZ

Reviewing Ideas, Terms, and Places

1. **a. Identify** What regions of the world have the highest levels of **population density**?
   b. Draw Conclusions What information can be learned by studying population density?
   c. Evaluate Would you prefer to live in a region with a dense or a sparse population? Why?
2. **a. Describe** What is natural increase? What can it tell us about a country?
   b. Analyze What effect does **migration** have on human populations?
   c. Predict What patterns do you think world population might have in the future?

Critical Thinking

3. **Summarizing** Draw a graphic organizer like the one here. Use your notes to write a sentence that summarizes each aspect of the study of population.

   Population Patterns

   Population Change

FOCUS ON WRITING

*my*WriteSmart

4. **Discussing Population** What effect does population have on our world? Write down some words and phrases that you might use on your poster to explain the importance of population.

Cultural Universals

If **YOU** lived there...

You're touring What the World Eats, a photography exhibit that shows families from 25 countries displaying the food they eat in a week. The food varies from image to image. Some foods—sheep meat soup, mutton dumpling—seem unusual. Still, each photo shows that families all over the world spend time together over food.

How can the world's people be so similar and so different?

> **BUILDING BACKGROUND** You have learned about how culture traits set cultures apart from one another. In this section, you will learn about features that people everywhere hold in common, including social institutions, cultural expressions, and technology.

What Do All Cultures Have in Common?

You may be wondering how cultures can be so different when all people have the same basic needs. All people need food, clothing, and shelter to survive. Geographers and other social scientists believe that some needs are so basic that societies everywhere have developed certain features to meet them. These features, common to all cultures, are called **cultural universals**. In this section, you will learn about three important cultural universals: social institutions, creative expressions, and technology.

READING CHECK Finding Main Ideas What can geographers learn from cultural universals?

What You Will Learn...

Main Ideas

1. The features common to all cultures are called cultural universals.
2. All societies have social institutions that help their groups survive.
3. Every culture expresses itself creatively in a variety of ways.
4. All societies use technology to help shape and control the environment.

The Big Idea

Geographers study cultural universals, features common to all societies, to understand similarities among the world's people.

Key Terms

cultural universal, p. 91
social institution, p. 92
heritage, p. 93
universal theme, p. 94
technology, p. 94
science, p. 94

hmhsocialstudies.com
TAKING NOTES

Use the graphic organizer online to compare features shared by all cultures.

Basic Social Institutions

Societies, like people, have basic needs that must be met for a group to survive. **Social institutions** are organized patterns of belief and behavior that focus on meeting these needs. They exist in all societies.

However, their specific characteristics vary from culture to culture. The most basic social institutions are family, education, religion, government, and economy.

Family

Family is the most basic social institution. In all societies, its purpose is the same. The family ensures that children are cared for until old enough to fend for themselves. Families provide emotional and physical support. They also teach the accepted norms, behaviors, and values of a culture.

Education

Societies rely on education to pass on knowledge to young people. For example, schools across the world teach reading, writing, math, and technical skills that prepare students to take on adult roles. Schools also teach the norms and values that sustain, or support, a society.

For instance, one goal of U.S. public schools is to develop informed citizens who contribute to the good of their communities.

Religion

The world's religions are incredibly diverse. Still, in all societies, religion helps explain the meanings of life and death and the difference between good and bad behavior. Over time, religion is passed down and supported by traditional practices, literature, sacred texts and stories, and sacred places. All of this makes religion a powerful force. It is often the foundation of a culture's philosophical beliefs and attitudes. Moreover, in all world regions, it has inspired and sustained itself through great works of devotion, including art and **monumental** architecture.

Government

To keep order and resolve conflicts, people need a government. A government is a system of leaders and laws that help people live safely together in their community or country. In Chapter 5 and throughout this book, you will learn about world governments and how they shape people's lives.

Education

In the United States (left) and in Peru (below), schools teach knowledge, skills, and cultural norms to prepare students for adult roles.

ANALYZING VISUALS What similarities and differences do you detect between the two classroom environments?

Economy

To support its people, a society must have an economy, or a system of using resources to meet needs. People must be able to make, buy, sell, and trade goods and services to get what they need and want. In Chapter 5, you will learn about and compare the features of various economic systems.

READING CHECK **Summarizing** What are the main social institutions?

Creative Expressions

All people are creative. Everyone has the ability to imagine, think, and create. Not surprisingly, all societies express themselves creatively, too. The main types of creative expression are:

- **Performing Arts**—art forms that combine sound and movement for an audience such as music, theater, and dance.
- **Visual Arts**—creative expressions that have both a visual and material form, such as painting, jewelry, sculpture, textiles, and architecture.
- **Literary Arts**—art forms rooted in words and language such as literature, folktales, and stories.

Creative Forces

Throughout this book, you will explore creative expressions from all world regions. As you discover them, note how they are influenced by the availability of natural materials and resources. Look, too, for how creative expressions reflect a specific **heritage,** or the wealth of cultural elements that has been passed down over generations.

Creative expressions also express individual choices. People use artistic forms to express individual, as well as cultural, ideas about what is pleasing, proper, and beautiful. They also use them to address contemporary issues such as politics, war, and social inequality. This is because the arts can inspire us. Creative forms communicate ideas and emotions that stir people to action.

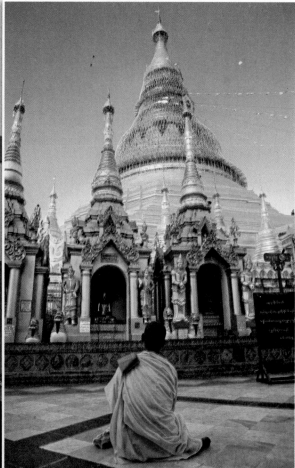

Monumental Architecture

Religion inspires creative expressions, including monumental architecture such as France's Notre Dame Cathedral (below) and Schwedagon Pagoda (right), a Buddhist temple in Myanmar.

ANALYZING VISUALS How do examples of monumental architecture express the power of religion?

Universal Themes

Some creative expressions communicate universal themes. A **universal theme** is a message about life or human nature that is meaningful across time and in all places. Because they express basic human truths, universal themes transcend, or move beyond, the boundaries of a particular society. They speak to people everywhere.

Masterpieces of art have qualities that are meaningful and timeless. Examples include Egyptian hieroglyphics and the sculptures of ancient Greece. The woodblock prints made by the Japanese painter Katsushika Hokusai are also an example of this type of art. They express a love of nature's beauty, simplicity, and power.

Other art forms also gain worldwide appreciation. For example, literature such as *The Lord of the Rings* contains a universal theme of a hero's search for truth, goodness, and honor. Blues music is another example. Derived from African American work songs and spirituals in the American South, blues songs express feelings of sadness and struggle in the face of great challenges.

READING CHECK **Describing** What are the main types of cultural expressions?

Science and Technology

All people use technology to shape and control their environments, and they use science to try and understand it. **Technology** refers to the use of knowledge, tools, and skills to solve problems. **Science** is a way of understanding the world through observation and the testing of ideas.

Factors Shaping Technology Use

Historically, the type of technology a culture developed has been strongly tied to environmental factors. Not only were tools and technology made from local resources, they were also designed to solve specific problems posed by nature. For example, farmers might build dams to prevent rivers from flooding and destroying their crops.

Other factors such as belief systems, political decisions, and economic factors can influence technology use, too. Some religious groups, like the Amish people of the United States, selectively use technology. They readily use gas and horse-drawn buggies. However, they reject technology they think will undermine their traditions, including cars and computers.

Nature's awesome power is a universal theme in the paintings of boats at sea created by Japanese artist Katsushika Hokusai (at left) and English artist Joseph Mallord William Turner (below).

Government decisions also affect technology use. North Korea, for example, restricts Internet use. To use the Internet, a North Korean must have special permission and may only use it for government purposes. Worldwide, however, the primary barrier between people and technology is economic. New technologies are simply too expensive for many of the world's people to access them.

Impact of Technology

Throughout time, advances in science and technology have made life easier. Some discoveries even changed the world.

Consider, for example, the work of French scientist Louis Pasteur. His work revolutionized health and medicine. In 1870 Pasteur discovered that germs caused infections. To prevent the spread of disease, he urged people to wash their hands. He also developed vaccines to prevent deadly diseases and a process for removing bacteria from food. Today most milk, cheese, and juice on our grocery shelves has been sterilized, or made germ-free, through pasteurization.

Inventors, too, change the world. For example, in 1879, Thomas Edison developed an affordable and practical light bulb. At the time, the invention caused a sensation. People no longer had to burn candles and oil lamps for light at night. Over time, electricity has transformed daily life and work for many of the world's people.

Today, scientists and inventors continue to identify and solve problems. They often work in groups to make discoveries or invent new devices or products that will benefit future generations. This involves careful thinking about the future and making predictions about the social, political, economic, cultural, and environmental impact of their work.

READING CHECK **Generalizing** What are the basic purposes of technology and science?

SUMMARY AND PREVIEW In this section you learned about the features that make cultures similar. Next you will learn how globalization is shaping world culture.

Section 3 Assessment

hmhsocialstudies.com
ONLINE QUIZ

Reviewing Ideas, Terms, and Places

1. **a. Identify and Explain** What are five basic **social institutions?** What purposes do they serve?
   b. Analyze What efforts and activities are most important for a religious institution to last over time? Explain.

2. **a. Explain** What is the relationship that exists between religious ideas, philosophical ideas, and cultures?
   b. Describe What forces influence cultural expressions?
   c. Identify List and explain examples of art, music, and literature with **universal themes**.

3. **a. Explain** How can factors related to belief systems, government, and economics affect technology use?
   b. Make Inferences How might a resource such as river water affect how farmers use technology?
   c. Explain Give an example of a scientific discovery and an example of a technological innovation that have changed the world. Discuss the role of scientists and inventors in making the discovery and innovation.

Critical Thinking

4. **Comparing** Draw a chart like the one here to organize your notes on the features of culture that all people share.

Social Institutions	Cultural Expressions	Science and Technology

FOCUS ON WRITING

my WriteSmart

5. **Describing Cultural Similarities** What kind of images could you use to show that all cultures have social institutions, cultural expressions, and science and technology?

Organizing Information

Learn

Remembering new information is easier if you organize it clearly. As you read and study, try to organize what you are learning. One way to do this is to create a graphic organizer. As you read;

- Identify the main idea of the text you are reading and write it in a circle.

- Look for subtopics under the main idea. Write the subtopics in the circles below the main idea.

- Below each subtopic, draw a big box. Look for facts and supporting details for each subtopic to list in the box.

- Organizing information is not limited to text. You can organize information found in visuals, too. Take a look at the High School Soccer participation map in Chapter 1, page 8. You could create a graphic organizer such as a chart showing the different rates in participation, or you could write a summary that organizes the information.

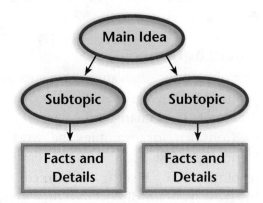

Practice

Study the chart to the right. Then create a graphic organizer or write a summary to organize the information.

Top Five Countries of Birth of New Legal Permanent Residents to the United States (by percent)	
Mexico	13.5
China	8.2
India	6.5
Philippines	5.4
Dominican Republic	4.3
Other	62.1

Apply

Turn to Section 1 and read the passage titled Culture Regions. Draw a graphic organizer like the one above. Then follow the steps to organize the information you have read. The passage will have two or more subtopics. Add additional circles and rectangles for each additional subtopic you find.

Global Connections

If YOU lived there...

You live in Louisville, Kentucky, and you have never traveled out of the United States. However, when you got ready for school this morning, you put on a T-shirt made in Guatemala and jeans made in Malaysia. Your shoes came from China. You rode to school on a bus with parts manufactured in Mexico. At school, your class even took part in a discussion with students in Canada.

What makes your global connections possible?

> **BUILDING BACKGROUND** Trade and technology have turned the world into a "global village." People around the world wear clothes, eat foods, and use goods made in other countries. Global connections are bringing people around the world closer than ever before.

Globalization

In just seconds an e-mail message sent by a teenager in India beams all the way to a friend in London. A band in Seattle releases a song that becomes popular in China. People from New York to Singapore respond to a crisis in Brazil. These are all examples of **globalization**, the process in which countries are increasingly linked to each other through culture and trade.

What caused globalization? Improvements in transportation and communication over the past 100 years have brought the world closer together. Airplanes, telecommunications, and the Internet allow us to communicate and travel the world with ease. As a result, cultural change happens faster and global culture and trade have increased.

Popular Culture

What might you have in common with a teenager in Japan? You probably have more in common than you think. You may use similar technology, wear similar clothes, and watch many of the same movies. You share the same global popular culture.

More and more, people around the world are linked through popular culture. **Popular culture** refers to culture traits that are well known and widely accepted. Food, sports, music, and movies are all examples of our popular culture.

The United States has great influence on global popular culture. For example, American soft drinks are sold in almost every country in the world. Many popular American television shows are broadcast internationally. English has become the major global language. One-quarter of the world's people speak English. It has become the main language for international music, business, science, and education.

At the same time, the United States is influenced by global culture. Martial arts movies from Asia attract large audiences in the United States. Radio stations in the United States play music by African, Latin American, and European musicians. We even adopt many foreign words, like *sushi* and *plaza*, into English.

Close-up

A Global Economy

The growth of the global economy has affected many businesses, especially the automobile industry. Automakers can now buy parts from countries all around the world, depending on where they can get the best price.

Many engines are manufactured in the United States and Canada.

Bumpers are often designed and produced in France, Germany, and the United States.

Tires come from a number of countries, including Mexico, South Korea, or Chile.

Global Trade

Globalization not only links the world's people, but it also connects businesses and affects trade. For centuries, societies have traded with each other. Improvements in transportation and communication have made global trade quicker and easier. For example, a shoe retailer in Chicago can order the sneakers she needs on a Web site from a company in China. The order can be flown to Chicago the next day and sold to customers that afternoon.

Many cars feature windows manufactured in Venezuela or the United States.

Seats are sometimes assembled in Japan from covers sewn in Mexico.

ANALYSIS SKILL **ANALYZING VISUALS**

From what different countries do automotive parts often originate?

The expansion of global trade has increased interdependence among the world's countries. **Interdependence** is a relationship between countries in which they rely on one another for resources, goods, or services. Many companies in one country often rely on goods and services produced in another country. For example, automakers in Europe might purchase auto parts made in the United States or Japan. Consumers also rely on goods produced elsewhere. For example, American shoppers buy bananas from Ecuador and tomatoes from Mexico. Global trade gives us access to goods from around the world.

READING CHECK **Finding Main Ideas** How has globalization affected the world?

A World Community

Some people call our world a global village. What do you think this means? Because of globalization, the world seems smaller. Places are more connected. What happens in one part of the world can affect the entire planet. Because of this, the world community works together to promote cooperation among countries in times of conflict and crisis.

The world community encourages cooperation by working to resolve global conflicts. From time to time, conflicts erupt among the countries of the world. Wars, trade disputes, and political disagreements can threaten the peace. Countries often join together to settle such conflicts. In 1945, for example, 51 nations created the United Nations. The **United Nations (UN)** is an organization of the world's countries that promotes peace and security around the globe.

The world community also promotes cooperation in times of crisis. A disaster may leave thousands of people in need.

FOCUS ON READING
What is the main idea of this paragraph? What facts are used to support that idea?

HISTORIC DOCUMENT
The Charter of the United Nations

Created in 1945, the United Nations is an organization of the world's countries that works to solve global problems. The Charter of the United Nations outlines the goals of the UN, some of which are included here.

We the Peoples of the United Nations Determined . . .

to save succeeding generations from the scourge [terror] of war . . .

to practice tolerance and live together in peace with one another as good neighbors, and

to unite our strength to maintain international peace and security, and

to ensure . . . that armed forces shall not be used, save [except] in the common interest, and

to employ international machinery [systems] for the promotion of the economic and social advancement of all peoples,

Have Resolved to Combine our Efforts to Accomplish these Aims.

—*from the Charter of the United Nations*

ANALYSIS SKILL **ANALYZING PRIMARY SOURCES**
What are some of the goals of the United Nations?

Earthquakes, floods, and drought can cause crises around the world. Groups from many nations often come together to provide **humanitarian aid**, or assistance to people in distress.

Organizations representing countries around the globe work to help in times of crisis. For example, in 2004 a tsunami, or huge tidal wave, devastated parts of Southeast Asia. Many organizations, like the United Nations Children's Fund (UNICEF) and the International Red Cross, stepped in to provide humanitarian aid to the victims of the tsunami. Some groups lend aid to refugees, or people who have been forced to flee their homes. Groups like Doctors Without Borders give medical aid to those in need around the world.

READING CHECK **Analyzing** How has globalization promoted cooperation?

SUMMARY In this section you learned how globalization links the countries of the world through shared culture and trade. Globalization allows organizations around the world to work together. They often solve conflicts and provide humanitarian aid.

Section 4 Assessment

hmhsocialstudies.com
ONLINE QUIZ

Reviewing Ideas, Terms, and Places

1. **a. Describe** What is **globalization**?
   b. Make Inferences How has **popular culture** influenced countries around the world?
   c. Evaluate Describe the impact of globalization and improved communication technology on cultures.
2. **a. Define** What is **humanitarian aid**?
   b. Draw Conclusions How has globalization promoted cooperation among countries?
   c. Predict What types of problems might lead to international cooperation?

Critical Thinking

3. **Identifying Cause and Effect** Use your notes and the graphic organizer at right to identify the effects that globalization has on our world.

Globalization	→	Effects
	→	Effects
	→	Effects

FOCUS ON WRITING

my WriteSmart

4. **Writing about Global Connections** What aspects of globalization could you include in your poster? Jot down your ideas in your notebook.

Chapter Review

Visual Summary

Use the visual summary below to help you review the main ideas of the chapter.

QUICK FACTS

The world has many different cultures, or shared beliefs and practices.

The world's people practice different economic activities and systems.

Globalization brings people around the world closer than ever before.

Reviewing Vocabulary, Terms, and Places

Choose one word from each word pair to correctly complete each sentence below.

1. Members of a/an _____ often share the same religion, traditions, and language. **(ethnic group/population)**

2. Music, art, and literature that transcend the boundaries of one society have _____. **(cultural universals/universal themes)**

3. Organizations like the International Red Cross provide _____ to people in need around the world. **(humanitarian aid/cultural diffusion)**

4. _____, the process of moving from one place to live in another, is a cause of population change. **(Population density/Migration)**

5. Family, education, religion, government, and economy are all examples of basic _____. **(technology/social institutions)**

Comprehension and Critical Thinking

SECTION 1 *(Pages 80–85)*

6. **a. Describe** What is a multicultural society?

   b. Identify What impact has cultural diffusion had on individuals? What impact has cultural diffusion had on world societies? Define these impacts.

   c. Elaborate Describe some of the culture traits practiced by people in your community.

SECTION 2 *(Pages 86–90)*

7. **a. Describe** What does population density tell us about a place?

   b. Draw Conclusions Why do certain areas attract large populations?

   c. Elaborate Why do you think it is important for geographers to study population trends?

SECTION 3 *(Pages 91–95)*

8. a. Evaluating Which social institution do you think is most important? Why?

b. Explain What relationship exists between a society and its art, music, literature, and architecture?

c. Predict Make a prediction about a future scientific discovery and a future technological innovation. What problem will each solve? What social, political, economic, cultural, or environmental impacts will each have?

SECTION 4 *(Pages 97–100)*

9. a. Describe How have connections among the world's countries improved?

b. Analyze What impact has globalization had on world trade and culture?

c. Evaluate What do you think has been the most important result of globalization? Why?

Social Studies Skills

10. Organizing Information Practice organizing information by creating a graphic organizer for Section 3. Use the main ideas on the first page of the section for your large circles. Then write the subtopics under each main idea. Finally, identify supporting details for each subtopic.

Using the Internet

11. Activity: Writing a Report Population changes have a huge impact on the world around us. Countries around the world must deal with shrinking populations, growing populations, and other population issues. Through your online textbook, explore the issues surrounding global population. Then imagine you have been asked to report on global population trends to the United Nations. Write a report in which you identify world population trends and their impact on the world today.

↗ **hmhsocialstudies.com**

Map Activity

Population Density *Use the map to the right to answer the questions that follow.*

12. What letter on the map indicates the least crowded area?

13. What letter on the map indicates the most densely crowded area?

14. Which letter indicates a region with 260–520 people per square mile (100–200 people per square km)?

Persons per square mile	Persons per square km
520	200
260	100
130	50
25	10
3	1
0	0

0   50   100 Miles
0   50   100 Kilometers
Projection: Albers Equal-Area

FOCUS ON READING AND WRITING   *my* **WriteSmart**

Understanding Main Ideas *Read the paragraph in question 15 below. Then, use myWriteSmart in your eBook to write out the main idea of the paragraph.*

15. The ancient Greeks were the first to practice democracy. Since then many countries have adopted democratic government. The United Kingdom, South Korea, and Ghana all practice democracy. Democracy is the most widely used type of government in the world today.

16. Creating a Poster Review your notes about the world's cultures, populations, governments, and economies. Then, select a topic for your poster. On large sheet of paper, write a title that identifies your topic. Illustrate your poster with images that support your topic. Write a short caption explaining each image.

Reading Social Studies

Understanding Main Ideas

Main ideas are like the hub of a wheel. The hub holds the wheel together, and everything circles around it. In a paragraph, the main idea holds the paragraph together and all the facts and details revolve around it. The main idea is usually stated clearly in a topic sentence, which may come at the beginning or end of a paragraph. Topic sentences always summarize the most important idea of a paragraph.

To find the main idea, ask yourself what one point is holding the paragraph together. See how the main idea in the following example holds all the details from the paragraph together.

A single country may also include more than one culture region within its borders. Mexico is one of many countries that is made up of different culture regions. People in northern Mexico and southern Mexico, for example, have different culture traits. The culture of northern Mexico tends to be more modern, while traditional culture remains strong in southern Mexico.

From Section 1, Culture

YOU TRY IT!

Read the following paragraph, and then use a graphic organizer like the one above to identify the main idea. Create as many circles as you need to list the supporting facts and details.

At the same time, the United States is influenced by global culture. Martial arts movies from Asia attract large audiences in the United States. Radio stations in the United States play music by African, Latin American, and European musicians. We even adopt many foreign words, like *sushi* and *plaza*, into English.

From Section 4, Global Connections

Government and Economic Systems

Essential Question

*my*Notebook

How do government systems, citizenship, and economic systems vary across the globe?

Texas Essential Knowledge and Skills (TEKS)

3A, 3C, 8A, 8B, 8C, 9A, 9B, 9C, 9D, 10A, 10B, 10C, 11A, 11B, 11C, 11D, 12A, 12B, 12C, 13A, 13B, 13C, 14A, 14B, 15E, 16A, 16B, 21B, 21C, 22A, 22D, 22E, 22F, 23A

FOCUS ON READING AND WRITING

my WriteSmart

Sequencing When you read, it is important to keep track of the sequence, or order, in which events happen. Look for dates and other clues to help you figure out the proper sequence. **See the lesson, Sequencing, on page 127.**

Writing an Online Article You are a journalist covering international affairs for a news site. You have been asked to compare the government systems, economic systems, and the roles of citizens that are found in different world regions. As you read, use the annotation tools in your eBook to gather information for your assignment.

Government
In democratic countries, leaders are elected by the people. Laura Chinchilla was elected president of Costa Rica in 2010.

The Palace of Westminster in London is where Parliament meets. Parliment is the United Kingdom's highest legislative authority.

What natural and human made features are located near the Palace of Westminster?

Citizenship Voting is an important responsibility for citizens of India and other free countries.

Economics People buy and sell goods in marketplaces around the world.

105

World Governments

TEKS 11A, 11B, 11C, 11D, 12A, 12B, 12C, 16A, 16B, 21B

What You Will Learn...

Main Ideas

1. Limited governments of the world include democracies.
2. Unlimited governments of the world include totalitarian governments.
3. Most human rights abuses occur under unlimited governments of the world.

The Big Idea

The world's countries have different governments and some countries struggle with human rights abuses.

Key Terms

democracy, *p. 106*
direct democracy, *p. 107*
limited government, *p. 107*
unlimited government, *p. 109*
totalitarian government, *p. 109*

hmhsocialstudies.com
TAKING NOTES

Use the graphic organizer online to take notes on different types of governments.

If YOU were there...

You live in Dallas, Texas. Your class at school is planning a presentation about life in the United States for a group of visitors from Japan. Your teacher wants you to discuss government in the United States. As you prepare for your speech, you wonder what you should say.

How does government affect your life?

BUILDING BACKGROUND Although you probably don't think about it every day, your country's government has a big influence on your life. That is true in every country in every part of the world. Governments affect everything from a person's individual rights to citizens' access to adequate health care.

Governments of the World

Can you imagine what life would be like if there were no rules? Without ways to establish order and ensure justice, life would be chaotic. This explains why societies have governments. Our governments make and enforce laws, regulate business and trade, and provide aid to people. Governments help shape the culture and economy of a country as well as the daily lives of the people who live there.

Limited Government

Many countries—including the United States, Canada, and Mexico—have democratic governments. A **democracy** is a form of government in which the people elect leaders and rule by majority. In most democratic countries, citizens are free to choose representatives to make and enforce the laws. Voters in the United States, for example, elect members of Congress, who make the laws, and the president, who enforces those laws.

Origins of Democracy

In a pure democracy, the people make decisions through a process of majority rule. Whatever the majority of voters wants becomes law. Such was the state of affairs in Athens and other ancient Greek city-states. Athenian democracy was a **direct democracy,** which means citizens met regularly in a popular assembly to discuss issues and vote for leaders. Athenians liked to boast that in their government everyone had equal say. In truth, Athenian democracy was an elite-based system. Only a small fraction of the male population was eligible to participate in political life. Neither women nor slaves, who formed the majority of the population, could participate.

A democracy, whether direct or indirect, is also a form of **limited government.** Limited government is a type of government that has legal limits on its power, usually in the form of a constitution.

Characteristics of Limited Governments

Because power can be misused, limiting government's reach reduces the chances of abuse and creates freer and fairer societies. Today nearly half of the more than 190 countries in the world are democratic or partly democratic with a limited system of government. Although the level of freedom in these nations varies they share some basic characteristics:

- Democratic systems tend to have social welfare policies that seek to improve the quality of their citizens' lives.
- Most democratic governments protect their citizens' rights and freedoms. For this reason, citizens of these countries generally enjoy a high degree of economic and political freedom.

Systems of Government	
Form	**Characteristics**
Dictatorship **Example: Cuba**	• Single dictator or a small group holds absolute authority and makes all decisions • Violence and force used to maintain rule
Totalitarian Regimes **Example: North Korea**	• Dictator holds ultimate authority • Government tightly controls all aspects of life—political, social, and economic • No formal or informal limits on government
Theocracy **Example: Iran**	• Government by officials regarded to have religious authority • Laws rooted in a particular religion or religious doctrine • Government power is unlimited
Direct Democracy **Example: ancient Greece (Athens)**	• Government by the people; citizens are the ultimate source of government authority • Citizens come together to discuss and pass laws and select leaders • Works best in small communities
Republic/ Representative Democracy **Example: ancient Rome, United States**	• Government by the people; citizens are the ultimate source of government authority • Indirect form of democracy; citizens elect representatives to make government decisions on their behalf • Representatives elected for set terms

- Strong democratic countries can generally withstand national crises such as war, economic troubles, or civil unrest without major changes to their basic systems or structures.

Comparing Limited Governments

National Congress, Brasilia

Brazil
- Presidential, federal system of government
- Three branches of government
- All legislative seats filled by direct election
- President elected directly by the people to a four-year term
- Voting compulsory for people 18 to 70

National Palace, Mexico City

Mexico
- Presidential, federal system of government
- Three branches of government
- Some legislative seats given to major parties
- President elected directly by the people to a six-year term
- Voting compulsory for people 18 and older

Comparing Mexico and Brazil

FOCUS ON READING
What happened in Mexico 100 years before the beginning of its civil war?

As you know, the United States is a democracy with a limited system of government. Mexico and Brazil are examples of other nations with limited systems. Their governments have much in common with our own.

Mexico's Government

After three centuries of control by Spain, in 1810 Mexican revolutionaries rose up against Spanish authority. In 1821 Mexico declared independence. The country's current governmental structure and constitution were established in 1917, after a civil war that began in 1910.

Mexico's federal government, like ours, has three branches: legislative, executive, and judicial. In a federal system, powers are divided between central and state governments. Mexico's central government is based in Mexico City, and its 31 states make up its state government.

Mexico's legislative branch has two houses. Three-fifths of the legislators in each house are elected, but the remaining seats are distributed to the major political parties in proportion to the parties' overall share of the popular vote.

The executive branch is led by a president elected directly by the people for one six-year term. By law, voting is compulsory for people over age 18, although no formal penalty is enforced. Mexico does not have the office of vice president.

Mexico has an independent judicial branch. Its highest court is the Supreme Court of Justice. Its judges are appointed by the president and must be approved by one of the houses of the legislature.

Brazil's Government

Brazil was a Portuguese colony for 300 years before gaining independence in 1822. The nation became a republic in 1889, but wealthy coffee planters held much of the political power until a series of military-led uprisings began in the 1920s. In 1930 Getúlio Vargas took power in a nonviolent revolution; by 1937 Vargas ruled as a dictator. After alternating attempts at democracy and at military rule, in 1985 the military finally turned over power to a civilian government. Three years later, Brazil enacted a constitution that is still in effect today.

Brazil has a federal system with 26 states and a federal district. In many ways, Brazil's government is similar to that of Mexico and the United States, with three branches and a separation of powers. Brazil's legislature is bicameral and includes a senate and a chamber of deputies. All members are elected.

The executive branch is led by the president. The president and vice president are elected by a direct vote of the people. Voting is compulsory for literate Brazilians between the ages of 18 and 70, and those who do not vote may be fined.

Brazil's Supreme Court is made up of two courts: the Superior Court of Justice, which deals with nonconstitutional issues, and the Supreme Federal Court, which handles cases involving constitutional interpretation.

READING CHECK **Comparing and Contrasting**
How are the governments of Mexico and Brazil similar and different?

Unlimited Governments

We categorize governments based on who holds governmental power, as well as by how much power they are allowed to execute. Recall that, in a limited government, everyone—including leaders—must obey the law. This form of government likely seems normal to you. That's because, in the United States, the Constitution and other laws limit what leaders can and cannot do. By contrast, an **unlimited government** is a government in which there are no limits set on a ruler's power.

Totalitarianism

Authoritarian governments are unlimited governments in which power is concentrated in the hands of a single person, such as a dictator, or a small group. Leaders can set laws without input from those they rule. They can also break laws without punishment because they answer to no one. At its most extreme, authoritarian rule becomes totalitarian. **Totalitarian governments** control all aspects of society—the government, the economy, and even people's personal beliefs and actions. The Soviet Union under Joseph Stalin, China under Mao Zedong, and North Korea under Kim Jong-un are examples of totalitarian regimes.

In these societies, citizens have no way to influence or change the government. The government sometimes maintains the appearance of democratic rule. For example, they may hold elections and have a written constitution. But these displays of democracy are nothing more than exhibitions to deceive the nation's people or outside observers.

Characteristics of Unlimited Governments

All forms of unlimited government share certain features. In authoritarian and totalitarian systems, ordinary citizens have limited political and economic freedoms. Their rights are rarely recognized or protected, and they may not be able to effectively take part in government or openly express their views.

Totalitarian rulers often use force to put down opposition, such as human rights or prodemocracy movements demanding change. Moreover, because they are not subject to law, totalitarian rulers can change or ignore constitutions or laws intended to restrict their power. For example, before Saddam Hussein of Iraq was overthrown in a 2003 U.S.-led invasion, he used torture and violence against his political opponents, even though torture was officially banned under Iraqi law.

Unlimited Government in China

China
A 1971 propaganda poster contrasts with a photo of prodemocracy demonstrators confronting Chinese troops in Tiananmen Square, Beijing, in 1989.

毛主席万岁！万万岁！

China's Government

In 1949 Chinese leader Mao Zedong created an authoritarian Communist system, imprisoning or killing those who spoke out against his policies. He instituted Soviet-style five-year plans for industrial development. Early efforts, begun in 1953, had some success, but widespread food shortages led to the deaths of tens of millions by 1961. In 1966, Mao began the Cultural Revolution, a violent effort to rid China of its pre-Communist customs and beliefs.

Mao's death in 1976 saw a gradual retreat from many of his policies. Deng Xiaoping eventually became China's leader and slowly introduced many economic and a few political reforms. There were limits to what officials would allow, however. In 1989 the government violently crushed a peaceful prodemocracy student demonstration in China's capital, Beijing, in what became known as the Tiananmen Square Massacre.

China's leaders today are balancing authoritarian rule, economic growth, and slow political reform. China continues to limit its citizens' basic freedoms and rights, and the government exercises strict control over the media and the Internet.

READING CHECK **Summarizing** What are the characteristics of unlimited government?

Human Rights Abuses

Despite international agreements such as the Universal Declaration of Human Rights, human rights abuses occur in both limited and unlimited countries. These abuses include torture, slavery, and murder, and are most common in countries that are not free or are partially free, as shown on the map on the next page. Human rights abuses are also common in countries in the process of establishing democracy. For example, in 2013 the Sudanese government demolished several Christian churches in Sudan as part of an effort to force Christians out of the country. As a result, many Sudanese Christians have fled to South Sudan to avoid persecution.

Abuses in democratic countries are far fewer, but they do occur, often as a result of inaction. For example, the European Union was criticized for not adequately helping asylum seekers fleeing the civil war in Syria in 2013, which left some refugees homeless and without food or water.

The United States recognizes that respect for human rights promotes peace and deters aggression. To that end, the United States has made promoting human rights a major part of its foreign policy. According to the U.S. Department of State, the United States uses a three-part approach

Freedom in Governments of the World

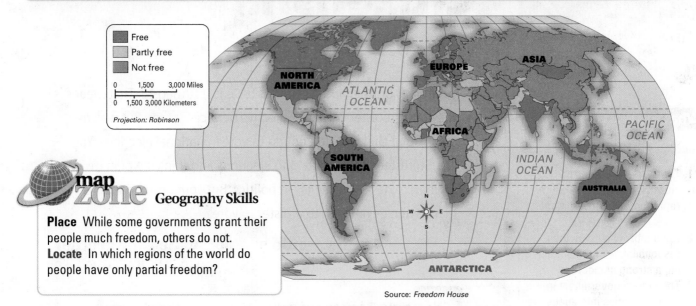

Free
Partly free
Not free

0   1,500   3,000 Miles
0 1,500 3,000 Kilometers

Projection: Robinson

NORTH AMERICA
ATLANTIC OCEAN
SOUTH AMERICA
EUROPE
ASIA
AFRICA
INDIAN OCEAN
PACIFIC OCEAN
AUSTRALIA
ANTARCTICA

Source: *Freedom House*

map zone Geography Skills

Place While some governments grant their people much freedom, others do not.
Locate In which regions of the world do people have only partial freedom?

in its work on human rights. Those three parts are: learning the truth and stating the facts, taking consistent positions about human rights abuses, and partnering with organizations and governments committed to human rights.

READING CHECK Drawing Conclusions
Why would human rights abuses occur more in countries with unlimited governments?

SUMMARY AND PREVIEW The world's countries have different governments. In the next section you will learn about citizenship in various countries.

Section 1 Assessment

Reviewing Ideas, Terms, and Places

1. **a. Define** What is a **direct democracy** and what are its origins?
   b. Elaborate Under which type of government would you most want to live? Why?
2. **a. Describe** What is life like in a country with a totalitarian leader?
   b. Contrast In what ways do **limited governments** differ from **unlimited governments**?
   c. Interpret What are some reasons for limiting the powers of government?
3. **a. Identify** What are some human rights abuses that occurred in Sudan?
   b. Elaborate How does the United States try to combat human rights abuses in other countries?
   c. Compare Look at the map on this page to compare regions. How does government in North America compare to government in Asia?

Critical Thinking

4. **Comparing** Review your notes on the limited and unlimited governments of the United States, Mexico, Brazil, and China. Then use a chart like this one to compare how each government functions and is organized.

United States	Mexico	Brazil	China

FOCUS ON WRITING

my WriteSmart

5. **Describing Government Systems** Take notes on the different systems of government covered in this section. Be sure to include details of the governments of the United States, Mexico, Brazil, and China. Your article should also describe human rights abuses around the world.

Citizenship

What You Will Learn...

Main Ideas

1. The duties and roles of citizenship help to make representative government work.
2. Good citizens accept their responsibilities for maintaining a strong democracy.
3. The type of government in some societies influences the roles of the citizens in those societies.

The Big Idea

Along with the rights and freedoms of citizenship in representative democracies like the United States come important duties and responsibilities.

Key Terms

representative government, *p. 112*
draft, *p. 113*
jury duty, *p. 113*
nonrepresentative government, *p. 115*

hmhsocialstudies.com
TAKING NOTES

Use the annotation tools in your eBook to take notes about the roles of citizens.

If **YOU** were there...

Your older brother and his friends have just turned 18. That means they must register with the Selective Service System. But it also means that they are old enough to vote in national elections. You are interested in the upcoming elections and think it would be exciting to have a real voice in politics. But your brother and his friends don't even plan to register to vote.

How would you persuade your brother that voting is important?

BUILDING BACKGROUND Imagine living in a society in which people did not take good citizenship seriously. For instance, what if people stayed home and did not vote? What would happen if people did not speak up when they saw an injustice? We cannot have a government "by the people"—as Abraham Lincoln said—unless people participate.

Duties and Roles of Citizenship

The United States has a democratic, **representative government**. In such a system, people are the ultimate source of government authority. Elections are free and fair. Elected representatives closely follow the wishes of the people. Citizens typically enjoy rights and privileges such as freedom of speech and freedom of religion. For a representative government to work well, citizens must participate actively and perform certain duties. Let's look at some duties of U.S. citizens.

Obeying the Law

Of course, all Americans must obey the law. Otherwise our society would collapse. To obey laws, you must know what they are. For example, if you are stopped for speeding, it will not help to claim that you did not know the speed limit. It is your duty to find out what the speed limit is and to obey it.

Attending School

You have to go to school, at least until age 16. A democracy cannot function without educated citizens. That is why we have free, public schools. People need good reading and thinking skills so they can wisely choose their leaders and understand issues that affect them. Education also provides workforce skills so people can get jobs and help the economy grow.

Paying Taxes

If you work or buy things, then you probably have to pay taxes. We might not love paying taxes, but we enjoy the services that result from them, such as police and fire protection, road maintenance, public schools, and countless other services. Tax money also pays the huge costs of national security and defense.

Serving in the Armed Forces

Volunteers have fought in every war in U.S. history. When the country's need has exceeded the number of volunteers, however, it sometimes has had to establish a **draft**. Draft laws require men of certain ages and qualifications to serve in the military.

The United States has not had a draft since 1973, during the Vietnam War. However, 18-year-old men must still register their names and addresses with the Selective Service System. If a crisis required that the country quickly expand its armed forces, a draft could be launched and registrated citizens could be called up.

Appearing in Court

Citizens must report to serve as members of a jury, if they are called to do so. This service is called **jury duty**. Jury duty often involves sacrifice. Many citizens must take time off work to serve on a jury, and they are paid very small sums. This sacrifice is necessary because the Constitution guarantees citizens the right to a trial by jury of their peers—that is, their fellow citizens. Citizens must also testify in court if called as witnesses. For our system of justice to function, citizens must fulfill their duty to serve on juries and appear as witnesses.

READING CHECK **Summarizing** Describe five duties of American citizenship.

Rights and Responsibilities

Civic participation in representative government includes both duties, or the things we *must* do, and responsibilities. Responsibilities are the things we *should* do as citizens. These tasks are not required by law; yet, in the United States, most people accept them as their responsibility. Several of these responsibilities are listed below.

Voting

United States government is based on the consent, or the approval, of the governed.

FOCUS ON READING
What things have to happen before we can benefit from government services?

Cadets from the U.S. Air Force Academy commit to several years of military service.

Therefore, we must let our legislators know when we approve or disapprove of their actions. One way to do this is by voting for people whose views we support and who we believe to be good, honest candidates.

Being Informed

To cast your vote wisely, you must be well informed about candidates, current events, and key issues. You also have a responsibility to tell your representatives what you think about topics of public concern. On occasion, you may even need to stand in protest for what you believe. Yet protest, like civic participation in any form, must also be peaceful, respectful of the law, and tolerant of others' rights and liberties.

Taking Part in Government

For a representative government to remain strong, people must participate in the political process at all levels. Citizens are needed to join political parties as well as lead, and educate others, and influence public opinion.

Especially needed are people to run for political office and serve wisely if elected. The quality of any democratic government depends on the quality of the people who serve it.

Helping Your Community

Have you ever volunteered to help your community? There are so many ways to help, from giving your time at the public library to participating in a walk for hunger. Citizens should volunteer to improve their communities. The government cannot be aware of every small problem, much less fix them all. Yet solving small problems is something volunteers can do in many ways. Think of how small acts of kindness—such as cheering up a sick person or caring for a stray animal—make community life better.

Respecting and Protecting Others' Rights

In return for performing civic duties and responsibilities, people in a representative government enjoy the privileges and rights of citizenship. The lasting success and the strength of the United States depends on the protection of its citizens' rights. You can play an important role in protecting these rights by knowing your own rights as an American citizen and knowing and respecting the rights of the people around you. For example, it is essential that community members respect others' property.

You should also know when people's rights are being violated. All Americans must help defend human rights. As a citizen, you have the responsibility to help make sure that our society works for everyone.

READING CHECK **Making Generalizations** How can U.S. citizens contribute to society?

Volunteers help citizens sign in to vote at a polling station.

By planting a tree, these volunteers are beautifying their community.

Citizenship in Other Societies

In other societies with representative governments, citizens' roles and rights are similar to, but not always the same as, those of U.S. citizens. For instance, German citizens are not called to serve on juries, because German courts do not use the jury system. The German constitution guarantees its citizens freedom of the press, but that freedom can be limited in order to protect youth or preserve a person's honor.

There are major differences, however, between the roles and rights of U.S citizens and those of citizens from societies with **nonrepresentative governments**. In such systems, government power is unlimited and citizens have few, if any, rights. For example, citizens of Iran do not have the right of freedom of speech. Without this freedom, Iranians cannot voice their concerns to their leaders.

Citizens' perception of opportunities to participate in and influence the political process vary greatly among contemporary societies. For example, in countries where citizens do not trust the people that run their governments, voting turnout is much lower than in countries where citizens tend to trust their governments.

READING CHECK **Contrasting** How does citizenship in nonrepresentative governments differ from citizenship in representational governments?

SUMMARY AND PREVIEW In this section, you learned about the rights, duties, and responsibilities of citizenship. In the next section you will learn how geographers study and understand world economies.

Section 2 Assessment

hmhsocialstudies.com
ONLINE QUIZ

Reviewing Ideas, Terms, and Places

1. a. Define What is **jury duty**?
 b. Explain How is registering for the **draft** part of being a good citizen?
 c. Predict What would happen in a representative government if only a small group of people performed their civic duties?

2. a. Identify In what ways can citizens participate in the political process?
 b. Interpret How are a citizen's duties, rights, and responsibilities connected?
 c. Evaluate Why is it important to respect other people's rights?

3. a. Identify What is an example of a **nonrepresentative government**?
 b. Explain Why do the levels of civic engagement vary among different contemporary societies?
 c. Compare and Contrast How are the roles and rights of German citizens and U.S. citizens alike? How are they different?

Critical Thinking

4. Evaluate Draw a chart like the one here to list and describe citizens' duties and responsibilities in representative governments. Use the chart to help answer this question: In your opinion, which duty or responsibility expected of citizens is the most important? Explain your answer.

DUTIES	RESPONSIBILITIES

FOCUS ON WRITING

my WriteSmart

5. Describing the Roles of Citizens Take notes on civic participation covered in this section. In your article, be sure to compare examples from the United States with those from various societies around the world.

Social Studies Skills

Chart and Graph | Critical Thinking | Geography | Study

Using a Problem-Solving Process

Learn

Solving problems is a process for finding solutions to difficult situations. Being able to use a problem-solving process is an important skill that will help you identify problems and solve challenges as they appear.

Practice

Use the following steps to solve problems.

1. **Identify the problem.** Study the issue to learn about the problem.

2. **Gather information.** Research and ask questions to learn more about the problem.

3. **List options.** Identify possible options for solving the problem.

4. **Evaluate your options.** Consider their advantages and disadvantages.

5. **Choose and implement a solution.** After comparing your options, choose the one that seems best and apply it to solve your problem.

6. **Evaluate the solution.** Once the solution has been tried, evaluate how effectively it solved the problem. If the solution does not work, go back to your list of options and start again.

Apply

With a partner, use the steps of a problem-solving process to address the issue of graffiti in a local park. Express your ideas orally based on your experiences. Also share information that you learn from research. Then, create a graphic organizer like the one above.

Problem

Voter turnout in elections for local government officials is decreasing in your hometown.

Facts

- In 2003, 51 percent of registered voters voted in local elections.

- By 2013, only 37 percent of registered voters voted in local elections.

- More people vote in local elections when they are held with state or national elections.

Possible Options

Option 1 Start a campaign to encourage voters to participate in local elections

Option 2 Hold local elections on the same day as state or national elections

Evaluation

Option 1 might persuade more people to vote, but could be expensive

Option 2 might increase voter turnout, but might not always be possible

Solution

An advertising campaign promoting voting in local elections increased voter turnout by 7 percent and cost an estimated $500,000.

World Economies

If YOU lived there...

You farm a small plot of land in southern India, and you have a decision to make. You can grow food for your family, or you can grow cassava, a cash crop that can be sold for profit if demand for the crop remains high.

What choice will you make?

 TEKS 3C, 8A, 8B, 8C, 9A, 9B, 9C, 9D, 10A, 10B, 10C, 15E, 21B

Main Ideas

1. Scarcity shapes how societies use factors of production.
2. There are three basic types of economic systems.
3. Contemporary societies have mixed economies.
4. The United States benefits from a free enterprise system.
5. Geographers categorize countries based on levels of economic development and range of economic activities.

The Big Idea

Geographers understand world economies by studying factors of production, economic activities, and levels of development.

Key Terms

scarcity, *p. 117*
factors of production, *p. 117*
free enterprise system, *p. 121*
agricultural industries, *p. 122*
manufacturing industries, *p. 122*
wholesale industries, *p. 122*
retail industries, *p. 122*
service industries, *p. 123*
developed countries, *p. 123*
developing countries, *p. 124*

hmhsocialstudies.com
TAKING NOTES

Use the graphic organizer online to compare economic systems.

BUILDING BACKGROUND Everyone has wants. The decisions you make to satisfy your wants are economic choices. Economists say that all societies face a basic problem: people's wants are unlimited. The resources to fulfill wants, however, are limited.

Scarcity and Resource Use

The conflict between people's unlimited wants and limited resources creates a condition called **scarcity**. Scarcity affects everybody. In fact, scarcity forces individuals, businesses, and societies to answer three basic questions: What will be produced? How will it be produced? For whom will it be produced?

Factors of Production

To understand how societies answer these questions, economists study **factors of production**, or the basic economic resources needed to produce goods and services. The four main factors of production are land, labor, capital, and entrepreneurship. These factors have one thing in common—their supply is limited.

In economic terms, land includes all the natural resources found on or under the ground that are used to produce goods and services. Labor refers to the human time, effort, and talent needed to produce goods and services. Capital refers to the resources used to make and distribute goods and services. Tools, factories, roads, and trains are all forms of capital. Finally, entrepreneurship is the combination of vision, skill, and willingness to take risks needed to start businesses.

If a factor of production is in short supply, problems can arise. Consider this example: a farmer uses skills (labor) and tools (capital) to grow strawberries on a farm (land), which he or she then sells at a market (role of entrepreneur). If a drought destroys farmland, the farmer might produce fewer, if any crops. The farmer's business would be hurt. Strawberries would be scarce. Consumers and businesses would likely have to buy them at a higher price.

The availability of resources influences economic activity. Rwanda's agricultural economy relies heavily on a large number of workers.

By contrast, the availability of capital resources, such as combine harvesters, helps a small number of U.S. farmers tend large fields.

Resources and Economies

The factors of production are not distributed equally. For this reason, countries decide what to produce based on the resources they have. For example, South Africa is rich in gold, diamonds, and mineral resources. Developing a mining industry has helped make South Africa one of the richest countries in Africa.

The availability of resources also shapes how a society produces goods and services. For example, Rwanda's economy is based on agriculture. Rwandans are rich in agricultural labor. In fact, about 90 percent of Rwandans work in agriculture. Farmers grow crops on small plots of land near their homes. In terms of capital, they have simple farming tools but few tractors and roads. By contrast, only about two percent of Americans work in agriculture. U.S. farmers rely heavily on capital. Using machinery and technology, they produce surplus crops on large farms.

Scarcity and Trade

When a resource is relatively scarce in one place, people may trade with others to get it. This happens within a society as well as between nations. In this way, scarcity contributes to economic interdependence. It is also a driving force behind international trade.

For instance, Japan manufactures cars, which requires a great deal of steel. However, Japan lacks the iron ore needed to make steel. To obtain iron ore, Japan has formed international trading relationships with Australia and Brazil.

READING CHECK **Analyzing** How does availability of the factors of production affect a society's economy?

Economic Systems

An economic system is the way in which a society organizes the production and distribution of goods and services. Economic systems can be divided into three types: traditional, market, and command.

In a traditional economy, the work that people do is based on long-established customs. People in these groups hunt, fish, and tend animals and crops. Often, the focus of work is survival. The good of the group is more important than individual desires. In earlier times, all societies had traditional economies.

Today traditional economies are rare and under pressure to change. Still, you can find this system in many places. For example, the Aymara people of the South American Andes and the Inuit people in northern Canada have traditional economies.

In a command economy, the government controls the economy. Command economies decide what goods and services to produce, how and how much to produce, and how goods and services are distributed. It also sets wages and prices. Some economists refer to command economies as centrally planned economies.

The most common economic system used today is a market economy. A market economy is based on private ownership, free trade, and competition. Individuals and businesses are free to buy and sell what they wish with little interference from government. Prices are determined by the supply of and demand for goods.

READING CHECK **Summarizing** What are the three basic types of economic systems?

Modern Economies

Few if any pure economic systems exist today. Most countries have mixed economies that combine elements of traditional, market, and command economic systems. The most common types of mixed economies are communist, capitalist, and socialist.

Communist Economies

Modern economies tend to emphasize features of one system over others. For

Traditional The Inuit of Canada use fishing techniques passed down over many generations.

Command Food was scarce and expensive in this store in the former Soviet Union, a command economy.

Market Advertisements, like these billboards in New York City, are a common sight in a market economy.

example, communist economies are closest to the command model. In a communist economy the government owns all the factors of production. There is no private ownership of property and little or no political freedom.

How do communist nations decide what, how, and for whom to produce? In countries such as North Korea and Cuba, the government collectivized, or took ownership, of the factors of production. Then government workers called central planners make long-term plans. They make all decisions about the production, price, and distribution of goods and services. They may even decide what types of work people are able to do.

Capitalist Economies

By contrast, capitalist economies emphasize features of market systems. In capitalist economies, individuals and businesses own the factors of production. They play a major role in answering the basic economic questions and no central government authority tells them what to do. Consumers buy goods and services that they like best. Their choices push producers to make better products at lower prices.

The economies of the United States, Canada, and Taiwan are capitalist. In these countries, government plays an important but limited role in the economy. For example, in the United States, government agencies enforce health and safety standards. These actions benefit U.S. workers and consumers but affect business planning in complicated ways. Regulations can increase the cost of running a business. On the other hand, the government spends money that it collects in taxes on services that support economic development, such as education, roads, and social welfare programs. Businesses save money by not having to pay for these services themselves.

Socialist Economies

The third type of economy falls between communism and capitalism. In socialist economies, the government controls some of the basic factors of production. In most cases, that control is limited to industries and services that are central to a nation's well being, such as electrical utilities, communications networks, and healthcare. Other industries are privately controlled.

Today, many nations with elements of a socialist economy, such as Sweden and India, have democratic governments. Still, central planners make decisions about government-owned industries. They also make decisions about other sectors, such as healthcare, to ensure that everyone has access to services.

Comparing Economic Systems			
	Communism	**Socialism**	**Free Enterprise**
Who owns resources?	Government	Government owns basic resources; the rest are privately owned	Individuals and businesses
Who distributes resources?	Government decides how resources are used	Government regulates basic resources; market allocates privately owned resources	Market allocates resources
What role does government play?	Government makes all economic decisions	Government makes decisions in the basic industries	Government has a limited role, acting mostly to ensure market forces are free to work

Trends Since the Fall of Communism

The record of collective, or communist, non-free market economies, is poor. From the 1940s until the 1990s, between one quarter and one third of the world's people lived under communist regimes. The former Soviet Union and several of its Eastern European neighbors, China and much of Southeast Asia, Cuba, and North Korea all had centrally planned economies.

The failure of these economies is due largely to the shortcomings of communism. Often, central planners had too many decisions to make and too little understanding of local conditions. With wages set, workers had little incentive to work hard. Communism's greatest failing, however, was the suffering that it caused. Shortages of food and goods were common. Millions of people died building huge collective farms in China and the Soviet Union. Millions more were imprisoned for criticizing government policies.

With the collapse of communism in the early 1990s, most communist countries adopted some form of market economy. Even the five communist countries that are left—China, Cuba, Laos, North Korea, and Vietnam—have adopted some features of market economies.

READING CHECK **Comparing** How are socialist economies similar to both communist and capitalist economies?

The Free Enterprise System

U.S. capitalism is sometimes called the **free enterprise system**. Under this system, Americans enjoy a number of freedoms. They are free to exchange goods and services and choose careers. They are also free to own and operate enterprises, or businesses, with little government intervention.

At age eight, Madison Robinson started a business selling flip-flops that she designed.

Let's take a look at one American who took advantage of these freedoms. In 2006 Eight-year-old Madison Robinson from Galveston, Texas, had an idea to sell light-up flip-flops for kids. With financing from friends and family, she started her own company, Fish Flops. By 2013 Fish Flops had over $1 million in sales, enough profit to cover Robinson's college tuition.

The ability to make a profit is one of the chief advantages of the free enterprise system. In this system, profit can reward hard work and innovation. The desire to make a profit also encourages competition, forcing producers to offer higher-quality products at lower prices. Another advantage is that people often have greater freedoms in societies with free enterprise systems. They can own property, make economic decisions, and participate in open elections.

Maintaining a functioning free enterprise system requires people to act in a morally responsible and ethical way. Businesses and individuals must obey laws, be truthful, and avoid behaviors harmful to others. Government regulations must be effective and fairly enforced.

Unethical behavior can lead to business failure and a loss of trust in the system. For example, if company officials begin to lie about a business's financial condition, then investors can lose thousands, even billions of dollars. Finally, the company itself could go bankrupt.

READING CHECK **Summarizing** How does the ability to make a profit help the economy?

Economic Activities and Development

Every nation's economy includes a variety of economic activities. Economic activities are the ways in which people make a living. Some people farm, others manufacture goods, and still others provide services. Geographers categorize these economic activities into four levels of industry.

Levels of Industry

The first level is called primary industry. People working at this level harvest products from the earth. **Agricultural industries** are primary activities that focus on growing crops and raising livestock. Fishing and mining are also primary activities. Raw materials such as grain, cattle, seafood, and coal are all products of primary activities.

At the next level, secondary industry, people use natural resources and raw materials to make products to sell. In **manufacturing industries**, people and businesses manufacture, or make, finished products from raw materials. For example, a furniture maker could use wood to make a table or a chair.

In the third level, or tertiary industry, people provide goods and services to customers. Workers at this level may sell goods and products from primary and secondary industries. Some work in **wholesale industries**, businesses that sell to businesses. They help move goods from manufacturer to market. Others work in **retail industries**, businesses that sell

Economic Activity

Primary Industry

Primary industries use natural resources to make money. This farmer sells milk from dairy cows to earn a living.

Secondary Industry

Secondary economic activities use raw materials to produce or manufacture something new. In this case, the milk from dairy cows is used to make cheese.

Tertiary Industry

Tertiary economic activities provide goods and services to people and businesses. This grocer selling cheese in a market is involved in a tertiary activity.

Quaternary Industry

Quaternary industries process and distribute information. Skilled workers research and gather information. Here, inspectors examine and test the quality of cheese.

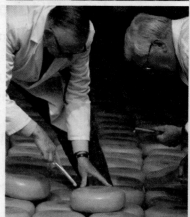

directly to final consumers. For example, a furniture wholesaler buys tables from a manufacturer. Then the wholesaler sells the tables to a retail store, such as a department store, that sells directly to consumers.

Still other tertiary workers, like health care workers and mechanics, work in **service industries**, businesses that provide services rather than goods. Teachers, store clerks, and doctors are all tertiary workers.

The fourth level of economic activity, quaternary industry, involves the research and distribution of information. People making a living at this level work with information rather than goods and often have specialized knowledge and skills. Architects, librarians, and scientists all work in quaternary industries.

Economic Indicators

Economic systems and activities affect a country's economic development, or the level of economic growth and quality of life. Geographers group countries into two basic categories: developed countries and developing countries. To decide if a country is developed or developing, geographers use economic indicators, or measures of a country's wealth.

One indicator, gross domestic product (GDP), is the value of all goods and services produced within a country in a single year. Another indicator is a country's per capita GDP, or the total GDP divided by the number of people in a country. As you can see in the chart, per capita GDP allows us to compare incomes among countries. Other indicators include literacy and life expectancy and the overall level of industrialization. We also look at the types of industries a country has and at its level of health care and education.

Developed and Developing Countries

Many of the world's wealthiest and most powerful nations are **developed countries**, countries with strong economies and a

A Developed and a Developing Country

Australia	Afghanistan
Per Capita GDP (U.S. $): $43,300	Per Capita GDP (U.S. $): $1,100
Life Expectancy at Birth: 82	Life Expectancy at Birth: 50.1
Literacy Rate: 99%	Literacy Rate: 28%
Physicians Per 10,000 People: 39	Physicians Per 10,000 People: 2

Contrasting How does the quality of life in Afghanistan differ from that in Australia?

high quality of life. Developed countries like Germany and the United States have a high per capita GDP and high levels of industrialization. Their health care and education systems are among the best in the world.

The world's poorer nations are known as **developing countries**, countries with less productive economies and a lower quality of life. Almost two-thirds of the world's people live in developing countries. These countries have a lower per capita GDP than developed countries. Most of their citizens work in farming or other primary industries. Although these countries typically have large cities, much of their population still lives in rural areas. People in developing countries usually have less access to health care and technology. Guatemala, Nigeria, and Afghanistan are all developing countries.

Often, a country's economic activities reflect its economic development.

In the poorest developing countries, the vast majority of people work in primary industries, such as farming. As a country becomes more developed, fewer people work in primary industries. In the mid-1800s about two thirds of U.S. workers worked in primary activities. Today, 80 percent work in tertiary industries, including wholesale, retail, and service industries. Only three percent of Americans work in primary industries.

READING CHECK **Analyzing** How does GDP differ in developed and developing countries?

SUMMARY AND PREVIEW In this section you learned about the economic activities, systems, and levels of development that characterize societies today. In the next chapter you will learn about citizenship in various countries.

Section 3 Assessment

Reviewing Ideas, Terms, and Places

1. **a. Describe** What are the **factors of production**?
   b. Predict What problems might a homebuilder face if one of the factors of production, such as land or labor, was in short supply?
   c. Explain Identify and explain an example of how the relative scarcity of resources might impact economic interdependence within a country.
2. **a. Compare** Who makes the economic decisions in a traditional economy? Compare this with market and command economies.
   b. Evaluate What explains the record of collective, non-free market economies in the world today?
3. **a. Identify** What are the advantages of the **free enterprise system**?
   b. Analyze How can unethical and immoral behavior hurt the free enterprise system?
4. **a. Define** Describe and give examples of **agricultural, wholesale, retail, manufacturing,** and **service industries**.

b. Explain What are **developed** and **developing countries**? Include examples of economic indicators in your answer.
c. Analyze How might economic factors affect the use of technology in a developing country?

Critical Thinking

5. **Comparing** Use your notes to complete a chart like the one below comparing economic systems. For each system, list how some societies organize the production and distribution of goods and services.

Free Enterprise	Socialist	Communist

FOCUS ON WRITING   *my*WriteSmart

6. **Describing Economic Systems** Use your notes on economic systems to write your article. Be sure to include definitions of different economic systems as well as details on the United States and Rwanda.

Chapter Review

Visual Summary

Use the visual summary below to help you review the main ideas of the chapter.

QUICK FACTS

World Governments
Governments around the world are categorized based on who holds power and how that power is distributed.

Citizenship
Active participation in civic life is critical in a representative democracy.

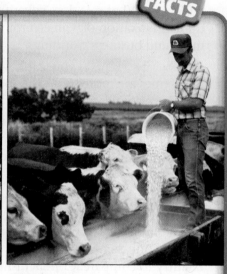

World Economies
The world's people practice different economic activities and systems.

Reviewing Vocabulary, Terms, and Places

For each group of terms below, write one or two sentences that shows how all the terms in the group are related.

1. democracy
   limited government

2. totalitarian government
   unlimited government

3. draft
   jury duty

4. scarcity
   factors of production

5. agricultural industries
   manufacturing industries
   wholesale industries
   retail industries

6. developed country
   developing country

Comprehension and Critical Thinking

SECTION 1 *(Pages 106–111)*

7. **a. Recall** What group created and practiced direct democracy?

   b. Analyze What are some ways that governments can misuse power?

   c. Elaborate Why does the United States promote human rights? Explain your answer. What arguments might someone with a different opinion use?

SECTION 2 *(Pages 112–115)*

8. **a. Describe** What is the purpose of a military draft?

   b. Analyze How does volunteering help your community?

   c. Elaborate Why would citizens in countries with a nonrepresentative government participate less in civic life?

9. a. Describe What is the relationship between scarcity and international trade?

b. Explain How do the factors of production influence a nation's economy? Give two examples.

c. Identify What role does government regulation and taxation play in economic development and business planning?

d. Elaborate Why do you think that market economies are more successful today than command economies are?

e. Analyze Study the images and text on page 118. How do economic factors affect how U.S. and Rwandan farmers use technology?

Using the Internet

10. Evaluating Government and Economic Systems Identify one democratic and one communist country to compare. Conduct Internet research to learn more about each nation's economy and government. For each, be sure to describe whether government is limited or unlimited and tell who holds power—one person, a few people, or many people. Then, research each country's human rights record and economic indicators including life expectancy, gross domestic product (GDP), per capita GDP, and literacy. Write a brief report summarizing your findings and evaluating the effectiveness of each country's political and economic system.

↗ hmhsocialstudies.com

Social Studies Skills

11. Using a Problem-Solving Process With a partner, use the steps of a problem-solving process to address the issue of overpopulation in China. Gather information about the problem and China's one child per family. Then create a graphic organizer like the one on page 116. List and consider options for solving the problem. Discuss the advantages and disadvantages of each. Express your ideas orally based on your experiences and on research. Be sure to address China's one-child per family policy and evaluate its effectiveness. Finally, choose the solution that you would implement.

Map Activity

Freedom in Governments of the World *Use the map below to answer the questions.*

12. Which letter indicates a country whose government does not allow its citizens any rights or freedoms?

13. Which letter indicates a country whose government allows its citizens only partial rights and freedoms?

14. List the countries whose governments allow their citizens rights and freedoms. What system of government do you think is practiced in these countries?

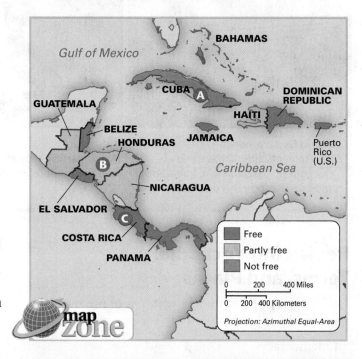

FOCUS ON READING AND WRITING *my* WriteSmart

15. Sequencing Describe the sequence of steps for moving goods from maker to consumer. Use sequence clue words in your answer.

16. Writing Your Online Article Choose two economic systems and two government systems. Your purpose is to compare the main characteristics of these systems. Write a headline and a brief introduction that expresses your main idea. Then write a paragraph comparing government systems and another comparing economic systems. Be sure to describe the roles of citizens and give examples of countries with these systems. Write a conclusion that summarizes your main points.

Reading Social Studies

Sequencing

Sequence is the order in which events follow one another. To show the order of events or steps in a process, writers use words like *before, after, next, first, then, later,* and *finally.* They also use words and phrases that indicate specific times, such as *the next day* and *on July 4, 1776.* Making a visual, such as a sequence chain or a timeline can help you sequence events.

Read the passage below, noting the underlined clue words and dates. Notice how they reveal the order of the events shown in the timeline at right.

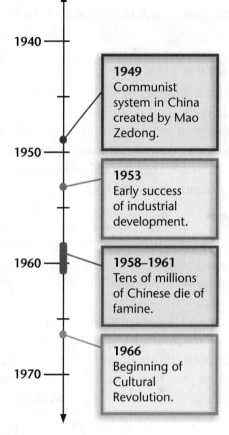

In 1949 Chinese leader Mao Zedong created an authoritarian Communist system, imprisoning or killing those who spoke out against his policies. He instituted Soviet-style five-year plans for industrial development. Early efforts, begun in 1953, had some success, but widespread food shortages led to the deaths of tens of millions by 1961. In 1966, Mao began the Cultural Revolution, a violent effort to rid China of its pre-Communist customs and beliefs.
From Section 1, World Governments

YOU TRY IT!

Read the following passage. Look for dates and clue words to help you figure out the sequence of steps described in it. Then make a timeline like the one above to show that order.

Brazil was a Portuguese colony for 300 years before gaining independence in 1822. The nation became a republic in 1889, but wealthy coffee planters held much of the political power until a series of military led uprisings began in the 1920s. In 1930 Getúlio Vargas took power in a nonviolent revolution; by 1937 Vargas ruled as a dictator. After alternating attempts at democracy and at military rule, in 1985 the military finally turned over power to a civilian government. Three years later, Brazil enacted a constitution that is still in effect today.
From Section 1, World Governments

Explaining a Process

How does soil renewal work? How do cultures change? Often the first question we ask about something is how it works or what process it follows. One way we can answer these questions is by writing an explanation.

Assignment *my*WriteSmart

Use *my*WriteSmart to write a paper explaining one of these topics:

- how water recycles on Earth
- how agriculture developed

1. Prewrite

Choose a Process

- Choose one of the topics above to write about.
- Turn your topic into a big idea, or thesis. For example, your big idea might be "Water continually circulates from Earth's surface to the atmosphere and back."

> **TIP** **Organizing Information** Explanations should be in a logical order. You should arrange the steps in the process in chronological order, the order in which the steps take place.

Gather and Organize Information

- Look for information about your topic in your textbook, in the library, or on the Internet.
- Start a plan to organize support for your big idea. For example, look for the individual steps of the water cycle.

2. Write

Use a Writer's Framework

> **A Writer's Framework**
>
> **Introduction**
> - Start with an interesting fact or question.
> - Identify your big idea.
>
> **Body**
> - Create at least one paragraph for each point supporting the big idea. Add facts and details to explain each point.
> - Use a variety of sentence structures to add interest to your writing.
> - Use chronological order or order of importance.
>
> **Conclusion**
> - Summarize your main points in your final paragraph.

3. Evaluate and Revise

Review and Improve Your Paper

- Re-read your paper and make sure you have followed the framework.
- Make the changes needed to improve your paper.

Evaluation Questions for Your Paper

1. Do you begin with an interesting fact or question?
2. Does your introduction identify your big idea?
3. Do you have at least one paragraph for each point you are using to support the big idea?
4. Do you use a variety of sentence structures?
5. Do you include facts and details to explain and illustrate each point?
6. Do you use chronological order or order of importance to organize your main points?

4. Proofread and Publish

Give Your Explanation the Finishing Touch

- Make sure to use standard grammar, spelling, punctuation, and sentence structure.
- Check for punctuation at the end of every sentence.
- Think of a way to share your explanation.
- Use social studies terminology correctly.

5. Practice and Apply

Use the steps and strategies outlined in this workshop to write your explanation. Present your paper to others and find out whether the explanation makes sense to them.

The Americas

The Great Lakes

Five huge lakes in North America known as the Great Lakes make up the largest group of freshwater lakes on Earth.

The Andes

Stretching along South America's western coast, the Andes are the longest mountain range in the world.

The Americas

The Amazon

In the heart of South America, the Amazon rain forest is home to millions of plant and animal species.

Explore the Satellite Image Forests, mountains, and plains stretch from north to south across the Americas. How do you think the features you can see on this satellite image influence life in the Americas?

The Satellite's Path

>44'56.08<

>>>>>>>>>>665.00'87<

456.094·

567.476·348   +799   +803   +966   +355

The Americas: Physical

Geography Skills

Place The Americas includes high mountains, major rivers, and large interior plains.

1. **Name** What are some major features of the Americas?
2. **Make Inferences** How do you think mountains have influenced settlement patterns in the region?

ELEVATION

Feet		Meters
13,120		4,000
6,560		2,000
1,640		500
656		200
(Sea level) 0		0 (Sea level)
Below sea level		Below sea level

0   600   1,200 Miles

0   600   1,200 Kilometers

Projection: Miller Cylindrical

Map labels:

ARCTIC OCEAN

Ellesmere Island

GREENLAND (DENMARK)

Victoria Island

Baffin Island

Yukon River

Alaska (U.S.)

Great Bear Lake

Mackenzie River

Great Slave Lake

Hudson Bay

CANADA

CANADIAN SHIELD

ROCKY MOUNTAINS

GREAT PLAINS

Lake Winnipeg

Missouri River

Great Lakes

Newfoundland

Ohio River

APPALACHIAN MTS.

ATLANTIC OCEAN

GREAT BASIN

UNITED STATES

Mt. Whitney 14,495 ft (4,418 m)

Mississippi River

Sierra Madre Occidental

Gulf of Mexico

Tropic of Cancer

Hawaii (U.S.)

Pico de Orizaba 18,855 ft (5,747 m)

MEXICO

BAHAMAS

CUBA

HAITI

DOMINICAN REPUBLIC

BELIZE

HONDURAS

GUATEMALA

NICARAGUA

EL SALVADOR

COSTA RICA

PANAMA

VENEZUELA

GUYANA

SURINAME

FRENCH GUIANA (FRANCE)

COLOMBIA

PACIFIC OCEAN

0° Equator

ECUADOR

PERU

AMAZON BASIN

Amazon River

BRAZIL

BRAZILIAN HIGHLANDS

ATLANTIC OCEAN

BOLIVIA

Paraguay River

ANDES MOUNTAINS

PARAGUAY

Uruguay River

Tropic of Capricorn

30°S

CHILE

Mt. Aconcagua 22,834 ft (6,960 m)

URUGUAY

ARGENTINA

Patagonia

Falkland Islands

60°N

30°N

150°W

120°W

90°W

60°W

30°W

Geographical Extremes: The Americas

Longest River	Amazon River, Brazil/Peru: 4,000 miles (6,435 km)
Highest Point	Mt. Aconcagua, Argentina: 22,834 feet (6,960 m)
Lowest Point	Death Valley, United States: 282 feet (86 m) below sea level
Highest Recorded Temperature	Death Valley, United States: 134°F (56.6°C)
Lowest Recorded Temperature	Snag, Canada: -81.4°F (-63°C)
Wettest Place	Lloro, Colombia: 523.6 inches (1,329.9 cm) average precipitation per year
Driest Place	Arica, Chile: .03 inches (.08 cm) average precipitation per year
Highest Waterfall	Angel Falls, Venezuela: 3,212 feet (979 m)
Most Tornadoes	United States: More than 1,000 per year

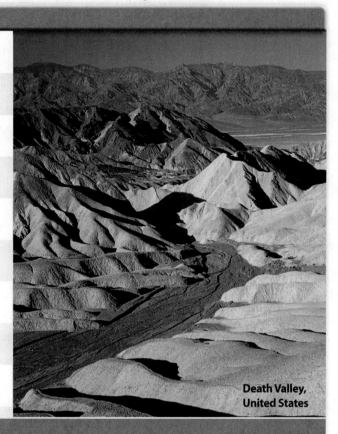

Death Valley, United States

Size Comparison: The United States and the Americas

North America: Political

ARCTIC OCEAN

GREENLAND (DENMARK)

Yukon River

Alaska (U.S.)

MacKenzie River

CANADA

Saskatchewan R.

Vancouver • Calgary

St. Lawrence River

Montreal
Ottawa ⊛
Toronto

Boston

Columbia River

UNITED STATES

Missouri River

Mississippi R.

Ohio R.

Chicago

New York
★ Washington, D.C.

PACIFIC OCEAN

Hawaii (U.S.)

Tropic of Cancer

Los Angeles

Houston

Rio Grande

ATLANTIC OCEAN

BAHAMAS
⊛ Nassau

Monterrey

MEXICO

Havana
⊛ CUBA

HAITI
DOMINICAN REPUBLIC

• Guadalajara

⊛ Mexico City

Santo Domingo
Port-au-Prince

BELIZE
Belmopan
⊛ HONDURAS
Tegucigalpa
GUATEMALA ⊛ ⊛ NICARAGUA
Guatemala City ⊛ ⊛ Managua
San Salvador
EL SALVADOR

Panama City

SOUTH AMERICA

San José
COSTA RICA PANAMA

⊛ National capital

0   300   600 Miles
0   300   600 Kilometers

Projection:
Lambert Azimuthal Equal-Area

Inset map (Caribbean):

ATLANTIC OCEAN

DOMINICAN REPUBLIC

VIRGIN IS. (U.S.)
BRITISH VIRGIN IS. (U.K.)
ANGUILLA (U.K.)

ANTIGUA AND BARBUDA

PUERTO RICO (U.S.)

Basseterre
St. John's
MONTSERRAT (U.K.)

ST. KITTS AND NEVIS

GUADELOUPE (FRANCE)

Roseau ⊛ DOMINICA

MARTINIQUE (FRANCE)

Caribbean Sea

Castries ⊛ ST. LUCIA

Kingstown
Bridgetown
⊛ BARBADOS

ST. VINCENT AND THE GRENADINES

St. George's ⊛ GRENADA

Port of Spain
⊛ TRINIDAD AND TOBAGO

VENEZUELA

0° Equator

map zone
Geography Skills

Place North America includes both large and small countries.
1. Locate Where are North America's smaller countries located?

2. Make Generalizations What are some advantages or disadvantages that countries might face because they are large or small?

The Americas

South America: Political

Cartagena

Caracas

VENEZUELA

Georgetown
Paramaribo

⊛ Bogotá

GUYANA

French Guiana
(FRANCE)

SURINAME

COLOMBIA

0° Equator

⊛ Quito
ECUADOR
Guayaquil

Manaus

Amazon River

*Galápagos
Islands*

PERU

BRAZIL

10°N

10°S

**PACIFIC
OCEAN**

Lima

Salvador

La Paz

⊛ Brasília

BOLIVIA

Sucre

**ATLANTIC
OCEAN**

20°S

Parana River

PARAGUAY

Rio de
Janeiro

CHILE

Asunción

São Paulo

Tropic of Capricorn

Córdoba

⊛ National capital

0   300   600 Miles

0   300   600 Kilometers

Projection:
Lambert Azimuthal Equal-Area

URUGUAY

Santiago

Buenos Aires

Montevideo

30°S

ARGENTINA

40°S

*Falkland
Islands*

*South Georgia
Island*

50°S

**map
zone**

Geography Skills

Place South America includes
12 countries and one overseas
department of France.

1. Name Which country is by far
the largest in South America?

2. Compare Compare this map to
the physical map of the Americas. What physical feature
separates Chile and Argentina?

100°W   90°W   80°W   70°W   60°W   50°W   40°W   30°W   20°W

The Americas: Population

ARCTIC OCEAN

60°N

Montreal
Toronto
Chicago
New York

ATLANTIC OCEAN

Los Angeles

30°N

Tropic of Cancer

Monterrey

Guadalajara
Mexico City

PACIFIC OCEAN

Caracas

Medellín
Bogotá

0° Equator

Lima

ATLANTIC OCEAN

Belo Horizonte
Rio de Janeiro
São Paulo

Tropic of Capricorn

30°S

Santiago

Buenos Aires

map zone

Geography Skills

Place Overall, population density in the Americas is not high, but many people live in large cities.

1. **Identify** Which areas of the United States have the highest population density?

2. **Make Inferences** Notice that most large cities in South America are located near the coast. Why do you think that is?

Persons per square mile	Persons per square km
520	200
260	100
130	50
25	10
3	1
0	0

● Major cities over 3 million

0   600   1,200 Miles

0   600   1,200 Kilometers

Projection: Miller Cylindrical

The Americas: Climate

ARCTIC
OCEAN

ATLANTIC
OCEAN

30°N

Tropic of Cancer

PACIFIC
OCEAN

0° Equator

ATLANTIC
OCEAN

Tropic of Capricorn

30°S

60°N

map zone

Geography Skills

Place The Americas has a huge variety of climates.

1. **Name** What are the main climates in North America and South America?

2. **Compare** Compare this map to the population map. How does climate relate to population distribution?

Climate Types

Humid tropical
Tropical savanna
Desert
Steppe
Mediterranean
Humid subtropical
Marine west coast
Humid continental
Subarctic
Tundra
Ice cap
Highland

0   600   1,200 Miles

0   600   1,200 Kilometers

Projection: Miller Cylindrical

Regional Database

The Americas

COUNTRY CAPITAL	FLAG	POPULATION	AREA (sq mi)	PER CAPITA GDP (U.S. $)	LIFE EXPECTANCY AT BIRTH	TVS PER 1,000 PEOPLE
Antigua and Barbuda St. John's		85,632	171	$19,600	74.3	493
Argentina Buenos Aires		40.9 million	1,068,302	$14,200	76.5	293
The Bahamas Nassau		309,156	5,382	$29,600	65.8	243
Barbados Bridgetown		284,589	166	$19,100	73.2	290
Belize Belmopan		307,899	8,867	$8,400	68.3	183
Bolivia La Paz, Sucre		9.8 million	424,164	$4,500	66.6	118
Brazil Brasília		198.7 million	3,286,488	$10,200	71.9	333
Canada Ottawa		33.5 million	3,855,101	$39,100	81.3	709
Chile Santiago		16.6 million	292,260	$14,900	77.3	240
Colombia Bogotá		45.6 million	439,736	$8,800	72.6	279
Costa Rica San José		4.3 million	19,730	$11,500	77.5	229
Cuba Havana		11.5 million	42,803	$9,500	77.3	248
Dominica Roseau		72,660	291	$9,900	75.4	232
Dominican Republic Santo Domingo		9.7 million	18,815	$8,200	73.4	96
Ecuador Quito		14.6 million	109,483	$7,500	76.9	213
United States Washington, D.C.		316.7 million	3,794,083	$50,700	78.6	844

COUNTRY Capital	FLAG	POPULATION	AREA (sq mi)	PER CAPITA GDP (U.S. $)	LIFE EXPECTANCY AT BIRTH	TVS PER 1,000 PEOPLE
El Salvador San Salvador		7.2 million	8,124	$6,200	72.2	191
Grenada Saint George's		90,739	133	$12,900	65.6	376
Guatemala Guatemala City		13.3 million	42,043	$5,300	70.1	61
Guyana Georgetown		772,298	83,000	$3,800	66.5	70
Haiti Port-au-Prince		9 million	10,714	$1,300	57.6	5
Honduras Tegucigalpa		7.8 million	43,278	$4,100	69.4	95
Jamaica Kingston		2.8 million	4,244	$7,500	73.7	191
Mexico Mexico City		111.2 million	761,606	$14,200	75.9	272
Nicaragua Managua		5.9 million	49,998	$2,900	71.3	69
Panama Panama City		3.4 million	30,193	$11,700	77	192
Paraguay Asunción		7 million	157,047	$4,200	75.7	205
Peru Lima		29.5 million	496,226	$8,500	70.5	147
Saint Kitts and Nevis Basseterre		40,131	101	$19,500	73.1	256
Saint Lucia Castries		160,267	238	$11,100	76.3	368
Saint Vincent and the Grenadines; Kingstown		104,574	150	$10,200	74.4	230
United States Washington, D.C.		316.7 million	3,794,083	$50,700	78.6	844

Regional Database

COUNTRY Capital	FLAG	POPULATION	AREA (sq mi)	PER CAPITA GDP (U.S. $)	LIFE EXPECTANCY AT BIRTH	TVS PER 1,000 PEOPLE
Suriname Paramaribo		481,267	63,039	$8,900	73.6	241
Trinidad and Tobago Port-of-Spain		1.2 million	1,980	$23,600	67.1	337
Uruguay Montevideo		3.5 million	68,039	$12,400	76.2	531
Venezuela Caracas		26.8 million	352,144	$13,500	73.6	185
United States Washington, D.C.		316.7 million	3,794,083	$50,700	78.6	844

ANALYSIS SKILL **ANALYZING TABLES**

1. Compare the information for the United States, Canada, Brazil, and Mexico. How do these four countries compare?
2. Which country has the lowest per capita GDP?

Largest Cities and Urban Populations

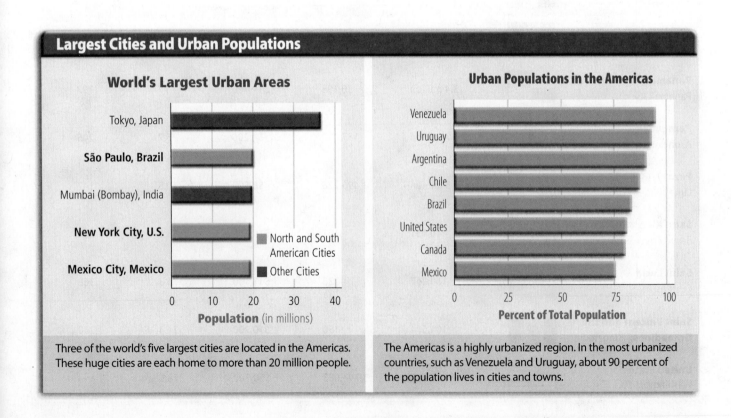

World's Largest Urban Areas

Tokyo, Japan
São Paulo, Brazil
Mumbai (Bombay), India
New York City, U.S.
Mexico City, Mexico

North and South American Cities
Other Cities

0   10   20   30   40
Population (in millions)

Three of the world's five largest cities are located in the Americas. These huge cities are each home to more than 20 million people.

Urban Populations in the Americas

Venezuela
Uruguay
Argentina
Chile
Brazil
United States
Canada
Mexico

0   25   50   75   100
Percent of Total Population

The Americas is a highly urbanized region. In the most urbanized countries, such as Venezuela and Uruguay, about 90 percent of the population lives in cities and towns.

Major Food Exports of the Americas

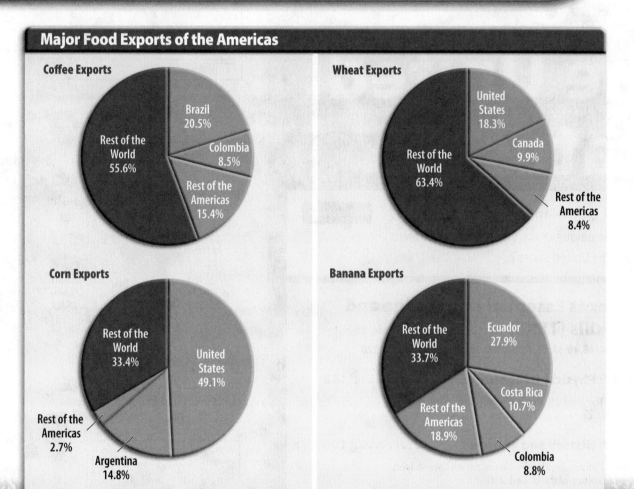

Coffee Exports

- Brazil 20.5%
- Colombia 8.5%
- Rest of the Americas 15.4%
- Rest of the World 55.6%

Wheat Exports

- United States 18.3%
- Canada 9.9%
- Rest of the Americas 8.4%
- Rest of the World 63.4%

Corn Exports

- United States 49.1%
- Argentina 14.8%
- Rest of the Americas 2.7%
- Rest of the World 33.4%

Banana Exports

- Ecuador 27.9%
- Costa Rica 10.7%
- Colombia 8.8%
- Rest of the Americas 18.9%
- Rest of the World 33.7%

The region of the Americas is a major exporter of some crops, like coffee, wheat, corn, and bananas. While the United States leads in wheat and corn exports, other crops like coffee and bananas are exported from Central and South America.

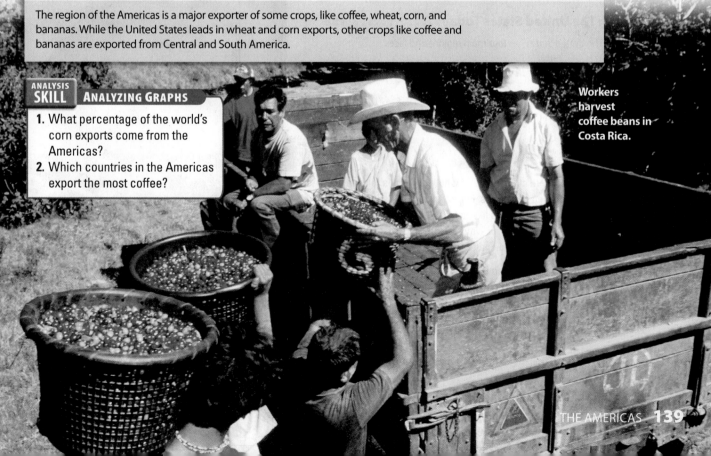

ANALYSIS SKILL | **ANALYZING GRAPHS**

1. What percentage of the world's corn exports come from the Americas?
2. Which countries in the Americas export the most coffee?

Workers harvest coffee beans in Costa Rica.

The United States

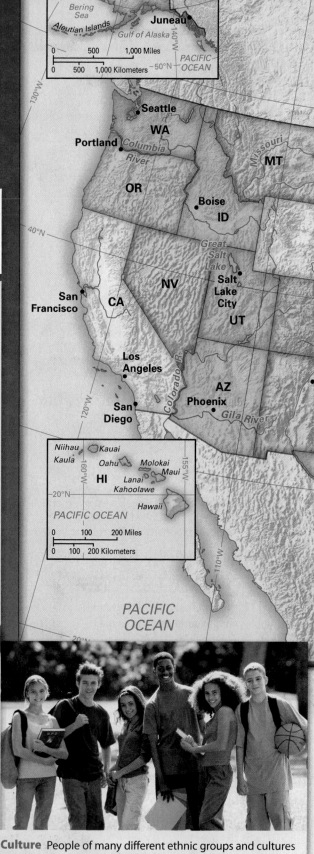

Essential Question
*my*Notebook

What are the unique characteristics of the different regions of the United States?

Texas Essential Knowledge and Skills (TEKS)

1A, 2B, 3A, 3B, 3C, 4B, 4D, 5A, 6B, 6C, 7B, 15D, 18D, 19B, 21A, 21B, 21C, 22D

FOCUS ON READING AND VIEWING
my WriteSmart

Categorizing A good way to make sense of what you read is to separate facts and details into groups, called categories. For example, you could sort facts about the United States into categories like natural resources, major cities, or rivers. As you read this chapter, look for ways to categorize details under each topic. **See the lesson, Categorizing, on page 167.**

Creating a Collage Artists create collages by gluing art and photographs onto a flat surface, such as a poster board. As you read this chapter, you will collect ideas for a collage about the United States. After you create your own collage, you will view and evaluate the collages of other students in your class. Use the annotation tools in your eBook to gather information for your assignment.

Culture People of many different ethnic groups and cultures make up the population of the United States.

The United States: Political

CANADA

MEXICO

HISTORY Paving America

↗ hmhsocialstudies.com | VIDEO

River

ND
Fargo
MN
SD
Minneapolis
WY
WI
L. Superior
MI
L. Michigan
L. Huron
L. Ontario
St. Lawrence R.
ME
VT
NH
Boston
MA
CT
RI
Milwaukee
Detroit
L. Erie
NY
New York
Cheyenne
IA
Chicago
Cleveland
PA
Philadelphia
NE
Des Moines
IN
OH
Baltimore
NJ
DE
MD
Lincoln
Missouri R.
Denver
CO
KS
Kansas City
MO
St. Louis
IL
Indianapolis
WV
Washington, D.C.
VA
Santa Fe
Ohio R.
Lexington
KY
NC
Charlotte
Nashville
TN
Memphis
OK
Oklahoma City
AR
Little Rock
SC
Charleston
NM
Mississippi R.
MS
AL
Atlanta
GA
Montgomery
TX
Dallas
Red R.
LA
Jacksonville
Houston
New Orleans
FL
Rio Grande
Gulf of Mexico
Lake Okeechobee
Miami

ATLANTIC OCEAN

40°N
30°N
80°W
90°W

N
W   E
S

○ National capital
● Other cities

0   200   400 Miles
0   200   400 Kilometers

Projection: Albers Equal Area

map zone

Geography Skills

Place The United States is made up of 50 states.

1. **Locate** What two countries border the United States?

2. **Contrast** How is Maryland's size and location different from California's size and location?

Geography The Grand Canyon in Arizona is one example of the many spectacular landscapes in the United States.

History The Statue of Liberty in New York Harbor symbolizes our freedom and our history as a democratic nation.

TEKS 3B, 4D, 6B, 6C, 21B, 21C, 22D

What You Will Learn...

Main Ideas

1. Major physical features of the United States include mountains, rivers, and plains.
2. The climate of the United States is wetter in the East and South and drier in the West.
3. The United States is rich in natural resources such as farmland, oil, forests, and minerals.

The Big Idea

The United States is a large country with diverse physical features, climates, and resources.

Key Terms and Places

Appalachian Mountains, *p. 142*
Great Lakes, *p. 143*
Mississippi River, *p. 143*
tributary, *p. 143*
Rocky Mountains, *p. 144*
continental divide, *p. 144*

TAKING NOTES

Use the graphic organizer online to take notes on the physical geography of the United States.

Physical Geography

If YOU lived there...

You live in St. Louis, Missouri, which is located on the Mississippi River. For the next few days, you will travel down the river on an old-fashioned steamboat. The Mississippi begins in Minnesota and flows south through 10 states in the heart of the United States. On your trip, you bring a video camera to film life along this great river.

What will you show in your video about the Mississippi?

BUILDING BACKGROUND The United States stretches from sea to sea across North America. To the north is Canada and to the south lies Mexico. Because it is so large, the United States has a great variety of landscapes and climates.

Physical Features

The United States is the third largest country in the world behind Russia and Canada. Our country is home to an incredible variety of physical features. All but two of the 50 states—Alaska and Hawaii—make up the main part of the country. Look at the physical map of the United States on the next page. It shows the main physical features of our country. Use the map as you read about America's physical geography in the East and South, the Interior Plains, and the West.

The East and South

If you were traveling across the United States, you might start on the country's eastern coast. This low area, which is flat and close to sea level, is called the Atlantic Coastal Plain. As you go west, the land gradually rises higher to a region called the Piedmont. The **Appalachian Mountains**, which are the main mountain range in the East, rise above the Piedmont. These mountains are very old. For many millions of years, rain, snow, and wind have

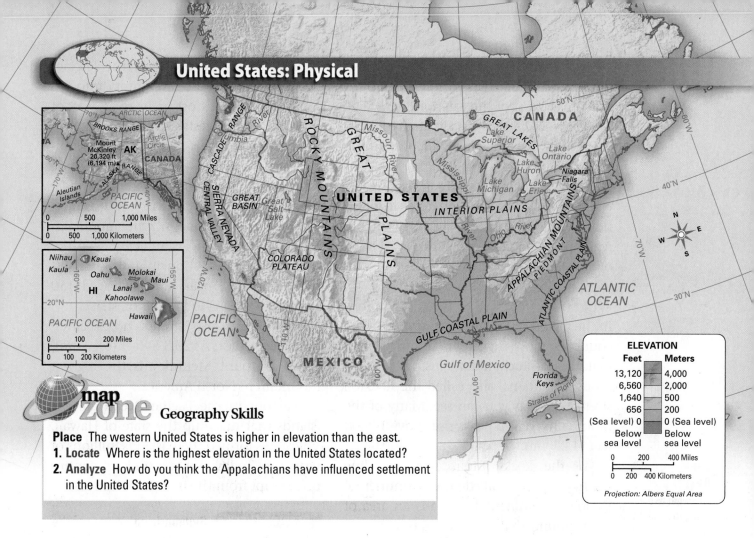

United States: Physical

ARCTIC OCEAN
BROOKS RANGE
Mount
McKinley
20,320 ft
(6,194 m) AK
Arctic
Circle
CANADA
Aleutian
Islands
PACIFIC
OCEAN

0   500   1,000 Miles
0   500   1,000 Kilometers

Niihau   Kauai
Kaula
Oahu   Molokai
HI   Lanai   Maui
Kahoolawe
PACIFIC OCEAN   Hawaii

0   100   200 Miles
0   100   200 Kilometers

PACIFIC
OCEAN

MEXICO

CASCADE RANGE
Columbia River
SIERRA NEVADA
CENTRAL VALLEY
GREAT
BASIN
Great
Salt
Lake
COLORADO
PLATEAU

ROCKY MOUNTAINS
GREAT PLAINS
UNITED STATES
Missouri River
Mississippi
INTERIOR PLAINS
Ohio River

GREAT LAKES
Lake
Superior
Lake
Michigan
Lake
Huron
Lake
Ontario
Lake
Erie
Niagara
Falls

CANADA

APPALACHIAN MOUNTAINS
PIEDMONT
ATLANTIC COASTAL PLAIN

GULF COASTAL PLAIN
Gulf of Mexico
Florida
Keys
Straits of Florida

ATLANTIC
OCEAN

50°N   60°N
40°N
70°W   30°N
60°W

map zone Geography Skills

Place The western United States is higher in elevation than the east.
1. **Locate** Where is the highest elevation in the United States located?
2. **Analyze** How do you think the Appalachians have influenced settlement in the United States?

ELEVATION

Feet		Meters
13,120		4,000
6,560		2,000
1,640		500
656		200
(Sea level) 0		0 (Sea level)
Below sea level		Below sea level

0   200   400 Miles
0   200   400 Kilometers

Projection: Albers Equal Area

eroded and smoothed their peaks. As a result, the highest mountain in the Appalachians is about 6,700 feet (2,040 m).

The Interior Plains

As you travel west from the Appalachians, you come across the vast Interior Plains that stretch to the Great Plains just east of the Rocky Mountains. The Interior Plains are filled with hills, lakes, and rivers. The first major water feature that you see here is called the **Great Lakes**. These lakes make up the largest group of freshwater lakes in the world. The Great Lakes are also an important waterway for trade between the United States and Canada.

West of the Great Lakes lies North America's largest and most important river, the **Mississippi River**. Tributaries in the interior plains flow to the Mississippi. A **tributary** is a smaller stream or river that flows into a larger stream or river.

Appalachians The smooth peaks of the Appalachian Mountains dominate the landscape of western North Carolina.

Along the way, these rivers deposit rich silt. The silt creates fertile farmlands that cover most of the Interior Plains. The Missouri and Ohio rivers are huge tributaries of the Mississippi. They help drain the entire Interior Plains.

Look at the map on the previous page. Notice the land begins to increase in elevation west of the Interior Plains. This higher region is called the Great Plains. Vast areas of grasslands cover these plains.

The West

In the region called the West, several of the country's most rugged mountain ranges make up the **Rocky Mountains**. These enormous mountains, also called the Rockies, stretch as far as you can see. Many of the mountains' jagged peaks rise above 14,000 feet (4,270 m).

FOCUS ON READING
Into what two categories might you group the details on rivers?

In the Rocky Mountains is a line of high peaks called the Continental Divide. A **continental divide** is an area of high ground that divides the flow of rivers towards opposite ends of a continent.

Rivers east of the divide in the Rockies mostly flow eastward and empty into the Mississippi River. Most of the rivers west of the divide flow westward and empty into the Pacific Ocean.

Farther west, mountain ranges include the Cascade Range and the Sierra Nevada. Most of the mountains in the Cascades are dormant volcanoes. One mountain, Mount Saint Helens, is an active volcano. A tremendous eruption in 1980 blew off the mountain's peak and destroyed 150 square miles (390 sq km) of forest.

Mountains also stretch north along the Pacific coast. At 20,320 feet (6,194 m), Alaska's Mount McKinley is the highest mountain in North America.

Far out in the Pacific Ocean are the islands that make up the state of Hawaii. Volcanoes formed these islands millions of years ago. Today, hot lava and ash continue to erupt from the islands' volcanoes.

READING CHECK **Summarizing** What are the major physical features of the United States?

Satellite View

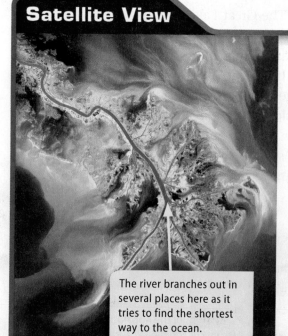

The river branches out in several places here as it tries to find the shortest way to the ocean.

The Mississippi River Delta

From its source in Minnesota, the Mississippi River flows south across the central United States. It ends at the tip of Louisiana, which is shown here. This satellite image shows the area where the Mississippi River meets the Gulf of Mexico. This area is called a delta. A river's delta is formed from sediment that a river carries downstream to the ocean. Sediment is usually made up of rocks, soil, sand, and dead plants. Each year, the Mississippi dumps more than 400 million tons of sediment into the Gulf of Mexico.

The light blue and green areas in this image are shallow areas of sediment. The deeper water of the Gulf of Mexico is dark blue. Also, notice that much of the delta land looks fragile. This is new land that the river has built up by depositing sediment.

Making Inferences What natural hazards might people living in the Mississippi Delta experience?

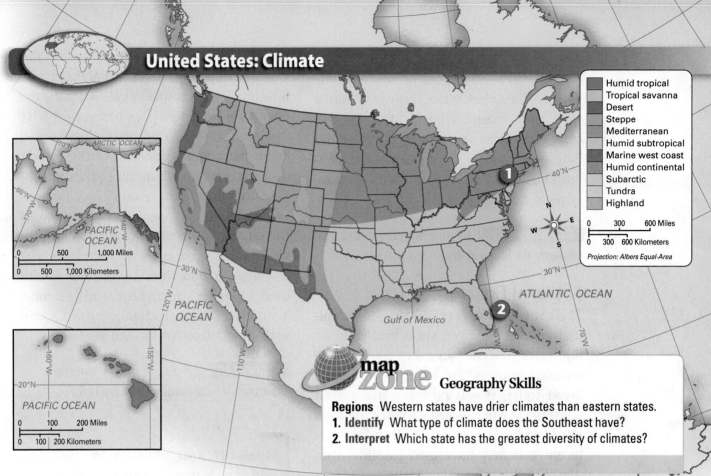

Humid tropical
Tropical savanna
Desert
Steppe
Mediterranean
Humid subtropical
Marine west coast
Humid continental
Subarctic
Tundra
Highland

0   300   600 Miles
0   300   600 Kilometers
Projection: Albers Equal-Area

ARCTIC OCEAN

PACIFIC OCEAN

0   500   1,000 Miles
0   500   1,000 Kilometers

PACIFIC OCEAN

0   100   200 Miles
0   100   200 Kilometers

PACIFIC OCEAN

ATLANTIC OCEAN

Gulf of Mexico

map zone Geography Skills

Regions Western states have drier climates than eastern states.
1. **Identify** What type of climate does the Southeast have?
2. **Interpret** Which state has the greatest diversity of climates?

Climate

Did you know that the United States has a greater variety of climates than any other country? Look at the map above to see the different climates of the United States.

The East and South

The eastern United States has three climate regions. In the Northeast, people live in a humid continental climate with snowy winters and warm, humid summers. Southerners, on the other hand, experience milder winters and the warm, humid summers of a humid subtropical climate. Most of Florida is warm all year.

The Interior Plains

Temperatures throughout the year can vary greatly in the Interior Plains. Summers are hot and dry in the Great Plains. However, most of the region has a humid continental climate with long, cold winters.

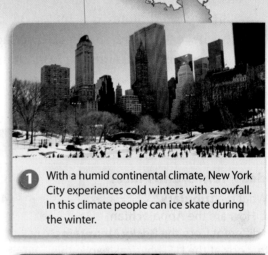

1 With a humid continental climate, New York City experiences cold winters with snowfall. In this climate people can ice skate during the winter.

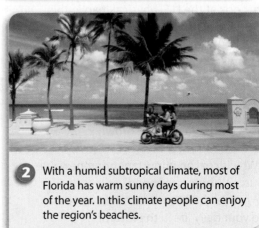

2 With a humid subtropical climate, most of Florida has warm sunny days during most of the year. In this climate people can enjoy the region's beaches.

The West

Climates in the West are mostly dry. The Pacific Northwest coast, however, has a wet, mild coastal climate. The region's coldest climates are in Alaska, which has both subarctic and tundra climates. In contrast, Hawaii is the only state with a warm, tropical climate.

READING CHECK **Identifying** What types of climates are found in the United States?

Natural Resources

The United States is extremely rich in natural resources. Do you know that your life is affected in some way every day by these natural resources? For example, if you ate bread today, it was probably made with wheat grown in the fertile soils of the Interior Plains. If you rode in a car or on a bus recently, it may have used gasoline from Alaska, California, or Louisiana.

The United States is a major oil producer but uses more oil than it produces. In fact, we import more than one half of the oil we need.

Valuable nonrenewable natural resources are mined in the Appalachians and Rockies. One resource, coal, supplies the energy for more than half of the electricity produced in the United States. The United States has about 25 percent of the world's coal reserves and is a major coal exporter.

Other important resources include forests and farmland, which cover much of the country. The trees in our forests provide timber that is used in constructing buildings. Wood from these trees is also used to make paper. Farmland produces a variety of crops including wheat, corn, soybeans, cotton, fruits, and vegetables.

READING CHECK **Summarizing** What are important natural resources in the U.S.?

SUMMARY AND PREVIEW In this section you learned about the geography, climates, and natural resources of the United States. In the next section, you will learn about the history and culture of the United States.

Section 1 Assessment

hmhsocialstudies.com
ONLINE QUIZ

Reviewing Ideas, Terms, and Places

1. a. **Define** What is a **tributary**?
   b. **Contrast** How are the **Appalachian Mountains** different from the **Rocky Mountains**?
   c. **Elaborate** Look at the U.S. physical map in this section to locate the **Great Lakes**. Why are the Great Lakes an important waterway?

2. a. **Describe** Look at the U.S. climate map in this section. What is the climate like in the Northeast?
   b. **Draw Conclusions** What would winter be like in Alaska?

3. a. **Recall** What kinds of crops are grown in the United States?
   b. **Explain** Why is coal an important nonrenewable natural resource? Where is it mined?
   c. **Predict** What natural resources might not be as important to your daily life in the future?

Critical Thinking

4. **Categorizing** Copy the graphic organizer below. Use it to organize your notes on physical features, climate, and resources by region of the country.

| East and South | Interior Plains | West |

FOCUS ON VIEWING

*my*WriteSmart

5. **Thinking about Physical Geography** Jot down key words that describe the physical features and climate of the United States. Think of at least three objects or images you might use to illustrate physical features and climate.

Using a Political Map

Learn

Many types of maps are useful in studying geography. Political maps are one of the most frequently used types of maps. These maps show human cultural features such as cities, states, and countries. Look at the map's legend to figure out how these features are represented on the map.

Most political maps show national boundaries and state boundaries. The countries on political maps are sometimes shaded different colors to help you tell where the borders of each country are located.

Practice

Use the political map here to answer the following questions.

- What countries does this map show?
- How does the map show the difference between state boundaries and national boundaries?
- What is the capital of Canada?

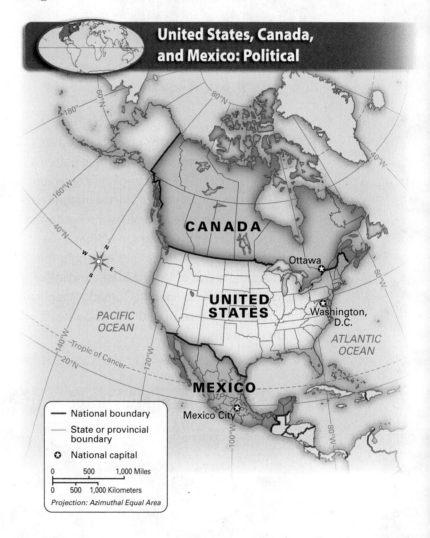

United States, Canada, and Mexico: Political

CANADA

Ottawa

UNITED STATES

Washington, D.C.

PACIFIC OCEAN

ATLANTIC OCEAN

MEXICO

Mexico City

— National boundary
— State or provincial boundary
✪ National capital

0   500   1,000 Miles
0   500   1,000 Kilometers
Projection: Azimuthal Equal Area

Apply

Using an atlas or the Internet, find a political map of your state. Use that map to answer the following questions.

1. What is the state capital and where is it located?

2. What other states or countries border your state?

3. What are two other cities in your state besides the capital and the city you live in?

Natural Hazards
in the United States

Essential Elements

The World in Spatial Terms
Places and Regions
Physical Systems
Human Systems
Environment and Society
The Uses of Geography

Background Earth's physical systems create patterns around us, and these patterns influence our lives. For example, every region of the United States has distinctive natural hazards. Volcanoes threaten the Pacific Northwest. Earthquakes rattle California. Wildfires strike forests in the West. Hurricanes endanger the Atlantic and Gulf of Mexico coasts, and major rivers are prone to flooding. Tornadoes regularly rip across flat areas of central and southeast United States.

In fact, the United States lies in danger of getting hit by an average of six hurricanes a year. Formed by the warm waters of the Atlantic Ocean and Caribbean Sea and the collision of strong winds, hurricanes are the most powerful storms on Earth. Most hurricanes look like large doughnuts with a hole, or eye, in the middle of the storm. Around the eye, high winds and rain bands rotate counterclockwise. Once the hurricane moves over land or cold water it weakens.

Natural Hazards in the United States

Tornado Alley

Earthquakes   Volcanoes
Wildfires   Tornadoes
Hurricanes   Tornado Risk
Flood areas   Moderate   High

map zone

After Hurricane Katrina hit New Orleans, people escaped the floodwaters by fleeing to rooftops and high-rise apartment buildings like this one.

Using satellite images like this one of Hurricane Katrina, scientists saw how large the storm was and warned people along the Gulf coast to evacuate.

Hurricane Katrina On August 29, 2005, one of the most destructive hurricanes ever hit the United States. Hurricane Katrina devastated coastal regions of Louisiana, the city of New Orleans, and the entire coast of Mississippi.

With winds as high as 145 mph (235 km), Katrina destroyed hundreds of thousands of homes and businesses. In addition, the force of Katrina's storm surge pushed water from the Gulf of Mexico onto land to a height of about two stories tall. As a result, low-lying areas along the Gulf coast experienced massive flooding.

The storm surge also caused several levees that protected New Orleans from the waters of Lake Pontchartrain to break. The loss of these levees caused the lake's waters to flood most of the city. About 150,000 people who did not evacuate before the storm were left stranded in shelters, high-rise buildings, and on rooftops. Using boats and helicopters, emergency workers rescued thousands of the city's people. Total damages from the storm along the Gulf coast was estimated to be nearly $130 billion. More than 1,300 people died and over a million were displaced.

What It Means Natural hazards can influence where we live, how we build our homes, and how we prepare for storms. In addition to hurricanes, other hazards affect the United States. For example, Tornado Alley is a region of the Great Plains that experiences a high number of tornadoes, or "twisters"—rapidly spinning columns of air that stay in contact with the ground. In Tornado Alley, special warning sirens go off when storms develop that might form a dangerous tornado.

Geography for Life Activity

1. How are hurricanes formed?

2. Many people train and volunteer as storm chasers. They may follow storms for hundreds of miles to gather scientific data, take photographs, or file news reports. What might be the risks and rewards of such activity? Would it interest you?

3. **Comparing Windstorms** Do some research to find out how tornadoes and hurricanes differ. Summarize the differences in a chart that includes information about how these storms start, where and when they tend to occur in the United States, and their wind strength.

History and Culture

 TEKS 1A, 2B, 4C, 15D, 18D, 19B, 21A, 21C

What You Will Learn...

Main Ideas

1. The United States is the world's first modern democracy.
2. The people and culture of the United States are very diverse.

The Big Idea

Democratic ideas and immigration have shaped the history and culture of the United States.

Key Terms and Places

colony, p. 150
Boston, p. 150
New York, p. 150
plantation, p. 151
pioneers, p. 152
bilingual, p. 155

hmhsocialstudies.com
TAKING NOTES

Use the graphic organizer online to take notes on the history and culture of the United States.

If YOU lived there...

It is 1803, and President Jefferson just arranged the purchase of a huge area of land west of the Mississippi River. It almost doubles the size of the United States. Living on the frontier in Ohio, you are a skillful hunter and trapper. One day, you see a poster calling for volunteers to explore the new Louisiana Territory. An expedition is heading west soon. You think it would be exciting but dangerous.

Will you join the expedition to the West? Why or why not?

BUILDING BACKGROUND From 13 colonies on the Atlantic coast, the territory of the United States expanded all the way to the Pacific Ocean in about 75 years. Since then, America's democracy has attracted immigrants from almost every country in the world. Looking for new opportunities, these immigrants have made the country very diverse.

First Modern Democracy

Long before Italian explorer Christopher Columbus sailed to the Americas in 1492, native people lived on the land that is now the United States. These Native Americans developed many distinct cultures. Soon after Columbus and his crew explored the Americas, other Europeans began to set up colonies there.

The American Colonies

Europeans began settling in North America and setting up colonies in the 1500s. A **colony** is a territory inhabited and controlled by people from a foreign land. By the mid-1700s the British Empire included more than a dozen colonies along the Atlantic coast. New cities in the colonies such as **Boston** and **New York** became major seaports.

Some people living in the British colonies lived on plantations. A **plantation** is a large farm that grows mainly one crop. Many of the colonial plantations produced tobacco, rice, or cotton. About 453,000 enslaved Africans were brought to the colonies and forced to work on plantations.

By the 1770s many colonists in America were unhappy with British rule. They wanted independence from Britain. In July 1776, the colonial representatives adopted the Declaration of Independence. The document stated that "all men are created equal" and have the right to "life, liberty, and the pursuit of happiness." Although not everyone in the colonies was considered equal, the Declaration was a great step toward equality and justice.

To win their independence, the American colonists fought the British in the Revolutionary War. First, colonists from Massachusetts fought in the early battles of the war in and around Boston. As the war spread west and south, soldiers from all the American colonies joined the fight against Britain.

In 1781 the American forces under General George Washington defeated the British army at the Battle of Yorktown in Virginia. With this defeat, Britain recognized the independence of the United States. As a consequence, Britain granted all its land east of the Mississippi River to the new nation.

Expansion and Industrial Growth

After independence, the United States gradually expanded west. Despite the challenges of crossing swift-moving rivers and traveling across rugged terrain and huge mountains, people moved west for land and plentiful resources.

BIOGRAPHY

George Washington
(1732–1799)

As the first president of the United States, George Washington is known as the Father of His Country. Washington was admired for his heroism and leadership as the commanding general during the Revolutionary War. Delegates to the Constitutional Convention chose him to preside over their meetings. Washington was then elected president in 1789 and served two terms.

Drawing Inferences Why do you think Washington was elected president?

Fight for Independence

This painting shows General George Washington leading American troops across the Delaware River to attack British forces.

These first settlers that traveled west were called **pioneers**. Many followed the 2,000-mile Oregon Trail west from Missouri to the Oregon Territory. Groups of families traveled together in wagons pulled by oxen or mules. The trip was harsh. Food, supplies, and water were scarce.

While many pioneers headed west seeking land, others went in search of gold. The discovery of gold in California in 1848 had a major impact on the country. The lure of gold brought hundreds of thousands of people to California.

By 1850 the population of the United States exceeded 23 million and the country stretched all the way to the Pacific Ocean. As the United States expanded, the nation's economy also grew. By the late 1800s, the country was a major producer of goods like steel, oil, and textiles, or cloth products. The steel industry grew around cities that were located near coal and iron ore deposits. Most of those new industrial cities were in the Northeast and Midwest. The country's economy also benefited from the **development** of waterways and railroads. This development helped industry and people move farther into the interior.

Attracted by a strong economy, millions of people immigrated, or came to, the United States for better jobs and land. Immigration from European countries was especially heavy in the late 1800s and early 1900s. As a result of this historical pattern of immigration, the United States is a culturally diverse nation today.

Western Expansion of the United States

map zone Geography Skills

Movement The United States expanded in about 100 years as the government gained territory and people moved west.
1. **Identify** What territory did the United States acquire in 1846?
2. **Analyzing** How were Louisiana and Alaska acquired?

Wars and Peace

The United States fought in several wars during the 1900s. Many Americans died in two major wars, World Wars I and II. After World War II, the United States and the Soviet Union became rivals in what was known as the Cold War. The Cold War lasted until the early 1990s, when the Soviet Union collapsed. U.S. troops also served in long wars in Korea in the 1950s and in Vietnam in the 1960s and 1970s. In 1991, the U.S. fought Iraq in the Persian Gulf War. In the early 2000s, the United States military fought long wars in Iraq and Afghanistan.

Today the United States is a member of many international organizations. The headquarters of one such organization, the United Nations (UN), is located in New York City. About 190 countries are UN members. The United States is one of the most powerful members.

Government and Citizenship

The United States is a representative democracy, whose limited government is based on the U.S. Constitution. This document spells out the powers and functions of the branches of the federal government. The federal government includes an elected president and Congress. In general, the federal government handles issues affecting the whole country, but many powers are left to the 50 state governments. Counties and cities also have their own local governments. Many local governments provide services to the community such as trash collection, road building, electricity, and public transportation.

Rights and Responsibilities

American citizens have many rights and responsibilities, including the right to vote. Starting at age 18, U.S. citizens are allowed to vote. They are also encouraged

Primary Source

HISTORIC DOCUMENT
The Constitution

On September 17, 1787, state delegates gathered in Philadelphia to create a constitution, a written statement of the powers and functions of the new government of the United States. The Preamble, or introduction, to the U.S. Constitution is shown below. It states the document's general purpose.

"*We the People* of the United States, in order to form a more perfect Union, establish justice, insure domestic tranquillity, provide for the common defense, promote the general welfare, and secure the blessings of liberty to ourselves and our posterity, do ordain and establish this Constitution for the United States of America."

Americans wanted peace within the United States and a national military force.

They wanted to ensure freedoms for themselves and for future generations.

ANALYSIS SKILL | **ANALYZING PRIMARY SOURCES**

How do you think the ideas that appear in the Preamble affect your daily life?

to play an active role in government. For example, Americans can call or write their public officials to ask them to help solve problems in their communities. Without people participating in their government, the democratic process suffers.

READING CHECK **Sequencing** What were some major events in the history of the United States?

People and Culture

About 7 out of 10 Americans are descended from European immigrants. However, the United States is also home to people of many other cultures and ethnic groups. As a result, the United States is a diverse nation where many languages are spoken and different religions and customs are practiced. The blending of these different cultures has helped produce a unique American culture.

Ethnic Groups in the United States

FOCUS ON READING
What details would be included under a category called *ethnic groups*?

Some ethnic groups in the United States include Native Americans, African Americans, Hispanic Americans, and Asian Americans. As you can see on the maps on the next page, higher percentages of these ethnic groups are concentrated in different areas of the United States.

For thousands of years, Native Americans were the only people living in the Americas. Today, most Native Americans live in the western United States. Many Native Americans are concentrated in Arizona and New Mexico.

Even though African Americans live in every region of the country, some areas of the United States have a higher percentage of African Americans. For example, a higher percentage of African Americans live in southern states. Many large cities also have a high percentage of African Americans. On the other hand, descendants of people who came from Asian countries, or Asian Americans, are mostly concentrated in California.

Many Hispanic Americans originally migrated to the United States from Mexico, Cuba, and other Latin American countries. As you can see on the map of Hispanic Americans, a higher percentage of Hispanic Americans live in the southwestern states. These states border Mexico.

Language

What language or languages do you hear as you walk through the hall of your school? Since most people in the United States speak English, you probably hear English spoken every day. However, in many parts of the country, English is just one of many languages you might hear. Are you or is someone you know bilingual? People who speak two languages are **bilingual**.

Today more than 57 million U.S. residents speak a language in addition to English. These languages include Spanish, French, Chinese, Vietnamese, Arabic, Tagalog, and many others.

After English, Spanish is the most widely spoken language in the United States. About 36 million Americans speak Spanish at home. Many of these people live near the border between the United States and Mexico and in Florida.

Religion

Americans also practice many religious faiths. The majority are Christians. However, some are Jewish or Muslim, and a smaller percentage are Hindu, Buddhist, or Sikh. Your community might have Christian churches, Jewish synagogues, Islamic mosques, Hindu temples, or Sikh gurdwaras, as well as other places of worship.

Many religious holidays are celebrated in the United States. Christians celebrate Jesus's birth on Christmas, and Jesus's resurrection at Easter. Jews observe Yom Kippur—also known as Day of Atonement—and Rosh Hashanah, the Jewish New Year. Muslims fast during the month of Ramadan, a time when they believe the Koran, their holy scripture, was revealed to Mohammed. Hindus celebrate Diwali, a festival of lights which symbolizes the victory of good over evil. Sikhs commemorate the establishment of a formalized Sikh community called the Khalsa in the 1690s with a festival called Vaisakhi.

Distribution of Selected Ethnic Groups, 2010

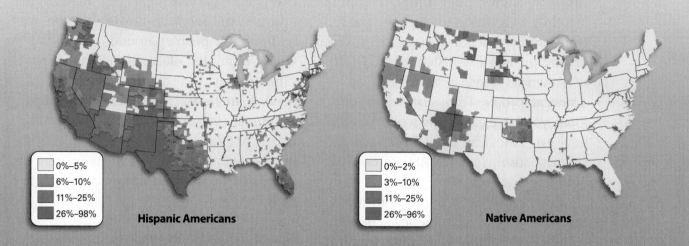

Hispanic Americans

- 0%–5%
- 6%–10%
- 11%–25%
- 26%–98%

Native Americans

- 0%–2%
- 3%–10%
- 11%–25%
- 26%–96%

Diverse America

People of different ethnic groups enjoy a parade in Washington, D.C. Like most large American cities, Washington has a very diverse population. About 50 percent of Washington's population is African American. Hispanic Americans make up about 10 percent of the city's population, and Asian Americans make up about four percent.

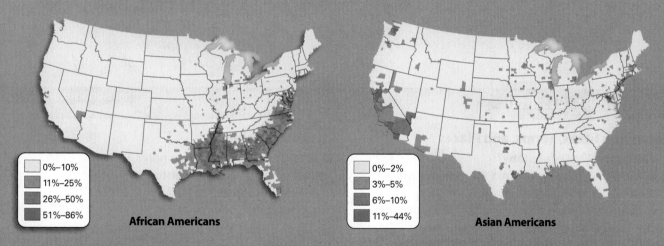

African Americans

- 0%–10%
- 11%–25%
- 26%–50%
- 51%–86%

Asian Americans

- 0%–2%
- 3%–5%
- 6%–10%
- 11%–44%

Source: U.S. Census Bureau, 2010

map zone
Geography Skills

Regions These maps show population information from the U.S. Census. Every 10 years, Americans answer census questions about their race or ethnic group.

1. **Locate** In what region of the United States does the highest percentage of African Americans live?
2. **Analyze** Why do you think many Hispanic Americans live in the southwestern United States?

Foods and Music

Diversity shows itself through cultural practices. In addition to language and religion, cultural practices include the food we eat and the music we listen to.

America's food is as diverse as the American people. Think about some of the foods you have eaten this week. You may have eaten Mexican tacos, Italian pasta, or Japanese sushi. These dishes are now part of the American diet.

Different types of music from around the world have also influenced American culture. For example, salsa music from Latin America is popular in the United States today. Many American musicians now combine elements of salsa into their pop songs. However, music that originated in the United States is also popular in other countries. American musical styles include blues, jazz, rock, and hip hop.

American Popular Culture

As the most powerful country in the world, the United States has tremendous influence around the world. American popular culture, such as movies, television programs, and sports, is popular elsewhere. For example, the *Star Wars* movies are seen by millions of people around the world. Other examples of American culture in other places include the popularity of baseball in Japan, Starbucks coffee shops in almost every major city in the world, and an MTV channel available throughout Asia. As you can see, Americans influence the rest of the world in many ways through their culture.

READING CHECK **Generalizing** How has cultural diversity enriched life in the United States?

SUMMARY AND PREVIEW The history of the United States has helped shape the democratic nation it is today. Drawn to the United States because of its democracy, immigrants from around the world have shaped American culture. In the next section, you will learn about the different regions of the United States and the issues the country is facing today.

Section 2 Assessment

hmhsocialstudies.com
ONLINE QUIZ

Reviewing Ideas, Terms, and Places

1. **a. Define** What is a **colony**?
   b. Make Inferences Why did the pioneers move west?
   c. Elaborate What is an example of the rights and responsibilities that American citizens have?
2. **a. Recall** What language other than English is widely spoken in the United States?
   b. Summarize What are some religious holidays celebrated in the United States?
   c. Predict How do you think American culture will be different in the future, and what contributions of diverse groups do you think will bring about the changes?

Critical Thinking

3. **Summarizing** Using your notes, write one descriptive sentence about the history, government, people, and culture of the United States.

People — History
Government — Culture

FOCUS ON VIEWING *my* WriteSmart

4. **Thinking about History and Culture** How would you describe the history and culture of the United States? Identify two images for your collage.

from
The Latehomecomer

memoir by Kao Kalia Yang

A Hmong American girl in traditional dress celebrates her culture at a festival in Minnesota.

About the Reading *In* The Latehomecomer: A Hmong Family Memoir, *an autobiographical novel, Kao Kalia Yang writes about her own immigrant experience as a Hmong American. In the novel, Yang's family immigrated to the United States by escaping persecution in Laos and fleeing to a refugee camp in Thailand. In the excerpt below, Yang reflects on her family's struggle to become accepted as Americans.*

AS YOU READ Notice how the author and her family feel about becoming American citizens.

A bill was being considered that would allow veterans of the Vietnam War, Hmong with documents, to apply for citizenship, and take the examination in Hmong. ❶ There was crazy studying everywhere. Aunt and Uncle Chue hovered over the pages that he read with his French accent as she tried to make out the letters of the alphabet one at a time, through her thick reading glasses. ❷

My own mother and father questioned themselves out loud, "What if we try to become Americans and fail?"

On the phone, Grandma said, "Lasting change cannot be forced, only inspired." For the Hmong, inspiration came in those that were born in this country, the ready-made Americans in our arms, the little faces of boys and girls who spoke Hmong with American stiffness.

We could not remain just Hmong any longer. For our children, we could not fail. We had to try, no matter what. Even if it meant moving. Thousands of Hmong families moved from the farming lands of California to the job possibilities in Minnesota companies and factories…A new chapter of our lives unfolded as we strived to become Americans.

GUIDED READING

❶ The Hmong are an ethnic group that live mostly in China, Laos, Thailand, and Vietnam.

❷ Before 1949 Laos was a territory of France. Today French is still spoken in the Laotian government and taught in schools as a second language.

Connecting Literature to Geography

1. **Describing** What details in the selection show us that the Hmong immigrants wanted to become American citizens? Which details describe the motivation behind their desire to become Americans?

2. **Drawing Inferences** Why do you think Yang's parents had doubts about being accepted as Americans? What was her grandmother's attitude about being American?

On September 17, Constitution Day, Americans celebrate the signing of the United States Constitution in 1787. In Texas, social studies classrooms also observe Celebrate Freedom Week. This important celebration focuses on the meaning and significance of the two foundational documents in United States history—the Declaration of Independence and the U.S. Constitution.

The Declaration of Independence

One of the most eloquent and influential documents ever written, the Declaration of Independence gave the reasons the American colonies were willing to fight for independence. Thomas Jefferson, the main author of the document, began by explaining the purpose of government. Part of this first section, known as the Preamble, must be recited by Texas students during Celebrate Freedom Week. It is perhaps the most famous statement from the document:

> *We hold these Truths to be self-evident, that all Men are created equal, that they are endowed by their Creator with certain unalienable Rights, that among these are Life, Liberty, and the Pursuit of Happiness. That to secure these Rights, Governments are instituted among Men, deriving their just Powers from the Consent of the Governed.*

—Declaration of Independence

IN CONGRESS, JULY 4, 1776.

The unanimous Declaration of the thirteen united States of America.

These powerful words established the idea that governments exist to serve their citizens, and that people have basic natural rights that government cannot take away. Throughout our history, these words have inspired Americans to fight for and expand the definitions of freedom, equality, and basic rights. For example, women's rights advocates echoed the language of the Declaration of Independence in 1848 when they demanded the right to vote by declaring that "all men and women are created equal." Abolitionists and civil rights leaders also looked to the Declaration of Independence in their struggles to end slavery and ensure that African Americans were guaranteed equal rights. Even beyond America, the Declaration of Independence has inspired independence and pro-democracy movements around the world. It continues to inspire us today.

Independence Day

Each 4th of July, Americans celebrate the adoption of the Declaration of Independence with parades, fireworks, picnics, fairs, and ceremonies honoring our freedoms and government.

KEY FACTS

DECLARATION OF INDEPENDENCE

Date
- Adopted July 4, 1776 by the Continental Congress

Key Author
- Thomas Jefferson

Intent
- To announce formally that the 13 American colonies considered themselves independent states no longer part of the British Empire
- To explain and justify the reasons for independence

Meaning and Importance
- Established in writing the principle that all people have certain fundamental rights that no government can take away
- Explained that the purpose of government is to serve citizens
- Influenced the U.S. Constitution and Bill of Rights
- Has inspired people throughout history in the struggle for equality, justice, and basic human rights

The U.S. Constitution

Building on the Declaration of Independence, the U.S. Constitution established the system of government that is still in effect today. Another truly ground-breaking document, the Constitution established the rule of law and made clear that no one, including the highest government official, is above it. The document's opening words, the Preamble, elegantly state its purpose:

> **We the People of the United States, in Order to form a more perfect Union, establish Justice, insure domestic Tranquility, provide for the common defense, promote the general Welfare, and secure the Blessings of Liberty to ourselves and our Posterity, do ordain and establish this Constitution for the United States of America.**
>
> **—United States Constitution**

The three opening words, *We the People*, which were written so much larger than the others, announced dramatically that in the United States the people are the source of all government power and authority.

To protect people's rights and to balance power, the Constitution set up a system that divides power among federal and state governments. Federal power is supreme, and certain powers are shared or reserved for the states. A system of checks and balances further divides power among three equal branches of government—legislative, executive, and judicial.

The Constitution also includes a process by which it can be amended, or changed. It is sometimes referred to as "a living document" for this reason; it can be added to and improved by the people to reflect changes in society. Since it was adopted in 1787, the Constitution has been amended 27 times. These amendments have abolished slavery, guaranteed women and minorities the right to vote and to receive equal treatment under the law, changed voting and election procedures, and made other improvements to our government.

One of the most important parts of the Constitution is the Bill of Rights—the first 10 amendments. The Bill of Rights helps protect the rights described in the Declaration of Independence. For example, the Bill of Rights protects such basic rights as freedom of speech, press, and religion as well as due process rights such as the right to a fair trial. The Bill of Rights was an important early addition to the Constitution because it stated in writing some of the specific individual rights and protections guaranteed for all Americans.

KEY FACTS

THE CONSTITUTION

Date
- Adopted September 17, 1787 by the Constitutional Convention

Key Author
- James Madison

Intent
- To establish a new national government of the United States
- To replace the Articles of Confederation
- To safeguard the freedoms of all Americans, present and future

Meaning and Importance
- Established the supreme law of the land for the United States that is still in effect today
- Identifies the people as the ultimate source of government power
- Sets up a system of power sharing among the federal and state government
- Divides power into three equal branches of government
- Includes an amendment process
- Includes the Bill of Rights and other amendments that have protected and expanded individual rights and freedoms

BILL OF RIGHTS

1st Amendment	Protects freedom of religion, speech, press, assembly, petition
2nd Amendment	Protects the right to keep and bear arms
3rd Amendment	Provides restrictions on quartering soldiers in citizens' homes
4th Amendment	Bans unreasonable searches or seizures
5th Amendment	Protects citizens against self-incrimination and being tried twice for the same crime; prohibits government from depriving citizens of life, liberty, or property without due process of law
6th Amendment	Protects citizens' right to a swift and fair trial
7th Amendment	Guarantees right to trial by jury
8th Amendment	Protects citizens against cruel and unusual punishment
9th Amendment	States that citizens have rights beyond those specifically written in the Constitution
10th Amendment	States that powers not given to the government are reserved to the states, or to the people

Research Activity

As part of Celebrate Freedom Week, conduct research on the two most influential documents in U.S. history. First, read the Declaration of Independence and explore how it influenced subsequent American history and has inspired people for generations. In your own words, explain how the Declaration of Independence is still relevant in our lives today. Then, review a copy of the U.S. Constitution to explore how it has been amended throughout our nation's history. Give an example of how the Constitution or Bill of Rights protects your rights, and the rights of others.

TEKS 4B, 5A, 6B, 7B, 21C

What You Will Learn...

Main Ideas

1. The United States has four regions—the Northeast, South, Midwest, and West.
2. The United States has a strong economy and a powerful military but is facing the challenge of world terrorism.

The Big Idea

The United States has four main regions and faces opportunities and challenges.

Key Terms and Places

megalopolis, *p. 159*
Washington, D.C., *p. 159*
Detroit, *p. 161*
Chicago, *p. 161*
Seattle, *p. 162*
terrorism, *p. 162*

hmhsocialstudies.com

TAKING NOTES

Use the graphic organizer online to take notes on the United States today.

The United States Today

If YOU lived there...

You and your family run a small resort hotel in Fort Lauderdale, on the east coast of Florida. You love the sunny weather and the beaches there. Now your family is thinking about moving the business to another region where the tourist industry is important. They have looked at ski lodges in Colorado, lake cottages in Michigan, and hotels on the coast of Maine.

How will you decide among these different regions?

BUILDING BACKGROUND Geography, history, climate, and population give each region of the United States its own style. Some differences between the regions are more visible than others. For example, people in each region speak with different accents and have their favorite foods. Even with some differences, however, Americans are linked by a sense of unity in confronting important issues.

Regions of the United States

Because the United States is such a large country, geographers often divide it into four main regions. These are the Northeast, South, Midwest, and the West. You can see the four regions on the map on the next page. Find the region where you live. You probably know more about your own region than you do the three others. The population, resources, and economies of the four regions are similar in some ways and unique in others.

The Northeast

The Northeast shares a border with Canada. The economy in this region is heavily dependent on banks, investment firms, and insurance companies. Education also contributes to the economy. The area's respected universities include Harvard and Yale.

map zone

Geography Skills

Regions The United States has four geographic and economic regions.
1. **Locate** What region is located on the Pacific Ocean?
2. **Analyze** What region does not border Canada?

Some natural resources of the Northeast states include rich farmland and huge pockets of coal. Used in the steelmaking process, coal remains very important to the region's economy. The steel industry helped make Pittsburgh, in western Pennsylvania, the largest industrial city in the Appalachians.

Today fishing remains an important industry in the Northeast. Major seaports allow companies to ship their products to markets around the world. Cool, shallow waters off the Atlantic coast are good fishing areas. Cod and shellfish such as lobster are the most valuable seafood.

The Northeast is the most densely populated region of the United States. Much of the Northeast is a **megalopolis**, a string of large cities that have grown together. This area stretches along the Atlantic coast from Boston to **Washington, D.C.** The three other major cities in the megalopolis are New York, Philadelphia, and Baltimore.

Population of Major U.S. Cities

	City	Population
1	New York	8,336,697
2	Los Angeles	3,857,799
3	Chicago	2,714,856
4	Houston	2,160,821
5	Philadelphia	1,547,607

New York, New York

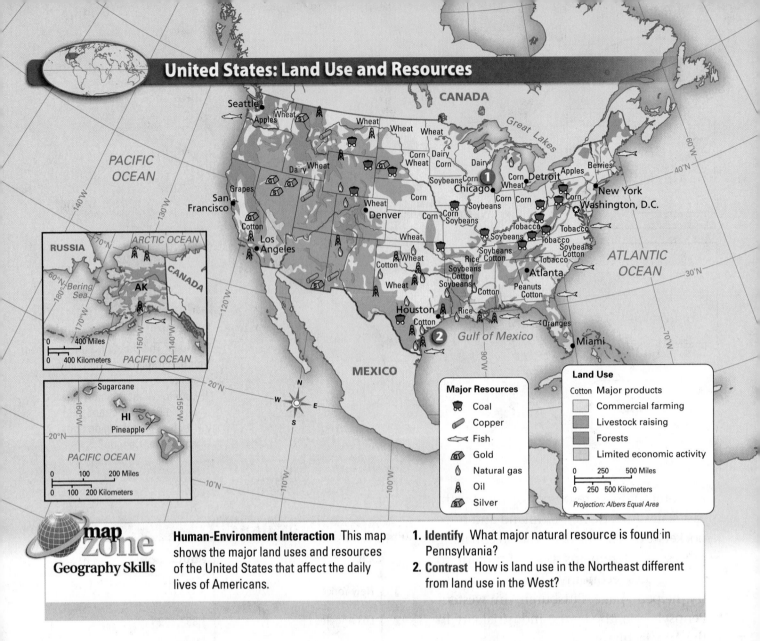

Human-Environment Interaction This map shows the major land uses and resources of the United States that affect the daily lives of Americans.

map zone
Geography Skills

1. **Identify** What major natural resource is found in Pennsylvania?
2. **Contrast** How is land use in the Northeast different from land use in the West?

At least 40 million people live in this urban area. All of these cities were founded during the colonial era. They grew because they were important seaports. Today these cities are industrial and financial centers.

The South

The South is a region that includes long coastlines along the Atlantic Ocean and the Gulf of Mexico. Along the coastal plains rich soils provide farmers with abundant crops of cotton, tobacco, and citrus fruit.

In recent years, the South has become more urban and industrial and is one of the country's fastest-growing regions. The South's cities, such as Atlanta, have grown along with the economy. The Atlanta metropolitan area has grown from a population of only about 1 million in 1960 to more than 5 million today.

Other places in the South have also experienced growth in population and industry. The Research Triangle in North Carolina is an area of high-tech companies and several large universities. The Texas Gulf Coast and the lower Mississippi River area have huge oil refineries and petrochemical plants. Their products, which include gasoline, are mostly shipped from the ports of Houston and New Orleans.

1 Farms with fertile soils like this one in Wisconsin cover much of the rural Midwest.

2 Large white containers, shown here at the Port of Houston, store oil from the Gulf Coast.

Millions of Americans vacation in the South, which makes the travel industry profitable in the region. Warm weather and beautiful beaches draw many vacationers to resorts in the South. You may not think of weather and beaches when you think about industry, but you should. Resort areas are an industry because they provide jobs and help local economies grow.

Many cities in the South trade goods and services with Mexico and countries in Central and South America. This trade is possible because several of the southern states are located near these countries. For example, Miami is an important trading port and travel connection with Caribbean countries, Mexico, and South America. Atlanta, Houston, and Dallas are also major transportation centers.

The Midwest

The Midwest is one of the most productive farming regions in the world. The Mississippi River and many of its tributaries carry materials that help create the region's rich soils, which are good for farming. Midwestern farmers grow mostly corn, wheat, and soybeans. Farmers in the region also raise livestock such as dairy cows.

The core of the Midwest's corn-growing region stretches from Ohio to Nebraska. Much of the corn is used to feed livestock, such as beef cattle and hogs.

To the north of the corn-growing region is an area of dairy farms. States with dairy farms are major producers of milk, cheese, and other dairy products. This area includes Wisconsin and most of Michigan and Minnesota. Much of the dairy farm region is pasture, but farmers also grow crops to feed dairy cows.

Many of the Midwest's farm and factory products are shipped to markets by water routes, such as those along the Ohio and Mississippi rivers. The other is through the Great Lakes and the Saint Lawrence Seaway to the Atlantic Ocean.

Most major cities in the Midwest are located on rivers or the Great Lakes. As a result, they are important transportation centers. Farm products, coal, and iron ore are easily shipped to these cities from nearby farms and mines. These natural resources support industries such as automobile manufacturing. For example, **Detroit**, Michigan, is the country's leading automobile producer.

One of the busiest shipping ports on the Great Lakes is **Chicago**, Illinois. The city also has one of the world's busiest airports. Chicago's industries attracted many immigrants in the late 1800s. People moved here to work in the city's steel mills. Today Chicago is the nation's third-largest city.

FOCUS ON READING
As you read about the Midwest, sort the details into three categories.

The West

The West is the largest region in the United States. Many western states have large open spaces with few people. The West is not all open spaces, however. Many large cities are on the Pacific coast.

One state on the coast, California, is home to more than 10 percent of the U.S. population. California's mild climate and wealth of resources attract people to the state. Most Californians live in Los Angeles, San Diego, and the San Francisco Bay area. The center of the country's entertainment industry, Hollywood, is in Los Angeles. Farming and the technology industry are also important to California's economy.

The economy of other states in the West is dependent on ranching and growing wheat. Wheat is grown mostly in Montana, Idaho, and Washington.

Much of the farmland in the West must be irrigated, or watered. One method of irrigation uses long sprinkler systems mounted on huge wheels. The wheels rotate slowly. This sprinkler system waters the area within a circle. From the air, parts of the irrigated Great Plains resemble a series of green circles.

The West also has rich deposits of coal, oil, gold, silver, copper, and other minerals. However, mining these minerals can cause problems. For example, coal miners in parts of the Great Plains use a **process** called strip mining, which strips away soil and rock. This kind of mining leads to soil erosion and other problems. Today laws require miners to restore mined areas.

In Oregon and Washington, forestry and fishing are two of the most important economic activities. **Seattle** is Washington's largest city. The Seattle area is home to many important industries, including a major computer software company. More than half of the people in Oregon live in and around Portland.

Alaska's economy is largely based on oil, forests, and fish. As in Washington and Oregon, people debate over developing

ACADEMIC
VOCABULARY

process a series of steps by which a task is accomplished

Olympic National Park

One of the largest sections of coastal wilderness in the United States, shown here, stretches along the Pacific coast in Washington's Olympic National Park.

these resources. For example, some people want to limit oil drilling in wild areas of Alaska. Others want to expand drilling to produce more oil.

Hawaii's natural beauty, mild climate, and fertile soils are its most important resources. The islands' major crops are sugarcane and pineapples. Millions of tourists visit the islands each year.

READING CHECK **Comparing** How is the economy of the West different from the economy of the South?

Changes in the Nation

Because of its economic and military strength, the United States is often called the world's only superpower. In recent years, however, the United States has faced many challenges and changes.

Economy

An abundance of natural resources, technology, and plentiful jobs have helped make the U.S. economy strong. The United States also benefits by cooperating with other countries. The three largest trading partners of the United States are Canada, China, and Mexico. In 1992 the United States, Mexico, and Canada signed the North American Free Trade Agreement, or NAFTA. This agreement made trade easier and cheaper between the three neighboring nations.

Still, the U.S. economy has experienced significant ups and downs since the 1990s. In the 1990s the nation experienced the longest period of economic growth in its history. By the end of 2007, the United States faced a recession, or a sharp decrease in economic activity. In this recession, the housing market collapsed, major banks and businesses failed, and an estimated 8.4 million jobs were lost in the United States.

The War on Terror

In the 1990s the United States began to experience acts of terrorism. **Terrorism** is the threat or use of violence against civilians to intimidate or cause fear for political or social reasons. Some terrorists have been from foreign countries, whereas others have been U.S. citizens.

On September 11, 2001, the United States suffered the deadliest terrorist attack in the country's history. Wanting to disrupt the U.S. economy, 19 Islamic extremist terrorists hijacked four American jets. They crashed two into the World Trade Center in New York City and one into the Pentagon.

In response, President George W. Bush declared a "war on terrorism." He sent military forces to Afghanistan, to kill or capture members of a terrorist group called al-Qaeda, which had planned the 9/11 attacks. The United States then turned its attention to Iraq. President Bush viewed Iraqi dictator Saddam Hussein as a serious threat to Americans. In March 2003 Bush sent U.S. troops into Iraq to remove Hussein from power.

Today world leaders are working with the United States to combat terrorism. In the United States, the Department of Homeland Security was established to prevent terrorist attacks on American soil. Many other countries have also increased security within their borders, especially at international airports.

Government

The 2008 U.S. presidential election pitted Republican senator John McCain of Arizona and his running mate, Alaska governor Sarah Palin, against the Democratic ticket of Senators Barack Obama of Illinois and Joe Biden of Delaware. McCain, a distinguished military veteran, was more experienced than Obama, but his support for the unpopular war in Iraq proved costly. Obama urged the

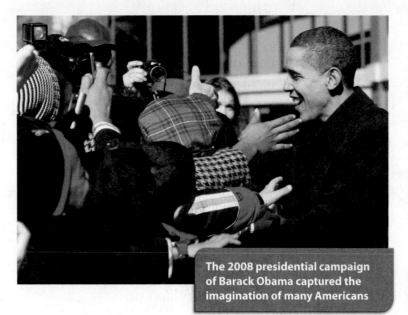

The 2008 presidential campaign of Barack Obama captured the imagination of many Americans

withdrawal of U.S. troops from Iraq as soon as possible. The two men also differed over how best to deal with the economic crisis and health care reform. Helped by record-setting voter turnout, Obama won the election, becoming the nation's first African American president.

President Obama succeeded in passing health care reform legislation and oversaw the withdrawal of U.S. troops from Iraq. Slow economic growth, unemployment, and high federal deficits were major issues during Obama's successful bid to win a second term in 2012.

READING CHECK **Summarizing** What issues were most important in the 2008 and 2012 presidential elections?

SUMMARY AND PREVIEW In this section, you learned about the geographic features, resources, and economic activities found in different regions of the United States. You also learned that the economy and terrorism are two important issues facing the country today. In the next chapter, you will learn about Canada, our neighbor to the north.

Section 3 Assessment

hmhsocialstudies.com
ONLINE QUIZ

Reviewing Ideas, Terms, and Places

1. a. Define What is a **megalopolis**? What major cities are part of the largest megalopolis in the United States?

b. Compare and Contrast How is the modification of the physical environment in the Midwest similar to and different from the modification of the physical environment in the South?

c. Elaborate How are the regions of the United States different from one another?

2. a. Define What is **terrorism**? What terrorist attack occurred in September 2001?

b. Explain How did a recession affect the U.S. economy in 2007?

c. Elaborate What steps are the United States and other countries taking in an attempt to combat world terrorism?

Critical Thinking

3. Finding Main Ideas Use your notes to help you list at least one main idea about the population, resources, and economy of each region.

	Northeast	South	Midwest	West
Population				
Resources				
Economy				

FOCUS ON VIEWING
my WriteSmart

4. Thinking about the United States Today Identify and explain the geographic factors responsible for the patterns of population in the regions of the United States that you have read about in this section. What key words, images, and objects might represent what you have learned?

Chapter Review

Visual Summary

Use the visual summary below to help you review the main ideas of the chapter.

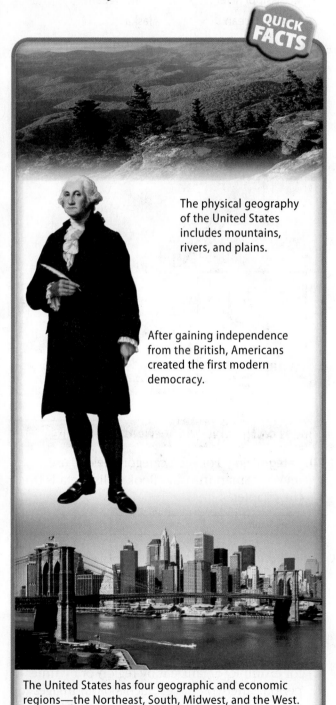

QUICK FACTS

The physical geography of the United States includes mountains, rivers, and plains.

After gaining independence from the British, Americans created the first modern democracy.

The United States has four geographic and economic regions—the Northeast, South, Midwest, and the West.

Reviewing Vocabulary, Terms, and Places

Match the terms or places with their definitions or descriptions.

a. Boston   **g.** pioneers
b. Great Lakes   **h.** bilingual
c. tributary   **i.** megalopolis
d. Rocky Mountains   **j.** Washington, D.C.
e. colony   **k.** Chicago
f. Appalachian Mountains   **l.** terrorism

1. a string of cities that have grown together
2. major seaport in the British colonies
3. stream or river that flows into a larger stream or river
4. violent attacks that cause fear
5. first settlers
6. largest freshwater lake system in the world
7. major mountain range in the West
8. capital of the United States
9. third-largest city in the United States
10. major mountain range in the East
11. having the ability to speak two languages
12. territory controlled by people from a foreign land

Comprehension and Critical Thinking

SECTION 1 *(Pages 142–146)*

13. **a. Identify** What river drains the entire Interior Plains and is the longest river in North America?

SECTION 1 (continued)

b. Contrast How are the Appalachians different from the Rocky Mountains?

c. Elaborate Imagine you live in Tornado Alley. How would your life be affected by the interaction of physical processes and the environment?

SECTION 2 (Pages 150–156)

14. a. Define Who were the pioneers?

b. Draw Conclusions Why do you think people immigrate to the United States?

c. Elaborate How has American culture influenced cultures around the world?

SECTION 3 (Pages 158–164)

15. a. Recall What are the four regions of the United States?

b. Compare Is corn grown mostly in the Midwest or the South?

c. Identify and Explain What is one example of the United States cooperating with another culture? Explain how the United States cooperates with this culture.

d. Make Inferences Look at the map and photos on pages 160–161. How might the location of natural resources affect technology use?

Using the Internet

16. Activity: Making a Brochure The United States has a diverse population. This diversity is seen in many of the holidays Americans celebrate. Through your online textbook, research and take notes on holidays celebrated in the United States. Then create an illustrated brochure about three holidays. Be sure to tell about the history, background, and traditions of each holiday.

↗ hmhsocialstudies.com

Social Studies Skills

Using a Political Map Look at the political map of the United States at the beginning of this chapter. Then answer the following questions.

17. What four states border Mexico?

18. What river forms the boundary between Illinois and Missouri?

Map Activity

19. The United States On a sheet of paper, match the letters on the map with their correct labels.

Great Lakes	Rocky Mountains
Mississippi River	Pacific Ocean
Atlantic Ocean	Alaska

FOCUS ON READING AND VIEWING | *my*WriteSmart

20. Categorizing For each category below, use *my*WriteSmart in your eBook to list details from the chapter.

Geography	People	Regions

21. Creating a Collage Gather valid primary and secondary sources and images you need to create a collage about the United States. Next, decide how to organize your collage. You might, for example, organize it by region or by time period. After you have attached your images to the poster board, create a label for each grouping. Finally, write a title for the entire collage. Be prepared to display your work and evaluate your classmates' collages for organization and clarity.

Reading Social Studies

Categorizing

When you sort things into groups of similar items, you are categorizing. When you read, categorizing helps you to identify the main groups of information. Then you can find and see the individual facts in each group. Notice how the information in the paragraph below has been sorted into three main groups, with details listed under each group.

If you were traveling across the United States, you might start on the country's eastern coast. This low area, which is flat and close to sea level, is called the Atlantic Coastal Plain. As you go west, the land gradually rises higher to a region called the Piedmont. The Appalachian Mountains, which are the main mountain range in the East, rise above the Piedmont.

From Section 1, Physical Geography

Category 1:
Atlantic Coastal Plain
Details: low, flat, close to sea level

Category 2:
Piedmont
Details: farther west & higher than Atlantic Coastal Plain

Category 3:
Appalachian Mountains
Details: main Eastern mountain range, higher than Piedmont

YOU TRY IT!

Read the following paragraph, and then use a graphic organizer like the one above to categorize the group and details in the paragraph. Create as many boxes as you need to list the main groups.

The eastern United States has three climate regions. In the Northeast, people live in a humid continental climate with snowy winters and warm, humid summers. Southerners, on the other hand, experience milder winters and the warm, humid summers of a humid subtropical climate. Most of Florida is warm all year.

From Section 1, Physical Geography

THE American REVOLUTION

The American Revolution led to the formation of the United States of America in 1776. Beginning in the 1760s, tensions grew between American colonists and their British rulers when Britain started passing a series of new laws and taxes for the colonies. With no representation in the British government, however, colonists had no say in these laws, which led to growing discontent. After fighting broke out in 1775, colonial leaders met to decide what to do. They approved the Declaration of Independence, announcing that the American colonies were free from British rule. In reality, however, freedom would not come until after years of fighting.

Explore some of the people and events of the American Revolution online. You can find a wealth of information, video clips, primary sources, activities, and more at ⏷ hmhsocialstudies.com.

"I know not what course others may take; but as for me, give me liberty or give me death!"

— Patrick Henry

"Give Me Liberty or Give Me Death"
Read an excerpt from Patrick Henry's famous speech, which urged the colonists to fight against the British.

Seeds of Revolution
Watch the video to learn about colonial discontent in the years before the Revolutionary War.

Independence!
Watch the video to learn about the origins of the Declaration of Independence.

Victory!
Watch the video to learn how the American colonists won the Revolutionary War.

Canada

Essential Question

myNotebook

How has geography and climate shaped the development of Canada's provinces?

Texas Essential Knowledge and Skills (TEKS)

1A, 1B, 2A, 2B, 3A, 3B, 3C, 3D, 4B, 4C, 4D, 4E, 4F, 5A, 5B, 5C, 6A, 6B, 15B, 18B, 21B, 21C, 22D

FOCUS ON READING AND SPEAKING

my WriteSmart

Understanding Lists Identifying a list of the interesting facts that you read about may help you understand the topic you are studying. For example, you could identify facts about Canada's physical features, regions, government, or economy. As you read this chapter, look for lists of facts. **See the lesson, Understanding Lists, on page 189.**

Creating a Radio Ad You are a member of the Canadian tourism board and your job is to develop a radio ad to attract visitors to Canada. Read about Canada in this chapter. Then, write a script for a one-minute radio ad. Be ready to present your ad to the class. Use the annotation tools in your eBook to gather information for your assignment.

Culture Ice hockey is Canada's national sport. Many Canadians grow up playing on frozen lakes.

Canada: Political

GREENLAND
(DENMARK)

Baffin
Bay

Arctic Circle

Iqaluit

Labrador
Sea

NUNAVUT

Hudson
Bay

NEWFOUNDLAND
AND LABRADOR

ATLANTIC
OCEAN

★ St. John's

SASKATCHEWAN

MANITOBA

QUEBEC

PRINCE EDWARD ISLAND

Saskatchewan R.

Lake
Winnipeg

Charlottetown

ONTARIO

Fredericton

NOVA SCOTIA

Regina ★

Quebec ★

★ Halifax

Winnipeg ★

Montreal ★

NEW BRUNSWICK

Lake
Huron

Ottawa ☆

St. Lawrence R.

UNITED STATES

Lake
Superior

Lake
Michigan

Toronto ●

Lake
Ontario

Lake
Erie

Windsor ●

HISTORY Technology of the Ice Road

↗ hmhsocialstudies.com VIDEO

map zone
Geography Skills

Place Ten provinces and three territories make up Canada.

1. **Locate** What is the provincial capital of Manitoba?
2. **Make Inferences** What do you think the climate is like in the Yukon Territory? Why?

History Since 1867, leaders of Canada's democratic government have met in the nation's parliament building in Ottawa.

Geography Canada's physical geography ranges from the rocky Atlantic coast shown here to vast interior plains and mountains in the west.

Physical Geography

 TEKS 3A, 3B, 3C, 4D, 4E, 4F, 5A, 5B, 5C, 6A, 6B, 21B, 21C, 22D

What You Will Learn...

Main Ideas

1. A huge country, Canada has a wide variety of physical features, including rugged mountains, plains, and swamps.
2. Because of its northerly location, Canada is dominated by cold climates.
3. Canada is rich in natural resources like fish, minerals, fertile soil, and forests.

The Big Idea

Canada is a huge country with a northerly location, cold climates, and rich resources.

Key Terms and Places

Rocky Mountains, *p. 170*
St. Lawrence River, *p. 170*
Niagara Falls, *p. 170*
Canadian Shield, *p. 171*
Grand Banks, *p. 172*
pulp, *p. 173*
newsprint, *p. 173*

hmhsocialstudies.com
TAKING NOTES

Use the graphic organizer online to take notes on the physical geography of Canada.

If **YOU** lived there...

You live in Winnipeg, Manitoba, in central Canada. Your hiking club is trying to decide where to go on a trip this summer. Since you live on the plains, some people want to visit the rugged Rocky Mountains in the west. Others want to travel north to Hudson Bay to see polar bears and other wildlife. Others would rather hike in the east near the Great Lakes and Niagara Falls.

Which place will you choose for this year's trip?

BUILDING BACKGROUND A long international boundary separates Canada and the United States. With the exception of the St. Lawrence River and the Great Lakes, there is no actual physical boundary between the two countries. Rivers, lakes, prairies, and mountain ranges cross the border.

Physical Features

Did you know that Canada is the second-largest country in the world? Russia is the only country in the world that is larger than Canada. The United States is the third-largest country in the world and shares many physical features with Canada.

Locate Canada on the map on the following page and see if you can find the physical features that the United States and Canada share. You may notice that mountains along the Pacific coast and the **Rocky Mountains** extend north into western Canada from the western United States. Broad plains stretch across the interiors of both countries. In the east, the two countries share a natural border formed by the **St. Lawrence River**. An important international waterway, the St. Lawrence links the Great Lakes to the Atlantic Ocean.

The United States and Canada also share a spectacular physical feature called **Niagara Falls**. The falls are located on the Niagara River between the province of Ontario and New York State.

Created by the waters of the Niagara River, the falls flow between two of the Great Lakes—Lake Erie and Lake Ontario. The falls here plunge an average of 162 feet (50 m) down a huge ledge. That is higher than many 15-story buildings!

Canada has a region of rocky uplands, lakes, and swamps called the **Canadian Shield**. See on the map how this feature curves around Hudson Bay. The Shield covers about half the country.

Farther north, Canada stretches all the way up to the Arctic Ocean. The land here is covered with ice year-round. Ellesmere Island is very rugged with snow-covered mountains and jagged coastlines. Very few people live this far north, but wildlife such as the polar bear and the Arctic wolf have adapted to the harsh environment.

READING CHECK **Summarizing** What are the major physical features of Canada?

Canada: Physical

map zone

Geography Skills

Place Canada is located between the United States and the Arctic Ocean.

1. **Locate** What mountain range has the highest elevation?
2. **Draw Conclusions** How does Canada's northerly location affect its climate?

ELEVATION

Feet		Meters
13,120		4,000
6,560		2,000
1,640		500
656		200
(Sea level) 0		0 (Sea level)
Below sea level		Below sea level

Projection: Lambert Azimuthal Equal-Area

Mist rises over Niagara Falls where the Niagara River forms a natural boundary between the United States and Canada.

Climate

FOCUS ON READING

What climates would you include in a list of the climates of Canada?

Canada's location greatly influences the country's climate. Canada is located far from the equator at much higher latitudes than the United States. This more northerly location gives Canada cool to freezing temperatures year-round.

The farther north you go in Canada, the colder it gets. The coldest areas of Canada are located close to the Arctic Circle. Much of central and northern Canada has a subarctic climate. The far north has tundra and ice cap climates. About half of Canada lies in these extremely cold climates.

The central and eastern parts of southern Canada have a much different climate. It is humid and relatively mild. However, the mildest area of Canada is along the coast of British Columbia. This location on the Pacific coast brings rainy winters and mild temperatures. Inland areas of southern Canada are colder and drier.

READING CHECK **Categorizing** What are Canada's climates?

Resources

Canada is incredibly rich in natural resources such as fish, minerals, and forests. Canada's Atlantic and Pacific coastal waters are among the world's richest fishing areas. Off the Atlantic coast lies a large fishing ground near Newfoundland and Labrador called the **Grand Banks**. Here, cold waters from the Labrador Sea meet the warm waters of the Gulf Stream. These conditions are ideal for the growth of tiny organisms, or plankton, that fish like to eat. As a result, large schools of fish gather at the Grand Banks. However, recent overfishing of this region has left many fishers in Canada unemployed.

Minerals are also valuable resources in Canada. The Canadian Shield contains many mineral deposits. Canada is a main source of the world's nickel, zinc, and uranium. Lead, copper, gold, and silver are also important resources. Saskatchewan has large deposits of potash, a mineral used to make fertilizer. Alberta produces most of Canada's oil and natural gas.

Banff National Park

Some of Canada's most spectacular scenery is found here in the Rockies at Banff National Park.

The city of Windsor, Ontario, lies across the Detroit River from Detroit, Michigan.

Agriculture in Ontario

In this satellite image, crop fields in different stages of growth appear scattered throughout the province of Ontario. These rectangular fields of vegetation appear red at their height of growth and white after the crops are harvested. Rich soils and a mild climate in this region, which lies north of Lake Erie, make it one of Canada's most fertile regions. Crops grown here include wheat, soybeans, corn, and a variety of vegetables. Some of these crops are exported to the United States through the Canadian port of Windsor to Detroit, Michigan, just across the Detroit River. Both cities appear in this image as shades of blue and brown.

Drawing Conclusions What is the economy of southern Ontario based on?

Vast areas of forests stretch across most of Canada from Labrador to the Pacific coast. These trees provide lumber and pulp. **Pulp**—softened wood fibers—is used to make paper. The United States, the United Kingdom, and Japan get much of their newsprint from Canada. **Newsprint** is cheap paper used mainly for newspapers.

READING CHECK **Drawing Conclusions** How do Canada's major resources affect its economy?

SUMMARY AND PREVIEW In this section, you learned that Canada shares many physical features with the United States. However, Canada's geography is also different. Due to its northerly location, Canada has a cold climate. Fish, minerals, fertile soil, and forests are all important natural resources. In the next section, you will learn about the history and culture of Canada.

Section 1 Assessment

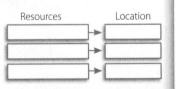
hmhsocialstudies.com
ONLINE QUIZ

Reviewing Ideas, Terms, and Places

1. **a. Recall** What river links the Great Lakes to the Atlantic Ocean?
   b. Explain What physical features does **Niagara Falls** flow between?
   c. Geographic Questions Look at the map in this section. Pose and answer a question about Canada's physical geography.
2. **a. Describe** How is Canada's climate related to its northerly location?
   b. Draw Conclusions Locate Canada on the map in this section. Where would you expect to find Canada's coldest climate? Why?
3. **a. Define** What is the **Grand Banks**?
   b. Interpret How are Canada's forests a valuable resource?

Critical Thinking

4. **Generalizing** Using your notes on Canada's resources, identify the location of each type of resource.

Resources		Location
	→	
	→	
	→	

FOCUS ON SPEAKING *my*WriteSmart

5. **Writing about Physical Geography** What information about Canada's physical features, climate, and resources might visitors find appealing? Jot down what descriptions you want to include in your radio ad.

History and Culture

What You Will Learn...

Main Ideas

1. Beginning in the 1600s, Europeans settled the region that would later become Canada.
2. Immigration and migration to cities have shaped Canadian culture.

The Big Idea

Canada's history and culture reflect Native Canadian and European settlement, immigration, and migration to cities.

Key Terms and Places

provinces, *p. 176*
Quebec, *p. 176*
British Columbia, *p. 176*
Toronto, *p. 178*

hmhsocialstudies.com
TAKING NOTES

Use the graphic organizer online to take notes on the history and culture of Canada.

If YOU lived there...

You own a general store in Calgary, Alberta, in the early 1880s. Your town is a center for agriculture and ranching on the prairies around you. Still, it sometimes feels very isolated. You miss your family in Ontario. Now the news comes that the Canadian Pacific Railway will soon reach Calgary. It will connect the town with all of central and eastern Canada.

How will the railroad change your life?

BUILDING BACKGROUND Canada is a close neighbor with the United States. The two countries are linked by a common language and a history of British colonial rule. But the two countries developed in different ways. Canada's diverse population developed its own culture and way of life.

History

As the ice sheets of the ice ages melted, people moved into all areas of what is now Canada. As they did elsewhere in the Americas, these ancient settlers adapted to the physical environment.

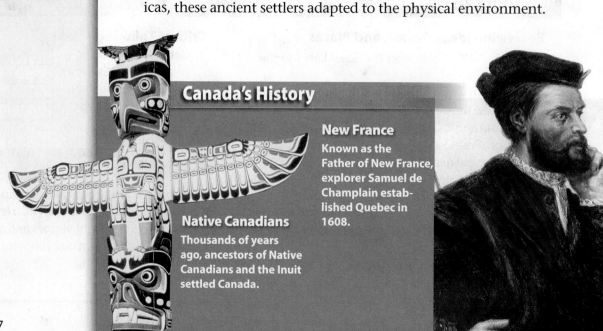

Canada's History

Native Canadians
Thousands of years ago, ancestors of Native Canadians and the Inuit settled Canada.

New France
Known as the Father of New France, explorer Samuel de Champlain established Quebec in 1608.

Native Canadians

Ancestors of Native Canadians and the Inuit (IH-nu-wuht) people were the first Canadians. Over time, native peoples divided into groups that became known as the First Nations. One group living on Canada's vast interior plains, the Cree, were skilled bison hunters. In the far north the Inuit adapted to the region's extreme cold, where farming was impossible. By hunting seals, whales, walruses, and other animals, the Inuit could feed, clothe, and house themselves. Today about 400,000 Native Canadians and Inuit live in Canada.

European Settlement

Other people migrated to Canada from Europe. The first Europeans in Canada were the Vikings, or Norse. They settled on Newfoundland Island in about AD 1000, but later abandoned their settlements. In the late 1400s other Europeans arrived and explored Canada. Soon more explorers and fishermen from western Europe began crossing the Atlantic.

Trade quickly developed between the Europeans and Native Canadians. Europeans valued the furs that Native Canadians supplied. The Canadians wanted European metal goods like axes and guns. Through trading, they began to also exchange foods, clothing, and methods of travel.

New France

France was the first European country to successfully settle parts of what would become Canada. The French **established** Quebec City in 1608. They called their new territories New France. At its height, New France included much of eastern Canada and the central United States.

New France was important for several reasons. It was part of the French Empire, which provided money and goods to French settlers. It also served as a base to spread French culture.

France had to compete with Britain, another European colonial power, for control of Canada. To defend their interests against the British, the French built trade and diplomatic relationships with Native Canadians. They exported furs, fish, and other products from New France to other parts of their empire. In addition, the French sent manufactured goods from France to New France. French missionaries also went to New France to convert people to Christianity.

All of these efforts protected French interests in New France for 150 years, until the British finally defeated the French. Although it did not last, New France shaped Canada's cultural makeup. The descendants of French settlers form one of Canada's major ethnic groups today.

ACADEMIC VOCABULARY

establish to set up or create

British Settlement
The British built forts throughout Canada like this one in Halifax, Nova Scotia.

Dominion of Canada
After 1867, Canadians created their own government and a mounted police force patrolled the border with the United States.

British Conquest

In the mid-1700s, the rivalry between France and England turned to war. The conflict was called the French and Indian War. This was the war that resulted in the British taking control of New France away from the French. A small number of French went back to France. However, the great majority stayed. For most of them, few changes occurred in their daily activities. They farmed the same land, prayed in the same churches, and continued to speak French. Few English-speaking settlers came to what is now called **Quebec**.

Canadian Pacific Railroad

Since 1885, the Canadian Pacific Railway has snaked through the Canadian Rockies on its way to the Pacific coast.

The British divided Quebec into two colonies. Lower Canada was mostly French-speaking, and Upper Canada was mostly English-speaking. The boundary between Upper and Lower Canada forms part of the border between the provinces of Quebec and Ontario today. **Provinces** are administrative divisions of a country. To the east, the colony of Nova Scotia (noh-vuh SKOH-shuh) was also divided. A new colony called New Brunswick was created where many of the British settlers lived.

Creation of Canada

For several decades these new colonies developed separately from each other. The colonists viewed themselves as different from other parts of the British Empire. Therefore, the British Parliament created the Dominion of Canada in 1867. A dominion is a territory or area of influence. For Canadians, the creation of the Dominion was a step toward independence from Britain. The motto of the new Dominion was "from sea to sea."

How would Canadians create a nation from sea to sea? With railroads. When the Dominion was established, Ontario and Quebec were already well served by railroads. **British Columbia**, on the Pacific coast, was not. To connect British Columbia with the provinces in the east, the Canadians built a transcontinental railroad. Completed in 1885, the Canadian Pacific Railway was Canada's first transcontinental railroad.

After the Canadian Pacific Railway linked the original Canadian provinces to British Columbia, Canada acquired vast lands in the north. Much of this land was bought from the Hudson's Bay Company, a large British fur-trading business. Most of the people living in the north were Native Canadians and people of mixed European and native ancestry. With the building

Canada's Major Languages

map zone Geography Skills

Place Canada's languages include English, French, and several Native Canadian languages.
1. **Locate** In what region do most Canadians speak French?
2. **Draw Conclusions** Why do you think few English speakers live in the Canadian North?

ARCTIC OCEAN

Greenland (DENMARK)

Baffin Bay

Beaufort Sea

ALASKA (U.S.)

Labrador Sea

Hudson Bay

PACIFIC OCEAN

UNITED STATES

ATLANTIC OCEAN

Concentrations of Speakers
- English
- French
- Cree
- Inuktitut
- Athapaskan

0   350   700 Miles
0   350   700 Kilometers

Projection: Lambert Azimuthal Equal-Area

of the railroad and the signing of treaties with Native Canadians, early Canadian settlers created a way for more people to settle Canada's new territories.

READING CHECK **Summarizing** How was Canada linked from sea to sea?

Canadian Ethnic Groups

- British Isles origin
- French origin
- Other European
- Native Canadians
- Mixed background
- Other, mostly Asian, African, Arab

6%
28%
26%
2%
15%
23%

Culture

Canada's people reflect a history of British and French colonial rule. In addition, the country has experienced waves of immigration. The country is home to a great variety of people who belong to different ethnic groups and cultures. Although individual groups still keep their own cultural ways, many Canadians have tried to create a single national identity.

Immigration

During the late 1800s and early 1900s, many immigrants came to Canada from Europe. Most were from Britain, Russia, and Germany. Some people also came from the United States. While most of these immigrants farmed, others worked in mines, forests, and factories.

Other immigrants were lured to Canada in 1897 by the discovery of gold in the Yukon Territory. Many people from the United States migrated north in search of Canada's gold.

Immigrants also came to Canada from Asian countries, especially China, Japan, and India. British Columbia became the first Canadian province to have a large Asian minority. Many Chinese immigrants migrated to Canada to work on the railroads. Chinese immigrants built most of the Canadian Pacific Railway, one of the railroad lines linking eastern Canada to the Pacific coast.

All of these immigrants played an important part in an economic boom that Canada experienced in the early 1900s. During these prosperous times, Quebec, New Brunswick, and Ontario produced wheat, pulp, and paper. British Columbia

FOCUS ON READING

What details of this paragraph could you add to a list of countries from which immigrants came?

and Ontario supplied the country with minerals and hydroelectricity. As a result, Canadians enjoyed one of the highest standards of living in the world by the 1940s.

Movement to Cities

After World War II, another wave of immigrants from Europe arrived in Canada. Many settled in Canada's large cities. For example, **Toronto** has become one of the most culturally diverse cities in the world. The Europeans were joined by other people from Africa, the Caribbean, Latin America, and particularly Asia. Asian businesspeople have brought a great deal of wealth to Canada's economy.

Many Canadians have recently moved from farms to the country's cities. Some settlements in rural Canada have even disappeared because so many people left. Many Canadians have moved to cities in

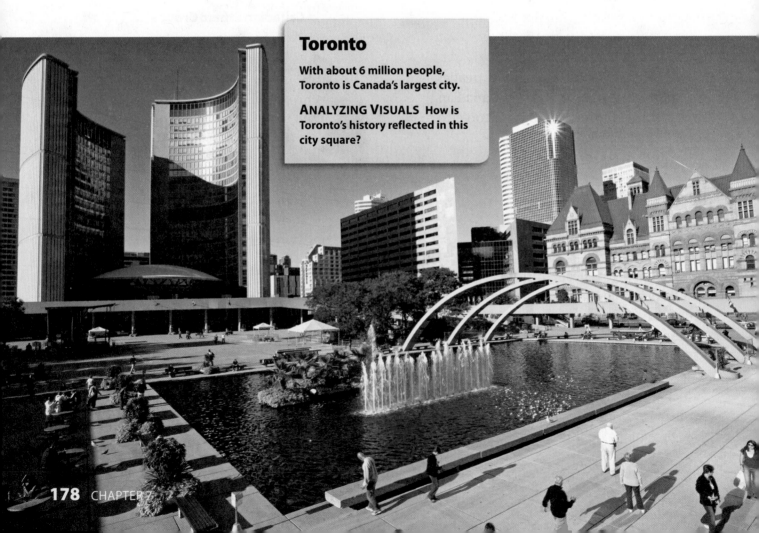

Toronto

With about 6 million people, Toronto is Canada's largest city.

ANALYZING VISUALS How is Toronto's history reflected in this city square?

Vancouver's Chinatown

If you walked around Vancouver, British Columbia, you would quickly realize when you entered the neighborhood of Chinatown. First you would notice that most signs are in Chinese and you would hear some people speaking Chinese. Then you would realize most restaurants serve Chinese food, and shops sell colorful silk clothing, herbs, and art imported from China. If you were in the city for the Chinese New Year, you would probably see a parade of people in traditional Chinese dress. Vancouver's Chinatown is a unique place where Chinese culture is kept alive in Canada today.

Drawing Conclusions How is Vancouver's Chinatown a unique neighborhood?

Ontario to find jobs. Others moved to Vancouver, British Columbia, for its good job opportunities, mild climate, and location near plentiful resources. Resources such as oil, gas, potash, and uranium have provided wealth to many cities in the Western Provinces. However, the political and economic center of power remains in the cities of Ottawa, Toronto, and Montreal.

READING CHECK **Analyzing** How has immigration changed Canada?

SUMMARY AND PREVIEW In this section, you learned that Canada was greatly influenced by British and French settlement, the building of the railroad to the Pacific coast, immigration, and movement to cities. In the next section you will learn about Canada's regions and economy today.

Section 2 Assessment

hmhsocialstudies.com
ONLINE QUIZ

Reviewing Ideas, Terms, and Places

1. **a. Recall** What is a **province**?
   b. Evaluate What are some cultural contributions of groups in Canada's past?
   c. Elaborate How do you think the Canadian Pacific Railway changed Canada?
2. **a. Identify** What immigrant group helped build the railroads?
   b. Draw Conclusions Why did people migrate to Canada?
   c. Elaborate Why do you think many Canadians moved from farms to the cities?

Critical Thinking

3. **Analyzing** Draw a diagram like the one below. Using your notes, write a sentence in each box about how each topic influenced the next topic.

Railroad	Immigration	Cities

FOCUS ON SPEAKING

4. **Adding Details** Add information about the history and culture of Canada to your notes. Which details would most interest potential visitors?

Canada Today

TEKS 1A, 1B, 2A, 2B, 3A, 3B, 3C, 3D, 4B, 4C, 4D, 4F, 4E, 15B, 18B, 21B, 21C, 22D

What You Will Learn...

Main Ideas

1. Canada has a democratic government with a prime minister and a parliament.
2. Canada has four distinct geographic and cultural regions.
3. Canada's economy is largely based on trade with the United States.

The Big Idea

Canada's democratic government oversees the country's regions and economy.

Key Terms and Places

regionalism, *p. 181*
maritime, *p. 181*
Montreal, *p. 182*
Ottawa, *p. 183*
Vancouver, *p. 184*

hmhsocialstudies.com
TAKING NOTES

Use the graphic organizer online to take notes on present-day Canada.

If YOU lived there...

You and your family live in Toronto, Ontario. Your parents, who are architects, have been offered an important project in Montreal. If they accept it, you would live there for two years. Montreal is a major city in French-speaking Quebec. You would have to learn a new language. In Montreal, most street signs and advertisements are written in French.

How do you feel about moving to a city with a different language and culture?

BUILDING BACKGROUND Canada today has been shaped by both history and geography. Canada's first European settlers were French, but the British eventually controlled the territory. Differences in culture still remain, however. In addition, the four regions of Canada are separated by vast distances, economic activities, and culture.

Canada's Government

"Peace, order, and good government" is a statement from Canada's constitution that Canadians greatly value. Canadians are proud of their democratic government, which is led by a prime minister. Similar to a president, a prime minister is the head of a country's government.

Canada's prime minister oversees the country's parliament, Canada's governing body. Parliament consists of the House of Commons and the Senate. Canadians elect members of the House of Commons. However, senators are appointed by the prime minister.

Canada's 10 provincial governments are each led by a premier. These provincial governments are much like our state governments. Canada's central government is similar to our federal government. The Canadian federal system lets people keep their feelings of loyalty to their own province.

READING CHECK **Comparing** How is Canada's government similar to that of the United States?

Canada's Regions

Canada's physical geography separates the country into different regions. For example, people living on the Pacific coast in British Columbia are isolated from Canadians living in the eastern provinces on the Atlantic coast. Just as geographic distance separates much of Canada, differences in culture also define regions.

Regionalism

The cultural differences between English-speaking and French-speaking Canadians have led to problems. English is the main language in most of Canada. In Quebec, however, French is the main language. When Canadians from different regions discuss important issues, they are often influenced by regionalism. **Regionalism** refers to the strong connection that people feel toward the region in which they live.

In some places, this connection is stronger than people's connection to their country as a whole. To better understand regionalism in Canada, we will now explore each region of the country. As you read, refer to the map below to locate each region.

The Eastern Provinces

The region called the Eastern Provinces is a region that lies on the Atlantic coast of Canada. The provinces of New Brunswick, Nova Scotia, and Prince Edward Island are often called the Maritime Provinces. **Maritime** means on or near the sea. The province of Newfoundland and Labrador is usually not considered one of the Maritime Provinces. It includes the island of Newfoundland and a large region of the mainland called Labrador.

A short growing season limits farming in the Eastern Provinces. However, farmers in Prince Edward Island grow potatoes.

Regions of Canada

Legend:
- The Eastern Provinces
- The Heartland
- The Western Provinces
- The Canadian North

0 — 500 — 1,000 Miles
0 — 500 — 1,000 Kilometers

Projection: Lambert Azimuthal Equal-Area

map zone

Geography Skills

Regions Canada has four distinct regions.

1. **Locate** What region is located on the Atlantic coast?
2. **Draw Conclusions** Why do you think few people live in the Canadian North?

Quebec's Winter Carnival

At the annual Winter Carnival in the city of Quebec, millions of Canadians and visitors from around the world brave below-freezing temperatures to celebrate French Canadian culture.

The Inuit people traditionally used dogsleds as a means of transportation. Today dogsledding is a popular sport in Canada and a highlight of the carnival.

Most of the economy in Canada's Eastern Provinces is related to the forestry and fishing industries.

Many people in the Eastern Provinces are descendants of immigrants from the British Isles. In addition, French-speaking families have moved from Quebec to New Brunswick. Most of the region's people live in coastal cities. Many cities have industrial plants and serve as fishing and shipping ports. Along the Atlantic coast lies Halifax, Nova Scotia, the region's largest city.

The Heartland

FOCUS ON READING
In the paragraphs under The Heartland sort the facts into different lists.

Inland from the Eastern Provinces are Quebec and Ontario, which together are sometimes referred to as the Heartland. More than half of all Canadians live in these two provinces. In fact, the chain of cities that extends from Windsor, Ontario, to the city of Quebec is the country's most urbanized region.

The provincial capital of Quebec is also called Quebec. The city's older section has narrow streets, stone walls, and French-style architecture. **Montreal** is Canada's second-largest city and one of the largest French-speaking cities in the world. About 3.8 million people live in the Montreal metropolitan area. It is the financial and industrial center of the province. Winters in Montreal are very cold. To deal with this harsh environment, Montreal's people use underground passages and overhead tunnels to move between buildings in the city's downtown.

In Canada many residents of Quebec, called Quebecois (kay-buh-KWAH), believe their province should be given a special status. Quebecois argue that this status would recognize the cultural differences between their province and the rest of Canada. Some even want Quebec to become an independent country.

Many of the city's buildings reflect French architecture.

From the clues you see in this scene, what do you think is unique about French Canadian culture?

Ice sculptures created by Canadian and international artists line the carnival's grounds.

The carnival's mascot is a snowman who wears a traditional Canadian sash and hat.

On the other hand, many English-speaking Canadians think Quebec already has too many privileges. Most Canadians, however, still support a united Canada. Strong feelings of regionalism will continue to be an important issue.

With an even larger population than Quebec, the province of Ontario is Canada's leading manufacturing province. Hamilton, Ontario, is the center of Canada's steel industry. Canada exports much of its steel to the United States.

Ontario's capital, Toronto, is a major center for industry, finance, education, and culture. Toronto's residents come from many different parts of the world, including China, Europe, and India.

Canada's national capital, **Ottawa**, is also in Ontario. In Ottawa many people speak both English and French. The city is known for its grand government buildings, parks, and several universities.

The Western Provinces

West of Ontario are the prairie provinces of Manitoba, Saskatchewan, and Alberta. On the Pacific coast is the province of British Columbia. Together, these four provinces make up Canada's Western Provinces.

More people live in Quebec than in all of the prairie provinces combined. The southern grasslands of these provinces are part of a rich wheat belt. Farms here produce far more wheat than Canadians need. The extra wheat is exported. Oil and natural gas production is a very important economic activity in Alberta. The beauty of the Canadian Rockies attracts many visitors to national parks in western Alberta and eastern British Columbia.

British Columbia is Canada's westernmost province and home to almost 4 million people. This mountainous province has rich natural resources, including forests, salmon, and valuable minerals.

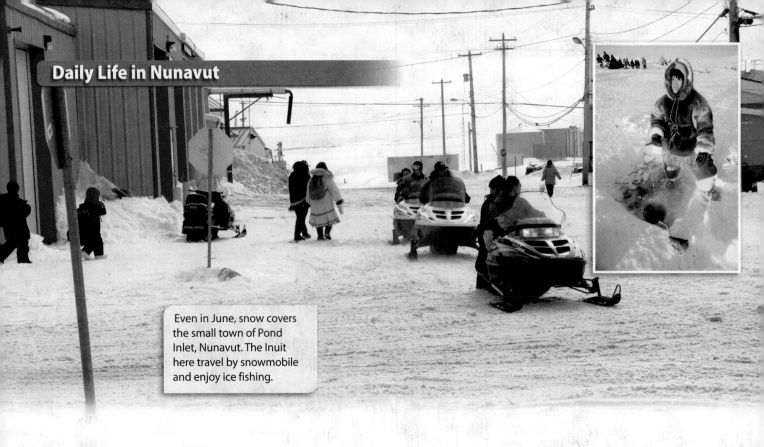

Even in June, snow covers the small town of Pond Inlet, Nunavut. The Inuit here travel by snowmobile and enjoy ice fishing.

Nearly half of British Columbia's population lives in and around the coastal city of **Vancouver**. The city's location on the Pacific coast helps it to trade with countries in Asia.

The Canadian North

Northern Canada is extremely cold because of its location close to the Arctic Circle. The region called the Canadian North includes the Yukon Territory, the Northwest Territories, and Nunavut (NOO-nuh-voot). These three territories cover more than a third of Canada but are home to only about 100,000 people.

Nunavut is a new territory created for the native Inuit people who live there. Nunavut means "Our Land" in the Inuit language. Even though Nunavut is part of Canada, the people there have their own **distinct** culture and government. About 30,000 people live in Nunavut.

The physical geography of the Canadian North includes forests and tundra. The frozen waters of the Arctic Ocean separate

ACADEMIC VOCABULARY
distinct separate

isolated towns and villages. During some parts of the winter, sunlight is limited to only a few hours.

READING CHECK Drawing Conclusions How does geography affect the location of economic activities in the Western Provinces?

Canada's Economy

As you learned in Section 1, Canada has many valuable natural resources. Canada's economy is based on the industries associated with these resources. In addition, Canada's economy also benefits from trade.

Industries

Canada is one of the world's leading mineral producers. Canadians mine valuable titanium, zinc, iron ore, gold, and coal. Canada's iron and steel industry uses iron ore to manufacture products like planes, automobiles and household appliances. However, most Canadians work in the services industry. For example, tourism is

Canada's fastest-growing services industry. Canada's economy also benefits from the millions of dollars visitors spend in the country each year.

Trade

Canada's economy depends on trade. Many of Canada's natural resources that you have learned about are exported to countries around the world. Canada's leading trading partner is the United States.

As the world's largest trading relationship, Canada and the United States rely heavily on each other. About 50 percent of Canada's imported goods are from the United States. About 75 percent of Canada's exports, such as lumber, goes to the United States.

However, the United States placed tariffs, or added fees, on Canadian timber. American lumber companies accused Canada of selling their lumber at unfairly low prices. Canada argued that the tariffs were unfair according to the North American Free Trade Agreement (NAFTA).

The export of cattle to the United States has also been an area of dispute between the two countries. When a Canadian cow was discovered with mad cow disease in 2003, the U.S. banned the import of all cattle from Canada. Canadian ranchers now claim that all their cows are free of the disease. As of 2012, about 70 percent of Canadian cattle and meat products are exported to the U.S.

READING CHECK Summarizing What goods does Canada export?

SUMMARY In this section you learned that Canada has distinct regions that are separated by both geography and culture. The U.S. and Canada share a common history, a border, and the English language. Next you will learn about the country of Mexico.

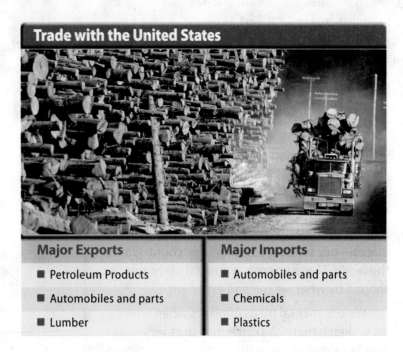

Trade with the United States

Major Exports	Major Imports
■ Petroleum Products	■ Automobiles and parts
■ Automobiles and parts	■ Chemicals
■ Lumber	■ Plastics

Section 3 Assessment

hmhsocialstudies.com
ONLINE QUIZ

Reviewing Ideas, Terms, and Places

1. a. Recall What office heads Canada's government?
   b. Summarize How is Canada's parliament structured?
2. a. Define What is **regionalism**?
   b. Contrast How are Canada's Western Provinces different from the Canadian North?
   c. Evaluate Why do you think the Quebecois want to break away from Canada?
3. a. Describe How are Canada's natural resources important to the country's economy?
   b. Draw Conclusions Why do Canada and the United States rely on each other as trading partners?

Critical Thinking

4. Comparing and Contrasting Use your notes to complete this chart. List the similarities and differences between the Eastern Provinces and Western Provinces.

Similarities	Differences
1.	1.
2.	

FOCUS ON SPEAKING *my* WriteSmart

5. Presenting Canada Today Add details about present-day Canada to your notes. Consider which images you will use to persuade your audience to visit Canada after they listen to your ad.

Drawing Sketch Maps

Learn

We create maps in our heads of all kinds of places—our schools, communities, country, and the world. These images, or mental maps, are shaped by what we see and experience.

We use mental maps of places when we draw sketch maps. A sketch map uses very simple shapes to show the relationship between places and regions and the relative size of places and regions. Notice the sketch map of the world shown here. It may not look like any other map in your book, but it does give you an idea of what the world looks like.

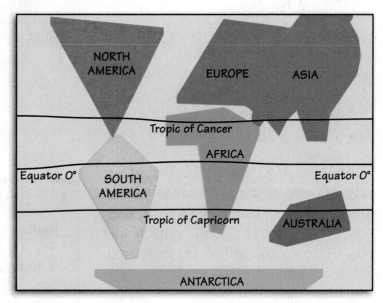

Practice

Does your mental map of the world look like the sketch map here? It is alright if they do not look exactly alike. Now think about the places in your own neighborhood. Use your mental map to draw a sketch map of your neighborhood. Then use your sketch map to answer the following questions and discuss your answers with a partner.

- What are the most important features of your map? Describe these features to your partner.
- What is the largest building in your neighborhood? Describe the building to your partner.
- What labels did you use on your map?

Apply

Draw a sketch map of Canada. Make sure to include the cities, regions, and physical features you learned about in this chapter. Then exchange your map with another student. Ask your partner to make corrections to your map if he or she does not understand it.

Chapter Review

Visual Summary

Use the visual summary below to help you review the main ideas of the chapter.

Native Canadian and European settlement has influenced Canadian culture.

Canada has cold climates and its physical features include rugged mountains.

Canada has distinctive cultural regions today.

Reviewing Vocabulary, Terms, and Places

Choose the letter of the answer that best completes each statement below.

1. A physical feature of rocky uplands, lakes, and swamps in Canada is called the
   - **a.** Niagara Falls.
   - **b.** Great Lakes.
   - **c.** Grand Banks.
   - **d.** Canadian Shield.

2. Which part of Canada did the French settle?
   - **a.** Ontario
   - **b.** New Brunswick
   - **c.** Quebec
   - **d.** British Colombia

3. What province was the first to have a large Asian population?
   - **a.** Manitoba
   - **b.** British Columbia
   - **c.** Quebec
   - **d.** Saskatchewan

4. A strong connection that people feel toward their region is called
   - **a.** maritime.
   - **b.** province.
   - **c.** heartland.
   - **d.** regionalism.

Comprehension and Critical Thinking

SECTION 1 *(Pages 170–173)*

5. **a. Define** What is pulp?

   b. Make Inferences What is the coldest area in Canada?

   c. Evaluate What makes the Grand Banks an ideal fishing ground?

SECTION 2 *(Pages 174–179)*

6. **a. Identify** Who were the first Canadians?

   b. Draw Conclusions Why did Canadians build a rail line across Canada?

   c. Predict Do you think Canada's cities will increase or decrease in population in the future? Explain your answers.

SECTION 3 *(Pages 180–185)*

7. **a. Recall** What kind of government does Canada have?

b. Compare and Contrast How are the Eastern Provinces different than the Western Provinces?

c. Evaluate Why do the Quebecois see themselves as different from other Canadians?

Using the Internet

8. **Activity: Writing Newspaper Articles** You are a reporter for The Quebec Chronicle assigned to write articles for the next issue of the newspaper. Through your online textbook, explore the people of Quebec and find background information for your articles covering Quebec. Use the links provided to conduct your research and then write three short articles. Go to press using the interactive template and publish your Canadian newspaper.

↗ **hmhsocialstudies.com**

Social Studies Skills

9. **Drawing Sketch Maps** Without looking at a map of Canada think about what the Eastern Provinces look like. Then create a sketch map of the Eastern Provinces. Make sure to include a compass rose and important physical features.

Map Activity

10. **Canada** On a separate sheet of paper, match the letters on the map with their correct labels.

Rocky Mountains	Manitoba
Nunavut	St. Lawrence River
Vancouver	

FOCUS ON READING AND SPEAKING *my* WriteSmart

11. **Understanding Lists** Use your notes about Canada to create a list of important facts for each section. Organize your lists using this chart.

Physical Geography	History and Culture	Canada Today

12. **Creating a Tourism Ad** Now that you have collected notes on Canada's geography, history, and culture, choose the information you think will most appeal to visitors. Write a one-minute radio script, using descriptive and persuasive language to convince your audience to visit Canada. Use *my*WriteSmart in your eBook to write your script. Describe Canada in a way that will capture your audience's imagination. Ask the class to listen carefully as you read your radio ad to them. Then ask the class to evaluate your ad on how persuasive it was or was not. When viewing other ads make sure to listen and take note of any basic or academic vocabulary terms you may hear.

Reading Social Studies

Understanding Lists

A to-do list can keep you focused on what you need to get done. Keeping lists while you read can keep you focused on understanding the main points of a text. In the example below, a list helps the reader identify and focus on the types of cold climates found in central and northern Canada.

> The farther north you go in Canada, the colder it gets. The coldest areas of Canada are located close to the Arctic Circle. Much of central and northern Canada has a subarctic climate. The far north has tundra and ice cap climates. About half of Canada lies in these extremely cold climates.
>
> *From Section 1, Physical Geography*

List of cold climates
1. subarctic
2. tundra
3. ice cap

YOU TRY IT!

Read the sentences and then list the territories that make up the Canadian North region.

> Northern Canada is extremely cold because of its location close to the Arctic Circle. The region called the Canadian North includes the Yukon Territory, the Northwest Territories, and Nunavut. These three territories cover more than a third of Canada but are home to only about 100,000 people.
>
> *From Section 3, Canada Today*

Mexico

Tijuana

30°N

Gulf of California

25°N

Tropic of Cancer

PACIFIC OCEAN

Essential Question

*my*Notebook

What are the major physical, cultural, and economic features of Mexico?

Texas Essential Knowledge and Skills (TEKS)

1A, 1B, 2A, 2B, 3A, 3B, 3C, 3D, 4B, 4C, 4D, 4E, 4F, 5A, 5B, 5C, 6A, 6B, 15B, 18B, 19B, 21B, 21C, 22D

FOCUS ON READING AND WRITING

my WriteSmart

Predicting Predicting is trying to guess what will happen next. As you read a chapter, stop along the way and consider what you have read. Does the text provide any clues about what will happen next? If it does, see if you can make a prediction about the text. **See the lesson, Predicting, on page 209.**

Writing an "I Am" Poem Countries have stories to tell, just like people do. As you read this chapter, gather details about Mexico—how it looks, what its history was like, and what it is like today. Then write an "I Am" poem from the point of view of Mexico telling what you have learned. Use the annotation tools in your eBook to gather information for your assignment.

map zone

Geography Skills

Location Mexico is located just south of the United States.
1. **Locate** What is the absolute location of Mexico's capital?
2. **Make Inferences** Do you think Tijuana or Mérida is more influenced by the United States? Why?

Culture Brightly costumed dancers perform a traditional dance in Cancún.

HISTORY

Mexico's Ancient
Civilizations

↗ hmhsocialstudies.com **VIDEO**

UNITED STATES

Ciudad
Juárez

Chihuahua

Río Grande

Río Bravo

Monterrey

MEXICO

Gulf of Mexico

○✪ National capital
● Other cities

0   100   200 Miles
0 100 200 Kilometers
Projection: Lambert Conformal Conic

25°N

Tropic of Cancer

N
W E
S

Yucatán
Channel

Cancún

Mérida

Cozumel
Island

20°N

Guadalajara

Río Lerma

Bay of
Campeche

Mexico City
Puebla

Veracruz

Balsas River

Caribbean
Sea

85°W

Oaxaca

Usumacinta R.

Acapulco

Grijalva River

Gulf of
Tehuantepec

**CENTRAL
AMERICA**

105°W

100°W

96°W

90°W

Geography
Much of Mexico's land-
scape is dry, with high
plateaus and mountains.

History The Spanish brought Christianity to
Mexico and built churches like this one.

SECTION 1

Physical Geography

TEKS 3A, 3B, 3C, 4D, 4E, 4F, 5A, 5B, 5C, 6A, 6B, 21B, 21C, 22D

What You Will Learn...

Main Ideas

1. Mexico's physical features include plateaus, mountains, and coastal lowlands.
2. Mexico's climate and vegetation include deserts, tropical forests, and cool highlands.
3. Key natural resources in Mexico include oil, silver, gold, and scenic landscapes.

The Big Idea

Mexico is a large country with different natural environments in its northern, central, and southern regions.

Key Terms and Places

Río Bravo (Rio Grande), *p. 192*
peninsula, *p. 192*
Baja California, *p. 192*
Gulf of Mexico, *p. 192*
Yucatán Peninsula, *p. 192*
Sierra Madre, *p. 193*

hmhsocialstudies.com
TAKING NOTES

Use the graphic organizer online to organize your notes on Mexico's physical geography.

If YOU lived there...

You live on Mexico's Pacific coast. Sunny weather and good beaches bring tourists year-round. Now you are on your way to visit a cousin in Puebla, in the highlands. To get there, you will have to take a bus along the winding roads of the steep Sierra Madre Occidental. This rugged mountain range runs along the coast. You have never been to the interior of Mexico before.

What landscapes will you see on your trip?

BUILDING BACKGROUND Mexico is part of Latin America, a region in the Western Hemisphere where Spanish and Portuguese culture shaped life. Mexico is also part of North America, along with the United States and Canada. Unlike its northern neighbors, Mexico's landscape consists mainly of highlands and coastal plains.

Physical Features

Mexico, our neighbor to the south, shares a long border with the United States. Forming part of this border is one of Mexico's few major rivers, the **Río Bravo**. In the United States this river is called the Rio Grande. At other places along the U.S.–Mexico border it is impossible to tell where one country ends and the other country begins.

Bodies of Water

Locate Mexico on the map on the following page and see that, except for its border with the United States, Mexico is mostly surrounded by water. Mexico's border in the west is the Pacific Ocean. Stretching south into the Pacific Ocean from northern Mexico is a narrow **peninsula**, or piece of land surrounded on three sides by water, called **Baja California**. To the east, Mexico's border is the **Gulf of Mexico**. The Gulf of Mexico is separated from the Caribbean Sea by a part of Mexico called the **Yucatán** (yoo-kah-TAHN) **Peninsula**.

UNITED STATES

30°N

Gulf of California

BAJA CALIFORNIA

Yaqui River

SIERRA MADRE OCCIDENTAL

Conchos R.

Rio Grande

Rio Bravo

SIERRA MADRE ORIENTAL

MEXICAN PLATEAU

25°N

Tropic of Cancer

20°N

Rio Santiago

Rio Lerma

Pánuco R.

Gulf of Mexico

90°W

95°W

YUCATÁN PENINSULA

Yucatán Channel

Cozumel Island

Caribbean Sea

ELEVATION

Feet	Meters
13,120	4,000
6,560	2,000
1,640	500
656	200
(Sea level) 0	0 (Sea level)
Below sea level	Below sea level

0   150   300 Miles
0 150 300 Kilometers

Projection: Lambert Conformal Conic

Popocatépetl
17,887 ft (5,452 m)

Balsas River

SIERRA MADRE DEL SUR

ISTHMUS OF TEHUANTEPEC

Bay of Campeche

Usumacinta R.

Grijalva River

Gulf of Tehuantepec

CENTRAL AMERICA

N W E S

PACIFIC OCEAN

15°N

115°W

105°W

100°W

85°W

map zone

Geography Skills

Regions The rugged Mexican Plateau covers much of Mexico.

1. **Name** What feature extends into the Gulf of Mexico?
2. **Analyze** Where in Mexico would it be easiest to cross from the Pacific Ocean to the Gulf of Mexico?

① Plateaus and mountains cover much of Mexico. Here, the volcano Popocatépetl rises above a mountain valley. Many people live and farm in the mountain valleys.

Plateaus and Mountains

Much of the interior landscape of Mexico consists of a high, mostly rugged region called the Mexican Plateau. The plateau's lowest point is more than a half mile above sea level. Its highest point is close to two miles above sea level. The entire plateau spreads between two mountain ranges that rise still higher. One range, the Sierra Madre Oriental, lies in the east. The other, the Sierra Madre Occidental, lies in the west. Together, these two mountain ranges and another shorter one in southern Mexico make up the **Sierra Madre** (SYER-rah MAH-dray), or "mother range."

Between the two ranges in the south lies the Valley of Mexico. Mexico City, the country's capital, is located there. The mountains south of Mexico City include towering, snowcapped volcanoes. Volcanic eruptions, as well as earthquakes, are a threat there. The volcano Popocatépetl (poh-puh-cah-TE-pet-uhl) near Mexico City has been active as recently as 2010.

FOCUS ON READING

What do you think the text will discuss next?

Coastal Lowlands

From the highlands in central Mexico, the land slopes down to the coasts. Beautiful, sunny beaches stretch all along Mexico's eastern and western coasts. The plain that runs along the west coast is fairly wide in the north. It becomes narrower in the south. On the east side of the country, the Gulf coastal plain is wide and flat. The soils and climate there are good for farming.

ACADEMIC VOCABULARY
vary to be different

Locate the Yucatán Peninsula on the map on the previous page. As you can see this region is also mostly flat. Limestone rock underlies much of the area. Erosion there has created caves and sinkholes, steep-sided depressions that form when the roof of a cave collapses. Many of these sinkholes are filled with water.

READING CHECK **Summarizing** What are Mexico's major physical features?

Climate and Vegetation

From snowcapped mountain peaks to warm, sunny beaches, Mexico has many different climates. You can see Mexico's climate regions on the map below. This great variety of climates results in several different types of vegetation.

In some areas, changes in elevation cause climates to **vary** widely within a short distance. For example, the areas of high elevation on the Mexican Plateau can have surprisingly cool temperatures. At times, freezing temperatures reach as far south as Mexico City—even though it is located in the tropics. Mexico's mountain valleys generally have mild climates, and many people have settled there.

The valleys along Mexico's southern coastal areas also have pleasant climates. Warm temperatures and a summer rainy season support the forests that cover about 25 percent of Mexico's land area. Tropical rain forests provide a home for jaguars, monkeys, anteaters, and other animals.

While most of southern Mexico is warm and humid, the climate in the northern part of the Yucatán Peninsula is hot and dry. The main vegetation there is scrub forest.

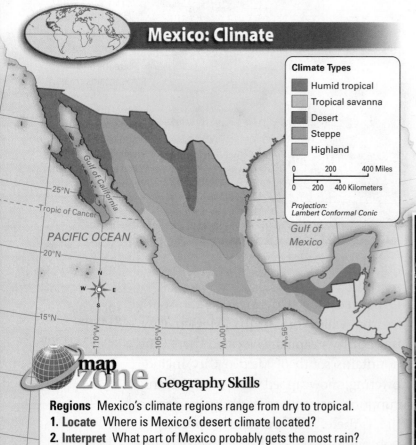

Mexico: Climate

Climate Types
- Humid tropical
- Tropical savanna
- Desert
- Steppe
- Highland

0   200   400 Miles
0   200   400 Kilometers

*Projection:
Lambert Conformal Conic*

25°N
Tropic of Cancer
PACIFIC OCEAN
20°N
15°N
Gulf of California
Gulf of Mexico

map zone **Geography Skills**

Regions Mexico's climate regions range from dry to tropical.
1. **Locate** Where is Mexico's desert climate located?
2. **Interpret** What part of Mexico probably gets the most rain?

A Tropical Climate
A tropical savanna climate supports lush vegetation along Mexico's southern beaches.

Like the Yucatán Peninsula in the south, most of northern Mexico is dry. The deserts in Baja California and the northern part of the plateau get little rainfall. Desert plants and dry grasslands are common in the north. Cougars, coyotes, and deer live in some areas of the desert.

READING CHECK **Analyzing** Why does Mexico City sometimes experience freezing temperatures even though it is in the tropics?

Natural Resources

Mexico is rich in natural resources. One of its most important resources is petroleum, or oil. Oil reserves are found mainly under the southern and Gulf coastal plains as well as offshore in the Gulf of Mexico. Mexico sells much of its oil to the United States.

Before oil was discovered in Mexico, minerals were the country's most valuable resource. Some gold and silver mines that were begun many centuries ago are still in operation. In addition, new mines have been developed in Mexico's mountains. Today Mexico's mines produce more silver than any other country in the world. Mexican mines also yield large amounts of copper, gold, lead, and zinc.

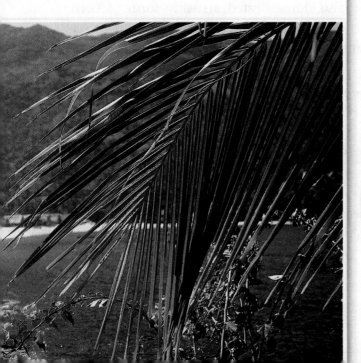

Another important resource is water. The refreshing water surrounding Mexico draws many tourists to the country's scenic beaches. Unfortunately, water is limited in many parts of Mexico. Water scarcity is a serious issue.

READING CHECK **Finding Main Ideas** What is one of Mexico's most important resources?

SUMMARY AND PREVIEW The natural environments of Mexico range from arid plateaus in the north to humid, forested mountains in the south. Next, you will study the history and culture of Mexico.

Section 1 Assessment

hmhsocialstudies.com
ONLINE QUIZ

Reviewing Ideas, Terms, and Places

1. **a. Describe** What is the interior of Mexico like?
   b. Analyze Locate Mexico on the climate map in this section. Do you think the **Yucatán Peninsula** is a good place for farming? Use your notes and the map to explain your answer.
2. **a. Recall** What is the climate like in the northern part of the Yucatán Peninsula?
   b. Explain Why can climates sometimes vary widely within a short distance?
   c. Elaborate How do you think climate and vegetation affect where people live in Mexico?
3. **a. Identify** Where are Mexico's oil reserves located?
   b. Make Inferences What problems might water scarcity cause for Mexican citizens?
   c. Geographic Questions Look at the physical map in this section. Pose and answer a question about Mexico's physical features.

Critical Thinking

4. **Categorizing** Draw a chart like the one here. Using your notes, list the geographical features found in northern Mexico and southern Mexico.

	Geography
Northern Mexico	
Southern Mexico	

FOCUS ON WRITING

my WriteSmart

5. **Telling What Mexico Looks Like** Locate major physical geographic features of places and regions in Mexico on the physical map in this section. What features will you include in your "I Am" poem? Write notes about the physical features, climate and vegetation, and natural resources of Mexico.

History and Culture

TEKS 1A, 1B, 2A, 2B, 3A, 3B, 3C, 3D, 4B, 4C, 4F, 15B, 18B, 19B, 21B, 21C, 22D

What You Will Learn...

Main Ideas

1. Early cultures of Mexico included the Olmec, the Maya, and the Aztec.
2. Mexico's period as a Spanish colony and its struggles since independence have shaped its culture.
3. Spanish and native cultures have influenced Mexico's customs and traditions today.

The Big Idea

Native American cultures and Spanish colonization shaped Mexican history and culture.

Key Terms

empire, *p. 197*
mestizos, *p. 198*
missions, *p. 198*
haciendas, *p. 198*

hmhsocialstudies.com
TAKING NOTES

Use the graphic organizer online to organize your notes on Mexico's history and culture.

If **YOU** lived there...

You belong to one of the native Indian peoples in southern Mexico in the early 1500s. Years ago, the Aztec rulers went to war against your people. They took many captives. They have always treated you cruelly. Now some strangers have come from across the sea. They want your people to help them conquer the Aztecs.

Will you help the strangers fight the Aztecs? Why or why not?

BUILDING BACKGROUND Mexico was home to several of the earliest advanced cultures in the Americas. Early farmers there developed crops that became staples in much of North America. Mexico also has valuable minerals, which drew Spanish conquerors and colonists. Spanish culture blended with native Mexican cultures.

Early Cultures

People first came to Mexico many thousands of years ago. As early as 5,000 years ago, they were growing beans, peppers, and squash. They also domesticated an early form of corn. Farming allowed these people to build the first permanent settlements in the Americas.

Early Cultures of Mexico

Olmec

- The Olmec made sculptures of giant stone heads.

- The heads may have represented rulers or gods.

Olmec

By about 1500 BC the Olmec people in Mexico were living in small villages. The Olmec lived on the humid southern coast of the Gulf of Mexico, where they built temples and giant statues. They also traded carved stones like jade and obsidian with other cultures in eastern Mexico.

Maya

A few hundred years later, the Maya built on the achievements of the Olmec. Between about AD 250 and 900, the Maya built large cities in Mexico and Central America. In these cities they built stone temples to worship their gods. They studied the stars and developed a detailed calendar. They also kept written records that scholars still study today to learn about Maya history. However, scholars do not fully understand why Maya civilization suddenly collapsed sometime after 900.

Aztec

After the decline of the Maya civilization, people called the Aztecs moved to central Mexico from the north. In 1325 they built their capital on an island in a lake. Known as Tenochtitlán (tay-nawch-teet-LAHN), this capital grew into one of the largest and most impressive cities of its time.

The Aztecs also built a large, powerful empire. An **empire** is a land with different territories and peoples under a single ruler.

CONNECTING TO Technology

Chinampas

The Aztecs practiced a form of raised-field farming in the swampy lake areas of central Mexico. They called these raised fields *chinampas*. To make them, Aztec farmers piled earth on rafts anchored to trees in the lake. There they grew the corn, beans, and squash that most people ate.

Analyzing Why do you think the Aztecs decided to build raised fields for their crops?

The Aztecs planted trees in the lake to anchor the rafts.

The Aztecs built their empire through conquest. They defeated their neighboring tribes in war. Then they forced the other people to pay taxes and to provide war captives for sacrifice to the Aztec gods.

READING CHECK **Summarizing** What were some achievements of Mexico's early cultures?

Maya

- The Maya had a trade network between cities.
- This Maya pyramid stands in Uxmal.

Aztec

- The Aztecs built the first empire in the Americas.
- Aztec artisans made art like this turquoise mask.

Colonial Mexico and Independence

FOCUS ON READING
What do you think will happen to the Aztec Empire?

In spite of its great size and power, the Aztec Empire did not last long after the first Europeans landed in Mexico. In 1519 Hernán Cortés, a Spanish soldier, arrived in Mexico with about 600 men. These conquistadors (kahn-KEES-tuh-dawrz), or conquerors, gained allies from other tribes in the region. They also had guns and horses, which the Aztecs had never seen before. The new weapons terrified the Aztecs and gave the Spanish an advantage.

The Spanish also unknowingly brought European diseases such as smallpox. The Aztecs had no resistance to these diseases, so many of them died. Greatly weakened by disease, the Aztecs were defeated. In 1521 Cortés claimed the land for Spain.

Colonial Times

After the conquest, Spanish and American Indian peoples and cultures mixed. This mixing formed a new Mexican identity. Spaniards called people of mixed European and Indian ancestry **mestizos** (me-STEE-zohs). When Africans were brought to America as slaves, they added to this mix of peoples. The Spaniards called people of mixed European and African ancestry mulattoes (muh-LAH-tohs). Africans and American Indians also intermarried.

Life in colonial Mexico was greatly influenced by the Roman Catholic Church. Large areas of northern Mexico were left to the church to explore and to rule. Church outposts known as **missions** were scattered throughout the area. Priests at the missions learned native languages and taught the Indians Spanish. They also worked to convert the American Indians to Catholicism.

In addition to spreading Christianity, the Spaniards wanted to find gold and silver in Mexico. American Indians and enslaved Africans did most of the hard physical labor in the mines. As a result, many died from disease and overwork.

Like mining, agriculture became an important part of the colonial economy. After the conquest, the Spanish monarch granted **haciendas** (hah-see-EN-duhs), or huge expanses of farm or ranch land, to some favored people of Spanish ancestry. Peasants, usually Indians, lived and worked on these haciendas. The haciendas made their owners very wealthy.

Hidalgo Calls for Independence

Miguel Hidalgo (center, in black) calls for independence from Spain in 1810. The famous Mexican painter Juan O'Gorman painted this image.

ANALYZING VISUALS What kinds of people joined Hidalgo in his revolt?

Independence

Spain ruled Mexico for almost 300 years before the people of Mexico demanded independence. The revolt against Spanish rule was led by a Catholic priest named Miguel Hidalgo. In 1810, he gave a famous speech calling for the common people to rise up against the Spanish. Hidalgo was killed in 1811, but fighting continued until Mexico won its independence in 1821.

Later Struggles

Fifteen years after Mexico gained its independence, a large area, Texas, broke away. Eventually, Texas joined the United States. As a result, Mexico and the United States fought over Texas and the location of their shared border. This conflict led to the Mexican-American War, in which Mexico lost nearly half its territory to the United States.

In the mid-1800s, Mexico faced other challenges. During this time, the popular president Benito Juárez helped Mexico survive a French invasion. He also changed Mexican society by making reforms that reduced the privileges of the church and the army.

In spite of these reforms, in the early 1900s the president helped the hacienda owners take land from peasants. Also, foreign companies owned huge amounts of land in Mexico and, in turn, influenced Mexican politics. Many Mexicans thought the president gave these large landowners too many privileges.

As a result, the Mexican Revolution broke out in 1910. The fighting lasted 10 years. One major result of the Mexican Revolution was land reform. The newly formed government took land from the large landowners and gave it back to the peasant villages.

READING CHECK **Sequencing** What events occurred after Mexico gained independence?

BIOGRAPHY

Benito Juárez
(1806–1872)

Benito Juárez was Mexico's first president of Indian heritage. A wise and passionate leader, Juárez stood up for the rights of all Mexicans. As the minister of justice, he got rid of special courts for members of the church and the military. As president, he passed reforms that laid the foundation for a democratic government. Today he is considered a national hero in Mexico.

Drawing Conclusions How may Juárez's heritage have affected his efforts for Mexico's citizens?

Culture

Mexico's history has **influenced** its culture. For example, one major influence from history is language. Most Mexicans speak Spanish because of the Spanish influence in colonial times. Another influence from Spain is religion. About 90 percent of all Mexicans are Roman Catholic.

However, Mexico's culture also reflects its American Indian heritage. For example, many people still speak American Indian languages. In Mexico, a person's language is tied to his or her ethnic group. Speaking an American Indian language identifies a person as Indian.

Mexicans also have some unique cultural practices that combine elements of Spanish influence with the influence of Mexican Indians. An example of this combining can be seen in a holiday called Day of the Dead. This holiday is a day to remember and honor dead ancestors.

ACADEMIC VOCABULARY

influence change or have an effect on

VIDEO
The Peasant Revolution
hmhsocialstudies.com

Day of the Dead

Everyone is sad when a loved one dies. But during Day of the Dead, Mexicans celebrate death as part of life. This attitude comes from the Mexican Indian belief that the souls of the dead return every year to visit their living relatives. To prepare for this visit, Mexican families gather in graveyards. They clean up around their loved one's grave and decorate it with flowers and candles. They also set out food and drink for the celebration. Favorite foods often include sugar candy skulls, chocolate coffins, and sweet breads shaped like bones.

Summarizing Why do Mexicans celebrate Day of the Dead?

Mexicans celebrate Day of the Dead on November 1 and 2. These dates are similar to the dates that the Catholic Church honors the dead with All Souls' Day. The holiday also reflects native customs and beliefs about hopes of life after death.

READING CHECK **Categorizing** What aspects of Mexican culture show the influence of Spanish rule?

SUMMARY AND PREVIEW Mexico's early cultures formed great civilizations, but after the conquest of the Aztec Empire, power in Mexico shifted to Spain. Spain ruled Mexico for nearly 300 years before Mexico gained independence. Mexico's history and its mix of Indian and Spanish backgrounds have influenced the country's culture. In the next section you will learn about life in Mexico today.

Section 2 Assessment

hmhsocialstudies.com
ONLINE QUIZ

Reviewing Ideas, Terms, and Places

1. a. Recall Where in Mexico did the Olmec live?
   b. Explain How did the Aztecs build and rule their **empire**?
   c. Elaborate Why do you think scholars are not sure what caused the end of Maya civilization?

2. a. Identify Who began the revolt that led to Mexico's independence?
   b. Evaluate What social contributions did Benito Juárez make to Mexican society?
   c. Predict How may history have been different if the Aztecs had defeated the Spanish?

3. a. Identify What Mexican holiday honors dead ancestors?
   b. Summarize How did Mexico's colonial past shape its culture?

Critical Thinking

4. Sequencing Draw a diagram like the one below. Then, using your notes, list the major events in Mexico's history in the order they happened.

FOCUS ON WRITING

my WriteSmart

5. Learning about History and Culture Mexico's history is full of fascinating stories. In your notebook, jot down ideas about relationships between past conflicts in Mexico's history. What effects do you think these past relationships have on current conditions in Mexico today?

Social Studies Skills

Taking Notes

Learn

Taking notes can help you remember what you have learned from your textbook or in class. To be effective, your notes must be clear and organized. One good way to organize your notes is in a chart like the one here. Use the following steps to help you take useful notes:

- Before you read or listen: Divide a page in your notebook into two columns as shown.

- While you read or listen: Write down your notes in phrases or sentences in the large column on the right.

- After you read or listen: Review your notes. Then in the small column on the left, jot down ideas, key terms, or questions in your own words based on the notes you took.

Recall	Notes
New Mexican identity	- Spanish and American Indian cultures mixed. - mestizos - Africans came as slaves.

Influence on Catholic Church	- Life in colonial Mexico was influenced by the Roman Catholic Church.
	  - missions
	  - Priests taught Spanish.

Economy: mining and agriculture	- Spaniards were interested in gold and silver.
	  - American Indians and enslaved Africans worked in mines.
	- Agriculture was important.
	  - haciendas

Practice

Answer the following questions about taking notes.

1. Where should you write your notes while you read or listen in class?

2. How can jotting down key ideas, terms, and questions help you clarify your notes after you take them?

Apply

Look back at Section 1 of this chapter. Divide your paper into two columns and take notes on the section using the suggestions above. Then answer the following questions.

1. What ideas or questions did you write in the Recall column on the left?

2. What are some advantages of taking notes?

TEKS 1A, 1B, 2A, 2B, 3A, 3B, 3C, 3D, 4B, 4C, 4F, 12B, 15A, 15B, 18B, 21B, 21C, 22D

What You Will Learn...

Main Ideas

1. Government has traditionally played a large role in Mexico's economy.
2. Mexico has four distinct culture regions.

The Big Idea

Mexico has four culture regions that all play a part in the country's government and economy.

Key Terms and Places

inflation, *p. 202*
slash-and-burn agriculture, *p. 203*
cash crop, *p. 203*
Mexico City, *p. 204*
smog, *p. 204*
maquiladoras, *p. 205*

hmhsocialstudies.com
TAKING NOTES

Use the graphic organizer online to take notes on Mexico's government and economy.

Mexico Today

If YOU lived there...

For many years, your family has lived in a small village in southern Mexico. Jobs are scarce there. Your older brother and sisters talk about moving to a larger city. Big cities may provide some more opportunities, but they can be crowded and noisy. Many people from your village have already gone to the city.

How do you feel about moving to the city?

BUILDING BACKGROUND After Mexico gained independence, many government leaders did not rule democratically. For years the Mexican people had little say in their government. But changes in the 1990s and 2000s led toward more democracy and prosperity.

Government and Economy

Today people in Mexico can vote in certain elections for the first time. People can find jobs in cities and buy their families a home. More children are able to attend school. In recent years, changes in Mexico's government and economy have made improvements like these possible.

Government

Mexico has a democratic government. However, Mexico is not like the United States where different political parties have always competed for power. In Mexico the same political party, the Institutional Revolutionary Party (PRI), controlled the government for 71 years. But this control ended in 2000 when Mexicans elected Vicente Fox their president. Fox represented a different political party. However, in 2012 the PRI assumed the office of president again when Mexicans elected Enrique Peña Nieto. As president, Peña Nieto hopes to improve Mexico's economy and reduce drug-related violence.

Economy

Mexico is a developing country. It has struggled with debts to foreign banks, unemployment, and inflation. **Inflation** is a rise in prices that occurs when currency loses its buying power.

Although living standards in Mexico are lower than in many other countries, Mexico's economy is growing. The North American Free Trade Agreement (NAFTA), which took effect in 1994, has made trade among Mexico, the United States, and Canada easier. Mexico's agricultural and industrial exports have increased since NAFTA went into effect.

Agriculture Agriculture has long been a key part of the Mexican economy. This is true even though just 13 percent of the land is good for farming. Many farmers in southern Mexico practice **slash-and-burn agriculture**, which is the practice of burning forest in order to clear land for planting.

The high market demand for food in the United States has encouraged many farmers in Mexico to grow cash crops. A **cash crop** is a crop that farmers grow mainly to sell for a profit. Trucks bring cash crops like fruits and vegetables from Mexico to the United States.

Industry Oil is also an important export for Mexico. Many Mexicans work in the oil, mining, and manufacturing industries. These industries are growing.

The fastest-growing industrial centers in Mexico lie along the U.S. border. Because wages are relatively low in Mexico, many U.S. and foreign companies have built factories in Mexico. Mexican workers in these factories assemble goods for export to the United States and other countries. Some Mexican workers also come to the United States to look for jobs that pay more than they can make at home.

Tourism Tourism is another important part of Mexico's economy. Many tourists visit old colonial cities and Maya and Aztec monuments. Coastal cities and resorts such as Cancún and Acapulco are also popular with tourists.

READING CHECK **Summarizing** How has NAFTA affected Mexico's economy?

VIDEO
Mexico in the Modern Era
hmhsocialstudies.com

Satellite View

Smoke

Fire

Many people in Mexico are subsistence farmers. They do not own much land and grow only enough food to feed their families. To gain more land, farmers in southern Mexico burn patches of forest. The fires clear the trees and kill weeds, and ash from the fires fertilizes the soil. However, growing the same crops year after year drains valuable nutrients from the soil. The farmers then have to burn new forest land.

In the satellite image here, agricultural fires appear as red dots. As you can see, the fires create a lot of smoke. Wind then blows the smoke great distances. Every few years, when the conditions are right, smoke from agricultural fires in Mexico reaches as far as the southern United States. The smoke can cause health problems for some people.

Analyzing What direction was the wind blowing in this image?

Northern Mexico Northern Mexico's land is generally too dry to be much good for farming, but ranching is an important part of the region's economy.

ANALYSIS SKILL **ANALYZING INFORMATION**

How do you think life in greater Mexico City differs from life in northern Mexico?

Central Mexico The architecture and cobblestone streets of many towns in central Mexico reflect the region's Spanish colonial heritage.

Mexico's Culture Regions

Although all Mexicans share some cultural characteristics, we can divide Mexico into four regions based on regional differences. These four culture regions differ from each other in their population, resources, climate, and other features.

Greater Mexico City

Greater Mexico City includes the capital and about 50 smaller cities near it. With a population of about 20 million, **Mexico City** is one of the world's largest and most densely populated urban areas. Thousands of people move there every year looking for work.

While this region does provide job and educational opportunities not so easily found in the rest of the country, its huge population causes problems. For example, Mexico City is very polluted. Factories and cars release exhaust and other pollutants into the air. The surrounding mountains trap the resulting **smog**—a mixture of smoke, chemicals, and fog. Smog can cause health problems like eye irritation and breathing difficulties.

Another problem that comes from crowding is poverty. Wealth and poverty exist side by side in Mexico City. The city has large urban slums. The slums often exist right next to modern office buildings, apartments, museums, or universities.

Greater Mexico City Traffic clogs Mexico City's busy streets. Taxis, buses, and private cars zoom past modern office buildings and old colonial government buildings.

Southern Mexico While poverty is a problem in much of southern Mexico, some people make money selling traditional handicrafts to tourists.

Central Mexico

North of greater Mexico City lies Mexico's central region. Many cities in this region were established as mining or ranching centers during the colonial period. Mexico's colonial heritage can still be seen today in these cities and towns. For example, small towns often have a colonial-style church near a main central square. The central square, or plaza, has served for hundreds of years as a community meeting spot and market area.

In addition to small colonial towns, central Mexico has many fertile valleys and small family farms. Farmers in this region grow vegetables, corn, and wheat for sale, mostly to cities in Mexico.

While central Mexico has always been a mining center, in recent years the region has also attracted new industries from overcrowded Mexico City. As a result, some cities in the region, such as Guadalajara, are growing rapidly.

Northern Mexico

Northern Mexico has become one of the country's richest and most modern areas. Trade with the United States has helped the region's economy grow. Monterrey and Tijuana are now major cities there. Many U.S.- and foreign-owned factories called **maquiladoras** (mah-kee-lah-DORH-ahs) have been built along Mexico's long border with the United States.

ACADEMIC VOCABULARY

affect to change or influence

Northern Mexico's closeness to the border has **affected** the region's culture as well as its economy. American television, music, and other forms of entertainment are popular there. Many Mexicans cross the border to shop, work, or live in the United States. While many people cross the border legally, the U.S. government tries to prevent Mexicans and others from crossing the border illegally.

Southern Mexico

Southern Mexico is the least populated and industrialized region of the country. Many people in this region speak Indian languages and practice traditional ways of life. Subsistence farming and slash-and-burn agriculture are common.

FOCUS ON READING

What do you think makes southern Mexico vital to the country's economy?

However, southern Mexico is vital to the country's economy. Sugarcane and coffee, two major export crops, grow well in the region's warm, humid climate. Also, oil production along the Gulf coast has increased in recent years. The oil business has brought more industry and population growth to this coastal area of southern Mexico.

Another place in southern Mexico that has grown in recent years is the Yucatán Peninsula. Maya ruins, beautiful sunny beaches, and clear blue water have made tourism a major industry in this area. Many cities that were just tiny fishing villages only 20 years ago are now booming with new construction for the tourist industry.

Mexico will continue to change in the future. Changes are likely to bring more development. However, maintaining the country's unique regional cultures may be a challenge as those changes take place.

READING CHECK **Comparing and Contrasting** What similarities and differences exist between greater Mexico City and southern Mexico?

SUMMARY AND PREVIEW Mexico has a democratic government and a growing economy. It also has distinct regions with different cultures, economies, and environments. In the next chapter you will learn about the countries to the south of Mexico.

Section 3 Assessment

hmhsocialstudies.com
ONLINE QUIZ

Reviewing Ideas, Terms, and Places

1. **a. Define** What is the term for the practice of burning forest in order to clear land for planting?
   b. Compare and Contrast How is Mexico's government similar to and different from the government of the United States?
2. **a. Identify** What is an environmental problem found in **Mexico City**?
   b. Make Inferences What conditions in Mexico lead some Mexicans to cross the border into the United States?
   c. Develop If you were to start a business in Mexico, what type of business would you start and where would you start it? Explain your decisions.

Critical Thinking

3. **Finding Main Ideas** Review your notes on Mexico's economy. Then use a chart like this one to identify the geographic factors responsible for the location of economic activities in each region of Mexico.

Greater Mexico City	Central Mexico	Northern Mexico	Southern Mexico

FOCUS ON WRITING

my WriteSmart

4. **Describing Mexico Today** Write some details about the four culture regions of Mexico. Which details will you include in your poem?

Chapter Review

Visual Summary

Use the visual summary below to help you review the main ideas of the chapter.

QUICK FACTS

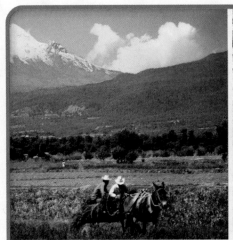

The physical geography of Mexico includes a high region of plateaus and mountains.

The Spanish conquered the Aztecs and ruled Mexico for about 300 years until the Mexicans gained independence.

Greater Mexico City, one of Mexico's four culture regions, is the center of Mexico's government and economy.

Reviewing Vocabulary, Terms, and Places

Unscramble each group of letters below to spell a term that matches the given definition.

1. **pmreie**—a land with different territories and peoples under a single ruler

2. **tflinnaoi**—a rise in prices that occurs when currency loses its buying power

3. **mogs**—a mixture of smoke, chemicals, and fog

4. **snipluane**—a piece of land surrounded on three sides by water

5. **ztosemsi**—people of mixed European and Indian ancestry

6. **hacs rpoc**—a crop that farmers grow mainly to sell for a profit

7. **ssnmiosi**—church outposts

8. **dqamiuarsloa**—U.S.- and foreign-owned factories in Mexico

9. **ndhceiasa**—expanses of farm or ranch land

Comprehension and Critical Thinking

SECTION 1 *(Pages 192–195)*

10. **a. Define** What is the Mexican Plateau? What forms its edges?

    b. Contrast How does the climate of Mexico City differ from the climate in the south?

    c. Evaluate What do you think would be Mexico's most important resource if it did not have oil? Explain your answer.

SECTION 2 *(Pages 196–200)*

11. **a. Recall** What early civilization did the Spanish conquer when they came to Mexico?

    b. Analyze How did Spanish rule influence Mexico's culture?

    c. Evaluate Which war—the war for independence, the Mexican War, or the Mexican Revolution—do you think changed Mexico the most? Explain your answer.

12. a. Describe What are Mexico's four culture regions? Describe a feature of each.

b. Analyze What regions do you think are the most popular with tourists? Explain your answer.

c. Evaluate What are two major drawbacks of slash-and-burn agriculture?

Using the Internet

13. Activity: Writing a Description Colorful textiles, paintings, and pottery are just some of the many crafts made throughout Mexico. Each region in Mexico has its own style of crafts and folk art. Through your online textbook, visit some of the different regions of Mexico and explore their arts and crafts. Pick a favorite object from each region. Learn about its use, its design, how it was made, and the people who made it. Then write a brief paragraph that describes each object and its unique characteristics.

↗ hmhsocialstudies.com

Social Studies Skills

14. Taking Notes With a partner read Section 3 about Mexico's government and economy to each other. As you listen to your partner, use a chart like this one to take notes on the information from your book.

Recall	Notes

Map Activity

15. Mexico On a separate sheet of paper, match the letters on the map with their correct labels.

Gulf of Mexico   Baja California

Río Bravo (Rio Grande)   Tijuana

Yucatán Peninsula   Mexico City

FOCUS ON READING AND WRITING   *my* WriteSmart

16. Predicting Now you can use your skills in predicting to think about events that might happen in the future. Reread the text in your book about Mexico's economy. Use *my*WriteSmart in your eBook to write three to four sentences about how you think the economy might change in the future.

17. Writing an "I Am" Poem Use myWriteSmart in your eBook to write your poem. Title your poem "I am Mexico" and make it six lines long. Use each line to give details about Mexico, such as "I have towering, snowcapped volcanoes." Make sure at least one line deals with physical geography, one line with history and culture, and one line with Mexico today. Your poem does not need to rhyme, but you should try to use vivid language. With a partner recite your poems to each other.

Predicting

FOCUS ON READING

Predicting is guessing what will happen next based on what you already know. In reading about geography, you can use what you know about the place you live to help you make predictions about other countries. Predicting helps you stay involved with your reading as you see whether your prediction was right. Your mind follows these four steps when you make predictions as you read:

Takes what you already know → Adds new information from your reading → Forms a prediction that makes sense → Confirms or adjusts your prediction based on what you just read

See how you might make a prediction from the following text:

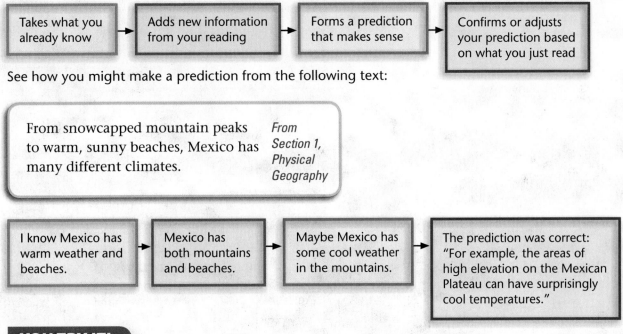

From snowcapped mountain peaks to warm, sunny beaches, Mexico has many different climates.

From Section 1, Physical Geography

I know Mexico has warm weather and beaches. → Mexico has both mountains and beaches. → Maybe Mexico has some cool weather in the mountains. → The prediction was correct: "For example, the areas of high elevation on the Mexican Plateau can have surprisingly cool temperatures."

YOU TRY IT!

Read the following sentences. Then use a graphic organizer like the one below to help you predict what you will learn in your reading. Check the text in Section 3 to see if your prediction was correct.

Mexico has a democratic government. However, Mexico is not like the United States where different political parties have always competed for power.

From Section 3, Mexico Today

What you already know → New information → Your prediction → Check your prediction

Mexico

Teotihuacán, established around 200 B.C., was the first great civilization of ancient Mexico. At its height around the middle of the first millennium A.D., the "City of the Gods" was one of the largest cities in the world. It covered 12 square miles and was home to some 200,000 people. The Pyramid of the Sun, above, was the largest building in Teotihuacán.

For centuries after the fall of Teotihuacán, present-day Mexico was home to a number of great empires, including the highly sophisticated Aztec civilization. The arrival of the Spanish in the early 1500s forever changed life for Mexico's ancient peoples, and Mexican culture today is dominated by a blend of indigenous and Spanish cultures.

Explore the history of Mexico from ancient to modern times online. You can find a wealth of information, video clips, primary sources, activities, and more at ⬈ hmhsocialstudies.com .

The Arrival of the Spanish

Watch the video to learn how the arrival of the conquistadors led to the fall of the Aztec Empire.

Miguel Hidalgo's Call to Arms

Watch the video to learn about Miguel Hidalgo's path from priest to revolutionary leader.

Mexico in the Modern Era

Watch the video to learn about the role of oil in the industrialization of Mexico's economy.

Mexico's Ancient Civilizations

Watch the video to learn about the great civilizations that arose in ancient Mexico.

Central America and the Caribbean

Gulf of Mexico

Essential Question

myNotebook

How have Central America and the Caribbean been shaped by geography and history?

Texas Essential Knowledge and Skills (TEKS)

1A, 1B, 2A, 2B, 3B, 3C, 3D, 4B, 4C, 4D, 4E, 4F, 15A, 15B, 15D, 18A, 18B, 21A, 21B, 21C, 22D

FOCUS ON READING AND WRITING

my WriteSmart

Understanding Comparison-Contrast When you compare, you look for ways in which things are alike. When you contrast, you look for ways in which things are different. As you read the chapter, look for ways you can compare and contrast information. **See the lesson, Understanding Comparison-Contrast, on page 233.**

Creating a Travel Guide People use travel guides to learn more about places they want to visit. As you read about Central America and the Caribbean in this chapter, you will collect information about places tourists might visit. Then you will create your own travel guide for visitors to one of these vacation spots. Use the annotation tools in your eBook to gather information for your assignment.

MEXICO

Usumacinta River

Belmopan
BELIZE

GUATEMALA
Guatemala City
Motagua R.

HONDURAS
Tegucigalpa
Coco River

San Salvador
EL SALVADOR

PACIFIC OCEAN

NICARAGUA
Managua
San Juan River

⊕ National capital

0   100   200 Miles
0 100 200 Kilometers

Projection: Azimuthal Equal-Area

COSTA RICA
San José

History The Spanish built forts like this one in Puerto Rico to defend their islands and protect the harbors from pirates.

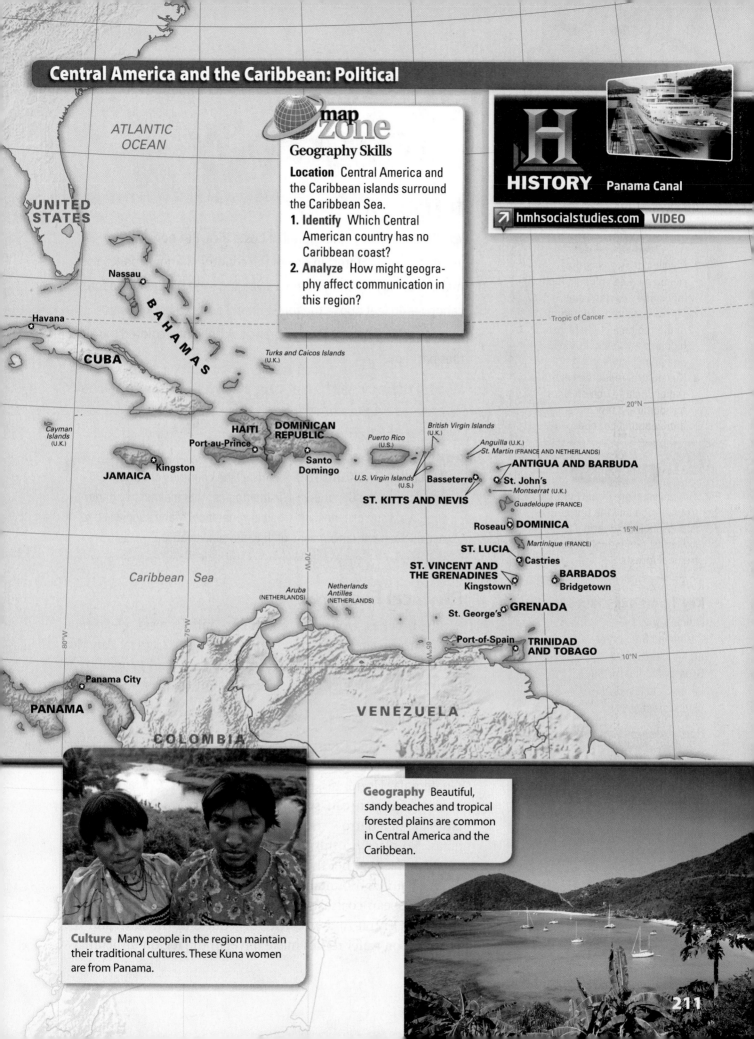

Central America and the Caribbean: Political

ATLANTIC OCEAN

UNITED STATES

map zone
Geography Skills

Location Central America and the Caribbean islands surround the Caribbean Sea.

1. **Identify** Which Central American country has no Caribbean coast?
2. **Analyze** How might geography affect communication in this region?

HISTORY Panama Canal

hmhsocialstudies.com VIDEO

Nassau

Havana

BAHAMAS

CUBA

Tropic of Cancer

Turks and Caicos Islands (U.K.)

20°N

Cayman Islands (U.K.)

HAITI

DOMINICAN REPUBLIC

Port-au-Prince

Santo Domingo

Puerto Rico (U.S.)

British Virgin Islands (U.K.)

Anguilla (U.K.)

St. Martin (FRANCE AND NETHERLANDS)

ANTIGUA AND BARBUDA

Kingston

JAMAICA

U.S. Virgin Islands (U.S.)

Basseterre

St. John's

Montserrat (U.K.)

ST. KITTS AND NEVIS

Guadeloupe (FRANCE)

Roseau **DOMINICA**

15°N

Caribbean Sea

Martinique (FRANCE)

ST. LUCIA

Castries

ST. VINCENT AND THE GRENADINES

Kingstown

BARBADOS

Bridgetown

Aruba (NETHERLANDS)

Netherlands Antilles (NETHERLANDS)

St. George's **GRENADA**

Port-of-Spain **TRINIDAD AND TOBAGO**

10°N

80°W

75°W

70°W

65°W

Panama City

PANAMA

VENEZUELA

COLOMBIA

Geography Beautiful, sandy beaches and tropical forested plains are common in Central America and the Caribbean.

Culture Many people in the region maintain their traditional cultures. These Kuna women are from Panama.

211

Physical Geography

TEKS 3A, 3B, 3C, 4D, 4E, 5A, 5B, 5C, 6A, 6B, 21B, 21C, 22D

What You Will Learn...

Main Ideas

1. Physical features of the region include volcanic highlands and coastal plains.
2. The climate and vegetation of the region include forested highlands, tropical forests, and humid lowlands.
3. Key natural resources in the region include rich soils for agriculture, a few minerals, and beautiful beaches.

The Big Idea

The physical geography of Central America and the Caribbean islands includes warm coastal lowlands, cooler highlands, and tropical forests.

Key Terms and Places

isthmus, *p. 212*
Caribbean Sea, *p. 212*
archipelago, *p. 213*
Greater Antilles, *p. 213*
Lesser Antilles, *p. 213*
cloud forest, *p. 214*

hmhsocialstudies.com
TAKING NOTES

Use the graphic organizer online to take notes on the physical geography of Central America and the Caribbean.

If YOU lived there...

You live in San José, the capital of Costa Rica. But now you are visiting a tropical forest in one of the country's national parks. You make your way carefully along a swinging rope bridge in the forest canopy—40 feet above the forest floor! You see a huge green iguana making its way along a branch. A brilliantly colored parrot flies past you.

What other creatures might you see in the forest?

BUILDING BACKGROUND Nearly all the countries of Central America and the Caribbean lie in the tropics. That means they generally have warm climates and tropical vegetation. Many people like to visit these countries because of their physical beauty.

Physical Features

Sandy beaches, volcanic mountains, rain forests, clear blue water—these are images many people have of Central America and the Caribbean islands. This region's physical geography is beautiful. This beauty is one of the region's greatest resources.

Central America

The region called Central America is actually the southern part of North America. Seven countries make up this region: Belize, Guatemala, Honduras, El Salvador, Nicaragua, Costa Rica, and Panama. As you can see on the map, Central America is an **isthmus**, or a narrow strip of land that connects two larger land areas. No place on this isthmus is more than about 125 miles (200 km) from either the Pacific Ocean or the **Caribbean Sea**.

A chain of mountains and volcanoes separates the Pacific and Caribbean coastal plains, and only a few short rivers flow through Central America. The ruggedness of the land and the lack of good water routes make travel in the region difficult.

ELEVATION

Feet	Meters
13,120	4,000
6,560	2,000
1,640	500
656	200
(Sea level) 0	0 (Sea level)
Below sea level	Below sea level

0   200   400 Miles
0   200   400 Kilometers

Projection: Azimuthal Equal-Area

Gulf of Mexico

ATLANTIC OCEAN

Tropic of Cancer

Straits of Florida

BAHAMAS

CUBA

20°N

Yucatán Peninsula

HAITI   DOMINICAN REPUBLIC

JAMAICA

Hispaniola

ANTIGUA AND BARBUDA

Greater Antilles

BELIZE

GUATEMALA

ST. KITTS AND NEVIS

DOMINICA

HONDURAS

Caribbean Sea

ST. LUCIA

Lesser Antilles

EL SALVADOR   NICARAGUA

BARBADOS

ST. VINCENT AND THE GRENADINES

GRENADA

10°N

Lake Nicaragua

Panama Canal

TRINIDAD AND TOBAGO

PACIFIC OCEAN   COSTA RICA

PANAMA

Gulf of Panama

Coastal plains, like this one in Cuba, are found in Central America and the Caribbean islands.

mapzone

Geography Skills

Location The countries of Central America and the Caribbean have easy access to the sea.

1. **Locate** On which island is Haiti located?
2. **Contrast** How do you think life in Honduras differs from life in the Bahamas?

The Caribbean Islands

Across the Caribbean Sea from Central America lie hundreds of islands known as the Caribbean islands. They make up an **archipelago** (ahr-kuh-PE-luh-goh), or large group of islands. Arranged in a long curve, the Caribbean islands stretch from the southern tip of Florida to northern South America. They divide the Caribbean Sea from the Atlantic Ocean.

There are two main island groups in the Caribbean. The four large islands of Cuba, Jamaica, Hispaniola, and Puerto Rico make up the **Greater Antilles** (an-TI-leez). Many smaller islands form the **Lesser Antilles**. They stretch from the Virgin Islands to Trinidad and Tobago. A third island group, the Bahamas, lies in the Atlantic Ocean southeast of Florida. It includes nearly 700 islands and thousands of reefs.

FOCUS ON READING

How are the Greater and Lesser Antilles different?

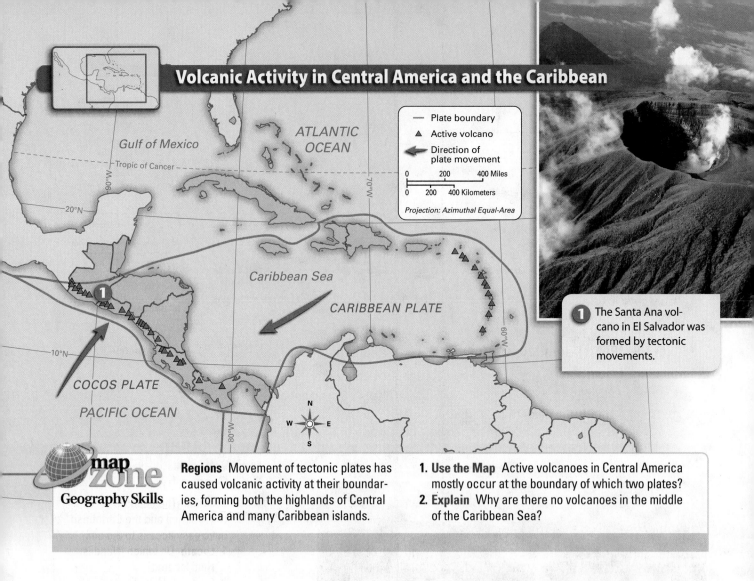

Volcanic Activity in Central America and the Caribbean

ATLANTIC OCEAN

Gulf of Mexico

Tropic of Cancer

20°N

Caribbean Sea

CARIBBEAN PLATE

COCOS PLATE

PACIFIC OCEAN

10°N

Plate boundary
▲ Active volcano
← Direction of plate movement

0   200   400 Miles
0   200   400 Kilometers

Projection: Azimuthal Equal-Area

1 The Santa Ana volcano in El Salvador was formed by tectonic movements.

map zone
Geography Skills

Regions Movement of tectonic plates has caused volcanic activity at their boundaries, forming both the highlands of Central America and many Caribbean islands.

1. **Use the Map** Active volcanoes in Central America mostly occur at the boundary of which two plates?
2. **Explain** Why are there no volcanoes in the middle of the Caribbean Sea?

Many Caribbean islands are actually the tops of underwater mountains and volcanoes. Others began as coral reefs that were gradually pushed up to become flat limestone islands. Colliding tectonic plates have pushed this region's land up out of the sea over several million years. You can see these tectonic plates on the map above. Notice how the land follows the boundaries of the plates. Earthquakes and volcanic eruptions occur frequently as these plates shift. When such events do occur, they can cause great damage to the region and its people.

READING CHECK **Comparing** What physical features do Central America and the Caribbean islands have in common?

Climate and Vegetation

Central America and the Caribbean islands are generally sunny and warm. Humid tropical and tropical savanna climates are common in the islands and on Central America's coastal plains. On the Pacific coast, much of the area's original savanna vegetation has been cleared. It has been replaced by plantations and ranches. The opposite coast, along the Caribbean, has areas of tropical rain forest.

Inland mountain areas contain cool, humid climates. Some mountainous parts of Central America are covered with dense cloud forest. A **cloud forest** is a moist, high-elevation tropical forest where low clouds are common. These forests are home to numerous plant and animal species.

Temperatures in most of Central America and the Caribbean do not change much from day to night or from summer to winter. Instead, the change in seasons is marked by a change in rainfall. Winters in the region are generally dry, while it rains nearly every day during the summers.

From summer to fall, hurricanes are a threat in the region. These tropical storms bring violent winds, heavy rain, and high seas. Most hurricanes occur between June and November. Their winds and flooding can cause destruction and loss of life.

READING CHECK **Generalizing** Where would one find the coolest temperatures in the region?

Resources

The region's best resources are its land and climate. These factors make tourism an important industry. They also influence agriculture. Agriculture in the region can be profitable where volcanic ash has enriched the soil. Coffee, bananas, sugarcane, and cotton grow well and are major crops. Timber is exported from the rain forests.

Although its land and climate make good agricultural resources, the region has few mineral resources. Energy resources are also limited. Central America and the Caribbean islands must rely on energy imports, which limits their development.

READING CHECK **Analyzing** Why would having few energy resources limit economic development?

SUMMARY AND PREVIEW Central America and the Caribbean islands share volcanic physical features and a warm, tropical climate good for agriculture. In the next section you will learn about the history and culture of Central America.

Satellite View

Strong hurricane winds spin around a calm center point called the eye.

Hurricane Isabel

Hurricanes are rotating storms that bring heavy rain and winds that can reach speeds higher than 155 miles per hour (249 kph). This image shows Hurricane Isabel sweeping through the Caribbean Sea in 2003. Strong hurricanes like this one can shatter houses and hurl cars through the air.

Analyzing How can you tell the storm is rotating?

Section 1 Assessment

hmhsocialstudies.com
ONLINE QUIZ

Reviewing Ideas, Terms, and Places

1. **a. Define** What is an **isthmus**?
   b. Explain How has tectonic activity affected Central America and the Caribbean islands?
2. **a. Describe** What is a **cloud forest**?
   b. Make Inferences Why do temperatures in the region change little from summer to winter?
3. **a. Recall** What crops grow well in the region?
   b. Evaluate Do you think tourists who want to go to the beach are more likely to visit Guatemala or the Bahamas? Explain your answer.

Critical Thinking

4. **Categorizing** Draw a diagram like the one here. Using your notes, write descriptive phrases about the physical features, climate, and resources of both places.

Central America	Caribbean Islands

FOCUS ON WRITING

5. **Writing about Geography** What information about the physical geography of the region might interest readers of your travel guide? Jot down some ideas.

TEKS 1A, 1B, 2B, 15A, 15B, 18A

Central America

If YOU lived there...

You live in El Salvador, in a town that is still living with the effects of a civil war 20 years ago. Your parents and your older neighbors still speak about those years with fear. One effect of the war was damage to the economy. Many people have gone to Mexico to try to make a better life. Now your parents are talking about going there to look for work. But you are not sure.

How do you feel about leaving your home?

BUILDING BACKGROUND All the countries of Central America were once colonies of European nations. Years of colonial rule made it hard for most of these countries to establish strong economies or democratic governments. Today things are slowly improving.

History

Many countries of Central America have a shared history. This shared history has been influenced by the Maya, the Spanish, and the United States.

Early History

In several Central American countries, the Maya were building large cities with pyramids and temples by about AD 250. The Maya abandoned most of their cities around 900, but the ruins of many ancient cities still stand in the region today. People of Maya descent still live in Guatemala and Belize. In fact, many ancient Maya customs still influence modern life there.

Hundreds of years later, in the early 1500s, most of Central America came under European control. Spain claimed most of the region. Britain claimed what is now Belize and also occupied part of Nicaragua's coast. The Spanish established large plantations in their colonies to grow crops like tobacco and sugarcane. They made Central American Indians work on the plantations or in gold mines elsewhere in the Americas. In addition, Europeans brought many enslaved Africans to the region to work on plantations and in mines.

One-Crop Economies

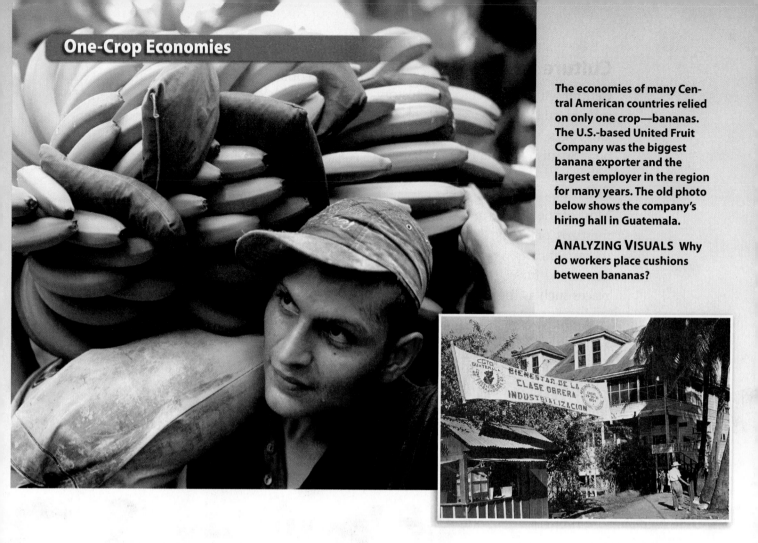

The economies of many Central American countries relied on only one crop—bananas. The U.S.-based United Fruit Company was the biggest banana exporter and the largest employer in the region for many years. The old photo below shows the company's hiring hall in Guatemala.

ANALYZING VISUALS Why do workers place cushions between bananas?

Central America Since Independence

The Spanish colonies of Central America declared independence from Spain in 1821, but much of the region remained joined together as the United Provinces of Central America. The countries of Costa Rica, Nicaragua, Honduras, El Salvador, and Guatemala separated from each other in 1838 to 1839. Panama remained part of Colombia until 1903. Belize did not gain independence from Britain until 1981.

For most countries in Central America, independence brought little change. The Spanish officials left, but wealthy landowners continued to run the countries and their economies. The plantation crops of bananas and coffee supported Central American economies.

In the early to mid-1900s, one landowner in particular, the U.S.-based United Fruit Company, controlled most of the banana production in Central America. To help its business, the company developed railroads and port facilities. This kind of development helped transportation and communications in the region.

Many people resented the role of foreign companies, however. They thought it was wrong that only a few people should own so much land while many people struggled to make a living. In the mid- to late 1900s, demands for reforms led to armed struggles in Guatemala, El Salvador, and Nicaragua. Only in recent years have these countries achieved peace.

READING CHECK **Evaluating** How did Spain influence the region's history?

Culture

Central America's colonial history has influenced its culture. The region's people, languages, religion, and festivals reflect both Spanish and native practices.

People and Languages

Most of the people in Central America are mestizos, or people of mixed European and Indian ancestry. Various Indian peoples descended from the ancient Maya live in places such as the Guatemalan Highlands.

People of African ancestry also make up a significant minority in this region. They live mostly along the Caribbean coast.

In some countries in Central America, many people still speak the native Indian languages. In places that were colonized by England, English is spoken. For example, it is the official language of Belize. In most countries, however, Spanish is the official language. The Spanish colonization of Central America left this lasting mark on the region.

Close-up

A Market in Guatemala

Villages in Guatemala and all over Central America hold weekly markets. On market day, people come from all around to buy and sell food and other items. The market is also an important gathering spot for the community. Scenes like this one are typical in the region.

The Catholic church is a major influence in most towns.

Patterns on women's clothing are unique to the village where the woman lives.

Religion, Festivals, and Food

Many Central Americans practice a religion brought to the region by Europeans. Most people are Roman Catholic because Spanish missionaries taught the Indians about Catholicism. However, Indian traditions have influenced Catholicism in return. Also, Protestant Christians are becoming a large minority in places such as Belize.

Religion has influenced celebrations in towns throughout the region. For example, to celebrate special saints' feast days, some people carry images of the saint in parades through the streets. Easter is a particularly important holiday. Some towns decorate whole streets with designs made of flowers and colorful sawdust.

During festivals, people eat **traditional** foods. Central America shares some of its traditional foods, like corn, with Mexico. The region is also known for tomatoes, hot peppers, and cacao (kuh-KOW), which is the source of chocolate.

READING CHECK **Contrasting** How is Belize culturally different from the rest of the region?

ACADEMIC VOCABULARY

traditional customary, time-honored

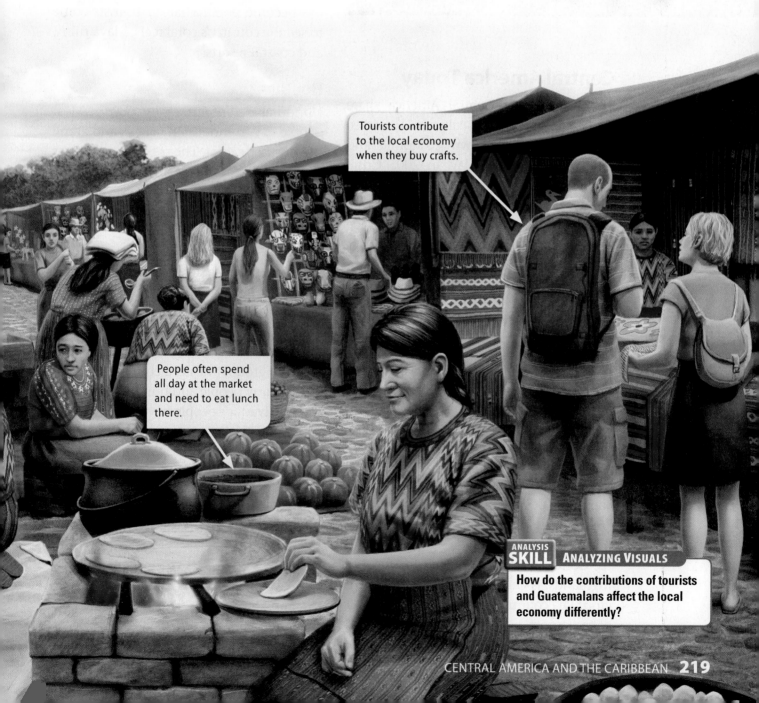

Tourists contribute to the local economy when they buy crafts.

People often spend all day at the market and need to eat lunch there.

ANALYSIS SKILL **ANALYZING VISUALS**

How do the contributions of tourists and Guatemalans affect the local economy differently?

Central America Today

The countries of Central America share similar histories and cultures. However, they all face their own economic and political challenges today. In 2005 Costa Rica, the Dominican Republic, El Salvador, Guatemala, Honduras, and Nicaragua signed the Central American Free Trade Agreement (CAFTA) with the United States to help increase trade among the countries.

Guatemala

Guatemala is the most populous country in Central America. More than 13 million people live there. About 60 percent of Guatemalans are mestizo and European. About 40 percent are Central American Indians. Many speak Maya languages.

Most people in Guatemala live in small villages in the highlands. Fighting between rebels and government forces there killed some 200,000 people between 1960 and 1996. Guatemalans are still recovering from this conflict.

Coffee, which grows well in the cool highlands, is Guatemala's most important crop. The country also is a major producer of cardamom, a spice used in Asian foods.

Belize

Belize has the smallest population in Central America. The country does not have much land for agriculture, either. But **ecotourism**—the practice of using an area's natural environment to attract tourists— has become popular lately. Tourists come to see the country's coral reefs, Maya ruins, and coastal resorts.

Honduras

Honduras is a mountainous country. Most people live in mountain valleys and along the northern coast. The rugged land makes transportation difficult and provides little land where crops can grow. However, citrus fruits and bananas are important exports.

El Salvador

In El Salvador, a few rich families own much of the best land while most people live in poverty. These conditions were a reason behind a long civil war in the 1980s. A **civil war** is a conflict between two or more groups within a country. The war killed many people and hurt the economy.

El Salvador's people have been working to rebuild their country since the end of the war in 1992. One advantage they have in this rebuilding effort is the country's fertile soil. People are able to grow and export crops such as coffee and sugarcane.

Nicaragua

Nicaragua has also been rebuilding since the end of a civil war. In 1979, a group called the Sandinistas overthrew a dictator.

Many Nicaraguans supported the Sandinistas, but rebel forces aided by the United States fought the Sandinistas for power. The civil war ended in 1990 when elections ended the rule of the Sandinistas. Nicaragua is now a democracy.

Costa Rica

Unlike most other Central American countries, Costa Rica has a history of peace. It also has a stable, democratic government. The country does not even have an army. Peace has helped Costa Rica make progress in reducing poverty.

Agricultural products like coffee and bananas are important to Costa Rica's economy. Also, many tourists visit Costa Rica's rich tropical rain forests.

Panama

Panama is the narrowest, southernmost country of Central America. Most people live in areas near the **Panama Canal**. Canal fees and local industries make the canal area the country's most prosperous region.

The Panama Canal provides a link between the Pacific Ocean, the Caribbean Sea, and the Atlantic Ocean. The United States finished building the canal in 1914. For years the Panama canal played an important role in the economy and politics of the region. The United States controlled the canal until 1999. Then, as agreed to in a treaty, Panama finally gained full control of the canal.

READING CHECK **Drawing Inferences** Why do you think Panama might want control of the canal?

FOCUS ON READING
What word in the paragraphs on Costa Rica signals contrast?

SUMMARY AND PREVIEW Native peoples, European colonizers, and the United States have influenced Central America's history and culture. Today most countries are developing stable governments. Their economies rely on tourism and agriculture. In the next section you will learn about the main influences on the Caribbean islands and life there today.

---

hmhsocialstudies.com
ONLINE QUIZ

Section 2 Assessment

Reviewing Ideas, Terms, and Places

1. **a. Recall** What parts of Central America did the British claim?
   b. Analyze How did independence affect most Central American countries?
   c. Elaborate What benefits and drawbacks might there be to the United Fruit Company's owning so much land?
2. **a. Identify** What language do most people in Central America speak?
   b. Explain How have native cultures influenced cultural practices in the region today?
3. **a. Define** What is a **civil war,** and where in Central America has a civil war been fought?
   b. Explain Why might some people practice **ecotourism**?
   c. Elaborate Why is the **Panama Canal** important to Panama? Why is it important to other countries?

Critical Thinking

4. **Summarizing** Copy the graphic organizer below. Using your notes, write at least one important fact about each Central American country today.

Guatemala	
Belize	
Honduras	
El Salvador	
Nicaragua	
Costa Rica	
Panama	

FOCUS ON WRITING *my* WriteSmart

5. **Describing Central America** Note details about the history, culture, and life today of people in Central America. Which details will appeal to people who are thinking of visiting the region?

The Panama Canal

The Panama Canal links the Atlantic and Pacific oceans. Built in the early 1900s, workers on the canal faced tropical diseases and the dangers of blasting through solid rock. The result of their efforts was an amazing feat of engineering. Today some 13,000 to 14,000 ships pass through the canal each year.

Routes Before and After the Panama Canal

map zone

San Francisco
New York
NORTH AMERICA
ATLANTIC OCEAN
5,200 MILES (8,368 KM)
Panama Canal
PACIFIC OCEAN
13,000 MILES (20,921 KM)
SOUTH AMERICA

N
W   E
S

— Route around South America
— Route through the Panama Canal

0   750   1,500 Miles
0   750   1,500 Kilometers

Projection: Azimuthal Equal-Area

The Panama Canal shortens a trip from the east coast of the United States to the west coast by about 8,000 miles (15,000 km).

Crossing a Continent

The Panama Canal takes ships from sea level, across a mountain range, and back to sea level.

Caribbean Sea

Gatún Locks

Pedro Miguel Locks

Miraflores Locks

Gatún Lake

Pacific Ocean

Trains help guide large ships through the canal.

These locks act as doors to different compartments of the canal. Underground pumps raise and lower the water in each compartment like an elevator.

H HISTORY. VIDEO **Panama Canal**

↗ hmhsocialstudies.com

ANALYSIS **SKILL** **ANALYZING VISUALS**

1. Why was Panama a good location for a canal?
2. Why must ships be raised and lowered in order to get through the canal?

The Caribbean Islands

TEKS 1A, 1B, 2B, 3D, 15A, 15B, 18A

What You Will Learn...

Main Ideas

1. The history of the Caribbean islands includes European colonization followed by independence.
2. The culture of the Caribbean islands shows signs of past colonialism and slavery.
3. Today the Caribbean islands have distinctive governments with economies that depend on agriculture and tourism.

The Big Idea

The Caribbean islands have a rich history and culture influenced by European colonization.

Key Terms and Places

dialect, *p. 226*
commonwealth, *p. 227*
refugee, *p. 227*
Havana, *p. 228*
cooperative, *p. 228*

hmhsocialstudies.com
TAKING NOTES

Use the graphic organizer online to organize your notes on the Caribbean islands.

If YOU lived there...

You are a young sailor on Christopher Columbus's second voyage to the New World. The year is 1493. Now that your ship is in the Caribbean Sea, you are sailing from island to island. You have seen volcanoes and waterfalls and fierce natives. Columbus has decided to establish a trading post on one of the islands. You are part of the crew who will stay there.

What do you expect in your new home?

BUILDING BACKGROUND In the late 1400s and early 1500s, European nations began to compete for colonies. Sailing for Spain, Christopher Columbus made four voyages to the Americas. He and his men discovered and explored many islands.

History

When Christopher Columbus discovered America in 1492, he actually discovered the Caribbean islands. These islands now include 13 independent countries. The countries themselves show the influence of those first European explorers.

Early History

Christopher Columbus first sailed into the Caribbean Sea from Spain in 1492. He thought he had reached the Indies, or the islands near India. Therefore, he called the Caribbean islands the West Indies and the people who lived there Indians.

Spain had little interest in the smaller Caribbean islands, but the English, French, Dutch, and Danish did. In the 1600s and 1700s, these countries established colonies on the islands. They built huge sugarcane plantations that required many workers. Most Caribbean Indians had died from disease, so Europeans brought Africans to work as slaves. Soon Africans and people of African descent outnumbered Europeans on many islands.

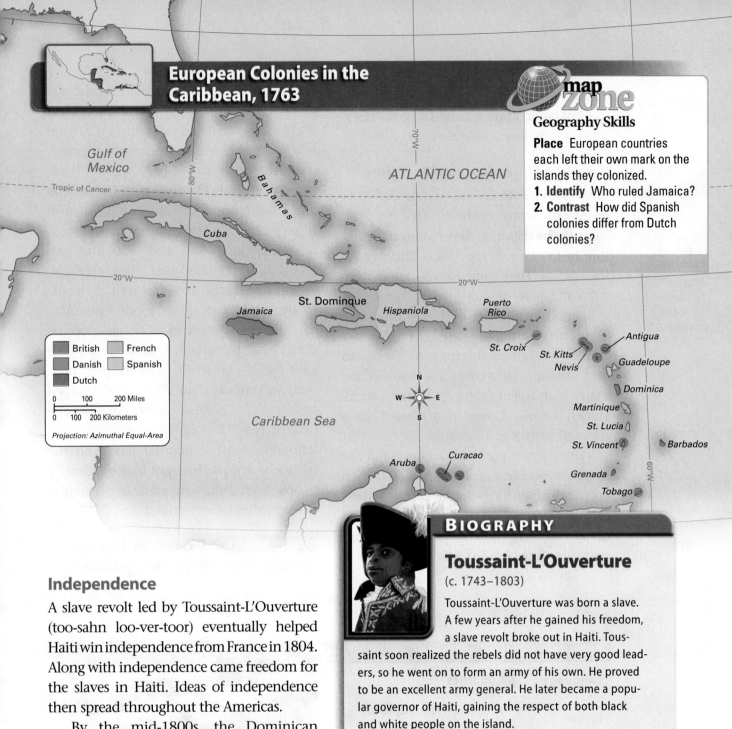

European Colonies in the Caribbean, 1763

map zone

Geography Skills

Place European countries each left their own mark on the islands they colonized.
1. **Identify** Who ruled Jamaica?
2. **Contrast** How did Spanish colonies differ from Dutch colonies?

Gulf of Mexico

Tropic of Cancer

ATLANTIC OCEAN

Bahamas

Cuba

St. Dominque

Jamaica

Hispaniola

Puerto Rico

St. Croix

Antigua

St. Kitts
Nevis

Guadeloupe

Dominica

Martinique

St. Lucia

St. Vincent

Barbados

Grenada

Tobago

Aruba

Curacao

Caribbean Sea

Legend: British · Danish · Dutch · French · Spanish

0   100   200 Miles
0   100   200 Kilometers

Projection: Azimuthal Equal-Area

BIOGRAPHY

Toussaint-L'Ouverture
(c. 1743–1803)

Toussaint-L'Ouverture was born a slave. A few years after he gained his freedom, a slave revolt broke out in Haiti. Toussaint soon realized the rebels did not have very good leaders, so he went on to form an army of his own. He proved to be an excellent army general. He later became a popular governor of Haiti, gaining the respect of both black and white people on the island.

Independence

A slave revolt led by Toussaint-L'Ouverture (too-sahn loo-ver-toor) eventually helped Haiti win independence from France in 1804. Along with independence came freedom for the slaves in Haiti. Ideas of independence then spread throughout the Americas.

By the mid-1800s, the Dominican Republic had gained independence. The United States won Cuba from Spain, but Cuba gained independence in 1902. The other Caribbean countries did not gain independence until more than 40 years later, after World War II. At that time, the Europeans transferred political power peacefully to most of the islands.

Many Caribbean islands still are not independent countries. For example, the islands of Martinique and Guadeloupe are still French possessions. Each has its own elected government and is also represented in the French government. Most people on these islands seem not to wish for independence from their ruling countries.

READING CHECK **Identifying Points of View**
Why might an island's people not be interested in gaining independence?

Culture

Today nearly all Caribbean islands show signs of past colonialism and slavery. These signs can be seen in the region's culture.

People, Languages, and Religion

Most islanders today are descended either from Europeans or from Africans who came to the region as slaves, or from a mixture of the two. Some Asians also live on the islands. They came to work on plantations after slavery ended in the region.

Languages spoken in the region reflect a colonial heritage. Spanish, English, or French as well as mixtures of European and African languages are spoken on many islands. For example, Haitians speak French Creole. Creole is a **dialect**, or a regional variety of a language.

The region's past is also reflected in the religions people practice. Former French and Spanish territories have large numbers of Catholics. People also practice a blend of Catholicism and traditional African religions. One blended religion is Santería.

Festivals and Food

People on the Caribbean islands celebrate a variety of holidays. One of the biggest and most widespread is Carnival. Carnival is a time of feasts and celebration before the Christian season of Lent begins. People usually celebrate Carnival with big parades and fancy costumes. Festivals like Carnival often include great music.

Caribbean food and cooking also reflect the region's past. For example, slave ships carried foods as well as people to the Caribbean. Now foods from Africa, such as yams and okra, are popular there. Also, in Barbados, people eat a dish called souse, which is made of pigs' tails, ears, and snouts. This dish was developed among slaves because slaveholders ate the best parts of the pig and gave slaves the leftovers. Another popular flavor on the islands, curry, was brought to the region by people from India who came as plantation workers after slavery ended.

READING CHECK **Generalizing** How does Caribbean culture reflect African influences?

FOCUS ON READING
What words in the paragraph on food signal comparison?

Languages of the Caribbean

Language	Countries
English	Antigua and Barbuda, Barbados, Trinidad and Tobago
Creole English	Saint Kitts and Nevis, Grenada, Jamaica, Bahamas
Creole French	Haiti, Dominica, Saint Lucia
Spanish	Cuba, Puerto Rico, Dominican Republic

Interpreting Charts What language do people speak in Barbados?

BIBLIOTHEQUE UNIVERSITAIRE

Caribbean Music

The Caribbean islands have produced many unique styles of music. For example, Jamaica is famous as the birthplace of reggae. Merengue is the national music and dance of the Dominican Republic. Trinidad and Tobago is the home of steel-drum and calypso music.

Here, a band in the Grenadines performs on steel drums. Steel-drum bands can include as few as 4 or as many as 100 musicians. The instruments are actually metal barrels like the kind used for shipping oil. The end of each drum is hammered into a curved shape with multiple grooves and bumps. Hitting different-sized bumps results in different notes.

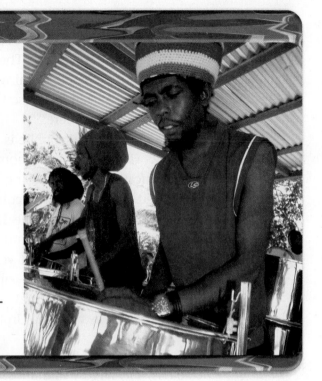

Drawing Inferences What role might trade have played in the development of steel-drum music?

The Caribbean Islands Today

Many Caribbean islands share a similar history. Still, each island has its own economy, government, and culture.

Puerto Rico

Once a Spanish colony, Puerto Rico today is a U.S. commonwealth. A **commonwealth** is a self-governing territory associated with another country. Puerto Ricans are U.S. citizens, but they do not have voting representation in Congress.

Overall, Puerto Rico's economy has benefitted from U.S. aid and investment. Still, wages are lower and unemployment is higher on the island than in the United States. Many Puerto Ricans have moved to the United States for better paying jobs. Today, Puerto Ricans debate whether their island should remain a U.S. commonwealth, become an American state, or become an independent nation.

Haiti

Haiti occupies the western part of the island of Hispaniola. Haiti's capital, Port-au-Prince, is the center of the nation's limited industry. Most Haitians farm small plots. Coffee and sugarcane are among Haiti's main exports.

Haiti is the poorest country in the Americas. Its people have suffered under a string of corrupt governments during the last two centuries. Violence, political unrest, and poverty have created many political refugees. A **refugee** is someone who flees to another country, usually for political or economic reasons. Many Haitian refugees have come to the United States.

On January, 12, 2010, a catastrophic earthquake struck close to Port-au-Prince. The quake devastated Haiti, leaving about 230,000 Haitians dead, 300,000 injured, and over a million homeless. Today, many Haitians continue working to rebuild their lives and nation.

Dominican Republic

The Dominican Republic occupies the eastern part of Hispaniola. The capital is Santo Domingo. Santo Domingo was the first permanent European settlement in the Western Hemisphere.

The Dominican Republic is not a rich country. However, its economy, health care, education, and housing are more developed than Haiti's. Agriculture is the basis of the economy in the Dominican Republic. The country's tourism industry has also grown in recent years. Beach resorts along the coast are popular with many tourists from Central and South America as well as from the United States.

Cuba

Cuba is the largest and most populous country in the Caribbean. It is located just 92 miles (148 km) south of Florida. **Havana**, the capital, is the country's largest and most important city.

Cuba has been run by a Communist government since Fidel Castro came to power in 1959. At that time, the government took over banks, large sugarcane plantations, and other businesses. Many of these businesses were owned by U.S. companies. Because of the takeovers, the U.S. government banned trade with Cuba and restricted travel there by U.S. citizens.

Today the government still controls the economy. Most of Cuba's farms are organized as cooperatives or government-owned plantations. A **cooperative** is an organization owned by its members and operated for their mutual benefit.

Besides controlling the economy, Cuba's government also controls all the newspapers, television, and radio stations. While many Cubans support these policies, others oppose them. Some people who oppose the government have become refugees in the United States. Many Cuban refugees have become U.S. citizens.

Cubans Divided

Government-sponsored rallies are a part of Cuban life. Meanwhile, some Cubans try to flee their country on tiny rafts.

ANALYZING VISUALS How can you tell that the people in the raft are trying to flee Cuba?

Other Islands

The rest of the Caribbean islands are small countries. Jamaica is the largest of the remaining Caribbean countries. The smallest country is Saint Kitts and Nevis. It is not even one-tenth the size of Rhode Island, the smallest U.S. state!

A number of Caribbean islands are not independent countries but territories of other countries. These territories include the U.S. and British Virgin Islands. The Netherlands and France also still have some Caribbean territories.

Some of these islands have enough land to grow some coffee, sugarcane, or spices. However, most islands' economies are based on tourism. Hundreds of people on the islands work in restaurants and hotels visited by tourists. While tourism has provided jobs and helped economies, not all of its effects have been positive. For example, new construction sometimes harms the same natural environment tourists come to the islands to enjoy.

READING CHECK **Contrasting** How are the governments of Puerto Rico and Cuba different?

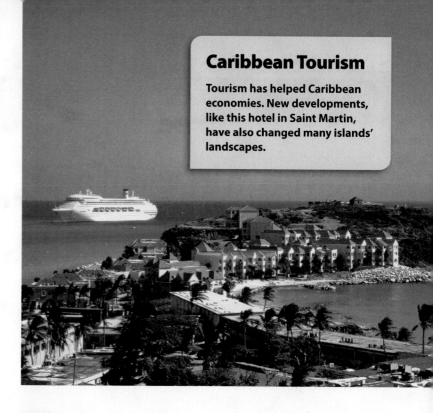

Caribbean Tourism

Tourism has helped Caribbean economies. New developments, like this hotel in Saint Martin, have also changed many islands' landscapes.

SUMMARY AND PREVIEW The Caribbean islands were colonized by European countries, which influenced the culture of the islands. Today the islands have different types of governments but similar economies. Next, you will read about countries in South America that are also located near the Caribbean Sea.

Section 3 Assessment

hmhsocialstudies.com
ONLINE QUIZ

Reviewing Ideas, Terms, and Places

1. **a. Describe** What crop was the basis of the colonial economy on the Caribbean islands?
   b. Make Inferences Why do you think most smaller Caribbean countries were able to gain independence peacefully?
2. **a. Define** What is a **dialect**?
   b. Explain In what ways have African influences shaped Caribbean culture?
3. **a. Recall** What is a **refugee**, and from what Caribbean countries have refugees come?
   b. Make Inferences Why do you think many Cubans support their government's policies?
   c. Evaluate What would be the benefits and drawbacks for Puerto Rico if it became a U.S. state?

Critical Thinking

4. **Summarizing** Look over your notes. Then use a diagram like this one to note specific influences on the region and where they came from in each circle. You may add more circles if you need to.

Caribbean Islands

FOCUS ON WRITING

my WriteSmart

5. **Telling about the Caribbean Islands** These islands have a fascinating history and a rich culture. Take notes and define the common culture traits that unify the region for your travel guide.

CENTRAL AMERICA AND THE CARIBBEAN **229**

Creating a Thematic Map

Learn

Thematic maps show specific information, or a theme, of a particular geographic area. When you draw a thematic map, it is easiest to use an existing map as a guide. On the map you draw, you can show geographical information. You can also draw other kinds of information, such as data on climates, population, disease, and economic activities. Often, this data comes from a graph or chart.

Practice

The first step in creating a thematic map is decide the theme or subject. Once you have the theme, you will need to find facts and data about that theme. Then, you will use your research to create the map. The thematic map on this page show the languages spoken in Central America. Follow these steps to create your own thematic map:

1. Decide what your thematic map will be about.

2. Find facts and data about your theme. Conduct research at the library or on the Internet to find facts and details about your theme. You may also want to find related maps to use as a guide.

3. Create a title that shows the purpose of the map.

4. Create a legend to explain any colors or symbols used.

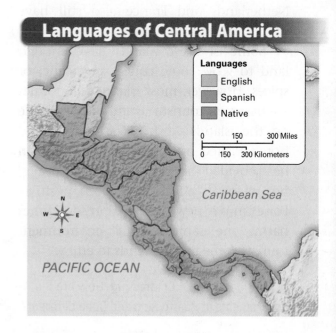

Languages of Central America

Languages
- English
- Spanish
- Native

0   150   300 Miles
0   150   300 Kilometers

Caribbean Sea

PACIFIC OCEAN

Apply

Create your own map. Turn to the chart titled "Languages of the Caribbean" in Section 3. Use the steps and the map on this page as a guide to help you draw a thematic map of the languages people speak in the Caribbean.

Chapter Review

Visual Summary

Use the visual summary below to help you review the main ideas of the chapter.

QUICK FACTS

The region's landscapes include warm coastal lowlands and cool highland regions with tropical forests.

Native cultures still influence Central America. Today governments and economies there are changing.

The Caribbean islands have a history of colonial rule. Today many countries' economies there depend on tourism.

Reviewing Vocabulary, Terms, and Places

Choose one word from each word pair to correctly complete each sentence below.

1. A(n) _____ is a narrow strip of land that connects two larger land areas. **(archipelago/isthmus)**

2. A _____ is a self-governing territory associated with another country. **(commonwealth/cooperative)**

3. A _____ is someone who flees to another country, usually for political or economic reasons. **(traditional/refugee)**

4. The United States controlled the _____ until 1999. **(Caribbean Sea/Panama Canal)**

5. The large islands of Cuba, Jamaica, Hispaniola, and Puerto Rico make up the _____. **(Greater Antilles/Lesser Antilles)**

6. _____ is found in the mountainous part of Central America. **(Cloud forest/Havana)**

Comprehension and Critical Thinking

SECTION 1 *(Pages 212–215)*

7. a. Describe What process has formed many of the Caribbean islands? Describe the effect this process has on the region today.

b. Compare and Contrast How are summer and winter similar in Central America and the Caribbean? How are the seasons different?

c. Elaborate What kinds of damage might hurricanes cause? What damage might earthquakes and volcanic eruptions cause?

SECTION 2 *(Pages 216–221)*

8. a. Identify In what Central American country is English the official language?

b. Make Inferences Why do you think people of African ancestry live mainly along the coast?

c. Elaborate How might recent political conflict have affected development in some countries?

9. a. Recall What country was the first to gain independence? Who led the revolt that led to independence?

b. Analyze Look at the Caribbean Music feature in this section. What is the relationship between some Caribbean cultures and their music?

c. Geographic Questions Look back at the data for Canada and Haiti in this unit's Regional Database. Based on the data, pose and answer a question about life expectancy in these countries.

Social Studies Skills

Creating a Thematic Map *Examine the thematic map titled* Volcanic Activity in Central America and the Caribbean *in Section 1 of this chapter. Then use the map to answer the following questions.*

10. What information, or theme, does the map show?

11. How does this map differ from a political map of the Caribbean?

12. Using information you have learned about in this chapter decide on a theme for a map. Create a thematic map depicting aspects of Central America and the Caribbean. Make sure to include a title and a legend on your map.

Using the Internet

13. Activity: Taking an Ecotour Ecotourism is all about visiting places to appreciate the environment. Through your online textbook, take your own Internet ecotour of Central America and the Caribbean islands. Visit the Web sites to learn more about some of the people and places you have read about in this chapter. Then create a postcard from a place you visited on your trip.

hmhsocialstudies.com

Map Activity

14. Central America and the Caribbean On a separate sheet of paper, match the letters on the map with their correct labels.

Guatemala	Caribbean Sea
Panama	Puerto Rico
Havana, Cuba	Lesser Antilles

FOCUS ON READING AND WRITING *my*WriteSmart

15. Understanding Comparison-Contrast Look back over the section on physical geography. Then use *my*WriteSmart in your eBook to write a paragraph comparing and contrasting Central America with the Caribbean islands. Consider their physical features, climates, landscapes, and resources.

16. Creating a Travel Guide Choose one place in this region to be the subject of your travel guide. Then look over your notes for facts about that place to interest your reader. Use myWriteSmart in your eBook to begin your guide with a paragraph describing the outstanding physical features of the place. Your second paragraph should identify interesting details about its history and culture. End with a sentence that might encourage your readers to visit. Include two images in your guide to show off the features of the place you have chosen.

Reading Social Studies

Understanding Comparison-Contrast

FOCUS ON READING

Comparing shows how things are alike. Contrasting shows how things are different. You can understand comparison-contrast by learning to recognize clue words and points of comparison. Clue words let you know whether to look for similarities or differences. Points of comparison are the main topics that are being compared or contrasted.

> Many Caribbean islands <u>share</u> a <u>similar</u> history and culture. <u>However</u>, today the islands' <u>different</u> economies, governments, and cultural landscapes encourage many <u>different</u> ways of life in the Caribbean.

Underlined words are clue words.

Highlighted words are points of comparison.

Clue Words	
Comparison	**Contrast**
share, similar, like, also, both, in addition, besides	however, while, unlike, different, but, although

YOU TRY IT!

Read the following passage to see how Haiti and the Dominican Republic are alike and different. Use a diagram like the one here to compare and contrast the two countries.

> Haiti occupies the western part of the island of Hispaniola. Haiti's capital, Port-au-Prince, is the center of the nation's limited industry. Most Haitians farm small plots. Coffee and sugarcane are among Haiti's main exports.
>
> The Dominican Republic occupies the eastern part of Hispaniola. The Dominican Republic is not a rich country. However, its economy, health care, education, and housing are more developed than Haiti's. Agriculture is the basis of the economy.

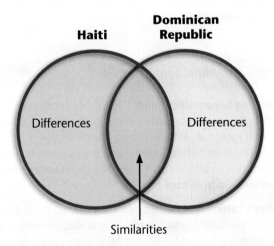

Haiti | Dominican Republic

Differences | Differences

Similarities

Caribbean South America

Caribbean Sea

Barranquilla
Cartagena
Maracaibo
Lake Maracaibo

PANAMA

Medellín

PACIFIC OCEAN

Cauca River

Magdalena River

⊛ **Bogotá**

Cali

C O L O M B I A

0° Equator

Putumayo River

ECUADOR

PERU

Essential Question

*my*Notebook

What challenges have the countries of Caribbean South America faced since gaining their independence?

Texts Essential Knowledge and Skills (TEKS)

Texas Essential Knowledge and Skills (TEKS)

1A, 1B, 2B, 3A, 3B, 3C, 4A, 4D, 4E, 4F, 5A, 5B, 6A, 6B, 15A, 15B, 15D, 18A, 21A, 21B, 21C, 22D

FOCUS ON READING AND WRITING

my WriteSmart

Identifying Supporting Details Supporting details are the facts and examples that provide information to support the main ideas of a chapter, section, or paragraph. At the beginning of each section in this book, there is a list of main ideas. As you read this chapter, look for the details that support each section's main ideas. **See the lesson, Identifying Supporting Details, on page 253.**

Writing a Letter You live in a country in Caribbean South America. Your pen pal in the United States has asked you to write a letter telling her about life in your region. As you read this chapter, collect details to include in your letter. Your friend will want to know about your country as well as the whole region. Use the annotation tools in your eBook to gather information for your assignment.

History The architecture of Cartagena, Colombia, reflects the city's Spanish colonial past.

National capital
★ Other capitals
• Other cities

0   100   200 Miles
0   100   200 Kilometers
Projection: Azimuthal Equal-Area

ATLANTIC OCEAN

W-60°

TRINIDAD AND TOBAGO

Caracas
Valencia

VENEZUELA

Orinoco River

Orinoco River

Georgetown

GUYANA

Paramaribo

Cayenne

SURINAME

FRENCH GUIANA
(FRANCE)

N
W   E
S

W-50°

Rio Negro

BRAZIL

Amazon River

map Zone

Geography Skills

Place Most of Caribbean South America is located on the Caribbean Sea.

1. **Identify** What is the capital of Venezuela?

2. **Contrast** How is Colombia's location different from Venezuela's location?

Culture Cowboys called llaneros work on the plains of Venezuela.

Geography Dense rain forest covers much of Suriname.

235

TEKS 3A, 3B, 3C, 4D, 4E, 4F, 5A, 5B, 5C, 6A, 6B, 21B, 21C, 22D

What You Will Learn...

Main Ideas

1. Caribbean South America has a wide variety of physical features and wildlife.
2. The region's location and elevation both affect its climate and vegetation.
3. Caribbean South America is rich in resources, such as farmland, oil, timber, and rivers for hydroelectric power.

The Big Idea

Caribbean South America is a region with diverse physical features, wildlife, climates, and resources.

Key Terms and Places

Andes, *p. 236*
cordillera, *p. 236*
Guiana Highlands, *p. 237*
Llanos, *p. 237*
Orinoco River, *p. 238*

hmhsocialstudies.com
TAKING NOTES

Use the graphic organizer online to take notes on the physical geography of Caribbean South America.

Physical Geography

If YOU lived there...

You live in Caracas, Venezuela, but this is your first visit to the great Orinoco River. You've heard about the fierce creatures that live in the river, so you think your guide is kidding when he says he's going to catch a piranha. You're expecting a monster and are surprised when he pulls up a small orange fish. It has many sharp teeth, but it's only seven inches long!

What other animals might you see in the region?

BUILDING BACKGROUND The narrow Isthmus of Panama joins the continent of South America at its northwestern corner, the country of Colombia. Like the countries of Central America, the five countries in Caribbean South America border the Caribbean Sea. They all vary in landscape, climate, and culture and have large rivers and rugged mountains.

Physical Features and Wildlife

If you were traveling through the region of Caribbean South America, you might see the world's highest waterfall, South America's largest lake, and even the world's largest rodent! As you can see on the map, the geography of this region includes rugged mountains, highlands, and plains drained by huge river systems.

Mountains and Highlands

The highest point in the region is in Colombia, a country larger than California and Texas combined. On the western side of Colombia the **Andes** (AN-deez) reach 18,000 feet (5,490 m). The Andes form a **cordillera** (kawr-duhl-YER-uh), a mountain system made up of roughly parallel ranges. Some of the Andes' snowcapped peaks are active volcanoes. Eruptions and earthquakes shake these mountains frequently.

Caribbean Sea

Pico Cristóbal Colón
18,947 ft (5,775 m)

PANAMA

Lake Maracaibo

Orinoco River

VENEZUELA

LLANOS

Angel Falls

GUIANA

GUYANA

SURINAME

French Guiana (FRANCE)

HIGHLANDS

ATLANTIC OCEAN

PACIFIC OCEAN

COLOMBIA

ANDES

Cauca River

Magdalena River

Orinoco River

BRAZIL

Equator 0°

ECUADOR

Putumayo River

AMAZON BASIN

Rio Negro

Amazon River

PERU

map zone Geography Skills

Place The region's landscapes include mountains, highlands, plains, and rivers.
1. **Name** What major river runs through Venezuela?
2. **Contrast** How is the elevation of Colombia different from that of the rest of Caribbean South America?

ELEVATION

Feet	Meters
13,120	4,000
6,560	2,000
1,640	500
656	200
(Sea level) 0	0 (Sea level)
Below sea level	Below sea level

0   200   400 Miles

0   200   400 Kilometers

Projection: Azimuthal Equal-Area

1 The Orinoco River flows through Venezuela's rain forests, plains, and highlands.

2 Stretching the entire length of western South America, the Andes is the longest mountain system in the world. Andean peaks fill the landscape here in western Colombia.

Lying on the Caribbean coast, Venezuela is located in the middle of the other countries in the region. Venezuela's highest elevation is in the **Guiana Highlands**, which stretch into Guyana and Suriname. For millions of years, wind and rain have eroded these highlands' plateaus. However, some of the steep-sided plateaus are capped by sandstone layers that have resisted erosion. These unusual flat-topped formations are sometimes called *tepuís* (tay-PWEEZ). The *tepuís* create a dramatic landscape as they rise about 3,000 to 6,000 feet (900 to 1,800 m) above the surrounding plains.

Plains, Rivers, and Wildlife

As you look at the map above, notice how much the elevation drops between the highlands and the Andes. This region of plains is known as the **Llanos** (YAH-nohs). The Llanos is mostly grassland with few trees. At a low elevation and not much vegetation, these plains flood easily.

FOCUS ON
READING
What details in
this paragraph
support this
section's first
main idea?

Flowing for about 1,600 miles (2,575 km), the **Orinoco** (OHR-ee-NOH-koh) **River** is the region's longest river. Snaking its way through Venezuela to the Atlantic Ocean, the Orinoco and its tributaries drain the plains and highlands. Two other important rivers, the Cauca and the Magdalena, drain the Andean region.

Caribbean South America is home to some remarkable wildlife. For example, hundreds of bird species, meat-eating fish called piranhas, and crocodiles live in or around the Orinoco River. Colombia has one of the world's highest concentrations of plant and animal species. The country's wildlife includes jaguars, ocelots, and several species of monkeys.

READING CHECK **Summarizing** What are the region's major physical features?

Venezuela's Canaima National Park

Covering almost 3 million acres of eastern Venezuela, Canaima National Park is one of the largest national parks in the world.

ANALYZING VISUALS What do you think attracts millions of people from around the world to visit Canaima National Park?

GUYANA

Angel Falls

Canaima
National
Park

Mt. Roraima ▲

Caroni River

VENEZUELA

BRAZIL

Dropping more than 3,200 feet (975 m), Angel Falls is the world's highest waterfall.

A rocky tepuí rises from the park's flat plains. Hundreds of these flat-topped mountains are scattered throughout the park.

The red-billed toucan is among the almost 500 species of birds that live in the park.

Climate and Vegetation

Caribbean South America's location near the equator means that most of the region has warm temperatures year-round. However, temperatures do vary with elevation. For example, in the Andes, as you go up in elevation, the temperature can drop rapidly—about four degrees Fahrenheit every 1,000 feet (305 m).

In contrast, the vast, flat landscape of the Llanos region has a tropical savanna climate. Here, both the wet and dry seasons provide favorable conditions for grasslands to grow.

Rain forests, another type of landscape, thrive in the humid tropical climate of southern Colombia. This area is a part of the Amazon Basin. Here, rain falls throughout the year, watering the forest's huge trees. These trees form a canopy where the vegetation is so dense that sunlight barely shines through to the jungle floor.

READING CHECK **Analyzing** What causes the region's temperatures to vary?

Resources

Good soil and moderate climates help make most of Caribbean South America a rich agricultural region. Major crops include rice, coffee, bananas, and sugarcane.

In addition, the region has other valuable resources, such as oil, iron ore, and coal. Both Venezuela and Colombia have large oil-rich areas. Forests throughout the region provide timber. While the seas provide plentiful fish and shrimp, the region's major rivers are used to generate hydroelectric power.

READING CHECK **Summarizing** How do geographic factors affect economic activities in Caribbean South America?

SUMMARY AND PREVIEW In this section you learned that the physical geography of Caribbean South America includes mountains, highlands, plains, and rivers. The region's location near the equator and its elevation affect the region's climate. In the next section you will learn about Colombia's history, people, and economy. You will also learn about the challenges Colombia is facing today, which include a civil war.

Section 1 Assessment

hmhsocialstudies.com
ONLINE QUIZ

Reviewing Ideas, Terms, and Places

1. **a. Recall** Where are the **Andes** located?
   b. Explain How are the rock formations called *tepuís* unusual?
   c. Elaborate Why do the **Llanos** in Colombia and Venezuela flood easily?
2. **a. Describe** In the Andes, how does the temperature change with elevation?
   b. Make Inferences How does the region's location near the equator affect its climate?
3. **a. Identify** What is a major resource in both Venezuela and Colombia?
   b. Explain Which resource provides hydroelectric power?

Critical Thinking

4. **Categorizing** Use your notes to identify four types of physical features in the region. Write each type in one of the small circles of the diagram.

Physical Features

FOCUS ON WRITING   *my* WriteSmart

5. **Describing Physical Geography** Take notes about the physical features, wildlife, climate, vegetation, and resources of the region. After you decide which country you are living in, collect more details about it.

TEKS 1A, 1B, 2B, 4A, 15A, 15B, 18A

What You Will Learn...

Main Ideas

1. Native cultures, Spanish conquest, and independence shaped Colombia's history.
2. In Colombia today, the benefits of a rich culture and many natural resources contrast with the effects of a long period of civil war.

The Big Idea

Spanish conquest, valuable resources, and civil war have shaped the history, culture, and economy of Colombia.

Key Terms and Places

Cartagena, *p. 241*
Bogotá, *p. 242*
guerrillas, *p. 243*

hmhsocialstudies.com
TAKING NOTES

Use the graphic organizer online to organize your notes on Colombia.

Colombia

If YOU lived there...

You live in the beautiful colonial city of Cartagena, on the coast of the Caribbean. Your family runs a small restaurant there. You're used to the city's wide beaches and old colonial buildings with wooden balconies that overhang the street. Now you are on your way to visit your cousins. They live on a cattle ranch on the inland plains region called the Llanos.

How do you think life on the ranch is different from yours?

BUILDING BACKGROUND Like most of the countries of Central and South America, Colombia was once a colony of Spain. Colombians gained their independence from Spain in 1819. The new country was then named after the explorer Christopher Columbus.

Colombia's History

Giant mounds of earth, mysterious statues, and tombs—these are the marks of the people who lived in Colombia more than 1,500 years ago. Colombia's history begins with these people. It also includes conquest by Spain and, later, independence.

The Chibcha

Have you heard of the legend of El Dorado (el duh-RAH-doh), or the Golden One? That legend about

This gold Chibcha artifact represents the ceremonial raft used by their king.

a land rich in gold was inspired by the Chibcha culture in Colombia. The Chibcha covered their new rulers in gold dust. Then they took each ruler to a lake to wash the gold off. As the new ruler washed, the Chibcha threw gold and emerald objects into the water. A well-developed civilization, they practiced pottery making, weaving, and metalworking. Their gold objects were among the finest in ancient America.

Spanish Conquest

In about 1500 Spanish explorers arrived on the Caribbean coast of South America. The Spaniards wanted to expand Spain's new empire. In doing so, the Spanish conquered the Chibcha and seized much of their treasure. Soon after claiming land for themselves, the Spaniards founded a colony and cities along the Caribbean coast.

One colonial city, **Cartagena**, was a major naval base and commercial port in the Spanish empire. By the 1600s Spaniards and their descendants had set up large estates in Colombia. Spanish estate owners forced South American Indians and enslaved Africans to work the land.

Independence

In the late 1700s people in Central and South America began struggling for independence from Spain. After independence was achieved, the republic of Gran Colombia was created. It included Colombia, Ecuador, Panama, and Venezuela. In 1830 the republic dissolved, and New Granada, which included Colombia and Panama, was created.

After independence, two different groups of Colombians debated over how Colombia should be run. One group wanted the Roman Catholic Church to participate in government and education. On the other hand, another group did not want the church involved in their lives.

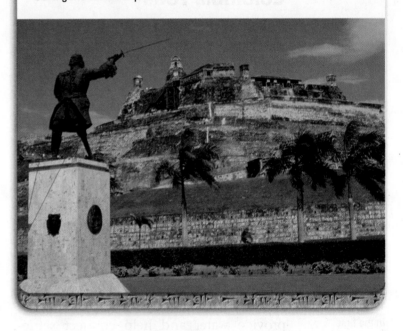

CONNECTING TO History

Cartagena's Spanish Fort

Imagine you are a Spanish colonist living in Cartagena, Colombia, in the 1600s. Your city lies on the Caribbean coast and has been attacked by English pirates several times. They have stolen tons of silver and gold that were waiting shipment to Spain. How do you protect your city from these pirates? Build an enormous fort, of course! You make sure to design the fort's walls to deflect the cannonballs that the pirates shoot from their ships. Today this fort still stands on a peninsula outside Cartagena. A statue commemorates one of the heroes that defended the city from attack.

Drawing Conclusions Why did the Spanish want to defend Cartagena from the pirates?

Outbreaks of violence throughout the 1800s and 1900s killed thousands. Part of the problem had to do with the country's rugged geography, which isolated people in one region from those in another region. As a result, they developed separate economies and identities. Uniting these different groups into one country was hard.

READING CHECK **Drawing Conclusions** How did Spanish conquest shape Colombia's history and culture?

Different regions of Colombia are home to diverse ethnic groups.

ANALYZING VISUALS What are some of the goods sold in this market?

Colombians of African descent unload their goods at a local market near the Pacific coast.

Colombia Today

Colombia is Caribbean South America's most populous country. The national capital is **Bogotá**, a city located high in the eastern Andes. Although Colombia is rich in culture and resources, more than 40 years of civil war have been destructive to the country's economy.

People and Culture

Most Colombians live in the fertile valleys and river basins among the mountain ranges, where the climate is moderate and good for farming. Rivers, such as the Cauca and the Magdalena, flow down from the Andes to the Caribbean Sea. These rivers provide water and help connect settlements located between the mountains and the coast. Other Colombians live on cattle ranches scattered throughout the Llanos. Few people live in the tropical rainforest regions in the south.

Because the physical geography of Colombia isolates some regions of the country, the people of Colombia are often known by the region where they live. For example, those who live along the Caribbean coast are known for songs and dances influenced by African traditions.

FOCUS ON READING
In the first paragraph under Economy, find at least three details to support the idea stated in the first sentence.

Colombian culture is an interesting mix of influences:

- Music: traditional African songs and dances on the Caribbean coast and South American Indian music in remote areas of the Andes
- Sports: soccer, as well as a traditional Chibcha ring-toss game called *tejo*
- Religion: primarily Roman Catholicism
- Official language: Spanish
- Ethnic groups: 58 percent mestizo; also Spanish, African, and Indian descent

Economy

Colombia's economy relies on several valuable resources. Rich soil, steep slopes, and tall shade trees produce world-famous Colombian coffee. Other major export crops include bananas, sugar cane, and cotton. Many farms in Colombia produce flowers that are exported around the world. In fact, 80 percent of the country's flowers are shipped to the United States.

Colombia's economy depends on the country's valuable natural resources. Recently oil has become Colombia's major export. Other natural resources include iron ore, gold, and coal. Most of the world's emeralds also come from Colombia.

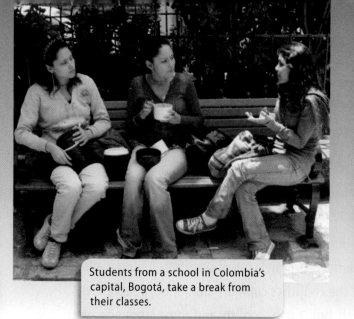

Students from a school in Colombia's capital, Bogotá, take a break from their classes.

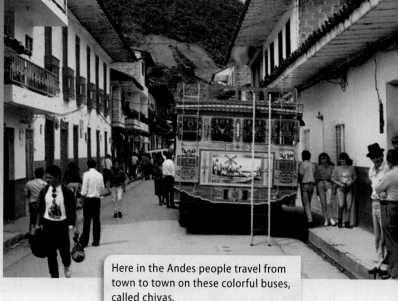

Here in the Andes people travel from town to town on these colorful buses, called chivas.

Civil War

Civil war is a major problem in Colombia today. Many different groups have waged war with each other and with Colombia's government. For more than 40 years, these heavily armed militant groups have controlled large areas of the country.

One of these groups is an army of **guerrillas**, or members of an irregular military force. These guerrillas want to overthrow the government. The guerrillas, as well as other militant groups, have forced farmers off their land and caused thousands of Colombians to flee the country. All of these groups are also involved in growing crops of the illegal coca plant. This plant is used to make cocaine, a dangerous drug.

Because of the instability caused by civil war, the future of Colombia is uncertain. However, the Colombian government has passed new laws that make it harder for the guerrillas and other militant groups to operate freely. In addition, the United States provides assistance to Colombia's government. Colombia is one of the top recipients of U.S. foreign aid.

READING CHECK **Drawing Conclusions** How do you think civil war affects daily life in Colombia?

SUMMARY AND PREVIEW Colombia's history includes the Chibcha, Spanish conquest, and independence. Today, Colombia's people are dealing with a long civil war. Next, you will learn about Colombia's neighbor, Venezuela.

hmhsocialstudies.com
ONLINE QUIZ

Section 2 Assessment

Reviewing Ideas, Terms, and Places

1. a. **Recall** Who were the Chibcha?
   b. **Draw Conclusions** Why did Spain want land in Colombia?
2. a. **Describe** What factors make Colombia ideal for growing coffee?
   b. **Interpret** In what part of the country do most Colombians live?
   c. **Predict** How might Colombia solve the problem of **guerrillas** trying to control the country?

Critical Thinking

3. **Analyzing** Using your notes, write a sentence about the topic of each box in a diagram like this one.

Music	→	
Sports	→	
Religion	→	
Language	→	

FOCUS ON WRITING

4. **Writing about Colombia** What information about the history, culture, and daily life of Colombia might your pen pal like to learn? Add these details to your notes.

CARIBBEAN SOUTH AMERICA **243**

TEKS 1A, 1B, 2B, 4A, 15A, 15B, 18A

What You Will Learn...

Main Ideas

1. Spanish settlement shaped the history and culture of Venezuela.
2. Oil production plays a large role in Venezuela's economy and government today.
3. The Guianas have diverse cultures and plentiful resources.

The Big Idea

European settlement, immigration, and natural resources have greatly influenced the culture and economy of Venezuela and the Guianas.

Key Terms and Places

llaneros, *p. 246*
Lake Maracaibo, *p. 246*
Caracas, *p. 247*
strike, *p. 248*
referendum, *p. 248*

hmhsocialstudies.com
TAKING NOTES

Use the graphic organizer online to organize your notes on Venezuela and the Guianas.

Venezuela and the Guianas

If YOU lived there...

You've come from your home in eastern Venezuela to visit the nearby country of Suriname. Your visit is full of surprises. As you walk along the streets of the country's capital, Paramaribo, people are not speaking Spanish, but Dutch, English, and some languages you don't even recognize. You see Hindu temples and Muslim mosques alongside Christian churches.

Why is Suriname so different from Venezuela?

BUILDING BACKGROUND Venezuela, like Colombia, was once a Spanish colony, but the Guianas were colonized by other nations—Great Britain, the Netherlands, and France. When these countries gained independence, British Guiana became Guyana and Dutch Guiana became Suriname.

History and Culture of Venezuela

Venezuela was originally the home of many small tribes of South American Indians. Those groups were conquered by the Spanish in the early 1500s. Though Venezuela became independent from Spain in the early 1800s, those three centuries of Spanish rule shaped the country's history and culture.

Spanish Settlement and Colonial Rule

The Spanish came to Venezuela hoping to find gold and pearls. They forced the native Indians to search for these treasures, but they finally realized there was little gold to be found. Then the Spanish turned to agriculture, once again forcing the Indians to do the work. They grew indigo (IN-di-goh), a plant used to make a deep blue dye. Because the work was very hard, many of the Indians died. Then the Spanish began bringing enslaved Africans to take the Indians' places. Eventually, some of the slaves escaped, settling in remote areas of the country.

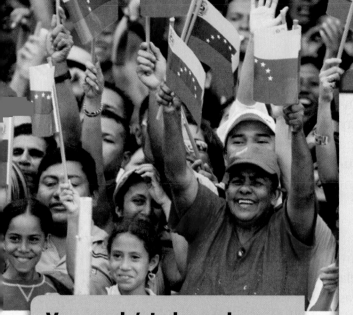

Venezuela's Independence

Each year, Venezuelans celebrate Simon Bolívar's efforts in achieving Venezuela's independence. Independence Day is filled with parades and parties.

Independence and Self-Rule

Partly because the colony was so poor, some people in Venezuela revolted against Spain. Simon Bolívar helped lead the fight against Spanish rule. Bolívar is considered a hero in many South American countries because he led wars of independence throughout the region. Bolívar helped win Venezuelan independence from Spain by 1821. However, Venezuela did not officially become independent until 1830.

Throughout the 1800s Venezuelans suffered from dictatorships and civil wars. Venezuela's military leaders ran the country. After oil was discovered in the early 1900s, some leaders kept the country's oil money for themselves. As a result, the people of Venezuela did not benefit from their country's oil wealth.

People and Culture

The people of Venezuela are descended from native Indians, Europeans, and Africans. The majority of Venezuelans are of mixed Indian and European descent. Indians make up only about 2 percent of the population. People of European descent tend to live in the large cities. People of African descent tend to live along the coast. Most Venezuelans are Spanish-speaking Roman Catholics, but the country's Indians speak 25 different languages and follow the religious practices of their ancestors.

Venezuelan culture includes dancing and sports. Venezuela's national dance, the *joropo*, is a lively foot-stomping couples' dance. Large crowds of Venezuelans attend rodeo events. Baseball and soccer are also popular throughout Venezuela.

READING CHECK **Summarizing** How did the Spanish contribute to Venezuela's history?

FOCUS ON READING

In the paragraphs under Venezuela Today, what details support the main idea that oil production plays a large role in Venezuela's economy and government?

Venezuela Today

Many Venezuelans make a living by farming and ranching. However, most wealthy Venezuelans have made money in the country's oil industry. In addition, Venezuela's government has also benefited from oil wealth.

Agriculture and Ranching

Rural areas of Venezuela are dotted by farms and ranches. Northern Venezuela has some small family farms as well as large commercial farms. **Llaneros** (yah-NAY-rohs)—or Venezuelan cowboys—herd cattle on the many ranches of the Llanos region. However, some small communities of Indians practice traditional agriculture.

Economy and Natural Resources

In the 1960s Venezuela began earning huge sums of money from oil production. This wealth allowed part of the population to buy luxuries. However, the vast majority of the population still lived in poverty. Many of Venezuela's poor people moved to the cities to try to find work. Some settled on the outskirts in communities of shacks. They had no running water, sewers, or electricity.

Venezuela's wealth attracted many immigrants from Europe and other South American countries. These immigrants, like most other Venezuelans, suffered in the 1980s when the price of oil dropped sharply. Without the money provided by high oil prices, the economy couldn't support the people. Oil prices recovered in the 1990s, and the Venezuelan economy continues to be based on oil production.

As you can see on the map on the next page, the Orinoco River basin and **Lake Maracaibo** (mah-rah-KY-boh) are rich in oil. Venezuela is the only South American member of the Organization of Petroleum

The Feast of Corpus Christi

One day each summer, men dressed as devils dance in the streets of the Venezuelan town of San Francisco de Yare. On this day, people here honor the Roman Catholic feast day of Corpus Christi. Spanish settlers brought the tradition of dressing up as devils to Venezuela. This tradition includes the making of elaborate, colorful masks that the dancers wear. These masks usually resemble pigs or jaguars. Dancing through the town's streets to the beat of drums, the dancers shake musical instruments called maracas. They believe their dancing, music, and scary masks will keep evil away from their town.

Summarizing How do some Venezuelans celebrate the Feast of Corpus Christi?

Venezuela's Major Resources

World's Top Oil Exporters		
	Country	**Oil Exports** (million barrels per day)
1	Saudi Arabia	6.8
2	Russia	4.9
3	Iran	2.4
4	Nigeria	2.3
5	United Arab Emirates	2.1
8	Venezuela	1.6

Oil fields
Oil pipelines
Gold
Coal

0 100 200 Miles
0 100 200 Kilometers
Projection: Azimuthal Equal-Area

map zone Geography Skills

Human-Environment Interaction Oil, gold, and coal are Venezuela's major resources.
1. **Locate** What resource is located near the Orinoco River?
2. **Draw Conclusions** What resource do you think is the most difficult to transport to port cities?

Exporting Countries (OPEC). The member countries in this organization attempt to control world oil production and keep oil prices from falling too low.

The Guiana Highlands in the southeast are rich in other minerals, such as iron ore for making steel. Gold is also mined in remote areas of the highlands. Dams on tributaries of the Orinoco River produce hydroelectricity.

Caracas (kah-RAH-kahs) is Venezuela's capital and the economic and cultural center of the country. It is a large city with a modern subway system, busy expressways, and tall office buildings. Still, neither Caracas nor Venezuela has escaped poverty.

Caracas is encircled by slums, and many Venezuelans living in the rural areas of the country are also poor.

Government

After years of suffering under military dictatorships, the people of Venezuela elected their first president in 1959. Since then, Venezuela's government has dealt with economic turmoil and political protests.

In 2002 Venezuela's president, Hugo Chavez, started to distribute the country's oil income equally among all Venezuelans. Before Chavez's presidency, only a small percentage of wealthy Venezuelans benefited from the country's oil income.

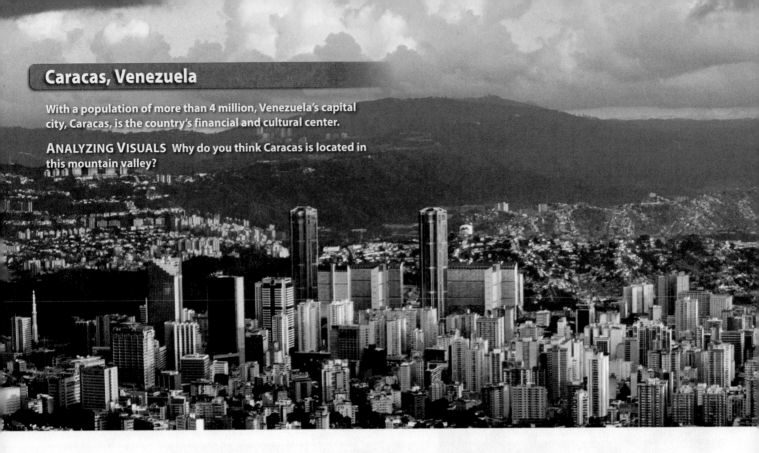

With a population of more than 4 million, Venezuela's capital city, Caracas, is the country's financial and cultural center.

ANALYZING VISUALS Why do you think Caracas is located in this mountain valley?

Thousands of Venezuelan oil workers went on strike to protest the president's actions. A **strike** is a group of workers stopping work until their demands are met. The strike lasted about two months. The protestors wanted Chavez to resign, but he refused. The strike caused Venezuela's economy to suffer as oil exports fell dramatically.

Venezuelans opposed to Chavez called for a **referendum**, a direct vote by the public, to remove him from office. The referendum was defeated. In 2006 about 63 percent of Venezuelans re-elected Chavez. In his second and third terms, Chavez adopted new **policies** aimed at bringing an end to poverty, illiteracy, and hunger. He supported changing his nation's constitution to end presidential term limits. In October 2012, Chavez was elected to a fourth term. A serious illness kept him from his January 2013 inauguration, and he died on March 5, 2013.

ACADEMIC VOCABULARY

policy rule, course of action

READING CHECK **Identifying Cause and Effect** What effect did the workers' strike have on Venezuela's economy?

The Guianas

The countries of Guyana, Suriname, and French Guiana are together known as the Guianas (gee-AH-nuhz). Dense tropical rain forests cover much of this region, which lies east of Venezuela.

Guyana

Guyana (gy-AH-nuh) comes from a South American Indian word that means "land of waters." About one-third of the country's population lives in Georgetown, the capital. Nearly all of Guyana's agricultural lands are located on the flat, fertile plains along the coast. Guyana's most important agricultural products are rice and sugar.

Guyana's population is diverse. About half of its people are descended from people who migrated to Guyana from India. These immigrants came to Guyana to work on the country's sugar plantations. Most Guyanese today farm small plots of land or run small businesses. About one-third of the population is descended from former African slaves. These people operate large businesses and hold most of the government positions.

Suriname

The resources and economy of Suriname (soohr-uh-NAHM) are similar to those of Guyana. Like Guyana, Suriname has a diverse population. The country's population includes South Asians, Africans, Chinese, Indonesians, and Creoles—people of mixed heritage. The capital, Paramaribo (pah-rah-MAH-ree-boh), is home to nearly half of the country's people.

French Guiana

French Guiana (gee-A-nuh) is a territory of France and sends representatives to the government in Paris. French Guiana's roughly 200,000 people live mostly in coastal areas. About two-thirds of the people are of African descent. Other groups include Europeans, Asians, and South American Indians. The country depends heavily on imports for its food and energy.

READING CHECK **Contrasting** How is French Guiana different from the rest of the Guianas?

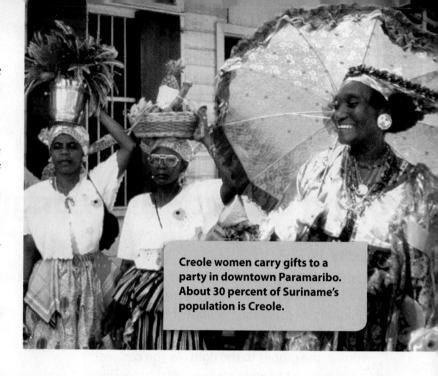
Creole women carry gifts to a party in downtown Paramaribo. About 30 percent of Suriname's population is Creole.

SUMMARY AND PREVIEW In this section, you learned that Venezuela's history was largely shaped by Spanish settlement. Today Venezuela's economy is based on oil. You also learned that to the east, the Guianas are home to a diverse population. In the next chapter, you will learn about the history and people of Atlantic South America.

Section 3 Assessment

hmhsocialstudies.com
ONLINE QUIZ

Reviewing Ideas, Terms, and Places

1. **a. Recall** What did Spanish settlers hope to find in Venezuela?
   b. Explain Who led Venezuela's revolt against Spain?
2. **a. Describe** What does the landscape of **Caracas** include?
   b. Explain How is oil important to Venezuela's economy?
   c. Elaborate Why did some Venezuelans go on **strike**?
3. **a. Describe** What are Guyana's agricultural lands and products like?
   b. Contrast How is population of the Guianas different from that of Colombia and Venezuela?

Critical Thinking

4. **Identifying Cause and Effect** Using your notes on Venezuela's natural resources and this diagram, list the effects of oil production on Venezuela's people, economy, and government.

Oil Production → People
Oil Production → Economy
Oil Production → Government

FOCUS ON WRITING

my WriteSmart

5. **Writing about Venezuela and the Guianas** Collect details about Venezuela and the Guianas for your letter. What is interesting about these cultures?

Social Studies Skills

Using Latitude and Longitude

Learn

The pattern of imaginary lines that circle the globe in east-west and north-south directions is called a grid. Geographers measure the distances between the lines of the grid in degrees.

Look at the globes to the right. As you can see, lines that run east to west are lines of latitude. These lines measure distance north and south of the equator. Lines that run north to south are lines of longitude. These lines measure distance east and west of the prime meridian. Reading lines of latitude and longitude on a map or globe helps you to find the absolute location of places.

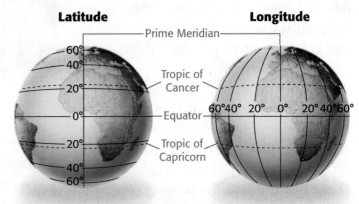

Practice

Look at the map to the right. Use these guidelines to read latitude and longitude to determine absolute location.

1. Pick a city on the map.

2. To find the latitude of the city you picked, first look at the equator. From there, look at the city's location. Then find the closest line of latitude to see how many degrees the city is north or south of the equator.

3. To find the longitude of the city, first look at the prime meridian. Then find the closest line of longitude to see how many degrees the city is east or west of the prime meridian.

Apply

Using a globe, find the United States. Then find the line of latitude that is located near your hometown. Look at the rest of the world on the globe and follow this line of latitude across the world. Which countries share the same latitude as your hometown?

Chapter Review

Visual Summary

Use the visual summary below to help you review the main ideas of the chapter.

QUICK FACTS

Caribbean South America's physical features include rivers, plains, mountains, and the world's highest waterfall.

A country rich in history and culture, Colombia is enduring a civil war today.

Venezuela is an oil-rich nation that has a population of mostly mixed Indian and European descent.

Reviewing Vocabulary, Terms, and Places

For each statement below, write T if it is true and F if it is false.

1. The Andes is a river system.

2. The Orinoco River flows 1,300 miles (2,100 km) through Venezuela.

3. Caribbean South America's location near the equator means that the region is very cold.

4. The Chibcha were the first people to settle Colombia.

5. Colombian culture includes traditional African songs and dances.

6. Most Venezuelans are of mixed Indian and European descent.

7. Venezuela gained its independence from France.

8. Venezuela's economy depends on oil production.

Comprehension and Critical Thinking

SECTION 1 *(Pages 236–239)*

9. **a. Recall** What is the region's longest river?

   b. Analyze How does the temperature vary in the Andes?

   c. Evaluate Why do you think it would be hard to live in the rain forest of Colombia?

SECTION 2 *(Pages 240–243)*

10. **a. Describe** How did the Chibcha treat their ruler?

    b. Draw Conclusions What created a problem for all Colombians after independence?

    c. Elaborate Why do most Colombians live in fertile valleys and river basins?

SECTION 3 *(Pages 244–249)*

11. **a. Define** What is a strike?

b. Draw Conclusions Why did people from India immigrate to Guyana?

c. Predict Do you think Venezuela's government will continue to use oil wealth to help the country's people? Explain your answer.

Using the Internet

12. Activity: Writing a Journal Entry Ride with the llaneros! Pack your bags and prepare for a trek through the South American countryside. Explore the vast grasslands, visit villages, and learn about the life and work of the cowboys, or llaneros, of the Venezuelan plains. Through your online textbook, research and take notes that will help you describe your adventure. Use the interactive template to write your journal entry. Describe what you have learned about the people and places you visited.

↗ hmhsocialstudies.com

Social Studies Skills

Using Latitude and Longitude *Use your knowledge of latitude and longitude to answer the questions below.*

13. Look at the physical map in Section 1. Find the lines of latitude and longitude. What line of latitude, shown on the map, runs through both Venezuela and Colombia? Using the latitude and longitude shown on the map, what is the absolute location of the Andes Mountains located in northwestern Venezuela?

14. Using a globe and your knowledge of latitude and longitude, determine the absolute location of Rio de Janeiro, Brazil; Madrid, Spain; Cape Town, South Africa; Tokyo, Japan; and Washington, D.C., United States.

Map Activity

15. Caribbean South America On a separate sheet of paper, match the letters on the map with their correct labels.

Llanos   Andes

Guiana Highlands   Orinoco River

Lake Maracaibo

FOCUS ON READING AND WRITING   *my*WriteSmart

16. Identifying Supporting Details Look back over Section 2 on Colombia. Then make a list of details you find to support the section's main ideas. Make sure you include details about the Spanish conquest, independence, culture, resources, and civil war.

17. Writing a Letter By now you have information about the region and the country you have chosen to live in. Use *my*WriteSmart in your eBook to begin your letter to your pen pal by describing the most interesting physical and cultural features of the whole region. Then write a second paragraph telling your pen pal about the special physical and cultural features of the country you've chosen to live in. Try to keep your pen pal interested in reading by including fascinating details and descriptions.

Reading Social Studies

Identifying Supporting Details

Why believe what you read? One reason is because of details that support or prove the main idea. These details might be facts, statistics, examples, or definitions. In the example below, notice what kind of proof or supporting details help you believe the main idea.

Colombia's economy relies on several valuable resources. Rich soil, steep slopes, and tall shade trees produce world-famous Colombian coffee. Other major export crops include bananas, sugarcane, and cotton. Many farms in Colombia produce flowers that are exported around the world. In fact, 80 percent of the country's flowers are shipped to the United States.

From Section 2, Colombia

Main Idea
Colombia's economy relies on several valuable resources.

Supporting Details			
Example	Fact	Fact	Statistic
Colombian coffee	Other export crops	Export flowers	80 percent shipped to U.S.

YOU TRY IT!

Read the following sentences. Then identify the supporting details in a graphic organizer like the one above.

Caribbean South America is home to some remarkable wildlife. For example, hundreds of bird species, meat-eating fish called piranhas, and crocodiles live in or around the Orinoco River. Colombia has one of the world's highest concentrations of plant and animal species. The country's wildlife includes jaguars, ocelots, and several species of monkeys.

From Section 1, Physical Geography

CHAPTER 11

Atlantic South America

Essential Question

myNotebook

How have the nations of Atlantic South America addressed economic and environmental challenges?

Texas Essential Knowledge and Skills (TEKS)

1A, 1B, 2B, 3A, 3B, 3C, 4D, 4E, 5A, 5B, 5C, 6A, 6B, 15D, 21A, 21B, 21C, 22D

FOCUS ON READING AND WRITING

myWriteSmart

Using Context Clues As you read, you may find some unknown words. You can usually figure out what a word means by using context clues. Look at the words and sentences around the unknown word—its context—to figure out the definition. **See the lesson, Using Context Clues, on page 275**

Creating a Web Site You are a Web designer at a travel agency. Read this chapter and then use what you learn to create a Web site about Atlantic South America. The goal of your Web site will be to convince viewers to visit the region. Use the annotation tools in your eBook to gather information for your assignment.

PACIFIC OCEAN

110°W   100°W

0° Equator

⊙ National capital
● Other cities

0   300   600 Miles
0   300   600 Kilometers

Projection:
Lambert Azimuthal Equal-Area

20°S

map zone

Geography Skills

Place Brazil and Argentina are South America's largest countries.

1. **Identify** What city lies on the Amazon River?
2. **Analyze** What would be some benefits of the location of Buenos Aires?

Culture During Carnival, Brazilians celebrate with music, dancing, and costumes.

COLOMBIA

VENEZUELA

GUYANA

SURINAME

FRENCH GUIANA
(FRANCE)

ECUADOR

PERU

Amazon River   • Manaus

B R A Z I L

BOLIVIA

• Salvador

☆ Brasília

CHILE

PARAGUAY

Asunción ☆

Rio de Janeiro
• São Paulo

Paraná River

Córdoba •

URUGUAY

Buenos Aires ☆   ☆ Montevideo

ARGENTINA

ATLANTIC
OCEAN

Falkland
Islands

Tropic of Capricorn

Tropic of Capricorn

0° Equator

10°S

20°S

30°S

40°S

50°S

80°W

70°W

60°W

50°W

40°W

30°W

20°W

10°W

0°

10°S

20°S

30°S

90°W

80°W

90°W

N W E S

Geography The Amazon Basin covers a huge forested region in northern Brazil.

History Colonial buildings, such as the Casa Rosada in Buenos Aires, reflect the region's colonial heritage.

Physical Geography

TEKS 3A, 3B, 3C, 4D, 4E, 5A, 5B, 5C, 6A, 6B, 21B, 21C, 22D

What You Will Learn...

Main Ideas

1. Physical features of Atlantic South America include large rivers, plateaus, and plains.
2. Climate and vegetation in the region range from cool, dry plains to warm, humid forests.
3. The rain forest is a major source of natural resources.

The Big Idea

The physical geography of Atlantic South America includes large river systems, plains and plateaus, and the Amazon rain forest.

Key Terms and Places

Amazon River, *p. 256*
Río de la Plata, *p. 257*
estuary, *p. 257*
Pampas, *p. 257*
deforestation, *p. 259*
soil exhaustion, *p. 259*

hmhsocialstudies.com
TAKING NOTES

Use the graphic organizer online to take notes on the physical geography of Atlantic South America.

If YOU lived there...

You live on the coast of Brazil, near the mouth of the Amazon River. Now you are taking your first trip up the river deep into the rain forest. The river is amazingly wide and calm. Trees on the riverbanks seem to soar to the sky. Your boat slows as you pass a small village. You notice that all the houses rest on poles that lift them 8 to 10 feet out of the water.

What would it be like to live in the rain forest?

BUILDING BACKGROUND While rugged mountains and highlands dominate the landscape of Caribbean South America, much of the Atlantic region is made up of broad interior plains. Landscapes in this region range from tropical rain forest to temperate, grassy plains.

Physical Features

The region of Atlantic South America includes four countries: Brazil, Argentina, Uruguay, and Paraguay. This large region covers about two-thirds of South America. Brazil alone occupies nearly half of the continent. Most of the physical features found in South America are found in these four countries.

Major River Systems

The world's largest river system, the Amazon, flows eastward across northern Brazil. The **Amazon River** is about 4,000 miles (6,440 km) long. It extends from the Andes Mountains in Peru to the Atlantic Ocean. Hundreds of tributaries flow into it, draining an area that includes parts of most South American countries.

Because of its huge drainage area, the Amazon carries more water than any other river in the world. About 20 percent of the water that runs off Earth's surface flows down the Amazon. Where it meets the Atlantic, this freshwater lowers the salt level of the Atlantic for more than 100 miles (160 km) from shore.

Atlantic South America: Physical

ELEVATION

Feet	Meters
13,120	4,000
6,560	2,000
1,640	500
656	200
(Sea level) 0	0 (Sea level)
Below sea level	Below sea level

0 500 1,000 Miles
0 500 1,000 Kilometers

Projection:
Lambert Azimuthal Equal-Area

Mt. Aconcagua
22,834 ft
(6,960 m)

① Iguazú Falls is part of the Paraná River system. Large rivers are a key physical feature in Atlantic South America.

② The wide, grassy plains of the Pampas in Argentina are good for raising cattle.

Geography Skills

Place Atlantic South America has several large river systems and plains.
1. **Name** What river flows through eastern Brazil?
2. **Analyze** Why do you think the Pampas are good for raising cattle?

The Paraná (pah-rah-NAH) River drains much of the central part of South America. Water from the Paraná River eventually flows into the **Río de la Plata** (REE-oh day lah PLAH-tah) and the Atlantic Ocean beyond. The Río de la Plata is an estuary. An **estuary** is a partially enclosed body of water where freshwater mixes with salty seawater.

Plains and Plateaus

As you can see on the map, this region's landforms mainly consist of plains and plateaus. The Amazon Basin in northern Brazil is a giant, flat floodplain. South of the Amazon Basin are the Brazilian Highlands, a rugged region of old, eroded mountains, and another area of high plains called the Mato Grosso Plateau.

Farther south, a low plains region known as the Gran Chaco (grahn CHAH-koh) stretches across parts of Paraguay and northern Argentina. In central Argentina are the wide, grassy plains of the **Pampas**. South of the Pampas is Patagonia—a region of dry plains and plateaus. All of these southern plains rise in the west to form the high Andes Mountains.

READING CHECK **Summarizing** What are the region's major landforms and rivers?

FOCUS ON READING
Where can you find the definition of *Pampas*?

The Amazon rain forest covers more than one-third of South America. Seen from the air, it looks like a big, green carpet. The top level of tree branches is called the canopy. Most action in the forest takes place in the canopy, but plenty of life also exists below.

Animals such as monkeys and sloths can spend their entire lives in the canopy.

People have cleared parts of the rain forest for farming, ranching, and logging.

Parts of the forest are flooded for half the year, and trees stand in water up to 40 feet (12 m) deep.

ANALYSIS SKILL ANALYZING VISUALS

What kinds of animals could not survive living in the canopy?

Climate and Vegetation

Atlantic South America has many climates. Generally, cool climates in southern and highland areas give way to tropical, moist climates in northern and coastal areas.

In southern Argentina Patagonia has a cool, desert climate. North of Patagonia, rich soils and a humid subtropical climate make parts of the Pampas good for farming. Farther north in Argentina, the Gran Chaco has a humid tropical climate. There, summer rains can turn some parts of the plains into marshlands.

North of Argentina, in Brazil, a large part of the central region has a tropical savanna climate with warm grasslands. The northeastern part of the country has a hot, dry climate, while the southeast is cooler and more humid.

In northern Brazil the Amazon Basin's humid tropical climate supports the world's largest tropical rain forest. Rain falls almost every day in this region. The Amazon rain forest contains the world's greatest variety of plant and animal life.

READING CHECK **Finding Main Ideas** What is the climate like in the rain forest?

Natural Resources

The Amazon rain forest is one of the region's greatest natural resources. It provides food, wood, rubber, plants for medicines, and other products. In recent years **deforestation**, or the clearing of trees, has become an issue in the forest.

The region's land is also a resource for commercial farming, which is found near coastal areas of Atlantic South America. In some areas, however, planting the same crop every year has caused **soil exhaustion**, which means the soil is infertile because it has lost nutrients needed by plants.

Atlantic South America also has good mineral and energy resources such as gold, silver, copper, iron, and oil. Dams on some of the region's large rivers also provide hydroelectric power.

READING CHECK **Summarizing** What resources does the rain forest provide?

SUMMARY AND PREVIEW Physical features of Atlantic South America include great river systems and plains. The Amazon rain forest makes up a huge part of the region. Next you will learn about Brazil, the country of the Amazon.

Section 1 Assessment

hmhsocialstudies.com
ONLINE QUIZ

Reviewing Ideas, Terms, and Places

1. **a. Define** What is an **estuary**?
   b. Explain How does the **Amazon River** affect the Atlantic Ocean at the river's mouth?
   c. Elaborate What benefits do you think the rivers might bring to Atlantic South America?

2. **a. Recall** What kind of climate does Patagonia have?
   b. Make Inferences Why are temperatures in the south generally cooler than temperatures in the north?

3. **a. Identify** What resources does the rain forest provide?
   b. Analyze What is one benefit and one drawback of practicing commercial agriculture in the rain forest?
   c. Elaborate **Soil exhaustion** might lead to what kinds of additional problems?

Critical Thinking

4. **Categorizing** Look back over your notes. Then use a table like this one to organize the physical geography of Atlantic South America by country.

	Geography
Brazil	
Argentina	

FOCUS ON WRITING

my WriteSmart

5. **Describing Physical Geography** Jot down notes about the physical features, climate and vegetation, landscapes, and resources of this area. Identify one or two images you could use for your Web site.

Brazil

TEKS 1A, 2B, 3B, 4D, 15D, 21A, 21C

What You Will Learn...

Main Ideas

1. Brazil's history has been affected by Brazilian Indians, Portuguese settlers, and enslaved Africans.
2. Brazil's society reflects a mix of people and cultures.
3. Brazil today is experiencing population growth in its cities and new development in rain forest areas.

The Big Idea

The influence of Brazil's history can be seen all over the country in its people and culture.

Key Terms and Places

São Paulo, *p. 262*
megacity, *p. 262*
Rio de Janeiro, *p. 262*
favelas, *p. 263*
Brasília, *p. 263*
Manaus, *p. 263*

hmhsocialstudies.com
TAKING NOTES

Use the graphic organizer online to take notes on Brazil.

If YOU lived there...

You live in Rio de Janeiro, Brazil's second-largest city. For months your friends have been preparing for Carnival, the year's biggest holiday. During Carnival, people perform in glittery costumes and there is dancing all day and all night in the streets. The city is packed with tourists. It can be fun, but it is hectic! Your family is thinking of leaving Rio during Carnival so they can get some peace and quiet, but you may stay in Rio with a friend if you like.

Would you stay for Carnival? Why or why not?

BUILDING BACKGROUND Carnival is a tradition that is not unique to Brazil, but it has come to symbolize certain parts of Brazilian culture. Brazilian culture differs from cultures in the rest of South America in many ways. Brazil's unique history in the region is responsible for most of the cultural differences.

History

Brazil is the largest country in South America. Its population of more than 188 million is larger than the population of all of the other South American countries combined. Most Brazilians are descended from three diverse groups of people whose experiences have contributed in different ways throughout Brazil's history.

Colonial Brazil

The first people in Brazil were American Indians. They arrived in the region many thousands of years ago and developed a way of life based on hunting, fishing, and small-scale farming.

In 1500 Portuguese explorers became the first Europeans to find Brazil. Soon Portuguese settlers began to move there. Good climates and soils, particularly in the northeast, made Brazil a large sugar-growing colony. Colonists brought a third group of people—Africans—to work as slaves on the plantations. Sugar plantations made Portugal rich, but they also eventually replaced forests along the Atlantic coast.

Other parts of Brazil also contributed to the colonial economy. Inland, many Portuguese settlers created cattle ranches. In the late 1600s and early 1700s, people discovered gold and precious gems in the southeast. A mining boom drew people to Brazil from around the world. Finally, in the late 1800s southeastern Brazil became a major coffee-producing region.

Brazil Since Independence

Brazil gained independence from Portugal without a fight in 1822. However, independence did not change Brazil's economy much. For example, Brazil was the last country in the Americas to end slavery.

Since the end of Portuguese rule, Brazil has been governed at times by dictators and at other times by elected officials. Today the country has an elected president and legislature. Brazilians can participate in politics through voting.

READING CHECK **Summarizing** What was Brazil's colonial economy like?

People and Culture

The people who came to Brazil over the years brought their own traditions. These traditions blended to create a unique Brazilian culture.

People

More than half of Brazilians consider themselves of European <u>descent</u>. These people include descendants of original Portuguese settlers along with descendants of more recent immigrants from Spain, Germany, Italy, and Poland. Nearly 40 percent of Brazil's people are of mixed African and European descent. Brazil also has the largest Japanese population outside of Japan.

Because of its colonial heritage, Brazil's official language is Portuguese. In fact, since Brazil's population is so huge, there are more Portuguese-speakers in South America than there are Spanish-speakers, even though Spanish is spoken in almost every other country on the continent. Other Brazilians speak Spanish, English, French, Japanese, or native languages.

FOCUS ON READING
What context clues in this paragraph help you understand the meaning of *descent*?

FOCUS ON CULTURE

Soccer in Brazil

To Brazilians, soccer is more than a game. It is part of being Brazilian. Professional stars are national heroes. The national team often plays in Rio de Janeiro, home of the world's largest soccer stadium. Some fans beat drums all through the games. But it is not just professional soccer that is popular. People all over Brazil play soccer—in cleared fields, on the beach, or in the street. Here, boys in Rio practice their skills.

Analyzing Why do you think soccer is so popular in Brazil?

Brazil's regions differ from each other in their people, climates, economies, and landscapes.

ANALYZING VISUALS Which region appears to be the wealthiest?

1 The southeast has the country's largest cities, such as Rio de Janeiro.

Religion

Brazil has the largest population of Roman Catholics of any country in the world. About 75 percent of Brazilians are Catholic. In recent years Protestantism has grown in popularity, particularly among the urban poor. Some Brazilians practice macumba (mah-KOOM-bah), a religion that combines beliefs and practices of African and Indian religions with Christianity.

Festivals and Food

ACADEMIC VOCABULARY

aspects parts

Other **aspects** of Brazilian life also reflect the country's mix of cultures. For example, Brazilians celebrate Carnival before the Christian season of Lent. The celebration mixes traditions from Africa, Brazil, and Europe. During Carnival, Brazilians dance the samba, which was adapted from an African dance.

Immigrant influences can also be found in Brazilian foods. In parts of the country, an African seafood dish called vatapá (vah-tah-PAH) is popular. Many Brazilians also enjoy eating feijoada (fay-ZHWAH-dah), a stew of black beans and meat.

READING CHECK **Analyzing** How has cultural borrowing affected Brazilian culture?

Brazil Today

Brazil's large size creates opportunities and challenges for the country. For example, Brazil has the largest economy in South America and has modern and wealthy areas. However, many Brazilians are poor.

While some of the same issues and characteristics can be found throughout Brazil, other characteristics are unique to a particular region of the country. We can divide Brazil into four regions based on their people, economies, and landscapes.

The Southeast

Most people in Brazil live in the southeast. **São Paulo** is located there. Almost 19 million people live in and around São Paulo. It is the largest urban area in South America and the fourth largest in the world. São Paulo is considered a **megacity**, or a giant urban area that includes surrounding cities and suburbs.

Rio de Janeiro, Brazil's second-largest city, lies northeast of São Paulo. Almost 12 million people live there. The city was the capital of Brazil from 1822 until 1960. Today Rio de Janeiro remains a major port city. Its spectacular setting and exciting culture are popular with tourists.

2 About one third of Brazilians live in the dry northeast, the nation's poorest region.

3 Rivers provide resources and transportation for people living in the Amazon region.

In addition to having the largest cities, the southeast is also Brazil's richest region. It is rich in natural resources and has most of the country's industries and productive farmland. It is one of the major coffee-growing regions of the world.

Although the southeast has a strong economy, it also has poverty. Cities in the region have huge slums called **favelas** (fah-VE-lahz). Many people who live in favelas have come to cities of the southeast from other regions of Brazil in search of jobs.

The Northeast

Immigrants to Brazil's large cities often come from the northeast, which is Brazil's poorest region. Many people there cannot read, and health care is poor. The region often suffers from droughts, which make farming and raising livestock difficult. The northeast has also had difficulty attracting industry. However, the region's beautiful beaches do attract tourists.

Other tourist attractions in northeastern Brazil are the region's many old colonial cities. These cities were built during the days of the sugar industry. They have brightly painted buildings, cobblestone streets, and elaborate Catholic churches.

The Interior

The interior region of Brazil is a frontier land. Its abundant land and mild climate could someday make it an important area for agriculture. For now, few people live in this region, except for those who reside in the country's capital, **Brasília**.

In the mid-1950s government officials hoped that building a new capital city in the Brazilian interior would help develop the region. Brasília has modern buildings and busy highways. More than 2 million people live in Brasília, although it was originally designed for only 500,000.

The Amazon

The Amazon region covers the northern part of Brazil. **Manaus**, which lies 1,000 miles (1,600 km) from the mouth of the Amazon, is a major port and industrial city. More than 1 million people live there. They rely on the river for transportation and communication.

Isolated Indian villages are scattered throughout the region's dense rain forest. Some of Brazil's Indians had little contact with outsiders until recently. Now, logging, mining, and new roads are bringing more people and development to this region.

Satellite View

Deforestation in the Amazon

Deforestation is changing the landscape of the Amazon rain forest. This satellite image shows new roads and cleared areas where people have taken resources from the forest.

Many people depend on the industries that result in deforestation. For example, people need wood for building and making paper. Also, farmers, loggers, and miners need to make a living. However, deforestation in the Amazon also threatens the survival of many plant and animal species. It also threatens hundreds of unique ecosystems.

Making Inferences What do you think might be some effects of building roads in the rain forest?

This new development provides needed income for some people. But it destroys large areas of the rain forest. It also creates tensions among the Brazilian Indians, new settlers, miners, and the government.

READING CHECK **Contrasting** How does the northeast of Brazil differ from the southeast?

SUMMARY AND PREVIEW In this section you read about Brazil—a huge country of many contrasts. Brazil reflects the mixing of people and cultures from its history. In the next section you will learn about Brazil's neighbors—Argentina, Uruguay, and Paraguay.

Section 2 Assessment

hmhsocialstudies.com
ONLINE QUIZ

Reviewing Ideas, Terms, and Places

1. **a. Recall** What European country colonized Brazil?
   b. Make Inferences Why did the colonists bring Africans to work on plantations as slaves?
   c. Analyze What diverse groups have contributed to Brazil's society? What were some of the experiences of these groups?

2. **a. Identify** What religion is most common in Brazil?
   b. Explain Why is so much of Brazil's culture influenced by African traditions?

3. **a. Define** What is a **megacity**, and what is an example of a megacity in Brazil?
   b. Make Inferences Why might development in the Amazon cause tensions between Brazilian Indians and new settlers?
   c. Elaborate How might life change for a person who moves from the northeast to the southeast?

Critical Thinking

4. **Finding Main Ideas** Review your notes on Brazil. Then, write a main idea statement about each region. Use a graphic organizer like this one.

	Main Idea
The Southeast	
The Northeast	
The Interior	
The Amazon	

FOCUS ON WRITING

my WriteSmart

5. **Writing about Brazil** What information about the history, people, and culture of Brazil will draw readers to the country? What regions do you think they would like to visit? List details and ideas for possible images for your Web site.

Connecting Ideas

Learn

You have already used several types of graphic organizers in this book. Graphic organizers are drawings that help you organize information and connect ideas.

One type of graphic organizer is a word web. A word web like the one at right helps you organize specific facts and details around a main topic. Notice that information gets more detailed as it gets farther away from the main topic.

Practice

Use the word web here to answer the following questions. You may also want to look back at the information on Brazilian culture in your textbook.

1. How can a graphic organizer help you connect ideas?

2. What is the main topic of this word web?

3. What three main ideas does this graphic organizer connect?

Apply

Copy the graphic organizer shown here in your notebook. Use the information on Brazilian culture in your textbook to fill in the blank circles with additional details about the main topic.

African — Vatapá

Brazilian culture — Native

European — Language

Carnival

Argentina, Uruguay, and Paraguay

TEKS 1A, 1B, 2B, 3B, 4D, 15D, 21A, 21C

What You Will Learn...

Main Ideas

1. European immigrants have dominated the history and culture of Argentina.
2. Argentina's capital, Buenos Aires, plays a large role in the country's government and economy today.
3. Uruguay has been influenced by its neighbors.
4. Paraguay is the most rural country in the region.

The Big Idea

Argentina, Uruguay, and Paraguay have been influenced by European immigration, a tradition of ranching, and large urban populations.

Key Terms and Places

gauchos, *p. 267*
Buenos Aires, *p. 268*
Mercosur, *p. 268*
informal economy, *p. 269*
landlocked, *p. 270*

hmhsocialstudies.com
TAKING NOTES

Use the graphic organizer online to organize your notes on Argentina, Uruguay, and Paraguay.

If YOU lived there...

You live in Montevideo, the capital of Uruguay. On weekends you like to visit the old part of the city and admire its beautiful buildings. You also enjoy walking along the banks of the Río de la Plata and watching fishers bring in their catch. Sometimes you visit the parks and beaches along the banks of the river.

How do you think the river has influenced Montevideo?

BUILDING BACKGROUND The southern countries of Atlantic South America—Argentina, Uruguay, and Paraguay—have all been influenced by their locations and European culture. Neither Spanish influence nor Indian culture is as strong in the southern part of South America as in other parts of the continent.

Argentina's History and Culture

Like most of South America, Argentina was originally home to groups of Indians. Groups living in the Pampas hunted wild game, while farther north Indians built irrigation systems for farming. However, unlike most of South America, Argentina has very few native peoples remaining. Instead, Argentina's culture has been mostly influenced by Europeans.

Early History

The first Europeans to come to Argentina were the Spanish. In the 1500s Spanish conquerors spread from the northern part of the continent into southern South America in search of silver and gold. They named the region Argentina. *Argentina* means "land of silver" or "silvery one."

Gauchos on the Pampas

Gauchos were a popular subject in Argentine art. In this painting from 1820, gauchos gather to watch a horse race.

ANALYZING VISUALS Why would horses be important to a gaucho?

The Spanish soon built settlements in Argentina. The Spanish monarch granted land to the colonists, who in turn built the settlements. These landowners were also given the right to force the Indians living there to work.

During the colonial era, the Pampas became an important agricultural region. Argentine cowboys, called **gauchos** (GOW-chohz), herded cattle and horses on the open grasslands. Although agriculture is still important on the Pampas, very few people in Argentina live as gauchos today.

In the early 1800s Argentina fought for independence from Spain. A period of violence and instability followed. Many Indians were killed or driven away by fighting during this time.

Modern Argentina

As the Indians were being killed off, more European influences dominated the region. New immigrants arrived from Italy, Germany, and Spain. Also, the British helped build railroads across the country. Railroads made it easier for Argentina to transport agricultural products for export to Europe. Beef exports, in particular, made the country rich.

Argentina remained one of South America's richest countries throughout the 1900s. However, the country also struggled under dictators and military governments during those years.

Some political leaders, like Eva Perón, were popular. But many leaders abused human rights. During the "Dirty War" in the 1970s, they tortured and killed many accused of disagreeing with the government. Both the country's people and its economy suffered. Finally, in the 1980s, Argentina's last military government gave up power to an elected government.

BIOGRAPHY

Eva Perón
(1919–1952)

Known affectionately as Evita, Eva Perón helped improve the living conditions of people in Argentina, particularly the poor. As the wife of Argentina's president, Juan Perón, Evita established thousands of hospitals and schools throughout Argentina. She also helped women gain the right to vote. After years of battling cancer, Evita died at age 33. All of Argentina mourned her death for weeks.

Analyzing Why was Eva Perón able to help many people?

People and Culture

Argentina's historical ties to Europe still affect its culture. Most of Argentina's roughly 40 million people are descended from Spanish, Italian, or other European settlers. Argentine Indians and mestizos make up only about 3 percent of the population. Most Argentines are Roman Catholic.

Beef is still a part of Argentina's culture. A popular dish is parrilla (pah-REE-yah), which includes grilled sausage and steak. Supper is generally eaten late.

READING CHECK **Generalizing** What kind of governments did Argentina have in the 1900s?

Argentina Today

Today many more of Argentina's people live in **Buenos Aires** (BWAY-nohs EYE-rayz) than in any other city. Buenos Aires is the country's capital. It is also the second-largest urban area in South America. Several geographic factors are responsible for the dense pattern of population in and around Buenos Aires. These factors include the location of most of Argentina's industry in and around the city, and its location on the coast and near the Pampas.

The Pampas are the country's most developed agricultural region. About 11 percent of Argentina's labor force works in agriculture. Large ranches and farms there produce beef, wheat, and corn for export to other countries.

Argentina's economy has always been affected by government policies. In the 1990s government leaders made economic reforms to help businesses grow. Argentina joined **Mercosur**—an organization that promotes trade and economic cooperation among the southern and eastern countries of South America. By the late 1900s and early 2000s, however, heavy debt and government spending brought Argentina into an economic crisis.

Argentina: Population

PARAGUAY
Tropic of Capricorn
San Miguel de Tucumán
CHILE
30°S
Córdoba
Mendoza
Rosario
Paraná River
BRAZIL
URUGUAY
Buenos Aires
PACIFIC OCEAN
ARGENTINA
ATLANTIC OCEAN
40°S
N W E S
50°S

• 10,000 people

0   300   600 Miles
0   300   600 Kilometers
Projection: Lambert Azimuthal Equal-Area

map zone **Geography Skills**

Place Buenos Aires is home to nearly a third of all Argentines.
1. **Interpreting Graphs** How many times bigger is Buenos Aires than Argentina's second-largest city?
2. **Analyze** What might be a benefit and a drawback of having most of the country's population in one area?

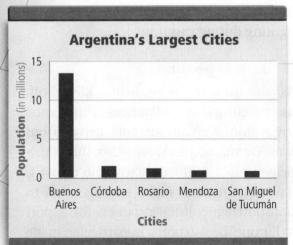

Argentina's Largest Cities

Population (in millions)

15

10

5

0

Buenos Aires   Córdoba   Rosario   Mendoza   San Miguel de Tucumán

Cities

The economic crisis caused a political crisis. As a result, during 2001, Argentina's government changed hands four times as its leaders tried to solve the problems. By 2003 the economy had stabilized somewhat, but thousands of people's lives had changed forever. The crisis caused many people who once had professional careers to lose their jobs and join the informal economy. The **informal economy** is a part of the economy based on odd jobs that people perform without government regulation through taxes. Today many Argentines are still searching for ways to improve their economy.

READING CHECK **Comparing and Contrasting** What are some similarities and differences between Buenos Aires and the Pampas?

Uruguay

Tucked between Argentina and Brazil lies Uruguay. Its capital, Montevideo (mawn-tay-vee-DAY-oh), is located on the north shore of the Río de la Plata, not far from Buenos Aires. Uruguay has always been influenced by its larger neighbors.

Portugal claimed Uruguay during the colonial era, but the Spanish took over in the 1770s. By that time, few Uruguayan Indians remained. A few years later, in 1825, Uruguay declared independence from Spain. Since then, military governments have ruled Uruguay off and on. In general, however, the country has a strong tradition of respect for political freedom. Today Uruguay is a democracy.

People

As in Argentina, people of European descent make up the majority of Uruguay's population. Only about 12 percent of the population is mestizo, Indian, or of African descent. Roman Catholicism is the main religion in the country. Spanish is the official language, but many people also speak Portuguese because of Uruguay's location near Brazil.

More than 90 percent of Uruguay's people live in urban areas. More than a third of Uruguayans live in and near Montevideo. The country has a high literacy rate. In addition, many people there have good jobs and can afford a wide range of consumer goods and travel to Europe. However, many young people leave Uruguay to explore better economic opportunities elsewhere.

Economy

FOCUS ON READING

Where can you find the definition of *landlocked*?

Just as Uruguay's culture is tied to its neighbors, its economy is tied to the economies of Brazil and Argentina. In fact, more than half of Uruguay's foreign trade is with these two Mercosur partners. Beef is an important export. As in Argentina, ranchers graze livestock on inland plains.

Agriculture, along with some limited manufacturing, is the basis of Uruguay's economy. Uruguay has few mineral resources. One important source of energy is hydroelectric power. Developing poor rural areas in the interior, where resources are in short supply, is a big challenge.

READING CHECK **Compare** In what ways is Uruguay similar to Argentina?

Paraguay

Paraguay shares borders with Bolivia, Brazil, and Argentina. It is a landlocked country. **Landlocked** means completely surrounded by land with no direct access to the ocean. The Paraguay River divides the country into two regions. East of the river is the country's most productive farmland. Ranchers also graze livestock in some parts of western Paraguay.

Paraguay was claimed by Spanish settlers in the mid-1530s. It remained a Spanish colony until 1811, when it won independence. From independence until 1989, Paraguay was ruled off and on by dictators. Today the country has elected leaders and a democratic government.

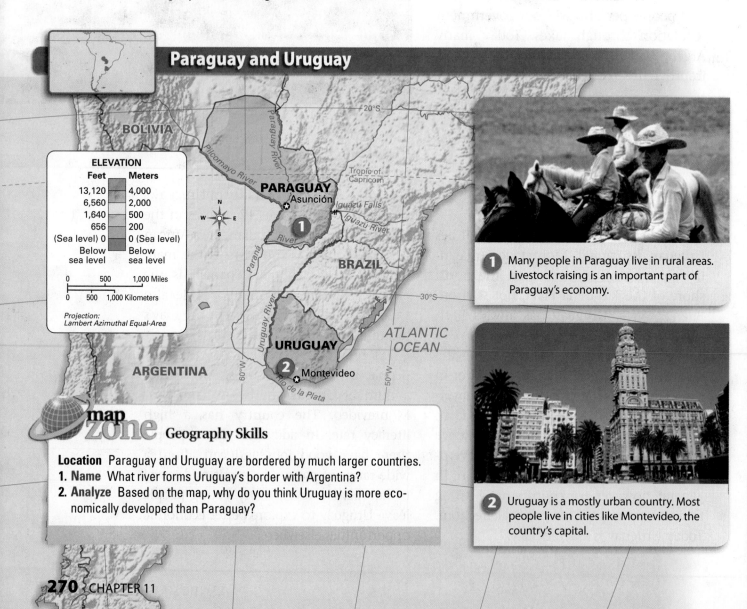

Paraguay and Uruguay

ELEVATION

Feet	Meters
13,120	4,000
6,560	2,000
1,640	500
656	200
(Sea level) 0	0 (Sea level)
Below sea level	Below sea level

0 500 1,000 Miles

0 500 1,000 Kilometers

Projection: Lambert Azimuthal Equal-Area

BOLIVIA

PARAGUAY
Asunción

1

Tropic of Capricorn

Iguazú Falls
Iguazú River

BRAZIL

ARGENTINA

URUGUAY

2 Montevideo

ATLANTIC OCEAN

Río de la Plata

Paraguay River

Pilcomayo River

Paraná River

Uruguay River

20°S

30°S

60°W

50°W

1 Many people in Paraguay live in rural areas. Livestock raising is an important part of Paraguay's economy.

2 Uruguay is a mostly urban country. Most people live in cities like Montevideo, the country's capital.

map zone Geography Skills

Location Paraguay and Uruguay are bordered by much larger countries.
1. **Name** What river forms Uruguay's border with Argentina?
2. **Analyze** Based on the map, why do you think Uruguay is more economically developed than Paraguay?

People

A great majority—about 95 percent—of Paraguayans are mestizos. Indians and people of mostly European descent make up the rest of the population. Paraguay has two official languages. Almost all people in Paraguay speak both Spanish and Guarani (gwah-ruh-NEE), an Indian language. As in Uruguay, most people are Roman Catholic.

Paraguay's capital and largest city is Asunción (ah-soon-SYOHN). The city is located along the Paraguay River near the border with Argentina.

Economy

Much of Paraguay's wealth is controlled by a few rich families and companies. These families and companies have tremendous influence over the country's government.

Agriculture is an important part of the economy. In fact, nearly half of the country's workers are farmers. Many of these farmers grow just enough food to feed themselves and their families. They grow crops such as corn, cotton, soybeans, and sugarcane. Paraguay also has many small businesses but not much industry.

Paraguay's future may be promising as the country learns how to use its resources more effectively. For example, the country has built large hydroelectric dams on the Paraná River. These dams provide more power than Paraguay needs, so Paraguay is able to sell the surplus electricity to Brazil and Argentina.

READING CHECK **Contrast** How are the people of Paraguay different from the people of Argentina and Uruguay?

SUMMARY AND PREVIEW The people of Paraguay, Argentina, and Uruguay share some aspects of their European heritage. Their economies are also closely tied. In the next chapter you will learn about these countries' neighbors to the west.

Section 3 Assessment

Reviewing Ideas, Terms, and Places

1. a. **Define** What is a **gaucho**?
   b. **Explain** Why is Argentina's population mostly of European descent?
2. a. **Identify** What is Argentina's biggest city?
   b. **Make Inferences** What benefits do you think being part of **Mercosur** brings to Argentina?
   c. **Elaborate** What are some benefits the **informal economy** provides, and what are some of its drawbacks?
3. a. **Recall** Where is Uruguay's capital located?
   b. **Summarize** How has Uruguay's location influenced its culture?
4. a. **Define** What does it mean to say a country is **landlocked**?
   b. **Explain** What is Paraguay's economy like?
   c. **Predict** What are some possible ways Paraguay may be able to improve its economy in the future?

Critical Thinking

5. **Comparing and Contrasting** Look over your notes on Uruguay and Paraguay. Then draw a diagram like the one here and use it to show similarities and differences between the two countries.

Uruguay   Paraguay

FOCUS ON WRITING *my* WriteSmart

6. **Thinking about Argentina, Uruguay, and Paraguay** Add details about these countries to your notes for your Web site. What information on history, culture, and specific locations will you include? For each country, think of one image that would best illustrate it.

from
The Gaucho Martín Fierro

by José Hernández

Gauchos spent a lot of time alone on the plains, but sometimes they got together for games and amusement.

About the Reading *José Hernández spent part of his childhood on Argentina's Pampas. The gauchos lived freely on the plains there, herding cattle. In 1872 he published an epic poem about his days as an Argentine cowboy. The passage below is an excerpt.*

AS YOU READ Notice the emotion with which Hernández writes.

Even the poorest gaucho
had a string of matching horses;
he could always afford some amusement,
and people were ready for anything . . .
Looking out across the land
you'd see nothing but cattle and sky. ❶

When the branding-time came round
that was work to warm you up!
What a crowd! lassoing the running steers
and keen to hold and throw them . . . ❷
What a time that was! in those days surely
there were champions to be seen . . .

And the games that would get going
when we were all of us together!
We were always ready for them,
as at times like those
a lot of neighbors would turn up
to help out the regular hands.

GUIDED READING

WORD HELP

lassoing catching with a rope
steers cattle
keen happy, eager

❶ Notice Hernández's description of the Pampas.

❷ Hernández describes the work of gauchos.

What were some activities of gauchos?

Connecting Literature to Geography

1. **Identifying Points of View** Hernández had happy memories of his days as a gaucho. What words and phrases demonstrate how Hernández felt?

2. **Analyzing** Although few people still work as gauchos, they are popular subjects in Argentine literature. What aspects of gaucho life do you think modern readers find appealing?

Chapter Review

Visual Summary

Use the visual summary below to help you review the main ideas of the chapter.

QUICK FACTS

The lush Amazon rain forest covers a huge part of the region.

Brazil has many large cities as well as large rural areas.

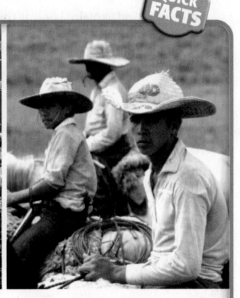

Argentina, Uruguay, and Paraguay have large plains that are good for ranching.

Reviewing Vocabulary, Terms, and Places

For each group of terms below, write a sentence that shows how all the terms in the group are related.

1. estuary
   Río de la Plata
   Buenos Aires
2. megacity
   favelas
   aspects
3. gauchos
   Pampas
4. soil exhaustion
   deforestation
   Amazon River
5. Rio de Janeiro
   São Paulo
   Manaus

Comprehension and Critical Thinking

SECTION 1 *(Pages 256–259)*

6. a. **Recall** What kind of climate does the Amazon Basin have?

   b. **Contrast** How are northern Brazil and southern Argentina different?

   c. **Elaborate** How might the region's major physical features have influenced development and daily life in Atlantic South America?

SECTION 2 *(Pages 260–264)*

7. a. **Describe** What parts of Brazilian culture reflect African influences?

   b. **Analyze** What factors lead people from the northeast of Brazil to move to the southeast?

   c. **Evaluate** Is deforestation of the Amazon rain forest necessary? Explain your answer. What arguments might someone with a different opinion use?

8. a. Describe How is Argentina's culture different from other South American countries?

b. Contrast What is one difference between Uruguay and Paraguay?

c. Identify and Explain Look at the population map of Argentina in Section 3. What patterns of population do you see? Explain how geographic factors affect these patterns.

Social Studies Skills

9. Connecting Ideas Draw a graphic organizer to help you organize information about the economy in Atlantic South America. One has been started for you below. You will need to add more ovals to contain the information.

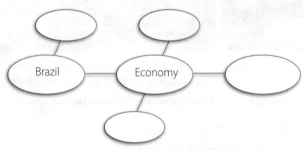

Brazil — Economy

Using the Internet

10. Activity: Creating a Poster The Amazon River is the world's second-longest river. Through your online textbook, explore the many aspects of the river, including its wildlife, the rain forest it cuts through, the people who live alongside it, and the environmental issues surrounding it. Use the information you find and the interactive template provided to create a poster about the amazing Amazon River.

hmhsocialstudies.com

Map Activity

11. Atlantic South America On a separate sheet of paper, match the letters on the map with their correct labels.

São Paulo	Pampas	Patagonia
Paraná River	Río de la Plata	Amazon River

Focus on Reading and Writing   *my*WriteSmart

12. Using Context Clues Look through the chapter and pick out two difficult words that you had to figure out by using context clues. Then, note the context clues you used to help you figure out the definitions of the difficult words.

13. Creating a Web Site You can create a real Web site or a paper version of a Web site. First, use *my*WriteSmart in your eBook to look back through your notes and choose key ideas about each country to include. In designing your site, first include a home page that briefly describes the region. Indicate links for pages about each of the countries in the region. Each of your country pages should include one short paragraph and one image. Remember to keep the pages simple—too much text might overwhelm your readers and send them off to another site!

Reading Social Studies

Using Context Clues

FOCUS ON READING

One practical way to tackle unfamiliar words you encounter is to look at the context. Reading the words and sentences surrounding the word will often help you because they give definitions, examples, or synonyms. For example, maybe you're not sure what the word *context* means. Just from reading the previous sentences, however, you probably understood that it means the "the part of a text surrounding a word or passage that makes its meaning clear." You have relied on the context to help you define the word. In reading geography, you may forget what some of the geographical terms mean. You can use context clues to figure them out. See how this process works in the example below with the word *tributary*.

> The Amazon River is about 4,000 miles long. It extends from the Andes Mountains in Peru to the Atlantic Ocean. Hundreds of tributaries flow into it, draining an area that includes parts of most South American countries.
>
> *From Section 1, Physical Geography*

1. Look at the surrounding words or sentences.
The passage talks about the Amazon River and what flows into it.

2. Make a guess at the word's meaning.
A tributary must be a smaller river or stream that flows into a bigger river.

3. Check your guess by inserting it into the passage.
Hundreds of smaller rivers flow into it.

YOU TRY IT!

Read the following sentences, and then use the three steps described above to help you define *hydroelectric*.

> Atlantic South America also has good mineral and energy resources such as gold, silver, copper, iron, and oil. Dams on some of the region's large rivers also provide hydroelectric power.
>
> *From Section 1, Physical Geography*

Pacific South America

Essential Question

*my*Notebook

How has political unrest shaped the nations of Pacific South America?

Texas Essential Knowledge and Skills (TEKS)

1A, 1B, 2A, 2B, 3A, 3B, 3C, 3D, 4B, 4C, 4D, 4E, 4F, 15B, 15D, 18B, 21B, 21C, 22D

FOCUS ON READING AND SPEAKING

*my*WriteSmart

Making Inferences An inference is a kind of guess. Sometimes an author does not give you complete information, and you have to make an inference. As you read, try to fill in gaps in information. Make guesses about things the writer does not tell you directly. **See the lesson, Making Inferences, on page 295.**

Interviewing Interviews with experts are a great way to learn new information. As you read about Pacific South America, you will identify questions for an interview. Then, with a partner, you will create a script for an interview about the region. One of you will play the role of the interviewer, and one will play the regional expert. Use the annotation tools in your eBook to gather information for your assignment.

0° Equator

Galápagos Islands
(ECUADOR)

10°S

PACIFIC OCEAN

20°S

Tropic of Capricorn

map zone

Geography Skills

Location The countries of Pacific South America lie on the western side of South America.

1. **Identify** Which country is landlocked?
2. **Analyze** How do you think Chile's shape affects life in that country?

30°S

40°S

Physical Geography The Andes are the second-highest mountain range in the world. These peaks are in a national park in Chile.

Pacific South America: Political

COLOMBIA

Quito ⊛
ECUADOR
Guayaquil •

PERU

Lima ⊛   Cuzco •

BOLIVIA
⊛ La Paz
• Santa Cruz
⊛ Sucre

BRAZIL

Amazon River

Equator—0°

10°S

CHILE   PARAGUAY

Valparaíso •
Santiago ⊛

URUGUAY

Tropic of Capricorn

20°S

ARGENTINA

ATLANTIC
OCEAN

30°S

HISTORY

Cliff Mummies of the
Andes: Unwrapped

↗ hmhsocialstudies.com   VIDEO

⊛ National capital

• Other cities

| 0 | 300 | 600 Miles |
| 0 | 300 | 600 Kilometers |

Projection:
Lambert Azimuthal Equal-Area

History Early
cultures made
beautiful gold
and silver art.

Culture Many people who live in the Andes still
wear traditional dress and speak native languages.
These women are from Peru.

277

Physical Geography

 TEKS 3A, 3B, 3C, 4D, 4E, 5A, 5B, 5C, 6A, 6B, 21B, 21C, 22D

What You Will Learn...

Main Ideas

1. The Andes are the main physical feature of Pacific South America.
2. The region's climate and vegetation change with elevation.
3. Key natural resources in the region include lumber, oil, and minerals.

The Big Idea

The Andes dominate Pacific South America's physical geography and influence the region's climate and resources.

Key Terms and Places

altiplano, *p. 279*
strait, *p. 279*
Atacama Desert, *p. 281*
El Niño, *p. 281*

hmhsocialstudies.com
TAKING NOTES

Use the graphic organizer online to take notes on the physical geography of Pacific South America.

If YOU lived there...

You and your family fish for herring in the cold waters off the coast of Peru. Last year, however, an event called El Niño changed both the weather and the water. El Niño made the nearby ocean warmer. Without cold water, all the herring disappeared. You caught almost no fish at all. El Niño also caused terrible weather on the mainland.

How might another El Niño affect you?

BUILDING BACKGROUND Although most of the countries of Pacific South America lie along the coast, their landscapes are dominated by the rugged mountain range called the Andes. These mountains influence climates in the region. Ocean winds and currents also affect coastal areas here.

Physical Features

The countries of Pacific South America stretch along the Pacific coast from the equator, for which the country of Ecuador is named, south almost to the Arctic Circle. One narrow country, Chile (CHEE-lay), is so long that it covers about half the Pacific coast by itself. Not all of the countries in Pacific South America have coastlines, however. Bolivia is landlocked. But all of the countries in this region do share one major physical feature—the high Andes mountains.

Mountains

The Andes run through Ecuador, Peru, Bolivia, and Chile. Some ridges and volcanic peaks in the Andes rise more than 20,000 feet (6,800 m) above sea level. Because two tectonic plates meet at the region's edge, earthquakes and volcanoes are a constant threat. Sometimes these earthquakes disturb Andean glaciers, sending ice and mud rushing down mountain slopes.

Landscapes in the Andes differ from south to north. In southern Chile, rugged mountain peaks are covered by ice caps. In the north, the Andes are more rounded than rugged, and there the range splits into two ridges. In southern Peru and Bolivia these ridges are quite far apart. A broad, high plateau called the **altiplano** lies between the ridges of the Andes.

Water and Islands

Andean glaciers are the source for many tributaries of the Amazon River. Other than the Amazon tributaries, the region has few major rivers. Rivers on the altiplano have no outlet to the sea. Water collects in two large lakes. One of these, Lake Titicaca, is the highest lake in the world that large ships can cross.

At the southern tip of the continent, the Strait of Magellan links the Atlantic and Pacific oceans. A **strait** is a narrow body of water connecting two larger bodies of water. The large island south of the strait is Tierra del Fuego, or "land of fire."

Chile and Ecuador both control large islands in the Pacific Ocean. Ecuador's volcanic Galápagos Islands have wildlife not found anywhere else in the world.

READING CHECK **Contrasting** How do the Andes differ from north to south?

Pacific South America: Physical

ELEVATION

Feet		Meters
13,120		4,000
6,560		2,000
1,640		500
656		200
(Sea level) 0		0 (Sea level)
Below sea level		Below sea level

0   400   800 Miles
0   400   800 Kilometers

Projection:
Lambert Azimuthal Equal-Area

map zone **Geography Skills**

Regions The Andes stretch all through the countries of Pacific South America.
1. **Identify** To what country do the Galápagos Islands belong?
2. **Interpret** How do you think the Andes affect life in the region?

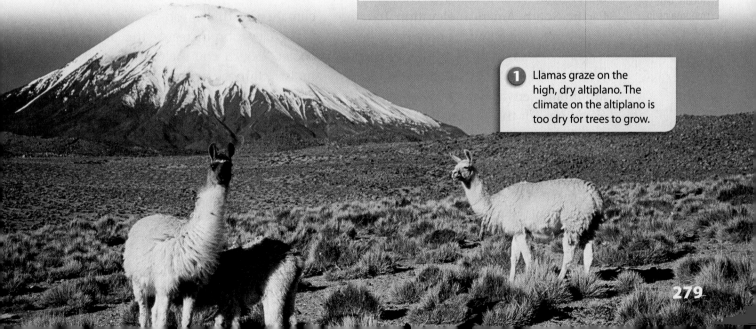

1 Llamas graze on the high, dry altiplano. The climate on the altiplano is too dry for trees to grow.

279

Climate Zones in the Andes

Five climate zones exist in the Andes. The different elevations support different types of plant and animal life.

- no vegetation
- shrubs, sheep, llamas
- potatoes, wheat, corn, sheep, llamas
- evergreens, coffee, wheat, cattle
- bananas, sugarcane

Snow line

15,000 ft (4550 m)

12,000 ft (3650 m)

6,000 ft (1850 m)

3,000 ft (900 m)

Sea Level

ANALYSIS SKILL **ANALYZING VISUALS**

Between what elevations do potatoes grow best?

Climate and Vegetation

FOCUS ON READING

What can you infer about the location of mountains in Ecuador?

Climate, vegetation, and landscapes all vary widely in Pacific South America. We usually think of latitude as the major factor that affects climate. However, in Pacific South America, elevation has the biggest effect on climate and vegetation.

Elevation

Mountain environments change with elevation. For this reason, we can identify five different climate zones in the Andes. You can see these different climate zones on the diagram above.

The lowest zone includes the hot and humid lower elevations near sea level. Crops such as sugarcane and bananas grow

well there. This first zone is often found along the coast, but it is also found inland in eastern Ecuador and Peru and northern Bolivia. These regions are part of the Amazon basin. They have a humid tropical climate with thick, tropical rain forests.

As elevation increases, the air becomes cooler. The second elevation zone has moist climates with mountain forests. This zone is good for growing coffee. In addition, many of Pacific South America's large cities are located in this zone.

Higher up the mountains is a third, cooler zone of forests and grasslands. Farmers grow potatoes and wheat there. Many people in Pacific South America live and farm in this climate zone.

At a certain elevation, the climate becomes too cool for trees to grow. This fourth climate zone above the tree line contains alpine meadows with grasslands and hardy shrubs. The altiplano region between the two ridges of the Andes lies mostly in this climate zone.

The fifth climate zone, in the highest elevations, is very cold. No vegetation grows in this zone because the ground is almost always covered with snow and ice.

Deserts

Pacific South America also has some climates that are not typical of any of the five climate zones. Instead of hot and humid climates, some coastal regions have desert climates.

Northern Chile contains the **Atacama Desert**. This desert is about 600 miles (965 km) long. Rain falls there less than five times a century, but fog and low clouds are common. They form when a cold current in the Pacific Ocean chills the warmer air above the ocean's surface. Cloud cover keeps the air near the ground from being warmed by the sun. As a result, coastal Chile is one of the cloudiest—and driest—places on Earth.

In Peru, some rivers cut through the dry coastal region. They bring snowmelt down from the Andes. Because they rely on melting snow, some of these rivers only appear at certain times of the year. The rivers have made some small settlements possible in these dry areas.

El Niño

About every two to seven years, this dry region experiences **El Niño**, an ocean and weather pattern that affects the Pacific coast. During an El Niño year, cool Pacific water near the coast warms. This change may cause extreme ocean and weather events that can have global effects.

As El Niño warms ocean waters, fish leave what is usually a rich fishing area. This change affects fishers. Also, El Niño <u>causes</u> heavy rains, and areas along the coast sometimes experience flooding. Some scientists think that air pollutants have made El Niño last longer and have more damaging effects.

ACADEMIC VOCABULARY
cause to make something happen

READING CHECK **Finding Main Ideas** How does elevation affect climate and vegetation?

Natural Resources

The landscapes of Pacific South America provide many valuable natural resources. For example, forests in southern Chile and in eastern Peru and Ecuador provide lumber. Also, as you have read, the coastal waters of the Pacific Ocean are rich in fish.

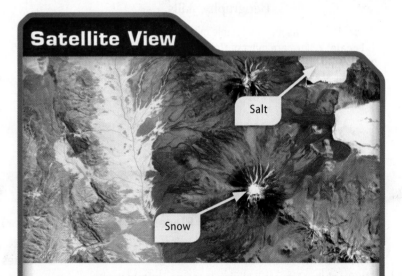

Satellite View

Salt

Snow

Atacama Desert

The Atacama Desert lies between the Pacific coast and the Andes in northern Chile. In this image you can see two snow-capped volcanoes. The salt in the top right part of the image is formed from minerals carried there by rivers that only appear during certain months of the year. These seasonal rivers also support some limited vegetation.

Drawing Conclusions Why do you think there is snow on the volcanoes even though the desert gets hardly any precipitation?

Bolivia: Resources

Gold
Lead
Silver
Tin
Zinc

0   100   200 Miles
0   100   200 Kilometers

Projection: Lambert
Azimuthal Equal-Area

BRAZIL

BOLIVIA

Madre de Dios
Madera R.
Beni River
Guapore River
Mamoré River
Picomayo River

Lake Titicaca
Lake Poopó

—20°S

N
W   E
S

CHILE   ARGENTINA   PARAGUAY

map zone Geography Skills

Place Bolivia has many valuable mineral resources.
1. **Locate** Where are most of Bolivia's gold resources found?
2. **Interpret** What do you notice about the location of the mineral resources and the rivers?

In addition, the region has valuable oil and minerals. Ecuador in particular has large oil and gas reserves, and oil is the country's main export. Bolivia has some deposits of tin, gold, silver, lead, and zinc. Chile has copper deposits. In fact, Chile exports more copper than any other country in the world. Chile is also the site of the world's largest open pit mine.

Although the countries of Pacific South America have many valuable resources, one resource they do not have much of is good farmland. Many people farm, but the region's mostly cool, arid lands make it difficult to produce large crops for export.

READING CHECK **Categorizing** What types of resources do the countries of Pacific South America have?

SUMMARY AND PREVIEW The Andes are the main physical feature of Pacific South America. Next, you will learn how the Andes have affected the region's history and how they continue to affect life there today.

Section 1 Assessment

hmhsocialstudies.com
ONLINE QUIZ

Reviewing Ideas, Terms, and Places

1. **a. Identify** What is the main physical feature of Pacific South America?
   b. Analyze How is Bolivia's location unique in the region?
2. **a. Define** What is **El Niño**, and what are some of its effects?
   b. Draw Conclusions Why are parts of Ecuador, in the tropics, cooler than parts of southern Chile?
3. **a. Identify** What country in this region has large oil reserves?
   b. Make Inferences Why do you think much of the region is not good for farming?
   c. Geographic Questions Look at the map on this page. Pose and answer a question about the distribution of mineral resources in Bolivia.

Critical Thinking

4. **Categorizing** Review your notes on climate. Then use a diagram like this one to describe the climate and vegetation in each of the five climate zones.

FOCUS ON SPEAKING

my WriteSmart

5. **Describing Physical Geography** Note information about the physical features, climate and vegetation, and resources of Pacific South America. Write two questions and answers you can use in your interview.

Avoiding Plagiarism

Learn

Plagiarism is the act of taking someone else's words and ideas and calling them your own. It is considered stealing. Whether plagiarizing is intentional or not, it is wrong.

Practice

Use the steps below to practice using proper citations and avoid plagiarizing someone else's work as you write your own research papers.

1. Carefully make a note of the exact quotations you want to use in your own paper. Use quotations marks and note the source so you won't forget the words belong to someone else.

2. Keep good notes about the sources you use for your paper in order to write proper citations. Include the title of the publication, the author, and the page number. A proper citation also includes the name of the publisher, the city of publication, and the year of publication.

3. When you refer to someone else's ideas, you have to give that author credit. Double-check your work to make sure your writing is your own and not a word-for-word copy of someone else's work.

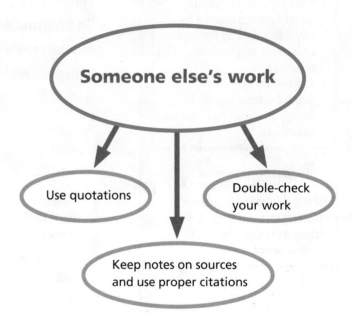

Apply

Using the information in Section 1 of this chapter, write a paragraph on the natural resources of Pacific South America. Use the steps above to create proper citations and to avoid plagiarizing your source material.

What You Will Learn...

Main Ideas

1. The countries of Pacific South America share a history influenced by the Inca civilization and Spanish colonization.
2. The culture of Pacific South America includes American Indian and Spanish influences.

The Big Idea

Native cultures and Spanish colonization have shaped the history and culture of Pacific South America.

Key Terms

viceroy, *p. 285*
Creoles, *p. 286*

hmhsocialstudies.com
TAKING NOTES

Use the graphic organizer online to take notes on the history and culture of Pacific South America.

History and Culture

If **YOU** lived there...

You live in Cuzco, the capital of the Inca Empire. You are required to contribute labor to the empire, and you have been chosen to work on a construction project. Hauling the huge stones will be difficult, but the work will be rewarding. You can either choose to help build a magnificent temple to the sun god or you can help build a road from Cuzco to the far end of the empire.

Which project will you choose? Why?

BUILDING BACKGROUND Before Spanish conquerors arrived in the early 1500s, a great American Indian empire ruled this region. Cuzco was the Inca capital. The Incas were such skilled engineers and builders that many of their forts and temples still stand today.

History

Thousands of years ago, people in Pacific South America tried to farm on mountainsides as steep as bleachers. Other people tried to farm where there was almost no rain. These early cultures learned how to adapt to and modify their environments.

Early Cultures

Peru's first advanced civilization reached its height in about 900 BC in the Andes. These people built stone terraces into the steep mountainside so they could raise crops. In coastal areas, people created irrigation systems to store water and control flooding.

Agriculture supported large populations, towns, and culture. In the Bolivian highlands one early culture, the Tiahuanaco (tee-uh-wuh-NAH-koh), made huge stone carvings near a lakeshore. In another civilization on the coast, people scratched outlines of animals and other shapes into the surface of the Peruvian desert. These designs, known as the Nazca lines, are so large they can only be recognized from the sky.

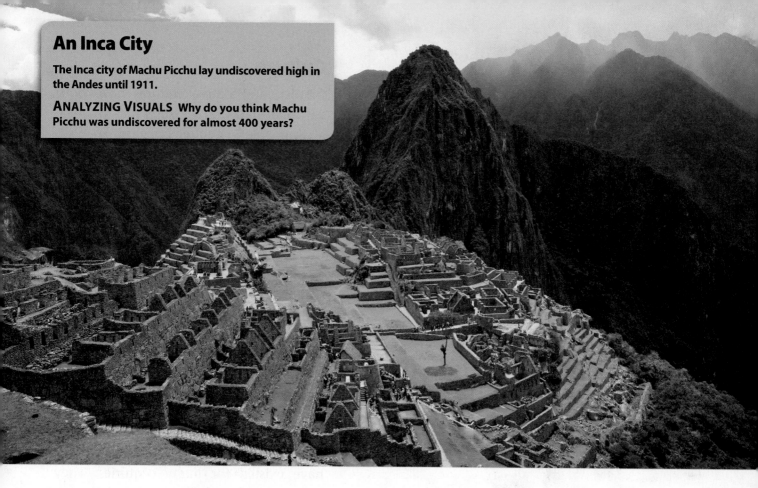

An Inca City

The Inca city of Machu Picchu lay undiscovered high in the Andes until 1911.

ANALYZING VISUALS Why do you think Machu Picchu was undiscovered for almost 400 years?

The Inca Empire

Eventually, one group of people came to rule most of the region. By the early 1500s, these people, the Incas, controlled an area that stretched from northern Ecuador to central Chile. The Inca Empire was home to as many as 12 million people.

The huge Inca Empire was highly organized. Irrigation projects turned deserts into rich farmland. Thousands of miles of stone-paved roads connected the empire. Rope suspension bridges helped the Incas cross the steep Andean valleys.

As advanced as their civilization was, the Incas had no wheeled vehicles or horses. Instead, relay teams of runners carried messages from one end of the empire to the other. Working together, a team of runners could carry a message up to 150 miles (240 km) in one day. The runners did not carry any letters, however, because the Incas did not have a written language.

Spanish Rule

In spite of its great organization, however, the Inca Empire did not last long. A new Inca ruler, on his way to be crowned king, met the Spanish explorer Francisco Pizarro. Pizarro captured the Inca king, who ordered his people to bring enough gold and silver to fill a whole room. These riches were supposed to be a ransom for the king's freedom. Instead, Pizarro ordered the Inca king killed. Fighting broke out, and by 1535 the Spaniards had conquered the Inca Empire.

The new Spanish rulers often dealt harshly with the South American Indians of the fallen Inca Empire. Many Indians had to work in gold or silver mines or on the Spaniards' plantations. A Spanish **viceroy**, or governor, was appointed by the king of Spain to make sure the Indians followed the Spanish laws and customs that had replaced native traditions.

VIDEO
Machu Picchu

hmhsocialstudies.com

FOCUS ON READING

How do you think the South American Indians felt about the viceroy?

Independence

By the early 1800s, people in Pacific South America began to want independence. They began to revolt against Spanish rule. **Creoles**, American-born descendants of Europeans, were the main leaders of the revolts. The success of the revolts led to independence for Chile, Ecuador, Peru, and Bolivia by 1825.

READING CHECK **Evaluating** How did Inca civilization influence the history of the region?

Culture

Spanish and native cultures have both left their marks on Pacific South America. Most people in the region speak Spanish, and Spanish is the official language in all of the countries of the region.

However, people in many parts of the region also maintain much of their native culture. Millions of South American Indians speak native languages in addition to or instead of Spanish. In Bolivia, two native languages are official languages in addition to Spanish.

The people and customs of Pacific South America also reflect the region's Spanish and Indian heritage. For example, Bolivia's population has the highest percentage of South American Indians of any country on the continent. Many Bolivian Indians follow customs and lifestyles that have existed for many centuries. They often dress in traditional styles—full skirts and derby hats for the women and colorful, striped ponchos for the men.

Another part of the region's culture that reflects Spanish and Indian influences is religion. Most people in Pacific

Languages in Pacific South America

map zone Geography Skills

Regions Spanish is an official language throughout the region, but many people speak native languages instead.

1. **Interpreting Graphs** Where do more people speak native languages than Spanish?
2. **Analyze** Why do you think many people do not speak Spanish?

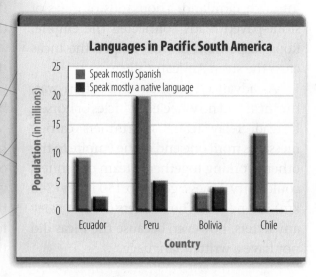

Languages in Pacific South America

- Speak mostly Spanish
- Speak mostly a native language

Andean Culture

Every May, high in the Andes, Bolivians gather in Macha, Bolivia for Tinku, a festival honoring *Pachamama*, or mother earth.

ANALYZING VISUALS
What do you think the climate is like in Macha?

Music played on wooden flutes like these is popular in the Andes.

South America practice the religion of the Spanish—Roman Catholicism. Some people in the Andes, however, also still practice ancient religious customs. Every June, for example, people participate in a festival that was celebrated by the Incas to worship the sun. During festivals people wear traditional costumes, sometimes with wooden masks. They also play traditional instruments, such as wooden flutes.

READING CHECK **Generalizing** What traditional customs do people in the region still practice today?

SUMMARY AND PREVIEW Pacific South America was home to one of the greatest ancient civilizations in the Americas—the Inca. The Spanish conquered the Incas. Today the region's culture still reflects Inca and Spanish influences. Next, you will learn more about the governments and economies of Ecuador, Bolivia, Peru, and Chile today.

Section 2 Assessment

hmhsocialstudies.com
ONLINE QUIZ

Reviewing Ideas, Terms, and Places

1. **a. Recall** What ancient empire built paved roads through the Andes?
   b. Explain What role did **Creoles** play in the history of Pacific South America?
   c. Identify How did the early Peruvians adapt to their physical environment?
2. **a. Recall** What country has the highest percentage of South American Indians in its population?
   b. Make Generalizations What aspects of culture in Pacific South America reflect Spanish influence, and what aspects reflect Indian heritage?

Critical Thinking

3. **Sequencing** Look over your notes on the region's history. Then draw a graphic organizer like the one here and use it to put major historical events in chronological order.

Nazca lines drawn

FOCUS ON SPEAKING

my WriteSmart

4. **Taking Notes on History and Culture** What information about the history and culture is important? Add two more questions, plus answers, to your notes.

TEKS 1A, 1B, 2A, 2B, 3A, 3B,
3C, 3D, 4B, 4C, 4F, 15B, 18B, 21B,
21C, 22D

What You Will Learn...

Main Ideas

1. Ecuador struggles with poverty and political instability.
2. Bolivia's government is trying to gain stability and improve the economy.
3. Peru has made progress against poverty and violence.
4. Chile has a stable government and a strong economy.

The Big Idea

The countries of Pacific South America are working to overcome challenges of poverty and political instability.

Key Terms and Places

Quito, *p. 289*
La Paz, *p. 289*
Lima, *p. 290*
coup, *p. 291*
Santiago, *p. 292*

hmhsocialstudies.com
TAKING NOTES

Use the graphic organizer online to take notes on Pacific South America today.

Pacific South America Today

If YOU lived there...

You are at a political rally in Valparaíso, Chile. Your family owns a vineyard nearby, so government policies about the economy affect you personally. You listen carefully to the speakers at the rally. Some politicians are in favor of more free trade with countries in North America. Others speak about different issues, such as housing and education.

What would you like to ask the politicians?

BUILDING BACKGROUND All the countries of Pacific South America have faced similar issues in recent years. These include poverty, unstable governments, economic development, and how to encourage development and still protect the environment. Several of these countries are making progress, while others still have problems.

Ecuador Today

In recent decades, the countries of Pacific South America have all experienced periods of political instability. Ecuador, in particular, has faced recent instability. Widespread poverty is a constant threat to a stable government in this country.

Government

Ecuador has been a democracy since 1979. Still, the country has experienced great political instability and corruption. From 1996–2007, the country had nine different presidents. In 2004, Ecuadorian president Lucio Gutiérrez fired the majority of the nation's supreme court judges because they did not support him. Soon after, to quiet his political opponents, Gutiérrez declared a state of emergency. In response, the Ecuadorian Congress forced Gutiérrez from power in 2005. In 2006, Ecuadorians elected Rafael Correa president. In 2009, Correa was the first Ecuadorian president to be re-elected in more than 30 years.

Economic Regions

Ecuador has three different economic regions. One region, the coastal lowlands, has agriculture and industry. The country's largest city, Guayaquil (gwy-ah-KEEL), is located there. It is Ecuador's major port and commercial center.

The Andean region of Ecuador is poorer. **Quito**, the national capital, is located there. Open-air markets and Spanish colonial buildings attract many tourists to Quito and other towns in the region.

A third region, the Amazon basin, has valuable oil deposits. The oil industry provides jobs that draw people to the region. Oil is also Ecuador's main export. But the oil industry has brought problems as well as benefits. The country's economy suffers if the world oil price drops. In addition, some citizens worry that drilling for oil could harm the rain forest.

READING CHECK **Generalizing** Why has Ecuador's government been unstable?

Bolivia Today

Like Ecuador, Bolivia is a poor country. Poverty has been a cause of political unrest in recent years.

Government

After years of military rule, Bolivia is a democracy. Bolivia's government is divided between two capital cities. The supreme court meets in Sucre (SOO-kray), but the congress meets in **La Paz**. Located at about 12,000 feet (3,660 m), La Paz is the highest capital city in the world. It is also Bolivia's main industrial center.

In the early 2000s, many Bolivians disagreed with their government's plans for fighting poverty. National protests forced several presidents to resign. Then in 2005, Bolivians elected an indigenous leader, Evo Morales, as president. Re-elected president in 2009, Morales continues to work to improve the lives of Bolivia's poor.

Economy

Bolivia is the poorest country in South America. In the plains of eastern Bolivia there are few roads and little money for investment. However, foreign aid has provided funds for some development. In addition, the country has valuable resources, including metals and natural gas.

READING CHECK **Analyzing** Why might political revolts slow development?

CONNECTING TO Economics

The Informal Economy

Many people in the countries of Pacific South America are part of the informal economy. Street vendors, like the ones shown here in Quito, are common sights in the region's cities. People visit street vendors to buy items like snacks, small electronics, or clothing. The informal economy provides jobs for many people. However, it does not help the national economy because the participants do not pay taxes. Without income from taxes, the government cannot pay for services.

Analyzing How does the informal economy affect taxes?

Lima has three main types of settlements. The wealthier people tend to live in houses and apartments in town. Poor people live mostly in slums or in recently built "young towns."

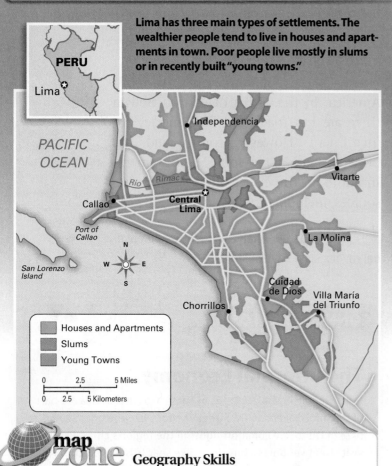

PERU

Lima

PACIFIC OCEAN

Independencia

Rio Rimac

Callao

Central Lima

Vitarte

Port of Callao

La Molina

San Lorenzo Island

Cuidad de Dios

Villa María del Triunfo

Chorrillos

N W E S

Houses and Apartments
Slums
Young Towns

0   2.5   5 Miles
0   2.5   5 Kilometers

map zone Geography Skills

Human-Environment Interaction People have built three different basic types of housing in and around Lima.
1. **Use the Map** What is the most common type of housing?
2. **Draw Conclusions** Why are most young towns built far from central Lima?

Houses and Apartments Most housing in Lima is made up of high-rise apartments and private houses, some of which are from the colonial era.

Peru Today

Peru is the largest and most populous country in Pacific South America. Today it is making some progress against political violence and poverty.

Lima

Peru's capital, **Lima** (LEE-muh), is the largest city in the region. Nearly one-third of all Peruvians live in Lima or the nearby port city of Callao (kah-YAH-oh). Lima has industry, universities, and government jobs, which attract many people from the countryside to Lima.

Lima was the colonial capital of Peru, and the city still contains many beautiful old buildings from the colonial era. It has high-rise apartments and wide, tree-lined boulevards. However, as in many big urban areas, a lot of people there live in poverty.

In spite of the poverty, central Lima has few slum areas. This is because most poor people prefer to claim land on the outskirts of the city and build their own houses. Often they can get only poor building materials. They also have a hard time getting water and electricity from the city.

Settlements of new self-built houses are called "young towns" in Lima. Over time, as people improve and add to their houses, the new settlements develop into large, permanent suburbs. Many of the people in Lima's young towns are migrants from the highlands. Some came to Lima to escape violence in their home villages.

Slums Just outside downtown and near the port area, many people live in slum housing. These buildings are permanent, but run-down.

Young Towns Many poor people in recent years have taken over land on the outskirts of Lima and have built their own shelters.

Government

In the 1980s and 1990s, a terrorist group called the Shining Path was active. This group carried out deadly attacks because it opposed government policies. Some 70,000 people died in violence between the Shining Path and government forces, and Peru's economy suffered. However, after the arrest of the group's leaders, Peru's government began making progress against political violence and poverty. The country has an elected president and congress.

Resources

Peru's resources are key factors in its economic progress. Some mineral deposits are located near the coast, and hydroelectric projects on rivers provide energy. Peru's highlands are less developed than the coastal areas. However, many Peruvian Indians grow potatoes and corn there.

READING CHECK **Identifying Cause and Effect** How did the Shining Path affect Peru?

Chile Today

Like Peru, Chile has ended a long violent period. Chile now has a stable government and a growing economy.

Government

In 1970 Chileans elected a president who had some ideas influenced by communism. A few years later he was overthrown and died in a U.S.-backed military coup (KOO). A **coup** is a sudden overthrow of a government by a small group of people.

In the years after the coup, military rulers tried to crush their political enemies. Chile's military government was harsh and often violent. It imprisoned or killed thousands of people.

In the late 1980s Chile's military dictatorship weakened and Chileans created a new, democratic government. In 2006 Chileans elected their first female president, Michelle Bachelet, and in 2010 they elected business leader Sebastián Piñera president.

FOCUS ON READING
What can you infer about the reason for the end of the military government?

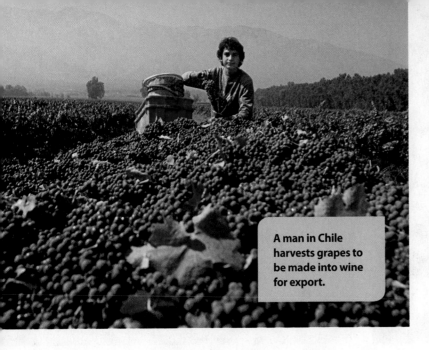

A man in Chile harvests grapes to be made into wine for export.

Mediterranean climate allows farmers to grow many crops. For example, grapes grow well there, and Chilean fruit and wine are exported around the world.

Farming, fishing, forestry, and mining form the basis of Chile's economy. Copper mining is especially important. It accounts for more than one-third of Chile's exports.

Chile's economic stability was rocked by a massive earthquake that struck on February 27, 2010. The quake killed about 500 Chileans and caused about $30 billion of damage to buildings, homes, and streets. Today, Chile's people and government continue to rebuild their nation.

READING CHECK **Identifying Points of View** Why might Chile want to join a free trade group?

SUMMARY AND PREVIEW In recent years Ecuador, Peru, Bolivia, and Chile have struggled with political violence and poverty. However, Peru and Chile are recovering. Next, you will study the culture and economy of Southern Europe.

Resources and Economy

Chile's economy is the strongest in the region. Poverty rates have decreased, and Chile's prospects for the future seem bright. Small businesses and factories are growing quickly. More Chileans are finding work, and wages are rising.

About one-third of all Chileans live in central Chile. This region includes the capital, **Santiago**, and a nearby seaport, Valparaíso (bahl-pah-rah-EE-soh). Its mild

Section 3 Assessment

Reviewing Ideas, Terms, and Places

1. **a. Identify** What is Ecuador's largest city?
   b. Make Generalizations Why have Ecuadorians been unhappy with their government in recent years?

2. **a. Identify** What are Bolivia's two capital cities?
   b. Analyze Why might Bolivia's economy improve in the future?

3. **a. Recall** Why did many Peruvians move to Lima from the highlands in the 1980s?
   b. Elaborate What challenges do you think people who move to **Lima** from the highlands face?

4. **a. Define** What is a **coup**?
   b. Make Inferences What might happen to Chile's economy if the world price of copper drops?

Critical Thinking

5. **Solving Problems** Review your notes. Then, in a diagram like the one here, write one sentence about each country, explaining how that country is dealing with poverty or government instability.

Ecuador	
Bolivia	
Peru	
Chile	

FOCUS ON SPEAKING

my WriteSmart

6. **Thinking about Pacific South America Today**
Add questions about each country in Pacific South America to your notes. How might you answer these questions in your interview? Write down the answer to each question.

Chapter Review

Visual Summary

Use the visual summary below to help you review the main ideas of the chapter.

QUICK FACTS

The high Andes affect the climates and landscapes of Pacific South America.

Many South American Indians maintain traditional customs and ways of life in the Andes.

Today the countries of Pacific South America are working toward development and improved economies.

Reviewing Vocabulary, Terms, and Places

Write each word defined below, circling each letter that is marked by a star. Then write the word these letters spell.

1. _ _ _ * _ _ _ _ _ _ _ _ _ _ _ _ _—a desert in northern Chile that is one of the cloudiest and driest places on Earth

2. * _ _ _ _ —the capital of Peru

3. _ _ _ _ * _ _—the capital of Ecuador

4. _ * _ _ _ _ _ _ _—a governor appointed by the king of Spain

5. _ _ _ * _ _ _—one of the capitals of Bolivia

6. _ _ _ _ _ * _ _—an American-born descendant of Europeans

7. _ _ _ _ * _ _ _—a narrow passageway that connects two large bodies of water

8. _ _ _ * _ _ _ _—an ocean and weather pattern that affects the Pacific coast

9. _ _ * _ _ _—a sudden overthrow of a government by a small group of people

Comprehension and Critical Thinking

SECTION 1 *(Pages 278–282)*

10. **a. Describe** What are climate and vegetation like on the altiplano?

b. Compare and Contrast What are two differences and one similarity between the Atacama Desert and the altiplano?

c. Geographic Questions Look back at the model of climate zones in the Andes in Section 1. Pose and answer a question about the geographic distribution of plants and animals in the Andes.

SECTION 2 *(Pages 284–287)*

11. **a. Describe** How did the Incas organize their huge empire?

b. Analyze How have Spanish and native cultures left their marks on culture in Pacific South America?

c. Elaborate Why do you think Pizarro killed the Inca king even though he had received riches as ransom?

12. a. Identify What country in Pacific South America has the healthiest economy?

b. Analyze What problems in Ecuador and Bolivia cause political unrest?

c. Evaluate What would be some benefits and drawbacks of moving from the highlands to one of Lima's "young towns"?

Using the Internet

13. Activity: Analyzing Climate Chile has steep mountains, volcanoes, a desert, a rich river valley, and thick forests. These diverse areas contain many different climates. Click on the links given in your online textbook to explore the many climates of Chile. Then test your knowledge by taking an online quiz.

 hmhsocialstudies.com

Social Studies Skills

Avoiding Plagiarism Practice avoiding plagiarism by reading the paragraph below carefully, then organize your notes in a graphic organizer like the one on the Social Studies Skills page. Make sure to use proper citations for this book.

> The people and customs of Pacific South America also reflect the region's Spanish and Indian heritage. For example, Bolivia's population has the highest percentage of South American Indians of any country on the continent. Many Bolivian Indians follow customs and lifestyles that have existed for many centuries. They often dress in traditional styles—full skirts and derby hats for the women and colorful, striped ponchos for the men.

Map Activity

14. Pacific South America On a separate sheet of paper, match the letters on the map with their correct labels.

Strait of Magellan	Santiago, Chile
Quito, Ecuador	Atacama Desert
Andes	La Paz, Bolivia

FOCUS ON READING AND SPEAKING *my*WriteSmart

Making Inferences *Use the information in this chapter to answer the following questions.*

15. What is an inference?

16. What can you infer about the size of the population in the Atacama Desert? What clues led you to make this inference?

17. Presenting an Interview Now that you have questions and answers, use *my*WriteSmart in your eBook to write your interview script. Read through your script several times so that you know it well enough to sound natural during the interview. Remember to use a lively tone as you speak so that your audience will pay attention.

Making Inferences

FOCUS ON READING

Sometimes reading effectively means understanding both what the writer tells you directly and what the writer doesn't tell you. When you fill in the gaps, you are making inferences, or educated guesses. Why worry about what the writer doesn't tell you? Making inferences can help you make connections with the text. It can also give you a fuller picture of the information. To make an inference, think about the text and what you know or can guess from the information. The example below shows you the process.

> At the southern tip of the continent, the Strait of Magellan links the Atlantic and Pacific oceans. A strait is a narrow body of water connecting two larger bodies of water. The large island south of the strait is Tierra del Fuego, or "land of fire."
>
> *From Section 1, Physical Geography*

1. Determine what the passage says:
The Strait of Magellan connects the Atlantic and Pacific oceans. There is an island south of it.

2. Determine what you know about the topic or what you can connect to your experience.
This sounds like a shortcut to me. It would keep boats from having to sail all the way around the island.

3. Make an inference.
Many ships probably use the Strait of Magellan because it is a shortcut.

YOU TRY IT!

Read the following sentences. Then use the three steps described above to make an inference about the Galápagos Islands.

> Chile and Ecuador both control large islands in the Pacific Ocean. Ecuador's volcanic Galápagos Islands have wildlife not found anywhere else in the world.
>
> *From Section 1, Physical Geography*

Describing a Place

What are the physical features of a country? What is the weather like? What drives the economy? The answers to questions like these are often cold, hard facts and statistics. But they can bring life to a description of a place.

Assignment *my*WriteSmart

Use *my*WriteSmart to write a paper describing one of these places in the Americas:
- a city
- a country

1. Prewrite

Identify a Topic and Big Idea
- Choose one of the topics above to write about.
- Turn your topic into a big idea, or thesis. For example, your big idea might be, "Cuba's government greatly influences life in the country."

> **TIP** **Precise Language** Describe your place with specific nouns, verbs, adjectives, and adverbs. For example, rather than writing "Buenos Aires is big," write "Buenos Aires is the largest city in Argentina."

Gather and Organize Information
- Look for information about your place in the library or on the Internet. Organize your notes in groupings such as physical features, economy, or culture. Decide which facts about the place you are describing are most important or unique.

2. Write

Use a Writer's Framework

> **A Writer's Framework**
>
> **Introduction**
> - Start with an interesting fact or question.
> - Identify your big idea and provide any necessary background information.
>
> **Body**
> - Write at least one paragraph for each category. Include facts that help explain each detail.
> - Write about each detail in order of importance.
>
> **Conclusion**
> - Summarize your description in your final paragraph.

3. Evaluate and Revise

Review and Improve Your Paper
- Re-read your paper and use the questions below to identify ways to revise your paper.
- Make the changes needed to improve your paper.

Evaluation Questions for a Description of a Place
1. Do you begin with an interesting fact or question?
2. Does your introduction identify your big idea? Do you provide background information to help your readers better understand your idea?
3. Do you have at least one paragraph for each category?
4. Do you use order of importance to organize the details of your description?
5. Are there more details you would like to know about your place? If so, what are they?

4. Proofread and Publish

Give Your Description the Finishing Touch
- Make sure you used commas correctly when listing more than two details in a sentence.
- Check your spelling of the names of places.
- Share your description with classmates or with students in another social studies class.

5. Practice and Apply

Use the steps and strategies outlined in this workshop to write your description of a place. Share your description with classmates. With your classmates, group the descriptions by country and then identify the places you would like to visit.

Europe, Russia, and the Eurasian Republics

The Alps

The Alps, one of Europe's major mountain ranges, stretch across the heart of central Europe.

Islands and Peninsulas

Islands and peninsulas surround the edges of Europe, drawing people to the sea to work, travel, and trade.

Northern European Plain

Rolling across northern Europe is a vast lowland called the Northern European Plain.

Europe, Russia, and the Eurasian Republics

Explore the Satellite Image
Land and sea are always close together in Europe. Islands and peninsulas are key features of this region. What can you learn about Europe's geography from this satellite image?

The Satellite's Path

>44'56.08<

>>>>>>>>>665.00'87<

+355   567.476.348   +799 +803 +996

456.094.

Europe, Russia, and the Eurasian Republics: Physical

Geographical Extremes: Europe, Russia, and the Eurasian Republics

Longest River	Volga River, Russia: 2,290 miles (3,685 km)
Highest Point	Qullai Ismoili Somoni, Tajikistan: 24,590 feet (7,495 m)
Lowest Point	Vpadina Kaundy, Kazakhstan: 132 feet (81m) below sea level
Highest Recorded Temperature	Seville, Spain: 122°F (50°C)
Lowest Recorded Temperature	Ust'Shchugor, Russia: -67°F (-55°C)
Wettest Place	Crkvica, Bosnia and Herzegovina: 183 inches (464.8 cm) average precipitation per year
Driest Place	Astrakhan, Russia: 6.4 inches (16.3 cm) average precipitation per year

ELEVATION

Feet		Meters
13,120		4,000
6,560		2,000
1,640		500
656		200
(Sea level) 0		0 (Sea level)
Below sea level		Below sea level

0   300   600 Miles

0   30   600 Kilometers

Projection: Robinson

Taymyr Peninsula

Laptev Sea

New Siberian Islands

ARCTIC OCEAN

75°N

165°W

East Siberian Sea

Central Siberian Plateau

RUSSIA

S I B E R I A

Yenisey River

Kuznetsk Basin

Angara River

Lena River

Kolyma R.

Kolyma Mountains

Bering Strait

60°N

Bering Sea

Yenisey River

Sayan Mts.

Lake Baikal

Yablonovy Range

Stanovoy Mts.

Amur River

Sea of Okhotsk

Kamchatka Peninsula

180°

Sakhalin Island

Kuril Islands

45°N

EAST ASIA

Sea of Japan (East Sea)

PACIFIC OCEAN

165°E

N
W E
S

Size Comparison: The United States and Europe, Russia, and the Eurasian Republics

map zone
Geography Skills

Place Europe is a small continent. Russia stretches from Eastern Europe across northern Asia. The Eurasian Republics include the Caucasus and Central Asia.

1. **Name** What is the large region located in eastern Russia called?
2. **Make Inferences** Based on its latitude, what do you think the environment of Siberia is like?

Europe: Political

National capital
Other city

0   200   400 Miles
0   200   400 Kilometers

Projection: Azimuthal Equal-Area

ARCTIC OCEAN

Denmark Strait

70°N

Reykjavik **ICELAND**

Norwegian Sea

Arctic Circle

Faeroe Islands
(DENMARK)

Shetland Islands
(U.K.)

60°N

NORWAY   **SWEDEN**   **FINLAND**

Oslo   Stockholm   Helsinki   **RUSSIA**

Tallinn   **ESTONIA**

North Sea

Baltic Sea

Riga   **LATVIA**

IRELAND   Kaliningrad (RUSSIA)

Dublin   **DENMARK**   **LITHUANIA**   Vilnius

Copenhagen   Minsk

UNITED KINGDOM   **NETHERLANDS**   Berlin   **POLAND**   **BELARUS**

50°N   London   Amsterdam   Warsaw

ATLANTIC OCEAN   Brussels   **GERMANY**   Kiev   *Dnieper River*

BELGIUM   **LUXEMBOURG**   Prague   **UKRAINE**

Paris   Luxembourg   **CZECH REPUBLIC**

Danube R.   **SLOVAKIA**   **MOLDOVA**

FRANCE   **LIECHTENSTEIN**   Bratislava

Bern   Vienna   Chişinău

SWITZERLAND   **AUSTRIA**   Budapest

Ljubljana   **SLOVENIA**   **HUNGARY**   **ROMANIA**

40°N   Zagreb   Belgrade   Bucharest

CROATIA   **ANDORRA**   **MONACO**   **BOSNIA AND HERZEGOVINA**   *Black Sea*

PORTUGAL   Madrid   **SAN MARINO**   Sarajevo   **SERBIA**

Lisbon   **ITALY**   Podgorica   **KOSOVO**   **BULGARIA**

SPAIN   Pristina   Sofia

Corsica (FRANCE)   **VATICAN CITY**   Rome   **MONTENEGRO**   Skopje

Gibraltar (U.K.)   **MACEDONIA**

Strait of Gibraltar   *Balearic Islands (SPAIN)*   *Sardinia (ITALY)*   Tirana   **GREECE**   *Aegean Sea*

AFRICA   **ALBANIA**

Sicily (ITALY)   Athens

MALTA   Valletta   *Crete (GREECE)*

Mediterranean Sea

20°E   30°E

ASIA

map zone
Geography Skills

Place Europe includes many small countries.

1. **Name** Which European countries are island countries?

2. **Make Generalizations** Based on this map, which countries do you think might have the largest populations? Why?

Europe, Russia, and the Eurasian Republics

Russia and the Eurasian Republics: Political

ATLANTIC OCEAN

ARCTIC OCEAN

Arctic Circle

Bering Strait

Bering Sea

North Sea

Barents Sea

Baltic Sea

Kaliningrad

St. Petersburg

EUROPE

Moscow

Nizhniy Novgorod

Volga River

Samara

Yekaterinburg

Ob River

Yenisey River

RUSSIA

Lena River

Sea of Okhotsk

Novosibirsk

Black Sea

GEORGIA

Tbilisi

ARMENIA

Yerevan

Baku

AZERBAIJAN

SOUTHWEST ASIA

Aral Sea

KAZAKHSTAN

Esil R.

Astana

Syr Darya

Lake Balkhash

Caspian Sea

UZBEKISTAN

Amu Darya

TURKMENISTAN

Ashgabat

Tashkent

Bishkek

Almaty

KYRGYZSTAN

Dushanbe

TAJIKISTAN

AFGHANISTAN

Kabul

SOUTH ASIA

MONGOLIA

CHINA

Vladivostok

JAPAN

PACIFIC OCEAN

Tropic of Cancer

Legend:

⊛ National capital

• Other city

0   300   600 Miles

0   300   600 Kilometers

Projection: Two-Point Equidistant

map zone

Geography Skills

Place Russia is the largest country in the world.

1. Use the Map About how many miles is Russia from west to east?

2. Analyze Where does Russia have access to the ocean? How do you think that affects trade?

Europe: Population

Persons per square mile	**Persons per square km**
520	200
260	100
130	50
25	10
3	1
0	0

● Major cities over 2 million

0   150   300 Miles
0   150   300 Kilometers
Projection: Azimuthal Equal-Area

ARCTIC OCEAN

Denmark Strait

70°N

Norwegian Sea

Arctic Circle

60°N

North Sea

Baltic Sea

Kaliningrad (RUSSIA)

RUSSIA

50°N

London ●

Berlin ●

Warsaw ●

Kiev ●

ATLANTIC OCEAN

Paris ●

Vienna ●

Bucharest ●

Madrid ●

Barcelona ●

Rome ●

Adriatic Sea

Black Sea

ASIA

Aegean Sea

40°N

Strait of Gilbraltar

AFRICA

Mediterranean Sea

30°W   20°W   10°W   10°E   20°E   30°E

N W E S

map zone

Geography Skills

Place Although Europe is small, it is densely populated.

1. Use the Map How does the population density of Northern Europe compare to the rest of Europe?

2. Compare Compare this map to the physical map. What large plain in Europe has a high population density?

Europe, Russia, and the Eurasian Republics

Russia and the Eurasian Republics: Climate

ATLANTIC OCEAN

North Sea

Baltic Sea

Arctic Circle

Barents Sea

ARCTIC OCEAN

Bering Strait

Bering Sea

Black Sea

Caspian Sea

Sea of Okhotsk

PACIFIC OCEAN

Tropic of Cancer

Climate Types

- Desert
- Steppe
- Mediterranean
- Humid subtropical
- Humid continental
- Subarctic
- Tundra
- Highland

0   300   600 Miles

0   300   600 Kilometers

Projection: Two-Point Equidistant

map zone

Geography Skills

Regions Russia is dominated by cold climates.

1. Name Which two climate types cover a large part of the Eurasian Republics?

2. Analyze Based on this map, where do you think Russia's population is concentrated? Why? Which areas would you expect to have a low population density?

Regional Database

Europe, Russia, and the Eurasian Republics

COUNTRY Capital	FLAG	POPULATION	AREA (sq mi)	PER CAPITA GDP (U.S. $)	LIFE EXPECTANCY AT BIRTH	TVS PER 1,000 PEOPLE
Afghanistan Kabul		31.1 million	250,001	$1,100	50.1	14
Albania Tirana		3 million	11,100	$8,200	77.7	146
Andorra Andorra la Vella		85,293	181	$37,200	82.6	440
Armenia Yerevan		3 million	11,506	$5,900	73.8	241
Austria Vienna		8.2 million	32,382	$43,100	80	526
Azerbaijan Baku		9.6 million	33,436	$10,700	71.6	257
Belarus Minsk		9.6 million	80,155	$15,900	71.8	331
Belgium Brussels		10.4 million	11,787	$38,500	79.8	532
Bosnia and Herzegovina: Sarajevo		3.9 million	19,741	$8,400	76.2	112
Bulgaria Sofia		7 million	42,823	$14,500	74	429
Croatia Zagreb		4.5 million	21,831	$18,100	76.2	286
Czech Republic Prague		10.2 million	30,450	$27,600	77.6	487
Denmark Copenhagen		5.6 million	16,639	$38,300	78.9	776
Estonia Tallinn		1.3 million	17,462	$22,100	73.8	567
Finland Helsinki		5.3 million	130,559	$37,000	78.9	643
United States Washington, D.C.		316.7 million	3,718,711	$50,700	78.6	844

COUNTRY Capital	FLAG	POPULATION	AREA (sq mi)	PER CAPITA GDP (U.S. $)	LIFE EXPECTANCY AT BIRTH	TVS PER 1,000 PEOPLE
France Paris		66 million	211,209	$36,100	81.6	620
Georgia T'bilisi		4.6 million	26,911	$6,000	77.5	516
Germany Berlin		81.1 million	137,847	$39,700	80.3	581
Greece Athens		10.8 million	50,942	$24,900	80.2	480
Hungary Budapest		9.9 million	35,919	$20,000	75.2	447
Iceland Reykjavik		315,281	39,769	$39,900	81.1	505
Ireland Dublin		4.8 million	27,135	$42,600	80.4	406
Italy Rome		61.5 million	116,306	$30,600	82	492
Kazakhstan Astana		17.7 million	1,049,155	$14,100	69.9	240
Kosovo Pristina		1.8 million	4,203	$3,455	70	Not available
Kyrgyzstan Bishkek		5.5 million	76,641	$2,400	69.8	49
Latvia Riga		2.2 million	24,938	$17,300	73.2	757
Liechtenstein Vaduz		37,009	62	$89,400	81.6	469
Lithuania Vilnius		3.5 million	25,174	$22,000	75.8	422
Luxembourg Luxembourg		514,862	998	$81,100	79.9	599
Macedonia Skopje		2.1 million	9,781	$10,800	75.6	273
Malta Valletta		411,277	122	$27,500	80	549
United States Washington, D.C.		316.7 million	3,718,711	$50,700	78.6	844

Regional Database

COUNTRY Capital	FLAG	POPULATION	AREA (sq mi)	PER CAPITA GDP (U.S. $)	LIFE EXPECTANCY AT BIRTH	TVS PER 1,000 PEOPLE
Moldova Chişinau		3.6 million	13,067	$3,500	69.8	297
Monaco Monaco		30,500	1	$70,700	89.6	758
Montenegro Cetinje, Podgorica		653,474	5,415	$12,000	74.5	Not available
Netherlands Amsterdam		16.8 million	16,033	$42,900	81	540
Norway Oslo		4.7 million	125,182	$55,900	80.4	653
Poland Warsaw		38.4 million	120,728	$20,900	76.5	387
Portugal Lisbon		10.8 million	35,672	$23,800	78.9	567
Romania Bucharest		21.8 million	91,699	$13,000	74.5	312
Russia Moscow		142.5 million	6,592,772	$18,000	69.9	421
San Marino San Marino		32,448	24	$36,200	83.1	875
Serbia Belgrade		7.2 million	39,518	$10,600	74.8	277
Slovakia Bratislava		5.5 million	18,859	$24,600	76.2	418
Slovenia Ljubljana		2 million	7,827	$28,700	77.7	362
Spain Madrid		47.4 million	194,897	$31,100	81.4	555
Sweden Stockholm		9.1 million	173,732	$41,900	81.3	551
United States Washington, D.C.		316.7 million	3,718,711	$50,700	78.6	844

COUNTRY Capital	FLAG	POPULATION	AREA (sq mi)	PER CAPITA GDP (U.S. $)	LIFE EXPECTANCY AT BIRTH	TVS PER 1,000 PEOPLE
Switzerland Bern		8 million	15,942	$46,200	82.2	457
Tajikistan Dushanbe		7.9 million	55,251	$2,300	66.7	328
Turkmenistan Ashgabat		5.1 million	188,456	$8,900	69.2	198
Ukraine Kiev		44.6 million	233,090	$7,500	68.9	433
United Kingdom London		63.4 million	94,526	$37,500	80.2	661
Uzbekistan Tashkent		28.7 million	172,742	$3,600	73	280
Vatican City Vatican City		826	0.17	Not available	Not available	Not available
United States Washington, D.C.		316.7 million	3,718,711	$50,700	78.6	844

World's Highest Per Capita GDPs

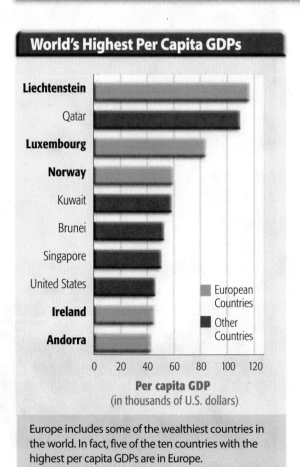

Per capita GDP
(in thousands of U.S. dollars)

Europe includes some of the wealthiest countries in the world. In fact, five of the ten countries with the highest per capita GDPs are in Europe.

Densely Populated Countries: Europe

Country	Population Density (per square mile)
Netherlands	1,278
Belgium	891
United Kingdom	655
Germany	611
Italy	512
Switzerland	495
Denmark	336
Poland	327
United States	87

Many European countries are densely populated, especially when compared to the United States.

ANALYSIS SKILL **ANALYZING INFORMATION**

1. In the chart above, what three European countries are the most densely populated? How do their densities compare to that of the United States?
2. Which countries in Europe seem to have the lowest per capita GDPs? Look at the atlas political map. Where are these countries located in Europe?

Southern Europe

Essential Question

myNotebook

How has climate influenced the land and people of Southern Europe?

Texas Essential Knowledge and Skills (TEKS)

1A, 1B, 2A, 2B, 3A, 3B, 3C, 3D, 4B, 4C, 4D, 4E, 4F, 5A, 5B, 5C, 6A, 6B, 15B, 18B, 21B, 21C, 22D

The Big Idea The peninsulas of southern Europe have rocky terrains and sunny, mild climates.

The Big Idea The home of one of the western world's oldest civilizations, Greece is trying to reclaim its place as a leading country in Europe.

The Big Idea Once the center of a huge empire, Italy grew to become a prosperous European country.

The Big Idea Spain and Portugal have rich cultures, stable governments, and struggling economies.

FOCUS ON READING AND WRITING

my **WriteSmart**

Asking Questions As you read a text, it can be helpful to ask yourself questions about what you are reading to be sure you understand it. One set of questions that you can use to test your understanding of a passage is the five *W*s—*who, what, when, where,* and *why.* **See the lesson Asking Questions on page 331.**

Writing a News Report You are a newspaper reporter on special assignment in Southern Europe. Your editor has told you that many readers know about Southern Europe's past but not about the region today. After you read this chapter, you will write a news report about an imaginary event in a Southern European country today. Use the annotation tools in your eBook to gather information for your assignment.

Geography Mountains cover large areas of Southern Europe. The Dolomites, shown here, are in northern Italy.

Southern Europe: Political

GERMANY

FRANCE

SWITZERLAND

AUSTRIA

Milan

Venice

Po River

Genoa

ITALY

ANDORRA

SAN MARINO

Florence

Tiber River

Barcelona

VATICAN CITY

Rome

Adriatic Sea

Balearic Islands

Sardinia

Naples

Thessaloníki

Tyrrhenian Sea

GREECE

TURKEY

Ionian Sea

Aegean Sea

Palermo

Athens

ALGERIA

Sicily

10°E

MALTA

Crete

TUNISIA

Mediterranean Sea

20°E

map zone Geography Skills

Place Southern Europe occupies three large peninsulas and thousands of small islands in the Mediterranean Sea.

1. Identify What is the capital of Greece?

2. Interpret Why is Southern Europe also called Mediterranean Europe?

History Greece was the home of Europe's first great civilization. The ruins in Delphi are more than 2,300 years old.

Culture Bullfights are popular events in parts of Spain. Bullfighters, called matadors, are honored members of society.

Physical Geography

 TEKS 3A, 3B, 3C, 4D, 4E, 5A, 5B, 5C, 6A, 6B, 21B, 21C, 22D

What You Will Learn...

Main Ideas

1. Southern Europe's physical features include rugged mountains and narrow coastal plains.
2. The region's climate and resources support such industries as agriculture, fishing, and tourism.

The Big Idea

The peninsulas of Southern Europe have rocky terrains and sunny, mild climates.

Key Terms and Places

Mediterranean Sea, *p. 310*
Pyrenees, *p. 311*
Apennines, *p. 311*
Alps, *p. 311*
Mediterranean climate, *p. 312*

hmhsocialstudies.com
TAKING NOTES

Use the graphic organizer online to take notes on the physical geography of Southern Europe.

If YOU lived there...

You are in a busy fish market in a small town on the coast of Italy, near the Mediterranean Sea. It is early morning. Colorful fishing boats have just pulled into shore with their catch of fresh fish and seafood. They unload their nets of slippery octopus and wriggling shrimp. Others bring silvery sea bass. You are looking forward to lunch—perhaps a tasty fish soup or pasta dish.

How does the Mediterranean affect your life?

BUILDING BACKGROUND The Mediterranean Sea has shaped the geography, climate, and culture of Southern Europe. All of these countries have long coastlines, with good harbors and beautiful beaches. Because much of the interior is rugged and mountainous, the sea has also been a highway for trade and travel.

Physical Features

The continent of Europe has often been called a peninsula of peninsulas. Why do you think this is so? Look at the map of Europe in this book's atlas to find out. Notice how Europe juts out from Asia like one big peninsula. Also, notice how smaller peninsulas extend into the many bodies of water that surround the continent.

Look at the map of Europe again. Do you see the three large peninsulas that extend south from Europe? From west to east, these are the Iberian Peninsula, the Italian Peninsula, and the Balkan Peninsula. Together with some large islands, they form the region of Southern Europe.

Southern Europe is also known as Mediterranean Europe. All of the countries of Southern Europe have long coastlines on the **Mediterranean Sea**. In addition to this common location on the Mediterranean, the countries of Southern Europe share many common physical features.

Landforms

The three peninsulas of Southern Europe are largely covered with rugged mountains. In Greece, for example, about three-fourths of the land is mountainous. Because much of the land is so rugged, farming and travel in Southern Europe can be a challenge.

The mountains of Southern Europe form several large ranges. On the Iberian Peninsula, the **Pyrenees** (PIR-uh-neez) form a boundary between Spain and France to the north. Italy has two major ranges. The **Apennines** (A-puh-nynz) run along the whole peninsula, and the **Alps**—Europe's highest mountains—are in the north. The Pindus Mountains cover much of Greece.

Southern Europe's mountains extend into the sea as well, where they rise above the water to form islands. The Aegean Sea east of Greece is home to more than 2,000 such islands. Southern Europe also has many larger islands formed by undersea mountains. These include Crete, which is south of Greece; Sicily, at the southern tip of Italy; and many others.

Not all of Southern Europe is rocky and mountainous, though. Some flat plains lie in the region. Most of these plains are along the coast and in the valleys of major rivers. It is here that most farming in Southern Europe takes place. It is also here that most of the region's people live.

FOCUS ON READING

As you read, ask yourself this question: Where are the Pyrenees?

Southern Europe: Physical

ELEVATION

Feet	Meters
13,120	4,000
6,560	2,000
1,640	500
656	200
(Sea level) 0	0 (Sea level)
Below sea level	Below sea level

0 150 300 Miles
0 150 300 Kilometers

Projection: Azimuthal Equal-Area

ATLANTIC OCEAN

Bay of Biscay

Cantabrian Mountains

PYRENEES

ANDORRA

A L P S

Po River Dolomites

ITALY

SAN MARINO

APENNINES

Tiber R.

Adriatic Sea

Douro River

40°N

SPAIN

Ebro River

PORTUGAL

Corisca

Tagus River

IBERIAN PENINSULA

VATICAN CITY

Sardinia

Pindus Mts.

Aegean Sea

GREECE

Guadiana River

Balearic Islands

Ionian Sea

Peloponnesus

Guadalquivir River

10°E

Sicily

20°E

Crete

Strait of Gibraltar

10°W

Mediterranean Sea

AFRICA

MALTA

map zone Geography Skills

Region The countries of Southern Europe lie on three peninsulas that extend into the Mediterranean Sea.

1. **Name** What mountain range separates Spain from the rest of Europe?
2. **Interpret** In what ways might mountains affect life in this region?

Southern Europe is known for mountains and seas. On Greece's coast, these two features come together to create a dramatic landscape.

311

Mediterranean Climate

Southern Europe is known for its Mediterranean climate, which features warm, dry summers and mild, wet winters. This climate affects nearly every aspect of life in the region.

SPAIN

PORTUGAL

1

2

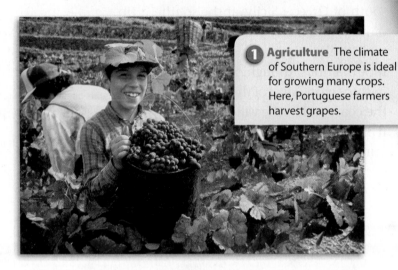

1 **Agriculture** The climate of Southern Europe is ideal for growing many crops. Here, Portuguese farmers harvest grapes.

2 **Tourism** The region's mild and sunny climate draws millions of tourists to places like this beach in Ibiza, Spain.

Water Features

Since Southern Europe is mostly peninsulas and islands, water is central to the region's geography. No place in Southern Europe is very far from a major body of water. The largest of these bodies of water is the Mediterranean, but the Adriatic, Aegean, and Ionian seas are also important to the region. For many centuries, these seas have given the people of Southern Europe food and a relatively easy way to travel around the region.

Only a few large rivers run through Southern Europe. The region's longest river is the Tagus (TAY-guhs), which flows across the Iberian Peninsula. In northern Italy, the Po runs through one of Southern Europe's most fertile and densely populated areas. Other rivers run out of the mountains and into the many surrounding seas.

READING CHECK **Finding Main Ideas** What are the region's major features?

Climate and Resources

Southern Europe is famous for its pleasant climate. Most of the region enjoys warm, sunny days and mild nights for most of the year. Little rain falls in the summer, falling instead during the mild winter. In fact, the type of climate found across Southern Europe is called a **Mediterranean climate** because it is common in this region.

The region's climate is also one of its most valuable resources. The mild climate is ideal for growing a variety of crops, from citrus fruits and grapes to olives and wheat. In addition, millions of tourists are drawn to the region each year by its climate, beaches, and breathtaking scenery.

ITALY

GREECE

3 **Vegetation** This field in Tuscany, a region of Italy, shows the variety of plants that thrive in Southern Europe's climate.

4 **Architecture** Climate also affects architecture in Southern Europe. Buildings, like these in Greece, are airy and made of light materials to reflect sunlight and heat.

ANALYSIS SKILL **ANALYZING VISUALS**

What are four ways in which the Mediterranean climate affects life in Southern Europe?

The sea is also an important resource in Southern Europe. Many of the region's largest cities are ports from which goods are shipped all over the world. In addition, the nearby seas are full of fish and shellfish, which provide the basis for profitable fishing industries.

READING CHECK **Generalizing** How is a mild climate important to Southern Europe?

SUMMARY AND PREVIEW In this section you learned about the physical features of Southern Europe. In the next section you will learn how those features affect life in one country—Greece.

Section 1 Assessment

hmhsocialstudies.com
ONLINE QUIZ

Reviewing Ideas, Terms, and Places

1. **a. Recall** Which three peninsulas are in Southern Europe?
   b. Explain Why is the sea important to Southern Europe?
   c. Elaborate Why do you think most people in Southern Europe live on coastal plains or in river valleys?
2. **a. Describe** What is the **Mediterranean climate** like?
   b. Generalize How is climate an important resource for the region?

Critical Thinking

3. **Finding Main Ideas** Draw a diagram like the one shown here. In the left oval, use your notes to explain how landforms affect life in Southern Europe. In the right oval, explain how climate affects life in the region.

Landforms   Climate

FOCUS ON WRITING

my WriteSmart

4. **Describing the Setting** Your news report will be about an imaginary event someplace in Southern Europe. That event might happen on a beach, in the mountains, or on a farm. Write some ideas in your notebook.

Reading a Climate Map

Learn

Geographers use many different types of maps to study a region. One type that can be very useful is a climate map. Because climate affects so many aspects of people's lives, it is important to know which climates are found in a region.

Practice

Use the climate map of Europe below to answer the following questions.

1. What does orange mean on this map?

2. What city has a highland climate?

3. What is the dominant climate in the countries of Southern Europe?

Europe: Climate

Climate Types
- Steppe
- Mediterranean
- Humid subtropical
- Marine west coast
- Humid continental
- Subarctic
- Tundra
- Ice cap
- Highland

0   300   600 Miles
0   300   600 Kilometers

Projection: Azimuthal Equal-Area

ATLANTIC OCEAN

Stockholm

London

Paris

Bern

Lisbon   Madrid

Rome

Mediterranean Sea

Athens

Black Sea

Apply

Choose one of the cities shown on the map above. Imagine that you are planning a trip to that city and need to know what the climate is like so you can prepare. Use the map to identify the type of climate found in your chosen city. Then use the library or the Internet to find out more about that type of climate. Write a short description of the climate and how you could prepare for it.

Greece

If YOU lived there...

You live in a small town on one of the many Greek islands. White houses perch on steep streets leading down to the sea. Many tourists come here by boat after visiting the busy capital city of Athens. They tell you about the beautiful ancient buildings they saw there. But your island has ancient statues and temple sites too. Still, some of your friends talk about moving to the city.

What might make people move to the city?

> **BUILDING BACKGROUND** In recent years, many people have moved out of Greece's small towns and villages into cities, especially Athens. Now the capital of Greece, Athens is an ancient city. It was home to one of Europe's greatest civilizations, one whose influence is still felt today all around the world.

History

Greece is a country steeped in history. Home to one of the world's oldest civilizations, it has been called the birthplace of Western culture. Even today, remnants of ancient Greece can be found all over the country, and ideas from ancient thinkers continue to affect people's lives today.

Ancient Greece

Theater. Philosophy. Democracy. These are just a few of the ideas that the modern world owes to ancient Greece. The Greeks were pioneers in many fields, and their contributions still affect how we live and think.

In art, the Greeks created lifelike paintings and statues that served as examples for later artists to imitate. In architecture, they built stately temples of marble that continue to inspire architects around the world.

An ancient Greek jar

 TEKS 1A, 1B, 2A, 2B, 3A, 3B, 3C, 3D, 4B, 4C, 15B, 18B, 21B, 21C, 22D

What You Will Learn...

Main Ideas

1. Early in its history, Greece was the home of a great civilization, but it was later ruled by foreign powers.
2. The Greek language, the Orthodox Church, and varied customs have helped shape Greece's culture.
3. In Greece today, many people are looking for new economic opportunities.

The Big Idea

The home of one of the Western world's oldest civilizations, Greece is trying to reclaim its place as a leading country in Europe.

Key Terms and Places

Orthodox Church, *p. 317*
Athens, *p. 318*

hmhsocialstudies.com
TAKING NOTES

Use the graphic organizer online to take notes on Greek history and culture.

Proportion

The ancient Greeks were great admirers of mathematics. They thought math could be used in many areas of their lives. For example, they used it to design temples and other buildings.

Greek builders believed in a concept called the Golden Mean. This concept said that the height of a building should be a particular fraction of the building's width. If the building were too tall, they thought it would look flimsy. If it were too wide, it would look squat and ugly. As a result, these builders were very careful in planning their buildings. The Parthenon, the temple pictured below, was built using the Golden Mean. Many consider it to be the greatest of all Greek temples.

Generalizing How did mathematical ideas influence ancient Greek architecture?

They invented new forms of literature, including history and drama, and made advances in geometry and other branches of math that we still study. In philosophy, they created a system of reasoning that is the foundation for modern science. In government, they created democracy, which inspired the government embraced by most people around the world today.

No ancient civilization lasted forever, though. In the 300s BC Greece became a part of Alexander the Great's empire, which also included Egypt and much of Southwest Asia. Under Alexander, Greek culture spread throughout his empire.

FOCUS ON READING
As you read, ask yourself this question: Who conquered Greece in the 300s BC?

The Romans and the Turks

Alexander's empire did not last very long. When it broke up, Greece became part of another empire, the Roman Empire. For about 300 years, the Greeks lived under Roman rule.

After about AD 400 the Roman Empire was divided into two parts. Greece became part of the Eastern, or Byzantine, Empire. The rulers of the Byzantine Empire admired Greek culture and encouraged people to adopt the Greek language and customs. They also encouraged people to adopt their religion, Christianity.

Greece was part of the Byzantine Empire for about 1,000 years. In the 1300s and 1400s, however, Greece was taken over by the Ottoman Turks from central Asia. The Turks were Muslim, but they allowed the people of Greece to remain Christian. Some elements of Greek culture, though, began to fade. For example, many people began speaking Turkish instead of Greek.

Independent Greece

Many Greeks were not happy under Turkish rule. They wanted to be free of foreign influences. In the early 1800s, they rose up against the Turks. The rebellion seemed likely to fail, but the Greeks received help from other European countries and drove the Turks out. After the rebellion, Greece became a monarchy.

Greece's government has changed many times since independence. The country's first kings took steps toward restoring democracy, but for most of the 1900s the nation experienced instability. A military dictatorship ruled from 1967 to 1974. More recently, democracy has once again taken root in the country where it was born nearly 2,500 years ago.

READING CHECK **Sequencing** What groups have ruled Greece throughout history?

Culture

Over the course of its history, many factors have combined to shape Greece's culture. These factors include the Greek language, Christianity, and customs adopted from the many groups who have ruled Greece.

Language and Religion

The people of Greece today speak a form of the same language their ancestors spoke long ago. In fact, Greek is one of the oldest languages still spoken in Europe today. The language has changed greatly over time, but it was never lost.

Although the Greeks maintained their language, their ancient religions have long since disappeared. Today nearly everyone in Greece belongs to the **Orthodox Church**, a branch of Christianity that dates to the Byzantine Empire. Religion is important to the Greeks, and holidays such as Easter are popular times for celebration.

Customs

Greek customs reflect the country's long history and its physical geography. Greek food, for example, is influenced both by products native to Greece and by groups who have ruled Greece over time.

Ingredients such as lamb, olives, and vegetables are easily available in Greece because they grow well there. As a result, the Greeks use lots of these ingredients in their cooking. Greek cuisine was later enhanced with ideas borrowed from other people. From the Turks, the Greeks learned to cook with yogurt and honey, and from the Italians they learned about pasta.

Greek meals are often eaten at family gatherings. For centuries, family has been central to Greek culture. Even as Greece is becoming more modernized, the family has remained the cornerstone of society.

READING CHECK **Summarizing** What are two dominant elements of Greek culture?

Easter in Greece

Easter is one of the most sacred days of the year for Orthodox Christians. All over Greece, people celebrate Easter with festivals, feasts, and special rituals.

ANALYZING VISUALS What evidence in this photo suggests that Easter is a major celebration?

The priests carry containers of holy water. Later, they will sprinkle this holy water on crowds as part of a blessing.

Priests wear richly decorated robes as part of their Easter celebration.

Many Easter ceremonies are led by an archbishop, a high-ranking official in the Orthodox Church.

map zone

Geography Skills

Place The most heavily populated regions in Greece lie along the coast.

1. **Locate** Which city in Greece has the highest population density?
2. **Draw Conclusions** How might Greece's physical geography influence where people live?

Persons per square mile		Persons per square km
520		200
260		100
130		50
25		10
3		1
0		0

⊕ National capital

0   50   100   150 Miles
0 50 100 200 Kilometers

Projection: Azimuthal Equal-Area

Thessaloníki

GREECE

Athens

Aegean Sea

Mediterranean Sea

① Many people in rural Greece raise sheep, goats, or other animals for a living.

② Athens, Greece's capital and largest city, is a busy economic and tourism center.

Greece Today

When many people think of Greece now, they think about the country's history. In fact, Greece's past often overshadows its present. Today, though, Greece is a largely urbanized society with a diverse economy.

Urban and Rural Greece

About three-fifths of all people in Greece today live in cities. Of these cities, **Athens**—the nation's capital—is by far the largest. In fact, almost one-third of the country's entire population lives in or around the city of Athens.

Athens is a huge city where old and new mix. Modern skyscrapers rise high above the ancient ruins of Greek temples. Most of the country's industry is centered there. However, this industry has resulted in air pollution, which damages the ancient ruins and causes health problems.

Outside of the city, Greek life is very different. People in rural areas still live largely as people have lived for centuries. Many live in isolated mountain villages, where they grow crops and raise sheep and goats. Village life often centers around the village square. People meet there to discuss local events and make decisions.

Greece's Economy

Greece's economic growth lags behind most other European nations. In 2009 an international economic crisis exposed the Greek government's huge debt. To avoid bankruptcy, Greek leaders in 2012 agreed to accept billions of dollars in loans from the International Money Fund and the European Union. In addition, Greece's parliament approved government spending cuts, which led to violent protests.

One industry in which Greece excels is shipping. Greece has one of the largest shipping fleets in the world. Greek ships can be found in ports all around the world, loaded with cargo from countries in Europe and other parts of the world.

Another profitable industry in Greece is tourism. Millions of people from around the world visit every year. Some are drawn to ancient ruins in Athens and other parts of the country. Others prefer the sunny, sandy beaches of Greece's many islands. Despite the boost that tourism provides, the country's debt crisis has slowed the economy.

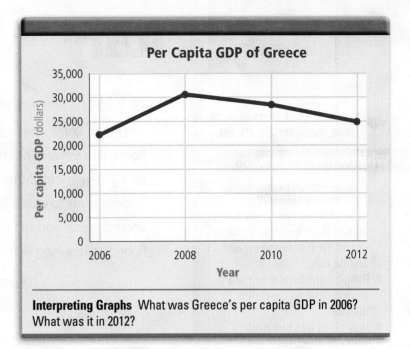

Per Capita GDP of Greece

Interpreting Graphs What was Greece's per capita GDP in 2006? What was it in 2012?

READING CHECK **Finding Main Ideas** What are the most important industries in Greece?

SUMMARY AND PREVIEW In this section you learned about Greece, a country with a long and varied history that still shapes its culture and economy today. In the next section you will learn about Italy, another country in the region that has been shaped by history.

Section 2 Assessment

Reviewing Ideas, Terms, and Places

1. **a. Identify** What were two major achievements of the ancient Greeks?
   b. Sequence What steps did the Greeks take to gain their independence?
2. **a. Define** What is the **Orthodox Church**?
   b. Generalize What is one way in which Greece's history affects its culture today?
3. **a. Describe** What is life like in **Athens** today?
   b. Explain Why is Greece's economic growth slower than most other European nations?
   c. Evaluate Would you rather live in Athens or in rural Greece? Why?

Critical Thinking

4. **Categorizing** Draw a table like the one here. Use the table to organize your notes into columns about Greece's history, its culture, and Greece today.

Greece		
History	Culture	Today

FOCUS ON WRITING

5. **Introducing Greece** If you choose Greece for the site of your news report, what would be a good topic? The movement of people to the cities? An event at a historic site? Jot down your ideas.

TEKS 1A, 1B, 2A, 2B, 3A, 3B, 3C, 3D, 4B, 4C, 4F, 15B, 18B, 21B, 21C, 22D

What You Will Learn...

Main Ideas

1. Italian history can be divided into three periods: ancient Rome, the Renaissance, and unified Italy.
2. Religion and local traditions have helped shape Italy's culture.
3. Italy today has two distinct economic regions—northern Italy and southern Italy.

The Big Idea

Once the center of a huge empire, Italy grew to become a prosperous European country.

Key Terms and Places

Christianity, *p. 320*
Catholicism, *p. 322*
pope, *p. 322*
Vatican City, *p. 322*
Sicily, *p. 323*
Naples, *p. 323*
Milan, *p. 323*
Rome, *p. 324*

hmhsocialstudies.com
TAKING NOTES

Use the graphic organizer online to take notes on Italian history, life, and culture.

If YOU lived there...

You live in Rome, the historic heart of Italy. Wherever you walk in Rome, you see reminders of the city's long and rich history. It may be a 600-year-old church or a 2,000-year-old market. One of your favorite spots to visit is the Colosseum. When you sit inside this ancient arena, you can imagine fierce gladiators and wild animals fighting there long ago.

How does history affect life in Italy?

BUILDING BACKGROUND Italian history continues to affect life in Italy today, but its influence extends far beyond that one country. All around the world, people owe their ideas about art, government, law, and language to Italy and its people. Many of these ideas are ancient, but even today Italians help shape the world's culture.

History

Locate Italy on the political map at the beginning of this chapter. As you can see on the map, Italy is located on the Mediterranean Sea near Greece. For centuries, Italy was the heart of one of the largest and most powerful states the world has ever seen. Even after that state collapsed, Italy remained a major influence on Europe and other parts of the world.

Ancient Rome

The great civilization that developed in Italy was Rome. Built in the 700s BC as a tiny village, Rome grew to control nearly all the land around the Mediterranean Sea. At the height of the Roman Empire, the Romans controlled an empire that stretched from Britain in the northwest to the Persian Gulf. It included most of Europe as well as parts of southwest Asia and northern Africa.

Roman influences in the world can still be seen today. The Romans' art, architecture, and literature are still admired. Their laws and political ideas have influenced the governments and legal systems of many countries. In addition, the Romans helped spread **Christianity**, a major world religion based on the life and teachings of Jesus of Nazareth.

The Renaissance

The Roman Empire collapsed in the AD 400s, largely due to weak leadership and invasions from outside. With no central government to unite them, Italy's cities formed their own states. Each had its own laws, its own government, and its own army. Wars between them were common.

As time passed, the cities of Italy became major centers of trade. Merchants from these cities traveled to far-off places like China to bring goods back to Europe.

Many merchants became very rich from this trade. With the money they made, these merchants sponsored artists and architects. Their support of the arts helped lead to the Renaissance, a period of great creativity in Europe. It lasted from about 1350 through the 1500s. During the Renaissance artists and writers—many of them Italian—created some of the world's greatest works of art and literature.

Unified Italy

Italy remained divided into small states until the mid-1800s. At that time, a rise in nationalism, or strong patriotic feelings for a country, led people across Italy to fight for unification. As a result of their efforts, Italy became a unified kingdom in 1861.

In the 1920s a new government came to power. Under Benito Mussolini, Italy became a dictatorship. That dictatorship was short-lived, however. Mussolini joined Hitler to fight other countries of Europe in World War II. In 1945 Italy was defeated.

After World War II, Italy became a democracy. Since that time, power has rested in an elected Parliament and prime minister. Also since the end of the war, Italy has developed one of the strongest economies in Europe.

READING CHECK **Summarizing** What are some key periods in the history of Italy?

Italian History

The history of Italy stretches back nearly 3,000 years. This long span includes several key periods.

Ancient Rome

- According to legend, the city of Rome was built in the 700s BC.
- The Romans created a huge empire. At its height, the empire included parts of Europe, Southwest Asia, and northern Africa.
- Roman art, architecture, literature, and law still influence people today.
- Christianity arose and spread in the Roman Empire.

Roman statue

The Renaissance

- The Renaissance was a period of great advances in art, architecture, and literature.
- The Renaissance began in the 1300s in cities like Florence.
- From Italy, the Renaissance spread to other parts of Europe.
- Some of the world's greatest works of art were created at this time.

Leonardo da Vinci's *Mona Lisa*

Unified Italy

- Since the Middle Ages, Italy had been divided into small states.
- In the mid-1800s, increased feelings of nationalism led people across Italy to fight for unification.
- The fight for unification was led by Giuseppe Garibaldi.
- Italy was officially unified in 1861.

Giuseppe Garibaldi

Culture

For centuries, people around the world have admired and borrowed from Italian culture. Italy's culture has been shaped by many factors. Among these factors are the Roman Catholic Church, local traditions, and regional geography.

Religion

Most Italians belong to the Roman Catholic Church. Historically, **Catholicism**, the largest branch of Christianity, has been the single strongest influence on Italian culture. This influence is strong in part because the **pope**, the spiritual head of the Roman Catholic Church, lives on the Italian Peninsula. He resides in **Vatican City**, an independent state located within the city of Rome.

The lasting importance of the church can be seen in many ways in Italy. For example, the city of Rome alone is home to hundreds of Catholic churches from all periods of history. In addition, religious holidays and festivals are major events.

ACADEMIC
VOCABULARY

contemporary
modern

Local Traditions

In addition to religion, local traditions have influenced Italian culture. Italian food, for example, varies widely from region to region. These variations are based on local preferences and products. All over Italy, people eat many of the same foods—olives, tomatoes, rice, pasta. However, the ways in which people prepare this food differ. In the south, for example, people often serve pasta with tomato sauces. In the north, creamy sauces are much more common.

Other traditions reflect Italy's past. For example, Italy has always been known as a center of the arts. The people of Italy have long been trendsetters, shaping styles that are later adopted by other people. As a result, the Italians are leaders in many **contemporary** art forms. For example, Italy has produced some of the world's greatest painters, sculptors, authors, composers, fashion designers, and filmmakers.

READING CHECK **Finding Main Ideas** What are two major influences on Italian culture?

Major Cities of Italy

Milan, Rome, and Naples are the three largest cities in Italy. Because of their varied histories and locations, each city has a distinct landscape and culture.

ANALYZING VISUALS **Which city would you most like to visit?**

Milan Milan, the largest city in Italy, is a global fashion capital. The clothes created there influence fashion designers around the world.

Italy Today

A shared language, the Roman Catholic Church, and strong family ties help bind Italians together. At the same time, though, major differences exist in the northern and southern parts of the country.

Southern Italy

Southern Italy is the country's poorer half. Its economy has less industry than the north and depends heavily on agriculture. Farming is especially important in **Sicily**, an island at the peninsula's tip. Tourism is also vital to the south's economy. Among the region's attractions are its dazzling beaches and ancient Roman ruins.

In recent decades, Italy's government has tried to promote industry in the south. It has offered <u>incentives</u>, such as lower taxes, to private companies that will build factories there. Many of these government efforts center on the city of **Naples**, a busy port and the largest city in southern Italy. Thanks to government programs, Naples is now also an industrial center.

Northern Italy

In contrast to southern Italy, the northern part of the country has a strong economy. The geographic factors responsible for the location of the region's economic activities includes Italy's most fertile farmlands, its major trade centers, and its most popular tourist destinations.

For decades, the Po River valley has been called the breadbasket of Italy because most of the country's crops are grown there. Despite its fertile soils, farmers cannot grow enough to support Italy's population. Italy has to import much of its food.

The north is also home to Italy's major industrial centers. Busy factories in such cities as Turin and Genoa make appliances, automobiles, and other goods for export. **Milan** is also a major industrial center as well as a worldwide center for fashion design. The location of these cities near central Europe helps companies sell their goods to foreign customers. Railroads, highways, and tunnels make the shipment of goods through the Alps easy.

ACADEMIC VOCABULARY

incentive something that leads people to follow a certain course of action

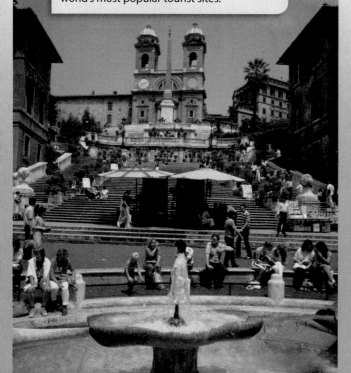

Rome Rome, the capital of Italy, is in the central part of the country. A major center of banking and industry, Rome is also one of the world's most popular tourist sites.

Naples Naples is the most important city in southern Italy. Less glamorous than many northern cities, it is a port and manufacturing center.

Venice

Venice, in northeastern Italy, is one of the country's most visited tourist attractions. Look at the image of Venice above, taken by an orbiting satellite. Does it look like other cities you have seen? What may not be obvious is that the paths that wind their way through the city are not roads, but canals. In fact, Venice has very few roads. This is because the city was built on islands—118 of them! People move about the city on boats that navigate along the canals. Every year, millions of tourists travel to Venice to see the sights as they are rowed along the scenic waterways.

Contrasting How is Venice unlike other cities you have studied?

Tens of millions of tourists visit the cities of northern Italy every year. They are drawn by the cities' rich histories and unique cultural features. Florence, for example, is a center of Italian art and culture. It was there that the Renaissance began in the 1300s. To the west of Florence is Pisa, famous for its Leaning Tower—the bell tower of the city's church. On the coast of the Adriatic Sea lies the city of Venice. Tourists are lured there by the romantic canals that serve as roads through the city.

Nestled in the center of the country is Italy's capital, **Rome**. With ties to both north and south, Rome does not fully belong to either region. From there, the country's leaders attempt to bring all the people of Italy together as one nation.

READING CHECK **Contrast** How are northern and southern Italy different?

SUMMARY AND PREVIEW In this section you read about Italy. The country's long history continues to affect life in Italy even today. Next, you will study two other countries whose pasts still affect life there—Spain and Portugal.

Section 3 Assessment

hmhsocialstudies.com
ONLINE QUIZ

Reviewing Ideas, Terms, and Places

1. a. **Describe** What was Renaissance Italy like?
   b. **Interpret** How did nationalism influence Italian history?
2. a. **Identify** What religion has had a major impact on Italian culture?
   b. **Explain** How have local traditions helped shape Italian culture?
3. a. **Recall** What is the main economic activity of southern Italy?
   b. **Contrast** How are the economies of **Milan**, **Rome**, and **Naples** different?
   c. **Rate** If you could visit any one city in Italy, which would it be? Why?

Critical Thinking

4. **Comparing and Contrasting** Draw two circles like the ones here. Using your notes, list details about southern Italy in the left circle and about northern Italy in the right circle. Where the circles overlap, list common features of the two.

Southern Italy — Northern Italy

FOCUS ON WRITING

*my*WriteSmart

5. **Investigating Italy** What Italian event could you report on? Perhaps it could be a fashion show or a religious service at the Vatican. Make a list of events that could make an interesting report.

Spain and Portugal

If **YOU** lived there...

You have just moved to southern Spain from a town in the far north. You cannot help noticing that many of the buildings here look different from those in your hometown. Many of the buildings here have rounded arches over the doorways and tall towers in front of them. In addition, some are decorated with ornate tiles.

Why do you think the buildings look different?

BUILDING BACKGROUND Throughout history, many different groups have ruled parts of Spain and Portugal. Each group brought elements of its own culture to the region. As a result, parts of the two countries have cultures unlike those found anywhere else.

History

Locate Spain and Portugal on the physical map in Section 1. As you can see, the two countries share the Iberian Peninsula, or **Iberia**, the westernmost peninsula in Europe. Although the two are different in many ways, they share a common history.

Across the centuries, several powerful empires controlled all or part of the Iberian Peninsula. By 700 BC, the Phoenicians, from the eastern Mediterranean, had colonized coastal areas of what is now Spain. After the Phoenicians came the Greeks. A few centuries later, all of Iberia became part of the Roman Empire.

After the Roman Empire fell apart, Iberia was invaded by the Moors, a group of Muslims from North Africa. For about 600 years, much of the Iberian Peninsula was under Muslim rule.

TEKS 1A, 1B, 2A, 2B, 3A, 3B, 3C, 3D, 4B, 4C, 4F, 15B, 18B, 21B, 21C, 22D

What You Will Learn...

Main Ideas

1. Over the centuries, Spain and Portugal have been part of many large and powerful empires.
2. The cultures of Spain and Portugal reflect their long histories.
3. Having been both rich and poor in the past, Spain and Portugal today have struggling economies.

The Big Idea

Spain and Portugal have rich cultures, stable governments, and struggling economies.

Key Terms and Places

Iberia, *p. 325*
parliamentary monarchy, *p. 328*
Madrid, *p. 328*
Barcelona, *p. 328*
Lisbon, *p. 328*

hmhsocialstudies.com
TAKING NOTES

Use the graphic organizer online to take notes on Spain and Portugal.

Moorish structures, such as this tower outside of Lisbon, Portugal, can still be seen all over Iberia.

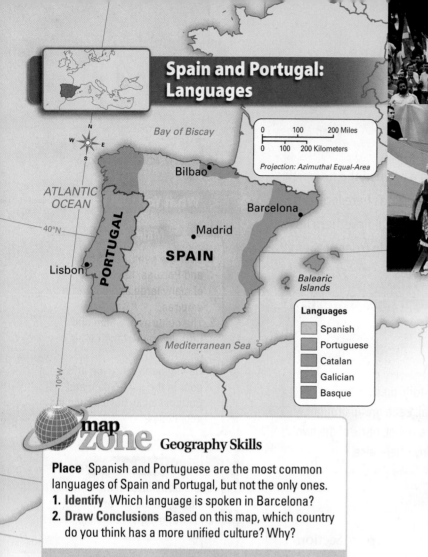

Spain and Portugal: Languages

Bay of Biscay

ATLANTIC OCEAN

Bilbao

Barcelona

PORTUGAL

40°N

Madrid

SPAIN

Lisbon

Balearic Islands

Mediterranean Sea

10°W

0   100   200 Miles
0   100   200 Kilometers
Projection: Azimuthal Equal-Area

Languages
- Spanish
- Portuguese
- Catalan
- Galician
- Basque

Many Basque speakers take part in rallies like this one in support of independence. The banner in this photo reads "Basque Nation Arise" in the Basque language.

map zone Geography Skills

Place Spanish and Portuguese are the most common languages of Spain and Portugal, but not the only ones.
1. **Identify** Which language is spoken in Barcelona?
2. **Draw Conclusions** Based on this map, which country do you think has a more unified culture? Why?

By the end of the 1400s, however, the Muslims were driven out of Iberia. The rulers of the Christian kingdoms of Spain and Portugal banded together to force non-Christians to leave Iberia. Those who refused to leave were made to convert or face severe punishments.

Spain and Portugal went on to build large empires that spanned the oceans. Both countries ruled huge territories in the Americas as well as smaller areas in Africa and Asia. These territories made the two kingdoms rich and powerful until most of their colonies broke away and became independent in the 1800s and 1900s.

READING CHECK **Summarizing** What empires have ruled Spain and Portugal?

Culture

In some ways, the cultures of Spain and Portugal are like those of other southern European countries. For example, the Spanish, Portuguese, Greeks, and Italians all cook with many of the same ingredients. The Catholic Church is very influential in Italy as well as Spain and Portugal. In other ways, Iberian cultures are unique.

Language

The most spoken languages in Iberia are, of course, Spanish and Portuguese. Various dialects of these languages are spoken in different parts of the peninsula. In addition, other languages are also spoken by many people in Iberia. The Catalan language of eastern Spain is similar to Spanish. Galician, which is spoken in northwest Spain, is more closely related to Portuguese.

In addition, the Basque (BASK) people of the Pyrenees have their own language, which is not related to either Spanish or Portuguese. The Basques also have their own customs and traditions, unlike those of the rest of Spain. As a result, many Basques have long wanted to form their own independent country.

Religion

Most people in both Spain and Portugal are Roman Catholic. People in both countries celebrate Christian holidays like Christmas and Easter. In addition, many towns hold fiestas, or festivals, in honor of their patron saints. At these festivals, people may gather to dance or to watch a bullfight.

Music and Art

Music and art have been central to Iberian culture for centuries. The Portuguese are famous for sad folk songs called fados. The Spanish are known for a style of song and dance called flamenco.

Many elements of Iberia's art and architecture reflect its Muslim past. Many buildings in the peninsula have elements of Muslim design, such as round arches and elaborate tilework.

READING CHECK **Comparing** What is one culture element that Spain and Portugal share?

Spain and Portugal Today

Compared to most other countries in Western Europe, Spain's and Portugal's economies are struggling. Their economic problems were brought on both by recent hardships and by past events.

Challenge of the Past

Spain and Portugal were once Europe's richest countries. Their wealth came from gold and silver found in their colonies.

When other countries in Europe began to build industrial economies, Spain and Portugal continued to rely on gold from their colonies. As those colonies became independent, that source of income was lost. As a result, Spain and Portugal were late in developing manufacturing.

Spain and Portugal are still poorer than other countries in Western Europe. Despite recent economic growth and vibrant industries such as tourism, their economies are struggling.

FOCUS ON READING

As you read, ask yourself this question: Why did Spain and Portugal fall behind other countries economically?

FOCUS ON CULTURE

Flamenco

Complex guitar rhythms, a heavy beat, and whirling dancers—these are all part of the traditional Spanish art form known as flamenco. The word *flamenco* refers both to a style of music and a style of dance. The most important instrument in the music is the guitar, which was itself a Spanish invention. Most of the time, the guitar is accompanied by other musical instruments and by singers.

When most people think of flamenco, however, they picture dancers. Flamenco dancers perform alone, in pairs, or in large groups. They wear brightly colored costumes as they perform complex steps. It is not unusual for dancers to clap their hands or snap their fingers to the beat or to play castanets as they dance. Castanets are small, hinged wooden instruments. The dancers clap the castanets together to make a clicking noise.

Finding Main Ideas What are the major elements of flamenco music and dancing?

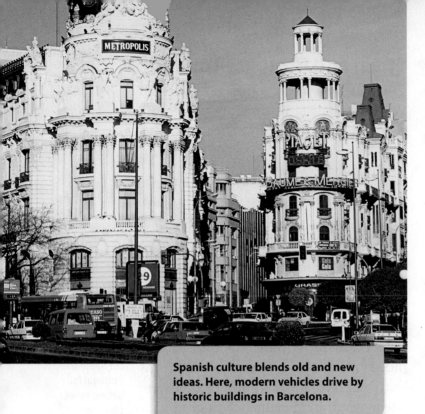

Spanish culture blends old and new ideas. Here, modern vehicles drive by historic buildings in Barcelona.

In other ways, Spain has become a more modern country. Agriculture was once the major economic activity, but factories now create automobiles and other high-tech products. Cities such as **Madrid**—the capital—and **Barcelona** are centers of industry, tourism, and culture.

Portugal Today

Unlike Spain, Portugal is not a monarchy. It is a republic with elected leaders. As in Spain, the economy is based largely on industries centered in large cities, especially **Lisbon**. In many rural areas, though, people depend on agriculture. Farmers there grow many crops but are most famous for grapes and cork. Farmers harvest cork from the bark of a particular type of oak tree. Once it is dried, the cork is used to make bottle stoppers and other products.

READING CHECK **Contrasting** How are Spain and Portugal's governments different?

Spain Today

The people of Spain have kept many aspects of their history alive. For example, Spain is still governed by a king, a descendant of the kings who ruled the country long ago. Unlike in the past, however, Spain today is a **parliamentary monarchy**, which means that the king shares power with an elected parliament and a prime minister.

SUMMARY AND PREVIEW You have just learned about the countries of Southern Europe. Next, you will move north to study West-Central Europe.

Section 4 Assessment

Reviewing Ideas, Terms, and Places

1. **a. Recall** What is **Iberia**? What two countries are located there?
   b. Sequence What people have ruled Iberia, and in what order did they rule it?
2. **a. Identify** What is the most common religion in Spain and Portugal?
   b. Generalize How is Spain's history reflected in its architecture?
   c. Elaborate Why do you think many Basques want to become independent from Spain?
3. **a. Identify** What are two crops grown in Portugal?
   b. Analyze What is Spain's government like?

Critical Thinking

4. **Categorizing** Draw a diagram like the one here. Using your notes, record information about the cultures and economies of Spain and Portugal.

	Spain	Portugal
Culture		
Economy		

FOCUS ON WRITING **my WriteSmart**

5. **Writing about Spain and Portugal** What details about Spain and Portugal will grab your readers' attention? Look back through your notes to choose the topic for your article.

Chapter Review

Visual Summary

Use the visual summary below to help you review the main ideas of the chapter.

QUICK FACTS

Greece
The birthplace of democracy, Greece is working to improve its economy.

Italy
Italy is one of Europe's leading cultural and economic countries.

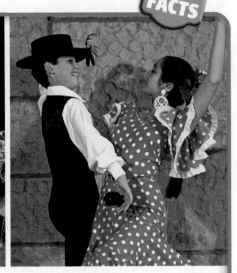

Spain and Portugal
The rich cultures of Spain and Portugal are shaped by their histories.

Reviewing Vocabulary, Terms, and Places

Fill in the blanks with the correct term or location from this chapter.

1. The climate found in most of Southern Europe is the _____.
2. The _____ is the head of the Roman Catholic Church.
3. The highest mountains in Europe are the _____.
4. _____ is the capital of Greece.
5. A _____ is a government in which a king rules with the help of an elected body.
6. Italy's capital, _____, was the birthplace of an ancient civilization.
7. _____ is an independent state located within the city of Rome.
8. Spain and Portugal are located on a peninsula known as _____.

Comprehension and Critical Thinking

SECTION 1 *(Pages 310–313)*

9. **a. Describe** What are two physical features that all the countries of Southern Europe have in common?

   b. Draw Conclusions Why has Southern Europe's climate been called its most valuable resource?

   c. Predict How would daily life in Southern Europe be different if it were not a coastal region?

SECTION 2 *(Pages 315–319)*

10. **a. Identify** What is the largest city in Greece? How would you describe the city?

   b. Generalize How has Greece's economy changed in the last decade? What is largely responsible for this change?

   c. Elaborate How does Greek history still affect the country today?

SECTION 3 (Pages 320–324)

11. a. Recall Which region of Italy has the stronger economy? Why?

b. Sequence What periods followed the Roman Empire in Italy? What happened during those periods?

c. Elaborate What are some ways in which the Italians have influenced world culture?

SECTION 4 (Pages 325–328)

12. a. Identify Who are the Basques?

b. Compare and Contrast How are Spain and Portugal alike? How are they different?

c. Elaborate How do you think Iberia's history makes it different from other places in Europe?

Social Studies Skills

Reading a Climate Map *Use the climate map from the Social Studies Skills lesson of this chapter to answer the following questions.*

13. What type of climate does London have?

14. What climate is found only in the far north?

15. Where in Europe would you find a humid subtropical climate?

Using the Internet

16. Activity: Exploring Italian Cuisine Pizza. Pasta. Mozzarella. Olive oil. These are some of the most popular elements of Italian food, one of the world's favorites. Through your online textbook, learn more about the history and variety of Italian cooking. Then test your knowledge with the interactive activity.

Map Activity

17. Southern Europe On a separate sheet of paper, match the letters on the map with their correct labels.

Mediterranean Sea	Lisbon, Portugal
Athens, Greece	Po River
Sicily	Rome, Italy
Spain	Aegean Sea

FOCUS ON READING AND WRITING *my* **WriteSmart**

Asking Questions *Read the passage below. After you read it, answer the questions below to be sure you have understood what you read.*

> Spain is a democracy, but it has not always been. From 1939 to 1975, a dictator named Francisco Franco ruled the country. He came to power as a result of a bloody civil war and was unpopular with the Spanish people.

18. Who is this paragraph about?

19. What did the people in this passage do?

20. When did the events described take place?

21. Where did the events described take place?

22. Why did the events happen?

Writing Your News Report *Use myWriteSmart in your eBook and your notes and the instructions below to help you create your news report.*

23. Select a topic for your news report. Create a plan for your report by answering these questions: What is the scene or setting of the event? Who is there? Why is it important enough to include in the news? What happened? Start your news report with a dateline, for example: Rome, May 5, 2009. Begin your first paragraph with an interesting observation or detail. Explain the event in two or three short paragraphs. Close with an important piece of information or interesting detail.

Reading Social Studies

Asking Questions

FOCUS ON READING

Reading is one place where asking questions will never get you in trouble. The five *W* questions—and—can help you be sure you understand the material you read. After you read a section, ask yourself the 5 *W*s: *Who* was this section about? *What* did they do? *When* and *where* did they live? *Why* did they do what they did? See the example below to learn how this reading strategy can help you identify the main points of a passage.

> Many Greeks were not happy under Turkish rule. They wanted to be free of foreign influences. In the early 1800s, they rose up against the Turks. The rebellion seemed likely to fail, but the Greeks received help from other European countries and drove the Turks out. After the rebellion, Greece became a monarchy.
>
> *From Section 2, Greece*

The 5 *W*s

| **Who?** Greeks | **What?** Led rebellion to become independent from Turks | **Where?** Greece | **When?** Early 1800s | **Why?** Wanted to be free of foreign influences |

YOU TRY IT!

With a partner, read the following passage to each other and answer the 5 *W*s to check your understanding of it.

> Italy remained divided into small states until the mid-1800s. At that time, a rise in nationalism, or strong patriotic feelings for a country, led people across Italy to fight for unification. As a result of their efforts, Italy became a unified kingdom in 1861.
>
> *From Section 3, Italy*

West-Central Europe

Essential Question

myNotebook

What geographic and cultural features characterize West-Central Europe?

Texas Essential Knowledge and Skills (TEKS)

1A, 1B, 2A, 2B, 3A, 3B, 3C, 3D, 4B, 4C, 4D, 4E, 4F, 5A, 5B, 5C, 6A, 6B, 15B, 18B, 21B, 21C, 22D

FOCUS ON READING AND SPEAKING

my **WriteSmart**

Recognizing Word Origins Many of the words we use today came into English from other languages, such as Latin, French, or German. As you read this chapter, think about the origin, or sources, of words. Knowing a word's origin can help you remember the word's meaning. **See the lesson, Recognizing Word Origins, on page 355.**

Writing a Persuasive Speech As you read about West-Central Europe, you will discover some issues. Issues are topics that people disagree about. Think about which of the issues seem important to you. Later, you will take a stand on one of these issues by writing and presenting a persuasive speech. Use the annotation tools in your eBook to gather information for your assignment.

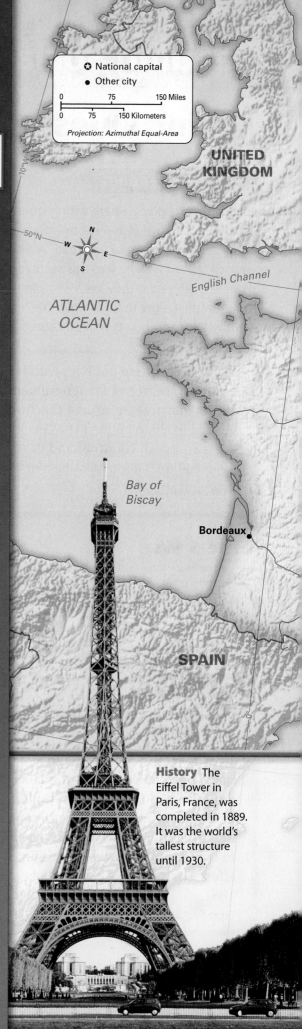

National capital
● **Other city**

0   75   150 Miles
0   75   150 Kilometers

Projection: Azimuthal Equal-Area

UNITED KINGDOM

ATLANTIC OCEAN

English Channel

Bay of Biscay

Bordeaux

SPAIN

History The Eiffel Tower in Paris, France, was completed in 1889. It was the world's tallest structure until 1930.

North Sea

Kiel Canal

Hamburg

NETHERLANDS
Amsterdam
Rotterdam

RUHR

Elbe River

Weser River

Oder River

Berlin

Neisse River

Antwerp
Lille   Brussels
BELGIUM

Rhine River

GERMANY

Frankfurt

CZECH REPUBLIC

Seine River

Paris

LUXEMBOURG
Luxembourg

Loire River

Danube River

Munich

Vienna

FRANCE

Zurich
Bern
SWITZERLAND

LIECHTENSTEIN

Innsbruck

Salzburg

AUSTRIA   HUNGARY

Lake Geneva
Geneva
Lyon

Rhone River

ITALY

Adriatic Sea

map zone Geography Skills

Regions The countries of West-Central Europe are some of the most industrialized and richest countries in the world.
1. **Identify** Which countries make up this region?
2. **Make Inferences** Why do you think some of the countries in this region might want to join together to promote economic growth?

Marseille

MONACO

Corsica (FRANCE)

Mediterranean Sea

10°E

20°E

Geography The Netherlands is famous for its fields of brightly colored tulips.

Culture A German teen participates in a Bavarian cow festival.

333

TEKS 3A, 3B, 3C, 4D, 4E, 5A, 5B, 5C, 6A, 6B, 21B, 21C, 22D

What You Will Learn...

Main Ideas

1. The physical features of West-Central Europe include plains, uplands, mountains, rivers, and seas.
2. West-Central Europe's mild climate and resources support agriculture, energy production, and tourism.

The Big Idea

West-Central Europe has a range of landscapes, a mild climate, and rich farmland.

Key Terms and Places

Northern European Plain, *p. 334*
North Sea, *p. 336*
English Channel, *p. 336*
Danube River, *p. 336*
Rhine River, *p. 336*
navigable river, *p. 336*

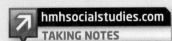
hmhsocialstudies.com
TAKING NOTES

Use the graphic organizer online to take notes on the physical geography of West-Central Europe.

Physical Geography

If YOU lived there...

You are a photographer planning a book about the landscapes of West-Central Europe. You are trying to decide where to find the best pictures of rich farmland, forested plateaus, and rugged mountains. So far, you are planning to show the colorful tulip fields of the Netherlands, the hilly Black Forest region of Germany, and the snow-covered Alps in Switzerland.

What other places might you want to show?

BUILDING BACKGROUND The countries of West-Central Europe are among the most prosperous and powerful countries in the world. The reasons include their mild climates, good farmland, many rivers, market economies, and stable governments. In addition, most of these countries cooperate as members of the European Union.

Physical Features

From fields of tulips, to sunny beaches, to icy mountain peaks, West-Central Europe offers a wide range of landscapes. Even though the region is small, it includes three major types of landforms—plains, uplands, and mountains. These landforms extend in wide bands across the region.

Plains, Uplands, and Mountains

Look at the map at right. Picture West-Central Europe as an open fan with Italy as the handle. The outer edge of this imaginary fan is a broad coastal plain called the **Northern European Plain**. This plain stretches from the Atlantic coast into Eastern Europe.

Most of this plain is flat or rolling and lies less than 500 feet (150 m) above sea level. In the Netherlands, parts of the plain dip below sea level. There, people must build walls to hold back the sea. In Brittany in northwestern France, the land rises to form a plateau above the surrounding plain.

The Northern European Plain provides the region's best farmland. Many people live on the plain, and the region's largest cities are located there.

The Central Uplands extend across the center of our imaginary fan. This area has many rounded hills, small plateaus, and valleys. In France, the uplands include the <u>Massif</u> Central (ma-SEEF sahn-TRAHL), a plateau region, and the Jura Mountains.

This range is on the French-Swiss border. In Germany, uplands cover much of the southern two-thirds of the country. Dense woodlands, such as the Black Forest, blanket many of the hills in this area.

The Central Uplands have many productive coalfields. As a result, the area is important for mining and industry. Some valleys provide fertile soil for farming, but most of the area is too rocky to farm.

FOCUS ON READING

Look up the origin of *massif* in a dictionary. How does its origin relate to the description of the Massif Central?

West-Central Europe: Physical

ELEVATION

Feet	Meters
13,120	4,000
6,560	2,000
1,640	500
656	200
(Sea level) 0	0 (Sea level)
Below sea level	Below sea level

0   100   200 Miles
0   100   200 Kilometers

Projection: Azimuthal Equal Area

DENMARK · Baltic Sea · IRELAND · North Sea · UNITED KINGDOM · NETHERLANDS · NORTHERN EUROPEAN PLAIN · BELGIUM · Rhine · GERMANY · LUXEMBOURG · CZECH REPUBLIC · Bohemian Forest · English Channel · Seine River · ATLANTIC OCEAN · BRITTANY · CENTRAL UPLANDS · Black Forest · Danube River · LIECHTENSTEIN · AUSTRIA · HUNGARY · FRANCE · JURA MTS. · ALPS · SWITZERLAND · Bay of Biscay · MASSIF CENTRAL · Rhône River · Mont Blanc 15,771 ft (4,807 m) · ❶ · FRENCH RIVIERA · MONACO · Adriatic Sea · ITALY · PYRENEES · SPAIN · Mediterranean Sea · 50°N · 10°W · 0° · 10°E

❶ Each summer, lavender blooms across Provence, a region of southern France. Lavender is used in perfumes and soaps.

map zone Geography Skills

Place The land of West-Central Europe rises from the low Northern European Plain to the Central Uplands to the high Alps.

1. **Name** What bodies of water surround the countries of West-Central Europe?
2. **Draw Conclusions** How might the elevation of the Netherlands affect life there?

Along the inner part of our imaginary fan, the land rises dramatically to form the alpine mountain system. This system includes the Alps and the Pyrenees, which you read about in the last chapter.

As you have read, the Alps are Europe's highest mountain range. They stretch from southern France to the Balkan Peninsula. Several of the jagged peaks in the Alps soar to more than 14,000 feet (4,270 m). The highest peak is Mont Blanc (mawn BLAHN), which rises to 15,771 feet (4,807 m) in France. Because of the height of the Alps, large snowfields coat some peaks.

Water Features

Several bodies of water are important to West-Central Europe's physical geography. The **North Sea** and **English Channel** lie to the north. The Bay of Biscay and Atlantic Ocean lie to the west. The Mediterranean Sea borders France to the south.

Several rivers cross the region as well. Look at the map on the previous page to identify them. Two important rivers are the **Danube** (DAN-yoob) and the **Rhine** (RYN). For centuries people and goods have traveled these rivers, and many cities, farms, and industrial areas line their banks.

Several of West-Central Europe's rivers are navigable. A **navigable river** is one that is deep and wide enough for ships to use. These rivers and a system of canals link the region's interior to the seas. These waterways are important for trade and travel.

READING CHECK Finding Main Ideas What are the region's three major landform areas?

Climate and Resources

A warm ocean current flows along Europe's northwestern coast. This current creates a marine west coast climate in most of West-Central Europe. This climate makes much of the area a pleasant place to live. Though winters can get cold, summers are mild. Rain and storms occur often, though.

At higher elevations, such as in the Alps, the climate is colder and wetter. In contrast, southern France has a warm Mediterranean climate. Summers are dry and hot, and winters are mild and wet.

West-Central Europe's mild climate is a valuable natural resource. Mild temperatures, plenty of rain, and rich soil have made the region's farmlands highly productive. Farm crops include grapes, grains, and vegetables. In the uplands and Alps, pastures and valleys support livestock.

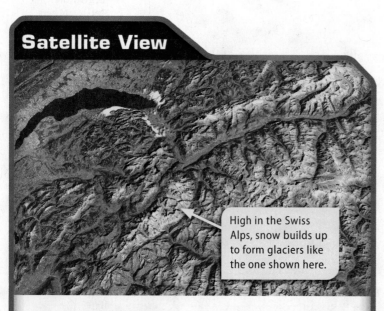

Satellite View

High in the Swiss Alps, snow builds up to form glaciers like the one shown here.

The Swiss Alps

At high elevations in the Alps, snow does not melt. For this reason, the snow builds up over time. As the snow builds up, it turns to ice and eventually forms glaciers. A glacier is a large, slow-moving sheet or river of ice. The satellite image above shows glaciers in the Swiss Alps. The white regions are the glaciers, and the blue areas are alpine lakes.

The buildup of snow and ice in the Alps can cause avalanches at lower elevations. An avalanche is a large mass of snow or other material that suddenly rushes down a mountainside. Avalanches pose a serious danger to people.

Analyzing Why do glaciers sometimes form at higher elevations in the Alps?

map zone **Geography Skills**

Human-Environment Interaction The land and resources of West-Central Europe support farming, mining, and industry.
1. **Identify** What cities serve as major manufacuturing centers?
2. **Draw Conclusions** Why is hydroelectric power found along alpine rivers?

Land Use

	Commercial farming
	Livestock raising
	Primarily forestland
	Manufacturing
	Limited economic activity

0   100   200   300 Miles
0 100 200 300 Kilometers
Projection: Azimuthal Equal-Area

Major Resources

	Coal
	Natural gas
	Oil
	Uranium
	Other minerals
	Fishing
	Nuclear power
	Hydroelectric power
	Major manufacturing and trade centers

Energy and mineral resources are not evenly distributed across the region, as the map shows. France has coal and iron ore, Germany also has coal, and the Netherlands has natural gas. Fast-flowing alpine rivers provide hydroelectric power. Even so, many countries must import fuels.

Another valuable natural resource is found in the breathtaking beauty of the Alps. Each year, tourists flock to the Alps to enjoy the scenery and to hike and ski.

READING CHECK **Summarizing** What natural resources contribute to the region's economy?

SUMMARY AND PREVIEW West-Central Europe includes low plains, uplands, and mountains. The climate is mild, and natural resources support farming, industry, and tourism. Next, you will read about France and the Benelux Countries.

Section 1 Assessment

hmhsocialstudies.com
ONLINE QUIZ

Reviewing Ideas, Terms, and Places

1. **a. Describe** What are the main physical features of the **Northern European Plain**?
   b. Analyze How does having many **navigable** rivers benefit West-Central Europe?
2. **a. Recall** What is the region's main climate?
   b. Make Inferences How might an uneven distribution of mineral resources affect the region?

Critical Thinking

3. **Categorizing** Draw a fan like this one. Label each band with the landform area in West-Central Europe it represents. Using your notes, identify each area's physical features, climate, and resources.

FOCUS ON SPEAKING

my WriteSmart

4. **Noting the Physical Geography** What issues related to land use and resources can you think of? Could mining coal or importing fuel be an issue? Jot down ideas.

France and the Benelux Countries

TEKS 1A, 1B, 2A, 2B, 3A, 3B, 3C, 3D, 4B, 4C, 4F, 7C, 15B, 18B, 21B, 21C, 22D

What You Will Learn...

Main Ideas

1. During its history France has been a kingdom, empire, colonial power, and republic.
2. The culture of France has contributed to the world's arts and ideas.
3. France today is a farming and manufacturing center.
4. The Benelux Countries have strong economies and high standards of living.

The Big Idea

France and the Benelux Countries have strong economies and rich cultural traditions.

Key Terms and Places

Paris, *p. 341*
Amsterdam, *p. 343*
The Hague, *p. 343*
Brussels, *p. 343*
cosmopolitan, *p. 343*

hmhsocialstudies.com
TAKING NOTES

Use the graphic organizer online to take notes on the Benelux countries.

If YOU lived there...

You are strolling through one of the many open-air markets in a Paris neighborhood. You stop to buy some fruit, then go into a bakery to buy bread, cheese, and lemonade. You sit on a park bench to eat lunch. You end your day with a stroll along the banks of the Seine River, where you look at books and postcards.

Why do you think people enjoy living in Paris?

BUILDING BACKGROUND For centuries, France has played a major role not only in Europe but also in the histories of the United Kingdom and the United States. The Norman Conquest in 1066 brought French influences into English language, law, and culture. France later helped the American colonists win their independence.

History of France

In southwest France, Lascaux (lah-SKOH) Cave holds a treasure from the past. Inside, prehistoric paintings of bulls run and jump along the stone walls. More than 15,000 years old, these paintings show how long people have lived in what is now France.

Early History

In ancient times, France was part of a region called Gaul (GAWL). Centuries ago, Celtic peoples from eastern Europe settled in Gaul. In the 50s BC, the Romans conquered the region. They introduced Roman law. The Romans also established a Latin-based language that in time developed into French.

Roman rule in Gaul lasted until the AD 400s. The Franks, a Germanic people, then conquered much of Gaul. It is from the Franks that France gets its name. The Franks' greatest ruler was Charlemagne (SHAHR-luh-mayn), who built a powerful Christian empire. After he had conquered much of the old Roman Empire, the pope crowned him Emperor of the Romans in 800.

After Charlemagne's death, many invaders attacked the Franks. One such group, the Normans, settled in northwestern France. This area is called Normandy.

In 1066 the Normans conquered England. William the Conqueror, the duke of Normandy, became king of England. He now ruled England as well as part of France. In the 1300s England's king tried to claim the French throne to gain control of the rest of France. This event led to the Hundred Years' War (1337–1453). The French eventually drove out the English.

Revolution and Empire

From the 1500s to the 1700s, France built a colonial empire. The French established colonies in the Americas, Africa, and Asia. At this time, most French people lived in poverty and had few rights. For these reasons, in 1789 the French people overthrew their king in the French Revolution.

A few years later a brilliant general named Napoleon took power. In time, he conquered much of Europe. Then in 1815 several European powers joined forces and defeated Napoleon. They exiled him and chose a new king to rule France.

Modern History

During both World War I and World War II, German forces invaded France. After each war, France worked to rebuild its economy. In the 1950s it experienced rapid growth.

During the 1950s and 1960s, many of of the French colonies gained their independence. Some people from these former colonies then moved to France.

France is now a republic with a parliament and an elected president. France still controls several overseas territories, such as Martinique in the West Indies.

READING CHECK **Summarizing** Which foreign groups have affected France's history?

France's History

During its long history, France has gone from strong kingdom to great empire, to colonial world power, to modern republic.

Early History

- Early Celtic peoples settle in Gaul.
- The Romans conquer Gaul and rule the region for hundreds of years.
- The Franks conquer Gaul. The ruler Charlemagne builds a powerful empire.
- Normans settle in northwestern France. In 1066 they conquer England and take the throne.
- France and England fight the Hundred Years' War.

Charlemagne

Revolution and Empire

- In the 1500s France begins to build a colonial empire.
- In 1789 the people rise up in the French Revolution.
- In 1799 Napoleon takes control. He soon conquers much of Europe.
- European powers unite to defeat Napoleon in 1815.

Arc de Triomphe

Modern History

- German forces invade France during World War I and World War II.
- Many French colonies declare independence in the 1950s and 1960s.
- Today France is a republic with a president and a democratic government.

WWII German occupation

The Culture of France

During their long history, the French have developed a strong cultural identity. Today French culture is admired worldwide.

FOCUS ON READING

Use a dictionary to find the origin of *cuisine*. How does the word's origin relate to the meaning of *cuisine* today?

Language and Religion

A common heritage unites the French. Most people speak French and are Catholic. At the same time, many immigrants have settled in France. These immigrants have their own languages, religions, and customs. For example, many Algerian Muslims have moved to France. This immigration is making France more culturally diverse.

Customs

The French have a phrase that describes their attitude toward life—*joie de vivre* (zhwah duh VEEV-ruh), meaning "enjoyment of life." The French enjoy good food, good company, and good conversation.

An enjoyment of food has helped make French cooking some of the best in the world. French chefs and cooking schools have worldwide reputations. The French have also contributed to the language of food. Terms such as *café*, *cuisine* (cooking), and *menu* all come from the French.

The French also enjoy their festivals. The major national festival is Bastille Day, held on July 14. On that date in 1789 a mob destroyed the Bastille, a Paris prison symbolizing the French king's harsh rule. The event began the French Revolution.

Ideas and the Arts

The French have made major contributions to the arts and ideas. In the Middle Ages, the French built majestic cathedrals in the Gothic style. This style has high pointed ceilings, stained-glass windows, and tall towers that reach heavenward. Notre Dame Cathedral in Paris is an example.

Close-up

Paris

Some 2,000 years old, Paris grew up along the banks of the Seine (SEN) River. Known as "the City of Light" for its gleaming beauty, Paris shines as one of Europe's most cultured cities. Wide tree-lined avenues, historic squares, and lovely gardens and parks grace the city center.

Notre Dame is France's most famous cathedral. It is a masterpiece of Gothic architecture.

The Seine River winds through the heart of Paris. Beautiful bridges cross the river, and in places booksellers line its banks.

In the 1700s France was a center of the Enlightenment, a period in which people used reason to improve society. French Enlightenment ideas about government inspired the American Revolution and the development of modern democracy.

In the 1800s France was the center of one of the most famous art movements of the modern age—impressionism. This style of painting uses rippling light to create an impression of a scene. During the same period, French authors wrote classics such as *The Three Musketeers* by Alexandre Dumas (doo-mah). Today France is known for art and its fashion and film industries.

READING CHECK **Summarizing** What are some main features of French culture?

France Today

France is now West-Central Europe's largest country. Locate France on the political map at the beginning of this chapter.

Today about 75 percent of the French live in cities. **Paris**, the capital, is by far the largest city, with about 10 million people.

Fashionable with a quick pace, Paris is a center of business, finance, learning, and culture. It boasts world-class museums, art galleries, and restaurants as well as famous landmarks such as the Eiffel Tower and Notre Dame Cathedral.

Other major cities include Marseille (mar-SAY), a Mediterranean seaport, and Lyon (LYAWN), located on the Rhone River. A modern system of highways, canals, and high-speed trains links France's cities.

France has a strong economy. It is the European Union's top agricultural producer, and its major crops include wheat and grapes. French workers are also highly productive. Rich soil and efficient workers have made France a major exporter of goods, such as its famous perfumes and wines.

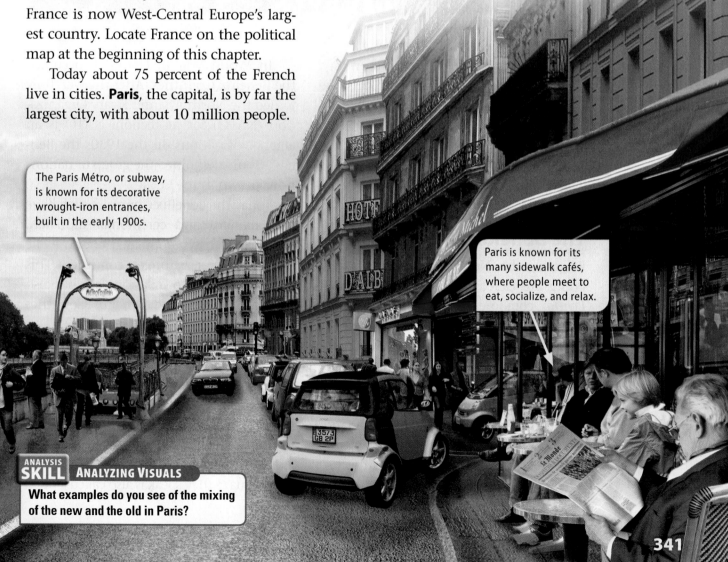

The Paris Métro, or subway, is known for its decorative wrought-iron entrances, built in the early 1900s.

Paris is known for its many sidewalk cafés, where people meet to eat, socialize, and relax.

ANALYSIS SKILL **ANALYZING VISUALS**

What examples do you see of the mixing of the new and the old in Paris?

341

Dutch Polders

More than 25 percent of the Netherlands lies below sea level. For centuries, the Dutch have reclaimed land from the sea. These reclaimed lands are called polders.

To create polders, the Dutch build dikes near the shoreline. They then use pumps to remove the water behind the dikes. A national system of dikes, dams, floodgates, and storm barriers now holds back the sea.

Unfortunately, creating polders has caused sinking lowlands and other environmental damage. The Dutch are working to address these problems. For example, they are considering restoring some of the polders to wetlands, lakes, and the seas.

Finding Main Ideas How have the Dutch modified their environment to live in a region that lies below sea level?

Tourism is also vital to the economy. Each year, millions of people visit Paris, the French Alps, and the sunny French Riviera, a resort area on the Mediterranean coast.

READING CHECK **Drawing Conclusions** Why do you think tourists might want to visit Paris?

The Benelux Countries

Belgium, the Netherlands, and Luxembourg are called the Benelux Countries. *Benelux* combines the first letters of each country's name. They are also called the Low Countries because of their elevation.

History

Many nations and empires dominated the Benelux region. In 1648 the Netherlands gained its independence. It ruled Belgium until 1830, and Luxembourg until 1867, when they gained independence.

In World War II, Germany occupied the Benelux Countries. After the war, they joined the North Atlantic Treaty Organization (NATO) for protection. NATO is an alliance of nations. In the 1950s the Benelux Countries joined the group of nations now known as the EU.

Today the Benelux Countries each have a parliament and ceremonial monarch. The tiny, densely populated countries lie between larger, stronger countries. This location has led to invasions but has also promoted trade. The Benelux Countries now have wealthy economies.

The Netherlands

Bordering the North Sea, the Netherlands is low and flat. Some of the land lies below sea level. The Netherlands includes the historical region of Holland and is sometimes called Holland. The people here are the Dutch, and the language they speak is also called Dutch.

Excellent harbors on the North Sea have made the Netherlands a center of international trade. The city of Rotterdam is one of the world's busiest seaports. It is also part of a highly industrial and urban, or city-based, area. This area includes **Amsterdam**, the capital, and **The Hague** (HAYG), the seat of government. Agriculture is also important to the Dutch economy, and Dutch cheese and tulips are world famous.

Belgium

Belgium is a highly urban country. More than 95 percent of the people of Belgium live in cities. The capital city, **Brussels**, serves as the headquarters for many international organizations, including the EU and NATO. The city of Brussels is as a result highly **cosmopolitan**, or characterized by many foreign influences.

Language divides Belgium. The coast and north are called Flanders. The people there speak Flemish. The southern interior is called Wallonia. The people there speak French and are called Walloons. These cultural differences have caused tensions.

Belgium is known for its cheeses, chocolate, cocoa, and lace. The city of Antwerp is a key port and diamond-cutting center.

Luxembourg

Luxembourg is a forested, hilly country. Although smaller than Rhode Island, it has one of the world's highest standards of living. Most of the people in Luxembourg are Roman Catholic and speak either French or German.

Luxembourg earns much of its income from services such as banking. The region also produces steel and chemicals. Its small cities are cosmopolitan centers of international business and government.

> **READING CHECK** **Comparing** What do the Benelux Countries have in common?

SUMMARY AND PREVIEW As you have learned, France and the Benelux Countries are modern and urban with strong economies. Next, you will read about Germany and the Alpine Countries.

Section 2 Assessment

hmhsocialstudies.com
ONLINE QUIZ

Reviewing Ideas, Terms, and Places

1. **a. Identify** Who was Charlemagne?
   b. Explain Why is Napoleon considered a significant figure in French history?
   c. Develop Why might the French be proud of their long history?
2. **a. Define** What is impressionism?
   b. Summarize What are some major contributions of French culture?
   c. Elaborate How has immigration influenced French culture?
3. **a. Describe** Why is **Paris** an important city?
   b. Summarize What is the French economy like?
4. **a. Describe** How does language divide Belgium?
   b. Draw Conclusions Why might **Brussels** be such a **cosmopolitan** city?
   c. Elaborate What are some ways in which technology influences human interactions with the environment in the Netherlands?

Critical Thinking

5. **Categorizing** Draw a chart like the one here. Use your notes and enter information into each category. Within each category, organize the information by country.

FOCUS ON SPEAKING
my WriteSmart

6. **Describing France and the Benelux Countries** For each country, note one possible issue for your persuasive speech. For example, one issue might be language in Belgium. Should all Belgians have to speak the same language?

The European Union

How can smaller countries compete with larger ones? One way is by working together. Since the 1950s, countries across Europe have been working to build a united community. Today this organization is called the European Union (EU). It promotes political and economic cooperation among member nations. The chart on the next page shows how the EU has changed life in Europe.

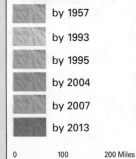

Member Country

	by 1957
	by 1993
	by 1995
	by 2004
	by 2007
	by 2013

0   100   200 Miles

0   100   200 Kilometers

Projection: Lambert's Az. Equal Area

IRELAND

UNITED KINGDOM

DENMARK

NETHERLANDS

BELGIUM

GERMANY

LUXEMBOURG

REP

FRANCE

AUSTRI

SLO

PORTUGAL

SPAIN

ITA

FINLAND

ESTONIA

LATVIA

LITHUANIA

POLAND

SLOVAKIA

HUNGARY

ROMANIA

ROATIA

BULGARIA

TURKEY

GREECE

CYPRUS

Benefits of Membership in the European Union

Trade

Before	After
■ European countries had to pay customs duties, or taxes, on goods they traded with other European countries. ■ Many European countries' economies were small compared to those of larger nations such as the United States.	■ EU countries are part of a common market. They can trade freely with each other without paying duties. ■ EU countries create a combined economy that is one of the largest in the world.

Currency

Before	After
■ Each European country had its own separate currency, or form of money. ■ European countries and their citizens had to exchange currencies to buy goods from other European countries.	■ Most EU countries share one currency, the euro. ■ EU countries and their citizens can use the euro to buy goods and trade throughout the EU.

Work and Travel

Before	After
■ Europeans had to have passports or other special permits to travel from one European country to another. ■ Europeans had to obtain permission to live and work in other countries in Europe.	■ Citizens of EU countries do not need passports or special permits to travel throughout most of the EU. ■ Citizens of EU countries can live and work anywhere in the EU without having to obtain permission.

The Euro The front sides of euro coins all have the same image, but the backs feature a unique symbol for each country. Euro bills show symbols of unity.

ANALYSIS SKILL **ANALYZING VISUALS**

1. **Name** Which six countries were the first to unite?
2. **Make Inferences** How do you think democracy's spread in Eastern Europe has affected the EU?
3. **Interpreting Charts** Based on the chart above, what are two benefits of EU membership?

Germany and the Alpine Countries

 TEKS 1A, 1B, 2A, 2B, 3A, 3B, 3C, 3D, 4B, 4C, 4F, 15B, 15D, 18B, 21B, 21C, 22D

What You Will Learn...

Main Ideas

1. After a history of division and two world wars, Germany is now a unified country.
2. German culture, known for its contributions to music, literature, and science, is growing more diverse.
3. Germany today has Europe's largest economy, but eastern Germany faces challenges.
4. The Alpine Countries reflect German culture and have strong economies based on tourism and services.

The Big Idea

Germany and the Alpine Countries are prosperous countries with similar cultures.

Key Terms and Places

Berlin, *p. 347*
Protestant, *p. 348*
chancellor, *p. 349*
Vienna, *p. 351*
cantons, *p. 351*
Bern, *p. 351*

hmhsocialstudies.com
TAKING NOTES

Use the graphic organizer online to take notes on Germany and the Alpine countries.

If YOU lived there...

You are walking with your grandfather through Berlin, Germany. He begins telling you about a time when Germany was divided into two countries—one democratic and one Communist. A large wall even divided the city of Berlin. Germans could not pass freely through the wall. You think of your friends who live in eastern Berlin. They would have been on the other side of the wall back then.

What do you think life in Berlin was like then?

BUILDING BACKGROUND Since the Middle Ages, Germany and France have been the dominant countries in West-Central Europe. Both are large and prosperous with hardworking people and good farmland. The two countries have often been at war, but today they are partners in building a cooperative European Union.

History of Germany

Some countries have had a strong influence on world events. Germany is one of these countries. Locate Germany on the political map on the next page. From its location in the heart of Europe, Germany has shaped events across Europe and the world—for both good and bad.

Growth of a Nation

In ancient times, tribes from northern Europe settled in the land that is now Germany. The Romans called this region Germania, after the name of one of the tribes. Over time, many small German states developed in the region. Princes ruled these states. With the support of the Roman Catholic Church, these states became part of the Holy Roman Empire.

For hundreds of years, Germany remained a loose association of small states. Then in 1871, Prussia, the strongest state, united Germany into one nation. As a unified nation, Germany developed into an industrial and military world power.

Germany: Political

The Brandenburg Gate, above, connects eastern and western Berlin. For 28 years, the Berlin Wall blocked the gate. It reopened in 1989.

map zone Geography Skills

Regions The former countries of East Germany and West Germany reunited in 1990 to form one country.
1. **Locate** Where is Germany's capital located?
2. **Contrast** How does river access to the sea differ between former East and West Germany?

War and Division

In 1914–1918, Germany fought and lost World War I. Payments for war damages and a major depression severely hurt the German economy. Looking for a strong leader, Germans found Adolf Hitler and his Nazi Party. Hitler promised the Germans to restore their country to its former glory.

In 1939 Germany attacked Poland, starting World War II. Soon, Germany had conquered much of Europe. The Nazis also sought to kill all European Jews in what is called the Holocaust. Germany lost the war, though. By 1945 it lay in ruins, defeated.

After the war, British, French, and U.S. troops occupied West Germany. The Soviet Union's troops occupied East Germany. Over time, two countries emerged.

The city of **Berlin** was in Communist East Germany. Even so, West Germany kept control of the western part of the city.

In 1961 Communist leaders built the Berlin Wall. The Wall's **purpose** was to prevent East Germans from fleeing to West Berlin.

ACADEMIC VOCABULARY
purpose the reason something is done

A Reunited Germany

After World War II, U.S. aid helped West Germany rebuild rapidly. It soon became an economic power. East Germany rebuilt as well, but its economy lagged. In addition, its people had limited freedoms.

In 1989 movements for democracy swept through Eastern Europe. Communist governments began collapsing. Joyful East Germans tore down the Berlin Wall. In 1990 East and West Germany reunited.

READING CHECK **Finding Main Ideas** What major challenges has Germany overcome?

German Culture

Germany's long history has enriched its culture. Historic castles dot the landscape, and long-held traditions continue. Blending with this history is a modern culture that includes a love of sports.

A Bavarian Castle King Ludwig II of Bavaria had the fairy-tale Neuschwanstein (noy-SHVAHN-shtyn) Castle built in the mid-1800s. The castle sits amid the Bavarian Alps in southern Germany.

Culture of Germany

Germans are known as hardworking and efficient people. At the same time, they enjoy their traditions and celebrating their cultural achievements.

People

Most Germans share a common heritage. About 90 percent are ethnic German, and most speak German. Due to a shortage in skilled labor, Germany has tried to attract highly-skilled workers from diverse groups to immigrate to Germany. As a result, the influence of these immigrants is making Germany more multicultural.

Religion

In 1517 the ideas of Martin Luther, a German monk, led to a religious protest movement called the Reformation. Those who protested against the Catholic Church became known as **Protestants.** Protestant churches arose in many Germanic states. Today in north and central Germany, most people are Protestant. In the south, most are Catholic. In eastern Germany, fewer Germans have religious ties, reflecting the area's Communist past.

Customs

Festivals and holidays tell us much about German culture. Religious festivals are very popular. For example, many areas hold festivals before the Christian season of Lent. In addition, Christmas is a major family event. The tradition of the Christmas tree even began in Germany.

Each region has local festivals as well. The best known is Oktoberfest in Bavaria, the region of southeast Germany. This festival is held each fall in Munich (MYOO-nik) to celebrate the region's food and drink.

The Arts and Sciences

Germany's contributions to the arts and sciences are widely admired. In music, Germany has produced famed classical composers, such as Johann Sebastian Bach and Ludwig van Beethoven. In literature, author Johann Wolfgang von Goethe (GOOH-tuh) ranks among Europe's most important writers. In science, Germans have made contributions in chemistry, engineering, medicine, and physics.

READING CHECK **Summarizing** What contributions have Germans made to world culture?

Soccer Fans
German soccer fans celebrate a victory. Soccer is the most popular sport in Germany. The country hosted the soccer World Cup in 2006.

Christmas Markets
German Christmas markets and fairs like this one have been popular for centuries. Booths sell trees, crafts, and food. Rides and music provide entertainment.

Germany Today

Despite a stormy history, Germany has endured. Today the country is a leading power in Europe and the world.

Government and Economy

Germany is a federal republic. A parliament chooses a **chancellor**, or prime minister, to run the government. The parliament also helps elect a president, whose duties are largely ceremonial. On the world stage, Germany belongs to the EU and NATO.

Germany's market economy has helped the country become an economic giant. It is Europe's largest economy, producing nearly one-fifth of all goods and services in the EU. The nation exports a wide range of products. You may be familiar with German cars, such as BMWs or Volkswagens.

The German economy is based on industry, such as chemicals, engineering, and steel. The main industrial district is the Ruhr, located in western Germany. Fewer Germans farm than in the past, but agriculture remains important. Major crops include grain, potatoes, and grapes. Timber is harvested in the south.

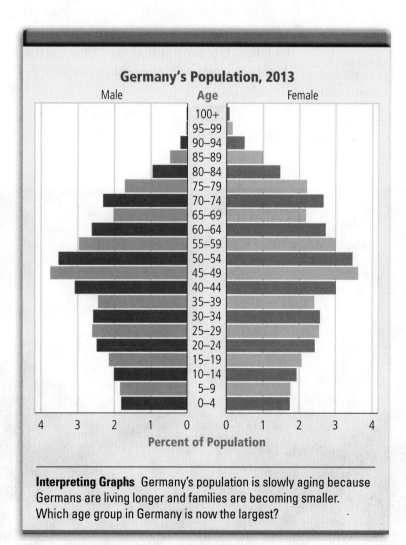

Germany's Population, 2013

Interpreting Graphs Germany's population is slowly aging because Germans are living longer and families are becoming smaller. Which age group in Germany is now the largest?

FOCUS ON READING

Use a dictionary to find the origin of *lag*. How does the word's origin relate to its meaning here?

Economic growth has slowed since East and West Germany reunited, however. The economy of former East Germany continues to <u>lag</u>. The region also suffers high unemployment. Germany's government is working to solve these problems.

Cities

Most Germans live in cities. The largest city is Berlin, the capital. During World War II, Berlin suffered major destruction. Today Germans have restored their capital to its former splendor. A historic city, it has wide boulevards and many parks.

Other major German cities include Hamburg, a key port city on the North Sea, and Munich, a cultural and manufacturing center. Like France, Germany has an excellent transportation system that links its cities. Germany's highway system, the Autobahn, is one of the best in the world.

ACADEMIC VOCABULARY

neutral (p. 351) unbiased, not favoring either side in a conflict

READING CHECK **Analyzing** How has the reunification of Germany affected its economy?

The Alpine Countries

The beauty of the Alps draws many tourists to Austria and Switzerland. These countries are called the Alpine Countries after the Alps, which cover much of them.

Austria and Switzerland have many similarities. Both are landlocked. Both are heavily influenced by German culture and were once part of the Holy Roman Empire. Yet, the countries have their differences.

Austria

Austria was once the center of one of the most powerful empires in Europe. The royal Habsburg family came to control this empire. At its height, the Habsburg line ruled the Netherlands, Spain, and much of Germany, Italy, and Eastern Europe.

In 1918, however, the Habsburgs were on the losing side of World War I. After the war, Austria became a republic. Since then, Austria has grown into a modern, industrialized nation. Today it is a federal republic and EU member.

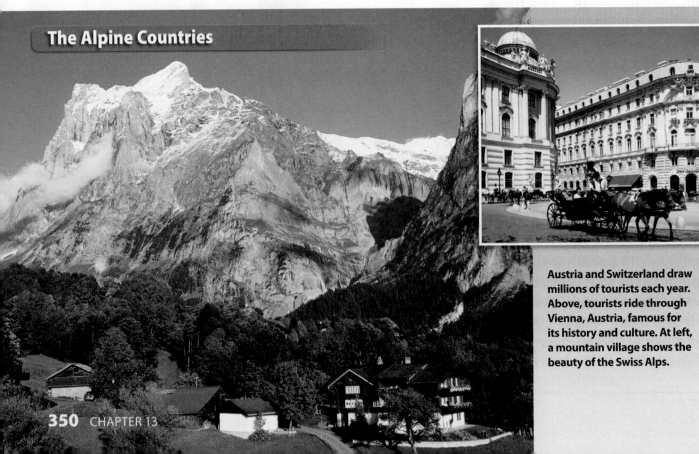

The Alpine Countries

Austria and Switzerland draw millions of tourists each year. Above, tourists ride through Vienna, Austria, famous for its history and culture. At left, a mountain village shows the beauty of the Swiss Alps.

Most Austrians speak German and are Roman Catholic. The city of **Vienna** is Austria's capital and largest city. Located on the banks of the Danube, Vienna was once the center of Habsburg rule. Today historic palaces grace the city, which is a center of music and the fine arts.

Austria has a prosperous economy with little unemployment. Service industries, such as banking, are important and employ more than half of Austria's workforce. Tourism is important as well.

Switzerland

Since the 1600s Switzerland has been an independent country. Today it is a federal republic with 26 districts called **cantons**. Citizens are active in local government. In addition, all male citizens serve for a period in the militia, a citizen army.

Switzerland's location in the Alps has helped it remain **neutral** for centuries. To stay neutral, Switzerland has not joined the EU or NATO. The Swiss are active in international organizations, however.

As the map shows, the Swiss speak several languages. The main languages are German and French. Switzerland's capital, **Bern**, is centrally located to be near both German- and French-speaking regions.

Switzerland has one of the world's highest standards of living. It is famous for its banks, watches and other precision devices, and chocolate and cheese.

READING CHECK **Contrasting** How are the countries of Austria and Switzerland different?

SUMMARY AND PREVIEW You have read that Germany is an economic power with a rich culture, while the Alpine Countries are prosperous with beautiful mountain scenery. In the next chapter you will learn about Northern Europe.

Switzerland: Language Regions

Legend:
- German
- French
- Italian
- Romansh
- ⊛ National capital
- • Other cities

0   25   50 Miles
0   25   50 Kilometers

Projection: Lambert Conformal Conic

map zone

Geography Skills

Place Each canton of Switzerland chooses its official language.
1. **Identify** What do they speak in Bern?
2. **Analyze** Why might the people in western Switzerland speak French?

Section 3 Assessment

hmhsocialstudies.com ONLINE QUIZ

Reviewing Ideas, Terms, and Places

1. **a. Identify** Why is Adolf Hitler significant in history?
   b. Sequence What events led to German reunification?
2. **a. Recall** What are some popular festivals in Germany?
   b. Evaluate What contributions are diverse groups making to Germany?
3. **a. Describe** What is the role of Germany's **chancellor**?
   b. Explain Why has Germany's economy slowed?
4. **a. Define** What are **cantons**, and where are they found?
   b. Analyze How are the Alps a valuable resource?

Critical Thinking

5. **Comparing and Contrasting** Draw a Venn diagram like this one. Use your notes to list the differences and similarities.

Germany — Alpine Countries

FOCUS ON SPEAKING

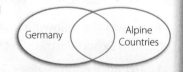

6. **Describing Germany and the Alpine Countries** For each country, note one issue for your speech. For example, you might argue that the Alps are the region's loveliest area.

Analyzing a Circle Graph

Learn

Circle graphs, also called pie charts, represent all the parts that make up something. Each piece of the circle, or "pie," shows what proportion that part is of the whole. Use the following guidelines to analyze circle graphs.

- Read the title to identify the circle graph's subject. The circle graph here shows the main languages spoken in Switzerland.

- Read the circle graph's other labels. Note what each part, or slice, of the circle graph represents. In the circle graph at right, each slice represents a different language.

- Analyze the data by comparing the size of the slices in the circle graph. Think about what the differences mean or imply.

Practice

1. Based on the circle graph at right, what are the three main languages spoken in Switzerland?

2. What language do less than 1 percent of the Swiss speak?

3. What percentage of the Swiss speak other languages not listed individually?

Source: Central Intelligence Agency, *The World Factbook 2002*

Apply

To answer the following questions, use the circle graph titled France's Current Export Partners in the Standardized Test Practice.

1. To which country does France send the highest percentage of its exports?

2. How many of France's main export partners belong to the European Union?

3. What percentage of French exports go to the United States?

Visual Summary

Use the visual summary below to help you review the main ideas of the chapter.

QUICK FACTS

France is a leading European nation and cultural center. The Benelux Countries are small, densely populated, and rich.

Germany is an industrial powerhouse with a rich culture. The landlocked Alpine Countries have stunning mountains.

Reviewing Vocabulary, Terms, and Places

Match each "I" statement below with the person, place, or thing that might have made the statement.

a. Berlin

b. Brussels

c. canton

d. chancellor

e. cosmopolitan city

f. Danube River

g. dike

h. navigable river

i. North Sea

j. Paris

1. "I am the capital of France and a center of business, finance, learning, and culture."

2. "I am an important waterway in the region of West-Central Europe."

3. "I am a prime minister in Germany."

4. "I am an earthen wall used to hold back water."

5. "I am a type of river that is wide and deep enough for ships to use."

6. "I am a district in Switzerland."

7. "I am a city that has many foreign influences."

8. "I am an international city and the capital of Belgium."

9. "I am a large body of water located to the north of the Benelux Countries and Germany."

10. "I was divided into two parts after World War II and am now the capital of Germany."

Comprehension and Critical Thinking

SECTION 1 *(Pages 334–337)*

11. **a.** Recall From southeast to northwest, what are the major landforms in West-Central Europe?

b. Analyze How have geographic features supported trade and travel across the region of West-Central Europe?

c. Elaborate How does West-Central Europe's mild climate serve as a valuable resource and contribute to the economy?

SECTION 2 *(Pages 338–343)*

12. a. Identify Where is the busiest seaport in the Netherlands located?

b. Summarize What are some products and cultural features for which France is famous?

c. Geographic Questions Use the map and chart of the European Union on pages 344 and 345 to pose and answer a question about geographic patterns associated with EU membership.

SECTION 3 *(Pages 346–351)*

13. a. Evaluate How did Johann Wolfgang von Goethe contribute to German culture?

b. Analyze How is Switzerland's position in European affairs unique?

c. Elaborate How has the royal Habsburg family shaped Austria's history?

Social Studies Skills

Analyzing a Circle Graph *Use the circle graph titled Languages in Switzerland in the Social Studies Skills to answer the following questions.*

14. Based on the circle graph, what percentage of the Swiss speak German?

15. What percentage of the Swiss speak French and Italian?

16. What fourth language do the Swiss speak?

Using the Internet

17. Activity: Researching Schools Imagine that your family is moving to Belgium or the Netherlands. In your new country you will be attending an international school. What kinds of classes will you have? What will your school day be like? What kinds of things might you see and do outside of school? Through your online textbook, research schools and daily life there. Then complete the online worksheet to record what you have learned. Finally, compare the schools you researched to the school you attend today.

hmhsocialstudies.com

Map Activity

18. West-Central Europe On a separate sheet of paper, match the letters on the map with their correct labels.

Alps	Paris, France
Berlin, Germany	Pyrenees
North Sea	Vienna, Austria
Northern European Plain	

FOCUS ON READING AND SPEAKING *my*WriteSmart

19. Recognizing Word Origins Find the key term cosmopolitan in Section 2. Write the word's definition. Then use a good dictionary to research the word's origins. Explain how the word's origins relate to its definition.

20. Writing a Persuasive Speech Choose one of the issues you identified as you read the chapter. Use *my*WriteSmart in your eBook to write an opinion statement about the issue, such as "The Dutch polders should be restored to wetlands." Next, list three facts or examples that support your opinion. Use the chapter and other sources to find information. Then use the list to write your short persuasive speech. After you present your speech respond to any questions your audience may have.

Reading Social Studies

Recognizing Word Origins

English is a language that loves to borrow words from other languages and cultures. From the French, we took faceon and changed it to fashion. From the German, we took strollen and changed it to stroll. From the Dutch, we took koekje and changed it to cookie. Below is a list of examples of other words that come from other languages.

English Words from French	English Words from German	English Words from Latin
conquer	muffin	culture
brilliant	dollar	defeat
restaurant	rocket	general
republic	kindergarten	forces
fashion	hamburger	join
parliament	noodle	president
several	pretzel	elect
power	snorkel	control
exiled	hex	territory

YOU TRY IT!

Read the following sentences. Refer to the above word lists and make a list of the words in the passage below that originally came from other languages. After each word, list the original language.

A few years later a brilliant general named Napoleon took power. In time, he conquered much of Europe. Then in 1815 several European powers joined forces and defeated Napoleon. They exiled him and chose a new king to rule France. . . .

France is now a republic with a parliament and an elected president. France still controls several overseas territories, such as Martinique in the West Indies.

From Section 2, France and the Benelux Countries

Northern Europe

✪ Reykjavik
ICELAND

❂ National capital
● Other city

0   100   200 Miles
0   100   200 Kilometers

Projection: Azimuthal Equal-Area

Faeroe Islands
(DENMARK)

60°N

N
W · E
S

ATLANTIC
OCEAN

Shetland Islands
(U.K.)

Orkney Islands
(U.K.)

Hebrides
(U.K.)

SCOTLAND

● Edinburgh

NORTHERN
IRELAND
Belfast ●

UNITED KINGDOM

Dublin ✪   ● Liverpool
              ● Leeds
IRELAND

● Birmingham

WALES   ENGLAND
Thames R.

50°N

London ❂

English Channel

Essential Question

myNotebook

How has location shaped the development of
nations in Northern Europe?

Texas Essential Knowledge and Skills (TEKS)

1A, 1B, 2A, 2B, 3A, 3B, 3C, 4B, 4C, 4D, 4E, 4F, 5A, 5B, 5C, 6A, 6B, 15A, 15B, 15F, 17D,
17E, 18B, 19A, 21B, 21C, 22D

FOCUS ON READING AND WRITING

my **WriteSmart**

Using Context Clues—Synonyms As you read, you may occasionally
encounter a word or phrase that you do not know. When that happens, use the
words and sentences around the unfamiliar word—context clues—to help you
determine the word's meaning. As you read this chapter, look for words that are
synonyms, or words that mean the same as the unfamiliar word. **See the lesson,
Using Context Clues—Synonyms, on page 375.**

Writing a Letter Letters are a great way to stay in touch with friends and
family. As you read this chapter, gather information about Northern Europe. Then
imagine you are traveling through this region. Write a letter to your friends and
family at home in which you describe what you have learned on your travels. Use
the annotation tools in your eBook to gather information for your assignment.

Geography Fertile plains like this one in Ireland
provide Northern Europe with much
of its farmland.

Northern Europe: Political

HISTORY Winston Churchill

↗ hmhsocialstudies.com VIDEO

70°N

ARCTIC OCEAN

Tromso

Arctic Circle

Norwegian Sea

FINLAND

RUSSIA

SWEDEN

NORWAY

Gulf of Bothnia

Bergen

Helsinki

Oslo

Gulf of Finland

Stockholm

ESTONIA

North Sea

Göteborg

LATVIA

DENMARK

LITHUANIA

Copenhagen

Baltic Sea

RUSSIA

BELARUS

NETHERLANDS

GERMANY

POLAND

map zone **Geography Skills**

Location Much of Northern Europe is separated from the rest of the continent by the English Channel and the North and Baltic seas.
1. Identify What countries extend north of the Arctic Circle?
2. Contrast How does Northern Europe differ physically from the rest of Europe?

History The Palace of Westminster in London has been home to the British Parliament for over 600 years.

Culture Skiing and other forms of outdoor recreation are popular throughout much of Scandinavia.

SECTION 1

Physical Geography

TEKS 3A, 3B, 3C, 4D, 4E, 4F, 5A, 5B, 5C, 6A, 6B, 21B, 21C, 22D

What You Will Learn...

Main Ideas

1. The physical features of Northern Europe include low mountain ranges and jagged coastlines.
2. Northern Europe's natural resources include energy sources, soils, and seas.
3. The climates of Northern Europe range from a mild coastal climate to a freezing ice cap climate.

The Big Idea

Northern Europe is a region of unique physical features, rich resources, and diverse climates.

Key Terms and Places

British Isles, *p. 358*
Scandinavia, *p. 358*
fjord, *p. 359*
geothermal energy, *p. 360*
North Atlantic Drift, *p. 360*

hmhsocialstudies.com
TAKING NOTES

Use the graphic organizer online to take notes on the physical geography of Northern Europe.

If YOU lived there...

Your family is planning to visit friends in Tromso, Norway. It is a city on the Norwegian Sea located 200 miles north of the Arctic Circle. You imagine a landscape covered in snow and ice. When you arrive, however, you discover green hills and ice-free harbors.

What might explain the mild climate?

BUILDING BACKGROUND Although located at high latitudes, Norway and the rest of Northern Europe have surprisingly mild temperatures. All the countries of Northern Europe are located on seas and oceans. As a result, they benefit from ocean currents that bring warm water north and keep the climate reasonably warm.

Physical Features

From Ireland's gently rolling hills to Iceland's icy glaciers and fiery volcanoes, Northern Europe is a land of great variety. Because of this variety, the physical geography of Northern Europe changes greatly from one location to another.

Two regions—the British Isles and Scandinavia—make up Northern Europe. To the southwest lie the **British Isles**, a group of islands located across the English Channel from the rest of Europe. Northeast of the British Isles is **Scandinavia**, a region of islands and peninsulas in far northern Europe. The island of Iceland, to the west, is often considered part of Scandinavia.

Hills and Mountains Rough, rocky hills and low mountains cover much of Northern Europe. Rugged hills stretch across much of Iceland, northern Scotland, and Scandinavia. The jagged Kjolen (CHUH-luhn) Mountains on the Scandinavian Peninsula divide Norway from Sweden. The rocky soil and uneven terrain in these parts of Northern Europe make farming there difficult. As a result, fewer people live there than in the rest of Northern Europe.

Denmark Strait

ARCTIC OCEAN

70°N

Norwegian Sea

ICELAND

20°W

Arctic Circle

KJOLEN MTS.

SCANDINAVIAN PENINSULA

FINLAND

60°N

NORWAY

Sogne Fjord

Gulf of Bothnia

Lake Vanern

1

ATLANTIC OCEAN

SCOTLAND

North Sea

SWEDEN

NORTHERN IRELAND

UNITED KINGDOM

DENMARK
JUTLAND PENINSULA

Baltic Sea

20°E

IRELAND

Irish Sea

WALES   ENGLAND

50°N

BRITISH ISLES

English Channel

10°E

EUROPE

1 Melting glaciers created Scandinavia's jagged coastline and many fjords.

ELEVATION	
Feet	**Meters**
13,120	4,000
6,560	2,000
1,640	500
656	200
(Sea level) 0	0 (Sea level)
Below sea level	Below sea level

ice cap

0   150   300 Miles
0   150   300 Kilometers
Projection: Azimuthal Equal-Area

map zone
Geography Skills

Place Northern Europe is made up of many islands and peninsulas.

1. **Identify** What countries are located on islands?
2. **Contrast** How is Norway's coastline different from Finland's?

Farmland and Plains Fertile farmland and flat plains stretch across the southern parts of the British Isles and Scandinavia. Ireland's rolling, green hills provide rich farmland. Wide valleys in England and Denmark also have plenty of fertile soil.

Effects of Glaciers Slow-moving sheets of ice, or glaciers, have left their mark on Northern Europe's coastlines and lakes. As you can see on the map above, Norway's western coastline is very jagged. Millions of years ago, glaciers cut deep valleys into Norway's coastal mountains. As the glaciers melted, these valleys filled with water,

creating deep fjords. A **fjord** (fee-AWRD) is a narrow inlet of the sea set between high, rocky cliffs. Many fjords are very long and deep. Norway's Sogne (SAWNG-nuh) Fjord, for example, is over 100 miles (160 km) long and more than three-quarters of a mile (1.2 km) deep. Melting glaciers also carved thousands of lakes in Northern Europe. Sweden's Lake Vanern, along with many of the lakes in the British Isles, were carved by glaciers thousands of years ago.

READING CHECK **Summarizing** What are some physical features of Northern Europe?

Natural Resources

ACADEMIC
VOCABULARY

primary
main, most
important

Natural resources have helped to make Northern Europe one of the wealthiest regions in the world. Northern Europe's **primary** resources are its energy resources, forests and soils, and surrounding seas.

Energy Northern Europe has a variety of energy resources. Norway and the United Kingdom benefit from oil and natural gas deposits under the North Sea. Hydroelectric energy is produced by the region's many lakes and rivers. In Iceland steam from hot springs produces **geothermal energy**, or energy from the heat of Earth's interior.

Satellite View

Norway's Fjords

Millions of years ago much of Norway was covered with glaciers. As the glaciers flowed slowly downhill, they carved long, winding channels, or fjords, into Norway's coastline.

As you can see in this satellite image, fjords cut many miles into Norway's interior, bringing warm waters from the North and Norwegian seas. As warm waters penetrate inland, they keep temperatures relatively mild. In fact, people have used these unfrozen fjords to travel during the winter when ice and snow made travel over land difficult.

Drawing Conclusions How do fjords benefit life in Norway?

Forests and Soils Forests and soils are two other important natural resources in Northern Europe. Large areas of timber-producing forests stretch across Finland and the Scandinavian Peninsula. Fertile soils provide rich farmland for crops, such as wheat and potatoes. Livestock like sheep and dairy cattle are also common.

Seas and Oceans The seas that surround Northern Europe are another important natural resource. For centuries, the North Sea, the Norwegian Sea, and the Atlantic Ocean have provided rich stocks of fish. Today, fishing is a key industry in Norway, Denmark, and Iceland.

READING CHECK **Summarizing** What natural resources are found in Northern Europe?

Climates

Locate Northern Europe on a map of the world. Notice that much of the region lies near the Arctic Circle. Due to the region's high latitude, you might imagine that it would be quite cold during much of the year. In reality, however, the climates in Northern Europe are remarkably mild.

Northern Europe's mild climates are a result of the **North Atlantic Drift**, an ocean current that brings warm, moist air across the Atlantic Ocean. Warm waters from this ocean current keep most of the region warmer than other locations around the globe at similar latitudes.

Much of Northern Europe has a marine west coast climate. Denmark, the British Isles, and western Norway benefit from mild summers and frequent rainfall. Snow and frosts may occur in winter but do not usually last long.

Central Norway, Sweden, and southern Finland have a humid continental climate. This area has four true seasons with cold, snowy winters and mild summers.

Northern Europe: Climate

ARCTIC OCEAN
70°N
Norwegian Sea
Arctic Circle
ICELAND
North Atlantic Drift
ATLANTIC OCEAN
60°N
NORWAY **1**
FINLAND
SWEDEN
North Sea
DENMARK
Baltic Sea
IRELAND UNITED KINGDOM
50°N
EUROPE

0   200   400 Miles
0   200   400 Kilometers
Projection: Azimuthal Equal-Area

Climate Types
- Marine west coast
- Humid continental
- Subarctic
- Tundra
- Ice cap

1 Skiers in Norway's Jotunheimen National Park make the most of the region's cold, snowy winters.

map zone Geography Skills

Regions The climates of Northern Europe range from mild marine west coast to freezing ice cap.
1. **Locate** What parts of Northern Europe have tundra climates?
2. **Make Inferences** What allows much of Northern Europe to have mild climates?

Far to the north are colder climates. Subarctic regions, like those in Northern Scandinavia, have long, cold winters and short summers. Iceland's tundra and ice cap climates produce extremely cold temperatures all year.

READING CHECK **Analyzing** How does the North Atlantic Drift keep climates mild?

SUMMARY AND PREVIEW Northern Europe has many different physical features, natural resources, and climates. Next, you will learn about the history and culture of the British Isles.

Section 1 Assessment

hmhsocialstudies.com
ONLINE QUIZ

Reviewing Ideas, Terms, and Places
1. a. **Describe** What are the physical features of this region?
   b. **Analyze** What role did glaciers play in shaping the physical geography of Northern Europe?
2. a. **Recall** What is **geothermal energy**?
   b. **Make Inferences** How do people in Northern Europe benefit from the surrounding seas?
3. a. **Identify** What climates exist in Northern Europe?
   b. **Predict** How might the climates of Northern Europe be different without the **North Atlantic Drift**?

Critical Thinking
4. **Comparing and Contrasting** Using your notes and a chart like the one below, compare and contrast the physical geography of the British Isles and Scandinavia.

	British Isles	Scandinavia
Physical Features		
Resources		
Climates		

Focus on Writing

my WriteSmart

5. **Describing the Physical Geography** Take notes on the physical features, resources, and climates of Northern Europe. In what season might you visit the region?

The British Isles

 TEKS 1A, 1B, 2A, 2B, 3A, 3B, 3C, 3D, 4B, 4C, 15B, 18B, 21B, 21C, 22D

What You Will Learn...

Main Ideas

1. Invaders and a global empire have shaped the history of the British Isles.
2. British culture, such as government and music, has influenced much of the world.
3. Efforts to bring peace to Northern Ireland and maintain strong economies are important issues in the British Isles today.

The Big Idea

Close cultural and historical ties link the people of the British Isles today.

Key Terms and Places

constitutional monarchy, *p. 364*
Magna Carta, *p. 364*
disarm, *p. 365*
London, *p. 366*
Dublin, *p. 366*

hmhsocialstudies.com
TAKING NOTES

Use the graphic organizer online to take notes on the British Isles.

If YOU lived there...

You have family and friends that live throughout the British Isles. On visits you have discovered that the people of England, Ireland, Scotland, and Wales share the same language, use the same type of government, and eat many of the same foods.

Why might culture in the British Isles be similar?

BUILDING BACKGROUND The people of the British Isles have had close ties for thousands of years. As a result, the people of England, Scotland, Ireland, and Wales share many of the same culture traits. Similar religions, languages, literary traditions, and even holidays are common throughout the British Isles.

History

Two independent countries—the Republic of Ireland and the United Kingdom—make up the British Isles. Locate the United Kingdom on the British Isles map in this section. As you can see, the countries of England, Scotland, Wales, and Northern Ireland make up the United Kingdom.

Time Line

History of the British Isles

1558–1603 England becomes a world power during the reign of Queen Elizabeth I.

3100 BC   1600

3100 BC Ancient settlers in England build Stonehenge.

Early History

The history of the British Isles dates back thousands of years. Early settlers built Stonehenge, an ancient monument, some 5,000 years ago. Around 450 BC, the Celts (KELTS) arrived in the British Isles and settled Scotland, Wales, and Ireland. Britain was even part of the ancient Roman Empire.

In the Middle Ages a series of invaders ruled the British Isles. The Angles, Saxons, and Vikings all established small kingdoms in Britain. Finally, in 1066, the Normans from northern France conquered England and established a strong kingdom there.

Over time, England grew in strength and power. It soon overshadowed its neighbors in the British Isles. By the 1500s strong rulers like Queen Elizabeth I had turned England into a world power.

Rise of the British Empire

A strong economy and mighty navy helped England build a vast empire. Over time, England joined with Wales and Scotland to create the United Kingdom of Great Britain. Eventually, Ireland was annexed too. England also launched an overseas empire. By the 1800s Britain had colonies in the Americas, India, and Australia.

The United Kingdom's economy soared in the 1700s and 1800s, thanks to the Industrial Revolution. Industries like iron, steel, and <u>textiles</u>, or cloth products, helped make the United Kingdom one of the world's richest countries.

Not everyone benefited, however. In the 1840s a severe food shortage devastated Ireland. Lack of support from the English government during the famine increased tensions between the two countries.

BIOGRAPHY

Sir Winston Churchill
(1874–1965)

One of Britain's greatest leaders, Sir Winston Churchill, guided the United Kingdom through the dark days of World War II. Churchill was appointed prime minister shortly after the beginning of World War II. He inspired the British to continue fighting despite Germany's defeat of much of Europe. During the Battle of Britain, Churchill gave fiery speeches. He encouraged British citizens to "never surrender." His creation of an alliance with the Soviet Union and the United States led to Germany's eventual defeat. Churchill's determination helped the Allies win the war.

Evaluating Do you think Churchill was important to British history? Why or why not?

VIDEO
Winston Churchill

hmhsocialstudies.com

FOCUS ON READING
What are *textiles*? How can you tell?

1730–1860
The Industrial Revolution brings great wealth to England.

1940
London is bombed during the Battle of Britain in World War II.

1700 **1800** **1900** **2000**

1858–1947
The British Empire controls India, its most valuable colony.

ANALYSIS SKILL **READING TIME LINES**

About how many years ago was Stonehenge built?

By the late 1800s the British Empire spanned the globe. Africa, Asia, Australia, and the Americas were all home to British colonies. At its height, the British Empire was the largest empire in history.

Decline of Empire

In the 1900s the British Empire began to fall apart. Both World War I and the Great Depression hurt the British economy. Rebellions in Ireland forced Britain to grant self-rule to all but the northern part of Ireland. In 1949 the Republic of Ireland gained full independence. Movements for independence also emerged in Britain's overseas colonies. After World War II, Great Britain gave up most of its colonies. The British Empire was no more.

READING CHECK **Sequencing** What major events mark the history of the British Isles?

Culture

People in different regions of the British Isles hold fast to regional traditions and customs. Here, Scots proudly display two symbols of Scottish culture—bagpipes and kilts.

Culture

For years the British ruled much of the world. As a result, the government, people, and popular culture of the British Isles have influenced people all around the globe.

Government

The government of the United Kingdom is a **constitutional monarchy**, a type of democracy in which a king or queen serves as head of state but a legislature makes the laws. The English first limited the power of monarchs in the Middle Ages. A document known as **Magna Carta**, or Great Charter, limited the powers of kings. It also required everyone to obey the law. Today, a prime minister leads the British government. Most members of Britain's legislative body, known as Parliament, are elected.

The Republic of Ireland has a president as head of state. The president, who has limited powers, appoints a prime minister. Together with the Irish parliament, the prime minister runs the government.

People

For hundreds of years, the countries of the British Isles have had close ties. As a result, the countries share many culture traits. One similarity is their common heritage. Many people in the British Isles can trace their heritage to the region's early settlers, such as the Celts, Angles, and Saxons. Sports like soccer and rugby are another shared trait among the people of Britain.

Although people in the British Isles share many culture traits, each region still maintains its own unique identity. This is particularly true in Ireland and Scotland. Unlike the rest of the British Isles, most Irish are Roman Catholic. Irish Gaelic, a Celtic language, is one of the country's official languages. The people of Scotland have also maintained their unique culture.

It is not unusual in Scotland to see people wearing kilts and playing bagpipes on special occasions.

Immigrants from all corners of the world have settled in Britain. Many immigrants from former British colonies, such as India and Jamaica, add to the rich culture of the British Isles.

Popular Culture

British popular culture influences people all around the globe. For example, English is the language of business, education, and the Internet in many places. British music and literature are also popular. Millions of people around the globe listen to music by bands like Ireland's U2 and England's The Beatles and read works by British authors like William Shakespeare.

READING CHECK **Summarizing** What parts of British culture have spread around the world?

British Isles Today

The British Isles face some challenges. Efforts to bring peace to Northern Ireland and to maintain a powerful economy are key issues in the British Isles today.

Northern Ireland

One of the toughest problems facing the British Isles today is conflict in Northern Ireland. Disputes between the people of Northern Ireland have a long history.

In the 1500s Protestants from England and Scotland began settling in Northern Ireland. Over time, they outnumbered Irish Catholics in the area. When Ireland became a separate state, Northern Ireland's Protestant majority chose to remain part of the United Kingdom.

Since then, many Catholics in Northern Ireland believe they have not been treated fairly by Protestants. Some Catholics hope

British Isles: Political

- National capital
- Other city

0   75   150 Miles
0   75   150 Kilometers

Projection: Azimuthal Equal-Area

Shetland Islands

Orkney Islands

ATLANTIC OCEAN

SCOTLAND

Edinburgh
Glasgow

North Sea

NORTHERN IRELAND
Belfast

UNITED KINGDOM

REPUBLIC OF IRELAND

Irish Sea
Liverpool

Leeds
Manchester

Dublin

Cork

WALES

Birmingham

ENGLAND
London

English Channel

Geography Skills

Regions The Republic of Ireland and the United Kingdom make up the British Isles.
1. **Identify** Which country is closer to mainland Europe?
2. **Make Inferences** How might the British Isles be affected by their location?

to unite with the Republic of Ireland. For years the two sides have waged a bitter and violent struggle. In the late 1990s peace talks between the two warring sides began. An **agreement** eventually led to a cease-fire and the creation of a national assembly in Northern Ireland. However, the refusal of some groups to **disarm**, or give up all weapons, stalled the peace talks. Recently, however, hopes are once again high that peaceful relations between the groups will bring about a long-lasting peace.

ACADEMIC VOCABULARY

agreement a decision reached by two or more people or groups

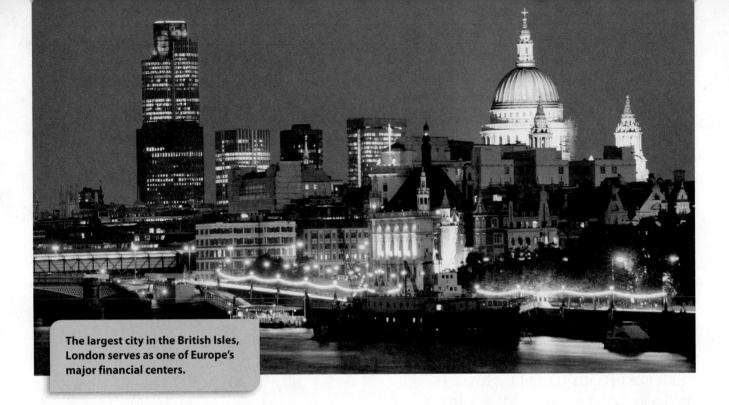

The largest city in the British Isles, London serves as one of Europe's major financial centers.

The Economy

The economies of the United Kingdom and the Republic of Ireland are among Europe's strongest. **London**, the capital of the United Kingdom, is a center for world trade and industry. North Sea energy reserves have made the United Kingdom a major producer of oil and natural gas. In Ireland, computer equipment and software have become major industries, especially near **Dublin**, Ireland's capital. The economies of the United Kingdom and the Republic of Ireland also rely on service industries like banking, tourism, and insurance.

READING CHECK **Summarizing** What has been the cause of conflict in Northern Ireland?

SUMMARY AND PREVIEW You have learned about the rich history and culture of the British Isles. Next, you will learn about the countries of Scandinavia.

Section 2 Assessment

hmhsocialstudies.com
ONLINE QUIZ

Reviewing Ideas, Terms, and Places

1. **a. Identify** What peoples invaded the British Isles?
   b. Make Inferences How did the Industrial Revolution strengthen the British Empire?
2. **a. Describe** What elements of British culture are found around the world?
   b. Explain How did **Magna Carta** affect British government?
3. **a. Define** What does **disarm** mean?
   b. Analyze What are the central issues of the conflict in Northern Ireland?
   c. Elaborate Why do you think the economy of the British Isles is so strong?

Critical Thinking

4. **Summarizing** Using your notes and a graphic organizer like the one here, summarize the history and culture of the British Isles in your own words.

History

Culture

FOCUS ON WRITING

my WriteSmart

5. **Writing about the British Isles** What information about the British Isles do you think is most interesting? Take notes on what you could include in a letter to someone who has never visited the area.

Social Studies Skills

Writing to Learn

Learn

Writing is an important tool for learning new information. When you write about what you read, you can better understand and remember information. For example, when you write a list of items you need from the grocery store, the act of writing can help you remember what to buy. Use the steps below to write to learn.

- Read the text carefully. Look for the main idea and important details.

- Think about the information you just read. Then summarize in your own words what you learned.

- Write a personal response to what you read. What do you think about the information? What questions might you have? How does this information affect you?

Practice

Use the steps you just learned to practice writing to learn. Read the paragraph below carefully, then complete a chart like the one here.

Tromso, Norway, is one of Europe's northern-most cities. Because of Earth's tilt and Tromso's location north of the Arctic Circle, the city experiences unusual conditions in both summer and winter. During the summer, the sun stays above the horizon continuously from late May to late July. In winter, residents of Tromso do not see the sun from November to January.

What I Learned	Personal Response

Apply

Read the information in Section 3 carefully. Then create a chart similar to the one above. In the first column, summarize the key ideas from the section in your own words. Use the second column to write your personal reaction to the information you learned.

Scandinavia

TEKS 1A, 1B, 2A, 2B, 3A, 3B, 3C, 3D, 4B, 4C, 15B, 18B, 21B, 21C, 22D

What You Will Learn...

Main Ideas

1. The history of Scandinavia dates back to the time of the Vikings.
2. Scandinavia today is known for its peaceful and prosperous countries.

The Big Idea

Scandinavia has developed into one of the most stable and prosperous regions in Europe.

Key Terms and Places

Vikings, *p. 368*
Stockholm, *p. 370*
neutral, *p. 370*
uninhabitable, *p. 371*
Oslo, *p. 371*
Helsinki, *p. 371*
geysers, *p. 372*

hmhsocialstudies.com
TAKING NOTES

Use the graphic organizer online to take notes on Scandinavia.

If **YOU** lived there...

You live in Copenhagen, the picturesque capital of Denmark. One of your favorite walks is along the waterfront, which is lined with colorful medieval buildings. Sailing boats of all sizes are anchored here. A famous statue in the harbor shows the Little Mermaid. But your favorite place of all is the huge amusement park called Tivoli Gardens, where you can enjoy fun and good food.

What sights would you show to a visitor?

BUILDING BACKGROUND After a long and warlike history, the modern countries of Scandinavia are models of peace and prosperity for the rest of Europe. Their cultures are similar in several ways, but each country has its own personality.

History

Hundreds of years ago, Scandinavia was home to warlike Vikings. The **Vikings** were Scandinavian warriors who raided Europe and the Mediterranean in the early Middle Ages. Excellent sailors, the Vikings used quick and powerful longboats to attack villages along coasts or rivers. The Vikings conquered the British Isles, Finland, and parts of France, Germany, and Russia. They were some of the most feared warriors of their time.

The Vikings were also great explorers. They established the first settlements in Iceland in the 800s and in Greenland in the 900s. A short time later, Vikings led by Leif Eriksson became the first Europeans to reach North America. The ruins of a Viking colony have been found in present-day Newfoundland, off the southeast coast of Canada.

In the 1100s the Viking raids ended. Powerful Scandinavian chiefs instead concentrated on strengthening their kingdoms. During the Middle Ages three kingdoms—Norway, Sweden, and Denmark—competed for power in the region.

Denmark was the first to gain the upper hand. By the late 1300s Denmark ruled a union of all the Scandinavian kingdoms and territories. Eventually, Sweden challenged Denmark's power.

In time, Sweden left the Danish-led union, taking Finland with it. Many years later, Sweden won control of Norway as well.

By the 1900s Scandinavian countries wanted their independence. Norway won its independence from Sweden in the early 1900s. Soon after, Finland became independent after centuries of foreign <u>domination</u>, or control, by Sweden and later by Russia. Iceland, then a Danish territory, declared its independence in 1944. To this day, however, Greenland remains a part of Denmark as a self-ruling territory.

READING CHECK **Analyzing** What historical ties do the countries of Scandinavia have?

FOCUS ON READING

What other word has the same meaning as *domination*? How can you tell?

Close-up

Viking Raids

The Vikings of Scandinavia launched raids on many European settlements in the early Middle Ages. Using powerful longships, Viking warriors attacked towns and villages near coasts and rivers. Vikings even sailed as far as North America in their longships.

A large woolen sail helped increase the ship's speed.

Sometimes as many as 30 oars spanned each side of a longship.

Viking longships were designed the same at each end. As a result, warriors did not have to turn the ship around to make a quick escape.

The longship's shallow design made river travel possible and allowed Viking raiders to sail their ships ashore.

ANALYSIS SKILL **ANALYZING VISUALS**

What aspects of Viking longships might have frightened Europeans who saw them approaching?

Scandinavia Today

Today the countries of Scandinavia have much in common. Similar political views, languages, and religion unite the region. The countries of Scandinavia have large, wealthy cities, strong economies, and well-educated workers. Scandinavians enjoy some of the world's highest standards of living. Each country provides its citizens with excellent social programs and services, such as free health care. Sweden, Denmark, Greenland, Norway, Finland, and Iceland are among the world's most peaceful, stable, and prosperous nations.

Sweden

Sweden is Scandinavia's largest and most populous country. Most Swedes live in the southern part of the country in large towns and cities. In fact, more than 85 percent of Swedes live in urban areas. **Stockholm**, Sweden's capital and largest city, is located on the east coast near the Baltic Sea. Often called a floating city, Stockholm is built on 14 islands and part of the mainland.

For almost 200 years, Sweden has been a neutral country. **Neutral** means that it has chosen not to take sides in an international conflict. Sweden does, however, play an active role in the United Nations as well as the European Union.

Denmark

Denmark, once the most powerful country in Scandinavia, is also the smallest. It is Scandinavia's most densely populated country, with some 338 people per square mile (131 per square km).

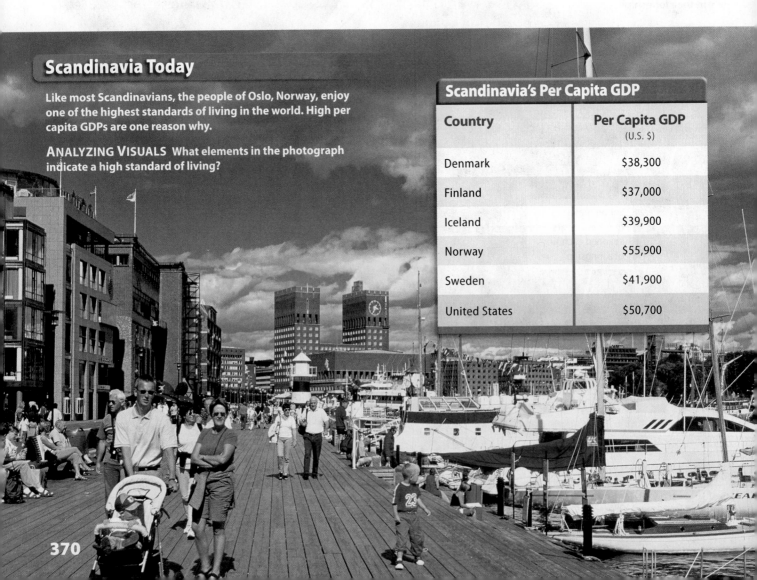

Scandinavia Today

Like most Scandinavians, the people of Oslo, Norway, enjoy one of the highest standards of living in the world. High per capita GDPs are one reason why.

ANALYZING VISUALS What elements in the photograph indicate a high standard of living?

Scandinavia's Per Capita GDP

Country	Per Capita GDP (U.S. $)
Denmark	$38,300
Finland	$37,000
Iceland	$39,900
Norway	$55,900
Sweden	$41,900
United States	$50,700

About 50 percent of Denmark's land is good for farming. Farm goods, especially meat and dairy products, are important Danish exports. Denmark also has modern industries, including iron, steel, textiles, and electronics industries.

Greenland

The island of Greenland is geographically part of North America. However, it is a territory of Denmark. A thick ice sheet covers about 80 percent of the island. Because of this, much of Greenland is **uninhabitable**, or not able to support human settlement. Most people have adapted to living on the island's southwest coast where the climate is warmest.

Recently, a movement for complete independence from Denmark has gained popularity. However, economic problems make independence unlikely, as Greenland relies heavily on imports and economic aid from Denmark.

Norway

With one of the longest coastlines in the world, Norway has adapted to its access to the sea. Fjords shelter Norway's many harbors. Its fishing and shipping fleets are among the largest in the world. **Oslo**, Norway's capital, is the country's leading seaport as well as its industrial center.

Norway has other valuable resources as well. Oil and natural gas provide Norway with the highest per capita GDP in Scandinavia. However, North Sea oil fields are expected to run dry over the next century. Despite strong economic ties to the rest of Europe, Norway's citizens have refused to join the European Union.

Finland

Finland is Scandinavia's easternmost country. It lies between Sweden and Russia. The capital and largest city is **Helsinki**, which is located on the southern coast.

As with other countries in the region, trade is important to Finland. Paper and other forest products are major exports. Shipbuilding and electronics are also important industries in Finland.

Iceland

Iceland is much greener than its name implies. Fertile farmland along the island's coast produces potatoes and vegetables and supports cattle and sheep.

Icelanders also make good use of their other natural resources. Fish from the rich waters of the Atlantic Ocean account for about 70 percent of Iceland's exports.

Iceland

Iceland's geysers and hot springs produce great amounts of energy. Geothermal plants like this one near the Blue Lagoon hot spring provide heat for buildings and homes throughout the country.

Icelanders have adapted to their physical environment by using steam from hot springs and geysers to produce geothermal energy. **Geysers** are springs that shoot hot water and steam into the air. Geothermal energy heats many of Iceland's buildings. Each year thousands of tourists flock to see Iceland's many geysers, volcanoes, and glaciers.

READING CHECK Comparing and Contrasting
In what ways are the countries of Scandinavia similar and different?

SUMMARY AND PREVIEW Scandinavia today is a region of relative peace and stability. A common history and culture link the people of the region. Today, Scandinavia is one of the wealthiest regions in Europe and in the world. In the next chapter, you will learn about the unique geography, history, and culture of another European region—Eastern Europe.

Section 3 Assessment

Reviewing Ideas, Terms, and Places

1. **a. Identify** Who were the **Vikings**?
   b. Analyze What effect did the Vikings have on Scandinavian history?
   c. Evaluate Do you think the Vikings helped or hurt the future of Scandinavia? Explain your answer.
2. **a. Define** What does the term **neutral** mean?
   b. Analyze How have some people in Scandinavia adapted to their physical environment?
   c. Elaborate In which Scandinavian country would you prefer to live? Why?

Critical Thinking

3. **Finding Main Ideas** Use your notes and this chart to identify two main ideas about Scandinavia's history and two about its culture today.

History	Today

FOCUS ON WRITING

my WriteSmart

4. **Writing about Scandinavia** Where would you travel and what would you see in Scandinavia? Take notes on the details you might include in your letter.

Chapter Review

Visual Summary

Use the visual summary below to help you review the main ideas of the chapter.

Low mountains and plentiful resources are key features of Northern Europe's physical geography.

The British Isles are known around the world for their rich history, vibrant culture, and healthy economies.

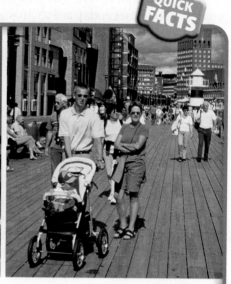

The countries of Scandinavia are among the most peaceful and prosperous in the world.

Reviewing Vocabulary, Terms, and Places

Write each word defined below, and circle each letter marked by a star. Then write the word these letters spell.

1. _ _ * _ _ _—to give up all weapons

2. _ _ _ _ _ _ _ _ _ *—a decision reached by two or more people or groups

3. _ _ * _ _—a narrow inlet of the sea set between high, rocky cliffs

4. _ * _ _ _ _ _ _ _ _ _—a region in far Northern Europe that crosses the Arctic Circle

5. _ _ * _ _ _ _—warriors from Northern Europe who raided much of Europe and the Mediterranean during the early Middle Ages

6. _ _ _ _ _ _ * _ _ _ _ _ _ _—unable to support human settlement

7. _ _ * _ _ _ _ _ _ _ _ energy—energy produced by the heat of the planet's interior

8. _ _ _ * _ _—the capital of the Republic of Ireland

9. _ _ _ * _ _ _—main or most important

Comprehension and Critical Thinking

SECTION 1 *(Pages 358–361)*

10. **a. Identify** What are the major resources found in Northern Europe?

b. Analyze Explain how the North Atlantic Drift is responsible for the relatively mild climates in Northern Europe.

c. Elaborate In which region of Northern Europe would you prefer to live—the British Isles or Scandinavia? Why?

SECTION 2 *(Pages 362–366)*

11. **a. Describe** What culture traits do the people of the British Isles share in common?

b. Interpret Study the time line of the history of the British Isles in this section. Then, organize the information from the time line into a written summary.

c. Predict How might the conflict in Northern Ireland affect the future of the United Kingdom?

12. **a. Recall** What countries make up Scandinavia?

    b. Compare and Contrast In what ways are the countries of Scandinavia similar and different?

    c. Elaborate Why do you think Scandinavian countries today are so prosperous and stable?

Social Studies Skills

13. **Writing to Learn** Read the paragraph below carefully, then summarize it in your own words. Finally, write a personal response to what you learned in the paragraph.

> In the mid-1800s Ireland was devastated by a severe famine. For many Irish, the potato was a key part of their diet. When a disease infected potato crops around the country, millions were left without enough to eat. About 1.5 million Irish died as a result of the Irish Potato Famine.

Map Activity

14. **Northern Europe** On a separate sheet of paper, match the letters on the map with their correct labels.

Dublin	Norway
English Channel	Reykjavik
Helsinki	Scandinavian Peninsula
London	Sweden

Using the Internet

15. **Activity: Creating a Poster** What does a medieval king have to do with modern democracy? Magna Carta was signed in 1215 by King John I of England. It established the principle that no one, including the king, is above the law. It also opened the door to a more democratic government in England. Centuries later, emerging democracies in the United States and France looked to Magna Carta for guidance. Through your online textbook, learn more about Magna Carta and its relationship with modern democracy. Then create a poster to display some of the ways this document has influenced modern governments.

↗ **hmhsocialstudies.com**

FOCUS ON READING AND WRITING *my* WriteSmart

Using Context Clues—Synonyms *Use context clues to determine the meaning of the underlined words in the sentences below. Make sure to ask for help if you do not understand a word.*

16. Wealthy in part because of its many natural resources, Scandinavia is one of the most <u>affluent</u> regions in Europe.

17. Thanks to the North Atlantic Drift, the British Isles are rarely affected by <u>inclement</u>, or harsh, weather.

18. <u>Dissent</u>, or disagreement, between Catholics and Protestants has caused years of conflict in Northern Ireland.

Writing a Letter *Use myWriteSmart in your eBook and your notes from the chapter and the directions below to write a letter.*

19. Tell your friends and family members what you have seen on your travels in the British Isles and Scandinavia. You may want to organize the information by country. For example, you could start with a flight into London and end in Iceland. Include descriptions of fascinating physical features as well as any cities or cultural activities that are unusual or interesting.

Reading Social Studies

Using Context Clues—Synonyms

FOCUS ON READING

You have probably discovered that geography is a subject with many new words and terms. What if you don't remember or don't know what a word means? You may be able to use context clues to determine its meaning. Context clues are words near the unfamiliar word that indicate its meaning.

One helpful context clue is the synonym—words or phrases that mean the same as the new word. Look for synonyms in the words and sentences surrounding an unfamiliar term. Synonyms can help you understand the meaning of the new word. They may come in the same sentence or in the sentence following the words they define. Notice how the following passage uses synonyms to define the word urban.

> Most Swedes live in the southern part of the country in large towns and cities. In fact, more than 80 percent of Swedes live in *urban* areas. Stockholm, Sweden's capital and largest city, is located on the east coast near the Baltic Sea.
>
> *From Section 3, Scandinavia*

1. Look for words or phrases that mean the same thing.
The first sentence uses the phrase large towns and cities to describe where most Swedes live.

2. Substitute the synonym for the new word to confirm its meaning.
More than 80 percent of Swedes live in large towns and cities.

YOU TRY IT!

As you read the following sentences, look for synonyms that mean the same as the italicized words. Then use a graphic organizer like the one below to define each italicized word. Make sure to ask your teacher or a classmate for help if you do not understand a word.

> Slow-moving sheets of ice, or *glaciers*, have left their mark on Northern Europe's coastlines and lakes.
>
> As the glaciers flowed slowly downhill, they carved long, winding channels, or *fjords*, into Norway's coastline.
>
> *From Section 1, Physical Geography*

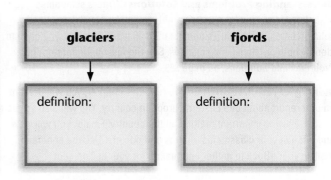

CHAPTER 16

Eastern Europe

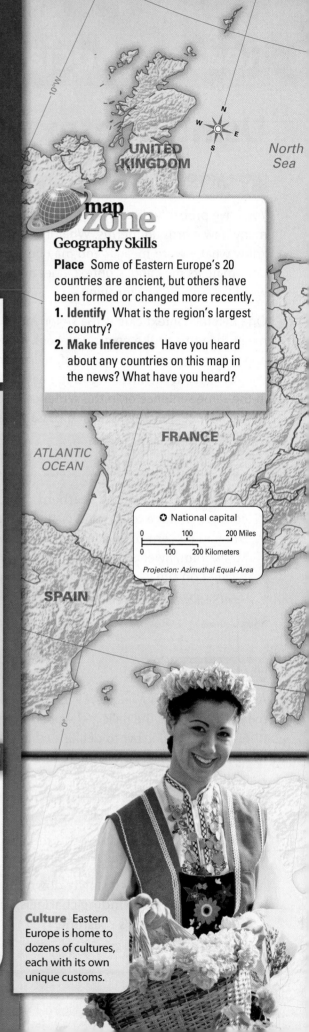

map zone
Geography Skills

Place Some of Eastern Europe's 20 countries are ancient, but others have been formed or changed more recently.
1. **Identify** What is the region's largest country?
2. **Make Inferences** Have you heard about any countries on this map in the news? What have you heard?

⊕ National capital

0   100   200 Miles
0 100 200 Kilometers

Projection: Azimuthal Equal-Area

Essential Question

*my*Notebook

What challenges has Eastern Europe faced since the breakup of the Soviet Union?

Texas Essential Knowledge and Skills (TEKS)

1A, 1B, 2A, 2B, 3A, 3B, 3C, 3D, 4B, 4C, 4D, 4E, 4F, 5A, 5B, 5C, 6A, 6B, 15A, 15B, 15F, 17D, 17E, 18B, 19A, 21B, 21C, 22D

FOCUS ON READING AND VIEWING

my WriteSmart

Understanding Problems and Solutions Writers sometimes organize information by stating a problem and then explaining the solution taken to solve it. To understand this type of writing, you need to identify both problems and solutions. **See the lesson, Understanding Problems and Solutions, on page 399.**

Making a Presentation After you read this chapter, you will present an oral report about one Eastern European country. You will also create a poster showing important features of the country. Finally, you will view and critique your classmates' reports and posters. Use the annotation tools in your eBook to gather information for your assignment.

Culture Eastern Europe is home to dozens of cultures, each with its own unique customs.

Tallinn
ESTONIA

Riga
LATVIA

Baltic Sea

LITHUANIA
Vilnius

RUSSIA

Minsk
BELARUS

RUSSIA

POLAND
Warsaw

GERMANY

Kiev

Prague
CZECH REPUBLIC

UKRAINE

SLOVAKIA
Bratislava

AUSTRIA

Budapest
HUNGARY

MOLDOVA
Chișinău

SLOVENIA
Ljubljana

Zagreb
CROATIA

ROMANIA

BOSNIA AND HERZEGOVINA
Sarajevo

Belgrade

SERBIA

Bucharest

Danube River

Black Sea

ITALY

Adriatic Sea

MONTENEGRO
Podgorica

KOSOVO
Pristina

Sofia
BULGARIA

Skopje

Tirana
MACEDONIA

ALBANIA

TURKEY

GREECE

Aegean Sea

20°E 50°N 30°E 40°E

HISTORY. Chernobyl

↗ hmhsocialstudies.com **VIDEO**

Geography Like the Danube River shown here, many rivers flow through the mountains and plains of Eastern Europe.

History Buildings in cities like Prague, Czech Republic, are symbols of Eastern Europe's long history.

377

What You Will Learn...

Main Ideas

1. The physical features of Eastern Europe include wide open plains, rugged mountain ranges, and many rivers.
2. The climate and vegetation of Eastern Europe differ widely in the North and the South.

The Big Idea

The physical geography of Eastern Europe varies greatly from place to place.

Key Places

Carpathians, *p. 378*
Balkan Peninsula, *p. 379*
Danube, *p. 380*
Chernobyl, *p. 381*

hmhsocialstudies.com

TAKING NOTES

Use the graphic organizer online to take notes on the physical geography of Eastern Europe.

Physical Geography

If YOU lived there...

You are traveling on a boat down the Danube River, one of the longest in Europe. As you float downstream, you pass through dozens of towns and cities. Outside of the cities, the banks are lined with huge castles, soaring churches, and busy farms. From time to time, other boats pass you, some loaded with passengers and some with goods.

Why do you think the Danube is so busy?

BUILDING BACKGROUND The physical geography of Eastern Europe varies widely from north to south. Many of the landforms you learned about in earlier chapters, including the Northern European Plain and the Alps, extend into this region.

Physical Features

Eastern Europe is a land of amazing contrasts. The northern parts of the region lie along the cold, often stormy shores of the Baltic Sea. In the south, however, are warm, sunny beaches along the Adriatic and Black seas. Jagged mountain peaks jut high into the sky in some places, while wildflowers dot the gently rolling hills of other parts of the region. These contrasts stem from the region's wide variety of landforms, water features, and climates.

Landforms

As you can see on the map, the landforms of Eastern Europe are arranged in a series of broad bands. In the north is the Northern European Plain. As you have already learned, this large plain stretches across most of Northern Europe.

South of the Northern European Plain is a low mountain range called the **Carpathians** (kahr-PAY-thee-uhnz). These rugged mountains are an extension of the Alps of West-Central Europe. They stretch in a long arc from the Alps to the Black Sea area.

South and west of the Carpathians is another plain, the Great Hungarian Plain. As its name suggests, this fertile area is located mostly within Hungary.

South of the plain are more mountains, the Dinaric (duh-NAR-ik) Alps and Balkan Mountains. These two ranges together cover most of the **Balkan Peninsula**, one of the largest peninsulas in Europe. It extends south into the Mediterranean Sea.

Water Features

Like the rest of the continent, Eastern Europe has many bodies of water that affect how people live. To the southwest is the Adriatic Sea, an important route for transportation and trade. To the east, the Black Sea serves the same <u>function</u>. In the far north is the Baltic Sea. It is another important trade route, though parts of the sea freeze over in the winter.

Eastern Europe: Physical

ELEVATION

Feet		Meters
13,120		4,000
6,560		2,000
1,640		500
656		200
(Sea level) 0		0 (Sea level)
Below sea level		Below sea level

0   150   300 Miles
0   150   300 Kilometers

Projection: Azimuthal Equal-Area

1 The Carpathian Mountains run through the center of Eastern Europe.

2 Many rivers flow across the plains of Eastern Europe. The Vistula, shown here, is one of them.

map zone Geography Skills

Place The physical features of Eastern Europe are arranged in alternating bands of rugged mountains and fertile plains.

1. **Locate** What large river flows through the southern part of the region?
2. **Interpret** Where do you think most of Eastern Europe's large cities are? Why?

In addition to these seas, Eastern Europe has several rivers that are vital paths for transportation and trade. The longest of these rivers, the **Danube** (DAN-yoob), begins in Germany and flows east across the Great Hungarian Plain. The river winds its way through nine countries before it finally empties into the Black Sea.

As you might expect, the Danube is central to the Eastern European economy. Some of the region's largest cities lie on the Danube's banks. Thousands of ships travel up and down the river every year, loaded with both goods and people. In addition, dams on the western parts of the river generate much of the region's electricity. Unfortunately, the high level of activity on the Danube has left it heavily polluted.

READING CHECK **Finding Main Ideas** What are the main bodies of water in Eastern Europe?

Climate and Vegetation

Like its landforms, the climates and natural vegetation of Eastern Europe vary widely. In fact, the climates and landscapes found across Eastern Europe determine which plants will grow there.

The Baltic Coast

The shores of the Baltic Sea are the coldest location in Eastern Europe. Winters there are long, cold, and harsh. This northern part of Eastern Europe receives less rain than other areas, but fog is common. In fact, some parts of the area have as few as 30 sunny days each year. The climate allows huge forests to grow there.

The Interior Plains

The interior plains of Eastern Europe are much milder than the far north. Winters there can be very cold, but summers are generally pleasant and mild. The western parts of these plains receive much more rain than those areas farther east.

Because of this variation in climate, the plains of Eastern Europe have many types of vegetation. Huge forests cover much of the north. South of these forests are open grassy plains. In the spring, these plains erupt with colorful wildflowers.

BOOK

The Plains of Ukraine

One of Russia's greatest novelists, Nikolai Gogol (gaw-guhl), was actually born in what is now Ukraine. Very fond of his homeland, he frequently wrote about its great beauty. In this passage from the short story "Taras Bulba," he describes a man's passage across the wide open fields of Ukraine.

"No plough had ever passed over the immeasurable waves of wild growth; horses alone, hidden in it as in a forest, trod it down. Nothing in nature could be finer. The whole surface resembled a golden-green ocean, upon which were sprinkled millions of different flowers. Through the tall, slender stems of the grass peeped light-blue, dark-blue, and lilac star-thistles; the yellow broom thrust up its pyramidal head; the parasol-shaped white flower of the false flax shimmered on high. A wheat-ear, brought God knows whence, was filling out to ripening. Amongst the roots of this luxuriant vegetation ran partridges with outstretched necks. The air was filled with the notes of a thousand different birds."

—from "Taras Bulba," by Nikolai Gogol

ANALYSIS SKILL **ANALYZING PRIMARY SOURCES**

What features does Gogol describe on the plains of Ukraine?

Radiation Cleanup

A nuclear accident in 1986 leaked dangerous amounts of radiation into Eastern Europe's soil. Ukraine's government and scientists are still working to repair the damage.

Unfortunately, Eastern Europe's forests were greatly damaged by a terrible accident in 1986. A faulty reactor at the **Chernobyl** (chuhr-NOH-buhl) nuclear power plant in Ukraine exploded, releasing huge amounts of radiation into the air. This radiation poisoned millions of acres of forest and ruined soil across much of the region.

The Balkan Coast

Along the Adriatic Sea, the Balkan coast has a Mediterranean climate, with warm summers and mild winters. As a result, its beaches are popular tourist destinations.

Because a Mediterranean climate does not bring much rain, the Balkan coast does not have many forests. Instead, the land there is covered by shrubs and hardy trees that do not need much water.

READING CHECK **Contrasting** How do the climates and vegetation of Eastern Europe vary?

SUMMARY AND PREVIEW The landforms of Eastern Europe vary widely, as do its cultures. Next you will study the cultures of the northernmost parts of the region.

FOCUS ON READING
What problems did the Chernobyl accident cause for Eastern Europe?

Section 1 Assessment

Reviewing Ideas, Terms, and Places

1. **a. Identify** What are the major mountain ranges of Eastern Europe?
   b. Make Inferences How do you think the physical features of Eastern Europe influence where people live?
   c. Elaborate Why is the **Danube** so important to the people of Eastern Europe?
2. **a. Describe** What is the climate of the **Balkan Peninsula** like?
   b. Explain Why are there few trees in the far southern areas of Eastern Europe?
   c. Predict How do you think the lingering effects of the **Chernobyl** accident affect the plant life of Eastern Europe?

Critical Thinking

3. **Categorizing** Draw a chart like the one shown here. In each column, identify the landforms, climates, and vegetation of each area in Eastern Europe.

	Landforms	Climates	Vegetation
Baltic coast			
Interior plains			
Balkan coast			

FOCUS ON VIEWING

my **WriteSmart**

4. **Presenting Physical Geography** Until you decide what country you will report on, take notes about all of them. Make a list of the countries of Eastern Europe and the physical features found in each.

TEKS 1A, 1B, 2A, 2B, 3A, 3B, 3C, 3D, 4B, 4C, 15B, 18B, 21B, 21C, 22D

What You Will Learn...

Main Ideas

1. History ties Poland and the Baltic Republics together.
2. The cultures of Poland and the Baltic Republics differ in language and religion but share common customs.
3. Economic growth is a major issue in the region today.

The Big Idea

The histories of Poland and the Baltic Republics, both as free states and as areas dominated by the Soviet Union, still shape life there.

Key Terms and Places

infrastructure, *p. 385*
Warsaw, *p. 385*

hmhsocialstudies.com
TAKING NOTES

Use the graphic organizer online to take notes on Poland and the Baltic Republics.

Poland and the Baltic Republics

If YOU lived there...

You live in the beautiful and historic city of Krakow, Poland. Over the centuries, terrible wars have damaged many Polish cities, but Krakow is filled with cobblestone streets, romantic castles, and elaborate churches. The city is home to one of Europe's oldest shopping malls, the 500-year-old Cloth Hall. Glorious old Catholic churches also rise high above many parts of the city.

What does the city suggest about Polish history?

BUILDING BACKGROUND Located on the Northern European Plain, Poland and the Baltic Republics are caught between east and west. As a result, the region has often been a battlefield. On the other hand, this location at a cultural crossroads has helped each country develop its own distinctive culture, traditions, and customs.

History

The area around the Baltic Sea was settled in ancient times by many different groups. In time, these groups developed into the people who live in the region today. One group became the Estonians, one became the Latvians and Lithuanians, and one became the Polish. Each of these groups had its own language and culture. Over the centuries, however, shared historical events have helped tie all these people together.

Early History

By the Middle Ages, the people of the Baltics had formed many independent kingdoms. The kingdoms of Lithuania and Poland were large and strong. Together they ruled much of Eastern and Northern Europe. The smaller kingdoms of Latvia and Estonia, on the other hand, were not strong. In fact, they were often invaded by their more powerful neighbors. These invasions continued through the 1800s.

Eastern Europe under Soviet Influence, 1988

Extent of Soviet influence

0   100   200 Miles
0   100   200 Kilometers

Projection: Azimuthal Equal-Area

SWEDEN
DENMARK
Baltic Sea
ESTONIA
LATVIA
LITHUANIA
SOVIET UNION
BELORUSSIA   RUSSIA
POLAND
Oder River
Elbe R.
EAST GERMANY
WEST GERMANY
Vistula R.
CZECHOSLOVAKIA
UKRAINE
AUSTRIA
MOLDOVA
HUNGARY
ROMANIA
Danube River
Black Sea
YUGOSLAVIA
Adriatic Sea
ITALY
BULGARIA
TURKEY
ALBANIA   GREECE

map zone

Geography Skills

Place From World War II until 1989, politics in Eastern Europe was dominated by the Soviet Union.
1. **Identify** Which modern countries were part of the Soviet Union?
2. **Name** What other countries have changed since 1988?

BIOGRAPHY

Pope John Paul II
(1920–2005)

Karol Wojtyła, later called Pope John Paul II, was born in Poland. Raised a Roman Catholic, he became a priest shortly after the Soviets took over the country. After becoming pope in 1978, he encouraged the Polish people to protest against their Communist government. Largely because of his efforts, Poland broke away from the Soviet Union in 1989.

The World Wars

Both World War I and World War II were devastating for the Baltic people. Much of the fighting in World War I took place in Poland. As a result, millions of Poles—both soldiers and civilians—died. Thousands more were killed in the Baltic countries.

World War II began when the Germans invaded Poland from the west. As the Germans pushed through Poland from the west, the army of the Soviet Union invaded Poland from the east. Once again, Poland suffered tremendously. Millions of people were killed, and property all over Poland was destroyed. Estonia, Latvia, and Lithuania also suffered. All three countries were occupied by the Soviet army.

Soviet Domination

As the map shows, the Soviet Union totally dominated Eastern Europe after World War II. Estonia, Latvia, and Lithuania became parts of the Soviet Union. Poland remained free, but the Soviets forced the Poles to accept a Communist government.

Many Eastern Europeans opposed Communist rule, and the Communist governments in the region eventually fell. Poland rejected Communism and elected new leaders in 1989. The Baltic Republics broke away from the Soviet Union in 1991 and became independent once more.

READING CHECK **Analyzing** How did the Soviet Union influence the region's history?

FOCUS ON READING

What problems were created in the Baltic region after World War II?

Culture

In some ways, the cultures of Poland and the Baltic Republics are very different from each other. For example, people in the area speak different languages and practice different religions. In other ways, however, their cultures are actually quite similar. Because the four countries lie near each other, common customs have taken root in all of them. People cook similar foods and enjoy the same types of entertainment.

CONNECTING TO the Arts

Baltic Embroidery

One of the crafts for which the people of the Baltic region are best known is embroidery. This type of decorative sewing lets people create beautiful designs. They use these designs on their clothing, tablecloths, and other cloth goods.

For centuries, people in the Baltic countries—both men and women—have embroidered the clothing they wear on special occasions, such as weddings. They use many colors of thread to sew intricate patterns of flowers, hearts, and geometric designs. Because the embroidery is done by hand, it can take hours of work to create a single garment.

Drawing Conclusions Why do you think people embroider only clothing for special occasions?

Cultural Differences

The most obvious differences between the cultures of the Baltic countries are their languages and religions. Because the countries were first settled by different groups, each has its own language today. Of these languages, only Latvian and Lithuanian are similar to each other. Polish is related to the languages of countries farther south. Estonian is similar to Finnish.

Trade patterns and invasions have affected religion in the area. Poland and Lithuania traded mostly with Roman Catholic countries, and so most people there are Catholic. Latvia and Estonia, on the other hand, were ruled for a long time by Sweden. Because the Swedish are mostly Lutheran, most people in Latvia and Estonia are Lutheran as well.

Cultural Similarities

Unlike language and religion, many of the customs practiced in the Baltic countries cross national boundaries. For example, people in these countries eat many of the same types of foods. Potatoes and sausage are very popular, as is seafood.

Other shared customs tie the Baltic countries together as well. For example, people in all three countries practice many of the same crafts. Among these crafts are pottery, painting, and embroidery.

Also common to the countries of the Baltic Sea area is a love of music and dance. For centuries, people of the Baltics have been famous for their musical abilities. Frédéric Chopin (1810–1849), for example, was a famous Polish pianist and composer. Today, people throughout Poland and the Baltic Republics gather at music festivals to hear popular and traditional tunes.

READING CHECK **Comparing** How are the cultures of the Baltic countries similar?

The Region Today

Estonia, Latvia, Lithuania, and Poland all still feel the effects of decades of Soviet rule. The economies of all four countries suffered because the Soviets did not build a decent infrastructure. An **infrastructure** is the set of resources, like roads, airports, and factories, that a country needs in order to support economic activities. The many factories built by the Soviets in Poland and the Baltics could not produce as many goods as those in Western Europe.

Today Poland and the Baltic Republics are working to rebuild and strengthen their economies. They are replacing the old and outdated factories built by the Soviets with new ones that take advantage of modern technology. As a result, cities like **Warsaw**, the capital of Poland, have become major industrial centers.

To further their economic growth, the countries of this region are also seeking new sources of income. One area in which they have found some success is tourism. Since the collapse of the Soviet Union in 1991, many Americans and Western Europeans have begun visiting. Polish cities like Warsaw and Krakow have long attracted tourists with their rich history and famous sites. Vilnius, Lithuania; Tallinn, Estonia; and Riga, Latvia, have also become tourist attractions. People are drawn to these cities by their fascinating cultures, cool summer climates, and historic sites.

READING CHECK **Generalizing** How has the region changed in recent years?

SUMMARY AND PREVIEW Poland and the Baltic Republics are still feeling the effects of decades of Soviet rule. In the next section, you will learn about more countries that feel the same effects.

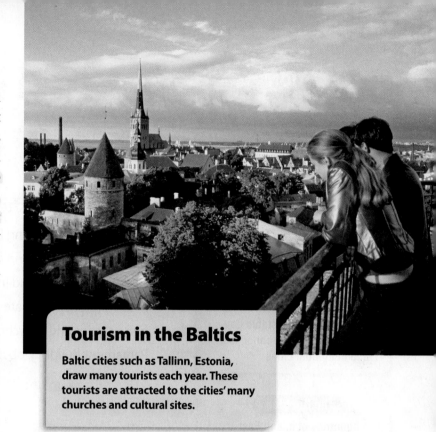

Tourism in the Baltics

Baltic cities such as Tallinn, Estonia, draw many tourists each year. These tourists are attracted to the cities' many churches and cultural sites.

Section 2 Assessment

hmhsocialstudies.com
ONLINE QUIZ

Reviewing Ideas, Terms, and Places

1. **a.** **Identify** What country ran the area after World War II?
   b. **Draw Conclusions** How do you think the two world wars affected the people of Poland?
2. **a.** **Describe** How do the languages spoken in Poland and the Baltic Republics reflect the region's history?
   b. **Elaborate** Why do you think that people across the region practice many of the same customs?
3. **a.** **Recall** What is one industry that has grown in the region since the fall of the Soviet Union?
   b. **Explain** How did Soviet rule hurt the area's economy?

Critical Thinking

4. **Identifying Cause and Effect** Draw a chart like the one shown here. In each box on the right, explain how the event affected the cultures or economies of the region.

Event	Effect
Soviet rule	
Breakup of the Soviet Union	
Growth of tourism	

FOCUS ON VIEWING   *my* WriteSmart

5. **Considering Poland and the Baltics** If you were to give your report about Poland or one of the Baltic Republics, what details would you include? Write down some ideas.

Inland Eastern Europe

What You Will Learn...

Main Ideas

1. The histories and cultures of inland Eastern Europe vary from country to country.
2. Most of inland Eastern Europe today has stable governments, strong economies, and influential cities.

The Big Idea

The countries of inland Eastern Europe have varied histories and cultures but face many of the same issues today.

Key Terms and Places

Prague, *p. 387*
Kiev, *p. 387*
Commonwealth of Independent States, *p. 388*
Budapest, *p. 389*

hmhsocialstudies.com
TAKING NOTES

Use the graphic organizer online to take notes on inland Eastern Europe.

If YOU lived there...

You are a tourist visiting Budapest, the capital of Hungary. Early one morning, you stand on a bridge over the glittering water of the Danube River. You read in your guidebook that the two banks of the river were once separate cities. On the bank to your right, you see huge castles and churches standing on a tall hill. To your left is the Parliament building, obviously a much newer building.

What might have brought the cities together?

BUILDING BACKGROUND The city of Budapest, like many of the cities of inland Eastern Europe, has a long, colorful history. Various parts of the city reflect wildly different eras in its past. Medieval churches, for example, stand near huge imperial fortresses and Soviet-built warehouses, all relics of the region's history.

History and Culture

Located on the Northern European and Hungarian plains, inland Eastern Europe consists of six countries. They are the Czech (CHEK) Republic, Slovakia, Hungary, Ukraine, Belarus, and Moldova. Throughout history, many different peoples ruled these countries. Each ruling group influenced the culture and customs of the area.

Czech Republic and Slovakia

The area that now includes the Czech Republic and Slovakia was once home to many small kingdoms. People called the Slavs founded these kingdoms. The Slavs were people from Asia who moved into Europe by AD 1000. Eventually, strong neighbors such as Austria conquered the Slavic kingdoms.

After World War I, the victorious Allies took land away from Austria to form a new nation, Czechoslovakia. About fifty years later, in 1993, it split into the Czech Republic and Slovakia.

Because of their location, these two countries have long had ties with Western Europe. As a result, Western influences are common. For example, many people in the two countries are Roman Catholic. The architecture of cities like **Prague** (PRAHG), the capital of the Czech Republic, also reflects Western influences.

Hungary

In the 900s, a group of fierce invaders called the Magyars swept into what is now Hungary. Although they were conquered by the Austrians, the Magyars continued to shape Hungarian culture. The Hungarian language is based on the language spoken by the Magyars. In fact, people in Hungary today still refer to themselves as Magyars.

Ukraine, Belarus, and Moldova

The Slavs also settled Ukraine, Belarus, and Moldova. Later other groups, including the Vikings of Scandinavia, invaded and conquered the Slavs.

A group called the Rus (RUHS) built a settlement in what is now **Kiev**, Ukraine, in the 800s. The rulers of Kiev eventually created a huge empire.

In the late 1700s, that empire became part of Russia. When the Soviet Union was formed in 1922, Ukraine and Belarus were made Soviet republics. Moldova became a republic two years later. They did not become independent until the breakup of the Soviet Union in 1991.

The long history of Russian influence in the region is reflected in the countries' cultures. For example, most people in these countries are Orthodox Christians, like the people of Russia. In addition, Ukrainian and Belarusian languages are written in the Cyrillic, or Russian, alphabet.

READING CHECK **Analyzing** Which groups have influenced the history of the region?

The Kievan Empire

Kiev, now the capital of Ukraine, was once the capital of a large and powerful empire. At its height, the Kievan Empire stretched across much of Eastern Europe and Central Asia.

Kiev

According to an old legend, the city of Kiev was built by three brothers and their sister. This monument built in the 1980s honors the city's legendary founders.

The people of Kiev built Saint Sophia Cathedral in the 1000s. By that time, nearly everyone who lived in the Kievan Empire was Orthodox Christian.

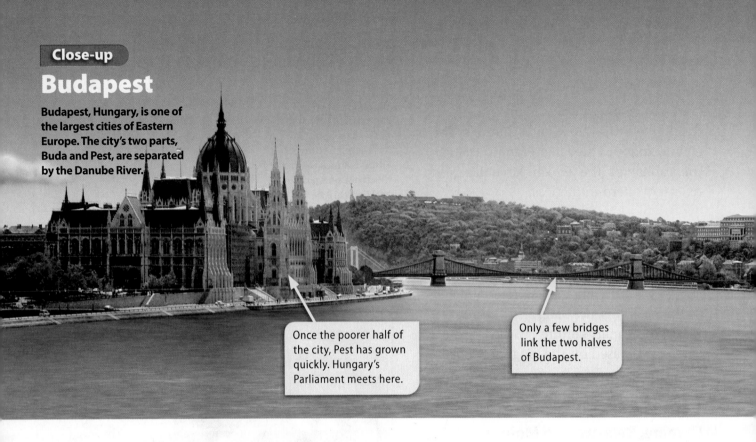

Close-up

Budapest

Budapest, Hungary, is one of the largest cities of Eastern Europe. The city's two parts, Buda and Pest, are separated by the Danube River.

Once the poorer half of the city, Pest has grown quickly. Hungary's Parliament meets here.

Only a few bridges link the two halves of Budapest.

Inland Eastern Europe Today

FOCUS ON READING

How might the CIS help solve problems in this region?

All of the countries of inland Eastern Europe were either part of the Soviet Union or run by Soviet-influenced governments. Since the end of Soviet domination, the people of inland Eastern Europe have largely overcome the problems created by the Soviets. Still, a few issues remain for the region's governments and economies.

Government

During the Soviet era, the countries of inland Eastern Europe had Communist governments. Under the Communists, people had few freedoms. In addition, the Soviets were poor economic planners, and their policies caused many hardships.

Since the collapse of the Soviet Union, the governments of inland Eastern Europe have changed. Hungary, Slovakia, the Czech Republic, Ukraine, and Moldova are now republics in which the people elect their leaders. Belarus also claims to be a republic, but it is really a dictatorship.

The countries of inland Eastern Europe belong to several international alliances. One such alliance, the **Commonwealth of Independent States**, or CIS, meets to discuss issues such as trade and immigration that affect former Soviet republics. The CIS is based in Minsk, the capital of Belarus. Ukraine and Moldova are also members, as are many countries in Asia.

The Czech Republic, Slovakia, Hungary, Romania, and Bulgaria are not part of the CIS. They have sought closer ties to the West than to the former Soviet Union. As a result, all five belong to the EU.

Economy

Economic development has been a major challenge for these countries since the collapse of the Soviet Union. The Czech Republic, Slovakia, Hungary, and Ukraine have been most successful. All four are thriving industrial centers. Ukraine, with rich, productive farmlands, grows grains, potatoes, and sugar beets.

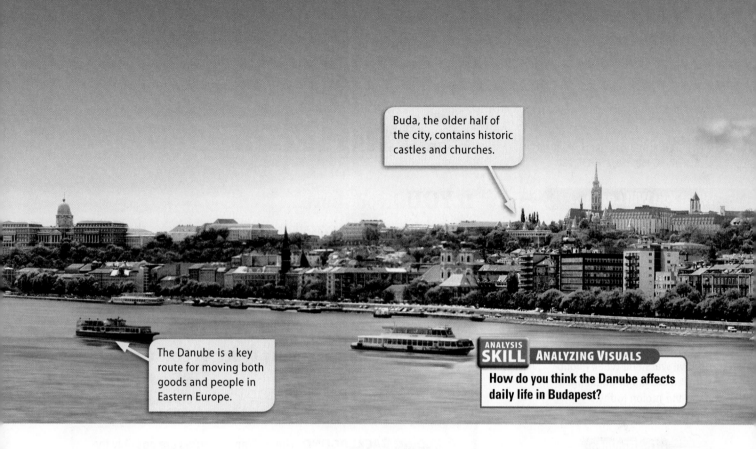

Buda, the older half of the city, contains historic castles and churches.

The Danube is a key route for moving both goods and people in Eastern Europe.

ANALYSIS SKILL **ANALYZING VISUALS**

How do you think the Danube affects daily life in Budapest?

Cities

Life in inland Eastern Europe is centered around cities, especially national capitals. In each country, the capital is both a key economic center and a cultural one.

Three cities in the region are especially important—Prague, Kiev, and **Budapest**, the capital of Hungary. They are the most prosperous cities in the region and home to influential leaders and universities. In addition, the cities are popular tourist destinations. People from all over the world visit Eastern Europe to see these cities' architectural and cultural sites.

READING CHECK **Generalizing** What are the countries of inland Eastern Europe like today?

SUMMARY AND PREVIEW Inland Eastern Europe has been successful in facing the challenges left by Soviet influence. Next, you will learn about a region that has faced more challenges, the Balkans.

Section 3 Assessment

hmhsocialstudies.com
ONLINE QUIZ

Reviewing Ideas, Terms, and Places

1. **a. Recall** In what country is **Prague** located?
   b. Sequence List the groups that ruled **Kiev** and the surrounding area in chronological order.
   c. Elaborate How has Hungary's history helped set it apart from other countries in inland Eastern Europe?
2. **a. Identify** What is the **Commonwealth of Independent States**? Which countries in this region are members?
   b. Draw Conclusions How have the economies of the region changed since the collapse of the Soviet Union?
   c. Develop Why do you think life is largely centered around cities in inland Eastern Europe?

Critical Thinking

3. **Generalizing** Draw a diagram like the one shown here.

   ( ) → Russia Today → ( )

   In the left oval, describe the government and economy of inland Eastern Europe under the Soviet Union. In the right oval, describe them since the Soviet Union's collapse.

FOCUS ON VIEWING

my **WriteSmart**

4. **Picturing Inland Eastern Europe** Which country sounds most interesting to you? Write down some details about it. Make a list of pictures you could use on your poster.

The Balkan Countries

TEKS 1A, 1B, 2A, 2B, 3A, 3B, 3C, 3D, 4B, 4C, 15B, 18B, 21B, 21C, 22D

What You Will Learn...

Main Ideas

1. The history of the Balkan countries is one of conquest and conflict.
2. The cultures of the Balkan countries are shaped by the many ethnic groups who live there.
3. Civil wars and weak economies are major challenges to the region today.

The Big Idea

Life in the Balkans reflects the region's troubled past and its varied ethnic makeup.

Key Terms

ethnic cleansing, *p. 392*

hmhsocialstudies.com
TAKING NOTES

Use the graphic organizer online to take notes on the physical geography of Central Asia.

If **YOU** lived there...

As part of your summer vacation, you are hiking across the Balkan Peninsula. As you hike through villages in the rugged mountains, you are amazed at the different churches you see. There are small Roman Catholic churches, huge Orthodox churches with onion-shaped domes, and Muslim mosques with tall minarets.

Why are there so many types of churches here?

BUILDING BACKGROUND The Balkan countries are possibly the most diverse area in Europe. In addition to practicing many religions, the people there speak many languages and have different customs. At times, the area's diversity has led to serious problems.

History

Like the rest of Eastern Europe, the Balkan Peninsula has been conquered and ruled by many different groups. The presence of these many groups continues to shape life in the area today.

Early History

By the 600s BC the ancient Greeks had founded colonies on the northern Black Sea coast. The area they settled is now part of Bulgaria and Romania. Later, the Romans conquered most of the area from the Adriatic Sea to the Danube River.

When the Roman Empire divided into west and east in the late AD 300s, the Balkan Peninsula became part of the Eastern, or Byzantine, Empire. Under Byzantine rule, many people of the Balkans became Orthodox Christians. More than 1,000 years later, Muslim Ottoman Turks conquered the Byzantine Empire. Under the Ottomans, many people became Muslims.

The Ottomans ruled the Balkan Peninsula until the 1800s. At that time, the people of the region rose up and drove the Ottomans out. They then created their own kingdoms.

World War I and After

Trouble between the Balkan kingdoms and their neighbors led to World War I. In the late 1800s the Austro-Hungarian Empire, which lay north of the Balkans, took over part of the peninsula. In protest, a man from Serbia shot the heir to the Austro-Hungarian throne, sparking the war.

After World War I, the Balkans changed dramatically. Europe's leaders divided the peninsula into new countries. Among these new countries was Yugoslavia, which combined many formerly independent countries under one government.

The nation of Yugoslavia lasted until the 1990s. The country eventually broke up, however, because of conflict between ethnic and religious groups.

READING CHECK **Summarizing** How did World War I affect the Balkan Peninsula?

Culture

Culturally, the Balkans are the most diverse area of Europe. This diversity is reflected in the large number of religions practiced and languages spoken there.

Religion

Most of the people of the Balkans, like most Europeans, are Christian. However, three types of Christianity are practiced in the area. Most Balkan Christians belong to the Orthodox Church. In the western part of the peninsula, there are many Roman Catholics. In addition, many countries also have large Protestant communities.

Christianity is not the only religion in the Balkans. Because of the Ottomans' long rule, Islam is also common. In fact, Albania is the only country in Europe in which most people are Muslims.

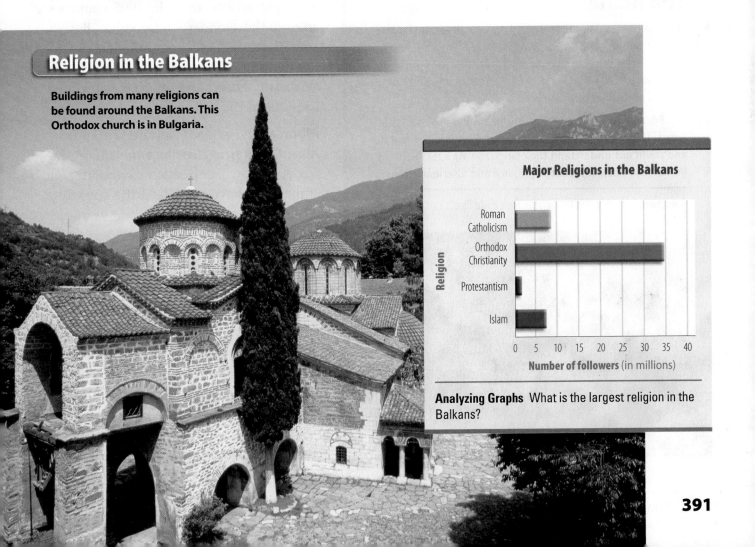

Religion in the Balkans

Buildings from many religions can be found around the Balkans. This Orthodox church is in Bulgaria.

Major Religions in the Balkans

Religion — Number of followers (in millions)
- Roman Catholicism
- Orthodox Christianity
- Protestantism
- Islam

Analyzing Graphs What is the largest religion in the Balkans?

Language

People in the Balkans speak languages from three major groups. Most languages in the region belong to the Slavic family and are related to Russian. In Romania, though, people speak a language that developed from Latin. It is more closely related to French, Italian, and Spanish than to Slavic languages. In addition, some people in Romania speak Germanic languages.

Some languages of the Balkans are not related to these groups. For example, Albanian is unlike any other language in the world. In addition, a group called the Roma have a language of their own.

ACADEMIC VOCABULARY

implications
consequences

READING CHECK **Drawing Conclusions** Why is Balkan culture so diverse?

FOCUS ON CULTURE

The Roma

The Roma are a nomadic people. For centuries, they have roamed from place to place in horse-drawn wagons, working as blacksmiths, animal trainers, and musicians. Although Roma live all over the world, the largest concentration of them is in southeastern Europe.

For centuries, many other Europeans did not trust the Roma. They were suspicious of the Roma's nomadic lifestyle and could not understand their language. As a result, many Roma have been subject to prejudice and discrimination.

Summarizing What is traditional Roma life like?

The Balkans Today

The countries of the Balkan Peninsula, like most of Eastern Europe, were once run by Communist governments. Weak economic planning has left most of them poor and struggling to improve their economies. This area is still the poorest in Europe today.

Relations among religious and ethnic groups have had serious **implications** for the Balkans. When Yugoslavia broke apart, violence broke out among groups in some of the newly formed countries. Members of the largest religious or ethnic group in each country tried to get rid of all other groups who lived there. They threatened those who refused to leave with punishments or death. This kind of effort to remove all members of a group from a country or region is called **ethnic cleansing**.

The violence in the former Yugoslavia was so terrible that other countries stepped in to put an end to it. In 1995 countries around the world sent troops to Bosnia and Herzegovina to help bring an end to the fighting. The fighting between groups eventually ended and, in 2008, ten countries shared the Balkan Peninsula:

Albania The poorest country in Europe, Albania has struggled since the end of the Soviet period. High unemployment and crime rates have prevented the country's economy from improving.

Macedonia Once a part of Yugoslavia, Macedonia broke away in 1991. It was the first country to do so peacefully.

Slovenia Slovenia also broke from Yugoslavia in 1991. In 2004 it became the first Balkan country to join the EU.

Croatia When Croatia broke away from Yugoslavia, fighting broke out within the country. Ethnic Croats and Serbs fought over land for many years. In the end, many Serbs left Croatia, and peace was restored.

Bosnia and Herzegovina Since the end of ethnic and religious violence, peace has returned to Bosnia and Herzegovina. The people there are working to rebuild.

Serbia Serbia is the largest nation to emerge from the former Yugoslavia. Like other Balkan countries, Serbia has seen fighting among ethnic groups.

Kosovo Formerly a province of Serbia, Kosovo declared independence in 2008. Its population is mostly ethnic Albanian.

Montenegro The mountainous country of Montenegro separated peacefully from Serbia in June 2006.

Romania Romania, the largest of the Balkan states, is working to recover from years of bad government. Poor leaders have left its government and economy in ruins.

Bulgaria Since the fall of the Soviet Union, Bulgaria has changed dramatically. People there are working to develop a capitalist economy based on industry and tourism.

FOCUS ON READING

What solutions are Bulgaria's leaders seeking to their economic problems?

READING CHECK **Generalizing** What issues does the Balkan region face today?

SUMMARY AND PREVIEW The Soviet Union had a huge effect on Eastern Europe. Next, you will read about the Soviet Union and Russia.

Section 4 Assessment

Reviewing Ideas, Terms, and Places

1. **a. Describe** What was Yugoslavia? When did it break apart?
   b. Explain What role did the Balkan countries play in starting World War I?
2. **a. Identify** What are the four most common religions in the Balkans?
   b. Analyze Why are so many different languages spoken in the Balkans?
3. **a. Define** What is **ethnic cleansing**?
   b. Elaborate Why do you think other countries sent troops to Bosnia and Herzegovina? How has the country changed since the war ended?

Critical Thinking

4. **Summarizing** Draw a chart like this one. Use your notes to write a sentence about how each topic listed in the left column affected life in the Balkans after the breakup of Yugoslavia.

   The Balkans Today

Soviet influence	
Ethnic diversity	
Religion	

FOCUS ON VIEWING

my WriteSmart

5. **Choosing a Country** Now that you have studied all of Eastern Europe, choose your topic. What information and pictures will you include?

The Breakup of Yugoslavia

Background A school playground has a limited amount of space. If many students want to use the playground at the same time, they have to work together and consider each other's feelings. Otherwise, conflict could break out.

Space on Earth is also limited. As a result, people are sometimes forced to live near people with whom they disagree. Like students on a playground, they must learn to work together to live in peace.

Yugoslavia The country of Yugoslavia was created after World War I. As a result, people from many ethnic groups—Serbs, Montenegrins, Bosnians, Croats, Slovenes, and Macedonians—lived together in one country. Each group had its own republic, or self-governed area, in the new country.

For decades, the republics of Yugoslavia worked together peacefully. People from various ethnic groups mixed within each republic. Then in 1991 Croatia, Macedonia, and Slovenia declared independence. The republic of Bosnia and Herzegovina did the same a year later. These republics were afraid Serbia wanted to take over Yugoslavia.

It appeared that they were right. Serbia's leader, Slobodan Milosevic (sloh-BOH-dahn mee-LOH-suh-vich), wanted to increase Serbia's power. He took land from other ethnic groups. He also called on Serbs who lived in other republics to vote to give Serbia more influence in the country.

Refugees Violence between ethnic groups led many people in Yugoslavia to leave their homes. The people in this photo are fleeing Bosnia to seek refuge in a safer area.

The Former Yugoslavia, 2000

Yugoslavia, 1991

Ethnic Groups
- Albanian
- Croat
- Macedonian
- Montenegrin
- Bosnian
- Serb
- Slovene
- Other or no majority

When the other republics broke away from Yugoslavia, Milosevic called on Serbs who lived there to rise up and demand that they rejoin the country. He also provided aid to Serbian military groups in these republics. In Bosnia and Herzegovina, Serbian rebels fought for three years against the Bosnian army in a destructive civil war.

Milosevic's actions caused other ethnic groups in Yugoslavia to resent the Serbs. As a result, additional violence broke out. In Croatia, for example, the army violently expelled all Serbs from their country. War raged in the area until 1995, when a peace accord was signed. As a result of that accord, Yugoslavia was dissolved. In its place were five countries that had once been Yugoslav republics.

What It Means The violent breakup of Yugoslavia has taught other countries some valuable lessons. First, it reinforced the idea that national borders are not permanent. Borders can and do change.

More importantly, however, the struggles in Yugoslavia have made some countries more aware of their people's needs. People want to feel that they have some say in their lives. When they feel as though another group is trying to take that say from them, as many in Yugoslavia felt the Serbs were doing, then trouble will often follow.

Geography for Life Activity

1. What led to the breakup of Yugoslavia?

2. Look at the maps on this page. How did the pattern of ethnic groups in Yugoslavia change between 1991 and 2000? Why do you think this is so?

3. **Investigating Ethnic Relationships** Yugoslavia is not the only country in which multiple ethnic groups lived together. Research another country in which multiple groups live together, such as Switzerland or Indonesia. How do the groups who live there live together?

Social Studies Skills

Creating a Benefits and Costs Chart

Learn

Decisions can be tough to make. A seemingly simple choice can have both positive effects, or benefits, and negative effects, or costs. Before you make a decision, it can be helpful to analyze all the possible benefits and costs that will result.

One way to analyze benefits and costs is to create a chart like the one below. On one side, list all the benefits that will result from your decision. On the other side, list the costs. Not all costs involve money. You must also consider opportunity costs, or the things that you might lose as a result of your decision. For example, going to a movie might mean that you have to miss a baseball game.

Practice

The chart to the right could have been written by an official considering whether to develop a tourism industry in Croatia. Decide whether each of the numbered items listed here should be added to the benefits column or the costs column. Once you have determined that, use the chart to decide whether the benefits of tourism outweigh the costs. Write a short paragraph to support your decision.

1. Would mean that tourist areas were not available for farming or industry

2. Would improve Croatia's image to people in other parts of the world

Tourism in Dalmatia, Croatia	
Benefits	**Costs**
■ Would create much-needed income for towns in the region	■ Would require building of hotels, airports, and roads
■ Would not require much new investment, since tourists are drawn to region's beaches and climate	■ Increase in tourism could lead to damaging of local environments
■	■
■	■

Apply

Imagine that city leaders in your area are trying to decide whether to build a new school. They cannot make a decision and have asked you to help analyze the benefits and costs of building the school. Create a chart like the one above to list those benefits and costs. Then write a brief paragraph stating whether the benefits of the plan outweigh its costs.

Chapter Review

Visual Summary

Use the visual summary below to help you review the main ideas of the chapter.

QUICK FACTS

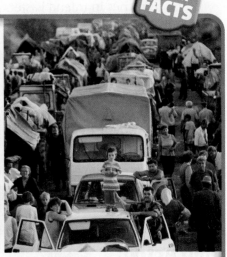

Poland and the Baltics
The history of Poland and the Baltic Republics still shapes their culture, government, and economy.

Inland Eastern Europe
Once Communist, the countries of inland Eastern Europe have stable governments and strong economies.

The Balkans
Since the breakup of Yugoslavia, the Balkans have been faced with conflict and economic challenges.

Reviewing Vocabulary, Terms, and Places

Unscramble each group of letters below to spell a term that matches the given definition.

1. **arwswa**—the capital of Poland

2. **neicht glncaenis**—the effort to remove all members of a group from a country or region

3. **ebndua**—the major river that flows through Eastern Europe, one of the longest on the continent

4. **ageurp**—the capital and largest city of the Czech Republic

5. **ncimlaitpiso**—consequences

6. **laknab**—the peninsula on which much of Eastern Europe is located

7. **ufrnrtriuacste**—the set of resources, like roads and factories, that a country needs to support economic activities

8. **nrhatcapias**—a mountain range in Eastern Europe

Comprehension and Critical Thinking

SECTION 1 *(Pages 378–381)*

9. **a. Identify** Name two major bodies of water that border Eastern Europe.

   b. Explain How do the Danube and other rivers affect life for people in Eastern Europe?

   c. Evaluate If you could live in any region of Eastern Europe, where would it be? Why?

SECTION 2 *(Pages 382–385)*

10. **a. Identify** What are the three Baltic Republics? Why are they called that?

    b. Compare and Contrast What are two cultural features that Poland and the Baltic Republics have in common? What are two features that are different in those countries?

    c. Elaborate How did the collapse of the Soviet Union affect people in Poland and the Baltic Republics?

SECTION 3 *(Pages 386–389)*

11. a. Describe What is the government of Belarus like? What type of government do the other countries of inland Eastern Europe have?

b. Draw Conclusions Why do you think that some countries in inland Eastern Europe have stronger economies than others?

c. Elaborate How has its location influenced the culture of the Czech Republic?

SECTION 4 *(Pages 390–393)*

12. a. Identify What religions are common in the Balkan countries?

b. Explain Why did countries from around the world send troops to Kosovo?

c. Predict How do you think peace will affect life in the Balkans?

Map Activity

13. Eastern Europe On a separate sheet of paper, match the letters on the map with their correct labels.

Great Hungarian Plain	Kiev, Ukraine
Latvia	Warsaw, Poland
Albania	Danube River

Using the Internet

14. Activity: Writing a Report For centuries the Balkans have been an arena of conflict. Through your online textbook, learn about the history and cultures of the Balkans and investigate recent conflicts there. Write a report on what you find.

 hmhsocialstudies.com

Social Studies Skills

15. Creating a Benefits and Costs Chart Imagine that you are a government official in Ukraine. Your country cannot produce enough energy to meet its needs and has to buy energy from Russia. A company in Kiev has expressed interest in building nuclear power plants, but many people are leery of nuclear power since the Chernobyl incident. Create a chart that lists the costs and benefits of nuclear power. Then write a statement that either supports or argues against the plan.

FOCUS ON READING AND VIEWING *my*WriteSmart

16. Understanding Problems and Solutions Re-read the first paragraph under the heading The Region Today in Section 2. Then write a short paragraph that explains the main problem facing Poland and the Baltics today. End your paragraph by suggesting a solution their governments might use to address the problem.

17. Making a Presentation Use *my*WriteSmart in your eBook to write a brief report about a country in Eastern Europe and prepare a poster that illustrates your main ideas. Find pictures of major features of your chosen country and arrange them on a poster board. Write a short caption that explains what each picture is. Present your report to the class. As you discuss each main idea, point out the pictures that illustrate it on your poster. Speak clearly and keep eye contact with your audience. Then, take notes to enhance and confirm your understanding of the main ideas as you listen to your peers present their reports and posters.

Reading Social Studies

Understanding Problems and Solutions

Throughout history, people have faced problems and found solutions to them. As a result, writers who describe historical events often structure their writing by identifying a problem and then describing its solution. The ability to identify this pattern of writing will help you understand what you read. Notice how the following passage presents one problem with a two-pronged solution.

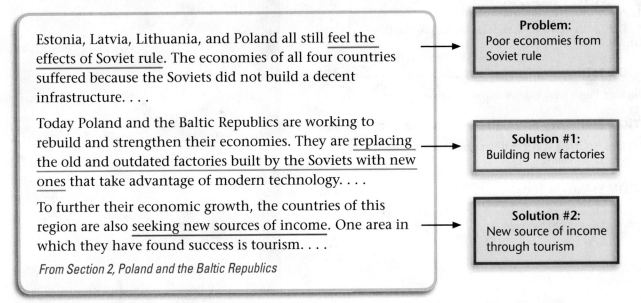

Estonia, Latvia, Lithuania, and Poland all still feel the effects of Soviet rule. The economies of all four countries suffered because the Soviets did not build a decent infrastructure. . . .

Today Poland and the Baltic Republics are working to rebuild and strengthen their economies. They are replacing the old and outdated factories built by the Soviets with new ones that take advantage of modern technology. . . .

To further their economic growth, the countries of this region are also seeking new sources of income. One area in which they have found success is tourism. . . .

From Section 2, Poland and the Baltic Republics

Problem:
Poor economies from Soviet rule

Solution #1:
Building new factories

Solution #2:
New source of income through tourism

YOU TRY IT!

Read the following passage, and then use the process shown above to identify the problems and solutions the writer presents. Create as many boxes as you need.

Many Eastern Europeans opposed Communist rule, and eventually the Communist governments in the region fell. Poland rejected Communism and elected new leaders in 1989. The Baltic Republics broke away from the Soviet Union in 1991 and became independent once more.

From Section 2, Poland and the Baltic Republics

17
Russia

Essential Question

myNotebook

What cultural and geographic features help define Russia?

Texas Essential Knowledge and Skills (TEKS)

1A, 1B, 2A, 2B, 3A, 3B, 3C, 4D, 4E, 4F, 5A, 5B, 5C, 6A, 6B, 15A, 15B, 15F, 17D, 17E, 19A, 21B, 21C, 21D, 22D

FOCUS ON READING AND WRITING

my WriteSmart

Making Generalizations A generalization is a broad, general idea drawn from new information combined with what you already know. As you read this chapter, stop now and then to make a generalization. It will help you pull the pieces of information together and make sense of them. **See the lesson, Making Generalizations, on page 419**.

Creating a Real Estate Ad As you read this chapter, imagine you work for a real estate agency in Russia. You are trying to sell a piece of property there. In order to sell the property, you must write an ad to be published in the newspaper and on the Internet. As you read, decide where your property would be located and what its characteristics would be. Use the annotation tools in your eBook to gather information for your assignment.

Geography A volcano created Crater Bay in the Kuril Islands off the east coast of Russia. The islands have several active volcanoes.

ARCTIC OCEAN

Barents Sea

Bering Strait

PACIFIC OCEAN

RUSSIA

Ob River

Yenisey River

Angara River

Lena River

Amur River

Novosibirsk

Lake Baikal

Sea of Okhotsk

Kuril Islands

Sakhalin Island

Vladivostok

Sea of Japan (East Sea)

JAPAN

MONGOLIA

CHINA

HISTORY   The Romanovs

hmhsocialstudies.com   VIDEO

map zone   Geography Skills

Regions Russia, the world's largest country, lies north and east of the Eurasian republics.

1. **Name** What ocean lies north of Russia?
2. **Contrast** How does the land and size of Russia differ from that of the other countries in this region?

Culture The Bolshoi Ballet in Moscow, Russia, is famous throughout the world. Above, dancers perform *Swan Lake*.

History The Kremlin complex houses Russia's government as well as gold-domed churches and beautiful, historical palaces.

TEKS 3A, 3B, 3C, 4D, 4E, 5A, 5B, 5C, 6A, 6B, 21B, 21C, 22D

Physical Geography

What You Will Learn...

Main Ideas

1. The physical features of Russia include plains, mountains, and rivers.
2. Climate and plant life change from north to south in Russia.
3. Russia has a wealth of resources, but many are hard to access.

The Big Idea

Russia is big and cold with vast plains and forests.

Key Terms and Places

Ural Mountains, *p. 402*
Moscow, *p. 402*
Siberia, *p. 402*
Volga River, *p. 404*
taiga, *p. 405*

hmhsocialstudies.com
TAKING NOTES

Use the graphic organizer online to take notes on the physical geography of Russia.

If YOU lived there...

You are making a documentary about the Trans-Siberian Railroad, a famous train that crosses the vast country of Russia. The train travels more than 5,700 miles across plains and mountains and through thick forests. As the train leaves the city of Moscow, you look out the window and see wheat fields and white birch trees.

What scenes might you include in your film?

BUILDING BACKGROUND Look at a globe, and you will see that Russia extends nearly halfway around the world. Russia is the world's largest country. It is so vast that it spans 11 time zones. While huge, much of Russia consists of flat or rolling plains.

Physical Features

Have you ever stood on two continents at once? In Russia's **Ural** (YOOHR-uhl) **Mountains**, you can. There, the continents of Europe and Asia meet. Europe lies to the west; Asia to the east. Together, Europe and Asia form the large landmass of Eurasia. On the map, you can see that a large chunk of Eurasia is the country of Russia. In fact, Russia is the world's largest country. Compared to the United States, Russia is almost twice as big.

Landforms

Locate Russia on the physical map on the following page. As the map shows, Russia's landforms vary from west to east. The Northern European Plain stretches across western, or European, Russia. This fertile plain forms Russia's heartland, where most Russians live. **Moscow**, Russia's capital, is located there.

To the east, the plain rises to form the Ural Mountains. These low mountains are worn down and rounded from erosion. The vast area between the Urals and the Pacific Ocean is **Siberia**. This area includes several landforms, as you can see on the physical map of Russia on the next page.

ARCTIC OCEAN

Bering Sea

PACIFIC OCEAN

KOLYMA MTS.

KAMCHATKA PENINSULA

North Sea

Barents Sea

TAYMYR PENINSULA

CHERSKIY RANGE

Sea of Okhotsk

Baltic Sea

NORTHERN EUROPEAN PLAIN

Sakhalin Island

Kuril Islands

EUROPE

SIBERIA

WEST SIBERIAN PLAIN

CENTRAL SIBERIAN PLATEAU

Yenisey R.

Ob River

RUSSIA

Lena R.

Lena River

Don R.

Volga R.

URAL MOUNTAINS

KUZNETSK BASIN

Black Sea

CAUCASUS MTS.

Lake Baikal

STANOVOY MTS.

Amur R.

Mt. Elbrus 18,510 ft (5,642 m)

Caspian Sea

SAYAN MTS.

YABLONOVY RANGE

Sea of Japan (East Sea)

SOUTHWEST ASIA

EAST ASIA

map zone **Geography Skills**

Regions The Ural Mountains in Russia separate the continents of Europe and Asia.

1. Locate What part of Russia is called Siberia?

2. Interpret In what ways might mountains affect life in eastern Russia?

ELEVATION

Feet	Meters
13,120	4,000
6,560	2,000
1,640	500
656	200
(Sea level) 0	0 (Sea level)
Below sea level	Below sea level

0   500   1,000 Miles

0   500   1,000 Kilometers

Projection: Two-Point Equidistant

The West Siberian Plain lies between the Urals and the Yenisey River and between the shores of the Arctic Ocean and the foothills of the Altay Mountains. Because the plain tilts northward, its rivers flow toward the Arctic Ocean. The West Siberian Plain is a flat, marshy area. It is one of the largest plains in the world.

East of this plain is an upland called the Central Siberian Plateau. Mountain ranges run through southern and eastern Siberia.

Eastern Siberia is called the Russian Far East. This area includes the Kamchatka (kuhm-CHAHT-kuh) Peninsula and several islands. The Russian Far East is part of the Ring of Fire, the area circling the Pacific.

1 The Kamchatka Peninsula on Russia's east coast has many old and active volcanoes.

The Ring of Fire is known for its volcanoes and earthquakes, and the Russian Far East is no exception. The Kamchatka Peninsula alone contains 120 volcanoes, 20 of which are still active. In some areas, steam from within Earth breaks free to form geysers and hot springs. The Sakhalin and Kuril islands lie south of the peninsula. Russia seized the islands from Japan after World War II. Japan still claims ownership of the Kuril Islands.

Bodies of Water

Some of the longest rivers in the world flow through the region. One of the most important is the **Volga** (VAHL-guh) **River** in western Russia. The longest river in Europe, the Volga winds southward to the Caspian Sea. The Volga has long formed the core of Russia's river network. Canals link the Volga to the nearby Don River and to the Baltic Sea.

Even longer rivers than the Volga flow through Siberia in the Asian part of Russia. The Ob (AWB), Yenisey (yi-ni-SAY), and Lena rivers flow northward to the Arctic Ocean. Like many of Russia's rivers, they are frozen for much of the year. The ice often hinders shipping and trade and closes some of Russia's ports for part of the year.

In addition to its rivers, Russia has some 200,000 lakes. Lake Baikal (by-KAHL), in south-central Siberia, is the world's deepest lake. Although not that large in surface area, Lake Baikal is deep enough to hold all the water in all five of the Great Lakes. Because of its beauty, Lake Baikal is called the Jewel of Siberia. Logging and factories have polluted the water, but Russians are now working to clean up the lake.

READING CHECK **Summarizing** What are the major landforms in Russia?

Russia's Climate and Plant Life

In the photo on the left, Russians bundled up in furs hurry through the snow and cold of Moscow, the capital. In the photo on the right, evergreen forest called *taiga* blankets a Russian plain. In the distance, the low Ural Mountains mark the division between Europe and Asia.

Climate and Plant Life

Russians sometimes joke that winter lasts for 12 months and then summer begins. Russia is a cold country. The reason is its northern location partly within the Arctic Circle. In general, Russia has short summers and long, snowy winters. The climate is milder west of the Urals and grows colder and harsher as one goes north and east.

Russia's northern coast is tundra. Winters are dark and bitterly cold, and the brief summers are cool. Much of the ground is permafrost, or permanently frozen soil. Only small plants such as mosses grow.

Distance from the sea affects the amount of precipitation the region gets, as well as its temperatures. Most of the region's moisture comes from the Atlantic Ocean. The air coming from the ocean loses its moisture as it travels farther and farther inland.

South of the tundra is a vast forest of evergreen trees called **taiga** (TY-guh). This huge forest covers about half of Russia. In Siberia, snow covers the taiga much of the year. South of the taiga is a flat grassland called the steppe (STEP). With rich, black soil and a warmer climate, the steppe is Russia's most important farming area.

READING CHECK **Finding Main Ideas** How does Russia's location affect its climate?

Natural Resources

Russia has a wealth of resources. The Northern European Plain and the steppe provide fertile soil for farming. The taiga provides wood for building and paper products. Metals such as copper and gold and precious gems such as diamonds provide useful raw materials.

Russia's main energy resources are coal, hydroelectricity, natural gas, and oil.

Russia has large oil and gas fields. Oil also lies beneath the Caspian Sea.

Russia's natural resources have been poorly managed, however. Until the early 1990s this region was part of the Soviet Union. The Soviet government put more importance on industry than on managing its resources. In Russia, many of the resources that were easy to access are gone. For example, most of the timber in western Russia has been cut down. Many remaining resources are in remote Siberia.

READING CHECK **Analyzing** Why are some of Russia's natural resources difficult to obtain?

SUMMARY AND PREVIEW Russia is big and cold, with vast plains and forests. The region also has many natural resources. Next, you will read about Russia's history and culture.

FOCUS ON READING

What general idea can you draw from the text about natural resources? What facts or details support that idea?

Section 1 Assessment

hmhsocialstudies.com
ONLINE QUIZ

Reviewing Ideas, Terms, and Places

1. **a. Describe** Why are the **Ural Mountains** significant?
   b. Draw Conclusions Why might the Russian Far East be a dangerous place to live?
2. **a. Describe** What are winters like in much of Russia?
   b. Analyze How does climate affect Russia's plant life?
3. **a. Recall** What valuable resource is in the Caspian Sea?
   b. Make Inferences Why might resources located in remote, cold areas be difficult to use?

Critical Thinking

4. **Generalizing** Draw a chart like the one here. Use your notes and enter one general idea for each topic in the chart.

Physical Features	
Climate and Plants	
Natural Resources	

FOCUS ON WRITING   *my* WriteSmart

5. **Describing the Physical Geography** Now that you know the physical geography of the region, make a list of possible locations for the house or land you are selling.

What You Will Learn...

Main Ideas

1. The Russian Empire grew under powerful leaders, but unrest and war led to its end.
2. The Soviet Union emerged as a Communist superpower with rigid government control.
3. Russia's history and diversity have influenced its culture.

The Big Idea

Strict rule, unrest, and ethnic diversity have shaped Russia's history and culture.

Key Terms and Places

Kiev, *p. 406*
Cyrillic, *p. 406*
czar, *p. 407*
Bolsheviks, *p. 407*
gulags, *p. 408*

hmhsocialstudies.com
TAKING NOTES

Use the graphic organizer online to take notes on the history and culture of Russia.

History and Culture of Russia

If YOU lived there...

It is 1992, an exciting time in your home town of Moscow. At the end of 1991 the Soviet Union fell apart. Russia became independent. You watched on TV as people pulled down the red Soviet flag and knocked down statues of former leaders. Everyone is talking about new freedoms and a new kind of government.

What new freedoms do you hope to have?

BUILDING BACKGROUND The fall of the Soviet Union was not the first time Russia had experienced change. For centuries Russia was part of a great empire. Then in the early 1900s Communists overthrew the empire. The Soviet Union was born. Today it too is gone.

The Russian Empire

Russia's roots lie in the grassy, windswept plains of the steppe. For thousands of years, people from Asia moved across the steppe. These groups of people included the Slavs. As you read in the last chapter, the Slavs settled in Eastern Europe, including what is now Ukraine and western Russia.

Early History and Empire

The Slavs developed towns and began trading with people from other areas. In the AD 800s, Viking traders from Scandinavia invaded the Slavs. These Vikings were called Rus (ROOS), and the word *Russia* probably comes from their name. The Vikings shaped the first Russian state among the Slavs. This Russian state, called Kievan (KEE-e-fuhn) Rus, centered around the city of **Kiev**. This city is now the capital of Ukraine.

Over time, missionaries introduced the Orthodox Christian faith to Kiev. In addition, the missionaries introduced a form of the Greek alphabet called **Cyrillic** (suh-RI-lik). The Russians adopted this Cyrillic alphabet and still use it today.

Russia, 1462–1533

Territory gained
- by 1689
- by 1725
- by 1801
- by 1945
— Russian boundary, 1993

0   250   500 Miles
0 250 500 Kilometers

*Projection:
Two-Point Equidistant*

Baltic republics: independent 1918–1940 and 1991

Finland: Russian territory 1809–1918

Poland: Russian territory 1815–1918

Russian territory 1871–1881

map zone Geography Skills

Location The colors in the map show the growth of the Russian Empire and of the Soviet Union over time.
1. **Name** What city is located in territory gained by 1725?
2. **Interpret** When was the period of greatest expansion?

In the 1200s, fierce Mongol invaders called Tatars (TAH-ters) swept out of Central Asia and conquered Kiev. The Mongols allowed Russian princes to rule over local states. In time, Muscovy became the strongest state. Its main city was Moscow.

After about 200 years Muscovy's prince, Ivan III, seized control from the Mongols. In the 1540s his grandson, Ivan IV, crowned himself **czar** (ZAHR), or emperor. *Czar* is Russian for "caesar." As czar, Ivan IV had total power. A cruel and savage ruler, he became known as Ivan the Terrible.

In time, Muscovy developed into the country of Russia. Strong czars such as Peter the Great (1682–1725) and Catherine the Great (1762–1796) built Russia into a huge empire and a world power. This empire included many conquered peoples.

In spite of its growth, Russia remained largely a country of poor farmers, while the czars and nobles had most of the wealth. In the early 1900s Russians began demanding improvements. The czar agreed to some changes, but unrest continued to grow.

War and Revolution

In 1914 Russia entered World War I. The country suffered huge losses in the war. In addition, the Russian people experienced severe shortages of food. When the czar seemed to ignore the people's hardship, they rose up against him. He was forced to give up his throne in 1917.

Later that year the **Bolsheviks**, a radical Russian Communist group, seized power in the Russian Revolution. They then killed the czar and his family. In 1922 the Bolsheviks formed a new country, the Union of Soviet Socialist Republics (USSR), or the Soviet Union. It soon included 15 republics, the strongest of which was Russia. The first leader was Vladimir Lenin.

READING CHECK **Sequencing** What series of events led to the creation of the Soviet Union?

HISTORY

VIDEO
The Romanovs

↗ hmhsocialstudies.com

The Soviet Union

The Soviet Union, led by Lenin, became a Communist country. In this political system, the government owns all property and controls all aspects of life. In 1924 Lenin died. Joseph Stalin took power, ruling as a brutal and paranoid dictator.

The Soviet Union under Stalin

FOCUS ON READING
Based on the Soviet Union's economy, what generalization might you make about command economies?

Under Stalin, the Soviet Union set up a command economy. In this system, the government owns all businesses and farms and makes all decisions. People were told what to make and how much to charge. Without competition, though, efficiency and the quality of goods fell over time.

The Soviet Union strictly controlled its people as well as its economy. Stalin had anyone who spoke out against the government jailed, exiled, or killed. Millions of people were sent to **gulags**, harsh Soviet labor camps often located in Siberia.

Cold War and Collapse

During World War II, the Soviet Union fought with the Allies against Germany. Millions of Soviet citizens died in the war. Stalin's <u>reaction</u> to the war was to build a buffer around the Soviet Union to protect it from invasion. To do so, he set up Communist governments in Eastern Europe.

ACADEMIC VOCABULARY
reaction
a response to something

The United States opposed communism and saw its spread as a threat to democracy. This opposition led to the Cold War, a period of tense rivalry between the Soviet Union and the United States. The two rival countries became superpowers as they competed to have superior weapons.

In part because of the high costs of weapons, the Soviet economy was near collapse by the 1980s. Mikhail Gorbachev (GAWR-buh-chawf), the Soviet leader, began making changes. He reduced government control and introduced some democracy.

Despite his actions, the Soviet republics began pushing for independence. In 1991 the Soviet Union collapsed. It broke apart into 15 independent countries, including Russia. The Soviet Union was no more.

READING CHECK Analyzing How did the Cold War help lead to the Soviet Union's collapse?

Culture

In the Soviet Union, the government had controlled culture just like everything else. Today, however, Russian culture is once again alive and vibrant.

People and Religion

Russia is big and diverse, with more than 140 million people. About 80 percent are ethnic Russians, or Slavs, but Russia also has many other ethnic groups. The largest are the Tatars and Ukrainians. Russia's many ethnic groups are once again taking great pride in their cultures.

Like ethnic culture, religious worship has seen a revival. The Soviet government opposed religion and closed many houses of worship. Today many have reopened, including historic Russian cathedrals with their onion-shaped domes. The main faith is Russian Orthodox Christian. Other religions include other forms of Christianity, Islam, Judaism, and Buddhism.

Customs

Russian history has shaped its customs, such as holidays. Religious holidays, like Easter and Christmas, are popular. The main family holiday is New Year's Eve. To celebrate this holiday, families decorate a tree where, according to Russian folklore, Grandfather Frost and his helper the Snow Maiden leave gifts. A newer holiday is Russian Independence Day, which marks the end of the Soviet Union on June 12.

St. Basil's Cathedral

Colorful St. Basil's Cathedral, in Moscow's Red Square, has become a symbol of Russia. Czar Ivan IV had the cathedral built between 1555 and 1561 in honor of Russian military victories. According to legend, Ivan had the architects blinded so they could never design anything else as magnificent.

Steeply sloped towers, called tent roofs, and onion-shaped domes easily shed snow.

Onion-shaped domes, based on Byzantine designs, decorate many early Russian churches.

St. Basil's Cathedral houses nine small, separate chapels.

In 1588 a chapel was added for the tomb of St. Basil the Blessed, a popular saint in Russia. In time, his name became linked to the cathedral.

ANALYSIS SKILL **ANALYZING VISUALS**

Besides onion domes, what other shapes and patterns are visible on the cathedral?

Communist-era Poster

The Soviet Union used posters as propaganda. Propaganda is information designed to promote a specific cause or idea by influencing people's thoughts and beliefs. For example, Soviet posters often promoted the greatness and power of the Soviet state, its leaders, and their Communist policies.

The message of this 1924 poster reads, "Long live the Young Communist League! The young are taking over the older generation's torch!"

The color red in this poster symbolizes communism and the Russian Revolution.

ANALYSIS SKILL **ANALYZING PRIMARY SOURCES**

How do you think the poster's images and message influenced Soviet teens at the time?

The Arts and Sciences

Russia has made great contributions in the arts and sciences. In the performing arts, Russia's ballet companies are world famous for their skill. In music, Peter Tchaikovsky (chy-KAWF-skee) is Russia's most famous composer. His many works include *The Nutcracker* ballet and the *1812 Overture.*

In the material arts, Russia's Fabergé eggs are priceless. Gifts for the czars, these eggs are made of precious metals and covered with gems such as emeralds and rubies. Each egg opens to reveal a tiny surprise.

In the sciences, Russia has contributed to space research. In 1957 the Soviet Union launched Sputnik, the first artificial satellite in space. Russian scientists now help work on the International Space Station.

READING CHECK **Generalizing** How did the end of the Soviet Union affect Russian culture?

SUMMARY AND PREVIEW The history of Russia, from a great empire to a Communist superpower to a new nation, has shaped its rich culture. Next, you will read about life in Russia today.

Section 2 Assessment

hmhsocialstudies.com
ONLINE QUIZ

Reviewing Ideas, Terms, and Places

1. **a. Define** Who were the **czars**?
   b. Analyze What role did the city of **Kiev** play in Russian history?
   c. Elaborate What problems and events caused the Russian Empire to decline?
2. **a. Identify** Why are Vladimir Lenin and Joseph Stalin significant in Russian history?
   b. Evaluate Do you think life in the Soviet Union was an improvement over life in the Russian empire? Why, or why not?
3. **a. Recall** What is the main religion in Russia?
   b. Summarize How has Russian culture changed since the collapse of the Soviet Union in 1991?

Critical Thinking

4. **Sequencing** Draw a chart like the one here. Use your notes to list the order of the major events leading up to the collapse of the Soviet Union.

   ○ → ○ → ○ → ○

FOCUS ON WRITING

my WriteSmart

5. **Considering Russia's History and Culture** Look at the locations you listed for Section 1. For the Russian locations, make notes about historical or cultural details you could include in your ad.

Social Studies Skills

Interpreting a Population Map

Learn

Population maps give you a snapshot of the distribution of people in a region or country. Each color on a population map represents an average number of people living within a square mile or square kilometer. Sometimes symbols identify the cities with populations of a certain size. The map's legend identifies what the colors and symbols in the map mean.

Practice

1. Based on the map below, in which region of Russia do most of the country's people live?

2. Which two cities in Russia have the largest population?

3. How many Russian cities have more than 1 million people?

Russia: Population

Persons per square mile	Persons per square km
520	200
260	100
130	50
25	10
3	1
0	0

Major cities
- Over 2 million
- 1 to 2 million
- Under 1 million

0   500   1,000 Miles
0   500   1,000 Kilometers

Projection: Two-Point Equidistant

Apply

Use an atlas to locate a current population map of the United States. Using the map, identify where the most and the least populated regions of the United States are. Then identify the number of U.S. cities or metropolitan areas with more than 2 million people.

Russia Today

TEKS 1A, 1B, 2A, 2B, 15A, 15B, 15F, 17D, 17E, 19A, 21B, 21C, 21D, 22D

What You Will Learn...

Main Ideas

1. The Russian Federation is working to develop democracy and a market economy.
2. Russia's physical geography, cities, and economy define its many culture regions.
3. Russia faces a number of serious challenges.

The Big Idea

Russia is a federal republic with a growing market economy but faces tough challenges.

Key Terms and Places

dachas, *p. 413*
St. Petersburg, *p. 414*
smelters, *p. 415*
Trans-Siberian Railroad, *p. 415*
Chechnya, *p. 416*

hmhsocialstudies.com
TAKING NOTES

Use the graphic organizer online to take notes on Russia today.

If YOU lived there...

You live in St. Petersburg, a city of beautiful palaces and canals. You are looking forward to the end of school, when your family will go to their dacha, a cottage in the country. In midsummer, when the nights are long and the sun never really sets, you will go to concerts and other celebrations of the "White Nights" in your city.

What do you like about living in St. Petersburg?

BUILDING BACKGROUND Russians have always had a special feeling for the countryside, from the wheat fields and birch forests in the west to the endless grasslands of the steppe. But Russia's great cities are exciting, too, with many shops, museums, and events.

The Russian Federation

For decades, the Soviet Union reigned as a superpower, with Russia as its strongest republic. Then in 1991 the Soviet Union broke apart. Russia's leaders had to create a new government as they struggled to change from communism to democracy.

Government

The Russian Federation is a federal republic, a system in which power is divided between national and local governments. The voters elect a president to serve as the country's chief executive, Russia's most powerful official. The president appoints a prime minister to serve as the head of the government. A legislature, called the Federal Assembly, makes the country's laws.

Increased democracy has led to more freedom for Russians. Voters can choose from several political parties. Information flows more freely. The government no longer seeks to control every aspect of life. In addition, the move toward democracy has improved relations between Russia and Western nations.

Changing to a democratic system has been difficult, though. Problems such as government corruption, or dishonesty, have slowed the development of a free society in Russia. Time will tell whether Russia will continue to grow as a democracy.

Economy

With the move to democracy, Russia also began shifting to a market economy. This type of economy is based on free trade and competition. Today the Russian government has greatly reduced its control of the economy, and most businesses and farms are now privately owned. These changes have led to economic growth. At the same time, most of Russia's wealth is now in the hands of a small number of people.

Today Russia produces and exports oil, natural gas, timber, metals, and chemicals. Heavy industry, such as machinery, is still important. However, light industry, such as clothing and electronics, has grown. Furthermore, service industries now make up the largest part of Russia's economy.

In agriculture, Russia is now a major grower and exporter of grains. Other major crops are fruits, potatoes, and sugar beets.

City and Rural Life

The changes sweeping Russia are visible in its cities. More restaurants and shopping centers are available. Stores offer a wider range of consumer goods, such as TVs. Some Russians have become wealthy and can afford luxuries. In fact, in 2005 Russia had more billionaires than any other European country. Nevertheless, the average Russian's standard of living remains low.

About 75 percent of all Russians live in cities. Most of these people live in small apartments in high-rise buildings. In rural areas, more people live in houses.

Although most Russians live in cities, they still have access to nature. Cities often have large parks and wooded areas in and around them. Many richer Russians own **dachas**, or Russian country houses, where they can garden and enjoy the fresh air.

READING CHECK **Summarizing** How has Russia changed since it became independent?

CONNECTING TO Economics

Kaliningrad

The small region of Kaliningrad—only slightly bigger than Connecticut—is more than 200 miles (320 km) from the rest of Russia. So why would Russia want this area? The reason has to do with the country's cold climate. Kaliningrad is Russia's only Baltic seaport that is free of ice all year. This important port provides Russia with year-round access to profitable European markets and trade. Railroads connect the port to Russia's major cities, as the map below shows.

Drawing Conclusions How do you think Russia's economy benefits from a Baltic seaport that is free of ice all year?

Culture Regions

You have learned that Russia is vast and diverse. For this reason, we divide Russia into several culture regions, as the map on the next page shows. These regions differ in **features** such as population, natural resources, and economic activity.

The four western culture regions make up Russia's heartland. This area is home to the vast majority of Russia's people as well as to the country's capital and largest cities. In addition, the fertile plains of Russia's heartland are the country's most productive farming area.

ACADEMIC VOCABULARY

features
characteristics

1 St. Petersburg's State Hermitage Museum, once the Winter Palace of the czars, now houses priceless works of art.

2 Moscow is Russia's capital and largest city. It is a political, cultural, and transportation center.

3 In Siberia, a Nenets woman leads a group of decorated reindeer as part of a village festival.

The Moscow Region

Moscow is Russia's capital and largest city. The sprawling, modern city has wide boulevards and large public squares. Its many cultural attractions include the world-famous Bolshoi Ballet and Moscow Circus.

At Moscow's heart is the Kremlin, the center of Russia's government. In Russian, *kremlin* means "fortress." The Kremlin consists of several buildings surrounded by a wall and towers. The buildings include not only government offices but also palaces, museums, and gold-domed churches.

Next to the Kremlin is Red Square, an immense plaza. It is lined by many famous landmarks, such as St. Basil's Cathedral.

The Moscow region is Russia's most important economic area, and its factories produce a wide range of goods. The city is also a transportation center and links by road, rail, and plane to all parts of Russia.

The St. Petersburg Region

St. Petersburg reflects Russians' desire for Western ways. Peter the Great founded the city and styled it after those of Western Europe. For some 200 years, St. Petersburg served as Russia's capital and home to the czars. It features wide avenues, grand palaces, and numerous canals. Theaters and museums enrich the city's cultural life.

PACIFIC OCEAN

Sea of Okhotsk

40°N

Culture Regions

- Moscow
- St. Petersburg
- Volga
- Urals
- Siberia
- Far East

0   300   600 Miles

0   300   600 Kilometers

Projection: Two-Point Equidistant

map zone **Geography Skills**

Regions Russia's culture regions differ in their resources, economic activity, and other features.
1. **Identify** What are the six culture regions?
2. **Interpret** Which geographic feature separates the Urals culture region from regions farther west?

The Ural Mountains are an important mining region and produce nearly every major mineral. **Smelters**, factories that process metal ores, process copper and iron. The Urals region is also known for gems and semiprecious stones.

Siberia

East of the Urals lies the vast expanse of Siberia. In the Tatar language, *Siberia* means "Sleeping Land." Siberian winters are long and severe. As you have read, much of the land lies frozen or buried under snow for most or all of the year. The remote region has many valuable resources, but accessing them in the harsh climate is difficult.

Siberia's main industries are lumber, mining, and oil production. Large coal deposits are mined in southwest Siberia. Rivers produce hydroelectric power. The southern steppes, where the weather is warmer, are Siberia's main farmlands.

Because of Siberia's harsh climate, jobs there pay high wages. Even so, few people choose to live in Siberia. Most towns and cities are in the western and southern parts of the region. These cities tend to follow the **Trans-Siberian Railroad**. This rail line runs from Moscow to Vladivostok on the east coast, and is the longest single rail line in the world.

The Russian Far East

Russia has a long coastline on the Pacific Ocean. There, in the Russian Far East, much land remains heavily forested. In the few cities, factories process forest and mineral resources. Farming occurs in the Amur River valley. The city of Vladivostok is a naval base and the area's main seaport. Islands off the coast provide oil, minerals, and commercial fishing.

READING CHECK **Finding Main Ideas** What areas make up Russia's culture regions?

FOCUS ON READING
Based on this description of Siberia, what generalization about human settlement can you make?

St. Petersburg's location on the Gulf of Finland has made the city a major port and trade center. This northern location also produces "White Nights," a period during summer when it never gets totally dark.

The Volga and Urals Regions

The Volga River and Ural Mountains are the third and fourth culture regions. The broad Volga is a major shipping route. Dams along its course form lakes and provide hydroelectric power. Factories in the area process oil and gas. In addition, a site on the Caspian Sea provides fish called sturgeon. The eggs of this fish are called black caviar, which is a costly delicacy, or rare and valued food.

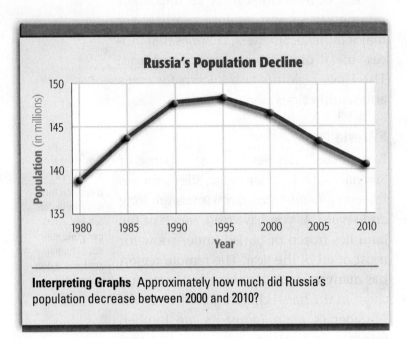

Russia's Population Decline

Population (in millions)

150

145

140

135

1980 1985 1990 1995 2000 2005 2010

Year

Interpreting Graphs Approximately how much did Russia's population decrease between 2000 and 2010?

Second, Russia's population is falling, as you can see in the graph. More Russians are dying than are being born. One reason is that many Russians cannot afford good health care.

Third, the Soviet government did little to prevent pollution. As a result pollution, such as industrial chemicals, has seriously harmed Russia's environment. The government must now repair the damage.

Last, Russia faces ethnic conflicts. One of the worst is in the Russian republic of **Chechnya** (CHECH-nyah) in the Caucasus Mountains. Some people in this Muslim area want independence. Fighting and terrorism there have caused many deaths.

READING CHECK **Categorizing** What social, economic, and political challenges face Russia?

Russia's Challenges

Although Russia has made great progress since 1991, challenges remain. First, Russia's shift to a market economy has not been without problems. For example, prices and unemployment have risen, and the gap between rich and poor has widened.

SUMMARY AND PREVIEW As you have read, Russia is a federal republic working to build a market economy. The west is Russia's heartland, but Siberia has many valuable resources. In the next section, you will read about the Eurasian Republics.

Section 3 Assessment

hmhsocialstudies.com
ONLINE QUIZ

Reviewing Ideas, Terms, and Places

1. **a. Recall** What type of government does Russia now have?
   b. Explain How is Russia's economy changing?
2. **a. Recall** From west to east, what are Russia's major culture regions?
   b. Draw Conclusions Why do you think most Siberian towns and cities are located along the **Trans-Siberian Railroad**?
   c. Rate Which of Russia's culture regions would you most want to live in, and why?
3. **a. Identify** What are the main challenges that face Russia today?
   b. Elaborate What difficulties does **Chechnya** pose for Russia's leaders?

Critical Thinking

4. **Categorizing** Draw a concept web like the one shown. Use your notes to list facts about each Russian culture region.

Russia's Culture Regions

FOCUS ON WRITING   *my* WriteSmart

5. **Collecting Details about Russia Today** Based on conditions in Russia today, what location would you choose for your property? Review your notes from Section 2 and this section. Then choose one location in Russia for the property you are selling.

Chapter Review

Visual Summary

Use the visual summary below to help you review the main ideas of the chapter.

QUICK FACTS

Russia is an immense, cold country with plains, mountains, and forest.

With a long history and a rich culture, Russia ranges from large modern cities to the vast plains and forests of Siberia.

Russia's six distinct culture regions differ in population, natural resources, and economic activity.

Reviewing Vocabulary, Terms, and Places

For each statement below, write T *if it is true and* F *if it is false. If the statement is false, replace the boldfaced term with one that makes the sentence a true statement.*

1. The **Caucasus Mountains** separate European Russia from Asian Russia.

2. Russia's capital and largest city is **St. Petersburg**.

3. Under the rule of the **Bolsheviks**, the Russian Empire expanded in size and power.

4. Many wealthier Russians have country houses, which are called **gulags**.

5. Russia's main government buildings are located in the **Kremlin** in Moscow.

6. Russia's culture regions differ in **features** such as cities, natural resources, and economic activity.

7. **Moscow** is a major port and was once home to Russia's czars.

Comprehension and Critical Thinking

SECTION 1 *(Pages 402–405)*

8. **a. Recall** What is Russia's most important river, and to what major bodies of water does it link?

b. Identify Cause and Effect How does Russia's location affect its climate?

c. Elaborate Why might developing the many natural resources in Siberia be difficult?

SECTION 2 *(Pages 406–410)*

9. **a. Identify** Who was Joseph Stalin?

b. Summarize How has Russia contributed to world culture?

c. Elaborate How was the end of the Soviet Union similar to the end of the Russian Empire?

10. **a. Identify** What four culture regions make up the Russian heartland?

    b. Compare and Contrast How are Moscow and St. Petersburg similar and different?

    c. Elaborate How might Siberia help make Russia an economic success?

Using the Internet

11. **Activity: Making a Map** The Trans-Siberian Railroad is the longest single rail line in the world. Climb aboard in Moscow and travel all the way across Russia. Through your online textbook, research the people, places, and history along the railroad's route. Then create an illustrated map of your journey. On the map, show the train's route, indicate the places where you stopped, and include images and descriptions about what you saw.

    ⤷ hmhsocialstudies.com

Social Studies Skills

Interpreting a Population Map *Use a good atlas to find a population map of Europe. The map does not need to include Russia. Use the map to answer the following questions. Do not include the country of Russia when answering the questions.*

12. Not including the cities of Russia, how many cities or metropolitan areas in Europe have more than 2 million people?

13. Not including Russia, which regions of Europe are the most populated? Which regions of Europe are the least populated?

Map Activity

14. **Russia** On a separate sheet of paper, match the letters on the map with their correct labels.

Caspian Sea	Ural Mountains
Kamchatka Peninsula	Vladivostok, Russia
Moscow, Russia	Volga River
St. Petersburg, Russia	West Siberian Plain

FOCUS ON READING AND WRITING *my* WriteSmart

15. **Making Generalizations** Examine the information in Section 3 about the four culture regions that make up Russia's heartland. Based on the specific information about these regions, make two generalizations about western Russia.

16. **Creating a Real Estate Ad** Review your notes about locations in Russia. Choose one location for the real estate you are selling. What are its best features? How would you describe the land and climate? What are the benefits of living there? If it is a building, what does it look like? What is nearby? Use *my*WriteSmart in your eBook to answer these questions in your real estate ad. Remember to include details that will make the property attractive to possible buyers.

Reading Social Studies

Making Generalizations

As you read about different people and cultures, you probably realize that people share some similarities. Seeing those similarities may lead you to make a generalization. A generalization is a broad, general idea drawn from new information combined with what you already know, such as your own experience. Notice how this process works with the following passage.

> Russians sometimes joke that winter lasts for 12 months and then summer begins. Russia is a cold country. The reason is its northern location partly within the Arctic Circle. In general, Russia has short summers and long, snowy winters. The climate is milder west of the Urals and grows colder and harsher as one goes north and east.
>
> *From Section 1, Physical Geography*

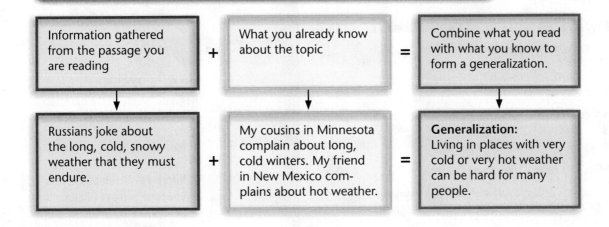

Information gathered from the passage you are reading	+	What you already know about the topic	=	Combine what you read with what you know to form a generalization.
Russians joke about the long, cold, snowy weather that they must endure.	+	My cousins in Minnesota complain about long, cold winters. My friend in New Mexico complains about hot weather.	=	**Generalization:** Living in places with very cold or very hot weather can be hard for many people.

YOU TRY IT!

Read the following passage. Using the process described above, form a general idea about holidays. Write your generalization in one sentence.

> Russian history has shaped its customs, such as holidays. Religious holidays, like Easter and Christmas, are popular. The main family holiday is New Year's Eve. To celebrate this holiday, families decorate a tree where, according to Russian folklore, Grandfather Frost and his helper the Snow Maiden leave gifts. A newer holiday is Russian Independence Day, which marks the end of the Soviet Union on June 12.
>
> *From Section 2, History and Culture of Russia*

The Eurasian Republics

Essential Question

myNotebook

How have foreign invasion and influence affected the societies and cultures of the Eurasian Republics?

Texas Essential Knowledge and Skills (TEKS)

1A, 1B, 2A, 2B, 3A, 3B, 3C, 3D, 4B, 4C, 4D, 4E, 5A, 5B, 5C, 6A, 6B, 15A, 15B, 18B, 18D, 19A, 19B, 21B, 21C, 21F, 22C, 22D

FOCUS ON READING AND VIEWING

my WriteSmart

Using Context Clues As you read, you may come across words in your textbook that you do not know. When this happens, look for context clues that restate the unknown word in other words that you know. **See the lesson, Using Context Clues, on page 445.**

Giving a Travel Presentation You work for a travel agency, and you are going to give a presentation encouraging people to visit the Eurasian Republics. Gather information from the chapter to help you prepare your presentation. Later you will view your classmates' presentations and provide feedback to them. Use the annotation tools in your eBook to gather information for your assignment.

National capital
• Other cities

0   100   200 Miles
0   100   200 Kilometers

Projection: Lambert Conformal Conic

Black Sea

TURKEY

SYRIA

map zone

Geography Skills

Regions Much of the Eurasian Republics is landlocked and has rugged terrain.

1. **Identify** What countries have coasts on the Caspian Sea?
2. **Interpret** Which country do you think is most influenced by Russia?

Geography Much of Central Asia's land is rugged. Here, mountains rise behind the city of Almaty, Kazakhstan.

RUSSIA

Ural River

Esil River

Astana

Irtysh River

Semey

KAZAKHSTAN

Aral Sea

Syr Darya

Lake Balkhash

Ili River

GEORGIA
Tbilisi

UZBEKISTAN

Almaty

Bishkek

KYRGYZSTAN

ARMENIA
Yerevan

Baku

Caspian Sea

Amu Darya

Tashkent

40°N

AZERBAIJAN

N
W   E
S

TURKMENISTAN

Bukhara

Samarqand

Dushanbe

TAJIKISTAN

CHINA

Ashgabat

Mary

IRAN

AFGHANISTAN

Kabul

INDIA

Herat

Helmand River

Qandahar

PAKISTAN

30°N

Culture There are many different cultures in Central Asia. This farm girl wears clothing typical of Uzbekistan.

History This mosque in Samarqand, Uzbekistan, shows Arab influence on the region.

421

Physical Geography of Central Asia

TEKS 3A, 3B, 3C, 4D, 4E, 5A, 5B, 5C, 6A, 6B, 21B, 21C, 22D

What You Will Learn...

Main Ideas

1. Key physical features of landlocked Central Asia include rugged mountains.
2. Central Asia has a harsh, dry climate that makes it difficult for vegetation to grow.
3. Key natural resources in Central Asia include water, oil and gas, and minerals.

The Big Idea

Central Asia, a dry, rugged, landlocked region, has oil and other valuable mineral resources.

Key Terms and Places

landlocked, *p. 422*
Pamirs, *p. 422*
Fergana Valley, *p. 423*
Kara-Kum, *p. 424*
Kyzyl Kum, *p. 424*
Aral Sea, *p. 425*

hmhsocialstudies.com
TAKING NOTES

Use the graphic organizer online to take notes on the physical geography of Central Asia.

If YOU lived there...

You are flying in a plane low over the mountains of Central Asia. You look down and notice that the area below you looks as if a giant hand has crumpled the land into steep mountains and narrow valleys. Icy glaciers fill some of the valleys. A few silvery rivers flow out of the mountains and across a green plain. This plain is the only green spot you can see in this rugged landscape.

How would this landscape affect people?

BUILDING BACKGROUND The physical geography of Central Asia affects the lives of the people who live there. This region has been shaped throughout its history by its isolated location, high mountains, dry plains, and limited resources.

Physical Features

Six of the Eurasian Republics are located in a region called Central Asia. As the name suggests, Central Asia lies in the middle of Asia. All of the countries in this region are landlocked. **Landlocked** means completely surrounded by land with no direct access to the ocean. This isolated location is just one challenge presented by the physical features of the region.

Mountains

Much of Central Asia has a rugged landscape. In the south, many high mountain ranges, such as the Hindu Kush, stretch through Afghanistan. Tajikistan and Kyrgyzstan are also very mountainous. Large glaciers are common in high mountains such as the **Pamirs**.

Like its landlocked location, Central Asia's rugged terrain presents a challenge for the region. Throughout history, the mountains have made travel and communication difficult and have contributed to the region's isolation. In addition, tectonic activity causes frequent earthquakes there.

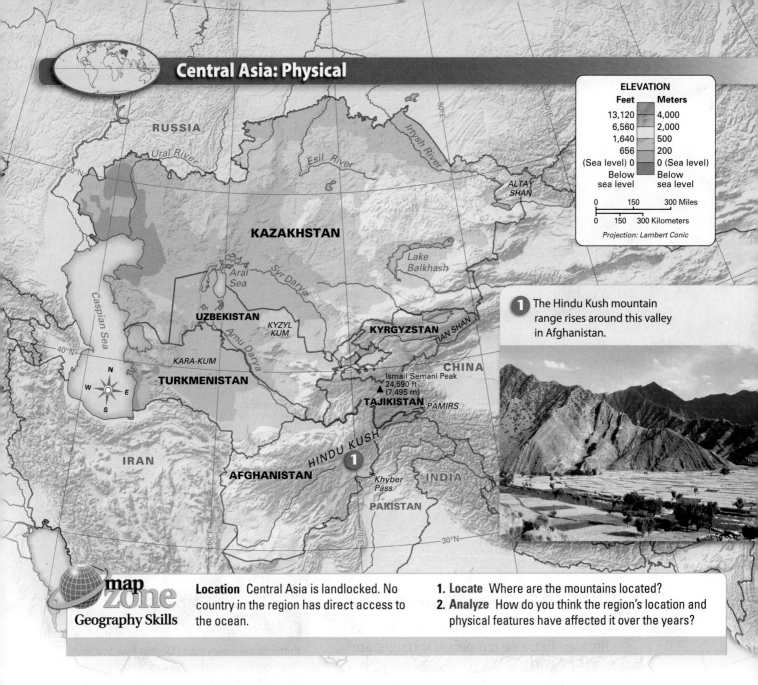

Central Asia: Physical

ELEVATION

Feet	Meters
13,120	4,000
6,560	2,000
1,640	500
656	200
(Sea level) 0	0 (Sea level)
Below sea level	Below sea level

0   150   300 Miles

0   150   300 Kilometers

Projection: Lambert Conic

RUSSIA

Ural River

Esil River

Irtysh River

ALTAY SHAN

KAZAKHSTAN

Lake Balkhash

Aral Sea

Syr Darya

Caspian Sea

UZBEKISTAN

KYZYL KUM

KYRGYZSTAN

TIAN SHAN

CHINA

Amu Darya

KARA-KUM

Ismail Semani Peak
24,590 ft
(7,495 m)

TURKMENISTAN

TAJIKISTAN

PAMIRS

IRAN

HINDU KUSH

①

INDIA

AFGHANISTAN

Khyber Pass

PAKISTAN

① The Hindu Kush mountain range rises around this valley in Afghanistan.

map zone
Geography Skills

Location Central Asia is landlocked. No country in the region has direct access to the ocean.

1. Locate Where are the mountains located?
2. Analyze How do you think the region's location and physical features have affected it over the years?

Plains and Plateaus

From the mountains in the east, the land gradually slopes toward the west. There, near the Caspian Sea, the land is as low as 95 feet (29 m) below sea level. The central part of the region, between the mountains and the Caspian Sea, is covered with plains and low plateaus.

The plains region is the site of the fertile **Fergana Valley**. This large valley has been a major center of farming in the region for thousands of years.

Rivers and Lakes

The Fergana Valley is fertile because of two rivers that flow through it—the Syr Darya (sir duhr-YAH) and the Amu Darya (uh-MOO duhr-YAH). These rivers flow from eastern mountains into the Aral Sea, which is really a large lake. Another important lake, Lake Balkhash, has freshwater at one end and salty water at the other end.

READING CHECK **Generalizing** What challenges do the mountains present to this region?

Geography Skills

Regions Central Asia's dry climate affects its land use.
1. **Locate** Where is most of Central Asia's oil?
2. **Draw Conclusions** What makes some places good for commercial farming?

KAZAKHSTAN

Caspian Sea

UZBEKISTAN

Alma-Ata

Tashkent

KYRGYZSTAN

TURKMENISTAN

TAJIKISTAN

AFGHANISTAN

N
W   E
S

Major Resources
- Coal
- Natural gas
- Oil
- Gold
- Silver
- Other minerals
- Fishing
- Major manufacturing and trade centers

Land Use
- Commercial farming
- Nomadic herding
- Livestock raising
- Subsistence farming
- Primarily forestland
- Limited economic activity

0   200   400 Miles
0   200   400 Kilometers

Projection: Lambert Conformal Conic

Cotton is the main crop in Central Asia. Students often have to take time off from school to help harvest the cotton.

Climate and Vegetation

Most places in Central Asia have harsh, dry climates. Extreme temperature ranges and limited rainfall make it difficult for plants to grow there.

One area with harsh climates in the region is the mountain area in the east. The high peaks in this area are too cold, dry, and windy for vegetation.

West of the mountains and east of the Caspian Sea is another harsh region. Two deserts—the **Kara-Kum** (kahr-uh-KOOM) in Turkmenistan and the **Kyzyl Kum** (ki-ZIL KOOM) in Uzbekistan and Kazakhstan—have extremely high temperatures in the summer. Rainfall is limited, though both deserts contain several settlements. Rivers crossing this dry region make settlements possible, because they provide water for irrigation. Irrigation is a way of supplying water to an area of land.

The only part of Central Asia with a milder climate is the far north. There, temperature ranges are not so extreme and rainfall is heavy enough for grasses and trees to grow.

READING CHECK **Generalizing** Why is it hard for plants to grow in much of Central Asia?

Natural Resources

In this dry region, water is one of the most valuable resources. Although water is scarce, or limited, the countries of Central Asia do have oil and other resources.

Water

The main water sources in southern Central Asia are the Syr Darya and Amu Darya rivers. Since water is so scarce there, different ideas over how to use the water from these rivers have led to conflict between Uzbekistan and Turkmenistan.

Today farmers use river water mostly to irrigate cotton fields. Cotton grows well in Central Asia's sunny climate, but it requires a lot of water. Irrigation has taken so much water from the rivers that almost no water actually reaches the **Aral Sea** today. The effect of this irrigation has been devastating to the Aral Sea. It has lost more than 75 percent of its water since 1960. Large areas of seafloor are now exposed.

In addition to water for irrigation, Central Asia's rivers supply power. Some countries have built large dams on the rivers to generate hydroelectricity.

Oil and Other Resources

The resources that present the best economic opportunities for Central Asia are oil and gas. Uzbekistan, Kazakhstan, and Turkmenistan all have huge reserves of oil and natural gas.

However, these oil and gas reserves cannot benefit the countries of Central Asia unless they can be exported. Since no country in the region has an ocean port, the only way to transport the oil and gas efficiently is through pipelines. But the rugged mountains, along with economic and political turmoil in some surrounding countries, make building and maintaining pipelines difficult.

In addition to oil and gas, some parts of Central Asia are rich in other minerals. They have deposits of gold, silver, copper, zinc, uranium, and lead. Kazakhstan, in particular, has many mines with these minerals. It also has large amounts of coal.

FOCUS ON READING
What context clues give you a restatement of the term *scarce*?

READING CHECK **Categorizing** What are three types of natural resources in Central Asia?

SUMMARY AND PREVIEW In this section you learned about Central Asia's rugged terrain, dry climate, and limited resources. In the next section you will learn about the geography, history, and culture of the Caucasus.

Section 1 Assessment

hmhsocialstudies.com
ONLINE QUIZ

Reviewing Ideas, Terms, and Places

1. **a. Identify** What fertile area has been a center of farming in Central Asia for many years?
   b. Make Inferences How does Central Asia's terrain affect life there?
2. **a. Describe** Where do people find water in the deserts?
   b. Make Generalizations What is the climate like in most of Central Asia?
3. **a. Recall** What mineral resources does Central Asia have?
   b. Explain How have human activities affected the **Aral Sea**?
   c. Elaborate What kinds of situations would make it easier for countries of Central Asia to export oil and gas?

Critical Thinking

4. **Finding Main Ideas** Look at your notes on this section. Then, using a chart like the one here, write a main idea statement about each topic.

	Main Idea
Physical Features	
Climate and Vegetation	
Natural Resources	

FOCUS ON VIEWING

my WriteSmart

5. **Describing Physical Geography** Note information about physical features, climates, and resources of this region. Highlight information to include in your presentation.

The Caucasus

TEKS 1A, 1B, 2A, 2B, 3A, 3B, 3C, 3D, 4B, 4C, 15B, 18B, 21B, 21C, 22D

What You Will Learn...

Main Ideas

1. Many groups have ruled and influenced the Caucasus during its long history.
2. Today the Caucasus republics are working to improve their economies, but they struggle with ethnic unrest and conflict.

The Big Idea

In an area long ruled by outside groups, the Caucasus republics are struggling to strengthen their economies and to deal with ethnic unrest.

Key Places

Caspian Sea, *p. 427*
Caucasus Mountains, *p. 427*
Tbilisi, *p. 428*
Yerevan, *p. 428*
Baku, *p. 429*

hmhsocialstudies.com
TAKING NOTES

Use the graphic organizer online to take notes on the Caucasus.

If YOU lived there...

You live in Tbilisi, the capital of the country of Georgia. Several years ago, your sister and her college friends joined the Rose Revolution, a political protest that forced a corrupt president to resign. The protestors' symbol was a red rose. Since the protest, you have become more interested in politics.

What kind of government do you want?

BUILDING BACKGROUND Georgia is one of three republics in the area called the Caucasus. In 1991, when the Soviet Union ended, the Caucasus republics gained independence. Since then, the republics have struggled to become democracies with market economies.

History

The Caucasus lies in the rugged Caucasus Mountains between the Black and Caspian seas. Located where Europe blends into Asia, the Caucasus reflects a range of cultural influences. At one time or another, Persians, Greeks, Romans, Arabs, Turks, and Mongols have all ruled or invaded the area. The Russians took control of much of the Caucasus in the early 1800s.

Russian control in the Caucasus did not include what is now western Armenia. The Ottoman Turks held this area. Over time, the Turks grew to distrust the Armenians, however; and in the late 1800s began abusing and killing them. During World War I (1914–1918), the Turks forced all Armenians to leave. Hundreds of thousands of Armenians died during this ethnic cleansing, or attempt to remove an ethnic group. The Turks lost World War I, though, and had to give up western Armenia.

After World War I, Armenia, Azerbaijan, and Georgia gained independence—but not for long. By the early 1920s they were part of the vast Soviet Union. Finally in 1991, when the Soviet Union fell, the Caucasus republics achieved true independence.

READING CHECK **Finding Main Ideas** Why do the countries in the Caucasus reflect a range of cultural influences?

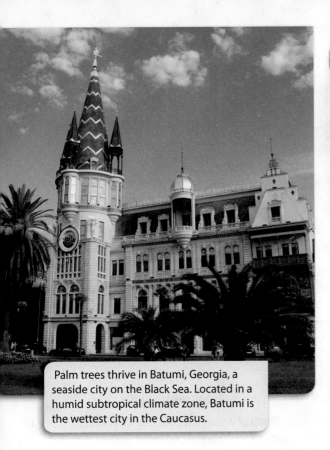

Palm trees thrive in Batumi, Georgia, a seaside city on the Black Sea. Located in a humid subtropical climate zone, Batumi is the wettest city in the Caucasus.

mapzone Geography Skills

Location The climates of the Caucasus range from steppe to highland.

1. **Name** Where are the region's Mediterranean climates located?
2. **Make Inferences** What part of the Caucasus is probably the coldest in the winter months?

Physical Geography

Georgia, Armenia (ahr-MEE-nee-uh), and Azerbaijan (a-zuhr-by-JAHN) lie south of Russia in the Caucasus (KAW-kuh-suhs), the area between the Black Sea and the **Caspian Sea.** This area, which includes part of southern Russia, is named for the **Caucasus Mountains.**

Landforms and Water Features

The Caucasus countries consist largely of rugged uplands. The Caucasus Mountains cover much of Georgia and extend into Armenia and Azerbaijan. These soaring mountains include Mount Elbrus (el-BROOS). At 18,510 feet (5,642 m), it is the highest peak in Europe. South of the Caucasus Mountains, a plateau covers much of Armenia. Gorges cut through this plateau, and earthquakes are common there. Lowlands lie along the Black and Caspian Seas. The Black Sea forms the region's western border. This sea connects to the Mediterranean Sea and is important for trade. To the east, the region is bordered by the Caspian Sea, which is actually a saltwater lake that stretches for nearly 750 miles from north to south. It is largest inland sea in the world.

Climate

Climate in the Caucasus ranges from warm and wet along the Black Sea to cooler in the uplands to hot and dry in much of Azerbaijan. Moist air from the Mediterranean Sea contributes to a humid subtropical climate zone. The region's health resorts were a favorite destination of tourists until ethnic conflict made traveling there dangerous.

READING CHECK **Summarizing** What are the major physical features in the Caucasus?

The snow-capped peaks of the Caucasus Mountains rise above a mountain village and the remains of a fortress built in the 900s.

Mount Elbrus
18,510 ft
(5,642 m)

RUSSIA

CAUCASUS MOUNTAINS

Black Sea

Ingur R.

GEORGIA

Tbilisi ✪

Kur River

TURKEY

ARMENIA

Lake Sevan

AZERBAIJAN

Baku ✪

Yerevan

40°N

✪ National capital

0   50   100 Miles

0   50   100 Kilometers

Projection: Lambert Equal-Area

IRAN

Aras River

Caspian Sea

map zone Geography Skills

Location South of western Russia, the Caucasus is located where Europe blends into Asia.

1. **Name** What two seas border the Caucasus?
2. **Contrast** Based on the map, how does Armenia differ from Azerbaijan and Georgia?

The Caucasus Today

The Caucasus may have a long history, but the Caucasus countries do not. Like other former Soviet republics, these young countries have had to create new governments and economies. Meanwhile, ethnic unrest and conflicts have slowed progress.

The Caucasus republics have similar governments. An elected president governs each nation, and an appointed prime minister runs each government. An elected parliament, or legislature, makes the laws.

Georgia

The country of Georgia lies in the Caucasus Mountains east of the Black Sea. **Tbilisi** is the capital. About 70 percent of the people are ethnic Georgians, and most belong to the Georgian Orthodox Church. The official language is Georgian, a unique language with its own alphabet. However, many other languages are also spoken.

Since 1991 Georgia has struggled with unrest and civil war. In 2003 Georgians forced out their president in the peaceful Rose Revolution. Meanwhile, ethnic groups in northern Georgia were fighting for independence. Because these groups now hold parts of northern Georgia, division and unrest continues.

Although unrest has hurt Georgia's economy, international aid is helping it improve. Georgia's economy is based on services and farming. Major crops include citrus fruits, grapes, and tea. In addition, Georgia produces steel and mines copper and manganese. Georgia is also famous for its wines. The Black Sea is a resort area, and tourism contributes to the economy, too.

Armenia

South of Georgia is the small, landlocked country of Armenia. The tiny country is slightly larger than the state of Maryland. **Yerevan** (yer-uh-VAHN) is the capital. Almost all the people are ethnic Armenian. Armenia prides itself as being the first country to adopt Christianity, and most people belong to the Armenian Orthodox Church.

In the early 1990s, Armenia fought a bitter war with its neighbor Azerbaijan. The war involved an area of Azerbaijan where most people are ethnic Armenian. Armenia wanted this area to become part of its country. Although a cease-fire stopped the fighting in 1994, Armenian armed forces still control the area. The issue remained unsettled as of the early 2000s.

This conflict has greatly hurt Armenia's economy. However, international aid is helping Armenia's economy recover and expand. For example, diamond processing is now a growing industry in Armenia.

Azerbaijan

East of Armenia is Azerbaijan. In contrast to the other Caucasus republics, Azerbaijan is largely Muslim. The Azeri (uh-ZE-ree) make up 90 percent of the population.

Azerbaijan's economy is based on oil, which is found along and under the Caspian Sea. **Baku**, the capital, is the center of a large oil-refining industry. This industry has led to strong economic growth. Corruption is high, though; and many of the country's people are poor. In addition,

Baku

Located on the Caspian Sea, the city of Baku is the capital and chief port of Azerbaijan.

Azerbaijan has many refugees as a result of its conflict with Armenia.

READING CHECK **Summarizing** What challenges do the Caucasus republics face?

FOCUS ON READING

What general statements can you make about the Caucasus as a whole?

SUMMARY AND PREVIEW In this section you learned about the geography and culture of the Caucasus. Next you will learn about the history and culture of Central Asia.

Section 2 Assessment

Reviewing Ideas, Terms, and Places

1. **a. Identify** Which country controlled much of the Caucasus for most of the 1800s?
   b. Identify Cause and Effect How did Turkish rule affect Armenians in the Ottoman Empire?
   c. Elaborate How has location affected the history and culture of the Caucasus area?

2. **a. Recall** How does **Baku** contribute to the economy of Azerbaijan?
   b. Compare and Contrast How is religion in Georgia and Armenia similar? How does religion in these countries differ from that in Azerbaijan?
   c. Elaborate How did the war between Armenia and Azerbaijan affect each country?

Critical Thinking

3. **Comparing and Contrasting** Draw a Venn diagram like the one here. Use your notes to identify the ways in which Georgia, Armenia, and Azerbaijan are similar and different.

FOCUS ON VIEWING

my WriteSmart

4. **Describing the Caucasus** Write notes about each country in the Caucasus. Which countries might you suggest travelers visit? What details might encourage them?

History and Culture of Central Asia

TEKS 1A, 1B, 2A, 2B, 15A, 15B, 15F, 17D, 17E, 19A, 21B, 21C, 21D, 22D

What You Will Learn...

Main Ideas

1. Throughout history, many different groups have conquered Central Asia.
2. Many different ethnic groups and their traditions influence culture in Central Asia.

The Big Idea

The countries of Central Asia share similar histories and traditions, but particular ethnic groups give each country a unique culture.

Key Terms and Places

Samarqand, *p. 430*
nomads, *p. 432*
yurt, *p. 432*

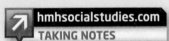

Use the graphic organizer online to take notes on the history and culture of Central Asia. Be sure to pay attention to the different peoples that influenced the region.

If YOU lived there...

Your family has always farmed a small plot of land. Most days you go to school and work in the fields. One day you get news that invaders have taken over your country. They don't look like you and they speak a different language, but now they are in charge.

How do you think your life will change under the new rulers?

BUILDING BACKGROUND You may have noticed that the names of the countries in this region all end with *stan*. In the language of the region, *stan* means "land of." So, for example, Kazakhstan means "land of the Kazakhs." However, throughout history many different groups have ruled these lands.

History

Central Asia has been somewhat of a crossroads for traders and invaders for hundreds of years. As these different peoples have passed through Central Asia, they have each left their own unique and lasting influences on the region.

Trade

At one time, the best trade route between Europe and India ran through Afghanistan. The best route between Europe and China ran through the rest of Central Asia. Beginning in about 100 BC, merchants traveled along the China route to trade European gold and wool for Chinese spices and silk. As a result, this route came to be called the Silk Road. Cities along the road, such as **Samarqand** and Bukhara, grew rich from the trade.

By 1500 the situation in Central Asia had changed, however. When Europeans discovered they could sail to East Asia through the Indian Ocean, trade through Central Asia declined. The region became more isolated and poor.

Invasions

Because of its location on the Silk Road, cultural diffusion occurred in Central Asia as group after group swarmed into the region. These groups left both positive and negative effects of their culture in the region. Among the first people to establish a lasting influence in the region were Turkic-speaking nomads who came from northern Asia in AD 500.

In the 700s Arab armies took over much of the region. They brought a new religion—Islam—to Central Asia. Many of the beautiful mosques in Central Asian cities date from the time of the Arabs.

Arabs, followed by other invaders, ruled Central Asia until the 1200s. Then, Mongol armies conquered Central Asia, destroying many cities with their violent attacks. Eventually, their empire crumbled. With the fall of the Mongols, various tribes of peoples, such as the Uzbeks, Kazakhs, and Turkmens moved into parts of the region.

Russian and Soviet Rule

In the mid-1800s the Russians became the next major group to conquer Central Asia. Although the Russians built railroads and expanded cotton and oil production, people began to resent their rule.

After the Russian Revolution in 1917, the new Soviet government wanted to weaken resistance to its rule. The new Soviet leaders did this by dividing the land into republics. The Soviets encouraged ethnic Russians to move to these areas and made other people settle on government-owned farms. The Soviets also built huge irrigation projects to improve cotton production.

The Soviet Union collapsed in 1991. As the Soviet government and economy fell apart, it could no longer control its huge territory. The Central Asian republics finally became independent countries.

READING CHECK **Generalizing** What groups of people influenced Central Asia?

Influences on Central Asia

The Arabs, Mongols, and Soviets all had a major influence on Central Asia.

Arab Influence

- The Arabs ruled Central Asia in the 700s and 800s.
- They introduced Islam and built beautiful mosques.
- They influenced styles of art and architecture in the region.

Mongol Influence

- The Mongols ruled from 1220 to the mid-1300s.
- They destroyed cities and irrigation systems.
- Eventually, they supported literature and the arts at Samarqand.

Soviet Influence

- The Soviet Union controlled Central Asia from 1922 to 1991.
- The Soviets separated ethnic groups and banned religious practices.
- They began growing cotton and constructed many useful but stark buildings.

Culture

The people who came through Central Asia influenced culture in the region. They brought new languages, religions, and ways of life that mixed with traditional ways of life in Central Asia.

Traditional Lives

For centuries, Central Asians have made a living by raising horses, cattle, sheep, and goats. Many herders live as **nomads**, people who move often from place to place. The nomads move their herds from mountain pastures in the summer to lowland pastures in the winter. Today most people in Central Asia live in more permanent settlements, but many others still live as nomads. The nomadic lifestyle is especially common in Kyrgyzstan.

Unique homes, called yurts, make moving with the herds possible. A **yurt** is a movable round house made of wool felt mats hung over a wood frame. Today the yurt is a symbol of the region's nomadic heritage. Even people who live in cities may put up yurts for special events such as weddings and funerals.

Close-up

Inside a Yurt

Historically, the nomadic life required that all possessions be portable—even houses. Nomads moved their yurts with them from place to place.

A hole at the top allows smoke from a fire to escape.

Nomads roll up part of the felt mat to create a door.

Traditional carpets provide decoration and warmth and are a yurt's main furniture.

ANALYSIS SKILL ANALYZING VISUALS

Why would a yurt be easier to move than another type of house?

Geography Skills

Regions People in Central Asia speak many different languages.

1. **Use the Map** What language is spoken in the largest area?
2. **Compare** How do language regions compare to political boundaries?

Legend:
- Kazakh
- Kyrgyz
- Pashto
- Russian
- Tajik
- Turkmen
- Uzbek
- Other

0   200   400 Miles
0   200   400 Kilometers

Projection: Lambert Conformal Conic

People, Languages, and Religion

Most people in Central Asia today belong to one of several ethnic groups that are part of a larger ethnic group called Turkic. Some of these ethnic groups are Kazakh (kuh-ZAHK), Kyrgyz (KIR-giz), Turkmen, and Uzbek (OOZ-bek). Another group, ethnic Russians, came to Central Asia when Russia conquered the region. They still live in every Central Asian country.

Each ethnic group speaks its own language. Look at the map above to see where a particular language is the primary language. In most countries in the region, more than one language is spoken.

When the Russians conquered Central Asia, they **established** their own language as the official language for business and government. It is still an official language in some Central Asian countries. The Russians also introduced the Cyrillic alphabet, the alphabet used to write the Russian language. Most countries in Central Asia now use the Latin alphabet, however, which is the one used to write English. Afghanistan also has its own alphabet. It is used for writing Pashto, one of that country's official languages.

Just as people in the region are of many ethnic groups and speak different languages, they also practice different religions. Traders and conquerors brought their religious beliefs and practices to the region. Islam, brought by the Arabs, is the main religion in Central Asia. Some people there also practice Christianity. Most of the region's Christians belong to the Russian Orthodox Church.

FOCUS ON READING
What context clues give a restatement of *Cyrillic alphabet?*

ACADEMIC VOCABULARY
establish to set up or create

Ethnic Groups of Central Asia

Traditional clothing, such as the hats men wear, distinguishes members of different ethnic groups in Central Asia.

ANALYZING VISUALS Why do you think men wear different hats?

Turkmen

Kyrgyz

Uzbek

During the Soviet era, the government closed or destroyed more than 35,000 religious buildings, such as mosques, churches, and Islamic schools. However, since the end of the Soviet Union in 1991, many religious buildings have reopened. They are in use once again and are also beautiful symbols of the region's past.

READING CHECK Summarizing How did Russian and Soviet rule influence culture in Central Asia?

SUMMARY AND PREVIEW Many different groups of people have influenced the countries of Central Asia over the years. As a result, the region has a mixture of languages and religions. In the next section you will learn about the governments and economies of the countries of Central Asia today. You will also study some of the challenges these countries face.

Section 3 Assessment

hmhsocialstudies.com
ONLINE QUIZ

Reviewing Ideas, Terms, and Places

1. **a. Identify** What people brought Islam to Central Asia?

   b. Analyze What impact did the Silk Road have on Central Asia?

   c. Elaborate How might Central Asia's history have been different without the influence of the Silk Road?

2. **a. Define** What is a **yurt**?

   b. Analyze What are some of the benefits of nomadic life, and what are some of the challenges of this lifestyle?

   c. Elaborate How might the mix of ethnic groups, languages, and religions in Central Asian countries affect life there today?

Critical Thinking

3. **Sequencing** Review your notes on the history of Central Asia. Then organize your information using a time line like the one below. You may add more dates if you need to.

   100 BC   1991

FOCUS ON VIEWING

my WriteSmart

4. **Taking Notes on History and Culture** What information about the history and culture of the region might encourage travelers to visit Central Asia? What sites might they be interested in visiting? Jot down a few notes.

Central Asia Today

If **YOU** lived there...

Your country, Kyrgyzstan, has just had an election. You listen to the radio with your brother, anxiously awaiting the results of the election. When the radio announcer says that the same president has won again, your brother is very angry. He says the election was unfair, and he is going to protest outside the president's palace. He expects there to be a big crowd.

Will you join your brother? Why or why not?

BUILDING BACKGROUND Political protests have been fairly common in some Central Asian countries in recent years. Political instability is just one of the challenges facing Central Asia today as the region learns to deal with independence.

Central Asia Today

A history of invasions and foreign rule has made an impact on Central Asia. Because of years of fighting and changes in the region, today many countries of Central Asia face similar issues in building stable governments and strong economies.

Afghanistan

The situation in Afghanistan today is in many ways a result of a long war with the Soviet Union in the 1980s. The Soviets left in 1989. However, turmoil continued under an alliance of Afghan groups. In the mid-1990s a radical Muslim group known as the **Taliban** arose. The group's leaders took over most of the country, including the capital, **Kabul**.

The Taliban used a strict interpretation of Islamic teachings to rule Afghanistan. For example, the Taliban severely limited the role of women in society. They forced women to wear veils and to stop working outside the home. They also banned all music and dancing. Although most Muslims sharply disagreed with the Taliban's policies, the group remained in power for several years.

TEKS 3B, 4B, 15A, 15B, 18B, 18D, 19A, 19B, 21B, 21C, 21F, 22C, 22D

What You Will Learn...

Main Ideas

1. The countries of Central Asia are working to develop their economies and to improve political stability in the region.
2. The countries of Central Asia face issues and challenges related to the environment, the economy, and politics.

The Big Idea

Central Asian countries are mostly poor, but they are working to create stable governments and sound economies.

Key Terms and Places

Taliban, *p. 435*
Kabul, *p. 435*
dryland farming, *p. 437*
arable, *p. 437*

hmhsocialstudies.com

TAKING NOTES

Use the graphic organizer online to take notes on governments, economies, and challenges in Central Asia today.

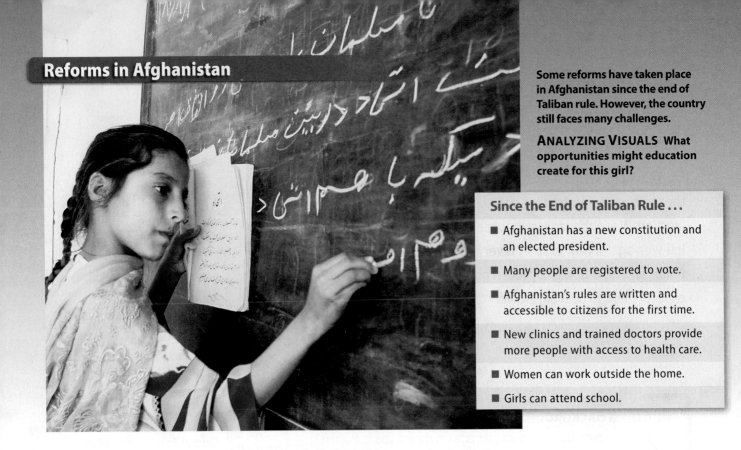

Reforms in Afghanistan

Some reforms have taken place in Afghanistan since the end of Taliban rule. However, the country still faces many challenges.

ANALYZING VISUALS What opportunities might education create for this girl?

Since the End of Taliban Rule . . .

- Afghanistan has a new constitution and an elected president.
- Many people are registered to vote.
- Afghanistan's rules are written and accessible to citizens for the first time.
- New clinics and trained doctors provide more people with access to health care.
- Women can work outside the home.
- Girls can attend school.

Eventually, the Taliban came into conflict with the United States. Investigation of the September 11, 2001, terrorist attacks on New York City and Washington, D.C., led to terrorist leader Osama bin Laden and his al Qaeda network, based in Afghanistan. U.S. and British forces attacked Taliban and al Qaeda targets and toppled Afghanistan's Taliban government.

Since the fall of the Taliban, Afghanistan's government has changed in many ways. The country has a new constitution. Also, all men and women age 18 and older can vote for the president and for the members of a national assembly. Some members of the assembly are appointed by the president, and the constitution requires that half of these appointees be women.

Many Afghans hope their government will be stable. However, since 2006 Afghans have experienced an organized rebellion, or insurgency, of the Taliban. Despite this threat, Afghan leaders are optimistic that they can defeat the insurgents.

Kazakhstan

Kazakhstan was the first part of Central Asia to be conquered by Russia. As a result, Russian influence remains strong in that country today. About one-third of Kazakhstan's people are ethnic Russians. Kazakh and Russian are both official languages. Many ethnic Kazakhs grow up speaking Russian at home and have to learn Kazakh in school.

Kazakhstan's economy was once tied to the former Soviet Union's. It was based on manufacturing. When the Soviet Union collapsed, the economy suffered. However, due to its valuable oil reserves and quick adaptation to the free market, Kazakhstan's economy is now growing steadily. The country is the richest in Central Asia.

Kazakhstan also has one of the more stable governments in Central Asia. The country is a democratic republic with an elected president and parliament. In 1998 Kazakhstan moved its capital from Almaty to Astana, which is closer to Russia.

Kyrgyzstan

The word *kyrgyz* means "forty clans." Throughout history, clan membership has been an important part of Kyrgyzstan's social, political, and economic life. Many people still follow nomadic traditions.

Many other people in Kyrgyzstan are farmers. Fertile soils there allow a mix of irrigated crops and **dryland farming**, or farming that relies on rainfall instead of irrigation. Farming is the most important industry in Kyrgyzstan. However, it does not provide much income for the country.

Although the standard of living in Kyrgyzstan is low, the economy shows signs of strengthening. Tourism might also help Kyrgyzstan's economy. The country has a Muslim pilgrimage site as well as the beautiful Lake Issyk-Kul.

Kyrgyzstan's government is changing. In 2010 opposition groups overthrew the president and adopted a new constitution. Soon after, the new government held the first-ever elections in Kyrgyzstan.

Tajikistan

Like other countries in Central Asia, Tajikistan is struggling to overcome its problems. In the mid-1990s the country's Communist government fought against a group of reformers. Some reformers demanded democracy. Others called for a government that ruled by Islamic law. The groups came together and signed a peace agreement in 1997. As a result, Tajikistan is now a republic with an elected president.

Years of civil war damaged Tajikistan's economy. Both industrial and agricultural production declined. Even with the decline in agricultural production, Tajikistan still relies on cotton farming for much of its income. However, only 7 percent of the country's land is **arable**, or suitable for growing crops. Lack of arable land makes progress there difficult.

Turkmenistan

Turkmenistan's president holds all power in the country. He was voted president for life by the country's parliament. He has used his power to bring about education and health care reforms, and offer free Web access at internet cafes in Ashgabat.

The Turkmen government supports Islam and has ordered schools to teach Islamic principles. However, it also views Islam with caution. It does not want Islam to become a political movement.

Turkmenistan's economy is based on oil, gas, and cotton. Although the country is a desert, about half of it is planted with cotton fields. Farming is possible because Turkmenistan has the longest irrigation channel in the world.

FOCUS ON CULTURE

Turkmen Carpets

Decorative carpets are an essential part of a nomad's home. They are also perhaps the most famous artistic craft of Turkmenistan. Carpet factories operate in cities all through Turkmenistan, but some women still weave carpets by hand. These weavers memorize hundreds of intricate designs so they can make rugs that look the same. Each of several different Turkmen tribes has its own rug design.

Analyzing Why are carpets good for a nomadic way of life?

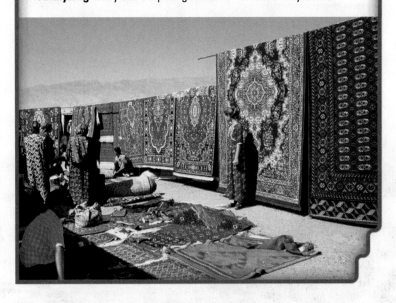

Uzbekistan

Uzbekistan has the largest population of the Central Asian countries. It also has the largest cities in the region. Two cities—Bukhara and Samarqand—are famous for their mosques and monuments.

As in Turkmenistan, Uzbekistan's elected president holds all the political power. The United States has criticized the government for not allowing political freedom or respecting human rights.

The government also closely controls the economy. Uzbekistan's economy, based on oil, gold, and cotton, is fairly stable even though it is growing only very slowly.

READING CHECK **Drawing Inferences** How does physical geography affect the economies of Kyrgyzstan and Tajikistan?

Issues and Challenges

As you have read, the countries of Central Asia face similar issues and challenges. Their greatest challenges are in the areas of environment, economy, and politics.

Environment

One of the most serious environmental problems is the shrinking of the Aral Sea. Winds sweep the dry seafloor and blow dust, salt, and pesticides hundreds of miles. Also, towns that once relied on fishing are now dozens of miles from the shore.

Another problem is the damage caused by Soviet military practices. The Soviets tested nuclear bombs in Central Asia. Now people there suffer poor health because of radiation left over from the tests.

Challenges for Central Asia

Most countries in Central Asia face environmental, economic, or political challenges. How the Central Asian countries face these challenges will shape their future.

Environmental
Industrial waste from old factories pollutes the air and groundwater.

Standard of Living in Central Asia

	TVs (Per 1,000 People)	**Radios** (Per 1,000 People)	**Per Capita GDP** (U.S. $)
Afghanistan	14	136	$1,100
Kazakhstan	240	395	$14,100
Kyrgyzstan	49	113	$2,400
Tajikistan	328	143	$2,300
Turkmenistan	198	289	$8,900
Uzbekistan	280	465	$3,600
United States	844	2,116	$50,700

Another environmental problem has been caused by the overuse of chemicals to increase crop production. These chemicals have ended up ruining some farmlands. Instead of increasing crop production, the chemicals have hurt the economy.

Economy

Many of Central Asia's economic problems are due to reliance on one crop—cotton. Suitable farmland is limited, so employment in the cotton industry is limited. Also, the focus on cotton has not encouraged countries to develop manufacturing.

Some countries have oil and gas reserves that may someday make them rich. For now, though, outdated equipment, lack of funds, and poor transportation systems slow development in Central Asia.

Politics

The other main challenge in Central Asia today is lack of political stability. In some countries, such as Kyrgyzstan, people do not agree on the best kind of government. People who are dissatisfied with their government sometimes turn to violence. These countries today are often faced with terrorist threats from different political groups within their own countries.

READING CHECK **Summarizing** What environmental challenges does Central Asia face?

SUMMARY Central Asia is recovering from a history of foreign rule. The region is struggling to develop sound economies and stable governments.

Political Protesters show their opposition to the government in Kyrgyzstan.

ANALYSIS SKILL ANALYZING VISUALS

What do you think could be done to improve the environment in Central Asia?

Section 4 Assessment

hmhsocialstudies.com
ONLINE QUIZ

Reviewing Ideas, Terms, and Places

1. **a. Describe** How did the **Taliban** affect Afghanistan?
   b. Contrast What are some major differences between Afghanistan and Kazakhstan?
   c. Elaborate What is one way a country might create more **arable** land?
2. **a. Identify** What three types of challenges does Central Asia face today?
   b. Make Generalizations Why does much of Central Asia face political instability?

Critical Thinking

3. **Categorizing** Using your notes and a chart like the one here, categorize your information on each Central Asian country. You will have to add more lines as needed.

	Government	Economy
Afghanistan		
Kazakhstan		

FOCUS ON VIEWING

my **WriteSmart**

4. **Describing Central Asia Today** Write notes about each country in Central Asia. Which countries might you suggest travelers visit? What details might encourage them?

The Aral Sea

In 1960 the Aral Sea was the world's fourth-largest lake. However, human activities over the years have caused the Aral Sea to shrink drastically. The lake's former seafloor is now a desert of sand and salt. Also, towns that once benefited from their lakeside location are now left without access to the water. Area governments have built dams to control the flow of water to restore parts of the lake, but so far their efforts have had little success.

Cause
Farmers have taken water from the Amu Darya and the Syr Darya to irrigate cotton fields. Now, less water flows into the sea than evaporates from it.

Effect
Stranded boats are a reminder of the fishing industry once based near the Aral Sea. The fishing industry is dying with the sea.

A Shrinking Sea

These satellite images show changes in the size of the Aral Sea over a period of 33 years.

Extent of Aral Sea, 1977

● Cities

0   25   50 Miles
0   35   70 Kilometers

Aral

Kokaral

Syr Darya

Aral Sea

Uchsay **Mŭynoq**

Amu Darya

1976

1997

2009

ANALYSIS SKILL **ANALYZING VISUALS**

1. **Place** How much wider was the Aral Sea in 1977 than it is now?
2. **Human-Environment Interaction** How might the shrinking of the sea affect towns that were once on its shore?

Social Studies Skills

Chart and Graph · Critical Thinking · Geography · Study

Using Math to Read Map Scales

Learn

Mapmakers use scales to represent distances between points on a map. On each map legend in this book, you will notice some lines marked to measure miles and kilometers. These lines are the map's scale.

To find distance on a map, use a ruler to measure the exact length of the scale bar in inches. Then read the scale's label. How many miles does that length stand for? Use your ruler to measure the distance between any two points. Then multiply the number of inches by the number of miles each inch represents in the map scale.

Practice

Use the maps here to practice using math to read map scales and to answer the following questions.

1. Which map shows a larger region?

2. About how many miles does one inch represent on the map of Kyrgyzstan? on the map of Bishkek?

3. How far is it from Dubovy Park to Victory Square in Bishkek?

Apply

Use the map of Southwest Asia in the unit opener to answer the following questions.

1. How many miles does one inch represent? How many kilometers does one inch represent?

2. How long is the Caspian Sea from north to south?

3. How far is Turkmenistan from the Persian Gulf?

Bishkek

Kyrgyzstan

Chapter Review

Visual Summary

Use the visual summary below to help you review the main ideas of the chapter.

QUICK FACTS

Central Asia is a dry, rugged region. However, people use irrigation to grow cotton, the region's main crop.

Some people follow traditional ways of life. For example, nomads move their yurts from place to place.

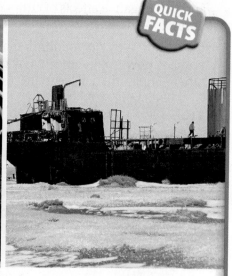

Central Asia faces environmental, economic, and political challenges. One challenge is the shrinking of the Aral Sea.

Reviewing Vocabulary, Terms, and Places

Unscramble each group of letters below to spell a term that matches the given definition.

1. **mnodsa**—people who move often from place to place

2. **yrddnal mrignaf**—farming that relies on rainfall, not irrigation

3. **tryu**—a moveable round house of wool felt mats hung over a wood frame

4. **ssblhieat**—to set up or create

5. **fgrenaa vlyela**—fertile region that has been a center of farming for thousands of years

6. **tlbania**—a radical Muslim group

7. **dknadclleo**—completely surrounded by land with no direct access to the ocean

8. **kluba**—the capital of Afghanistan

9. **aabler**—suitable for growing crops

10. **aalr sae**—body of water that is shrinking because of use of water for irrigation

Comprehension and Critical Thinking

SECTION 1 *(Pages 422–425)*

11. **a. Describe** How are farmers able to grow crops in Central Asia's dry landscapes?

   b. Analyze What factors make it difficult for the countries of Central Asia to export their oil and gas resources?

   c. Evaluate Do you think Central Asia's location or its mountains do more to keep the region isolated? Explain your answer.

SECTION 2 *(Pages 426–429)*

12. **a. Recall** What is the capital of each of the Caucasus republics?

   b. Compare What do the three Caucasus countries have in common?

   c. Elaborate What issues and challenges do the Caucasus countries need to address to improve their economies?

SECTION 3 (Pages 430–434)

13. a. Describe How did life in Central Asia change under Russian and Soviet rule?

b. Identify How did culture groups influence Central Asia? List at least two positive effects and two negative effects of cultural diffusion in Central Asia.

c. Evaluate Why do you think many former nomads now live in cities? Why do you think other people still choose to live as nomads?

SECTION 4 (Pages 435–439)

14. a. Identify What are some reforms that have taken place in Afghanistan since the fall of the Taliban?

b. Analyze How does having a limited amount of arable land affect Tajikistan's economy?

c. Elaborate How do you think political and environmental challenges in Central Asia affect the region's economy?

Map Activity

15. The Eurasian Republics On a separate sheet of paper, match the letters on the map with their correct labels.

Aral Sea	Pamirs
Caspian Sea	Astana, Kazakhstan
Afghanistan	Tashkent, Uzbekistan

Social Studies Skills

Using Math to Read Map Scales *Use the physical map of Central Asia in Section 1 to answer the following questions.*

16. How many miles does one inch represent?

17. How far is it from the shore of the Caspian Sea to Ismail Samani Peak?

18. How many kilometers long is the Amu Darya?

Using the Internet

19. Activity: Writing Home For thousands of years, nomads have traveled the lands of Central Asia. They move their herds to several different pasture areas as the seasons change. Through the online book, join a caravan of nomads. Find out what it is like to pack up your house, clothes, and all you own as you move from place to place. Then create a postcard to share your adventures with friends and family back home in the United States.

> 🡕 hmhsocialstudies.com

FOCUS ON READING AND VIEWING　*my*WriteSmart

20. Using Context Clues Look through your book for examples of restatement. Note one or two examples of restatement for each section of the chapter.

21. Giving a Travel Presentation Review your notes and select one country in Central Asia your audience might want to visit. Look for pictures of at least five locations in that country: buildings, monuments, or other interesting places. As you plan your presentation, use *my*WriteSmart in your eBook to create a brief introduction, a brief description of each location and its picture, and a conclusion. Use connecting words in your presentation, such as first, next, and finally, to help students follow along. Hold up each picture and point out important features as you make your presentation. After you have listened to all of your classmates' presentations, choose one of the presentations to retell to a partner. Make sure to retell the main ideas of the presentation.

Reading Social Studies

Using Context Clues

FOCUS ON READING

One way to figure out the meaning of an unfamiliar word or term is by finding clues in its context, the words or sentences surrounding it. A common context clue is a restatement. Restatements simply define the new word using ordinary words you already know. Notice how the following passage uses a restatement to define nomads.

> For centuries, Central Asians have made a living by raising horses, cattle, sheep, and goats. Many herders live as <u>nomads</u>, people who move often from place to place. The nomads move their herds from mountain pastures in the summer to lowland pastures in the winter.
>
> *From Section 3, History and Culture of Central Asia*

Restatement: people who move often from place to place

YOU TRY IT!

Read the following sentences and identify the restatement for each underlined term.

> Many other people in Kyrgyzstan are farmers. Fertile soils there allow a mix of irrigated crops and <u>dryland farming</u>, or farming that relies on rainfall instead of irrigation. . . .
>
> . . . Even with the decline in agricultural production, Tajikistan still relies on cotton farming for much of its income. However, only 7 percent of the country's land is <u>arable</u>, or suitable for growing crops.
>
> *From Section 4, Central Asia Today*

An Oral Report

People have shaped the world. Who are the important people in history? How do individuals contribute to societies, past and present? These are questions we ask as we try to understand our world.

Assignment

Use *my*WriteSmart to write an oral report about the individual achievements of a historical figure such as Queen Isabella, Martin Luther, Napoleon, or Mikhail Gorbachev.

1. Prewrite

Choose a Topic

- Choose a person who affected the history of Europe or Russia.
- Choose a specific achievement in the person's life. For example, you might choose to explain how Mikhail Gorbachev contributed to the end of the Cold War.

> **TIP** Think about why you chose this person. Is there something from your own personal experience or knowledge that makes this person interesting?

Gather and Organize Information

- Look for information about your person in the library or on the Internet. Identify the important main ideas and details about your person's life.
- Organize the main ideas and details in an outline or note cards. Speaking from an outline or note cards will make your speech sound more natural.

2. Write

Use a Writer's Framework

> **A Writer's Framework**
>
> **Introduction**
> - Introduce the person and the event.
> - Identify the importance of the event.
>
> **Body**
> - Write at least one paragraph for each major part of the event. Include specific details.
> - Use chronological, or time, order to organize the parts of the event.
>
> **Conclusion**
> - Summarize the importance of the person and event in the final paragraph.

3. Evaluate and Revise

Review and Improve Your Report

- Read your first draft at least twice, and then use the questions below to evaluate your report.
- Make the changes needed to improve your report.

Evaluation Questions for an Oral Report

1 Do you introduce the person and identify their importance?
2 Do you have one paragraph for each main idea?
3 Do you include specific details about the person?
4 Do you use chronological order, the order in time, to organize the person's achievement?
5 Do you end the paper with a summary of the importance of the person?

4. Proofread and Present

Give Your Oral Report the Finishing Touch

- Make sure your central idea or theme is clear and your oral report supports it.
- Use words or images that reflect your oral report's theme
- Maintain eye contact with your audience and pace yourself. Do not rush to finish your oral report.
- Vary your tone of voice to help bring out the meaning of your words.

5. Practice and Apply

Use the steps and strategies outlined in this workshop to write your oral report. Share your oral report with a partner. As you listen to your partner's report, organize and interpret the information by creating an outline of the report.

Southwest Asia and North Africa

The Nile River Valley

Since ancient times, the Nile River Valley has provided North Africans with fertile farm land, fresh water, and food.

The Sahara

The world's largest desert, the Sahara, dominates land and life in North Africa.

The Persian Gulf

The shallow waters of the Persian Gulf are home to the world's largest offshore oilfields.

Southwest Asia and North Africa

Explore the Satellite Image
Vast deserts, high mountains, and large rivers stand out clearly on this satellite image of Southwest Asia and North Africa. How do you think these features influence life in the region?

The Satellite's Path

>44'56.08<

>>>>>>>>>665.00'87<

567.476.348

+355

+799

+803

+999

456.094.

Southwest Asia and North Africa: Physical

ATLANTIC OCEAN

EUROPE

CENTRAL ASIA

Black Sea

Caspian Sea

PONTIC MOUNTAINS

Mount Ararat
16,945 ft (5,165 m)

KOPET DAG

TURKEY

TAURUS MTS.

Lake Urmia

ELBURZ MTS.

GREAT SALT DESERT

IRAN

PLATEAU OF IRAN

Strait of Gibraltar

CYPRUS

SYRIA

ZAGROS MOUNTAINS

MOROCCO

TUNISIA

Mediterranean Sea

LEBANON
ISRAEL

SYRIAN DESERT

IRAQ

Tigris R.

Euphrates R.

JORDAN

KUWAIT

ATLAS MOUNTAINS

Gulf of Sidra

Suez Canal

Dead Sea

AN NAFUD

Persian Gulf

OMAN

Gulf of Aqaba

BAHRAIN
QATAR

Gulf of Oman

ALGERIA

LIBYA

EGYPT

Arabian Desert

Gulf of Aqaba

UNITED ARAB EMIRATES

Western Sahara
(Claimed by Morocco)

S A H A R A

Aswan High Dam

Red Sea

SAUDI ARABIA

ARABIAN PENINSULA

OMAN

Ahaggar Mountains

Nile River

Nubian Desert

RUB' AL-KHALI

Arabian Sea

S A H E L

Libyan Desert

YEMEN

Blue Nile R.

Gulf of Aden

Socotra (YEMEN)

White Nile R.

AFRICA

ELEVATION

Feet		Meters
13,120		4,000
6,560		2,000
1,640		500
656		200
(Sea level) 0		0 (Sea level)
Below sea level		Below sea level

0   200   400 Miles

0   200   400 Kilometers

Projection: Lambert Conformal

ATLANTIC OCEAN

Geography Skills

Place Southwest Asia and North Africa are separated by a human feature, the Suez Canal.

1. **Name** What is the name of the large peninsula in Southwest Asia?
2. **Explain** What country has a mountain with an elevation greater than 16,000 feet (7,300m)?

Southwest Asia and North Africa

Geographical Extremes: Southwest Asia and North Africa

Longest River	**Nile River, northeastern Africa:** 4,132 miles (6,650 kilometers)
Highest Point	**Kuh-e Damavand, Iran:** 18,606 feet (5,671 m)
Lowest Point	**Dead Sea, Israel/Jordan:** 1,348 feet (411 m) below sea level
Highest Recorded Temperature	**Kebili, Tunisia:** 131°F (55°C)
Driest Place	**Aden, Yemen:** 1.8 inches (4.6 cm) average precipitation per year
Largest Country	**Algeria:** 919,595 square miles (2,381,741 square km)
Smallest Country	**Bahrain:** 257 square miles (666 square km)
Saltiest Lake	**Dead Sea, Israel/Jordan:** 33 percent salt content
Most Powerful Earthquake	**Erzincan, Turkey, 1939:** 7.8 magnitude

A high salt content keeps people afloat in the Dead Sea.

Size Comparison: The U.S. and Southwest Asia and North Africa

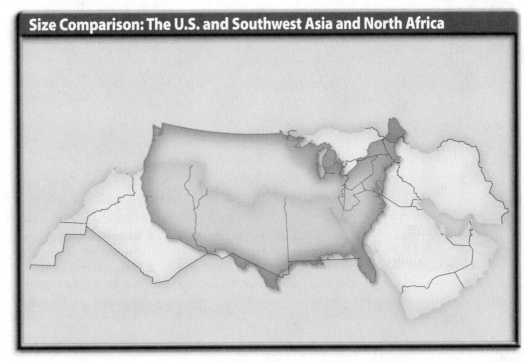

Southwest Asia and North Africa: Political

map zone
Geography Skills

Place All countries in this region have access to the sea. Even Jordan has a small strip of shoreline that provides access to the Red Sea.

1. **Name** What are the five largest countries in this region?
2. **Make Inferences** How do you think a country's size relates to its population?

Southwest Asia and North Africa

Southwest Asia and North Africa: Resources

Major Resources

- Coal
- Natural gas
- Oil
- Hydroelectric power
- Uranium
- Silver
- Other minerals
- Seafood

Land Use

- Major manufacturing and trade centers
- Oil pipelines
- Shipping lanes

0   250   500 Miles

0   250   500 Kilometers

Projection: Azimuthal Equal-Area

map Zone Geography Skills

Place The key resource of this region is oil.

1. **Name** Which resource is heavily concentrated between Abu Dhabi and Baghdad?

2. **Explain** Based on the map, how is oil transported out of Southwest Asia and North Africa? How can you tell?

Southwest Asia and North Africa: Population

EUROPE

CENTRAL ASIA

ATLANTIC OCEAN

50°N

40°N

Black Sea

Caspian Sea

Istanbul

Mashhad

Izmir

Aegean Sea

Tehran

Aleppo

Baghdad

Strait of Gibraltar

Algiers

Damascus

Casablanca

Mediterranean Sea

Tel Aviv

Kuwait City

30°N

Alexandria

Persian Gulf

Cairo

Gulf of Suez

Gulf of Oman

Riyadh

Red Sea

Jeddah

20°N

Arabian Sea

Sanaa

Gulf of Aden

10°N

AFRICA

ATLANTIC OCEAN

0°

10°S

Persons per square mile / **Persons per square km**

Persons per square mile	Persons per square km
520	200
260	100
130	50
25	10
3	1
0	0

● Major cities over 2 million

0   250   500 Miles

0   250   500 Kilometers

Projection: Azimuthal Equal-Area

map zone

Geography Skills

Place In this region, most people live in plains and valleys.

1. **Identify** What is the population density in the area surrounding Cario?

2. **Compare** Compare this map to the physical map. How do physical features influence where people live in the region?

Southwest Asia and North Africa

EUROPE

CENTRAL ASIA

ATLANTIC OCEAN

50°N

40°N

Black Sea

Caspian Sea

30°N

Strait of Gibraltar

Mediterranean Sea

Aegean Sea

Gulf of Suez

Persian Gulf

Gulf of Oman

Red Sea

20°N

Arabian Sea

Gulf of Aden

10°N

0°

ATLANTIC OCEAN

10°S

AFRICA

10°W

0°

10°E

Climate Types
- Desert
- Steppe
- Mediterranean
- Humid subtropical

0   250   500 Miles

0   250   500 Kilometers

Projection: Azimuthal Equal-Area

map zone

Geography Skills

Regions Hot and dry climates dominate Southwest Asia and North Africa.

1. Locate Which climates are found in this region?

2. Make Generalizations How do you think the region's climate influences people's daily lives?

Regional Database

Southwest Asia and North Africa

COUNTRY Capital	FLAG	POPULATION	AREA (sq mi)	PER CAPITA GDP (U.S. $)	LIFE EXPECTANCY AT BIRTH	TVS PER 1,000 PEOPLE
Algeria Algiers		37.4 million	919,595	$7,600	74.7	107
Bahrain Manama		1.2 million	257	$29,200	78.3	446
Cyprus Nicosia		1.1 million	3,571	$27,500	78	154
Egypt Cairo		83.7 million	386,662	$6,700	72.9	170
Iran Tehran		78.9 million	636,296	$13,300	70.4	154
Iraq Baghdad		31.1 million	168,754	$7,200	70.9	82
Israel Jerusalem		7.6 million	8,019	$32,800	81.1	328
Jordan Amman		6.5 million	35,637	$6,100	80.2	83
Kuwait Kuwait City		2.6 million	6,880	$40,500	77.3	480
Lebanon Beirut		4.1 million	4,015	$16,000	75.2	355
Libya Tripoli		5.6 million	679,362	$12,300	77.8	139
Morocco Rabat		32.3 million	172,414	$5,400	76.1	165
Oman Muscat		3.1 million	82,031	$29,600	74.5	575
Qatar Doha		2 million	4,416	$103,900	78.1	866
United States Washington, D.C.		316.7 million	3,794,083	$50,700	78.6	844

COUNTRY Capital	FLAG	POPULATION	AREA (sq mi)	PER CAPITA GDP (U.S. $)	LIFE EXPECTANCY AT BIRTH	TVS PER 1,000 PEOPLE
Saudi Arabia Riyadh		26.5 million	756,985	$31,800	74.4	263
Syria Damascus		22.5 million	71,498	$5,100	74.9	68
Tunisia Tunis		10.7 million	63,170	$9,900	75.2	190
Turkey Ankara		79.7 million	301,384	$15,200	72.8	328
United Arab Emirates Abu Dhabi		5.3 million	32,000	$49,800	76.7	309
Yemen Sanaa		24.8 million	2,300	$2,400	64.1	286
United States Washington, D.C.		316.7 million	3,794,083	$50,700	78.6	844

ANALYSIS SKILL **ANALYZING TABLES**

1. How does the per capita GDP of countries in this region compare to the per capita GDP of the United States?
2. Based on the table, which countries seem to have the highest standard of living?

Oil Giants

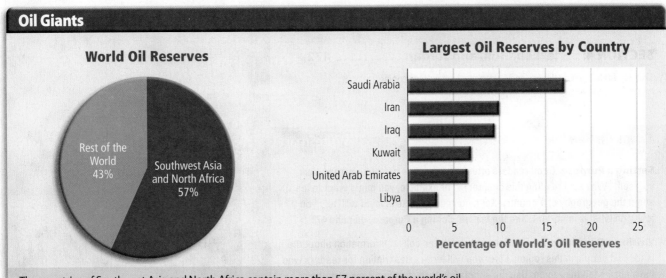

World Oil Reserves

- Rest of the World 43%
- Southwest Asia and North Africa 57%

Largest Oil Reserves by Country

Saudi Arabia, Iran, Iraq, Kuwait, United Arab Emirates, Libya

Percentage of World's Oil Reserves

The countries of Southwest Asia and North Africa contain more than 57 percent of the world's oil. Saudi Arabia has by far the most oil, with about 17 percent of the world's total.

The Eastern Mediterranean

Essential Question
*my*Notebook

How has religion shaped the development of the nations of the Eastern Mediterranean?

Texas Essential Knowledge and Skills (TEKS)

1A, 1B, 2A, 2B, 3A, 3B, 3C, 3D, 4B, 4C, 4D, 4F, 5A, 6B, 15B, 15C, 15D, 15F, 18B, 19B, 21A, 21B, 21C, 22B, 22C, 22D

The Big Idea The Eastern Mediterranean, a region with a dry climate and valuable resources, sits in the middle of three continents.

The Big Idea Although Turkey has historically been more Asian than European, its leaders are seeking to develop closer economic ties to Europe.

The Big Idea Israel and the Palestinian Territories are home to Jews and Arabs who continue to struggle over the region's land.

The Big Idea Syria, Lebanon, and Jordan are Arab nations coping with religious diversity.

FOCUS ON READING AND WRITING
my WriteSmart

Setting a Purpose Good readers often set a purpose before they read. Ask yourself, "Why am I reading this chapter?" For example, you might want to learn about the geography of a country. Keeping your purpose in mind will help you focus on what is important. **See the lesson, Setting a Purpose, on page 479.**

Writing a Description As you read this chapter, collect information about the lands and people in this region. Later you will write a description for readers who have not visited the region. Use the annotation tools in your eBook to gather information for your assignment.

EUROPE

Istanbul
Sea of Marmara

40°N

Izmir

Gediz River

Menderes River

Aegean Sea

○ National capital
• Other cities
⬚ Some areas controlled by the Palestinian Authority

0   50   100 Miles
0   50   100 Kilometers

Projection: Lambert Azimuthal Equal-Area

Mediterranean Sea

EGYPT

30°E

Geography The Jordan River valley in Israel provides fertile soils for farming.

Black Sea

N
W · E
S

HISTORY Jesus' Jerusalem

↗ hmhsocialstudies.com VIDEO

Sakarya River

Kızıl River

★ Ankara

T U R K E Y

Lake Van

Adana

Aleppo

Euphrates River

Orontes River

Gulf of Antalya

CYPRUS
★
Nicosia

S Y R I A

Tigris River

I R A N

Tripoli

LEBANON
Beirut ★

Damascus ★

Haifa

Sea of Galilee

Jordan R.

I R A Q

ISRAEL

West Bank

Tel Aviv
Jerusalem ★ ★ Amman
Gaza Jericho

Dead Sea

J O R D A N

**S A U D I
A R A B I A**

Elat
Aqaba

map zone

Geography Skills

Place The Eastern Mediterranean region is located at the crossroads between Europe and Asia.

1. Locate What is Turkey's capital?

2. Interpret Why is the region called the Eastern Mediterranean?

History Carved completely out of a sandstone cliff in Jordan, the ancient city of Petra dates back more than 2,000 years.

Culture In Turkey, a Muslim dervish spins around in a circle during a ritual dance.

Physical Geography

 TEKS 3A, 3B, 3C, 4D, 4F, 5A, 6B, 21C, 22D

What You Will Learn...

Main Ideas

1. The Eastern Mediterranean's physical features include the Bosporus, the Dead Sea, rivers, mountains, deserts, and plains.
2. The region's climate is mostly dry with little vegetation.
3. Important natural resources in the Eastern Mediterranean include valuable minerals and the availability of water.

The Big Idea

The Eastern Mediterranean, a region with a dry climate and valuable resources, sits in the middle of three continents.

Key Terms and Places

Dardanelles, *p. 458*
Bosporus, *p. 458*
Sea of Marmara, *p. 458*
Jordan River, *p. 459*
Dead Sea, *p. 459*
Syrian Desert, *p. 460*

hmhsocialstudies.com
TAKING NOTES

Use the graphic organizer online to take notes on the physical features, climate and vegetation, and natural resources of the region.

If YOU lived there...

You live in Izmir, Turkey, on the Aegean Sea, but are traveling into the far eastern part of the country called eastern Anatolia. At home you are used to a warm, dry Mediterranean climate. You are surprised by the colder and wetter climate you're experiencing. Two mountain ranges come together here, and you notice that the peaks are covered with snow.

How does geography affect climate in these two places?

BUILDING BACKGROUND The Eastern Mediterranean region lies at the crossroads of Europe, Africa, and Asia. In ancient times, Greek colonists settled here, and it was later part of the Roman Empire. Geographically, however, it is almost entirely in Southwest Asia.

Locate Israel, Lebanon, Turkey, Cyprus, Syria, and Jordan on the map on the next page. The countries of the Eastern Mediterranean make up part of a larger region called Southwest Asia. This region is sometimes referred to as the Middle East. Europeans first called the region the Middle East to distinguish it from the Far East, which included China and Japan.

Physical Features

As you can see on the physical map on the next page, a narrow waterway separates Europe from Asia. This waterway is made up of the **Dardanelles** (dahrd-uhn-ELZ), the **Bosporus** (BAHS-puh-ruhs), and the **Sea of Marmara** (MAHR-muh-ruh). Large ships travel through the waterway, which connects the Black Sea to the Mediterranean Sea. The Bosporus also splits the country of Turkey into two parts, a small part lies in Europe and the rest in Asia. The Asian part of Turkey includes the large peninsula called Anatolia (a-nuh-TOH-lee-uh).

The Eastern Mediterranean: Physical

Black Sea

Bosporus
Sea of Marmara
Dardanelles
Gediz R.
Menderes R.
Aegean Sea
Sakarya
Kızıl R.
PONTIC MOUNTAINS
Mount Ararat
16,945 ft (5,165 m)
Lake Van
Tigris River

T U R K E Y

TAURUS MOUNTAINS
Gulf of Antalya

CYPRUS
Mediterranean Sea

Orontes R.
SYRIA
LEBANON MOUNTAINS
LEBANON
Jordan River
Sea of Galilee
Euphrates River
ISRAEL
SYRIAN DESERT
IRAQ
Dead Sea
NEGEV DESERT
JORDAN
SAUDI ARABIA
EGYPT

40°E
40°N
30°E
30°N

ELEVATION

Feet	Meters
13,120	4,000
6,560	2,000
1,640	500
656	200
(Sea level) 0	0 (Sea level)
Below sea level	Below sea level

0   100   200 Miles
0   100   200 Kilometers
Projection: Lambert Azimuthal Equal-Area

map zone

Geography Skills

Place Turkey's elevation is higher than the rest of the region.

1. **Locate** Where is the Dead Sea located?
2. **Draw Conclusions** Notice the physical features in Jordan and Israel. What do you think the climate is like here?

Mount Ararat's snowcapped peak rises about 17,000 feet (5,180 m) in eastern Turkey.

Rivers and Lakes

The **Jordan River** begins in Syria and flows south through Israel and Jordan. The river finally empties into a large lake called the **Dead Sea**. As its name suggests, the Dead Sea contains little life. Only bacteria lives in the lake's extremely salty water. The world's saltiest lake, its surface is 1,312 feet (400 m) below sea level—the lowest point on any continent.

Mountains and Plains

As you can see on the map, two mountain systems stretch across Turkey. The Pontic Mountains run east–west along the northern edge. The Taurus Mountains run east–west along the southern edge.

Heading south from Turkey and into Syria lies a narrow plain. The Euphrates River flows southeast from Turkey through the plains to Syria and beyond.

Dead Sea

Because of its high salt content, swimmers do not sink in the Dead Sea.

ANALYZING VISUALS
What appears on the shore of the Dead Sea?

Farther inland lies plateaus, hills, and valleys. A rift valley that begins in Africa extends northward into Syria. Hills rise on both sides of the rift. Two main mountain ridges run north–south. One runs from southwestern Syria through western Jordan. The other, closer to the coast, runs through Lebanon and Israel.

READING CHECK Summarizing What are the region's main physical features?

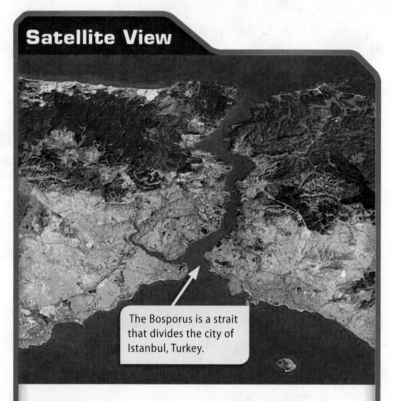

Satellite View

The Bosporus is a strait that divides the city of Istanbul, Turkey.

Istanbul and the Bosporus

Throughout history, geography has almost always determined the location of a city. Istanbul, Turkey, which sits between Europe and Asia, is no exception. In this satellite image the city of Istanbul appears light brown and white. The body of water that cuts through the city is a strait called the Bosporus. It separates the Sea of Marmara in the south with the Black Sea in the north. Historically, the Bosporus has served as a prized area for empires that have controlled the city. Today, the strait is a major shipping route.

Drawing Conclusions Why do you think the Bosporus has been seen as a strategic location?

Climate and Vegetation

The Eastern Mediterranean is a mostly dry region. However, there are important variations. As you can see on the map on the next page, Turkey's Black Sea coast and the Mediterranean coast all the way to northern Israel have a Mediterranean climate. Much of interior Turkey experiences a steppe climate. Central Syria and lands farther south have a desert climate. A small area of northeastern Turkey has a humid subtropical climate.

The region's driest areas are its deserts. Much of Syria and Jordan is covered by the **Syrian Desert**. This desert of rock and gravel usually receives less than five inches (12.7 cm) of rainfall a year. Another desert, the Negev (NE-gev), lies in southern Israel. Here the temperatures can reach as high as 114°F (46°C), and annual rainfall totals barely two inches.

In such dry conditions, only shrubs grow scattered throughout the region's deserts. However, in other areas vegetation is plentiful. In Israel, more than 2,800 species of plants thrive throughout the country's various environments.

READING CHECK Generalizing What are climates like in the Eastern Mediterranean?

Natural Resources

Because the Eastern Mediterranean is so dry, water is a valuable resource. The people of this region are mostly farmers. The region lacks oil resources, but does have valuable minerals.

Land and Water

In this dry region the limited availability of water limits how land is used. Commercial farms can only grow crops where rain or irrigation provides enough water.

Black Sea

TURKEY

CYPRUS

Mediterranean Sea

SYRIA

LEBANON

ISRAEL

JORDAN

Aegean Sea

Persian Gulf

Climate Types

- Desert
- Steppe
- Mediterranean
- Humid subtropical

0   150   300 Miles

0   150   300 Kilometers

Projection: Lambert Azimuthal Equal-Area

map zone

Geography Skills

Place The region has mostly desert, Mediterranean, and steppe climates.

1. **Locate** What countries experience a desert climate?
2. **Contrast** How does Turkey's climate differ from the rest of the region?

In drier areas, subsistence farming and livestock herding are common. In the desert areas, available water supports a few nomadic herders, but no farming.

Mineral Resources

The region's resources include many minerals, including sulfur, mercury, and copper. Syria, Jordan, and Israel all produce phosphates—mineral salts that contain the element phosphorus. Phosphates are used to make fertilizers. This region also produces asphalt—the dark tarlike material used to pave streets.

READING CHECK **Drawing Conclusions** How do people use the region's mineral resources?

SUMMARY AND PREVIEW In this section you learned about the physical geography of the Eastern Mediterranean. Next, you will learn about Turkey.

Section 1 Assessment

hmhsocialstudies.com
ONLINE QUIZ

Reviewing Ideas, Terms, and Places

1. **a. Describe** What makes the **Dead Sea** unusual?
   b. Explain What physical features separate Europe and Asia?
2. **a. Recall** What desert covers much of Syria and Jordan?
   b. Make Generalizations What is the climate of the Eastern Mediterranean like?
3. **a. Identify** What mineral resource is produced by Syria, Jordan, and Israel?
   b. Draw Conclusions Why must farmers in the region rely on irrigation?
   c. Geographic Questions Look at the map on this page. Pose and answer a question about climate patterns in the Eastern Mediterranean.

Critical Thinking

4. **Comparing** Using your notes, summarize the physical geography of Israel and Turkey. Use this chart to organize your notes.

Physical Features	
Turkey	Israel

Focus on Writing

my WriteSmart

5. **Describing Physical Geography** What physical features would you include in your description? How would you describe the climate? Note your ideas.

Turkey

 TEKS 1A, 1B, 2A, 2B, 3A, 3B, 3C, 3D, 4B, 4C, 15B, 18B, 21B, 21C, 22D

What You Will Learn...

Main Ideas

1. Turkey's history includes invasion by the Romans, rule by the Ottomans, and a twentieth-century democracy.
2. Turkey's people are mostly ethnic Turks, and its culture is a mixture of modern and traditional.
3. Today, Turkey is a democratic nation seeking economic opportunities and considering European Union membership.

The Big Idea

Although Turkey has historically been more Asian than European, its leaders are seeking to develop closer economic ties to Europe.

Key Terms and Places

Ankara, *p. 464*
Istanbul, *p. 465*
secular, *p. 465*

TAKING NOTES

Use the graphic organizer online to take notes on Turkey.

If YOU lived there...

Your cousins from central Turkey are coming to visit your hometown, Istanbul. You think your city is both beautiful and interesting. You like to stroll in the Grand Bazaar and smell the spices for sale. You admire the architecture of the Blue Mosque, whose walls are lined with thousands of tiny tiles. You also like to visit the elegant Topkapi Palace, where sultans once lived.

What sights will you show your cousins?

BUILDING BACKGROUND Many sites in Turkey reflect the country's long and diverse cultural history. Throughout the country you will find the ruins of ancient Greek temples and Roman palaces. You can also see magnificent early Christian buildings and art, as well as the palaces and mosques of Ottoman rulers.

Close-up

Early Farming Village

The village of Çatal Hüyük in modern Turkey is one of the earliest farming villages discovered. Around 8,000 years ago, the village was home to about 5,000–6,000 people living in more than 1,000 houses. Villagers farmed, hunted and fished, traded with distant lands, and worshipped gods in special shrines.

Villagers used simple channels to move water to their fields.

Wheat, barley, and peas were some of the main crops grown outside the village.

History

Around 8,000 years ago the area that is now Turkey was home to one of the world's earliest farming villages. For centuries invasions from powerful empires shaped the region. By the 1920s Turkey was a democratic nation.

Invasions

Byzantium was an ancient Greek city located on the site of present-day Istanbul. When the Romans invaded the area, they captured the city of Byzantium and later renamed it Constantinople. Recall how this site is at the crossroads between Europe and Asia. This made Constantinople an important trading port. After the fall of Rome, Constantinople became the capital of the Byzantine Empire.

In the AD 1000s a nomadic people from central Asia called the Seljuk Turks invaded the area. In 1453 another Turkish people, the Ottoman Turks, captured the city of Constantinople and made it the capital of their Islamic empire.

BIOGRAPHY

Kemal Atatürk
(1881–1938)

Known as the Father of the Turks, Kemal Atatürk was Turkey's first president. As president, he modernized Turkey, which dramatically changed the Turkish way of life. Atatürk separated all aspects of Islam from Turkey's government. He even closed Islamic schools. Turkey's people were also encouraged to wear Western dress and adopt surnames.

Generalizing How did Atatürk change Turkey's government?

The Ottoman Empire

During the 1500s and 1600s the Ottoman Empire was very powerful. The empire controlled territory in northern Africa, southwestern Asia, and southeastern Europe.

In World War I the Ottomans fought on the losing side. When the war ended, they lost most of their territory. Military officers then took over the government, led by a war hero, Mustafa Kemal.

Houses were made of wood covered with mud. Since they didn't have doors, people entered on ladders through rooftop openings.

Inside their houses, villagers made the earliest-known wooden bowls and cups, pottery, and mirrors.

Some houses were built as shrines and had small statues of goddesses and large sculpted bulls' heads.

ANALYSIS SKILL ANALYZING VISUALS

How did farmers get water to their fields?

Turkey: Population

map zone **Geography Skills**

Place About 77 million people live in Turkey.
1. **Identify** What is the population density of Ankara?
2. **Contrast** How does the population density around major cities differ from the rest of the country?

Persons per square mile / **Persons per square km**

Persons per square mile	Persons per square km
520	200
260	100
130	50
25	10
3	1

0   500   1000 Miles
0   500   1000 Kilometers
Projection:
Lambert Azimuthal Equal-Area

FOCUS ON READING

Set a purpose for reading by asking yourself what you want to learn about Turkey's people and culture.

ACADEMIC VOCABULARY

method a way of doing something

Kemal later adopted the name Kemal Atatürk, which means Father of Turks. Atatürk created the democratic nation of Turkey and moved the capital to **Ankara** from Constantinople, which was renamed Istanbul.

Modern Turkey

Atatürk believed Turkey needed to modernize and adopt Western **methods** in order to be a strong nation. To achieve this, he focused on making cultural changes. For example, he banned the fez, the traditional hat of Turkish men, and required that they wear European-style hats. Reforms urged women to stop wearing traditional veils. Women were also encouraged to vote, work, and hold office. Other ways Atatürk modernized Turkey included replacing the Arabic alphabet with the Latin alphabet, and adopting the metric system.

READING CHECK **Finding Main Ideas** How did Atatürk modernize Turkey?

People and Culture

Most of Turkey's people are mostly ethnic Turks. Kurds are the largest minority and make up 20 percent of the population.

Turkey's culture today is a reflection of some of Kemal Atatürk's changes. He created a cultural split between Turkey's urban middle class and rural villagers. The lifestyle and attitudes of middle-class Turks have much in common with those of the European middle class. In contrast, most rural Turks are more traditional. Islam strongly influences their attitudes on matters such as the role of women.

Turkish cooking features olives, vegetables, cheese, yogurt, and bread. Kebabs—grilled meats on a skewer—are a favorite Turkish dish.

READING CHECK **Contrasting** How are urban Turks different from rural Turks?

With about 10 million people, Istanbul, shown here, is Turkey's largest city.

Turkey Today

Turkey's government meets in the capital of Ankara, but **Istanbul** is Turkey's largest city. Istanbul's location will serve as an economic bridge to Europe as Turkey plans to join the European Union.

Government

Turkey's legislature is called the National Assembly. A president and a prime minister share executive power.

Although most of its people are Muslim, Turkey is a secular state. **Secular** means that religion is kept separate from government. For example, the religion of Islam allows a man to have up to four wives. However, by Turkish law a man is permitted to have just one wife. In recent years Islamic political parties have attempted to increase Islam's role in Turkish society.

Economy and Resources

As a member of the European Union, Turkey's economy and people would benefit by increased trade with Europe. Turkey's economy includes modern factories as well as village farming and craft making.

Among the most important industries are textiles and clothing, cement, and electronics. About 25 percent of Turkey's labor force works in agriculture. Grains, cotton, sugar beets, and hazelnuts are major crops.

Turkey is rich in natural resources, which include oil, coal, and iron ore. Water is also a valuable resource in the region. Turkey has spent billions of dollars building dams to increase its water supply. On one hand, these dams provide hydroelectricity. On the other hand, some of these dams have restricted the flow of river water into neighboring countries.

READING CHECK **Finding Main Ideas** What kind of government does Turkey have?

SUMMARY AND PREVIEW In this section you learned about Turkey's history, people, government, and economy. Next, you will learn about Israel.

Section 2 Assessment

hmhsocialstudies.com
ONLINE QUIZ

Reviewing Ideas, Terms, and Places

1. **a. Recall** What city did both the Romans and Ottoman Turks capture?
   b. Identify How did Atatürk's achievements help modernize Turkey?
   c. Explain How was the character of Turkey influenced by the Ottomans?
2. **a. Recall** What ethnic group makes up 20 percent of Turkey's population?
   b. Draw Conclusions What makes Turkey **secular**?
   c. Elaborate Why do you think some Turks want Turkey to join the European Union?

Critical Thinking

3. **Summarizing** Using the information in your notes, summarize Turkey's history and Turkey today.

Turkey's History	Turkey Today

Focus on Writing

4. **Describing the Human Geography Turkey** A description of Turkey might include details about its people, culture, government, and economy. Take notes on the details you think are important human features.

Israel

 TEKS 1A, 1B, 2A, 2B, 3A, 3B, 3C, 3D, 4D, 15B, 15C, 15D, 15F, 18B, 19B, 21A, 22B, 22C, 22D

What You Will Learn...

Main Ideas

1. Israel's history includes the the ancient Israelites and the creation of the State of Israel.
2. In Israel today, Jewish culture is a major part of daily life.
3. The Palestinian Territories are areas next to Israel—Gaza and the West Bank—controlled partly by Palestinian Arabs.

The Big Idea

Israel and the Palestinian Territories are home to Jews and Arabs who continue to struggle over the region's land.

Key Terms and Places

Judaism, *p. 466*
Diaspora, *p. 466*
Jerusalem, *p. 466*
Zionism, *p. 467*
kosher, *p. 468*
kibbutz, *p. 468*
Gaza, *p. 469*
West Bank, *p. 469*

hmhsocialstudies.com
TAKING NOTES

Use the graphic organizer online to take notes on Israel and the Palestinian Territories.

If YOU lived there...

When you were only six years old, your family moved to Israel from Russia. You are learning Hebrew in school, but your parents and grandparents still speak Russian at home. When you first moved here, your parents worked in an office building, but you now live on a farm where you grow oranges and tomatoes.

What do you like about living in Israel?

BUILDING BACKGROUND Modern Israel was formed in 1948. Since then immigrants from many parts of the world have made the population of Israel very diverse. Many Jews emigrated to Israel from Russia, Europe, the Middle East, and the Americas.

History

Israel is often referred to as the Holy Land because it is home to sacred sites for three major religions—Judaism, Christianity, and Islam. **Judaism** is the religion of the Jewish people. It is the world's oldest monotheistic religion. Many events in Jewish history and in the life of Jesus happened in Israel.

The Holy Land

The Israelites, the descendants of the Hebrews and ancestors of the Jews, first established the kingdom of Israel about 1000 BC. It covered roughly the same area as the modern state of Israel. In the 60s BC the Roman Empire conquered the region, which was called Judea. After several Jewish revolts, the Romans forced many Jews to leave the region and renamed it Palestine in AD 135. This dispersal of the Jewish population is known as the **Diaspora**.

Muslims conquered Palestine in the mid-600s. However, from the late 1000s to the late 1200s, Christians from Europe launched a series of invasions of Palestine called the Crusades. The Crusaders captured the city of **Jerusalem** in 1099. In time the Crusaders were pushed out of the area. Palestine then became part of the Ottoman Empire. After World War I, it came under British control.

Creation of Israel

Zionism, a nationalist movement calling for Jews to reestablish a Jewish state in their ancient homeland, began in Europe in the late 1800s. Tens of thousands of Jews and Arabs began moving to the region.

In 1947 the United Nations voted to divide the Palestine Mandate, then under British control, into Jewish and Arab states. While Arab countries rejected this plan, the Jews accepted it, and a year later created the State of Israel. Five Arab armies then invaded Israel. Against the odds, the Israelis defeated the Arabs.

After Israel's victory, many Palestinians fled to neighboring Arab countries. Israel and Arab countries have fought each other in several wars since then. Disputes between the two sides continue today.

READING CHECK **Summarizing** What two groups played a large role in Israel's history?

Israel Today

Jews from all over the world, including many who fled from Arab lands, have migrated to Israel hoping to find peace and stability. Yet, they have faced continual conflicts with neighboring countries. Despite these problems, Israelis have built a modern, democratic country.

Primary Source

HISTORIC DOCUMENT
The Dead Sea Scrolls

Written by Jews about 2,000 years ago, the Dead Sea Scrolls include prayers, commentaries, letters, and passages from the Hebrew Bible. Hidden in caves near the Dead Sea, these scrolls were not found until 1947. Here are two passages from a prayer written on one of the scrolls.

" With knowledge shall I sing out my music, only for the glory of God, my harp, my lyre for His holiness established; the flute of my lips will I lift, His law its tuning fork. **"**

" When first I begin campaign or journey, His name shall I bless; when first I set out or turn to come back; when I sit down or rise up, when I spread my bed, then shall I rejoice in Him. **"**

ANALYSIS SKILL **ANALYZING PRIMARY SOURCES**
What does this prayer from the Dead Sea Scrolls reveal about the people who wrote it?

Government and Economy

Israel has a prime minister and a parliament—the Knesset. There are several major political parties and many smaller ones.

Israel's government has built a strong military. At age 18 most Israeli men and women must serve at least one year.

FOCUS ON READING
What do you want to find out about Israel today?

Jerusalem

The city of Jerusalem is sacred to three world religions—Judaism, Christianity, and Islam.

Israel's economy is modern and diverse. Important exports include high-tech equipment and cut diamonds. Israel has increased food production by irrigating farmland. Israel's economy also benefits from the millions of visitors who come to Israel to see the country's historic sites.

Cities, Diversity, and Languages

Most of Israel's population lives in cities. Jerusalem, the capital, and Tel Aviv are Israel's largest cities.

About 75 percent of Israel's population is Jewish. The rest of the country's people are mostly Arab. About three-fourths of Israeli Arabs are Muslim, but some are Christian. Israel's Jewish population includes Jews from all parts of the world. Many arrive not knowing Hebrew, one of Israel's official languages. To assist these new citizens, the government provides language classes. Israeli Arabs speak Arabic, Israel's other official language.

Culture and Rural Settlements

Israeli Jewish culture is rich in holidays and special foods. For Jews, the Sabbath, from sunset Friday until sundown Saturday, is a holy day. Yom Kippur, a very important holiday, is celebrated in the fall. Passover, in the spring, celebrates the Israelites' escape from captivity in ancient Egypt.

Because Judaism is a way of life, religious laws address every aspect of daily life, including what Jews should eat. These laws come from the Hebrew Bible. **Kosher**, which means "fit" in Hebrew, is the term used for food allowed under Jewish dietary laws. Not all Jews in Israel eat a kosher diet, but all government and army kitchens serve kosher food. This enables both religious and secular Jews to participate together in these core institutions.

Some Israeli Jews live in a collective community known as a **kibbutz** (ki-BOOHTS). Traditionally, a kibbutz is a large farm where people shared everything in common. About 100,000 Israeli Jews live in more than 250 diverse kibbutzim.

READING CHECK **Generalizing** What is Jewish culture in Israel like?

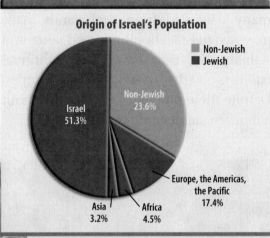

Origin of Israel's Population

- Non-Jewish
- Jewish

Israel 51.3%

Non-Jewish 23.6%

Europe, the Americas, the Pacific 17.4%

Asia 3.2%

Africa 4.5%

Jews from all over the world have settled in Israel. The graph above shows the percentages of Jews who migrated from different places. Non-Jews in Israel include Arabs who are Muslims, Christians, and Druze. This photo shows a Jewish teenager celebrating his bar mitzvah—a ceremony that acknowledges 13-year-old Jewish boys as adults in the community.

ANALYZING VISUALS According to the graph, what is the origin of most Israeli Jews?

Israel's Population

The Palestinian Territories

In 1967, during the Six-Day War, Israel captured areas from Jordan and Egypt inhabited by Palestinian Arabs—Gaza, the West Bank, and East Jerusalem. In the 1990s Israel agreed to turn over parts of these territories to the Palestinians. In return, the Palestine Liberation Organization (PLO) agreed to recognize Israel's right to exist and pledged to renounce terrorism. These territories have continued to be central to ongoing conflicts between Israelis and Arabs.

Gaza and the West Bank

Gaza is a small, crowded coastal area where more than a million Palestinians live. The area has few resources. However, citrus fruit is grown in irrigated fields. Unemployment is high for the Palestinians living in Gaza. In 2005 Israel transferred control of Gaza to the Palestinians.

The **West Bank** is much larger than Gaza and has a population of about 2.7 million. It is mostly rural, but the territory has three large cities—Nablus, Hebron, and Ramallah. The West Bank's economy is mostly based on agriculture. Farmers rely on irrigation to grow their crops.

Since Israel gained control of the West Bank in 1967, 280,000 Israelis have moved there. Israelis and Palestinians dispute the territory. Peace agreements have tried to divide the land fairly. This conflict over land and terrorist attacks against Israel are the greatest sources of tension between Arabs and Israelis.

East Jerusalem

Other disputed land includes Israel's capital, Jerusalem. Control of Jerusalem is a difficult and emotional issue for Jews, Muslims, and Christians. The city has sites that are holy to all three religions. Areas of the old city are divided into Jewish, Muslim, and Christian neighborhoods.

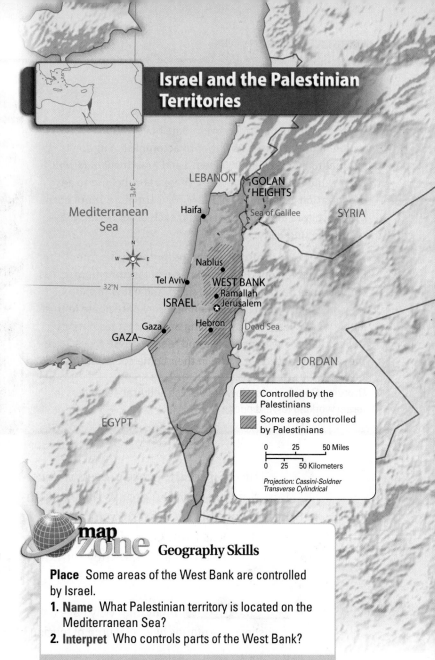

Israel and the Palestinian Territories

Controlled by the Palestinians

Some areas controlled by Palestinians

0   25   50 Miles
0   25   50 Kilometers

Projection: Cassini-Soldner Transverse Cylindrical

map zone **Geography Skills**

Place Some areas of the West Bank are controlled by Israel.
1. Name What Palestinian territory is located on the Mediterranean Sea?
2. Interpret Who controls parts of the West Bank?

After the 1948 war, Israel controlled West Jerusalem and Jordan controlled East Jerusalem. Israel captured East Jerusalem in 1967. Jerusalem is the ancient and modern capital of Israel. Palestinians also claim Jerusalem as their capital.

The Territories Today

In 2006, control of the territories was split between two opposing Palestinian political groups. The West Bank was governed by a group called Fatah, and Gaza by the group Hamas. Today political tensions in the region remain high.

Teenagers for Peace

Peace between Israeli Jews and Palestinian Arabs has not been easy in the past. Moreover, some believe peace in the region might be impossible ever to accomplish. But don't tell that to a group of 2,000 Jewish and Arab teenagers who are making a difference in Israel. These teens belong to an organization called Seeds of Peace. To learn more about each other's culture and thus understand each other better, these teens meet regularly.

Seeds of Peace also hosts camps for teenagers from high-conflict regions. Participating students come from across conflict lines. At camp they live, sleep, and eat with those they have believed are their enemies. They participate in trust activities and learn peace-building and conflict resolution skills. Equipped with new skills and friends, these teens hope they can plant seeds of peace in their home communities.

Drawing Conclusions How are Jewish and Arab teenagers in Israel working toward peace?

The future of the peace process is uncertain. Some Palestinian groups have continued to commit acts of terrorism, including rocket attacks from Gaza. Israelis fear they would be open to attack if they withdrew from the West Bank.

READING CHECK **Analyzing** Why have the Palestinian Territories been a source of tension?

SUMMARY AND PREVIEW In this section you learned about Israel's history, people, government and economy, and the future of the Palestinian Territories. In the next section you will learn about the history and culture of Israel's neighbors—Syria, Lebanon, and Jordan.

Section 3 Assessment

hmhsocialstudies.com
ONLINE QUIZ

Reviewing Ideas, Terms, and Places

1. **a. Define** What is the **Diaspora**?
   b. Explain How did **Zionism** help create the nation of Israel?
2. **a. Explain** As a religious observance, what is the significance of a kosher diet?
   b. Draw Conclusions Why have Israeli leaders built up a strong military?
   c. Explain How has the migration of Jews influenced the character of Israel?
3. **a. Identify** Which territory is fully controlled by Palestinians and which is partly controlled?
   b. Identify and Explain Read the Teenagers for Peace feature on this page. What conflict are these teens trying to resolve?

Critical Thinking

4. **Categorizing** Use the chart below to separate your notes on Israel into categories.

Israel Today	
Government	
Economy	
Diversity and Languages	
Jewish Culture	

FOCUS ON WRITING

my WriteSmart

5. **Describing Israel's Cultural Traits** What cultural traits define culture in Israel? What are some of the positive and negative qualities of multiculturalism in Israel? Take notes on how you might describe these traits for your readers.

Social Studies Skills

Creating a Cartogram

Learn

For statistical information like population figures, geographers sometimes create a special map called a cartogram. A cartogram displays information about countries by the size shown for each country. In contrast, a political map like the one on the right reflects countries' actual physical size. Here are some guidelines for reading and analyzing a cartogram.

- Read the title of the map to determine the subject area covered.

- Compare the political map to the cartogram. Notice how some countries are much different in size on the cartogram compared to the map.

- Read the cartogram's legend and think about what the information means.

Practice

1. Which country has the largest population?

2. How is the size of Saudi Arabia's land area different from the size of its population?

3. Using the cartogram legend, what is the approximate population of Lebanon?

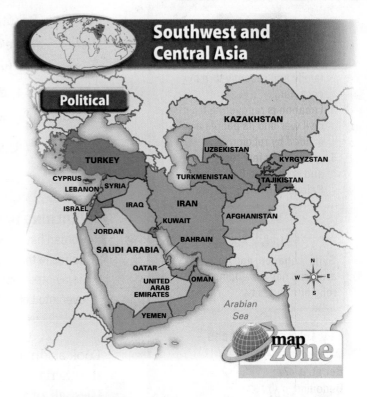

Southwest and Central Asia

Political

Cartogram

An area this size represents 1 million people

Apply

Draw your own cartogram using the gross domestic product, or GDP, of each country in Southwest and Central Asia. Use a reference source or the Internet to find these statistics. Then determine the scale for sizing each country by GDP. For example, you might use one square unit of area per $10 billion or $100 billion. Countries with a high GDP should appear larger than countries with a low GDP.

Syria, Lebanon, and Jordan

TEKS 1A, 1B, 2A, 2B, 15B, 15D, 15F, 18B, 19B, 21B, 21C, 22B, 22D

What You Will Learn...

Main Ideas

1. Syria is an Arab country that has been ruled by a powerful family and recently torn by civil war.
2. Lebanon is recovering from civil war and its people are divided by religion.
3. Jordan has few resources and is home to Bedouins and Palestinian refugees.

The Big Idea

Syria, Lebanon, and Jordan are Arab nations coping with religious diversity.

Key Terms and Places

Damascus, *p. 472*
Beirut, *p. 474*
Bedouins, *p. 474*
Amman, *p. 475*

hmhsocialstudies.com
TAKING NOTES

Use the graphic organizer online to take notes on Syria, Lebanon, and Jordan.

If YOU lived there...

You live in Beirut, Lebanon. Your grandparents often tell you about the years before civil wars destroyed the heart of Beirut. The city then had wide boulevards, parks, and elegant shops. It was popular with tourists. Even though much of Beirut has been rebuilt, you find it hard to imagine what the city used to look like.

What hopes do you have for your country?

BUILDING BACKGROUND The histories of Lebanon, Syria, and Jordan have been entangled since the countries gained independence in the 1940s. Syria is a large nation with a strong military. It has dominated Lebanon's political life. Conflicts in the region have spilled over into Lebanon. In 2011, Syria too was torn by conflict.

Look again at the map at the beginning of this chapter. Notice that Syria, Lebanon, and Jordan all border Israel. These countries, all of which have majority Arab populations, have been involved in conflicts with Israel. In addition, Syria, Lebanon, and Jordan also share a similar history, religion, and culture.

Syria

The capital of Syria, **Damascus**, is believed to be the oldest continuously inhabited city in the world. For centuries it was a leading regional trade center. Syria became part of the Ottoman Empire in the 1500s. After World War I, France controlled Syria. Syria finally became independent in the 1940s.

History and Government

From 1971 to 2000, the Syrian government was led by a dictator, Hafiz al-Assad. As president, Assad increased the size of Syria's military. He wanted to match Israel's military strength and protect his rule from his political enemies within Syria. After Assad's death in 2000, his son, Bashar, was elected president.

One of Bashar al-Assad's main goals was to improve Syria's economy.

In 2011, anti-government protestors challenged Bashar al-Assad's rule. Syria used brutal force—tanks, gunfire, and mass arrests—to crush the protests. By 2012, the protests had grown into an uprising. Syria was divided by a civil war.

Syria's People

Nearly 90 percent of Syria's 23 million people are culturally Arab. About 10 percent are Kurd and Armenian. Of Syria's Muslims, about 74 percent are Sunni. About 16 percent are Druze and Alawite, members of small religious groups related to Islam. About 10 percent of Syrians are Christian. There are also small Jewish communities in some cities.

Syria's civil war drastically affected its people. By September 2013, more than 120,000 had died as a result of the fighting, and more than 6 million had lost their homes. More than 2 million refugees have left the country.

READING CHECK **Analyzing** How has recent conflict affected Syria's people?

Lebanon

Lebanon is a small, mountainous country on the Mediterranean coast. It is home to several different groups of people. At times these different groups have fought.

Lebanon's History and People

During the Ottoman period, many religious and ethnic minority groups settled in Lebanon. After World War I, France controlled Lebanon and Syria. Lebanon finally gained independence in the 1940s. Even so, some aspects of French culture influenced Lebanese culture. For example, in addition to Arabic, many Lebanese also speak French.

Lebanon's people are overwhelmingly Arab, but they are divided by religion. Most Lebanese are either Muslim or Christian. Each of those groups is divided into several smaller groups. Muslims are divided into Sunni, Shia, and Druze.

The Maronites are the largest of the Christian groups in the country. Over time, however, Muslims have become Lebanon's majority religious group.

FOCUS ON READING
Look at the headings under Lebanon to set your purpose for reading these paragraphs.

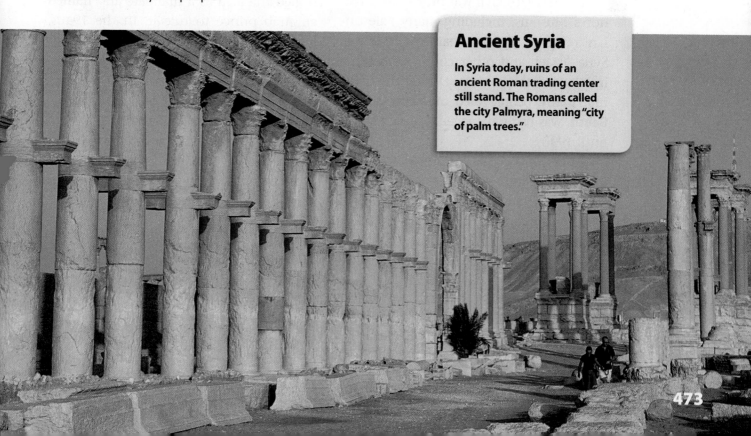

Ancient Syria

In Syria today, ruins of an ancient Roman trading center still stand. The Romans called the city Palmyra, meaning "city of palm trees."

People of Syria, Lebanon, and Jordan

The people of Syria, Lebanon, and Jordan share many cultural traits. For example, most people living in this region are Arab and practice Islam.

ANALYZING VISUALS What can you see in these photos that tells you about daily life in the region?

Syria In Syria drinking tea is an important part of Arab culture. Many Syrians, like this carpet seller, drink tea every day with family and friends.

Conflict and Civil War

After independence, Christians and Muslims shared power in Lebanon. Certain government positions were held by different religious groups. For example, the president was always a Maronite. However, over time tensions between Christians and Muslims mounted.

In the 1970s civil war broke out. Lebanon's Muslims, including many Palestinian refugees, fought against Christians. Syria, Israel, and other countries became involved in the conflict. During the fighting, many people died and the capital, **Beirut**, was badly damaged. Warfare lasted until 1990.

After 1990, Syria continued to maintain a strong influence in Lebanon. In fact, Syrian troops stayed in Lebanon until they were pressured to leave in 2005. In 2006, cross border attacks by Lebanese guerrillas against Israel led to fighting between the two countries.

READING CHECK Drawing Conclusions
What has caused divisions in Lebanese society?

Jordan

Jordan's short history has been full of conflict. The country has few resources and several powerful neighbors.

Jordan's History and Government

The borders of what is now Jordan were created after World War I. The British controlled the area as a mandate and named an Arab prince to rule it. In the 1940s, Jordan became an independent country.

At the time of its independence, Jordan's population was small. Most Jordanians lived a nomadic or semi-nomadic life. Hundreds of thousands of Palestinian Arab refugees fled Israel and came to live in Jordan. From 1952 to 1999 Jordan was ruled by King Hussein. The king enacted some democratic reforms in the 1990s.

Jordan's People and Resources

Many of Jordan's people are **Bedouins**, or Arabic-speaking nomads who mostly live in the deserts of Southwest Asia. Jordan produces phosphates, cement, and potash. Tourism and banking are becoming impor-

Lebanon After more than two decades of civil war, Lebanon's people are rebuilding their capital, Beirut. The city's people now enjoy a new public square.

Jordan Jordan's people value education and equal rights for women. Jordanian teenagers like these girls are required to attend school until age 15.

tant industries. Jordan depends on economic aid from the oil-rich Arab nations and the United States. **Amman**, the capital, is Jordan's largest city. Jordanian farmers grow fruits and vegetables and raise sheep and goats. A shortage of water is a crucial resource issue for Jordan.

READING CHECK **Summarizing** How did King Hussein affect Jordan's history?

SUMMARY AND PREVIEW In this section you learned about the history, government, and people of Syria, Lebanon, and Jordan. In the next chapter you will learn about Iraq and Iran and the countries of the Arabian Peninsula—Saudi Arabia, Kuwait, Bahrain, Qatar, the United Arab Emirates, Yemen, and Oman.

Section 4 Assessment

hmhsocialstudies.com
ONLINE QUIZ

Reviewing Ideas, Terms, and Places

1. **a. Recall** What is the capital of Syria?
   b. Explain What does Syria's government own?
   c. Elaborate Why did Hafiz al-Assad want to increase the size of Syria's military?
2. **a. Identify** What European country ruled Lebanon after World War I?
   b. Analyze How was **Beirut** damaged?
   c. Identify and Explain What is the history of political divisions between religious groups in Lebanon's government? What conflict did this lead to?
3. **a. Define** Who are the **Bedouins**?
   b. Summarize Who provides economic aid to Jordan?

Critical Thinking

4. **Comparing and Contrasting** Use your notes to identify similarities and differences among the people in the three countries.

	Similarities	Differences
Syria		
Lebanon		
Jordan		

FOCUS ON WRITING

my WriteSmart

5. **Describing Syria, Lebanon, and Jordan** If you could only include two details about these countries, what would they be?

from
Red Brocade

by Naomi Shihab Nye

Drinking tea with guests is a traditional Arab custom.

About the Poem *In "Red Brocade," Arab-American writer Naomi Shihab Nye tells about an Arab custom. As a part of this custom, strangers are given a special welcome by those who meet them at the door. Since the poet is Arab-American, she is suggesting that we go "back to that" way of accepting new people.*

AS YOU READ Identify the special way that Arab people in Southwest Asia greet strangers at their door.

GUIDED READING

WORD HELP

pine nuts a small sweet edible seed of some pine trees

brocade a heavy fabric of silk, cotton, or wool woven with a raised design, often using metallic threads

mint a plant with aromatic leaves that grows in northern temperate regions and is often used for flavoring

❶ Arabs are a cultural group that speak Arabic. They live mostly in Southwest Asia and North Africa.

❷ When entertaining, Arabs often sit on pillows on the floor.

The Arabs ❶ used to say,
When a stranger appears at your
    door,
feed him for three days
before asking who he is,
where he's come from,
where he's headed.
That way, he'll have strength
enough to answer.
Or, by then you'll be
such good friends
you don't care.

Let's go back to that.
Rice? Pine nuts?

Here, take the red brocade
    pillow. ❷
My child will serve water
to your horse.

No, I was not busy when you
    came!
I was not preparing to be busy.
That's the armor everyone put
    on to pretend they had a purpose
in the world.

I refuse to be claimed.
Your plate is waiting.
We will snip fresh mint
into your tea.

Connecting Literature to Geography

1. **Describing** What details in the second verse show us that the Arab speaker is extending a warm welcome to the stranger?

2. **Comparing and Contrasting** Do you think this poem about greeting a stranger at the door would be different if it had taken place in another region of the world? Explain your answer.

Chapter Review

Visual Summary

Use the visual summary below to help you review the main ideas of the chapter.

QUICK FACTS

The eastern Mediterranean is a dry region, and water is a key resource.

The region's history includes conflict between three major religions.

Most people living in the eastern Mediterranean are Arab Muslims.

Reviewing Vocabulary, Terms, and Places

Fill in the blanks with the correct term or place from this chapter.

1. The_____ is the lowest point on any continent and the world's saltiest body of water.

2. A desert located in southern Israel is called the_____.

3. A_____is a way of doing something.

4. Turkey's largest city is_____.

5. _____means that religion is kept separate from government.

6. The dispersal of the Jewish population is known as_____.

7. A_____is a large farm where people share everything in common.

8. _____is Lebanon's capital that was badly damaged during the country's civil war.

Comprehension and Critical Thinking

SECTION 1 *(Pages 458–461)*

9. **a. Describe** How is the Eastern Mediterranean considered a part of the Middle East?

   b. Draw Conclusions How would the region's dry climates affect where people lived?

   c. Predict What would happen if the region's people did not have access to water?

SECTION 2 *(Pages 462–465)*

10. **a. Recall** How was control of Constantinople important?

    b. Evaluate How did Atatürk's efforts to modernize Turkey contribute to cultural change there?

    c. Elaborate How might Turkey benefit from joining the European Union?

SECTION 3 *(Pages 466–470)*

11. **a. Define** What is Zionism?

SECTION 3 (continued)

b. Make Inferences Why does Israel need a strong military?

c. Elaborate How has Israel's history affected the country today?

d. Explain What is the significance of Passover?

SECTION 4 *(Pages 472–475)*

12. a. Identify What is the capital of Syria? Why is it historically significant?

b. Identify and Explain Identify and describe examples of conflict within Syria and Lebanon that led to civil war.

c. Evaluate How do you think Jordan survives with so few resources?

Using the Internet

13. Creating an Exhibit Jerusalem is a city rich in tradition, history, and culture dating back thousands of years. Through the online book, travel back in time to historic Jerusalem. Explore its history, archaeology, buildings, daily life, food, and more. Then create a museum exhibit to highlight the artifacts, information, and stories you encounter in your journey through Jerusalem's past. Some things you may want to include are artifacts, models, time lines, maps, small placards providing information, and an exhibit guide for viewers.

⌐ hmhsocialstudies.com

Social Studies Skill

14. Creating a Cartogram Draw your own cartogram using the life expectancy at birth data listed for each country in the Unit 4 Regional Atlas. Then determine a scale for sizing each country by age. For example, you might use one square unit of area for every 10 years of age. Countries with higher numbers for life expectancy at birth should appear larger than countries with lower life expectancy numbers.

15. Geographic Questions Use your cartogram to pose and answer a question that compares population patterns in Southwest Asia to those in North Africa.

Map Activity

16. The Eastern Mediterranean On a separate sheet of paper, match the letters on the map with their correct labels.

Bosporus   Negev

Israel   Euphrates River

Dead Sea

FOCUS ON READING AND WRITING   *my*WriteSmart

Setting a Purpose *Use the information in this chapter to answer the following questions.*

17. How does setting a purpose before you read help you become a better reader?

18. How is your purpose in reading this chapter different from your purpose when you read a newspaper comic strip?

19. How can looking at headings and main idea statements help you set a purpose for reading?

20. Writing a Description Look over your notes and choose one Eastern Mediterranean country to describe. Organize your notes by topic—physical features, people, culture and government. Then, write a one-to-two-paragraph description of the country. Include information you think would be interesting to someone who knows nothing about the country. Add details that will help your readers picture the country. Use *my*WriteSmart in your eBook to write your description.

Reading Social Studies

Setting a Purpose

When you start on a trip, you have a purpose or a destination in mind. When you read, you should also have a purpose in mind before you start. This purpose keeps you focused and moving toward your goal. To decide on a purpose, look over the headings, pictures, and study tips before you read. Then pose questions that can guide your reading. See how a heading suggested a purpose for the passage below.

Teenagers for Peace

Peace between Israeli Jews and Palestinian Arabs has not been easy in the past. Moreover, some believe peace in the region might be impossible ever to accomplish. But don't tell that to a group of more than 2,000 Jewish and Arab teenagers who are making a difference in Israel. These teens belong to an organization called Seeds of Peace. To learn more about each other's culture and thus understand each other better, these teens meet regularly.

From Section 3, Israel

Notice Headings, Pictures or Tips
Here's a heading about teenagers and a picture.

Set a Purpose
I wonder who these teenagers are and what they're doing for peace. I'll read to find out.

Pose Questions
Why are these teens working for peace?

YOU TRY IT!

Read the following introduction to the section on Israel. Pose questions that can set a purpose for your reading. Following the steps given above, develop a purpose for reading about Israel. State this purpose in one to two sentences.

Do you know that Israel is often referred to as the Holy Land? Some people call Israel the Holy Land because it is home to sacred sites for three of the world's major religions—Judaism, Christianity, and Islam. According to the Bible, many events in Jewish history and in the life of Jesus happened in Israel.

From Section 3, Israel

The Arabian Peninsula, Iraq, and Iran

Essential Question What are the common cultural and geographic characteristics of the Islamic Middle East?

myNotebook

Texas Essential Knowledge and Skills (TEKS)

1A, 1B, 2A, 2B, 3A, 3B, 3C, 4D, 4F, 5A, 5B, 5C, 6B, 7B, 7C, 11A, 15B, 15E, 18A, 19A, 21B, 21C, 21D, 22B, 22D

FOCUS ON READING AND WRITING

my **WriteSmart**

Re-Reading Sometimes a single reading is not enough to understand a passage of text. If you feel like you do not fully understand something you have read, it may help to re-read the passage more slowly. **See the lesson, Re-Reading, on page 503.**

Creating a Geographer's Log You are a geographer taking a journey of discovery through the Arabian Peninsula, Iraq, and Iran. As you travel from place to place, create a geographer's log, a written record of what you see on your journey. Use the annotation tools in your eBook to gather information for your assignment.

AFRICA

⊗ National capital
● Other cities

0   150   300 Miles
0   150   300 Kilometers

Projection: Lambert Conformal Conic

map Zone

Geography Skills

Place The countries of the Arabian Peninsula, Iraq, and Iran are centered around the Persian Gulf.

1. **Locate** What is the capital of Saudi Arabia?
2. **Analyze** Approximately how many miles would you have to travel from Baghdad to Kuwait City?

Culture Islam is a major part of the culture in every country in the region. These women pray at a mosque in Mecca, Saudi Arabia.

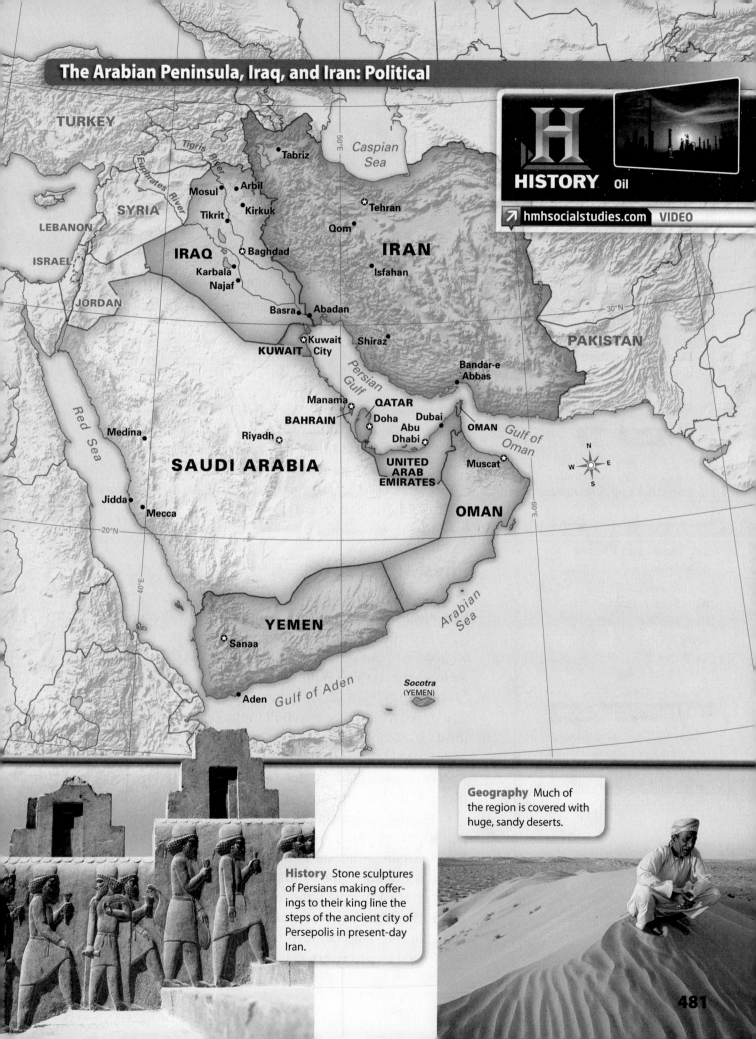

The Arabian Peninsula, Iraq, and Iran: Political

TURKEY

SYRIA

LEBANON

ISRAEL

JORDAN

Tigris River

Euphrates River

Tabriz

Mosul • Arbil
Tikrit • Kirkuk

IRAQ
Baghdad
Karbala
Najaf

Basra • Abadan

Caspian Sea

Tehran

Qom

IRAN

Isfahan

Shiraz

Bandar-e Abbas

PAKISTAN

KUWAIT
Kuwait City

Persian Gulf

Manama
BAHRAIN

QATAR
Doha

Dubai
Abu Dhabi

OMAN

Gulf of Oman

Medina

Riyadh

SAUDI ARABIA

UNITED ARAB EMIRATES

Muscat

OMAN

Red Sea

Jidda
Mecca

20°N

40°E

YEMEN

Sanaa

Arabian Sea

Aden
Gulf of Aden

Socotra (YEMEN)

N
W • E
S

30°N

50°E

60°E

HISTORY Oil

↗ hmhsocialstudies.com VIDEO

Geography Much of the region is covered with huge, sandy deserts.

History Stone sculptures of Persians making offerings to their king line the steps of the ancient city of Persepolis in present-day Iran.

481

TEKS 3A, 3B, 3C, 4D, 4F, 5A, 5B, 7B, 7C, 21B, 21C, 22D

Physical Geography

If YOU lived there...

You are in a plane flying over the vast desert areas of the Arabian Peninsula. As you look down, you see some tents of desert nomads around trees of an oasis. Sometimes you can see a truck or a line of camels crossing the dry, rocky terrain. A shiny oil pipeline stretches for miles in the distance.

What is life like for people in the desert?

BUILDING BACKGROUND Iran, Iraq, and the countries of the Arabian Peninsula are part of a region sometimes called the "Middle East." This region lies at the intersection of Africa, Asia, and Europe. Much of the region is dry and rugged.

Physical Features

Did you know that not all deserts are made of sand? The **Arabian Peninsula** has the largest sand desert in the world. It has huge expanses of desert covered with bare rock or gravel. These wide desert plains are a common landscape in the region that includes the Arabian Peninsula, Iraq, and Iran. Locate the countries of this region on the map. Notice how they appear in a semicircle, with the **Persian Gulf** in the center. The Arabian Peninsula is also bounded by the Gulf of Oman, the Arabian Sea, and the Red Sea. The Caspian Sea borders Iran to the north.

The region contains four main landforms: rivers, plains, plateaus, and mountains. The **Tigris** (TY-gruhs) and **Euphrates** (yooh-FRAY-teez) rivers flow across a low, flat plain in Iraq. They join together before they reach the Persian Gulf. The Tigris and Euphrates are what are known as exotic rivers, or rivers that begin in humid regions and then flow through dry areas. The rivers create a narrow fertile area, which in ancient times gave rise to the world's first civilization. The area is called Mesopotamia, or the "land between the rivers." The Arabian Peninsula has no permanent rivers.

The vast, dry expanse of the Arabian Peninsula is covered by plains in the east. The peninsula's desert plains are covered with sand in the south and volcanic rock in the north. As you can see on the map, the surface of the peninsula rises gradually from the Persian Gulf to the Red Sea. Near the Red Sea the landscape becomes one of plateaus and mountains, with almost no coastal plain. The highest point on the peninsula is in the mountains of Yemen.

Plateaus and mountains also cover most of Iran. In fact, Iran is one of the world's most mountainous countries. In the west, the land climbs sharply to form the Zagros Mountains. The Elburz Mountains and the Kopet-Dag lie in the north. Historically, the mountains have been a barrier, isolating towns and helping them control their territories.

FOCUS ON READING

After you read this paragraph, re-read it to make sure you understand Iran's landscape.

READING CHECK **Summarizing** What are the major physical features of this area?

Arabian Peninsula, Iraq, and Iran: Physical

map zone

Geography Skills

Location This region lies at the intersection of Europe, Africa, and Asia.

1. **Locate** Where are the Elburz Mountains?
2. **Make Inferences** How might the region's location have affected its history?

ELEVATION

Feet	Meters
13,120	4,000
6,560	2,000
1,640	500
656	200
(Sea level) 0	0 (Sea level)
Below sea level	Below sea level

0   200   400 Miles
0   200   400 Kilometers

Projection: Lambert Conformal Conic

TURKEY
Mediterranean Sea
LEBANON
SYRIA
ISRAEL
JORDAN
Euphrates River
Tigris River
Lake Urmia
Caspian Sea
ELBURZ MOUNTAINS
KOPET DAG
TURKMENISTAN
ZAGROS MOUNTAINS
IRAN
GREAT SALT DESERT
PLATEAU OF IRAN
IRAQ
SYRIAN DESERT
Shatt al Arab
Gulf of 'Aqaba
AN NAFUD
KUWAIT
Persian Gulf
BAHRAIN
QATAR
OMAN
UNITED ARAB EMIRATES
Gulf of Oman
PAKISTAN
INDIA
Arabian Sea
AFRICA
Red Sea
SAUDI ARABIA
ARABIAN PENINSULA
OMAN
RUB' AL-KHALI
YEMEN
Gulf of Aden
Socotra (YEMEN)

① The Elburz Mountains in Iran are the highest land in the region.

② The Euphrates River creates a narrow, fertile area in Iraq.

483

1 Sand dunes in the Rub' al-Khali are constantly shifting as the wind blows.

map zone Geography Skills

Regions Most of this region has a desert climate.
1. **Identify** Which countries have only desert climates?
2. **Interpret** Look back at the physical map. How do landforms in the region influence climate?

Climate Types
- Desert
- Steppe
- Mediterranean

0   300   600 Miles
0   300   600 Kilometers
Projection: Lambert Conformal Conic

Climate and Vegetation

As you have already read, most of this region has a desert climate. The desert can be both very hot and very cold. In the summer, afternoon temperatures regularly climb to over 100°F (38°C). During the night, however, the temperature may drop quickly. Nighttime temperatures in the winter sometimes dip below freezing.

The world's largest sand desert, the Rub' al-Khali (ROOB ahl-KAH-lee), covers much of southern Saudi Arabia. *Rub' al-Khali* means "Empty Quarter," a name given to the area because there is so little life there. Sand dunes in the desert can rise to 800 feet (245 m) high and stretch for nearly 200 miles! In northern Saudi Arabia is the An Nafud (ahn nah-FOOD), another large

desert. These deserts are among the driest places in the world. The Rub' al-Khali receives an average of less than 4 inches (10 cm) of rainfall each year.

Some plateau and mountain areas do get winter rains or snow. These higher areas generally have semiarid steppe climates. Some mountain peaks receive more than 50 inches (130 cm) of rain per year.

Rainfall supports vegetation in some parts of the region. Trees are common in mountain regions and in scattered desert oases. An **oasis** is a wet, fertile area in a desert that forms where underground water bubbles to the surface. Most desert plants have adapted to survive without much rain. For example, the shrubs and grasses that grow on the region's dry plains have roots that either grow deep or spread out far to capture as much water as possible. Still, some places in the region are too dry or too salty to support any vegetation.

READING CHECK Finding the Main Idea
What climate dominates this region?

Resources

Water is one of the region's two most valuable resources. However, water is very scarce. In some places in the desert, springs provide water. At other places, water comes from wells dug into dry streambeds called **wadis**. Modern wells can reach water deep underground called fossil water. **Fossil water** is water that is not replaced by rainfall. The image at right shows how farmers modify the environment by using fossil water. Wells that pump fossil water will eventually run dry.

While water is scarce, the region's other important resource, oil, is plentiful. Oil exports bring great wealth to the countries that have oil fields. Most of the oil fields are located near the shores of the Persian Gulf. However, although oil is plentiful now, it cannot be replaced once it is taken from Earth. Too much drilling for oil now may cause problems in the future because most countries of the region are not rich in other resources. Iran is an exception with its many mineral deposits.

READING CHECK **Summarizing** What are the region's important resources?

Satellite View

Irrigated areas

Pivot-Irrigated Fields

This satellite image shows how fossil water has converted desert land into farmers' fields. Each circular plot of land has a water source at its center. An irrigation device extends out and pivots around the center.

Drawing Inferences Why are the fields circular?

SUMMARY AND PREVIEW The Arabian Peninsula, Iraq, and Iran form a desert region with significant oil resources. Next, you will learn more about the countries of the Arabian Peninsula.

Section 1 Assessment

hmhsocialstudies.com
ONLINE QUIZ

Reviewing Ideas, Terms, and Places

1. **a. Geographic Questions** Where was the world's first civilization located? Why was it there? What was significant about its location?
   b. Identify Where are the region's mountains? Which mountains influence Iran's ability to control it's territory?

2. **a. Recall** What parts of the region receive the most rainfall?
   b. Explain How have desert plants adapted to their environment?

3. **a. Define** What is **fossil water**? How do farmers modify, or change, the land to access this water?
   b. Make Inferences How do you think resources in the region influence where people live?
   c. Predict What might happen to the oil-rich countries if their oil was used up or if people found a new energy source to replace oil?

Critical Thinking

4. **Comparing and Contrasting** Using your notes and a graphic organizer like the one here, note physical characteristics unique to each area. Then list characteristics shared by all three areas.

Arabian Peninsula	Iraq	Iran
All		

FOCUS ON WRITING *my* WriteSmart

5. **Describing Physical Geography** Take notes on the physical features, climate and vegetation, and resources that you could record in your log. What would you see and feel if you were in this region?

The Arabian Peninsula

TEKS 5A, 5C, 6B, 21B, 21C, 22B, 22D

What You Will Learn...

Main Ideas

1. Islamic culture and an economy greatly based on oil influence life in Saudi Arabia.
2. Most Arabian Peninsula countries other than Iraq and Iran are monarchies influenced by Islamic culture and oil resources.

The Big Idea

Most countries of the Arabian Peninsula share three main characteristics: Islamic religion and culture, monarchy as a form of government, and valuable oil resources.

Key Terms

Islam, *p. 486*
Shia, *p. 486*
Sunni, *p. 486*
OPEC, *p. 487*

hmhsocialstudies.com
TAKING NOTES

Use the graphic organizer online to take notes on the countries of the Arabian Peninsula.

If **YOU** lived there...

You are a financial adviser to the ruler of Oman. Your country has been making quite a bit of money from oil exports. However, you worry that your economy is too dependent on oil. You think Oman's leaders should consider expanding the economy. Oman is a small country, but it has beautiful beaches, historic palaces and mosques, and colorful markets.

How would you suggest expanding the economy?

BUILDING BACKGROUND Oman and all the countries of the Arabian Peninsula have valuable oil resources. In addition to oil, these countries share two basic characteristics: Islamic religion and monarchy as a form of government. The largest country, and the one with the most influence in the region, is Saudi Arabia.

Saudi Arabia

Saudi Arabia is by far the largest of the countries of the Arabian Peninsula. It is also a major religious and cultural center and has one of the region's strongest economies.

People and Customs

Nearly all Saudis are Arab and speak Arabic. Their culture is strongly influenced by **Islam**, a religion founded around AD 622 in Arabia by Muhammad. It is based on submitting to God (Allah) and on messages Muslims believe Muhammad received from God. These messages are written in the Qur'an, the holy book of Islam.

Nearly all Saudis follow one of two main branches of Islam. **Shia** Muslims believe that true interpretation of Islamic teaching can only come from certain religious and political leaders called imams. **Sunni** Muslims believe in the ability of the majority of the community to interpret Islamic teachings. About 85 percent of Saudi Muslims are Sunni.

$$y = -2x(x^2 - 2x + 4) + 3x^3$$

Muslim Contributions to Math

During the early centuries of the Middle Ages, European art, literature, and science declined. However, during this same period, Muslim scholars made important advances in literature, art, medicine, and mathematics.

Our familiar system of numerals, which we call Arabic, was first created in India. However, it was Muslim thinkers who introduced that system to Europe. They also developed algebra and made advances in geometry. Muslims used math to advance the study of astronomy and physics. Muslim geographers calculated distances between cities, longitudes and latitudes, and the direction from one city to another. Muslim scientists even defined ratios and used mathematics to explain the appearance of rainbows.

Drawing Inferences Why do we need math to study geography?

$6 + x - 54 - 102 - 9y \pm \mp \pi 8 + x^2 - 33 \times 157 + x^3 - ab \div 102 \div 8n \mp \pi 4 + x - 21 \times 76 \pm x - 637$

Islam influences Saudi Arabia's culture in many ways. In part because Islam requires modesty, Saudi clothing keeps arms and legs covered. Men wear a long, loose shirt and a cotton headdress held in place with a cord. Saudi women wear a black cloak and veil in public, although some wear Western-style clothing.

Saudi laws and customs limit women's activities. For example, a woman rarely appears in public without her husband or a male relative. Also, women are not allowed to drive cars. However, women can own and run businesses in Saudi Arabia.

Government and Economy

Saudi Arabia is a monarchy. Members of the Saud family have ruled Saudi Arabia since 1932. Most government officials are relatives of the king. The king may ask members of his family, Islamic scholars, and tribal leaders for advice on decisions.

Local officials are elected. For many years only men were allowed to vote.

Starting in 2015 Saudi Arabian women will be able to vote and run for local offices.

Saudi Arabia's economy and foreign policy is influenced strongly by one geographic factor: oil. Saudi Arabia has the world's largest oil reserves, or supplies. It is also the world's leading exporter of oil. Because it has so much oil, Saudi Arabia is an influential member of OPEC, the Organization of Petroleum Exporting Countries. **OPEC** is an international organization whose members work to influence the price of oil on world markets by controlling the supply.

Oil also shapes the country's domestic policy. In the 1970s, oil industry profits helped Saudi Arabia build roads, schools, hospitals and universities. Today, Saudi Arabia has a sizable middle class and provides its people with free health care and education.

Despite these gains, Saudi Arabia's oil-based economy faces some challenges. Because oil is a nonrenewable resource,

FOCUS ON
READING

After you read
this paragraph,
re-read it to make
sure you
understand
Saudi Arabia's
economic
challenges.

many Saudi Arabians think their nation should develop other industries. Others think that new industries would provide important opportunities for Saudi youth. In 2012, about one third of Saudi workers under 30 was unemployed. To secure its future, Saudi Arabia must create jobs for its young people.

READING CHECK **Finding Main Ideas** What religion influences Saudi Arabia's culture?

Other Countries of the Arabian Peninsula

Saudi Arabia shares the Arabian Peninsula with six smaller countries. Like Saudi Arabia, these countries are all influenced by Islam. Also like Saudi Arabia, most have monarchies and economies based on oil.

Kuwait

Oil was discovered in Kuwait in the 1930s. Since then it has made Kuwait very rich. In 1990 Iraq invaded Kuwait to try to control its oil, starting the Persian Gulf War. The United States and other countries defeated Iraq, but the war caused major destruction to Kuwait's oil fields.

Although Kuwait's government is dominated by a royal family, the country did elect a legislature in 1992. Only men from certain families—less than 15 percent of Kuwait's population—had the right to vote in these elections. However, Kuwait recently gave women the right to vote.

Bahrain and Qatar

Bahrain is a group of islands in the Persian Gulf. It is a monarchy with a legislature. Bahrain is a rich country. Most people there live well in big, modern cities. Oil made Bahrain wealthy, but in the 1990s the country began to run out of oil. Now banking and tourism are major industries.

Qatar occupies a small peninsula in the Persian Gulf. Like Bahrain, Qatar is ruled by a powerful monarch. In 2003 men and women in Qatar voted to approve a new constitution that would give more power to elected officials. Qatar is a wealthy country. Its economy relies on its oil and natural gas.

Oil Wealth

Big, modern cities such as Dubai, UAE, were built with money from oil exports. Many people in the region's cities can afford to buy luxury items.

ANALYZING VISUALS What kind of luxury items is this man selling?

The United Arab Emirates

The United Arab Emirates, or UAE, consists of seven tiny kingdoms. Profits from oil and natural gas have created a modern, comfortable lifestyle for the people of the UAE. Partly because it is so small, the UAE depends on foreign workers. In fact, it has more foreign workers than citizens.

Oman and Yemen

Oman covers most of the southeastern part of the Arabian Peninsula. Oman's economy is also based on oil. However, Oman does not have the great oil wealth of Kuwait or the UAE. Therefore, the government is attempting to develop new industries.

Yemen is located on the southwestern part of the Arabian Peninsula. The country has an elected government, but it has suffered from corruption. Oil was not discovered in Yemen until the 1980s. Oil and coffee generate much of the national income, but Yemen is still the poorest country on the Arabian Peninsula.

READING CHECK **Summarizing** How has oil affected the countries of the Arabian Peninsula?

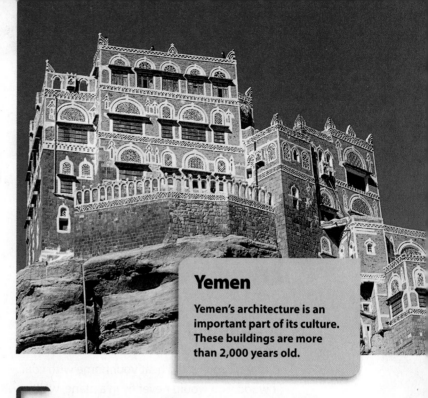

Yemen
Yemen's architecture is an important part of its culture. These buildings are more than 2,000 years old.

SUMMARY AND PREVIEW Islam is a major influence on the people and culture of Saudi Arabia and the other countries of the Arabian Peninsula. The other major influence in the region is oil. Oil has brought wealth to most countries on the peninsula. In the next section you will learn about Iraq, a neighboring country with similar influences.

Section 2 Assessment

hmhsocialstudies.com
ONLINE QUIZ

Reviewing Ideas, Terms, and Places

1. **a. Evaluate** What is **OPEC** and how does its work contribute to the economies of its member nations?
   b. Compare and Contrast How are **Sunni** and **Shia** Muslims similar, and how are they different from each other?
   c. Elaborate What do you think Saudi Arabia would be like if it did not have such huge oil reserves?
2. **a. Identify** Which geographic factor has been the most important to the economic development of countries on the Arabian Peninsula?
   b. Analyze How does its small size affect the United Arab Emirates?
   c. Predict How might Yemen change now that oil is a major part of its economy?
   d. Geographic Questions Look back at the Oil Giants graph on page 455. Pose and answer a question about the geographic distribution of oil in Southwest Asia and North Africa.

Critical Thinking

3. **Summarizing** Look at your notes on the countries of the Arabian Peninsula. Then copy the graphic organizer here and for each topic, write a one-sentence summary about the region.

	Summary
Culture	
Government	
Economy	

FOCUS ON WRITING   *my* WriteSmart

4. **Writing About the Arabian Peninsula** If you were traveling through these lands, what would you see or experience? Take notes on the region's physical and human features.

Oil in Saudi Arabia

Essential Elements

The World in Spatial Terms
Places and Regions
Physical Systems
Human Systems
Environment and Society
The Uses of Geography

Background Try to imagine your life without oil. You would probably walk or ride a horse to school. You would heat your home with coal or wood. You would never fly in a plane, walk in rubber-soled shoes, or even drink out of a plastic cup.

We live in a world that is dependent on oil. In fact, more than 35 percent of the world's energy comes from crude oil products.

However, oil is a nonrenewable resource. This means that supplies are limited, and we may one day run out of oil. How might this affect countries that have economies based on oil production?

Oil Reserves in Saudi Arabia

Saudi Arabia has the world's largest supply of oil. This important resource, found naturally in the environment, has had a huge impact on Saudi Arabia's society.

Before the discovery of oil there in the 1930s, Saudi Arabia was a poor country. But income from oil exports has given the government money to invest in improvements such as new apartments, communications systems,

Saudi Arabia's Oil Fields

IRAN
IRAQ
KUWAIT
OMAN
QATAR
Persian Gulf
Riyadh
UNITED ARAB EMIRATES
SAUDI ARABIA

● Oil fields
— Oil pipelines

Saudi Arabia's Oil Production

Oil Production (millions of barrels per day): 12, 10, 8, 6, 4, 2, 0

Year: 1940, 1950, 1960, 1970, 1980, 1990, 2000, 2010

map zone

Saudi Arabia's oil is pumped through pipelines to tankers that ship the oil around the world. The oil industry has made Saudi Arabia a rich country.

Saudi Arabia's Exports

Oil Products 91%

Other 9%

airports, oil pipelines, and roads. For example, in 1960 Saudi Arabia had only about 1,000 miles (1,600 km) of roads. By 2005 it had over 94,000 miles (152,000 km) of roads. These improvements have helped modernize Saudi Arabia's economy.

Oil exports have also affected Saudi society. Rising incomes have given many people there more money to spend on consumer goods. New stores and restaurants have opened, and new schools have been built throughout the country. Education is now available to all citizens. Increased education means the literacy rate has increased also—from about 3 percent when oil was discovered to about 85 percent today. Health care there has also improved.

The oil industry has also increased Saudi Arabia's importance in the world. Since it is a member of the Organization of Petroleum Exporting Countries (OPEC), Saudi Arabia influences the price of oil on the world market. Countries around the world want to have good relations with Saudi Arabia because of its vast oil reserves.

What It Means Today Saudi Arabia's government has a lot of money. This wealth has come almost entirely from the sale of oil. However, since the world's oil supplies are limited, Saudi Arabia's economy may be at risk in the future. Many countries are beginning to research other types of energy that can one day be used in place of oil. Until then, the many countries buying oil from Saudi Arabia will continue to pump wealth into Saudi society.

Geography for Life Activity

1. How has oil contributed to the economic development of Saudi Arabia?

2. What are some advantages and disadvantages for a society that relies on oil?

3. **Other Types of Energy** Research other types of energy we can get from the environment. Based on your findings, do you think other types of energy will replace oil in the near future? Why or why not?

Iraq

TEKS 1A, 1B, 2A, 2B, 3B, 5C, 6B, 15B, 19A, 21B, 21C, 22D

What You Will Learn...

Main Ideas

1. Iraq's history includes rule by many conquerors and cultures. Its recent history includes wars.
2. Most of Iraq's people are Arab, and Iraqi culture includes the religion of Islam.
3. Iraq today must rebuild its government and economy, which have suffered from years of conflict.

The Big Idea

Iraq, a country with a rich culture and natural resources, faces the challenge of rebuilding after years of conflict.

Key Terms and Places

embargo, *p. 493*
Baghdad, *p. 495*

TAKING NOTES

Use the graphic organizer online to take notes on Iraq's history and on Iraq today.

If YOU lived there...

You are a student in a school in Iraq's capital, Baghdad. During the war, your school and its library were badly damaged. Since then, you and your friends have had few books to read. Now your teachers and others are organizing a project to rebuild your library. They want to include books from all countries of the world as well as computers so students can use the Internet.

What would you like to have in the new library?

BUILDING BACKGROUND In spite of its generally harsh climate, the area that is now Iraq was one of the ancient cradles of civilization. Mesopotamia—the "land between the rivers"—was part of the "Fertile Crescent." Thousands of years ago, people there developed farming, domesticated animals, and organized governments.

History

Did you know that the world's first civilization was located in Iraq? Thousands of years ago people known as Sumerians settled in Mesopotamia—a region that is part of Iraq today. The country's recent history includes wars and a corrupt leader.

Early Civilization

Throughout Mesopotamia's history, different cultures and empires conquered the region. As you can see on the map on the next page, the Sumerians settled in southern Mesopotamia. By about 3000 BC, the Sumerians built the world's first known cities there. The Persians then conquered Mesopotamia in the 500s BC. By 331 BC Alexander the Great made it part of his empire. In the AD 600s Arabs conquered Mesopotamia, and the people gradually converted to Islam.

In the 1500s Mesopotamia became part of the Ottoman Empire. During World War I Great Britain took over the region. The British set up the kingdom of Iraq in 1932 and placed a pro-British ruler in power. In the 1950s a group of Iraqi army officers overthrew this government.

Saddam Takes Power

In 1968, after several more changes in Iraq's government, the Baath (BAHTH) Party took power. In 1979, a Baath leader named Saddam Hussein became Iraq's president. Saddam Hussein was a harsh ruler. He controlled Iraq's media, restricted personal freedoms, and killed an unknown number of political enemies.

Invasions of Iran and Kuwait

Under Saddam's leadership, Iraq invaded Iran in 1980. The Iranians fought back, and the Iran-Iraq War dragged on until 1988. Both countries' economies were seriously damaged, and many people died.

In 1990 Iraq invaded Kuwait, Iraq's oil-rich neighbor to the south. This event shocked and worried many world leaders. They were concerned that Iraq might gain control of the region's oil. In addition, they worried about Iraq's supply of weapons of mass destruction, including chemical and biological weapons.

War and Its Effects

In 1991, an alliance of countries led by the United States forced the Iraqis out of Kuwait. This six week event was called the Persian Gulf War. Saddam, who remained in power after the war, would not accept all the United Nations' (UN) terms for peace. In response, the UN placed an **embargo**, or limit on trade, on Iraq. As a result, Iraq's economy suffered.

Soon after the fighting ended, Saddam faced two rebellions from Shia Muslims and Kurds. He brutally put down these uprisings. In response, the UN forced Iraq to end all military activity. The UN also required that Iraq allow inspectors into the country. They wanted to make sure that Saddam had destroyed the weapons of mass destruction. Iraq later refused to cooperate completely with the UN.

Ten years after the Persian Gulf War, the terrorist attacks of September 11, 2001, led to new tensions between the United States and Iraq. U.S. government officials believed that Iraq aided terrorists. In March 2003, President George W. Bush ordered U.S. forces to attack Iraqi targets. Within a few weeks the Iraqi army was defeated and Saddam's government was crushed. Saddam went into hiding, but U.S. soldiers later found Saddam hiding in an underground hole in Iraq. Saddam was arrested, tried, and executed for his crimes.

READING CHECK **Summarizing** What are some key events in Iraq's history?

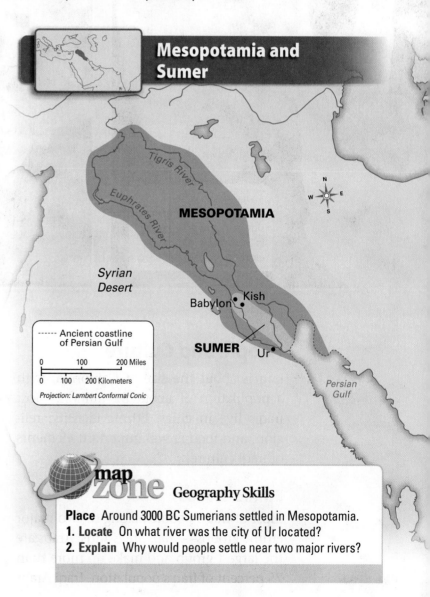

Mesopotamia and Sumer

map zone Geography Skills

Place Around 3000 BC Sumerians settled in Mesopotamia.
1. **Locate** On what river was the city of Ur located?
2. **Explain** Why would people settle near two major rivers?

With help from the United States, Iraqis worked to establish peace and security after the overthrow of Saddam Hussein.

ANALYZING VISUALS How did the United States support Iraqis in rebuilding their nation?

U.S. soldiers in Iraq searching for suspected terrorists

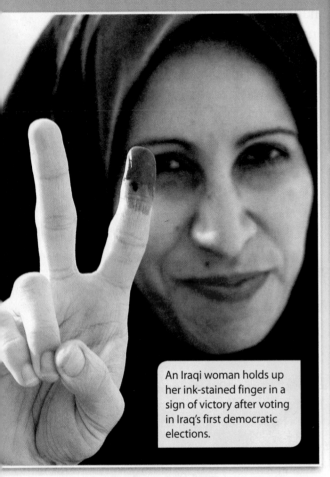

An Iraqi woman holds up her ink-stained finger in a sign of victory after voting in Iraq's first democratic elections.

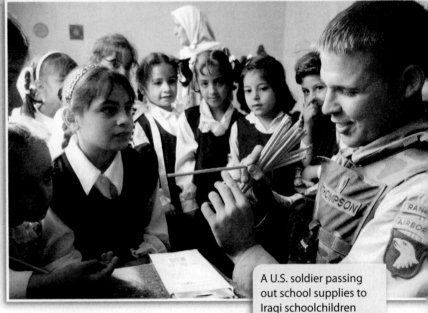

A U.S. soldier passing out school supplies to Iraqi schoolchildren

People and Culture

Iraq is about the size of California, with a population of about 32 million. Most Iraqis live in cities. Ethnic identity, religion, and food are all important elements of Iraqi culture.

Ethnic Groups

Most of Iraq's people belong to two major ethnic groups—Arabs and Kurds. Arabs are the largest group and make up more than 75 percent of Iraq's population. Iraqi Arabs speak the country's official language, Arabic. The smaller group, the Kurds, make up some 15 to 20 percent of the population. The Kurds are mostly farmers and live in a large region of northern Iraq. Most Iraqi Kurds speak Kurdish in addition to Arabic.

Religion

Like ethnic identity, religion plays a large role in the lives of most Iraqis. Nearly all Iraqis, both Arab and Kurdish, are Muslim. Within Iraq, the two different branches of Islam—Shia and Sunni—are practiced. About 60 percent of Iraqis are Shia and live in the south. Some 35 percent of Iraqis are Sunnis and live in the north.

READING CHECK **Summarizing** What ethnic groups do most Iraqis belong to?

Iraq Today

Despite years of war, Iraq is slowly rebuilding. However, the country faces many challenges, such as ongoing fighting.

Rebuilding Baghdad

Iraq's capital, **Baghdad**, was severely damaged in the overthrow of Saddam's government. For example, the city's 6 million people lost electricity and running water. To help the city's residents, U.S. military and private contractors worked with the Iraqis to restore electricity and water and to rebuild homes, businesses, and schools. However, violence in Baghdad continued, disrupting efforts to rebuild.

Government and Economy

In January 2005 Iraqis participated in democracy for the first time. Millions of Iraqis went to the polls to elect members to the National Assembly. One of the Assembly's first tasks was to create a new constitution. Deep divisions among Iraqis led to fierce internal fighting, however, and threatened the new government's stability.

Iraqis also began trying to rebuild their once strong economy. In the 1970s Iraq was the world's second-largest oil exporter. Time will tell if Iraq can again be a major oil producer.

Oil isn't Iraq's only resource. From earliest times, Iraq's wide plains and fertile soils have produced many food crops. Irrigation from the Tigris and Euphrates rivers allows farmers to grow barley, cotton, and rice.

After years of harsh government and wars, Iraq's future remains uncertain. After the United States military transferred control back to the Iraqis, the country's government faced huge challenges in creating a free and prosperous society.

READING CHECK **Drawing Conclusions** What happened to Iraq's oil industry?

SUMMARY AND PREVIEW In this section, you have learned about Iraq's ancient history, rich culture, and efforts to rebuild. Next, you will learn about Iran, which also has an ancient history but is otherwise quite different from Iraq.

FOCUS ON READING
Do you understand everything you just read? If not, try re-reading the paragraphs that you do not understand.

Section 3 Assessment

hmhsocialstudies.com
ONLINE QUIZ

Reviewing Ideas, Terms, and Places

1. **a. Recall** Where was the world's first civilization located?
   b. Sequence What events led to the **embargo** on Iraq by the United Nations?
2. **a. Identify** What are two major ethnic groups in Iraq?
   b. Contrast What is one difference between Shia Muslims and Sunni Muslims?
3. **a. Describe** How was **Baghdad** damaged by war?
   b. Draw Conclusions What natural resource may help Iraq's economy recover?
   c. Predict What kind of country do you think Iraq will be in five years?

Critical Thinking

4. **Summarizing** Use your notes on Iraq today to fill in this table by summarizing what you have learned about Baghdad and Iraq's government and economy.

Baghdad	Government	Economy

FOCUS ON WRITING

my WriteSmart

5. **Writing about Iraq** Add details about Iraq's people, culture, and the country today to your notes. Which characteristics can be traced to conquests, invasion, and trade?

Iran

TEKS 1A, 1B, 2A, 2B, 3C, 11A, 15B, 15E, 18A, 19A, 21B, 21C, 22D

What You Will Learn...

Main Ideas

1. Iran's history includes great empires and an Islamic republic.
2. In Iran today, Islamic religious leaders restrict the rights of most Iranians.

The Big Idea

Islam is a huge influence on government and daily life in Iran.

Key Terms and Places

shah, *p. 497*
revolution, *p. 497*
Tehran, *p. 497*
theocracy, *p. 498*

hmhsocialstudies.com
TAKING NOTES

Use the graphic organizer online to take notes on Iran's history and life in the country today.

If **YOU** lived there...

You are a student in Tehran, the capital of Iran. In school, you are taught that the way of life in the West—countries of Europe and the Americas—is bad. News reports and newspapers are filled with negative propaganda about Western countries. Yet you know that some of your friends secretly listen to Western popular music and watch American television programs that they catch using illegal satellite dishes at home. This makes you very curious about Western countries.

What would you like to know about life in other countries?

BUILDING BACKGROUND Like Iraqis, Iranians have a proud and ancient history. While most people living in the Arabian Peninsula and Iraq are Arabs, the majority of Iranians are Persian. They have a distinct culture and language.

History

The early history of the country we now call Iran includes the Persian Empire and a series of Muslim empires. Iran's recent history includes an Islamic revolution. Today Iran is an Islamic republic, which limits the rights of many Iranians.

Persian Empire

Beginning in the 500s BC, the Persian Empire ruled the region around present-day Iran. For centuries Persia was a great center of art and learning. The Persian Empire was known for its spectacular paintings, carpets, metalwork, and architecture. In the empire's capital, Persepolis, walls and statues throughout the city glittered with gold, silver, and precious jewels.

The Persian Empire was later conquered by several Muslim empires. Muslims converted the Persians to Islam, but most people retained their Persian culture. They built beautiful mosques with colorful tiles and large domes.

The Shah and Islamic Revolution

In 1921 an Iranian military officer took power and encouraged change in Iran's government. He claimed the old Persian title of **shah**, or king. In 1941 the shah's son took control. This shah became an ally of the United States and Great Britain and tried to modernize Iran. His programs were unpopular with many Iranians.

In 1978 Iranians began a revolution. A **revolution** is a drastic change in a country's government and way of life. By 1979, Iranians overthrew the shah and set up an Islamic republic. This type of government follows strict Islamic law.

Soon after Iran's Islamic Revolution began, relations with the United States broke down. A mob of students attacked the U.S. Embassy in Iran's capital, **Tehran**. With the approval of Iran's government, the students took Americans working at the embassy hostage. More than 50 Americans were held by force for over a year.

READING CHECK **Drawing Conclusions** How did Iran's history lead to the Islamic Revolution?

Iran Today

Iranian culture differs from many other cultures of Southwest Asia. Unlike most of the Arab peoples living in the region, more than half of all Iranians are Persian. They speak Farsi, the Persian language.

People and Culture

With about 80 million people, Iran has one of the largest populations in Southwest Asia. Iran's population is very young. The average age in Iran is about 28 years old. It is also ethnically diverse. Iranian ethnic groups other than the Persian majority include Azeris, Lurs, Kurds, Arabs, and Turks.

Most Iranians belong to the Shia branch of Islam. Only about 10 percent are Sunni Muslim. The rest of Iran's people practice Christianity, Judaism, or other religions.

In addition to the Islamic holy days, Iranians celebrate Nowruz—the Persian New Year. Iranians tend to spend this holiday outdoors. As a part of this celebration, they display goldfish in their homes to symbolize life.

Iranian culture also includes close-knit families and respect for elders. Most family

FOCUS ON READING

Re-read the paragraphs under The Shah and Islamic Revolution to better understand important parts of Iran's recent history.

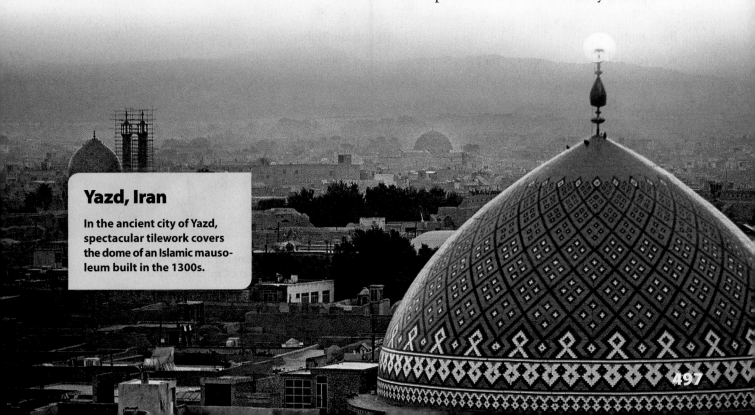

Yazd, Iran

In the ancient city of Yazd, spectacular tilework covers the dome of an Islamic mausoleum built in the 1300s.

gatherings in Iran are centered around Persian food, which includes rice, bread, vegetables, fruits, lamb, and tea.

Economy and Government

Huge oil reserves make Iran a wealthy country. In addition to oil, the production of beautiful woven carpets contributes to Iran's economy. The country's strong agricultural sector employs nearly one-third of the Iranian workforce.

The chart below compares life in Iran to life in the United States. Many of the differences highlighted are related to forms of government. Today, Iran is led by a **theocracy**—a government ruled by religious leaders. These religious leaders, or *ayatollahs*, control Iran's government. The head of the *ayatollahs,* or supreme leader, has unlimited power. Even though religious leaders control Iran, its government has an elected president and parliament.

Life in Iran and the United States

Iran	United States
Daily Life	**Daily Life**
■ An Iranian woman has to cover her head and most of her body with clothing in public.	■ Americans are free to wear any type of clothing.
■ Iranians are forbidden to view most Western Web sites, and Internet use is monitored by the government.	■ Americans are free to surf the Internet and view most Web sites.
■ Boys and girls have separate schools, and they cannot be alone with each other without adult supervision.	■ Boys and girls can attend the same school.
Government	**Government**
■ Iran is a theocracy.	■ The United States is a democracy.
■ A supreme religious leader rules Iran.	■ A president is the leader of our country.
■ Only candidates approved by the government can run for political office.	■ Any U.S. citizen can run for political office.
Basic Rights	**Basic Rights**
■ Freedom of speech, religion, and the press is limited.	■ Freedom of speech, religion, and the press is allowed.

Iranian teenagers can shop for computers, but a girl must wear clothing that covers most of her body.

Americans enjoy freedom of speech. Here, a teen speaks at the Texas State Capitol in Austin.

Contrasting In what ways does Iran's government differ from the U.S. government?

Iran's government has supported many hard-line policies. For example, it has called for the destruction of Israel. It has also supported terrorist groups in other countries. With a newly elected president in 1997, some signs indicated that Iran's government might adopt democratic reforms. This government attempted to improve Iran's economy and rights for women.

However, in 2005 Iranians moved away from democratic reforms by electing Mahmoud Ahmadinejad (mah-MOOD ah-mah-di-nee-ZHAHD) president. He wanted Iranians to follow strict Islamic law. After the election, a reporter asked the new president if he had any plans for reforms. He responded, "We did not have a revolution in order to have a democracy."

More recently, international debate arose over Iran's expansion of its nuclear program. The United States and some of its allies feared that Iran was building nuclear weapons, which could threaten world security. Iran claimed it was using nuclear technology to create energy.

READING CHECK **Analyzing** What are Iran's government and people like?

BIOGRAPHY

Shirin Ebadi
(1947–)

Iranians hoping for more democratic reforms were encouraged in 2003 when Shirin Ebadi received the Nobel Peace Prize. Ebadi is a lawyer, judge, and author. However, her work attempting to improve human rights in Iran has at times made her unpopular with the country's government leaders. Ebadi's goals include to attain better conditions for women, children, and refugees.

Drawing Inferences Why would Iran's government be opposed to Ebadi's human rights efforts?

SUMMARY AND PREVIEW In this section you learned about Iran's history, people, culture, economy, and government. In the next chapter, you will learn about the region of North Africa.

Section 4 Assessment

hmhsocialstudies.com
ONLINE QUIZ

Reviewing Ideas, Terms, and Places

1. **a. Define** What is a **revolution**?
   b. Explain What was the Persian Empire known for?
   c. Elaborate What changes were made in Iran after the Islamic Revolution?
2. **a. Recall** What kind of leaders have authority over their people in a **theocracy**?
   b. Compare In what ways does Iran's culture differ from cultures in other countries of Southwest Asia and from culture in the United States?
   c. Identify and Explain What are some examples of conflict that have shaped current conditions in Iran?
   d. Explain What is the relationship between religion, government, and daily life in Iran?

Critical Thinking

3. **Finding Main Ideas** Use your notes on Iran today to fill in this diagram with the main ideas of Iran's people, culture, economy, and government.

People — Iran Today — Culture
Economy — Iran Today — Government

FOCUS ON WRITING

my WriteSmart

4. **Writing About Iran** What types of things would you see if you were traveling in Iran? Record information about the cultural traits that define Iranian culture in your log.

Social Studies Skills

Using and Creating Databases

Learn

Geographers use databases to learn about people and places and to identify patterns in various regions. A **database** is a collection of information about a topic that is organized so that it can be easily found. A database could be in print or electronic form, and it could be simple or complex. Almost any kind of information can be stored in electronic databases, including statistics, text, images, audio, and video. The table at right is a database. So too is your library's electronic catalog. Learning how to read a database will help you learn how to create one.

Literacy Rates in Southwest Asia			
	Literacy Rate (%)		
Country	Male	Female	Total
Iran	89.3	80.7	85
Iraq	86	71.2	78.5
Oman	90.2	81.8	86.9
Qatar	96.5	95.4	96.3
Saudi Arabia	90.8	82.2	87.2

Source: Central Intelligence Agency, *World Factbook 2013*

- Look at the title to identify the topic.
- Read the column and row headings. These keywords tell what kind of data is included.
- Locate specific data where rows and columns intersect by reading across rows and down columns.
- Use critical thinking skills to organize and interpret data, identify relationships, and note patterns.

Practice

Use the database to answer the following questions.

1. Which country has the highest total literacy rate?

2. Which country has the largest difference between the literacy rate among men and the literacy rate among women?

3. Organize information from the database into a list that shows the countries in order of highest literacy rate to lowest literacy rate.

Apply

Using the Internet, an encyclopedia, or an electronic database, locate information on the population density, birthrate, and death rate for each country listed in the table above. Then create a print or electronic database to organize your information.

Visual Summary

Use the visual summary below to help you review the main ideas of the chapter.

QUICK FACTS

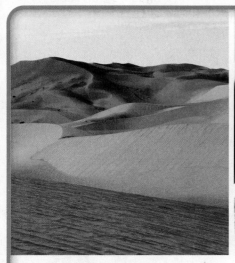

Deserts cover much of the Arabian Peninsula. The region also has a lot of valuable oil reserves.

Many people in Iraq, such as this woman, enjoy more freedoms now that the country has a new government.

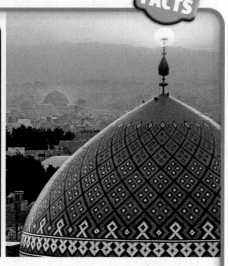

Iran is a theocracy. Islam is an important part of the country's government and culture.

Reviewing Vocabulary, Terms, and Places

Match the words in the columns with the correct definitions listed below.

1. wadis
2. revolution
3. embargo
4. procedure
5. fossil water
6. OPEC
7. shah
8. theocracy

a. the Persian title for a king

b. dry streambeds

c. a limit on trade

d. a series of steps taken to accomplish a task

e. water that is not being replaced by rainfall

f. an organization whose members try to influence the price of oil on world markets

g. a drastic change in a country's government

h. a government ruled by religious leaders

Comprehension and Critical Thinking

SECTION 1 *(Pages 482–485)*

9. a. Identify Through what country do the Tigris and Euphrates rivers flow?

b. Identify and Explain Compare the population map on page 452 to the physical map on page 448. Which geographic factors are most responsible for population patterns in this region? Why?

c. Evaluate Do you think oil or water is a more important resource in the region? Explain your answer.

SECTION 2 *(Pages 486–489)*

10. a. Describe What kind of government does Saudi Arabia have?

b. Analyze In what ways does religion affect Saudi Arabia's culture and economy?

c. Explain What impact has oil had on Saudi Arabia's economy, foreign policy, and domestic policy?

SECTION 3 *(Pages 492–495)*

11. a. Recall What is Mesopotamia known for?

b. Draw Conclusions Why did Iraq invade Kuwait in 1990?

c. Analyze Which past conflicts are most important to understanding current conditions in Iraq? Explain.

SECTION 4 *(Pages 496–499)*

12. a. Describe What occurred at the U.S. Embassy in Tehran after the Islamic Revolution?

b. Compare and Contrast How is Iran similar to or different from the United States?

c. Predict Do you think Iran's government will ever become more democratic? Why or why not?

Social Studies Skills

13. Geographic Questions Look back at the Regional Database for this unit. Examine the data for Per Capita GDP and TVs per Thousand People. Based on the data, pose and answer a question about the distribution of TVs in Southwest Asia and North Africa.

14. Creating a Database Create a database comparing a topic in different world regions. First select one country for each regional unit in this book. Then select one of the following topics: population, disease, or economic activities. Use the Internet or an electronic database to locate information about your topic. Then create a print or digital database to organize your information.

Using the Internet

15. Activity: Charting Democracy Some countries face challenges as they become more democratic. How does democracy in Iraq, or elections in Saudi Arabia and Lebanon, affect the people of those countries? How do the media, literature, and arts in those areas reflect life in a democratic society? In what ways does democracy in Southwest Asia differ from democracy in the United States? Through the online book, create a chart that compares democratic life in the United States with democratic life in Southwest Asia.

Map Activity

16. The Arabian Peninsula, Iraq, and Iran On a separate sheet of paper, match the letters on the map with their correct labels.

Rub' al-Khali   Tehran, Iran

Persian Gulf   Riyadh, Saudi Arabia

Baghdad, Iraq

FOCUS ON READING AND WRITING   *my* WriteSmart

17. Re-Reading Read the passage titled Resources in Section 1. After you read, write down the main ideas of the passage. Then go back and re-read the passage carefully. Identify at least one thing you learned from the passage when you re-read it and add it to your list of main ideas.

18. Creating a Geographer's Log Imagine that you began your journey in Saudi Arabia. Use *my*WriteSmart to create a geographer's log. Write the name of the country at the top of your log. Under the country's name, record details about what you saw as you traveled through the country. Then choose another country and do the same until you have created an entry in your log for each country. Be sure to include descriptions of the land and people.

Reading Social Studies

Re-Reading

FOCUS ON READING

Re-reading can help you understand the vocabulary terms, main ideas, and details in a passage. Follow these steps in re-reading. First, read the whole passage. Look over the passage and identify the vocabulary terms, main ideas, and details that you need help understanding. Then re-read the passage slowly. As you read, make sure you understand new information by summarizing a passage silently. For especially difficult texts, you may wish to take turns reading aloud and checking understanding with a friend. Finally, if necessary, seek help from a teacher to clarify understanding.

1. Read the passage.

2. Identify the main details to focus on.
Persian Empire, Muslims, culture

3. Re-read and restate the details silently.
The Persian Empire was first. Then it was conquered by Muslims. Persian and Muslim cultures blended. Mosques show the region's culture.

4. Re-read with a friend or seek help from a teacher.

> The Persian Empire was later conquered by several Muslim empires. Muslims converted the Persians to Islam, but most people retained their Persian culture. They built beautiful mosques with colorful tiles and large domes.
>
> *From Section 4, Iran*

YOU TRY IT!

Read the following sentences. Then, following the three steps above, write down the main details to focus on. After you re-read the paragraph, write down the information restated in your own words to show that you understood what you read. As needed, seek help from a teacher or friend to clarify meaning.

> The Tigris and Euphrates rivers flow across a low, flat plain in Iraq. They join together before they reach the Persian Gulf. The Tigris and Euphrates are what are known as exotic rivers, or rivers that begin in humid regions and then flow through dry areas. The rivers create a narrow fertile area, which in ancient times was called Mesopotamia, or the "land between rivers."
>
> *From Section 1, Physical Geography*

North Africa

map zone Geography Skills

Regions North Africa is a region of countries located on the Mediterranean Sea.
1. **Locate** What is the capital of Egypt?
2. **Draw Conclusions** Why do you think many countries in Europe have influenced the countries of North Africa?

Essential Question

*my*Notebook

How have deserts and rivers affected the development of North African civilization?

Texas Essential Knowledge and Skills (TEKS)

1A, 1B, 2A, 2B, 3A, 3B, 3C, 3D, 4B, 4C, 4D, 4F, 6B, 7C, 15B, 15D, 18A, 18D, 19A, 19B, 21B, 21C, 22D

FOCUS ON READING AND WRITING

my **WriteSmart**

Summarizing To better understand what you read, it is sometimes helpful to stop and summarize the information you have read. A summary is a short restatement of important events or main ideas. As you read this chapter, stop now and then to summarize what you have read. **See the lesson, Summarizing, on page 525.**

Writing a Myth Ancient peoples created stories called myths to explain things about the world. For example, they created myths to explain the seasons and to explain the powers of their gods. As you read this chapter, look for information that might have seemed mysterious to ancient peoples. Later you will write your own myth to explain something about North Africa. Use the annotation tools in your eBook to gather information for your assignment.

ATLANTIC OCEAN

Strait of Gibraltar

Rabat
Casablanca

MOROCCO

30°N

Canary Islands
(SPAIN)

Western Sahara
(Claimed by MOROCCO)

Tropic of Cancer

20°N

MAURITANIA

Culture Most North Africans are Muslims and speak Arabic.

North Africa: Political

EUROPE

HISTORY How Does the Nile Measure Up?

➚ hmhsocialstudies.com VIDEO

SOUTHWEST ASIA

Algiers

Tunis

TUNISIA

Mediterranean Sea

Tripoli

Alexandria

30°E

30°N

Cairo

ALGERIA

LIBYA

EGYPT

Nile River

Red Sea

Lake Nasser

20°N

* National capital

• Other cities

| 0 | 150 | 300 Miles |

| 0 | 150 | 300 Kilometers |

Projection: Azimuthal Equal-Area

MALI

NIGER

10°E

CHAD

20°E

SUDAN

Geography Most of North Africa is covered by the world's largest desert—the Sahara.

History Artifacts like this one from King Tutankhamen's tomb have revealed clues about the daily lives of ancient Egyptians.

505

TEKS 3A, 3B, 3C, 4B, 4D, 4F, 7C, 21B, 21C, 22D

What You Will Learn...

Main Ideas

1. Major physical features of North Africa include the Nile River, the Sahara, and the Atlas Mountains.
2. The climate of North Africa is hot and dry, and water is the region's most important resource.

The Big Idea

North Africa is a dry region with limited water resources.

Key Terms and Places

Sahara, *p. 506*
Nile River, *p. 506*
silt, *p. 506*
Suez Canal, *p. 507*
oasis, *p. 508*
Atlas Mountains, *p. 508*

hmhsocialstudies.com
TAKING NOTES

Use the graphic organizer online to take notes on the physical geography of North Africa.

Physical Geography

If YOU lived there...

As your airplane flies over Egypt, you look down and see a narrow ribbon of green—the Nile River Valley—with deserts on either side. As you fly along North Africa's Mediterranean coast, you see many towns scattered across rugged mountains and green valleys.

What are the challenges of living in a mainly desert region?

BUILDING BACKGROUND Even though much of North Africa is covered by rugged mountains and huge areas of deserts, the region is not a bare wasteland. Areas of water include wet, fertile land with date palms and almond trees.

Physical Features

The region of North Africa includes Morocco, Algeria, Tunisia, Libya, and Egypt. Locate these countries on the map on the next page. From east to west the region stretches from the Atlantic Ocean to the Red Sea. Off the northern coast is the Mediterranean Sea. In the south lies the **Sahara** (suh-HAR-uh), a vast desert. Both the desert sands and bodies of water have helped shape the cultures of North Africa.

The Nile

The **Nile River** is the world's longest river. It is formed by the union of two rivers, the Blue Nile and the White Nile. Flowing northward through the eastern Sahara for about 4,000 miles, the Nile finally empties into the Mediterranean Sea.

For centuries, rain far to the south caused floods along the northern Nile, leaving rich silt in surrounding fields. **Silt** is finely ground fertile soil that is good for growing crops.

The Nile River Valley is like a long oasis in the desert. Farmers use water from the Nile to irrigate their fields. The Nile fans out near the Mediterranean Sea, forming a large delta. A delta

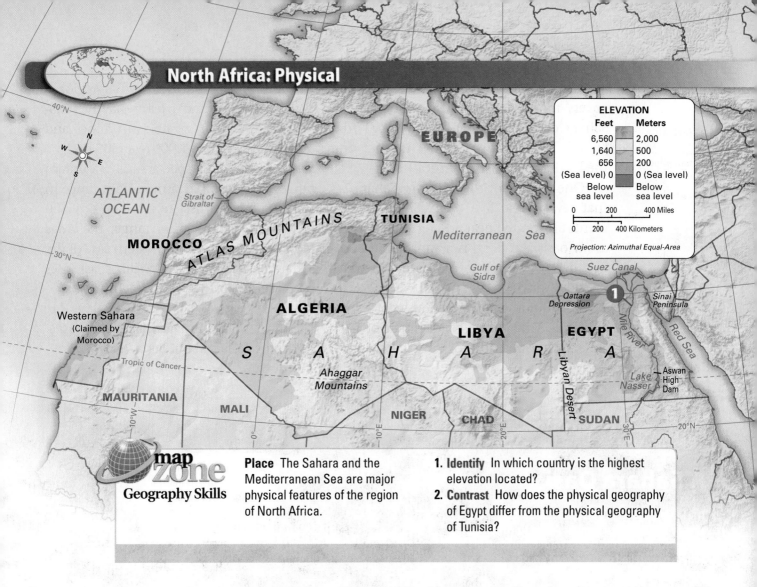

EUROPE

ATLANTIC OCEAN

Strait of Gibraltar

MOROCCO

ATLAS MOUNTAINS

TUNISIA

Mediterranean Sea

Gulf of Sidra

ELEVATION

Feet		Meters
6,560		2,000
1,640		500
656		200
(Sea level) 0		0 (Sea level)
Below sea level		Below sea level

0   200   400 Miles

0   200   400 Kilometers

Projection: Azimuthal Equal-Area

Suez Canal

Western Sahara (Claimed by Morocco)

ALGERIA

Qattara Depression

Sinai Peninsula

EGYPT

Red Sea

LIBYA

S A H A R A

Tropic of Cancer

Ahaggar Mountains

Libyan Desert

Nile River

Lake Nasser

Aswan High Dam

MAURITANIA

MALI

NIGER

CHAD

SUDAN

map zone
Geography Skills

Place The Sahara and the Mediterranean Sea are major physical features of the region of North Africa.

1. **Identify** In which country is the highest elevation located?
2. **Contrast** How does the physical geography of Egypt differ from the physical geography of Tunisia?

is a landform at the mouth of a river that is created by the deposit of sediment. The sediment in the Nile delta makes the area extremely fertile.

The Aswan High Dam controls flooding along the Nile. However, the dam also traps silt, preventing it from being carried downriver. Today some of Egypt's farmers must use fertilizers to enrich the soil.

The Sinai and the Suez Canal

East of the Nile is the triangular Sinai Peninsula. Barren, rocky mountains and desert cover the Sinai. The **Suez Canal,** a narrow waterway, connects the Mediterranean Sea with the Red Sea. The French built the canal in the 1860s to make trade and transportation easier. Today large cargo ships carry oil and goods through the canal.

1 Flowing for 4,132 miles, the Nile is the longest river in the world.

507

The Sahara

The Sahara, the largest desert in the world, covers most of North Africa. The name Sahara comes from the Arabic word for "desert." It has an enormous **impact** on the landscapes of North Africa.

One impact of the very dry Sahara is that few people live there. Small settlements are located near a water source such as an oasis. An **oasis** is a wet, fertile area in a desert where a natural spring or well provides water.

In addition to broad, windswept gravel plains, sand dunes cover much of the Sahara. Dry streambeds are also common.

ACADEMIC VOCABULARY
impact effect, result

Mountains

Do you think of deserts as flat regions? You may be surprised to learn that the Sahara is far from flat. Some sand dunes and ridges rise as high as 1,000 feet (305 m). The Sahara also has spectacular mountain ranges. For example, a mountain range in southern Algeria rises to a height of 9,800 feet (3,000 m). Another range, the **Atlas Mountains** on the northwestern side of the Sahara near the Mediterranean coast, rises even higher, to 13,600 feet (4,160 m).

READING CHECK **Summarizing** What are the major physical features of North Africa?

Close-up

A Sahara Oasis

The largest desert in the world, the Sahara, spans almost 4 million square miles across North Africa. From ancient times to today, traders crossing the Sahara have relied on the desert's oases. These oases provide water and shade.

Date palms thrive on the banks of this natural spring, which provides water to travelers and irrigated fields.

By carrying supplies, camels help the nomadic Tuareg people travel from oasis to oasis.

Climate and Resources

North Africa is very dry. However, rare storms can cause flooding. In some areas these floods as well as high winds have carved bare rock surfaces out of the land.

North Africa has three main climates. A desert climate covers most of the region. Temperatures range from mild to very hot. How hot can it get? Temperatures as high as 136°F (58°C) have been recorded in Libya. However, the humidity is very low. As a result, temperatures can drop quickly after sunset. In winter temperatures can fall below freezing at night.

The second climate type in the region is a Mediterranean climate. Much of the northern coast west of Egypt has this type of climate. Winters there are mild and moist. Summers are hot and dry. Areas between the coast and the Sahara have a steppe climate.

Oil and gas are important resources, particularly for Libya, Algeria, and Egypt. Morocco mines iron ore and minerals used to make fertilizers. The Sahara has natural resources such as coal, oil, and natural gas.

READING CHECK **Generalizing** What are North Africa's major resources?

FOCUS ON READING
Summarize the details of what you just read about North Africa's climate.

Shelters like this one provide a place for travelers to rest.

SUMMARY AND PREVIEW In this section, you learned about the physical geography of North Africa. Next, you will learn about the history and cultures of the countries of North Africa.

ANALYSIS SKILL **ANALYZING VISUALS**

Why do you think an oasis would be important to people traveling through the Sahara?

Section 1 Assessment

hmhsocialstudies.com
ONLINE QUIZ

Reviewing Ideas, Terms, and Places

1. **a. Define** What is an **oasis**?
   b. Analyze How did the French modify the Sinai Peninsula? Why?
   c. Elaborate Would it be possible to farm in Egypt if the **Nile River** did not exist? Explain your answer.
2. **a. Recall** What is the climate of most of North Africa?
   b. Draw Conclusions What resources of North Africa are the most valuable?

Critical Thinking

3. **Categorizing** Draw a diagram like the one shown here. Use your notes to list two facts about each physical feature of North Africa.

   Nile — Sinai and Suez Canal — Physical Features — Sahara — Mountains

FOCUS ON WRITING

my WriteSmart

4. **Writing About Physical Geography** What physical feature could you choose as the subject of your myth? How will you describe this feature? Note your ideas.

History and Culture

TEKS 1A, 1B, 2A, 2B, 4C, 15B, 15D, 18A, 18D, 19A, 19B, 21B, 21C, 22D

What You Will Learn...

Main Ideas

1. North Africa's history includes ancient Egyptian civilization.
2. Islam influences the cultures of North Africa and most people speak Arabic.

The Big Idea

North Africa is rich in history and Islamic culture.

Key Terms and Places

Alexandria, *p. 511*
Berbers, *p. 513*

hmhsocialstudies.com
TAKING NOTES

Use the graphic organizer online to take notes on the history and culture of North Africa.

If YOU lived there...

You live in a village in ancient Egypt in about 800 BC. Your family grows wheat and date palms along the banks of the Nile River, which brings water for your crops. You and your friends like to explore the marshy areas along the banks of the river, where many kinds of birds live in the tall reeds.

How is the Nile River important in your life?

BUILDING BACKGROUND Some of the world's earliest civilizations began in river valleys in Asia and Africa. One of these civilizations was the Nile Valley in Egypt. Egypt was called the "gift of the Nile," because the river's floods brought rich soil to the valley. The soil built up a fertile delta where the Nile emptied into the sea.

Egypt's Nile River Valley was home to some of the world's oldest civilizations. These ancient Egyptians built large monuments, participated in trade, and developed a writing system.

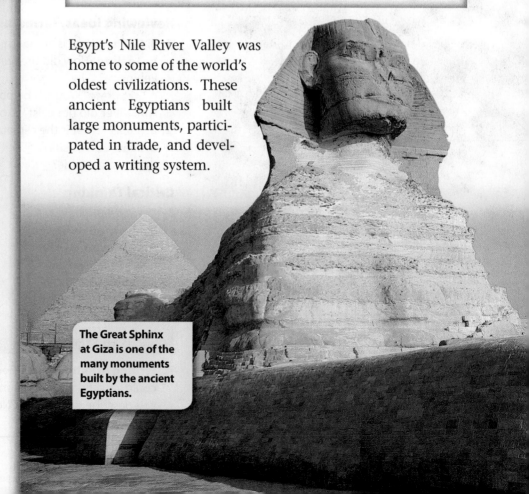

The Great Sphinx at Giza is one of the many monuments built by the ancient Egyptians.

North Africa's History

Sometime after 3200 BC people along the northern Nile united into one Egyptian kingdom. The ancient Egyptians built large stone monuments and developed a written system. Later Greeks and Arabs, who wanted to expand their empires, invaded North Africa.

The Ancient Egyptians

What is the first thing that comes to mind when we think of the ancient Egyptians? Most of us think of the great stone pyramids. The Egyptians built these huge monuments as tombs, or burial places, for pharaohs, or kings.

How did the Egyptians build these huge monuments? Scholars believe thousands of workers cut large blocks of stone far away and rolled them on logs to the Nile. From there the blocks were moved on barges. At the building site, the Egyptians finished carving the blocks. They built dirt and brick ramps alongside the pyramids. Then they hauled the blocks up the ramps.

One of the largest pyramids, the Great Pyramid, contains 2.3 million blocks of stone. Each stone averages 2.5 tons (2.25 metric tons) in weight. Building the Great Pyramid probably required from 10,000 to 30,000 workers. They finished the job in about 20 years, and the pyramid still stands thousands of years later.

Egyptian Writing

The ancient Egyptians developed a sophisticated writing system, or hieroglyphics (hy-ruh-GLIH-fiks). This writing system used pictures and symbols that stood for ideas or words. Each symbol represented one or more sounds in the Egyptian language. The Egyptians carved hieroglyphics on their temples and stone monuments. Many of these writings recorded the words and achievements of the pharaohs.

Greek and Arab Civilizations

Because of North Africa's long Mediterranean coastline, the region was open to invaders over the centuries. Those invaders included people from the eastern Mediterranean, Greeks, and Romans. For example, one invader was the Macedonian king Alexander the Great. Alexander founded the city of **Alexandria** in Egypt in 332 BC.

BIOGRAPHY

Cleopatra
(69–30 BC)

After the death of the Egyptian king Ptolemy XII in 51 BC, his daughter, Cleopatra, and her brother became co-rulers of Egypt. From the age of 17, Cleopatra ruled ancient Egypt for more than 20 years. Her reign was during a period of Egyptian history when Egypt was dominated by Rome. Even though she was of Greek descent, Cleopatra was worshipped by ancient Egyptians.

Cleopatra tried to drive out the Romans from Egypt. She feared the Romans would arrest her and take over Egypt. Rather than see them ruling her kingdom, Cleopatra chose to commit suicide. According to tradition, she poisoned herself at the age of 39 with the venom of a deadly snake.

Analyzing What did Cleopatra fear?

FOCUS ON READING

What details would you use to summarize the ancient Egyptians and their writing?

Ancient Egypt's King Tut

More than 3,300 years ago a 19-year-old named King Tutankhamen ruled ancient Egypt. Since the discovery of Tut's mummy in 1922, many have wondered how he died. Scientists have used modern technology to help find possible clues to King Tut's cause of death.

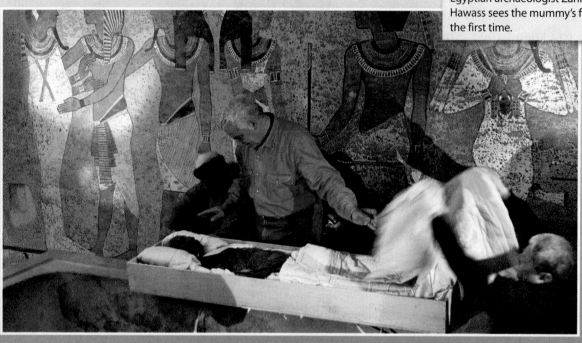

Mummy Unveiled
Inside King Tut's burial chamber, Egyptian archaeologist Zahi Hawass sees the mummy's face for the first time.

Analyzing the Mummy
A CT scanner created detailed images of the mummy's skeleton and remaining soft tissues. These images showed that Tut broke his left thigh soon before he died, which may have contributed to his death. DNA testing revealed that Tut had suffered from a deformed left foot for most of his life and from diseases such as malaria, a blood disease spread by mosquitoes.

Tut's Face Revealed
Using images from the CT scan, an artist reconstructed the mummy's face with clay and plastic.

ANALYSIS SKILL **ANALYZING VISUALS**

By looking at King Tut's burial chamber, how can you tell that King Tut was an important person?

Alexandria became an important seaport and trading center. The city was also a great center of learning.

Beginning in the AD 600s, Arab armies from Southwest Asia swept across North Africa. They brought the Arabic language and Islam to the region. Under Muslim rule, North African cities became major centers of learning, trade, and craft making. These cities included Cairo in Egypt and Fès in Morocco.

European Influence

In the 1800s European countries began to take over the region. By 1912 they had authority over all of North Africa. In that year Italy captured Libya. Spain already controlled northern Morocco. France ruled the rest of Morocco as well as Tunisia and Algeria. The British controlled Egypt.

The countries of North Africa gradually gained independence. Egypt gained limited independence in 1922. The British kept military bases there and maintained control of the Suez Canal until 1956. During World War II the region was a major battleground. Libya, Morocco, and Tunisia each won independence in the 1950s.

Algeria was the last North African country to win independence. Many French citizens had moved to the country, and they considered Algeria part of France. Algeria finally won independence in 1962.

Modern North Africa

Since independence, the countries of North Africa have tried to build stronger ties with other Arab countries. Before signing a peace treaty in 1979, Egypt led other Arab countries in several wars against Israel. In 1976 Morocco took over the former Spanish colony of Western Sahara.

READING CHECK **Evaluating** What was one significant event in North Africa's history?

Cultures of North Africa

As you have just read, many of the countries of North Africa share a common history. Likewise, the people of North Africa share many aspects of culture—language, religion, foods, holidays, customs, and arts and literature.

People and Language

Egyptians, Berbers, and Bedouins make up nearly all of Egypt's population. Bedouins are nomadic herders who travel throughout the deserts of Egypt.

Most people in the other countries of North Africa are of mixed Arab and Berber ancestry. The **Berbers** are an ethnic group who are native to North Africa and speak Berber languages. The majority of North Africans speak Arabic.

Most ethnic Europeans left North Africa after the region's countries became independent. However, because of the European influence in the region, some North Africans also speak French, Italian, and English.

Religion

Most North Africans are Muslims who practice the religion of Islam. Islam plays a major role in North African life. For example, North African Muslims stop to pray five times a day. In addition, Fridays are special days when Muslims meet in mosques for prayer. About 10 percent of Egyptians are Christians or practice other religions.

Foods

What kinds of food would you eat on a trip to North Africa? Grains, vegetables, fruits, and nuts are common foods.

You would also notice that most meals in North Africa include couscous (KOOS-koos). This dish is made from wheat and looks like small pellets of pasta.

Couscous is usually steamed over boiling water or soup. Often it is served with vegetables or meat, butter, and olive oil.

Egyptians also enjoy a dish called *fuul*. It is made with fava beans mashed with olive oil, salt, pepper, garlic, and lemons. It is often served with hard-boiled eggs and bread. Many Egyptians eat these foods on holidays and at family gatherings.

FOCUS ON CULTURE

The Berbers

Before the AD 600s when Arabs settled in North Africa, a people called the Berbers lived in the region. The descendants of these ancient peoples live throughout North Africa today—mostly in Morocco and Algeria. Some Berbers are nomadic and live in goat-hair tents. Other Berbers farm crops that include wheat, barley, fruits, and olives. Some also raise cattle, sheep, or goats.

Berber culture is centered on a community made up of different tribes. Once a year, Berber tribes gather at large festivals. At these gatherings Berbers trade goods, and many couples get married in elaborate ceremonies.

Drawing Conclusions How have Berbers kept their culture alive?

Holidays and Customs

Important holidays in North Africa include the birthday of Muhammad, the prophet of Islam. This holiday is marked with lights, parades, and special sweets of honey, nuts, and sugar. During the holy month of Ramadan, Muslims abstain from food and drink during the day.

Gathering at cafes is a custom practiced by many men in North Africa. The cafes are a place where they go to play chess or dominoes. Most women in North Africa socialize only in their homes.

A certain way of greeting each other on the street is another North African custom. People greet each other by shaking hands and then touching their hand to their heart. If they are family or friends, they will kiss each other on the cheek. The number of kisses varies from country to country.

Many North Africans wear traditional clothes, which are long and loosely fitted. Such styles are ideal for the region's hot climate. Many North African women dress according to Muslim tradition. Their clothing covers all of the body except the face and hands.

The Arts and Literature

North Africa has a rich and varied tradition in the arts and literature. Traditional arts include wood carving and weaving. The region is famous for beautiful hand-woven carpets. The women who weave these carpets use bright colors to create complex geometric patterns. Beautifully detailed handpainted tilework is also a major art form in the region.

Other arts in Egypt include its growing movie industry. Egyptian films in Arabic have become popular throughout Southwest Asia and North Africa.

Many North Africans also enjoy popular music based on singing and poetry. The musical scale there has many more notes

Fès, Morocco

At a tannery in the city of Fès, men dye sheepskins in large vats of dyes. The city's craftspeople use yellow-dyed leather to make distinctive leather shoes.

ANALYZING VISUALS What other colors are the sheepskins dyed?

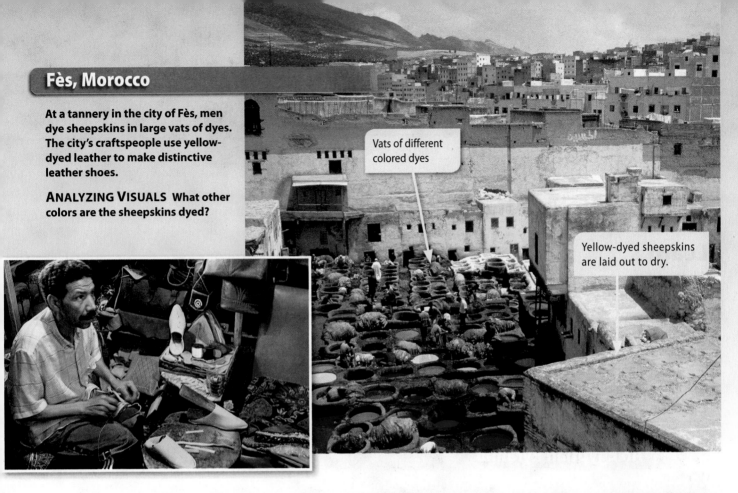

Vats of different colored dyes

Yellow-dyed sheepskins are laid out to dry.

than are common in Western music. As a result of this difference, North African tunes seem to wail or waver. Musicians in Morocco often use instruments such as the three-stringed sintir.

The region has also produced important writers and artists. For example, Egyptian poetry and other writing date back thousands of years. One of Egypt's most famous writers is Naguib Mahfouz. In 1988 he became the first Arab writer to win the Nobel Prize for Literature.

READING CHECK Analyzing What are some important facts about the people and culture of North Africa?

SUMMARY AND PREVIEW In this section you learned about the history and culture of North Africa. Next, you will learn about the region today.

Section 2 Assessment

hmhsocialstudies.com
ONLINE QUIZ

Reviewing Ideas, Terms, and Places

1. **a. Define** What are hieroglyphics?
   b. Make Inferences What made the city of **Alexandria** important?
   c. Evaluate Why do you think European countries wanted to take over countries in North Africa?
2. **a. Recall** What language do most North Africans speak?
   b. Summarize What is one religious holiday or observance followed in North Africa? Why is it significant?
   c. Elaborate How is Islam a major part of the daily lives of many North Africans?

Critical Thinking

3. **Describing** Use your notes to describe the cultural traits that are common in North Africa.

Language	
Religion	
Food	
The Arts	
Literature	

FOCUS ON WRITING

my WriteSmart

4. **Choosing Details** Which details about North Africa's history and culture will you include in your myth? Write a sentence or two about each detail.

Creating a Model

Learn

When you create a model, you show a place, process, relationship, or event in a visual way. A model might be a sketch, poster, or diagram that explains how something works. Or, it could be a three-dimensional model, such as a globe or a diorama. The model below is a diagram that shows the interior of an Egyptian pyramid. Notice how the title and labels identify important information and features.

Practice

Use the model below to answer the following questions.

1. Where is the air shaft located? Why is it there?

2. What labels in the model suggest what this pyramid was used for?

3. Where is the pyramid located? How can you tell?

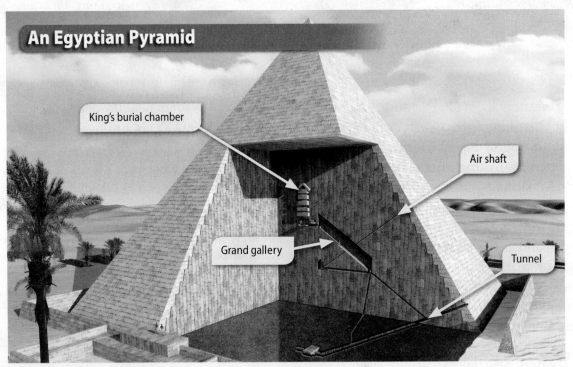

An Egyptian Pyramid

King's burial chamber

Air shaft

Grand gallery

Tunnel

Apply

With a partner, create a model to explain a day in your life at school. Brainstorm a list of signs that label places in your school, such as offices, the cafeteria, and classrooms. Add to the list other important places, activity areas, and classroom features, such as desks, doors, a chalkboard, computers, and bookshelves. Work with your partner to create your model. Finally, present your model to the class. Use the model to tell a story about what a typical day is like for you at school. Use connecting words like first, next, and finally to help students follow along.

North Africa Today

If YOU lived there...

You live in Tunis, Tunisia. The city is known for its architecture, a mix of French and Arab styles. Ordinarily, you could stroll a maze of streets in the city's ancient, walled center, where blacksmiths and leather tanners still work. But today, the streets are filled with protestors demanding change.

What might cause you to join a protest?

BUILDING BACKGROUND The countries of North Africa have deep historical and cultural ties to Europe, the Arab world, and Sub-Saharan Africa. Most recently, North Africa has been shaped by a series of anti-government protests.

The Arab Spring

In 2011, a wave of pro-democracy uprisings called the **Arab Spring** shook North Africa and Southwest Asia. Tired of living under authoritarian regimes, people took to the streets. Some demanded the right to vote and an end to political corruption. Others wanted better living conditions, better jobs, and the freedom to write and say what they wanted.

In different countries, protestors used similar strategies. They held strikes and mostly non-violent protests. They used the Internet, cell phones, and social media to unite people and promote their cause. Likewise, different governments acted similarly to stop the protests. For example, they used violence against their own people and blocked Internet and mobile network access.

Each country touched by the Arab Spring has had a different outcome. Some protests were successful. Dictators were forced out of power in Tunisia, Egypt, and Libya. By contrast, Bahrain and Syria used brutal force to stop the protests. Regardless, the Arab Spring gave hope to millions of people in the region. Only time will tell the extent to which these hopes will be met.

TEKS 1A, 1B, 2A, 2B, 3B, 6B, 15A, 15B, 21B, 21C, 22D

What You Will Learn...

Main Ideas

1. In 2011, a pro-democracy movement called the Arab Spring brought change to North Africa.
2. Many of Egypt's people are farmers and live along the Nile River.
3. People in the other countries of North Africa are mostly pastoral nomads or farmers, and oil is an important resource in the region.

The Big Idea

Countries in North Africa face great change due to popular protests and political instability.

Key Terms and Places

Arab Spring, *p. 517*
Cairo, *p. 519*
Maghreb, *p. 520*
souks, *p. 521*
free port, *p. 521*
dictator, *p. 521*

hmhsocialstudies.com
TAKING NOTES

Use the graphic organizer online to take notes on the governments, economies, and cities in Egypt and the other countries of North Africa.

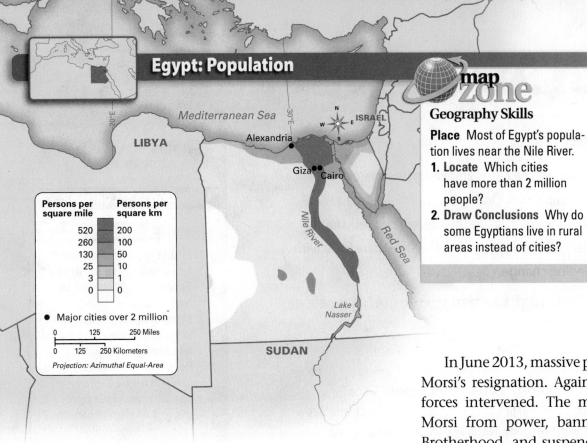

Mediterranean Sea

LIBYA

Alexandria

Giza ● ● Cairo

ISRAEL

Nile River

Red Sea

Lake Nasser

SUDAN

Persons per square mile	Persons per square km
520	200
260	100
130	50
25	10
3	1
0	0

● Major cities over 2 million

0   125   250 Miles

0   125   250 Kilometers

Projection: Azimuthal Equal-Area

map zone

Geography Skills

Place Most of Egypt's population lives near the Nile River.

1. **Locate** Which cities have more than 2 million people?
2. **Draw Conclusions** Why do some Egyptians live in rural areas instead of cities?

Egypt

With more than 85 million people, Egypt is North Africa's most populous country. Most Egyptians are poor farmers living with political instability and limited resources.

Government and Society

In 2011, massive popular protests broke out across Egypt. Poverty, unemployment, rising prices, and political corruption stirred the unrest. Egypt's military forced President Hosni Mubarak from power, ending 30 years of autocratic rule.

After a heated presidential campaign, Egyptians elected Mohamed Morsi in May 2012. Morsi had the support of the Muslim Brotherhood, a multinational activist political organization that believes Egypt's government, laws, and society should be based on Islamic law.

Still, Egyptians were divided and unhappy. They debated the role of Islam in government and society. Many feared losing personal freedoms. Others were concerned by Egypt's weak economy and failing social services.

In June 2013, massive protests called for Morsi's resignation. Again, Egypt's armed forces intervened. The military removed Morsi from power, banned the Muslim Brotherhood, and suspended Egypt's constitution. Today, Egypt's government and society continue to face many challenges.

Many Egyptians live in poverty, without clean water for cooking or washing. The spread of disease in cities is also a problem. In addition, about 30 percent of Egyptians cannot read or write. Still, Egypt has made progress. Today Egyptians live longer and are much healthier than they were 50 years ago.

Resources and Economy

In addition to political instability, Egypt is challenged by its limited resources. The country's only farmland is in the Nile River Valley and Delta. To keep the land productive, farmers must use more and more fertilizer. In addition, salt water drifting up the Nile from the Mediterranean has been harmful to crops. These problems and a rapidly growing population force Egypt to import much of its food.

About 32 percent of Egyptians are farmers, but less than 3 percent of the land is used for farming. Most farming is located along the Nile Delta, which is extremely fertile. A warm, sunny climate and water for irrigation make the delta ideal for growing cotton. Farmlands along the Nile River are used for growing vegetables, grain, and fruit.

The Suez Canal is an important part of Egypt's economy. The canal makes about $5 billion a year by requiring tolls from ships that pass through the canal. Thousands of ships use the canal each year to avoid making long trips around Southern Africa. This heavy traffic makes the canal one of the world's busiest waterways.

Egypt's economy depends mostly on agriculture, petroleum exports, and tourism. Unfortunately, in 2011, civil unrest caused a decline in tourism. To provide for its people, Egypt is working to rebuild tourism and expand other industries. Recently, the government has invested in the country's communications and natural gas industries.

Many Egyptians depend on money sent home by family members working in Europe or oil-rich countries in Southwest Asia. Often Egyptians work abroad because there are not enough jobs in Egypt.

Cities and Rural Life

Most North Africans live in cities along the Mediterranean coast or in villages in the foothills of the Atlas Mountains. However, 99 percent of Egyptians live in the Nile Valley and Delta. Egypt's capital, **Cairo**, is located in the Nile Delta.

With almost 12 million people, Cairo is the largest urban area in North Africa. The city is crowded, poor, and polluted. Cairo continues to grow as people move into the city from Egypt's rural areas in search of work. For centuries, Cairo's location at the southern end of the Nile Delta helped the city grow. The city also lies along old trading routes.

Satellite View

The Nile River

From space, the Nile looks like a river of green. Actually, the areas that appear green in this satellite image are thousands of irrigated fields that line the banks of the river. The river deposits silt along its banks, which makes the land extremely fertile. Farmers also depend on the Nile's waters to irrigate their crops. Without water, they could not farm in the desert.

Notice how the river appears smaller at the bottom of this image. The Aswan High Dam controls the river's flow here, which prevents flooding and provides electricity.

Drawing Conclusions How is the Nile important to Egypt's people?

Today the landscape of Cairo is a mixture of modern buildings, historic mosques, and small, mud-brick houses. However, there is not enough housing in Cairo for its growing population. Many people live in makeshift housing in the slums or boats along the Nile. Communities have even developed in cemeteries, where people convert tombs into bedrooms and kitchens.

VIDEO
Lake Nassar

hmhsocialstudies.com

Impact of the Arab Spring

TURKEY

ATLANTIC OCEAN

TUNISIA

CYPRUS

SYRIA

IRAN

MOROCCO

Mediterranean Sea

LEBANON

IRAQ

ISRAEL

JORDAN

KUWAIT

Western Sahara (Claimed by Morocco)

ALGERIA

LIBYA

EGYPT

Red Sea

BAHRAIN QATAR

OMAN

SAUDI ARABIA

UNITED ARAB EMIRATES

OMAN

YEMEN

Arabian Sea

Gulf of Aden

Socotra (YEMEN)

INDIAN

Legend
- Government overthrown
- Civil war
- Major protests
- Minor protests

map zone
Geography Skills

Movement In 2011 pro-democracy protests spread throughout North Africa and Southwest Asia. The protests had varying results.

1. **Identify** Which country experienced a civil war following the Arab Spring?
2. **Contrast** How did the Arab Spring affect Libya and Saudi Arabia differently?

FOCUS ON READING

Think about what details are important in a summary of Egypt's government, economy, and cities.

Alexandria is Egypt's second-largest city. The city was founded by Alexander the Great. Known in ancient times for its spectacular library, it is now the home to a large university and many industries. Its location on the Mediterranean Sea has made it a major seaport. The home of some 4 million people, Alexandria is as poor and crowded as Cairo.

More than half of all Egyptians live in small villages and other rural areas. Most rural Egyptians are farmers called fellahin (fel-uh-HEEN). These farmers own very small plots of land along the Nile River. Some fellahin also work large farms owned by powerful families.

READING CHECK **Finding Main Ideas** What are some of the challenges Cairo faces today?

Other Countries of North Africa

Western Libya, Tunisia, Algeria, and Morocco are often called the **Maghreb** (MUH-gruhb). This Arabic word means "west" or "the direction of the setting sun." Since most of the Maghreb is covered by the Sahara, cities and farmland are located in narrow bands along the coast.

Government and Economy

Major political changes have occurred in the Maghreb since 2011. Following the Arab Spring, Tunisia and Libya experienced revolutions and new governments. Political unrest still challenges the region, as does conflict over the role of Islam in society.

1 **Tunisia** Protests in Tunisia, the birthplace of the Arab Spring uprisings, led to a revolution that ousted a dictator.

2 **Egypt** Hundreds of thousands of protestors gathered in Cairo's Tahrir Square, the center point of pro-democracy protests in Egypt.

Oil, mining, and tourism are important industries for the countries of North Africa. Oil is the most important resource, particularly in Libya and Algeria. Money from oil pays for schools, health care, food, social programs, and military equipment. The region's countries also have large deposits of natural gas, iron ore, and lead. The largest trade partners of Algeria, Libya, and Morocco are European Union members.

Agriculture is a major economic activity in North Africa. About one in six workers in Libya, Tunisia, and Algeria is a farmer. In Morocco, farmers make up about 40 percent of the labor force. North Africa's farmers grow and export wheat, olives, fruits, and nuts. Tourism is also an important economic activity in the region, especially in Morocco and Tunisia.

Cities

Many North African cities have large marketplaces, or **souks**. The souks are located in the old district of a city called the Casbah. These souks sell various goods such as spices, carpets, and copper teapots. The Casbah in Algeria's capital, Algiers, is a maze of winding alleys and tall walls.

Libya and Tunisia's cities and most of its population are found in the coastal areas. Libya is the most urbanized country in the region. About 77 percent of Libya's roughly 6 million people live in cities. The largest cities are Benghazi and the capital, Tripoli. Tunisia's capital and largest city, Tunis, lies on the Mediterranean coast.

Morocco's largest city, Casablanca, has about 3.2 million people. Another Moroccan city, Tangier, overlooks the Strait of Gibraltar. This beautiful city was once a Spanish territory. Today tourists can take a quick ferry ride from Spain across the strait to Tangier, a free port. A **free port** is a city in which almost no taxes are placed on goods sold there.

The Countries Today

In addition to sharing similar economies, the countries of North Africa also share similar challenges. Some countries are dealing with violence, while others are strengthening their trading relationships with the United States and Europe.

Libya From 1969 to 2011, Libya was ruled by a dictator, Colonel Muammar Gaddafi. A **dictator** is someone who rules a country with complete power. In 2011, pro-democracy protests broke out in Libya. Gaddafi's crackdown on protesters led to civil war. An international air and naval intervention sealed the dictator's fate. Gaddafi's regime toppled. In 2012, Libya formed a new parliament and elected Ali Zaydan prime minister.

Algiers, Algeria

Algeria's capital and major port, Algiers, sits on the Mediterranean Sea.

Algeria Following a series of protests in 2011, Algeria's government made reforms. It lifted a 19-year state of emergency. It also eased restrictions on the media, political parties, and the ability of women to serve in elected office.

Tunisia The protests of the Arab Spring started in Tunisia in December 2010. By January 2011, protestors had forced long-time President Zine al-Abidine Ben Ali from power. Since that time, Tunisians have held democratic elections and struggled with the role of Islam in government and society.

Morocco Morocco is the only North African country with little oil. Today, the country is an important producer and exporter of fertilizer.

READING CHECK Summarizing What are some of the challenges these countries face?

SUMMARY AND PREVIEW In this section you learned about North Africa today. In the next chapter you will learn about the region of West Africa.

Section 3 Assessment

hmhsocialstudies.com
ONLINE QUIZ

Reviewing Ideas, Terms, and Places

1. **a. Identify and Explain** Which geographic factor is responsible for Egypt's population pattern? Explain.
   b. Draw Conclusions Why is housing scarce in **Cairo**?
   c. Analyze How have conflicts associated with the **Arab Spring** shaped current conditions in Egypt?
2. **a. Recall** What countries in North Africa make up the **Maghreb**?
   b. Analyze How do you think the countries of North Africa can improve their economies?
   c. Evaluate What do you think are the most important political contributions made by the Arab Spring protestors?

Critical Thinking

3. **Comparing** Use your notes to compare Egypt with the other countries of North Africa.

Egypt — Other Countries of North Africa

FOCUS ON WRITING

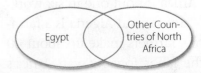

4. **Taking Notes on North Africa** Are there any characteristics of North Africa today that you might feature in your myth? Write down your ideas.

Chapter Review

Visual Summary

Use the visual summary below to help you review the main ideas of the chapter.

QUICK FACTS

The Sahara is a major physical feature of North Africa.

One of the world's earliest civilizations thrived on the Nile River in ancient Egypt.

Most major cities in North Africa are located on the Mediterranean Sea.

Reviewing Vocabulary, Terms, and Places

Unscramble each group of letters below to spell a term or place that matches the given definition.

1. **sasoi**—wet, fertile area in a desert where a spring or well provides water

2. **ashraa**—the largest desert in the world that covers most of North Africa

3. **ipmtac**—effect, result

4. **enli virer**—the world's longest river that empties into the Mediterranean Sea in Egypt

5. **oicar**—a city founded more than 1,000 years ago on the Nile and is the capital of Egypt today

6. **uahtroyti**—power; right to rule

7. **tidrotca**—someone who rules a country with complete power

8. **ksuos**—marketplaces

9. **efer tpro**—a city in which almost no taxes are placed on goods sold there

Comprehension and Critical Thinking

SECTION 1 *(Pages 506–509)*

10. **a. Describe** What is the Nile River Valley like? Describe the river and the landscape.

   b. Elaborate Why do you think few people live in the Sahara? What role does climate play in where people live? Explain your answer.

   c. Geographic Questions Look back at the model of A Sahara Oasis on pages 508 and 509. Pose and answer a geographic question about how physical features shape patterns of human movement in the Sahara.

SECTION 2 *(Pages 510–515)*

11. **a. Recall** What types of monuments did the ancient Egyptians build?

   b. Make Inferences Why did European countries want to control most of North Africa?

   c. Elaborate Why do you think some groups living in North Africa are nomadic people?

12. a. Define What is the Maghreb? What physical feature covers this region?

b. Contrast How did Egypt's experience of the Arab Spring differ from Libya's?

c. Predict Think about the goals shared by the Arab Spring protestors. Do you think they will achieve these goals? Explain.

Using the Internet

13. Activity: Exploring the Sahara The Sahara is the largest desert in the world and is covered by great seas of sand dunes. One of the most inhospitable, hostile places on Earth, few people live in the Sahara, and few people even travel through it. Through the online book, take a journey through the Sahara. Imagine what it would be like to cross the desert. Then create a PowerPoint presentation or a visual display that summarizes your adventures across the great Sahara.

↗ hmhsocialstudies.com

Social Studies Skills

14. Creating a Model of Economic Activity Oil, agriculture, and tourism are important economic activities in North Africa. Select one activity as a topic. Conduct research to learn more about your topic. Then, create a model that explains an important feature related to your topic, such as a place, process, relationship, or event.

15. Creating a Model to Compare Regions The ancient Maya of Mexico also built pyramids. Create a model that compares Egyptian and Mayan pyramids. Conduct research to learn more about both types of pyramids. Be sure to use clear labels on your model. Also include maps showing the distribution of pyramids in each region. Use your model to pose and answer a geographic question about the distribution of pyramids in each region. Finally, present your model and pose your question to the class.

Map Activity

16. North Africa On a separate sheet of paper, match the letters on the map with their correct labels.

Nile River   Tripoli

Atlas Mountains   Strait of Gibraltar

Cairo

FOCUS ON READING AND WRITING *my*WriteSmart

17. Summarizing Re-read the paragraphs under Physical Features in Section 1. Create a short summary of each paragraph, then combine these paragraph summaries into a summary of the whole passage.

18. Writing a Myth Identify one major physical or human feature in North Africa to be the subject of your myth. Use *my*WriteSmart to write two to three paragraphs describing the characteristics of your feature and how you think ancient peoples would find it important. Use your imagination! For example, your myth might explain why it rarely rains in the Sahara, how the Nile brings water to the region, or why pyramids have been built.

Reading Social Studies

Summarizing

FOCUS ON READING

Summarizing is one way to help you handle large amounts of information. A summary is a short restatement of the most important ideas in a text. The example below shows three steps you can use to write a summary. First underline important details. Then write a short summary of each paragraph. Finally, combine your summaries into a summary of the whole passage.

With more than 10 million people, <u>Cairo is the largest urban area in North Africa</u>. The <u>city is crowded</u>, poor, and polluted. <u>Cairo continues to grow</u> as people move into the city from Egypt's rural areas in search of work. For centuries, Cairo's location at the southern end of the Nile Delta helped the city grow. The city also lies along old trading routes.

Today the landscape of Cairo is a mixture of modern buildings, historic mosques, and small, mud-brick houses. However, <u>there is not enough housing in Cairo for its growing population.</u> Many <u>people live in makeshift housing in the slums or boats</u> along the Nile. <u>Communities have even developed in cemeteries</u>, where people convert tombs into bedrooms and kitchens.

From Section 3, North Africa Today

Summary of Paragraph 1
The crowded city of Cairo is North Africa's largest city and continues to grow.

Summary of Paragraph 2
Without enough housing, people in Cairo live in slums, boats and cemeteries.

Combined Summary
Cairo is North Africa's largest city, and it is so crowded that people live in houses, boats and cemeteries.

YOU TRY IT!

Read the following paragraphs. First, write a summary for each paragraph and then write a combined summary of the whole passage.

Even though Egypt is a republic, its government is heavily influenced by Islamic law. Egypt's government has a constitution and Egyptians elect their government officials. Power is shared between Egypt's president and the prime minister.

Many Egyptians debate over the role of Islam in the country. Some Egyptian Muslims believe Egypt's government, laws, and society should be based on Islamic law. However, some Egyptians worry that such a change in government would mean fewer personal freedoms.

Compare and Contrast

How are two countries or regions alike? How are they different? Comparing the similarities and contrasting the differences between places can teach us more than we can learn by studying each one individually.

Assignment *my*WriteSmart

Use *my*WriteSmart in your eBook to write a paper comparing and contrasting two countries or regions. Consider physical geography, government, and/or culture.

1. Prewrite

Choose a Topic

- Choose two countries or regions to write about.
- Create a big idea, or thesis, about the two countries. For example, your big idea might be "Iran and Iraq both have oil-based economies, but they also have many differences."

> **TIP** **Organizing Information** A Venn diagram (two overlapping circles) can help you plan your paper. Write similarities in the overlapping area and differences in the areas that do not overlap.

Gather and Organize Information

- Conduct research and use data from geographic tools, including maps, graphs, charts, databases, and models to identify at least three similarities or differences between the countries.
- Decide how to organize your main ideas and details, for example, by each place or by each similarity or difference.

2. Write

Use a Writer's Framework

> **A Writer's Framework**
>
> **Introduction**
> - Start with a fact or question relating to both countries.
> - Identify your big idea.
>
> **Body**
> - Write at least one paragraph for each country or each point of similarity or difference. Include facts and details to help explain each point.
> - Use block style or point-by-point style.
>
> **Conclusion**
> - Summarize the process in your final paragraph.

3. Evaluate And Revise

Review and Improve Your Paper

- Re-read your draft, then ask yourself the questions below to see if you have followed the framework.
- Make any changes needed to improve your comparison and contrast paper.

Evaluation Questions for a Compare and Contrast Paper

1. Do you begin with an interesting fact or question that relates to both places?
2. Does your first paragraph clearly state your big idea and provide background information?
3. Do you discuss at least three similarities and differences between the places?
4. Do you include main ideas and details from your research?
5. Is your paper clearly organized by country and region or by similarities and differences?

4. Proofread And Publish

Give Your Paper the Finishing Touch

- Make sure you have capitalized the names of countries and cities.
- Reread your paper to check that you have used standard grammar, spelling, sentence structures, and punctuation.
- Share your compare-and-contrast paper by reading it aloud in class or in small groups.

5. Practice And Apply

Use the steps outlined in this workshop to write a compare-and-contrast paper. Compare and contrast your paper to those of your classmates.

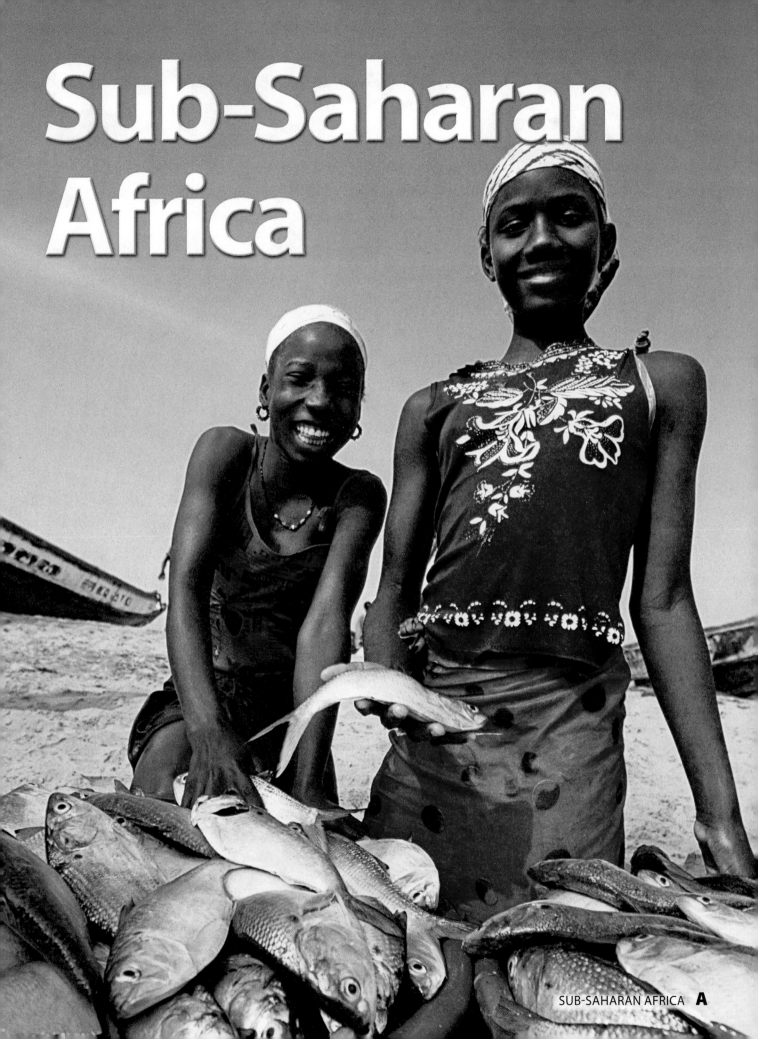

Sub-Saharan Africa

The Sahel

Ancient civilizations such as that of Djenné thrived in the Sahel, a narrow strip of semi-arid land just south of the Sahara desert.

Savannas

Grassy plains called savannas stretch across large parts of the continent and are home to much African wildlife.

Sub-Saharan Africa

Rift Valleys

In East Africa, Earth's crust is slowly being pulled apart. This causes hills, long lakes, and wide "rift valleys" to form.

Explore the Satellite Image
Africa south of the Sahara is home to many different kinds of physical features. Based on this satellite image, how would you describe Africa's physical geography?

The Satellite's Path

>44'56.08<

>>>>>>>>>665.00'87<

+799   +603   +996   +355

567.476.348

456.094.

Sub-Saharan Africa: Physical

ELEVATION

Feet		Meters
13,120		4,000
6,560		2,000
1,640		500
656		200
(Sea level) 0		0 (Sea level)
Below sea level		Below sea level

0   250   500 Miles

0   250   500 Kilometers

Projection: Azimuthal Equal-Area

map zone
Geography Skills

Place Africa is a huge continent with a great variety of physical features.

1. **Name** What major rivers can you see on the map, and where are they located?

2. **Compare** How does the average elevation of southern Africa compare to that of western Africa?

Sub-Saharan Africa

Geographical Extremes: Sub-Saharan Africa

Longest River	**Congo River, Democratic Republic of the Congo:** 2,900 miles (4,700 km)	**Driest Place**	Wadi Halfa, Sudan: .1 inches (.3 cm) average precipitation per year
Highest Point	**Mount Kilimanjaro, Tanzania:** 19,340 feet (5,895 m)	**Largest Country**	**Democratic Republic of the Congo:** 905,430 square miles (2,344,858 sq km)
Lowest Point	**Lake Assal, Djibouti:** 512 feet (156 m) below sea level	**Smallest Country**	**Seychelles:** 176 square miles (455 square km)
Highest Recorded Temperature	**Timbuktu, Mali:** 130°F (54.4°C)	**Largest Desert**	**Kalahari Desert:** 360,000 square miles (930,000 sq km)
Lowest Recorded Temperature	**Buffelsfontein, South Africa:** −4.2°F (−20.1°C)	**Largest Island**	**Madagascar:** 226,658 square miles (587,044 square km)
Wettest Place	**Debundscha, Cameroon:** 405 inches (1,028.7 cm) average precipitation per year	**Highest Waterfall**	**Tugela, South Africa:** 2,800 feet (853 m)

Size Comparison: The U.S. and Sub-Saharan Africa

Mount Kilimanjaro, Tanzania

Sub-Saharan Africa: Political

SOUTHWEST ASIA

Strait of Gibraltar

Mediterranean Sea

30°N

MOROCCO   TUNISIA

Western Sahara
(Claimed by Morocco)

ALGERIA   LIBYA   EGYPT

Tropic of Cancer

20°N

CAPE VERDE   MAURITANIA   MALI
                    ✪ Nouakchott   Timbuktu   SUDAN   ERITREA
✪ Praia   NIGER   ✪ Asmara   DJIBOUTI
SENEGAL   Bamako   BURKINA Niamey   ✪ Khartoum   ✪ Djibouti
Dakar ✪   FASO   • Nyala   10°N
GAMBIA   ✪ Bissau GUINEA   Ouagadougou Kano •   N'Djamena   Addis
Banjul   Ababa ✪
GUINEA-BISSAU Conakry ✪ CÔTE   BENIN NIGERIA   SOUTH   ETHIOPIA   SOMALIA
Freetown ✪   D'IVOIRE TOGO ✪ Abuja   SUDAN
SIERRA LEONE   GHANA Porto   CENTRAL
Monrovia ✪ Yamoussoukro Novo Lagos   AFRICAN REPUBLIC ✪ Juba
LIBERIA   Accra Lomé   CAMEROON Bangui   Mogadishu •
Gulf of Guinea ✪ Malabo ✪ Yaoundé
EQUATORIAL GUINEA   Congo River   UGANDA   KENYA
SÃO TOMÉ AND PRÍNCIPE   Kampala ✪   SEYCHELLES
0° Equator   ✪ Libreville REPUBLIC Kigali ✪ RWANDA Nairobi ✪   ✪ Victoria
  São Tomé •   GABON   OF THE DEMOCRATIC BURUNDI
              Brazzaville ✪ CONGO REPUBLIC OF Bujumbura Mombasa •
              Cabinda   THE CONGO Dodoma • Zanzibar • INDIAN
              (ANGOLA) ✪ Kinshasa   Dar es Salaam • OCEAN
ATLANTIC   TANZANIA
OCEAN   ✪ Luanda   COMOROS
10°S   MALAWI ✪ Moroni
                        ANGOLA   ZAMBIA Lilongwe ✪
                                     Lusaka ✪ MOZAMBIQUE   Antananarivo ✪ MAURITIUS
                                     Harare ✪   ✪ Port
                        NAMIBIA BOTSWANA ZIMBABWE Beira •   MADAGASCAR   Louis
20°S   Walvis Bay • Windhoek ✪ Gaborone ✪
                                              Pretoria ✪ Maputo ✪
                                     Johannesburg • Mbabane ✪
                                     Bloemfontein • SWAZILAND
Tropic of Capricorn   LESOTHO
                                     ✪ Maseru
       ✪ National capital   SOUTH
       • Other cities   AFRICA
   0   250   500 Miles   Cape Town ✪ • Port Elizabeth
   0   250   500 Kilometers
   Projection: Azimuthal Equal-Area

30°S

30°W   20°W   10°W   0°   10°E   20°E   30°E   40°E   50°E   60°E

map zone
Geography Skills

Location Africa is located south of Europe and Southwest Asia.
1. Name What island countries can you see on this map?

2. Analyze Which physical features might help explain the locations of the capitals of South Africa and Sudan?

Sub-Saharan Africa: Resources

SOUTHWEST ASIA

Mediterranean Sea

Red Sea

Gulf of Aden

30°N

Tropic of Cancer

20°N

10°N

0° Equator

Gulf of Guinea

INDIAN OCEAN

10°S

ATLANTIC OCEAN

Mozambique Channel

20°S

Tropic of Capricorn

30°S

Major Resources

- Coal
- Oil
- Hydroelectric power
- Gold
- Silver
- Platinum
- Diamonds
- Uranium
- Other minerals
- Seafood

0   250   500 Miles

0   250   500 Kilometers

Projection: Azimuthal Equal-Area

N / W / E / S

30°W 20°W 10°W 0° 10°E 20°E 30°E 40°E 50°E 60°E

map zone

Geography Skills

Place Africa south of the Sahara is rich in resources.

1. **Identify** What are some of the key resources in southern Africa?

2. **Make Generalizations** Where in Sub-Saharan Africa are oil resources found? How do you think oil affects the economies of these regions?

Sub-Saharan Africa: Population

SOUTHWEST ASIA

Strait of Gibraltar

Mediterranean Sea

Tropic of Cancer

30°N

20°N

Nile River

Red Sea

Khartoum

Gulf of Aden

10°N

Niger River

Kano

Lagos

Abidjan

Gulf of Guinea

0° Equator

Nairobi

INDIAN OCEAN

ATLANTIC OCEAN

N
W   E
S

Kinshasa

10°S

Mozambique Channel

Persons per square mile | **Persons per square km**

Persons per square mile	Persons per square km
520	200
260	100
130	50
25	10
3	1
0	0

● Major cities over 2 million

0   125   250 Miles
0   125   250 Kilometers

Projection: Azimuthal Equal-Area

20°S

Tropic of Capricorn

Johannesburg

30°S

30°W   20°W   10°W   0°   10°E   20°E   30°E   40°E   50°E   60°E

map zone
Geography Skills

Regions Many areas of Africa have a relatively even population density.

1. Name Which parts of Sub-Saharan Africa have the highest population density?

2. Analyze Compare this map to the climate map. How does climate seem to influence population patterns in Sub-Saharan Africa?

Sub-Saharan Africa

Sub-Saharan Africa: Climate

SOUTHWEST ASIA

Strait of Gibraltar

Mediterranean Sea

Red Sea

Gulf of Aden

30°N

Tropic of Cancer

20°N

10°N

Gulf of Guinea

0° Equator

ATLANTIC OCEAN

INDIAN OCEAN

N W E S

10°S

Mozambique Channel

20°S

Climate Types
- Humid tropical
- Tropical savanna
- Desert
- Steppe
- Mediterranean
- Humid subtropical
- Marine west coast
- Highland

Tropic of Capricorn

0   300   600 Miles
0   300   600 Kilometers
Projection: Azimuthal Equal-Area

30°S

30°W   20°W   10°W   0°   10°E   20°E   30°E   40°E   50°E   60°E

map zone
Geography Skills

Location Africa's location around the equator influences its climates.

1. Name Which climates dominate large parts of Sub-Saharan Africa?

2. Explain Africa's climates are sometimes said to "mirror each other around the equator." What do you think is meant by this statement?

Sub-Saharan Africa

COUNTRY Capital	FLAG	POPULATION	AREA (sq mi)	PER CAPITA GDP (U.S. $)	LIFE EXPECTANCY AT BIRTH	TVS PER 1,000 PEOPLE
Angola Luanda		18.6 million	481,354	$6,500	55	15
Benin Porto-Novo		9.9 million	43,483	$1,700	60.7	44
Botswana Gaborone		2.1 million	231,804	$17,100	54.5	21
Burkina Faso Ouagadougou		17.8 million	105,869	$1,400	54.4	11
Burundi Bujumbura		10.9 million	10,745	$600	59.7	15
Cameroon Yaoundé		20.6 million	183,568	$2,400	55	34
Cape Verde Praia		531,046	1,557	$4,200	71.3	5
Central African Republic; Bangui		5.2 million	240,535	$800	51	6
Chad N'Djamena		11.2 million	495,755	$2,000	49	1
Comoros Moroni		752,288	838	$1,300	63	4
Congo, Democratic Republic of the; Kinshasa		75.5 million	905,568	$400	56.1	2
Congo, Republic of the; Brazzaville		4.5 million	132,047	$4,700	55.6	13
Côte d'Ivoire Yamoussoukro		22.4 million	124,503	$1,800	57.7	65
Djibouti Djibouti		792,198	8,880	$2,700	62	48
United States Washington, D.C.		316.7 million	3,794,083	$50,700	78.6	844

COUNTRY Capital	FLAG	POPULATION	AREA (sq mi)	PER CAPITA GDP (U.S. $)	LIFE EXPECTANCY AT BIRTH	TVS PER 1,000 PEOPLE
Equatorial Guinea Malabo		704,001	10,831	$26,400	63.1	116
Eritrea Asmara		6.2 million	46,842	$800	63.2	16
Ethiopia Addis Ababa		93.9 million	435,186	$1,200	60	5
Gabon Libreville		1.6 million	103,347	$16,800	52.2	251
Gambia, The Banjul		1.9 million	4,363	$1,900	64.1	3
Ghana Accra		25.2 million	92,456	$3,400	65.3	115
Guinea Conakry		11.2 million	94,926	$1,100	59.1	47
Guinea-Bissau Bissau		1.7 million	13,946	$1,200	49.5	43
Kenya Nairobi		44 million	1,049,155	$1,800	63.3	240
Lesotho Maseru		1.9 million	11,720	$2,200	52.3	16
Liberia Monrovia		4 million	76,641	$700	57.8	49
Madagascar Antananarivo		22.6 million	226,657	$1,000	64.9	23
Malawi Lilongwe		16.8 million	45,745	$900	52.8	3
United States Washington, D.C.		316.7 million	3,794,083	$50,700	78.6	844

Regional Database

COUNTRY Capital	FLAG	POPULATION	AREA (sq mi)	PER CAPITA GDP (U.S. $)	LIFE EXPECTANCY AT BIRTH	TVS PER 1,000 PEOPLE
Mali Bamako		16 million	478,767	$1,100	54.6	13
Mauritania Nouakchott		3.4 million	397,955	$2,200	61.2	95
Mauritius Port Louis		1.3 million	788	$15,800	74.9	248
Mozambique Maputo		24 million	309,496	$1,200	52.3	5
Namibia Windhoek		2.2 million	318,696	$7,900	52	38
Niger Niamey		16.9 million	489,191	$800	54.3	15
Nigeria Abuja		174.5 million	356,669	$2,800	52.5	69
Rwanda Kigali		12 million	10,169	$1,500	58.9	0.09
São Tomé and Príncipe; São Tomé		186,817	387	$2,400	63.9	229
Senegal Dakar		13.3 million	75,749	$2,100	60.6	41
Seychelles Victoria		90,846	176	$25,600	70	214
Sierra Leone Freetown		5.6 million	27,699	$1,400	57	13
Somalia Mogadishu		10.3 million	246,201	$600	51.2	14
United States Washington, D.C.		316.7 million	3,794,083	$50,700	78.6	844

COUNTRY Capital	FLAG	POPULATION	AREA (sq mi)	PER CAPITA GDP (U.S. $)	LIFE EXPECTANCY AT BIRTH	TVS PER 1,000 PEOPLE
South Africa; Pretoria, Cape Town, Bloemfontein		48.6 million	471,011	$11,600	49.5	138
South Sudan Juba		11 million	248,777	$1,000	61.5	—
Sudan Khartoum		34.8 million	718,723	$2,600	63	173
Swaziland Mbabane		1.4 million	6,704	$5,900	50	112
Tanzania Dar es Salaam, Dodoma		48.3 million	364,900	$1,600	60.8	21
Togo Lomé		7.2 million	55,251	$1,100	63.6	328
Uganda Kampala		34.8 million	91,136	$1,400	54	28
Zambia Lusaka		14.2 million	290,586	$1,700	51.5	145
Zimbabwe Harare		13.2 million	172,742	$600	53.9	280
United States Washington, D.C.		316.7 million	3,794,083	$50,700	78.6	844

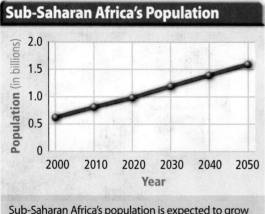

Sub-Saharan Africa's Population

Population (in billions) vs Year (2000–2050)

Sub-Saharan Africa's population is expected to grow dramatically in the next 40 years.

Sub-Saharan Africa and the World

	Average Age	Life Expectancy at Birth	Per Capita GDP (in U.S. $)
Sub-Saharan Africa	19.8 years	58.4	$5,090
Rest of the World	29.4 years	68.1	$12,700

Compared to the rest of the world, Sub-Saharan Africa's population is younger, has a shorter life expectancy, and has less money.

ANALYSIS SKILL **ANALYZING INFORMATION**

1. Based on the information above, what do you think are some key challenges in Sub-Saharan Africa today?

West Africa

Essential Question

myNotebook

How is West Africa shaped by its diverse climates and people groups?

Texas Essential Knowledge and Skills (TEKS)

1A, 1B, 2A, 2B, 3A, 3B, 4D, 5A, 5C, 6A, 6B, 6C, 7B, 15B, 15C, 15F, 18A, 18C, 21A, 21B, 21C, 22A, 22D

FOCUS ON READING AND SPEAKING

my WriteSmart

Understanding Comparison-Contrast Comparing and contrasting, or looking for similarities and differences, can help you more fully understand the subject you are studying. Create a comparison-contrast chart to help you take notes as you read. **See lesson, Understanding Comparison-Contrast, on page 559.**

Presenting an Oral Description Storytelling is an important part of West Africa's history and culture. Storytellers pass along information to the community about events, places, and people. As you read this chapter, imagine that you are a storyteller. You are going to pass on some information about a person who lives, or has lived, in this region. Use the annotation tools in your eBook to gather information for your assignment.

National capital
Other city

0   150   300 Miles
0   150   300 Kilometers
Projection: Azimuthal Equal-Area

30°N

WESTERN SAHARA (MOROCCO)

Tropic of Cancer

20°N

N
W   E
S

CAPE VERDE

Nouakchott ⊕

Dakar ⊕   SENEGAL
Gambia R.
Banjul ⊕
GAMBIA

Praia

Bissau ⊕
GUINEA-BISSAU

10°N

GUINEA

Conakry ⊕

Freetown ⊕
SIERRA LEONE

ATLANTIC OCEAN

20°W

History People such as the Dogon cliff dwellers have been living in Mali for hundreds of years.

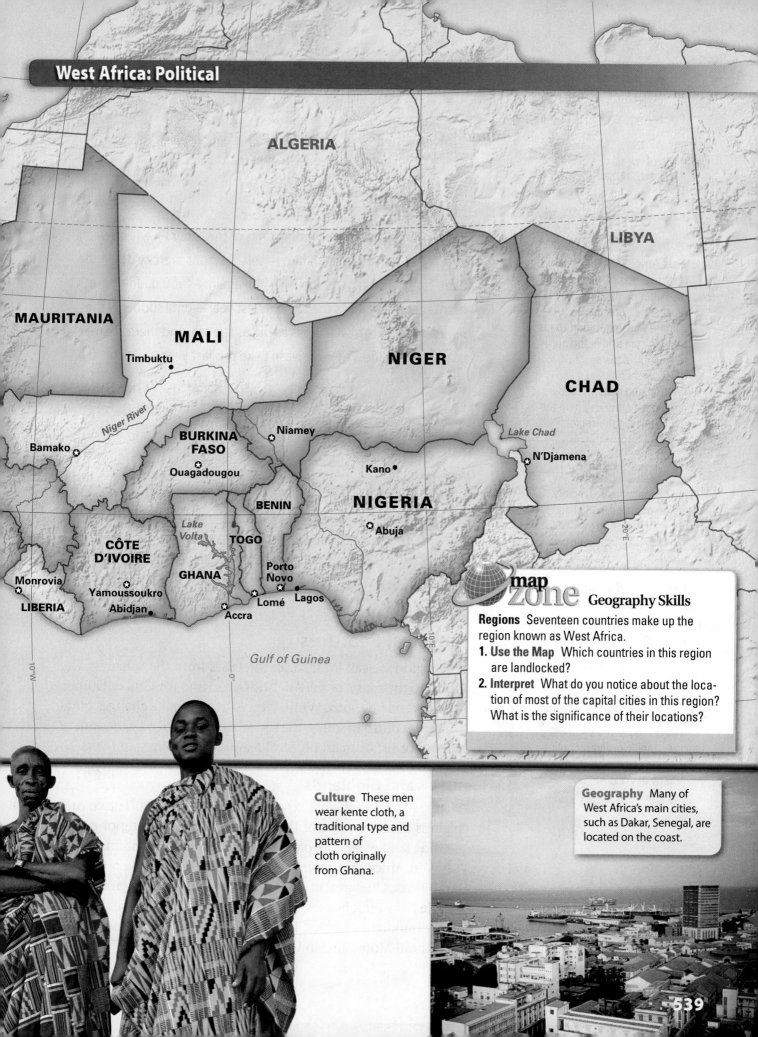

West Africa: Political

ALGERIA

LIBYA

MAURITANIA

MALI

Timbuktu

NIGER

CHAD

Niger River

Bamako •

BURKINA
FASO

Niamey

Lake Chad

N'Djamena •

Ouagadougou

Kano •

NIGERIA

BENIN

Abuja

Lake
Volta

TOGO

CÔTE
D'IVOIRE

GHANA

Porto
Novo

Monrovia •

Yamoussoukro

Lomé

Lagos

LIBERIA

Abidjan

Accra

Gulf of Guinea

10°W

0°

10°E

20°E

map zone Geography Skills

Regions Seventeen countries make up the region known as West Africa.

1. Use the Map Which countries in this region are landlocked?

2. Interpret What do you notice about the location of most of the capital cities in this region? What is the significance of their locations?

Culture These men wear kente cloth, a traditional type and pattern of cloth originally from Ghana.

Geography Many of West Africa's main cities, such as Dakar, Senegal, are located on the coast.

SECTION 1

TEKS 3A, 3B, 4D, 6A, 6B, 6C, 7B, 21B, 21C, 22A, 22D

What You Will Learn...

Main Ideas

1. West Africa's key physical features include plains and the Niger River.
2. West Africa has distinct climate and vegetation zones that go from arid in the north to tropical in the south.
3. West Africa has good agricultural and mineral resources that may one day help the economies in the region.

The Big Idea

West Africa, which is mostly a region of plains, has climates ranging from arid to tropical and has important resources.

Key Terms and Places

Niger River, *p. 541*
zonal, *p. 542*
Sahel, *p. 542*
desertification, *p. 542*
savanna, *p. 542*

hmhsocialstudies.com
TAKING NOTES

Use the graphic organizer online to take notes on the physical geography of West Africa.

Physical Geography

If YOU lived there...

Your family grows crops on the banks of the Niger River. Last year, your father let you go with him to sell the crops in a city down the river. This year you get to go with him again. As you paddle your boat, everything looks the same as last year—until suddenly the river appears to grow! It looks as big as the sea, and there are many islands all around. The river wasn't like this last year.

What do you think caused the change in the river?

BUILDING BACKGROUND The Niger River is one of West Africa's most important physical features. It brings precious water to the region's dry plains. Much of the interior of West Africa experiences desertlike conditions, but the region's rivers and lakes help to support life there.

Physical Features

The region we call West Africa stretches from the Sahara in the north to the coasts of the Atlantic Ocean and the Gulf of Guinea in the west and south. While West Africa's climate changes quite a bit from north to south, the region does not have a wide variety of landforms. Its main physical features are plains and rivers.

Plains and Highlands

Plains, flat areas of land, cover most of West Africa. The coastal plain is home to most of the region's cities. The interior plains provide land where people can raise a few crops or animals.

West Africa's plains are vast, interrupted only by a few highland areas. One area in the southwest has plateaus and cliffs. People have built houses directly into the sides of these cliffs for many hundreds of years. The region's only high mountains are the Tibesti Mountains in the northeast.

The Niger River

As you can see on the map below, many rivers flow across West Africa's plains. The most important river is the Niger (NY-juhr). The **Niger River** starts in some low mountains not too far from the Atlantic Ocean. From there, it flows 2,600 miles (4,185 km) into the interior of the region before emptying into the Gulf of Guinea.

The Niger brings life-giving water to West Africa. Many people farm along its banks or fish in its waters. It is also an important transportation route, especially during the rainy season. At that time, the river floods and water flows smoothly over its rapids.

Part of the way along its route the river divides into a network of channels, swamps, and lakes. This watery network is called the inland delta. Although it looks much like the delta where a river flows into the sea, this one is actually hundreds of miles from the coast in Mali.

READING CHECK **Summarizing** Why is the Niger River important to West Africa?

FOCUS ON READING
The word *although* signals contrast in this paragraph. What is being contrasted?

West Africa: Physical

ELEVATION

Feet	Meters
13,120	4,000
6,560	2,000
1,640	500
656	200
(Sea level) 0	0 (Sea level)
Below sea level	Below sea level

0   250   500 Miles
0   250   500 Kilometers

Projection: Azimuthal Equal-Area

map zone
Geography Skills

Regions West Africa is mainly a region of plains with a few highland areas. Many rivers flow across West Africa's plains.

1. **Identify** What is the longest river in West Africa?
2. **Make Inferences** How do you think the rivers affect life in West Africa?

1 The wide Niger River flows past Bamako, the capital of Mali, seen here in the distance.

West Africa: Climate

MAURITANIA
MALI
NIGER
CHAD
SENEGAL
GAMBIA
GUINEA
BURKINA FASO
BENIN
NIGERIA
GUINEA-BISSAU
CÔTE D'IVOIRE
SIERRA LEONE
LIBERIA
TOGO
GHANA
Gulf of Guinea
Niger River
0° Equator
ATLANTIC OCEAN

Climate Types
- Humid tropical
- Tropical savanna
- Desert
- Steppe

0   400   800 Miles
0   400   800 Kilometers
Projection: Azimuthal Equal-Area

map zone   Geography Skills

Regions Four climate types stretch across West Africa in horizontal bands.
1. **Identify** What countries have desert climates?
2. **Make Inferences** What areas do you think get the most rainfall?

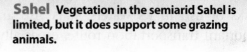

Sahel Vegetation in the semiarid Sahel is limited, but it does support some grazing animals.

Climate and Vegetation

West Africa has four different climate regions. As you can see on the map above, these climate regions stretch from east to west in bands or zones. Because of this, geographers say the region's climates are **zonal**, which means "organized by zone."

The northernmost zone of the region lies within the Sahara, the world's largest desert. Hardly any vegetation grows in the desert, and large areas of this dry climate zone have few or no people.

South of the Sahara is the semiarid **Sahel** (SAH-hel), a strip of land that divides the desert from wetter areas. It has a steppe climate. Rainfall there varies greatly from year to year. In some years it never rains. Although the Sahel is quite dry, it does have enough vegetation to support hardy grazing animals.

However, the Sahel is becoming more like the Sahara. Animals have overgrazed the land in some areas. Also, people have cut down trees for firewood. Without these plants to anchor the soil, wind blows soil away. These conditions, along with drought, are causing desertification in the Sahel. **Desertification** is the spread of desertlike conditions.

To the south of the Sahel is a savanna zone. A **savanna** is an area of tall grasses and scattered trees and shrubs. When rains fall regularly, farmers can do well in this region of West Africa.

The fourth climate zone lies along the coasts of the Atlantic and the Gulf of Guinea. This zone has a humid tropical climate. Plentiful rain supports tropical forests. However, many trees have been cut from these forests to make room for the region's growing populations.

READING CHECK **Categorizing** What are the region's four climate zones?

Savanna Grasses and scattered trees grow on the savanna. This region can be good for farming.

Tropical Forest Thick forests are found along the coasts of West Africa. The tall trees provide homes for many animals.

Resources

West Africa has a variety of resources. These resources include agricultural products, oil, and minerals.

The climate in parts of West Africa is good for agriculture. For example, Ghana is the world's leading producer of cacao, which is used to make chocolate. Coffee, coconuts, and peanuts are also among the region's main exports.

Oil, which is found off the coast of Nigeria, is the region's most valuable resource. Nigeria is a major exporter of oil. West Africa also has mineral riches, such as diamonds, gold, iron ore, and bauxite. Bauxite is the main source of aluminum.

READING CHECK **Summarizing** What are some of the region's resources?

SUMMARY AND PREVIEW West Africa is mostly covered with plains. Across these plains stretch four different climate zones, most of which are dry. In spite of the harsh climate, West Africa has some valuable resources. Next, you will learn about West Africa's history and culture.

Reviewing Ideas, Terms, and Places

1. a. Describe What is the inland delta on the **Niger River** like?

b. Summarize What is the physical geography of West Africa like?

c. Elaborate Why do you think most of West Africa's cities are located on the coastal plain?

2. a. Recall Why do geographers say West Africa's climates are **zonal**?

b. Compare and Contrast What is one similarity and one difference between the **Sahel** and the **savanna**?

c. Evaluate How do you think **desertification** affects people's lives in West Africa?

3. a. Identify What is the most valuable resource in West Africa?

b. Make Inferences Where do you think most of the crops in West Africa are grown?

Critical Thinking

4. Identifying Cause and Effect
Review your notes on climate. Using a graphic organizer like the one here, identify the causes and effects of desertification.

| Causes | → | Desertification | → | Effects |

FOCUS ON SPEAKING *my* WriteSmart

5. Describing the Physical Geography The person you will describe will live or have lived in this region. How might the physical geography have affected his or her life?

History and Culture

TEKS 1A, 1B, 2A, 2B, 3A, 3B, 15A, 15B, 18A, 18C, 21B, 22D

What You Will Learn...

Main Ideas

1. In West Africa's history, trade made great kingdoms rich, but this greatness declined as Europeans began to control trade routes.
2. The culture of West Africa includes many different ethnic groups, languages, religions, and housing styles.

The Big Idea

Powerful early kingdoms, European slave trade and colonization, and traditions from a mix of ethnic groups have all influenced West African culture.

Key Terms and Places

Timbuktu, *p. 545*
animism, *p. 546*
extended family, *p. 547*

hmhsocialstudies.com
TAKING NOTES

Use the graphic organizer online to take notes on West Africa's history and culture.

If YOU lived there...

When you were a small child, your family moved to Lagos, the largest city in Nigeria. You live in a city apartment now, but you still visit your aunts and uncles and cousins in your home village. There are more types of activities in the city, but you also remember that it was fun to have all your family members around.

Do you want to stay in the city or move back to your village? Why?

BUILDING BACKGROUND West African societies are changing as people like this family move to cities where they meet people whose habits and language are strange to them. West Africa has been home to many different ethnic groups throughout its history.

History

Much of what we know about West Africa's early history is based on archaeology. Archaeology is the study of the past based on what people left behind. Oral history—a spoken record of past events—offers other clues.

Merchants from North Africa crossed the Sahara to trade for West African gold and salt.

Great Kingdoms

Ancient artifacts suggest that early trading centers developed into great kingdoms in West Africa. One of the earliest kingdoms was Ghana (GAH-nuh). By controlling the Sahara trade in gold and salt, Ghana became rich and powerful by about 800.

According to legend, Ghana fell to a mighty warrior from a neighboring kingdom in about 1300. Under this leader, the empire of Mali (MAH-lee) replaced Ghana. Mali gained control of the Sahara trade routes. Mali's most famous king, Mansa Musa, used wealth from trade to support artists and scholars. However, invasions caused the decline of Mali by the 1500s.

As Mali declined, the kingdom of Songhai (SAWNG-hy) came to power. With a university, mosques, and more than 100 schools, the Songhai city of **Timbuktu** was a cultural center. By about 1600, however, invasions had weakened this kingdom.

The great West African trade cities also faded when the Sahara trade decreased. Trade decreased partly because Europeans began sailing along the west coast of Africa. They could trade for gold on the coast rather than with the North African traders who carried it through the desert.

The Slave Trade

For a while, both Europeans and Africans profited from trade with each other. However, in the 1500s the demand for labor in Europe's American colonies changed this relationship. European traders met the demand for labor by selling enslaved Africans to colonists.

The slave trade was profitable for these traders, but it devastated West Africa. Many families were broken up when members were kidnapped and enslaved. Africans often died on the voyage to the Americas. By the end of the slave trade in the 1800s, millions of Africans had been enslaved.

Colonial Era and Independence

Even with the end of the slave trade, Europeans wanted access to West Africa's resources. To ensure that access, France, Britain, Germany, and Portugal all claimed colonies in the region in the 1800s.

Some Europeans moved to West Africa to run the colonies. They built schools, roads, and railroads. However, they also created new and difficult problems for the people of West Africa. For example, many West Africans gave up farming and instead earned only low wages working in the new commercial economy.

After World War II, Africans worked for independence. Most of the colonies became independent during the 1950s and 1960s. All were independent by 1974.

READING CHECK **Summarizing** What impact did Europeans have on West Africa?

FOCUS ON READING

What words in the discussion of the slave trade signal comparison or contrast?

Culture

West African societies are very diverse. Their culture reflects three main influences —traditional African cultures, European culture, and Islam.

People and Languages

West Africa's people belong to hundreds of different ethnic groups. In fact, Nigeria alone is made up of more than 250 ethnic groups. The biggest ethnic groups there are Hausa and Fulani, Yoruba, and Igbo. Members of some ethnic groups in West Africa still live in their traditional villages. Other ethnic groups mix with each other in the region's cities.

Because of the way the European colonizers drew political boundaries, country borders sometimes separated members of the same ethnic group. Other borders grouped together peoples that did not get along. As a result, many West Africans are more loyal to their own ethnic groups than they are to their countries.

Because of the huge number of ethnic groups, hundreds of different languages are spoken in West Africa. In some areas, using the colonial languages of French, English, or Portuguese helps people from different groups communicate with each other. Also, West African languages that many people share, such as Fula and Hausa, help with communication in the region.

Religion

Like peoples and languages, many forms of religion exist in West Africa. Traditional religions of West Africa have often been forms of animism. **Animism** is the belief that bodies of water, animals, trees, and other natural objects have spirits. Animists also honor the memories of ancestors.

The two most common religions came from outside the region. They are Islam and Christianity. North African traders brought Islam to West Africa. Europeans introduced Christianity. Today most West Africans of the Sahel practice Islam. Many towns there have mosques built of mud. Christianity is the most common religion south of the Sahel.

Clothing, Families, and Homes

West Africans wear a mix of traditional and modern clothing styles. Some West Africans, particularly in the cities, wear Western-style clothing. Traditional robes, pants, blouses, and skirts are made from colorful cotton fabrics. Women often wear beautiful wrapped headdresses. Because of the warm climate, most clothing is loose.

CONNECTING TO the Arts

Masks

Masks are one of the best-known West African arts. They are traditionally carved out of wood only by skilled and respected men. The colors and shape of a mask have specific meanings. For example, the color white represents the spirit world.

Masks are used in ceremonies to call spirits or to prepare boys and girls for adulthood. Ceremony participants often wear a mask as part of a costume that completely hides the body. The wearer is believed to become what the mask represents.

Drawing Inferences Why would someone want to wear a mask?

A West African Village

These homes are in Burkina Faso. Trees are scarce in the Sahel and savanna so there is little wood for construction.

Women are responsible for painting and decorating the walls of the homes.

These homes are made of a mixture of mud, water, and cow dung.

Rural homes are small and simple. Many homes in the Sahel and savanna zones are circular. Straw or tin roofs sit atop mud, mud-brick, or straw huts. Large extended families often live close together in the same village. An **extended family** includes the father, mother, children, and close relatives in one household.

In urban areas also, members of an extended family may all live together. However, in West Africa's cities you will find modern buildings. People may live in houses or high-rise apartments.

READING CHECK **Generalizing** What are some features of West African culture?

SUMMARY AND PREVIEW Great kingdoms and European colonists once ruled West Africa. These historical influences still affect West Africa's diverse cultures. Next, you will learn about the countries of West Africa today.

Section 2 Assessment

hmhsocialstudies.com
ONLINE QUIZ

Reviewing Ideas, Terms, and Places

1. **a. Identify** What was the significance of **Timbuktu**?
   b. Explain How did the slave trade affect West Africa?
   c. Evaluate Do you think West Africans mostly appreciated or disliked the European colonizers? Explain your answer.
2. **a. Recall** What do people who believe in **animism** think about natural objects?
   b. Analyze How did European colonizers affect tension between ethnic groups?

Critical Thinking

3. **Sequencing** Look over your notes on the history of West Africa. Then, using a diagram like the one here, put major events in chronological order.

FOCUS ON SPEAKING

my WriteSmart

4. **Describing History and Culture** What details about West Africa's history might affect the daily life of someone in the area? Many aspects of culture in the region would affect someone in West Africa. What religion would this person practice? How would he or she dress? List some ideas for your description.

The Atlantic Slave Trade

Between 1500 and 1870, British, French, Dutch, Portuguese, and Spanish traders sent millions of enslaved Africans to colonies in the Americas. The highest number of slaves went to British and French colonies in the West Indies. The climate in the colonies was good for growing crops like cotton, tobacco, and sugarcane. These crops required a great deal of labor to grow and process. The colonists relied on enslaved Africans to meet this demand for labor.

NORTH AMERICA

ATLANTIC OCEAN

453,000

Tropic of Cancer

20° N

WEST INDIES

3,793,000

1,553,000

The Americas Most Africans were brought to the Americas to work on plantations. This painting from 1823 shows slaves cutting sugarcane on a sugar plantation in the West Indies.

SOUTH AMERICA

3,596,000

120° W
100° W
80° W
40° W

West Africa Africans were captured in the interior and then brought to forts like this one on the coast. The slave forts held the Africans until a ship arrived to take them to the Americas.

■ St. Luis de Senegal

■ James Fort

AFRICA

Accra
Elmina
Assinie ■ ■ ■ Whydah

Kidnapped and Taken to a Slave Ship

Mahommah G. Baquaqua was captured and sold into slavery as a young man. In this 1854 account, he recalls being taken to the African coast to board a slave ship.

"I was taken down to the river and placed on board a boat; the river was very large and branched off in two different directions, previous to emptying itself into the sea . . . We were two nights and one day on this river, when we came to a . . . place . . . [where] the slaves were all put into a pen, and placed with our backs to the fire . . . When all were ready to go aboard, we were chained together, and tied with ropes round about our necks, and were thus drawn down to the sea shore."

Slave forts began as trading posts. They were built near river mouths to provide easy access to both the sea and inland areas.

■ Fort

0   250   500 Miles
0   250   500 Kilometers

Projection: Miller Cylindrical

ANALYSIS SKILL **ANALYZING VISUALS**

1. **Location** Why were slave forts located where they were?
2. **Human-Environment Interaction** What geographic factors influenced the development of the Atlantic slave trade?

West Africa Today

 TEKS 1A, 1B, 2B, 3A, 3B, 4D, 5A, 5C, 6C, 15A, 15B, 15C, 15F, 21A, 21B, 21C, 22A, 22D

What You Will Learn...

Main Ideas

1. Nigeria has many different ethnic groups, an oil-based economy, and one of the world's largest cities.
2. Most coastal countries of West Africa have struggling economies and weak or unstable governments.
3. Lack of resources in the Sahel countries is a main challenge to economic development.

The Big Idea

Many countries in West Africa struggle with poor economies and political instability.

Key Terms and Places

secede, *p. 550*
Lagos, *p. 551*
famine, *p. 553*

TAKING NOTES

Use the annotation tools in your eBook to take notes on the governments and economies of the different regions of West Africa.

If **YOU** lived there...

You live in the Sahel country of Niger, where your family herds cattle. You travel with your animals to find good grazing land for them. In the past few years, however, the desert has been expanding. It is getting harder and harder to find good grass and water for your cattle. You worry about the coming years.

How does this environment affect your life and your future?

> **BUILDING BACKGROUND** The countries of West Africa are very different from one another. Some, such as Niger, have poor soils, little rain, and few resources. Others, such as Nigeria, have good natural resources. None of these countries is wealthy, however.

Nigeria

Nigeria is the second largest country in West Africa. With almost 175 million people, it has Africa's largest population, Sub-Saharan Africa's largest city, and one of the strongest economies.

People and Government

Like many other former colonies, Nigeria has many different ethnic groups within its borders. Conflicts have often taken place among those ethnic groups. In the 1960s one conflict became so serious that one ethnic group, the Igbo, tried to secede from Nigeria. To **secede** means to break away from the main country. This action led to a bloody civil war, which the Igbo eventually lost.

Ethnic and regional conflicts have continued to be an issue in Nigeria. Avoiding conflict was important in choosing a site for a new capital in the 1990s. Leaders chose Abuja (ah-BOO-jah) because it was centrally located in an area of low population density. A low population density meant that there would be fewer people to cause conflicts. Nigeria's government is now a democracy after years of military rule.

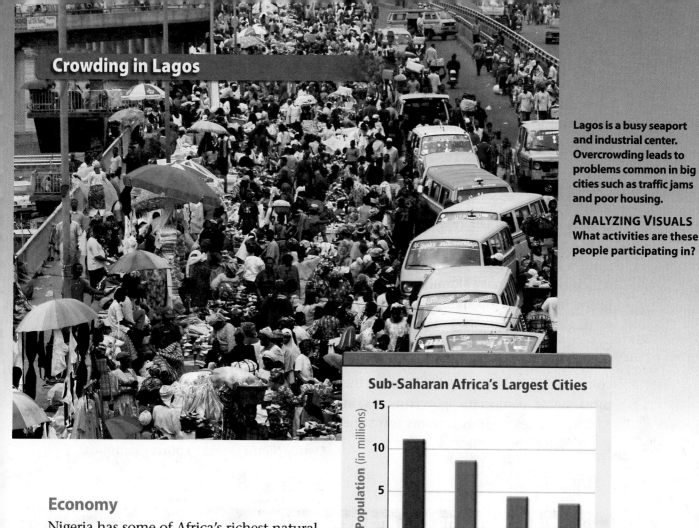

Crowding in Lagos

Lagos is a busy seaport and industrial center. Overcrowding leads to problems common in big cities such as traffic jams and poor housing.

ANALYZING VISUALS What activities are these people participating in?

Sub-Saharan Africa's Largest Cities

Population (in millions) — Cities: Lagos, Kinshasa, Khartoum, Johannesburg

Economy

Nigeria has some of Africa's richest natural resources. Major oil fields, the country's most important resource, are located in the Niger River delta and just off the coast. Oil accounts for about 95 percent of the country's export earnings. Income from oil exports has allowed Nigeria to build good roads and railroads for transporting oil. The oil industry is centered around **Lagos** (LAY-gahs). Also the former capital, Lagos is the most populous city in West Africa.

Although Nigeria is rich in resources, many Nigerians are poor. One cause of the poverty there is a high birthrate. Nigeria cannot produce enough food for its growing population. Another cause of Nigeria's poverty is a history of bad government. Corrupt government officials have used their positions to enrich themselves.

READING CHECK **Drawing Inferences** What are some obstacles to progress in Nigeria?

Other Coastal Countries

Several West African countries lie along the Atlantic Ocean and the Gulf of Guinea. Many of these countries have struggling economies and unstable governments.

Senegal and Gambia

Senegal wraps around Gambia. The odd border was created by French and British diplomats during the colonial era. Senegal is larger and richer than Gambia, but the two countries do have many similarities. For example, peanuts are their major crops. Also, tourism is becoming more important in both countries.

FOCUS ON READING
How are Senegal and Gambia similar?

Many people in Senegal and Gambia speak a language called Wolof (WOH-lawf). Griots (GREE-ohz), or storytellers, are important to the Wolof speakers there and to other West Africans.

Guinea, Guinea-Bissau, and Cape Verde

Guinea and its small neighbor, Guinea-Bissau (GI-nee bi-SOW), are poor countries. Guinea's main natural resource is bauxite, which is used to make aluminum. Guinea-Bissau has undeveloped mineral resources.

Cape Verde (VUHRD) is a group of volcanic islands in the Atlantic. It is West Africa's only island country. Once a Portuguese colony, Cape Verde now has one of the most stable democratic governments in Africa. Services such as tourism form the main part of the country's economy.

Liberia and Sierra Leone

Liberia is Africa's oldest republic. Americans founded it in the 1820s as a home for freed slaves. The freed slaves who settled in Liberia and their descendants lived in towns on the coast. They often clashed with Africans already living there. Those Africans were usually poorer and lived in rural areas. In the 1980s these conflicts led to a civil war, which ended in 2003.

Sierra Leone (lee-OHN) also experienced violent civil war, from 1991 to 2002. The fighting wrecked the country's economy, killed thousands of people, and forced millions from their homes.

Now, both Liberia and Sierra Leone are trying to rebuild. They do have natural resources on which to build stronger economies. Liberia exports rubber and iron ore while Sierra Leone exports diamonds.

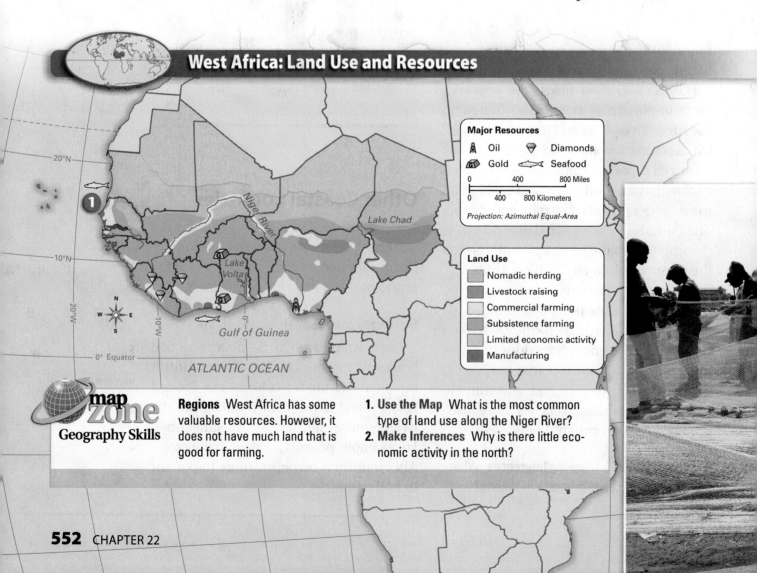

West Africa: Land Use and Resources

Major Resources
- Oil
- Gold
- Diamonds
- Seafood

0   400   800 Miles
0   400   800 Kilometers
Projection: Azimuthal Equal-Area

Land Use
- Nomadic herding
- Livestock raising
- Commercial farming
- Subsistence farming
- Limited economic activity
- Manufacturing

Niger River
Lake Chad
Lake Volta
Gulf of Guinea
ATLANTIC OCEAN
20°N
10°N
20°W
10°W
0°
0° Equator

map zone
Geography Skills

Regions West Africa has some valuable resources. However, it does not have much land that is good for farming.

1. **Use the Map** What is the most common type of land use along the Niger River?
2. **Make Inferences** Why is there little economic activity in the north?

Ghana and Côte d'Ivoire

Ghana is named for an ancient kingdom. Côte d'Ivoire (koht-dee-VWAHR) is a former French colony whose name means "Ivory Coast" in English. Côte d'Ivoire boasts Africa's largest Christian church building.

These two countries have rich natural resources. Gold, timber, and cacao (kuh-KOW) are major products of Ghana. Côte d'Ivoire is a world leader in export of cacao and coffee. However, civil war there has hurt the economy.

Togo and Benin

Unstable governments have troubled Togo and Benin (buh-NEEN) since independence. These two countries have experienced periods of military rule. Their fragile economies have contributed to their unstable and sometimes violent politics.

Both Togo and Benin are poor. The people depend on farming and herding for income. Palm products, cacao, and coffee are the main crops in both countries.

READING CHECK **Generalizing** What are the economies of the coastal countries like?

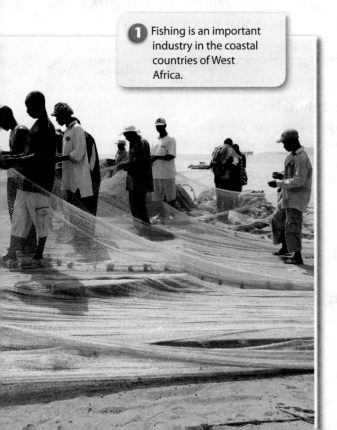

1 Fishing is an important industry in the coastal countries of West Africa.

Sahel Countries

The Sahel region of West Africa includes some of the poorest and least developed countries in the world. Drought and the expanding desert make feeding the people in these countries difficult.

Mauritania, Niger, and Chad

Most Mauritanians were once nomadic herders. Today the expanding Sahara has driven more than half of the nomads into cities. People in these cities, as well as the rest of the country, are very poor. Only in the far south, near the Senegal River, can people farm. Near the Atlantic Ocean, people fish for a living. Corrupt governments and ethnic tensions between blacks and Arabs add to Mauritania's troubles.

In Niger, only about 11 percent of the land is good for farming. The country's only farmland lies along the Niger River and near the Nigerian border. Farmers there grow staple, or main, food crops, such as millet and sorghum.

In 2005, locusts and drought destroyed Niger's crops. The loss of crops caused widespread **famine**, or an extreme shortage of food. International groups provided some aid, but it was impossible to **distribute** food to all who needed it. In 2007, fighting broke out between Tuareg rebels and government forces. In 2009, President Mamadou Tandja used his emergency powers to dissolve the government. He then instituted changes that would allow him to serve a third term as president.

Chad has more land for farming than Mauritania or Niger, and conditions there are somewhat better than in the other two countries. In addition to farming, Lake Chad once had a healthy fishing industry and supplied water to several countries. However, drought has evaporated much of the lake's water in the past several years.

ACADEMIC VOCABULARY
distribute to divide among a group of people

Water well

Dry Croplands

This aerial view shows how, with just a little water, people can farm in the dry Sahel.

The future may hold more promise for Chad. A long civil war finally ended in the 1990s. Also, oil was recently discovered there, and Chad began to export this valuable resource in 2004.

Mali and Burkina Faso

The Sahara covers about 40 percent of the land in Mali. The scarce amount of land available for farming makes Mali among the world's poorest countries. The available farmland lies in the southwest, along the Niger River. Most people in Mali fish or farm in this small area along the river. Cotton and gold are Mali's main exports.

Mali's economy does have some bright spots, however. A fairly stable democratic government has begun economic reforms. Also, the ancient cities of Timbuktu and Gao (GOW) continue to attract tourists.

Burkina Faso is also a poor country. It has thin soil and few mineral resources. Few trees remain in or near the capital, Ouagadougou (wah-gah-DOO-goo), because they have been cut for firewood and building material. Jobs in the city are also scarce. To support their families many men try to find work in other countries. Thus, when unrest disrupts work opportunities in other countries, Burkina Faso's economy suffers.

READING CHECK **Summarizing** What are the challenges facing Chad and Burkina Faso?

SUMMARY AND PREVIEW Countries in West Africa struggle with poor economies. In addition, many have faced political instability since independence. In the next chapter, you will learn about how the countries in East Africa face some similar issues.

Section 3 Assessment

hmhsocialstudies.com
ONLINE QUIZ

Reviewing Ideas, Terms, and Places

1. **a. Recall** Why did the Igbo try to **secede**?
   b. Evaluate What do you think were some benefits and drawbacks to Nigeria's leaders moving the capital from **Lagos** to Abuja?
2. **a. Compare** What are some similarities between Togo and Benin?
   b. Elaborate Why do you think countries with poor economies often have unstable governments?
3. **a. Describe** What caused **famine** in Niger?
   b. Evaluate What do you think is the biggest problem facing the Sahel countries? Explain.
   c. Identify and Explain Which geographic factors best explain the patterns of land use and economic activity shown on the Land Use and Resources map on page 552?

Critical Thinking

4. **Compare and Contrast** Review your notes on the coastal countries and the Sahel countries. Then use a diagram like the one here to compare and contrast the two regions.

Coastal   Sahel

FOCUS ON SPEAKING

5. **Describing Countries of West Africa** Think about the countries of West Africa. Which one might be a good location for the person you are going to describe? Take some notes about that place.

BOOK

I Speak of Freedom

In his book I Speak of Freedom, *Kwame Nkrumah writes about the need for African nations to unite. In this excerpt from the preface, Nkrumah describes the value of Africa's natural resources and the importance of coming together to benefit from these resources.*

Although most Africans are poor, our continent is potentially extremely rich. Our mineral resources, which are being exploited[1] with foreign capital[2] only to enrich foreign investors, range from gold and diamonds to uranium and petroleum. Our forests contain some of the finest woods to be grown anywhere. Our cash crops[3] include cocoa, coffee, rubber, tobacco and cotton . . . This is one of the reasons why we have in Africa the paradox[4] of poverty in the midst of plenty, and scarcity in the midst of abundance.

Never before have a people had within their grasp so great an opportunity for developing a continent endowed[5] with so much wealth. Individually, the independent states of Africa, some of them potentially rich, others poor, can do little for their people. Together, by mutual help, they can achieve much. But the economic development of the continent must be planned and pursued as a whole.

Notice the detailed list of resources Nkumrah includes to illustrate Africa's abundance.

In 1960, the year before Nkumrah's book was published, 17 African countries became independent nations.

[1] **exploited**: taken advantage of; manipulated

[2] **foreign capital**: money invested from another country

[3] **cash crops**: crops grown for direct sale to make money

[4] **paradox**: something that seems contradictory

[5] **endowed**: enriched

Women sort coffee beans near Bonga, Ethiopia, where coffee production is the main source of income. Nkrumah (inset) argued that Africa's future depended on its ability to control such resources.

ANALYSIS SKILL ANALYZING PRIMARY SOURCES

1. **Identifying** What does Nkumrah mean when he calls Africa a "paradox of poverty in the midst of plenty"? What is one cause of this poverty?
2. **Analyzing** How does Nkumrah view Africa's future?

Social Studies Skills

Differentiating Valid Sources

Learn

How can you tell the difference between a valid primary source and a valid secondary source? **Primary sources** are materials written or made by people who took part in or saw a historical event. Examples include letters, diaries, interviews, artifacts, and photographs. **Secondary sources** are historical records that are produced by people who were not there. History books, computer software, biographies, paintings, and encyclopedia entries are examples of secondary sources.

Practice

Read the passage below. It contains a primary and a secondary source. Use these tips to tell the difference between valid primary and secondary sources.

- Determine whether the source is primary or secondary.
- Consider the author or producer of the source.
- Assess the level of bias in the source.
- Think about the context of the source, including why, where, and when the source was produced.

Kidnapped and Taken to a Slave Ship

Mahommah G. Baquaqua was captured and sold into slavery as a young man. In this 1854 account, he recalls being taken to the African coast to board a slave ship.

"I was taken down to the river and placed on board a boat; the river was very large and branched off in two different directions, previous to emptying itself into the sea . . . We were two nights and one day on this river, when we came to a . . . place . . . [where] the slaves were all put into a pen, and placed with our backs to the fire . . . When all were ready to go aboard, we were chained together, and tied with ropes round about our necks, and were thus drawn down to the sea shore."

Distinguish the secondary source. The first paragraph is not a first-hand account of a historical event.

Distinguish the primary source. The quotation is a first-hand account of the slave trade.

Identify the author and context of the source. Consider why the author produced it, what the document was supposed to achieve, and who would read it.

Apply

1. Which part of the excerpt is the primary source, and which is a secondary source?

2. What was Baquaqua's purpose in giving this account? What does it tell about the time in which it was written?

3. What information is available only in the secondary source?

Visual Summary

Use the visual summary below to help you review the main ideas of the chapter.

QUICK FACTS

West Africa has four distinct climate zones. In the dry Sahel, people try to farm or herd cattle.

Masks are just one example of traditional African culture that can be seen in West Africa today.

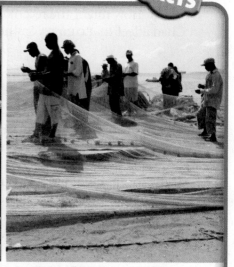

Most West African countries are poor. Fishing is important to the economy along rivers and in coastal areas.

Reviewing Vocabulary, Terms, and Places

For each statement below, write T if it is true and F if it is false. If the statement is false, write the correct term that would make the sentence a true statement.

1. West Africa's climate is described as <u>savanna</u> because it is organized by zone.

2. <u>Animism</u>, a belief that natural objects have spirits, is a traditional religion in West Africa.

3. An <u>extended family</u> is one that includes a mother, father, children, and close relatives in one household.

4. International aid agencies have tried to <u>distribute</u> food in Niger.

5. <u>Timbuktu</u> is the largest city in Nigeria.

6. The <u>Niger River</u> flows through many countries in West Africa and empties into the Gulf of Guinea.

7. The spread of desertlike conditions is <u>famine</u>.

8. Some animals can graze in the <u>Sahel</u>.

Comprehension and Critical Thinking

SECTION 1 *(Pages 540–543)*

9. **a. Geographic Questions** With a partner, pose and answer the following: Where is the Sahel located? Why is it there? How is its location related to the location of other environments?

   b. Make Inferences What are some problems caused by desertification?

   c. Elaborate West Africa has valuable resources such as gold and diamonds. Why have these resources not made West Africa rich?

SECTION 2 *(Pages 544–547)*

10. **a. Recall** What religion do most people in the Sahel practice?

   b. Analyze What role did trade play in the early West African kingdoms and later in West Africa's history?

   c. Elaborate What might be some advantages of living with an extended family?

SECTION 3 *(Pages 550–554)*

11. a. Identify Which country in West Africa has an economy based nearly entirely on oil?

b. Compare and Contrast What is one similarity and one difference between the cause of civil war in Nigeria and its cause in Liberia?

c. Predict How might the recent discovery of oil in Chad affect that country in the future?

Using the Internet

12. Activity: Creating a Postcard Come and learn about the mighty baobab tree. This unique tree looks as if it has been plucked from the ground and turned upside down. These trees are known not only for their unique look but also for their great size. Some are so big that a chain of 30 people is needed to surround one tree trunk! Through the online book, visit Web sites about baobab trees in West Africa. Then create a postcard about this strange wonder of nature.

Map Activity

13. West Africa On a separate sheet of paper, match the letters on the map with their correct labels.

Niger River	Senegal River
Lagos, Nigeria	Mali
Gulf of Guinea	

Social Studies Skills

Differentiating Valid Sources *Use the Primary Source feature on page 555 to answer the following questions.*

14. Which part of the feature is a primary source, and which part is a secondary source? How can you tell?

15. Who is the author of the primary source?

16. What is the purpose of each source?

FOCUS ON READING AND SPEAKING *my* WriteSmart

Understanding Comparison-Contrast *Look over your notes or re-read Section 1. Use the information on climate and vegetation to answer the following questions.*

17. How are the Sahara and the Sahel similar?

18. How are the Sahara and the Sahel different?

19. Compare the Sahel and the savanna zone. How are they similar?

20. Contrast the savanna region and the humid tropical region along the coast. How are these areas different?

21. Presenting an Oral Description Read over your notes. Then prepare a brief oral presentation about a day in the life of someone from West Africa. Tell about the land, climate, and vegetation. Describe the culture, including family life. Tell what this person does for a living. With a partner, practice your presentation. As you present, make eye contact and speak clearly. Plainly state your topic and main ideas. For supporting ideas and details, use descriptive language that will interest your audience. Then listen as your partner presents. Practice active listening and take notes. Ask questions to clarify anything that was unclear or confusing. Review your notes right away to make sure that you understand what was said. Finally, summarize aloud your partner's main points.

Reading Social Studies

Understanding Comparison-Contrast

Geographers compare and contrast to understand how various world regions and countries are alike and different. They may describe similarities and differences in text or show them in a visual such as a chart. You can understand comparison-contrast by learning to recognize clue words and points of comparison. Clue words let you know whether to look for similarities or differences. Points of comparison are the main topics that are being compared or contrasted. Notice how the passage below compares and contrasts life in rural and urban areas.

Highlighted words are points of comparison.

Rural homes are small and simple. Many homes in the Sahel and savanna zones are circular. Straw or tin roofs sit atop mud, mud-brick, or straw huts. Large extended families often live close together in the same village . . .

In urban areas, also, members of an extended family may all live together. However, in West Africa's cities you will find modern buildings. People may live in houses or high rise apartments.

From Section 2, History and Culture

Underlined words are clue words.

Clue Words	
Comparison	**Contrast**
share, similar, like, also, both, in addition, besides	however, while, unlike, different, but, although

YOU TRY IT!

Read the following passage with a partner. Use your knowledge of clue words to help you identify similarities and differences between Liberia and Sierra Leone. Create a chart like the one here to compare and contrast the two countries.

Now, both Liberia and Sierra Leone are trying to rebuild. They do have natural resources on which to build stronger economies. Liberia has rubber and iron ore while Sierra Leone exports diamonds.

From Section 3, West Africa Today

Liberia   Sierra Leone

Differences   Differences

Similarities

East Africa

Essential Question *my*Notebook

What challenges and conflicts does East Africa face today?

Texas Essential Knowledge and Skills (TEKS)

1A, 1B, 2A, 2B, 3A, 3B, 4D, 5A, 5B, 6A, 6B, 6C, 7A, 7B, 7C, 15B, 15D, 15E, 15F, 16A, 17A, 19A, 21B, 21C, 22D, 22E

FOCUS ON READING AND WRITING *my* **Write**Smart

Identifying Supporting Details Supporting details are the facts and examples that provide information to support the main ideas of a chapter, section, or paragraph. At the beginning of each section in this book, there is a list of main ideas. As you read this chapter, look for the details that support each section's main ideas. **See the lesson, Identifying Supporting Details, on page 579.**

Writing a Letter Home Imagine that you are spending your summer vacation visiting the countries of East Africa. You want to write a letter home to a friend in the United States describing the land and its people. As you read this chapter, you will gather information that you can include in your letter. Use the annotation tools in your eBook to gather information for your assignment.

History This gold artifact is from the early Nubian civilization of northern Sudan.

East Africa: Political

LIBYA

EGYPT

CHAD

SUDAN

Nile *River*

Port Sudan

Red Sea

ERITREA

Khartoum

Asmara

White Nile

Blue Nile

Lake Tana

DJIBOUTI

Djibouti

Gulf of Aden

CENTRAL AFRICAN REPUBLIC

SOUTH SUDAN

Addis Ababa

ETHIOPIA

SOMALIA

10°N

Lake Turkana

Juba

Lake Albert

UGANDA

KENYA

Mogadishu

N

Kampala

Nairobi

W   E

0° Equator

DEMOCRATIC REPUBLIC OF THE CONGO

RWANDA   Kigali

S

Bujumbura   BURUNDI

Lake Victoria

Mombasa

INDIAN OCEAN

50°E

TANZANIA

Dodoma

Zanzibar

Lake Tanganyika

Dar es Salaam

Lake Malawi

ZAMBIA

10°S

MOZAMBIQUE

20°E   30°E   40°E   60°E

map zone

Place East Africa is located on the Red Sea and the Indian Ocean.

1. **Locate** What is the capital of Ethiopia?
2. **Analyze** How do you think the economies of the landlocked countries in East Africa are affected by their location?

Culture Masai women of East Africa wear colorful jewelry and traditional clothing.

Geography The plains surrounding Mount Kilimanjaro are rich in wildlife. Millions of tourists come to visit this part of East Africa each year.

561

SECTION **1**

Physical Geography

TEKS 3A, 3B, 4D, 6A, 6C, 7A, 7B, 7C, 21B, 21C, 22D, 22E

What You Will Learn...

Main Ideas

1. East Africa's physical features range from rift valleys to plains.
2. East Africa's climate is influenced by its location and elevation, and the region's vegetation includes savannas and forests.

The Big Idea

East Africa is a region of diverse physical features, climates, and vegetation.

Key Terms and Places

rift valleys, *p. 562*
Great Rift Valley, *p. 562*
Mount Kilimanjaro, *p. 563*
Serengeti Plain, *p. 563*
Lake Victoria, *p. 564*
droughts, *p. 564*

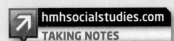

hmhsocialstudies.com
TAKING NOTES

Use the graphic organizer online to take notes on East Africa's physical features and climate and vegetation.

If YOU lived there...

You and your friends are planning to hike up Mount Kilimanjaro, near the equator in Tanzania. It is hot in your camp at the base of the mountain. You're wearing shorts and a T-shirt, but your guide tells you to pack a fleece jacket and jeans. You start your climb, and soon you understand this advice. The air is much colder, and there's snow on the nearby peaks.

Why is it cold at the top of the mountain?

BUILDING BACKGROUND The landscapes of East Africa have been shaped by powerful forces. The movement of tectonic plates has stretched the Earth's surface here, creating steep-sided valleys and huge lakes.

Physical Features

East Africa is a region of spectacular landscapes and wildlife. Vast plains and plateaus stretch throughout the region. In the north lie huge deserts and dry grasslands. In the southwest, large lakes dot the plateaus. In the east, sandy beaches and colorful coral reefs run along the coast.

The Rift Valleys

Look at the map on the next page. As you can see, East Africa's rift valleys cut from north to south across the region. **Rift valleys** are places on Earth's surface where the crust stretches until it breaks. Rift valleys form when Earth's tectonic plates move away from each other. This movement causes the land to arch and split along the rift valleys. As the land splits open, volcanoes erupt and deposit layers of rock in the region.

Seen from the air, the **Great Rift Valley** looks like a giant scar. The Great Rift Valley is the largest rift on Earth and is made up of two rifts—the eastern rift and the western rift.

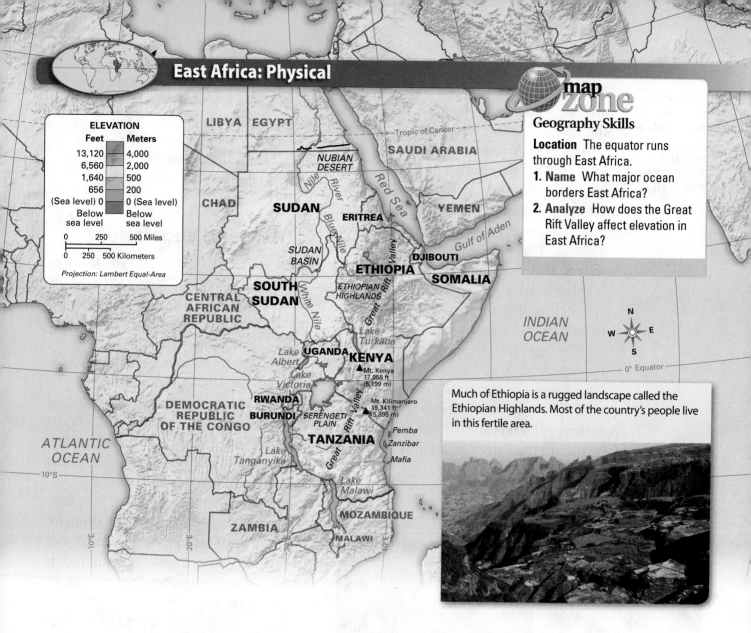

East Africa: Physical

ELEVATION

Feet	Meters
13,120	4,000
6,560	2,000
1,640	500
656	200
(Sea level) 0	0 (Sea level)
Below sea level	Below sea level

0   250   500 Miles

0   250   500 Kilometers

Projection: Lambert Equal-Area

LIBYA   EGYPT

Tropic of Cancer

SAUDI ARABIA

NUBIAN DESERT

Nile River

Red Sea

YEMEN

CHAD

SUDAN

ERITREA

Blue Nile

SUDAN BASIN

Gulf of Aden

DJIBOUTI

ETHIOPIA

SOMALIA

SOUTH SUDAN

White Nile

ETHIOPIAN HIGHLANDS

CENTRAL AFRICAN REPUBLIC

Great Rift Valley

INDIAN OCEAN

Lake Turkana

Lake Albert

UGANDA

KENYA

0° Equator

Mt. Kenya 17,058 ft (5,199 m)

Lake Victoria

DEMOCRATIC REPUBLIC OF THE CONGO

RWANDA

BURUNDI

Mt. Kilimanjaro 19,341 ft (5,895 m)

Great Rift Valley

SERENGETI PLAIN

Pemba

Zanzibar

TANZANIA

Mafia

ATLANTIC OCEAN

10°S

Lake Tanganyika

Great Rift Valley

Lake Malawi

ZAMBIA

MALAWI

MOZAMBIQUE

10°E   20°E   30°E   40°E

map zone

Geography Skills

Location The equator runs through East Africa.
1. **Name** What major ocean borders East Africa?
2. **Analyze** How does the Great Rift Valley affect elevation in East Africa?

Much of Ethiopia is a rugged landscape called the Ethiopian Highlands. Most of the country's people live in this fertile area.

The rift walls are usually a series of steep cliffs. These cliffs rise as much as 6,000 feet (2,000 m).

Mountains and Highlands

The landscape of East Africa has many high volcanic mountains. The highest mountain in Africa, **Mount Kilimanjaro** (ki-luh-muhn-JAHR-oh), rises to 19,340 feet (5,895 m). Despite Kilimanjaro's location near the equator, the mountain's peak has long been covered in snow. This much colder climate is caused by Kilimanjaro's high elevation.

Other areas of high elevation in East Africa include the Ethiopian Highlands.

These highlands, which lie mostly in Ethiopia, are very rugged. Deep river valleys cut through this landscape.

Plains

Even though much of East Africa lies at high elevations, some areas are flat. For example, plains stretch as far as the eye can see along the eastern rift in Tanzania and Kenya. Tanzania's **Serengeti Plain** is one of the largest plains. It is here that an abundance of wildlife thrives. The plain's grasses, trees, and water provide nutrition for wildlife that includes elephants, giraffes, lions, and zebras. To protect this wildlife, Tanzania established a national park.

Rivers and Lakes

FOCUS ON READING
What details in this paragraph support this section's second main idea?

East Africa also has a number of rivers and large lakes. The world's longest river, the Nile, begins in East Africa and flows north to the Mediterranean Sea. The Nile is formed by the meeting of the Blue Nile and the White Nile at Khartoum, Sudan. The White Nile is formed by the water that flows into Africa's largest lake, **Lake Victoria**. The Blue Nile is formed from waters that run down from Ethiopia's highlands. As the Nile meanders through Sudan, it provides a narrow, fertile lifeline to farmers in the desert.

The region has a number of great lakes in addition to Lake Victoria. One group of lakes forms a chain in the western rift valleys. There are also lakes along the drier eastern rift valleys. Near the eastern rift, heat from the Earth's interior makes some lakes so hot that no human can swim in them. In addition, some lakes are extremely salty. However, some of these rift lakes provide algae for the region's flamingos.

READING CHECK **Evaluating** What river is the most important in this region? Why?

Climate and Vegetation

When you think of Africa, do you think of it as being a hot or cold place? Most people usually think all of Africa is hot. However, they are mistaken. Some areas of East Africa have a cool climate.

East Africa's location on the equator and differences in elevation influence the climates and types of vegetation in East Africa. For example, areas near the equator receive the greatest amount of rainfall. Areas farther from the equator are much drier and seasonal droughts are common. **Droughts** are periods when little rain falls, and crops are damaged. During a drought, crops and the grasses for cattle die and people begin to starve. Several times in recent decades droughts have affected the people of East Africa.

Further south of the equator the climate changes to tropical savanna. Tall grasses and scattered trees make up the savanna landscape. Here the greatest climate changes occur along the sides of the rift valleys. The rift floors are dry with grasslands and thorn shrubs.

North of the equator, areas of plateaus and mountains have a highland climate and dense forests. Temperatures in the highlands are much cooler than temperatures on the savanna. The highlands experience heavy rainfall because of its high elevation, but the valleys are drier. This mild climate makes farming possible. As a result, most of the region's population lives in the highlands.

Satellite View

Great Rift Valley

This satellite image of part of the Great Rift Valley in Ethiopia was created by using both infrared light and true color. The bright blue dots are some of the smaller lakes that were created by the rifts. Once active volcanoes, some of these lakes are very deep. Vegetation appears as areas of green. Bare, rocky land appears pink and gray.

Analyzing How were the lakes in the Great Rift Valley created?

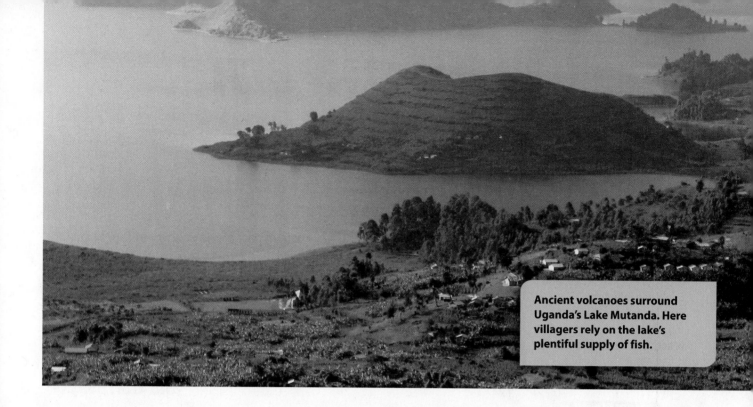

Ancient volcanoes surround Uganda's Lake Mutanda. Here villagers rely on the lake's plentiful supply of fish.

Areas east of the highlands and on the Indian Ocean coast are at a much lower elevation. These areas have desert and steppe climates. Vegetation is limited to shrubs and hardy grasses that are adapted to water shortages.

READING CHECK **Categorizing** What are some of East Africa's climate types?

SUMMARY AND PREVIEW In this section you learned about East Africa's rift valleys, mountains, highlands, plains, rivers, and lakes. You also learned that the region's location and elevation affect its climate and vegetation. In the next section you will learn about East Africa's history and culture.

Section 1 Assessment

hmhsocialstudies.com
ONLINE QUIZ

Reviewing Ideas, Terms, and Places

1. **a. Define** What are **rift valleys**?
   b. Explain Why is there snow on **Mount Kilimanjaro**?
   c. Elaborate What are some unusual characteristics of the lakes in the **Great Rift Valley**?
2. **a. Recall** What is the climate of the highlands in East Africa like?
   b. Draw Conclusions What are some effects of **drought** in the region?
   c. Develop How are the climates of some areas of East Africa affected by elevation?
   d. Geographic Questions Use the physical map on page 563 to pose and answer a question about the distribution of physical features in the various countries of East Africa.

Critical Thinking

3. **Categorizing** Using your notes and this chart, place details about East Africa's physical features into different categories.

Physical Features			
Rift Valleys	Mountains and Highlands	Plains	Rivers and Lakes

FOCUS ON WRITING

my WriteSmart

4. **Describing the Physical Geography** Note the physical features of East Africa that you can describe in your letter. How do these features compare to the features where you live?

History and Culture

TEKS 1A, 1B, 2A, 2B, 3A, 3B, 15A, 15B, 15F, 16A, 17A, 21B, 21

What You Will Learn...

Main Ideas

1. The history of East Africa is one of religion, trade, and European influence.
2. East Africans speak many different languages and practice several different religions.

The Big Idea

East Africa is a region with a rich history and diverse cultures.

Key Terms and Places

Nubia, *p. 566*
Zanzibar, *p. 567*
imperialism, *p. 567*

hmhsocialstudies.com
TAKING NOTES

Use the graphic organizer online to take notes on East Africa's history and culture.

If **YOU** lived there...

You live on the island of Zanzibar, part of the country of Tanzania. Your hometown has beautiful beaches, historic palaces, and sites associated with the East African slave trade. Although you and your friends learn English in school, you speak the African language of Swahili to each other.

How has your country's history affected your life today?

BUILDING BACKGROUND For almost a century, nearly all the countries of East Africa were controlled by European countries. Before that, however, the region's people had close trade ties with Arabs from Southwest Asia. This Arab influence blended with native African cultures to form a new culture and language.

History

Early civilizations in East Africa were highly developed. Later, Christianity and Islam influenced the lives of many East Africans. Other influences included trade, the arrival of Europeans, ethnic conflict, and independence.

Cultural Diffusion of Christianity and Islam

Christian missionaries from Egypt first introduced Christianity to Ethiopia as early as the AD 300s. About 200 years later Christianity spread into **Nubia**, an area of Egypt and Sudan today.

In the early 1200s, a powerful Christian emperor named Lalibela ruled Ethiopia. Lalibela is best known for the 11 rock churches he built during his reign. He claimed that God told him to carve the churches out of the rocky ground. Today, the town where the churches are located is called Lalibela.

By about AD 700, Islam was a major religion in Egypt and other parts of North Africa. Gradually, Muslim Arabs from Egypt

Lalibela, Ethiopia

In the 1200s, highly skilled Ethiopian architects and craftspeople built this Christian church at Lalibela.

ANALYZING VISUALS What Christian symbol does the church resemble?

Workers dug deep trenches to carve out the church.

Craftspeople used special tools to carve windows and doors out of solid rock.

spread into northern Sudan and brought their Islamic faith with them. At the same time, Islam spread to the Indian Ocean coast of what is now Somalia. City-states such as Mogadishu and Mombasa became major Islamic centers and controlled trade on the coast.

The Slave Trade

The slave trade along the Indian Ocean coast dates back more than 1,000 years. East Africans, Arabs, and Europeans all participated in the slave trade in East Africa. They kidnapped Africans, enslaved them, and shipped them to ports throughout Africa and Southwest Asia. Most of these slaves went to Islamic countries. By the early 1500s the Portuguese had begun setting up forts and settlements on the East African coast to support the slave trade.

In the late 1700s the East African island of **Zanzibar** became an international slave-trading center. Later, large plantations with slave labor were set up by Europeans in the interior. They grew crops of cloves and sugarcane.

European Influence and Conflict

Most European nations ended slavery in the early 1800s. They focused instead on trading products such as gold, ivory, and rubber. To get these goods, Europeans believed they needed to dominate regions of Africa rich in these natural resources. Europeans also wanted to expand their empires by establishing more colonies. The British were the most aggressive, and they gained control over much of East Africa.

In the 1880s Britain and other European powers divided up most of Africa. They drew boundaries that separated some ethnic groups. To maintain power over their colonies, Europeans used **imperialism**, a practice that tries to dominate other countries' government, trade, and culture.

Within East Africa, just Kenya was settled by large numbers of Europeans. Under imperialism, colonial rulers usually controlled their countries through African deputies. Many of the deputies were traditional chiefs. These chiefs were loyal to their own peoples, which tended to strengthen ethnic rivalries. Today governments are trying to influence feelings of national identity, but ethnic conflict is still strong in many countries.

FOCUS ON READING

In the second paragraph under Languages, find at least two details to support the main idea in the first sentence.

In the early 1960s, most East African countries gained independence from European colonizers. Ethiopia was never colonized. Its mountains provided natural protection, and its peoples resisted European colonization.

Independence, however, did not solve all of the problems of the former colonies. In addition, new challenges faced the newly independent countries. For example, some countries experienced ethnic conflicts.

READING CHECK **Evaluating** Why was Ethiopia never a European colony?

Culture

Over thousands of years of human settlement, East Africa developed a great diversity of people and ways of life. As a result, East Africans speak many different languages and practice several religions.

Language

East Africa's history of European imperialism influenced language in many countries in the region. For example, French is an official language in Rwanda, Burundi, and Djibouti today. English is the primary language of millions of people in Uganda, Kenya, and Tanzania.

In addition to European languages, many East Africans also speak African languages. Swahili is the most widely spoken African language in the region. As East Africans traded with Arabic speakers from Southwest Asia, Swahili developed. In fact, Swahili comes from the Arabic word meaning "on the coast." Today about 80 million people speak Swahili. Ethiopians speak Amharic, and Somalians speak Somali.

FOCUS ON CULTURE

The Swahili

For more than 1,000 years, a culture unlike any other has thrived along the coast of modern-day Kenya and Tanzania. In the AD 700s, trade contacts between East Africans and Arab traders began. Over time these interactions led to the creation of a unique language and culture known as Swahili.

The Swahili adopted some cultural traits from Arab traders. For example, many East Africans converted to the religion of the Arab traders—Islam. African languages blended with Arabic to form the Swahili language.

Generalizing What effects did Arab traders have on Swahili culture?

Major Languages of East Africa

Legend:
- Amharic
- Arabic
- English
- French
- Somali
- Swahili
- English and Swahili
- Arabic and French

LIBYA, CHAD, SUDAN, ERITREA, SAUDI ARABIA, YEMEN, Red Sea, Gulf of Aden, DJIBOUTI, SOMALIA, 10°N, SOUTH SUDAN, ETHIOPIA, DEMOCRATIC REPUBLIC OF THE CONGO, UGANDA, KENYA, 0° Equator, RWANDA, BURUNDI, INDIAN OCEAN, ATLANTIC OCEAN, TANZANIA, 10°S, ZAMBIA

N W E S

0   300   600 Miles
0   300   600 Kilometers
Projection: Lambert Equal-Area

map zone
Geography Skills

Regions A number of major languages are spoken in East Africa.
1. **Name** What major languages are spoken in Kenya?
2. **Draw Conclusions** How might the languages spoken in Rwanda and Burundi reflect each country's history?

Religion

Religion is an important aspect of culture for many East Africans. While the religions in East Africa vary greatly, most of them place emphasis on honoring ancestors.

Many East Africans are followers of animist religions. Animists believe the natural world contains spirits. Some people also combine animist worship with religions such as Christianity. Most Christians in East Africa live in Ethiopia. Islam is also practiced in the region. Sudan and Somalia are predominantly Muslim.

READING CHECK **Analyzing** Why might people in East Africa speak a European language?

SUMMARY AND PREVIEW In this section you learned about the history and culture of East Africa. Next, you will learn about the countries of East Africa today.

Section 2 Assessment
hmhsocialstudies.com
ONLINE QUIZ

Reviewing Ideas, Terms, and Places

1. **a. Define** What is **imperialism**?
   b. Explain What did the emperor Lalibela have architects build in Ethiopia?
   c. Evaluate Why do you think Europeans wanted colonies in East Africa?
2. **a. Identify** What language do most Ugandans speak?
   b. Explain What do animists believe?
   c. Describe Explain the factors behind and the impact of the cultural diffusion of Christianity and Islam to East Africa.

Critical Thinking

3. **Summarizing** Using your notes and this chart, write two sentences that summarize what you learned about the region's languages and religions.

Language	
Religion	

FOCUS ON WRITING
my WriteSmart

4. **Geographic Questions** Pose and answer the following questions about East Africa: What is significant about its location? How is its location related to the location of other people, places, and environments? How has location shaped history and culture in the region?

East Africa Today

TEKS 5A, 5B, 6B, 6C, 15A, 15B, 15D, 15E, 15F, 19A, 21B, 21C

What You Will Learn...

Main Ideas

1. National parks are a major source of income for Tanzania and Kenya.
2. Rwanda and Burundi are densely populated rural countries with a history of ethnic conflict.
3. Both Sudan and Uganda have economies based on agriculture, but Sudan has suffered from years of war.
4. The countries of the Horn of Africa are among the poorest in the world.

The Big Idea

East Africa has abundant national parks, but most of the region's countries are poor and recovering from conflicts.

Key Terms and Places

safari, *p. 571*
geothermal energy, *p. 571*
genocide, *p. 573*
Darfur, *p. 573*
Mogadishu, *p. 575*

hmhsocialstudies.com
TAKING NOTES

Use the graphic organizer online to take notes on East Africa's people and economies.

If YOU lived there...

You are a safari guide in one of Kenya's amazing national parks. Your safari van, filled with tourists, is parked at the edge of the vast savanna. It is early evening, and you are waiting for animals to come to a water hole for a drink. As it grows darker, a huge lion appears and then stalks away on huge paws.

What benefits do tourists bring to your country?

BUILDING BACKGROUND Many of the countries of East Africa are rich in natural resources—including wildlife—but people disagree about the best way to use them. Droughts can make life here difficult. In addition, political and ethnic conflicts have led to unrest and violence in some areas of the region.

Close-up

Serengeti National Park

The Serengeti Plain is home to one of the world's greatest concentrations of wildlife. In Tanzania, part of the plain is a national park. About 100,000 tourists visit the Serengeti each year to view its diverse wildlife.

Each year huge herds of wildebeest migrate across the Serengeti.

ANALYSIS SKILL **ANALYZING VISUALS**

How would you describe the Serengeti landscape?

Tanzania and Kenya Today

The economies of both Tanzania and Kenya rely heavily on tourism and agriculture. However, both countries are among the poorest in the world.

Economy and Resources

Tanzania and Kenya are popular tourist destinations. With about 2 million tourists visiting each year, tourism is a major source of income for both countries. Today many tourists visit Tanzania and Kenya to go on a safari in the countries' numerous national parks. A **safari** is an overland journey to view African wildlife.

In addition to tourism, Tanzania is particularly rich in gold and diamonds. However, it is still a poor country of mainly subsistence farmers. Poor soils and limited technology have restricted productivity.

In Kenya, much of the land has been set aside as national parkland. Many people would like to farm these lands, but farming would endanger African wildlife. Kenya's economy and tourism industry would likely be **affected** as well.

Kenya's economy relies mostly on agriculture. Mount Kilimanjaro's southern slopes are a rich agricultural region. The rich soils here provide crops of coffee and tea for exports.

Kenya's economy also benefits from another natural resource—geothermal energy. **Geothermal energy** is energy produced from the heat of Earth's interior. This heat—in the form of extremely hot steam—comes up to the surface through cracks in the rift valleys.

ACADEMIC VOCABULARY

affect to change or influence

READING CHECK **Finding Main Ideas** What activity supports the economies of both Tanzania and Kenya?

Tanzanian guides take visitors on a safari to view Serengeti's wildlife.

Watering holes attract wildlife, which includes flamingos, hippos, and giraffes.

Population Density in East Africa	
Country	**Population Density** (per square mile)
Burundi	908
Kenya	178
Rwanda	1087
Sudan	45
Tanzania	120
Uganda	420
United States	87

Nairobi, Kenya

map Zone Geography Skills

Place Most of East Africa's people live near rivers or lakes.
1. **Interpreting Charts** What country has the highest population density?
2. **Contrast** How does Somalia's population differ from Ethiopia's population?

Cities

Imagine a large city with businesspeople hurrying to work, colorful outdoor markets, soaring skyscrapers, and beautiful parks. The capitals of Tanzania and Kenya both fit this description of a vibrant, modern African city.

Tanzania's official capital is Dodoma. The Tanzanian government began moving its capital from Dar es Salaam to Dodoma in the mid-1970s. Dar es Salaam, a port city with about 3.5 million people, is located on the Indian Ocean and is Tanzania's business center.

Kenya's capital, Nairobi, also serves as the country's industrial center. In addition,

Nairobi is well connected with the rest of East Africa by a network of railways. By rail, Kenya transports tea and other major crops to the major port of Mombasa.

Even though Kenya and Tanzania are peaceful countries, Dar es Salaam and Nairobi have both endured terrorist attacks. In 1998 members of the al Qaeda terrorist group bombed the U.S. embassies in Dar es Salaam and Nairobi. Most of the more than 250 people killed and the thousands injured were Africans.

READING CHECK **Draw Conclusions** Why do you think it would be important for the railroad to link Kenya's cities?

Rwanda and Burundi

Rwanda and Burundi are mostly populated by two ethnic groups—the Tutsi and the Hutu. Since gaining their independence from Belgium, Rwanda and Burundi have experienced conflict between the Tutsi and Hutu ethnic groups. These conflicts have roots in the region's history. The colonial borders of Rwanda and Burundi drawn by Europeans often lumped different ethnic groups into one country.

In Rwanda in the 1990s, hatred between the Hutu and the Tutsi led to genocide. A **genocide** is the intentional destruction of a people. The Hutu tried to completely wipe out the Tutsi. Armed bands of Hutu killed hundreds of thousands of Tutsi.

Rwanda and Burundi are two of the most densely populated countries in all of Africa. These two countries are located in fertile highlands and share a history as German and, later, Belgian colonies. Both countries lack resources and rely on coffee and tea exports for economic earnings.

READING CHECK **Analyzing** What contributed to the region's ethnic conflict?

Sudan and Uganda

Sudan is a mix of Arab, Afro-Arab, and African cultures. Its people follow Muslim, animist, and Christian traditions. Sudanese Arabs are Sudan's majority population, and they hold all political power.

Sudan's government has abused the human rights of ethnic and religious minorities, including Christians. It has supported the Janjaweed, a violent Arab militia. From 2003 to 2008, the Janjaweed killed hundreds of thousands of ethnically African Sudanese in a region called **Darfur.** Millions more fled Darfur as refugees. Since 1984, the Janjaweed has also killed an estimated 1.5 million Christians.

In 2011, South Sudan gained independence, becoming Africa's newest country. South Sudan's population is mostly African and follows animist or Christian faiths.

Today Uganda is still recovering from several decades of a military dictatorship. Since 1986 Uganda has become more democratic, but economic progress has been slow. About 80 percent of Uganda's workforce is employed in agriculture, with coffee as the country's major export.

READING CHECK **Summarizing** What ethnic group dominates Sudan?

FOCUS ON READING

In the paragraphs under Rwanda and Burundi, what details support the main idea that these countries have a history of ethnic conflict?

Refugees in Sudan

People from Sudan who fled the country's Darfur region receive food and aid at a refugee camp.

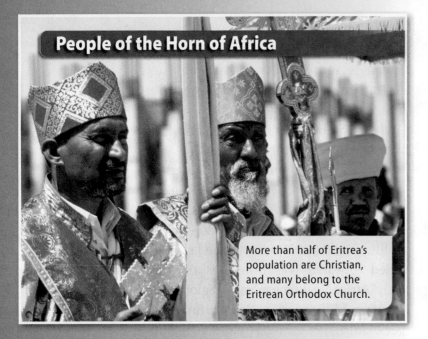

People of the Horn of Africa

More than half of Eritrea's population are Christian, and many belong to the Eritrean Orthodox Church.

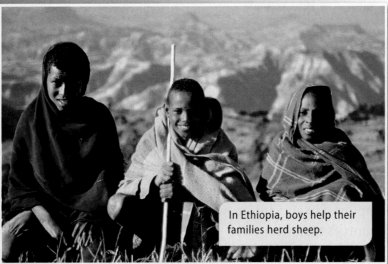

In Ethiopia, boys help their families herd sheep.

A teacher in Somalia shows a student how to use the school's new computer.

The Horn of Africa

Four East African countries along the Red Sea and the Indian Ocean are called the Horn of Africa. On a map, these countries resemble the horn of a rhinoceros.

Ethiopia

Unlike the other countries of the Horn of Africa, Ethiopia has never been under foreign rule. The country's mountains have protected it from invasion.

In addition to providing a natural defense barrier, Ethiopia's rugged mountain slopes and highlands have rich volcanic soil. As a result, agriculture is Ethiopia's chief economic activity. The country's top exports include coffee, livestock, and oilseeds. Many people also herd sheep and cattle.

Ethiopia suffers from harsh droughts. In 2011 East Africa faced what many called the worst drought in 60 years. The drought killed crops, causing a severe food crisis for about 9.5 million people living in Ethiopia, Somalia, Kenya, and Djibouti.

Most Ethiopians living in the highlands are Christian, while most of the lowland people are Muslim. Many Ethiopians speak Amharic, one of the country's official languages.

Eritrea

In the late 1800s the Italians made Eritrea a colony. In the 1960s it became an Ethiopian province. After years of war with Ethiopia, Eritrea gained independence in 1993. Since then the economy has slowly improved. The country's Red Sea coastline has spectacular coral reefs that attract tourists. Most Eritreans are farmers or herders. The country's economy relies largely on cotton exports.

Somalia

Somalia is a country of deserts and dry savannas. Much of the land is not suitable for farming. As a result, most Somalis are nomadic herders. Somalia also has a thriving telecommunications industry.

Somalia is less diverse than most other African countries. Most people in the country are members of a single ethnic group, the Somali. In addition, most Somalis are Muslim and speak the same African language, also called Somali.

Somalia has been troubled by violence in the past. In addition, the country has often had no central government of any kind. Different clans have fought over grazing rights and control of port cities such as **Mogadishu**.

In the 1990s Somalis experienced widespread starvation caused by a civil war and a severe drought. The United Nations sent aid and troops to the country. U.S. troops also assisted with this operation. In recent years, Somali pirates have captured several cargo ships off the coast of Somalia. The pirates have demanded and received millions of dollars in ransom money.

Djibouti

Djibouti (ji-BOO-tee) is a small, desert country. It lies on the Bab al-Mandab, which is the narrow strait that connects the Red Sea and the Indian Ocean. The strait lies along a major shipping route.

In the 1860s the French took control of Djibouti. It did not gain independence from France until 1977. The French government still contributes economic and military support to the country. As a result, French is one of Djibouti's two official languages. The other is Arabic.

The country's capital and major port is also called Djibouti. The capital serves as a port for landlocked Ethiopia. Since Djibouti has very few resources, the port is a major source of the country's income.

The people of Djibouti include two major ethnic groups—the Issa and the Afar. The Issa are closely related to the people of Somalia. The Afar are related to the people of Ethiopia. Members of both groups are Muslim. In the early 1990s, a civil war between the Afar and Issa broke out. In 2001 the two groups signed a peace treaty, which ended the fighting.

READING CHECK **Generalizing** What do the people of Djibouti have in common with people from other countries in East Africa?

SUMMARY AND PREVIEW The countries of East Africa are poor, but rich in wildlife and resources. Next, you will learn about the region of Central Africa.

Section 3 Assessment

Reviewing Ideas, Terms, and Places

1. **a. Define** What is **geothermal energy**?
   b. Make Generalizations Why are Kenyans not allowed to farm in national parks?
2. **a. Define** What is **genocide**?
   b. Compare and Contrast How have recent conflicts in Rwanda and Sudan been similar and different?
   c. Interpret Look back at the chart on page 572. Which country has a population density lower than that of the United States?
3. **a. Identify** What is the newest country in Africa?
   b. Analyze Why are millions of Sudanese refugees?
4. **a. Recall** What two major world religions are practiced in Ethiopia?
   b. Analyze How do you think Djibouti's location has helped its economy?
   c. Geographic Questions Look back at the Regional Database for this unit. Use the data to pose and answer a question about patterns of life expectancy in East Africa.

Critical Thinking

5. **Summarize** Draw a chart like this one. Using your notes, summarize in at least two sentences what you learned about each country.

FOCUS ON WRITING

my WriteSmart

6. **Writing About East Africa Today** Think about what it would be like to travel through the East African countries. What would you want to tell your friend about their people, their governments, and their economies? Make a list of details you would share.

Creating an Outline

Learn

When you read a report or your textbook, how can you make sense of new information? One way is to organize information into an outline. An outline shows the relationship between a text's main ideas and its supporting details. In an outline, you use roman numerals to show main ideas and capital letters to point out supporting details. If you need to add another level of details, use arabic numerals to indicate those.

Practice

This is a partial outline of Section 1 of this chapter. Use the following strategies to outline as you read.

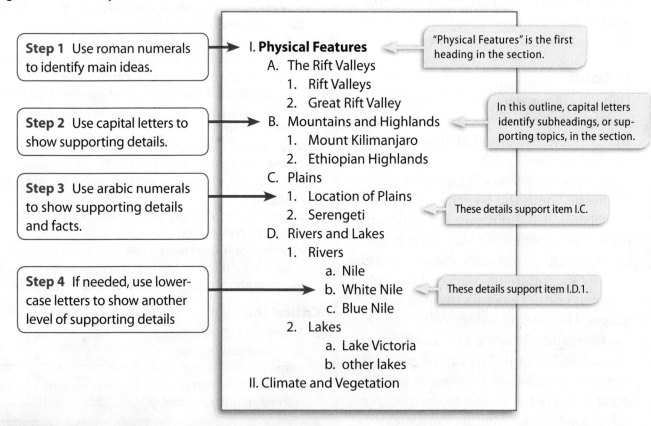

Step 1 Use roman numerals to identify main ideas.

Step 2 Use capital letters to show supporting details.

Step 3 Use arabic numerals to show supporting details and facts.

Step 4 If needed, use lower-case letters to show another level of supporting details

I. **Physical Features**
  A. The Rift Valleys
     1. Rift Valleys
     2. Great Rift Valley
  B. Mountains and Highlands
     1. Mount Kilimanjaro
     2. Ethiopian Highlands
  C. Plains
     1. Location of Plains
     2. Serengeti
  D. Rivers and Lakes
     1. Rivers
        a. Nile
        b. White Nile
        c. Blue Nile
     2. Lakes
        a. Lake Victoria
        b. other lakes
II. Climate and Vegetation

"Physical Features" is the first heading in the section.

In this outline, capital letters identify subheadings, or supporting topics, in the section.

These details support item I.C.

These details support item I.D.1.

Apply

Create an outline for Section 3: East Africa Today. Scan the text for features that help you identify the main ideas and details. Once you have completed your outline, use it to organize information into a written summary of the section.

CHAPTER 23

Chapter Review

Visual Summary

Use the visual summary below to help you review the main ideas of the chapter.

QUICK FACTS

East Africa is a land of spectacular mountains, highlands, and lakes.

East Africa's history includes European imperialism and independence.

Even though many countries in East Africa are very poor, they are trying to improve educational opportunities.

Reviewing Vocabulary, Terms, and Places

Choose one word from each word pair to correctly complete each sentence below.

1. A_____(rift valley/plain) is a place on Earth's surface where the crust stretches until it breaks.

2. The tallest mountain in Africa is_____. (Mount Kilimanjaro/Mount Kenya)

3. _____means to change or influence. (geothermal energy/affect)

4. A_____is an overland journey that is taken to view African wildlife. (drought/safari)

5. _____has experienced serious droughts over the past 30 years. (Ethiopia/Kenya)

6. _____are periods when little rain falls and crops are damaged. (flood/drought)

7. The intentional destruction of a people is called_____. (murder/genocide)

8. _____is a practice which tries to dominate other countries' government, trade, and culture. (imperialism/influence)

9. A genocide committed by an Arab militia occured in the region of Sudan known as _____. (Darfur/Khartoum)

10. _____is an East African island that was an international slave-trading center in the late 1700s. (Madagascar/Zanzibar)

Comprehension and Critical Thinking

SECTION 1 *(Pages 562–565)*

11. a. **Identify** What is the Great Rift Valley? What is it made of?

   b. **Draw Conclusions** How is the Nile necessary for farming in the desert?

   c. **Predict** How do you think the effects of drought can be avoided in the future?

SECTION 2 (Pages 566–569)

12. a. Recall In which East African country did an emperor build 11 rock churches?

b. Contrast How does the major religion practiced in Ethiopia differ from other religions practiced in East Africa?

c. Elaborate How did the African language of Swahili develop?

SECTION 3 (Pages 570–575)

13. a. Define What is a safari?

b. Draw Conclusions What economic activity do both Kenya and Tanzania rely on?

c. Evaluate Why do you think the al Qaeda terrorist group bombed U.S. embassies in Dar es Salaam and Nairobi?

Using the Internet

14. Activity: Understanding Cultures In the East African countries you read about in this chapter, there are hundreds of different ethnic groups. Through the online book, discover some ethnic groups of East Africa as you visit Web sites about their culture. Then create a graphic organizer or chart that compares East African ethnic groups. It might include comparisons of language, beliefs, traditions, foods, and more.

Social Studies Skills

15. Creating an Outline Conduct research to locate a news report on a current issue related to conflict or the environment in East Africa. Scan the report for text features that help you identify main ideas and details. Use these features to help you interpret and organize information from the report into an outline.

16. Organizing Information from an Outline Exchange your outline with a partner. Organize information from your partner's outline into a written summary. Once you have completed your summary, confirm your understanding of the main ideas and details with your partner.

Map Activity

17. East Africa On a separate sheet of paper, match the letters on the map with their correct labels.

Great Rift Valley   Mount Kilimanjaro

Lake Victoria   Nile River

Indian Ocean

| FOCUS ON READING AND WRITING | *my* WriteSmart |

18. Identifying Supporting Details Look back over the paragraphs under the Culture heading in Section 2. Then make a list of details you find to support the section's main ideas. Make sure you include details about the different languages spoken in East Africa today.

19. Writing a Letter Now that you have information about East Africa, you need to organize it. Think about your audience, a friend at home, and what would feel natural if you had been traveling. Would you organize by topics like physical geography and culture? Or would you organize by country? After you organize your information, write a one-page letter. Be sure to use standard grammar, spelling, sentence structure, and punctuation.

Reading Social Studies

Identifying Supporting Details

FOCUS ON READING

Why believe what you read? One reason is because of details that support or prove the main idea. These details might be facts, statistics, examples, or definitions. In the example below, notice what kind of proof or supporting details help you believe the main idea.

> The landscape of East Africa has many high volcanic mountains. The highest mountain in Africa, Mount Kilimanjaro, rises to 19,340 feet. Despite Kilimanjaro's location near the equator, the mountain's peak has long been covered in snow. This much colder climate is caused by Kilimanjaro's high elevation.
>
> *From Section 1, Physical Geography*

Main Idea
The landscape of East Africa has many high volcanic mountains.

Supporting Details			
Example	**Statistic**	**Fact**	**Fact**
The highest mountain is Mount Kilimanjaro.	Mount Kilimanjaro is 19,340 feet high.	Kilimanjaro has a cold climate.	It is near the equator, but its peak is snow covered.

YOU TRY IT!

Read the following sentences, and then use a graphic organizer like the one above to identify the supporting details.

> Somalia is less diverse than most other African countries. Most people in the country are members of a single ethnic group, the Somali. In addition, most Somalis are Muslim and speak the same African language, also called Somali.
>
> *From Section 3, East Africa Today*

Central Africa

Essential Question

myNotebook

How is poverty affecting the nations of Central Africa?

Texas Essential Knowledge and Skills (TEKS)

1A, 1B, 2A, 2B, 3A, 3B, 4C, 4D, 5C, 6B, 15B, 15F, 21B, 21C, 22D

FOCUS ON READING AND WRITING

*my*WriteSmart

Using Word Parts Many English words have little word parts at the beginning (prefixes) or the end (suffixes) of the word. When you come to an unfamiliar word in your reading, see if you can recognize a prefix or suffix to help you figure out the meaning of the word. **See the lesson, Using Word Parts, on page 601.**

Writing an Acrostic An acrostic is a type of poem in which the first letters of each line spell a word. The lines of the poem describe that word. As you read the chapter, think of a word—maybe a country name or a physical feature—that you would like to describe in your acrostic. Use the annotation tools in your eBook to gather information for your assignment.

ATLANTIC
OCEAN

0° Equator

⊙ National capital
• Other cities

0   200   400 Miles
0   200   400 Kilometers

Projection: Lambert Azimuthal Equal-Area

map zone Geography Skills

Regions The region we call Central Africa consists of 10 countries.
1. **Identify** Which country includes land on the mainland and on islands?
2. **Make Inferences** Why do you think a small part of Angola is separated from the main part of the country?

Culture Drums and horns are used in traditional music from Central Africa. These musicians are from Cameroon.

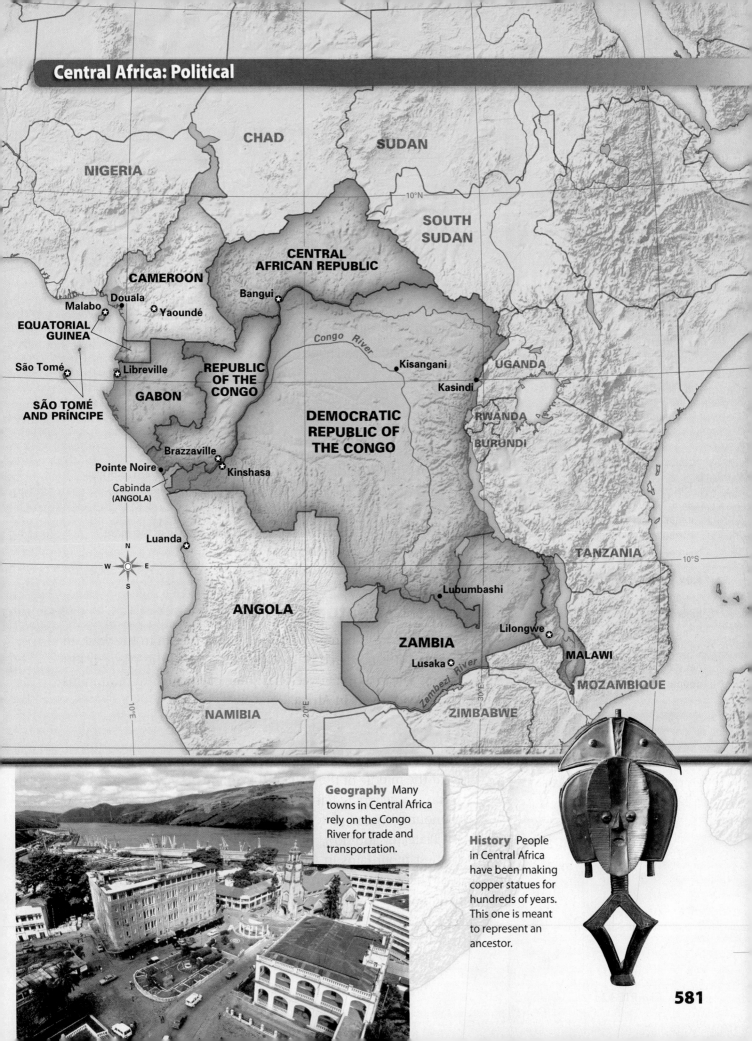

CHAD

SUDAN

NIGERIA

10°N

SOUTH
SUDAN

CENTRAL
AFRICAN REPUBLIC

CAMEROON

Bangui

Douala

Malabo

Yaoundé

EQUATORIAL
GUINEA

Congo River

Kisangani

UGANDA

São Tomé

Libreville

REPUBLIC
OF THE
CONGO

Kasindi

SÃO TOMÉ
AND PRÍNCIPE

GABON

RWANDA

DEMOCRATIC
REPUBLIC OF
THE CONGO

BURUNDI

Brazzaville

Pointe Noire

Kinshasa

Cabinda
(ANGOLA)

Luanda

TANZANIA

10°S

N
W   E
S

Lubumbashi

ANGOLA

Lilongwe

ZAMBIA

MALAWI

Lusaka

Zambezi River

MOZAMBIQUE

NAMIBIA

20°E

30°E

ZIMBABWE

10°E

Geography Many
towns in Central Africa
rely on the Congo
River for trade and
transportation.

History People
in Central Africa
have been making
copper statues for
hundreds of years.
This one is meant
to represent an
ancestor.

581

Physical Geography

 TEKS 3A, 3B, 4D, 6B, 21B, 21C, 22D

What You Will Learn...

Main Ideas

1. Central Africa's major physical features include the Congo Basin and plateaus surrounding the basin.
2. Central Africa has a humid tropical climate and dense forest vegetation.
3. Central Africa's resources include forest products and valuable minerals such as diamonds and copper.

The Big Idea

The Congo River, tropical forests, and mineral resources are important features of Central Africa's physical geography.

Key Terms and Places

Congo Basin, *p. 582*
basin, *p. 582*
Congo River, *p. 583*
Zambezi River, *p. 583*
periodic market, *p. 585*
copper belt, *p. 585*

hmhsocialstudies.com
TAKING NOTES

Use the graphic organizer online to note characteristics of Central Africa's physical geography.

If YOU lived there...

You are on a nature hike with a guide through the forests of the Congo Basin. It has been several hours since you have seen any other people. Sometimes your guide has to cut a path through the thick vegetation, but mostly you try not to disturb any plants or animals. Suddenly, you reach a clearing and see a group of men working hard to load huge tree trunks onto big trucks.

How do you feel about what you see?

BUILDING BACKGROUND Much of Central Africa, particularly in the Congo Basin, is covered with thick, tropical forests. The forests provide valuable resources, but people have different ideas about how the forests should be used. Forests are just one of the many types of landscapes in Central Africa.

Physical Features

Central Africa is bordered by the Atlantic Ocean in the west. In the east, it is bordered by a huge valley called the Western Rift Valley. The land in between has some of the highest mountains and biggest rivers in Africa.

Landforms

You can think of the region as a big soup bowl with a wide rim. Near the middle of the bowl is the **Congo Basin**. In geography, a **basin** is a generally flat region surrounded by higher land such as mountains and plateaus.

Plateaus and low hills surround the Congo Basin. The highest mountains in Central Africa lie farther away from the basin, along the Western Rift Valley. Some of these snowcapped mountains rise to more than 16,700 feet (5,090 m). Two lakes also lie along the rift—Lake Nyasa and Lake Tanganyika (tan-guhn-YEE-kuh). Lake Nyasa is also called Lake Malawi.

Rivers

The huge **Congo River** is fed by hundreds of smaller rivers. They drain the swampy Congo Basin and flow into the river as it runs toward the Atlantic. Many rapids and waterfalls lie along its route, especially near its mouth. These obstacles make it impossible for ships to travel from the interior of Central Africa all the way to the Atlantic. The Congo provides an important transportation route in the interior, however.

In the southern part of the region, the **Zambezi** (zam-BEE-zee) **River** flows eastward toward the Indian Ocean. Many rivers in Angola and Zambia, as well as water from Lake Nyasa, flow into the Zambezi. The Zambezi also has many waterfalls along its route, the most famous of which are the spectacular Victoria Falls.

READING CHECK **Finding Main Ideas** Where is the highest land in Central Africa?

Central Africa: Physical

map zone

Geography Skills

Regions Central Africa has two major river systems.
1. **Identify** What river flows through the Congo Basin?
2. **Analyze** How do you think Central Africa's rivers have affected country borders?

ELEVATION

Feet		Meters
13,120		4,000
6,560		2,000
1,640		500
656		200
(Sea level) 0		0 (Sea level)
Below sea level		Below sea level

0   250   500 Miles
0   250   500 Kilometers
Projection: Lambert Azimuthal Equal-Area

1 Local people call Victoria Falls Mosi-oa-Tunya, which means "the smoke that thunders." The Zambezi River plunges 343 feet (105 m) over a cliff between Zambia and Zimbabwe.

CENTRAL AFRICA **583**

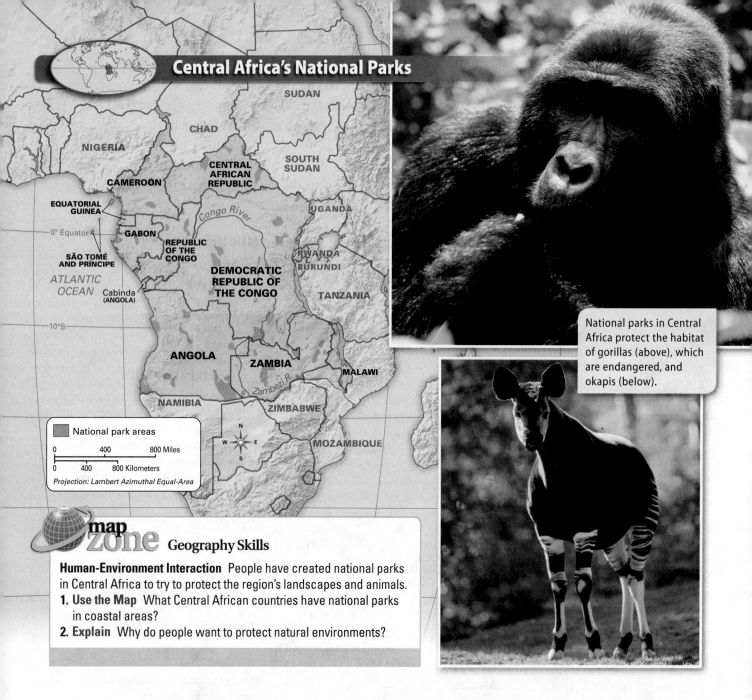

Central Africa's National Parks

National parks in Central Africa protect the habitat of gorillas (above), which are endangered, and okapis (below).

map zone Geography Skills

Human-Environment Interaction People have created national parks in Central Africa to try to protect the region's landscapes and animals.

1. **Use the Map** What Central African countries have national parks in coastal areas?
2. **Explain** Why do people want to protect natural environments?

Climate, Vegetation, and Animals

Central Africa lies along the equator and in the low latitudes. Therefore, the Congo Basin and much of the Atlantic coast have a humid tropical climate. These areas have warm temperatures all year and receive a lot of rainfall.

This climate supports a large, dense tropical forest. The many kinds of tall trees in the forest form a complete canopy. The canopy is the uppermost layer of the trees where the limbs spread out. Canopy leaves block sunlight to the ground below.

Such animals as gorillas, elephants, wild boars, and okapis live in the forest. The okapi is a short-necked relative of the giraffe. However, since little sunlight shines through the canopy, only a few animals live on the forest floor. Some animals, such as birds, monkeys, bats, and snakes, live in the trees. Many insects also live in Central Africa's forest.

The animals in Central Africa's tropical forests, as well as the forests themselves, are in danger. Large areas of forest are being cleared rapidly for farming and logging. Also, people hunt the large animals in the forests to get food. To promote protection of forests and other natural environments, governments have set up national park areas in their countries.

North and south of the Congo Basin are large areas with a tropical savanna climate. Those areas are warm all year, but they have distinct dry and wet seasons. There are grasslands, scattered trees, and shrubs. The high mountains in the east have a highland climate. Dry steppe and even desert climates are found in the far southern part of the region.

READING CHECK **Summarizing** What are the climate and vegetation like in the Congo Basin?

Resources

The tropical environment of Central Africa is good for growing crops. Most people in the region are subsistence farmers. However, many farmers are now beginning to grow crops for sale. Common crops are coffee, bananas, and corn. In rural areas, people trade agricultural and other products in periodic markets. A **periodic market** is an open-air trading market that is set up once or twice a week.

Central Africa is rich in other natural resources as well. The large tropical forest provides timber, while the rivers provide a way to travel and to trade. Dams on the rivers produce hydroelectricity, an important energy resource. Other energy resources in the region include oil, natural gas, and coal.

Central Africa also has many valuable minerals, including copper, uranium, tin, zinc, diamonds, gold, and cobalt. Of these, copper is the most important. Most of

Africa's copper is found in an area called the **copper belt**. The copper belt stretches through northern Zambia and southern Democratic Republic of the Congo. However, poor transportation systems and political problems have kept the region's resources from being fully developed.

READING CHECK **Analyzing** Why are Central Africa's rivers an important natural resource?

FOCUS ON READING
What prefix do you recognize in *promote*?

SUMMARY AND PREVIEW Mighty rivers, tropical forests and mineral resources characterize the physical geography of Central Africa. Next, you will read about Central Africa's history and culture.

Section 1 Assessment

hmhsocialstudies.com
ONLINE QUIZ

Reviewing Ideas, Terms, and Places

1. **a. Describe** What is the **Congo Basin**?
   b. Elaborate How do you think the **Congo River**'s rapids and waterfalls affect the economy of the region?
2. **a. Recall** What part of Central Africa has a highland climate?
   b. Explain Why have governments in the region set up national parks?
   c. Evaluate Is it more important to use the forest's resources or to protect the natural environment? Why?
3. **a. Define** What is a **periodic market**?
   b. Elaborate What kinds of political problems might keep mineral resources from being fully developed?

Critical Thinking

4. **Contrasting** Use your notes and a graphic organizer like this one to list differences between the Congo Basin and the areas surrounding it in Central Africa.

Congo Basin   Surrounding Areas

FOCUS ON WRITING   *my* WriteSmart

5. **Describing Physical Geography** What topics in this section might work well in your acrostic? Jot down notes on one or two topics you could feature in your poem.

Mapping Central Africa's Forests

Essential Elements

The World in Spatial Terms

Places and Regions

Physical Systems

Human Systems

Environment and Society

The Uses of Geography

Background Imagine taking a walk along a street in your neighborhood. Your purpose is to see the street in spatial terms and gather information to help you make a map. While you walk, you ask the kinds of questions geographers ask. How many houses, apartment buildings, or businesses are on the street? What kinds of animals or trees do you see? Your walk ends, and you organize your data. Now imagine that you are going to gather data on another walk. This walk will be 2,000 miles long.

A 2,000-Mile Walk In September 1999, an American scientist named Michael Fay began a 465-day, 2,000-mile walk through Central Africa's forests. He and his team followed elephant trails through thick vegetation. They waded through creeks and mucky swamps.

On the walk, Fay gathered data on the number and kinds of animals he saw. He counted elephant dung, chimpanzee nests, leopard tracks, and gorillas. He counted the types of trees and other plants along his route.

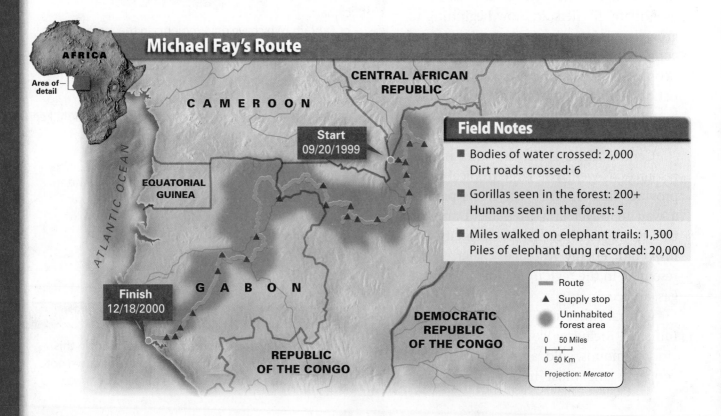

Michael Fay's Route

AFRICA

Area of detail

CAMEROON

CENTRAL AFRICAN REPUBLIC

Start 09/20/1999

EQUATORIAL GUINEA

ATLANTIC OCEAN

GABON

Finish 12/18/2000

REPUBLIC OF THE CONGO

DEMOCRATIC REPUBLIC OF THE CONGO

Field Notes

- Bodies of water crossed: 2,000
  Dirt roads crossed: 6

- Gorillas seen in the forest: 200+
  Humans seen in the forest: 5

- Miles walked on elephant trails: 1,300
  Piles of elephant dung recorded: 20,000

Route
▲ Supply stop
⬤ Uninhabited forest area

0   50 Miles
0   50 Km
Projection: *Mercator*

Michael Fay (above) and his team had to chop their way through thick forest vegetation. In a clearing, they spotted this group of elephants.

He also counted human settlements and determined the effect of human activities on the environment.

Fay used a variety of tools to record the data he gathered on his walk. He wrote down what he observed in waterproof notebooks. He shot events and scenes with video and still cameras. To measure the distance he and his team walked each day, he used a tool called a Fieldranger. He also kept track of his exact position in the forest by using a GPS, or global positioning system.

What It Means Michael Fay explained the purpose of his long walk. "The whole idea behind this is to be able to use the data we've collected as a tool." Other geographers can compare Fay's data with their own. Their comparison may help them create more accurate maps. These maps will show where plants, animals, and humans are located in Central Africa's forests.

Fay's data can also help scientists plan the future use of land or resources in a region. For example, Fay has used his data to convince government officials in Gabon to set aside 10 percent of its land to create 13 national parks. The parks will be protected from future logging and farming. They also will preserve many of the plants and animals that Fay and his team observed on their long walk.

Geography for Life Activity

1. Why did Michael Fay walk 2,000 miles?

2. In what practical way has Michael Fay used his data?

3. **Read More about Fay's Walk** Read the three-part article on Michael Fay's walk in *National Geographic* October 2000, March 2001, and August 2001. After you read the article, explain why Fay called his walk a "megatransect."

History and Culture

TEKS 1A, 1B, 2A, 2B, 4C, 15B, 21B, 21C, 22D

What You Will Learn...

Main Ideas

1. Great African kingdoms and European colonizers have influenced the history of Central Africa.
2. The culture of Central Africa includes many ethnic groups and languages, but it has also been influenced by European colonization.

The Big Idea

Central Africa's history and culture have been influenced by native traditions and European colonizers.

Key Terms and Places

Kongo Kingdom, *p. 588*
dialects, *p. 590*

hmhsocialstudies.com
TAKING NOTES

Use the graphic organizer online to take notes on Central Africa's history and culture.

If **YOU** lived there...

You live in Central Africa in the 1300s. Over the past year, many new people have moved to your village. They speak a different language—one that you don't understand. They also have some customs that seem strange to you. But they have begun bringing fancy items such as animal skins and shells to your village. Now your village seems very rich.

How do you feel about these new people?

BUILDING BACKGROUND Different groups of people have influenced Central Africa throughout its history. Whether they came from near or far, and whether they stayed in Central Africa for only a few decades or for more than a hundred years, these groups brought their own cultures and customs to the region.

History

Early humans lived in Central Africa many thousands of years ago. However, the descendants of these people have had less impact on the region's history than people from the outside. Tribes from West Africa, and later European colonists, brought their customs to the region and changed the way people lived.

Early History

About 2,000 years ago new peoples began to migrate to Central Africa from West Africa. They eventually formed several kingdoms in Central Africa. Among the most important was the **Kongo Kingdom**. Founded in the 1300s, it was located near the mouth of the Congo River.

The Kongo people established trade routes to western and eastern Africa. Their kingdom grew rich from the trade of animal skins, shells, slaves, and ivory. Ivory is a cream-colored material that comes from elephant tusks.

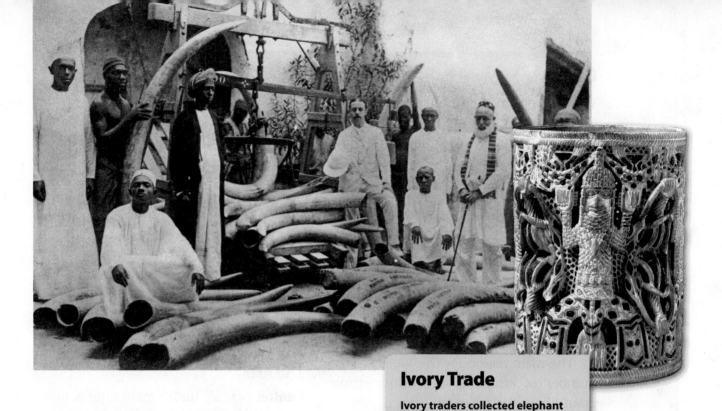

Ivory Trade

Ivory traders collected elephant tusks for export to Europe.

ANALYZING VISUALS Who was involved in the ivory trade?

In the late 1400s, Europeans came to the region. They wanted the region's forest products and other resources such as ivory. They used ivory for fine furniture, jewelry, statues, and piano keys. Europeans also began to trade with some Central African kingdoms for slaves. Over a span of about 300 years, the Europeans took millions of enslaved Africans to their colonies in the Americas.

Some African kingdoms became richer by trading with Europeans. However, all were gradually changed and weakened by European influence. In the late 1800s, European countries divided all of Central Africa into colonies. The colonial powers were France, Belgium, Germany, Spain, the United Kingdom, and Portugal.

These European powers drew colonial borders that ignored the homelands of different ethnic groups. Many different ethnic groups were lumped together in colonies where they had to interact. These groups spoke different languages and had different customs. Their differences caused conflicts, especially after the colonies won independence.

Modern Central Africa

Central African colonies gained their independence from European powers after World War II. Some of the colonies fought bloody wars to win their independence. The last country to become independent was Angola. It won freedom from Portugal in 1975.

Independence did not bring peace to Central Africa, however. Ethnic groups continued to fight one another within the borders of the new countries. Also, the United States and the Soviet Union used Central Africa as a battleground in the Cold War. They supported different allies in small wars throughout Africa. The wars in the region killed many people and caused great damage.

FOCUS ON READING
What prefix do you recognize in *interact*?

READING CHECK **Summarizing** What role did Europeans play in Central Africa's history?

Culture

Today about 137 million people live in Central Africa. These people belong to many different ethnic groups and have different customs.

People and Language

The people of Central Africa speak hundreds of different languages. They also speak different **dialects**, regional varieties of a language. For example, although many Central Africans speak Bantu languages, those languages can be quite different from one another.

The main reason for this variety is the number of ethnic groups. Most ethnic groups have their own language or dialect. Most people in the region speak traditional African languages in their daily lives. However, the official languages of the region are European because of the influence of the colonial powers. For example, French is the official language of the Democratic Republic of the Congo. Portuguese is the language of Angola. English is an official language in Zambia and Malawi.

Religion

Central Africa's colonial history has also influenced religion. Europeans introduced Christianity to the region. Now many people in the former French, Spanish, and Portuguese colonies are Roman Catholic. Protestant Christianity is most common in former British colonies.

Two other religions came to parts of Central Africa from other regions. Influenced by the Muslim countries of the Sahel, the northern part of Central Africa has many Muslims. Zambia is the home of Muslims as well as Hindus.

The Arts

Central Africa's traditional cultures influence the arts of the region. The region is famous for sculpture, carved wooden masks, and beautiful cotton gowns dyed in bright colors.

Christianity in Central Africa

Major Religions of Central Africa

- Traditional religions/other 23%
- Christianity 64%
- Islam 13%

Analyzing Graphs What is the second most common religion in Central Africa?

Christian missionaries established churches and schools throughout Central Africa. These students attend a Catholic school in Malawi.

Bantu Languages

About 2,000 years ago people who spoke Bantu languages migrated out of West Africa. They moved to Central Africa as well as eastern and southern Africa. The Bantu speakers mixed with peoples who already lived in these lands.

The migration of Bantu speakers had important effects on African life. They brought new ways for growing food. They used tools made of iron, which others also began to use. The Bantu speakers also brought their languages.
Today many Central Africans speak one or more of the some 500 Bantu languages such as Rundi, Bemba, or Luba.

Drawing Inferences How do you think the number of languages affects communication in the region?

Central Africa also has popular styles of music. The *likembe*, or thumb piano, was invented in the Congo region. Also, a type of dance music called *makossa* originated in Cameroon and has become popular throughout Africa. It can be played with guitars and electric keyboards.

READING CHECK **Generalizing** What are characteristics of culture in Central Africa?

SUMMARY AND PREVIEW Central Africa's history was influenced by great kingdoms that controlled trade and by Europeans, who originally came to the region looking for trade goods. European and traditional African influences have shaped the region's culture. Next, you will learn about the countries of Central Africa and what life is like there today.

Section 2 Assessment

hmhsocialstudies.com
ONLINE QUIZ

Reviewing Ideas, Terms, and Places

1. **a. Recall** What Central African resource did Europeans value for making jewelry and crafts?
   b. Explain How did the **Kongo Kingdom** become important?
   c. Elaborate How do you think the colonial borders affected Central African countries' fights for independence?
2. **a. Summarize** How did the colonial era affect Central Africa's culture?
   b. Elaborate How might Central Africa's culture be different today if the region had not been colonized by Europeans?
   c. Geographic Questions Use the graph on page 590 to pose and answer a question about patterns of religion in Central Africa.

Critical Thinking

3. **Sequencing** Review your notes on Central Africa's history. Using a graphic organizer like this one, put major events in chronological order.

FOCUS ON WRITING

4. **Taking Notes on History and Culture** Your acrostic could describe the region's history and culture as well as physical geography. Take notes on interesting information you might include in your poem.

TEKS 1A, 1B, 2B, 5C, 15B, 15F, 21B, 21C, 21D

What You Will Learn...

Main Ideas

1. The countries of Central Africa are mostly poor, and many are trying to recover from years of civil war.
2. Challenges to peace, health, and the environment slow economic development in Central Africa.

The Big Idea

War, disease, and environmental problems have made it difficult for the countries of Central Africa to develop stable governments and economies.

Key Terms and Places

Kinshasa, *p. 593*
inflation, *p. 595*
malaria, *p. 596*
malnutrition, *p. 597*

hmhsocialstudies.com
TAKING NOTES

Use the graphic organizer online to take notes on the countries of Central Africa and the challenges facing those countries.

Central Africa Today

If YOU lived there...

You are an economic adviser in Zambia. Your country is poor, and most people are farmers. But scientists say Zambia has a lot of copper under ground. With a new copper mine, you could sell valuable copper to other countries. However, the mine would destroy a lot of farmland.

Do you support building the mine? Why or why not?

BUILDING BACKGROUND You have already read about Central Africa's great resources. Many countries in the region have the potential for great wealth. However, several factors throughout history have made it difficult for Central African countries to develop their resources.

Countries of Central Africa

Most of the countries in Central Africa are very poor. After years of colonial rule and then civil war, they are struggling to build stable governments and strong economies.

Democratic Republic of the Congo

The Democratic Republic of the Congo was a Belgian colony until 1960. When the country gained independence, many Belgians left. Few teachers, doctors, and other professionals remained in the former colony. In addition, various ethnic groups fought each other for power. These problems were partly to blame for keeping the new country poor.

A military leader named Joseph Mobutu came to power in 1965. He ruled as a dictator. One way Mobutu used his power was to change the name of the country to Zaire—a name that was traditionally African rather than European. He also changed his own name to Mobutu Sese Seko.

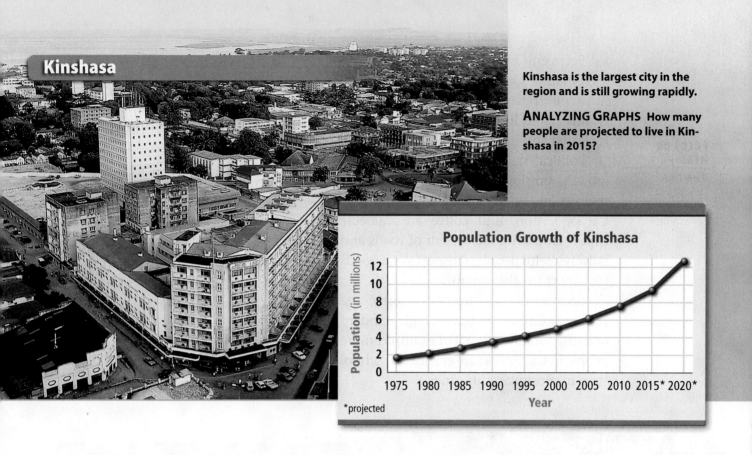

Kinshasa

Kinshasa is the largest city in the region and is still growing rapidly.

ANALYZING GRAPHS How many people are projected to live in Kinshasa in 2015?

Population Growth of Kinshasa

Population (in millions)

12
10
8
6
4
2
0

1975 1980 1985 1990 1995 2000 2005 2010 2015* 2020*

Year

*projected

During his rule, the government took over foreign-owned industries. It borrowed money from foreign countries to try to expand industry. However, most farmers suffered, and government and business leaders were corrupt. While the economy collapsed, Mobutu became one of the richest people in the world and used violence against people who challenged him.

In 1997, after a civil war, a new government took over. The new government renamed the country the Democratic Republic of the Congo.

The Democratic Republic of the Congo is a treasure chest of minerals that could bring wealth to the country. The south is part of Central Africa's rich copper belt. The country also has gold, diamonds, and cobalt. In addition, the tropical forest provides wood, food, and rubber. However, civil war, bad government, and crime have scared many foreign businesses away. As a result, the country's resources have helped few of its people.

Most people in the Democratic Republic of the Congo are poor. They usually live in rural areas where they must farm and trade for food. Many people are moving to the capital, **Kinshasa**. This crowded city has some modern buildings, but most of the city consists of poor slums.

Central African Republic and Cameroon

North of the Democratic Republic of the Congo is the landlocked country of Central African Republic. Since independence, this country has struggled with military coups, corrupt leaders, and improper elections.

In addition to political instability, the country suffers from a weak economy. Most people there are farmers. Although the country has diamonds and gold, it does not have railroads or ports needed to transport the resources for export. Central African Republic receives some aid from foreign countries, but this is not enough to meet the needs of its people.

Between Central African Republic and the Atlantic Ocean is Cameroon. Unlike most countries in Central Africa, Cameroon is fairly stable. It is a republic. The president is elected and holds most of the power.

Political stability has made economic growth possible. The country has oil reserves and good conditions for farming. Cacao, cotton, and coffee are valuable export crops. A good system of roads and railways helps people transport these goods for export to other countries.

Because of the steady economy, the people of Cameroon have a high standard of living for the region. For example, more people in Cameroon are enrolled in school than in most places in Africa.

FOCUS ON READING

If –al means "relating to," what does *political* mean?

Equatorial Guinea and São Tomé and Príncipe

Tiny Equatorial Guinea is divided between the mainland and five islands. The country is a republic. It has held elections, but many have seen the elections as being flawed. These elections have kept the same president ruling the country for more than 25 years. Although the discovery of oil has produced economic growth, living conditions for most people are still poor.

The island country of São Tomé and Príncipe has struggled with political instability. In addition, it is a poor country with few resources. It produces much cacao but has to import food. The recent discovery of oil in its waters may help the economy.

Village Architecture

Although Central Africa has several big cities, many people still live in rural villages. Different groups of people have different styles of architecture for their villages. Building materials vary depending on the resources available in the geographic setting.

An extended family lives together in these adobe homes in the mountains of Cameroon.

The strong tropical sun provides power for this hut in Angola.

Gabon and Republic of the Congo

Gabon has had only one president since 1967. For many years, Gabon held no multi-party elections. Gabon's economy provides the highest standard of living in the region. More than half the country's income comes from oil.

Like Gabon, the Republic of the Congo receives much of its income from oil. It also receives income from forest products. Despite these resources, a civil war in the late 1990s hurt the economy.

The Republic of the Congo is mostly urban and growing more so. Many people are moving from villages to cities. The biggest city is the capital, Brazzaville.

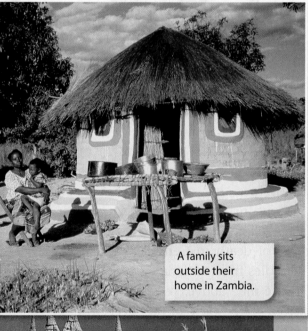

A family sits outside their home in Zambia.

ANALYSIS SKILL | **ANALYZING VISUALS**

How does the construction of the huts help you recognize different climates in Central Africa?

Angola

Angola won independence from Portugal in 1975. The country then plunged into a long civil war. Fighting finally ended in 2002, and the country has been more stable since then. Angola is now a republic with an elected president.

Even with peace, Angola's economy is struggling. For about 85 percent of the population, subsistence farming is the only source of income. Even worse, land mines left over from the civil war endanger the farmers. A high rate of **inflation**, the rise in prices that occurs when currency loses its buying power, hurt Angola's economy during the early 2000s. Finally, corrupt officials have taken large amounts of money meant for public projects.

Angola does have potential, however. The country has diamonds and oil. The oil is found offshore and in Cabinda. Cabinda is a part of Angola that is separated from the rest of the country by the Democratic Republic of the Congo.

Zambia and Malawi

The southernmost countries in Central Africa are Zambia and Malawi. About 85 percent of Zambia's workers are farmers. Though rich with copper mines, Zambia's economy is growing very slowly. It is hurt by high levels of debt and inflation.

Nearly all of Malawi's people farm for a living. About 83 percent of the people live in villages in rural areas. Aid from foreign countries and religious groups has been important to the economy. However, the country has been slow to build factories and industries. In the future, Malawi will probably have to develop its own industries rather than rely on aid from foreign countries.

READING CHECK **Generalizing** What are the economies like in Central African countries?

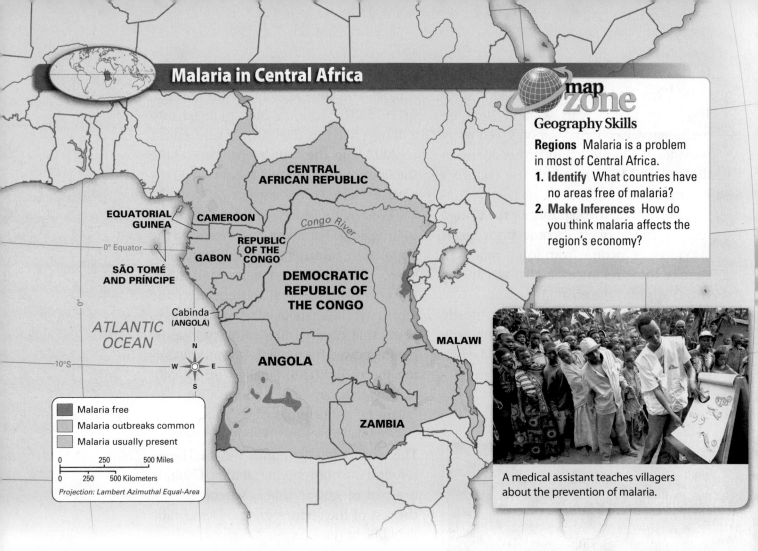

map zone

Geography Skills

Regions Malaria is a problem in most of Central Africa.
1. **Identify** What countries have no areas free of malaria?
2. **Make Inferences** How do you think malaria affects the region's economy?

CENTRAL AFRICAN REPUBLIC

EQUATORIAL GUINEA

CAMEROON

Congo River

0° Equator

GABON

REPUBLIC OF THE CONGO

SÃO TOMÉ AND PRÍNCIPE

DEMOCRATIC REPUBLIC OF THE CONGO

Cabinda (ANGOLA)

ATLANTIC OCEAN

MALAWI

ANGOLA

ZAMBIA

Malaria free

Malaria outbreaks common

Malaria usually present

0   250   500 Miles
0   250   500 Kilometers

Projection: Lambert Azimuthal Equal-Area

A medical assistant teaches villagers about the prevention of malaria.

Issues and Challenges

As you have read, many of the countries in Central Africa have unstable governments and poor economies. These circumstances have been either the cause or effect of the grave challenges that face the region today.

Ethnic and Regional Conflict

A mix of ethnic groups and competing desires for power has led to civil war in many of the region's countries. Millions of people have been killed in these wars, especially in the Democratic Republic of the Congo.

Wars have also contributed to poor economies in the region. The people killed or injured in the fighting can no longer work. In addition, the fighting destroys land and other resources that could be used in more productive ways.

ACADEMIC VOCABULARY

implement to put in place

Health

Like war, disease kills many people in the region. **Malaria** is a disease spread by mosquitoes that causes fever and pain. Without treatment it can lead to death. In fact, malaria is by far the most common cause of death in Central Africa. A child there dies from malaria every 45 seconds. On the map above, you can see that this disease is a problem almost everywhere.

International health organizations and some national governments have begun to **implement** strategies to control malaria. These strategies include educating people about the disease and passing out nets treated with insecticide. The nets and medicine are expensive, and not everyone can afford them. However, people who sleep under these nets will be protected from mosquitoes and malaria.

While some countries are beginning to control malaria, another disease is spreading rapidly. HIV, the virus that causes AIDS, is very common in Central Africa. Hundreds of thousands of people die of AIDS each year in Central Africa. There is no cure for HIV infection, and medicines to control it are very expensive. International groups are working hard to find a cure for HIV and to slow the spread of the disease.

Partly because so many people die of disease, Central Africa has a very young population. Almost 45 percent of people living in Central Africa are under age 15. For comparison, only about 20 percent of the people in the United States are under age 15. Although many young people in Central Africa work, they do not contribute to the economy as much as older, more experienced workers do.

Resources and Environment

To help their economies and their people, the countries of Central Africa must begin to develop their natural resources more effectively. Agricultural land is one resource that must be managed more effectively. In some places, partly because of war, food production has actually declined. Also, food production cannot keep up with the demands of the growing population. The results are food shortages and malnutrition. **Malnutrition** is the condition of not getting enough nutrients from food.

The environment is another important resource that must be managed. Some of Central Africa's most important industries are destroying the environment. Lumber companies cut down trees in the tropical forest, threatening the wildlife that lives there. Mining is also harming the environment. Diamonds and copper are mined in huge open pits. This mining process removes large areas of land and destroys the landscape.

Many people in Central Africa and around the world are working hard and spending billions of dollars to improve conditions in the region. National parks have been set up to protect the environment. Projects to provide irrigation and prevent erosion are helping people plant more crops. Central Africa's land and people hold great potential for the future.

READING CHECK **Summarizing** What are some threats to Central Africa's environment?

SUMMARY AND PREVIEW Countries in Central Africa are trying to build stable governments and strong economies after years of civil war. Next, you will learn about Southern Africa.

Section 3 Assessment

hmhsocialstudies.com
ONLINE QUIZ

Reviewing Ideas, Terms, and Places

1. a. Summarize What effect did Mobutu Sese Seko's rule have on the Democratic Republic of the Congo?
   b. Evaluate Do you think Central African countries would benefit more from a stable government or from a strong economy? Explain your answer.
2. a. Identify What causes **malaria**?
   b. Explain How are some countries coping with environmental challenges?
   c. Geographic Questions Look back at the Regional Database for this unit. Based on the data, pose and answer a question about life expectancy for the various countries in this region.

Critical Thinking

3. Evaluating Look over your notes on Central Africa. Using a graphic organizer like the one here, rank the challenges facing Central Africa.

Challenges
1.
2.

FOCUS ON WRITING   *my* WriteSmart

4. Describing Countries You can focus on one country or on the whole region in your acrostic. Review your notes and jot down some ideas for the focus of your acrostic.

Interpreting a Population Pyramid

Learn

A population pyramid is a graph that shows the percentages of males and females by age group in a country's population. The pyramids are split into two sides. Each bar on the left shows the percentage of a country's population that is male and of a certain age. The bars on the right show the same information for females.

Population pyramids help us understand population trends in countries. Countries that have large percentages of young people have populations that are growing rapidly. Countries with more older people are growing slowly or not at all.

Practice

Interpret information from the population pyramid graph of Angola to answer the following questions.

1. What age group is the largest?

2. What percent of Angola's population is made up of 15- to 19-year-old males?

3. What does this population pyramid tell you about the population trend in Angola?

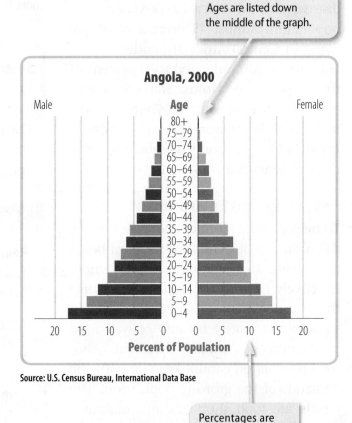

Ages are listed down the middle of the graph.

Source: U.S. Census Bureau, International Data Base

Percentages are labeled across the bottom of the graph.

Apply

Do research at the library or on the Internet to find age and population data for the United States. Use that information to answer the following questions.

1. What age group is the largest?

2. Are there more males or females over age 80?

3. How would you describe the shape of the population pyramid?

Chapter Review

Visual Summary

Use the visual summary below to help you review the main ideas of the chapter.

QUICK FACTS

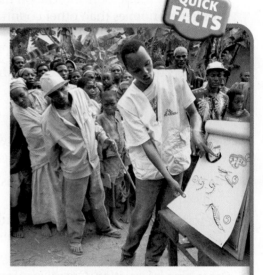

The forests of Central Africa's Congo Basin are home to gorillas and many other kinds of animals.

Ivory attracted Europeans to Central Africa. They left their influence on the region's history and culture.

Countries of Central Africa are looking for ways to solve many of their challenges, such as preventing disease.

Reviewing Vocabulary, Terms, and Places

Using your own paper, complete the sentences below by providing the correct term for each blank.

1. The _____ is a low area near the middle of Central Africa.

2. _____ is a disease spread by mosquitoes that causes fever and aching.

3. People who do not get enough nutrients from their food suffer from _____.

4. To _____ a system is to put it in place.

5. _____ is the rise in prices that occurs when currency loses its buying power.

6. A _____ is a regional variety of a language.

7. The river that flows through Central Africa and into the Atlantic Ocean is the _____.

8. A _____ is an open-air market set up once or twice a week.

9. Much of the copper in Central Africa comes from a region known as the _____.

Comprehension and Critical Thinking

SECTION 1 *(Pages 582–585)*

10. **a. Describe** What are the main landforms in Central Africa?

    b. Make Inferences Why would people in rural areas be more likely to shop at periodic markets than at grocery stores?

    c. Elaborate How does the development of national parks affect people in the region? How does it affect people around the world?

SECTION 2 *(Pages 588–591)*

11. **a. Recall** When did European countries divide Central Africa into colonies?

    b. Analyze What factors besides European colonization influenced where different religions are most common in Central Africa today?

    c. Evaluate What do you think was the most significant influence or effect the Europeans had on Central Africa? Explain your answer.

12. a. Identify What are the diseases that affect many people in Central Africa?

b. Analyze Which geographic factors help explain why Cameroon and Gabon have stronger economies than other countries in the region?

c. Evaluate What are the benefits and possible drawbacks of foreign aid to Central Africa?

Social Studies Skills

Interpreting a Population Pyramid *Use the graph on page 598 to answer the following questions.*

13. Interpreting Graphs What age group is the smallest?

14. Geographic Questions Use the population pyramid graph to pose and answer a question about population patterns in Angola.

15. Organizing Information Organize information from the population pyramid graph into a written summary of population trends in Angola.

Map Activity

16. Central Africa Match the letters on the map with their correct labels.

Congo River Congo Basin Angola

Zambezi River Lake Nyasa

Using the Internet

17. Activity: Making a Scrapbook Central Africa is home to many different ethnic groups. Although there are similarities among them, they each have unique characteristics as well. Through the online book, take a journey to Central Africa. Research some of the many groups that live there. Then create an illustrated scrapbook that documents some of the groups that you have met in your travels. Include information on their towns, ways of life, and environments. You may also want to include maps, souvenirs, and pictures from your journey.

↗ **hmhsocialstudies.com**

FOCUS ON READING AND WRITING   *my*WriteSmart

Using Word Parts *Look at the list of prefixes and suffixes and their meanings below. Then answer the questions that follow.*

mal- (bad)	-ous (characterized by)
in- (not)	-ment (result, action)
re- (again)	-ion (action, condition)

18. Which of the following words means "getting only poor nutrients"?

a. nutriment **c.** renutrition

b. malnutrition **d.** nutrious

19. Which of the following words means "the condition of being protected"?

a. reprotect **c.** protection

b. protectment **d.** protectous

20. Writing Your Acrostic Your poem will describe Central Africa or a part of it. Choose the place you want to describe and write the letters of that word vertically, with one letter on each line of your paper. For each letter, use your notes to write a descriptive word or phrase that tells about your subject. Make a final copy of your acrostic to share with classmates. Use *my*WriteSmart in your eBook to write your acrostic.

Reading Social Studies

Using Word Parts

Many English words are made up of several word parts: roots, prefixes, and suffixes. A root is the main part of the word. A prefix is a letter or syllable added before the root. A suffix is a word part added after the root. Knowing the meanings of common prefixes and suffixes may help you figure out unfamiliar words. Below are some common prefixes and suffixes along with their meanings and examples of their use.

Common Prefixes		
Prefix	**Meaning**	**Sample Words**
en-	to cause to be	enforce
in-	not	ineffective
inter-	between, among	interpersonal
mal-	bad	malfunction
pro-	for, in front	proclaim
re-	again	rerun, rebuild

Common Suffixes		
Suffix	**Meaning**	**Sample Words**
-al	relating to	directional
-dom	state, condition	freedom
-ion	action, condition	rotation, selection
-ous	characterized by	victorious
-ment	result, action	development, entertainment

YOU TRY IT!

Read the following words from the chapter. Underline any prefixes or suffixes. Use the chart above to find the meaning of the prefix or the suffix. Define each word. Then exchange your work with a partner to confirm your understanding. With your partner, take turns using the words correctly in questions about Africa.

independence	instability	malnutrition
interact	re-elected	enslaved
industrial	endanger	migration

Southern Africa

Essential Question

*my*Notebook

What role did European imperialism play in the development of Southern Africa?

Texas Essential Knowledge and Skills (TEKS)

1A, 1B, 2A, 2B, 3A, 3B, 4C, 4D, 5C, 6B, 15B, 18A, 21B, 21C, 22D, 23B

FOCUS ON READING AND VIEWING

my WriteSmart

Making Generalizations A generalization is a broad, general conclusion drawn from examples, facts, or other information. As you read this chapter, try to make generalizations about the facts and information in the text. Making generalizations will help you understand the meaning of what you are reading. **See the lesson, Making Generalizations, on page 623.**

Viewing a TV News Report You are a TV journalist on assignment in Southern Africa. As you read this chapter, collect information about the region and plan your report. Also pay careful attention during classroom instruction. Listen especially for the social studies terms, basic vocabulary, and academic vocabulary that your teacher uses to explain Southern Africa. Write down their meanings. Later you and your classmates will use this information to create, present, and evaluate TV news reports. Use the annotation tools in your eBook to gather information for your assignment.

0° Equator

10°S

ATLANTIC OCEAN

20°S

-- Tropic of Capricorn --

⊙ National capital
•   Other cities

0   150   300 Miles
0   150   300 Kilometers

Projection: Azimuthal Equidistant

10°W

0°

Geography In northern Botswana, the Okavango River forms an enormous inland delta.

Southern Africa: Political

ANGOLA

TANZANIA

INDIAN OCEAN

ZAMBIA

MALAWI

MOZAMBIQUE

Moroni ✪ COMOROS

Zambezi River

Harare ✪

ZIMBABWE

Mozambique Channel

MADAGASCAR

Antananarivo ✪

NAMIBIA

BOTSWANA

Windhoek ✪

Limpopo River

Gaborone ✪

Pretoria ✪

Johannesburg ●

Mbabane ✪ Maputo
SWAZILAND

Orange River

Bloemfontein ✪ ✪ Maseru
LESOTHO

SOUTH AFRICA

INDIAN OCEAN

Cape Town ✪

10°E   30°E   50°E

mapzone Geography Skills

Place Southern Africa is located between the Indian Ocean and the Atlantic Ocean.

1. **Locate** What is the capital of Botswana?
2. **Draw Conclusions** What are some of the disadvantages of being a landlocked country like Zimbabwe and Botswana?

History Ancient rock art of southern Africa often includes hunters and animals.

Culture South Africa's culture is a reflection of the country's diverse population.

What You Will Learn...

Main Ideas

1. Southern Africa's main physical feature is a large plateau with plains, rivers, and mountains.
2. The climate and vegetation of Southern Africa is mostly savanna and desert.
3. Southern Africa has valuable mineral resources.

The Big Idea

Southern Africa's physical geography includes a high, mostly dry plateau, grassy plains and rivers, and valuable mineral resources.

Key Terms and Places

escarpment, *p. 604*
veld, *p. 606*
Namib Desert, *p. 606*
pans, *p. 606*

hmhsocialstudies.com
TAKING NOTES

Use the graphic organizer online to take notes on the physical geography of Southern Africa.

Physical Geography

If YOU lived there...

You are a member of the San, a people who live in the Kalahari Desert. Your family lives with several others in a group of circular grass huts. You are friends with the other children. Sometimes you help your mom look for eggs or plants to use for carrying water. Your water containers, clothes, carrying bags, and weapons all come from the resources you find in the desert. Next year you will move away to attend school in a town.

How will your life change next year?

BUILDING BACKGROUND Parts of Southern Africa have a desert climate. Little vegetation grows in these areas, but some people do live there. Most of Southern Africa's people live in cooler and wetter areas, such as on the high, grassy plains in the south and east.

Physical Features

Southern Africa has some amazing scenery. On a visit to the region, you might see grassy plains, steamy swamps, mighty rivers, rocky waterfalls, and steep mountains and plateaus.

Plateaus and Mountains

Most of the land in Southern Africa lies on a large plateau. Parts of this plateau reach more than 4,000 feet (1,220 m) above sea level. To form the plateau, the land rises sharply from a narrow coastal plain. The steep face at the edge of a plateau or other raised area is called an **escarpment**.

In eastern South Africa, part of the escarpment is made up of a mountain range called the Drakensberg (DRAH-kuhnz-buhrk). The steep peaks rise as high as 11,425 feet (3,482 m). Farther north, another mountain range, the Inyanga (in-YANG-guh) Mountains, separates Zimbabwe and Mozambique. Southern Africa also has mountains along its western coast.

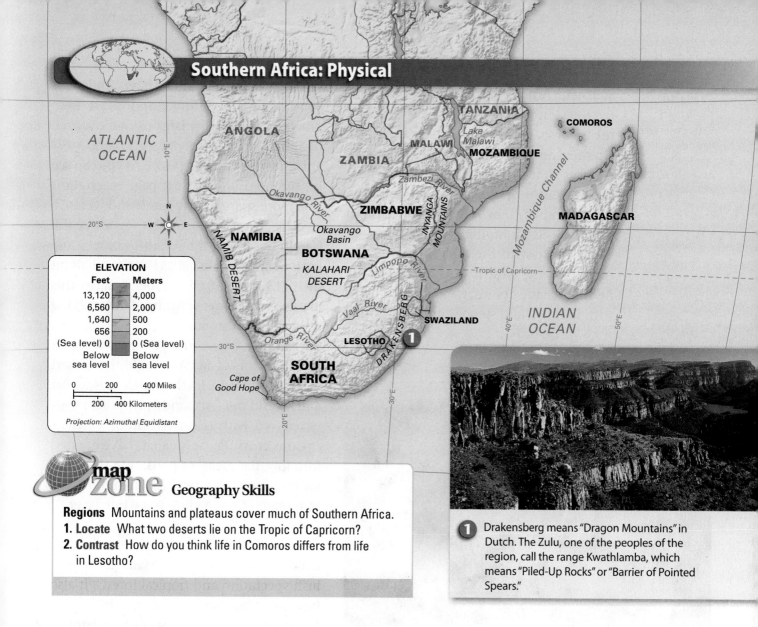

Southern Africa: Physical

ATLANTIC OCEAN

ANGOLA

NAMIBIA

NAMIB DESERT

ZAMBIA

MALAWI

Lake Malawi

TANZANIA

MOZAMBIQUE

COMOROS

Okavango River

ZIMBABWE

Okavango Basin

BOTSWANA

KALAHARI DESERT

Zambezi River

INYANGA MOUNTAINS

Mozambique Channel

MADAGASCAR

Limpopo River

Tropic of Capricorn

INDIAN OCEAN

Vaal River

DRAKENSBERG

SWAZILAND

Orange River

LESOTHO

SOUTH AFRICA

Cape of Good Hope

ELEVATION

Feet	Meters
13,120	4,000
6,560	2,000
1,640	500
656	200
(Sea level) 0	0 (Sea level)
Below sea level	Below sea level

0   200   400 Miles
0   200   400 Kilometers

Projection: Azimuthal Equidistant

map zone Geography Skills

Regions Mountains and plateaus cover much of Southern Africa.
1. **Locate** What two deserts lie on the Tropic of Capricorn?
2. **Contrast** How do you think life in Comoros differs from life in Lesotho?

① Drakensberg means "Dragon Mountains" in Dutch. The Zulu, one of the peoples of the region, call the range Kwathlamba, which means "Piled-Up Rocks" or "Barrier of Pointed Spears."

Plains and Rivers

Southern Africa's narrow coastal plain and the wide plateau are covered with grassy plains. These flat plains are home to animals such as lions, leopards, elephants, baboons, and antelope.

Several large rivers cross Southern Africa's plains. The Okavango River flows from Angola into a huge basin in Botswana. This river's water never reaches the ocean. Instead it forms a swampy inland delta that is home to crocodiles, zebras, hippos, and other animals. Many tourists travel to Botswana to see these wild animals in their natural habitat.

The Orange River passes through the rocky Augrabies (oh-KRAH-bees) Falls as it flows to the Atlantic Ocean. When the water in the river is at its highest, the falls are several miles wide. The water tumbles down 19 separate waterfalls. The Limpopo River is another of the region's major rivers. It flows into the Indian Ocean. **Features** such as waterfalls and other obstacles block ships from sailing up these rivers. However, the rivers do allow irrigation for farmland in an otherwise dry area.

READING CHECK **Generalizing** What are Southern Africa's main physical features?

ACADEMIC VOCABULARY

features
characteristics

Climate and Vegetation

FOCUS ON READING
What generalization can you make about Southern Africa's climate?

Southern Africa's climates vary from east to west. The wettest place in the region is the east coast of the island of Madagascar. On the mainland, winds carrying moisture blow in from the Indian Ocean. Because the Drakensberg's high elevation causes these winds to blow upward, the eastern slopes of these mountains are rainy.

In contrast to the eastern part of the continent, the west is very dry. From the Atlantic coast, deserts give way to plains with semiarid and steppe climates.

Satellite View

Namib Desert

One of the world's most unusual deserts, the Namib lies on the Atlantic coast in Namibia. As this satellite image shows, the land there is extremely dry. Some of the world's highest sand dunes stretch for miles along the coast.

In spite of its harsh conditions, some insects have adapted to life in the desert. They can survive there because at night a fog rolls in from the ocean. The insects use the fog as a source of water.

Drawing Conclusions How have some insects adapted to living in the Namib Desert?

Savanna and Deserts

A large savanna region covers much of Southern Africa. Shrubs and short trees grow on the grassy plains of the savanna. In South Africa, these open grassland areas are known as the **veld** (VELT). As you can see on the map on the next page, vegetation gets more sparse in the south and west.

The driest place in the region is the **Namib Desert** on the Atlantic coast. Some parts of the Namib get as little as a half an inch (13 mm) of rainfall per year. In this dry area, plants get water from dew and fog rather than from rain.

Another desert, the Kalahari, occupies most of Botswana. Although this desert gets enough rain in the north to support grasses and trees, its sandy plains are mostly covered with scattered shrubs. Ancient streams crossing the Kalahari have drained into low, flat areas, or **pans**. On these flat areas, minerals left behind when the water evaporated form a glittering white layer.

Tropical Forests

Unlike the mainland, Madagascar has lush vegetation and tropical forests. It also has many animals found nowhere else. For example, some 50 species of lemurs, relatives of apes, live only on this island. However, the destruction of Madagascar's forests has endangered many of the island's animals.

READING CHECK **Summarizing** What is the climate and vegetation like in Southern Africa?

Resources

Southern Africa is rich in natural resources. Madagascar's forests provide timber. The region's rivers supply hydroelectricity and water for irrigation. Where rain is plentiful or irrigation is possible, farmers can grow a wide range of crops.

Southern Africa: Vegetation

ATLANTIC OCEAN

ANGOLA

TANZANIA

COMOROS

MALAWI   MOZAMBIQUE

ZAMBIA

Mozambique Channel

MADAGASCAR

ZIMBABWE

NAMIBIA

BOTSWANA

Tropic of Capricorn

SWAZILAND

LESOTHO

SOUTH AFRICA

INDIAN OCEAN

Broadleaf trees
Grass with trees
Grass
Shrubs
Barren land

0   250   500 Miles
0   250   500 Kilometers

Projection: Azimuthal Equidistant

map zone

Geography Skills

Regions Southern Africa has several different vegetation types.
1. **Identify** What area has the least vegetation?
2. **Contrast** How does Botswana's vegetation differ from Mozambique's vegetation?

The region's most valuable resources, however, are minerals. Mines in South Africa produce most of the world's gold. In addition, South Africa, Botswana, and Namibia have productive diamond mines. Other mineral resources in Southern Africa include coal, platinum, copper, uranium, and iron ore. Although mining is very important to the economy of the region, the mines can have damaging effects on the surrounding natural environments.

READING CHECK Finding Main Ideas What are the main resources of Southern Africa?

SUMMARY AND PREVIEW Southern Africa is mainly covered with grassy plains and deserts atop a large plateau. Minerals are among the region's main resources. In the next section, you will learn about Southern Africa's history and culture.

Section 1 Assessment

hmhsocialstudies.com
ONLINE QUIZ

Reviewing Ideas, Terms, and Places

1. **a. Define** What is an **escarpment**?
   b. Elaborate How is the Okavango River different from most other rivers you have studied?
2. **a. Recall** Where in Southern Africa is the driest climate?
   b. Explain What caused minerals to collect in **pans** in the Kalahari Desert?
3. **a. Identify** What are Southern Africa's most valuable resources?
   b. Elaborate How do you think the gold and diamond mines have affected South Africa's economy?

Critical Thinking

4. **Categorizing** Review your notes and use a graphic organizer like this one to sort characteristics by location.

	East	West
Physical Features		
Climate and Vegetation		

Focus on Viewing

5. **Telling about the Physical Geography** Your TV news report might focus on some part of the geography of Southern Africa. Could you focus on the destruction of the rain forest or life in the desert?

History and Culture

TEKS 1A, 1B, 2A, 2B, 4C, 5C, 15B, 18A, 21B, 21C, 22D

What You Will Learn...

Main Ideas

1. Southern Africa's history began with hunter-gatherers, followed by great empires and European settlements.
2. The cultures of Southern Africa are rich in different languages, religions, customs, and art.

The Big Idea

Native African ethnic groups and European settlements influenced the history and culture of Southern Africa.

Key Terms and Places

Great Zimbabwe, *p. 609*
Cape of Good Hope, *p. 609*
Afrikaners, *p. 610*
Boers, *p. 610*
apartheid, *p. 610*
township, *p. 611*

hmhsocialstudies.com
TAKING NOTES

Use the graphic organizer online to take notes on the history and culture of Southern Africa.

If YOU lived there...

You are a hunter living in Southern Africa 10,000 years ago. The animals you hunt include antelope, rhinoceros, and ostrich. A spear is your only weapon. You spend several days following herds of animals until you and several other people are able to surround them. After the hunt, you decide to paint your hunting experience on a rock overhang near where you live.

Why do you paint these images of animals?

BUILDING BACKGROUND Southern Africa's fertile land and its abundance of wildlife have supported different peoples for tens of thousands of years. Hunter-gatherers were the first peoples to thrive in the region. Much later, peoples from West Africa migrated to the region, and then eventually Europeans.

History

As you learned in the previous chapter, Bantu farmers migrated from West Africa to Central Africa as early as 2,000 years ago. These peoples also migrated to Southern Africa at about the same time. Much later, Europeans arrived on the coast of Southern Africa and forever changed the landscape and ways of life of the people in the region.

Early History

For many centuries the Khoisan peoples lived in Southern Africa. Divided into several ethnic groups, the Khoisan were hunter-gatherers and herders. When the early Bantu peoples migrated from West and Central Africa, they brought new languages and iron tools.

One Bantu group, the Shona, built an empire that reached its height in the 1400s. The Shona Empire included much of what is now the countries of Zimbabwe and Mozambique.

The Shona farmed, raised cattle, and traded gold with other groups on the coast.

The Shona are best known for **Great Zimbabwe**, their stone-walled capital. In fact, the name Zimbabwe is the Shona word for stone-walled towns. The builders of Great Zimbabwe used huge granite boulders and rectangular blocks of stone to build the capital's walls.

Founded in the late 1000s, Great Zimbabwe was a small trading and herding center. In the 1100s, the population grew, and both gold mining and farming grew in importance. Great Zimbabwe may have had 10,000 to 20,000 residents. With these resources, the city eventually became the center of a large trading network.

Trade made Great Zimbabwe's rulers wealthy and powerful. However, in the 1400s the gold trade declined. Deprived of its main source of wealth, Great Zimbabwe weakened. By 1500 it was no longer a capital and trading center.

Archaeologists have found Chinese porcelain and other artifacts from Asia at Great Zimbabwe. These artifacts suggest that the Shona traded widely. In addition to trading with peoples of Asia, the Shona apparently traded with the Swahili. The Swahili were Muslim Africans living along the East Africa coast. In effect, all of these peoples were once connected by an Indian Ocean trade network.

Europeans in Southern Africa

In the late 1400s traders from Portugal explored the Southern African coast on their way to Asia to trade for spices. To get to Asia from Portugal, they had to sail around the southern tip of Africa and then cross the Indian Ocean. The trip was long and difficult, so they set up bases on the Southern African coast. These bases provided the ships with supplies.

The Dutch Other Europeans arrived in Southern Africa after the Portuguese. People from the Netherlands, or the Dutch, were the first Europeans to settle in the region. In 1652 the Dutch set up a trade station at a natural harbor near the **Cape of Good Hope.**

Highly skilled craftspeople built several stone walls that surrounded the Shona capital of Great Zimbabwe. Today the ruins are a World Heritage Site.

ANALYZING VISUALS Why do you think Great Zimbabwe was made of stone?

Great Zimbabwe

The Cape sits at the tip of Africa. The land around the Cape lacked the gold and copper of the interior. However, it had a mild climate, similar to the climate the Dutch were used to back home.

This small colony on the Cape provided supplies to Dutch ships sailing between Dutch colonies in the East Indies and the Netherlands. The Dutch eventually brought in slaves from the region and Southeast Asia to work in the colony.

The Afrikaners and the Boers The people of the colony were very diverse. In addition to the Dutch, other Europeans also settled on the Cape. Dutch, French, and German settlers and their descendants in South Africa were called **Afrikaners**. Over time, a new language called Afrikaans emerged in the Cape colony. This language combined Dutch with Khoisan and Bantu words. German, French, and English also influenced the language's development.

Dutch Settlers

This painting shows Dutch settlers arriving at the Cape of Good Hope in Southern Africa.

In the early 1800s, Great Britain took over the area of the Cape. The **Boers**, Afrikaner frontier farmers who had spread out from the original Cape colony, resisted the British. Many Boers packed all their belongings into wagons and soon moved farther east and north.

The Zulu and the British At about the same time, a Bantu-speaking group, the Zulu, became a powerful fighting force in the region. They conquered the surrounding African peoples, creating their own empire. When the Boers moved north of the Cape, they entered Zulu territory. The two sides clashed over control of the land. Eventually the British also wanted Zulu land. After a series of battles, the British defeated the Zulu.

The ending of slavery in the British Empire in the 1830s brought changes to the economy of colonial settlements in the region. Instead of slaves, people traded ivory—the tusks of elephants. Over time, however, hunters wiped out the entire elephant population in some parts of Southern Africa. With ivory in short supply, trade shifted to diamonds and gold, which were discovered in South Africa in the 1860s.

Apartheid

In the early 1900s South Africa's government, which was dominated by white Afrikaners, became increasingly racist. As a result, black South Africans opposed the government. To defend their rights, they formed the African National Congress (ANC) in 1912.

However, the trend toward racial division and inequality continued. South Africa's government set up a policy of separation of races, or **apartheid**, which means "apartness." This policy divided people into four groups: whites, blacks, Coloureds, and Asians.

Music of South Africa

Stomping. Spinning. Swaying. This is the kind of dancing you might see at a performance of South African music. In addition, musicians playing drums, guitars, and traditional flutes provide a rhythmic beat that makes it impossible to stand still.

One of the groups that does it the best are the Mahotella Queens. They are grandmothers who have been singing together for over 40 years. Their songs mix gospel with traditional African music. Performing all over the world, the Queens give unforgettable performances of nonstop singing and dancing.

Drawing Conclusions Why do you think South African music is popular around the world?

Coloureds and Asians were only allowed to live in certain areas. Each African tribe or group was given its own rural "homeland." These homelands generally did not include good farmland, mines, or other natural resources. Those resources were owned by the whites, and blacks had no rights in white areas.

Housing, health care, and schools for blacks were poor compared to those for whites. Schools for Coloureds were poor, but slightly better than the black schools.

During apartheid, many blacks found work in white-owned industries, mines, shops, and farms. Blacks had to live in separate areas called **townships**, which were often crowded clusters of tiny homes. The townships were far from the jobs in the cities and mines.

Independence

Beginning in the 1960s, many colonies gained independence from the European countries that had once colonized them. Some gained independence rather peacefully, but others struggled. For example, the British colonists in Rhodesia fought native Africans for years. Fighting broke out after the colonists declared their own white-dominated republic in 1970. Finally, in 1980, the Africans won independence and renamed their country Zimbabwe.

Independence also did not come easy for other countries. Despite violent resistance, Namibia continued to be ruled by South Africa until 1990. Mozambique was granted independence in 1975 after 10 years of war against Portuguese rule.

READING CHECK **Generalizing** Why did Europeans settle Southern Africa?

Culture

Over time, many groups of people created a diverse culture in Southern Africa. As a result, the region's culture reflects both European and African influence.

Ndebele Village

The Ndebele are one of many ethnic groups in South Africa who have kept their traditional culture alive. Many live in villages of brightly painted houses.

ANALYSIS SKILL ANALYZING VISUALS

What aspect of Ndebele culture do you see in these two photographs?

People

The people of Southern Africa belong to hundreds of different ethnic groups. Some groups are very large. For example, about 11 million people in South Africa are Zulu. Nearly 1.6 million of Botswana's 2 million people belong to a single ethnic group, the Tswana.

Other ethnic groups are small and usually not native to Africa. For example, about 6 percent of Namibia's population is of European descent. In Madagascar people are a mix of 18 small ethnic groups. These Malagasy groups descended from people who migrated across the Indian Ocean from Indonesia.

Languages

FOCUS ON READING

What generalization can you make about the languages spoken in Southern Africa?

Because people in Southern Africa belong to hundreds of different ethnic groups, they speak many languages. Most of the African languages spoken in Southern Africa are related to one of two language families—Khoisan or Bantu.

The early peoples of Southern Africa spoke different Khoisan languages. Khoisan speakers are known for the "click" sounds they make when they speak. Today, the majority of Khoisan speakers belong to the San ethnic group and live in remote areas of Botswana and Namibia.

Most people in Southern Africa speak one of the more than 200 Bantu languages. For example, most of South Africa's 11 official languages are Bantu languages.

In countries with European influence, European languages are also spoken. For example, English is the official language of Namibia and Zimbabwe. The official language of Mozambique is Portuguese.

Religion

In addition to language, Europeans brought the religion of Christianity to Southern Africa. As a result, millions of people in Southern Africa are Christians. In Namibia and South Africa the majority of the population is Christian.

Painting houses is traditionally the role of Ndebele women. They use colorful geometric patterns.

Artists in Zimbabwe are known for their beautiful stone sculptures of birds and other animals. Traditional crafts of Botswana include ostrich-eggshell beadwork and woven baskets with complex designs. People there also produce colorful wool rugs.

READING CHECK **Analyzing** Why do you think the people of Southern Africa speak several different languages?

SUMMARY AND PREVIEW Southern Africa's ancient history and later European settlement greatly influenced the region's culture. Next, you will learn about the governments and economies of the region's countries today.

Many people in Southern Africa who are not Christian practice traditional African religions. Some of these people believe that ancestors and the spirits of the dead have divine powers. In Zimbabwe, traditional beliefs and Christianity have been mixed together. About half of the people in Zimbabwe practice a combination of traditional beliefs and Christianity.

Celebrations and Art

Southern Africans celebrate many holidays. On Heritage Day, South Africans celebrate their country's diverse population. Most countries in Southern Africa celebrate their countries' independence day. Many Christian holidays such as Christmas Day are also celebrated throughout the region.

Southern Africa's art reflects its many cultures. For example, South African artists make traditional ethnic designs for items such as clothing, lamps, linens, and other products. Artists in Lesotho are famous for their woven tapestries of daily life.

Section 2 Assessment

hmhsocialstudies.com
ONLINE QUIZ

Reviewing Ideas, Terms, and Places

1. **a. Define** What was **apartheid**?
   b. Draw Conclusions Why did the Shona capital of **Great Zimbabwe** decline as a trading center?
   c. Elaborate Why do you think the language of Afrikaans developed among the European colonists?
2. **a. Recall** What ethnic group in Southern Africa speaks languages that use click sounds?
   b. Draw Conclusions How do the religions practiced in Southern Africa reflect the region's history?
   c. Evaluate Why do you think Heritage Day is a national holiday in South Africa?

Critical Thinking

3. **Sequencing** Review your notes on the history of Southern Africa. Then organize your information using a time line like the one below. You may add more dates if you need to.

AD 1000   1990

FOCUS ON VIEWING

my WriteSmart

4. **Discussing History and Culture** Which information about the history and culture of Southern Africa might make a good TV news report? What visuals would be interesting?

Southern Africa Today

TEKS 1A, 1B, 2B, 15B, 21B, 21C, 22D

What You Will Learn...

Main Ideas

1. South Africa ended apartheid and now has a stable government and strong economy.
2. Some countries of Southern Africa have good resources and economies, but several are still struggling.
3. Southern African governments are responding to issues and challenges such as drought, disease, and environmental destruction.

The Big Idea

Countries of Southern Africa today are trying to use their governments and resources to improve their economies and deal with challenges.

Key Terms and Places

sanctions, *p. 614*
Cape Town, *p. 616*
enclave, *p. 616*

hmhsocialstudies.com
TAKING NOTES

Use the graphic organizer online to take notes on the countries of Southern Africa today and the challenges they face.

If YOU lived there...

You are an economic adviser in Botswana. In recent years your country has made progress toward improving people's lives, but you think there is room for improvement. One way you plan to help the economy is by promoting tourism. Botswana already has amazing natural landscapes and fascinating animals.

What could your country do to attract more tourists?

BUILDING BACKGROUND Some of the countries in Southern Africa are relatively well off, with plentiful resources and good jobs and transportation systems. Others lack these positive conditions. One of the most successful countries in the region is South Africa.

South Africa

Today South Africa has a stable government and the strongest economy in the region. In addition, many South Africans are enjoying new rights and freedoms. The country has made great progress in resolving the problems of its past, but it still faces many challenges.

End of Apartheid

Ending apartheid, the separation of races, has probably been South Africa's biggest challenge in recent years. Many people around the world objected to the country's apartheid laws. For that reason, they put **sanctions**—economic or political penalties imposed by one country on another to force a change in policy—on South Africa. Some countries banned trade with South Africa. Several companies in the United States and Europe refused to invest their money in South Africa. In addition, many international scientific and sports organizations refused to include South Africans in meetings or competitions.

Celebrating Mandela's Freedom

South Africans in Soweto warmly welcomed Nelson Mandela after he was released from prison in 1990.

The sanctions isolated South Africa. As other countries in Southern Africa gained independence, South Africa became even more isolated. Protest within the country increased. In response, the government outlawed the African National Congress (ANC). This group had been formed to protect the rights of black South Africans. Many ANC members were jailed or forced to leave the country.

The antiapartheid protests continued, however. In the late 1980s, the efforts of the ANC and antiapartheid protestors contributed to social and political change. In 1990 the government released its political prisoners, including Nelson Mandela. Mandela was elected president in 1994 after South Africans of all races were given the right to vote.

Today all races have equal rights in South Africa. The country's public schools and universities are open to all people, as are hospitals and transportation. However, economic equality has come more slowly. White South Africans are still wealthier than the vast majority of black South Africans. Still, South Africans now have opportunities for a better future.

Government and Economy

South Africa's government and economy are well positioned to create a better future for the country. South Africa's new government is a republic with an elected president. The country's constitution emphasizes equality and human rights.

In working toward equality, the government is trying to create jobs and better conditions for black workers and farmers. Currently, most of South Africa's wealth and industries are still controlled by whites. However, even some officials who favor reform are afraid to **execute** new policies. They fear that rapid change will weaken the economy. They are also concerned that it might cause educated and wealthy whites to leave the country.

ACADEMIC VOCABULARY

execute to perform, to carry out

South Africa's strong economy may help bring economic opportunities to the entire population. The country has more resources and industry than most African countries. For example, South Africa is one of the world's leading producers of several valuable minerals—gold, platinum, and chromium. The country is also a major exporter of gold and diamonds.

Large cities in South Africa also contribute to the country's economy. Africa's largest industrial area is located in Johannesburg. In addition, beautiful cities such as **Cape Town** attract many tourists.

READING CHECK **Analyzing** Why and how did South Africa do away with apartheid?

Other Countries of Southern Africa

The eight other countries in the region share some characteristics with South Africa. Some, but not all, have strong economies and stable governments.

Lesotho and Swaziland

These two countries are particularly influenced by South Africa. Lesotho and Swaziland are both enclaves. An **enclave** is a small territory surrounded by foreign territory. Lesotho and Swaziland are both located completely, or almost completely, within South Africa. Swaziland shares part of its border with Mozambique.

Close-up

Cape Town

Founded by the Dutch in 1652, Cape Town is a bustling international port city today. It lies on the South Atlantic Ocean and is home to about 3 million people.

Hiking trails lead to the top of Lion's Head for an amazing view of the city.

ANALYSIS SKILL **ANALYZING VISUALS**

What can you see in this photograph that might reveal why Cape Town is popular with tourists?

Because it is so small, Lesotho has few resources or agricultural land. As a result, it is a poor country. Many of its people work in nearby South Africa. In spite of its poverty, Lesotho has the highest female literacy rate in Africa. Most children, including females, get at least a primary education in free schools run by Christian churches.

Swaziland has some important mineral deposits and industry. Cattle raising and farming are also common there. A good transportation system helps Swaziland to participate in foreign trade.

Lesotho and Swaziland are both kingdoms. Although each country has a king as head of state, each is governed by an elected prime minister and a parliament.

The city's buildings are a mix of modern and Dutch colonial architecture.

People jog, bike, and rollerblade on this trail along the ocean.

Namibia

Namibia gained its independence from South Africa as recently as 1990. Now it is a republic with an elected president and legislature. Its capital, Windhoek, is located in the central highlands.

Very few people live in Namibia's deserts in the east and the west, but these areas are the sites of some of the richest mineral deposits in Africa. Most of the country's income comes from the mining of diamonds, copper, uranium, lead, and zinc. Fishing in the Atlantic Ocean and sheep ranching are also important sources of income. In spite of this strong economy, however, most people are still poor.

Botswana

Botswana is one of Africa's success stories, thanks to mineral resources and a stable democratic government. The main economic activities in Botswana are cattle ranching and diamond mining. Recently, international companies have built factories there, and tourism is increasing. Although unemployment is high, the country has had one of the world's highest rates of economic growth since the 1960s.

Zimbabwe

Zimbabwe has suffered from a poor economy and political instability. Zimbabwe does not lack resources. It has gold and copper mines as well as productive agriculture and manufacturing. However, high inflation, debts, and war have hurt the economy.

In addition, there is much inequality. Although white residents made up less than 1 percent of the population, they owned most of the large farms and ranches. In 2000 the president began a program to take farmland from white farmers and give the land to black residents. This action led many white farmers to leave the country and caused food shortages.

FOCUS ON READING
In general, what is Botswana's economy like?

Tourism in Southern Africa

Tourism is a rapidly growing industry in a number of countries in Southern Africa. The region's wildlife is its main attraction. People come from all over the world to see lions, elephants, zebras, and giraffes in their natural habitats. Many countries have established huge parks to protect these habitats.

Analyzing How do you think tourism affects a country?

	Country	Numbers of Visitors in 2012
1	South Africa	18.7 million
2	Zimbabwe	1.9 million
3	Botswana	2.1 million
4	Mozambique	1.8 million
5	Namibia	931,000

Interpreting Charts How many people visited Zimbabwe?

The attempt at land reform, the poor economy, and violent acts against political opponents have made people in Zimbabwe unhappy with the president. Although he was re-elected in 2002 and 2008, most people think the elections were flawed.

Mozambique

Mozambique is one of the world's poorest countries. The economy has been badly damaged by civil war, but it is improving. Mozambique's ports ship many products from the interior of Africa. Taxes collected on these shipments are an important source of income. Also, plantations grow cashews, cotton, and sugar for export. The country must import more than it exports, however, and it relies on foreign aid.

Madagascar and Comoros

Madagascar was ruled for more than 20 years by a socialist dictator. Today the elected president is working to improve the struggling economy. Most of the country's income comes from exports of coffee, vanilla, sugar, and cloves. Madagascar also has some manufacturing, and the country is popular with tourists who come to see the unique plants and animals.

Comoros is a country made up of four tiny islands. It suffers from a lack of resources and political instability. The government of Comoros is struggling to improve education and promote tourism.

READING CHECK **Contrasting** In what ways are Botswana and Zimbabwe different?

Issues and Challenges

Although conditions in many countries of Southern Africa are better than they are on much of the continent, the region has its own challenges. One of the most serious problems facing Southern Africa is poverty. Terrible droughts often destroy food crops. In addition, many of Southern Africa's people are unemployed.

Disease is another problem. Southern Africa has high numbers of people infected with HIV. The region's governments are trying to educate people to slow the spread of disease.

Another challenge is environmental destruction. For example, in Madagascar, deforestation leads to erosion. There is hope for the future, though. Namibia was the first country in the world to put environmental protection in its constitution. Also, the African Union (AU) works to promote cooperation among African countries. The AU tries to solve problems across the continent.

READING CHECK **Generalizing** What main challenges does Southern Africa face?

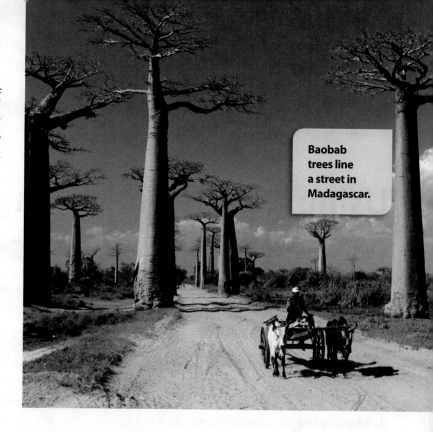

Baobab trees line a street in Madagascar.

SUMMARY Southern Africa has valuable mineral resources and landscapes popular with tourists. Some countries have more stable governments and economies than much of Africa. However, the region still faces many challenges.

Section 3 Assessment

hmhsocialstudies.com
ONLINE QUIZ

Reviewing Ideas, Terms, and Places

1. **a. Describe** What effect did **sanctions** have on South Africa?
   b. Evaluate What social and political contributions did the African National Congress and antiapartheid protestors make in South Africa?
2. **a. Recall** Which country's president began a program to take farmland from white farmers?
   b. Make Inferences Why might being an **enclave** affect a country's economy?
   c. Rank Besides South Africa, which two countries in the region seem to have the best economies?
3. **a. Describe** How can drought lead to poverty?
   b. Explain How are people in Southern Africa addressing the challenges in the region?
   c. Geographic Questions Use the chart on page 618 to pose and answer a question about the distribution of tourists among the various countries of Southern Africa.

Critical Thinking

4. **Summarizing** Review your notes on South Africa. Then using a graphic organizer like this one, describe what the country has been like at each different period.

Before the 1990s	The 1990s	Today

FOCUS ON VIEWING

my WriteSmart

5. **Telling about Southern Africa Today** Would you try to include information about all of Southern Africa in your report? Or would you just focus on one country? Take notes on your ideas.

Social Studies Skills

Using a Decision-Making Process

Learn

Making decisions is a process for choosing a course of action between two or more options. Understanding the steps in the process can help you to make more thoughtful decisions.

Practice

Use the following steps to make decisions.

1. **Identify the situation.** Determine if the situation requires a decision.

2. **Gather information.** Do research and ask questions to learn more about the situation.

3. **Identify options.** Use your information to develop a list of options for addressing the situation.

4. **Predict Consequences.** Identify the possible outcome of each option. Think about which option will have the best result.

5. **Take action to implement a decision.** Use the information you gathered and your analysis of options to help you a make a decision. Then take steps to put the decision in action.

Apply

With a partner, use the steps of a decision-making process to make a decision about a proposal to build a garbage dump in your community. Express your ideas orally based on experiences and share information that you learn through research. Create a graphic organizer like the one at right.

Situation

In 2002, facing a water shortage, senior leaders in South Africa's government considered building a dam on the Berg River.

Facts

- The Berg River Basin is home to 8% of South Africans, but only provides 3% of the country's water.

- The dam would collect and store winter rains and supply the water during the dry summer season.

- The Department of Water Affairs and Forestry (DWAF) has requested the dam to help solve a water shortage.

- To keep the river's downstream environments healthy, a plan for releasing water from the dam would have to be put in place.

Option 1

Agree to the building the dam.

- The dam would help secure water for Cape Town.

- Building the dam would create a significant number of new job.

- The cost of building the dam is about $180 million.

- The DWAF's based its request on the results of a study that evaluated 24 options for solving the water shortage problem.

Option 2

Promote a water awareness campaign.

- Based on current rates of usage, the dam would not meet all the area's water needs.

- Building the dam would destroy some pine plantations and might harm farming and tourist industries.

- Critics argue that less expensive conservation efforts have not been considered. These include reducing water use and pollution.

Decision and Action Taken

In 2002, the Berg Dam project was approved, under the condition that Cape Town reduce its water use by 20%.

Chapter Review

Visual Summary

Use the visual summary below to help you review the main ideas of the chapter.

QUICK FACTS

The Drakensberg rises to meet a high plateau that dominates the physical geography of Southern Africa.

Traditional African and European cultures mix in Southern Africa. Music and dance are very important.

Countries such as South Africa have strong economies and modern cities. Other countries struggle with poverty.

Reviewing Vocabulary, Terms, and Places

Match the words with their definitions.

1. Great Zimbabwe
2. features
3. Boers
4. apartheid
5. sanctions
6. townships
7. escarpment
8. enclave

a. the steep face at the edge of a plateau or other raised area

b. economic or political penalties imposed by one country on another to force a change in policy

c. a large, stone-walled town built by the Shona

d. Afrikaner frontier farmers in South Africa

e. a small territory surrounded by foreign territory

f. characteristics

g. South Africa's policy of separation of races

h. separate areas with clusters of tiny homes for black South Africans

Comprehension and Critical Thinking

SECTION 1 *(Pages 604–607)*

9. **a. Identify** What are the two main deserts in Southern Africa?

   b. Contrast How is the eastern part of Southern Africa different from the western part?

   c. Elaborate How do you think the geography of Southern Africa has affected settlement patterns in the region?

SECTION 2 *(Pages 608–613)*

10. **a. Define** Who are the Afrikaners? What country do they live in?

    b. Contrast How does the origin of Khoisan languages differ from Bantu languages? What is unusual about Khoisan languages?

    c. Elaborate What was life like for non-whites under the policy of apartheid? What rights were blacks, Coloureds, and Asians denied?

SECTION 3 *(Pages 614–619)*

11. a. Analyze In what ways has South Africa changed with the end of apartheid? In what ways has it stayed the same?

b. Evaluate Poverty is the most serious challenge facing Southern Africa. Do you agree or disagree with this statement? Explain your answer.

Social Studies Skills

12. Using a Decision-Making Process In an effort to protect its resources, Madagascar has periodically banned the sale of rosewood, a precious wood used to make furniture, guitars, and other items. With a partner, use a decision-making process and a graphic organizer like the one on page 620 to address whether a ban should be lifted or put in place. Gather information, identify options, and predict consequences. Express your ideas orally based on your experiences and on research. Finally, identify the actions necessary to implement your decision.

Map Activity

13. Southern Africa Match the letters on the map with their correct labels.

Cape of Good Hope	Namib Desert
Okavango Basin	Drakensberg
Orange River	

Using the Internet

14. Activity: Researching Apartheid From 1948 until 1994, many people in South Africa were legally discriminated against under the policy known as apartheid. Imagine that you are a reporter writing an article on the history of apartheid. Through the online book, use both primary and secondary sources to research who started apartheid, how people struggled against it, and when it finally came to an end. Using that information, create an outline for your article. Be sure to include details from your research that support the main ideas.

↗ **hmhsocialstudies.com**

FOCUS ON READING AND VIEWING | *my* **WriteSmart**

15. Making Generalizations Re-read the information about South Africa today in Section 3. Based on the specific information you read, make one generalization about the country's economy and one about its resources.

16. Presenting a TV News Report Review your notes and decide on a topic for your report. Your purpose may be to share interesting information—a recently celebrated holiday, for example. Or your purpose may be more serious—perhaps the need to reduce poverty. Decide what images you will show and what you will say to make your point.

Write a script and identify which visuals go with your content. Include social studies terms, basic vocabulary, and academic vocabulary from your notes. Be sure to use standard grammar, spelling, sentence structure, and punctuation. Present your report to the class using visuals, just as though you were on the TV news. Listen and watch your classmates' reports. Evaluate their reports based on accuracy of the content and visual interest.

Reading Social Studies

Making Generalizations

As you read about different people and cultures, you probably notice many similarities. Seeing those similarities may lead you to make a generalization. A generalization is a statement that applies to many different situations or people even though it is based on a few specific situations or people. In the following example, a generalization is made from combining new information with information from personal experience. Sometimes you might also make a generalization from reading about several new situations, even though you don't have personal experience with the situation.

> Several large rivers cross Southern Africa's plains. The Okavango River flows from Angola into a huge basin in Botswana. This river's water never reaches the ocean. Instead it forms a swampy inland delta that is home to crocodiles, zebras, hippos, and other animals. Many tourists travel to Botswana to see these wild animals in their natural habitat.
>
> *From Section 1, Physical Geography*

1. What you read:
Tourists will travel to see wild animals.

2. What you know from personal experience:
My family loves to see wild animals in the zoo.

Generalization:
Many people enjoy seeing wild animals in person.

YOU TRY IT!

Read the following sentences about four South African countries. Then make a generalization from these four situations about political instability and a country's economy.

> Zimbabwe has suffered from a poor economy and political instability.
>
> Mozambique is one of the world's poorest countries. The economy has been badly damaged by civil war, but it is improving.
>
> Comoros suffers from a lack of resources and political instability. The government of Comoros is struggling to improve education and promote tourism.
>
> Madagascar was ruled for more than 20 years by a socialist dictator. Today the elected president is working to improve the struggling economy.
>
> *From Section 3, Southern Africa Today*

Explaining Cause or Effect

"Why did it happen?" "What were the results?" Questions like these help us identify causes and effects. This, in turn, helps us understand the relationships among physical geography, history, and culture.

Assignment

Use *my*WriteSmart in your eBook to write a paper about:

- the causes of economic problems in West Africa
- the effects of colonization in Southern Africa

1. Prewrite

Choose a Topic

- Choose one of the topics above to write about.
- Turn that topic into a big idea, or thesis. For example, "Three main factors cause most of the economic problems in West Africa."

> **TIP** **What Relationships?** Transitional words like *as a result, because, since,* and *so* can help make connections between causes and effects.

Gather and Organize Information

- Depending on the topic you have chosen, identify at least three causes or three effects. Use your textbook, the library, or the Internet.
- Organize causes or effects in their order of importance. To have the most impact on your readers, put the most important cause or effect last.

2. Write

Use a Writer's Framework

> **A Writer's Framework**
>
> **Introduction**
> - Start with an interesting fact or question related to your big idea, or thesis.
> - State your big idea and provide background information.
>
> **Body**
> - Write at least one paragraph, including supporting facts and examples, for each cause or effect.
> - Organize your causes or effects by order of importance.
>
> **Conclusion**
> - Summarize the causes or effects.
> - Restate your big idea.

3. Evaluate and Revise

Review and Improve Your Paper

- Re-read your paper and use the questions below to determine how to make your paper better.
- Make changes to improve your paper.

Evaluation Questions for a Cause and Effect Explanation

1. Do you begin with a fact or question related to your big idea, or thesis?
2. Does your introduction identify your big idea and provide any needed background?
3. Do you have at least one paragraph for each cause or effect?
4. Do you include facts and details to support the connections between causes and effects?
5. Do you explain the causes or effects in order of importance?
6. Do you summarize the causes or effects and restate your big idea?

4. Proofread and Publish

Give Your Explanation the Finishing Touch

- Make that you use social studies terminology correctly and that transitional words clearly connect causes and effects.
- Check for the use of standard grammar, spelling, sentence structure, and punctuation.
- Confirm your understanding by having someone provide feedback on your paper.

5. Practice and Apply

Use the steps and strategies outlined in this workshop to write your cause-and-effect paper. Share your paper with other students who wrote on the same topic. Compare your lists of causes or effects.

South and East Asia and the Pacific

Himalayas

The highest mountain range in the world, the Himalayas, separates the Indian Subcontinent from the rest of Asia.

The Outback

About 75 to 80 percent of Australia is covered by the Outback, a dry interior region of ancient rocks and plains.

South and East Asia and the Pacific

Rain Forest

The rich green color of Southeast Asia is caused by tropical rain forests. They are home to rare animals like the orangutan, found only in this region.

Explore the Satellite Image
Towering mountains, dense rain forests, and dry plains are all features of this large region in Asia and the Pacific. What other physical features can you see in this satellite image?

The Satellite's Path

>44'56.08<

>>>>>>>>>665.00'87<

567.476.348

+355

+799

+803

+996

456.094.

South and East Asia: Physical

CENTRAL ASIA

Altay Mountains

MONGOLIA

Mongolian Plateau

GOBI DESERT

Tian Shan

Tarim Basin

K2
28,250 ft
(8,610 m)

Taklimakan Desert

Kunlun Shan

CHINA

Plateau of Tibet

PAKISTAN

Mount Everest
29,035 ft
(8,850 m)

NEPAL   BHUTAN

H I M A L A Y A S

Thar Desert

Ganges River

Indus River

BANGLADESH

INDIA

Godavari River

Deccan Plateau

Western Ghats

Krishna R.

Eastern Ghats

Malabar Coast

Ganges Delta

MYANMAR (BURMA)

Qinling Shandi

Huang He (Yellow River)

Sichuan Basin

Chang Jiang (Yangzi River)

North China Plain

Yellow Sea

NORTH KOREA

SOUTH KOREA

Sea of Japan (East Sea)

JAPAN

Hokkaido

Honshu

Shikoku

Kyushu

Ryukyu Islands

East China Sea

Tropic of Cancer

Xi River

TAIWAN

LAOS

THAILAND

VIETNAM

CAMBODIA

Mekong River

Hainan

South China Sea

Luzon

PHILIPPINES

Mindanao

PACIFIC OCEAN

Lakshadweep Islands (INDIA)

Bay of Bengal

Andaman Islands (INDIA)

Gulf of Thailand

BRUNEI

New Guinea

MALDIVES

SRI LANKA

Nicobar Islands (INDIA)

Strait of Malacca

MALAYSIA

SINGAPORE

Borneo

Sulawesi (Celebes)

Moluccas

INDIAN OCEAN

I N D O N E S I A

Sumatra

Java

Timor

TIMOR-LESTE

AUSTRALIA

40°N
30°N
20°N
10°N
0° Equator
10°S

160°
150°E
140°E
130°E
110°E
100°E
70°E

ELEVATION

Feet	Meters
13,120	4,000
6,560	2,000
1,640	500
656	200
(Sea level) 0	0 (Sea level)
Below sea level	Below sea level

0   250   500   750 Miles
0 250 500 750 Kilometers

Projection: Two-Point Equidistant

map zone
Geography Skills

Regions South and East Asia includes many major rivers, long coastal plains, and large islands.

1. **Identify** What major rivers can you see in China and India?

2. **Make Inferences** How do you think rivers influence where people live in this region?

Geographical Extremes: South and East Asia

Longest River	**Chang Jiang (Yangzi River), China:** 3,450 miles (5,552 km)
Highest Point	**Mount Everest, Nepal/China:** 29,035 feet (8,850 m)
Lowest Point	**Turpan Depression, China:** 505 feet (154 m) below sea level
Highest Recorded Temperature	**Turpan Depression, China** 118˚F (48˚C)
Wettest Place	**Mawsynram, India:** 467.4 inches (1,187.2 cm) average precipitation per year
Largest Country	**China:** 3,705,407 square miles (9,596,960 square km)
Smallest Country	**Maldives:** 116 square miles (300 square km)
Largest Rain Forest	**Indonesia:** 386,000 square miles (999,740 square km)
Strongest Earthquake	**Off the coast of Sumatra, Indonesia, on December 26, 2004:** Magnitude 9.1

Mount Everest

Size Comparison: The United States and South and East Asia

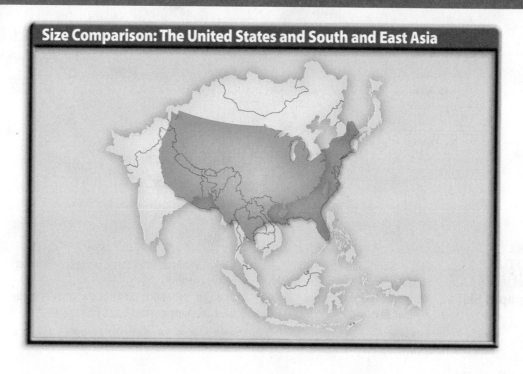

South and East Asia: Political

RUSSIA

CENTRAL ASIA

MONGOLIA
Ulaanbaatar ✪

NORTH KOREA
Pyongyang ✪
✪ Seoul
SOUTH KOREA

Sea of Japan (East Sea)

Tokyo ✪
JAPAN

PACIFIC OCEAN

40°N

30°N

Beijing ✪

Yellow Sea

Islamabad ✪
KASHMIR

CHINA

Shanghai

Huang He (Yellow River)

East China Sea

150°E

PAKISTAN

Chongqing
Chang Jiang (Yangzi River)

Tropic of Cancer

Karachi
New Delhi ✪
NEPAL
Kathmandu ✪
BHUTAN
Thimphu ✪

Taipei
TAIWAN

Indus River
Ganges River
Dhaka ✪
Kolkata (Calcutta)
MYANMAR (BURMA)

Hong Kong

N
W E
S

20°N

INDIA

BANGLADESH
Naypyidaw
LAOS
Vientiane ✪
Hanoi ✪

Manila ✪

140°E

Mumbai (Bombay)
Hyderabad

Bay of Bengal

Yangon (Rangoon)
THAILAND ✪
VIETNAM

South China Sea

PHILIPPINES

130°E

Bangalore
Chennai (Madras)

Bangkok ✪
CAMBODIA
Phnom Penh ✪

10°N

MALDIVES
Colombo
SRI LANKA
Male ✪

BRUNEI
Bandar Seri Begawan ✪

MALAYSIA

0° Equator

INDIAN OCEAN

Kuala Lumpur ✪
Singapore ✪ SINGAPORE

INDONESIA

Dili ✪
TIMOR-LESTE

120°E

10°S

✪ National capital
• Other cities

0   250   500   750 Miles
0 250 500 750 Kilometers

Projection: Two-Point Equidistant

Jakarta ✪

AUSTRALIA

20°S

70°E
80°E
90°E
100°E
110°E

30°S

map zone
Geography Skills

Place South and East Asia includes several large countries, many smaller ones, and a number of island countries.

1. **Name** What are the three largest countries in this region?

2. **Analyze** What do you notice about the locations of many capital cities?

South and East Asia and the Pacific

South and East Asia: Population

CENTRAL ASIA

Harbin

Shenyang

Pyongyang

Dalian

Beijing

Seoul

Pusan

Qingdao

Jinan

Zhengzhou

Nanjing

Shanghai

Xi'an

Wuhan

Hangzhou

Chengdu

Chongqing

Taipei

Guangzhou

Hong Kong

Lahore

Delhi

Kanpur

Karachi

Ahmadabad

Kolkata (Calcutta)

Dhaka

Hanoi

Manila

Mumbai (Bombay)

Hyderabad

Yangon (Rangoon)

Bangalore

Chennai (Madras)

Bangkok

Ho Chi Minh City (Saigon)

Colombo

Singapore

Jakarta

Surabaya

Bandung

Sea of Japan (East Sea)

Tokyo

Yokohama

Nagoya

Osaka

Tropic of Cancer

PACIFIC OCEAN

South China Sea

Bay of Bengal

INDIAN OCEAN

AUSTRALIA

40°N

30°N

150°E

140°E

130°E

120°E

110°E

100°E

70°E

20°N

10°N

0° Equator

10°S

20°S

30°S

Persons per square mile	Persons per square km
520	200
260	100
130	50
25	10
3	1
0	0

● Major cities over 2 million

0   250   500   750 Miles

0   250 500 750 Kilometers

Projection: Two-Point Equidistant

map zone
Geography Skills

Regions This region has very large populations.
1. **Name** Based on the map, which two countries do you think have the largest populations?

2. **Compare** Compare this map to the physical map. How does China's physical geography relate to its population patterns?

South and East Asia: Climate

Climate Types

- Humid tropical
- Tropical savanna
- Desert
- Steppe
- Humid subtropical
- Humid continental
- Subarctic
- Highland

0   250   500 Miles

0   250   500 Kilometers

Projection: Two-Point Equidistant

PACIFIC OCEAN

Sea of Japan (East Sea)

Yellow Sea

East China Sea

South China Sea

Tropic of Cancer

Bay of Bengal

INDIAN OCEAN

map zone
Geography Skills

Location Climates in South and East Asia are very different depending on an area's location.

1. **Identify** What is the main climate in the islands of Southeast Asia?

2. **Analyze** Does most of this region have warm climates or cold climates?

South and East Asia and the Pacific

South and East Asia: Land Use and Resources

CENTRAL ASIA

Ürümqi

Islamabad
Lahore
New Delhi
Karachi
Ahmadabad
Mumbai (Bombay)
Hyderabad
Bangalore
Chennai (Madras)
Colombo
Kathmandu
Kolkata (Calcutta)
Dhaka
Naypyidaw
Yangon (Rangoon)

Shenyang
Beijing
Tianjin
Huang He (Yellow River)
Nanjing
Wuhan
Chang Jiang (Yangzi River)
Chongqing
Guangzhou
Hong Kong
Hanoi
Bangkok
Ho Chi Minh City
Kuala Lumpur
Singapore
Jakarta

Pyongyang
Seoul
Pusan
Shanghai
Taipei
Manila

Sea of Japan (East Sea)
Tokyo-Yokohama
Nagoya
Osaka-Kobe-Kyoto

Tropic of Cancer

PACIFIC OCEAN

South China Sea

Bay of Bengal

Indus River
Ganges River
Mekong River

INDIAN OCEAN

0° Equator

AUSTRALIA

Major Resources
- Coal
- Natural gas
- Oil
- Gold
- Silver
- Other minerals
- Fishing
- Major manufacturing and trade centers

Land Use
- Commercial farming
- Nomadic herding
- Forestland
- Subsistence farming
- Limited economic activity

0   250   500   750 Miles
0 250 500 750 Kilometers

Projection: Two-Point Equidistant

map zone Geography Skills

Human-Environment Interaction
People have converted much of this region to farmland. South and East Asia is also rich in resources.

1. **Locate** In which part of China is commercial farming found?
2. **Explain** Why do you think interior parts of Asia have only limited economic activity?

The Pacific Realm: Physical

Islands (U.S.)
— Saipan

MARSHALL ISLANDS

SOUTHEAST ASIA

MICRONESIA

Melekeok
PALAU

Caroline Islands
Palikir

FEDERATED STATES OF MICRONESIA

Majuro

Howland Island (U.S.)

Tarawa

Baker I. (U.S.)

New Ireland

NAURU

New Guinea

PAPUA NEW GUINEA

Bougainville I.

Port Moresby

Honiara

SOLOMON ISLANDS

TUVALU

Funafuti

Wallis & Futuna (FR.)

M E L A N E S I A

Darwin

Cape York Peninsula

Great Barrier Reef

Coral Sea

VANUATU

Port-Vila

FIJI

Suva

New Caledonia (FRANCE)

Noumea

Loyalty Islands (FRANCE)

A U S T R A L I A

O U T B A C K

WESTERN PLATEAU

MACDONNELL RANGES

Uluru (Ayers Rock) 2,845 ft (867 m)

Lake Eyre

Great Artesian Basin

GREAT DIVIDING RANGE

Brisbane

Norfolk Island (AUSTRALIA)

Kermadec Islands (N.Z.)

NULLARBOR PLAIN

Darling R.

Lachlan R.

Sydney

Adelaide

Murray River

Canberra

Mount Kosciusko 7,310 ft (2,228 m)

Melbourne

North Island

Auckland

NEW ZEALAND

Tasman Sea

Mount Cook 12,349 ft (3,764 m)

Wellington

Tasmania

Hobart

Christchurch

South Island

Chatham Islands (N.Z.)

Stewart Island

Auckland Islands (NEW ZEALAND)

ELEVATION

Feet	Meters
13,120	4,000
6,560	2,000
1,640	500
656	200
(Sea level) 0	0 (Sea level)
Below sea level	Below sea level

Ice cap

⊙ National capital

● City

Island boundaries are for convenience only and do not represent international boundaries.

0 — 500 — 1,000 Miles

0 — 500 — 1,000 Kilometers

Projection: Mercator

N
W ✦ E
S

map zone
Geography Skills

Place The continent of Australia dominates the geography of the Pacific realm.

1. **Name** What large island country is located southeast of Australia?

2. **Make Inferences** How do you think this region's island geography influences travel and trade?

South and East Asia and the Pacific

PACIFIC OCEAN

Hawaiian Islands (U.S.)

Midway Islands (U.S.)

Johnston Atoll (U.S.)

Kingman Reef (U.S.)

Palmyra Atoll (U.S.)

Jarvis I. (U.S.)

Tropic of Cancer

20°N

0° Equator

K I R I B A T I

P O L Y N E S I A

Tokelau (N.Z.)

SAMOA

American Samoa (U.S.)

Apia

Cook Islands (NEW ZEALAND)

French Polynesia (FRANCE)

ONGA

Niue (N.Z.)

uku'alofa

Tahiti

20°S

Pitcairn Island (U.K.)

Geographical Extremes: The Pacific Realm

Highest Point	**Mount Wilhelm, Papua New Guinea:** 14,793 feet (4,509 m)
Lowest Point	**Lake Eyre, Australia:** 52 feet (16 m) below sea level
Highest Recorded Temperature	**Cloncurry, Australia:** 128°F (53°C)
Lowest Recorded Temperature	**Charlotte Pass, Australia:** -9°F (-22°C)
Wettest Place	**Bellenden Ker, Australia:** 340 inches (863.6 cm) average precipitation per year
Driest Place	**Mulka, Australia:** 4.1 inches (10.4 cm) average precipitation per year
Largest Country	**Australia:** 2,967,908 square miles (7,686,882 square km)
Smallest Country	**Nauru:** 8 square miles (20.7 square km)
Largest Rain Forest	**Papua New Guinea:** 130,000 square miles (336,700 square km)
Longest Coral Reef	**Great Barrier Reef, Australia:** (1,600 miles (2,600 km)

Antarctica

SOUTHERN OCEAN

Antarctic Circle

Weddell Sea

ANTARCTICA

Antarctic Peninsula

Ronne Ice Shelf

EAST ANTARCTICA

Vinson Massif 16,067 ft (4,897 m)

South Pole

TRANSANTARCTIC MOUNTAINS

WEST ANTARCTICA

Ross Ice Shelf

Ross Sea

SOUTHERN OCEAN

0   500   1,000 Miles

0   500   1,000 Kilometers

Projection: Polar Azimuthal Equidistant

Australia's Great Barrier Reef

Regional Database

South and East Asia and the Pacific

COUNTRY Capital	FLAG	POPULATION	AREA (sq mi)	PER CAPITA GDP (U.S. $)	LIFE EXPECTANCY AT BIRTH	TVS PER 1,000 PEOPLE
Australia Canberra		22.3 million	2,967,909	$43,000	82	716
Bangladesh Dhaka		163.7 million	55,599	$2,100	70.4	7
Bhutan Thimphu		725,296	18,147	$6,800	68.4	6
Brunei Bandar Seri Begawan		415,717	2,228	$55,300	76.6	637
Cambodia Phnom Penh		15.2 million	69,900	$2,400	63.4	9
China Beijing		1,350 million	3,705,407	$9,300	75	291
Fiji Suva		896,758	7,054	$4,900	71.9	110
India New Delhi		1,221 million	1,269,346	$3,900	67.5	75
Indonesia Jakarta		251.2 million	741,100	$5,100	71.9	143
Japan Tokyo		127.3 million	145,883	$36,900	84.2	719
Kiribati Tarawa		103,248	313	$6,100	65.1	23
Laos Vientiane		6.7 million	91,429	$3,100	63.1	10
Malaysia Kuala Lumpur		29.6 million	127,317	$17,200	74.3	174
Maldives Male		393,989	116	$9,400	74.9	38
Marshall Islands Majuro		69,747	70	$8,800	72.3	NA
United States Washington, D.C.		316.7 million	3,794,083	$50,700	78.6	844

COUNTRY / Capital	FLAG	POPULATION	AREA (sq mi)	PER CAPITA GDP (U.S. $)	LIFE EXPECTANCY AT BIRTH	TVS PER 1,000 PEOPLE
Micronesia, Federated States of Palikir		106,104	271	$7,500	72	20
Mongolia Ulaanbaatar		3.2 million	603,909	$5,500	69	58
Myanmar (Burma); Yangon (Rangoon) Naypyidaw		55.2 million	261,970	$1,400	65.6	7
Nauru No official capital		9,434	8	$5,000	66	1
Nepal Kathmandu		30.4 million	54,363	$1,300	66.7	6
New Zealand Wellington		4.4 million	103,738	$30,200	80.8	516
North Korea Pyongyang		24.7 million	46,541	$1,800	69.6	55
Pakistan Islamabad		193.2 million	310,403	$2,900	66.8	105
Palau Melekeok		21,108	177	$10,500	72.3	98
Papua New Guinea Port Moresby		6.4 million	178,704	$2,800	66.7	13
Philippines Manila		105.7 million	115,831	$4,500	72.2	110
Samoa Apia		195,476	1,137	$6,300	72.9	56
Singapore Singapore		5.5 million	268	$61,400	84	341
Solomon Islands Honiara		597,248	10,985	$3,400	74.7	16
South Korea Seoul		49 million	38,023	$32,800	79.6	364
United States Washington, D.C.		316.7 million	3,794,083	$50,700	78.6	844

Regional Database

COUNTRY Capital	FLAG	POPULATION	AREA (sq mi)	PER CAPITA GDP (U.S. $)	LIFE EXPECTANCY AT BIRTH	TVS PER 1,000 PEOPLE
Sri Lanka Colombo		21.7 million	25,332	$6,200	76.2	102
Taiwan Taipei		23.3 million	13,892	$39,400	79.8	327
Thailand Bangkok		67.4 million	198,457	$10,300	74	274
Timor-Leste Dili		1.2 million	5,743	$10,000	67	NA
Tonga Nuku'alofa		106,322	289	$7,700	75.6	61
Tuvalu Funafuti		10,698	10	$3,400	65.5	9
Vanuatu Port-Vila		261,565	4,710	$5,000	72.4	12
Vietnam Hanoi		92.5 million	127,244	$3,600	72.7	184
United States Washington, D.C.		316.7 million	3,794,083	$50,700	78.6	844

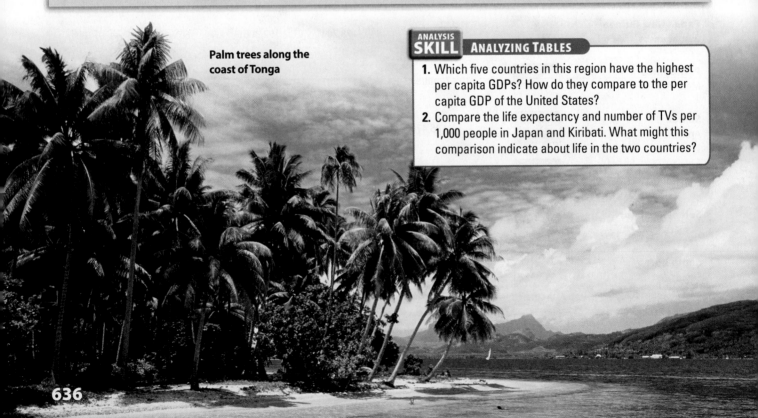

Palm trees along the coast of Tonga

ANALYSIS SKILL **ANALYZING TABLES**

1. Which five countries in this region have the highest per capita GDPs? How do they compare to the per capita GDP of the United States?
2. Compare the life expectancy and number of TVs per 1,000 people in Japan and Kiribati. What might this comparison indicate about life in the two countries?

Population Giants

World's Largest Populations

Country	Population
China	1.350 billion
India	1.221 billion
United States	316.7 million
Indonesia	251.2 million
Brazil	201 million
Pakistan	193.2 million
Nigeria	174.5 million
Bangladesh	163.7 million
Russia	142.5 million
Japan	127.3 million

■ Asian Countries
■ Other Countries

Of the ten countries with the largest populations, six are located in South and East Asia.

Percent of World Population

- Rest of the world 40%
- China 19%
- India 18%
- Rest of Asia 23%

The large populations of China and India help make Asia home to about 60 percent of the world's people.

Economic Powers

Japan

- World's third-largest economy
- $773.9 billion in exports
- Gross Domestic Product $4.7 trillion
- Major exports: transportation equipment, cars, semiconductors, electronics

Japan is one of the most technologically advanced countries and is a leading producer of hi-tech goods.

China

- World's second-largest economy
- $1.6 trillion in exports
- Gross Domestic Product $12.6 trillion
- Major exports: machinery and electronics, clothing, plastics, furniture, toys

China is an emerging economic powerhouse with a huge population and a fast-growing economy.

ANALYSIS SKILL ANALYZING VISUALS

1. Which two countries have the largest populations?
2. What kinds of exports help make Japan and China economic powers?

CHAPTER 26

The Indian Subcontinent

Essential Question

myNotebook

What are the unique geographic and cultural features of the Indian Subcontinent?

Texas Essential Knowledge and Skills (TEKS)

1A, 1B, 2A, 2B, 3A, 3B, 3C, 4B, 4D, 4E, 5A, 5B, 5C, 6A, 6B, 15B, 15D, 15F, 17D, 17E, 18B, 18D, 19A, 19B, 21B, 21C, 21D, 22D

SECTION 1: Physical Geography

FOCUS ON READING AND VIEWING

myWriteSmart

Visualizing As you read, try to visualize the people, place or events that the text describes. Visualizing, or creating mental images, helps you to better understand and remember the information that is presented. Use your senses to imagine how things look, sound, smell, and feel. **See the lesson, Visualizing, on page 661.**

Presenting and Viewing a Travelogue You are journeying through the Indian Subcontinent, noting the sights and sounds of this beautiful and bustling region of the world. As you read this chapter you will gather details about this region. Then you will create an oral presentation of a travelogue, or traveler's journal. After you present your travelogue, you will watch and listen as your classmates present their travelogues. Use the annotation tools in your eBook to gather information for your assignment.

IRAQ

IRAN

○ National capital
● Major city
--- Disputed boundary

0   150   300 Miles
0   150   300 Kilometers

Projection: Albers Equal-Area

SAUDI ARABIA

OMAN

YEMEN

map zone

Geography Skills

Place The Indian Subcontinent is a large landmass in South Asia.

1. **Locate** What bodies of water border the Indian Subcontinent?
2. **Analyze** What separates the Indian Subcontinent from the rest of Asia?

Culture The people of the subcontinent represent the many cultures and religions of the region.

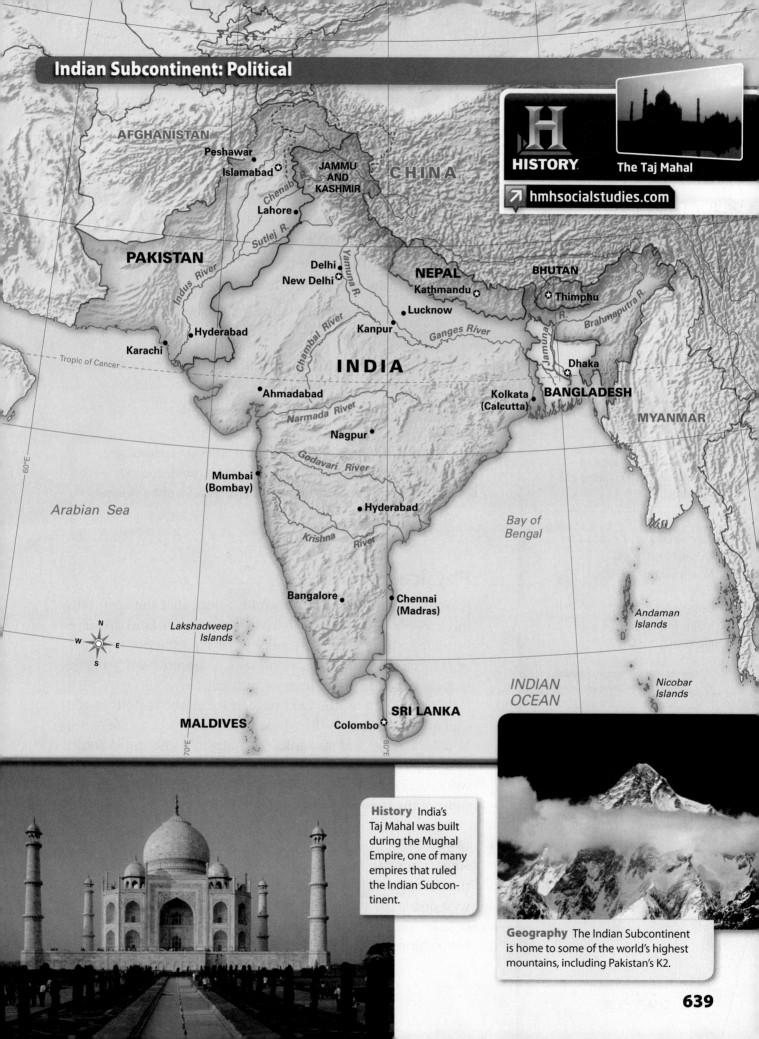

Indian Subcontinent: Political

AFGHANISTAN

Peshawar

Islamabad ✪

JAMMU AND KASHMIR

CHINA

Chenab R.

Lahore

Sutlej R.

PAKISTAN

Indus River

Hyderabad

Karachi

Tropic of Cancer

Delhi

New Delhi ✪

Yamuna R.

NEPAL

Kathmandu ✪

BHUTAN

Thimphu ✪

Brahmaputra R.

Lucknow

Kanpur

Chambal River

Ganges River

INDIA

Jamuna R.

Dhaka ✪

BANGLADESH

Ahmadabad

Narmada River

Kolkata (Calcutta)

MYANMAR

Nagpur

Godavari River

Mumbai (Bombay)

Hyderabad

Bay of Bengal

Arabian Sea

Krishna River

60°E

Andaman Islands

Bangalore

Chennai (Madras)

INDIAN OCEAN

Nicobar Islands

N W E S

Lakshadweep Islands

70°E

80°E

SRI LANKA

MALDIVES

Colombo ✪

639

History India's Taj Mahal was built during the Mughal Empire, one of many empires that ruled the Indian Subcontinent.

Geography The Indian Subcontinent is home to some of the world's highest mountains, including Pakistan's K2.

Physical Geography

 TEKS 3A, 3B, 3C, 4D, 4E, 5A, 5B, 5C, 6A, 6B, 21B, 21C, 22D

What You Will Learn...

Main Ideas

1. Towering mountains, large rivers, and broad plains are the key physical features of the Indian Subcontinent.
2. The Indian Subcontinent has a great variety of climate regions and resources.

The Big Idea

The physical geography of the Indian Subcontinent features unique physical features and a variety of climates and resources.

Key Terms and Places

subcontinent, *p. 640*
Mount Everest, *p. 641*
Ganges River, *p. 641*
delta, *p. 641*
Indus River, *p. 642*
monsoons, *p. 643*

hmhsocialstudies.com
TAKING NOTES

Use the graphic organizer online to take notes on the physical features, climates, and resources of the Indian Subcontinent.

If YOU lived there...

You live in a small farming village in central India. Every year your father talks about the summer monsoons, winds that can bring heavy rains to the region. You know that too much rain can cause floods that may threaten your house and family. Too little rain could cause your crops to fail.

How do you feel about the monsoons?

BUILDING BACKGROUND Weather in the Indian Subcontinent, a region in southern Asia, is greatly affected by monsoon winds. Monsoons are just one of the many unique features of the physical geography of the Indian Subcontinent.

Physical Features

Locate Asia on a map of the world. Notice that the southernmost portion of Asia creates a triangular wedge of land that dips into the Indian Ocean. The piece of land jutting out from the rest of Asia is the Indian Subcontinent. A **subcontinent** is a large landmass that is smaller than a continent.

Use the map on the next page to locate the nations of the Indian Subcontinent—Bangladesh, Bhutan, India, Maldives, Nepal, Pakistan, and Sri Lanka. This region is also called South Asia and it is one of the most diverse geographic regions in the world. Soaring mountains, powerful rivers, and fertile plains are some of the region's dominant features.

Mountains

Huge mountain ranges separate the Indian Subcontinent from the rest of Asia. The rugged Hindu Kush mountains in the northwest divide the subcontinent from Central Asia. For thousands of years, peoples from Asia and Europe have entered the Indian Subcontinent through mountain passes in the Hindu Kush.

Indian Subcontinent: Physical

K2
28,251 ft
(8,611 m)

Hindu Kush
Karakoram Range
HIMALAYAS

IRAN

AFGHANISTAN

CHINA

30°N

Chenab River

Indus River

Sutlej R.

PAKISTAN

Mount
Everest
29,035 ft
(8,850 m)

NEPAL

BHUTAN

Thar
Desert

Gangetic Plain

Tarai

Yamuna R.

Indus
River
Valley

Ganges River

Brahmaputra River

Tropic of Cancer

Chambal R.

BANGLADESH

Narmada River

Ganges
Delta

MYANMAR

20°N

INDIA

N
W   E
S

Godavari River

Gulf of
Khambhat

Deccan
Plateau

Ghats

Bay of
Bengal

Arabian Sea

Krishna River

Western Ghats

Eastern

Coromandel Coast

60°E

70°E

ELEVATION

Feet	Meters
13,120	4,000
6,560	2,000
1,640	500
656	200
(Sea level) 0	0 (Sea level)
Below sea level	Below sea level

0   250   500 Miles
0   250   500 Kilometers

Projection: Albers Equal-Area

Malabar Coast

Gulf of
Mannar

SRI LANKA

10°N

MALDIVES

INDIAN OCEAN

80°E

90°E

Geography Skills

Regions The Indian Subcontinent is separated from the rest of Asia.

1. **Identify** What landforms separate the Indian Subcontinent from the rest of Asia?
2. **Draw Conclusions** How might physical features divide the countries of the Indian Subcontinent?

1 The Himalayas and the Indus River are two key physical features on the Indian Subcontinent.

Two smaller mountain ranges stretch down India's coasts. The Eastern and Western Ghats (GAWTS) are low mountains that separate India's east and west coasts from the country's interior.

Perhaps the most impressive physical features in the subcontinent, however, are the Himalayas. These enormous mountains stretch about 1,500 miles (2,415 km) along the northern border of the Indian Subcontinent. Formed by the collision of two massive tectonic plates, the Himalayas are home to the world's highest mountains. On the border between Nepal and China is **Mount Everest**, the highest mountain on the planet. It measures some 29,035 feet (8,850 m). K2 in northern Pakistan is the world's second highest peak.

Rivers and Plains

Deep in the Himalayas are the sources of some of Asia's mightiest rivers. Two major river systems—the Ganges (GAN-jeez) and the Indus—originate in the Himalayas. Each carries massive amounts of water from the mountains' melting snow and glaciers. For thousands of years, these rivers have flooded the surrounding land, leaving rich soil deposits and fertile plains.

India's most important river is the Ganges. The **Ganges River** flows across northern India and into Bangladesh. There, the Ganges joins with other rivers and creates a huge delta. A **delta** is a landform at the mouth of a river created by sediment deposits. Along the length of the Ganges is a vast area of rich soil and fertile farmland.

FOCUS ON
READING
What words in this paragraph help you to visualize the information?

Indian Subcontinent: Precipitation

0 — 250 — 500 Miles
0 — 250 — 500 Kilometers
Projection: Albers Equal-Area

PAKISTAN

NEPAL BHUTAN

INDIA

BANGLADESH

20°N

Arabian
Sea

Bay
of
Bengal

10°N

MALDIVES

70°E

SRI
LANKA

INDIAN OCEAN

ANNUAL PRECIPITATION

Inches		Centimeters
Over 80		Over 203
60–80		152–203
40–60		102–152
20–40		51–102
10–20		25–51
Under 10		Under 25

← Dry monsoon air flow (Winter)

→ Wet monsoon air flow (Summer)

Summer monsoons often bring heavy rains and fertile growing conditions to many places in the Indian Subcontinent.

During the winter, monsoons change direction, bringing dry air from the north to the subcontinent. Little rain falls during this time of year.

map zone Geography Skills

Place Monsoons bring both wet and dry conditions to the Indian Subcontinent.

1. **Identify** Which country receives the least precipitation?
2. **Draw Conclusions** How do monsoons affect the amount of precipitation in the Indian Subcontinent?

Known as the Ganges Plain, this region is India's farming heartland.

Likewise, Pakistan's **Indus River** also creates a fertile plain known as the Indus River Valley. This valley was once home to the earliest Indian civilizations. Today, it is Pakistan's most densely populated region.

Other Features

Other geographic features are scattered throughout the subcontinent. South of the Ganges Plain, for example, is a large, hilly plateau called the Deccan. East of the Indus Valley is the Thar (TAHR), or Great Indian Desert. Marked by rolling sand dunes, parts of this desert receive as little as 4 inches (100 mm) of rain per year. Still another geographic region is the Tarai (tuh-RY) in southern Nepal. It has fertile farmland and tropical jungles.

READING CHECK Summarizing What are the physical features of the Indian Subcontinent?

Climates and Resources

Just as the physical features of the Indian Subcontinent differ, so do its climates and resources. A variety of climates and natural resources exist throughout the region.

Climate Regions

From the Himalayas' snow-covered peaks to the dry Thar Desert, the climates of the Indian Subcontinent differ widely. In the Himalayas, a highland climate brings cool temperatures to much of Nepal and Bhutan. The plains south of the Himalayas have a humid subtropical climate. Hot, humid summers with plenty of rainfall are common in this important farming region.

Tropical climates dominate much of the subcontinent. The tropical savanna climate in central India and Sri Lanka keeps temperatures there warm all year long. This region experiences wet and dry seasons during the year. A humid tropical climate brings warm temperatures and heavy rains to parts of southwest India, Sri Lanka, Maldives, and Bangladesh.

The remainder of the subcontinent has dry climates. Desert and steppe climates extend throughout southern and western India and most of Pakistan.

Monsoons have a huge influence on the weather and climates in the subcontinent. **Monsoons** are seasonal winds that bring either moist or dry air to an area. From June to October, summer monsoons bring moist air up from the Indian Ocean, causing heavy rains. Flooding often accompanies these summer monsoons. In 2005, for example, the city of Mumbai (Bombay), India received some 37 inches (94 cm) of rain in just 24 hours. However, in winter the monsoons change direction, bringing dry air from the north. Because of this, little rain falls from November to January.

Natural Resources

A wide variety of resources are found on the Indian Subcontinent. Agricultural and mineral resources are the most plentiful.

Perhaps the most important resource is the region's fertile soil. Farms produce many different crops, such as tea, rice, nuts, and jute, a plant used for making rope. Timber and livestock are also key resources in the subcontinent, particularly in Nepal and Bhutan.

The Indian Subcontinent also has an abundance of mineral resources. Large deposits of iron ore and coal are found in India. Pakistan has natural gas reserves, while Sri Lankans mine many gemstones.

READING CHECK **Summarizing** What climates and resources are located in this region?

SUMMARY AND PREVIEW In this section you learned about the wide variety of physical features, climates, and resources in the Indian Subcontinent. Next, you will learn about the rich history and culture of this unique region.

Section 1 Assessment

Reviewing Ideas, Terms, and Places

1. **a. Define** What is a **subcontinent**?
   b. Make Inferences Why do you think the **Indus River** Valley is so heavily populated?
   c. Rank Which physical features in the Indian Subcontinent would you most want to visit? Why?
2. **a. Identify** What natural resources are found in the Indian Subcontinent?
   b. Analyze What are some of the benefits and drawbacks of **monsoons**?

Critical Thinking

3. **Drawing Inferences** Draw a chart like the one shown here. Using your notes, write a sentence explaining how each aspect affects life on the Indian Subcontinent.

	Effect on Life
Physical Features	
Climates	
Natural Resources	

FOCUS ON VIEWING

my WriteSmart

4. **Telling about Physical Geography** What information and images of the region's physical geography might you include in your travelogue? Jot down some ideas.

History and Culture of India

 TEKS 1A, 1B, 2A, 2B, 15A, 15B, 15F, 17D, 17E, 19A, 21B, 21C, 21D, 22D

What You Will Learn...

Main Ideas

1. Advanced civilizations and powerful empires shaped the early history of India.
2. Powerful empires controlled India for hundreds of years.
3. Independence from Great Britain led to the division of India into several countries.
4. Indian culture is shaped by many things, including religion and a caste system.

The Big Idea

Ancient civilizations and powerful empires have shaped the history and culture of India.

Key Terms and Places

Delhi, *p. 646*
colony, *p. 646*
partition, *p. 647*
Hinduism, *p. 648*
Buddhism, *p. 648*
caste system, *p. 648*

hmhsocialstudies.com
TAKING NOTES

Use the graphic organizer online to take notes on the history and culture of India.

If YOU lived there...

You live in New Delhi, India's capital city. Museums in your city display artifacts from some of India's oldest civilizations. People can visit beautiful buildings built by powerful empires. Statues and parades celebrate your country's independence.

How does your city celebrate India's history?

BUILDING BACKGROUND The Indian Subcontinent has a rich and interesting history. Ancient civilizations, powerful empires, rule by foreigners, and the struggle for independence have shaped not only the history, but also the culture of India and its neighbors.

Early Civilizations and Empires

India, the largest country on the Indian Subcontinent, is one of the world's oldest civilizations. Early civilizations and empires greatly influenced the history of the Indian Subcontinent.

India's History

Ancient Civilizations

- Around 2300 BC the Harappan civilization begins in the Indus River Valley.

- Beginning in about 1500, Indo-Aryan language speakers from Central Asia move into the Indus Valley, bringing their language, Sanskrit, with them.

Harappan artifact

Early Empires

- By 233 BC the Mauryan Empire controls most of the Indian Subcontinent.

- Emperor Asoka helps spread Buddhism in India.

- Indian trade and culture flourish during the Gupta Empire.

Mauryan troops atop a war elephant

Ancient Civilizations

The Indus River Valley in Pakistan supported one of the world's largest ancient civilizations. It is often called the Harappan civilization after its first discovered city, Harappa. Harappa was one of at least eight major Harappan cities that flourished between 3000 BC and 1700 BC. All were trade centers located along waterways. Archaeologists believe that over 30,000 people may have lived in Mohenjo-Daro, the best-known Indus city.

Archaeologists have uncovered a wealth of Harappan artifacts and ruins. Still the end of Harappan civilization is shrouded in mystery. Some scholars believe the Indus River may have changed its course. This could have caused destructive floods in some cities, and water shortages and transportation problems for others.

There is also little evidence to explain how Sanskrit, an Indo-Aryan language, spread into the region. Some scholars believe that, beginning in about 1500 BC, small groups of Indo-Aryan language speakers began to migrate into the Indus Valley from Central Asia. They likely encountered and mixed with the descendants of the Indus Valley civilizations. Over time their language, Sanskrit, became the main language in northern India.

Early Empires

In about 320 BC a ruler by the name of Chandragupta Maurya united nearly all of northern India, Afghanistan, and parts of Asia into the Mauryan Empire. Under Chandragupta, trade flourished, farming improved, and weights and measures were made standard. Asoka, one of the greatest Mauryan emperors, helped expand the empire and improve trade. Asoka also encouraged the acceptance of other religions. After his death, however, the empire slowly crumbled. Power struggles and invasions destroyed the Mauryan Empire.

After the fall of the Mauryan Empire, India split into many small kingdoms. Eventually, however, a strong new empire gained **influence**. In the AD 300s, the Gupta Empire united much of northern India. Under Gupta rulers, trade and culture thrived. Scholars made important advances in math, medicine, and astronomy. Indian mathematicians, for example, first introduced the concept of zero.

Gradually, the Gupta Empire also declined. Attacks by invaders such as the Hun from Central Asia weakened the empire. By about 550, India was once again divided.

> **READING CHECK** **Summarizing** How did early civilizations and empires influence India?

ACADEMIC VOCABULARY

influence
the ability to change, or have an effect on

The Mughal Empire

- Babur establishes the Mughal Empire in northern India in 1526.

- Indian trade, culture, and religion thrive under the rule of Akbar the Great.

- By 1700 the Mughal Empire rules almost all of the Indian Subcontinent.

The first Mughal emperor, Babur

The British Empire

- The British East India Company establishes trade in northern India in the early 1600s.

- Indian troops trigger a massive revolt against the East India Company.

- The British government takes direct control of India in 1858.

- India and Pakistan gain independence in 1947.

Indian troop in the British Army

Mohandas Gandhi
(1869–1948)

Considered by many to be the father of modern India, Mohandas Gandhi led the struggle for Indian independence. As a leading member of the Indian National Congress, Gandhi introduced a policy of nonviolent resistance to British rule. He led millions in fasts, peaceful protest marches, and boycotts of British goods. His devotion to nonviolence earned him the name *Mahatma*, or "Great Soul." Gandhi's efforts proved successful. In 1947 India won its independence from Britain.

Drawing Conclusions Why did people call Gandhi *Mahatma*?

VIDEO
Gandhi

hmhsocialstudies.com

Powerful Empires

Powerful empires controlled India for much of its history. First the Mughal Empire and then the British Empire ruled India for hundreds of years.

The Mughal Empire

In the late 600s Muslim armies began launching raids into India. Some Muslims tried to take over Indian kingdoms. Turkish Muslims, for example, established a powerful kingdom at **Delhi** in northern India. In the 1500s a new group of Muslim invaders swept into the subcontinent. Led by the great warrior Babur (BAH-boohr), they conquered much of India. In 1526 Babur established the Mughal (MOO-guhl) Empire.

Babur's grandson, Akbar, was one of India's greatest rulers. Under Akbar's rule, trade flourished. Demand for Indian goods like spices and tea grew. The Mughal Empire grew rich from trade.

Akbar and other Mughal rulers also promoted culture. Although the Mughals were Muslim, most Indians continued to practice Hinduism. Akbar's policy of religious tolerance, or acceptance, encouraged peace throughout his empire. Architecture also thrived in the Mughal Empire. One of India's most spectacular buildings, the Taj Mahal, was built during Mughal rule.

The British Empire

The Mughals were not the only powerful empire in India. As early as the 1500s Europeans had tried to control parts of India. One European country, England, rose to power as the Mughal Empire declined.

The English presence in India began in the 1600s. At the time, European demand for Indian goods, such as cotton and sugar, was very high. Mughal rulers granted the East India Company, a British trading company, valuable trading rights.

At first, the East India Company controlled small trading posts. However, the British presence in India gradually grew. The East India Company expanded its territory and its power. By the mid-1800s the company controlled more than half of the Indian Subcontinent. India had become a British **colony**, a territory inhabited and controlled by people from a foreign land.

British rule angered and frightened many Indians. The East India Company controlled India with the help of an army made up mostly of Indian troops commanded by British officers. In 1857 Indian troops revolted, triggering violence all across India. The British government crushed the rebellion and took control of India away from the East India Company. With that, the British government began to rule India directly.

READING CHECK **Analyzing** How did powerful empires affect Indian history?

Independence and Division

By the late 1800s many Indians had begun to question British rule. Upset by their position as second-class citizens, a group of Indians created the Indian National Congress. Their goal was to gain more rights and opportunities.

As more and more Indians became dissatisfied with British rule, they began to demand independence. Mohandas Gandhi was the most important leader of this Indian independence movement. During the 1920s and 1930s his strategy of nonviolent protest convinced millions of Indians to support independence.

Finally, Great Britain agreed to make India independent. However, tensions between the Hindu and Muslim communities caused a crisis. Fearing they would have little say in the new government, India's Muslims called for a separate nation.

In part to avoid a civil war, the British government agreed to the **partition**, or division, of India. In 1947 two countries were formed. India was mostly Hindu. Pakistan, which included the area that is now Bangladesh, was mostly Muslim. As a result, some 10 million people rushed to cross the border. To avoid religious persecution, Muslims and Hindus wanted to live in the country where their religion held a majority.

Soon after India and Pakistan won their independence, other countries in the region gradually did too. Sri Lanka and Maldives gained their independence from Great Britain. In 1971, after a bloody civil war that killed almost 1 million people, East Pakistan broke away to form the country of Bangladesh.

READING CHECK **Identifying Cause and Effect** What were the effects of Indian independence from Great Britain?

FOCUS ON READING
As you read this paragraph, visualize the events described. Draw a rough sketch to depict what you imagine.

The Partition of India

Following the partition, riots claimed the lives of as many as one million Indians and created a massive refugee crisis. Hindus and Muslims who found themselves on the wrong side of the new border crowded onto trains that would take them to their new homelands in India and Pakistan.

Indian Culture

India's rich culture has been shaped by many factors. History, geography, language, the arts, and interactions with other cultures have all played a part. So too have religion and a social class system.

Religion

Religion has played a very important role in Indian history. In fact, India is the birthplace of several major religions, including Hinduism and Buddhism.

Hinduism One of the world's oldest religions is **Hinduism**, the dominant religion of India. According to Hindu beliefs, everything in the universe is part of a single spirit called Brahman. Hindus believe that their ultimate goal is to reunite their souls with that spirit. Hinduism teaches that souls are reincarnated, or reborn, many times before they join with Brahman.

Buddhism Another Indian religion is Buddhism, which began in northern India in the late 500s BC. **Buddhism** is a religion based on the teachings of Siddhartha Gautama—the Buddha. According to the Buddha's teachings, people can rise above their desire for material goods and reach nirvana. Nirvana is a state of perfect peace in which suffering and reincarnation end.

Caste System

India's social class system dates to ancient times. Ancient India was organized into many social classes called castes. Over centuries, these groups developed into a **caste system**, a class structure that divided Indian society into groups based on a person's birth or occupation. This system has four main classes, each of which is further divided into many castes. Moreover, a number of castes exist below this structure. Some people in these castes are considered untouchables because they hold unpleasant jobs that are seen as impure.

READING CHECK **Analyzing** How do religion and the caste system influence Indian culture?

SUMMARY AND PREVIEW In this section you learned about the rich history and culture of the Indian Subcontinent. Next, you will learn about India today.

Section 2 Assessment

Reviewing Ideas, Terms, and Places

1. **a. Identify** What different peoples ruled India?
   b. Analyze How did these early civilizations and empires influence Indian culture?
2. **a. Describe** What were some accomplishments of the Mughal Empire?
   b. Predict How might Indian history have been different if the British had not ruled India?
3. **a. Recall** Who was the leader of India's independence movement?
   b. Explain What led to the **partition** of India?
4. **a. Define** What is the **caste system**?
   b. Elaborate Why do you think India is home to some of the world's oldest religions?

Critical Thinking

5. **Summarizing** Use your notes and a diagram like the one here to write a sentence summarizing each aspect of Indian history and culture.

| Early History | Foreign Rule |
| Self-Rule | Culture |

Focus on Viewing

my WriteSmart

6. **Discussing History and Culture** Which details about India's history and culture will you use? How will you explain and illustrate them?

Creating a Line Graph

Learn

Line graphs are drawings that display information in a clear, visual form. People often use line graphs to track changes over time. For example, you may want to see how clothing prices change from year to year. Line graphs also provide an easy way to see patterns, like increases or decreases, that emerge over time. Use the following guidelines to analyze a line graph.

- Read the title. The title will tell you about the subject of the line graph.

- Examine the labels. Note the type of information in the graph, the time period, and the units of measure.

- Analyze the information. Be sure to look for patterns that emerge over time.

Average Monthly Precipitation, Dhaka, Bangladesh

Source: *National Geographic Atlas of the World, Seventh Edition*

Practice

Examine the line graph carefully, then answer the questions below.

1. What is the subject of this line graph?

2. What units of measure are used? What period of time does the line graph reflect?

3. What pattern does the line graph indicate? How can you tell?

Apply

Create a line graph that tracks your grades in a particular class. Start by organizing your grades by the date of the assignment. Then plot your grades on a line graph. Be sure to use labels and a title to identify the subject and information presented in your line graph. Finally, organize information from the graph into a summary statement that describes any patterns that you see in your grades.

India Today

TEKS 3B, 4B, 15B, 18B, 18D, 19A, 19B, 21B, 21C, 22D

What You Will Learn...

Main Ideas

1. Daily life in India is centered around cities, villages, and religion.
2. Today India faces many challenges, including a growing population and economic development.

The Big Idea

India today features a blend of modern and traditional culture, a rapidly growing population, and a developing economy.

Key Terms and Places

Mumbai (Bombay), *p. 650*
Kolkata (Calcutta), *p. 650*
Sikhism, *p. 651*
urbanization, *p. 652*
green revolution, *p. 653*

hmhsocialstudies.com
TAKING NOTES

Use the graphic organizer online to take notes about daily life and challenges in India today.

If YOU lived there...

You live in Mumbai, India's largest city. A major port, Mumbai is home to many industries, such as textiles and electronics. Museums and theaters offer entertainment. Every year, thousands of people flock to Mumbai in search of jobs or to enroll in its universities. The streets are crowded, and pollution is often heavy.

Do you enjoy living in Mumbai? Why or why not?

BUILDING BACKGROUND India has undergone many changes since gaining its independence from Great Britain. Cities have grown dramatically, new businesses and industries have developed, and the population has exploded. India today faces many challenges.

Daily Life in India

Nearly 1.2 billion people live in India today. This huge population represents modern India's many different ethnic groups, religions, and lifestyles. Despite these many differences, city life, village life, and religion all help unite the people of India.

Cities

Millions of Indians live in large, bustling cities. In fact, India's three largest cities, **Mumbai (Bombay),** Delhi, and **Kolkata (Calcutta),** are among the world's most populous cities. Many people in Indian cities work in factories and offices. Some cities, like Bangalore and Mumbai, are home to universities, research centers, and high-tech businesses. Most city-dwellers, however, struggle to earn a living. Those who live in slums often live in makeshift shacks with no plumbing and little access to clean water.

Villages

Most Indians still live in rural areas. Hundreds of thousands of villages are home to more than 70 percent of India's population. Most villagers work as farmers and live with an extended family in simple homes.

Religion

In Indian cities and villages, religion plays a key role in daily life. While most Indians practice Hinduism, many people follow other religions such as Islam and traditional religions. In addition, millions of Indians practice three native religions, Sikhism, Buddhism, and Jainism. **Sikhism embraces equality for all, belief in one God, service to humanity, and honest labor.**

Religious celebrations are an important part of Indian life. One of India's most popular holidays is Diwali. Called the festival of lights, Diwali is a new year celebration marked by festivals, gift giving and family gatherings. As part of the festival, Hindus light small oil lamps that symbolize the victory of good over evil.

Vaisakhi is one of the most popular days in the Sikh calendar. The holiday originated as a harvest festival in Punjab. All Punjabis celebrate the day with parades, dancing, and singing. For Sikhs, however, Vaisakhi also has special religious significance. It marks the Sikh New Year and honors the establishment of the *Khalsa*, or the community of initiated Sikhs.

READING CHECK Contrasting How does life in Indian cities and villages differ?

Close-up

Diwali: The Festival of Lights

Diwali, or the festival of lights, is one of the most important celebrations in India. A variety of activities on each of the five days of Diwali celebrate Hindu, Sikh, and Jain beliefs.

Beautiful firework displays are common during Diwali.

Elaborate chalk designs, called *rangolis*, often decorate floors and walls.

Diwali is a time to spend with friends and family. Cards and small gifts, such as sweets and candles, are often exchanged.

ANALYSIS SKILL ANALYZING VISUALS

What elements of Indian daily life do you see in the illustration?

Small oil lamps, or *diyas*, decorate homes inside and out.

India's Challenges

India has undergone drastic changes since gaining independence. Today the country faces several challenges, such as dealing with a growing population and managing its economic development.

Population

With more than 1 billion people, India is the world's second most populous country. Only China has a larger population. India's population has grown rapidly, doubling since 1947. This huge population growth places a strain on India's environment and many of its resources, including food, housing, and schools.

India's cities are particularly affected by the growing population. As the country's population has grown, urbanization has taken place. **Urbanization** is the increase in the percentage of people who live in cities. Many millions of people have moved to India's cities in search of jobs.

Government and Economy

Since India gained independence, its leaders have strengthened the government and economy. Today India is the world's

India: Population

map zone

Geography Skills

Regions India is one of the world's most densely populated countries.
1. **Identify** What regions in India are the least populated?
2. **Draw Conclusions** What geographic feature in northeastern India attracts high population densities?

CHINA

PAKISTAN

Delhi

NEPAL

BHUTAN

INDIA

Kolkata (Calcutta)

BANGLADESH

Ahmadabad

Mumbai (Bombay)

Hyderabad

Bay of Bengal

Arabian Sea

Bangalore

Chennai (Madras)

SRI LANKA

INDIAN OCEAN

0° Equator

Streets like this one in Delhi are crowded due to India's rapid urbanization.

Major Cities
- ● Over 10 million inhabitants
- ● 5 to 9 million inhabitants
- · 100,000 people

0   250   500 Miles
0   250   500 Kilometers

Projection: Lambert Conformal Conic

largest democracy and one of the strongest nations in Asia. The greatest challenges facing India's government are providing for a growing population and resolving conflicts with its neighbor, Pakistan. Both India and Pakistan have nuclear weapons.

India's gross domestic product (GDP) places it among the world's top 5 industrial countries. However, its per capita, or per person, GDP is only $3,900. As a result, millions of Indians live in poverty.

India's government has taken steps to reduce poverty. In the 1960s and 1970s the **green revolution**, a program that encouraged farmers to adopt modern agricultural methods, helped farmers produce more food. Recently, the government has succeeded in attracting many high-tech businesses to India.

READING CHECK **Finding Main Ideas** What are India's government and economy like?

SUMMARY AND PREVIEW India today faces many challenges as it continues to modernize. Next, you will learn about India's neighbors on the subcontinent.

CONNECTING TO Economics

Bollywood

One of India's largest industries is its moviemaking industry. Much of India's film industry is located in Mumbai (Bombay). Many people refer to the industry as Bollywood—a combination of Bombay and Hollywood. Bollywood produces more films every year than any other country. In fact, each year India produces almost twice the number of films produced in the United States. In recent years, Bollywood films have become increasingly popular outside of India—particularly in the United Kingdom and the United States.

Drawing Conclusions How might the film industry affect India's economy?

Section 3 Assessment

hmhsocialstudies.com
ONLINE QUIZ

Reviewing Ideas, Terms, and Places

1. **a. Explain** What is the significance of Diwali? Vaisakhi?
   b. Compare and Contrast In what ways are Indian cities similar to cities in the United States? How are they different from U.S. cities?
   c. Elaborate Why do you think that a majority of Indians live in villages?

2. **a. Recall** What is **urbanization**? What is one cause of urbanization?
   b. Make Inferences How did the **green revolution** affect India's economy?
   c. Predict What effects might India's growing population have on its resources and environment in the future?

Critical Thinking

3. **Finding Main Ideas** Using your notes and the web diagram, write the main idea for each element of India today.

Cities and Villages · Population · India Today · Government · Economy

FOCUS ON VIEWING

my WriteSmart

4. **Telling about India Today** You will need some images, or pictures, for your travelogue. What images can you use to tell about India today?

SECTION 4

What You Will Learn...

Main Ideas

1. Many different ethnic groups and religions influence the culture of India's neighbors.
2. Rapid population growth, ethnic conflicts, and environmental threats are major challenges to the region today.

The Big Idea

Despite cultural differences, the countries that border India share similar challenges.

Key Terms and Places

Sherpas, *p. 654*
Kashmir, *p. 655*
Dhaka, *p. 656*
Kathmandu, *p. 656*

hmhsocialstudies.com

TAKING NOTES

Use the graphic organizer online to take notes on the culture and issues in the countries that border India.

India's Neighbors

If YOU lived there...

You live in the mountainous country of Bhutan. For many years Bhutan's leaders kept the country isolated from outsiders. Recently, they have begun to allow more tourists to enter the country. Some of your neighbors believe that tourism will greatly benefit the country. Others think it could harm the environment.

How do you feel about tourism in Bhutan?

BUILDING BACKGROUND After years of isolation or control by Great Britain, the 1900s brought great changes to the countries on the Indian Subcontinent. Today these countries face rapid population growth and economic and environmental concerns.

Culture

Five countries—Pakistan, Bangladesh, Nepal, Bhutan, and Sri Lanka—share the subcontinent with India. Though they are neighbors, these countries have significantly different cultures.

People

The cultures of the countries that border India reflect the customs of many ethnic groups. For example, the **Sherpas**, an ethnic group from the mountains of Nepal, often serve as guides through the Himalayas. Members of Bhutan's largest ethnic group originally came from Tibet, a region in southern China. Many of Sri Lanka's Tamil (TA-muhl) people came from India to work the country's huge plantations.

Religion

As you can see on the map on the next page, a variety of religions exist on the Indian Subcontinent. Most countries, like India, have one major religion. In Pakistan and Bangladesh, for example, most people practice Islam and small portions of the population follow Hinduism, Christianity, and tribal religions. In Nepal, the dominant religion is Hinduism, although Buddhism is practiced in some parts of the country. Buddhism dominates both Bhutan and Sri Lanka.

READING CHECK **Contrasting** In what ways are the cultures of this region different?

Religions of the Indian Subcontinent

0   250   500 Miles
0   250   500 Kilometers
Projection: Albers Equal-Area

map zone **Geography Skills**

Regions People in the Indian Subcontinent practice a variety of religions.
1. **Identify** Which religion dominates Pakistan?
2. **Analyze** In which country are the most religions practiced?

Legend:
- Buddhism
- Christianity
- Hinduism
- Islam
- Jainism
- Sikhism
- Traditional religions

PAKISTAN
NEPAL
BHUTAN
BANGLADESH
INDIA
SRI LANKA

Tropic of Cancer
Arabian Sea
20°N
Bay of Bengal
10°N
70°E
90°E

Religions of the Indian Subcontinent

- Hinduism — 58%
- Islam — 29%
- Christianity — 3%
- Traditional religions — 5%
- Buddhism — 2%
- Sikhism — 2%
- Jainism — >1%

The Region Today

Like India, the other nations of the subcontinent face a variety of challenges. Two of the greatest challenges are population growth and poverty.

Pakistan

One of the greatest challenges Pakistan faces is the lack of government stability. Since its creation in 1947, Pakistan has suffered from rebellions and assassinations of government leaders. In 2001, General Pervez Musharraf came to power in a military coup. Under pressure from protestors calling for democracy, Musharraf resigned in 2008. Pakistanis then elected Asif Ali Zardari as president.

Another challenge is Pakistan's rapid population growth. The country's government struggles to manage resources and to reduce poverty.

Relations with India are another important issue in Pakistan today. Since the partition in 1947, the two countries have clashed over the territory of **Kashmir**. Both India and Pakistan claim control of the region. Today Pakistan controls western Kashmir while India controls the east. Armed troops from both countries guard a "line of control" that divides Kashmir.

Since 2001 Pakistan has aided the United States in its war on terrorism. Pakistan's military has arrested hundreds of terrorists and provided information about suspected terrorists. Despite this crackdown, however, many people believe that there are still terrorists within Pakistan's borders.

FOCUS ON READING
Visualize the information described in this paragraph. Describe what mental images you see.

Bangladesh

Bangladesh is a small country about the same size as the state of Wisconsin. Despite its small size, Bangladesh's population is almost half the size of the U.S. population. As a result, it is one of the world's most densely populated countries with some 3,018 people per square mile (1,165 per square km). The capital and largest city, **Dhaka** (DA-kuh), is home to more than 13 million people. Overcrowding is not limited to urban areas, however. Rural areas are also densely populated.

Flooding is one of Bangladesh's biggest challenges. Many <u>circumstances</u> cause these floods. The country's many streams and rivers flood annually, often damaging farms and homes. Summer monsoons also cause flooding. For example, massive flooding in 2004 left more than 25 million people homeless. It also destroyed schools, farms, and roads throughout the country.

Nepal

The small kingdom of Nepal also faces many challenges today. Its population is growing rapidly. In fact, the population has more than doubled in the last 30 years. **Kathmandu** (kat-man-DOO), the nation's capital and largest city, is troubled by overcrowding and poverty. Thousands have moved to Kathmandu in search of jobs and better opportunities. As a result of population growth and poor resources, Nepal is one of the world's least-developed nations.

Nepal also faces environmental threats. As the population grows, more and more land is needed to grow enough food. To meet this need, farmers clear forests to create more farmland. This deforestation causes soil erosion and harms the wildlife in the region. Nepal's many tourists add to the problem as they use valuable resources and leave behind trash.

Bhutan

Bhutan is a small mountain kingdom that lies in the Himalayas between India and China. Because of the rugged mountains, Bhutan has been isolated throughout much of its history. This isolation limited outside influences until the 1900s, when Bhutan's king established ties first with Great Britain and later with India. By the mid-1900s Bhutan had ended its long isolation. Efforts to modernize Bhutan resulted in the construction of new roads, schools, and hospitals.

Today Bhutan continues to develop economically. Most Bhutanese earn a living as farmers, growing rice, potatoes, and corn. Some raise livestock like yaks, pigs,

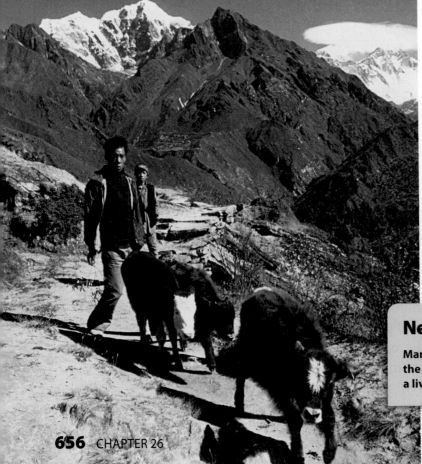

Nepal

Many of Nepal's people live in the rugged Himalayas and earn a living herding animals.

and horses. Another important industry is tourism. The government, however, limits the number of visitors to Bhutan to protect Bhutan's environment and way of life.

Sri Lanka

Sri Lanka is a large island country located some 20 miles (32 km) off India's southeast coast. As a result of its close location, India has greatly influenced Sri Lanka. In fact, Sri Lanka's two largest ethnic groups—the Tamil and the Sinhalese (sin-huh-LEEZ)—are descended from Indian settlers.

Conflicts between the Sinhalese and the Tamil divide Sri Lanka today. The Tamil minority has fought for years to create a separate state. In 2009, government troops declared an end to the fighting after the Tamil leader was killed.

Parts of Sri Lanka were devastated by the 2004 tsunami in the Indian Ocean. Thousands of Sri Lankans were killed, and more than 500,000 people were left homeless. The tsunami also damaged Sri Lanka's fishing and agricultural industries, which are still struggling to rebuild.

READING CHECK **Summarizing** What key issues affect India's neighbors today?

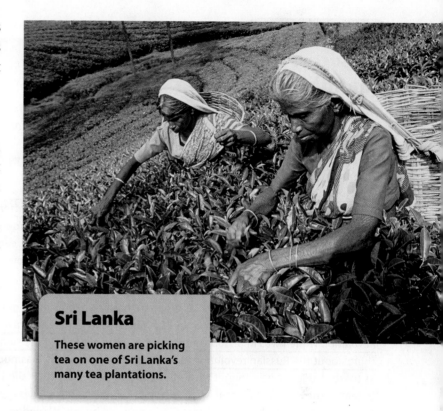

Sri Lanka
These women are picking tea on one of Sri Lanka's many tea plantations.

SUMMARY AND PREVIEW You have learned about the important challenges that face India's neighbors on the subcontinent. In the next chapter, you will learn about the physical geography, history, and culture of China, Mongolia, and Taiwan.

Section 4 Assessment

Reviewing Ideas, Terms, and Places

1. **a. Geographic Questions** Use the map and graph on page 655 to pose and answer a question about the geographic distribution of religion in the Indian Subcontinent.
   b. Summarize What cultural differences exist among India's neighbors?
   c. Elaborate Why do you think there are so many different religions in this region?
2. **a. Compare and Contrast** In what ways are the countries of this region similar and different?
   b. Predict How might conflict over **Kashmir** cause problems in the future?
   c. Analyze How do summer monsoons affect people living in Bangladesh?

Critical Thinking

3. **Solving Problems** Using your notes and a chart like the one here, identify one challenge facing each of India's neighbors. Then develop a solution for each challenge.

Challenges	Solutions

FOCUS ON VIEWING

my WriteSmart

4. **Telling about India's Neighbors** Your travels include voyages to India's neighbors. Include important or intriguing details and images in your travelogue.

PERSUASIVE SPEECH
Gandhi's "Quit India" Speech

On August 8, 1942, Gandhi delivered this speech before the All India Congress Committee. At the time, the committee was considering a resolution demanding the British "quit," or leave, India.

Ours is not a drive for power, but purely a non-violent fight for India's independence. In a violent struggle, a successful general has been often known to effect a military coup[1] and to set up a dictatorship. But under the Congress scheme of things, essentially non-violent as it is, there can be no room for dictatorship. A non-violent soldier of freedom will covet nothing for himself, he fights only for the freedom of his country. . . .

I believe that in the history of the world, there has not been a more genuinely democratic struggle for freedom than ours. I read Carlyle's *French Revolution* while I was in prison, and Pandit Jawaharlal has told me something about the Russian revolution. But it is my conviction that inasmuch as these struggles were fought with the weapon of violence they failed to realize the democratic ideal. In the democracy which I have envisaged[2], a democracy established by non-violence, there will be equal freedom for all. Everybody will be his own master. It is to join a struggle for such democracy that I invite you today.

As you read, look for main ideas and details related to how Gandhi thinks India should achieve independence.

Here, Gandhi refers to two violent revolutions that did not result in a lasting democracy, the French Revolution (1789–1799) and the Russian Revolution (1917).

[1] **military coup** a sudden seizure of political power by a nation's armed forces.

[2] **envisaged** imagined

Gandhi's "Quit India Speech" helped unite India's people against British rule.

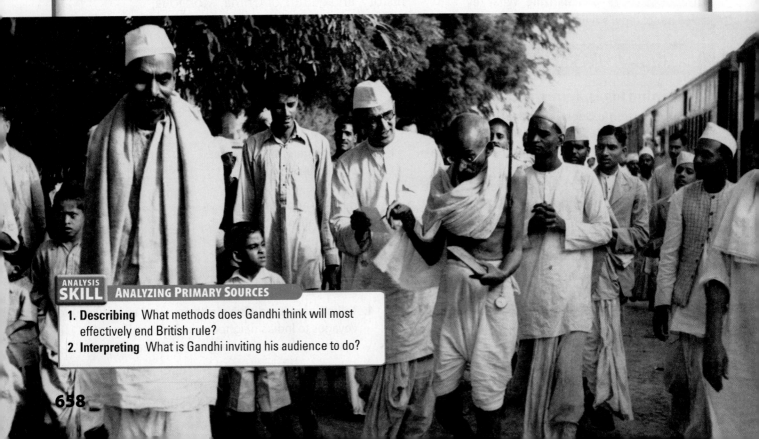

ANALYSIS SKILL ANALYZING PRIMARY SOURCES

1. **Describing** What methods does Gandhi think will most effectively end British rule?
2. **Interpreting** What is Gandhi inviting his audience to do?

Visual Summary

Use the visual summary below to help you review the main ideas of the chapter.

QUICK FACTS

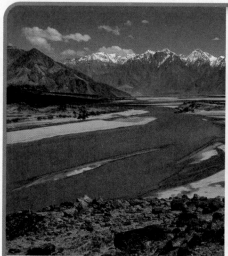

Towering mountains and powerful monsoons characterize the physical geography of the Indian Subcontinent.

India's Taj Mahal represents the subcontinent's rich history and culture.

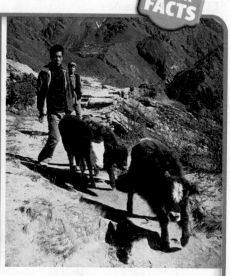

The nations that border India face many economic, political, and environmental challenges today.

Reviewing Vocabulary, Terms, and Places

Choose one word from each word pair to correctly complete each sentence below.

1. _____ often bring heavy rains to the Indian Subcontinent in summer. **(Monsoons/Ghats)**

2. The most popular religion in India today is _____. **(Buddhism/Hinduism/Islam)**

3. A _____ is a condition that influences an event or activity. **(feature/circumstance)**

4. _____ are an ethnic group from the mountains of Nepal. **(Tamil/Sherpas)**

5. The highest peak in the Indian Subcontinent and the world is _____. **(Mount Everest/K2)**

6. India's _____ system divides society based on a person's birth, wealth, and job. **(caste/colonial)**

7. Pakistan is located on the Indian _____, a large landmass. **(Peninsula/Subcontinent)**

Comprehension and Critical Thinking

SECTION 1 *(Pages 640–643)*

8. **a. Recall** What are the major physical features of the Indian Subcontinent?

   b. Draw Conclusions Why are rivers important to the people of the Indian Subcontinent?

   c. Evaluate Do you think monsoons have a positive or negative effect on India? Why?

SECTION 2 *(Pages 644–648)*

9. **a. Describe** What was the partition of India? When and why did it take place?

   b. Compare and Contrast In what ways were Mughal and British rule of India similar and different?

   c. Evaluate In your opinion, was partitioning India a good decision? Why or why not?

SECTION 3 *(Pages 650–653)*

10. **a. Explain** What is the significance of Vaisakhi?

SECTION 3 (continued)

b. Analyze How has population growth affected India's economy?

c. Elaborate If you lived in India, would you prefer to live in a city or a village? Why?

SECTION 4 (Pages 654–657)

11. a. Identify What countries share the subcontinent with India?

b. Analyze How was Sri Lanka affected by the 2004 tsunami?

c. Predict How might conflict between India and Pakistan lead to problems in the future?

Social Studies Skills

Creating a Line Graph *Use the information in the chart to answer the question below.*

Population Growth in India	
Year	**India's Population**
1951	361,088,000
1961	439,235,000
1971	548,160,000
1981	683,329,000
1991	846,387,888
2001	1,028,737,436
2011	1,210,193,422

Source: *Census of India*

12. Plot the data from the chart on a line graph. Be sure to use labels and a title to identify the subject and information presented in your line graph. Finally, organize information from your line graph into a brief summary that identifies any patterns that you see in the data.

Using the Internet

13. Touring India Pack your bags and experience India! It's a country where you can climb towering mountains, journey across vast deserts, and even hike through rain forests. Through the online book, discover the regions of India. Then make an illustrated travel brochure that features some of the regions you have explored.

Map Activity

14. The Indian Subcontinent Locate major human and geographic features of this region. On a sheet of paper, match the letters on the map with their correct labels.

Deccan   Mount Everest   Indus River

Himalayas   Mumbai (Bombay)   Sri Lanka

Kashmir   New Delhi

FOCUS ON READING AND VIEWING   *my* WriteSmart

15. Visualizing Read the primary source feature *Gandhi's "Quit India" Speech*. As you read, visualize the scenes that Gandhi describes. Then make a list of words from the passage that help you create a mental image of a nonviolent soldier fighting for freedom. Lastly, draw a rough sketch of your soldier.

16. Presenting and Viewing a Travelogue Use your notes to write a short script describing your travels in the Indian Subcontinent. Gather images to illustrate your script. Present your travelogue to a partner. Then, listen actively and take notes as your partner presents. Ask questions to clarify anything that is unclear or confusing. Review your notes right away to make sure that you understand what was said. Finally, summarize aloud your partner's main points.

Reading Social Studies

Visualizing

FOCUS ON READING

Maybe you have heard the saying "a picture is worth a thousand words." That means a picture can show in a small space what might take many words to describe. Visualizing, or creating mental pictures, can help you see and remember what you read. When you read, try to imagine what a snapshot of the images in the passage might look like. First, form the background or setting in your mind. Then keep adding specific details that can help you picture the rest of the information.

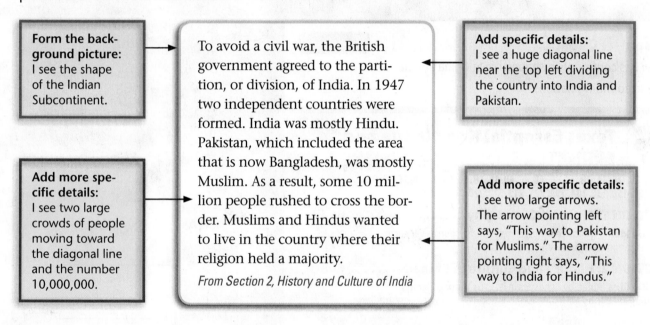

Form the background picture: I see the shape of the Indian Subcontinent.

Add more specific details: I see two large crowds of people moving toward the diagonal line and the number 10,000,000.

To avoid a civil war, the British government agreed to the partition, or division, of India. In 1947 two independent countries were formed. India was mostly Hindu. Pakistan, which included the area that is now Bangladesh, was mostly Muslim. As a result, some 10 million people rushed to cross the border. Muslims and Hindus wanted to live in the country where their religion held a majority.

From Section 2, History and Culture of India

Add specific details: I see a huge diagonal line near the top left dividing the country into India and Pakistan.

Add more specific details: I see two large arrows. The arrow pointing left says, "This way to Pakistan for Muslims." The arrow pointing right says, "This way to India for Hindus."

YOU TRY IT!

Read the following sentences. Then, using the process explained above, describe the images you see.

Flooding is one of Bangladesh's biggest challenges. Many circumstances cause these floods. The country's many streams and rivers flood annually, often damaging farms and homes. Summer monsoons also cause flooding. For example, massive flooding in 2004 left more than 25 million people homeless. It also destroyed schools, farms, and roads throughout the country.

From Section 4, India's Neighbors

CHAPTER 27

China, Mongolia, and Taiwan

CENTRAL
ASIA

Ürümqi

XIZANG
(TIBET)

SOUTH
ASIA

Brahmaputra River

Lhasa

✪ National capital
● Other cities

0   250   500 Miles
0   250   500 Kilometers

Projection: Two-Point Equidistant

Essential Question

*my*Notebook

How has communism shaped life in China and in the surrounding nations?

Texas Essential Knowledge and Skills (TEKS)

1A, 1B, 2A, 2B, 3A, 3B, 3C, 3D, 4B, 4C, 4D, 5A, 5B, 5C, 6B, 6C, 7B, 7C, 9B, 9D, 11D, 12B, 15B, 15C, 18A, 19A, 20A, 21B, 21C, 22B, 22D

FOCUS ON READING AND WRITING

*my*WriteSmart

Identifying Implied Main Ideas The main idea in a piece of writing is sometimes stated directly. Other times, you must figure out the main idea. As you read, look for key details or ideas to help you identify the implied main ideas. **See the lesson, Identifying Implied Main Ideas, on page 687.**

Writing a Legend Since ancient times, people have passed along legends. These stories often tell about supernatural people or events from the past. Read the chapter. Then write your own legend describing the creation of a physical feature in this region. Use the annotation tools in your eBook to gather information for your assignment.

Geography Horses play an important role in Mongolian life and culture. Many Mongolians are nomads and use horses to travel across the country's large plains.

China, Mongolia, and Taiwan: Political

RUSSIA

Heilong (Amur River)

MONGOLIA

Ulaanbaatar

Harbin

Shenyang

KOREA

Sea of Japan (East Sea)

JAPAN

40°N

30°N

Great Wall of China

Beijing

Tianjin

Huang He (Yellow River)

Yellow Sea

PACIFIC OCEAN

CHINA

Zhengzhou

Nanjing

Shanghai

East China Sea

Wuhan

Chang Jiang (Yangzi River)

Chengdu

Chongqing

Mekong River

Nu River

Xi River

Guangzhou

Hong Kong

Taipei
TAIWAN

Tropic of Cancer

20°N

130°E

120°E

110°E

SOUTHEAST ASIA

South China Sea

HISTORY Guarding Against Invaders

hmhsocialstudies.com **VIDEO**

map zone Geography Skills

Regions China is the largest country in East Asia and is closely linked with Mongolia and Taiwan.

1. **Name** What are the capitals of China, Mongolia, and Taiwan?
2. **Contrast** Based on the map, how do the countries of Mongolia and Taiwan differ?

History The Great Wall of China stretches for many miles across China's northern lands.

Culture Chinese opera uses music and symbolism to tell stories. The actors wear bold and colorful makeup that has special meanings.

Physical Geography

TEKS 3A, 3B, 4D, 5A, 6B, 6C, 21B, 21C, 22D

What You Will Learn...

Main Ideas

1. Physical features of China, Mongolia, and Taiwan include mountains, plateaus and basins, plains, and rivers.
2. China, Mongolia, and Taiwan have a range of climates and natural resources.

The Big Idea

Physical features, climate, and resources vary across China, Mongolia, and Taiwan.

Key Terms and Places

Himalayas, *p. 664*
Plateau of Tibet, *p. 665*
Gobi, *p. 665*
North China Plain, *p. 666*
Huang He, *p. 666*
loess, *p. 666*
Chang Jiang, *p. 666*

hmhsocialstudies.com
TAKING NOTES

Use the graphic organizer online to take notes on the physical features, climate, and resources of China, Mongolia, and Taiwan.

If YOU lived there...

You are a young filmmaker who lives in Guangzhou, a port city in southern China. You are preparing to make a documentary film about the Huang He, one of China's great rivers. To make your film, you will follow the river across northern China. Your journey will take you from the Himalayas to the coast of the Yellow Sea.

What do you expect to see on your travels?

BUILDING BACKGROUND China, Mongolia, and Taiwan make up a large part of East Asia. They include a range of physical features and climates—dry plateaus, rugged mountains, fertile plains. This physical geography has greatly influenced life in each country.

Physical Features

Have you seen the view from the top of the world? At 29,035 feet (8,850 m), Mount Everest in the **Himalayas** is the world's highest mountain. From atop Everest, look east. Through misty clouds, icy peaks stretch out before you, fading to land far below. This is China. About the size of the United States, China has a range of physical features. They include not only the world's tallest peaks but also some of its driest deserts and longest rivers.

Two other areas are closely linked to China. To the north lies Mongolia (mahn-GOHL-yuh). This landlocked country is dry and rugged, with vast grasslands and desert. In contrast, Taiwan (TY-WAHN), off the coast of mainland China, is a green tropical island. Look at the map to see the whole region's landforms.

Mountains

Much of the large region, including Taiwan, is mountainous. In southwest China, the Himalayas run along the border. They are Earth's tallest mountain range. Locate on the map the region's other ranges. As a tip, the Chinese word *shan* means "mountain."

map zone

Geography Skills

Place Physical features vary across the region.
1. **Identify** What major rivers begin in the Plateau of Tibet?
2. **Make Generalizations** In general, how does China's elevation differ from west to east?

MONGOLIA
Mongolian Plateau
Altay Mountains
GOBI DESERT
Greater Khingan Range
Manchurian Plain
Sea of Japan (East Sea)
Tian Shan
Turpan Depression -505 ft (-154 m)
Tarim Basin
Taklimakan Desert
CHINA
Kunlun Shan
Qinling Shandi
Huang He (Yellow River)
North China Plain
Yellow Sea
Plateau of Tibet
Nu River
Sichuan Basin
Chang Jiang (Yangzi River)
East China Sea
HIMALAYAS
Brahmaputra River
Mount Everest 29,035 ft (8,850 m)
Xi River
TAIWAN
Tropic of Cancer
PACIFIC OCEAN
Hainan
South China Sea

ELEVATION

Feet		Meters
13,120		4,000
6,560		2,000
1,640		500
656		200
(Sea level) 0		0 (Sea level)
Below sea level		Below sea level

0   250   500   750 Miles

0   250   500   750 Kilometers

Projection: Two-Point Equidistant

1 The Himalayas are the world's highest mountain range.

Other Landforms

Many of the mountain ranges are separated by plateaus, basins, and deserts. In southwest China, the **Plateau of Tibet** lies north of the Himalayas. The world's highest plateau, it is called the Roof of the World.

Moving north, we find a low, dry area. A large part of this area is the Taklimakan (tah-kluh-muh-KAHN) Desert, a barren land of sand dunes and blinding sandstorms.

In fact, sandstorms are so common that the desert's Turkish name, Taklimakan, has come to mean "Enter and you will not come out." To the northeast, the Turpan (toohr-PAHN) Depression is China's lowest point, at 505 feet (154 m) below sea level.

Continuing northeast, in Mongolia we find the **Gobi**. This harsh area of gravel and rock is the world's coldest desert. Temperatures can drop to below –40°F (–40°C).

2 Hills that are called karst towers line the Li River in southeast China. These dramatic hills formed over time as rainwater eroded limestone.

In east China, the land levels out into low plains and river valleys. These fertile plains, such as the **North China Plain**, are China's main population centers and farmlands. On Taiwan, a plain on the west coast is the island's main population center.

Rivers

FOCUS ON READING

Which details help you identify the main idea of the paragraph to the right?

In China, two great rivers run west to east. The **Huang He** (HWAHNG HEE), or the Yellow River, flows across northern China. Along its course, this river picks up large amounts of **loess** (LES), or fertile, yellowish soil. The soil colors the river and gives it its name.

In summer, the Huang He often floods. The floods spread layers of loess, enriching the soil for farming. However, such floods have killed millions of people. For this reason, the river is called China's Sorrow.

The mighty **Chang** (CHAHNG) **Jiang**, or the Yangzi (YAHNG-zee) River, flows across central China. It is Asia's longest river and a major transportation route.

READING CHECK **Summarizing** What are the main physical features found in this region?

Climate and Resources

Climate varies widely across the region. The tropical southeast is warm to hot, and monsoons bring heavy rains in summer. In addition, typhoons can strike the southeast coast in summer and fall. Similar to hurricanes, these violent storms bring high winds and rain. As we move to the northeast, the climate is drier and colder. Winter temperatures can drop below 0°F (–18°C).

China, Mongolia, and Taiwan: Precipitation

ANNUAL PRECIPITATION

Inches	Centimeters
Over 80	Over 203
60–80	152–203
40–60	102–152
20–40	51–102
10–20	25–51
Under 10	Under 25

0   300   600 Miles
0   300   600 Kilometers
Projection: Two-Point Equidistant

MONGOLIA

CHINA

Huang He (Yellow River)

Chang Jiang (Yangzi River)

Xi River

TAIWAN

PACIFIC OCEAN

map zone
Geography Skills

Regions In general, precipitation decreases from the southeast to the northwest. Deserts and dry steppes cover the northwest.

1. **Use the Map** How much precipitation does the lower Chang Jiang average each year?
2. **Contrast** How does annual precipitation in Mongolia differ from that in Taiwan?

Flooding in China

China's rivers and lakes often flood during the summer rainy season. The satellite images here show Lake Dongting Hu in southern China. The lake appears blue, and the land appears red. Soon after the Before image was taken, heavy rains led to flooding. The After image shows the results. Compare the two images to see the extent of the flood, which killed more than 3,000 people and destroyed some 5 million homes.

Before

After

For comparison, these arrows are pointing to the same place in each image.

Drawing Inferences Why might people continue to live in areas that often flood?

In the north and west, the climate is mainly dry. Temperatures vary across the area and can get both very hot and cold.

Like the climate, the region's natural resources cover a wide range. China has a wealth of natural resources. The country is rich in mineral resources and is a leading producer of coal, lead, tin, and tungsten. China produces many other minerals and metals as well. China's forestland and farmland are also valuable resources.

Mongolia's natural resources include minerals such as coal, iron, and tin as well as livestock. Taiwan's major natural resource is its farmland. Important crops include sugarcane, tea, and bananas.

READING CHECK **Contrasting** Which of these three countries has the most natural resources?

SUMMARY AND PREVIEW As you have read, China, Mongolia, and Taiwan have a range of physical features, climate, and resources. Next, you will read about the history and culture of China.

Section 1 Assessment

hmhsocialstudies.com
ONLINE QUIZ

Reviewing Ideas, Terms, and Places

1. **a. Identify** What two major rivers run through China?
   b. Explain How does the **Huang He** both benefit and hurt China's people?
   c. Elaborate Why do you think many people in China live on the **North China Plain**?
2. **a. Define** What is a typhoon?
   b. Contrast What are some differences between the climates of southeast and northwest China?
   c. Rate Based on the different climates in this region, which part of the region would you prefer to live in? Why?

Critical Thinking

3. **Categorizing** Look back over your notes for this section. Then use a chart like the one shown here to organize, identify, and describe the main physical features of China, Mongolia, and Taiwan.

   - Mountains
   - Plateaus, basins, deserts
   - Physical Features
   - Plains and river valleys
   - Rivers

FOCUS ON WRITING

my WriteSmart

4. **Writing about Physical Geography** Note the main physical features of this region. Consider which feature you might want to explain in your legend. Features to consider include mountains, plateaus, and deserts.

History and Culture of China

TEKS 1A, 1B, 2A, 2B, 5B, 12B,
15B, 15C, 18A, 19A, 20A,
21B, 21C, 22A

What You Will Learn...

Main Ideas

1. Family lines of emperors ruled China for most of its early history.
2. In China's modern history, revolution and civil war led to a communist government.
3. China has the world's most people and a rich culture shaped by ancient traditions.

The Big Idea

Ruled by dynasties in its early history, China is a communist country with an enormous population and ancient traditions.

Key Terms

dynasty, *p. 669*
dialect, *p. 671*
Daoism, *p. 672*
Confucianism, *p. 672*
pagodas, *p. 673*

hmhsocialstudies.com
TAKING NOTES

Use the graphic organizer online to take notes on China's history, people, and culture.

If YOU lived there...

Your parents own a small farm in the Chinese countryside in the mid-1950s. China's new leaders are making changes, however. They are taking people's farms and combining them to create large government-run farms. Your family and neighbors will now work a large farm together. China's leaders will tell you what to grow and pay you based on how much the farm produces.

How do you feel about these changes?

BUILDING BACKGROUND In 1949 China established a strong central government. This new government changed many familiar patterns of life. For much of its history, though, China had been ruled by family lines of emperors. During this period, China developed one of the world's most advanced civilizations.

China's Early Dynasties

Dynasties ruled China for some 3,500 years. The major achievements of the early dynasties are shown here.

Shang, c. 1500–1050 BC

- First recorded Chinese dynasty
- Strongest in the Huang He valley
- Developed China's first writing system, a calendar, and chopsticks
- Skilled at bronze casting

Shang bronze tigress container

Zhou, c. 1050–400 BC

- Longest-lasting Chinese dynasty
- Expanded China but declined into a period of disorder
- Influenced by the new teachings of Confucianism, Daoism, and Legalism
- Began using iron tools and plows

Confucius, a Zhou thinker

China's Early History

When we enjoy the colorful fireworks on the Fourth of July, we can thank the early Chinese people. They invented fireworks. China's early civilization was one of the most advanced in the world. Its many achievements include the magnetic compass, gunpowder, paper, printing, and silk.

Today China can boast a civilization some 4,000 years old, older than any other. Understanding this long history is central to understanding China and its people.

China's Dynasties

For much of its history, China was ruled by dynasties. A **dynasty** is a series of rulers from the same family line. The rulers of China's dynasties were called emperors. Over time, many dynasties rose and fell in China. Between some dynasties, periods of chaos occurred as kingdoms or warlords fought for power. At other times, invaders came in and took control. Through it all, Chinese culture endured and evolved.

One of the most important dynasties is the Qin (CHIN), or Ch'in. It was the first dynasty to unite China under one empire. The greatest Qin ruler was Shi Huangdi (SHEE hwahng-dee). He ordered the building of much of the Great Wall of China. Made to keep out invaders, the wall linked many older walls in northern China. In addition, Shi Huangdi had thousands of terra-cotta, or clay, warriors made to guard his tomb. These life-size warriors, each of which is unique, are skillful works of art.

The last dynasty in China was the Qing (CHING). Invaders called the Manchu ruled this dynasty starting in 1644. In time, outside influences would help lead to its end.

Outside Influences in China

Throughout history, China often limited contact with the outside world. The Chinese saw their culture as superior and had little use for foreigners. The tall mountains, deserts, and seas around China further limited contact and isolated the region. These geographic factors also helped China control its territory.

Yet, other people increasingly wanted Chinese goods such as silk and tea. To gain access to the goods, some European powers forced China to open up trade in the 1800s. Europeans took control of parts of the country as well. These actions angered many Chinese, some of whom blamed the emperor. At the same time, increased contact with the West exposed the Chinese to new ideas.

READING CHECK **Drawing Conclusions** How did geography affect China's early history?

Qin, c. 221–206 BC

- First unified Chinese empire
- Strong central government with strict laws
- Created standardized money and writing systems
- Built a network of roads and canals and much of the Great Wall

Qin life-size terra-cotta warrior

Han, c. 206 BC–AD 220

- Based government on Confucianism
- Began trading over Silk Road
- Spread of Buddhism from India
- Invented paper, sundial, and acupuncture

Han bronze oil lamp

China's Modern History

As foreign influences increased, China's people grew unhappy with imperial rule. This unhappiness sparked a revolution.

Revolution and Civil War

In 1911, rebels forced out China's last emperor. They then formed a republic, a political system in which voters elect their leaders. Power struggles continued, however. In time, two rival groups emerged—the Nationalists, led by Chiang Kai-shek (chang ky-SHEK), and the Communists, led by Mao Zedong (MOW ZUH-DOOHNG).

The two groups fought a violent civil war. That war ended in October 1949 with the Communists as victors. They founded a new government, the People's Republic of China. The Nationalists fled to Taiwan, where they founded the Republic of China.

FOCUS ON READING

What is the main idea of the second paragraph under Population and Settlement on the next page?

Communist China under Mao

Mao, the Communists' leader, became the head of China's new government. In a Communist system, the government owns most businesses and land and controls all areas of life. China's new Communist government began by taking over control of the economy. The government seized all private farms and organized them into large, state-run farms. It also took over all businesses and factories.

While some changes improved life, others did not. On one hand, women gained more rights and were able to work. On the other hand, the government limited freedoms and imprisoned people who criticized it. In addition, many economic programs were unsuccessful, and some were outright disasters. In the early 1960s, for example, poor planning and drought led to a famine that killed millions.

China: Population

map zone

Geography Skills

Place Most Chinese live in the east, China's farming and industrial heartland.

1. **Use the Map** Which areas have the fewest people?
2. **Make Inferences** Based on this map, what can you infer about China's eastern cities?

Major cities
- ● Over 10 million people
- ● 7 to 9 million people
- · 100,000 people

0   300   600 Miles
0   300   600 Kilometers

Projection: Two-Point Equidistant

MONGOLIA

Beijing
Tianjin

CHINA

Shanghai   30°N
Wuhan

Tropic of Cancer

TAIWAN   20°N

Guangzhou Hong Kong

PACIFIC OCEAN

Communist China Since Mao

Mao died in 1976, and Deng Xiaoping (DUHNG SHOW-PING) soon rose to power. Deng admitted the government had made mistakes. He then worked to modernize and improve China's economy. He allowed some private businesses and encouraged countries to invest in China. As a result, the economy began growing rapidly. Leaders after Deng continued economic reforms.

READING CHECK Summarizing How did communism change life in China?

China's People and Culture

One of China's best known features is its people—all 1.3 billion of them. China has the world's largest population. More people live there than in all of Europe, Russia, and the United States combined.

Population and Settlement

As the map shows, this huge population is not evenly spread out. Only 10 percent of the people live in the west, while the rest are jam-packed into the east. In fact, more people live in the Manchurian and North China Plains than in the United States!

Meanwhile, China's population continues to grow—by about 6 million each year. China's officials have worked to slow this growth. Officials have urged people to delay having children and have tried to limit each couple to one child. These actions have succeeded in slowing China's population growth.

Ethnic Groups and Language

Of China's millions of people, 92 percent identify their ancestry as Han Chinese. These people share the same culture and traditions. Many Han speak Mandarin, one of China's official languages. Others speak a **dialect**, a regional version of a language.

Ethnic Groups

The majority of Chinese are Han. However, China includes 55 other ethnic groups. Most of these people live in western and southern China.

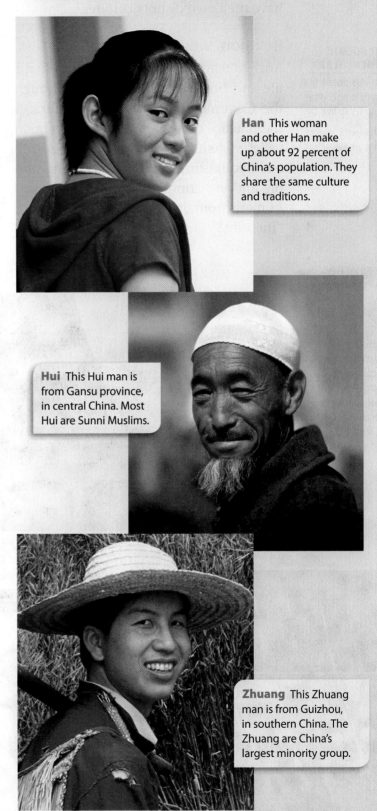

Han This woman and other Han make up about 92 percent of China's population. They share the same culture and traditions.

Hui This Hui man is from Gansu province, in central China. Most Hui are Sunni Muslims.

Zhuang This Zhuang man is from Guizhou, in southern China. The Zhuang are China's largest minority group.

Some 55 other ethnic groups make up the remaining 8 percent of China's population. Most of these minority groups live in western and southern China, where they have their own distinct cultures.

ACADEMIC
VOCABULARY

values ideas that people hold dear and try to live by

elements parts of a whole

Religion, Values, and Beliefs

Ancient religions, **values**, and beliefs shape life for China's many people, even though the Communist government discourages the practice of religion. China's two main belief systems are Daoism (DOW-i-zuhm) and Buddhism. **Daoism** stresses living simply and in harmony with nature. It takes its name from the word *Dao,* which means "the way."

Buddhism came to China from India about AD 100. This religion is based on the teachings of Siddhartha Gautama—the Buddha, who lived from 563 to 483 BC. Buddhists believe moral behavior, kindness, and meditation can lead to peace.

Many Chinese blend **elements** of Daoism and Buddhism with **Confucianism**, a philosophy based on the ideas and teachings of Confucius. This philosophy stresses the importance of family, moral values, and respect for one's elders.

Other major religions in China include Christianity and Islam. Ancestor worship and fortune-telling are popular among the Chinese as well.

Close-up

Beijing's National Day

China celebrates National Day on October 1 with huge parades in Tiananmen Square. This square is one of the world's largest public gathering places. The space is needed because parades can include more than 500,000 participants.

Beijing

CHINA

PACIFIC OCEAN

The Gate of Heavenly Peace displays Mao Zedong's portrait above the entrance.

The parades include couples married on National Day, a popular time to wed.

中华   万岁

A military parade of soldiers, tanks, and other equipment shows China's power.

The Arts and Popular Culture

China has a rich artistic tradition. Chinese crafts include items made of bronze, jade, ivory, silk, or wood. Chinese porcelain, which the ancient Chinese developed, is highly prized for its quality and beauty.

Traditional Chinese painting is done on silk or fine paper and reflects a focus on balance and harmony with nature. Popular subjects are landscapes, such as scenes of rugged mountains, trees, and lakes.

Chinese art often includes calligraphy, or decorative writing. Chinese writing uses symbols, or characters, instead of letters. This writing makes beautiful art, and some paintings feature just Chinese calligraphy.

In literature, the Chinese are known for their beautiful poetry. The Chinese highly value poetry, and poems appear on paintings and in novels and plays.

In theater, traditional Chinese opera is popular. These operas tell stories through spoken words, music, and dance. Actors wear elaborate costumes and makeup that have special meanings.

Traditional Chinese architecture features wooden buildings on stone bases. Large tiled roofs curve upward at the edge. Also common are **pagodas**, Buddhist temples that have multi-storied towers with an upward curving roof at each floor. Many cities are a mix of traditional and modern.

ANALYSIS
SKILL **ANALYZING VISUALS**

Why might China's government include so many different groups in the National Day parades?

The Chinese believe dragon dances bring good fortune to important events.

世界人民大团结万岁

Lion dances are performed to spread good blessings to the community.

Chinese Martial Arts

Can you imagine getting up each day at 5 AM and exercising for 12 hours or more? Chinese teenagers who attend martial arts schools do just that. Many of the schools' instructors are Buddhist monks trained in the Chinese martial art of kung fu. These instructors teach their students self-defense techniques as well as the importance of hard work, discipline, and respect for one's elders. These values are important in Chinese culture and religion.

Starting as early as age 6, students memorize up to several hundred martial arts movements. These movements include different kicks, jumps, and punches. Some students dream of one day using their martial arts skills to star in a Chinese or American action movie.

Drawing Conclusions Why do you think discipline, hard work, and respect might be important for learning martial arts?

Popular culture includes many activities. Popular sports are martial arts and table tennis. A popular game is mah-jongg, played with small tiles. People also enjoy karaoke clubs, where they sing to music.

READING CHECK **Evaluating** Which aspect of Chinese culture most interests you? Why?

SUMMARY AND PREVIEW After centuries of imperial rule under dynasties, China became a Communist country. China has a rich and ancient culture and is the world's most populous country. In the next section you will read about China's economy, government, and cities.

Section 2 Assessment

hmhsocialstudies.com
ONLINE QUIZ

Reviewing Ideas, Terms, and Places

1. a. **Define** What is a **dynasty**?
   b. **Summarize** How did outside influences affect China's early history?
2. a. **Recall** Which two groups fought for power during China's civil war, and which group won?
   b. **Evaluate** How did Mao contribute to the economic and political history of China?
3. a. **Recall** What are some popular pastimes in China today?
   b. **Explain** What are China's population problems, and how is China addressing them?
   c. **Elaborate** What is the relationship between religious and philosophical ideas such as Buddhism, **Confucianism**, and **Daoism** and Chinese culture?

Critical Thinking

4. **Sequencing** Look back over your notes and then create a chart like this one. List the main events in China's history in the order in which they occurred.

FOCUS ON WRITING

*my*WriteSmart

5. **Collecting Information about China's Culture** You may wish to use your legend to explore the relationship between art and culture. China is well known for its art, music, literature, and architecture. Take notes on the significance of each form of cultural expression to Chinese culture.

China Today

If YOU lived there...

For many years your parents have been farmers, growing tea plants. Since the government began allowing private businesses, your parents have been selling tea in the market as well. Now, they are considering opening a tea shop.

What do you think your parents should do?

> **BUILDING BACKGROUND** When a Communist government took over China in 1949, it began strictly controlling all areas of life. Over time, China's government has loosened control of the economy. Control over politics and other areas of life remains strict, however.

China's Economy

Think ahead to the day you start working. Would you rather choose your career or have the government choose it for you? The first situation describes a market economy, which we have in the United States. In this type of economy, people can choose their careers, decide what to make or sell, and keep the profits they earn. The second situation describes a **command economy**, an economic system in which the government owns all the businesses and makes all decisions, such as where people work. Communist China used to have a command economy. Then in the 1970s, China began allowing aspects of a market economy.

Farmers near Yunnan, in southern China, use traditional methods to work rice paddies.

TEKS 1A, 1B, 3B, 4B, 5A, 5C, 7B, 7C, 9B, 9D, 11D, 15B, 21B, 21C, 22A, 22B, 22D

What You Will Learn...

Main Ideas

1. China's booming economy is based on agriculture, but industry is growing rapidly.
2. China's government controls many aspects of life and limits political freedom.
3. China is mainly rural, but urban areas are growing.
4. China's environment faces a number of serious problems.

The Big Idea

China's economy and cities are growing rapidly, but the Chinese have little political freedom and many environmental problems.

Key Terms and Places

command economy, *p. 675*
Beijing, *p. 676*
Tibet, *p. 677*
Shanghai, *p. 678*
Hong Kong, *p. 678*

hmhsocialstudies.com
TAKING NOTES

Use the graphic organizer online to take notes on China today.

China developed a mixed economy because it had major economic problems. For example, the production of goods had fallen. In response, the government closed many state-run factories and began allowing privately owned businesses. In addition, the government created special economic zones where foreign business-people could own companies. A mixed economic approach has helped China's economy boom. Today China has the world's second largest economy.

Agriculture and Industry

More Chinese work in farming than in any other economic activity. The country is a leading producer of several crops, such as rice, wheat, corn, and potatoes. China's main farmlands are in the eastern plains and river valleys. To the north, wheat is the main crop. To the south, rice is.

Only about 12 percent of China's land is good for farming. So how does China produce so much food? More than a third of all Chinese workers are farmers. This large labor force can work the land at high levels. In addition, farmers cut terraces into hillsides to make the most use of the land.

Although China is mainly agricultural, industry is growing rapidly. Today China produces everything from satellites and chemicals to clothing and toys. Moreover, industry and manufacturing are now the most profitable part of China's economy.

Results of Economic Growth

Economic growth has improved wages and living standards in China. Almost all homes now have electricity, even in rural areas. More and more Chinese can afford goods such as TVs, computers, and even cars. At the same time, many rural Chinese remain poor, and unemployment is high.

READING CHECK **Summarizing** How has China changed its economy in recent times?

China's Government

More economic freedom in China has not led to more political freedom. The Communist government tightly controls most areas of life. For example, the government controls newspapers and Internet access, which helps to restrict the flow of information and ideas.

In addition, China harshly punishes people who oppose the government. In 1989 more than 100,000 pro-democracy protestors gathered in Tiananmen Square in **Beijing**, China's capital. The protestors were demanding more political rights and freedoms. The Chinese government tried to get the protestors to leave the square. When they refused, the government used troops and tanks to make them leave. Hundreds of protestors were killed, and many more were injured or imprisoned.

China's Urban Growth

China has taken harsh actions against ethnic rebellions as well. As an example, since 1950 China has controlled the Buddhist region of **Tibet**, in southwest China. When the Tibetans rebelled in 1959, the Chinese quickly crushed the revolt. The Dalai Lama (dah-ly LAH-muh), Tibet's Buddhist leader, had to flee to India. China then cracked down on Tibetans' rights.

Because of actions such as these, many other countries have accused China of not respecting human rights. Some of these countries have considered limiting or stopping trade with China. For example, some U.S. politicians want our government to limit trade with China until it shows more respect for human rights.

READING CHECK **Analyzing** What adjectives might you use to describe China's government?

Rural and Urban China

China is a land in the midst of change. Although its countryside remains set in the past, China's cities are growing rapidly and rushing headlong toward the future.

Rural China

Most of China's people live in small, rural villages. Farmers work the fields using the same methods they have used for decades. In small shops and along the streets, sellers cook food and offer goods. Although some villagers' standards of living are improving, the modern world often seems far away.

Urban China

Many people are leaving China's villages for its booming cities, however. The graph below shows how China's urban population is expected to rise in the future.

FOCUS ON READING
What is the implied main idea of the text under Rural China?

China's Projected Urban Population

Urban population
Rural population

Many of China's rapidly growing cities are severely crowded, as can be seen in this Shanghai shopping area. Overcrowding is expected to worsen as China's cities continue to grow.

INTERPRETING GRAPHS About when is China's urban population expected to be larger than its rural population?

CHINA, MONGOLIA, AND TAIWAN **677**

China's Environmental Challenges

Forest areas
Forest destroyed
Desertification
Soil erosion
High risk of flooding
• **Poor urban air quality**

0 250 500 750 Miles
0 250 500 750 Kilometers

Projection: Two-Point Equidistant

CHINA

Shenyang
Baotou Beijing
Lanzhou
Xi'an
Shanghai
Guangzhou

Liao He
Huang He (Yellow River)
Huai He
Chang Jiang (Yangzi River)
Min Jiang
Nu River
Brahmaputra River
Xi River
Mekong River

PACIFIC OCEAN
Tropic of Cancer

map zone **Geography Skills**

Human-Environment Interaction China faces a number of serious environmental challenges.
1. **Identify** Which rivers does the map show as having a high risk of flooding?
2. **Interpret** Which environmental problem has had the most impact on southern China?

China's growing economy has led to its rapid city growth. Look at the population map in Section 2 and find the cities with more than 7 million people. Most are on the coast or along major rivers. These areas have benefited from growing industry and trade. Places that were rice fields not long ago are now bustling urban centers with skyscrapers, factories, and highways.

China's largest city is **Shanghai**, with some 16.5 million people. Located where the Chang Jiang meets the East China Sea, it is China's leading seaport and an industrial and commercial center. The city is also known for its European feel and nightlife.

China's second-largest city is its capital, Beijing. Also known as Peking, this historic city has many beautiful palaces and temples. A mix of the old and new, Beijing is China's political and cultural center.

In central Beijing, large walls hide the golden-roofed palaces of the Forbidden City, former home of China's emperors. Once off-limits to all but the emperor's household, the city is now a museum open to the public. Nearby, Tiananmen Square is the site of many parades and other public events. Government buildings and museums line this immense square.

In southern China, **Hong Kong** and Macao (muh-KOW) are major port cities and centers of trade and tourism. Both cities were European colonies until recently. The United Kingdom returned Hong Kong to China in 1997, and Portugal returned Macao in 1999. The two modern, crowded cities provide a mix of cultures.

READING CHECK **Contrasting** In what ways might rural life differ from city life in China?

① Residents of Baotou, in north-central China, wear masks to keep from inhaling harmful particles in the city's polluted air.

② These children are planting trees to help create new forestland north of Beijing.

China's Environment

China's economic and urban growth has created serious environmental problems. A major problem is pollution. The country's rising number of cars and factories pollute the air and water. At the same time, China burns coal for much of its electricity, which further pollutes the air.

Another serious problem is the loss of forestland and farmland. For centuries the Chinese cut down trees without replanting more. In addition, many of China's expanding cities are in its best farmlands.

The Chinese are working to address such problems. For example, China hopes to lessen pollution by using more hydro-electric power, electricity produced from dams. China has built the Three Gorges Dam on the Chang Jiang.

It is the world's largest dam and generates as much power as 15 coal-burning power plants. However, the water of the dam's reservoir now covers hundreds of towns and huge amounts of farmland. Millions of people have had to move, and plant and animal habitats have been harmed.

READING CHECK **Finding Main Ideas** What are some of China's environmental problems?

SUMMARY AND PREVIEW China's economy and cities are growing rapidly, but its government restricts political freedom and faces environmental problems. In the next section you will learn about Mongolia and Taiwan.

Section 3 Assessment

ONLINE QUIZ

Reviewing Ideas, Terms, and Places

1. **a. Define** What is a **command economy**?
   b. Identify Cause and Effect What changes have helped lead to China's rapid economic growth?
2. **a. Describe** In what ways does China's government restrict freedom?
   b. Evaluate What is your opinion of China's handling of the 1989 demonstration at Tiananmen Square?
3. **a. Identify and Explain** Which geographic factor best explains why Shanghai is a major center for shipping, industry, and commerce? Why?
   b. Compare How are **Hong Kong** and Macao similar?
4. **a. Recall** What are China's environmental problems?
   b. Evaluate Do you think building the Three Gorges Dam was beneficial to China?

Critical Thinking

5. **Categorizing** Create a table like the one shown to organize the challenges that China faces today.

Challenges Facing China		
Economic	Political	Environmental

FOCUS ON WRITING

my WriteSmart

6. **Collecting Information about China Today** Note any details about China's current economy, government, cities, or environment that you might include in your legend.

Mongolia and Taiwan

 TEKS 1A, 1B, 2A, 2B, 3A, 3B, 3C, 3D, 4C, 15B, 21B, 21C, 22B, 22D

What You Will Learn...

Main Ideas

1. Mongolia is a sparsely populated country where many people live as nomads.
2. Taiwan is a small island with a dense population and a highly industrialized economy.

The Big Idea

Mongolia is a rugged land with a nomadic way of life and growing cities, while Taiwan is a densely settled and industrialized island.

Key Terms and Places

gers, *p. 681*
Ulaanbaatar, *p. 681*
Taipei, *p. 682*
Kao-hsiung, *p. 682*

hmhsocialstudies.com
TAKING NOTES

Use the graphic organizer online to take notes on the history and culture of Mongolia and Taiwan, as well as life in these countries today.

If YOU lived there...

Like many Mongolians, you have loved horses since you were a small child. You live in an apartment in the city of Ulaanbaatar, however. Some of your family are talking about leaving the city and becoming nomadic herders like your ancestors were. You think you might like being able to ride horses more. You're not sure you would like living in a tent, though, especially in winter.

Do you want to move back to the land?

BUILDING BACKGROUND While Mongolia is a rugged land where some people still live as nomads, Taiwan is a modern and highly industrialized island. The two regions do have a few things in common, however. Mongolia and Taiwan are both neighbors of China, both are becoming more urban, and both are democracies.

Mongolia

A wild and rugged land, Mongolia is home to the Mongol people. They have a proud and fascinating history. This history includes conquests and empires and a culture that prizes horses.

Mongolia's History

Today when people discuss the world's leading countries, they do not mention Mongolia. However, 700 years ago Mongolia was perhaps the greatest power in the world. Led by the ruler Genghis Khan, the Mongols conquered much of Asia, including China. Later Mongol leaders continued the conquests. They built the greatest empire the world had seen at the time.

The Mongol Empire reached its height in the late 1200s. During that time, the empire stretched from Europe's Danube River in the west to the Pacific Ocean in the east. As time passed, however, the Mongol Empire declined. In the late 1600s China conquered Mongolia and ruled it for more than 200 years.

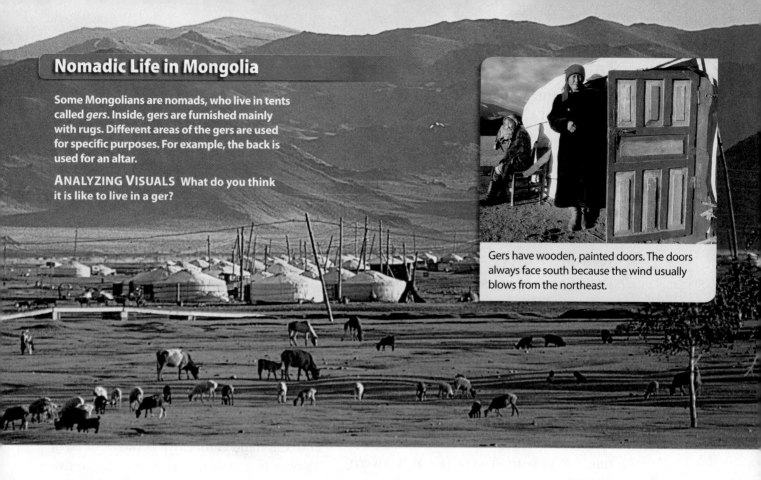

Nomadic Life in Mongolia

Some Mongolians are nomads, who live in tents called *gers*. Inside, gers are furnished mainly with rugs. Different areas of the gers are used for specific purposes. For example, the back is used for an altar.

ANALYZING VISUALS What do you think it is like to live in a ger?

Gers have wooden, painted doors. The doors always face south because the wind usually blows from the northeast.

With Russia's help, Mongolia declared independence from China in 1911. Soon Communists gained control and in 1924 formed the Mongolian People's Republic. Meanwhile, Russia had become part of the Soviet Union, a large Communist country north of Mongolia. The Soviet Union strongly influenced Mongolia and gave it large amounts of economic aid. This aid ended, however, after the Soviet Union collapsed in 1991. Since then, Mongolians have struggled to build a democratic government and a free-market economy.

Mongolia's Culture

In spite of years of Communist rule, many Mongolians follow a way of life that is traditional and adapted to the landscape. Nearly half of Mongolia's people live as nomads. They herd livestock across Mongolia's vast grasslands and make their homes in **gers** (GUHRZ). These are large, circular, felt tents that are easy to put up, take down, and move.

Since many Mongols are nomadic, horses play a major **role** in Mongolian life. As a result, Mongolian culture highly prizes horse skills, and Mongolian children often learn to ride when they are quite young.

Mongolia Today

Mongolia is sparsely populated. Slightly larger than Alaska, it has about 3 million people. More than a quarter of them live in **Ulaanbaatar** (oo-lahn-BAH-tawr), the capital and only large city. Mongolia's other cities are quite small. However, Mongolia's urban population is slowly growing.

The country's main industries include textiles, carpets, coal, copper, and oil. The city of Ulaanbaatar is the main industrial and commercial center. Mongolia produces little food other than from livestock, however, and faces food and water shortages.

READING CHECK **Summarizing** What are some features of Mongolian culture?

ACADEMIC VOCABULARY
role part or function

FOCUS ON READING
Read the second paragraph under Mongolia Today. Determine the topic of each sentence. What is the implied main idea?

Taiwan

When Portuguese sailors visited the island of Taiwan in the late 1500s, they called it *Ilha Formosa*, or "beautiful island." For many years, Westerners called Taiwan by the name Formosa. Today the loveliness of Taiwan's green mountains and waterfalls competes with its modern, crowded cities.

Taiwan's History

The Chinese began settling Taiwan in the 600s. At different times in history, both China and Japan have controlled Taiwan. In 1949, though, the Chinese Nationalists took over Taiwan. Led by Chiang Kai-shek, the Nationalists were fleeing the Communists, who had taken control of China's mainland. The Chinese Nationalist Party ruled Taiwan under martial law, or military rule, for 38 years. Today Taiwan's government is a multiparty democracy.

As the chart below explains, tensions remain between China and Taiwan. The Chinese government claims that Taiwan is a rebel part of China. In contrast, Taiwan's government claims to be the true government of China. For all practical purposes, though, Taiwan functions as an independent country.

Taiwan's Culture

Taiwan's history is reflected in its culture. Its population is about 85 percent native Taiwanese. These people are descendants of Chinese people who migrated to Taiwan largely in the 1700s and 1800s. As a result, Chinese ways dominate Taiwan's culture.

Other influences have shaped Taiwan's culture as well. Because Japan once ruled Taiwan, Japanese culture can be seen in some Taiwanese buildings and foods. More recently, European and American practices and customs are becoming noticeable in Taiwan, particularly in larger cities.

Taiwan Today

Taiwan is a modern country with a population of about 23 million. These people live on an island about the size of Delaware and Maryland combined. Because much of Taiwan is mountainous, most people live on the island's western coastal plain. This region is home to Taiwan's main cities.

The two largest cities are **Taipei** (TY-PAY) and **Kao-hsiung** (KOW-SHYOOHNG). Taipei, the capital, is Taiwan's main financial center. Because it has grown so quickly, it faces serious overcrowding and environmental problems. Kao-hsiung is a center of heavy industry and Taiwan's main seaport.

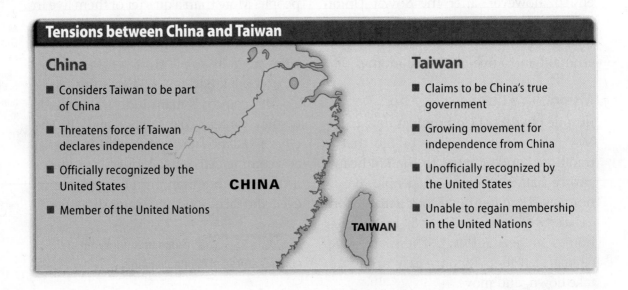

Tensions between China and Taiwan

China
- Considers Taiwan to be part of China
- Threatens force if Taiwan declares independence
- Officially recognized by the United States
- Member of the United Nations

Taiwan
- Claims to be China's true government
- Growing movement for independence from China
- Unofficially recognized by the United States
- Unable to regain membership in the United Nations

CHINA

TAIWAN

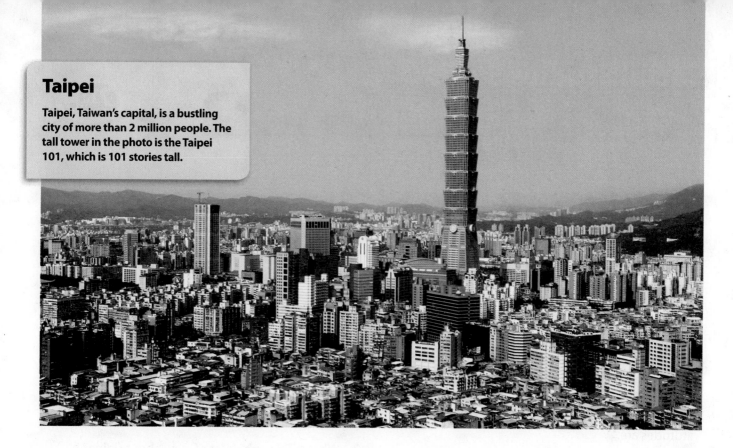

Taipei

Taipei, Taiwan's capital, is a bustling city of more than 2 million people. The tall tower in the photo is the Taipei 101, which is 101 stories tall.

Taiwan is one of Asia's richest and most industrialized countries. It is a leader in the production and export of computers and sports equipment. Taiwan's farmers grow many crops as well, such as sugarcane.

READING CHECK **Contrasting** How does Taiwan's economy differ from Mongolia's?

SUMMARY AND PREVIEW Mongolia and Taiwan are smaller countries bordering China. Mongolia is a wild land with a nomadic people who prize horses. In contrast, Taiwan is a modern and industrialized island. In the next chapter, you will learn about Japan and the Koreas.

Section 4 Assessment

hmhsocialstudies.com
ONLINE QUIZ

Reviewing Ideas, Terms, and Places

1. **a. Identify and Analyze** What is one way that Mongolia's people have adapted to their environment? Explain its significance.
   b. Make Inferences Why might many Mongolians be proud of their country's history?
   c. Elaborate Why does Mongolia's culture prize horses?

2. **a. Recall** Why is **Taipei** an important Taiwanese city, and what problems does the city face?
   b. Summarize What is the significance of Chiang Kai-shek in Taiwan's history?
   c. Evaluate Would you rather live in Taiwan or Mongolia? Provide information about each place to explain your answer.

Critical Thinking

3. **Comparing and Contrasting** Create a Venn diagram like the one shown. Use your notes and compare and contrast the histories, cultures, and societies of Mongolia and Taiwan.

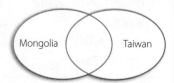

Mongolia — Taiwan

FOCUS ON WRITING

my WriteSmart

4. **Collecting Information about Mongolia and Taiwan** Consider Mongolia and Taiwan as settings for your legend. For example, your legend might explain the creation of the Gobi, a large desert located partly in Mongolia.

Social Studies Skills

Chart and Graph | **Critical Thinking** | Geography | Study

Identifying Points of View

Learn

Geography often involves the study of issues and current events that affect people, places, and regions. The way people look at an issue is their **point of view**. To analyze points of view, use these tips:

- Consider **frame of reference**, or the elements of a person's background that shapes how they see the world. Think about where the person lives, what the person does, and what his or her beliefs and attitudes are.

- Look for emotional language, such as name calling or biased terms. Emotional language often reveals a person's point of view.

- Look at the evidence, or facts and statistics, to see what point of view they support.

- Put it all together to identify the point of view.

Practice

Read the passage below about a law forbidding any part of China to declare independence. Then answer the questions that follow.

1. What is China's point of view about Taiwan?

2. What is Taiwan's point of view about China?

New Law Angers Taiwan

Taiwan's government has warned that China's new anti-secession [anti-independence] law . . . will have a "serious impact" on security in the region. . .

Taiwan officials were quick to call the measure a "war bill," coming as China boosts its military spending by 13 percent to $30 billion. . .

But Chinese Premier Wen Jiabao said the new legislation [law] was not a "war bill" and warned outsiders not to get involved . . . "It is not targeted at the people of Taiwan, nor is it a war bill," Wen said at a news conference.

Source: *CNN International,* March 14, 2005

Consider frame of reference—China considers Taiwan a rebel province. Taiwan has a growing movement for independence.

Look for emotional language—The phrase "war bill" appeals to the emotions. People have strong feelings about war.

Look at the evidence—The information about military spending is evidence supporting one point of view.

Put it all together to identify each point of view.

Apply

1. In the passage above, how might the elements of each side's frame of reference affect its point of view?

2. Which point of view does the evidence about China's military spending support?

Chapter Review

Visual Summary

Use the visual summary below to help you review the main ideas of the chapter.

QUICK FACTS

China is a large communist country with a rich culture. Both its economy and population are growing rapidly.

Mongolia lies to the north of China. It is a harsh, wild land. Many Mongolians are nomads who herd livestock.

Taiwan is an island off the southern coast of China. It is a modern and industrialized region.

Reviewing Vocabulary, Terms, and Places

Match the words or places below with their definitions or descriptions.

1. command economy
2. North China Plain
3. pagodas
4. gers
5. Tibet
6. dialect
7. Himalayas
8. Taipei

a. Buddhist region in southwest China

b. world's highest mountain range

c. regional version of a language

d. capital city of Taiwan

e. system in which the government owns most businesses and makes most economic decisions

f. fertile and highly populated region in eastern China

g. circular, felt tents in which Mongol nomads live

h. Buddhist temples with multiple stories

Comprehension and Critical Thinking

SECTION 1 *(Pages 664–667)*

9. **a. Recall** What physical features separate many of the mountain ranges in this region?

b. Explain What is the Huang He called in English, and how did the river get its name?

c. Elaborate What physical features might you see on a trip from the Himalayas to Beijing?

SECTION 2 *(Pages 668–674)*

10. **a. Identify** Which geographic and human features help China control its territory?

b. Summarize What are some of China's artistic traditions, and how have they contributed to world culture?

c. Explain Compare the population map on page 670 to the physical map on page 665. What population patterns can you identify for China? Which geographic factors do you think are responsible for these patterns?

SECTION 3 *(Pages 675–679)*

11. a. Recall What do more than half of China's workers do for a living?

b. Summarize What elements of free enterprise does China's command economy now include?

c. Evaluate What is your opinion about China's treatment of Tibet?

SECTION 4 *(Pages 680–683)*

12. a. Identify What is the capital of Mongolia?

b. Analyze How is Taiwan's history reflected in the island's culture today?

c. Predict Do you think China and Taiwan can resolve their disagreements? Why or why not?

Using the Internet

13. Activity: Touring China's Great Wall The construction of the Great Wall of China began more than 2,000 years ago. The wall was built over time to keep out invaders and to protect China's people. Through the online book, explore this wonder of the world. Take notes on the wall's history, myths and legends, and other interesting facts. Then make a brochure about your virtual visit to the Great Wall of China.

↗ hmhsocialstudies.com

Social Studies Skills

Identifying Points of View *Read the following passage from this chapter. Then answer the questions below.*

> "In 1989 more than 100,000 pro-democracy protestors gathered in Tiananmen Square in Beijing, China's capital. The protestors were demanding more political rights and freedoms. The Chinese government tried to get the protestors to leave the square. When they refused, the government used troops and tanks to make them leave. Hundreds of protestors were injured or killed."

14. What was the point of view of the protestors toward China's government? What elements shaped their frame of reference?

15. What was the point of view of China's government toward the protestors? What elements shaped its frame of reference?

Map Activity

16. China, Mongolia, and Taiwan Locate major human and geographic features of this region. On a separate sheet of paper, match the letters on the map with their correct labels below.

Beijing, China	Hong Kong, China	Taipei, Taiwan
Chang Jiang	Huang He	Himalayas
Great Wall of China	Ulaanbaatar, Mongolia	

FOCUS ON READING AND WRITING *my* WriteSmart

17. Identifying Implied Main Ideas Read the first paragraph under the heading Revolution and Civil War in Section 2. What is the implied main idea of this paragraph? What words and phrases help signal the implied main idea?

18. Writing a Legend Choose one physical or cultural feature and decide how you will explain its creation. Then review your notes and choose characters, events, and settings for your legend. Your legend should be two to three paragraphs. It should include (a) a beginning; (b) a middle that includes a climax, or high point of the story; and (c) a conclusion, or end. Remember, legends tell about extraordinary events, so you should use your imagination and creativity.

Reading Social Studies

Identifying Implied Main Ideas

FOCUS ON READING

Main ideas are often stated in a paragraph's topic sentence. When the main idea is not stated directly, however, you can find it by looking at the details in the paragraph. First, read the text carefully and think about the topic. Next, look at the facts and details and ask yourself what details are repeated. What points do those details make? Then create a statement that sums up the main idea. Examine how this process works for the paragraph below.

> Yet, other people increasingly wanted Chinese goods such as silk and tea. To gain access to the goods, some European powers forced China to open up trade in the 1800s. Europeans took control parts of the country as well. These actions angered many Chinese, some of whom blamed the emperor. At the same time, increased contact with the West exposed the Chinese to new ideas.
>
> *From Section 2, History and Culture of China*

1. What is the topic?
China's contact with Europe

↓

2. What are the facts and details?
• Europe forced China to trade.

• Europeans took over some parts of China.

• Some Chinese blamed the emperor.

• The Chinese heard new ideas.

↓

3. What details are repeated?
Increased contact with Europe

↓

4. What is the main idea?
Increased contact with Europe had both positive and negative effects on China.

YOU TRY IT!

Read the following sentences. Then use the steps listed to the right to develop a statement that expresses the main idea of the paragraph. Exchange your statement with a partner to check your understanding of the implied main idea.

> Only about 12 percent of China's land is good for farming. So how does China produce so much food? More than a third of all Chinese workers are farmers. This large labor force can work the land at high levels. In addition, farmers cut terraces into hillsides to make the most use of the land.
>
> *From Section 3, China Today*

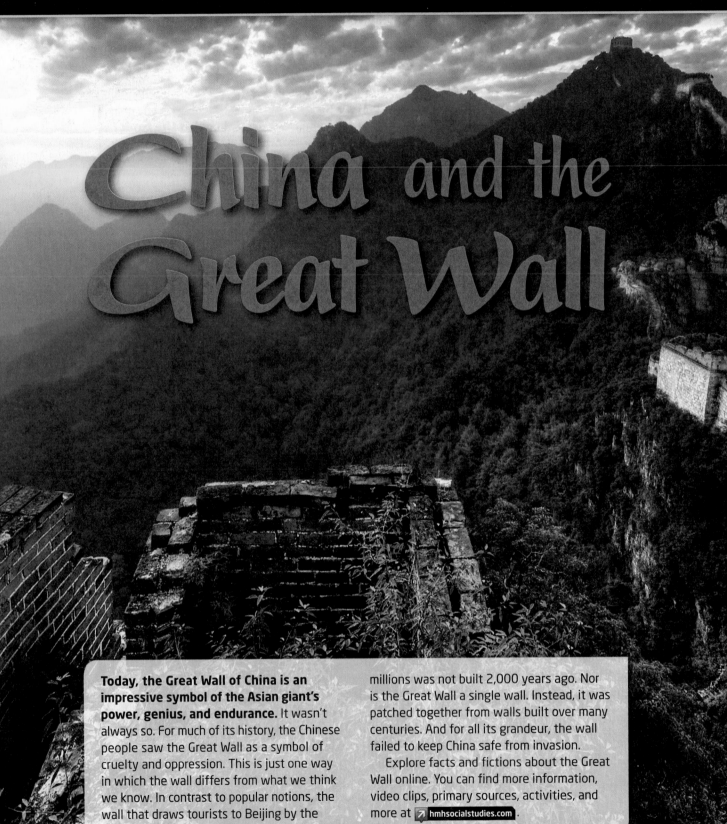

China and the Great Wall

Today, the Great Wall of China is an impressive symbol of the Asian giant's power, genius, and endurance. It wasn't always so. For much of its history, the Chinese people saw the Great Wall as a symbol of cruelty and oppression. This is just one way in which the wall differs from what we think we know. In contrast to popular notions, the wall that draws tourists to Beijing by the millions was not built 2,000 years ago. Nor is the Great Wall a single wall. Instead, it was patched together from walls built over many centuries. And for all its grandeur, the wall failed to keep China safe from invasion.

Explore facts and fictions about the Great Wall online. You can find more information, video clips, primary sources, activities, and more at ↗ **hmhsocialstudies.com**.

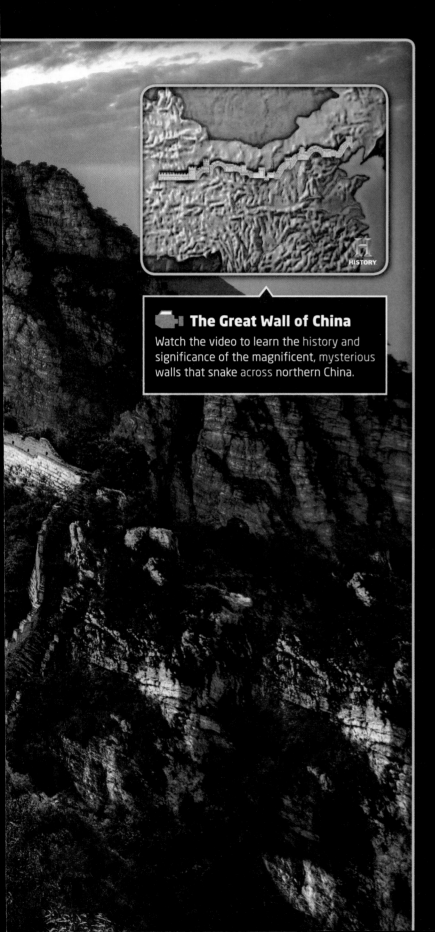

The Great Wall of China

Watch the video to learn the history and significance of the magnificent, mysterious walls that snake across northern China.

A Land of Walls Within Walls

Watch the video to learn how the Great Wall fits within the ancient Chinese tradition of wall-building.

The Human Costs of Building

Watch the video to learn about the miseries that awaited the men who built the wall.

Twentieth-Century China

Watch the video to examine the role that the wall has played in modern Chinese history.

CHAPTER 28

Japan and the Koreas

Essential Question

myNotebook

How does geography affect daily life in Japan and the Koreas?

Texas Essential Knowledge and Skills (TEKS)

1A, 1B, 2A, 2B, 3A, 3B, 3C, 4B, 4C, 4D, 4F, 5A, 5C, 6A, 6B, 7A, 7B, 8C, 9A, 9B, 9D, 15B, 15F, 17A, 17D, 18A, 18B, 18D, 19A, 20A, 20B, 20C, 21B, 21C, 22B, 22C, 22D

FOCUS ON READING AND WRITING

my **WriteSmart**

Understanding Fact and Opinion A fact is a statement that can be proved true. An opinion is someone's belief about something. When you read a textbook, you need to recognize the difference between facts and opinions. **See the lesson, Understanding Fact and Opinion, on page 713.**

Composing a Five-Line Poem For centuries, Japanese poets have written five-line poems called *tankas*. Most tanka poems describe a single image or emotion in very few words. After you read this chapter, you will choose one image of Japan or the Koreas to use as the subject of your own five-line poem. Use the annotation tools in your eBook to gather information for your assignment.

★ National capital

0   100   200 Miles
0   100   200 Kilometers

Projection: Lambert Conformal Conic

CHINA

map zone

Geography Skills

Location Japan and the Koreas are on the eastern edge of Asia.

1. **Identify** What narrow body of water separates Japan from the Koreas?
2. **Draw Conclusions** How do you think the sea may have affected life in Japan?

History For many years, Japan was ruled by warriors and generals.

Japan and the Koreas: Political

RUSSIA

Tumen R.

Yalu River

NORTH KOREA

Pyongyang

Nampo

Sea of Japan (East Sea)

Seoul

Inchon

SOUTH KOREA

Yellow Sea

Taegu

Pusan

JAPAN

Tokyo

Kyoto Nagoya Yokohama

Hiroshima

Osaka

PACIFIC OCEAN

Korea Strait

Nagasaki

40°N

130°E

140°E

120°E

30°N

N
W E
S

East China Sea

Philippine Sea

Geography Mount Fuji, a common symbol of Japan, is one of the thousands of mountains found in the region.

Culture Under Kim Il Sung, North Korea became a Communist country.

689

Physical Geography

What You Will Learn...

Main Ideas

1. The main physical features of Japan and the Koreas are rugged mountains.
2. The climates and resources of Japan and the Koreas vary from north to south.

The Big Idea

Japan and the Koreas are rugged, mountainous areas surrounded by water.

Key Terms and Places

Fuji, *p. 691*
Korean Peninsula, *p. 691*
tsunamis, *p. 692*
fishery, *p. 693*

hmhsocialstudies.com
TAKING NOTES

Use the graphic organizer online to take notes about the physical geography of Japan and the Korean Peninsula.

If YOU lived there...

You are a passenger on a very fast train zipping its way across the countryside. If you look out the window to your right, you can see the distant sparkle of sunlight on the ocean. If you look to the left, you see rocky, rugged mountains. Suddenly the train leaves the mountains, and you see hundreds of trees covered in delicate pink flowers. Rising above the trees is a single snowcapped volcano.

How does this scenery make you feel?

BUILDING BACKGROUND The train described above is one of the many that cross the islands of Japan every day. Japan's mountains, trees, and water features give the islands a unique character. Not far away, the Korean Peninsula also has a distinctive landscape.

Physical Features

Japan, North Korea, and South Korea are on the eastern edge of the Asian continent, just east of China. Separated from each other only by a narrow strait, Japan and the Koreas share many common landscape features.

Physical Features of Japan

Japan is an island country. It is made up of four large islands and more than 3,000 smaller islands. These islands are arranged in a long chain more than 1,500 miles (2,400 km) long. This is about the same length as the eastern coast of the United States, from southern Florida to northern Maine. All together, however, Japan's land area is slightly smaller than the state of California.

About 95 percent of Japan's land area is made up of four large islands. From north to south, these major islands are Hokkaido (hoh-KY-doh), Honshu (HAWN-shoo), Shikoku (shee-KOH-koo), and Kyushu (KYOO-shoo). Together they are called the home islands. Most of Japan's people live there.

Rugged, tree-covered mountains are a common sight in Japan. In fact, mountains cover some 75 percent of the country. For the most part, Japan's mountains are very steep and rocky. As a result, the country's largest mountain range, the Japanese Alps, is popular with climbers and skiers.

Japan's highest mountain, **Fuji**, is not part of the Alps. In fact, it is not part of any mountain range. A volcano, Mount Fuji rises high above a relatively flat area in eastern Honshu. The mountain's cone-shaped peak has become a symbol of Japan. In addition, many Japanese consider Fuji a sacred place. As a result, many shrines have been built at its foot and summit.

Physical Features of Korea

Jutting south from the Asian mainland, the **Korean Peninsula** includes both North Korea and South Korea. Like the islands of Japan, much of the peninsula is covered with rugged mountains. These mountains form long ranges that run along Korea's eastern coast. The peninsula's highest mountains are in the north.

Unlike Japan, Korea also has some large plains. These plains are found mainly along the peninsula's western coast and in river valleys. Korea also has more rivers than Japan does. Most of these rivers flow westward across the peninsula and pour into the Yellow Sea.

FOCUS ON READING

Are these sentences facts or opinions? How can you tell?

Japan and the Koreas: Physical

map zone

Geography Skills

Place Rugged mountains cover much of Japan and the Koreas with only a few plains areas.

1. **Locate** On which island are the Japanese Alps located?
2. **Analyze** Do you think more people live in the eastern or western part of Korea? Why?

Both Japan and the Koreas have rugged landscapes. This rocky coast is in South Korea.

ELEVATION

Feet	Meters
13,120	4,000
6,560	2,000
1,640	500
656	200
(Sea level) 0	0 (Sea level)
Below sea level	Below sea level

0   100   200 Miles
0   100   200 Kilometers

Projection: Lambert Conformal Conic

Japan and the Koreas: Volcanoes and Earthquakes

Legend
- City
- Volcano
- Earthquake
- Plate boundary

0   100   200 Miles
0   100   200 Kilometers
Projection: Miller Cylindrical

RUSSIA

Hokkaido

NORTH KOREA

Sea of Japan (East Sea)

SOUTH KOREA

Honshu

JAPAN

Kobe

Korea Strait

Shikoku

Kyushu

East China Sea

Ryukyu Islands

Philippine Sea

PACIFIC OCEAN

map zone Geography Skills

Human-Environment Interaction More than 1,000 earthquakes hit Japan every year. Most are minor, but some cause huge amounts of damage.

1. **Locate** On which large island did the 1995 Kobe earthquake occur?
2. **Compare** How does volcanic activity in Korea compare to activity in Japan?

A devastating earthquake struck Kobe (KOH-bay), Japan, in 1995. It caused more than $100 billion in damages and left thousands homeless.

Natural Disasters

Because of its location, Japan is subject to many sorts of natural disasters. Among these disasters are volcanic eruptions and earthquakes. As you can see on the map, these disasters are common in Japan. They can cause huge amounts of damage in the country. In addition, large underwater earthquakes sometimes cause destructive waves called **tsunamis** (sooh-NAH-mees).

Korea does not have many volcanoes or earthquakes. From time to time, though, huge storms called typhoons sweep over the peninsula from the Pacific. These storms cause great damage in both the Korean Peninsula and Japan.

READING CHECK **Contrasting** How are the physical features of Japan and Korea different?

Climate and Resources

Just as Japan and the Koreas have many similar physical features, they also have similar climates. The resources found in each country, however, differ greatly.

Climate

The climates of Japan and the Koreas vary from north to south. The northern parts of the region have a humid continental climate. This means that summers are cool, but winters are long and cold. In addition, the area has a short growing season.

To the south, the region has a humid subtropical climate with mild winters and hot, humid summers. These areas see heavy rains and typhoons in the summer. Some places receive up to 80 inches (200 cm) of rain each year.

Resources

Resources are not evenly distributed among Japan and the Koreas. Neither Japan nor South Korea, for example, is very rich in mineral resources. North Korea, on the other hand, has large deposits of coal, iron, and other minerals.

Although most of the region does not have many mineral resources, it does have other resources. For example, the people of the Koreas have used their land's features to generate electricity. The peninsula's rocky terrain and rapidly flowing rivers make it an excellent location for creating hydroelectric power.

In addition, Japan has one of the world's strongest fishing economies. The islands lie near one of the world's most productive fisheries. A **fishery** is a place where lots of fish and other seafood can be caught. Swift ocean currents near Japan carry countless fish to the islands. Fishers then use huge nets to catch the fish and bring them to Japan's many bustling fish markets. These fish markets are among the busiest in the world.

READING CHECK **Analyzing** What are some resources found in Japan and the Koreas?

This fish market in Tokyo, Japan, is the busiest in the world. People gather here every morning to buy freshly caught fish.

SUMMARY AND PREVIEW The islands of Japan and the Korean Peninsula share many common features. In the next section, you will see how the people of Japan and Korea also share some similar customs and how their histories have been intertwined for centuries.

Section 1 Assessment

hmhsocialstudies.com
ONLINE QUIZ

Reviewing Ideas, Terms, and Places

1. **a. Identify** What types of landforms cover Japan and the **Korean Peninsula**?
   b. Compare and Contrast How are the physical features of Japan and Korea similar? How are they different?
   c. Predict How do you think natural disasters affect life in Japan and Korea?

2. **a. Describe** What kind of climate is found in the northern parts of the region? What kind of climate is found in the southern parts?
   b. Draw Conclusions Why are **fisheries** important to Japan's economy?

Critical Thinking

3. **Categorizing** Draw a chart like this one. In each row, describe the region's landforms, climate, and resources.

	Japan	Korean Peninsula
Landforms		
Climate		
Resources		

FOCUS ON WRITING

my WriteSmart

4. **Thinking about Nature** Many Japanese poems deal with nature—the beauty of a flower, for example. What could you write about the region's physical environment in your poem?

Social Studies Skills

Using a Topographic Map

Learn

Topographic maps show elevation, or the height of land above sea level. They do so with contour lines, lines that connect points on the map that have equal elevation. Every point on a contour line has the same elevation. In most cases, everything inside that line has a higher elevation. Everything outside the line is lower. Each contour line is labeled to show the elevation it indicates.

An area that has lots of contour lines is more rugged than an area with few contour lines. The distance between contour lines shows how steep an area is. If the lines are very close together, then the area has a steep slope. If the lines are farther apart, then the area has a much gentler incline. Other symbols on the map show features such as rivers and roads.

Practice

Use the topographic map on this page to answer the following questions.

1. Is Awaji Island more rugged in the south or the north? How can you tell?

2. Does the land get higher or lower as you travel west from Yura?

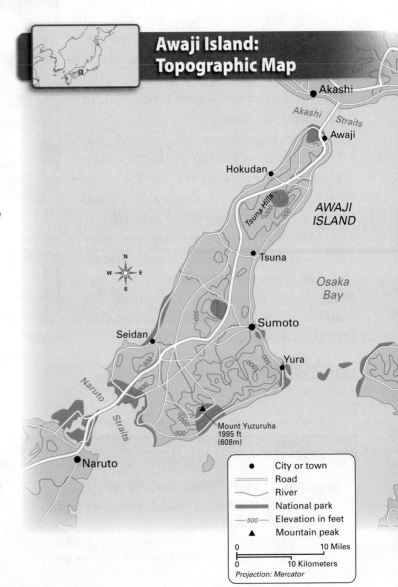

Awaji Island: Topographic Map

●	City or town
	Road
	River
	National park
—500—	Elevation in feet
▲	Mountain peak

0 — 10 Miles
0 — 10 Kilometers
Projection: Mercator

Mount Yuzuruha
1995 ft
(608m)

Apply

Search the Internet or look in a local library to find a topographic map of your area. Study the map to find three major landmarks and write down their elevations. Then pose and answer two geographic questions about the landmarks or patterns that you see on the map.

History and Culture

If YOU lived there...

You live in Kyoto, one of the most beautiful cities in Japan. Your class is visiting a museum to see an amazing demonstration by a sword maker. You all stare in amazement as he hammers red-hot metal into a curved sword, then plunges it into cold water. He tells you that his family has been making swords for 300 years.

What kind of craft would you like to know?

BUILDING BACKGROUND Even though Japan is an industrial nation, the Japanese still respect and admire traditional arts and crafts and the people who make them, such as this sword maker. In fact, traditions continue to shape life in Japan and the Koreas today.

History

Both Japan and the Koreas have very long histories. Early in these histories, their cultures were intertwined. As time passed, though, Japan and the Koreas developed very differently.

Early History

Early in their histories, both Japan and the Koreas were influenced by China. Since the Korean Peninsula borders China, and Japan lies just across the sea, elements of Chinese culture seeped into both places.

Among the elements of Chinese culture that influenced Japan and Korea was Buddhism. Scholars and missionaries first brought Buddhism into Korea. From there, visitors carried it to Japan. Before long, Buddhism was the main religion in both countries.

What You Will Learn...

Main Ideas

1. The early histories of Japan and Korea were closely linked, but the countries developed very differently.
2. Japanese culture blends traditional customs with modern innovations.
3. Though they share a common culture, life is very different in North and South Korea.

The Big Idea

History and tradition are very important to the people of Japan and the Koreas.

Key Terms and Places

Kyoto, *p. 696*
shoguns, *p. 696*
samurai, *p. 696*
kimonos, *p. 698*
kimchi, *p. 699*

hmhsocialstudies.com
TAKING NOTES

Use the graphic organizer online to take notes about the history and culture of Japan and the Koreas.

Japanese Buddha statue

Emperors, Shoguns, and Samurai

FOCUS ON
READING
Where could you
look to find out
whether these
facts are true?

The first central government in Japan was based on China's government. For many centuries, emperors ruled in Japan just as they did in China. The imperial capital at Heian, now called **Kyoto**, was a center of art, literature, and learning. At times, some of Japan's emperors were more concerned with art than with running the country. Eventually, their power slipped away.

As the emperors' power faded, Japan fell under the control of military leaders called **shoguns**. Powerful generals, the shoguns ruled Japan in the emperor's name. Only one shogun could hold power at a time.

Serving under the shogun were armies of **samurai**, or highly trained warriors. They were fierce in battle and devoted to their leaders. As a result, the samurai were very respected in Japanese society. With their support, the shoguns continued to rule Japan well into the 1800s.

BIOGRAPHY

Hirohito
(1901–1989)

Hirohito was Japan's emperor for most of the 1900s. As such, he led the country through periods of great crisis and change. He was emperor when Japan launched wars against China and Russia in the 1930s. He was also in power in 1945 when the United States bombed Hiroshima and Nagasaki. After World War II ended, Hirohito led Japan through changes in its government and economy. Many of these changes affected Hirohito personally. For example, he gave up much of the power he had once held as emperor in favor of a democratic government.

Drawing Conclusions Why might a ruler give up much of his power?

Later Japan

Not everyone was happy with the rule of the shoguns. In 1868 a group of samurai overthrew the shogun and gave power back to the emperor.

When World War II began, Japan allied itself with Germany and Italy. It wanted to build an empire in Southeast Asia and the Pacific. The Japanese drew the United States into the war in 1941 when they bombed the naval base at Pearl Harbor, Hawaii. After many years of fighting, the Americans took drastic measures to end the war. They dropped devastating atomic bombs on two Japanese cities, Hiroshima and Nagasaki. Shocked by these terrible weapons, the Japanese surrendered.

Korea

Like Japan, the Korean Peninsula has long been influenced by China. Although Korea remained independent, it was considered part of China's empire. Later, the Japanese invaded the Korean Peninsula. They were harsh rulers, and the Korean people grew to resent the Japanese.

After World War II, Korea was taken away from Japan and once again made independent. Rather than forming one country, though, the Koreans formed two. Aided by the Soviet Union, North Korea created a Communist government. In South Korea, the United States helped build a democratic government.

In 1950 North Korea invaded South Korea, starting the Korean War. The North Koreans wanted to unify all of Korea under a Communist government. With the aid of many other countries, including the United States, the South Koreans drove the invaders back. The Korean War was costly, and its effects linger in the Koreas today.

READING CHECK **Analyzing** How did the Koreas change after World War II?

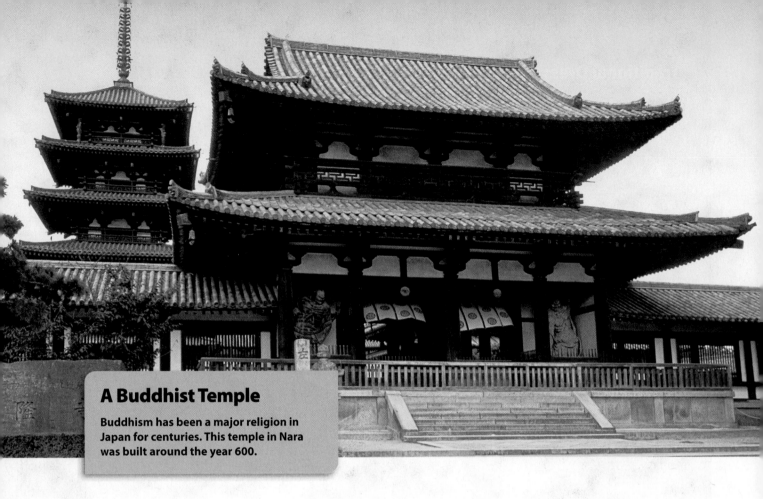

A Buddhist Temple

Buddhism has been a major religion in Japan for centuries. This temple in Nara was built around the year 600.

Japanese Culture

Japan's culture reflects the country's long and varied history. For example, some elements of the culture reflect the influence of the Chinese, while others are native to Japan. Since World War II, Western ideas and innovations have also helped shape Japanese life.

Language

Nearly everyone in Japan speaks Japanese. The Japanese language is complicated and can be difficult for other people to learn. This difficulty stems in large part from the Japanese writing system. Japanese writing uses two different types of characters. Some characters, called kanji, represent whole words. There are about 2,000 kanji characters in common use today. Other characters, called kana, stand for parts of words. Most texts written in Japanese use both kanji and kana characters.

Religion

Religion can also be complicated in Japan. Most people who live there blend elements of two religions—Shinto and Buddhism.

Unlike Buddhism, which was brought to Japan from Korea, Shinto is native to the islands. According to Shinto teachings, nature spirits called *kami* (KAH-mee) live in the world. Shintoists believe everything in nature—the sun, the moon, trees, rocks, waterfalls, and animals—has *kami*. They also believe that some *kami* help people live and keep them from harm. As a result, they build shrines to the *kami* and perform ceremonies to ask for their blessings.

Buddhists have also built shrines and temples all over Japan. Some temples, like the one pictured above, are very old. They date back to the earliest days of Buddhism in Japan. People visit these temples to seek peace and enlightenment. The search for enlightenment is Buddhists' main goal.

These Korean dancers are wearing traditional costumes to perform a fan dance. Most of the time, people in both South Korea and North Korea wear Western-style clothes.

Customs and Traditions

Japan's history lives on in its customs and traditions. For example, many Japanese wear traditional robes called **kimonos** on special occasions, just as samurai did long ago. Most of the time, though, people in Japan wear Western-style clothing.

Traditional forms of art are also still popular in Japan. Among these art forms are two types of drama, Noh and Kabuki. Noh plays use music and dance to tell a story. Actors do not move much and wear masks, using their gestures to convey their tale. Kabuki actors, on the other hand, are much more active. Kabuki plays tell stories, but they often teach lessons about duty and other **abstract** ideas as well.

READING CHECK **Summarizing** How did Japan's history affect its culture today?

ACADEMIC VOCABULARY

abstract expressing a quality or idea without reference to an actual thing

Korean Culture

Like Japan's, Korea's culture reflects the peninsula's long history. Traditional ways of life influence how people act and think.

Language and Religion

People in both North Korea and South Korea speak Korean. Unlike Japanese, Korean is written with an alphabet. People combine letters to form words, rather than using symbols to represent entire words or syllables as in Japanese.

In the past, most people in Korea were Buddhists and Confucianists. Recently, though, Christianity has also become widespread. About one-fourth of South Korea's people are Christian. North Korea, like many Communist countries, discourages people from practicing any religion.

Kimonos are the traditional clothing style in Japan. Both men and women wear kimonos for special occasions, such as weddings.

Customs and Traditions

Like the Japanese, the people of Korea have kept many ancient traditions alive. Many Korean foods, for example, have been part of the Korean diet for centuries.

One example of a long-lasting Korean food is **kimchi**, a dish made from pickled cabbage and various spices. First created in the 1100s, kimchi is still served at many Korean meals. In fact, many people think of it as Korea's national dish.

Traditional art forms have also remained popular in parts of the Koreas. This is true especially in North Korea. Since World War II, the Communist government of North Korea has encouraged people to retain many of their old customs and traditions. The Communists think that Korean culture is the best in the world and do everything they can to preserve it.

In South Korea, urbanization and the spread of modern lifestyles have led to a decline in some traditional customs. Rural areas are still very traditional, but people in urban areas have adopted new ways of life. Many of these ways are combinations of old and new ideas. For example, Korean art today combines traditional themes such as nature with modern forms, like film.

READING CHECK **Contrasting** How are North and South Korea's cultures different?

SUMMARY AND PREVIEW In this section, you learned that the cultures of Japan and the Koreas have been shaped by the countries' histories. In the next section you will see how traditional cultures continue to influnce life in Japan today.

Section 2 Assessment
hmhsocialstudies.com
ONLINE QUIZ

Reviewing Ideas, Terms, and Places

1. **a. Define** Who were **shoguns**?
   b. Elaborate How did World War II affect life in Japan?
2. **a. Identify** What is one traditional style of clothing in Japan? What do people wear most of the time?
   b. Elaborate How does Japan's religion reflect its history?
3. **a. Recall** What is **kimchi**? Why is it important in Korea?
   b. Explain What has led to many of the differences between modern culture in North and South Korea?

Critical Thinking

4. **Analyzing** Draw a diagram like this one. Using your notes, list two features of Japanese culture in the left box and of Korean culture in the right box. Below each box, write a sentence about how each country's culture reflects its history.

Japanese Culture	Korean Culture

FOCUS ON WRITING

my WriteSmart

5. **Evaluating Cultural Contributions** What cultural contributions from Japanese and Korean culture do you think are the most important?

Japan Today

TEKS 4B, 5C, 7A, 7B, 8C, 15B, 15F, 21B, 21C, 22D

What You Will Learn...

Main Ideas

1. Since World War II, Japan has developed a democratic government and one of the world's strongest economies.
2. A shortage of open space shapes daily life in Japan.
3. Crowding, competition, and pollution are among Japan's main issues and challenges.

The Big Idea

Japan has overcome many challenges to become one of the most highly developed countries in Asia.

Key Terms and Places

Diet, *p. 700*
Tokyo, *p. 700*
work ethic, *p. 701*
trade surplus, *p. 701*
tariff, *p. 701*
Osaka, *p. 704*

hmhsocialstudies.com
TAKING NOTES

Use the graphic organizer online to take notes about Japan's government, economy, and daily life.

If YOU lived there...

You and your family live in a small apartment in the crowded city of Tokyo. Every day you and your friends crowd into jammed subway trains to travel to school. Since your work in school is very hard and demanding, you really look forward to weekends. You especially like to visit mountain parks where there are flowering trees, quiet gardens, and ancient shrines.

Do you like your life in Tokyo? Why or why not?

BUILDING BACKGROUND Although Japan has become an economic powerhouse, it is still a small country in area. Its cities have become more and more crowded with high-rise office and apartment buildings. Most people live in these cities today, though many feel a special fondness for natural areas like mountains and lakes.

Government and Economy

Do you own any products made by Sony? Have you seen ads for vehicles made by Honda, Toyota, or Mitsubishi? Chances are good that you have. These companies are some of the most successful in the world, and all of them are Japanese.

Since World War II, Japan's government and economy have changed dramatically. Japan was once an imperial state that was shut off from the rest of the world. Today Japan is a democracy with one of the world's strongest economies.

Government

Since the end of World War II, Japan's government has been a constitutional monarchy headed by an emperor. Although the emperor is officially the head of state, he has little power. His main role is to act as a symbol of Japan and of the Japanese people. In his place, power rests in an elected legislature called the **Diet** and in an elected prime minister. From the capital city of **Tokyo**, the Diet and the prime minister make the laws that govern life in Japan today.

Economy

Today Japan is an economic powerhouse. However, this was not always the case. Until the 1950s, Japan's economy was not that strong. Within a few decades, though, the economy grew tremendously.

The most successful area of Japan's economy is manufacturing. Japanese companies are known for making high-quality products, especially cars and electronics. Japanese companies are among the world's leading manufacturers of televisions, DVD players, CD players, and other electronic items. The methods that companies use to make these products are also celebrated. Many Japanese companies are leaders in new technology and ideas.

Reasons for Success Many factors have contributed to Japan's economic success. One factor is the government. It works closely with business leaders to control production and plan for the future.

Japan's workforce also contributed to its success. Japan has well-educated, highly trained workers. As a result, its companies tend to be both efficient and productive. Most workers in Japan also have a strong work ethic. A **work ethic** is the belief that work in itself is worthwhile. Because of their work ethic, most Japanese work hard and are loyal to their companies. As a result, the companies are successful.

Trade Japan's economy depends on trade. In fact, many products manufactured in the country are intended to be sold outside of Japan. Many of these goods are sent to China and the United States. The United States is Japan's major trading partner.

Japan's trade has been so successful that it has built up a huge trade surplus. A **trade surplus** exists when a country exports more goods than it imports. Because of this surplus, many Japanese companies have become very wealthy.

CONNECTING TO **Technology**

Building Small

The Japanese are known as masters of technology. Companies use this technology in many ways to create new products and improve existing ones. One way many Japanese companies have sought to improve their products—especially personal electronics products—is by making them smaller.

Since Sony released the first personal stereo system in the late 1970s, making small products has been a major business in Japan. Now shoppers can buy tiny radios, video games, cell phones, and cameras. Some of these products are smaller than the palm of your hand.

Generalizing Why might people want to buy small versions of products?

Japan is able to export more than it imports in part because of high tariffs. A **tariff** is a fee that a country charges on imports or exports. For many years, Japan's government has placed high tariffs on goods brought into the country. This makes imported goods more expensive, and so people buy Japanese goods rather than imported ones.

Resources Although its economy is based on manufacturing, Japan has few natural resources. As a result, the country must import raw materials. In addition, Japan has little arable land. Farms cannot grow enough food for the country's growing population. Instead, the Japanese have to buy food from other countries, including China and the United States.

READING CHECK **Summarizing** What have the Japanese done to build their economy?

Daily Life

Japan is a densely populated country. Slightly smaller than California, it has nearly three times as many people! Most of these people live in crowded cities such as the capital, Tokyo.

Life in Tokyo

FOCUS ON READING

How can you tell that the statements in this paragraph are facts?

Besides serving as the national capital, Tokyo is the center of Japan's banking and communication industries. As a result, the city is busy, noisy, and very crowded. About 36 million people live in a relatively small area. Because Tokyo is so densely populated, land is scarce. As a result, Tokyo's real estate prices are among the highest in the world. Some people save up for years to buy homes in Tokyo. They earn money by putting money in savings accounts or by investing in stocks and bonds.

Because space is so limited in Tokyo, people have found creative ways to adapt. Buildings tend to be fairly tall and narrow so that they take less land area. People also use space under ground. For example, shops and restaurants can be found below the streets in subway stations. Another way the Japanese have found to save space is the capsule hotel. Guests in these hotels—mostly traveling businesspeople—crawl into tiny sleeping chambers rather than having rooms with beds.

Many people work in Tokyo but live outside the city. So many people commute to and from Tokyo that trains are very crowded. During peak travel times, commuters are crammed into train cars.

Tokyo is not all about work, though. During their leisure time, people can visit Tokyo's many parks, museums, and stores. They can also take short trips to local amusement parks, baseball stadiums, or other attractions. Among these attractions are a huge indoor beach and a ski resort filled with artificial snow.

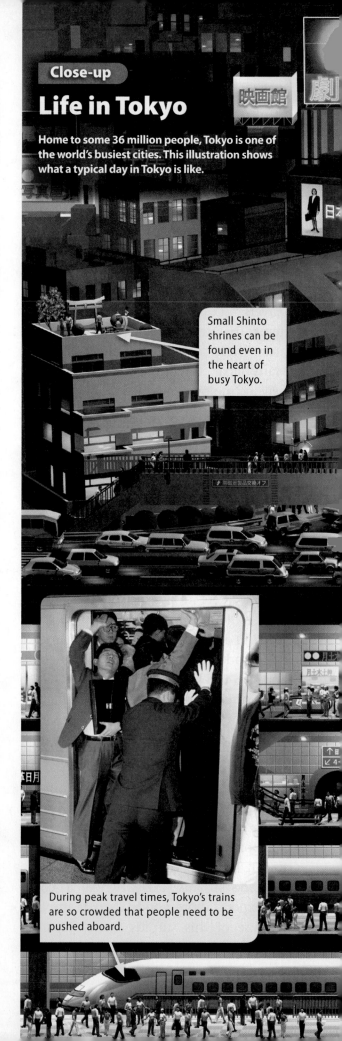

Close-up

Life in Tokyo

Home to some 36 million people, Tokyo is one of the world's busiest cities. This illustration shows what a typical day in Tokyo is like.

Small Shinto shrines can be found even in the heart of busy Tokyo.

During peak travel times, Tokyo's trains are so crowded that people need to be pushed aboard.

Gardens planted on the roofs of buildings help keep Tokyo's temperature down.

To save space, the Japanese build capsule hotels. Each guest sleeps in his or her own tiny chamber.

Bustling shopping centers can be found below many of Tokyo's streets.

ANALYSIS SKILL **ANALYZING VISUALS**

Based on this image, how does life in Tokyo compare to daily life where you are?

Life in Other Cities

Most of Japan's other cities, like Tokyo, are crowded and busy. Many of them serve as centers of industry or transportation.

The second largest city in Japan, **Osaka**, is located in western Honshu. In Osaka—as in Tokyo and other cities—tall, modern skyscrapers stand next to tiny Shinto temples. Another major city is Kyoto. Once Japan's capital, Kyoto is full of historic buildings.

Transportation between Cities

To connect cities that lie far apart, the Japanese have built a network of rail lines. Some of these lines carry very fast trains called *Shinkansen*, or bullet trains. They can reach speeds of more than 160 miles per hour (250 kph). Japan's train system is very **efficient**. Trains nearly always leave on time and are almost never late.

ACADEMIC
VOCABULARY

efficient
productive and
not wasteful

Rural Life

Not everyone in Japan lives in cities. Some people live in the country in small villages. The people in these villages own or work on farms.

Relatively little of Japan's land is arable, or suitable for farming. Much of the land is too rocky or steep to grow crops on. As a result, most farms are small. The average Japanese farm is only about 2.5 acres (1 hectare). In contrast, the average farm in the United States is 175 times that size.

Because their farms are so small and Japan imports so much of its food, many farmers cannot make a living from their crops. As a result, many people have left rural areas to find jobs in cities.

READING CHECK **Finding Main Ideas** What are Japanese cities like?

Japan: Population

100,000 people

| 0 | 100 | 200 Miles |
| 0 | 100 | 200 Kilometers |

Projection: Lambert Conformal Conic

Sapporo

Sea of Japan
(East Sea)

JAPAN

Tokyo
Kyoto Nagoya
Osaka

Korea Strait

PACIFIC
OCEAN

Population Growth in Japan

Japan

Tokyo Area

map zone **Geography Skills**

Place Most of Japan's people live in crowded cities on the country's few coastal plains.
1. **Locate** Where are Japan's most crowded cities?
2. **Analyze** According to the chart, what was Japan's population in 2000?

Issues and Challenges

Many people consider Japan one of the world's most successful countries. In recent years, however, a few issues have arisen that present challenges for Japan's future.

One of these issues is Japan's lack of space. As cities grow, crowding has become a serious issue. It is not uncommon for a family of four to live in a one-bedroom apartment. To escape overcrowded city life, some move to distant suburbs. Unfortunately, many suburban dwellers must travel back to the city for work. For commuters, two to three hour daily trips to and from work are normal.

To make space, some people have begun to construct taller buildings. Such buildings have to be carefully planned, though, to withstand earthquakes.

Japan also faces economic challenges. For many years, it had the only strong economy in East Asia. Recently, however, other countries have challenged Japan's economic dominance. Competition from China and South Korea has begun taking business from some Japanese companies.

Pollution has also become a problem in Japan. In 1997 officials from more than 150 countries met in Japan to discuss the pollution problem. They signed the Kyoto Protocol, an agreement to cut down on pollution and improve air quality.

Japan's stability was deeply shaken on March 11, 2011, when a massive earthquake struck northeastern Japan, unleashing a savage tsunami. More than 18,000 people were killed; most died by drowning. To make matters worse, the tsunami caused a cooling system failure at the Fukushima Daiichi Nuclear Power Plant, resulting in a nuclear meltdown and release of radioactive materials. Today, Japan's people and government continue to rebuild their nation.

READING CHECK **Finding Main Ideas** What are three issues facing Japan?

SUMMARY AND PREVIEW Since World War II, Japan has created a democratic government and a strong, highly technological economy. In the next section, you will learn about changes that have occurred in South Korea and North Korea in the same time period.

Section 3 Assessment

Reviewing Ideas, Terms, and Places

1. **a. Identify** What are some goods made in Japan?
   b. Explain How has Japan's government changed since World War II?
   c. Elaborate Why do you think a **work ethic** is so important to the Japanese economy?
2. **a. Describe** How have people tried to save space in Japanese cities?
   b. Geographic Questions Look back at the model of Daily Life in Tokyo. Use the model to pose and answer a question about population patterns in Japan.
3. **a. Identify** What is one issue that crowding has caused for Japan?
   b. Analyze How are other countries presenting challenges to Japan's economy?

Critical Thinking

4. **Analyzing** Draw a graphic organizer like the one shown here. In one circle, write two sentences about city life in Japan. In another, write two sentences about rural life. In the third, write two sentences about issues facing the Japanese.

   (City Life) (Rural Life) (Issues)

FOCUS ON WRITING *my* WriteSmart

5. **Thinking about Japan** What image, or picture, of life in Japan could you write about in your poem? List two or three ideas. Then decide which is the most promising idea for your poem.

The Koreas Today

 TEKS 1B, 2B, 4B, 5C, 9A, 9B, 9D, 15B, 15F, 21B, 21C, 22C, 22D

What You Will Learn...

Main Ideas

1. The people of South Korea today have freedom and economic opportunities.
2. The people of North Korea today have little freedom or economic opportunity.
3. Some people in both South and North Korea support the idea of Korean reunification.

The Big Idea

Though they share a common history and culture, the two Koreas have very different governments and economies.

Key Terms and Places

Seoul, *p. 707*
demilitarized zone, *p. 707*
Pyongyang, *p. 709*

hmhsocialstudies.com
TAKING NOTES

Use the graphic organizer online to take notes about South Korea and North Korea.

If YOU lived there...

You live in Inchon, one of South Korea's largest cities. Sometimes your grandparents tell you about the other family members who still live in North Korea. You have never met them, of course, and your grandparents have not seen them since they were children, more than 50 years ago. After hearing stories about these family members, you are curious about their lives.

Would you like to visit North Korea?

BUILDING BACKGROUND A truce ended the Korean War in 1953, but it left the Korean Peninsula divided into two very different countries. The conflict separated families from their relatives on the other side of the zone that divides South Korea from North Korea. Since then, the countries have developed in very different ways.

South Korea Today

Japan's closest neighbor is both a major economic rival and a key trading partner. That neighbor is South Korea. Like Japan, South Korea is a democratic country with a strong economy. Unlike Japan, South Korea shares a border with a hostile neighbor—North Korea.

Government and Economy

The official name of South Korea is the Republic of Korea. As the name suggests, South Korea's government is a republic. It is headed by a president and an assembly elected by the people, much like the United States is. In fact, the United States helped create South Korea's government after World War II.

The United States also helped make South Korea's economy one of the strongest in East Asia. In addition, Korean business leaders and government officials have worked together to ensure that the economy stays strong. In recent years, South Korea has become a major manufacturing country, exporting goods to places all around the world.

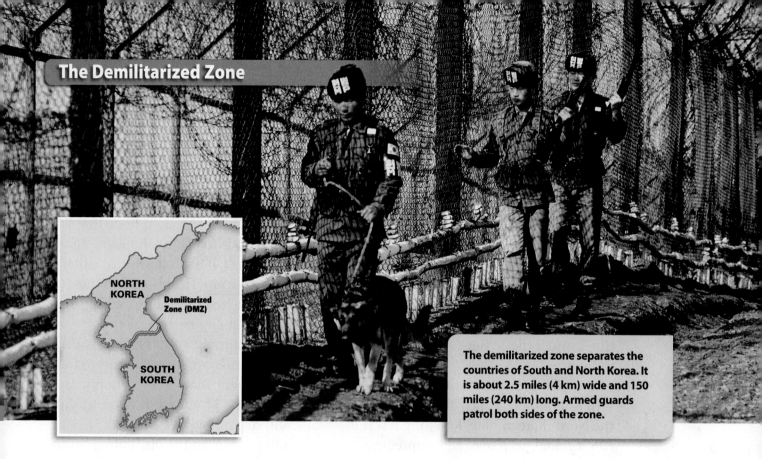

The Demilitarized Zone

NORTH KOREA

Demilitarized Zone (DMZ)

SOUTH KOREA

The demilitarized zone separates the countries of South and North Korea. It is about 2.5 miles (4 km) wide and 150 miles (240 km) long. Armed guards patrol both sides of the zone.

Daily Life

Like Japan, South Korea is very densely populated. The capital city, **Seoul** (SOHL), is one of the most densely populated cities in the world. It has more than 44,000 people per square mile (17,000/sq km).

Although parts of South Korea are densely populated, very few people live in the mountainous interior. Most people live near the coast. A coastal plain in western South Korea is the most crowded part of the country.

In South Korea's cities, most people live in small apartments. Because space is scarce, housing is expensive. Also, cities sometimes suffer from pollution from the many factories, cars, and coal-fired heating systems found there. In some cities, industrial waste has also polluted the water.

Outside the cities, many South Koreans still follow traditional ways of life. Most of them are farmers who grow rice, beans, and cabbage they can use to make kimchi. They usually live on small farms.

Issues and Challenges

Government policies and international politics have led to some challenges for South Korea. Although South Korea has a successful economy, some people feel that its government is corrupt. For many years, four families have controlled much of the country's industry. As a result, wealth and power became concentrated in the hands of big business. This led to corruption of government officials, but efforts are being made to reform business practices.

A bigger challenge to South Korea is its relationship with North Korea. Since the end of the Korean War in the 1950s, the two countries have been separated. Between them is a **demilitarized zone**, an empty buffer zone created to keep the two countries from fighting. Although troops are not allowed in the demilitarized zone, guards patrol both sides.

READING CHECK **Summarizing** What issues face South Korea today?

North Korea Today

The official name of North Korea is the Democratic People's Republic of Korea. Its name, however, is misleading. North Korea is neither a democracy nor a republic. It is a totalitarian, communist state.

Government and Economy

ACADEMIC VOCABULARY

policies rules, courses of action

The government of North Korea was created soon after World War II. Its first leader, Kim Il Sung, ruled from 1948 until his death in 1994. During this time North Korea was a communist dictatorship, at times under the Soviet Union's sphere of influence.

Kim Il Sung was succeeded by his eldest son, Kim Jong Il. Called "Dear Leader" by the North Korean state, Kim Jong Il was in fact a brutal, secretive, and unpredictable dictator. He tightly controlled life in North Korea. Under his rule, North Koreans suffered human rights abuses, poverty, and widespread hunger. He also developed long-range missiles and nuclear weapons that he used to threaten neighboring countries.

When Kim Jong Il died in December 2011, his son Kim Jong Un took over. The rise of a new leader brought hope that life would improve for North Koreans. However, Kim Jong Un has followed his father's domestic policies. He also continues to develop and test weapons, which has threatened stability in the region.

As a Communist country, North Korea has a command economy. This means that the government plans the economy and decides what is produced. It also owns all land and controls access to jobs.

Unlike Japan and South Korea, North Korea is rich in mineral resources. With

Life in South and North Korea

these resources, factories in North Korea make machinery and military supplies. However, most factories use out-of-date technology. As a result, North Korea is much poorer than Japan and South Korea.

Because it is so rocky, very little of North Korea's land can be farmed. The farmland that does exist is owned by the government. It is farmed by cooperatives—large groups of farmers who work the land together. These cooperatives are not able to grow enough food for the country. As a result, the government has to import food. This can be a difficult foreign policy task because North Korea's relations with most other countries are strained.

Daily Life

Like Japan and South Korea, North Korea is largely an urban society. Most people live in cities. The largest city is the capital,

The differences between life in South Korea and North Korea can be seen in their capitals. Seoul, South Korea (shown to the left), is a busy, modern city and a major commercial center. In comparison, North Korea's capital, Pyongyang (shown above), has little traffic or commercial development.

ANALYZING VISUALS What do these photos suggest about life in Seoul and Pyongyang?

Pyongyang (PYUHNG-YAHNG), in the west. Pyongyang is a crowded urban area. About 3 million people live in the city.

Life in Pyongyang is very different from life in Tokyo or Seoul. For example, few people in Pyongyang own private cars. The North Korean government allows only top Communist officials to own cars. Most residents have to use buses or the subway to get around. At night, many streets are dark because of electricity shortages.

North Koreans have fewer rights than the people of Japan or South Korea. For example, the government controls individual speech and the press. Because the government feels that religion conflicts with Communist ideas, it also discourages people from practicing religion.

Issues and Challenges

Why does North Korea, which is rich in resources, have shortages of electricity and food? These problems are due in part to North Korea's foreign policies. For years, North Korea had ties with other Communist countries. Since the breakup of the Soviet Union, North Korea has isolated itself from the rest of the world. It has closed its markets to foreign goods, which means that other countries cannot sell their goods there. At the same time, North Korea lacks the technology to take advantage of its resources. As a result, many people suffer and resources go unused.

In addition, many countries worry about North Korea's possession of nuclear weapons. In 2006 North Korea declared that it had successfully conducted its first underground nuclear test. It has conducted two more nuclear tests, one in 2009 and another 2013. These developments concern countries in Asia and around the world.

READING CHECK **Generalizing** What is North Korea's relationship with the world?

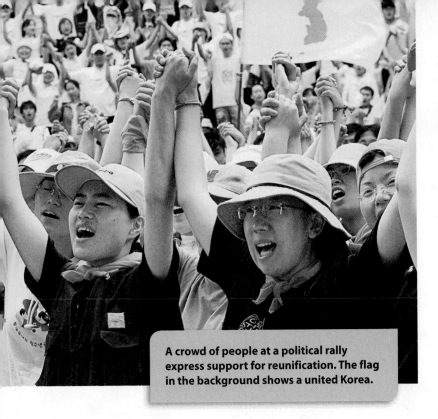

A crowd of people at a political rally express support for reunification. The flag in the background shows a united Korea.

At times, the governments of both South Korea and North Korea have expressed their support for reunification. Leaders from the two countries met in 2000 for the first time since the Korean War. As part of their meeting, they discussed ways to improve relations between the two countries. For example, they agreed to build a road through the demilitarized zone to connect the two Koreas.

The question of government is an obstacle to reunification. South Koreans want democracy while North Korean leaders insist on communism. Another obstacle is generational. As time passes, fewer young South Koreans support reunification. Some even fear that they will inherit the social and political problems of North Korea.

READING CHECK **Summarizing** What issues stand in the way of Korean reunification?

Korean Reunification

FOCUS ON READING

What opinion do many Koreans hold toward reunification?

For years, many South and North Koreans wanted their country to be reunited. The creation of two Koreas split friends and family. It also divided people that shared a common culture and history. Many believed that reunification would heal families and Korean culture as a whole.

SUMMARY AND PREVIEW In this chapter you learned about the history, cultures, and people of Japan and the Koreas. In the next chapter, you will examine a region that lies farther south, a region called Southeast Asia.

Section 4 Assessment

 hmhsocialstudies.com
ONLINE QUIZ

Reviewing Ideas, Terms, and Places

1. **a. Define** What is the **demilitarized zone**? Why does it exist?
   b. Summarize What factors have helped South Korea develop a strong economy?
2. **a. Explain** Which geographic factor explains why North Korea must import food? Why is this a difficult foreign policy task?
   b. Compare How is North Korea's government different from South Korea's?
3. **a. Recall** Why do many Koreans support the idea of reunification?
   b. Evaluate If you lived in North or South Korea, do you think you would support the reunification of the countries? Why or why not?

Critical Thinking

4. **Analyze** Draw a diagram like the one below to analyze the differences between the societies of South and North Korea. Write three statements about South Korea and three statements about North Korea. In the oval, list one factor that supports reunification and one that hinders it.

South Korea | Reunification | North Korea

FOCUS ON WRITING *my* WriteSmart

5. **Considering Korea** As you read about the Koreas, did you think of an image, or picture, that would work in a poem? List your ideas.

Chapter Review

Visual Summary

With a partner, use the visual summary to discuss the chapter's main ideas.

QUICK FACTS

Japan and the Korean Peninsula have rugged landscapes that are largely covered by mountains.

Japan has one of the world's strongest economies, due in large part to its superior technology.

Since World War II, life in democratic South Korea has been very different from life in Communist North Korea.

Reviewing Vocabulary, Terms, and Places

Imagine these terms from the chapter are correct answers to items in a crossword puzzle. Write the clues for the answers.

1. Tokyo
2. abstract
3. trade surplus
4. tariff
5. kimono
6. efficient
7. work ethic
8. Seoul
9. fishery
10. Pyongyang
11. kimchi
12. policy

Comprehension and Critical Thinking

SECTION 1 *(Pages 690–693)*

13. **a. Identify** What physical feature covers most of Japan and the Korean Peninsula? What is one famous example of this landform?

   b. Draw Conclusions Fish and seafood are very important in the Japanese diet. Why do you think this is so?

   c. Predict How do you think earthquakes and typhoons would affect your life if you lived in Japan?

SECTION 2 *(Pages 695–699)*

14. **a. Identify** Who were the shoguns? What role did they play in Japanese history?

   b. Explain What caused the Korean War? What happened as a result of the war?

   c. Elaborate How have the histories of Japan and Korea affected their cultures?

SECTION 3 *(Pages 700–705)*

15. **a. Recall** What is the most important aspect of Japan's economy?

   b. Make Inferences Why is Tokyo such a busy and crowded city?

   c. Develop How might Japan try to address the problem of crowding in its cities?

SECTION 4 *(Pages 706–710)*

16. a. Recall What type of government does South Korea have? What type of government does North Korea have?

b. Contrast How is South Korea's economy different from North Korea's? Which has been more successful?

c. Predict Do you think the reunification of the Koreas will happen in the near future? Why or why not?

Social Studies Skills

Using a Topographic Map *Use the topographic map in this chapter's Social Studies Skills lesson to answer the following questions.*

17. What elevations do the contour lines on this map show?

18. Where are the highest points on Awaji Island located? How can you tell?

19. Is the city of Sumoto located more or less than 500 feet above sea level?

Using the Internet

20. Activity: Comparing Schools Have you ever wondered what it would be like to live in Japan? How would your life be different if you lived there? What would you learn about in school? What would you eat for lunch? Learn about Japan and about Japanese culture by exploring the Web links provided through the online book. Look for ways that your life would be the same and different if you grew up in Japan. Then record what you learned in a chart or a graphic organizer.

hmhsocialstudies.com

Map Activity

21. Japan and the Koreas On a separate sheet of paper, match the letters on the map with their correct labels.

North Korea	Tokyo, Japan
South Korea	Hokkaido
Korea Strait	Sea of Japan (East Sea)

map zone

FOCUS ON READING AND WRITING *my*WriteSmart

Understanding Fact and Opinion *Decide whether each of the following statements is a fact or an opinion.*

22. Japan would be a great place to live.

23. Japan is an island country.

24. North Korea should give up communism.

25. The Koreas should reunify.

Writing Your Five-Line Poem *Use your notes and the instructions below to create your poem.*

26. Review your notes and decide on a topic to write about. Remember that your poem should describe one image or picture—an object, a place, etc.—from Japanese or Korean culture.

The first three lines of your poem should describe the object or place you have chosen. The last two should express how it makes you feel. Try to use the traditional Tanka syllable count in your poem: five syllables in lines 1 and 3; seven in lines 2, 4, and 5. Remember that your poem does not have to rhyme. Use *my*WriteSmart in your eBook to write your poem.

Reading Social Studies

Understanding Fact and Opinion

When you read, it is important to distinguish facts from opinions. A fact is a statement that can be proved or disproved. An opinion is a personal belief or attitude, so it cannot be proved true or false. When you are reading a social studies text, you want to read only facts, not the author's opinions. To determine whether a sentence is a fact or an opinion, ask if it can be proved using outside sources. If it can, the sentence is a fact. The following pairs of statements show the difference between facts and opinions.

Fact: Hirohito was Japan's emperor for most of the 1900s. *(This fact can be proved through research.)*

Opinion: I believe Hirohito was Japan's best emperor. *(The word* best *signifies that this is the writer's judgment, or opinion.)*

Fact: One example of a long-lasting Korean food is kimchi, a dish made from pickled cabbage and various spices. *(The ingredients in kimchi can be checked for accuracy.)*

Opinion: Kimchi is a delicious dish made from pickled cabbage and various spices. *(No one can prove kimchi is delicious, because it is a matter of personal taste.)*

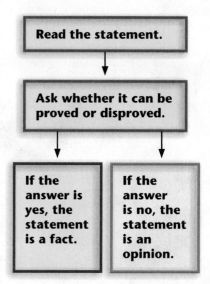

Read the statement.

Ask whether it can be proved or disproved.

If the answer is yes, the statement is a fact.

If the answer is no, the statement is an opinion.

YOU TRY IT!

Read the following sentences and identify each as a fact or an opinion.

1. The second largest city in Japan, Osaka, is located in western Honshu.

2. In Osaka—as in Tokyo and other cities—tall modern skyscrapers stand next to tiny Shinto temples.

3. Osaka is more beautiful than Tokyo.

4. Another major city is Kyoto, which all tourists should visit.

5. Once Japan's capital, Kyoto is full of historic buildings.

6. Tokyo has the country's best restaurants.

Japan and the Samurai Warrior

For over a thousand years, the samurai—an elite warrior class—were a powerful force in Japanese society. The way of life of the samurai lords and warriors was, in many ways, like those of the medieval lords and knights of Europe. The great samurai warlords ruled large territories and relied on the fighting skills of their fierce samurai warriors to battle their enemies. But samurai warriors were more than just soldiers. Samurai were expected to embrace beauty and culture, and many were skilled artists. They also had a strict personal code that valued personal honor above all things—even life itself.

Explore the fascinating world of the samurai warrior online. You can find a wealth of information, video clips, primary sources, activities, and more at ↗ **hmhsocialstudies.com** .

Rise of the Samurai Class

Watch the video to learn how the samurai developed from armed tax collectors into warlords and armies that ruled Japan.

A New Way of Life in Japan

Watch the video to learn how peace and isolation took hold in Japan and changed the role of the samurai in society.

> *I have no eyes;*
> *   I make the Flash of Lightning my Eyes.*
> *I have no ears; I make Sensibility my Ears.*
> *I have no limbs;*
> *   I make Promptitude my Limbs.*
> *I have no laws;*
> *   I make Self-Protection my Laws.*

A Code for Samurai Living

Read the document to learn about the strict but lyrical code of the samurai warrior.

Death of the Samurai Class

Watch the video to see how the end of Japan's isolation from the outside world signaled the beginning of the end of the samurai class.

CHAPTER 29
Southeast Asia

Essential Question   *my*Notebook

What characteristics unite the diverse nations of Southeast Asia?

Texas Essential Knowledge and Skills (TEKS)

1A, 1B, 2A, 2B, 3A, 3B, 3C, 4B, 4C, 4D, 4F, 5A, 5B, 5C, 6A, 6B, 6C, 7A, 7B, 7C, 11D, 15B, 15D, 15E, 15F, 18A, 21B, 21C, 21D, 22A, 22B, 22C, 22D

FOCUS ON READING AND SPEAKING   *my* WriteSmart

Using Context Clues–Definitions As you read, you may run across words you do not know. You can often figure out the meaning of an unknown word by using context clues. One type of context clue is a definition of a word, or a restatement of its meaning. To use these clues, look at the words and sentences around the unknown word—its context. **See the lesson, Using Context Clues–Definitions, on page 739.**

Presenting an Interview With a partner, you will role-play a journalist interviewing a regional expert on Southeast Asia. First, read about the region. Then, with your partner create a question-and-answer interview script about the region to present to your classmates. Use the annotation tools in your eBook to gather information for your assignment.

Geography Boats lie along the shore of Phi Phi Don Island in Thailand. The island's beauty makes it a popular vacation spot.

Tropic of Cancer

Luzon
Quezon City
Manila **PHILIPPINES**

South China Sea

Philippine Sea

Palawan

Mindanao

map zone Geography Skills

Regions The region of Southeast Asia includes 11 countries—some quite small.
1. **Name** What are the names of the 11 countries located in Southeast Asia?
2. **Make Inferences** The countries of Indonesia and the Philippines consist of many islands. How do you think this fact affects life there?

BRUNEI
Bandar Seri Begawan

MALAYSIA

Celebes Sea

Sulawesi (Celebes)

PACIFIC OCEAN

Borneo

INDONESIA   Moluccas

IRIAN JAYA

Java Sea   New Guinea

Java Bali

TIMOR-LESTE

Lesser Sunda Islands   Dili

Timor

Culture Traditional dances remain an important part of the culture of Bali. *Barong* dancers use their hands, arms, and eyes to tell a traditional story.

History The golden Shwedagon Pagoda is a Buddhist shrine in Yangon, Myanmar. Pagodas have been on this site since the 500s BC.

715

TEKS 3A, 3B, 3C, 4D, 5A, 6A, 6B, 7B, 21B, 21C, 21D

What You Will Learn...

Main Ideas

1. Southeast Asia's physical features include peninsulas, islands, rivers, and many seas, straits, and gulfs.
2. The tropical climate of Southeast Asia supports a wide range of plants and animals.
3. Southeast Asia is rich in natural resources such as wood, rubber, and fossil fuels.

The Big Idea

Southeast Asia is a tropical region of peninsulas, islands, and waterways with diverse plants, animals, and resources.

Key Terms and Places

Indochina Peninsula, *p. 716*
Malay Peninsula, *p. 716*
Malay Archipelago, *p. 716*
archipelago, *p. 716*
New Guinea, *p. 717*
Borneo, *p. 717*
Mekong River, *p. 717*

TAKING NOTES

Use the graphic organizer online to take notes on the physical geography of Southeast Asia.

Physical Geography

If **YOU** lived there...

Your family lives on a houseboat on a branch of the great Mekong River in Cambodia. You catch fish in cages under the boat. Your home is part of a floating village of houseboats and houses built on stilts in the water. Boats loaded with fruits and vegetables travel from house to house. Even your school is on a nearby boat.

How does water shape life in your village?

BUILDING BACKGROUND Waterways, such as rivers, canals, seas, and oceans, are important to life in Southeast Asia. Waterways are both "highways" and sources of food. Where rivers empty into the sea, they form deltas, areas of rich soil good for farming.

Physical Features

Where can you find a flower that grows up to 3 feet across and smells like rotting garbage? How about a lizard that can grow up to 10 feet long and weigh up to 300 pounds? These amazing sights as well as some of the world's most beautiful tropical paradises are all in Southeast Asia.

The region of Southeast Asia is made up of two peninsulas and two large island groups. The **Indochina Peninsula** and the **Malay** (muh-LAY) **Peninsula** extend from the Asian mainland. We call this part of the region Mainland Southeast Asia. The two island groups are the Philippines and the **Malay Archipelago**. An **archipelago** (ahr-kuh-PE-luh-goh) is a large group of islands. We call this part of the region Island Southeast Asia.

Landforms

In Mainland Southeast Asia, rugged mountains fan out across the countries of Myanmar (MYAHN-mahr), Thailand (TY-land), Laos (LOWS), and Vietnam (vee-ET-NAHM). Between these mountains are low plateaus and river floodplains.

Southeast Asia: Physical

map zone **Geography Skills**

Regions Southeast Asia is a region of islands and peninsulas surrounded by water.
1. **Identify** What two major peninsulas are located in this region?
2. **Contrast** Almost all the countries in this region have coastlines. How does the country of Laos differ from this pattern?

Hkakabo Razi
19,300 ft
(5,885 m)

MYANMAR
(BURMA)

CHINA

Tropic of Cancer

20°N

LAOS

Gulf of
Tonkin

Indochina
Peninsula

THAILAND

South
China
Sea

Luzon

Philippine
Sea

PHILIPPINES

CAMBODIA   VIETNAM

Mindoro

Tonle
Sap

10°N   Isthmus
of Kra

Palawan

Mindanao

Strait of
Malacca

BRUNEI

Celebes Sea

PACIFIC
OCEAN

Sumatra   MALAYSIA

Malay

Archipelago
Sulawesi
(Celebes)

0° Equator

SINGAPORE

Borneo

Moluccas

INDONESIA

INDIAN
OCEAN

Java Sea

Jaya Peak ▲
16,500 ft (5,030 m)

New
Guinea

10°S

Krakatau
2,667 ft
(813 m)

Java   Bali Sumbawa

Flores

Lombok   Sumba

Timor

TIMOR-LESTE

ELEVATION

Feet	Meters
13,120	4,000
6,560	2,000
1,640	500
656	200
(Sea level) 0	0 (Sea level)
Below sea level	Below sea level

0   400   800 Miles

0   400   800 Kilometers

Projection: Miller Cylindrical

① Mist hovers over the Mekong River as it flows through the forested mountains of northern Thailand.

Island Southeast Asia consists of more than 20,000 islands, some of them among the world's largest. **New Guinea** is Earth's second largest island, and **Borneo** its third largest. Many of the area's larger islands have high mountains. A few peaks are high enough to have snow and glaciers.

Island Southeast Asia is a part of the Ring of Fire as well. As a result, earthquakes and volcanic eruptions often rock the area. When such events occur underwater, they can cause tsunamis, or giant series of waves. In 2004 a tsunami in the Indian Ocean killed hundreds of thousands of people, many in Southeast Asia.

Bodies of Water

Water is a central part of Southeast Asia. Look at the map to identify the many seas, straits, and gulfs in this region.

In addition, several major rivers drain the mainland's peninsulas. Of these rivers, the mighty **Mekong** (MAY-KAWNG) **River** is the most important. The mainland's fertile river valleys and deltas support farming and are home to many people.

READING CHECK **Finding Main Ideas** What are Southeast Asia's major physical features?

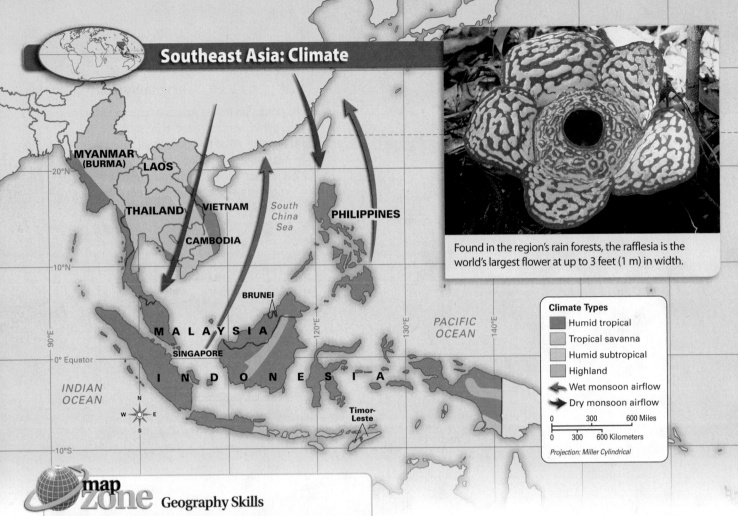

Southeast Asia: Climate

Found in the region's rain forests, the rafflesia is the world's largest flower at up to 3 feet (1 m) in width.

Climate Types
- Humid tropical
- Tropical savanna
- Humid subtropical
- Highland
- ← Wet monsoon airflow
- → Dry monsoon airflow

0   300   600 Miles
0   300   600 Kilometers

Projection: Miller Cylindrical

map zone Geography Skills

Location Southeast Asia's location on and around the equator affects the region's climate.
1. **Identify** What is the main climate found in Indonesia, Malaysia, and the Philippines?
2. **Interpret** Based on the map, how do monsoons affect the climate of this region?

Climate, Plants, and Animals

Southeast Asia lies in the tropics, the area on and around the equator. Temperatures are warm to hot year-round, but become cooler to the north and in the mountains.

Much of the mainland has a tropical savanna climate. Seasonal <u>monsoon</u> winds from the oceans bring heavy rain in summer and drier weather in winter. Severe flooding is common during wet seasons. This climate supports savannas—areas of tall grasses and scattered trees and shrubs.

FOCUS ON READING

What context clues help you figure out the definition of *monsoon?*

The islands and the Malay Peninsula mainly have a humid tropical climate. This climate is hot, muggy, and rainy all year. Showers or storms occur almost daily. In addition, huge storms called typhoons can bring heavy rains and powerful winds.

The humid tropical climate's heat and heavy rainfall support tropical rain forests. These lush forests are home to a huge number of different plants and animals. About 40,000 kinds of flowering plants grow in Indonesia alone. These plants include the rafflesia, the world's largest flower. Measuring up to 3 feet (1 m) across, this flower produces a horrible, rotting stink.

Rain forest animals include elephants, monkeys, tigers, and many types of birds. Some species are found nowhere else. They include orangutans and Komodo dragons, lizards that can grow 10 feet (3 m) long.

Orangutans live in the rain forests of Borneo and Sumatra. Deforestation has seriously reduced their habitat.

Natural Resources

Southeast Asia has a number of valuable natural resources. The region's hot, wet climate and rich soils make farming highly productive. Rice is a major crop, and others include coconuts, coffee, sugarcane, palm oil, and spices. Some countries, such as Indonesia and Malaysia (muh-LAY-zhuh), also have large rubber tree plantations.

The region's seas provide fisheries, and its tropical rain forests provide valuable hardwoods and medicines. The region also has many minerals and fossil fuels, including tin, iron ore, natural gas, and oil. For example, the island of Borneo sits atop an oil field.

READING CHECK **Summarizing** What are the region's major natural resources?

Many of these plants and animals are endangered because of loss of habitat. People are clearing the tropical rain forests for farming, wood, and mining. These actions threaten the area's future diversity.

READING CHECK **Analyzing** How does climate contribute to the region's diversity of life?

SUMMARY AND PREVIEW Southeast Asia is a tropical region of peninsulas, islands, and waterways with diverse life and rich resources. Next, you will read about the region's history and culture.

Section 1 Assessment

hmhsocialstudies.com
ONLINE QUIZ

Reviewing Ideas, Terms, and Places

1. **a. Define** What is an **archipelago**?
   b. Compare and Contrast How do the physical features of Mainland Southeast Asia compare and contrast to those of Island Southeast Asia?
2. **a. Recall** What type of forest occurs in the region?
   b. Summarize What is the climate like across much of Southeast Asia?
   c. Predict What do you think might happen to the region's wildlife if the tropical rain forests continue to be destroyed?
3. **a. Identify** Which countries in the region are major producers of rubber?
   b. Analyze How does the region's climate contribute to its natural resources?

Critical Thinking

4. **Summarizing** Draw a chart like this one. Use your notes to provide information about the climate, plants, and animals in Southeast Asia. In the left-hand box, also note how climate shapes life in the region.

Climate of Southeast Asia → Plants
Climate of Southeast Asia → Animals

FOCUS ON SPEAKING

*my*WriteSmart

5. **Writing Questions about the Region's Physical Geography** Note information about the region's physical features, climate, plants, animals, and natural resources. Write two questions and answers for your interview. For example, you might ask a question about the region's tropical rain forests.

Tsunami!

Essential Elements

The World in Spatial Terms
Places and Regions
Physical Systems
Human Systems
Environment and Society
The Uses of Geography

Background "Huge Waves Hit Japan." This event is a tsunami (soo-NAH-mee), a series of giant sea waves. Records of deadly tsunamis go back 3,000 years. Some places, such as Japan, have been hit time and again.

Tsunamis occur when an earthquake, volcanic eruption, or other event causes seawater to move in huge waves. The majority of tsunamis occur in the Pacific Ocean because of the region's many earthquakes.

Warning systems help alert people to tsunamis. The Pacific Tsunami Warning Center monitors tsunamis in the Pacific Ocean. Sensors on the ocean floor and buoys on the water's surface help detect earthquakes and measure waves. When a tsunami threatens, radio, TV, and sirens alert the public.

Indian Ocean Catastrophe

On December 26, 2004, a massive earthquake erupted below the Indian Ocean. The earthquake launched a monster tsunami. Within half an hour, walls of water up to 65 feet high came barreling ashore in Indonesia. The water swept away boats, buildings, and people. Meanwhile, the tsunami kept traveling in ever-widening rings across the ocean. The waves eventually wiped out coastal communities in a dozen countries. Some 200,000 people eventually died.

At the time, the Indian Ocean did not have a tsunami warning system. Tsunamis are rare in that part of the world. As a result, many countries there had been unwilling to invest in a warning system.

1 A 9.0 underwater earthquake caused the 2004 Indian Ocean tsunami. The event pushed up millions of tons of water.

2 The water surged up and outward in huge waves. The waves moved at speeds of about 500 mph.

Indian Ocean Tsunami

map zone

Estimated deaths as of 2005

0   300   600 Miles

0   300 600 Kilometers

Arabian Sea

INDIA
10,872 dead

BANGLADESH
2 dead

MYANMAR
at least 2,500 dead

SOMALIA
at least 150 dead

MALDIVES
82 dead

Bay of Bengal

THAILAND
5,392 dead

TANZANIA
10 dead

SRI LANKA
30,959 dead

MALAYSIA
68 dead

8   **6**   **4**   **2**

SEYCHELLES
3 dead

Arrival time of first wave (hours)

Epicenter

Sumatra

INDONESIA
166,760 dead

INDIAN OCEAN

A large wave smashes into the beach on Penang Island in Malaysia during the 2004 Indian Ocean tsunami.

In 2004 these countries paid a terrible price for their decision. As the map shows, the 2004 tsunami hit countries from South Asia to East Africa. Most people had no warning of the tsunami. In addition, many people did not know how to protect themselves. Instead of heading to high ground, some people went to the beach for a closer look. Many died when later waves hit.

Tilly Smith, a 10-year-old on vacation in Thailand, was one of the few who understood the danger. Two weeks earlier, her geography teacher had discussed tsunamis. As the water began surging, Smith warned her family and other tourists to flee. Her geographic knowledge saved their lives.

What It Means No one can prevent tsunamis. Yet, by studying geography, we can prepare for these disasters and help protect lives and property. The United Nations is now working to create a global tsunami warning system. People are also trying to plant more mangroves along coastlines. These bushy swamp trees provide a natural barrier against high waves.

3 When they strike, tsunamis often look like a rapidly rising tide or swell of water. The water then rushes far inland and back out.

Geography for Life Activity

1. What steps are being taken to avoid another disaster such as the Indian Ocean tsunami in 2004?

2. About 75 percent of tsunami warnings since 1948 were false alarms. What might be the risks and benefits of early warnings to move people out of harm's way?

3. **Creating a Survival Guide** Create a tsunami survival guide. List the dos and don'ts for this emergency.

History and Culture

TEKS 1A, 1B, 2A, 2B, 4B, 4C, 15A, 15B, 15D, 21B, 22A, 22D

What You Will Learn...

Main Ideas

1. Southeast Asia's early history includes empires, colonial rule, and independence.
2. The modern history of Southeast Asia involves struggles with war and communism.
3. Southeast Asia's culture reflects its Chinese, Indian, and European heritage.

The Big Idea

People, ideas, and traditions from China, India, Europe, and elsewhere have shaped Southeast Asia's history and culture.

Key Terms and Places

Timor, *p. 623*
domino theory, *p. 724*
wats, *p. 724*

hmhsocialstudies.com
TAKING NOTES

Use the graphic organizer online to take notes on the history and culture of Southeast Asia.

If YOU lived there...

You and your friends are strolling through the market in Jakarta, Indonesia, looking for a snack. You have many choices—tents along the street, carts called gerobak, and vendors on bicycles all sell food. You might choose satay, strips of chicken or lamb grilled on a stick. Or you might pick one of many rice dishes. For dessert, you can buy fruit or order an ice cream cone.

What do you like about living in Jakarta?

BUILDING BACKGROUND Colonial rule helped shape Southeast Asia's history and culture—including foods. Throughout the region you can see not only a blend of different Asian influences but also a blend of American, Dutch, French, and Spanish influences.

Early History

Southeast Asia lies south of China and east of India, and both countries have played a strong role in the region's history. Over time, many people from China and India settled in Southeast Asia. As settlements grew, trade developed with China and India.

Early Civilization

The region's most advanced early civilization was the Khmer (kuh-MER). From the AD 800s to the mid-1200s the Khmer controlled a large empire in what is now Cambodia. The remains of Angkor Wat, a huge temple complex the Khmer built in the 1100s, reflect their advanced civilization and Hindu religion.

In the 1200s the Thai (TY) from southern China settled in the Khmer area. Around the same time, Buddhism, introduced earlier from India and Sri Lanka, began replacing Hinduism in the region.

Colonial Rule and Independence

As in many parts of the world, European powers started colonizing Southeast Asia during the 1500s. Led by Portugal, European powers came to the region in search of spices and other trade goods.

In 1521 explorer Ferdinand Magellan reached the Philippines and claimed the islands for Spain. The Spaniards who followed came to colonize, trade, and spread Roman Catholicism. This religion remains the main faith in the Philippines today.

In the 1600s and 1700s Dutch traders drove the Portuguese out of much of the region. Portugal kept only the small island of **Timor**. The Dutch gained control of the tea and spice trade on what became the Dutch East Indies, now Indonesia.

In the 1800s the British and French set up colonies with plantations, railroads, and mines. Many people from China and India came to work in the colonies. The British and French spread Christianity as well.

In 1898 the United States entered the region when it won the Philippines from Spain after the Spanish-American War. By the early 1900s, colonial powers ruled most of the region, as the map on the next page shows. Only Siam (sy-AM), now Thailand, was never colonized, although it lost land.

In World War II (1939–1945), Japan invaded and occupied most of Southeast Asia. After Japan lost the war, the United States gave the Philippines independence. Soon, other people in the region began to fight for their independence.

One of the bloodiest wars for independence was in French Indochina. In 1954 the French left. Indochina then split into the independent countries of Cambodia, Laos, and Vietnam. By 1970, most of Southeast Asia had thrown off colonial rule.

READING CHECK **Identifying Cause and Effect** What reasons led other countries to set up colonies across most of Southeast Asia?

Angkor Wat

The stone towers of Angkor Wat rise from the rain forest in what is now Cambodia. To the Khmer, Angkor Wat symbolized the center of the universe.

ANALYZING VISUALS
What conclusions can you draw about the Khmer based on Angkor Wat?

The towers represent the peaks of Mount Meru, the home of the gods in Hindu mythology.

The pathway represents the rainbow bridge, the link between the gods and people in Hindu mythology.

Angkor Wat was built in the mid-1100s as a Hindu temple. It later became a Buddhist temple.

723

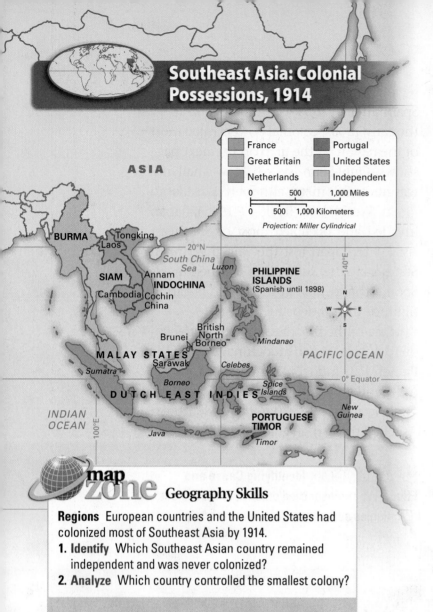

Southeast Asia: Colonial Possessions, 1914

ASIA

France
Great Britain
Netherlands
Portugal
United States
Independent

0   500   1,000 Miles
0 500 1,000 Kilometers
Projection: Miller Cylindrical

BURMA
Tongking
Laos
20°N
South China Sea
Luzon
SIAM
Annam
INDOCHINA
PHILIPPINE ISLANDS
(Spanish until 1898)
Cambodia
Cochin China
140°E
Brunei
British North Borneo
Mindanao
MALAY STATES
Sarawak
Celebes
PACIFIC OCEAN
Sumatra
Borneo
Spice Islands
0° Equator
DUTCH EAST INDIES
INDIAN OCEAN
100°E
Java
PORTUGUESE TIMOR
New Guinea
Timor

map zone Geography Skills

Regions European countries and the United States had colonized most of Southeast Asia by 1914.
1. **Identify** Which Southeast Asian country remained independent and was never colonized?
2. **Analyze** Which country controlled the smallest colony?

Modern History

FOCUS ON READING

How does the context help explain the meaning of the term *oust* in the paragraph to the right?

ACADEMIC VOCABULARY

criterion rule or standard for defining

The move toward independence was not easy. In Vietnam, the fighting to <u>oust</u> the French left the country divided into North and South Vietnam. A civil war then broke out in the South. To defend South Vietnam from Communist forces in that war, the United States sent in troops in the 1960s.

The United States based its decision to send troops on one **criterion**—the potential spread of communism. According to the **domino theory**, if one country fell to communism, other countries nearby would follow like falling dominoes.

Years of war caused millions of deaths and terrible destruction. In the end, North and South Vietnam reunited as one Communist country. As the Communists took over, about 1 million refugees fled South Vietnam. Many went to the United States.

Civil wars also raged in Cambodia and Laos. In 1975 Communist forces took over both countries. The government in Cambodia was brutal, causing the deaths of more than 1 million people there. Then in 1978 Vietnam helped to overthrow Cambodia's government. This event sparked further fighting, which continued off and on until the mid-1990s. The United Nations then helped Cambodia achieve peace.

READING CHECK **Summarizing** What are some key events in the region's modern history?

Culture

The many groups that influenced Southeast Asia's history also shaped its culture. This diverse culture blends native, Chinese, Indian, and European ways of life.

People and Languages

The countries in Southeast Asia have many ethnic groups. As an example, Indonesia has more than 300 ethnic groups. Most of the countries have one main ethnic group plus many smaller ethnic groups.

Not surprisingly, many languages are spoken in Southeast Asia. These languages include native languages and dialects as well as Chinese and European languages.

Religions

The main religions in Southeast Asia are Buddhism, Christianity, Hinduism, and Islam. Buddhism is the main faith on the mainland. This area features many beautiful **wats**, Buddhist temples that also serve as monasteries.

Islam is the main religion in Malaysia, Brunei, and Indonesia. In fact, Indonesia has more Muslims than any other country. In the Philippines, most people are Roman Catholic. Hinduism is practiced in Indian communities and on the island of Bali.

Customs

Customs differ widely across the region, but some similarities exist. For example, religion often shapes life, and people celebrate many religious festivals. Some people continue to practice traditional customs, such as dances and music. These customs are especially popular in rural areas. In addition, many people wear traditional clothing, such as sarongs, strips of cloth worn wrapped around the body.

READING CHECK **Generalizing** How has Southeast Asia's history influenced its culture?

SUMMARY AND PREVIEW Southeast Asia has a long history that has helped shape its diverse culture. Next, you will read about Mainland Southeast Asia.

Thai Teenage Buddhist Monks

Would you be willing to serve as a monk for a few months? In Thailand, many Buddhist boys and young men serve as monks for a short period. This period might last from one week to a few months. These temporary monks follow the lifestyle of actual Buddhist monks, shaving their heads, wearing robes, and maintaining a life of simplicity. During their stay, the teenage monks learn about Buddhism and practice meditation. Some Thai teens decide to become Buddhist monks permanently. This decision is considered a great honor for their families.

Summarizing What are some of the things that Thai boys and young men do while serving as Buddhist monks?

Section 2 Assessment

Reviewing Ideas, Terms, and Places

1. **a. Describe** What was the significance of the Khmer Empire?
   b. Identify Cause and Effect What was the result of the war for independence in French Indochina?
   c. Elaborate How did European colonization shape Southeast Asia's history?
2. **a. Define** What was the **domino theory**?
   b. Summarize What role has communism played in Southeast Asia's modern history?
3. **a. Define** What is a **wat**?
   b. Contrast How does religion in the mainland and island countries differ?
   c. Elaborate How has the history of Southeast Asia shaped the region's culture?

Critical Thinking

4. **Sequencing** Copy the time line shown below. Using your notes, identify on the time line the important people, periods, events, and years in Southeast Asia's history.

800s   2000

FOCUS ON SPEAKING   *my* WriteSmart

5. **Writing Questions about History and Culture** What interesting questions could you ask about the history and culture of Southeast Asia? Write two questions and their answers to add to your notes.

Social Studies Skills

Interpreting Visuals

Learn

Geographers get information from many sources. These sources include text and data. They also include visuals, such as photographs, diagrams, charts, timelines, maps, and graphs. Use these tips to interpret information from visuals.

- **Identify the subject.** Read the title and caption, if available. If not, look at the content of the image. What does it show? Where is it located?

- **Analyze the content.** What is the purpose of the image? What information is in the image? What conclusions can you draw from this information? Write your conclusions in your notes.

- **Summarize your analysis.** Write a summary of the information in the visual and of the conclusions you can draw from it.

Practice

Analyze the photograph at right. Then answer the following questions.

1. What is the title of the photograph?

2. Where is this scene, and what is happening?

3. What conclusions can you draw from the information in the photograph?

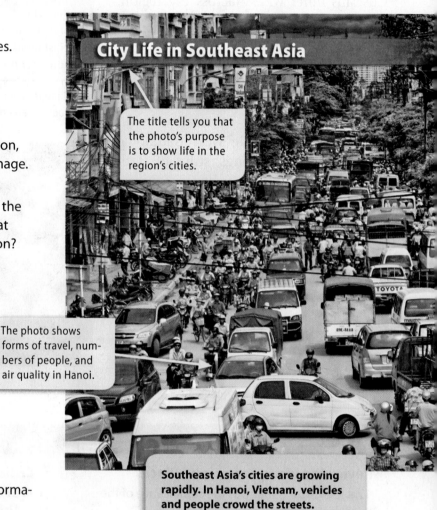

City Life in Southeast Asia

The title tells you that the photo's purpose is to show life in the region's cities.

The photo shows forms of travel, numbers of people, and air quality in Hanoi.

Southeast Asia's cities are growing rapidly. In Hanoi, Vietnam, vehicles and people crowd the streets.

Apply

Work with a partner to analyze the images of the rubber tree plantation in Section 4. Then answer the following questions.

1. What is the purpose of the two photos?

2. What do the photos show about rubber tree farming?

3. Based on the information in the images, write a summary of the steps involved in collecting rubber from trees. Then, with your partner, take turns retelling how a worker collects rubber from trees.

Mainland Southeast Asia Today

SECTION 3

If YOU lived there...

You live in Vietnam, where your family works on a collective state-run farm. On the side, your family also sells vegetables. Now your older brother wants to start his own business—a bicycle repair shop. The communist government allows this, but your parents think it is safer for him to keep working on the farm.

What do you think your brother should do?

> **BUILDING BACKGROUND** After decades of war and hardship, most countries in Mainland Southeast Asia are moving forward. Even those countries with communist governments, such as Vietnam and Laos, are working to develop freer and stronger economies.

The Area Today

Look at the map at the start of the chapter and identify the countries of Mainland Southeast Asia. These countries include Myanmar, Thailand, Cambodia, Laos, and Vietnam.

War, harsh governments, and other problems have slowed progress in most of Mainland Southeast Asia. However, the area's countries have rich resources and are working to improve their futures. For example, as of 2010 all the countries of Southeast Asia except Timor-Leste had joined the Association of Southeast Asian Nations (ASEAN). This organization promotes political, economic, and social cooperation throughout the region.

Rural Life

Mainland Southeast Asia is largely rural. Most people are farmers who live in small villages and work long hours in the fields. Most farm work is done by hand or using traditional methods. Farmers grow rice, the region's main crop, on fertile slopes along rivers and on terraced shelves of land. The wet, tropical climate enables farmers to grow two or three crops each year.

TEKS 2B, 4B, 4F, 5A, 6B, 6C, 7A, 7B, 11D, 15B, 15F, 21B, 21C, 22A, 22D

What You Will Learn...

Main Ideas

1. The area today is largely rural and agricultural, but cities are growing rapidly.
2. Myanmar is poor with a harsh military government, while Thailand is a democracy with a strong economy.
3. The countries of Indochina are poor and struggling to rebuild after years of war.

The Big Idea

Many of the farming countries in Mainland Southeast Asia are poor but are working to improve their economies.

Key Terms and Places

Yangon, *p. 728*
human rights, *p. 728*
Bangkok, *p. 728*
klongs, *p. 728*
Phnom Penh, *p. 731*
Hanoi, *p. 731*

hmhsocialstudies.com
TAKING NOTES

Use the graphic organizer online to take notes on each country in Mainland Southeast Asia.

Most rural people live in the area's fertile river valleys and deltas, which have the best farmland. A delta is an area of fertile land around the mouth of a river. A few people live in remote villages in the rugged, forested mountains. These areas have poor soils that make farming difficult. Many of the people who live there belong to small ethnic groups known as hill peoples.

Urban Life

FOCUS ON READING
What words in the paragraph to the right tell you the definition of *pedicabs*?

Although most people live in rural areas, Mainland Southeast Asia has several large cities. Most are growing rapidly as people move to them for work. Rapid growth has led to crowding and pollution. People, bicycles, scooters, cars, and buses clog city streets. Smog hangs in the still air. Growing cities also mix the old and new. Skyscrapers tower over huts, and cars zip past pedicabs, taxicabs that are pedaled like bikes.

READING CHECK Finding Main Ideas Where do most people in Mainland Southeast Asia live?

BIOGRAPHY

Aung San Suu Kyi
(1945–)

Aung San Suu Kyi has dedicated herself to making life better in her native Myanmar. Suu Kyi is the best-known opponent of the country's harsh military government. Her party, the National League for Democracy (NLD), won control of the country's parliament in 1990. The military government refused to give up power, however. The government then placed Aung San Suu Kyi and other NLD members under house arrest. For her efforts to bring democracy to Myanmar, Suu Kyi received the Nobel Peace Prize in 1991. Even though she has been repeatedly placed under house arrest, Suu Kyi continues to fight for democratic reform and free elections. Her efforts have led the United States and some Asian countries to press Myanmar's government to change.

Identifying Points of View What does Aung San Suu Kyi hope to achieve through her efforts in Myanmar?

Myanmar and Thailand

Myanmar and Thailand form the northwestern part of Mainland Southeast Asia. While Myanmar is poor, Thailand boasts the area's strongest economy.

Myanmar

Myanmar lies south of China on the Bay of Bengal. Also known as Burma, the country gained independence from Great Britain in 1948. The capital is **Yangon**, or Rangoon, and the administrative capital is Naypyidaw.

Most of the people in Myanmar are Burmese. Many live in small farming villages in houses built on stilts. Buddhism is the main religion, and village life often centers around a local Buddhist monastery.

Life is difficult in Myanmar because a harsh military government rules the country. The government abuses **human rights**, rights that all people deserve such as rights to equality and justice. A Burmese woman, Aung San Suu Kyi (awng sahn soo chee), has led a movement for more democracy and rights. She and others have been jailed and harassed for their actions.

Myanmar's poor human-rights record has isolated the country and hurt its economy. Some countries, such as the United States, will no longer trade with Myanmar. Despite rich natural resources—such as oil, timber, metals, jade, and gems—Myanmar and most of its people remain poor.

Thailand

To the southeast of Myanmar is Thailand, once known as Siam. The capital and largest city is **Bangkok**. Modern and crowded, it lies near the mouth of the Chao Phraya (chow PRY-uh) River. Bangkok is known for its many spectacular palaces and Buddhist wats. The city is also famous for its **klongs**, or canals. Klongs are used for transportation and trade and to drain floodwater.

A Bangkok Canal

Sick of crowded roads? In Bangkok, you can use a network of canals, called klongs, to travel through parts of the city. Water taxis and boats transport people and goods. At floating markets, vendors sell fish, fruit, and other foods to locals and tourists.

To move around the klongs, people use narrow, shallow boats and poles.

ประกาศ
ห้ามเรือทุกชนิดใช้เครื่องยนต์
ตั้งแต่เวลา 08.00-12.00 น.
ฝ่าฝืนมีโทษปรับไม่เกิน 1,000 บาท
สภ.อ.ดำเนินสะดวก

Many sellers wear bamboo hats with wide brims to block the sun and rain.

Small bananas, called finger bananas, are displayed on green banana leaves.

Vendors sell both cooked food and raw produce, such as the pomelos shown here.

ANALYSIS SKILL ANALYZING VISUALS

What advantages do you think klongs provide to both travelers and people selling goods?

729

Southeast Asia: Land Use and Resources

map zone Geography Skills

Regions The countries of Southeast Asia have rich farmland and many other natural resources.
1. **Identify** Which cities in the region are major manufacturing centers?
2. **Draw Conclusions** Why might timber be an important product in the region?

Major Resources
- Coal
- Natural gas
- Oil
- Nuclear power
- Hydroelectric power
- Gold
- Silver
- Other minerals
- Seafood

Land Use
- Farming
- Forest
- Manufacturing
- Major manufacturing and trade centers

0 250 500 Miles
0 250 500 Kilometers
Projection: Miller Cylindrical

A Vietnamese woman gathers and washes carrots in traditional woven baskets.

A woman uses traditional methods to carry sea salt across the salt pans in Doc Let Beach in Vietnam.

Thailand is a constitutional monarchy. A monarch, or king, serves as a ceremonial head of state. A prime minister and elected legislature hold the real power, however.

A democratically elected government and rich resources have helped Thailand's economy to grow. Industry, farming, fishing, mining, and tourism fuel this growth.

Farms produce rice, pineapples, and rubber. Factories produce computers, textiles, and electronics. Magnificent Buddhist wats and unspoiled beaches draw tourists.

READING CHECK Comparing and Contrasting
What are some similarities and differences between Myanmar and Thailand?

The Countries of Indochina

The former countries of French Indochina lie to the east and south of Thailand. They are struggling to overcome decades of war.

Cambodia

Cambodia lies to the northeast of the Gulf of Thailand. **Phnom Penh** (puh-NAWM pen) is the capital and chief city. Located in the Mekong River valley, it is a center of trade.

Some 20 years of war, terror, and devastation in Cambodia finally ended in the early 1990s. Today the country has a stable, elected government similar to Thailand's. Years of conflict left their mark, however. Although farming has improved, the country has little industry. In addition, many land mines remain hidden in the land.

Laos

Laos is landlocked with rugged mountains. Poor and undeveloped, it has few roads, no railroads, and limited electricity.

The Communist government of Laos has been increasing economic freedom in hopes of improving the economy. Even so, Laos remains the area's poorest country.

The economy is based on farming, but good farmland is limited. Most people are subsistence farmers, meaning they grow just enough food for their families.

Vietnam

Like Laos, Vietnam is rugged and mountainous. The capital, **Hanoi**, is located in the north in the Hong (Red) River delta. The largest city, Ho Chi Minh City, is in the south in the Mekong delta.

Vietnam's Communist government has been allowing more economic freedom and private business. The changes have helped the economy grow. Most people still farm, but industry and services are expanding. Fishing and mining are also important.

READING CHECK **Evaluating** How would you rate the economies of these three countries?

SUMMARY AND PREVIEW The mainland countries are rural and agricultural with fast-growing cities. Most of the countries are poor despite rich resources. Next, you will read about Island Southeast Asia.

Section 3 Assessment

Reviewing Ideas, Terms, and Places

1. **a. Recall** In what areas do most people in Mainland Southeast Asia live?
   b. Identify Cause and Effect How has rapid growth affected the area's cities?
2. **a. Define** What are **klongs**, and in what ways are they used?
   b. Predict How might Myanmar's economy change if the country had a government that respected **human rights**? Explain your answer.
3. **a. Identify and Locate** Use the map and key on page 730 to make a list of the region's renewable and nonrenewable resources. Then, locate those resources on the map.
   b. Summarize What issues and challenges face Cambodia, Laos, and Vietnam?

Critical Thinking

4. **Categorizing** Draw a chart like the one shown. Use your notes to provide information for each category in the chart.

FOCUS ON SPEAKING

my WriteSmart

5. **Writing Questions about Mainland Southeast Asia** Write one interview question about each country covered in this section. Your questions might highlight differences among the countries or focus on similarities across the area.

Island Southeast Asia Today

TEKS 3A, 3B, 3C, 5A, 5B, 5C, 6B, 7A, 15B, 15D, 15E, 15F, 18A, 21B, 21C, 22D

What You Will Learn...

Main Ideas

1. The area today has rich resources and growing cities but faces challenges.
2. Malaysia and its neighbors have strong economies but differ in many ways.
3. Indonesia is big and diverse with a growing economy, and East Timor is small and poor.
4. The Philippines is ethnically diverse and has a strengthening economy.

The Big Idea

The countries of Island Southeast Asia range from wealthy and urban to poor and rural.

Key Terms and Places

kampong, *p. 733*
Jakarta, *p. 733*
Kuala Lumpur, *p. 733*
free ports, *p. 734*
sultan, *p. 735*
Java, *p. 735*
Manila, *p. 736*

hmhsocialstudies.com
TAKING NOTES

Use the graphic organizer online to take notes on each country in Island Southeast Asia.

If YOU lived there...

You live in Canada but are visiting your cousins in Singapore. You start to cross the street in the middle of a block, but your cousin quickly stops you. "You have to pay a big fine if you do that!" he says. Singapore has many strict laws and strong punishments, he explains. These laws are meant to make the city safe.

What do you think about Singapore's laws?

BUILDING BACKGROUND Singapore and the other countries of Island Southeast Asia present many contrasts. You can quickly go from skyscrapers to rice paddies to tropical rain forests. Many ethnic groups may live in one country, which can lead to unrest.

The Area Today

Island Southeast Asia lies at a crossroads between major oceans and continents. The area's six countries are Malaysia, Singapore, Brunei (brooh-NY), Indonesia, Timor-Leste, and the Philippines.

The future for these countries could be bright. They have the potential for wealth and good standards of living, such as rich resources and a large, skilled labor force. The region's economies are growing, and all but Timor-Leste belong to ASEAN. This organization promotes cooperation in Southeast Asia.

Island Southeast Asia faces challenges, however. First, violent ethnic conflicts have hurt progress in some countries. Second, many people live in poverty, while a few leaders and businesspeople control much of the money. Third, the area has many environmental problems, such as pollution.

Rural and Urban Life

Many people in Island Southeast Asia live in rural areas, where they farm or fish. As on the mainland, rice is the main crop. Others include coffee, spices, sugarcane, tea, and tropical fruit.

Rubber is a major crop as well, and Indonesia and Malaysia are the world's largest producers of natural rubber. Seafood is the area's main source of protein.

As on the mainland, many people in Island Southeast Asia are leaving rural villages to move to cities for work. The largest cities, the major capitals, are modern and crowded. Common problems in these cities include smog and heavy traffic. Some cities also have large slums.

In Malaysia, Indonesia, and other parts of the area, many people live in kampongs. A **kampong** is a village or city district with traditional houses built on stilts. The stilts protect the houses from flooding, which is common in the area. The term *kampong* also refers to the slums around the area's cities such as **Jakarta**, Indonesia's capital.

READING CHECK **Summarizing** Why could the future be bright for Island Southeast Asia?

Malaysia and Its Neighbors

Malaysia and its much smaller neighbors, Singapore and Brunei, were all once British colonies. Today all three countries are independent and differ in many ways.

Malaysia

Malaysia consists of two parts. One is on the southern end of the Malay Peninsula. The other is on northern Borneo. Most of the country's people live on the peninsula. **Kuala Lumpur** (KWAH-luh LOOHM-poohr), Malaysia's capital, is there as well. The capital is a cultural and economic center.

Malaysia is ethnically diverse. The Malays are the main ethnic group, but many Chinese and other groups live in Malaysia as well. As a result, the country has many languages and religions. Bahasa Malay is the main language, and Islam and Buddhism are the main religions.

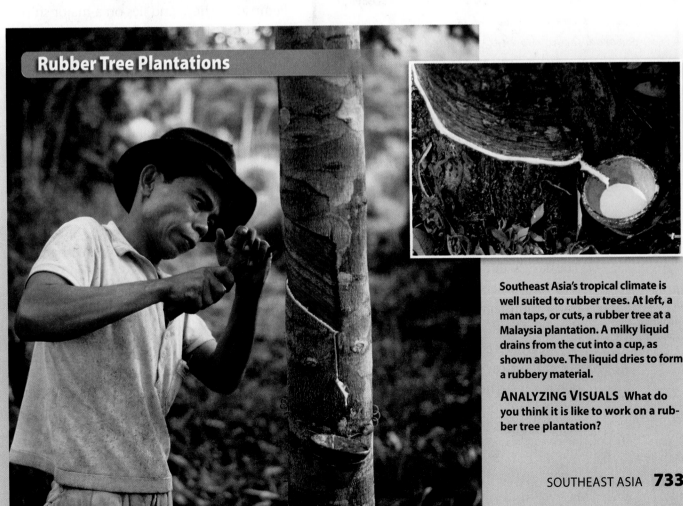

Rubber Tree Plantations

Southeast Asia's tropical climate is well suited to rubber trees. At left, a man taps, or cuts, a rubber tree at a Malaysia plantation. A milky liquid drains from the cut into a cup, as shown above. The liquid dries to form a rubbery material.

ANALYZING VISUALS What do you think it is like to work on a rubber tree plantation?

INTERVIEW

Lee Kuan Yew on Singapore

Lee Kuan Yew was Singapore's prime minister from 1959 to 1990. He remade the tiny country into an economic power. In a 1994 interview, Lee discussed Singapore's strict laws.

" The expansion of the right of the individual to behave or misbehave as he pleases has come at the expense of orderly society. In the East the main object is to have a well-ordered society so that everybody can have maximum enjoyment of his freedoms. This freedom can exist only in an ordered state."

—from "A Conversation with Lee Kuan Yew"

ANALYSIS SKILL ANALYZING PRIMARY SOURCES

Do you agree with Lee that freedom for all can exist only in a society with strict order? Why or why not?

ACADEMIC VOCABULARY

concrete
specific, real

Malaysia is a constitutional monarchy. The king's duties are largely ceremonial, and local rulers take turns being king. A prime minister and elected legislature hold the real power.

Malaysia's economy is one of the stronger in the area. Well-educated workers and rich resources help drive this economy. The country produces and exports natural rubber, palm oil, electronics, oil, and timber.

Singapore

A populous country, Singapore is squeezed onto a tiny island at the tip of the Malay Peninsula. The island lies on a major shipping route. This location has helped make Singapore a rich country.

Today Singapore is one of the world's busiest **free ports**, ports that place few if any taxes on goods. It is also an industrial center, and many foreign banks and high-tech firms have located offices there.

Singapore sparkles as the gem of Southeast Asia. The country is modern, wealthy, orderly, and clean. Crime rates are low.

How has Singapore achieved such success? The government has worked hard to clean up slums and improve housing. In addition, laws are extremely strict. To provide **concrete** examples, fines for littering are stiff, and people caught with illegal drugs can be executed. Moreover, the government strictly controls politics and the media. Certain movies are banned, as are satellite dishes. Recently, however, Singapore has loosened up some restrictions.

Brunei

The tiny country of Brunei is on the island of Borneo, which it shares with Malaysia and Indonesia. A **sultan**, the supreme ruler of a Muslim country, governs Brunei.

The country has grown wealthy from large oil and gas deposits. Because of this wealth, Brunei's citizens do not pay income tax and receive free health care and other benefits. Brunei's oil will run out around 2020, however. As a result, the government is developing other areas of the economy.

READING CHECK Contrasting How do Malaysia, Singapore, and Brunei differ?

Indonesia and Timor-Leste

Indonesia is the largest of the island countries. Timor-Leste, once part of Indonesia, is one of the area's smallest countries.

Indonesia

Indonesia has several claims to fame. It is the world's largest archipelago, with some 13,500 islands. It has the fourth-largest population of any country as well as the largest Muslim population. Indonesia is extremely diverse as well, as you have read. It has more than 300 ethnic groups who speak more than 250 languages.

Indonesia's main island is **Java**. The capital, Jakarta, is there, as are more than half of Indonesia's people. For this reason, Java is extremely crowded. To reduce the crowding, the government has been moving people to less-populated islands. Many people on those islands dislike that policy.

Indonesia's rich resources have helped its economy to grow. The main resources include rubber, oil and gas, and timber. The country also has good farmland for rice and other crops. Factories turn out clothing and electronics. Islands such as Bali draw thousands of tourists each year.

At the same time, problems have hurt Indonesia's economy. Many of the people are poor, and unemployment is high. In some areas, ethnic and religious conflicts have led to fighting and terrorism.

Timor-Leste

Timor-Leste is located on the small island of Timor. In 1999 Timor-Leste declared independence from Indonesia. The island then plunged into violence. Timor-Leste only gained its independence after the United Nations sent in troops to restore peace. Years of fighting have left Timor-Leste one of the region's poorest countries. Most people farm, and coffee is the main export.

READING CHECK Generalizing How has violence affected Indonesia and Timor-Leste?

FOCUS ON READING
How does the highlighted text help you understand the meaning of *sultan?*

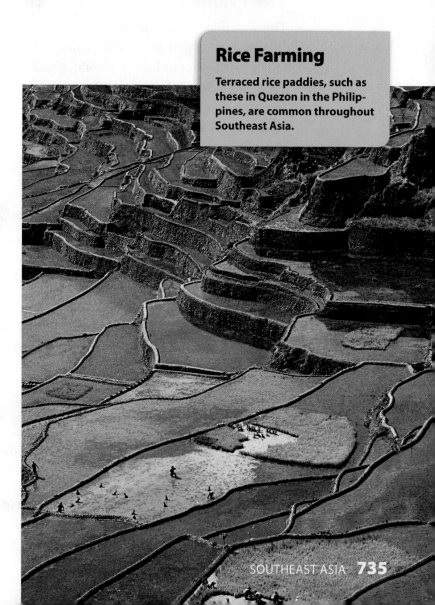

Rice Farming

Terraced rice paddies, such as these in Quezon in the Philippines, are common throughout Southeast Asia.

Per Capita GDP in Island Southeast Asia

Per Capita GDP (thousands of U.S. dollars)

Interpreting Graphs Compare the per capita GDP of Brunei and the United States. What does it imply about Brunei and its people?

The Philippines has many resources to fuel economic growth. Natural resources include copper and other metals, oil, and tropical wood. Farmers grow coconuts, sugarcane, rice, and corn. Factories produce and export clothing and electronics.

The Philippine economy has recently improved, but a wide gap exists between the rich and the poor. A few Filipinos are wealthy. Most, however, are poor farmers who do not own the land they work.

The Philippines has experienced religious conflict as well. Although the country is mainly Roman Catholic, some areas are largely Muslim and want independence.

READING CHECK **Summarizing** What kinds of challenges do the Philippine people face?

The Philippines

The Philippines includes more than 7,000 islands. The largest and most populated is Luzon, which includes the capital, **Manila**. These islands are home to 10 major ethnic groups and large communities of foreigners, making the Philippines one of the most diverse countries in the region.

SUMMARY AND PREVIEW You have read that Island Southeast Asia has many contrasts. While some countries are wealthy, others are poor. While some countries are modern and urban, others are more traditional and rural. In the next chapter you will read about the Pacific World.

Section 4 Assessment

Reviewing Ideas, Terms, and Places

1. **a. Identify** What problems does the area face?
   b. Compare How does urban life compare between the island and mainland countries?
2. **a. Define** What is a **sultan**?
   b. Explain How have Singapore and Brunei become rich countries?
3. **a. Recall** What island is **Jakarta** located on?
   b. Sequence What series of events led to Timor-Leste's independence?
4. **a. Identify** What are the capital city and the main island in the Philippines?
   b. Analyze Why is the Philippines' economic improvement not benefiting many of its people?

Critical Thinking

5. **Categorizing** Draw a chart like the one shown. Use your notes to provide information for each category in the chart.

FOCUS ON SPEAKING

my WriteSmart

6. **Writing Questions about Island Southeast Asia Today** Write one interview question about each country covered in this section. Your questions might highlight differences among the countries or focus on similarities across the area.

Chapter Review

Visual Summary

Use the visual summary below to help you review the main ideas of the chapter.

QUICK FACTS

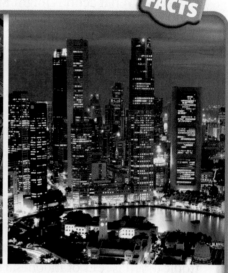

Southeast Asia is a tropical region of peninsulas, islands, and water. Its history includes empires and colonization.

Mainland Southeast Asia is rural with growing cities. Many of the countries are poor but have rich resources.

Island Southeast Asia is more urban, and some countries are wealthy. Many of the area's people are poor, though.

Reviewing Vocabulary, Terms, and Places

For each group of terms below, write a sentence that shows how all the terms in the group are related.

1. archipelagos
   Indonesia
   Philippines

2. Aung San Suu Kyi
   human rights
   Myanmar

3. Bangkok
   klongs

4. Indochina
   domino theory

5. Jakarta
   kampongs

6. Singapore
   free port

7. Brunei
   sultan

Comprehension and Critical Thinking

SECTION 1 *(Pages 716–719)*

8. **a. Identify** What are the two peninsulas and the two archipelagos that make up the region of Southeast Asia?

   b. Compare and Contrast In what ways are the main climate of Mainland Southeast Asia and of Island Southeast Asia similar and different?

   c. Develop What different needs should people weigh when considering how best to protect the region's tropical rain forests?

SECTION 2 *(Pages 722–725)*

9. **a. Recall** What theory led the U.S. military to become involved in Southeast Asia?

   b. Identify Cause and Effect Why are so many languages spoken in Southeast Asia?

   c. Predict How do you think Southeast Asia might be different today if Europeans had never explored and colonized the area?

SECTION 3 *(Pages 727–731)*

10. a. Describe Where do most people live and work in Mainland Southeast Asia?

b. Summarize What factors have slowed economic progress in Mainland Southeast Asia?

c. Develop What actions might Myanmar take to try to improve its economy?

SECTION 4 *(Pages 732–736)*

11. a. Identify Which two countries in Island Southeast Asia have wealthy economies?

b. Compare What are some ways in which Indonesia and the Philippines are similar?

c. Elaborate How has ethnic diversity affected the countries of Island Southeast Asia?

Using the Internet

12. Activity: Writing a Report on Rain Forests The tropical rain forests of Indonesia are home to a rich diversity of life. Research these rain forests through the online book. Take notes on the main and supporting ideas that help explain challenges to Indonesia's rain forests. Then use your notes to write a short report that summarizes the threats they face. Organize information from your report into a brief summary to present to the class.

↗ hmhsocialstudies.com

Social Studies Skills

Interpreting Visuals *Use the tips for interpreting visuals on page 726 to answer the following questions.*

13. Analyze the photograph on page 729. What can you learn from the title and captions? What activities are taking place? What conclusions can you draw about the use of canals in Bangkok?

14. Select two different types of visuals from your textbook. For example, you might select a photograph, chart, time line, map, or graph. Analyze the subject, purpose, and content of each visual. Then organize information from the visuals into a written summary.

Map Activity

15. Southeast Asia On a separate sheet of paper, match the letters on the map with their correct labels below.

Bangkok, Thailand   Jakarta, Indonesia

Borneo   Malay Peninsula

Hanoi, Vietnam   Manila, Philippines

Indochina Peninsula   Singapore

FOCUS ON READING AND SPEAKING *my* WriteSmart

Using Context Clues–Definitions *Add a phrase or sentence to provide a definition for the underlined word.*

16. In Thailand, many young men serve for short periods in Buddhist <u>monasteries</u>.

17. Much of the <u>cultivated</u> land in Southeast Asia is used to grow rice.

Presenting an Interview *Use your interview notes to complete the activity below.*

18. With your partner, choose the five best questions and answers for your interview. Use *my*WriteSmart in your eBook to write a brief introduction and conclusion. Try to include questions of varying difficulty. Decide who will play the journalist and who will play the expert. Practice listening to and responding to questions until the interview sounds natural. Then present it to your class.

Reading Social Studies

Using Context Clues— Definitions

One way to figure out the meaning of an unfamiliar word or term is by finding clues in its context, the words or sentences surrounding the word or term. A common context clue is a restatement. Restatements are simply a definition of the new word using ordinary words you already know. Notice how the following passage uses a restatement to define archipelago. Some context clues are not as complete or obvious. Notice how the following passage provides a description that is a partial definition of peninsula.

The region of Southeast Asia is made up of two *peninsulas* and two large island groups. The Indochina *Peninsula* and the Malay (muh-LAY) *Peninsula* extend from the Asian mainland. . . . The two island groups are the Philippines and the Malay Archipelago. An *archipelago* (ahr-kuh-PE-luh-goh) is a large group of islands.

From Section 1, Physical Geography

Peninsula: land that extends from a mainland out into water

Archipelago: large group of islands

YOU TRY IT!

Read the following passages and identify the meaning of the italicized words by using definitions, or restatements, in context. Seek help from a classmate or a teacher to confirm your understanding.

The many groups that influenced Southeast Asia's history also shaped its culture. This *diverse* culture blends native, Chinese, Indian, and European ways of life.

From Section 2, History and Culture

The economy is based on farming, but good farmland is limited. Most people are *subsistence farmers,* meaning they grow just enough food for their families.

From Section 3, Mainland Southeast Asia Today

The Pacific Realm

Essential Question

How has the Pacific realm been shaped by the mixture of native cultures and Western influence?

Texas Essential Knowledge and Skills (TEKS)

1A, 1B, 2A, 2B, 3A, 3B, 3C, 4B, 4C, 4D, 4F, 5A, 6A, 6B, 7A, 7B, 15A, 15B, 15D, 15E, 16A, 16B, 21B, 21C, 22A, 22D

The Big Idea Australia and New Zealand share a similar history and culture but have unique natural environments.

The Big Idea The Pacific Islands have tropical climates, rich cultures, and unique challenges.

The Big Idea Antarctica's unique environment has made it an important site for research.

FOCUS ON READING AND WRITING

Drawing Conclusions When you read, you discover new information. However, to find out what that information means, you have to draw conclusions. Conclusions are judgments we make as we combine new information with what we already know. As you read about the Pacific realm, draw conclusions about the information you come across. **See the lesson, Drawing Conclusions, on page 763.**

Creating a Brochure You work for an advertising agency, and your assignment is to create a brochure about the natural resources in the Pacific realm. Your goal is to encourage people to invest money in developing the local economies. As you read this chapter, collect information to use in your brochure. Use the annotation tools in your eBook to gather information for your assignment.

Geography From Uluru in the dry Australian Outback to freezing Antarctica, the Pacific realm is a land of great geographic variety.

The Pacific Realm: Political

Midway Islands

Hawaiian Islands (U.S.)

Wake Island

Johnston Atoll

MARSHALL ISLANDS

Kingman Reef

Palmyra Atoll

PACIFIC OCEAN

Howland Island

0° Equator

NAURU

Gilbert Islands

Line Islands

Bougainville

SOLOMON ISLANDS **TUVALU**

K I R I B A T I

Marquesas Islands

Wallis and Futuna (FRANCE) **SAMOA**

American Samoa (U.S.)

French Polynesia (FRANCE)

VANUATU

Cook Islands (NEW ZEALAND)

Tahiti

New Caledonia (FRANCE)

Loyalty Islands

FIJI **TONGA**

Niue

Tasman Sea

● Auckland

NEW ZEALAND

☆ Wellington

Chatham Islands

Auckland Islands

Legend:
- ✪ National capital
- ● Other cities

Island boundaries are for convenience only and do not represent international boundaries.

0 300 600 Miles

0 300 600 Kilometers

Projection: Miller Cylindrical

160°E *180°* *160°W* *140°W*

The Amazing Story of Shackleton

HISTORY

hmhsocialstudies.com **VIDEO**

map zone Geography Skills

Regions Three main regions make up the Pacific realm—Australia and New Zealand, the Pacific Islands, and Antarctica.

1. **Identify** What two continents are part of the Pacific realm?
2. **Make Inferences** Why do you think only the eastern half of New Guinea is considered part of this region?

SOUTHERN OCEAN

Antarctic Circle

30°W *30°E* *60°E*

Weddell Sea

Antarctic Peninsula

Ronne Ice Shelf

ANTARCTICA

90°W *South Pole* *90°E*

Transantarctic Mountains

120°W *120°E*

Ross Ice Shelf

Ross Sea

SOUTHERN OCEAN

150°W *180°* *150°E*

History The famous *moai* statues on Easter Island reflect the rich history of the Pacific realm.

Culture Sydney's Opera House is one example of the vibrant culture that exists throughout the Pacific realm.

TEKS 1A, 2A, 2B, 3A, 3B, 3C, 4B, 4C, 4D, 4F, 5A, 6A, 6B, 7A, 7B, 15B, 15D, 15E, 16A, 16B, 21B, 21C, 22A, 22D

What You Will Learn...

Main Ideas

1. The physical geography of Australia and New Zealand is diverse and unusual.
2. Native peoples and British settlers shaped the history of Australia and New Zealand.
3. Australia and New Zealand today are wealthy and culturally diverse countries.

The Big Idea

Australia and New Zealand share a similar history and culture but have unique natural environments.

Key Terms and Places

Great Barrier Reef, *p. 743*
coral reef, *p. 743*
Aborigines, *p. 745*
Maori, *p. 745*
Outback, *p. 746*

hmhsocialstudies.com
TAKING NOTES

Use the graphic organizer online to take notes on Australia and New Zealand's physical geography, history, and situation today.

Australia and New Zealand

If YOU lived there...

You have just taken a summer job working at a sheep station, or ranch, in Australia's Outback. You knew the Outback would be hot, but you did not realize how hot it could get! During the day, temperatures climb to over 100°F (40°C), and it hardly ever rains. In addition, you have learned that there are no towns nearby. Your only communication with home is by radio.

How will you adapt to living in the Outback?

BUILDING BACKGROUND Australia and New Zealand are very different. Much of Australia, such as the Outback, is hot, dry, and flat. In contrast, New Zealand has much milder climates, fertile valleys, and a variety of landforms.

Physical Geography

Locate Australia and New Zealand on the map on the next page. These countries are quite unlike most places on Earth. The physical features, variety of climates, unusual wildlife, and plentiful resources make the region truly unique.

Physical Features

The physical features of the region differ widely. Australia is home to wide, flat stretches of dry land. On the other hand, New Zealand features beautiful green hills and tall mountains.

Australia Similar to an island, Australia is surrounded by water. However, due to its immense size—almost 3 million square miles (7.7 million square km)—geographers consider Australia a continent.

A huge plateau covers the western half of Australia. Mostly flat and dry, this plateau is home to Uluru, a rock formation also known as Ayers Rock. Uluru is one of Australia's best-known landforms. Low mountains, valleys, and a major river system cover much of Eastern Australia. Fertile plains lie along the

INDIAN OCEAN

10°S

20°S

30°S

40°S

AUSTRALIA

O U T B A C K

Great Sandy Desert

Uluru (Ayers Rock) 2,844 ft (867 m)

Simpson Desert

Eastern Highlands

Great Victoria Desert

Central Lowlands

Lake Eyre

Darling River

Nullarbor Plain

Great Dividing Range

Great Australian Bight

Murray River

Mount Kosciusko 7,310 ft (2,228 m)

Tasmania

Coral Sea

Great Barrier Reef

Norfolk Island

PACIFIC OCEAN

North Island

Tasman Sea

NEW ZEALAND

Mount Cook 12,316 ft (3,754 m)

Southern Alps

South Island

Stewart Island

Chatham Islands

110°E 120°E 130°E 140°E 150°E 160°E 170°E 180°

ELEVATION

Feet	Meters
13,120	4,000
6,560	2,000
1,640	500
656	200
(Sea level) 0	0 (Sea level)
Below sea level	Below sea level

0   300   600 Miles

0   300   600 Kilometers

Projection: Miller Cylindrical

map zone

Geography Skills

Regions Australia and New Zealand are two of the southernmost countries in the Pacific region.

1. **Locate** What is the highest point in Australia?

2. **Analyze** About how far is New Zealand from Australia?

① Hot and dry, much of the western portion of Australia is covered in low trees and shrubs.

② New Zealand's fertile soil and long coastline provide the country with rich farmland and many harbors.

coasts. Off Australia's northeastern coast is the **Great Barrier Reef**, the world's largest coral reef. A **coral reef** is a collection of rocky material found in shallow, tropical waters. The Great Barrier Reef is home to an incredible variety of marine animals.

New Zealand New Zealand, located some 1,000 miles southeast of Australia, includes two main islands, North Island and South Island. North Island is covered by hills

and coastal plains. It is also home to volcanoes, geysers, and hot springs. One of the key features on South Island is a large mountain range called the Southern Alps. Thick forests, deep lakes, and even glaciers are found in the Southern Alps. The rest of the island is covered by fertile hills and rich plains. Fjords, or narrow inlets of the sea, create many natural harbors along the coasts of both islands.

Climates

The climates of Australia and New Zealand differ greatly. Because much of Australia has desert and steppe climates, temperatures are warm and rainfall is limited. However, along the coasts the climate is more temperate. Unlike Australia, New Zealand is mild and wet. A marine climate brings plentiful rainfall and mild temperatures to much of the country.

Wildlife and Resources

Both Australia and New Zealand are home to many unique animals. Some of the region's most famous native animals are Australia's kangaroo and koala and New Zealand's kiwi, a flightless bird.

Australia is rich in resources. It is the world's top producer of bauxite and opals, and is a leading producer of diamonds and lead. Australia is also home to energy resources like coal, natural gas, and oil. Despite poor soil, farms and ranches raise wheat, cotton, and sheep.

Unlike Australia, New Zealand has a great deal of fertile land but few mineral resources. New Zealand's main resources are wool, timber, and gold.

READING CHECK **Contrasting** How does the physical geography of the two countries differ?

Close-up

Maori Culture

The Maori, the descendants of New Zealand's earliest settlers, lived in small settlements throughout the islands. Their rich culture and traditions are still alive in New Zealand today.

Beautifully decorated store-houses served as a sign of a village's wealth and power. They often held weapons, tools, and foods.

The *moko*, or tattoos, of Maori warriors were symbols of a warrior's bravery. They also helped intimidate the enemy during battle.

The Maori used elaborately carved war canoes to launch attacks on their enemies.

History

Despite their many geographic differences, Australia and New Zealand have both been influenced by similar waves of human migration. Both countries were originally inhabited by settlers who migrated from other parts of the Pacific. Later, both Australia and New Zealand were colonized by the British.

Early Settlers

The first settlers in Australia likely migrated there from Southeast Asia at least 40,000 years ago. These settlers, the **Aborigines** (a-buh-RIJ-uh-nees), were the first humans to live in Australia. Early Aborigines were nomads who gathered various plants and hunted animals with boomerangs and spears. Nature played an important role in the religion of the early Aborigines, who believed that it was their duty to preserve the land.

New Zealand's first settlers came from other Pacific islands more recently, about 1,200 years ago. The descendants of these early settlers, the **Maori** (MOWR-ee), settled throughout New Zealand. Like Australia's Aborigines, the Maori were fishers and hunters. Unlike the Aborigines, however, the Maori also used farming to survive.

The Arrival of Europeans

European explorers first sighted Australia and New Zealand in the 1600s. It wasn't until later, however, that Europeans began to explore the region. In 1769 British explorer James Cook explored the main islands of New Zealand. The following year, Cook landed on the east coast of Australia and claimed the land for Britain.

Within 20 years of Cook's claim, the British began settling in Australia. Many of the first to arrive were British prisoners, but other settlers came, too. As the settlers built farms and ranches, they took over the Aborigines' lands. Many Aborigines died of diseases introduced by the Europeans.

In New Zealand, large numbers of British settlers started to arrive in the early 1800s. After the British signed a treaty with the Maori in 1840, New Zealand became a part of the British Empire. However, tensions between the Maori and British settlers led to a series of wars over land.

Australia and New Zealand both gained their independence in the early 1900s. Today the two countries are members of the British Commonwealth of Nations and are close allies of the United Kingdom.

FOCUS ON READING
What conclusions can you draw about why European settlers were attracted to Australia?

Maori life centered around a village meetinghouse, where important gatherings like weddings and funerals were held.

ANALYSIS SKILL **ANALYZING VISUALS**
Based on the illustration, what elements were important in Maori culture?

READING CHECK **Finding Main Ideas** How did early settlers influence the region?

Australian Sports

Outdoor sports are tremendously popular in sunny Australia. Some of Australia's most popular activities include water sports, such as swimming, surfing, and water polo. In recent years, many Australians have dominated the swimming competition at the summer Olympic Games.

Australia's national sport is cricket, a game played with a bat and ball. Cricket was first introduced to Australia by British settlers. Other popular sports with British roots are rugby and Australian Rules football. These two sports allow players to kick, carry, or pass the ball with their hands or feet. Every year hundreds of thousands of Australians attend professional rugby matches like the one in the photo below.

Drawing Conclusions Why do you think outdoor sports are so popular in Australia?

Australia and New Zealand Today

Despite their isolation from other nations, Australia and New Zealand today are rich and well-developed. Their governments, economies, and people make them among the world's most successful countries.

Government

As former British colonies, the British style of government has influenced both Australia and New Zealand. As a result, both countries have similar governments.

For example, the British monarch is the head of state in both Australia and New Zealand. Both countries are parliamentary democracies, a type of government in which citizens elect members to represent them in a parliament. Each country has a prime minister. The prime minister, along with Parliament, runs the government.

The governments of Australia and New Zealand have many features in common with the U.S. government. For example, Australia has a federal system like that of the United States. In this system, a central government shares power with the states. Australia's Parliament, similar to the U.S. Congress, consists of two houses—a House of Representatives and a Senate. A Bill of Rights also protects the individual rights of New Zealand's citizens.

Economy

Australia and New Zealand are both rich, economically developed countries. Agriculture is a major part of their economies. The two countries are among the world's top producers of wool. In fact, Australia regularly supplies about one-quarter of the wool used in clothing. Both countries also export meat and dairy products.

Australia and New Zealand also have other important industries. Mining is one of Australia's main industries. Companies mine bauxite, gold, and uranium throughout the **Outback**, Australia's interior. Other industries include steel, heavy machines, and computers. New Zealand has also become more industrialized in recent years. Factories turn out processed food, clothing, and paper products. Banking, insurance, and tourism are also important industries.

People

Today Australia and New Zealand have diverse populations. Most Australians and New Zealanders are of British ancestry. In recent years, however, peoples from around the world have migrated to the region. For example, since the 1970s Asians and Pacific Islanders have settled in Australia and New Zealand in growing numbers.

Native Maori and Aborigines make up only a small percentage of New Zealand's and Australia's populations. One challenge facing both countries today is improving the economic and political status of the those populations. Many of the region's Maori and Aborigines trail the rest of the population in terms of education, land ownership, and employment.

Most Australians and New Zealanders live in urban areas. About 90 percent of Australia's population lives in large cities along the coasts. Sydney and Melbourne, Australia's two largest cities, are home to about 8 million people. Rural areas like the Outback, on the other hand, have less than 10 percent of the population. In New Zealand, a majority of the population lives on the North Island. There, large cities like Auckland are common.

READING CHECK **Summarizing** What are the economic strengths of these countries?

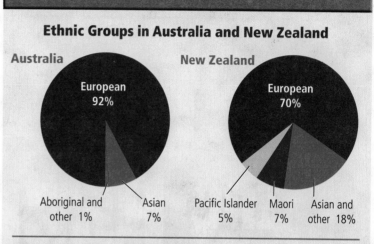

Ethnic Groups in Australia and New Zealand

Australia
European 92%
Aboriginal and other 1%
Asian 7%

New Zealand
European 70%
Pacific Islander 5%
Maori 7%
Asian and other 18%

Comparing and Contrasting In what ways are the ethnic populations of Australia and New Zealand similar and different?

SUMMARY AND PREVIEW Despite their geographical differences, Australia and New Zealand have much in common. The two countries share a similar history, culture, and economy. In the next section you will learn about another region in the Pacific world—the Pacific Islands.

Section 1 Assessment

Reviewing Ideas, Terms, and Places

1. **a. Identify** What is the **Great Barrier Reef**? Where is it located?
   b. Elaborate Given its harsh climate, why do you think so many people have settled in Australia?
2. **a. Describe** Who are the **Maori**? From where did they originate?
   b. Draw Conclusions How does religion shape the **Aborigines**' relationship with nature? How might this differ from other peoples?
3. **a. Explain** How have Australia and New Zealand been influenced by the migration of different people?
   b. Compare and Contrast How are the governments of Australia and New Zealand similar to and different from that of the United States?

Critical Thinking

4. **Comparing and Contrasting** Use your notes and a diagram like the one here to compare and contrast the geography, history, and culture of Australia and New Zealand.

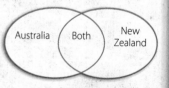

Australia | Both | New Zealand

FOCUS ON WRITING

my WriteSmart

5. **Describing Australia and New Zealand** What natural resources do these two countries produce? Make a list of the ones people might want to invest in. What illustrations could you include.

Settling the Pacific

For years scholars have puzzled over a mystery in the Pacific. How exactly did humans reach the thousands of islands scattered throughout the Pacific world? While we don't know all the details, evidence suggests that people from Southeast Asia originally settled the Pacific Islands. Over tens of thousands of years these people and their descendants slowly migrated throughout the Pacific. Thanks to expert canoe-building and navigational skills, these settlers reached islands many thousands of miles apart.

Many long-distance voyages were likely made on double canoes built with two hulls carved from huge logs.

Stick Charts Stick charts like this one from the Marshall Islands were probably used to navigate from island to island. The sticks show the direction of waves and ocean currents. Shells indicate the location of islands and other landmarks.

Settling the Pacific

map zone

Pacific Ocean

Hawaiian Islands

PHILIPPINES

Mariana Islands

MICRONESIA

Marshall Islands

MELANESIA

INDONESIA

NEW GUINEA

Solomon Islands

POLYNESIA

Samoa

Fiji   Tonga

Tahiti

Coral Sea

AUSTRALIA

Easter Island

NEW ZEALAND

c. 50,000 BC–25,000 BC
c. 1500 BC–AD 1
c. AD 1–1000

Double canoes used one or two sails and could reach speeds of up to 25 miles per hour (41 km per hour).

Double-hulled canoes likely included a shelter to store food, seeds, and other essentials.

Three Waves The Pacific world was settled in three main waves. People from Southeast Asia migrated first to Australia and New Guinea. Over thousands of years migrations took place from Southeast Asia and New Guinea to the islands of Micronesia and western Polynesia. In the last great wave of migration, Polynesians settled New Zealand, Hawaii, and Easter Island.

Settlers took along food items, such as dried bananas, and animals such as pigs and chickens.

ANALYSIS SKILL ANALYZING VISUALS

1. What were the last Pacific islands to be settled?
2. Why might the settlers have taken seeds and animals on their journey?

21ST CENTURY

Locating and Using Sources

Learn

Your teacher has asked you to locate valid primary and secondary sources about the Maori of New Zealand. Where do you look? What do you look for? The best place to start your search is in the library. The chart below will help you locate and identify the differences between primary and secondary sources.

Practice

Use information from the chart to answer the questions below.

1. What makes a primary source different from a secondary source?

2. Your teacher wants you to find images of traditional Maori dress. Which library tool would you use? What type of source would you use?

3. You want to find background information on Maori culture and history. Which library tool would you use? What type of source would you use?

Apply

Create a poster that shows a feature of Maori culture, such as art, food, or sport. Locate and use a primary source for your topic and a secondary source that you can use to write a paragraph explaining the significance of your topic to Maori culture. Present your poster to the class. Explain your topic and how you located and selected your sources. Help your classmates understand your key points by explaining culturally specific terms and by inviting and answering questions.

Library Tools

Electronic database	A computer software program that stores a collection of information about a topic, such as climate or population
Online catalog	An electronic database of books, videos, and other resources that can be searched by title, author, keyword, or subject
World Wide Web	A collection of Web sites and pages that can be accessed through the Internet, a huge system of linked computers

Primary and Secondary Sources

Primary Sources **Definition:** firsthand accounts created by people who took part in or witnessed events	Oral histories, music, photographs, videos, artifacts (clothing, tools, weapons, pottery, houses), census data, government documents, letters, speeches, autobiographies, firsthand newspaper and magazine stories
Secondary Sources **Definition:** records of events created by people who were not present at the event	Textbooks, reference books (encyclopedias, biographies, dictionaries, almanacs, atlases), computer software, videos, newspaper and magazine articles published after an event

The Pacific Islands

If **YOU** lived there...

You live on a small island in the South Pacific. For many years, the people on your island have made their living by fishing. Now, however, a European company has expressed interest in building an airport and a luxury hotel on your island. It hopes that tourists will be drawn by the island's dazzling beaches and tropical climate. The company's leaders want your permission before they build.

Will you give them permission? Why or why not?

BUILDING BACKGROUND Thousands of islands are scattered across the Pacific Ocean. Many of these islands are tiny and have few mineral resources. Among the resources they do have are pleasant climates and scenic landscapes. As a result, many Pacific islands have become popular tourist destinations.

Physical Geography

The Pacific Ocean covers more than one-third of Earth's surface. Scattered throughout this ocean are thousands of islands with similar physical features, climates, and resources.

Island Regions

We divide the Pacific Islands into three regions—Micronesia, Melanesia, and Polynesia—based on their culture and geography. **Micronesia**, which means "tiny islands," is located just east of the Philippines. Some 2,000 small islands make up this region. South of Micronesia is **Melanesia**, which stretches from New Guinea in the west to Fiji in the east. Melanesia is the most heavily populated Pacific Island region. The largest region is **Polynesia**, which means "many islands." Among Polynesia's many islands are Tonga, Samoa, and the Hawaiian Islands.

Physical Features

The Pacific Islands differ greatly. Some islands, like New Guinea (GI-nee), cover thousands of square miles. Other islands are tiny. For example, Nauru covers only 8 square miles (21 square km).

 TEKS 1A, 1B, 3A, 3B, 3C, 4C, 4F, 6A, 7B, 15D, 21B, 21C, 22A

What You Will Learn...

Main Ideas

1. Unique physical features, tropical climates, and limited resources shape the physical geography of the Pacific Islands.
2. Native customs and contact with the western world have influenced the history and culture of the Pacific Islands.
3. Pacific Islanders today are working to improve their economies and protect the environment.

The Big Idea

The Pacific islands have tropical climates, rich cultures, and unique challenges.

Key Terms and Places

Micronesia, *p. 751*
Melanesia, *p. 751*
Polynesia, *p. 751*
atoll, *p. 752*
territory, *p. 753*

hmhsocialstudies.com
TAKING NOTES

Use the graphic organizer online to take notes on the Pacific Islands.

Geographers classify the islands of the Pacific as either high islands or low islands. High islands tend to be mountainous and rocky. Most high islands are volcanic islands. They were formed when volcanic mountains grew from the ocean floor and reached the surface. The islands of Tahiti and Hawaii in Polynesia are examples of high islands. Other high islands, such as New Guinea, are formed from continental rock rather than volcanoes. For example, the country of Papua (PA-pyooh-wuh) New Guinea, located on the eastern half of the island of New Guinea, has rocky mountains that rise above 13,000 feet (3,960 m).

Low islands are typically much smaller than high islands. Most barely rise above sea level. Many low islands are atolls. An **atoll** is a small, ring-shaped coral island that surrounds a lagoon. Wake Island, west of the Hawaiian Islands, is an example of an atoll. Wake Island rises only 21 feet (6.4 m) above sea level and covers only 2.5 square miles (6.5 square km).

High and Low Islands

Many high islands, like the island of Hawaii, often have mountainous terrain, rich soils, and dense rain forests. Many low islands, like this small island in the Society Islands chain, are formed from coral reefs. Because most low islands have poor soils, agriculture is limited.

Climate and Resources

All but two of the Pacific Island countries lie in the tropics. As a result, most islands have a humid tropical climate. Rain falls all year and temperatures are warm. Tropical savanna climates with rainy and dry seasons exist in a few places, such as New Caledonia. The mountains of New Guinea are home to a cool highland climate.

Resources in the Pacific Islands vary widely. Most low islands have thin soils and little vegetation. They have few trees other than the coconut palm. In addition, low islands have few mineral or energy resources. Partly because of these conditions, low islands have small populations.

In contrast to low islands, the Pacific's high islands have many natural resources. Volcanic soils provide fertile farmland and dense forests. Farms produce crops such as coffee, cocoa, bananas, and sugarcane. Some high islands also have many mineral resources. Papua New Guinea, for example, exports gold, copper, and oil.

READING CHECK **Contrasting** How do the Pacific's low islands differ from high islands?

The Formation of an Atoll

The Pacific Islands are home to many atolls, or small coral islands that surround shallow lagoons. Coral reefs are formed from the skeletons of many tiny sea animals. When a coral reef forms on the edges of a volcanic island, it often forms a barrier reef around the island.

As the volcanic island sinks, the coral remains. Sand and other debris gradually collects on the reef's surface, raising the land above sea level. Eventually, all that remains is an atoll.

Sequencing Describe the process in which atolls form.

Coral reefs will sometimes form along the edges of a volcanic island, creating a ring around the island.

As the island sinks into the ocean floor, the coral reef grows upward and forms an offshore barrier reef.

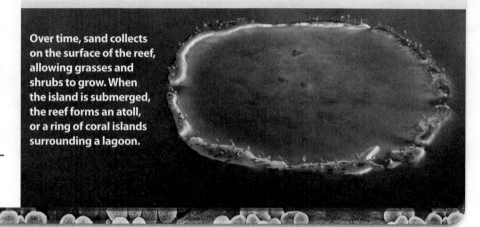

Over time, sand collects on the surface of the reef, allowing grasses and shrubs to grow. When the island is submerged, the reef forms an atoll, or a ring of coral islands surrounding a lagoon.

History and Culture

The Pacific Islands were one of the last places settled by humans. Because of their isolation from other civilizations, the islands have a unique history and culture.

Early History

Scholars believe that people began settling the Pacific Islands at least 35,000 years ago. The large islands of Melanesia were the first to be settled. Over time, people spread to the islands of Micronesia and Polynesia.

Europeans first encountered the Pacific Islands in the 1500s. Two centuries later, British captain James Cook explored all the main Pacific Island regions. By the late 1800s European powers such as Spain, Great Britain, and France controlled most of the Pacific Islands.

Modern History

By the early 1900s, other countries were entering the Pacific as well. In 1898 the United States defeated Spain in the Spanish-American War. As a result, Guam became a U.S. territory. A **territory** is an area that is under the authority of another government. Japan also expanded its empire into the Pacific Ocean in the early 1900s. In World War II, the Pacific Islands were the scene of many tough battles between Allied and Japanese forces. After Japan's defeat in 1945, the United Nations placed some islands under the control of the United States and other Allies.

In the last half of the 1900s many Pacific Islands gained their independence. However, several countries—including the United States, France, and New Zealand—still have territories in the Pacific Islands.

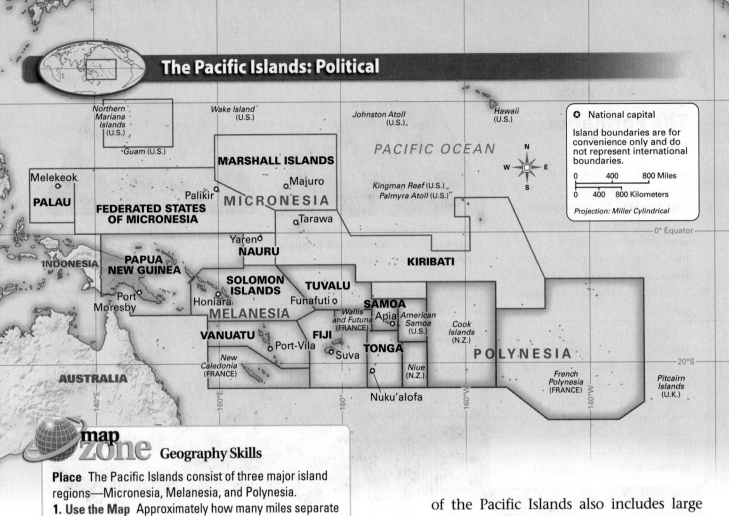

The Pacific Islands: Political

map zone Geography Skills

Place The Pacific Islands consist of three major island regions—Micronesia, Melanesia, and Polynesia.

1. **Use the Map** Approximately how many miles separate the islands of Palau and French Polynesia?
2. **Contrast** Based on the map, how do the Melanesian islands differ from those of French Polynesia?

Pacific Islands gained their independence. However, several countries—including the United States, France, and New Zealand—still have territories in the Pacific Islands.

Culture

A variety of cultures thrive throughout the Pacific Islands. Some culture traits, such as fishing, are common throughout the entire region. Others are only found on a specific island or island chain.

People More than 10 million people live in the Pacific Islands today. Most Pacific Islanders are descendants of the region's original settlers. However, the population

of the Pacific Islands also includes large numbers of ethnic Europeans and Asians, particularly Indians and Chinese. Many ethnic Asians are descended from people brought to the islands to work on colonial plantations. On the Melanesian island of Fiji, for example, Indians make up nearly half of the population.

Before the arrival of Europeans, the people of the Pacific Islands practiced hundreds of different religions. Today most Pacific Islanders are Christian. In Melanesia, however, some people continue to practice traditional local religions.

Traditions Although modern culture exists throughout the Pacific Islands, many people continue to practice traditional customs. In parts of Polynesia, for example, people still construct their homes from bamboo and palm leaves. Many Pacific Islanders today continue to live in ancient villages, practice customary art styles, and hold ceremonies that feature traditional

FOCUS ON READING

What can you conclude about the influence other cultures have had on the Pacific Islands?

The Pacific Islands Today

Many people imagine sunny beaches and tourists when they think of the Pacific Islands today. Despite the region's healthy tourism industry, however, Pacific Island countries face important challenges.

The countries of the Pacific Islands have developing economies. Fishing, tourism, and agriculture are key industries. Some countries, particularly Papua New Guinea, export minerals and timber. The region's isolation from other countries, however, hinders its ability to trade.

The environment is an important concern in the Pacific Islands. The Pacific Islands were used for nuclear testing grounds from the 1940s to the 1990s. Many people fear that one **effect** of these tests may be health problems for people in the region. Global warming also concerns Pacific Islanders. Some researchers believe that rising temperatures may cause polar ice to melt. The rise in ocean levels would threaten low-lying Pacific Islands.

READING CHECK **Summarizing** What are some challenges Pacific Islanders face today?

Villagers on Tanna Island in Vanuatu perform a traditional dance.

SUMMARY AND PREVIEW The Pacific Islands are one of the most isolated regions in the world. As a result, unique cultures and challenges exist in the region. In the next section you will learn about another isolated part of the globe—Antarctica.

ACADEMIC VOCABULARY

effect the results of an action or decision

Section 2 Assessment

hmhsocialstudies.com
ONLINE QUIZ

Reviewing Ideas, Terms, and Places

1. **a. Describe** Into what regions are the Pacific Islands divided?
   b. Draw Conclusions Why might high islands have larger populations than low islands?
2. **a. Define** What is a **territory**?
   b. Make Inferences Why did other countries seek to control the Pacific Islands?
   c. Elaborate Why do you think that many Pacific Islanders continue to practice traditional customs?
3. **a. Recall** What economic resources are available to the Pacific Islands?
   b. Predict How might the Pacific Islands be affected by global warming in the future?

Critical Thinking

4. **Finding Main Ideas** Draw a chart like the one shown. Using your notes, identify the main idea of each topic and write a sentence for each.

Physical Geography	History	Culture	Issues Today

FOCUS ON WRITING

*my*WriteSmart

5. **Telling about the Resources of the Pacific** Add to your list by noting the natural resources of the Pacific Islands. Which resources will you describe in your brochure? How might you describe them.

Antarctica

TEKS 1A, 1B, 2A, 2B, 3A, 3B,
4D, 7B, 21B, 21C, 22A, 22D

What You Will Learn...

Main Ideas

1. Freezing temperatures, ice, and snow dominate Antarctica's physical geography.
2. Explorations in the 1800s and 1900s led to Antarctica's use for scientific research.
3. Research and protecting the environment are key issues in Antarctica today.

The Big Idea

Antarctica's unique environment has made it an important site for research.

Key Terms and Places

ice shelf, *p. 757*
icebergs, *p. 757*
Antarctic Peninsula, *p. 757*
polar desert, *p. 757*
ozone layer, *p. 758*

hmhsocialstudies.com
TAKING NOTES

Use the graphic organizer online to take notes on Antarctica's physical geography, early exploration, and issues today.

If **YOU** lived there...

You are a scientist working at a research laboratory in Antarctica. One day you receive an e-mail message from a friend. She wants to open a company that will lead public tours through Antarctica so people can see its spectacular icy landscapes and wildlife. Some of your fellow scientists think that tours are a good idea, while others think that they could ruin the local environment.

What will you tell your friend?

BUILDING BACKGROUND Antarctica, the continent surrounding the South Pole, has no permanent residents. The only people there are scientists who research the frozen land. For many years, people around the world have debated the best way to use this frozen land.

Physical Geography

In the southernmost part of the world is the continent of Antarctica. This frozen land is very different from any other place on Earth.

The Land

Ice covers about 98 percent of Antarctica's 5.4 million square miles (14 million square km). This ice sheet contains more than 90 percent of the world's ice. On average the ice sheet is more than 1 mile (1.6 km) thick.

Penguins live in the icy waters around Antarctica, a continent almost completely covered in ice.

The weight of Antarctica's ice sheet causes ice to flow slowly off the continent. As the ice reaches the coast, it forms a ledge over the surrounding seas. This ledge of ice that extends over the water is called an **ice shelf**. Antarctica's ice shelves are huge. In fact, the Ross Ice Shelf, Antarctica's largest, is about the size of France.

Sometimes parts of the ice shelf break off into the surrounding water. Floating masses of ice that have broken off a glacier are **icebergs**. When one iceberg recently formed, it was approximately the size of the country of Luxembourg.

In western Antarctica, the **Antarctic Peninsula** extends north of the Antarctic Circle. As a result, temperatures there are often warmer than in other parts of the continent.

Climate and Resources

Most of Antarctica's interior is dominated by a freezing ice-cap climate. Temperatures can drop below –120°F (–84°C), and very little precipitation falls. As a result, much of Antarctica is considered a **polar desert**, a high-latitude region that receives very little precipitation. The precipitation that does fall does not melt due to the cold temperatures. Instead, it remains as ice.

Because of Antarctica's high latitude, the continent is in almost total darkness during winter months. Seas clog with ice as a result of the extreme temperatures.

In the summer, the sun shines around the clock and temperatures rise to near freezing.

Plant life only survives in the ice-free tundra areas. Insects are the frozen land's only land animals. Penguins, seals, and whales live in Antarctica's waters. Antarctica has many mineral resources, including iron ore, gold, copper, and coal.

READING CHECK **Summarizing** What are the physical features and resources of Antarctica?

Primary Source

BOOK

Crossing Antarctica

In 1989 a six-person team set off to cross Antarctica on foot. The 3,700-mile journey took seven months to complete. Team member Will Steger describes his first view of the continent.

> Now, flying over the iceberg-laden Weddell Sea, the biggest adventure of my life was about to begin . . .
>
> To the south I could barely pick out the peaks of mountains, mountains I knew jutted three thousand feet into the air. They lined the peninsula's coast for hundreds of miles. Leading up to them was a two-mile-wide sheet of snow and ice, preceded by the blue of the sea. It was a picture of purity, similar to many I had seen in the picture books . . .

—from *Crossing Antarctica*, by Will Steger and John Bowermaster

 ANALYSIS SKILL **ANALYZING PRIMARY SOURCES**

What physical features does the author notice on his trip over Antarctica?

BIOGRAPHY

Sir Ernest Shackleton
(1874–1922)

Irish-born Ernest Shackleton was one of several early explorers of Antarctica. Shackleton led a British expedition in 1907–1909 that climbed Mt. Erebus, an active volcano, discovered the Beardmore Glacier, and came within 97 miles of the South Pole—the farthest south anyone had ever been.

In the early 1900s several expeditions set out to find the South Pole. The first to reach the pole were members of a Norwegian expedition led by Roald Amundsen. In this photo a member of the Norwegian expedition poses with his team of dogs near the flag that marks the South Pole.

VIDEO
The Amazing Story of Shackleton

hmhsocialstudies.com

ACADEMIC VOCABULARY

motive
a reason for doing something

FOCUS ON READING

What conclusions can you draw about why some countries wanted to preserve Antarctica for research?

Early Explorations

The discovery of Antarctica is a fairly recent one. Although explorers long believed there was a southern continent, it was not until 1775 that James Cook first sighted the Antarctic Peninsula. In the 1800s explorers first investigated Antarctica. One **motive** of many explorers was to discover the South Pole and other new lands. In 1911 a team of Norwegian explorers became the first people to reach the South Pole.

Since then, several countries—including the United States, Australia, and Chile—have claimed parts of Antarctica. In 1959 the international Antarctic Treaty was signed to preserve the continent "for science and peace." This treaty banned military activity in Antarctica and set aside the entire continent for research.

READING CHECK Making Inferences Why do you think Antarctica is set aside for research?

Antarctica Today

Today Antarctica is the only continent without a permanent human population. Scientists use the continent to conduct research and to monitor the environment.

Scientific Research

While they are conducting research in Antarctica, researchers live in bases, or stations. Several countries, including the United States, the United Kingdom, and Russia, have bases in Antarctica.

Antarctic research covers a wide range of topics. Some scientists concentrate on the continent's plant and animal life. Others examine weather conditions. One group of researchers is studying Earth's ozone layer. The **ozone layer** is a layer of Earth's atmosphere that protects living things from the harmful effects of the sun's ultraviolet rays. Scientists have found a thinning in the ozone layer above Antarctica.

Environmental Threats

Many people today are concerned about Antarctica's environment. Over the years, researchers and tourists have left behind trash and sewage, polluting the environment. Oil spills have damaged surrounding seas. In addition, companies have hoped to exploit Antarctica's valuable resources.

Some people fear that any mining of the resources in Antarctica will result in more environmental problems. To prevent this, a new international agreement was reached in 1991. This agreement forbids most activities that do not have a scientific purpose. It bans mining and drilling and limits tourism.

READING CHECK **Finding Main Ideas** What are some issues that affect Antarctica today?

SUMMARY In this section, you have learned about Antarctica's unusual physical geography and harsh climates. Despite the difficulty of living in such harsh conditions, Antarctica remains an important place for scientific research.

Satellite View

Antarctica's Ice Shelves

Antarctica is home to many large ice shelves. An ice shelf is a piece of a glacier that extends over the surrounding seas. In recent years, scientists have become concerned that rising temperatures on the planet are causing the rapid disintegration of some of Antarctica's ice shelves. This satellite image from 2002 shows the breakup of a huge portion of Antarctica's Larsen B Ice Shelf, located on the Antarctic Peninsula. The breakup of this ice shelf released some 720 billion tons of ice into the Weddell Sea.

Identifying Cause and Effect What do scientists believe has led to growing disintegration of Antarctica's ice shelves?

Section 3 Assessment

hmhsocialstudies.com
ONLINE QUIZ

Reviewing Ideas, Terms, and Places

1. **a. Define** What are **ice shelves** and **icebergs**?
   b. Contrast How does Antarctica differ from most other continents?
   c. Elaborate What aspects of Antarctica's physical geography would you most like to see? Why?
2. **a. Compare** How do the geographic factors responsible for population patterns in Antarctica compare to those that shape the rest of the Pacific Realm?
   b. Predict What might have happened if countries had not agreed to preserve Antarctica for research?
3. **a. Recall** What is Antarctica used for today?
   b. Analyze How has Antarctic research benefited science?
   c. Elaborate Do you agree with bans on tourism and mining in Antarctica? Why or why not?

Critical Thinking

4. **Summarizing** Draw a diagram like the one here. Use your notes to list three facts about each aspect of Antarctica's physical geography.

Physical Geography	→	
Early Explorers	→	
Antarctica Today	→	

FOCUS ON WRITING

my WriteSmart

5. **Describing Antarctica** In your notebook, describe the natural resources of Antarctica. Decide which to include in your brochure. What illustrations might you include.

PERSONAL ACCOUNT

The South Pole

In this book, Norwegian explorer Roald Amundsen describes winter camp during the first expedition to reach the South Pole, which he led from 1911–1912.

The sun left us on April 22, and we did not see it again for four months. We spent the winter in altering our whole equipment, which our depot journeys had shown to be too heavy and clumsy for the smooth barrier surface[1]. At the same time we carried out all the scientific work for which there was opportunity. We made a number of surprising meteorological observations. There was very little snow, in spite of there being open water in the neighbourhood. We had expected to observe higher temperatures in the course of the winter, but the thermometer remained very low. During five months temperatures were observed varying between −58° and −74° F. We had the lowest (−74° F.) on August 13; the weather was calm. On August 1 we had −72° F. with a wind of thirteen miles an hour. The mean temperature for the year was −15° F. We expected blizzard after blizzard, but had only two moderate storms . . . Our bill of health was the best possible throughout the whole winter. When the sun returned on August 24 it shone upon men who were healthy in mind and body, and ready to begin the task that lay before them.

> Amundsen's team had already spent months storing supplies along the route they would later take to the Pole.

> Notice the detailed measurements included here.

[1] **depot**: a place where supplies are kept

[2] **barrier surface**: the top layer of snow and ice

[3] **meteorological**: related to the atmosphere and weather

Roald Amundsen (right) was the first explorer to reach both the North and South Poles within a lifetime.

ANALYSIS SKILL **ANALYZING PRIMARY SOURCES**

1. **Describing** What types of details about Antarctica does Amundsen include?
2. **Analyzing** This account was written after Amundsen had successfully reached the Pole and left Antarctica. Do you think he had any written sources on which to base his account? Why?

Visual Summary

Use the visual summary below to help you review the main ideas of the chapter.

QUICK FACTS

Australia and New Zealand
Despite different physical features, Australia and New Zealand have much in common.

The Pacific Islands
The Pacific Islands are home to tropical climates and beautiful beaches.

Antarctica
Antarctica's unique environment makes it an important site for scientific research.

Reviewing Vocabulary, Terms, and Places

Work in a small group to identify the term that best completes each statement and discuss why the other terms are incorrect.

1. The original inhabitants of Australia are the
   - **a.** Aborigines
   - **b.** Maori
   - **c.** Papuans
   - **d.** Polynesians

2. A floating mass of ice that has broken off a glacier is a(n)
   - **a.** atoll
   - **b.** coral reef
   - **c.** iceberg
   - **d.** polar desert

3. Located off the northeast coast of Australia, this is the world's largest coral reef
   - **a.** Australian Reef
   - **b.** Great Barrier Reef
   - **c.** Kiwi Reef
   - **d.** Reef of the Coral Sea

4. The result of an action or decision is a(n)
   - **a.** agreement
   - **b.** effect
   - **c.** motive
   - **d.** purpose

Comprehension and Critical Thinking

SECTION 1 *(Pages 742–747)*

5. **a. Describe** What is the physical geography of Australia like?

   b. Compare and Contrast In what ways are the countries of Australia and New Zealand similar and different?

   c. Elaborate Why do you think the economies of Australia and New Zealand are so strong?

SECTION 2 *(Pages 751–755)*

6. **a. Identify** What two types of islands are commonly found in the Pacific Ocean? How are they different?

   b. Analyze How were the islands of the Pacific Ocean originally settled? How has migration influenced the character of this region?

   c. Elaborate Many Pacific Islands are isolated from other societies. Would you want to live in such a place?

SECTION 3 *(Pages 756–759)*

7. a. Describe What types of wildlife are found in and around Antarctica?

b. Draw Conclusions Why do you think many of the world's countries supported setting aside Antarctica for scientific research?

c. Predict What effects might the thinning of the ozone layer have on Antarctica?

Social Studies Skills

Locating and Using Sources *Use your knowledge about locating and using sources to answer the question below.*

8. You have two recently published newspaper articles on exploring Antarctica. One is written by a scientist currently living there. The other describes Roald Amundsen's 1911 expedition. Which is a primary source? Explain.

9. Look at the Primary Source feature on page 760. Create your own Primary Source page for one of the cultures described in this chapter. Locate and use at least one primary source and one secondary source to create your page.

Using the Internet

10. Creating a Visual Display Learn more about Australia's original people, the Aborigines, through your online book. Take notes and use your research to create a visual display of an important event or cultural feature. Present your display to the class. Be sure to define any unfamiliar terms. Then, invite and answer questions from your classmates to make sure they understand your key points.

Map Activity

11. The Pacific Realm On a sheet of paper, match the letters on the map with their correct labels.

Great Barrier Reef	Perth, Australia	Outback
Papua New Guinea	Sydney, Australia	North Island
Melbourne, Australia	Pacific Ocean	

FOCUS ON READING AND WRITING *my* WriteSmart

Drawing Conclusions *Read the paragraph below. Then answer the questions that follow.*

> Getting an education can be a challenge in the Outback, where students are spread across vast distances. Basic education comes from the School of the Air, which broadcasts classes via radio. Other lessons are conducted by video or mail. The internet, e-mail, and videoconferencing have also been used in recent years.

12. What did you know about education and Australia before you read this paragraph?

13. What conclusion(s) can you draw about education in Australia's Outback?

Writing a Brochure *Use your notes and the directions below to create a brochure.*

14. Divide your brochure into sections—one on Australia and New Zealand, one on the Pacific Islands, and one on Antarctica. Identify the renewable and nonrenewable resources located in each region and try to convince the reader to invest in them. Use illustrations to support the points you want to make. Finally, design a cover page for your brochure.

Drawing Conclusions

FOCUS ON READING

You have probably heard the phrase, "Put two and two together." When people say that, they don't mean "2 + 2 = 4." They mean, "put the information together." When you put together information you already know with information you have read, you can draw a conclusion. To make a conclusion, read the passage carefully. Then think about what you already know about the topic. Put the two together to draw a conclusion.

> Off Australia's northeastern coast is <u>the Great Barrier Reef, the world's largest coral reef.</u> A coral reef is a collection of rocky material found in wshallow, tropical waters. The Great Barrier Reef is home to an incredible variety of marine animals.
>
> *From Section 1, Australia and New Zealand*

Information gathered from the passage: Australia has the world's largest coral reef.	**+**	**What you already know:** I know many people like to snorkel or scuba dive at coral reefs.	**=**	**Add the information up to reach your conclusion:** Australia probably has many tourists who come to visit the Great Barrier Reef.

YOU TRY IT!

Read the following paragraphs. Think about what you know about living in a very cold climate. Then use the process described above to draw a conclusion about the following passage.

> Because of Antarctica's high latitude, the continent is in almost total darkness during winter months. Seas clog with ice as a result of the extreme temperatures. In the summer, the sun shines around the clock and temperatures rise to near freezing.
>
> Plant life only survives in the ice-free tundra areas. Insects are the frozen land's only land animals. Penguins, seals, and whales live in Antarctica's waters.
>
> *From Section 3, Antarctica*

Persuasion

Persuasion is about convincing others to act or believe in a certain way. Just as you use persuasion to convince your friends to see a certain movie, people use persuasion to convince others to help them solve the world's problems.

Assignment   *my*WriteSmart

Use *my*Write Smart to write a persuasive paper about an issue faced by the people of Asia and the Pacific. Choose an issue related to the region's environment or culture.

1. Prewrite

Choose an Issue

- Choose an issue to write about. For example, you might choose the danger of tsunamis or the role of governments.
- Create a statement of opinion. For example, you might say, "Countries in this region must create a warning system for tsunamis."

Gather and Organize Information

- Search your textbook, the library, or the Internet for evidence that supports your opinion.
- Identify at least two reasons to support your opinion. Find facts, examples, and expert opinions to support each reason.

> **TIP** **That's a Reason** Convince your readers by presenting reasons to support your opinion. For example, one reason to create a warning system for tsunamis is to save lives.

2. Write

Use a Writer's Framework

A Writer's Framework

Introduction
- Start with a fact or question related to the issue you will discuss.
- Clearly state your opinion in a sentence.

Body
- Write one paragraph for each reason. Begin with the least important reason and end with the most important.
- Include facts, examples and expert opinions as support.

Conclusion
- Restate your opinion and summarize your reasons.

3. Evaluate and Revise

Review and Improve Your Paper

- As you review your paper, use the questions below to evaluate it.
- Make changes to improve your paper.

Evaluation Questions for a Persuasive Essay

1. Do you begin with an interesting fact or question related to the issue?
2. Does your introduction clearly state your opinion and provide any necessary background information?
3. Do you discuss your reasons from least to most important?
4. Do you provide facts, examples, or expert opinions to support each of your reasons?
5. Does your conclusion restate your opinion and summarize your reasons?

4. Proofread and Publish

Give Your Paper the Finishing Touch

- Make sure that you have used standard grammar, spelling, sentence structure, and punctuation.
- Check for correct comma usage when presenting a list of reasons or evidence.
- Decide how to share your paper. For example, could you publish it in a school paper or in a classroom collection of essays?

5. Practice and Apply

Use the steps and strategies outlined in this workshop to write your persuasive essay. Share your opinion with others to see whether they find your opinion convincing.

References

Available @

 hmhsocialstudies.com

- Facts About the World
- Regions of the World Handbook
- Standardized Test-Taking Strategies
- Economics Handbook

United States: Physical

Strait of Juan de Fuca

Puget Sound

Mount Rainier
14,410 ft
(4,392 m)

45°N

COAST RANGES

CASCADE RANGE

Columbia River

Willamette River

Franklin D. Roosevelt Lake

Pend Oreille River

Clark Fork

Flathead River

Flathead Lake

LEWIS RANGE

Milk River

Missouri River

Lake Sakakawea

Fort Peck Lake

ROCKY

GREAT

Salmon River

Bitterroot Range

Salmon River Mts.

CONTINENTAL

Yellowstone River

Bighorn Mts.

Powder River

Lake Oahe

40°N

Cape Mendocino

Klamath River

Goose Lake

Shasta Lake

Pyramid Lake

Columbia Plateau

Sawtooth Mts.

Snake River

GREAT

Great Salt Lake

Utah Lake

Grand Tetons

Gannett Peak
13,804 ft
(4,207 m)

Wind River Range

Yellowstone Lake

Bighorn River

DIVIDE

Front Range

Wind River

North Platte River

Black Hills

Cheyenne River

White River

Niobrara River

James River

WINTER

PLAINS

San Francisco Bay

125°W

Sacramento River

Central Valley

San Joaquin River

SIERRA NEVADA

Lake Tahoe

BASIN

Wasatch Range

Uinta Mts.

Green River

Colorado River

Mount Elbert
14,433 ft
(4,400 m)

DIVIDE

South Platte River

Pikes Peak
14,110 ft
(4,301 m)

Republican River

Platte River

MOUNTAINS

35°N

Monterey Bay

Coast Ranges

Mount Whitney
14,494 ft
(4,419 m)

Death Valley

Mojave Desert

Lake Mead

Colorado River

Lake Powell

Grand Canyon

COLORADO

PLATEAU

Painted Desert

San Juan River

San Luis Valley

Rio Grande

Sangre De Cristo Mts.

Smoky Hill River

PACIFIC

OCEAN

Channel Islands

Salton Sea

Imperial Valley

120°W

Gila River

Sonoran Desert

DIVIDE

CONTINENTAL

Rio Grande

Canadian River

30°N

Gulf of California

Pecos River

Colorado River

MEXICO

To understand the relative locations of Alaska and Hawaii, as well as the vast distances separating them from the rest of the United States, see the world map.

Amistad Reservoir

Rio Grande

Nueces River

Padre Island

HAWAII

Kauai

Niihau

Oahu

Molokai

Maui

Lanai

Kahoolawe

Mauna Kea
13,796 ft
(4,206 m)

Hawaii

22°N

155°W

PACIFIC OCEAN

19°N

| 0 | 75 | 150 Miles |
| 0 | 75 | 150 Kilometers |

Projection: Mercator

160°W

ARCTIC OCEAN

Arctic Circle

BROOKS RANGE

RUSSIA

Bering Strait

St. Lawrence Island

St. Matthew Island

Nunivak Island

Yukon River

Kuskokwim River

Tanana River

ALASKA RANGE

Mount McKinley
20,320 ft
(6,194 m)

CANADA

170°E

Bering Sea

55°N

50°N

Attu Island

ALEUTIAN ISLANDS

PACIFIC OCEAN

180°

170°W

160°W

150°W

Kodiak Island

Gulf of Alaska

Alexander Archipelago

55°N

| 0 | 250 | 500 Miles |
| 0 | 250 | 500 Kilometers |

Projection: Albers Equal Area

CANADA

Red River
Mesabi Range
Isle Royale
Lake Superior
Minnesota River
Mississippi River
Wisconsin River
Lake Michigan
Lake Huron
Lake Ontario
Lake Erie
St. Lawrence River
St. Lawrence Seaway
St. John River
Lake Champlain
Adirondack Mts.
Green Mts.
White Mts.
Longfellow Mts.
Penobscot River
Connecticut River
Hudson R.
Catskill Mts.
Cape Cod
Long Island Sound
Long Island
ALLEGHENY PLATEAU
Allegheny R.
Susquehanna River
Delaware R.
APPALACHIAN MOUNTAINS
40°N

Missouri River
Des Moines River
Illinois River
Wabash River
Scioto River
Ohio River
P L A I N S
Kansas R.
Lake of the Ozarks
OZARK PLATEAU
Keystone Lake
Eufaula Lake
Arkansas River
White River
Lake Barkley
Cumberland River
Kentucky Lake
Lake Texoma
Ouachita Mts.
Cumberland Plateau
Great Smoky Mts.
BLUE RIDGE MOUNTAINS
Monongahela R.
Kanawha R.
Potomac River
James River
Roanoke River
P I E D M O N T
Delaware Bay
Chesapeake Bay
ATLANTIC OCEAN
70°W
Pamlico Sound
Cape Hatteras
35°N

Trinity River
Brazos River
Saline River
Red River
Toledo Bend Reservoir
Mississippi River
Pearl River
Tombigbee River
Tennessee River
Coosa River
Alabama R.
Chattahoochee River
Oconee River
Savannah River
Altamaha River
Sea Islands
C O A S T A L   P L A I N
GULF
Chandeleur Islands
Mississippi Delta
Okefenokee Swamp
Cape Canaveral
FLORIDA PENINSULA
80°W

Gulf of Mexico
N E W S (compass)
95°W
90°W
85°W
75°W
Lake Okeechobee
The Everglades
Cape Sable
Florida Keys
Straits of Florida
BAHAMAS
25°N

ELEVATION

Feet	Meters
13,120	4,000
6,560	2,000
1,640	500
656	200
(Sea level) 0	0 (Sea level)
Below sea level	Below sea level

0   100   200 Miles
0   100   200 Kilometers

Projection: Albers Equal Area

United States: Political

WASHINGTON
Strait of Juan de Fuca
Puget Sound
Seattle
Tacoma
Olympia ★
Spokane ●
Franklin D. Roosevelt Lake
Pend Oreille
Portland ●
Columbia River
Salem ★
Eugene ●
OREGON

Flathead Lake
Great Falls ●
Helena ★
MONTANA
Fort Peck Lake
Missouri River
Yellowstone River
Billings ●

NORTH DAKOTA
Lake Sakakawea
Bismarck ★

Cape Mendocino
Goose Lake
Shasta Lake
Sacramento River
Pyramid Lake
IDAHO
Boise ★
Sun Valley ●
Snake River
Pocatello ●
Yellowstone Lake
WYOMING
Cheyenne ★

Lake Oahe
SOUTH DAKOTA
Pierre ★
Rapid City ●

Berkeley
Oakland
San Francisco
San Francisco Bay
San Jose ●
Sacramento ★
Reno ●
Carson City ★
Lake Tahoe
NEVADA
Great Salt Lake
Ogden ●
Salt Lake City ★
Provo ●
Utah Lake
Green River
UTAH
NEBRASKA
Platte River

Monterey Bay
San Joaquin River
Fresno ●
CALIFORNIA
Las Vegas ●
Lake Mead
Colorado River
Lake Powell
Aspen ●
Vail ●
Boulder ●
Denver ★
Colorado Springs ●
Pueblo ●
COLORADO
Arkansas River
KANSAS

PACIFIC OCEAN
Santa Barbara ●
Ventura ●
Los Angeles ●
Long Beach ●
Riverside ●
Palm Springs ●
Anaheim ●
Santa Ana ●
Channel Islands
San Diego ●
Salton Sea
Flagstaff ●
ARIZONA
Phoenix ★
Casa Grande ●
Tucson ●
Gila River
Taos ●
Santa Fe ★
Albuquerque ●
NEW MEXICO
Las Cruces ●
El Paso ●
OKLAHOMA
Amarillo ●
Oklahoma City ★
Lawton ●
Canadian River

Gulf of California
Lubbock ●
Abilene ●
Fort Worth
Brazos River
Midland ●
Odessa ●
TEXAS
Pecos River
Colorado River
Rio Grande
Amistad Reservoir
Austin ★
San Antonio ●
Corpus Christi ●
Laredo ●
Padre Island

MEXICO

To understand the relative locations of Alaska and Hawaii, as well as the vast distances separating them from the rest of the United States, see the world map.

Kauai
Niihau
Oahu
Molokai
HAWAII
Honolulu ★
PACIFIC OCEAN
Lanai
Maui
Kahoolawe
Hilo ●
Hawaii
22°N
155°W
160°W

0   75   150 Miles
0   75   150 Kilometers
Projection: Mercator
19°N

ARCTIC OCEAN
Arctic Circle
RUSSIA
Bering Strait
St. Lawrence Island
St. Matthew Island
Nunivak Island
Nome ●
Yukon River
Fairbanks ●
ALASKA
CANADA
Anchorage ●
Valdez ●
Skagway ●
Juneau ★
Kodiak Island
Gulf of Alaska
Alexander Archipelago
55°N

Attu Island
Bering Sea
55°N
50°N
170°E
180°
170°W
160°W
150°W
140°W
ALEUTIAN ISLANDS
PACIFIC OCEAN

0   250   500 Miles
0   250   500 Kilometers
Projection: Albers Equal Area

45°N
40°N
35°N
30°N
125°W
120°W

CANADA

MAINE

Augusta ★

Grand Forks
Red River
Fargo
Duluth
Superior
Marquette
Sault Ste. Marie

MINNESOTA

Lake Superior

St. Lawrence River

Burlington
Montpelier
Portland
Lake Champlain
VT Concord
NH Manchester

WISCONSIN

MICHIGAN

Lake Huron

Hudson R.
Connecticut R.

Minneapolis
★ St. Paul
Green Bay
Madison
Milwaukee

Grand Rapids
Saginaw
Lansing ★ Detroit
Ann Arbor

Lake Michigan

Lake Ontario
Rochester
Syracuse
Albany
Springfield
MA Boston
Worcester
Providence
CT **RI**
Hartford ★
New Haven
Cape Cod

Minnesota River
Mississippi River

Sioux Falls
Sioux City

IOWA

Cedar Rapids
Davenport
★ Des Moines

Rockford
Chicago
Gary
South Bend
Fort Wayne

Buffalo
Lake Erie
Cleveland
Youngstown
Akron

NEW YORK

Bridgeport
Yonkers
Long Island Sound
Long Island
Jersey City
Newark
New York City

40°N

Omaha
Lincoln
Missouri River

MISSOURI

Peoria
Springfield

ILLINOIS

Indianapolis ★

INDIANA

Dayton
Cincinnati

Columbus ★

OHIO

PENNSYLVANIA

Allentown
Harrisburg
Pittsburgh
Philadelphia
Trenton
Camden
NJ
Atlantic City

Susquehanna River

Kansas City
Topeka ★
Kansas City

St. Louis
East St. Louis

Jefferson City
Lake of the Ozarks

Frankfort ★
Louisville
Evansville
Lexington

WEST VIRGINIA
★ Charleston

Washington, D.C. ⊛
Baltimore
MD Annapolis ★
Dover ★
DE

Delaware Bay

Wichita

Ohio River
Lake Barkley

KENTUCKY

VIRGINIA
Richmond ★

Chesapeake Bay

ATLANTIC OCEAN

70°W

Keystone Lake
Tulsa
Fayetteville

Kentucky Lake
Kentucky River

Nashville ★
Knoxville

Newport News
Norfolk
Virginia Beach

35°N

Cape Hatteras

Eufaula Lake

Mississippi River

Memphis

TENNESSEE
Chattanooga

Asheville

Winston-Salem
Greensboro
Durham
Raleigh ★

NORTH CAROLINA

Charlotte

Lake Texoma

ARKANSAS

Little Rock ★
Pine Bluff

Huntsville

Greenville

SOUTH CAROLINA
★ Columbia

Dallas

Atlanta ★

Savannah River

Charleston

Waco

MISSISSIPPI

Vicksburg
Jackson ★

Meridian
Montgomery ★

ALABAMA

Birmingham

GEORGIA

Macon
Columbus

Sea Islands

Savannah

30°N

Toledo Bend Reservoir

LOUISIANA

Shreveport
Red River

Baton Rouge ★
Biloxi

Mobile
Pensacola
Tallahassee ★

Chattahoochee R.

Jacksonville

80°W

Beaumont
Houston

New Orleans
Chandeleur Islands

Gainesville

FLORIDA

Galveston

Gulf of Mexico

N
W ⊛ E
S

St. Petersburg

Orlando
Tampa

Cape Canaveral

Lake Okeechobee

BAHAMAS

25°N

Fort Myers
Fort Lauderdale
Miami

Cape Sable
Florida Keys

Straits of Florida

75°W

Legend:
⊛ National capital
★ State capitals
• Other cities

0   100   200 Miles
0   100   200 Kilometers

Projection: Albers Equal Area

95°W   90°W   85°W

ARCTIC 80°N OCEAN
Greenland
Beaufort Sea
Victoria Island
Baffin Bay
Baffin Island
Davis Strait
Denmark Strait
Iceland
Arc
Bering Strait
Yukon River
Great Bear Lake
Mackenzie River
Great Slave Lake
Hudson Bay
60°N
Bering Sea
Gulf of Alaska
ROCKY MOUNTAINS
Lake Winnipeg
Great Lakes
St. Lawrence River
Aleutian Islands
Vancouver Island
Missouri River
Bay of Bisca
NORTH AMERICA
APPALACHIAN MTS.
40°N
Colorado River
ATLANTIC OCEAN
Strait of Gibraltar
ATL
SIERRA MADRE
Rio Grande
Gulf of Mexico
Bahamas
Tropic of Cancer
Hawaiian Islands
Niger
20°N
Greater Antilles
Caribbean Sea
Lesser Antilles
PACIFIC OCEAN
Isthmus of Panama
GUIANA HIGHLANDS
ANDES MOUNTAINS
Amazon River
N
0° Equator
W E
S
SOUTH AMERICA
BRAZILIAN HIGHLANDS
20°S
Tropic of Capricorn
River
ANDES MOUNTAINS
ATLANTIC OCEAN
Parana
40°S
Strait of Magellan
Falkland Islands
Tierra del Fuego
Cape Horn
60°S
160°W 140°W 120°W
SOUTHERN OCEAN
60°W 40°W 20°W
Antarctic Circle
Weddell Sea

ELEVATION

Feet		Meters
13,120		4,000
6,560		2,000
1,640		500
656		200
(Sea level) 0		0 (Sea level)
Below sea level		Below sea level

 Ice cap

0   500   1,000   1,500   2,000 Miles
0   1,000   2,000 Kilometers

Projection: Mollweide

ARCTIC—80°N—OCEAN
North Cape
Barents Sea
Kara Sea
Laptev Sea
East Siberian Sea
Kolyma River
Lena River
Yenisei River
Ob River
URAL MOUNTAINS
Volga River
Baltic Sea
EUROPE
LPS
Black Sea
Caspian Sea
Aral Sea
Balqash Lake
Lake Baikal
ALTAY
60°N
Sea of Okhotsk
KAMCHATKA PENINSULA
Amur River
Sakhalin Island
Hokkaido
40°N
Honshu
Shikoku
Kyushu
ASIA
GOBI
Huang He (Yellow River)
Chang Jiang (Yangzi) River
East China Sea
HIMALAYAS
Mediterranean Sea
HARA
ARABIAN PENINSULA
Tigris River
Euphrates River
Persian Gulf
Nile River
Red Sea
Indus River
Thar Desert
Ganges River
AFRICA
Arabian Sea
Bay of Bengal
Mekong River
South China Sea
Taiwan
Tropic of Cancer
20°N
Philippine Islands
PACIFIC OCEAN
Sri Lanka
Strait of Malacca
MALAY PENINSULA
Borneo
0° Equator
Congo River
Lake Tanganyika
Lake Victoria
INDIAN OCEAN
Sumatra
Java
Celebes
New Guinea
Solomon Islands
Coral Sea
New Hebrides
Fiji Islands
Madagascar
Mozambique Channel
GREAT SANDY DESERT
New Caledonia
20°S
KALAHARI DESERT
GREAT VICTORIA DESERT
AUSTRALIA
Darling River
GREAT DIVIDING RANGE
Tropic of Capricorn
Cape of Good Hope
Tasman Sea
North Island
NEW ZEALAND
Tasmania
South Island
SOUTHERN OCEAN
60°S
120°E
140°E
160°E
ANTARCTICA
20°E
40°E

ATLAS

Denmark Strait
0°
10°E
20°E
30°E
40°E
North Cape
Kara Sea
Barents Sea
N
W E
S
KJØLEN MTS.
Iceland
URAL MTS.
0   250   500 Miles
0   250   500 Kilometers
Projection: Mollweide
60°N
North Sea
Baltic Sea
Volga River
NORTHERN EUROPEAN PLAIN
British Isles
50°N
Rhine
Danube
ALPS
ATLANTIC OCEAN
Bay of Biscay
10°W
Black Sea
40°N
IBERIAN PENINSULA
Mediterranean Sea
Strait of Gibraltar
Crete

ATLAS

National capital
Other city

| 0 | 500 | 1,000 Miles |
| 0 | 500 1,000 Kilometers | |

Projection: Mollweide

ARCTIC OCEAN

Greenland
(DENMARK)

ALASKA
(U.S.)

Godthåb

ICELA

CANADA

Aleutian Islands

Vancouver   Winnipeg

NORTH
AMERICA

Ottawa   Montreal
Chicago   Toronto
UNITED   New York City
STATES   Washington,
                    D.C.

ATLANTIC
OCEAN

Los Angeles

Houston

Bermuda
(U.K.)

Rabe
Casablanca
MOROCC

MEXICO

Western
Sahara
(Claimed by
Morocco)

Tropic of Cancer

Mexico
City

MAURITANIA

Nouakchott

HAWAII
(U.S.)

CAPE VERDE   SENEGAL
Dakar
GAMBIA
GUINEA-BISSAU   GUINEA
Ban

Caracas

SIERRA
LEONE   D'I
LIBERIA

PACIFIC
OCEAN

VENEZUELA GUYANA
Georgetown   SURINAME
Bogotá   Paramaribo French Guiana
COLOMBIA   (FRANCE)

KIRIBATI

Galápagos
Islands
(ECUADOR)

Quito
ECUADOR

N
W   E
S

PERU

SOUTH
AMERICA

SAMOA

American
Samoa

Lima

BRAZIL

Brasília

BOLIVIA
La Paz

TONGA

Sucre

Rio de Janeiro

PARAGUAY

São Paulo

CHILE

Asunción

ATLANTIC
OCEAN

URUGUAY
Santiago   Buenos
                Aires   Montevideo

ARGENTINA

Falkland
Islands
(U.K.)

South
Georgia
(U.K.)

South Sandwic
Islands

SOUTHERN OCEAN

Antarctic Circle

| 0 | 200 | 400 Miles |
| 0 | 200 | 400 Kilometers |

Projection: Mercator

FLORIDA
(U.S.)

Nassau

BAHAMAS

Gulf of
Mexico

Havana

CUBA

Tropic of Cancer

Turks and Caicos Is.
(U.K.)

ATLANTIC   OCEAN

Virgin Islands
(U.S. and U.K.)

Cayman Is.
(U.K.)

HAITI   DOMINICAN
            REPUBLIC

1

MEXICO

BELIZE
Belmopan

JAMAICA
Kingston

Port-au-Prince
Santo
Domingo

Puerto Rico
(U.S.)

2

Guadeloupe (FRANCE)

3

Caribbean Sea

Martinique (FRANCE)

GUATEMALA   HONDURAS
Guatemala City Tegucigalpa
San Salvador
EL SALVADOR   NICARAGUA
                Managua

Netherlands
Antilles
(NETHERLANDS)
Aruba
(NETHERLANDS)

4
5   6

7

Port-of-
Spain   TRINIDAD AND
            TOBAGO

N
W   E
S

COSTA RICA
San José

Panama
City

10°N

PACIFIC   OCEAN

PANAMA

COLOMBIA

VENEZUELA

GUYANA

COUNTRY	CAPITAL
1 Antigua and Barbuda	St. Johns
2 St. Kitts and Nevis	Basseterre
3 Dominica	Roseau
4 St. Lucia	Castries
5 St. Vincent and the Grenadines	Kingstown
6 Barbados	Bridgetown
7 Grenada	St. George's

	COUNTRY	CAPITAL
1	Czech Republic	Prague
2	Slovakia	Bratislava
3	Slovenia	Ljubljana
4	Croatia	Zagreb
5	Bosnia and Herzegovina	Sarajevo
6	Macedonia	Skopje
7	Serbia	Belgrade
8	Montenegro	Podgorica
9	Lithuania	Vilnius
10	Latvia	Riga
11	Estonia	Tallinn
12	Kosovo	Pristina

North America: Physical

ASIA

ARCTIC OCEAN

EUROPE

+North Pole

POLAR ICE PACK

Queen
Elizabeth
Islands

Greenland

Cape
Farewell

Beaufort
Sea

Banks
Island

Baffin
Bay

Ellesmere Island

Denmark Strait

Arctic Circle

St. Lawrence Island

Bering Strait

Nunivak Island

BROOKS RANGE

Victoria
Island

Baffin Island

Davis Strait

Labrador
Sea

ALASKA

Mt. McKinley
20,320 ft
(6,194 m)

Yukon River

RANGE

YUKON PLATEAU

Mackenzie River

Great
Bear
Lake

Southampton
Island

Hudson Strait

Kodiak Island

Gulf of Alaska

Great
Slave
Lake

Peace River

Lake
Athabasca

Coats
Island

Mansel
Island

Hudson
Bay

CANADIAN

SHIELD

Anticosti
Island

Newfoundland

Alexander Archipelago

Athabasca River

Cape
Breton
Island

Queen
Charlotte
Islands

PACIFIC
OCEAN

Vancouver
Island

ROCKY

Fraser River

Nelson River

Saskatchewan
River

Lake
Winnipeg

Lake
Superior

Prince
Edward
Island

Gulf of
St. Lawrence

St. Lawrence River

Mount Rainier
14,410 ft
(4,392 m)

CASCADE RANGE

Columbia River

GREAT

MOUNTAINS

Missouri River

Lake
Huron

Lake
Ontario

Cape
Cod

Cape Mendocino

Snake River

BLACK
HILLS

Lake
Michigan

Lake
Erie

Long
Island

ATLANTIC
OCEAN

SIERRA NEVADA

CENTRAL VALLEY

GREAT
BASIN

Great
Salt
Lake

PLAINS

Platte
River

Ohio River

APPALACHIAN

MOUNTAINS

Cape
Hatteras

Bermuda

COAST RANGES

DEATH
VALLEY

Mount Whitney
14,494 ft
(4,419 m)

COLORADO
PLATEAU

Colorado River

Arkansas River

Red River

INTERIOR PLAINS

OZARK
PLATEAU

Cumberland R.

Tennessee
River

Mississippi River

PIEDMONT

ATLANTIC COASTAL PLAIN

Cape
Canaveral

Guadalupe
Island

Gulf of
California

BAJA CALIFORNIA

SIERRA MADRE OCCIDENTAL

Rio Grande

Brazos River

GULF COASTAL PLAIN

FLORIDA
PENINSULA

Bahamas

Tropic of Cancer

SIERRA MADRE ORIENTAL

Gulf of
Mexico

Florida
Keys

Straits of
Florida

Cuba

Greater

Antilles

Jamaica

Hispaniola

Puerto
Rico

Lesser
Antilles

Popocatépetl
17,887 ft (5,452 m)

YUCATÁN
PENINSULA

Caribbean Sea

Trinidad

SIERRA MADRE DEL SUR

CENTRAL
AMERICA

Lake
Nicaragua

ISTHMUS OF
PANAMA

0° Equator

SOUTH
AMERICA

ELEVATION

Feet	Meters
13,120	4,000
6,560	2,000
1,640	500
656	200
(Sea level) 0	0 (Sea level)
Below sea level	Below sea level

Ice cap

0   300   600 Miles

0   300   600 Kilometers

Projection: Azimuthal Equal Area

North America: Political

ASIA

ARCTIC OCEAN

+ North Pole

EUROPE

160°E
170°E
180°
170°W
160°W
150°W
140°W
130°W
120°W
110°W
100°W
90°W
10°E
0°
10°W
20°W
30°W
40°W
50°W
60°N
50°N
40°N
30°N
20°N
10°N

St. Lawrence Island
Nunivak Island
Bering Strait
Bering Sea

Point Barrow
Beaufort Sea

Banks Island
Victoria Island
Great Bear Lake

Queen Elizabeth Islands
Ellesmere Island

Greenland (DENMARK)

Arctic Circle

ICELAND

Denmark Strait

ALASKA (U.S.)
Anchorage
Gulf of Alaska
Kodiak Island
Alexander Archipelago
Juneau
Queen Charlotte Islands

Great Slave Lake

Baffin Bay
Baffin Island

Davis Strait

Cape Farewell

PACIFIC OCEAN

Vancouver Island
Vancouver
Seattle
Portland

Edmonton
Calgary

Winnipeg

CANADA

Lake Winnipeg

Southampton Island
Coats Island
Mansel Island

Hudson Bay

Hudson Strait

Labrador Sea

San Francisco
San Jose

Salt Lake City
Great Salt Lake

Lake Superior

Minneapolis
Milwaukee
Chicago

Lake Michigan
Lake Huron

Detroit

Lake Ontario
Lake Erie

Ottawa
Toronto

Montreal
Quebec

Cleveland
Columbus

Boston
Cape Cod
New York City
Philadelphia
Baltimore
Washington, D.C.

Anticosti Island
Newfoundland
Gulf of St. Lawrence
Prince Edward Island
Cape Breton Island
St. Pierre and Miquelon (FRANCE)

ATLANTIC OCEAN

Los Angeles
San Diego
Tijuana

Phoenix

Denver
Kansas City

Indianapolis
St. Louis

Memphis

UNITED STATES

Atlanta
Birmingham

Norfolk

Bermuda (U.K.)

Dallas
Austin
San Antonio
Houston

New Orleans

Jacksonville

Gulf of California

Monterrey

Gulf of Mexico

MEXICO

Florida Keys

Miami
Nassau

BAHAMAS

Turks and Caicos Islands (U.K.)

Tropic of Cancer

Havana
Straits of Florida

CUBA

DOMINICAN REPUBLIC
San Juan

Puerto Rico (U.S.)

ST. KITTS & NEVIS
ANTIGUA & BARBUDA
Guadeloupe (FRANCE)
DOMINICA

Guadalajara
Mexico City
Puebla

Mérida

Cayman Is. (U.K.)

Kingston
JAMAICA

HAITI
Port-au-Prince

Santo Domingo

Virgin Is. (U.S. & U.K.)
Martinique (FRANCE)
ST. LUCIA
ST. VINCENT AND THE GRENADINES

BARBADOS
GRENADA

Belmopan
BELIZE
GUATEMALA
Guatemala City
San Salvador
EL SALVADOR

HONDURAS
Tegucigalpa
NICARAGUA
Managua

San José
COSTA RICA

Caribbean Sea

Panama Canal

Aruba (NETHERLANDS)
Netherlands Antilles (NETHERLANDS)

TRINIDAD AND TOBAGO

Panama City
PANAMA

SOUTH AMERICA

0° Equator
90°W

Legend
✪ National capital
● Other city

0   300   600 Miles
0   300   600 Kilometers

Projection: Azimuthal Equal-Area

South America: Physical

CENTRAL
AMERICA

Caribbean Sea

Panama
Canal

Gulf
of
Panama

Malpelo
Island

Galápagos
Islands

Gulf of Guayaquil

PACIFIC
OCEAN

Margarita
Island

Tobago

Trinidad

Orinoco River
Delta

Lake
Maracaibo

LLANOS

Cauca River

Magdalena River

Orinoco River

Meta
River

Angel Falls

GUIANA

Orinoco River

Mount Tolima
18,425 ft
(5,616 m)

Caquetá River

Río Negro

Japurá
River

AMAZON

Amazon River

Negro

GUIANA
HIGHLANDS

Devil's Island
Cape Orange

Amazon
River Delta

0° Equator

Mount Chimborazo
20,561 ft
(6,267 m)

ANDES

Marañón River

Ucayali River

Amazo
River

Juruá River

Purus

BASIN

Madeira River

Tapajós River

Amazon

Xingu River

Tocantins River

Araguaia

Parnaíb River

ATLANTIC
OCEAN

N
W   E
S

10°N

Mount Huascarán
22,205 ft
(6,768 m)

Beni River

Mamoré

MATO GROSSO
PLATEAU

BRAZILIAN

HIGHLANDS

10°S

Lake
Titicaca

Ancohuma Peak
20,958 ft
(6,388 m)

Pilcomayo

São Francisco River

PACIFIC
OCEAN

Lake
Poopó

ATACAMA DESERT

ANDES

CHACO

Paraguay River

BRAZILIAN
PLATEAU

Tropic of Capricorn

20°S

San Félix Island

San Ambrosio
Island

Salado River

Paraná River

Uruguay River

Tropic of Capricorn

Juan Fernández
Islands

Mount Aconcagua
22,834 ft
(6,960 m)

Salado River

Rio de la Plata

ATLANTIC
OCEAN

30°S

PAMPAS

Colorado

Río de la Plata

Chiloé
Island

Chonos
Archipelago

PATAGONIA

Gulf of San Matías

40°S

Gulf of
San Jorge

Cape Tres Puntas

50°S

Bahía
Grande

Strait of
Magellan

Tierra del
Fuego

Cape Horn

Falkland
Islands

South
Georgia
Islands

ELEVATION

Feet		Meters
13,120		4,000
6,560		2,000
1,640		500
656		200
(Sea level) 0		0 (Sea level)
Below sea level		Below sea level

0   250   500 Miles

0   250   500 Kilometers

Projection: Azimuthal Equal Area

South America: Political

Central America

Caribbean Sea

Barranquilla
Cartagena
Lake Maracaibo
Caracas
VENEZUELA
Georgetown
Paramaribo
GUYANA
Cayenne
SURINAME
French Guiana (FRANCE)
ATLANTIC OCEAN

Medellín
Bogotá
COLOMBIA
Cali

Malpelo Island (COLOMBIA)

Quito
ECUADOR
Guayaquil

Galápagos Islands (ECUADOR)

Belém

0° Equator

PERU

BRAZIL

Recife

Trujillo

Callao
Lima

PACIFIC OCEAN

Arequipa

Lake Titicaca
La Paz
Lake Poopó
BOLIVIA
Sucre

Brasília

Salvador

Belo Horizonte

PARAGUAY
Asunción

Campinas
São Paulo
Curitiba
Rio de Janeiro
Tropic of Capricorn

Tropic of Capricorn

San Ambrosio Island (CHILE)
San Félix Island (CHILE)

CHILE

Pôrto Alegre

Juan Fernández Islands (CHILE)

Córdoba
Rosario
Valparaíso
Santiago
Buenos Aires
URUGUAY
Montevideo

ATLANTIC OCEAN

ARGENTINA

○ National capital
● Other city

0   250   500 Miles
0   250   500 Kilometers

Projection: Azimuthal Equal-Area

Strait of Magellan
Falkland Islands (U.K.)

Tierra del Fuego

South Georgia Island (U.K.)

ATLAS

ASIA

URAL MOUNTAINS

River

River

Kama

Pechora

Volga

Don River

Caspian Sea

Mt. Elbrus 15,642 ft
(5,642 m)

CAUCASUS MTS.

SOUTHWEST
ASIA

NORTHERN

EUROPEAN PLAIN

Barents Sea

KOLA
PENINSULA

White
Sea

North
Dvina

River

Lake
Onega

Lake
Ladoga

Rybinsk
Reservoir

Volga
River

Dnipro

Sea of
Azov

CRIMEAN
PENINSULA

Black Sea

Sea of
Marmara

Aegean Sea

Rhodes

Crete

PLAINS

BALTIC

North Cape

ARCTIC OCEAN

Gulf of Bothnia

Gulf of Finland

Daugava

Western Dvina

River

Dniester River

Nistru River

CARPATHIAN

Prut

Danube

TRANSYLVANIAN
ALPS

BALKAN

PENINSULA

KJOLEN MOUNTAINS

Lake
Vänern

Lake
Vättern

Skagerrak

Kattegat

Baltic Sea

Oder River

Vistula River

Elba River

DINARIC ALPS

Adriatic Sea

Sea

Malta

Norwegian
Sea

N
E
W
S

North
Sea

Rhine River

Danube River

Po

River

A L P S

APENNINES

Tiber River

Tyrrhenian Sea

Sicily

Iceland

Arctic Circle

Shetland
Islands

Orkney
Islands

Faeroe
Islands

Hebrides

British
Isles

Irish Sea

PENNINES

Thames
River

English Channel

Seine
River

Loire
River

15,781 ft
(4,810 m)

Mont Blanc

Lake
Geneva

Rhône
River

Corsica

Sardinia

Balearic Islands

Mediterranean

AFRICA

ATLANTIC
OCEAN

Cape Finisterre

Bay of
Biscay

Garonne River

PYRENEES

Ebro River

IBERIAN

PENINSULA

Duero
River

Tejus
River

Guadiana
River

Guadalquivir
River

Strait of
Gibraltar

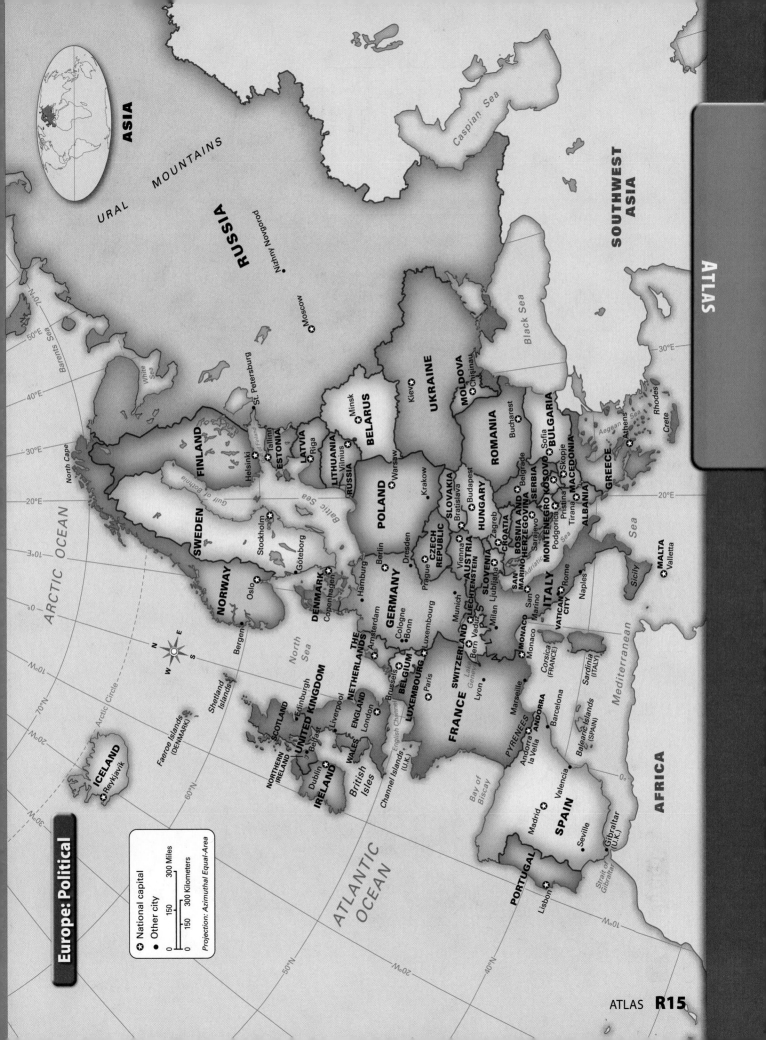

Europe: Political

National capital
• Other city

300 Miles
0   150   300 Kilometers
0   150   300

Projection: Azimuthal Equal-Area

ASIA

URAL MOUNTAINS

RUSSIA

Nizhny Novgorod •

Moscow

SOUTHWEST ASIA

Caspian Sea

Black Sea

30°E

St. Petersburg

White Sea

Barents Sea

North Cape

ARCTIC OCEAN

ARCTIC OCEAN

Arctic Circle

70°N

Gulf of Bothnia

FINLAND

Helsinki

Tallinn
ESTONIA

Riga
LATVIA

LITHUANIA
Vilnius

Minsk
BELARUS

Kiev

UKRAINE

MOLDOVA
Chisinau

ROMANIA
Bucharest

Sofia
BULGARIA

RUSSIA

Warsaw

POLAND

Krakow

SLOVAKIA
Bratislava

HUNGARY
Budapest

Belgrade
SERBIA

KOSOVO
Pristina

Skopje
MACEDONIA

GREECE

Athens

Aegean Sea

Rhodes

Crete

SWEDEN

Stockholm

Göteborg

Baltic Sea

Berlin

Dresden

CZECH REPUBLIC
Prague

Vienna
AUSTRIA

LIECHTENSTEIN
Vaduz

SLOVENIA
Ljubljana

CROATIA
Zagreb

BOSNIA AND HERZEGOVINA
Sarajevo

MONTENEGRO
Podgorica

Tirana
ALBANIA

Adriatic Sea

NORWAY

Oslo

Bergen

DENMARK
Copenhagen

Hamburg

GERMANY

Cologne
Bonn

Munich

SWITZERLAND
Bern
Lake Geneva

SAN MARINO
San Marino

MONACO
Monaco

VATICAN CITY

ITALY
Rome

Naples

Sicily

MALTA
Valletta

North Sea

Amsterdam
THE NETHERLANDS

Brussels
BELGIUM

LUXEMBOURG
Luxembourg

Paris

FRANCE

Lyon

Marseille

Corsica
(FRANCE)

Sardinia
(ITALY)

Mediterranean Sea

Shetland Islands

Faeroe Islands
(DENMARK)

SCOTLAND
Edinburgh

Liverpool

WALES
ENGLAND
London

UNITED KINGDOM

NORTHERN IRELAND
Belfast

IRELAND
Dublin

British Isles

Channel Islands
(U.K.)

English Channel

Bay of Biscay

PYRENEES

ANDORRA
Andorra la Vella

Barcelona

Balearic Islands
(SPAIN)

AFRICA

ICELAND
Reykjavik

ATLANTIC OCEAN

PORTUGAL
Lisbon

SPAIN
Madrid

Valencia

Seville

Gibraltar
(U.K.)

Strait of Gibraltar

30°W

20°W

10°W

0°

10°E

20°E

30°E

40°E

50°E

70°N

60°N

50°N

40°N

Asia: Physical

ELEVATION

Feet	Meters
13,120	4,000
6,560	2,000
1,640	500
656	200
(Sea level) 0	0 (Sea level)
Below sea level	Below sea level

Ice cap

750 Miles
750 Kilometers
0 250 500
0 250 500

Projection: Two-Point Equidistant

North Pole

AUSTRALIA

PACIFIC OCEAN

New Guinea

MAOKE MOUNTAINS

Arafura Sea

Molucca Sea

Banda Sea

Celebes Sea

Celebes

Borneo

Java Sea

Java

Bangka

Sumatra

Mentawai Islands

MALAY PENINSULA

Mindanao

Philippines

Luzon

Luzon Strait

Taiwan

South China Sea

Hainan

Gulf of Thailand

INDOCHINA PENINSULA

Chao Phraya River

Mekong River

Andaman Sea

Nicobar Islands

Andaman Islands

Irrawaddy River

Bay of Bengal

Maldives

Lakshadweep Islands

Sri Lanka

EASTERN GHATS

WESTERN GHATS

DECCAN PLATEAU

Godavari River

THAR DESERT

INDO-GANGETIC PLAIN

Ganges River

Sutlej River

Brahmaputra River

HIMALAYAS

Mount Everest 29,035 ft (8,850 m)

Nu River

PLATEAU OF TIBET

KUNLUN MOUNTAINS

TARIM BASIN

TAKLIMAKAN DESERT

TIAN SHAN

HINDU KUSH

KYZYL KUM

KARA KUM

Amu Darya

Syr Darya

TURAN LOWLAND

Aral Sea

USTYURT PLATEAU

KAZAKH UPLANDS

Balqash Lake

Ishim River

Ob River

Irtysh River

URAL MOUNTAINS

WEST SIBERIAN PLAIN

Yenisey River

Lower Tunguska River

Angara River

CENTRAL SIBERIAN PLATEAU

TAYMYR PENINSULA

North Land

Franz Josef Land

Novaya Zemlya

Kara Sea

Barents Sea

Laptev Sea

New Siberian Islands

Wrangel Island

East Siberian Sea

KOLYMA MTS.

CHERSKIY RANGE

VERKHOYANSKY RANGE

Lena River

Aldan River

STANOVOY MOUNTAINS

YABLONOV RANGE

Lake Baykal

Shilka River

GREATER KHINGAN RANGE

MONGOLIAN PLATEAU

GOBI

SAYAN MOUNTAINS

ALTAY MOUNTAINS

Amur River

Huang He (Yellow River)

Yellow River

QIN LING

NORTH CHINA PLAIN

BOHEA HILLS

Xi River

Hong River

Chang Jiang (Yangtze River)

East China Sea

Yellow Sea

Sea of Japan (East Sea)

Korea Strait

Kyushu

Shikoku

Honshu

Hokkaido

Sakhalin Island

Kuril Islands

Sea of Okhotsk

KAMCHATKA PENINSULA

CENTRAL RANGE

Bering Sea

Aleutian Islands

Ryukyu Islands

Okinawa

Tropic of Cancer

EUROPE

Black Sea

Bosporus

Mediterranean Sea

Cyprus

ANATOLIAN PLATEAU

Mount Ararat 16,945 ft (5,165 m)

CAUCASUS MTS.

Caspian Sea

ZAGROS MTS.

Tigris River

Euphrates River

SYRIAN DESERT

AN-NAFUD

SINAI PENINSULA

Red Sea

RUB' AL-KHALI

GREAT SALT DESERT

Persian Gulf

Gulf of Oman

Gulf of Aden

Socotra Island

Arabian Sea

INDIAN OCEAN

AFRICA

National capitals
Other cities

750 Miles
750 Kilometers

Projection: Two-Point Equidistant

PACIFIC OCEAN

AUSTRALIA

New Guinea

Arafura Sea

TIMOR-LESTE

Dili

PHILIPPINES

Manila

INDONESIA

Celebes Sea

Java Sea   Ujung Pandang

Surabaya

Jakarta

Bandung

BRUNEI

Bandar Seri Begawan

MALAYSIA

SINGAPORE

Singapore

Kuala Lumpur

Medan

South China Sea

Hainan (CHINA)

VIETNAM

Ho Chi Minh City

CAMBODIA

Phnom Penh

LAOS

Vientiane

THAILAND

Bangkok

Gulf of Thailand

Hanoi

Guangzhou

Macao

Hong Kong

Andaman Sea

Andaman Islands (INDIA)

Nicobar Islands (INDIA)

MYANMAR (BURMA)

Yangon (Rangoon)

Mandalay

Bay of Bengal

BHUTAN

Thimphu

BANGLADESH

Dhaka

Kolkata (Calcutta)

Chennai (Madras)

SRI LANKA

Colombo

Male

MALDIVES

INDIAN OCEAN

Bangalore

Lakshadweep Islands (INDIA)

INDIA

Mumbai (Bombay)

Ahmadabad

Arabian Sea

Socotra (YEMEN)

Gulf of Aden

AFRICA

YEMEN

Sanaa

Mecca

Jidda

Red Sea

Mediterranean Sea

EUROPE

RUSSIA

Moscow

Aleutian Islands

Bering Sea

Sea of Okhotsk

Kuril Islands (RUSSIA)

Sakhalin Island

JAPAN

Sapporo

Vladivostok

Tokyo

Yokohama

Osaka

Kobe

Hiroshima

Nagasaki

NORTH KOREA

Pyongyang

SOUTH KOREA

Seoul

Pusan

Dalian

Yellow Sea

East China Sea

Ryukyu Islands (JAPAN)

Tropic of Cancer

TAIWAN

Taipei

Luzon Strait

Shanghai

Nanjing

Qingdao

Beijing

Fushun

Harbin

Wuhan

Chongqing

Chengdu

CHINA

MONGOLIA

Ulaanbaatar

Yakutsk

Lake Baykal

Irkutsk

Novosibirsk

Omsk

Yekaterinburg

Chelyabinsk

URAL MOUNTAINS

RUSSIA

KAZAKHSTAN

Astana

Lake Balkhash

Aral Sea

Almaty

Bishkek

KYRGYZSTAN

Tashkent

UZBEKISTAN

TAJIKISTAN

Dushanbe

TURKMENISTAN

Ashgabat

AFGHANISTAN

Kabul

Islamabad

PAKISTAN

Lahore

Karachi

Delhi

New Delhi

Jaipur

NEPAL

Kathmandu

Caspian Sea

IRAN

Tehran

Shiraz

Baku

AZERBAIJAN

ARMENIA

Yerevan

GEORGIA

Tbilisi

Black Sea

TURKEY

Ankara

Istanbul

Izmir

CYPRUS

Nicosia

LEBANON

Beirut

ISRAEL

Tel Aviv

Jerusalem

SYRIA

Damascus

JORDAN

Amman

IRAQ

Baghdad

Mosul

Basra

KUWAIT

Kuwait City

Persian Gulf

BAHRAIN

Manama

QATAR

Doha

Riyadh

SAUDI ARABIA

UNITED ARAB EMIRATES

Abu Dhabi

OMAN

Masqat (Muscat)

North Pole

Arctic Circle

Barents Sea

Kara Sea

Laptev Sea

ATLAS R17

Africa: Physical

EUROPE

SOUTHWEST ASIA

Azores

Madeira Islands

Canary Islands

Strait of Gibraltar

ATLAS MOUNTAINS

Mediterranean Sea

Gulf of Sidra

Suez Canal

Persian Gulf

Tropic of Cancer

Cape Blanc

EL DJOUF

S A H A R A

AHAGGAR MOUNTAINS

AIR MTS.

TIBESTI MOUNTAINS

LIBYAN DESERT

QATTARA DEPRESSION

Nile River

Lake Nasser

Red Sea

20°N

Cape Verde Islands

S A H E L

Niger River

Senegal R.

NUBIAN DESERT

Cape Verde

FOUTA DJALLON

S U D A N

White Volta

Black Volta

Lake Volta

Benué River

CHAD BASIN

Lake Chad

A N

Blue Nile

White Nile

Lake Tana

Gulf of Aden

10°N

Cape Palmas

Gulf of Guinea

ADAMAWA MTS.

Ubangi River

SUDAN BASIN

ETHIOPIAN HIGHLANDS

RIFT VALLEY

HORN OF AFRICA

SOMALI PENINSULA

Cape Lopez

CONGO BASIN

Congo River

Kasai River

Lake Albert

Lake Edward

Lake Victoria

Lake Kivu

MITUMBA MOUNTAINS

WESTERN RIFT VALLEY

Lake Turkana

Mount Kenya 17,058 ft (5,199 m)

SERENGETI PLAIN

MASAI STEPPE

EASTERN RIFT VALLEY

Mount Kilimanjaro 19,340 ft (5,895 m)

INDIAN OCEAN

0° Equator

Ascension

ATLANTIC OCEAN

Cuanza River

Lake Tanganyika

Lake Rukwa

Zanzibar

Lake Mweru

Lake Malawi (Nyasa)

Cape Delgado

Seychelles

10°S

Comoro Islands

Lake Kariba

Zambezi River

Madagascar

Mozambique Channel

Mauritius

Okavango Delta

Victoria Falls

Réunion

NAMIB DESERT

KALAHARI BASIN

KALAHARI DESERT

Limpopo River

Tropic of Capricorn

Vaal River

Orange River

DRAKENSBERG MOUNTAINS

GREAT KARROO

Cape of Good Hope

ELEVATION

Feet	Meters
13,120	4,000
6,560	2,000
1,640	500
656	200
(Sea level) 0	0 (Sea level)
Below sea level	Below sea level

0   250   500 Miles

0   250   500 Kilometers

Projection: Azimuthal Equal-Area

Africa: Political

EUROPE

SOUTHWEST ASIA

Azores (PORTUGAL)

Madeira (PORTUGAL)

Canary Islands (SPAIN)

El Aaiún

WESTERN SAHARA (Claimed by Morocco)

Strait of Gibraltar

Casablanca • Rabat ✪

Algiers ✪ Tunis ✪

Mediterranean Sea

TUNISIA

Tripoli ✪

Alexandria •

Giza • Cairo ✪

MOROCCO

ALGERIA

LIBYA

EGYPT

Red Sea

Gulf of Aden

Tropic of Cancer

CAPE VERDE

✪ Praia

MAURITANIA

✪ Nouakchott

MALI

NIGER

CHAD

SUDAN

Khartoum ✪

ERITREA
✪ Asmara

DJIBOUTI
Djibouti •

SENEGAL
Dakar ✪

GAMBIA
Banjul ✪

Bamako ✪

BURKINA FASO

Niamey ✪

Lake Chad

N'Djamena ✪

Bissau ✪

GUINEA-BISSAU

GUINEA

Conakry ✪
Freetown ✪

SIERRA LEONE

Monrovia ✪

LIBERIA

CÔTE D'IVOIRE

Yamoussoukro ✪

Abidjan •

Ouagadougou ✪

GHANA

Accra ✪

BENIN
TOGO

Lomé ✪

NIGERIA

✪ Abuja

Lagos •

Porto-Novo ✪

Malabo •

Gulf of Guinea

CAMEROON

Bangui ✪

CENTRAL AFRICAN REPUBLIC

SOUTH SUDAN

Juba ✪

ETHIOPIA

Addis Ababa ✪

SOMALIA

Mogadishu •

EQUATORIAL GUINEA

SÃO TOMÉ AND PRÍNCIPE

São Tomé ✪

Yaoundé ✪

Libreville ✪

GABON

REPUBLIC OF THE CONGO

Kisangani •

DEMOCRATIC REPUBLIC OF THE CONGO

RWANDA
Kigali ✪

Bujumbura ✪

BURUNDI

UGANDA

Kampala ✪

Lake Victoria

KENYA

Nairobi ✪

INDIAN OCEAN

Victoria ✪

SEYCHELLES

0° Equator

Brazzaville ✪

CABINDA (ANGOLA)

Kinshasa ✪

TANZANIA

Dodoma ✪

Lake Tanganyika

Mombasa •
Pemba
Zanzibar

Dar es Salaam •

Luanda ✪

ATLANTIC OCEAN

St. Helena (U.K.)

ANGOLA

Lubumbashi •

ZAMBIA

Lusaka ✪

Lake Malawi (Nyasa)

MALAWI

Lilongwe ✪

COMOROS
Moroni •

Harare ✪

ZIMBABWE

Bulawayo •

MOZAMBIQUE

Antananarivo ✪

MADAGASCAR

MAURITIUS

Port Louis ✪

Réunion (FRANCE)

Tropic of Capricorn

NAMIBIA

Windhoek ✪

BOTSWANA

Gaborone ✪

Pretoria ✪

Johannesburg •

Bloemfontein •

Maputo ✪

Mbabane ✪

SWAZILAND

Maseru ✪

LESOTHO

SOUTH AFRICA

Cape Town •

Legend

✪ National capital

• Other city

| 0 | 250 | 500 Miles |
| 0 | 250 | 500 Kilometers |

Projection: Azimuthal Equal-Area

NORTH
AMERICA

The Pacific: Political

ASIA

NORTH PACIFIC OCEAN

SOUTH PACIFIC OCEAN

Tropic of Cancer

0° Equator

Tropic of Capricorn

International Date Line

30°N
15°N
15°S
30°S
45°S

135°W
150°W
165°W
180°
165°E
150°E
135°E
120°E
120°W

National capital
● Other city

1,000 Miles
1,000 Kilometers
500
500
0
0

Projection: Azimuthal Equal-Area

Marquesas
Islands
(FRANCE)

Tuamotu
Archipelago
(FRANCE)

Easter Island
(CHILE)

Pitcairn (U.K.)
Pitcairn
Island
Ducie
Island

French Polynesia

Rapa Island
(FRANCE)

Society
Islands
(FRANCE)
Tahiti
(FRANCE)
Papeete

Tubuai Islands
(FRANCE)

P O L Y N E S I A

Starbuck
Island

Manihiki
Island
Cook
Islands
(NEW ZEALAND)

Rarotonga
Island

KIRIBATI

Palmyra Island (U.S.)
Fanning
Island
Washington
Island
Kingman Reef
(U.S.)

Jarvis I.
(U.S.)

Phoenix
Islands

Tokelau (N.Z.)
American
Samoa
Pago
Pago
Niue
(N.Z.)

Hawaiian Islands
Hawaii
(U.S.)

Midway
Island
(U.S.)

Johnston
Island
(U.S.)

Howland I.
(U.S.)
Baker I. (U.S.)

McKean I.
Gardner

SAMOA
Apia
Wallis &
Futuna (FR.)

TONGA
Nuku'alofa

Kermadec
Islands
(N.Z.)

Chatham
Islands
(N.Z.)

MARSHALL ISLANDS
Eniwetok I.
Kwajalein Island
Majuro

Wake Island
(U.S.)

Tarawa
Gilbert
Islands

TUVALU
Funafuti

FIJI
Suva

M E L A N E S I A

Loyalty
Islands
(FRANCE)

Norfolk
Island
(AUSTRALIA)

Auckland
Wellington
Christchurch

North
Island
South
Island

Bounty
Islands
(N.Z.)

Auckland Islands
(NEW ZEALAND)

NEW
ZEALAND

NAURU
SOLOMON
ISLANDS

MICRONESIA

Palikir
Truk Is.
FEDERATED STATES
OF MICRONESIA

Bonin Islands
(JAPAN)

Volcano Islands
(JAPAN)

Northern
Marianas
(U.S.)

Agana
Guam
(U.S.)

Bismarck
Archipelago

PAPUA
NEW GUINEA
Port
Moresby

VANUATU
Port-
Vila

Espiritu Santo I.
Malekula I.

New
Caledonia
(FRANCE)
Noumea

Coral
Sea

Honiara
Guadalcanal I.

New Guinea

PALAU
Melekeok

AUSTRALIA

Brisbane
Sydney
Canberra
Hobart
Melbourne
Adelaide
Perth
Darwin

Tasman
Sea

Arafura
Sea
Timor
Sea

Philippine
Sea

South
China
Sea

Christmas
Island
(AUSTRALIA)

INDIAN OCEAN

N E
W S

The North Pole

0   200   400 Miles
0   200   400 Kilometers

Projection:
Polar Azimuthal Equidistant

Kara
Sea

Barents
Sea

EUROPE

Norwegian
Sea

Laptev
Sea

ASIA

ARCTIC
OCEAN

Greenland
Sea

Arctic Circle

North
Pole

POLAR ICE PACK

Greenland
(DENMARK)

ATLANTIC
OCEAN

International Date Line

North
Magnetic
Pole

Baffin
Bay

Beaufort
Sea

Bering Sea

NORTH
AMERICA

ATLAS

150°E
120°E
90°E
60°E
30°E
0°
30°W
60°N
80°N
70°N
150°W
60°W
120°W
90°W
180°
50°N

The South Pole

SOUTHERN   OCEAN

SOUTH
AMERICA

International Date Line

Antarctic Circle

Amundsen
Sea

Bellingshausen Sea

Antarctic
Peninsula

PACIFIC
OCEAN

POLAR ICE PACK

Ross
Sea

Marie Byrd Land

Vinson Massif
16,067 ft
(4,897 m)

Ellsworth Land

POLAR ICE PACK

Ross
Ice Shelf

Ronne
Ice Shelf

Weddell
Sea

Edith Ronne Land

Filchner
Ice Shelf

Mount Markham
over 14,275 ft
(over 4,351 m)

South
Pole

Coats
Land

Adelie
Land

South
Magnetic
Pole

ANTARCTICA

WILKES LAND

ICE CAP

QUEEN MAUD LAND

ATLANTIC
OCEAN

Shackleton
Ice Shelf

American
Highland

Enderby
Land

INDIAN OCEAN

0   250   500 Miles
0   250   500 Kilometers

Projection:
Polar Azimuthal Equidistant

SOUTHERN   OCEAN

180°
150°W
120°W
90°W
60°W
30°W
150°E
120°E
90°E
60°E
30°E
0°
70°S
80°S
60°S
50°S

ATLAS **R21**

Gazetteer

A

Abuja (ah-BOO-jah) (9°N, 7°E) the capital of Nigeria (p. 539)

Acapulco (17°N, 100°W) a resort on the Pacific Ocean in southwest Mexico (p. 203)

Accra (6°N, 0°) the capital of Ghana (p. 539)

Addis Ababa (AH-dis AH-bah-bah) (9°N, 39°E) the capital of Ethiopia (p. 561)

Adelaide (35°S, 139°E) a city in southern Australia (p. 740)

Afghanistan a landlocked country in Central Asia (p. 421)

Africa the second-largest continent; surrounded by the Atlantic Ocean, Indian Ocean, and Mediterranean Sea (p. R18)

Alabama (AL) a state in the southern United States; admitted in 1819 (pp. R4–R5)

Alaska (AK) a state in northwestern North America; admitted in 1959 (pp. R4–R5)

Albania a country on the Balkan Peninsula in south-eastern Europe (p. 377)

Alberta a province in western Canada (p. 181)

Alexandria an ancient city in Egypt built by Alexander the Great (p. 511)

Algeria a country in North Africa between Morocco and Libya; it is the largest country in Africa (p. 505)

Algiers (37°N, 3°E) the capital of Algeria (p. 505)

Almaty (ahl-mah-TUH) (43°N, 77°E) the former capital of Kazakhstan (p. 436)

Alps a great mountain system in central Europe (p. 311)

Amazon Basin a huge basin in the heart of South America (p. R12)

Amazon River the major river in South America (p. R12)

Amman (32°N, 36°E) the capital of Jordan (p. 475)

Amsterdam (52°N, 5°E) the capital and largest city of the Netherlands (p. 343)

Amu Darya (uh-MOH duhr-YAH) a river in Central Asia that flows along Afghanistan's border with Tajikistan, Uzbekistan, and Turkmenistan to the Aral Sea (p. 423)

Amur River a river in Asia that forms part of the Russia-China border (p. 415)

Anatolia (a-nuh-TOH-lee-uh) a mountainous region in Southwest Asia forming most of Turkey; also referred to as Asia Minor (p. 458)

Andes Mountains (AN-deez) a long mountain range along the west coast of South America (p. R12)

Angola a country in Central Africa that borders the Atlantic Ocean (p. 581)

Ankara (40°N, 33°E) the capital and second-largest city of Turkey (p. 464)

An Nafud (ahn nah-FOOD) a large desert in northern Saudi Arabia; known for its giant sand dunes (p. 484)

Antananarivo (19°S, 48°E) the capital of Madagascar (p. 603)

Antarctica a continent around the South Pole (p. R21)

Antarctic Circle the line of latitude located at 66.5° south of the equator; parallel beyond which no sunlight shines on the June solstice (pp. R6–R7)

Antarctic Peninsula a large peninsula in Antarctica (p. R21)

Apennines (A-puh-nynz) the major mountain range on the Italian Peninsula (p. 311)

Apia (14°S, 172°W) the capital of Western Samoa (p. 754)

Appalachian Mountains a mountain system in eastern North America (p. 142)

Arabia or Arabian Peninsula the world's largest peninsula; located in Southwest Asia (p. 481)

Arabian Sea a large arm of the Indian Ocean between India and Arabia (p. R17)

Aral Sea an inland sea in Central Asia fed by the Syr Darya and Amu Darya rivers; it has been steadily shrinking (p. 440)

Arctic Circle the line of latitude located at 66.5° north of the equator; parallel beyond which no sunlight shines on the December solstice (pp. R6–R7)

Arctic Ocean the ocean north of the Arctic Circle; the world's fourth-largest ocean (p. R21)

Argentina a country in South America (p. 268)

Arizona (AZ) a state in the southwestern United States; admitted in 1912 (pp. R4–R5)

Arkansas (AR) a state in the south-central United States; admitted in 1836 (pp. R4–R5)

Armenia a country in the Caucasus Mountains (p. 427)

Ashgabat (38°N, 58°E) the capital of Turkmenistan (p. 421)

Asia the world's largest continent; located between Europe and the Pacific Ocean (p. R16)

Asmara (15°N, 39°E) the capital of Eritrea (p. 561)

Astana (51°N, 72°E) the capital of Kazakhstan (p. 436)

Asunción (ah-soon-SYOHN) (25°N, 58°W) the capital of Paraguay (p. 271)

Atacama Desert a desert located in northern Chile near the border with Peru (p. 281)

Athens (38°N, 24°E) an ancient city and the modern capital of Greece (p. 318)

Atlanta (33°N, 84°W) capital of Georgia (p. 160)

Atlantic Ocean the ocean between the continents of North and South America and the continents of Europe and Africa (p. R6)

Atlas Mountains a high mountain range in northwestern Africa (p. 507)

Australia a country and continent in the Pacific (p. 740)

Austria a country in West-Central Europe (p. 333)

Azerbaijan (a-zuhr-by-JAHN) a country in the Caucasus Mountains (p. 427)

B

Baghdad (33°N, 44°E) the capital of Iraq (p. 481)

Bahamas a country and group of islands located east of Florida in the Atlantic Ocean (p. 213)

Bahrain a small country on the Persian Gulf (p. 481)

Baja California a peninsula in Mexico (p. 192)

Baku (40°N, 48°E) the capital of Azerbaijan (p. 427)

Balkan Peninsula a peninsula in Southern Europe (p. 379)

Baltic Sea a shallow arm of the Atlantic Ocean in northern Europe (p. 359)

Baltimore (39°N, 76°W) a large city in Maryland northeast of Washington, D.C. (p. R13)

Bamako (BAH-mah-koh) (13°N, 8°W) the capital of Mali (p. 539)

Bandar Seri Begawan (5°N, 115°E) capital of Brunei (p. 715)

Bangkok (14°N, 100°E) the capital of Thailand (p. 714)

Bangladesh a country in South Asia (p. 639)

Bangui (bahn-GEE) (4°N, 19°E) the capital of the Central African Republic (p. 581)

Banjul (BAHN-jool) (13°N, 17°W) the capital of Gambia (p. 538)

Barbados island country in the Caribbean (p. 226)

Barcelona (41°N, 2°E) a large port city in Spain on the Mediterranean Sea (p. 326)

Basseterre (16°N, 62°W) the capital of St. Kitts and Nevis (p. 211)

Bavaria a state and region in southern Germany (p. 348)

Bay of Bengal a large bay of the Indian Ocean between India and Southeast Asia (p. 639)

Beijing (40°N, 116°E) the capital of China (p. 663)

Beirut (34°N, 36°E) the capital of Lebanon (p. 474)

Belarus a country in Eastern Europe (p. 377)

Belgium a country in West-Central Europe (p. 151)

Belgrade (45°N, 21°E) the capital of Serbia (p. 395)

Belize a country in Central America (p. 213)

Belmopan (17°N, 90°W) capital of Belize (p. 210)

Benelux a term that refers to Belgium, the Netherlands, and Luxembourg (p. 342)

Benin a country in West Africa between Togo and Nigeria (p. 539)

Berlin (53°N, 13°E) the capital of Germany (p. 347)

Bern (47°N, 7°E) the capital of Switzerland (p. 333)

Bhutan a country in South Asia north of India (p. 639)

Bishkek (43°N, 75°E) the capital of Kyrgyzstan (p. 421)

Bissau (bis-OW) (12°N, 16°W) the capital of Guinea-Bissau (p. 538)

Bloemfontein (BLOOM-fahn-tayn) (29°S, 26°E) the judicial capital of South Africa (p. 603)

Bogotá (4°N, 72°W) capital of Colombia (p. 234)

Bolivia a country in South America (p. 279)

Borneo the world's third-largest island; located in Southeast Asia (p. 717)

Bosnia and Herzegovina a country on the Balkan Peninsula (p. 377)

Bosporus (BAHS-puh-ruhs) a narrow strait in Turkey that connects the Mediterranean Sea with the Black Sea (p. 459)

Boston (42°N, 71°W) the capital of Massachusetts (p. 150)

Botswana a country in Southern Africa between Namibia and Zimbabwe (p. 603)

Brasília (10°S, 55°W) the capital of Brazil (p. 263)

Bratislava (48°N, 17°E) the capital of Slovakia (p. 377)

Brazil a country in South America (p. 255)

Brazilian Highlands a region of rugged, old, eroded mountains in eastern Brazil (p. 257)

Brazzaville (4°S, 15°E) the capital of the Republic of the Congo (p. 581)

British Columbia a province in Canada (p. 181)

British Isles a group of islands off the northwestern coast of Europe including Britain and Ireland (p. 359)

Brunei (brooh-NY) a country in Southeast Asia on the northern coast of Borneo (p. 715)

Brussels (51°N, 4°E) the capital of Belgium (p. 333)

Bucharest (44°N, 26°E) the capital of Romania (p. 377)

Budapest (48°N, 19°E) the capital of Hungary (p. 389)

Buenos Aires (BWAY-nohs EYE-rayz) (36°S, 60°W) the capital of Argentina (p. 268)

Bujumbura (booh-juhm-BOOHR-uh) (3°S, 29°E) the capital of Burundi (p. 561)

Bukhara (40°N, 64°E) an ancient city along the Silk Road in Central Asia; it has long been an important trade and cultural center in the region (p. 430)

Bulgaria a country in the Balkans (p. 377)

Burkina Faso (boor-KEE-nuh FAH-soh) a landlocked country in West Africa (p. 539)

Burundi (buh-ROON-dee) a landlocked country in East Africa (p. 561)

C

Cairo (30°N, 31°E) the capital of Egypt (p. 505)

Calgary (51°N, 114°W) a large city in the province of Alberta in Canada (p. 168)

California (CA) a state in the western United States; admitted in 1850 (pp. R4–R5)

Callao (kah-YAH-oh) (12°S, 77°W) a port city in Peru west of Lima (p. 290)

Cambodia a country in Southeast Asia (p. 714)

Cameroon a country in Central Africa south of Nigeria (p. 581)

Canada a country in North America (p. 168–169)

Canadian Shield a region of ancient rock that covers more than half of Canada (p. 171)

Canberra (35°S, 149°E) the capital of Australia (p. 740)

Cancún (21°N, 87°W) a popular resort on Mexico's Caribbean coast (p. 203)

Cape of Good Hope a cape at the southern tip of Africa (p. 605)

Cape Town (34°S, 18°E) the legislative capital of South Africa (p. 603)

Cape Verde (VUHRD) an island country off the coast of West Africa (p. 538)

Caracas (11°N, 67°W) the capital of Venezuela (p. 235)

Caribbean Islands a group of islands in the Caribbean Sea (p. 213)

Caribbean Sea an arm of the Atlantic Ocean between North and South America (p. 211)

Carpathians (kahr-PAY-thee-uhnz) a major mountain chain in central and eastern Europe (p. 378)

Cartagena (kahr-tah-HAY-nuh) (10°N, 74°W) a coastal city in northern Colombia (p. 234)

Cascade Range a mountain range in western North America (p. 143)

Caspian Sea an inland sea located between Europe and Asia; it is the largest inland body of water in the world (p. 423)

Cauca River a river in Colombia (p. 237)

Caucasus Mountains a mountain system in southeastern Europe between the Black Sea and Caspian Sea (p. 402)

Cayenne (4°N, 53°W) the capital of French Guiana (p. 235)

Central African Republic a landlocked country in Central Africa south of Chad (p. 581)

Central America a region in North America south of Mexico (p. 212)

Central Uplands an area of hills, plateaus, and valleys in central Europe (p. 335)

Chad a landlocked country in West Africa located east of Niger (p. 539)

Chang Jiang (Yangzi River) a major river in China (p. 665)

Chao Phraya (chow PRY-uh) a river in Thailand (p. R16)

Chechnya (CHECH-nyuh) a republic in Russia that is fighting a violent struggle for independence (p. 416)

Chernobyl (51°N, 30°E) a city in Ukraine; the world's worst nuclear reactor accident occurred there in 1986 (p. 381)

Chicago (42°N, 88°W) a major U.S. city and port in northeastern Illinois on Lake Michigan (p. 159)

Chile (CHEE-lay) a country in western South America (p. 277)

China a large country in East Asia (p. 663)

Chişinau (47°N, 29°E) the capital of Moldova (p. 377)

Coast Mountains a mountain range in North America along the Pacific coast (p. 171)

Colombia a country in South America (p. 234)

Colombo (7°N, 80°E) the capital of Sri Lanka (p. 639)

Colorado (CO) a state in the southwestern United States; admitted in 1876 (pp. R4–R5)

Comoros (KAH-muh-rohz) an island country in the Indian Ocean off the coast of Africa (p. 603)

Conakry (KAH-nuh-kree) (10°N, 14°W) the capital of Guinea (p. 538)

Congo Basin a large flat area on the Congo River in Central Africa (p. 583)

Congo, Democratic Republic of the the largest and most populous country in Central Africa (p. 581)

Congo, Republic of the a country in Central Africa on the Congo River (p. 581)

Congo River the major river of Central Africa (p. 583)

Connecticut (CT) a state in the northeastern United States; admitted in 1788 and one of the original 13 colonies (pp. R4–R5)

Copenhagen (56°N, 13°E) the capital of Denmark (p. 357)

Costa Rica a country in Central America (p. 210)

Côte d'Ivoire (KOHT dee-VWAHR) a country in West Africa between Liberia and Ghana (p. 539)

Croatia a country in the Balkans (p. 377)

Cuba an island country in the Caribbean Sea south of Florida (p. 211)

Czech Republic a country in Eastern Europe (p. 377)

D

Dakar (15°N, 17°W) the capital of Senegal (p. 538)

Dallas (33°N, 97°W) a major U.S. city and transportation and financial center in Texas (pp. R4–R5)

Damascus (34°N, 36°E) the capital of Syria (p. 457)

Danube (DAN-yoob) the second-longest river in Europe; it flows from Germany east to the Black Sea (p. 335)

Dardanelles (dahrd-uhn-ELZ) a strait between the Aegean Sea and the Sea of Marmara; part of a waterway that connects the Black Sea and the Mediterranean Sea (p. 459)

Dar es Salaam (7°S, 39°E) the capital of Tanzania (p. 561)

Darfur a region in western Sudan; because of genocide, millions of people have fled from Darfur (p. 573)

Dead Sea the saltiest lake and lowest point on Earth; located on the border between Israel and Jordan and fed by the Jordan River (p. 459)

Deccan a large plateau in southern India (p. 641)

Delaware (DE) a state in the eastern United States; admitted in 1787 and one of the original 13 colonies (pp. R4–R5)

Delhi a city in northern India that was the capital of the Mughal Empire (p. 639)

Denmark a country in Northern Europe (p. 357)

Detroit (42°N, 83°W) a large U.S. city in Michigan (p. R5)

Dhaka (DA-kuh) (24°N, 90°E) the capital of Bangladesh (p. 639)

Dili (8°N, 125°E) the capital of Timor-Leste (p. 715)

District of Columbia (39°N, 77°W) a federal district between Maryland and Virginia; the capital of the United States (p. 141)

Djibouti (ji-BOO-tee) a country in East Africa on the Horn of Africa (p. 561)

Djibouti (12°N, 43°E) the capital of Djibouti (p. 561)

Dodoma (6°S, 36°E) the capital of Tanzania (p. 561)

Doha (26°N, 51°E) the capital of Qatar (p. 481)

Dominican Republic a country in the Caribbean (p. 211)

Drakensberg a mountain range in Southern Africa (p. 605)

Dublin (53°N, 6°W) the capital of Ireland (p. 365)

Dushanbe (39°N, 69°E) the capital of Tajikistan (p. 421)

E

Eastern Ghats (gawts) a mountain range in India (p. 641)

Eastern Hemisphere the half of the globe between the prime meridian and 180° longitude that includes most of Africa and Europe as well as Asia, Australia, and the Indian Ocean (p. H3)

Ecuador a country in South America (p. 277)

Edinburgh (56°N, 3°W) the capital of Scotland (p. 365)

Egypt a country in North Africa on the Mediterranean Sea; home to one of the world's oldest civilizations (p. 505)

Elburz Mountains a mountain range in northern Iran south of the Caspian Sea (p. 483)

El Salvador a country in Central America (p. 210)

England a part of the United Kingdom occupying most of the island of Great Britain (p. 365)

English Channel a strait of the Atlantic Ocean between England and France (p. 336)

equator the imaginary line of latitude that circles the globe halfway between the North and South Poles (p. H2)

Equatorial Guinea a country in Central Africa between Cameroon and Gabon (p. 581)

Eritrea (er-uh-TREE-uh) an East African country north of Ethiopia (p. 561)

Estonia a Baltic country in Eastern Europe (p. 377)

Ethiopia an East African country located on the Horn of Africa (p. 561)

Euphrates River a river in Southwest Asia (p. 483)

Europe the continent between the Ural Mountains and the Atlantic Ocean (p. R14)

F

Fergana Valley a fertile plains region of Uzbekistan in Central Asia (p. 423)

Fertile Crescent a large arc of fertile lands between the Persian Gulf and the Mediterranean Sea; the world's earliest civilizations began in the region (p. 482)

Fiji an island country in the Pacific (p. 741)

Finland a country in Northern Europe (p. 357)

Florida (FL) a state in the southeastern United States; admitted in 1845 (pp. R4–R5)

France a country in West-Central Europe (p. 333)

Freetown (9°N, 13°W) the capital of Sierra Leone (p. 538)

French Guiana (gee-A-nuh) a region of France in northern South America (p. 235)

Fuji (FOO-jee) (35°N, 135°E) a volcano and Japan's highest peak (p. 691)

Funafuti (9°S, 179°E) the capital of Tuvalu (p. 754)

G

Gabon (gah-BOHN) a country in Central Africa between Cameroon and the Democratic Republic of the Congo (p. 581)

Gaborone (24°S, 26°E) the capital of Botswana (p. 603)

Galápagos Islands a group of islands in the Pacific Ocean that are part of Ecuador (p. 279)

Gambia a country in West Africa surrounded on three sides by Senegal (p. 538)

Ganges River (GAN-jeez) a major river in northern India (p. 641)

Gangetic Plain a broad plain in northern India formed by the Ganges River (p. 641)

Gaza (32°N, 34°E) a city in southwestern Israel on the Mediterranean Sea (p. 469)

Georgetown (5°N, 59°W) capital of Guyana (p. 235)

Georgia (GA) a state in the southeastern United States; admitted in 1788 and one of the original 13 colonies (pp. R4–R5)

Georgia a country in the Caucasus Mountains (p. 427)

Germany a country in West-Central Europe (p. 333)

Ghana a country in West Africa between Côte d'Ivoire and Togo (p. 539)

Gobi (GOH-bee) a desert in China and Mongolia (p. 665)

Gran Chaco (grahn CHAH-koh) a region of lowlands in South America (p. 257)

Grand Banks (47°N, 52°W) a rich fishing ground near Newfoundland, Canada (p. 171)

Great Barrier Reef a huge coral reef off the northeastern coast of Australia (p. 743)

Greater Antilles an island group in the Caribbean that includes Cuba, Jamaica, Hispaniola, and Puerto Rico (p. 213)

Great Lakes a group of five large freshwater lakes in North America; they are Lake Superior, Lake Michigan, Lake Huron, Lake Erie, and Lake Ontario (p. 143)

Great Plains a large region of plains and grasslands in central North America (p. 143)

Great Rift Valley a series of valleys in East Africa caused by the stretching of Earth's crust (p. 563)

Great Zimbabwe an ancient walled town in Southern Africa (p. 609)

Greece a country in Southern Europe (p. 309)

Greenland a large island in North America controlled by Denmark (p. 169)

Guadalajara (21°N, 103°W) the second-largest city in Mexico (p. 191)

Guadeloupe a group of islands in the Caribbean that are part of France (p. 211)

Guatemala a country in Central America (p. 210)

Guatemala City (15°N, 91°W) the capital of Guatemala (p. 210)

Guayaquil (gwah-ah-KEEL) (2°S, 80°W) a city in Ecuador (p. 277)

Guiana Highlands (gee-YAH-nah) a large plateau region in northern South America (p. 237)

Guinea a country in West Africa north of Sierra Leone (p. 538)

Guinea-Bissau a country in West Africa north of Guinea (p. 538)

Gulf of Mexico a large gulf off the southeastern coast of North America (p. 191)

Gulf Stream a warm ocean current that flows north along the east coast of the United States (p. 52)

Guyana (gy-AH-nuh) a country in northern South America (p. 235)

Haiti a country in the Caribbean (p. 211)

Hanoi (21°N, 106°E) the capital of Vietnam (p. 714)

Harare (hah-RAH-ray) (18°S, 31°E) the capital of Zimbabwe (p. 603)

Havana (23°N, 82°W) the capital of Cuba (p. 211)

Hawaii (HI) state in the Pacific Ocean comprised of the Hawaiian Islands; admitted in 1959 (pp. R4–R5)

Helsinki (60°N, 25°E) the capital of Finland (p. 357)

Himalayas the highest mountains in the world; they separate the Indian Subcontinent from China (p. 641)

Hindu Kush a mountain system that stretches from northern Pakistan into northeastern Afghanistan (p. 423)

Hispaniola (ees-pah-nee-O-lah) an island in the Caribbean (p. 213)

Ho Chi Minh City a large city in southern Vietnam (p. 714)

Hokkaido (hoh-KY-doh) the northernmost of Japan's four major islands (p. 691)

Holland a region in the Netherlands (p. 342)

Honduras a country in Central America (p. 210)

Hong Kong (22°N, 115°E) a city in southern China (p. 663)

Honiara (9°S, 160°E) the capital of the Solomon Islands (p. 754)

Honshu (HAWN-shoo) the largest of Japan's four major islands (p. 691)

Houston (30°N, 95°W) a major U.S. port city in Texas (p. 159)

Huang He (Yellow River) a major river in northern China (p. 665)

Hudson Bay a large bay in central Canada (p. 171)

Hungary a country in central Europe (p. 377)

Iberian Peninsula a large peninsula in Southern Europe; Spain and Portugal are located there (p. 325)

Iceland an island country in Northern Europe (p. 356)

Idaho (ID) a state in the northwestern United States; admitted in 1890 (pp. R4–R5)

Illinois (IL) a state in the north-central United States; admitted in 1819 (pp. R4–R5)

India a country in South Asia (p. 639)

Indiana (IN) a state in the north-central United States; admitted in 1816 (pp. R4–R5)

Indian Ocean the world's third-largest ocean; it is located between Asia and Antarctica (p. R7)

Indochina Peninsula a large peninsula in Southeast Asia (p. 717)

Indonesia the largest country in Southeast Asia (p. 715)

Indus River a major river in Pakistan (p. 641)

Indus Valley a river valley in Pakistan that was home to the ancient Harappan civilization (p. 641)

Interior Plains a large plains region of North America (p. 143)

Iowa (IA) a state in the north-central United States; admitted in 1846 (pp. R4–R5)

Iran a country in the Persian Gulf region; it includes the ancient region of Persia (p. 481)

Iraq a country in the Persian Gulf region; it includes the ancient region of Mesopotamia (p. 481)

Ireland a country west of Britain in the British Isles (p. 356)

Islamabad (34°N, 73°E) the capital of Pakistan (p. 639)

Israel a country between the Mediterranean Sea and Jordan (p. 457)

Istanbul (41°N, 29°E) the largest city in Turkey; formerly known as Constantinople (p. 465)

Italy a country in Southern Europe (p. 309)

Jakarta (6°S, 107°E) the capital of Indonesia (p. 714)

Jamaica an island country in the Caribbean (p. 211)

Japan an island country in East Asia (p. 689)

Java a large island in Indonesia (p. 717)

Jerusalem (32°N, 35°E) the capital of Israel; it contains holy sites of Judaism, Christianity, and Islam (p. 468)

Jordan a country east of Israel and the Jordan River (p. 457)

Jordan River a river between Israel and Jordan that empties into the Dead Sea (p. 459)

Juba (5°N, 32°E) the capital of South Sudan (p. 561)

Jura Mountains a mountain range in West-Central Europe in Switzerland and France (p. 335)

K

Kabul (35°N, 69°E) the capital of Afghanistan (p. 421)

Kaliningrad (55°N, 21°E) a strategic city and port controlled by Russia (p. 413)

Kamchatka Peninsula a large, mountainous peninsula in eastern Russia on the Pacific Ocean (p. 403)

Kampala (0°, 32°E) the capital of Uganda (p. 561)

Kansas (KS) a state in the central United States; admitted in 1861 (pp. R4–R5)

Kara-Kum (kahr-uh-koom) a desert in Central Asia east of the Caspian Sea (p. 424)

Kashmir a disputed region between India and Pakistan (p. 639)

Kathmandu (kat-man-DOO) (28°N, 85°E) the capital of Nepal (p. 639)

Kazakhstan a country in Central Asia; it was part of the Soviet Union until 1991 (p. 424)

Kentucky (KY) a state in the east-central United States; admitted in 1792 (pp. R4–R5)

Kenya a country in East Africa south of Ethiopia (p. 561)

Khartoum (16°N, 33°E) the capital of Sudan (p. 561)

Kiev (50°N, 31°E) the capital of Ukraine (p. 387)

Kigali (2°S, 30°E) the capital of Rwanda (p. 561)

Kinshasa (4°S, 15°E) the capital of the Democratic Republic of the Congo (p. 581)

Kiribati an island country in the Pacific (p. 741)

Kjolen Mountains a mountain range in Scandinavia along the Norway-Sweden border (p. 358)

Kobe (KOH-bay) (35°N, 135°E) a major port city in Japan (p. 692)

Kolkata (Calcutta) a major city in eastern India (p. 639)

Kopet-Dag a group of mountains in northern Iran bordering Turkmenistan (p. 483)

Korean Peninsula a peninsula on the east coast of Asia (p. 689)

Kuala Lumpur (3°N, 102°E) the capital of Malaysia (p. 714)

Kuwait a small country on the Persian Gulf (p. 481)

Kyoto (KYOH-toh) (35°N, 136°E) the ancient capital of Japan (p. 689)

Kyrgyzstan a country in Central Asia; it was part of the Soviet Union until 1991 (p. 424)

Kyushu (KYOO-shoo) the southernmost of Japan's four major islands (p. 691)

Kyzyl Kum (ki-ZIL KOOM) a vast desert region in Uzbekistan and Kazakhstan (p. 424)

L

Lagos (6°N, 3°E) a city in Nigeria; the most populous city in West Africa (p. 539)

Lake Baikal a huge freshwater lake in Russia; it is the deepest lake in the world (p. 404)

Lake Maracaibo (mah-rah-KY-boh) (10°N, 72°W) an oil-rich body of water in Venezuela (p. 247)

Lake Victoria the largest lake in Africa (p. 563)

Laos (LOWS) a landlocked country in Southeast Asia (p. 714)

La Paz (17°S, 65°W) the capital of Bolivia (p. 289)

Latvia a Baltic country in Eastern Europe (p. 377)

Lebanon a country on the Mediterranean Sea north of Israel (p. 457)

Lena River a long river in central Russia that flows north to the Arctic Sea (p. 403)

Lesotho (luh-SOH-toh) a country completely surrounded by South Africa (p. 603)

Lesser Antilles a group of small islands in the Caribbean; they stretch from the Virgin Islands in the north to Trinidad in the south (p. 213)

Liberia a country in West Africa between Sierra Leone and Côte d'Ivoire (p. 539)

Libreville (0°, 9°E) the capital of Gabon (p. 581)

Libya a country in North Africa between Egypt and Algeria (p. 505)

Lilongwe (li-LAWN-gway) (14°S, 34°E) the capital of Malawi (p. 581)

Lima (10°S, 75°W) the capital of Peru (p. 277)

Lisbon (39°N, 9°W) the capital of Portugal (p. 308)

Lithuania a Baltic country in Eastern Europe (p. 377)

Ljubljana (46°N, 15°E) the capital of Slovenia (p. 377)

Llanos a plains region in South America (p. 237)

Lomé (6°N, 1°E) the capital of Togo (p. 539)

London (51°N, 1°W) the capital of England and the United Kingdom (p. 366)

Louisiana (LA) a state in the southeastern United States; admitted in 1812 (pp. R4–R5)

Luanda (9°S, 13°E) the capital of Angola (p. 581)

Lusaka (15°S, 28°E) the capital of Zambia (p. 581)

Luxembourg a country in West-Central Europe (p. 333)

Luxembourg City (45°N 6°E) capital of Luxembourg (p. 333)

M

Macedonia a country on the Balkan Peninsula in southeastern Europe (p. 395)

Madagascar a large island country off the southeastern coast of Africa (p. 603)

Madrid (40°N, 4°W) the capital of Spain (p. 308)

Magdalena River a river in Colombia (p. 234)

Maghreb a region in North Africa that includes western Libya, Tunisia, Algeria, and Morocco; it means "west" in Arabic (p. 520)

Maine (ME) a state in the northeastern United States; admitted in 1820 (pp. R4–R5)

Majuro (7°N, 171°E) the capital of the Marshall Islands (p. 754)

Malabo (mah-LAH-boh) (4°N, 9°E) the capital of Equatorial Guinea (p. 581)

Malawi a landlocked country in Central Africa located south of Tanzania (p. 581)

Malay Archipelago (muh-LAY) a large group of islands in Southeast Asia (p. 717)

Malay Peninsula (muh-LAY) a narrow peninsula in Southeast Asia (p. 717)

Malaysia a country in Southeast Asia (p. 714)

Maldives an island country south of India (p. R17)

Male (5°N, 72°E) the capital of the Maldives (p. R17)

Mali a country in West Africa on the Niger River (p. 539)

Manama (26°N, 51°E) capital of Bahrain (p. 481)

Manaus (3°S, 60°W) a major port and industrial city in Brazil's Amazon rain forest (p. 255)

Manila (15°N, 121°E) the capital of the Philippines (p. 715)

Manitoba a province in central Canada (p. 169)

Maputo (27°S, 33°E) the capital of Mozambique (p. 603)

Marseille (mar-SAY) (43°N, 5°E) a port city in France on the Mediterranean Sea (p. 333)

Marshall Islands an island country in the Pacific (p. 741)

Martinique a group of islands in the Caribbean that are part of France (p. 211)

Maryland (MD) a state in the eastern United States; admitted in 1788 and one of the original 13 colonies (pp. R4–R5)

Maseru (29°S, 27°E) the capital of Lesotho (p. 603)

Massachusetts (MA) a state in the northeastern United States; admitted in 1788 and one of the original 13 colonies (pp. R4–R5)

Massif Central (ma-SEEF sahn-TRAHL) an upland region in south-central France (p. 335)

Mato Grosso Plateau a high plateau area in Brazil (p. 257)

Mauritania a country in West Africa located between Mali and the Atlantic Ocean (p. 539)

Mauritius (maw-RI-shuhs) an island country east of Madagascar (p. R19)

Mbabane (uhm-bah-BAH-nay) (26°S, 31°E) the capital of Swaziland (p. 603)

Mecca (21°N, 40°E) an ancient city in Arabia and the birthplace of Muhammad (p. 481)

Mediterranean Sea a sea between Europe and Africa (p. 311)

Mekong River a major river in Southeast Asia (p. 717)

Melanesia a huge group of Pacific islands that stretches from New Guinea to Fiji (p. 751)

Melbourne (38°S, 145°E) a city in southeastern Australia (p. 740)

Melekeok (muh-LAY-kay-ohk) (7°N, 134°E) the capital of Palau (p. 754)

Mesopotamia (mes-uh-puh-TAY-mee-uh) the region in Southwest Asia between the Tigris and Euphrates rivers; it was the site of some of the world's earliest civilizations (p. 482)

Mexican Plateau a high, mostly rugged region covering much of the interior of Mexico (p. 193)

Mexico a country in North America (p. 191)

Mexico City (23°N, 104°W) the capital of Mexico (p. 204)

Michigan (MI) a state in the north-central United States; admitted in 1837 (pp. R4–R5)

Micronesia a large group of Pacific islands located east of the Philippines (p. 751)

Micronesia, Federated States of an island country in the western Pacific (p. 740)

Mid-Atlantic Ridge a mid-ocean ridge located in the Atlantic Ocean (p. 37)

Middle East the region around the eastern Mediterranean, northeastern Africa, and Southwest Asia that links the continents of Europe, Asia, and Africa (p. 482)

Minnesota (MN) a state in the north-central United States; admitted in 1858 (pp. R4–R5)

Mississippi (MS) a state in the southeastern United States; admitted in 1817 (pp. R4–R5)

Mississippi River a major river in the United States (p. 143)

Missouri (MO) a state in the central United States; admitted in 1821 (pp. R4–R5)

Mogadishu (2°N, 45°E) the capital of Somalia (p. 561)

Moldova a country in Eastern Europe (p. 377)

Monaco a small country in West-Central Europe (p. 333)

Mongolia a landlocked country in East Asia (p. 663)

Monrovia (6°N, 11°W) the capital of Liberia (p. 539)

Montana (MT) a state in the northern United States; admitted in 1889 (pp. R4–R5)

Mont Blanc (mawn BLAHN) (46°N, 7°E) a mountain peak in France; highest of the Alps (p. 336)

Montenegro (43°N, 19°E) a country in the Balkans (p. 377)

Monterrey (26°N, 100°W) a large city and industrial center in northern Mexico (p. 191)

Montevideo (mawn-tay-vee-DAY-oh) (35°S, 56°W) the capital of Uruguay (p. 255)

Montreal (46°N, 74°W) a major Canadian city in Quebec; founded by the French in 1642 (p. 169)

Morocco a country in North Africa south of Spain (p. 504)

Moroni (12°S, 43°E) the capital of Comoros (p. 603)

Moscow (56°N, 38°E) the capital of Russia (p. 414)

Mount Elbrus (el-BROOS) the highest peak of the Caucasus Mountains (p. 403)

Mount Everest the highest mountain in the world at 29,035 feet (8,850 km); it is located in India and Nepal (p. 641)

GAZETTEER

Mount Kilimanjaro (3°S, 37°E) the highest mountain in Africa at 19,341 feet (5,895 m); it is in Tanzania near the Kenya border (p. 563)

Mount Saint Helens (46°N, 122°W) a volcano in Washington State; it erupted in 1980 (p. 43)

Mozambique a country in Southern Africa south of Tanzania (p. 603)

Mumbai (Bombay) a major city in western India (p. 639)

Muscat (24°N, 59°E) the capital of Oman (p. 481)

Myanmar (Burma) (MYAHN-mahr) a country in Southeast Asia (p. 714)

N

Nairobi (1°S, 37°E) the capital of Kenya (p. 561)

Namib Desert a desert in southwestern Africa (p. 605)

Namibia a country on the Atlantic coast of Southern Africa (p. 603)

Nassau (25°N, 77°W) the capital of the Bahamas (p. 211)

Nauru an island country in the Pacific (p. 741)

Naypyidaw (20°N, 98°E) the administrative capital of Myanmar (Burma) (p. 714)

N'Djamena (uhn-jah-MAY-nah) (12°N, 15°E) the capital of Chad (p. 539)

Nebraska (NE) a state in the central United States; admitted in 1867 (pp. R4–R5)

Negev (NE-gev) an arid region of southern Israel (p. 459)

Nepal a landlocked country in South Asia (p. 639)

Netherlands a country in West-Central Europe (p. 333)

Nevada (NV) a state in the western United States; admitted in 1864 (pp. R4–R5)

New Brunswick a province in Canada (p. 169)

New Delhi (29°N, 77°E) the capital of India (p. 639)

Newfoundland and Labrador an island province in eastern Canada (p. 169)

New Guinea the world's second-largest island; located in Southeast Asia (p. 717)

New Hampshire (NH) a state in the northeastern United States; admitted in 1788 and one of the original 13 colonies (pp. R4–R5)

New Jersey (NJ) a state in the northeastern United States; admitted in 1787 and one of the original 13 colonies (pp. R4–R5)

New Mexico (NM) a state in the southwestern United States; admitted in 1912 (pp. R4–R5)

New Orleans (30°N, 90°W) a major U.S. port city located in southeastern Louisiana (p. 141)

New York (NY) a state in the northeastern United States; admitted in 1788 and one of the original 13 colonies (pp. R4–R5)

New York City (41°N, 74°W) the largest city in the United States (p. 141)

New Zealand an island country southeast of Australia (p. 741)

Niamey (14°N, 2°E) the capital of Niger (p. 539)

Nicaragua a country in Central America (p. 210)

Niger (NY-juhr) a country in West Africa north of Nigeria (p. 539)

Nigeria a country on the Atlantic coast of West Africa (p. 539)

Niger River the major river of West Africa (p. 541)

Nile River the longest river in the world; located in North Africa (p. 507)

North America a continent including Canada, the United States, Mexico, Central America, and the Caribbean islands (p. R41)

North Carolina (NC) a state in the southeastern United States; admitted in 1789 and one of the original 13 colonies (pp. R4–R5)

North China Plain a plains region of northeastern China (p. 665)

North Dakota (ND) a state in the north-central United States; admitted in 1889 (pp. R4–R5)

Northern European Plain a large plain across central and northern Europe (p. 335)

Northern Hemisphere the northern half of the globe, between the equator and the North Pole (p. H3)

Northern Ireland a part of the United Kingdom occupying the northeastern portion of the island of Ireland (p. 365)

North Korea a country in East Asia (p. 689)

North Pole (90°N) the northern point of Earth's axis (p. R21)

North Sea a shallow arm of the Atlantic Ocean in Northern Europe (p. 336)

Northwest Territories a territory in Canada (p. 181)

Norway a country in Northern Europe (p. 357)

Nouakchott (nooh-AHK-shaht) (18°N, 16°W) the capital of Mauritania (p. 538)

Nova Scotia (noh-vuh SKOH-shuh) a province in eastern Canada (p. 169)

Nuku'alofa (21°N, 174°E) the capital of Tonga (p. 754)

Nunavut (NOO-nah-VOOT) a territory in northern Canada created as a homeland for Canada's Inuit people (p. 169)

O

Ob River a long river in central Russia (p. 403)

Ohio (OH) a state in the north-central United States; admitted in 1803 (pp. R4–R5)

Oklahoma (OK) a state in the south-central United States; admitted in 1907 (pp. R4–R5)

Oman a country on the Arabian Peninsula (p. 481)

Ontario a province in east-central Canada (p. 169)

Oregon (OR) a state in the northwestern United States; admitted in 1859 (pp. R4–R5)

Orinoco River (OHR-ee-NOH-koh) a major river in Venezuela (p. 235)

Osaka (oh-SAH-kuh) (35°N, 135°E) a city in Japan (p. 704)

Oslo (60°N, 11°E) the capital of Norway (p. 357)

GAZETTEER

Ottawa (45°N, 76°W) capital of Canada (p. 169)

Ouagadougou (wah-gah-DOO-goo) (12°N, 2°W) the capital of Burkina Faso (p. 539)

Outback the dry interior region of Australia (p. 743)

P

Pacific Ocean the world's largest ocean; located between Asia and the Americas (p. R20)

Pakistan a country in South Asia northwest of India (p. 639)

Palau an island country in the Pacific (p. 740)

Palestine a region between the Jordan River and the Mediterranean Sea in modern Israel (p. 467)

Palikir (6°N, 158°E) the capital of the Federated States of Micronesia (p. 754)

Pamirs a highland region in Central Asia, mainly in Tajikistan (p. 422)

Pampas a fertile plains region in southern South America located mainly in Argentina (p. 257)

Panama a country in Central America (p. 211)

Panama Canal (26°N, 80°W) a canal built by the United States in the early 1900s across the Isthmus of Panama (p. 222)

Panama City (8°N, 81°W) capital of Panama (p. 211)

Papua New Guinea a country on the island of New Guinea (p. 740)

Paraguay a country in South America (p. 270)

Paraguay River a river in South America (p. 270)

Paramaribo (6°N, 55°W) the capital of Suriname (p. 235)

Paraná River a river in South America (p. 255)

Paris (46°N, 0°) the capital of France (p. 333)

Patagonia a region of dry plains and plateaus east of the Andes in southern Argentina (p. 257)

Pennsylvania (PA) a state in the eastern United States; admitted in 1787 and one of the original 13 colonies (pp. R4–R5)

Persian Gulf a body of water located between the Arabian Peninsula and the Zagros Mountains in Iran; it has enormous oil deposits along its shores (p. 481)

Perth (32°S, 116°E) a city in western Australia (p. 740)

Peru a country in western South America (p. 277)

Philadelphia (40°N, 75°W) a major U.S. city located in southeastern Pennsylvania; it was the capital of the United States from 1790 to 1800 (p. 159)

Philippines an island country in Southeast Asia (p. 715)

Phnom Penh (puh-NAWM pen) (12°N, 105°E) the capital of Cambodia (p. 714)

Podgorica (43°N, 19°E) capital of Montenegro (p. 377)

Poland a country in Eastern Europe (p. 377)

Polynesia the largest group of islands in the Pacific Ocean (p. 751)

Pontic Mountains a group of mountains in northern Turkey bordering the Black Sea (p. 459)

Popocatépetl (poh-poh-cah-TE-pet-uhl) (19°N, 99°W) a volcano near Mexico City (p. 193)

Po River a major river in northern Italy (p. 311)

Port-au-Prince (pohr-toh-PRINS) (19°N, 72°W) the capital of Haiti (p. 211)

Port Louis (20°S, 58°E) the capital of Mauritius (p. R19)

Port Moresby (10°S, 147°E) the capital of Papua New Guinea (p. 740)

Port-of-Spain (11°N, 61°W) the capital of Trinidad and Tobago (p. 211)

Porto-Novo (6°N, 3°E) the capital of Benin (p. 539)

Portugal a country in Southern Europe on the Iberian Peninsula (p. 308)

Port-Vila (18°S, 169°E) the capital of Vanuatu (p. 754)

Prague (50°N, 14°E) capital of the Czech Republic (p. 377)

Praia (PRY-uh) (15°N, 24°W) the capital of Cape Verde (p. 538)

Pretoria (26°S, 28°E) the administrative capital of South Africa (p. 603)

prime meridian an imaginary line that runs through Greenwich, England, at 0° longitude (p. H2)

Prince Edward Island (46°N, 64°W) a small province in eastern Canada (p. 169)

Pristina (43°N, 21°E) capital of Kosovo (p.377)

Puerto Rico an island east of Cuba and southeast of Florida; it is a U.S. territory (p. 211)

Pyongyang (pyuhng-YANG) (39°N, 126°E) the capital of North Korea (p. 689)

Pyrenees (PIR-uh-neez) a high mountain range between Spain and France (p. 311)

Q

Qatar (KUH-tahr) a country on the Arabian Peninsula (p. 481)

Quebec a province in eastern Canada (p. 169)

Quito (2°S, 78°W) the capital of Ecuador (p. 277)

R

Rabat (34°N, 7°W) the capital of Morocco (p. 504)

Red Sea a sea between the Arabian Peninsula and Africa (p. 483)

Reykjavik (64°N, 22°W) the capital of Iceland (p. 356)

Rhine a major river in Europe; it begins in Switzerland and flows north to the North Sea (p. 335)

Rhode Island (RI) a state in the northeastern United States; admitted in 1790 and one of the original 13 colonies (pp. R4–R5)

Riga (57°N, 24°E) the capital of Latvia (p. 377)

Ring of Fire a region that circles the Pacific Ocean; known for its earthquakes and volcanoes (p. 42)

Río Bravo the Mexican name for the river known as the Rio Grande in the United States; it forms the border between Mexico and Texas (p. 191)

Rio de Janeiro (23°N, 43°W) the second-largest city in Brazil; it is a major port city and Brazil's former capital (p. 255)

Río de la Plata (REE-oh day lah PLAH-tah) a body of water in South America (p. 257)

Riyadh (25°N, 47°E) the capital of Saudi Arabia (p. 481)

Rocky Mountains a major mountain range in western North America (p. 143)

Romania a country in Eastern Europe (p. 377)

Rome (42°N, 13°E) the capital of Italy; it was the capital of the ancient Roman Empire (p. 309)

Ross Ice Shelf the largest ice shelf in Antarctica (p. 741)

Rub' al-Khali (ROOB ahl-KAH-lee) a huge sandy desert on the Arabian Peninsula; its name means "empty quarter" (p. 484)

Ruhr a major industrial region in Germany (p. 349)

Russia a huge country that extends from Eastern Europe to the Pacific Ocean (p. 403)

Rwanda a country in East Africa between Tanzania and the Democratic Republic of the Congo (p. 561)

S

Sahara the world's largest desert; it dominates much of North Africa (p. 507)

Sahel a semiarid region between the Sahara and wetter areas to the south (p. 542)

St. Kitts and Nevis country in the Caribbean (p. 211)

St. Lawrence River a river in North America that flows from the Great Lakes to the Atlantic Ocean (p. 141)

Samarqand (40°N, 67°E) an ancient city on the Silk Road in modern Uzbekistan (p. 430)

Samoa an island country in the Pacific (p. 741)

San Francisco (37°N, 122°W) a major U.S. port city in Northern California (p. 140)

San Jose (10°N, 84°W) capital of Costa Rica (p. 210)

San Salvador (14°N, 89°W) the capital of El Salvador (p. 210)

Santiago (33°S, 71°W) the capital of Chile (p. 277)

Santo Domingo (19°N, 71°W) the capital of the Dominican Republic (p. 211)

São Paulo (24°S, 47°W) the largest city in Brazil and South America (p. 255)

São Tomé (sow too-MAY) (1°N, 6°E) the capital of São Tomé and Príncipe (p. 581)

São Tomé and Príncipe (PREEN-see-pee) an island country located off the Atlantic coast of Central Africa (p. 581)

Sarajevo (44°N, 18°E) the capital of Bosnia and Herzegovina (p. 395)

Saskatchewan a province in Canada (p. 169)

Saudi Arabia a country occupying much of the Arabian Peninsula in Southwest Asia (p. 481)

Scandinavian Peninsula a large peninsula in Northern Europe that includes Norway and Sweden (p. 359)

Scotland a part of the United Kingdom located in the northern part of Great Britain (p. 356)

Seattle (48°N, 122°W) a major U.S. port and city in Washington State (p. 140)

Senegal a country in West Africa south of Mauritania (p. 538)

Seoul (38°N, 127°E) the capital of South Korea (p. 689)

Serbia a country in the Balkans (p. 377)

Serengeti Plain a large plain in East Africa that is famous for its wildlife (p. 563)

Seychelles an island country located east of Africa in the Indian Ocean (p. R19)

Shanghai (31°N, 121°E) a major port city in eastern China (p. 670)

Shikoku (shee-koh-koo) the smallest of Japan's four major islands (p. 691)

Siberia a huge region in eastern Russia (p. 403)

Sierra Leone a West African country located south of Guinea (p. 538)

Sierra Madre (SYER-rah MAH-dray) the chief mountain range in Mexico (p. 193)

Sierra Nevada a large mountain range mainly in California (p. 143)

Silk Road an ancient trade route from China through Central Asia to the Mediterranean Sea (p. 430)

Singapore an island country at the tip of the Malay Peninsula in Southeast Asia (p. 714)

Slovakia a country in Eastern Europe (p. 377)

Slovenia a country in Eastern Europe (p. 377)

Sofia (43°N, 23°E) the capital of Bulgaria (p. 377)

Solomon Islands an island country in the Pacific (p. 741)

Somalia an East African country located on the Horn of Africa (p. 561)

South Africa a country located at the southern tip of Africa (p. 603)

South America a continent in the Western and Southern hemispheres (p. R12)

South Carolina (SC) a state in the southeastern United States; admitted in 1788 and one of the original 13 colonies (pp. R4–R5)

South Dakota (SD) a state in the north-central United States; admitted in 1889 (pp. R4–R5)

Southern Hemisphere the southern half of the globe, between the equator and the South Pole (p. H3)

South Korea a country in East Asia (p. 689)

South Pole (90°S) the southern point of Earth's axis (p. R21)

South Sudan a country in East Africa, newly independent in 2011 (p. 573)

Soviet Union a former country that included Russia and the former Soviet Republics; it broke up in 1991 (p. 383)

Spain a country in Southern Europe on the Iberian Peninsula (p. 308)

Sri Lanka an island country located south of India (p. 639)

Stockholm (59°N, 18°E) the capital of Sweden (p. 357)

Sucre (SOO-kray) (19°S, 65°W) the capital of Bolivia (p. 277)

Sudan a country in East Africa (p. 561)

Suez Canal a canal in Egypt that links the Mediterranean and Red seas (p. 507)

Sumatra a large island in Indonesia (p. 717)

Suriname (soohr-uh-NAHM) a country in northern South America (p. 235)

Suva (19°S, 178°E) the capital of Fiji (p. 754)

Swaziland a country in Southern Africa almost completely surrounded by South Africa (p. 598)

Sweden a country in Northern Europe (p. 357)

Switzerland a country in West-Central Europe (p. 151)

Sydney (34°S, 151°E) the largest city in Australia (p. 740)

Syr Darya (sir duhr-YAH) the longest river in Central Asia; it flows through the Fergana Valley and Kazakhstan, Tajikistan, and Uzbekistan on its way to the Aral Sea (p. 423)

Syria a country on the eastern Mediterranean Sea (p. 457)

Syrian Desert a desert in Southwest Asia covering much of the Arabian Peninsula between the Mediterranean coast and the Euphrates River (p. 459)

Taipei (25°N, 122°E) the capital of Taiwan (p. 663)

Taiwan (ty-wahn) an island country southeast of China (p. 663)

Tajikistan a country in Central Asia; it was part of the Soviet Union until 1991 (p. 423)

Tallinn (59°N, 25°E) the capital of Estonia (p. 385)

Tanzania (tan-zuh-NEE-uh) an East African country south of Kenya (p. 561)

Tarawa the capital of Kiribati (p. 754)

Tashkent (41°N, 69°E) the capital of Uzbekistan (p. 421)

Tasmania a large island off the southern coast of Australia (p. 740)

Taurus Mountains a mountain range in southern Turkey along the Mediterranean Sea (p. 459)

Tbilisi (42°N, 45°E) the capital of Georgia (p. 427)

Tegucigalpa (15°N, 87°W) the capital of Honduras (p. 210)

Tehran (36°N, 51°E) the capital of Iran (p. 481)

Tennessee (TN) a state in the south-central United States; admitted in 1796 (pp. R4–R5)

Texas (TX) a state and former independent republic in the south-central United States; admitted in 1845 (pp. R4–R5)

Thailand (TY-land) a country in Southeast Asia (p. 714)

Thar Desert (TAHR) a desert in western India and eastern Pakistan (p. 641)

Thimphu (28°N, 90°E) the capital of Bhutan (p. 639)

Tierra del Fuego a group of islands in southern South America (p. 279)

Tigris River (ty-gruhs) a major river in Southwest Asia; with the Euphrates River it defined the "land between the rivers" known as Mesopotamia (p. 483)

Timor-Leste an island country in Southeast Asia (p. 715)

Tirana (41°N, 20°E) the capital of Albania (p. 377)

Togo a country in West Africa between Ghana and Benin (p. 539)

Tokyo (36°N, 140°E) the capital of Japan (p. 689)

Tonga an island country in the Pacific (p. 741)

Toronto (44°N, 79°W) Canada's largest city (p. 169)

Trinidad and Tobago a country in the Caribbean just north of Venezuela (p. 211)

Tripoli (33°N, 13°E) the capital of Libya (p. 505)

Tropic of Cancer the parallel 23.5° north of the equator; parallel on the globe at which the sun's most direct rays strike Earth during the June solstice (pp. R6–R7)

Tropic of Capricorn the parallel at 23.5° south of the equator; parallel on the globe at which the sun's most direct rays strike Earth during the December solstice (pp. R6–R7)

Tunis (37°N, 10°E) the capital of Tunisia (p. 505)

Tunisia a country in North Africa on the Mediterranean Sea (p. 505)

Turkey a country on the eastern Mediterranean (p. 464)

Turkmenistan a country in Central Asia; it was part of the Soviet Union until 1991 (p. 424)

Tuvalu an island country in the Pacific (p. 741)

Uganda a country in East Africa located west of Kenya (p. 561)

Ukraine a country in Eastern Europe (p. 377)

Ulaanbaatar (oo-lahn-BAH-tawr) (48°N, 107°E) the capital of Mongolia (p. 663)

Uluru a huge natural rock formation in central Australia; also called Ayers Rock (p. 743)

United Arab Emirates a country on the Arabian Peninsula (p. 481)

United Kingdom a country in the British Isles that includes England, Wales, Scotland, and Northern Ireland (p. 365)

United States of America a country in North America located between Canada and Mexico (pp. 140–141)

Ural Mountains (YOOHR-uhl) a mountain range in Russia that separates Europe and Asia (p. 402)

Uruguay a country in South America (p. 255)

Utah (UT) a state in the western United States; admitted in 1896 (pp. R4–R5)

Uzbekistan a country in Central Asia; it was part of the Soviet Union until 1991 (p. 424)

Valley of Mexico a large plateau region in central Mexico (p. 193)

Valparaíso (bahl-pah-rah-EE-soh) (33°S, 72°W) a city and major port in Chile (p. 277)

Vancouver (49°N, 123°W) a city in western Canada just north of the U.S. border (p. 168)

Vanuatu an island country in the Pacific (p. 741)

Vatican City (42°N, 12°E) a small country in Rome that is the head of the Roman Catholic Church (p. 322)

Venezuela a country in South America (p. 235)

Vermont (VT) a state in the northeastern United States; admitted in 1791 (pp. R4–R5)

Victoria (1°S, 33°E) the capital of Seychelles (p. R19)

Vienna (45°N, 12°E) the capital of Austria (p. 333)

Vientiane (vyen-THAN) (18°N, 103°E) the capital of Laos (p. 714)

Vietnam (vee-ET-NAHM) a country in Southeast Asia (p. 714)

Vilnius (55°N, 25°E) the capital of Lithuania (p. 377)

Virginia (VA) a state in the eastern United States; admitted in 1788 and one of the original 13 colonies (pp. R4–R5)

Virgin Islands a group of small islands in the Caribbean (p. 211)

Volga (VAHL-guh) the longest river in Europe and Russia's most important commercial river (p. 403)

Wales a part of the United Kingdom located west of England on the island of Great Britain (p. 359)

Warsaw (52°N, 21°E) the capital of Poland (p. 377)

Washington (WA) a state in the northwestern United States; admitted in 1889 (pp. R4–R5)

Washington, D.C. (39°N, 77°W) the capital of the United States (p. 141)

Wellington (41°S, 175°E) the capital of New Zealand (p. 741)

West Bank a disputed territory in eastern Israel (p. 469)

Western Ghats (GAWTS) a mountain range in India (p. 641)

Western Hemisphere the half of the globe between 180° and the prime meridian that includes North and South America and the Pacific and Atlantic oceans (p. H3)

West Indies a group of more than 1,200 islands in the Caribbean Sea (p. 224)

West Virginia (WV) a state in the east-central United States; admitted in 1863 (pp. R4–R5)

Windhoek (VINT-hook) (22°S, 17°E) the capital of Namibia (p. 603)

Windsor (42°N, 83°W) a city in Canada near the U.S. border (p. 169)

Wisconsin (WI) a state in the north-central United States; admitted in 1848 (pp. R4–R5)

Wyoming (WY) a state in the northwestern United States; admitted in 1890 (pp. R4–R5)

Y

Yamoussoukro (yah-moo-SOO-kroh) (7°N, 5°W) the capital of Côte d'Ivoire (p. 539)

Yangon (Rangoon) (17°N, 96°E) the capital of Myanmar (Burma) (p. 714)

Yaoundé (yown-DAY) (4°N, 12°E) the capital of Cameroon (p. 581)

Yellow Sea a body of water between northeastern China and the Korean Peninsula (p. 665)

Yemen a country on the Arabian Peninsula bordering the Red Sea and the Gulf of Aden (p. 481)

Yenisey River a long river in central Russia that flows north to the Arctic Ocean (p. 403)

Yerevan (40°N, 45°E) the capital of Armenia (p. 427)

Yucatán Peninsula (yoo-kah-TAHN) a large peninsula that separates the Caribbean Sea from the Gulf of Mexico (p. 192)

Yugoslavia a former country in the Balkans that broke apart in the 1990s (p. 394)

Yukon Territory a territory in Canada (p. 168)

Z

Zagreb (46°N, 16°E) the capital of Croatia (p. 395)

Zagros Mountains a mountain range in Iran; it forms the western boundary of the Plateau of Iran (p. 483)

Zambezi River a river in Central Africa that flows into the Indian Ocean (p. 583)

Zambia a country in Central Africa east of Angola (p. 581)

Zanzibar an island in Tanzania; once a major trading center (p. 563)

Zimbabwe a country in Southern Africa between Botswana and Mozambique (p. 603)

Zurich (47°N, 9°E) a city in Switzerland (p. 333)

GAZETTEER

English and Spanish Glossary

MARK	AS IN	RESPELLING	EXAMPLE
a	<u>a</u>lphabet	a	*AL-fuh-bet
ā	<u>A</u>sia	ay	AY-zhuh
ä	c<u>a</u>rt, t<u>o</u>p	ah	KAHRT, TAHP
e	l<u>e</u>t, t<u>e</u>n	e	LET, TEN
ē	<u>e</u>ven, l<u>ea</u>f	ee	EE-vuhn, LEEF
i	<u>i</u>t, t<u>i</u>p, Br<u>i</u>t<u>i</u>sh	i	IT, TIP, BRIT-ish
ī	s<u>i</u>te, b<u>uy</u>, Oh<u>i</u>o	y	SYT, BY, oh-HY-oh
ə	<u>i</u>ris	eye	EYE-ris
k	<u>c</u>ard	k	KAHRD
kw	<u>qu</u>est	kw	KWEST
ō	<u>o</u>ver, rainb<u>o</u>w	oh	OH-vuhr, RAYN-boh
u̇	b<u>oo</u>k, w<u>oo</u>d	ooh	BOOHK, WOOHD
ȯ	<u>a</u>ll, <u>o</u>rchid	aw	AWL, AWR-kid
ȯi	f<u>oi</u>l, c<u>oi</u>n	oy	FOYL, KOYN
au̇	<u>ou</u>t	ow	OWT
ə	c<u>u</u>p, b<u>u</u>tter	uh	KUHP, BUHT-uhr
ü	r<u>u</u>le, f<u>oo</u>d	oo	ROOL, FOOD
yü	f<u>ew</u>	yoo	FYOO
zh	vi<u>s</u>ion	zh	VIZH-uhn

*A syllable printed in small capital letters receives heavier emphasis than the other syllable(s) in a word.

Phonetic Respelling and Pronunciation Guide

Many of the key terms in this textbook have been respelled to help you pronounce them. The letter combinations used in the respelling throughout the narrative are explained in this phonetic respelling and pronunciation guide. The guide is adapted from *Merriam-Webster's Collegiate Dictionary, Eleventh Edition; Merriam-Webster's Geographical Dictionary;* and *Merriam-Webster's Biographical Dictionary.*

A

Aborigines (a-buh-rij-uh-nees) the original inhabitants of Australia (p. 745)
aborígenes habitantes originales de Australia (pág. 745)

absolute location a specific description of where a place is located; absolute location is often expressed using latitude and longitude (p. 12)
ubicación absoluta descripción específica del lugar donde se ubica un punto; con frecuencia se define en términos de latitud y longitud (pág. 12)

Afrikaners (a-fri-KAH-nuhrz) Dutch, French, and German settlers and their descendants in South Africa (p. 610)
afrikaners colonizadores holandeses, franceses y alemanes y sus descendientes en Sudáfrica (pág. 610)

agricultural industries businesses that focus on growing crops and raising livestock (p. 122)
industrias agrícolas empresas dedicadas al cultivo de la tierra y la ganadería (pág. 122)

altiplano a broad, high plateau that lies between the ridges of the Andes (p. 279)
altiplano meseta amplia y elevada que se extiende entre las cadenas montañosas de los Andes (pág. 279)

animism the belief that bodies of water, animals, trees, and other natural objects have spirits (p. 546)

animismo creencia de que las masas de agua, los animales, los árboles y otros objetos de la naturaleza tienen espíritu (pág. 546)

apartheid South Africa's government policy of separation of races that was abandoned in the 1980s and 1990s; apartheid means "apartness" (p. 610)
apartheid política gubernamental de Sudáfrica de separar las razas, abandonada en las décadas de 1980 y 1990; apartheid significa "separación" (pág. 610)

Arab Spring a wave of pro-democracy uprisings that spread throughout Northern Africa and Southwest Asia in 2011. (p. 517)
revolución democrática árabe una serie de levantamientos en favor de la democracia que comenzaron en Túnez en el 2010 y se extendieron hasta el norte de África y el suroeste de Asia en el 2011 (pág. 517)

arable land that is suitable for growing crops (p. 437)
cultivable tierra buena para el cultivo (pág. 437)

archipelago a large group of islands (pp. 213, 716)
archipiélago gran grupo de islas (págs. 213, 716)

Association of Southeast Asian Nations (ASEAN) an organization that promotes economic development and social and cultural cooperation among the countries of Southeast Asia (p. 727)
Asociación de Naciones de Asia del Sudeste (ASEAN por sus siglas en inglés) organización que promueve el desarrollo económico y social y la cooperación cultural entre los países del sureste asiático (pág. 727)

atoll a ring-shaped coral island that surrounds a lagoon (p. 752)

atolón isla de coral en forma de anillo que rodea una laguna (pág. 752)

B

basin a generally flat region surrounded by higher land such as mountains and plateaus (p. 582)

cuenca región generalmente llana rodeada de tierras más altas, como montañas y mesetas (pág. 582)

Bedouins Arabic-speaking nomads that live mostly in the deserts of Southwest Asia (p. 474)

beduinos nómadas que hablan árabe y viven principalmente en los desiertos del suroeste de Asia (pág. 474)

Berbers members of an ethnic group who are native to North Africa and speak Berber languages (p. 513)

bereberes miembros de un grupo étnico del norte de África que hablan lenguas bereberes (pág. 513)

bilingual a term used to describe people who speak two languages (p. 154)

bilingüe término utilizado para describir a las personas que hablan dos idiomas (pág. 154)

birthrate the annual number of births per 1,000 people (p. 88)

índice de natalidad número de nacimientos por cada 1,000 personas en un año (pág. 88)

Boers Afrikaner frontier farmers in South Africa (p. 610)

bóers agricultores afrikaners de la frontera en Sudáfrica (pág. 610)

Bolsheviks a radical Russian Communist group that seized power in 1917 (p. 407)

bolcheviques grupo comunista ruso radical que obtuvo el poder en 1917 (pág. 407)

Buddhism a religion based on the teachings of the Buddha that developed in India in the 500s BC (p. 648)

budismo religión basada en las enseñanzas de Buda, originada en la India en el siglo VI a. C. (pág. 648)

C

canton one of 26 districts in the republic of Switzerland (p. 351)

cantón uno de los 26 distritos de la república de Suiza (pág. 351)

cartography the science of making maps (p. 19)

cartografía ciencia de crear mapas (pág. 19)

cash crop a crop that farmers grow mainly to sell for a profit (p. 203)

cultivo comercial cultivo que los agricultores producen principalmente para vender y obtener ganancias (pág. 203)

caste system the division of Indian society into groups based on birth or occupation (p. 648)

sistema de castas división de la sociedad india en grupos basados en el nacimiento o la profesión (pág. 648)

Catholicism the faith of Roman Catholics; the largest branch of Christianity (p. 322)

Catolicismo la fe de los católicos romanos; rama más grande del cristianismo (pág. 322)

chancellor a German prime minister (p. 349)

canciller primer ministro alemán (pág. 349)

Christianity a major world religion based on the life and teachings of Jesus of Nazareth (p. 320)

cristianismo una de las pincipales religions del mundo, basada en las enseñanzas de Jesús (pág. 320)

civil war a conflict between two or more groups within a country (p. 220)

guerra civil conflicto entre dos o más grupos dentro de un país (pág. 220)

climate a region's average weather conditions over a long period of time (p. 50)

clima condiciones del tiempo promedio de una región durante un período largo de tiempo (pág. 50)

cloud forest a moist, high-elevation tropical forest where low clouds are common (p. 214)

bosque nuboso bosque tropical de gran elevación y humedad donde los bancos de nubes son muy comunes (pág. 214)

colony a territory inhabited and controlled by people from a foreign land (pp. 150, 646)

colonia territorio habitado y controlado por personas de otro país (págs. 150, 646)

command economy an economic system in which the central government makes all economic decisions (pp. 94, 675)

economía autoritaria sistema económico en el que el gobierno central toma todas las decisiones económicas (págs. 94, 675)

commonwealth a self-governing territory associated with another country (p. 227)

mancomunidad o estado libre asociado territorio autogobernado asociado con otro país (pág. 227)

Commonwealth of Independent States (CIS) a union of former Soviet republics that meets about issues such as trade and immigration (p. 388)

Comunidad de Estados Independientes (CEI) unión de ex repúblicas soviéticas que se reúne para tratar temas como el comercio y la inmigración (pág. 388)

communism a political system in which the government owns all property and dominates all aspects of life in a country (p. 92)

comunismo sistema político en el que el gobierno es dueño de toda la propiedad y controla todos los aspectos de la vida de un país (pág. 92)

Confucianism a philosophy based on the ideas of Confucius that focuses on morality, family order, social harmony, and government (p. 672)

confucianismo filosofía basada en las ideas de Confucio que se concentra en la moralidad, el orden familiar, la armonía social y el gobierno (pág. 672)

constitutional monarchy a type of democracy in which a monarch serves as head of state but a legislature makes the laws (p. 364)

monarquía constitucional tipo de democracia en la cual un monarca sirve como jefe de estado, pero una asamblea legislativa hace las leyes (pág. 364)

continent a large landmass that is part of Earth's crust; geographers identify seven continents (p. 36)

continente gran masa de tierra que forma parte de la corteza terrestre; los geógrafos identifican siete continentes (pág. 36)

continental divide an area of high ground that divides the flow of rivers towards opposite ends of a continent (p. 144)

línea divisoria de aguas zona de terreno elevado que divide el flujo de los ríos en dos direcciones, hacia los extremos opuestos de un continente (pág. 144)

cooperative an organization owned by its members and operated for their mutual benefit (p. 228)

cooperativa organización cuyos miembros son los propietarios y que es operada para beneficio de todos (pág. 228)

coral reef a chain of rocky material found in shallow tropical waters (p. 743)

arrecife de coral cadena de material rocoso que se encuentra en aguas tropicales de poca profundidad (pág. 743)

cordillera (kawr-duhl-YER-uh) a mountain system made up of roughly parallel ranges (p. 236)

cordillera sistema de cadenas montañosas aproximadamente paralelas entre sí (pág. 236)

cosmopolitan characterized by many foreign influences (p. 343)

cosmopolita caracterizado por muchas influencias extranjeras (pág. 343)

coup (KOO) a sudden overthrow of a government by a small group of people (p. 291)

golpe de estado derrocamiento repentino de un gobierno por parte de un grupo reducido de personas (pág. 291)

Creole an American-born descendant of Europeans (p. 286)

criollo persona de ascendencia europea y nacida en América (pág. 286)

cultural diffusion the spread of culture traits from one region to another (p. 85)

difusión cultural difusión de rasgos culturales de una región a otra (pág. 85)

cultural diversity having a variety of cultures in the same area (p. 83)

diversidad cultural existencia de una variedad de culturas en la misma zona (pág. 83)

cultural universal a cultural feature found in all societies (p. 91)

rasgo cultural universal rasgo de la cultura que es común a todos los grupos sociales (pág. 91)

culture the set of beliefs, values, and practices that a group of people have in common (p. 80)

cultura conjunto de creencias, valores y costumbres compartidas por un grupo de personas (pág. 80)

culture region an area in which people have many shared culture traits (p. 82)

región cultural región en la que las personas comparten muchos rasgos culturales (pág. 82)

culture trait an activity or behavior in which people often take part (p. 81)

rasgo cultural actividad o conducta frecuente de las personas (pág. 81)

Cyrillic (suh-RIHL-ihk) a form of the Greek alphabet (p. 406)

cirílico forma del alfabeto griego (pág. 406)

czar (ZAHR) a Russian emperor (p. 407)

zar emperador ruso (pág. 407)

D

dachas Russian country houses (p. 413)

dachas casas de campo rusas (pág. 413)

Daoism a philosophy that developed in China and stressed the belief that one should live in harmony with the Dao, the guiding force of all reality (p. 672)

taoísmo filosofía que se desarrolló en China y que enfatizaba la creencia de que se debe vivir en armonía con el Tao, la fuerza que guía toda la realidad (pág. 672)

deforestation the clearing of trees (pp. 69, 259)

deforestación tala de árboles (págs. 69, 259)

delta a landform at the mouth of a river created by sediment deposits (p. 641)

delta accidente geográfico que se forma en la desembocadura de un río, creado por depósitos de sedimento (pág. 641)

demilitarized zone an empty buffer zone created to keep two countries from fighting (p. 707)

zona desmilitarizada zona vacía que se crea como barrera entre dos países para evitar que luchen (pág. 707)

democracy a form of government in which the people elect leaders and rule by majority (p. 106)

democracia sistema de gobierno en el que el pueblo elige a sus líderes y gobierna por mayoría (pág. 91)

desertification the spread of desert-like conditions (pp. 65, 542)

desertización ampliación de las condiciones desérticas (págs. 65, 542)

developed countries countries with strong economies and a high quality of life (p. 95)

países desarrollados países con economías sólidas y una alta calidad de vida (pág. 123)

developing countries countries with less productive economies and a lower quality of life (p. 124)
  países en vías de desarrollo países con economías menos productivas y una menor calidad de vida (pág. 95)

dialect a regional version of a language (pp. 226, 590)
  dialecto versión regional de una lengua (págs. 226, 590)

Diaspora the dispersal of the Jewish population outside of Israel (p. 466)
  Diáspora dispersión de la población judía fuera de Israel (pág. 466)

dictator a ruler who has almost absolute power (p. 521)
  dictador gobernante que tiene poder casi absoluto (pág. 521)

Diet the name for Japan's elected legislature (p. 700)
  Dieta nombre de la asamblea legislativa electa de Japón (pág. 700)

direct democracy a form of government in which citizens meet regularly in a popular assembly to discuss issues, pass laws, and vote for leaders (p. 107)
  democracia directa forma de gobierno caracterizada por asambleas populares en las que los ciudadanos se reúnen periódicamente para debatir problemas, aprobar leyes y elegir funcionarios públicos (pág. 107)

disarm to give up all weapons (p. 365)
  desarmarse renunciar a todas las armas (pág. 365)

domino theory the idea that if one country fell to Communism, neighboring countries would follow like falling dominoes (p. 724)
  teoría del efecto dominó idea de que si un país cae en manos del comunismo, los países vecinos lo seguirán como fichas de dominó que caen una tras otra (pág. 724)

draft law requiring men of certain ages and qualification to serve in the military (p. 113)
  servicio militar obligatorio ley que establece que los varones de edades y calificaciones determinadas deben prestar servicio militar (pág. 113)

droughts periods when little rain falls and crops are damaged (p. 564)
  sequías períodos en los que los cultivos sufren daños por la falta de lluvia (pág. 564)

dryland farming farming that relies on rainfall instead of irrigation (p. 437)
  cultivo de secano cultivo que depende de la lluvia en vez de la irrigación (pág. 437)

dynasty a series of rulers from the same family (p. 669)
  dinastía serie de gobernantes de la misma familia (pág. 669)

E

earthquake a sudden, violent movement of Earth's crust (p. 38)
  terremoto movimiento repentino y violento de la corteza terrestre (pág. 38)

ecosystem a group of plants and animals that depend on each other for survival, and the environment in which they live (p. 63)
  ecosistema grupo de plantas y animales que dependen unos de otros para sobrevivir, y el ambiente en el que estos viven (pág. 63)

ecotourism the practice of using an area's natural environment to attract tourists (p. 220)
  ecoturismo uso de regiones naturales para atraer turistas (pág. 220)

El Niño an ocean and weather pattern that affects the Pacific coast of the Americas; about every two to seven years, it warms normally cool ocean water and causes extreme ocean and weather events (p. 281)
  El Niño patrón oceánico y del tiempo que afecta a la costa del Pacífico de las Américas; aproximadamente cada dos a siete años, calienta las aguas normalmente frías del océano, y provoca sucesos oceánicos y climatológicos extremos (pág. 281)

embargo a limit on trade (p. 493)
  embargo límite impuesto al comercio (pág. 493)

empire a land with different territories and peoples under a single ruler (p. 197)
  imperio zona que reúne varios territorios y pueblos bajo un solo gobernante (pág. 197)

enclave a small territory surrounded by foreign territory (p. 616)
  enclave territorio pequeño rodeado de territorio extranjero (pág. 616)

environment the land, water, climate, plants, and animals of an area; surroundings (pp. 12, 62)
  ambiente la tierra, el agua, el clima, las plantas y los animales de una zona; los alrededores (págs. 12, 62)

erosion the movement of sediment from one location to another (p. 39)
  erosión movimiento de sedimentos de un lugar a otro (pág. 39)

escarpment a steep face at the edge of a plateau or other raised area (p. 604)
  acantilado cara empinada en el borde de una meseta o de otra área elevada (pág. 604)

estuary a partially enclosed body of water where freshwater mixes with salty seawater (p. 257)
  estuario masa de agua parcialmente rodeada de tierra en la que el agua de mar se combina con agua dulce (pág. 257)

ethnic cleansing the effort to remove all members of an ethnic group from a country or region (p. 392)
  limpieza étnica esfuerzo por eliminar a todos los miembros de un grupo étnico de un país o región (pág. 392)

ethnic group a group of people who share a common culture and ancestry (p. 83)
  grupo étnico grupo de personas que comparten una cultura y una ascendencia (pág. 83)

extended family a family group that includes the father, mother, children, and close relatives (p. 547)
  familia extendida grupo familiar que incluye al padre, la madre, los hijos y los parientes cercanos (pág. 547)

extinct no longer here; a species that has died out has become extinct (p. 64)

extinto que ya no existe; una especie que ha desaparecido está extinta (pág. 64)

F

factors of production the basic economic resources needed to produce goods and services. The four main factors of production are land, labor, capital, and entrepreneurship. (p. 117)

factores de producción los diferentes recursos que se necesitan para la creación de un bien o servicio. Los cuatro factores de producción principales son: la tierra, la mano de obra, el capital y la capacidad empresarial. (pág. 117)

famine an extreme shortage of food (p. 553)

hambruna grave escasez de alimentos (pág. 553)

favela (fah-VE-lah) a huge slum in Brazil (p. 263)

favela enorme barriada en Brasil (pág. 263)

fishery a place where lots of fish and other seafood can be caught (p. 693)

pesquería lugar donde suele haber muchos peces y mariscos para pescar (pág. 693)

fjord (fyawrd) a narrow inlet of the sea set between high, rocky cliffs (p. 359)

fiordo entrada estrecha del mar entre acantilados altos y rocosos (pág. 359)

fossil fuels nonrenewable resources that formed from the remains of ancient plants and animals; coal, petroleum, and natural gas are all fossil fuels (p. 69)

combustibles fósiles recursos no renovables formados a partir de restos de plantas y animales antiguos; el carbón, el petróleo y el gas natural son combustibles fósiles (pág. 69)

fossil water water underground that is not being replaced by rainfall (p. 485)

aguas fósiles agua subterránea que no es reemplazada por el agua de lluvia (pág. 485)

free enterprise system an economic system in which businesses can compete freely with one another with little government intervention; capitalism (p. 121)

libre empresa sistema económico basado en la competencia libre entre las empresas con una intervención estatal mínima; también conocida como capitalismo (pág. 121)

free port a city in which almost no taxes are placed on goods (pp. 521, 734)

puerto libre ciudad donde hay muy pocos impuestos sobre los bienes (págs. 521, 734)

freshwater water that is not salty; it makes up only about 3 percent of our total water supply (p. 31)

agua dulce agua que no es salada; representa sólo alrededor del 3 por ciento de nuestro suministro total de agua (pág. 31)

front the place where two air masses of different temperatures or moisture content meet (p. 53)

frente lugar en el que se encuentran dos masas de aire con diferente temperatura o humedad (pág. 53)

G

gaucho (GOW-choh) an Argentine cowboy (p. 267)

gaucho vaquero argentino (pág. 267)

genocide the intentional destruction of a people (p. 573)

genocidio destrucción intencional de un grupo de personas (pág. 573)

geography the study of the world, its people, and the landscapes they create (p. 4)

geografía estudio del mundo, de sus habitantes y de los paisajes creados por el ser humano (pág. 4)

geothermal energy energy produced from the heat of Earth's interior (pp. 360, 571)

energía geotérmica energía producida a partir del calor del interior de la Tierra (págs. 360, 571)

ger a large, circular, felt tent used in Mongolia and Central Asia (p. 681)

ger gran tienda circular de fieltro usada en Mongolia y Asia Central (pág. 681)

geyser a spring that shoots hot water and steam into the air (p. 372)

géiser manantial que lanza agua caliente y vapor al aire (pág. 372)

glacier a large area of slow moving ice (p. 31)

glaciar gran bloque de hielo que avanza con lentitud (pág. 31)

globalization the process in which countries are increasingly linked to each other through culture and trade (p. 97)

globalización proceso por el cual los países se encuentran cada vez más interconectados a través de la cultura y el comercio (pág. 97)

globe a spherical, or ball-shaped, model of the entire planet (p. 8)

globo terráqueo modelo esférico, o en forma de bola, de todo el planeta (pág. 8)

green revolution a program that encouraged farmers to adopt modern agricultural methods to produce more food (p. 653)

revolución verde programa que animó a los agricultores a adoptar métodos de agricultura modernos para producir más alimentos (pág. 653)

gross domestic product (GDP) the value of all goods and services produced within a country in a single year (p. 95)

producto interior bruto (PIB) valor de todos los bienes y servicios producidos en un país durante un año (pág. 95)

groundwater water found below Earth's surface (p. 32)

agua subterránea agua que se encuentra debajo de la superficie de la Tierra (pág. 32)

guerrilla a member of an irregular military force (p. 243)
  guerrillero miembro de una fuerza militar irregular (pág. 243)

gulag a soviet labor camp (p. 408)
  gulag campo soviético de trabajos forzados (pág. 408)

H

habitat the place where a plant or animal lives (p. 64)
  hábitat lugar en el que vive una planta o animal (pág. 64)

hacienda (hah-see-EN-duh) a huge expanse of farm or ranch land in the Americas (p. 198)
  hacienda granja o rancho de gran tamaño en las Américas (pág. 198)

heritage the wealth of cultural elements that has been passed down over generations (p. 93)
  patrimonio cultural riqueza cultural que se pasa de una generación a otra (pág. 93)

Hinduism the main religion of India; it teaches that everything is part of a universal spirit called Brahman (p. 648)
  hinduismo religión principal de la India; sus enseñanzas dicen que todo forma parte de un espíritu universal llamado Brahma (pág. 648)

human geography the study of the world's human geographic features— people, communities, and landscapes (p. 18)
  geografía humana estudio de los habitantes, las comunidades y los paisajes del mundo (pág. 18)

human rights rights that all people deserve, such as rights to equality and justice (p. 728)
  derechos humanos derechos que toda la gente merece como derechos a la igualdad y la justicia (pág. 728)

humanitarian aid assistance to people in distress (p. 100)
  ayuda humanitaria ayuda a personas en peligro (pág. 100)

humus (HYOO-muhs) decayed plant or animal matter; it helps soil support abundant plant life (p. 65)
  humus materia animal o vegetal descompuesta; contribuye a que crezca una gran cantidad de plantas en el suelo (pág. 65)

hydroelectric power the production of electricity from waterpower, such as from running water (p. 70)
  energía hidroeléctrica producción de electricidad generada por la energía del agua, como la del agua corriente (pág. 70)

I

iceberg a floating mass of ice that has broken off a glacier (p. 757)

iceberg masa de hielo flotante que se ha desprendido de un glaciar (pág. 757)

ice shelf a ledge of ice that extends over the water (p. 757)
  banco de hielo saliente de hielo que se extiende sobre el agua (pág. 757)

imperialism an attempt to dominate a country's government, trade, and culture (p. 567)
  imperialismo intento de dominar el gobierno, el comercio y la cultura de un país (pág. 567)

inflation the rise in prices that occurs when currency loses its buying power (pp. 202, 595)
  inflación aumento de los precios que ocurre cuando la moneda de un país pierde poder adquisitivo (págs. 202, 595)

informal economy a part of the economy that is based on odd jobs that people perform without government regulation through taxes (p. 269)
  economía informal parte de la economía basada en trabajos pequeños que se realizan sin el pago de impuestos regulados por el gobierno (pág. 269)

infrastructure the set of resources, like roads and factories, that a country needs to support economic activities (p. 385)
  infraestructura conjunto de recursos, como carre-teras o fábricas, que necesita un país para sostener su actividad económica (pág. 385)

interdependence a relationship between countries in which they rely on one another for resources, goods, or services (p. 99)
  interdependencia una relación entre países en que dependen unos de otros para obtener recursos, bienes, o servicios (pág. 99)

Islam a religion founded in Arabia by Muhammad based on submitting to God (Allah) and on messages Muslims believe God gave to Muhammad (p. 486)
  Islam una religión fundada por Mahoma en Arabia, basada en la sumisión a Dios (Alá) y en los mensajes que los musulmanes creen Dios le dio a Mahoma (pág. 486)

isthmus a narrow strip of land that connects two larger land areas (p. 212)
  istmo franja estrecha de tierra que une dos zonas más grandes (pág. 212)

J

Judaism (JOO-dee-i-zuhm) the religion of the ancient Israelites (practiced by Jews today); the oldest monotheistic religion (p. 466)
  judaísmo religión de los israelitas (practicada por los judíos hoy en dia); la relgión monoteista más antigua (pág. 466)

jury duty obligation to serve as a juror (p. 113)
  servicio de jurado obligación que tiene un ciudadano de desempeña la función de jurado (pág. 113)

K

kampong a traditional village in Indonesia; also the term for crowded slums around Indonesia's large cities (p. 733)
kampong aldea tradicional de Indonesia; término que también se usa para los barrios pobres y superpoblados que rodean las grandes ciudades de Indonesia (pág. 733)

kibbutz (kih-BOOTS) in Israel, a large farm where people traditionally shared everything in common (p. 468)
kibbutz en Israel, granja grande donde las personas comparten tradicionalmente todo (pág. 468)

kimchi a traditional Korean food made from pickled cabbage and spices (p. 699)
kimchi comida tradicional coreana hecha con repollo en vinagre y especias (pág. 699)

kimono a traditional robe worn in Japan (p. 698)
kimono bata tradicional usada en Japón (pág. 698)

klong a canal in Bangkok (p. 728)
klong canal de Bangkok (pág. 728)

kosher a term used to refer to the food allowed under Jewish dietary laws; it means "fit" in Hebrew (p. 468)
kosher término utilizado para referirse a la comida que es permitida bajo las leyes alimenticias judías; significa "ser sano/a" en hebreo (pág. 468)

L

landform a shape on the planet's surface, such as a mountain, valley, plain, island, or peninsula (p. 35)
accidente geográfico forma de la superficie terrestre, como una montaña, un valle, una llanura, una isla o una península (pág. 35)

landlocked completely surrounded by land with no direct access to the ocean (pp. 270, 422)
sin salida al mar que está rodeado completamente por tierra, sin acceso directo al océano (págs. 270, 422)

landscape all the human and physical features that make a place unique (p. 4)
paisaje todas las características humanas y físicas que hacen que un lugar sea único (pág. 4)

latitude the distance north or south of Earth's equator (p. 27)
latitud distancia hacia el norte o el sur desde el ecuador (pág. 27)

lava magma that reaches Earth's surface (p. 37)
lava magma que llega a la superficie terrestre (pág. 37)

limited government a type of government that has legal limits on its power, usually in the form of a constitution (p. 107)
gobierno limitado forma de gobierno cuyo poder está restringido por la ley, comúnmente la constitución (pág. 107)

llanero (yah-NAY-roh) Venezuelan cowboy (p. 246)
llanero vaquero venezolano (pág. 246)

loess (LES) fertile, yellowish soil (p. 666)
loess suelo amarillento y fértil (pág. 666)

M

Magna Carta a document signed in 1215 by King John of England that required the king to honor certain rights (p. 364)
Carta Magna documento firmado por el rey Juan de Inglaterra en 1215 que exigía que el rey respetara ciertos derechos (pág. 364)

malaria a disease spread by mosquitoes that causes fever and pain (p. 596)
malaria enfermedad transmitida por los mosquitos que causa fiebre y dolor (pág. 596)

malnutrition a condition of not getting enough nutrients from food (p. 597)
desnutrición estado producido al no obtener suficientes nutrientes de los alimentos (pág. 597)

manufacturing industries businesses where people make finished products from raw materials (p. 122)
industria manufacturera actividad económica en la cual las personas transforman materias primas en artículos de consumo (pág. 122)

Maori (MOWR-ee) the original inhabitants of New Zealand (p. 745)
maoríes primeros habitantes de Nueva Zelanda (pág. 745)

map a flat drawing that shows all or part of Earth's surface (p. 8)
mapa representación plana que muestra total o parcialmente la superficie de la Tierra (pág. 8)

maquiladora (mah-kee-lah-DORH-ah) a U.S. or other foreign-owned factory in Mexico (p. 205)
maquiladora fábrica estadounidense o de otro país establecida en México (pág. 205)

maritime on or near the sea (p. 181)
marítimo en o cerca del mar (pág. 181)

market economy an economic system based on free trade and competition (p. 94)
economía de mercado sistema económico basado en el libre comercio y la competencia (pág. 94)

Mediterranean climate the type of climate found across Southern Europe; it features warm and sunny summer days, mild evenings, and cooler, rainy winters (p. 312)
clima mediterráneo tipo de clima de todo el sur europeo; se caracteriza por días de verano cálidos y soleados, noches templadas e inviernos lluviosos y más frescos (pág. 312)

megacity a giant urban area that includes surrounding cities and suburbs (p. 262)
megaciudad zona urbana enorme que incluye los suburbios y ciudades de alrededor (pág. 262)

megalopolis a string of large cities that have grown together (p. 159)
megalópolis serie de ciudades grandes que han crecido hasta unirse (pág. 159)

Mercosur an organization that promotes trade and economic cooperation among the southern and eastern countries of South America (p. 268)

Mercosur organización que promueve el comercio y la cooperación económica entre los países del sur y el este de América del Sur (pág. 268)

mestizo (me-STEE-zoh) a person of mixed European and Indian ancestry (p. 198)

mestizo persona de origen europeo e indígena (pág. 198)

meteorology the study of weather and what causes it (p. 20)

meteorología estudio de las condiciones del tiempo y sus causas (pág. 20)

migration the movement of people from one place to live in another (p. 89)

migración movimiento de personas de un lugar para ir a vivir a otro lugar (pág. 89)

mission a church outpost (p. 198)

misión asentamiento de la Iglesia (pág. 198)

monsoon a seasonal wind that brings either dry or moist air (p. 643)

monzón viento estacional que trae aire seco o húmedo (pág. 643)

multicultural society a society that includes a variety of cultures in the same area (p. 83)

sociedad multicultural área de la sociedad en la que convergen culturas diversas (pág. 83)

N

natural resource any material in nature that people use and value (p. 68)

recurso natural todo material de la naturaleza que las personas utilizan y valoran (pág. 68)

navigable river a river that is deep and wide enough for ships to use (p. 336)

río navegable río que tiene la profundidad y el ancho necesarios para que pasen los barcos (pág. 336)

neutral not taking sides in an international conflict (p. 370)

neutral que no toma partido en un conflicto internacional (pág. 370)

newsprint cheap paper used mainly for newspapers (p. 173)

papel de prensa papel económico utilizado principalmente para imprimir periódicos (pág. 173)

nomads people who move often from place to place (p. 432)

nómadas personas que se trasladan frecuentemente de un lugar a otro (pág. 432)

nonrenewable resource a resource that cannot be replaced naturally; coal and petroleum are examples of nonrenewable resources (p. 69)

recurso no renovable recurso que no puede reemplazarse naturalmente; el carbón y el petróleo son ejemplos de recursos no renovables (pág. 69)

nonrepresentative government a system of government where power is unlimited and citizens have few, if any, rights (p. 115)

gobierno sin representación sistema de gobierno con poder ilimitado, en el que los ciudadanos tienen pocos o ningún derecho (pág. 115)

North Atlantic Drift a warm ocean current that brings warm, moist air across the Atlantic Ocean to Northern Europe (p. 360)

Corriente del Atlántico Norte corriente oceánica cálida que trae aire cálido y húmedo a través del océano Atlántico al norte de Europa (pág. 360)

O

oasis a wet, fertile area in a desert where a spring or well provides water (pp. 484, 508)

oasis zona húmeda y fértil en el desierto con un manantial o pozo que proporciona agua (págs. 484, 508)

ocean currents large streams of surface seawater; they move heat around Earth (p. 52)

corrientes oceánicas grandes corrientes de agua de mar que fluyen en la superficie del océano; transportan calor por toda la Tierra (pág. 52)

OPEC an international organization whose members work to influence the price of oil on world markets by controlling the supply (p. 487)

OPEP organización internacional cuyos miembros trabajan para influenciar el precio del petróleo en los mercados mundiales controlando la oferta (pág. 487)

Orthodox Church a branch of Christianity that dates to the Byzantine Empire (p. 317)

Iglesia ortodoxa rama del cristianismo que data del Imperio bizantino (pág. 317)

ozone layer a layer of Earth's atmosphere that protects living things from the harmful effects of the sun's ultraviolet rays (p. 758)

capa de ozono capa de la atmósfera de la Tierra que protege a los seres vivos de los efectos dañinos de los rayos ultravioleta del sol (pág. 758)

P

pagoda a Buddhist temple based on Indian designs (p. 673)

pagoda templo budista basado en diseños de la India (pág. 673)

pans low, flat areas (p. 606)

depresiones áreas bajas y planas (pág. 606)

ENGLISH AND SPANISH GLOSSARY

parliamentary monarchy a type of government in which a king shares power with an elected parliament and a prime minister (p. 328)

monarquía parlamentaria tipo de gobierno en el que un rey rige conjuntamente con un parlamento elegido por votación y un primer ministro (pág. 328)

partition division (p. 647)

partición división (pág. 647)

peninsula a piece of land surrounded on three sides by water (p. 192)

península pedazo de tierra rodeado de agua por tres lados (pág. 192)

periodic market an open-air trading market that is set up once or twice a week (p. 585)

mercado periódico mercado al aire libre que funciona una o dos veces a la semana (pág. 585)

permafrost permanently frozen layers of soil (p. 61)

permafrost capas de tierra congeladas permanentemente (pág. 61)

phosphate a mineral salt containing the element phosphorus (p. 461)

fosfato sal mineral que contiene el elemento fósforo (pág. 461)

physical geography the study of the world's physical geographic features—its landforms, bodies of water, climates, soils, and plants (p. 16)

geografía física estudio de las características físicas de la Tierra: sus accidentes geográficos, sus masas de agua, sus climas, sus suelos y sus plantas (pág. 16)

pioneer an early settler; in the United States, people who settled the interior and western areas of the country were known as pioneers (p. 152)

pionero poblador; en Estados Unidos, las personas que se establecieron en el interior y el oeste del país se llamaron pioneros (pág. 152)

plantation a large farm that grows mainly one crop (p. 151)

plantación granja muy grande en la que se produce principalmente un solo tipo de cultivo (pág. 151)

plate tectonics a theory suggesting that Earth's surface is divided into a dozen or so slow-moving plates, or pieces of Earth's crust (p. 36)

tectónica de placas teoría que sugiere que la superficie terrestre está dividida en unas doce placas, o fragmentos de corteza terrestre, que se mueven lentamente (pág. 36)

polar desert a high-latitude region that receives little precipitation (p. 757)

desierto polar región a una latitud alta que recibe pocas precipitaciones (pág. 757)

pope the spiritual head of the Roman Catholic Church (p. 322)

papa jefe espiritual de la Iglesia Católica Romana (pág. 322)

popular culture culture traits that are well known and widely accepted (p. 98)

cultura popular rasgos culturales conocidos y de gran aceptación (pág. 98)

population the total number of people in a given area (p. 86)

población número total de personas en una zona determinada (pág. 86)

population density a measure of the number of people living in an area (p. 86)

densidad de población medida del número de personas que viven en una zona (pág. 86)

precipitation water that falls to Earth's surface as rain, snow, sleet, or hail (p. 31)

precipitación agua que cae a la superficie de la Tierra en forma de lluvia, nieve, aguanieve o granizo (pág. 31)

prevailing winds winds that blow in the same direction over large areas of Earth (p. 51)

vientos preponderantes vientos que soplan en la misma dirección sobre grandes zonas de la Tierra (pág. 51)

Protestant a Christian who protested against the Catholic Church, or whose faith is rooted in the Reformation (p. 348)

protestante un cristiano que protestó en contra del la Iglesia Católica, o cuya fe tiene sus raíces en la Reforma (pág. 348)

province an administrative division of a country (p. 176)

provincia división administrativa de un país (pág. 176)

pulp softened wood fibers; used to make paper (p. 173)

pulpa fibras ablandadas de madera; usadas para hacer papel (pág. 173)

R

referendum a direct vote of the public (p. 248)

referéndum voto directo del pueblo (pág. 248)

reforestation planting trees to replace lost forestland (p. 69)

reforestación siembra de árboles para reemplazar los bosques que han desaparecido (pág. 69)

refugee someone who flees to another country, usually for political or economic reasons (p. 227)

refugiado persona que escapa a otro país, generalmente por razones económicas o políticas (pág. 227)

region a part of the world that has one or more common features that distinguish it from surrounding areas (p. 6)

región parte del mundo que tiene una o más características comunes que la distinguen de las áreas que la rodean (pág. 6)

regionalism the strong connection that people feel toward the region in which they live (p. 181)

regionalismo gran conexión que las personas sienten con la región en la que viven (pág. 181)

relative location a general description of where a place is located; a place's relative location is often expressed in relation to something else (p. 12)
  ubicación relativa descripción general de la posición de un lugar; la ubicación relativa de un lugar suele expresarse en relación con otra cosa (pág. 12)

renewable resource a resource that Earth replaces naturally, such as water, soil, trees, plants, and animals (p. 69)
  recurso renovable recurso que la Tierra reemplaza por procesos naturales, como el agua, el suelo, los árboles, las plantas y los animales (pág. 69)

representative government a system of government where people are the ultimate source of government authority (p. 112)
  gobierno representativo sistema de gobierno en el que los ciudadanos son la fuente de autoridad absoluta (pág. 112)

retail industries businesses that sell directly to final customers (p. 122)
  distribuidores minoristas empresas comerciales que venden directamente a los consumidores finales (pág. 122)

revolution the 365 ¼ day trip Earth takes around the sun each year (p. 27)
  revolución viaje de 365 ¼ días que la Tierra hace alrededor del Sol cada año (pág. 27)

revolution a drastic change in a country's government and way of life (p. 497)
  revolución cambio drástico en el gobierno y la forma de vida de un país (pág. 497)

rift valleys places on Earth's surface where the crust stretches until it breaks (p. 562)
  valles de fisura puntos de la superficie de la Tierra en los que la corteza se estira hasta romperse (pág. 562)

rotation one complete spin of Earth on its axis; each rotation takes about 24 hours (p. 26)
  rotación giro completo de la Tierra sobre su propio eje; cada rotación toma 24 horas (pág. 26)

S

safari an overland journey to view African wildlife (p. 571)
  safari excursión por tierra con el fin de ver animales salvajes en África (pág. 571)

Sahel (SAH-hel) a strip of land that divides the Sahara from wetter areas (p. 542)
  Sahel franja de tierra que divide el Sahara de zonas más húmedas (pág. 542)

samurai (SA-muh-ry) a trained professional warrior in feudal Japan (p. 696)
  samurai guerrero profesional entrenado del Japón feudal (pág. 696)

sanctions economic or political penalties imposed by one country on another to try to force a change in policy (p. 614)
  sanciones penalizaciones económicas o políticas que un país impone a otro para obligarlo a cambiar su política (pág. 614)

savanna an area of tall grasses and scattered trees and shrubs (pp. 58, 542)
  sabana zona de pastos altos con arbustos y árboles dispersos (págs. 58, 542)

scarcity conflict that exists because wants are unlimited and resources are limited (p. 117)
  escasez conflicto que resulta cuando existe una demanda ilimitada y una oferta limitada de productos (pág. 117)

Science a way of understanding the world through observation and the testing of ideas (p. 94)
  ciencia manera de comprender el mundo por medio de la observación y la experimentación (pág. 94)

secede to break away from the main country (p. 550)
  separarse dividirse del territorio principal del país (pág. 550)

secular the separation of religion and government; nonreligious (p. 465)
  secular separación entre la religión y el gobierno; no religioso (pág. 465)

service industries businesses that provide services rather than goods (p. 123)
  empresas de servicios empresas que proveen servicios pero no bienes (pág. 123)

shah a Persian title that means "king" (p. 497)
  sha título persa que significa "rey" (pág. 497)

Sherpas an ethnic group from the mountains of Nepal (p. 654)
  sherpas grupo étnico de las montañas de Nepal (pág. 654)

Shia Muslims who believe that true interpretation of Islamic teaching can only come from certain religious and political leaders called imams; they make up one of the two main branches of Islam (p. 486)
  chiítas musulmanes que creen que la interpretación correcta de las enseñanzas islámicas solo puede provenir de ciertos líderes religiosos y políticos llamados imanes; forman una de las dos ramas principales del Islam (pág. 486)

shogun a general who ruled Japan in the emperor's name (p. 696)
  shogun general que gobernaba a Japón en nombre del emperador (pág. 696)

Sikhism a religion native to India that embraces equality for all, belief in one God, service to humanity, and honest labor (p. 651)
  sijismo una religión originaria de la India, que abarca la igualdad para todos, la creencia en un solo Dios, el servicio a la humanidad y el trabajo honesto (pág. 651)

silt finely ground fertile soil that is good for growing crops (p. 506)
  cieno tierra fértil de partículas finas que es buena para el crecimiento de los cultivos (pág. 506)

slash-and-burn agriculture the practice of burning forest in order to clear land for planting (p. 203)
agricultura de tala y quema práctica de quemar los bosques para despejar el terreno y sembrar en él (pág. 203)

smelters factories that process metal ores (p. 415)
fundiciones fábricas que tratan menas de metal (pág. 415)

smog a mixture of smoke, chemicals, and fog (p. 204)
smog mezcla de humo, sustancias químicas y niebla (pág. 204)

social science a field that focuses on people and the relationships among them (p. 5)
ciencias sociales campo de estudio que se enfoca en las personas y en las relaciones entre ellas (pág. 5)

soil exhaustion the process of soil becoming infertile because it has lost nutrients needed by plants (p. 259)
agotamiento del suelo proceso por el cual el suelo se vuelve estéril porque ha perdido los nutrientes que necesitan las plantas (pág. 259)

solar energy energy from the sun (p. 26)
energía solar energía del Sol (pág. 26)

souk (SOOK) a marketplace or bazaar in the Islamic world (p. 521)
zoco mercado o bazar del mundo islámico (pág. 521)

steppe a semidry grassland or prairie; steppes often border deserts (p. 59)
estepa pradera semiárida; las estepas suelen encontrarse en el límite de los desiertos (pág. 59)

strait a narrow passageway that connects two large bodies of water (p. 279)
estrecho paso angosto que une dos grandes masas de agua (pág. 279)

strike a work stoppage by a group of workers until their demands are met (p. 248)
huelga interrupción del trabajo por parte de un grupo de trabajadores hasta que se cumplan sus demandas (pág. 248)

subcontinent a large landmass that is smaller than a continent (p. 640)
subcontinente gran masa de tierra, más pequeña que un continente (pág. 640)

sultan the supreme ruler of a Muslim country (p. 735)
sultán gobernante supremo de un país musulmán (pág. 735)

Sunni Muslims who believe in the ability of the majority of the community to interpret Islamic teachings; they make up one of the two main branches of Islam (p. 486)
sunitas musulmanes que creen en la capacidad de la mayor parte de la comunidad de interpretar las enseñanzas islámicas; forman una de las dos ramas principales del Islam (pág. 486)

surface water water that is found in Earth's streams, rivers, and lakes (p. 31)
agua superficial agua que se encuentra en los arroyos, ríos y lagos de la Tierra (pág. 31)

T

taiga (TY-guh) a forest of mainly evergreen trees covering much of Russia (p. 405)
taiga bosque de árboles de hoja perenne principalmente que cubre gran parte de Rusia (pág. 405)

Taliban a radical Muslim group that rose to power in Afghanistan in the mid-1990s (p. 435)
talibanes grupo radical musulmán que llegó al poder en Afganistán a mediados de la década de 1990 (pág. 435)

tariff a fee that a country charges on imports or exports (p. 701)
arancel tarifa que impone un país a las importaciones y exportaciones (pág. 701)

technology the use of knowledge, tools, and skills to solve problems (p. 94)
tecnología el uso de herramientas, destrezas y conocimientos necesarios para resolver problemas (pág. 94)

territory an area that is under the authority of another government (p. 753)
territorio zona que está bajo el control de otro go-bierno (pág. 753)

terrorism Violent attacks against civilians to create fear (p. 164)
terrorismo ataques violentos contra civiles que provocan miedo (pág. 164)

theocracy a government ruled by religious leaders (p. 498)
teocracia gobierno dirigido por líderes religiosos (pág. 498)

totalitarian government a type of government that exercises control over all aspects of society (p. 109)
gobierno totalitario forma de gobierno que ejerce control sobre todos los aspectos de una sociedad (pág. 109)

townships crowded clusters of small homes in South Africa outside of cities where black South Africans live (p. 611)
distritos segregados grupos de pequeñas viviendas amontonadas ubicadas en las afueras de las ciudades de Sudáfrica, donde vivían los sudafricanos negros (pág. 611)

trade surplus when a country exports more goods than it imports (p. 701)
excedente comercial cuando un país exporta más bienes de los que importa (pág. 701)

Trans-Siberian Railroad a rail line in Russia that extends about 5,800 miles (9,330 km) from Moscow to Vladivostok; it is the longest single rail line in the world (p. 415)
Ferrocarril Transiberiano línea de ferrocarril rusa de 5,800 millas (9,330 km) de largo, desde Moscú hasta Vladivostok; es la vía de ferrocarril más larga del mundo (pág. 415)

tributary a smaller stream or river that flows into a larger stream or river (p. 143)

   tributario río o corriente más pequeña que fluye hacia un río o una corriente más grande (pág. 143)

tropics regions close to the equator (p. 29)

   trópicos regiones cercanas al ecuador (pág. 29)

tsunami (sooh-NAH-mee) a destructive and fast-moving wave (p. 692)

   tsunami ola rápida y destructiva (pág. 692)

U

uninhabitable unable to support human settlement (p. 371)

   inhabitable que no puede sustentar asentamientos humanos (pág. 371)

United Nations an organization of countries that promotes peace and security around the world (p. 99)

   Naciones Unidas organización de países que promueve la paz y la seguridad en todo el mundo (pág. 99)

unlimited government a type of government in which there are no legal limits set on its power (p. 109)

   gobierno ilimitado forma de gobierno en el que no hay límites legales establecidos en su poder (pág. 109)

universal theme is a message about life or human nature that is meaningful across time and in all places (p. 94)

   tema universal mensaje significativo sobre la vida o la naturaleza humana que se conoce en todo tiempo y lugar (pág. 94)

urbanization the increase in the percentage of people who live in cities (p. 652)

   urbanización aumento del porcentaje de personas que vive en las ciudades (pág. 652)

V

veld (VELT) open grassland areas in South Africa (p. 606)

   veld praderas descampadas en Sudáfrica (pág. 606)

viceroy governor (p. 285)

   virrey gobernador (pág. 285)

Vikings Scandinavian warriors who raided Europe in the early Middle Ages (p. 368)

   vikingos guerreros escandinavos que atacaron Europa al principio de la Edad Media (pág. 368)

W

wadi a dry streambed (p. 485)

   uadi cauce seco de un río o arroyo (pág. 485)

wat a Buddhist temple that also serves as a monastery (p. 724)

   wat templo budista que sirve también como monasterio (pág. 724)

water cycle the movement of water from Earth's surface to the atmosphere and back (p. 33)

   ciclo del agua circulación del agua desde la superficie de la Tierra hacia la atmósfera y de regreso a la Tierra (pág. 33)

water vapor water occurring in the air as an invisible gas (p. 32)

   vapor de agua agua que se encuentra en el aire en estado gaseoso e invisible (pág. 32)

weather the short-term changes in the air for a given place and time (p. 50)

   tiempo cambios a corto plazo en la atmósfera en un momento y lugar determinados (pág. 50)

weathering the process by which rock is broken down into smaller pieces (p. 39)

   meteorización proceso de desintegración de las rocas en pedazos pequeños (pág. 39)

wholesale industries businesses that sell to businesses (p. 122)

   distribuidores mayoristas empresas comerciales que venden productos a otras empresas comerciales (pág. 122)

work ethic a belief that work in itself is worthwhile (p. 701)

   ética de trabajo creencia de que el trabajo tiene valor propio (pág. 701)

Y

yurt a movable round house made of wool felt mats hung over a wood frame (p. 432)

   yurt tienda redonda y portátil de fieltro de lana que se coloca sobre una armazón de madera (pág. 432)

Z

Zionism a nationalist movement that began in the late 1800s and called for Jews to reestablish a Jewish state in their original homeland (p. 467)

   sionismo movimiento nacionalista que comenzó a finales del siglo XIX y que alentaba a los judíos a reestablecer un estado judío en su tierra natal (pág. 467)

zonal organized by zone (p. 542)

   zonal organizado por zonas (pág. 542)

ENGLISH AND SPANISH GLOSSARY

Index

H

INDEX

INDEX

P

INDEX

Y

Z

INDEX

Credits and Acknowledgments

HISTORY Unless otherwise indicated below, all video reference screens are © 2010 A&E Television Networks, LLC. All rights reserved.

For permission to reproduce copyrighted material, grateful acknowledgment is made to the following sources:

Excerpt from "A Conversation with Lee Kuan Yew" by Fareed Zakaria from *Foreign Affairs Quarterly, March/April 1994.* Copyright © 2004 by Council on Foreign Relations. Reprinted by permission of Council on Foreign Relations.

"National Geography Standards 1994" from *Geography for Life by* National Geographic. Text copyright © 1994 by National Geographic. Reprinted by permission of National Geographic.

Excerpt from "Quit India" Speech by Mohandas Gandhi. Reprinted by permission of the Navajivan Trust India.

Excerpt from "Red Brocade" from *19 Varieties of Gazelle: Poems of the Middle East* by Naomi Shihab Nye. Copyright © 1994, 1995, 2002 by Naomi Shihab Nye. Reprinted by permission of Naomi Shihab Nye.

"Taiwan: War Bill a Big Provocation" from *CNN.com,* March 14, 2005. Text Copyright © 2005. Reprinted by permission of PARS International.

Excerpt from "Charter of the United Nations." Text copyright © the United Nations. Reprinted by permission of the United Nations.

Excerpt from *The Latehomecomer: A Hmong Family Memoir* by Kao Kalia Yang. Text copyright © 2008 by Kao Kalia Yang. Reprinted by permission of Coffee House Press.

Illustrations and Photo Credits

Cover: ©Ocean/Corbis.

Front Matter: ii (t) ©Sam Dudgeon/Houghton Mifflin Harcourt; (b) ©Houghton Mifflin Harcourt; iv ©Frans Lemmens/The Image Bank/Getty Images; v (t) ©Sharna Balfour/Gallo Images/Corbis; (b) ©Penny Tweedie/The Image Bank/Getty Images; vii (c) ©Juan Silva/The Image Bank/Getty Images; viii ©James Cheadle/Alamy; ix ©SIME s.a.s./eStock Photo; x ©Robbie Jack/Corbis; xi ©Danny Lehman/Corbis; xii ©David Beatty/Robert Harding Picture Library Ltd/Alamy; xiii ©Indianapolis Museum of Art, USA/Gift of Mr and Mrs Harrison Eiteljorg/The Bridgeman Art Library; xiv ©R. Philips/Arco Images GmbH/Alamy; (l) ©Gregory Johnston/Alamy; (cl) ©J. Griffs Smith/Texas Department of Transportation, Travel and Information D; (cr) ©Scott Vallance VIP/Houghton Mifflin Harcourt; xv ©Wally Santana/AP Images; xvi ©David Gray/Reuters/Corbis; xviii ©2010 A&E Television Networks, LLC. All rights reserved; xix ©2010 A&E Television Networks, LLC. All rights reserved; TEKS1 ©LMPphoto/Shutterstock; TEKS2 (l) ©David Ponton/Design Pics/Corbis; (cl) ©Bill Draker/Getty Images; (cr) ©Glowimages/Getty Images; (r) ©Texas Department of Transportation (TxDOT); TEKS3 (cl) ©Corbis; (cr) ©TX DOT/Texas Department of Transportation; (r) ©Steve Hamblin/Alamy Images; TEKS4 (cr)

©Kushal Bose/Shutterstock; TEKS5 (cr) ©Peter Tsai Photography/Alamy; (cr) ©Texas Stock Photo/Alamy; (r) ©Texas Department of Transportation (TxDOT); blind ©L. Clarke/Corbis; H12 (t) ©ESA/K. Horgan/The Image Bank/Getty Images; (tc) ©Frans Lemmens/The Image Bank/Getty Images; (b) ©Harvey Schwartz/Index Stock Imagery/Fotosearch; (b) ©Tom Nebbia/Corbis; (c) ©Sandy Stockwell/Skyscan/Corbis; ELL1 ©Alamy; ELL3 ©Alamy; ELL5 ©Alamy; ELL7 ©Alamy; ELL8 (t) ©C Squared Studios/Photodisc/Getty Images; (cr) ©Ingram Publishing/Superstock; (bl) ©Johannes Hendrik Snyman/E+/Getty Images.

Unit 1: A ©Anne-Marie Weber/The Image Bank/Getty Images; B (bg) Planetary Visions; (tr) ©Frans Lemmens/The Image Bank/Getty Images; (b) ©Michael Melford/The Image Bank/Getty Images; 1 (b) ©Robert Harding/Digital Vision/Getty Images.

Chapter 1: 2 (bg) ©age fotostock/SuperStock; (b) ©M. Colonel/Photo Researchers/Science Source; 3 (t) ©2010 A&E Television Networks, LLC. All rights reserved; (br) ©Anthony Cassidy/The Image Bank/Getty Images; (bl) ©Digital Vision/Getty Images; 5 ©Frans Lemmens/The Image Bank/Getty Images; 6 ©Kim Sayer/Corbis; 7 (r) ©ESA/K. Horgan/The Image Bank/Getty Images; (l) ©Sandy Stockwell/Skyscan/Corbis; 8 ©D. Hurst/Alamy; 11 (bl) ©Kevin Burke/Corbis; (tl) ©David R. Frazier/Photo Researchers/Science Source; (tr) ©Miles Ertman/Masterfile; (bc) ©Paul Buck/AFP/Getty Images; (br) ©Morton Beebe/Corbis; 12 ©Tom Nebbia/Corbis; 17 (l) ©Torleif Svensson/Corbis; (r) ©Penny Tweedie/The Image Bank/Getty Images; 19 ©Donna Cox and Robert Patterson/NCSA; 20 ©Joe Raedle/Getty Images; 21 (l) ©Frans Lemmens/The Image Bank/Getty Images; (r) ©Donna Cox and Robert Patterson/NCSA; (c) ©Penny Tweedie/The Image Bank/Getty Images.

Chapter 2: 24 (b) ©Pete Saloutos/Corbis; (bg) ©ESC/Science Source; 25 (t) © 2010 A&E Television Networks, LLC. All rights reserved; (bl) ©George H.H. Huey/Corbis; (br) ©Mark Karrass/Corbis; 29 ©Paul A. Souders/Corbis; 31 (r) ©Terje Rakke/The Image Bank/Getty Images; 32 ©Doug Wilson/Corbis; 34 (r) ©Alan Sirulnikoff/Photo Researchers/Science Source; (l) ©Rick Doyle/Corbis; 36 ©Earth Satellite Corporation/Science Photo Library/Science Source; 37 ©Bettmann/Corbis; 38 (b) ©Marta/Fotolia; (t) ©Yann Arthus-Bertrand/Corbis; 39 ©age fotostock/Superstock; 40 ©Owaki - Kulla/Corbis; 41 ©age fotostock/Superstock; 43 (l) ©David Weintraub/Science Source; (r) ©Gary Braasch/Corbis; 45 (c) ©Rick Doyle/Corbis; (r) ©Marta/Fotolia; (l) ©Werner H. Mueller/Corbis.

Chapter 3: 48 (br) ©Kate Thompson/National Geographic/Getty Images; (bg) ©Minerva Studio/Shutterstock; 49 (bl) ©L. Clarke/Corbis; (t) ©2010 A&E Television Networks, LLC. All rights reserved; (br) ©Bill Ross/Corbis; 53 (t) ©William Thomas Cain/Getty Images; (b) ©Eric Meola/The Image Bank/Getty Images; 56 ©age fotostock/Superstock; 57 (b) ©Robert Marien/Corbis; (t) ©Robert Glusic/Corbis; 58 ©Ariadne Van Zandbergen/Lonely Planet Images/Getty Images; 59 ©Ingram/PictureQuest/Jupiterimages; 60 ©Sharna Balfour/Gallo Images/Corbis; 64 ©Carl and Ann Purcell/

Corbis; 69 (b) ©Adrian Arbib/Corbis; (t) ©Peter Arnold, Inc./Alamy; 71 (t) ©James L. Amos/Corbis; (b) ©Charles Bowman/Photolibrary; 72 ©Sarah Leen/National Geographic Stock; 73 ©Layne Kennedy/Corbis; 75 (r) ©James L. Amos/Corbis; (r) ©Robert Marien/Corbis.

Chapter 4: 78 (bg) ©Gary M. Prior/Getty Images; (b) ©Jerry Kobalenko/Alamy; 79 (br) ©Shahn Rowe/Stone/Getty Images; (bl) ©Richard I'Anson/Lonely Planet Images; 81 (l) ©TWPhoto/Corbis; (r) ©Knut Mueller/Das Fotoarchiv/Photolibrary New York; 83 (l) ©Photononstop/Superstock; (l) ©Peter Armenia; 84 (c) ©Timothy A. Clary/AFP/Getty Images; (l) ©Reuters/Corbis; (r) Library of Congress Prints & Photographs Division; 89 The Granger Collection, NYC — All rights reserved; 90 (t) ©Peter Beck/Corbis; (b) ©Jewel Samad/AFP/Getty Images; 92 (r) ©Mike Theiss/National Geographic/Corbis; (l) ©David Coates/The Detroit News/AP Images; 93 (l) ©Corbis; (r) ©MasterLu/Fotolia; 94 (l) Library of Congress Prints & Photographs Division; (l) ©Universal Images Group/Getty Images; 101 (l) ©Photononstop/Superstock; (r) ©Reuters/Corbis; (c) ©MasterLu/Fotolia.

Chapter 5: 104 (bg) ©Jose Fuste Raga/Corbis; (b) ©Monica Quesada/AP Images; 105 (bl) ©Narinder Nanu/AFP/Getty Images; (br) ©Godong/Universal Images Group/Getty Images; 108 (l) ©J. D. Heaton/Picture Finders/age fotostock; (r) ©VISION/easyFotostock/age fotostock; 110 (r) ©Jeff Widener/AP Images; (l) ©Swim Ink/Corbis; 113 U.S. Air Force; 114 (l) ©Blend Images/Hill Street Studios/Getty Images; (r) ©Kidstock/Blend Images/Getty Images; 118 (t) ©Tony Camacho/Science Source; ©Artville/Getty Images; 119 (l) ©White Fox/Tips Images/age fotostock; (c) ©Peter Turnley/Corbis; (r) ©Francisco Diez Photography/Getty Images; 121 ©Fish Flops; 122 (tl) ©Owaki-Kulla/Corbis; (tr) ©Jack Sullivan/Alamy; (br) ©Michelle Garrett/Corbis; (bl) ©Kevin Fleming/Corbis; 123 (l) ©Glen Allison/The Image Bank/Getty Images; (r) ©Carl & Ann Purcell/Corbis; 125 (l) ©Jose Fuste Raga/Corbis; (c) ©Kidstock/Blend Images/Getty Images; (r) ©Owaki-Kulla/Corbis.

Unit 2: A ©Ocean/Corbis; B (cl) ©Ryan/Beyer/Photographer's Choice/Getty Images; (bg) ©Planetary Visions; (bc) ©David W. Hamilton/The Image Bank/Getty Images; 129 (c) ©John Wang/Photodisc/Getty Images; 131 ©Gavin Hellier/Robert Harding Picture Library; 138 (c) ©Globe Turner/Shutterstock; 139 (b) ©Russell Gordon/Das Fotoarchiv/Photolibrary New York.

Chapter 6: 140 ©eStock Photo/PictureQuest/Photolibrary New York; 141 (t) ©2010 A&E Television Networks, LLC. All rights reserved; (bl) ©Ron Watts/Corbis; (br) ©Tom Grill/Photographer's Choice RF/Getty Images; 143 ©Altrendo Panoramic/Altrendo/Getty Images; 144 ©NASA/Science Photo Library/Science Source; 145 (c) ©Alan Schein Photography/Corbis; (b) ©Kord.com/age fotostock; 149 (r) ©NASA/Corbis; (l) ©Eric Gay/AP Images; 151 ©The Metropolitan Museum of Art/Bridgeman Art Library; 153 ©Hall of Representatives, Washington, DC/Bridgeman Art Library; 155 ©Saul Loeb/AFP/Getty Images; 157 ©Steve Skjold/Alamy; 157 CF1 (b) ©Houghton Mifflin Harcourt; 157 CF2 (t)

R66 CREDITS AND ACKNOWLEDGMENTS

Staff Credits

The people who contributed to *Holt McDougal: Contemporary World Studies* are listed below. They represent editorial, design, production, emedia, and permissions.

Amy Bono, Melanie Baccus, Angela Beckmann, Julie Beckman-Key, Genick Blaise, Ed Blake, Jennifer Campbell, Henry Clark, Grant Davidson, Nina Degollado, Rose Degollado, Christine Devall, Michelle Dike, Lydia Doty, Chase Edmond, Mescal Evler, Susan Flurry, Stephanie Friedman, Bob Fullilove, Matthew Gierhart, Bill Gillis, Ann Gorbett, Janet Harrington, Betsy Harris, Wendy Hodge, Tim Hovde, Cathy Jenevein, Carrie Jones, Kadonna Knape, Laura Lasley, Sarah Lee, Sean McCormick, Joe Melomo, Richard Metzger, Andrew Miles, Debra O'Shields, Jarred Prejean, Paul Provence, Shelly Ramos, Curtis Riker, Michael Rinella, Michelle Rimsa, Jennifer Rockwood, Carole Rollins, Beth Sample, Annette Saunders, Jenny Schaeffer, Kay Selke, Chris Smith, Jeremy Strykul, Jeannie Taylor, Terri Taylor, Joni Wackwitz, Mary Wages, Diana Holman Walker, Nadyne Wood, Robin Zaback